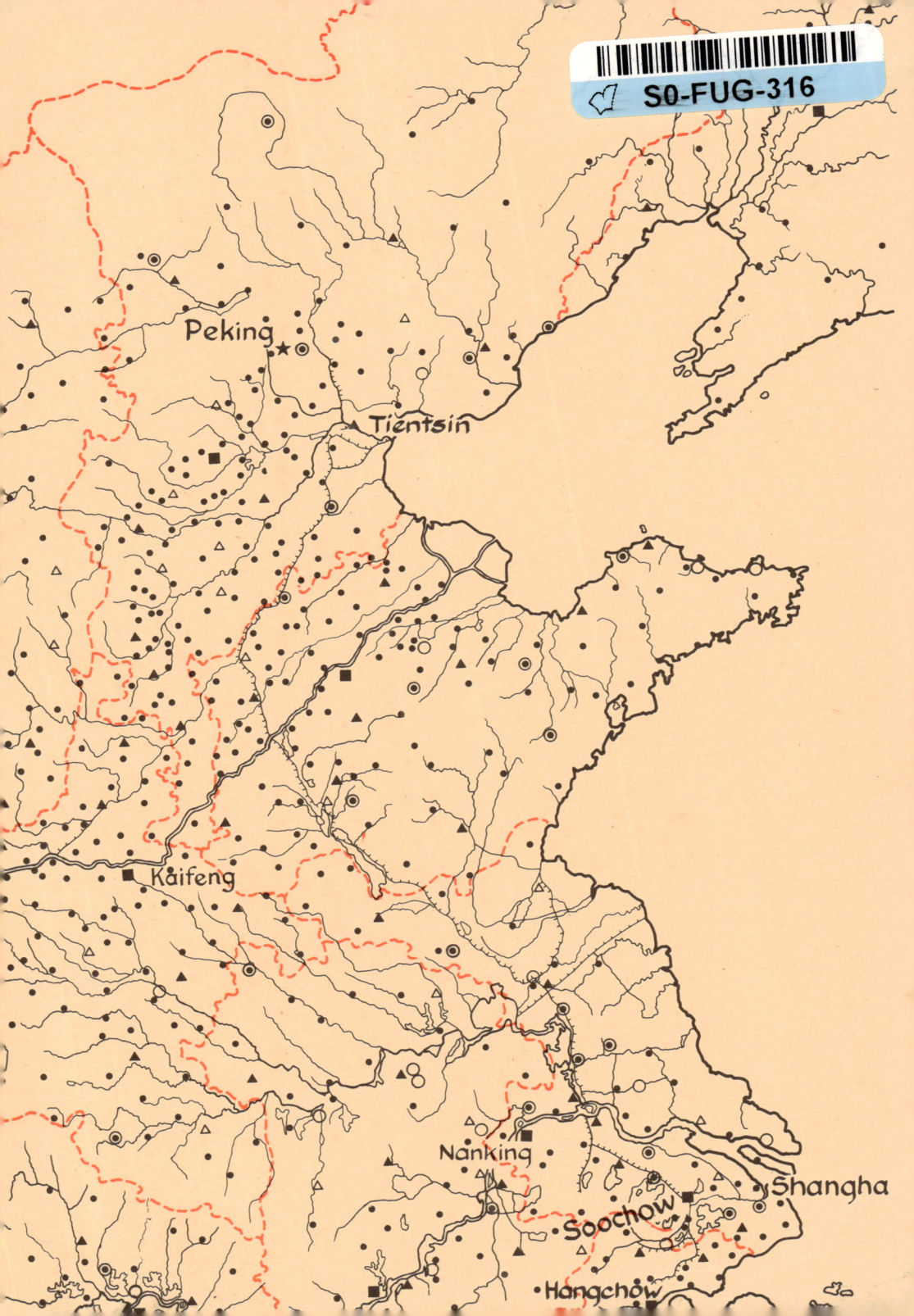

THE CITY IN
LATE IMPERIAL CHINA

Contributors

Hugh D. R. Baker
Sen-dou Chang
Donald R. DeGlopper
Mark Elvin
Stephan Feuchtwang
Peter J. Golas
Tilemann Grimm
Harry J. Lamley

F. W. Mote
Kristofer M. Schipper
Yoshinobu Shiba
G. William Skinner
Sybille van der Sprenkel
John R. Watt
Arthur F. Wright

THE CITY IN
LATE IMPERIAL CHINA

Edited by G. WILLIAM SKINNER

SMC PUBLSHING INC., Taipei

STUDIES IN CHINESE SOCIETY

Sponsored by the Subcommittee on Research on Chinese Society
of the Joint Committee on Contemporary China of the Social
Science Research Council and the American Council of
Learned Societies, 1967–68

G. WILLIAM SKINNER, *Chairman*
MORTON H. FRIED
IRENE B. TAEUBER
EZRA F. VOGEL
BRYCE WOOD, *Staff*

Previously published in this series
Maurice Freedman, ed., *Family and Kinship in Chinese Society*
John Wilson Lewis, ed., *The City in Communist China*
W. E. Willmott, ed., *Economic Organization in Chinese Society*
Mark Elvin and G. William Skinner, eds., *The Chinese City Between Two Worlds*
Arthur P. Wolf, ed., *Religion and Ritual in Chinese Society*
Margery Wolf and Roxane Witke, eds., *Women in Chinese Society*

© 1977 by the Board of Trustees of the Leland Stanford Junior University.
All rights reserved. Reprinted and published in 1995, by arrangement with
Stanford University Press.

ISBN 957-638-310-2

Preface

In 1968–69 the Subcommittee on Research on Chinese Society—financed by the Carnegie Corporation of New York, administered by the Social Science Research Council, and overseen by the Joint Committee on Contemporary China of that Council and the American Academy of Learned Societies—devoted two of its research conferences to the Chinese city. In the wake of these conferences, the Subcommittee planned three volumes, of which this is the last to appear. *The City in Communist China* (edited by John Wilson Lewis) and *The Chinese City Between Two Worlds* (edited by Mark Elvin and myself) were published in 1971 and 1974, respectively. These three volumes in turn form part of a larger series, Studies in Chinese Society, on which particulars are given opposite.

Thirteen of the papers in this volume were presented in preliminary form at a conference held at Wentworth-by-the-Sea, Portsmouth, New Hampshire, in August-September 1968. In addition to the authors of these papers—Hugh D. R. Baker, Mark Elvin, Stephan Feuchtwang, Peter J. Golas, Tilemann Grimm, Harry J. Lamley, F. W. Mote, Kristofer M. Schipper, Yoshinobu Shiba, G. William Skinner, Sybille van der Sprenkel, John R. Watt, and Arthur F. Wright—the following China specialists attended the conference and participated in discussions relevant to the volume: Kwang-chih Chang, Lawrence W. Crissman, John Wilson Lewis, William L. Parish, Jr., Gilbert Rozman, Irene B. Taeuber, Ezra F. Vogel, Edwin A. Winckler, and Lien-sheng Yang. A full and cogent record of the discussion, prepared by Messrs. Parish and Rozman, was placed at the disposal of the contributors to assist them in revising their papers, and I have been able to draw on that record in writing my introductions. Charles Tilly and John Whitney Hall, invited to attend by reason of their expertise on premodern European and Japanese cities, respectively, provided more than the requisitioned comparative perspective; we all left wiser for their pungent criticisms and fresh insights. Three contributions were later solicited to supplement the thirteen Wentworth papers: Sen-dou Chang's on urban morphology, Donald R. DeGlopper's on nineteenth-century Lu-kang, and mine on regional urbanization.

The participants in this endeavor mourn the loss of two of our number. Irene B. Taeuber, a pioneer in demographic studies of China and Japan, died in February 1974, and among our many losses we must count the paper intended for this volume on patterns of migration and urban growth in premodern China. Arthur F. Wright's death in August 1976 robs sinological history of a distinguished scholar and indefatigable leader. In the present context, I need only stress that Professor Wright, champion of humanistic studies, did more than any other sinologist of his generation to make the dialogue between history and social science both respectable and exciting.

I want also to record here the deep sense of loss occasioned by the death of Maurice Freedman in July 1975—a loss felt by all those associated with the larger enterprise of which this book is a part. Professor Freedman helped design the Subcommittee's research conferences and, in organizing the first in the series, set their standards and tone. His ecumenical vision of sinological scholarship left its mark on this volume, whose contributors include representatives of five disciplines and six nations. The introductions to the volume's three parts were written under the heavy shadow of Freedman's passing, and in them I have endeavored to do some of what he would have accomplished much more deftly in a review article. That we shall never again benefit from his perspicacious reaction to our ideas is difficult to accept.

The endpaper maps show China's cities as of 1894. The two frames—North China at the front and South China at the back—cover virtually all parts of the empire that were dominated by Han Chinese. Within these frames, all capitals of county- and higher-level administrative units are plotted, together with some of the most important nonadministrative cities. (A key to the symbols will be found overleaf from the back endpaper.) Standing alone, these maps serve especially to point up the ubiquity of cities in that heavily agrarian society, their comparatively dense concentration in the areas that my analysis takes to constitute the cores of regional urban systems, and the distinctive distribution of different kinds of administrative centers—in particular, capitals of prefectures (*fu*) and of autonomous departments (*chih-li chou*). Subse-

Preface

quent changes in the spatial patterning of cities of different types may be appreciated by comparing these endpaper maps with those in *The Chinese City Between Two Worlds*, which show data for 1930 in comparable frames.

I felt it essential to the purpose of this book to include a wide variety of maps, and I am grateful to the Joint Committee on Contemporary China for a subsidy that helped defray the cost of their preparation. Jill Leland did virtually all of the volume's cartographic work under my direction, and I wish to record my pleasure in working with her over the years. Her drafting skill, her ability to translate visionary concepts into visual effects, and her cheerful flexibility deserve special tribute. I am also grateful to Albert Burkhardt and J. G. Bell of Stanford University Press for assistance in designing the maps and for ensuring technical excellence in their reproduction.

Special thanks are due to Bryce Wood for his competent staff work for the Subcommittee, and to J. G. Bell for advice on the overall design and general editorial guidance. Without their continual support and understanding patience, this book might well have fallen victim to extraneous pressures. I am also grateful to Peter J. Kahn for bringing to the press editing not only meticulousness but also intelligence and sensitivity. The Character List owes much to the research of Wei-ming Chen and John R. Ziemer; the characters were written by Elsie L. Young.

For the unconscionable delay in the publication of this volume, I offer my heartfelt apologies to its contributors and readers alike. Extenuating circumstances and explanations are now beside the point, but I do wish to absolve all others from blame; for better or worse the decisions and the priorities were mine, and I accept full responsibility for the consequences. For the gaps in the coverage of this book I do not apologize; comprehensiveness in a volume of this kind is unattainable in practice and undesirable in principle. We have aimed to open up a new field of study—the historical sociology of Chinese urbanism. I think we have succeeded in establishing the main dimensions of the subject, in suggesting the intellectual excitement it affords, and in demonstrating its importance for social science as well as for sinology. As the intellectual quest quickens, we shall be pleased to see these essays superseded.

G.W.S.

August 1976

Contents

List of Maps and Figures   xi

Contributors   xv

PART ONE: *The City in History*

Introduction: Urban Development in Imperial China   3
G. WILLIAM SKINNER

The Cosmology of the Chinese City   33
ARTHUR F. WRIGHT

The Morphology of Walled Capitals   75
SEN-DOU CHANG

The Transformation of Nanking, 1350–1400   101
F. W. MOTE

The Formation of Cities: Initiative and Motivation in Building Three Walled Cities in Taiwan   155
HARRY J. LAMLEY

Regional Urbanization in Nineteenth-Century China   211
G. WILLIAM SKINNER

PART TWO: *The City in Space*

Introduction: Urban and Rural in Chinese Society   253
G. WILLIAM SKINNER

Cities and the Hierarchy of Local Systems G. WILLIAM SKINNER	275
The Yamen and Urban Administration JOHN R. WATT	353
Ningpo and Its Hinterland YOSHINOBU SHIBA	391
Market Towns and Waterways: The County of Shang-hai from 1480 to 1910 MARK ELVIN	441
Academies and Urban Systems in Kwangtung TILEMANN GRIMM	475
Extended Kinship in the Traditional City HUGH D. R. BAKER	499

PART THREE: *The City as a Social System*

Introduction: Urban Social Structure in Ch'ing China G. WILLIAM SKINNER	521
Early Ch'ing Guilds PETER J. GOLAS	555
School-Temple and City God STEPHAN FEUCHTWANG	581
Urban Social Control SYBILLE VAN DER SPRENKEL	609
Social Structure in a Nineteenth-Century Taiwanese Port City DONALD R. DEGLOPPER	633
Neighborhood Cult Associations in Traditional Tainan KRISTOFER M. SCHIPPER	651
Notes	679
Character List	777
Index	799

List of Maps and Figures

PART ONE: *The City in History*

Introduction: Urban Development in Imperial China

Fig. 1. P'ing-chiang T'u Pei. Map of Soochow, 1229	14
Fig. 2. Aerial Photograph of Soochow, 1945	15

The Cosmology of the Chinese City

Map 1. T'ang Ch'ang-an	58
Map 2. Northern Sung Kaifeng	61
Map 3. Southern Sung Hangchow	65
Map 4. Ming Peking	68
Fig. 1. The Walls of Peking	69
Fig. 2. Hsi-chih Men, Peking	70
Map 5. Four Capitals, a Comparison of Sizes and Shapes	72

The Morphology of Walled Capitals

Fig. 1. City Wall and Corner Tower of T'ai-ku, Shansi	76
Map 1. Ta-t'ung-fu, Shansi	78
Fig. 2. Lu-lung, Chihli	80
Fig. 3. Loyang	81
Map 2. Chou-chia-k'ou, Honan	82
Fig. 4. Ling-t'ai, Kansu	84
Map 3. Feng-yang-fu and Capital of Feng-yang *hsien*, Anhwei	89
Fig. 5. Models of Street Grids in Cities with Four Gates	97
Fig. 6. T'ung-ch'uan-fu, Szechwan	98

The Transformation of Nanking, 1350–1400

Map 1. Ming Nanking, ca. 1390	135
Map 2. Ming Nanking, ca. 1390, Detail Showing Major Built-Up Areas	140

The Formation of Cities: Initiative and Motivation in Building Three Walled Cities in Taiwan

Map 1. Taiwan, 1810–75	159
Map 2. Northern Taiwan, ca. 1888	160
Map 3. Hsin-chu City, ca. 1843	163
Map 4. I-Lan City, ca. 1835	165
Map 5. Urban Growth in the Taipei Area to 1894	169
Map 6. T'ai-pei-fu and Environs, ca. 1894	171

Regional Urbanization in Nineteenth-Century China

Map 1. Physiographic Macroregions of Agrarian China in Relation to Major Rivers, with Regional Cores Indicated by Shading	214
Map 2. Physiographic Macroregions in Relation to Provinces, and Showing Metropolitan Cities, 1843	215
Fig. 1. Rank-Size Distribution of Urban Central Places, by Region, 1843	238
Fig. 2. Rank-Size Distribution of Cities with a Population of 10,000 or more, Agrarian China Except Manchuria and Taiwan, 1843	248

PART TWO: *The City in Space*

Cities and the Hierarchy of Local Systems

Fig. 1. A Regular Central-Place Hierarchy, Boundless and Bounded	279
Map 1. The Upper Yangtze Region, 1893, Showing Regional-City Trading Systems	289
Fig. 2. Greater-City Trading Systems in Relation to Rivers and Major Roads (Schematized), Upper Yangtze Region, 1893	291
Map 2. The Upper Yangtze Region, 1893, Showing Greater-City Trading Systems	292
Map 3. A Small Portion of the Upper Yangtze Region, 1893	294
Map 4. A Still Smaller Portion of the Upper Yangtze Region, 1893	295

The Yamen and Urban Administration

Fig. 1. Shao-hsing-fu, Chekiang	354
Fig. 2. The Shan-yin County Yamen, Shao-hsing-fu, Chekiang	380

Ningpo and Its Hinterland

Map 1. Waterworks on the Ningpo Plain	394
Map 2. Market Towns in the Ningpo Area, ca. 1227	398
Map 3. Growth of Market Towns in the Ningpo Area, ca. 1227–ca. 1560	400
Map 4. Market Towns in the Ningpo Area, ca. 1730	402

List of Maps and Figures   xiii

    Map 5. Market Towns in the Ningpo Area, ca. 1900   404
    Map 6. Ningpo, 1877   406
    Map 7. Local Specialization in the Ningpo Area, Late Nineteenth
            Century   425

Market Towns and Waterways: The County of Shang-hai
from 1480 to 1910

    Fig. 1. Waterways, Walled Cities, and Military Stations in
           Northeastern Sung-chiang Prefecture   442
    Fig. 2. Shanghai Before the Building of Its Walls   443
    Map 1. Southeastern Kiangnan, ca. 1600   446
    Map 2. Market Towns in the Vicinity of Shanghai, ca. 1470   470
    Map 3. Market Towns in the Vicinity of Shanghai, ca. 1600   470
    Map 4. Market Towns in the Vicinity of Shanghai, ca. 1750   471
    Map 5. Market Towns in the Vicinity of Shanghai, ca. 1870   471
    Map 6. Market Towns in the Vicinity of Shanghai, ca. 1910   471

PART THREE: *The City as a Social System*

Introduction: Urban Social Structure in Ch'ing China

    Fig. 1. Ward in the Major Business District of Peking, ca. 1750   530
    Fig. 2. Ward in an Upper-Class District of Peking, ca. 1750   531
    Fig. 3. Demographic Characteristics of Peking, 1917–18   532
    Fig. 4. Chiang-lan Chieh, Canton, 1890's   534

Neighborhood Cult Associations in Traditional Tainan

    Map 1. Tainan in 1907   658

MAP SYMBOLS

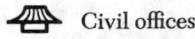

    Civil offices

    Military offices and installations

    Religious institutions

    Academic institutions

    Charitable institutions

    Granary

Contributors

HUGH D. R. BAKER received his Ph.D. from the University of London in 1967, and since then has been Lecturer in Chinese at the School of Oriental and African Studies there. He is the author of *A Chinese Lineage Village: Sheung Shui* (Stanford, 1968).

SEN-DOU CHANG was born in Chekiang and received his Ph.D. from the University of Washington in 1961. He is now Professor of Geography at the University of Hawaii in Honolulu. He has published articles on various aspects of urbanization and the growth of cities in China from ancient times to the present. His current research interests focus on changes in the structure of Chinese cities since 1949.

DONALD R. DEGLOPPER received his M.A. from the University of London in 1965 and his Ph.D. from Cornell University in 1973. He is Assistant Professor of Anthropology and Asian Studies at Cornell University. Articles on economic organization and religion in contemporary Lu-kang have been published in W. E. Willmott, ed., *Economic Organization in Chinese Society* (Stanford, 1972), and Arthur P. Wolf, ed., *Religion and Ritual in Chinese Society* (Stanford, 1974), respectively.

MARK ELVIN is a Fellow of St. Antony's College and Lecturer in Chinese History at the University of Oxford. He received his Ph.D. from the University of Cambridge in 1968 and taught for several years at the University of Glasgow. He is the author of *The Pattern of the Chinese Past* (Stanford, 1973) and coeditor of *The Chinese City Between Two Worlds* (Stanford, 1974). His current research is on China's premodern population.

STEPHAN FEUCHTWANG is Lecturer in Sociology at the City University, London. He received his Ph.D. in 1975 from the University of London in

Social Anthropology for a dissertation on Chinese religion in Taiwan. Articles on Chinese religion have been published in Arthur P. Wolf, ed., *Religion and Ritual in Chinese Society* (Stanford, 1974) and in Mark Elvin and G. William Skinner, eds., *The Chinese City Between Two Worlds* (Stanford, 1974). He is also the author of *An Anthropological Analysis of Chinese Geomancy* (1974).

PETER J. GOLAS received his M.A. in History from Stanford in 1964, and his Ph.D. in History and Far Eastern Languages from Harvard in 1972. He is Chairman of the Chinese Studies Program at the University of Denver and Co-Director of the Colorado East Asian Consortium. His major interest is the social and economic history of the Sung dynasty.

TILEMANN GRIMM is Professor of Chinese, Seminar für Ostasiatische Philologie, Universität Tübingen. Earlier appointments were at Hamburg, where he took his doctorate in 1953, Münster, and Bochum. He is the author of *Erziehung und Politik im konfuzianischen China der Ming-Zeit* (1960), *China und Südostasien in Geschichte und Gegenwart* (1966), and *Chinas Traditionen im Umbrach der Zeit* (1971).

HARRY J. LAMLEY, Professor of History at the University of Hawaii, received his Ph.D. from the University of Washington in 1964. His specialty is local Chinese history of the Ch'ing period and the twentieth century. Since his first stay in Taiwan (1956–59), much of his research has related to that island's history. He has published articles on the Taiwanese gentry, early Japanese rule, and the Taiwan Republic and Japanese takeover of 1895.

F. W. MOTE, Professor of Chinese History, Princeton University, was trained at the University of Nanking and Peking National University, and at the University of Washington, where he received his Ph.D. He is the author of *The Poet Kao Ch'i, 1336–1374* (1962) and *Intellectual Foundations of China* (1971).

KRISTOFER M. SCHIPPER devoted many years in Taiwan to the study of Taoism, combining textual research with intimate participant observation of current practices. Formerly a member of l'Ecole Française d'Extrême-Orient, he is now Professor at the Centre Documentaire d'Histoire des Religions, Ecole Pratique des Haute Etudes, Paris.

YOSHINOBU SHIBA studied economic history at Tokyo University, where he received his Ph.D. in 1962. His publications include *Sōdai shōgyōshi kenkyū* (1968), of which an abridged English translation prepared by Mark Elvin was published in 1970 as *Commerce and Society in Sung China*. His current research concerns processes of urbanization and commercialization within regional systems during the centuries from early Sung times to late Ming.

Contributors

G. WILLIAM SKINNER, Professor of Anthropology, Stanford University, received his Ph.D. from Cornell in 1954. A research interest in Chinese market towns and cities stems from fieldwork in the Chengtu area of Szechwan in 1949–50. He is the author of two books on the Chinese in Bangkok and coeditor of *The Chinese City Between Two Worlds* (Stanford, 1974) and *Change and Persistence in Thai Society* (1975). Other publications include *Modern Chinese Society: An Analytical Bibliography*, 3 vols. (Stanford, 1973).

SYBILLE VAN DER SPRENKEL is Lecturer in Sociology at the University of Leeds, England. Her interest in the sociology of Chinese law was kindled when she spent 1948–49 in North China. She is the author of *Legal Institutions in Manchu China* (1962).

JOHN R. WATT has studied at Oxford and Harvard, and at Columbia, where he received his Ph.D. in Chinese and Japanese History in 1967. He has taught at MIT and at Johnston College. In 1974 he was appointed Academic Dean at Windham College, Putney, Vt. Among his published works are *The District Magistrate in Late Imperial China* (1972) and articles in *Ch'ing-shih Wen-t'i* and the *China Quarterly*.

ARTHUR F. WRIGHT was trained at Stanford, Oxford, and Harvard, and had some eight years' study in China and Japan. A onetime Editor of the *Far Eastern Quarterly* and former President of the Association for Asian Studies, he served as Chairman of the Committee on Studies of Chinese Civilization of the American Council of Learned Societies from 1963 to 1973. He published widely on Chinese social and intellectual history. From 1961 until his death on 11 August 1976, he was Charles Seymour Professor of History at Yale University.

Part One
THE CITY IN HISTORY

Introduction: Urban Development in Imperial China

G. WILLIAM SKINNER

No book on traditional Chinese cities can remain wholly aloof from the preconceptions and paradigms that dominate the sociological literature on premodern cities.[1] Though I may not avoid them entirely, I mean to chart a course that skirts them very cautiously. Still, since scholarship in any field is supposed to build on what has gone before, a word is in order about how this book relates to synthetic theorizing in comparative urbanism and why it does not relate more closely.

The dominant approach may be characterized by reference to four scholars. Wirth and Redfield, in quite different ways, sought to characterize *the* city irrespective of time and place, to isolate what is typically and specifically urban in contrast to what are rural or folk phenomena.[2] Sjoberg, dichotomizing all cities known to history, contrasted the preindustrial with the industrial city and sought a generic characterization of each type by abstracting from phenomena in a wide range of "disparate cultural settings."[3] Weber, contemplating a somewhat restricted subset of preindustrial cities, constructed the Occidental and the Oriental cities as types, once again seeking contrastive generic characterizations.[4]

These efforts vary considerably in theoretical respectability. Wirth's procedures were admirable in that he derived the specific features of the urban "way of life" from what he took to be generic or defining characteristics of cities (size, density, and heterogeneity); in retrospect, however, the logic of several deductions appears faulty. Weber's construct, sociologically sound if not always historically accurate, was given intellectual point by the special role of the Occidental type of city in his larger developmental scheme. Redfield's basic framework can only be characterized as misconceived, and the folk-urban continuum has by now been thoroughly discredited.[5] The intellectual rationale that Sjoberg gave the "preindustrial city" is badly flawed in several respects, and there is little to recommend his methodology for arriving at the specific features of his constructed type.[6]

Specialists in the cities of particular places and times have had little trouble disproving the universality of features specified for these various ideal types of cities, and indeed have found it great sport to shoot down universal schemes. As might be expected, the more extensive the domain covered by a given constructed type, the more poorly its diagnostic features have fared. The lists provided by Wirth and Redfield have been pretty well demolished;[7] rather more of Sjoberg's "features" have withstood assault; whereas of Weber's two constructs the "Occidental city" has stood up better than the more inclusive "Oriental city." The cities of late imperial China were on the whole not distinctively "urban" in Wirth's or Redfield's sense; they were wretched examples of "preindustrial cities"; and they were only very imperfectly "Oriental." To document these assertions today would be a largely sterile exercise.

Where can we take the tradition of constructed ideal types that once figured so importantly in the sociological literature on premodern urbanism? For one thing, the inherited types can be subdivided, refined, and developed into a logically constructed hierarchical typology. Sjoberg's scheme, which derives ultimately from a typology of societies, in effect holds that all nonindustrial cities were found in societies of a single basic type. Other analysts posit two, three, or even four basic societal types where Sjoberg sees one,[8] and at the very least his "preindustrial city" should be subdivided into the cities of agrarian civilizations (with literate elites) and those of primitive states (without them). Each of the three (or more) basic types of cities might then be dichotomized into autonomous/enclaved versus dependent/integrated. These subtypes in turn could then be subdivided on a cultural/geographic basis, whereby the dependent/integrated category occurring in primitive states would be broken down into its New World examples (Inca, Aztec, etc.) and its African examples, and the dependent/integrated category in agrarian civilizations would be broken down (initially) into East European, Middle Eastern, Hindic, Sinic, etc. Finally, the Sinic grouping (to take the relevant case) would at the next level down in the hierarchy be subdivided into its Chinese, Vietnamese, Korean, Japanese, and other variants. With a refined hierarchical typology of this kind, we could reasonably test as contingency generalizations propositions alleged to hold for Chinese cities, for all Sinic cities, for dependent/integrated cities in agrarian civilizations everywhere, for all cities in agrarian civilzations, and finally for all cities. The result would be a hierarchical set of verified generalizations, with urban universals at the top and contrastive generalizations at each lower level, becoming ever more specific as we descended the typological ladder. This book hazards a number of generalizations that would have a place in such a comprehensive scheme.

But are generalizations the sole or even the most important objective of the intellectual quest? Is the point to categorize the Chinese case so that it can be placed unambiguously in the proper cell of particular cross-cultural contingency tables? Should we aim here at a set of conclusions in the form of generalizations about *the* Chinese city—statements that by their very nature can reflect only the lowest common denominator of all empirical cases? I think not. The "Chinese" city is no less a constructed ideal type than the "preindustrial" or the "Oriental" city. And when we survey the range of premodern Chinese cities—from imperial capitals to lowly subprefectural seats on remote frontiers; from great commercial emporia such as Soochow, Canton, and Hankow to central market towns; from the relatively spacious cities of the Lower Yangtze region to the congested cities of the Lingnan region,* where intramural areas were on the average one-sixth as large—when we comprehend this varied array, we run into the same difficulties that beset generalizations about more inclusive constructed types. Unless we are prepared to fudge, almost any general propositions about Chinese cities must be specified, and qualified, and so burdened with exceptions and contingencies as to frustrate sinologist and comparativist alike.

The fact is that the constructed-types approach assumes a coincidence in covariation among key variables that seldom obtains in the real world. In my view, a more productive approach to understanding phenomena within any domain is to ask what covaries with what. To what extent does a particular function vary with scale? How do morphological features change along with the different types of urban functions? If we could ascertain which empirical and analytical features of urban phenomena in China varied together in space and time, we would be in a better position to say something about cause and effect, about the direction of change, and about systemic relationships within the domain of Chinese cities. We would find, furthermore, that many propositions concerning covariation that hold for Chinese cities would also hold, or on first principles ought to hold, for analytically or geographically more inclusive urban domains.

The contributors to this book are largely historians. None of them is

---

* Lingnan refers to a physiographic region (defined at p. 212) that corresponds roughly to the provinces of Kwangtung and Kwangsi.

by inclination or training a Cliometrician, so that the brave words just enunciated should not be thought to herald a harvest of multivariate analyses. And apart from my own contributions, the smaller number of papers written by anthropologists and sociologists largely eschew quantitative manipulations. Nonetheless, every paper in this book contributes directly to the quest for differentiation, and to our understanding of the significance of differences, among Chinese cities. And, though this book has something to say about the proposition that premodern Chinese cities are in comparative perspective a distinct cultural type, its more important contributions are to point up the ways in which variation among Chinese cities is systematic and significant, thereby bringing a semblance of order to the domain as a field of study.

The book is organized around three aspects of cities in late imperial China. Part One treats the establishment and spread of cities and the factors affecting their form and growth. Part Two emphasizes the embeddedness of cities in their respective hinterlands and regions, treating linkages among cities as well as between city and countryside. Part Three deals with the internal social structure of cities. Each part has a separate introduction.

In addition to pointing up a number of issues raised by the five papers in Part One, the present introduction aims to provide an overview of urban development in late imperial times—by which in this volume is generally meant the Ming and Ch'ing periods down to 1895. It will be helpful to begin with a brief characterization of the five contributions that follow.

Professor Wright opens the volume with a detailed and fascinating account of how the bits and pieces of practical and religious lore that had accumulated on aspects of city building during China's preimperial antiquity were during the Han period systematized into a consistent cosmology. After calling our attention to geomantic elements as the single subsequent addition to the Han synthesis—a contribution of southern regions to a tradition that had developed entirely in North and Northwest China—he then follows the influence of the classical cosmology on the building of selected capitals from Sui to Ming. His ironic conclusion is that of all the imperial capitals considered, it was the last—Ming Peking—that accorded most closely with the canonical cosmology. The particular relevance of Wright's contribution to the cities of late imperial China becomes clear when we realize that in this respect Peking was representative of a host of less exalted cities whose construction or rebuilding occurred during the Ming period. The restorationism of the Ming was classical in part because Sung Neo-Confucianism had driven men back to classical models and in part because the trauma of Mongol conquest had stimulated a nativistic cultural chauvinism that included the ancient cosmology. To the very end of the empire, the elaborate urban symbolism synthesized before the time of Christ persisted in the midst of secular change.

Professor Chang's informative survey of the morphology of walled cities in Ch'ing China discusses a number of elements that illustrate the persistence of this traditional urban symbolism. His treatment of city siting emphasizes the preference for level land near waterways—a pattern that, on Wright's telling, was already apparent in Shang and early Chou times. Chang's discussion of gate patterns emphasizes the orientation of cities to the four cardinal points and the priority given the south gate and the thoroughfare leading north from it—once again elements of Chinese city planning that predate even the Han synthesis. One result of these two ancient practices in conjunction, Chang points out, is an empirical preference for sites that face waterways to the south, as shown by the widespread occurrence in city names of *yang* (indicating the sunny north bank) as opposed to *yin* (evoking the shady south bank). Chang's paper provides an important analysis of the internal transport grids that are so closely associated with the patterning of city gates. His comprehensive treatment of multiple cities is in some respects a deviant-case analysis that highlights the normative and empirical regularities of form in late imperial cities.

The introduction provided by Professor Mote to his authoritative case study of Ming Nanking—an essay rich in insights that have come of long immersion in the data on Chinese urbanism—provides a wide-ranging analysis of traditional Chinese cities as a distinct cultural type. Those parts of his study that touch on the embeddedness of cities in their hinterlands and on the internal organization of cities I discuss in the introductions to Parts Two and Three of this volume, respectively. Most of the points made in his remarkably well-rounded analysis of Ming Nanking are relevant here. In respect of Wright's arguments, Mote shows how Nanking was heir to earlier city-building traditions and emphasizes the ways in which it served as a model for the rebuilding of Peking during the Yung-lo reign. His paper places the Nanking case firmly in the context of the great institutional changes of the late medieval period, of which more below, and makes a provocative case for the symbolic significance of city walls in China. Finally, his paper points up historical fluctuations in the size and role of great cities in the Lower Yangtze region, noting the leading role of Soochow and Yangchow in the T'ang and of Hangchow in the Southern Sung, and emphasizing the dramatic rise of Nanking after its capture by the Ming founder, its subsequent decline in the fifteenth century, and its revival in the sixteenth. Patterns of this kind are given preliminary interpretation later in this introduction.

Professor Lamley's paper is also a case study, and in a number of respects it constitutes a neat foil to Mote's. By contrast with Ming Nanking, a renowned city in China's most urbanized and strategically central region, two of the three cities Lamley examines were at the lowest administrative level in northern Taiwan, an unurbanized area at the very periphery of the empire. Mote emphasizes the role of government in shaping a city at the beginning of the late imperial era, Lamley the role of local nonofficial leadership in shaping three cities as that era drew to a close. The chief contribution of Lamley's study is the light it throws on such particular aspects of the city-building process as the interaction between local and imperial goals and expectations, the complementary interdigitation of responsibilities and tasks between bureaucrats and the local elite, and the variations that arise out of the specifics of time and place. In pointing to the founding of temples and religious institutions as essential elements in the city-building process, Lamley echoes a point made by Wright about preimperial cities, thereby underlining the singular persistence of China's city-building tradition in the face of secularizing change. Finally, Lamley provides useful data for appraising the overall meaning of city walls in imperial China.

The last paper in Part One is my own on urbanization in nineteenth-century China. Perhaps its most important argument is that separate urban systems developed in each of the major physiographic regions into which agrarian China may be subdivided (see Maps 1 and 2, pp. 214–15), and that even as late as the mid-nineteenth century, economic and administrative transactions between these discrete systems of cities were too attenuated to bind the parts into an integrated empire-wide urban system. The relative discreteness of these regional systems seemed sufficient cause for analyzing urbanization separately for each region, which the paper does in preliminary fashion for 1843 and 1893. In accounting for regional differences in urbanization rates—ranging from around 4 percent to nearly 8 percent (1843) or more than 10 percent (1893)—and in the rank-size distribution of cities in the different regions, I bring into focus some of the more important factors that affected urban development.

In the remainder of this introduction I take up three problems: the influence of China's physiographic structure on the spread of cities and the development of urban systems, the reasons for the limited prolifera-

Introduction: Urban Development in Imperial China

tion of capital cities from T'ang times on, and the causes of the medieval "urban revolution." Finally, I show the significance of these topics—physiographic constraints, administrative retrenchment, and medieval patterns of transformation—for urban development in late imperial times.

Regional Citification and Urban Systems

The process whereby administrative cities spread throughout agrarian China is little studied and fraught with interpretive problems. A general picture of the geographic and temporal sequences of city building may be obtained from Table 1, where data on the initial founding of *hsien* capitals, collected by Sen-dou Chang, are grouped in accordance with the physiographic regions introduced in this volume (see Map 2, p. 215). For reasons that will become apparent below, the Middle Yangtze region is subdivided into its five major subregions—the Yangtze corridor; the basin of the Han River to the north; and the basins of the three great tributaries to the south, the Kan, the Hsiang, and the Yüan.*

In Table 1, the five subregions of the Middle Yangtze and the seven other macroregions are arranged by the proportion of the full Ch'ing complement of *hsien* capitals that had already been founded by the end of the Han dynasty. This arrangement points up the basic north-to-south sequence of regional citification. The earliest Chinese cities were limited to the North and Northwest; the first cities elsewhere were established in the upper reaches of the Han Basin during the Ch'un-ch'iu period (722–481 B.C.). During the Han dynasty, the most important migration route was that from Northwest China, then the metropolitan region, down the Han River valley and on southward up the Hsiang River valley into Lingnan. Accordingly, city building within the Middle Yangtze region was most advanced in the Han Basin and next most advanced in the Hsiang Basin. The Kan Basin to the east was somewhat further behind, while in the Corridor proper, where drainage problems slowed settlement, city-building activity accelerated only in the post-Han era (221–589). In the Yüan basin, the last of the Middle Yangtze subregions to be settled by Chinese, city building lagged and little progress was made until the medieval period.

Meanwhile, the Upper Yangtze had been settled from the Han Basin

---

* Chang's data are less than ideal for the purpose at hand. They omit entirely cities whose status in late Ch'ing was that of *chou* or *t'ing* capitals, and say nothing about the founding of capitals that by late Ch'ing times had lost their administrative status. However, rectification of these shortcomings would not greatly change the picture.

TABLE 1. HSIEN CAPITALS AS OF 1911 BY HISTORICAL PERIOD OF FIRST ESTABLISHMENT AND BY REGION, AGRARIAN CHINA EXCEPT MANCHURIA AND TAIWAN

Macroregion or subregion	A.D. 221		221–589		589–1280		1280–1911		Total	
	No.	Pct.	No.	Pct.	No.	Pct.	No.	Pct.	No.	Pct.
North China	305	78%	20	5%	48	12%	16	4%	389	100%
MY[a]: Han Basin	27	68	9	23	1	3	3	8	40	100
Northwest China	103	59	27	15	32	18	14	8	176	100
MY: Hsiang Basin	26	58	9	20	9	20	1	2	45	100
MY: Kan Basin	28	41	13	19	21	30	7	10	69	100
Lower Yangtze	49	40	23	19	35	28	17	14	124	100
Upper Yangtze	43	32	43	32	25	19	22	17	133	100
MY: Corridor	19	30	28	44	13	20	4	6	64	100
MY: Yüan Basin	8	23	3	9	8	23	16	46	35	100
Lingnan	27	19	32	22	50	35	35	24	144	100
Southeast Coast	10	11	20	21	33	35	32	34	95	100
Yun-Kwei	2	2	1	1	4	5	78	92	85	100

SOURCE: Data from the provincial maps included in Sen-dou Chang, "The Historical Trend of Chinese Urbanization," *Annals of the Association of American Geographers*, 53, no. 2 (June 1963). For the definition of the regions, see pp. 212–13 and the maps on pp. 214–15.

[a] MY = Middle Yangtze.

Introduction: Urban Development in Imperial China

as well as directly from Northwest China, and city building in the Upper Yangtze made particularly rapid progress when the Shu-Han kingdom was centered there (221–65) and again under the Eastern Chin (317–420). The Lower Yangtze had been settled gradually over a period of centuries by migrants from North China, but it was above all during the T'ang that its city system was fleshed out and showed rapid growth. Of the three southern regions, Lingnan, the first to be settled, had the largest complement of cities in A.D. 221. The Southeast Coast, which was settled primarily from the Lower Yangtze, but also from Lingnan and the Kan Basin, saw a rapid development of its city system during the medieval period. By Northern Sung times, the major north-south route for migration and trade went from North China, then the metropolitan region, to the Lower Yangtze, southward up the Kan River valley, and across the pass to Lingnan. This axis of development is reflected in the 589–1280 column by high percentages for the Lower Yangtze (28 percent), the Kan Basin (30 percent), and Lingnan (35 percent). Yun-Kwei was citified only after its incorporation in the empire by the Yüan.* In accounting for the heavy concentration of city building indicated for the Yüan basin in the late imperial era, we must remember that its population, like that of Yun-Kwei and western Lingnan, was only very partially sinified in the Ming-Ch'ing period.

In a sense, we can think of the physiographic subregions and macroregions as the "natural" vessels for territorially based socioeconomic systems—"empty" vessels whose potential for shaping and integrating human interaction was realized only as their space was "filled up" by Chinese settlement. But this metaphor should not be taken to imply historical inevitability or geographic determinism. As the imperial era ended, each of the nine physiographic regions I have delineated supported a socioeconomic system whose spatial structure was articulated more or less closely by an interrelated cluster of Chinese-style cities. This description of the outcome, however, in no sense implies that these nine geographic entities and no others were somehow predestined to become Chinese. To be sure, regions to the west and north of the river basins that are included in my macroregions were for reasons of climate unsuited to the Chinese form of sedentary agriculture and hence to Chinese settlement on any scale. But there is no reason of geography why the Yun-Kwei plateau should have ended up Chinese and Tonkin not;

---

* There can be no doubt that walled cities were built in Yun-Kwei during the Nan-chao and Ta-li periods. The extent to which they were Chinese-style cities is not entirely clear, but, as F. W. Mote has pointed out in a personal communication, experience with city building during preceding centuries may well have facilitated the remarkably rapid citification of the region after the Yüan conquest.

and whether much of Manchuria was "suited" to Chinese-style agriculture became clear only around the turn of the century, when Chinese pioneers cleared the forests and laid out their farms. Geographic conditions set limits to Chinese settlement and expansion, but so did the demography of neighboring peoples and the power of neighboring states. One can easily imagine scenarios that would have precluded Chinese dominance in Yun-Kwei and Manchuria or have yielded in Lingnan a Chuang state that was no more sinicized than the Vietnamese state in Tonkin. And of course mention of the Chuang reminds us that the physiographic "vessels" of what became agrarian China had by no means been empty of people prior to Han Chinese settlement.

Nonetheless, knowing in advance the extent of the domain within which the Chinese were destined during the imperial era to achieve and sustain both numerical and political dominance, one is struck by the overwhelming importance of physiographic structure in shaping regional economies and regional social systems. Such systems developed first in smaller physiographic units, often the basins of short rivers or tributaries; such isolated systems were subsequently linked with others to form larger systems, again contained in and constrained by the hierarchical physiographic structure. The processes whereby subregional socioeconomic systems were integrated to form the great regional economies that eventually developed within macroregions were gradual and, for most of agrarian China, still very much under way in the nineteenth century. What makes these processes seem inexorable in geographic terms is not only that a single autonomous socioeconomy eventually grew up in each of the nine macroregions* but also that the subregional systems that came to dominate regions, and the regional systems that eventually dominated macroregions, were in most cases those endowed by physiography with superior potential for production and exchange.

Having said this, I must qualify it in two directions. First, what constituted superior potential was very much a function of the Chinese cultural repertoire—above all, the technology and social organization of

---

* In understanding why regional economies in China came to correspond closely with physiographic regions, we should keep in mind the unity of the empire throughout most of the centuries since the Sui reunification. The contrast with Europe is instructive. The development of an integrated regional economy and of a single urban system within the basin of the Danube or of the Rhine was hindered throughout most of European history by the subdivision of these physiographic macroregions among the jurisdictions of several often antagonistic states. But in China, international frontiers, with their potential for obstructing trade and political transactions, almost never cut across physiographic regions. Even during the period of division from 1127 to 1280, the Southern Sung empire consisted essentially of five intact macroregions—Lingnan, the Southeast Coast, and the three Yangtze regions.

Introduction: Urban Development in Imperial China 13

production and exchange. One thinks in this regard of the ability eventually to drain and tame swampy lowlands, of a technology more sophisticated in its application to water transport than to overland transport, and of the preference for siting cities and towns on waterways—a predilection resting on ideological considerations as well as on practical requirements of the peculiarly Chinese modes of defending and provisioning cities. Second, internal physiographic structure was far more sharply defined in some macroregions than in others. The Middle Yangtze and the Southeast Coast were strongly subregionalized by topography, as to a lesser extent were Lingnan, the Upper Yangtze, and Northwest China. In two of these regions, the Upper Yangtze and the Southeast Coast, the location of major cities appears virtually preordained by the structure of the river systems. By contrast, physiographic constraints on the development of socioeconomic subregions were weak in the Lower Yangtze and negligible in North China. In consequence, the number and extent of subregions, as well as their internal structure, have been unstable in these two macroregions during medieval and late imperial times. The dominance of particular regions and their central cities has shifted from one period to another, and the scope for politico-military factors in the determination of superior potential has been correspondingly great. In North China and to a lesser extent in the Lower Yangtze, the superior potential for production and exchange enjoyed by particular subregional systems has depended as much on imperial favor as on physiographic endowment.

China's first urban systems developed in North and Northwest China with centers in the western flood plains of the Yellow River and in the lower Wei River valley, respectively. But these systems were initially quite circumscribed, and it was not until Han times, after nearly a millennium of urban development, that they had expanded to the point where each served the macroregion as a whole. Arguably, a *well-integrated* macroregion-wide urban system may have been achieved in Northwest China only during the T'ang and in North China only during the Northern Sung. In the development of other macroregional systems—everywhere a gradual process apart from late-blooming Manchuria—we may discern two distinctive patterns. In three regions—the Upper Yangtze, Lingnan, and Manchuria—the central city of the first urban system to emerge was destined to retain its supremacy and become the macroregional metropolis. Despite radical differences in timing, the development of an integrated urban system in these cases can be characterized as the gradual extension of the maximal hinterland of the original central city—Chengtu, Canton, and Mukden, respectively—

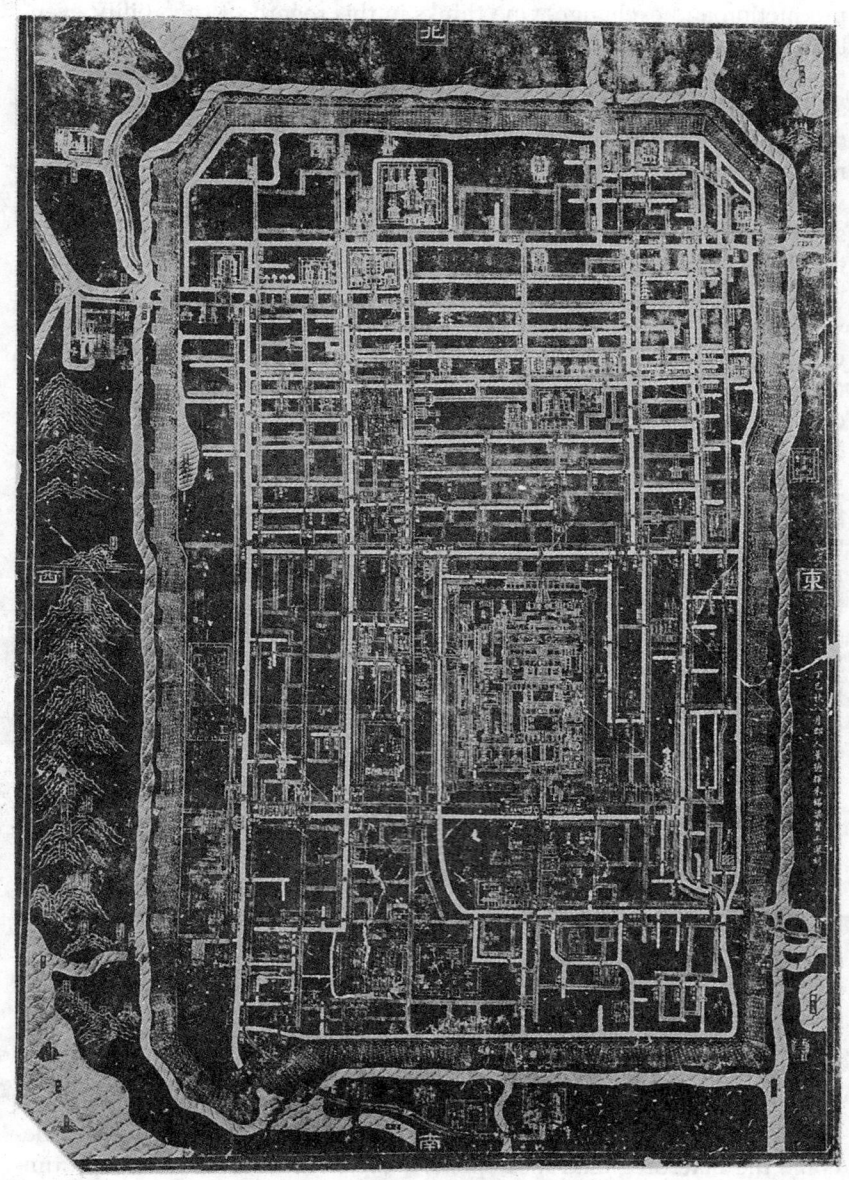

FIG. 1. P'ING-CHIANG T'U PEI. MAP OF SOOCHOW, 1229. Rubbing in possession of the Academia Sinica, Taiwan.

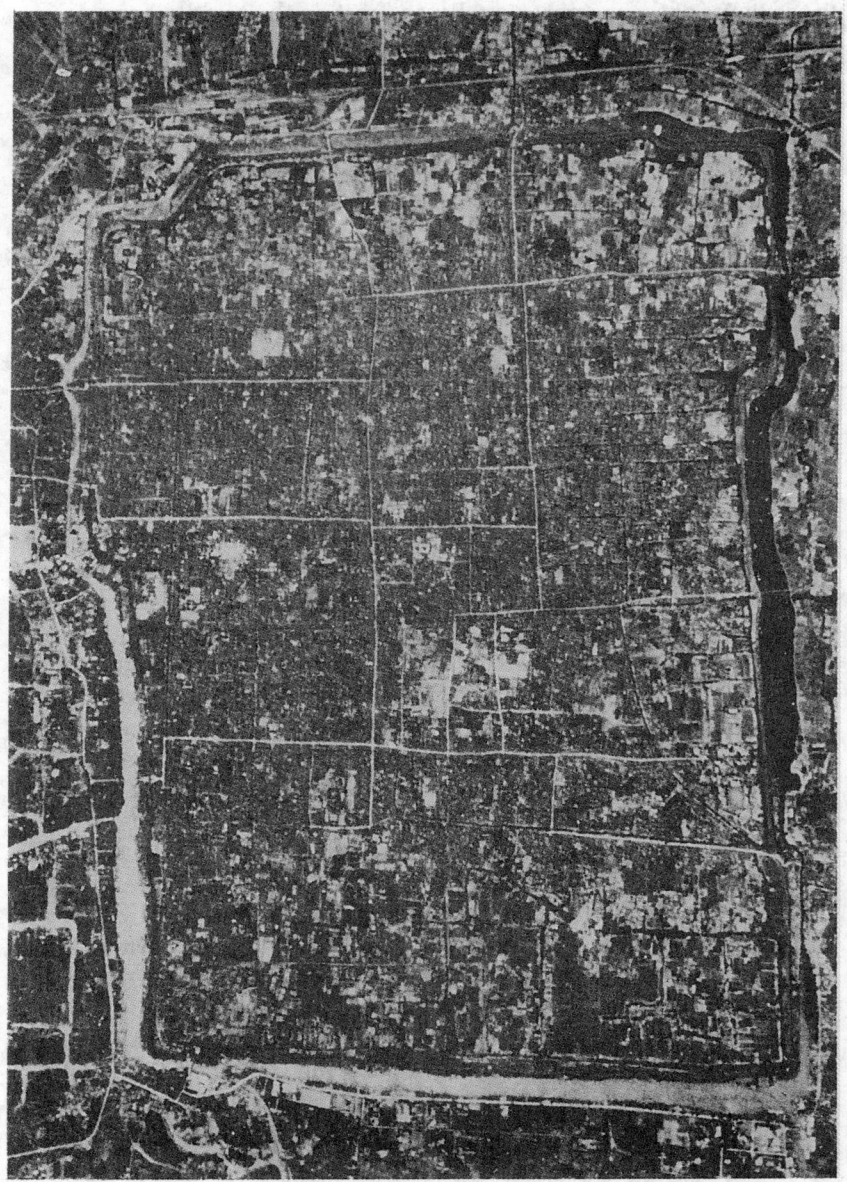

FIG. 2. AERIAL PHOTOGRAPH OF SOOCHOW, 1945. From U.S. Army, Fourteenth Air Force, World War II Archives, courtesy Department of Defense and F. W. Mote.

to the limits of the macroregion. By contrast, in the Middle Yangtze, the Southeast Coast, and Yun-Kwei, the problematic historical process was the integration of the essentially autonomous economies that developed in the sharply defined subregions. Thus, for instance, despite the antiquity of Chinese settlement in at least two subregions of the Middle Yangtze, it was not until the Ch'ing period that Wuhan's commercial hegemony was extended throughout most of the macroregion.

I am prepared to argue, although space does not permit me to do so here, that much of the flux of economic and social history in imperial China, urban phenomena included, falls into meaningful temporal patterns when the data are first specified by physiographic region. In a word, it seems to me that the economic development, demographic history, and sociopolitical dynamics of each region have displayed a distinctive rhythm. These regional cycles were associated in medieval and late imperial times with the buildup of an urban system centered on a particular apex city and with its subsequent (at least partial) breakdown. We may illustrate by brief reference to two regions.

North China experienced a prototypical cycle of urban development between the eighth and the thirteenth centuries.[9] Its upswing was marked by the growth of a complex regional economy and an elaborate transport network centered on Kaifeng, by a regional population increase from approximately 20 million to over 33 million, and by a 15-fold increase in the population of Kaifeng.[10] Its downswing involved the disruption of trade and transport, the collapse of the Kaifeng market, and the eventual destruction of most of the region's cities at the hands of Mongol invaders. At the cycle's nadir, the regional population had fallen to approximately 11 million and Kaifeng's population had been reduced to 90,000 from a previous high of nearly ten times that.[11] In the subsequent history of the North China region, Peking assumed the central integrating role that had been Kaifeng's during the medieval cycle, and changes in trading patterns and the transport grid clearly reflected this radical shift. The region experienced two major developmental cycles during the late imperial era. The first, which got under way in the mid-fifteenth century, was checked by epidemics, rebellions, and invasion during the decades from 1580 to 1660; and the second was brought to a close by the Taiping and Nien rebellions and by subsequent disasters after 1850. Each of these developmental cycles was accompanied by a demographic cycle—the region's population peaked at about 25 million in the 1580's and at about 120 million in the 1850's—and an urban cycle, in the course of which the region's city trading systems were subject to recurring transformation and reorientation.

Developmental cycles in the Lower Yangtze, though less pronounced

Introduction: Urban Development in Imperial China

than those in North China, were likewise associated with the ascendancy of particular cities.[12] During the cycle of late T'ang and Northern Sung, the relatively complex urban system that developed was focused on Yangchow as the central metropolis. The designation of Hangchow as the Southern Sung capital touched off the upswing of a developmental cycle during which the urban structure was reoriented toward the imperial capital. Hangchow remained the regional metropolis until the fourteenth century, when the far-reaching changes effected by the Ming founder, described in detail in Mote's paper below, initiated yet another cycle of development, one in which a vastly enlarged Nanking played the central role. The longer and somewhat more dramatic developmental cycle that began in the sixteenth century and was brought to a disastrous conclusion by the Taiping Rebellion in the nineteenth saw Soochow rise to prominence as the regional metropolis. And the post-Taiping cycle, which very quickly moved into the modern era of mechanized transport and industry, was intimately associated with the rise of Shanghai.

The Lower Yangtze case is notable in that repeated restructuring of the region's urban system never entailed the eclipse of any one of its several great cities. A notable case in point is Soochow. A picture map of that city engraved on stone in 1229 is juxtaposed with an aerial photograph made in 1945 in Figures 1 and 2 (pp. 14 and 15).[13] The stability of urban form they document is extraordinary. Walls, moats, streets, and canals are very nearly identical. A few minor differences can be detected in the number and location of gates, but the only major change is the removal of an inner-city wall originally built to enclose the offices of civil government—a change ordered in 1368 by the Ming founder to eradicate the associations of that seat of power with a recently eliminated rival. In fact, the Soochow walls had been rebuilt in 922 in the precise location and approximate size maintained throughout the subsequent millennium. During these centuries the city's population rose and fell—from approximately 200,000 in 922 to some 700,000 in 1850, declining thereafter to perhaps 400,000 at the time of the 1945 photograph. But both before and after its heyday as the Lower Yangtze's central metropolis, Soochow maintained its standing as a commercial and political center of major importance.

The Limited Proliferation of Capital Cities

The spread of cities throughout agrarian China has been described as an amoebalike process.[14] According to conventional wisdom, the *hsien* of the Ch'in unifiers, direct descendants of feudal town-hinterland compartments, resembled cells, each a self-contained economic as well as political unit in which virtually all central functions were concentrated in the *hsien* capital. As settlement spread outward, the cells proliferated; and as population grew, the cells subdivided. Thus the county-level unit has been the great constant of Chinese society, its late imperial manifestation being basically similar to that of Ch'in China, though found on a subcontinental scale.

One of the many deficiencies of this metaphor is that it says nothing about the process of replication, not even which came first, the nucleus or the protoplasm. In Wright's account, the protoplasm preceded the nucleus, that is, the settlement and growth of an agricultural population preceded the establishment of a walled city. The sharp contrast he draws with Roman practice in this regard may be a bit overdone. Walled "centers of imperial authority" were also built to deny the control of frontier areas to powerful enemies and to pacify unruly aboriginal populations. Moreover, in many instances of military colonization, the construction of a walled city accompanied rather than followed the founding of the colony of soldier-farmers;[15] and some of the fortress cities built in coastal areas to control pirates subsequently attracted agricultural settlement and were eventually converted into *hsien* capitals. Nonetheless, the usual pattern is that described by Wright and illustrated by Lamley's accounts of Hsin-chu and I-lan. The site of the new capital was less likely to be a "stockaded village," as Wright puts it, and more likely to be a substantial town, as Mote points out, as we move from north to south and from earlier to later centuries in the imperial era.

The kernel of truth in the cell-replication metaphor is that, as one would expect on first principles, new seats of government were established as settlement expanded into the frontier. G. Edward Stephan has recently developed a theory about the government's ability to enforce its regulations over distance and has applied it to the historical process of dividing American states into county jurisdictions.[16] A comparable model of the economics of revenue extraction has been developed by Joseph B. R. Whitney for application to county-level units in China.[17] Both theories predict that as the settled area expands into the frontier beyond the range of governmental effectiveness, new counties will be created in the outlying area unless transport improvements make this no longer necessary. In general, segmental growth has proceeded in China in accordance with this expectation, with the important exception that from late medieval times on, the number of new counties established in outlying areas has been consistently smaller than predicted by theory. No known transport improvements could account for this growing discrepancy.

To understand this discrepancy we must first confront a more serious difficulty with the cell-replication view of territorial expansion in China. This view implies a steady increase in the number of county-level units as settlement expanded and population grew in previously settled areas. Yet the record shows a remarkable stability in the number of county-level units throughout imperial history. Taking the approximate figure that applied during the heyday of each dynasty, we find 1,180 in Han, 1,255 in Sui, 1,235 in T'ang, 1,230 in Sung, 1,115 in Yüan, 1,385 in Ming, and 1,360 in Ch'ing.[18] If new counties were continually being founded as the frontier expanded, then clearly the number of counties in the already settled areas was being regularly reduced. And that is exactly what the history of Chinese field administration shows: the continual consolidation of county-level units in the regional cores. Not only were counties seldom subdivided (in amoebalike fashion or otherwise), but they actually grew larger across dynasties. North China counties inherited from the feudal era were consolidated during the Han; counties established in the Han were merged during the T'ang; and so on. The stability of the county-level unit in Chinese history is illusory.

In theory, the average area of counties in China should have declined steadily over the centuries. In fact, the average gradually increased, for the total area incorporated within the 1,360 county-level units of 1730 was far greater than that incorporated within the 1,235 counterpart units a millennium earlier. Why the discrepancy between theoretical expectations and the Chinese record? The explanation is simple enough. The theory assumes a constant level of government effectiveness—ongoing administrative services that remain steady on a per capita basis. It fails precisely because Chinese history saw a secular decline in governmental effectiveness from mid-T'ang on to the end of the imperial era, a steady reduction in basic-level administrative central functions from one era to the next.

And why did that occur? The answer almost certainly relates to problems of control within the governmental apparatus. We may get an idea of the growing magnitude of the problem by considering the population increase that accompanied settlement expansion. In a wavelike growth pattern that subsumed the various regional rhythms, the population of the empire peaked out roughly as follows: 60 million in A.D. 180, 80 million in 875, 110 million in 1190, 200 million in 1585, and 425 million in 1850.[19] In A.D. 180 the empire was divided into approximately 1,180 county-level units, yielding an average county population of approximately 50,000. To have maintained bureaucratic administration at the intensity of a basic-level yamen for every 50,000 of the population on the average would have required 1,600 counties in 875, 2,200 counties in 1190, 4,000 counties in 1585, and 8,500 counties in 1850. A corresponding increase in the number of higher-level yamens would also have been necessary to maintain a reasonable level of supervision over the basic-level yamens. For instance, if the average number of county-level units within each prefectural-level unit were held constant at six, then somewhat fewer than 200 prefectural-level yamens would have been required for 1,180 counties, whereas over 1,400 would have been needed for 8,500 counties. Applied to late Ch'ing, then, these assumptions imply a field administration with nearly 10,000 subprovincial yamens, not counting those of circuit intendants.

My argument is that such growth in the scale of field administration, involving not only a proliferation of yamens but also an expansion of the ranked bureaucracy and of subbureaucratic personnel, would have taxed communication facilities to the breaking point and posed problems of coordination and control beyond the capabilities of any agrarian state.* Moreover, the enlarged officialdom could only have been supported by raising the extraction rate in the form of extralegal exactions as well as agricultural and business taxes. Higher extraction rates across the board would have served not only to depress peasant living standards but also to reduce the take of local gentry and traders; and problems of controlling the consequent disaffection at the local level would doubtless have been the undoing of any ruling house. These considerations, then, can account for the fact that new counties established on the expanding frontier fell increasingly short of the number predicted by theory during the last millennium of the imperial era. Had counties been established at the rate needed (1) to maintain the government's ability to enforce its regulations at the local level (Stephan's theory) or (2) to achieve revenue extraction at a level commensurate with the

* The issues are complex, but the gist of the argument is apparent from Blau's generalizations that in organizations "increasing size generates structural differentiation," which in turn "enlarges the administrative component"; from Downs's Law of Diminishing Control ("The larger any organization becomes, the weaker is the control over its actions exercised by those at the top") and Law of Decreasing Coordination ("The larger any organization becomes, the poorer is the coordination among its actions"); and from Kasarda's conclusions that the most prominent of the organizational changes that accompany increasing size concern communication, and that any economies of scale are normally exceeded by "the marginal costs (in terms of manpower) of larger clerical and professional staffs." See Peter M. Blau, "A Formal Theory of Differentiation in Organizations," *American Sociological Review*, 35, no. 2 (Apr. 1970): 201–18; Anthony Downs, *Inside Bureaucracy* (Boston: Little, Brown, 1967), pp. 140–43; and John D. Kasarda, "The Structural Implications of Social Systems Size: A Three-Level Analysis," *American Sociological Review*, 39, no. 1 (Feb. 1974): 26–27.

administrative costs of collecting it (Whitney's theory), problems of both bureaucratic and popular control would have grown intolerable owing to the overlarge absolute size of the field administration. Thus counties were established on the peripheries at lower than expected rates for the same reason that counties were consolidated at the cores. On this reading, a unified empire could be maintained on into the late imperial era only by systematically reducing the scope of basic-level administrative functions and countenancing a decline in the effectiveness of bureaucratic government within local systems.

The historical record provides circumstantial evidence in support of this argument. In the case of several dynasties, the initial reorganization of field administration divided the imperial domain into over 1,500 county-level units, but within a few decades consolidation brought their number down within the magic range already cited. Thus (using approximate figures only), the 1,580 units of early Han were reduced to 1,180 in 143 B.C.; the 1,550 units of early T'ang were down to 1,235 by 713; and the 1,510 units of early Ch'ing were down to 1,360 by 1730.[20] It is as though each of these "strong" dynastic regimes attempted at first to maintain the same level of administrative intensity as its predecessor only to be forced by bureaucratic problems within the augmented field administration to retrench to a level appropriate to an expanded domain and larger population. Further telling evidence comes from periods of disunity, when the country was divided into two or more empires, each with its own bureaucracy. If constraints of organizational scale were the operative factor, repeatedly frustrating the court's desire to maintain earlier levels of governmental effectiveness and administrative intensity at the local level, then we would expect the number of county-level units in the various coexisting empires to exceed the levels that obtained during the universal empires. In at least one case this expectation is borne out. During the sixth century, China was divided among three kingdoms, known to history as Ch'en, Northern Chou, and Northern Ch'i. County-level units in the three kingdoms together totaled approximately 2,300, in sharp contrast to the 1,255 *hsien* in the unified field administration of the Sui after the reorganization of 605.[21]

Whether or not my explanation is the whole story, the fact is that the number of administrative cities throughout the empire—periods of disunity aside—remained more or less constant throughout the medieval and late imperial eras.[22] The implications for urban development may be pointed up by returning to the hypothetical cellular *hsien* of the early empire. Let us assume that economic as well as administrative functions were largely confined to the county capital. In the case of larger counties, at least, this would have been possible only if villages at any distance from the capital were largely self-sufficient; and one would expect their few needs for exogenous products (salt, plowshares, etc.) to have been met by itinerant peddlers based in the county capital. It should be clear that secular growth in population, other things being equal, would raise the total demand within the county. If we also posit a rise in commercialization whereby an increasing proportion of village households became dependent on commercial channels for consumption goods or production factors (or the same proportion became more dependent), then the demand density would increase that much more rapidly than the population density. If the population of the cell increased in the course of a few centuries by 50 percent and the level of commercialization doubled (a change that might well have occurred in the average North China county during the Northern Sung or in the average Lower Yangtze county during the Southern Sung), then the demand density would have tripled. How would such a growth in demand be met? Even in the relatively densely settled core areas of North and Northwest China, county capitals were spaced quite far apart, and elsewhere the county "cells" were on the average much larger.[23] Since it would have been quite impracticable for villagers in outlying districts to visit markets in the county capitals for their everyday needs, one would expect new trading centers to have sprung up near the borders of counties where the untapped demand was greatest. In the absence of any reduction in the size of the administrative cells—or, to put it another way, if the new economic central places were not also co-opted to serve as capitals of newly formed counties—the economic integrity of the county cell would be shattered.

Even during early T'ang the facts are at odds with the model of uniform, self-contained county cells. As Denis Twitchett makes clear, a number of higher-order capitals served hinterlands that extended far beyond the metropolitan counties, and such cities, like the imperial capital, normally supported more than one market.[24] In sparsely peopled and peripheral areas, on the other hand, many county capitals and even some prefectural capitals had no markets at all.[25] Nonetheless, in many respects the typical county in the core of a developing region was an economic as well as an administrative unit, and central functions in both realms tended to be monopolized by the county capital.[26] By government regulations, an officially controlled market was to be located in the capital and none was permitted outside it. Since local taxes were largely collected in kind, and a good deal of local revenue was disbursed locally, a certain portion of the county's surplus production found its way back into circulation within the county. Moreover, since local officials were responsible for the upkeep, improvement, and regulation of communications, the network of local roads and waterways was more strictly town-centered than might otherwise have been the case. The county capital, then, with its concentration of nonproductive consumers and its nodal position in the local transport network, was normally both the natural collecting and distributing center for local produce and the point of connection with longer-distance trade flows.

The official market system of the early T'ang, in large part a continuation of Han institutions, was part of an elaborate apparatus for regulating the commercial activities of the empire.[27] In capital cities of any considerable size, the official markets were walled, forming an integral part of the walled-ward system, which enabled officials to regulate the hours of trading and the movements of buyers and sellers alike. The market director, a ranked bureaucrat in the case of first-class prefectural and higher-order capitals, was charged with responsibility for virtually all aspects of commerce: the quality of money, the accuracy of weights and measures, the prevention of unfair business practices, the registration and control of brokers, and the control of prices. Twitchett has mustered data indicating that in the first half of the eighth century the official regulations relating to markets were carefully enforced in at least some small and fairly remote towns.[28]

The Medieval Urban Revolution

We have introduced the major considerations that provide a context for the key institutional changes described by scholars of medieval China as having begun during the second half of the eighth century and culminated during the Southern Sung. Mote refers in his paper to the pioneering work of Katō Shigeshi in identifying many of these changes and pointing up their significance. The subsequent masterly analyses of Denis Twitchett for the T'ang and Shiba Yoshinobu for the Sung provide a solid basis for understanding what Mark Elvin calls the "medieval revolution in market structure and urbanization."[29] Its salient features[30] were (1) a relaxation of the requirement that each county could maintain only one market, which had to be located in the capital city; (2) the breakdown and eventual collapse of the official marketing organization; (3) the disappearance of the enclosed marketplace, along with the walled-ward system, and their replacement by "a much freer street plan in which trade and commerce could be conducted anywhere within the city or its outlying suburbs";[31] (4) the rapid expansion of particular walled cities and the growth of commercial suburbs outside their gates; and (5) the emergence of "great numbers of small and intermediate-sized towns" with important economic functions.³² These changes, as Twitchett shows,³³ were accompanied by the increased monetization of taxation and trade; by a growth in the numbers, wealth, and power of merchants; and by a softening of social and official attitudes disparaging trade and the merchant class.*

These trends are well and convincingly documented in the literature, but it is worth specifying the spatial and temporal coordinates of the evidence. Imperial policy aside, the developments on which these analyses rest—i.e., the specific facts documented by primary sources—almost all relate to the upswing and heyday of regional cycles. The great majority of examples are drawn from the Northwest during the ascendant phases of the Ch'ang-an cycle (up to 900), from North China during the ascendant phases of the Kaifeng cycle (up to 1100), from the Lower Yangtze during the ascendant phases of the successive Yangchow and Hangchow cycles (up to 1300), and from the Southeast Coast during the ascendant phases of its Ch'üan-chou cycle (also up to 1300).† During the upswing of each of these regional cycles, population and commercialization increased dramatically, both approximating a logistic growth curve. Meanwhile, the reorganization of the field administrative system effected by the T'ang in A.D. 713 had involved considerable consolidation of counties in the cores of the regions in question, and to the end of the medieval period there was if anything a trend toward further reduction in the number of county-level units in the more developed regions. The predominant trends in these regions during the specified periods, then, were demographic and commercial expansion coupled with administrative consolidation.

What happened, it seems to me, is just what might be expected. Given the growing scale of commerce and the decline in the number of yamens per unit of population, the system of administered trade became increasingly arduous and expensive to enforce. Through a process of trial and error—the secular trend was punctuated by the periodic reimposition of controls—there occurred a general withdrawal by government from

---

* Professor Shiba would doubtless add to this list the development of a national market. I agree that the growth in specialized production for export and the increase in extraregional trade were critical components of the late medieval economic revolution and can be said to have moved the Chinese economy in the direction of a national market. But I follow conventional usage in speaking of the emergence of a national market in China only after 1895, when the economic centrality of Shanghai began to expand decisively beyond the Lower Yangtze region.

† During the thirteenth century, the heyday of an extraordinarily long cycle of development in the Southeast Coast, Ch'üan-chou was the region's central metropolis and, in all probability, the largest port in China.

Introduction: Urban Development in Imperial China 25

the minute regulation of commercial affairs. By late T'ang, Twitchett argues, it was generally accepted that "since trade could neither be suppressed nor adequately controlled, such control had best be abandoned and commerce exploited as a source of revenue."[34] With the wraps off, and under conditions of accelerating commercialization, the specifics of the medieval urban revolution logically follow. It is necessary only to specify in somewhat more analytical terms the changes listed above as (4) and (5). The cities that grew most rapidly were those that emerged as important economic central places for their regions, and it was outside the gates of these cities—in particular, of course, the gates providing access to major trade routes—that the more spectacular commercial suburbs developed. Not all cities grew at the same rate, nor did all cities acquire new central functions. What these changes reflect is not uniform increased growth in size and complexity but rather differentiation of higher-level central places by economic function. Functional differentiation also characterized the proliferation of rural markets, as the more advantageously situated towns grew to considerable size and began providing central services to their smaller (and usually more recently established) neighbors. A fundamental component of the urban revolution, then, was the development of a more fully differentiated hierarchy of economic central places articulating the various regional economies.

Much of what happened has been summed up by saying that "commerce spilled out of cities"; but one could also say, and thereby come closer to the whole truth, that all kinds of central functions and services spilled out of walled capitals for the simple reason that new capitals were not created "as needed." In his study of the T'ang system of marketing, Twitchett concludes that "official involvement in the organization of commerce can . . . be shown to exemplify the way in which the T'ang administration deliberately delimited its involvement in local matters to a restricted area in which its authority could be exercised effectively."[35] My point is that this area, which was by no means limited to commercial matters, grew increasingly restricted in subsequent dynastic eras. That is, I see a long-term secular trend beginning in the T'ang whereby the degree of official involvement in local affairs—not only in marketing and commerce but also in social regulation (e.g., dispute resolution) and administration itself—steadily declined, a retrenchment forced by the growing scale of empire.

The new central places that emerged on the landscape were not only market towns, i.e., not only economic central places; other "urban" functions that had once been largely limited to capitals devolved on them as well. We can turn the whole matter around and say that the level of intensity of urban functions held steady or even increased from early T'ang to the end of the medieval cycle, and that the really significant change was a steady retrenchment of the bureaucratic government's role in all of those functions—administrative and social as well as economic. The urban systems that had developed by the eve of the Mongol conquest included a far greater number of central places than had existed in the sixth century—perhaps 6,000 as against 1,500. The great cities were greater, the urban population vastly enlarged, the integration of city systems much tighter; but perhaps the most significant change of all was the greatly reduced proportion of central places that were capitals. For this feature of urban development signaled an ongoing revolution in the manner in which the entire society was managed.

Late Imperial Urban Development

Those components of the "medieval urban revolution" that involved official policy were forced, it seems to me, by the burgeoning commercialization of China's most "advanced" regional economies during ascendant phases of their developmental cycles. In arguing that the retreat from administered trade was part of a governmental retrenchment that was comprehensive (i.e., affected all aspects of local affairs) and persistent (i.e., continued on through the late imperial era, being a response to the growing scale of empire), I mean to account for the essential irreversibility of the policy shift that occurred between the eighth century and the thirteenth. Under conditions of premodern technology and imperial unity, commerce outside capital cities would never again be suppressed, nor would a system of administered trade be reinstituted.

At the same time, it would be a grievous error to imagine that, *policy aside*, the medieval urban revolution had been completed or even had taken place in all or even most of China during medieval times. Levels of commercialization comparable to those achieved in the core areas of the Lower Yangtze during the Southern Sung were attained in the central areas of other macroregions only during the Ming or the Ch'ing. Not only did the interior regions generally lag behind those on the coast, but regional developments were often poorly synchronized. For instance, in the tenth century Northwest China suffered an economic depression while North China's economy boomed, and in the twelfth century the Lower Yangtze prospered while North China languished, with the result that urbanization was delayed in most of North and Northwest China. Finally, the urbanizing effects of commercialization varied with the internal structure of each macroregion, being far weaker

Introduction: Urban Development in Imperial China 27

in the peripheral areas at any given time than in the regional heartland. Thus, at a time in the tenth century, say, when market towns were springing up like mushrooms in the hinterland of Yangchow, there were counties around the periphery of the Lower Yangtze region that could support no market at all, not even in the county capital. We come down, then, to the paradox that, apart from the relaxation of governmental regulation, most parts of China experienced the "medieval" urban revolution only during late imperial times. Urban development during the Ming-Ch'ing period was largely an extension and intensification of processes already manifest during medieval times at the cores of the economically most advanced regions.

The regional developmental cycles that I have illustrated above and that I characterize more fully in my Part One paper were no less prominent in late imperial than in medieval times. As of early Ming, however, they had been brought into extraordinary if deleterious synchrony. The Mongol invasions of the thirteenth century had brought regional development to a halt in three macroregions and had had an adverse if less severe impact in all but three of the remainder. Then, beginning early in the fourteenth century under the Yüan and continuing through the fifteenth century under the Ming, there occurred a basic shift in imperial policy in the direction of reducing foreign contact and foreign trade.[36] Though the impact of this official isolationism was heaviest in the Southeast Coast, it was also substantial in Lingnan and significant in the Lower Yangtze and the Northwest. These two factors, the Mongol invasion and mid-Ming foreign policy, largely account for the devolutionary trend of the centuries from 1200 to 1500.[37] The most important of the linkages among China's regional economies was of course trade, and the combined effect of these two factors was an overall decline and stagnation in interregional as well as foreign trade. Thus, devolutionary trends in one region tended to corrode development in its neighbors, and the baleful influence of economic isolation came to be felt everywhere. Even in the Lower Yangtze, where interdynastic devastation was minor and where the centuries in question witnessed the peak years of two resplendent capitals, Hangchow and Nanking, a certain stagnation in the economy was evident. As Professor Shiba demonstrates in Part Two of this volume, the number of market towns in Ning-po prefecture remained practically unchanged between 1227 and 1465. There is every indication that in agrarian China as a whole this was the rule rather than the exception.

There is some justification, then, for periodizing the history of urban and regional development since the Sui reunification into two great eras separated by a dark age of devolution and depression, and even for speaking of two great macrocycles of development in agrarian China as a whole. A systematic comparison of the two eras, taking regional differences into account and controlling for phases in the two developmental macrocycles, suggests a number of propositions, some of which are addressed by the contributors to this volume. First, as Wright indicates, the medieval era saw a progressive departure from cosmologically proper principles of city planning, whereas the late imperial era was characterized by a deliberately restorationist adherence to orthodox norms. Second, the regional city systems that developed in the medieval era were immature and uneven: capitals and market towns were only very imperfectly meshed into an integrated system, and the urban population as a whole was concentrated in the largest cities. By contrast, city systems of the late imperial era were more mature and more fully fleshed out: capitals and market towns were better integrated into a single hierarchical system, and the total urban population was more evenly distributed throughout the hierarchy.[38] Third, foreign trade and technological advance, although the most important urbanizing factors throughout the imperial era, were far more significant in medieval times than in late imperial times, when the development of urban systems was more closely dependent on population growth, rural commercialization, and interregional as opposed to foreign trade. Fourth, the levels of urbanization achieved in the most advanced regions were higher in the medieval era than in late imperial times.

This last generalization may appear paradoxical, but the evidence points strongly in that direction, and a secular decline is by no means implausible. The estimates presented in my paper below indicate an urbanization rate for the Lower Yangtze, the most urbanized region, of less than 8 percent in the 1840's. Rather extensive circumstantial evidence for the same region as of the thirteenth century suggests a rate of at least 10 percent and probably a good deal more. In 1100, nearly 3 percent of the population of North China lived in Kaifeng, the regional metropolis.[39] In the 1840's, with the regional population swollen to approximately 120 million, the combined population of North China's top ten cities came to less than 2 percent of the total.[40] Not every region attained higher levels of urbanization prior to the late imperial era than during it; Yun-Kwei surely, and Lingnan probably, did not. But it is reasonable to expect (and indeed what evidence I have mustered suggests) that other regions more nearly followed the pattern of the Lower Yangtze and North China, where the evidence seems overwhelming for medieval rates surpassing anything attained in the late imperial era.

Introduction: Urban Development in Imperial China

If this conclusion is sustained, the explanation must lie chiefly in the declining stimulus to city development provided by foreign trade and by technological advance. These are certainly the factors on which Elvin would lay the heaviest emphasis.[41] Further, it seems probable, for reasons suggested earlier, that in the late imperial era growth in agricultural output outran the capacity of the state to extract a steady proportion as revenue. The number of yamens required to extract per-capita revenues in the Ch'ing comparable to those extracted in the T'ang could not have been supported without jeopardizing the survival of the state; thus the "surplus" itself declined as a proportion of total output and the government's share of that surplus declined relative to the share retained by local systems.[42] The medieval patterns of governmental expenditure favored urban growth, I argue, whereas the late imperial patterns of investment and redistribution within local systems favored balanced growth between market towns and villages. Thus urbanization suffered on two counts. First, in the absence of any appreciable increase in the number of capitals, the proportion of all central places that experienced the urbanizing effects of the presence of government offices steadily declined. And second, the urbanizing effects of governmental expenditure were less pronounced in late imperial times, having declined substantially in per-capita terms.

Interestingly enough, the greatest cities in late imperial China were little if any larger than those of medieval China. In my Part One paper, I estimate that in the 1840's China's four largest cities—Peking, Soochow, Canton, and the Wuhan conurbation—ranged in size from 850,000 down to 575,000. Contemporary population estimates for each of these cities do range up to or even exceed one million, but there are good reasons to prefer my more conservative figures. Each of these four metropolises was more populous in the 1840's than ever before. In the late imperial era, only Nanking was ever larger than these four cities; according to Mote, its population may have reached a peak of about one million in the second decade of the fifteenth century. Since Mote also believes that the population of Soochow in 1850 "may have been close to one million,"[43] whereas my considered estimate of Soochow's population in the 1840's is only 700,000, his scale of reference for city populations is seemingly more bullish across the board than mine. Either way, few would argue that in the late imperial era any city's population exceeded one million.[44]

The largest medieval cities were almost certainly larger. Once again, hyperbole in the sources is a problem, and enthusiastic writers have argued that at least a half dozen Chinese cities attained a population of a million or more during the medieval period.[45] But to my mind the evidence indicates that during medieval times only three cities could have been larger than fifteenth-century Nanking or nineteenth-century Peking. Nonetheless, even the moderately conservative figures that seem plausible to me—1.0 million for eighth-century Ch'ang-an; 850,000 for Kaifeng on the eve of the Jurchen invasion; and 1.2 million for Hangchow on the eve of the Mongol invasion—point to the paradoxical conclusion that the greatest cities of medieval China were if anything larger than their late imperial counterparts.

Why? The three cities in question, like fifteenth-century Nanking and nineteenth-century Peking, were imperial capitals at the time of their greatest size, and the effects of administrative centrality should have increased with growth over the centuries in the extent and population of the empire. Moreover, in considering the role of these cities as regional metropolises, we must recognize that the population of the metropolitan region was smaller for each of the medieval capitals than for either of the late imperial capitals.

One factor that might be thought relevant is the court's practice of forcibly transferring large populations to the recently established capital. However, though these transfers unquestionably accelerated the capital's rate of growth in the early decades, it is doubtful that they had much effect on the eventual maximum size of the city. In this regard, the population transfers to Nanking ordered by the Ming founder may have had a significant impact on that city's maximum size precisely because of its short life as an imperial capital. Moreover, Peking benefited from an analogous infusion of population after 1644 when large numbers of Manchus were installed in its northern city.

Probably the most important explanatory factor (apart from the general points made above concerning technology and foreign trade) is the capital's location in relation to its region. In a word, the medieval capitals were more centrally situated than their late imperial counterparts. Ch'ang-an was located near the center of the regional core in the Northwest; Kaifeng was far closer than Peking to the geographic center of North China; and Hangchow, at the southern terminus of the Grand Canal between Kiangnan's Golden Triangle and the rich prefectures of northeastern Chekiang, was more advantageously situated than Nanking, whose immediate hinterland, as Mote points out, "lacked the sources of wealth that characterize the Lower Yangtze generally." In fact, both Nanking and Peking were selected as imperial capitals primarily for strategic reasons, as Mote's paper makes clear. Kaifeng and Hangchow were far better situated than Peking and Nanking to serve

Introduction: Urban Development in Imperial China

as regional centers of trade, industry, and finance; moreover, each was already a thriving economic center at the time it was designated the capital. Thus location greatly enhanced the economic centrality of Kaifeng and Hangchow within their respective regions, making these cities truly multifunctional metropolises.[46] When we recall that the medieval era was far more cosmopolitan than the succeeding era, and that foreign trade was encouraged during the heydays of Ch'ang-an, Kaifeng, and Hangchow but discouraged by the dynasts of the Ming and Ch'ing, the importance for city growth of locating the imperial capital in a "natural" economic center is underlined.

Meanwhile, Great Han chauvinists may reflect with satisfaction that Nanking and Peking each ranked during its prime as the world's largest city, just as medieval Ch'ang-an, Kaifeng, and Hangchow had before them.[47] Nanking overtook Cairo as the largest city in the world within a decade or so of its rebuilding by the Ming founder, to be succeeded at some point in the fifteenth century by Peking. Except perhaps for short periods during the seventeenth century, when Agra, Constantinople, and Delhi challenged its preeminence, Peking remained the world's largest city until overtaken by London around 1800.[48]

The Cosmology of the Chinese City

ARTHUR F. WRIGHT

All civilizations have traditions for choosing a fortunate site for a city and symbol systems for relating the city and its various parts to the gods and to the forces of nature. In ancient times, when old religions are strong, a people's beliefs and value system are reflected in where they locate a city and how they design it. Generally, as a civilization develops, the authority of the ancient beliefs wanes and secular concerns—economic, strategic, and political—come to dominate the location and design of cities. In most societies, then, the influence of early religious concerns is only accidentally reflected in their later cities. But the history of Chinese civilization offers an exception to this general pattern. Throughout the long record of Chinese city building we find an ancient and elaborate symbolism for the location and design of cities persisting in the midst of secular change.

Before considering the long history of Chinese cities and their symbolism, we should mention several important facts that may help the reader both to differentiate Chinese cities from their better known Western counterparts and to locate the city and its cosmology within the total pattern of Chinese civilization. First, in taming a subcontinent over three millennia, the Chinese did not regard the city as the prime unit—practical or symbolic—of their penetration of new territory. The important step was the expansion of Chinese agriculture, which was centered in peasant villages. Later, when the land was tamed and the population stable and numerous, one stockaded village or another would be reconstructed as a center of imperial authority. (The Romans, by contrast, established a new *urbs* wherever their arms gained them the barest foothold in hostile territory.) Second, the Chinese city was constructed mainly of ephemeral materials; there was little effort, even in the building of capitals, to make of a city an "eternal" monument. Sites came in time to be revered for the accumulated memories of great events that had occurred there, but few physical reminders of the distant past survived in any city. Third, the cosmology of Chinese cities was made up of elements drawn from the core ideology of the Great Tradition—enriched at times by borrowings from the Little Traditions of the peasant villages, but scarcely at all by elements from alien civilizations. This core ideology was perpetuated by the literate elite, which survived the vicissitudes of time and clung to the body of norms embodied in its Classics. Yet it would seem that the cosmological ideas of the elite relating to the city were shared by other groups in society as well. In the second century A.D., for example, popular Taoist writings theorized about a utopian city, and a substratum of Taoist ideas persisted in the cosmology of the city. The artisans, the largely anonymous perpetuators of a continuous architectural tradition, were charged with applying these cosmological ideas to city building and undoubtedly influenced them in ways we have yet to discover.[1] Thus the ideas we shall consider were part of the world view of the Chinese of the Little Traditions and were not solely the property of the elite that systematized them.

What place did theories of the city have in the systematic writings of the elite? It was a cliché of imperial Confucianism that rural life fostered virtue while cities were centers of vice and corruption. This standard view was belied by the behavior of the elite in later dynasties, when they came to use cities as bases of their wealth and power; but perhaps this cliché accounts in part for the relatively insignificant place of city theory in the literary tradition. We have seen that the elite apparently did not monopolize this body of ideas, which was diffused among other classes and groups. This fact may have made the subject less attractive than those connected with morality, statecraft, history, and the arts—subjects of high prestige on which one could write with hope of renown and possibly immortality. Whether or not these are the reasons, theorizing about the city and its cosmology was a minor concern of the elite, though it is only from their records that we can reconstruct something of the evolution of cities and their symbolism.

This paper is divided into five parts. In the first, I consider evidences of city building from the earliest times to the end of the period of the Warring States, when a considerable body of lore and practice had accumulated. Next, after showing how this heritage fared in the upheavals of imperial unification, I deal briefly with the first capital of an enduring Chinese empire: Han Ch'ang-an. Third, I attempt to show how ancient traditions of cosmology and of the city were systematized by the Han Confucian synthesists. Fourth, I consider the mutations in city building and its theory in South China during the centuries following the collapse of the Han. Finally, I deal with the influence of earlier traditions on the building of selected cities from Sui to Ming.

Cosmological Elements in the Building of Early Cities

The legendary beginnings of Chou city building are evoked in the ode called "Mien" in the *Book of Songs*. There it is recounted that T'an-fu, grandfather of King Wen, led his people—who had previously lived in loess caves—to the foot of Mt. Ch'i on the north bank of the Wei River. On this site (the traditional date is 1352 B.C.) he took the oracle by tortoiseshell, and the answer was that the Chou people should build their houses there. Having divided the surrounding land among his people, he called in his builders and ordered them to build houses. "Dead straight was the plumb line." They used the pounded earth method to build the walls of the first building mentioned—the ancestral hall. Then came the work of building the city walls, and there is evidence of both an inner and an outer enclosure, each with a gate. Finally, "They raised the great earth-mound, whence excursions of war might start."[2] Although the ode was written down in a period much later than that of its subject, it evokes a fairly primitive stage of city building. The ritual-symbolic elements to be noticed are the taking of the oracle, the building in straight lines (this was also practical), the ancestral hall, and the great earth-mound.

The Chou people stayed here for a time, and then King Wen moved southeast across the Wei River to establish his capital of Feng. This is celebrated in the ode "Wen-wang yu sheng."[3] Feng may well have been a conquered city, for Legge remarks on the absence of any mention of divination before its establishment as capital, and this probably indicates that it was a preexisting city. There is no addition to the ritual-symbolic lore in this part of the ode. However, Feng did have a *ling-t'ai*, or magic tower.[4] In addition, there was at Feng a "hall with a circlet of water" (*pi-yung*), as Legge calls it, or a "moated mound" as Waley translates it in his version of "Ling-t'ai." Waley's note says that it "was a holy place surrounded by water, where the sons of the Chou royal house were trained in the accomplishments of manhood."[5] Legge has a similar explanation and adds that "the whole thing resembled a *peih* (= *pi*, the round jade symbol of rank), with a pavilion rising in the center of it."[6] At Feng it was the scene of music and festivity. Waley cites an inscription describing the king shooting wildfowl from a boat on the waters of the moated mound.[7]

King Wu, who succeeded King Wen, built his capital at Hao, to the east of the Feng River. According to the ode "Wen-wang yu sheng," he divined by the tortoise regarding the site. Further details, even of the legendary type found in the *Songs*, are few. King Wu, like King Wen before him, had his "hall with a circlet of water."

We should note that in these early and admittedly legendary accounts there are missing a good many ritual-symbolic elements later associated with the founding of cities: animal sacrifice, orientation, disposition in relation to hills and rivers, disposition in relation to astral phenomena, relation of palace to market, and so forth. Although this proves nothing, it is worth keeping in mind. For example, "Wen-wang yu sheng" says, apropos of Feng, "The Feng River flowed to the east of the city." This is simply a topographical statement and has no symbolic meaning.

At the next stage of the evolution of the ritual-symbolic complex we are on somewhat firmer, though by no means certain, ground. Two probably authentic books of the *Book of History* deal with the establishment of a second Chou capital at Lo, in what was formerly Shang territory. This is momentous historically, for it provides the precedent for establishing capitals in conquered country as a means of controlling both territory and people. The Duke of Chou is about to give up his regency, since King Ch'eng has come of age. The conquest of Shang has been accomplished, a revolt has been put down, and the consolidation of power must now begin. The tone of these two books is portentous, suited to the claims to dominion that the Chou were now making. Let us quote a solemn speech, which the Duke of Chou addresses to young King Ch'eng: "I report to you my son and bright sovereign. If the King will not settle in the place where Heaven founded the mandate and fixed the mandate [i.e., the western capital at Hao], I have...made a great survey of the eastern regions in order to found a place where he shall be the people's bright sovereign."[8]

The events relating to the choice and sanctification of the site and to the building of the city may be summarized from the "Shao kao" and "Lo kao" chapters.[9] The Grand Guardian, Duke of Shao, went ahead to search for auspicious sites. He arrived at Lo, took a tortoise oracle and, finding it favorable, planned the new city, determining the dimensions of the walls, the palace, the ancestral hall, and so forth. Then he put the Shang people (resettled here and now used as forced labor) to work laying out the city, "marking out on the ground the foundations of the various structures." The Duke of Chou arrived the day after this was completed to inspect it. Two days later he sacrificed two oxen[10] on the suburban altar, following this the next day with another sacrifice of one ox, one sheep, and one pig to the god of the soil in the new city. Six days later the Duke of Chou gave orders in writing regarding the recruitment of a labor force and the apportionment of work to the local chiefs of the Shang people. The laborers then began work. In his report to King Ch'eng, which is given in the "Lo kao" chapter, the Duke of Chou adds a few details. He recounts how he followed the Grand Guardian to Lo and then conducted an elaborate series of oracles, the results of which, together with a map, he had sent to the king. The king duly acknowledges all this, and says: "We two men have both verified the reading of the oracles." The Duke of Chou then says, "May the king in accordance with the rites of the Yin [Shang] make sacrifice in the new city. Range everything in order without confusion."

This sequence adds substantially to what could be learned from the legendary accounts. The Chou at Lo were establishing a city in former Shang territory, and some of the new elements of symbolism and ritual were almost certainly of Shang origin. Note the reference to "the rites of Yin" in the Duke of Chou's speech. There are four elements appearing for the first time in this text. First, the city was preplanned, and the plan was reduced to written form. Second, the proposed city was staked out on its site according to the plan. Third, when this had been completed, there were two sets of animal sacrifices. One set—probably to Heaven and the Chou primordial ancestor—took place at the altar outside the limits of the planned city, whereas the other set—fertility sacrifices—took place at the earth-mound that had been raised within. Fourth, the labor force was charged in advance with specific parts of the work.

It is with the building of this new city in the eastern plain that Chou and Shang ritual-symbolic practices are fully merged. Professor Kwang-chih Chang, in his notable book *The Archeology of Ancient China*, discusses the physical features and distribution of the several categories of early towns.[11] In their outlines we can discern several elements that are of ritual-symbolic significance. The first of these is the placing of the city in precise alignment with the four directions.[12] The second, which follows from the first, is the building of city walls in the form of a square or a rectangle. South is the ritually favored orientation of important excavated temples, halls, and tombs; we may infer that the cities, too, "faced south" and that their principal gate was in the south wall. The oracle bone inscriptions tell us nothing about rituals for the dedication of new cities, but the excavations at Anyang indicate the elaborate use of sacrificial victims, both human and animal, in the consecration of important buildings.[13] It is safe to infer that analogous ceremonies were conducted for the consecration of new walled cities. A third element that shows the merging of Chou and Shang ritual-symbolic practices is the use of divination. We know that divination was intensively used by the Shang in determining the auspices for undertakings of all kinds. Although we have no Shang oracle bone inscriptions concerned with siting a new city, such oracles were probably taken. The practice of bone and shell divination was borrowed by the Chou during their long period of development as a client civilization of the Shang. Thus the use of this technique for choosing city sites that we noted in the early Chou texts was probably a common Shang practice.

In the Eastern Chou period, from 771 B.C. on, the building of cities spread all over the North China Plain. Some of the cities were capitals of the various states—capitals frequently moved, destroyed, and rebuilt. Others were lesser towns, and some were basically citadels against "barbarian" incursions. In this period the number of walled towns within a state became a measure of its strength. In the building of these hundreds of urban centers there are clearly continuities with Shang and early Chou patterns as well as some important innovations. Among the continuities are the following: location of cities on level land near waterways; consistent use of pounded earth walls; use of pounded earth platforms as foundations of politically or religiously important buildings; adherence to a rectangular or square form, with some notable exceptions; orientation of the city to the four cardinal points with emphasis on the north-south axis.[14] A poem from the *Book of Songs* evokes the scene of the building of a new capital in 658.[15]

> The Ting-star is in the middle of the sky;
> We begin to build the palaces at Ch'u
> Orienting them by the rays of the sun
> We set to work on the houses at Ch'u
> . . .
> We take the omens and they are lucky,
> All of them are truly good.

Among the innovations of this period the most important is the articulation of city plans into functional zones or areas—a development prefigured perhaps in the Shang capitals but now fully realized. In these Eastern Chou cities there was a central area, usually walled, that contained the palaces and important buildings used by the aristocracy. Surrounding this was a second walled area that included industrial and artisan quarters, residences of the people, some farmland, commercial streets, and markets. Outside the wall there was often a moat, with additional farmlands beyond.[16] This double enclosure, purely functional in origin, was to have an important place in the normative theories of city building developed at a later time.

The early Eastern Chou period also saw the elaboration of various ancient cults, of which we need consider here only those closely connected with the design of cities. We should remember that for the men of Chou the universe was peopled with divinities, spirits, and forces that only worship, sacrifices, and propitiatory rites could control. Specialists in the management of all these unseen forces appeared in great variety: ritualists; interpreters of dreams; diviners by the tortoise and by the milfoil; specialists in the interpretation of such divinations; witches; exorcists; shamans; and astrologers, who drew their prognostications from steadily deepening knowledge of the heavenly bodies.[17]

One of the most ubiquitous cults was that of the god of the soil, a personification of the forces of fertility and self-renewal that reside in the earth. The gods of the soil were localized, so that the potency of any individual god was coterminous with the extent of the state, town, or village where it was worshiped. Every locality had its earth-mound, often topped by a tree, where sacrifices to the local god were conducted to assure the harmonious working of natural forces for the community's good. The public earth-mound (*kung-she*) of each of the various state capitals not only was the scene of fertility rites but also became in effect the locus of each state's guardian god. There the armies of a state sacrificed before the start of a campaign, and there they presented captives and offered sacrifices after a victory. Before these altars rulers took solemn vows and swore to covenants. The altar became in turn the symbol of the continuing power of the state, whose extinction—as we see in countless texts—was expressed as "the ruin of their altars of earth and of crops."[18] There is inconclusive evidence in what Karlgren calls the "free" texts that the altar of the land and grain was located to the right, i.e. the west, of the lord's palace, and the ancestral temple (*tsung-miao*) to the left, or east. On the fact that the two were paired the texts are clear.

The location of the ancestral temple shows the importance to city building of a second prominent Chou cult—ancestor worship. The cult of ancestors is perhaps as old as Chinese culture itself, and in Chou times ancestor veneration was no doubt practiced in every humble village. But it is the public and political aspect of the ancestor cult that concerns us here. The *Tso-chuan* attests its central importance: "All walled towns having an ancestral hall containing the tablets of former rulers were called capitals [*tu*]."[19] All the territorial nobles of Chou times worshiped their ancestors in a fixed temple where the commemorative tablets of their lineage were enshrined; the high ancestor of the lineage was the focus of the cult. The lord's ancestors, like his god of the soil, were believed to have the power (if properly propitiated) to help assure good crops, victory in war, the timely appearance of rain and sunshine, the chastisement of the state's enemies, and the punishment of the unrighteous. All significant events had to be reported at the *tsung-miao* in appropriate formulas, and an elaborate annual calendar of sacrifices was followed.

The ancestral temple thus shared with the altar of the land and grain symbolic significance as the locus of the state's power. This may be seen in the following passage from the *Tso-chuan* recording the behavior of a defeated lord in 548: "The Marquis of Ch'en ordered his Master of the Horse, Huan Tzu, to offer the utensils of the ancestral temple to the victors, while he himself, wearing mourning, carried in his arms the tablet of his god of earth; he caused the multitude of his sons and of his daughters to be separated into two groups and chained together to wait in the court for the victors."[20] The early texts are full of references to the threatened or real destruction of the ancestral temples of princely lineages; and when a state was destroyed, the conquerors often built special temples where the ancestral spirits of the defeated could be propitiated. The First Sovereign Emperor is said to have built near his capital ancestral temples for the various lineages he had conquered on his way to supreme power.[21] Thus we can see that the ancestral temple was a building of the highest importance in religious and political terms. Paired with the altar of earth, this sacred structure figures in the later theories of city design and in the long history of capital building in China.

The third Chou cult relating to cities is the worship of Heaven, or the God on High. This divinity was a fusion of the supreme god of the Shang, *Shang-ti*, and that of the Chou, *T'ien* or *Hao-t'ien*. He was believed to be the chief of all the gods and spirits, the master of men and gods alike. He supervised and judged the actions of men, rewarded virtue, and punished vice. He gave the mandate to rule to those who deserved it, and when their line showed signs of vice or incompetence he sent natural calamities to warn them; if these warnings were not heeded, he awarded the Heavenly Mandate (*T'ien-ming*) to a more virtuous prince. In the making of covenants it was this god who was solemnly invoked, as in this oath of 548: "If I do not adhere to those who are loyal to the prince and seek the good of his altar of the land and grain, may God on High witness it." Whereupon the man who took this vow smeared his lips with the blood of the sacrificial victim.[22] In theory it was the Chou overlord, holder of the Mandate of Heaven, who should worship Heaven, the God on High. In practice, though, as Maspero notes, the princes of the states of Lu and Sung, and perhaps other princes, carried on sacrifices to Heaven.[23] The place for such solemn rites was a round altar, possibly in three tiers, in the southern suburbs of the capital.[24] Whatever its early form (and this was later the subject of much theorizing), an altar for the worship of Heaven became a common feature of capital plans.

In the preceding paragraphs we have seen some of the elements of ritual and symbolism that entered into the design of early cities. Down to perhaps the beginning of the third century B.C., these elements were not systematized but were parts of a slowly growing body of traditional practice—sometimes followed, sometimes not—that varied with the time and the region. Underlying all was a kind of primitive organicism: a belief that the worlds of the gods and of men were interconnected, that it behooved men to respect the natural forces and natural features over which the gods presided in locating cities and their parts, and that the ancestors, particularly those of great lineages, continued to play an important role in the affairs of their descendants as surrogates of the God on High. Thus gods, men, and nature, the living and the dead—all were seen as interacting in a seamless web.

Far-reaching changes occurred in the last centuries of Eastern Chou. Social and political transformations helped produce the first great flowering of Chinese philosophy, and the representatives of different schools and doctrines moved from state to state offering their analyses and their nostrums to the various princes. No school or thinker left the corpus of inherited beliefs and practices untouched: Confucius moralized the traditional ways; Mo-tzu developed a universalistic ethic; the early Taoists subjected traditional institutions to a primitivistic critique that was (in George Boas's words) "a record of civilized man's doubts about his own performance"; the Legalists proposed to sweep away the incubus of tradition and build a new system on the basis of rational social, economic, and political principles.

Toward the end of Chou still other schools appeared that influenced the cosmology and symbolism of cities. One was the school of the Dual Forces (*yin-yang*), another the school of the Five Elements (*wu-hsing*). The two schools were closely related, and they developed the model of the universe and its forces that is at the heart of the organicism that appeared in early times and remained a constant in Chinese thought. The school of the Dual Forces elaborated the idea of complementary energies that, if properly perceived and controlled, kept all phenomena in smooth oscillating motion. The school of the Five Elements analyzed phenomena into five categories (*hsing*) that appeared in a cyclical sequence—of which there were two variants. Members of these two schools—and people who drew from both—offered analyses of events and prognostications, estimates of character, and appraisals of the natural forces at work in a given segment of nature, whether a river valley, a mountain slope, a proposed building site, or a grave site.

Even as the philosophers were analyzing and breaking down the components of the ancient religion, the ritualists—less a school than an occupational group of those who served the feudal lords in their diverse observances—set about to preserve and codify the oral tradition. The rituals were no doubt written down at different times in different states, though the state of Lu, the homeland of Confucius, figures largely in the transmission of the surviving texts. Despite the fact that the writings of the ritualists were fragmented and in large part lost in the destruction of traditional books by the First Sovereign Emperor, enough survived of them—as of the *yin-yang* and Five Elements writings—that they could be incorporated into the synthesis known as Han Confucianism.

Thus, at the time of the founding of a unified empire there was a large and heterogeneous body of lore, practices, and ideas connected with city building. Parts of it were the property of surviving ritualists, and parts were known to archivist-historians; other aspects were perhaps kept alive in the families of hereditary builders and artisans. This corpus was not the property of any one group, and it was not systematized; despite the fact that some of the ideas had been appropriated and developed by one school or another, the whole complex belonged to no single school. Already segmented and dispersed among various social groups, this body of ideas and practices was most likely further attenuated and diffused by the great upheavals that accompanied the Ch'in unification.

The traveler across the North China Plain in the century before unification would have had to look far to find a symmetrical and perfectly oriented city, with all its religiously important buildings placed in accordance with ancient tradition. Incessant war, explosive economic development, and the increasing agnosticism of the elite had brought many changes; sieges and sacks had destroyed cities, which were then hurriedly rebuilt; and the need to expand one functional quarter or another—whether for palaces, residential areas, or markets—had resulted in ad hoc protrusions in, and extensions of, the original city plans. Of the cities excavated thus far, only two seem to preserve their basic sym-

The Cosmology of the Chinese City

metry.²⁵ At any event, all inner and outer city walls in the formal feudal states were ordered razed by the First Sovereign Emperor prior to 215 B.C.²⁶

The First Imperial Capital

It is against this background that the first emperor of the Han decided to make his capital in the Kuan-chung Plain, across the Wei River from the Ch'in capital of Hsien-yang and a short distance east of the sites of the early Chou capitals of Feng and Hao. His trusted minister Hsiao Ho began the preparations. First he repaired a Ch'in detached palace, and then he built a new palace complex to the west of it. He built eastern and northern gatetowers, which were given names symbolizing the two directions; a reception hall; a great storehouse; and, somewhere between the two palaces, an arsenal.²⁷ It was not until the reign of Han Kao-tsu's successor (in 192 B.C.) that masses of forced labor were recruited to build a city wall around these early buildings and the growing settlements that had sprung up around them.²⁸ Satō estimates that the completion of the pounded earth walls of the new capital, Ch'ang-an, took approximately five years and nine months.²⁹ The walls were highly irregular, bulging out to accommodate preexisting settlements and, on the north, sloping toward the southwest to accommodate the course of the Wei River. (For the shape of Han Ch'ang-an, see Map 5.) The site survey published in 1957 gave wall lengths as follows: east wall, 5,940 meters (3.69 miles); south wall, 6,250 meters (3.88 miles); west wall, 4,550 meters (2.83 miles); and north wall, 5,950 meters (3.70 miles). The walls were about 52.5 feet thick at the base, and were about 27.3 feet high.³⁰ The original palaces were in the extreme south of the city, whereas the main gate (called the Heng Men, and off-center) was in the north. Commercial activity was supervised by the government, and there were at least nine markets, many of which were located outside the walls; one of the most important was outside the Heng Men.³¹ Han Kao-tsu built his ancestral hall somewhere near the Wei-yang palace, but it was later moved near his tomb on the north bank of the Wei River. The ancestral halls of his descendants were also built there, adjoining their tombs.³² Those streets in the capital that led to the palaces were probably straight, and the city was divided into 160 wards, but much of Ch'ang-an was simply a random growth of streets, lanes, and alleys. The city and its suburbs were adorned with new palaces in the reign of the great Wu-ti (r. 140–87 B.C.), but it remained very much the bustling, untidy, dusty capital of a young empire. Some scholars have called it *tou-ch'eng* ("city of the dippers") and have maintained that the north and south walls were built in the shape of the northern and southern dippers. However, though astral symbolism in building had a venerable pedigree and had been used as recently as the reign of the First Sovereign Emperor, there was none in the haphazard building of Ch'ang-an.[33] Though the central gate in the east wall was called Ch'ing-ming Men after the appropriate one of the five old directional gods (Fang-ti), the other gates were built where they were needed, and their names were without symbolic referents. Thus the Han capital reflected few of those unsystematized norms for important cities that had descended from the Shang and the Chou; nor did it conform to the symbolism and cosmology evolved by the ritualists, by the practitioners of the *yin-yang* or the Five Elements systems, or by any of the lesser schools.

How, then, did an elaborate and detailed cosmology of the city emerge during the later years of the Former or Western Han dynasty and impose itself on dynasts and builders for more than two millennia?

The early years of Western Han were a period of intense political and military struggle for the consolidation of imperial rule during which philosophic and scholarly activity was at low ebb. Han Kao-tsu decreed, no doubt as a practical measure, that city walls destroyed by the Ch'in should be rebuilt,[34] and he submitted to some traditional court rituals devised under the direction of Shu-sun T'ung. But the effects of the draconian Ch'in regime and of the bitter civil war that followed were palpable and far-reaching. They were particularly severe in their effects on the transmission of texts and of living traditions from the preceding age. The various feudal states' archives had been destroyed or scattered, and their professional ritualists and archivists killed or transported. Local enclaves of the masters and disciples of different schools had been broken up and their followers dispersed. The Ch'in burning of the ancient books was followed by the destruction of the remaining great repository of such works in the sack of their capital at Hsien-yang.

The Emergence of an Imperial Ideology of the City

A half century after the establishment of Han rule, many of the ancient books had been partially reconstructed, and scholars were beginning their controversies over the relative authenticity of various versions. How slow and tenuous this recovery of the past was is illustrated by the history of the texts on the rituals. The "Essay on Rites and Music" of the *Han shu* says that the rituals which the ubiquitous Shu-sun T'ung had compiled while he served the Ch'in were stored with the state statutes in the Office of Punishments and did not survive the fall of that dynasty. The Han ritual canon (which Shu-sun T'ung improvised for the Han founder from old practices) was not made known, and "among the people there was none who had kept the words of it." The "Essay" goes on to say that after Shu-sun T'ung's death, the Prince of Ho-chien (d. 132 B.C.) began to collect old accounts of music and rituals and bit by bit pieced them together in more than five hundred sections.[35]

It was with such materials that the Han ideologues in the service of the great Emperor Wu began to put together a synthesis that offered a coherent view of the world and of the place of China and the imperial system in it. Let us discuss a few of the characteristic themes of this Han synthesis.

Archaism is prevalent with Tung Chung-shu and the other builders of the Han synthesis. This theme took Confucius's idealization of the early Chou and transformed it into an elaborate scholastic system in which the ancient provenance of desirable ideas and institutions was invoked to justify them to the men of Han. And this in turn meant that the surviving texts of the early Chou had to be expanded, interpolated, and explained at great cost (we would say) to their historical truth and literary integrity.

Another theme is organicism—not of the primitive sort we referred to earlier, but of the kind that elaborates and explains all the elements of the human and natural world in terms of their interaction. To develop this theme the Han syncretists had to pull in texts and ideas that had been quite separate from the Confucian tradition; since the new ideology aspired to complete dominance and (as Tung Chung-shu recommended) the extirpation of all competing schools, it had to encompass a field far larger than the moralism of the primitive Confucians. Thus in 136 B.C., the *I-ching* or *Book of Changes*, originally a manual for the interpretation of milfoil auguries, was made a "Confucian" classic because its images could be used to explain the interrelations among many phenomena. Ideas from the school of *Tao*, from the school of *yin-yang*, and from the school of the Five Elements were drawn into the synthesis for the same purpose.

A third important theme is that of centralism, which we may use to cover both the centrality of the emperor in the world of men and the centrality of China, the Central Kingdom, in the universe. Here the ritual sanctions were found both in the reconstructed and greatly idealized institutional plan of the early Chou and in the theories of the ritualists, enriched by borrowings from the other schools. Theories of China's centrality were enormously strengthened by the realities of Han power: an expansive and seemingly invincible system, great and growing productive strength, and ignorance of any civilization of comparable achievements.

Finally, there is the theme of moralism. This involved belief in the moral right of the emperor to rule, in the moral rightness of the social hierarchy, and in the inalienable right of the classically educated to interpret the moral as well as the physical universe to emperor above and commoners below. A corollary to this idea was the belief that the Classics contained the basis of morality and offered both the norms for proper social behavior among the masses and the standards by which the literate could perfect themselves.

Let us turn now to consider the characteristic features of the cosmology of the city that emerged in Han times. Although there are scattered references to this subject in the *Huai-nan-tzu* and in the *Li-chi*, the classical source for city theory is the *Chou li* or *Chou kuan*—particularly the last section, known as the "K'ao-kung chi." Controversies on the authenticity and date of the *Chou li* have continued for two millennia. I take the view that whereas some passages, or their underlying ideas, may be of early date, the basic structure—and particularly the numerical-symbolic references—date from about the time of Han Wu-ti.[36] This view is based on the conviction that the text as it now stands was arranged, interpolated, and partly invented by the architects of the Han syncretic ideology described in the preceding paragraphs. As Karlgren says, these texts "represent the endeavors of the Confucian school to determine what the beliefs and rites *should properly be*."[37] In other words, they are normative and prescriptive, not historical. Yet the archaistic bias—the belief that ancient models alone had authority— was so strong among the Han ideologues that the *Chou li* was attributed by them to the Duke of Chou, that peerless statesman of early Chou idolized by Confucius. In what follows I consider one by one the elements of city planning that emerge from the *Chou li*. In each case I note the genuinely ancient elements that are attested by the "free" texts and by archaeology, and call attention to the symbolism that was probably of Han origin.

Choice of a site. Each of the four main sections of the *Chou li*—corresponding to the four seasons—opens with the following passage: "It is the sovereign alone who establishes the states of the empire, gives to the four quarters their proper positions, gives to the capital its form and to the fields their proper divisions. He creates the offices and apportions their functions in order to form a center to which the people may look."[38] This clearly expresses the centralism so characteristic of Han ideology, and it makes of the capital the epicenter of an orderly spatial grid extending to the boundaries of civilization. Elsewhere the *Chou li* goes into great detail on the taking of auguries by the tortoise-

The Cosmology of the Chinese City

shell and by the milfoil, and then specifies that a major shift in the site of the capital is an occasion for consulting the tortoise.[39] Again, the *Chou li* prescribes that in the event of a major shift of capital, the official known as the *ta-shih* shall take the plan and study it in advance.[40] Thus the systematizers of Han times elaborated on, but did not basically change, what we know to be ancient practices of site selection.

Preparation of the site. The *Chou li* says that when construction workers start to build a capital, they calculate the contours of the site by the use of plumb lines and water levels. (They then grade the site to the calculated level.)[41] This is a straightforward description of procedures for preparing a building site that were no doubt of great antiquity.

Orientation. The *Chou li* describes the method of determining the four directions on the site by taking at various times the shadow of the sun as cast by a pole whose verticality has been assured by the use of multiple plumb lines. This method is supplemented by night observations of the polestar.[42] Again, these are clearly tested procedures of great antiquity. We have noted the strict orientation of many early cities: the poem from the *Book of Songs* cited earlier refers to the use of the sun's rays for orienting a new city in 658 B.C.; and the ode on the building of the first Chou capital refers to the plumb line.[43] There is nothing arcane or symbolic in these procedures, and nothing to cast doubt on their workaday use in antiquity and in subsequent ages.[44] But elsewhere the *Chou li* prescribes a far more elaborate procedure for establishing a capital at the very center of the earth's surface by the use of five gnomons. "Here, where Heaven and Earth are in perfect accord, where the four seasons come together, where the winds and the rains gather, where the forces of *yin* and *yang* are harmonized, one builds a royal capital."[45] In this passage, the siting of a capital is seen in relation to the forces of nature and to the hypostasized powers that govern all phenomena. This, I believe, is an expression of the systematized organicism characteristic of Han Confucian ideology; further, it makes of a capital city a cosmic focal point—a center from which the forces of nature may be adapted to or controlled in the interests of the whole realm.

Layout of the city. After the proper location is achieved, the *Chou li* then directs the construction workers to lay out the city in the form of a square.[46] As nearly as we know, a square or a rectangle was the traditional form of the Chinese city. But the *Chou li*'s prescription of a square form has a symbolic significance as well. For the men of Han, the earth was a perfect square; thus it was fitting that the ruler of all under heaven should live in a structure that was a replica and a symbol of the earth. The *Chou li* continues, the wall "shall measure nine *li* on each side, and in each side there shall be three gates. Within the capital there shall be nine north-south streets and nine east-west streets. The north-south streets shall accommodate nine chariot-ways." Here we encounter the theory of emblematic numbers that had developed before the Han but that was then incorporated into official Confucianism. As Granet put it in his brilliant essay on the subject, "It is by means of numbers that one finds a suitable way to represent the logical sectors and the concrete categories that make up the universe.... In choosing for them one or another disposition which permits them to demonstrate their interplay, one believes he has succeeded in rendering the universe at once intelligible and manageable."[47] Three, nine, and twelve are, within this mode of thinking, particularly significant numbers: three because it represents the three sectors of the intelligible universe (heaven, earth, and man); nine because it represents three times three and is also the number that represents the ancient Chinese world (the nine provinces as established by the Emperor Yü); twelve because it is the sum of three and nine *and* the number of months in a year. Thus it follows that the ruler, who is seen by the Han theorizers as uniting in his person the three sectors of the universe and presiding over the nine provinces during the sequence of twelve months in each year, should have the numbers three, nine, and twelve in the symbolism of his capital. This systematizing element in the cosmology of city planning is, in my view, a product of the second half of the Western Han.

There are further points in these prescriptions: the greater width of the north-south streets emphasizes the orientation of the city toward the south; and the fact that the streets are nine in number by implication gives importance to the central avenue approaching from the south (an importance that we find in all later capital building). Moreover, the prescription of a grid plan as a norm for capital cities is but one example of the ordering of space by the use of grid schemes. It belongs to the same group as the *ching-t'ien* or well-field system, which was believed by Mencius and later Confucians to have been the land system of the early Chou; the basic pattern is, of course, nine equal squares arranged in a larger square. It also recalls the mythological division of the empire into nine provinces by the Emperor Yü.

Disposition of the principal structures. The *Chou li* states that the ancestral hall of the prince shall be on the left, i.e. the east, and the altar of the god of the soil on the right, i.e. the west.[48] We have seen that these were the two principal cult centers in early cities, but there is inconclusive evidence that they were placed in this way. The palace of the prince occupies the very center of the city; to the south of his residence is his audience hall, and to the north, the market. This prescription reflects to a degree the value system of the Han Confucians. The center of mercantile activity is given the place of least honor and minimum *yang* influence by being located in the northern extremity of the city.

Under the rubric "Market Supervisor" the *Chou li* provides a circumstantial picture of a highly supervised and controlled market that may well be close to the way capital markets were managed in the latter half of Western Han.[49] In this passage the hierarchy of officials and the detailed duties prescribed for each reflect the Legalist ideas that were incorporated into Han Confucianism as they were into the machinery of the Han state. In another passage, under the duties of the *nei-tsai*, the *Chou li* tells us that this official is to assist the empress in establishing a market, to attend to its layout and regulations, and then to dedicate it by the *yin-li* or female ritual.[50] The commentary of Cheng Hsüan (2d century A.D.) explains that in establishing the capital of a state the emperor builds the palaces whereas the empress establishes the market, and that this is to represent the harmonious complementarity of the male and female principles (*yang* and *yin*). That this ever happened is doubtful, to say the least, but the additional theorizing tends to underscore the *yin* character of the market location in the classical plan.

The Hall of Light. The *ming-t'ang* (hall of light, or cosmic house) has been the subject of endless theorizing by Chinese scholars from the Han onward. Bits of the nomenclature associated with it are drawn from quite ancient sources—e.g. the *ling-t'ai* or "magic tower," and the *pi-yung* or "moated mound," both of which we encountered in the *Book of Songs*. But the coalescence of earlier elements, the additions to them, and the full symbolic elaboration of the whole into a microcosm of the universe is, I believe, to be attributed to the Han systematizers. The *Chou li* gives us the different names and measurements of the cosmic houses of the Hsia, the Shang, and the Chou, but there is no solid evidence that any of the early dynasties built such structures, or that their rulers performed seasonal rituals in their various rooms and fanes.[51] The conception and the terminology of this building belong to the systematized centralism of the imperial period and only took form after several generations of scholiasts had worked on them. Han Wu-ti considered building a cosmic house, but in 140 B.C., when he wanted to build one at the foot of Mt. T'ai, "they did not know the measurements for it." In 110 he finally built one according to plans—allegedly of the time of the Yellow Emperor—presented to him by a Shantung scholar.[52] Although the *ming-t'ang* is a fascinating illustration of the cosmological and political ideas of the Han and later periods, it never became a fixed part of the capital plans, and each proposal to build one evoked storms of conflicting views from the scholars. Nonetheless, we shall find echoes of its symbolism in later practices.

Many cults of great antiquity are mentioned in the *Chou li* and figured in the Han ritual calendar, but their locations are not given precisely and they are not related to the city plan. For example, one of the many officials is given the responsibility not only for placing the altar of the land and grain on the west and the ancestral hall on the east, but also for setting up altars to the five directional gods in the four suburbs.[53] There are many references to sacrifices to the God on High and to the spirits of the mountains and rivers, but urban locales for these cults are not specified.

By the end of the Western Han, a core cosmology of the capital city had been put together partly out of ancient lore and practice and partly out of the systematizing imaginations of the architects of Han imperial Confucianism. Surrounding this core ideology, and in a loose relation to it, are bits of nomenclature and symbolism from the early Classics, as well as other elements (such as the *ming-t'ang*), that are symbolically consistent with the core cosmology but not always associated with capital cities.

Wang Mang, who succeeded the Western Han emperors in A.D. 6, was the heir and in a sense the victim of the imperial ideology. As the *Han shu* says, "Wang Mang believed that if institutions were fixed, the world would pacify itself. Hence he gave detailed attention to geographical arrangements, the institution of rites, and the composition of music. To expound the harmonizing of the theories of the Six Classics, the ministers came into the palace at dawn and left at dusk. The discussions went on for years on end."[54] The record of his reign is filled with portents and their interpretation; with attention to element, numerical, and color symbolism; and with repeated changes of official nomenclature, place names, and so on. In this frenetic ritual and symbolic activity, we see clearly the efforts of a usurper to justify himself and legitimize his rule.

Wang Mang inherited the Han capital of Ch'ang-an and seems to have done little to it beyond making changes in nomenclature. He appeared repeatedly at the *ming-t'ang* south of the city, reenacting with great attention to detail various ceremonies sanctioned by the *Chou li*. Then in A.D. 20, having several times been dissuaded from founding, in the manner of the Duke of Chou, an eastern capital at Loyang, he announced elaborate building plans south of Ch'ang-an. Posing himself at center stage, he said, "Day and night I have reflected long and have not presumed to rest. . . . I then divined by the tortoise-shell concerning the

The Cosmology of the Chinese City

region north of the Po River and south of the Lang Pool, and it was judged fit to produce imperial sustenance. I also divined by the tortoise-shell concerning the region south of the Chin River and west of the Ming-t'ang, and it was also judged fit to produce imperial sustenance."[55] In this passage Wang Mang is echoing the divinations of the Duke of Chou preparatory to building the capital at Lo, as recorded in the *Book of History*. He proceeded to plan a layout to cover a hundred *ch'ing* (about 1,500 acres). Later he went to inspect the progress of the work and symbolically pounded three times on the earth being used for walls or for platform foundations. He then spoke of the magnificence of the plan, saying that it should be made known to all within the four seas and that it all should be of such perfection that "after ten thousand generations there would be nothing to be added."[56] Here he is echoing the speech of Hsiao Ho to the first Han emperor justifying his work on the beginnings of Ch'ang-an. Wang Mang demolished a number of buildings in the Shang-lin park to use their materials, rounded up artisans from the whole empire, levied a special tax for the construction, and assembled a labor force of convicts and those subject to the corvée. The buildings consisted of nine great halls honoring the Yellow Emperor, the Sage Emperor Shun—whom Wang Mang claimed as the ancestor of his house—and the more recent ancestors of Wang Mang. Recent excavations south of Han Ch'ang-an have uncovered the remains of an elaborate building. A lower foundation of pounded earth is round, a second layer is square, and on the square are the remains of structures disposed symmetrically in the shape of a Greek cross roughly 138 feet in each direction. Around the whole is a square wall of pounded earth 700 feet in circumference with a gate in the center of each side. Surrounding all this was a circular watercourse ("hall with a circlet of water"?). Since the structural remains indicate nine divisions of the building, this may well be Wang Mang's hall.[57]

Whether this is confirmed or not, Wang Mang appears in the record as the captive of the imperial ideology and its interpreters. He built the archaic buildings, acted out the ancient rituals, and echoed in his speeches the words of exemplary emperors of the past. He may well be unique among Chinese emperors not only for the fervor of his commitment to imperial Confucianism but also for his infatuation with the whole range of its symbolism.

City Building in the South and the Mutations of Theory and Practice in New Terrain

All the normative ideas and techniques of city building were developed in the North China Plain, the nuclear area of Chinese civilization. The availability of flat sites made orientation to the cardinal points easy, and construction with pounded earth or mud brick was universal. During and after the Han dynasty, the area of Chinese culture was greatly increased as the Chinese moved into the Yangtze Valley and, farther to the south and east, into a mountainous and heavily watered region. City building was inevitably adapted to irregular and hilly sites as well as to large bodies of water and different climatic conditions.[58] This process of adaptation can be seen in the early history of southern Chinese cities in the period from the fall of the Han to the reunification of the empire in 589.

The initial history of cities in the Yangtze Valley and beyond is the history of long years of effort to sinicize the aborigines, to colonize, and to establish Chinese-type agriculture. The centers of this activity were military outposts established at favorable points. As the process continued, these strongpoints were enlarged; their earlier wooden stockades were replaced by more permanent walls. In the course of time, population grew, trade and industry increased, and at some of these early sites the great southern cities grew up.

In the Ch'in and Han some of the larger centers became garrison headquarters or provincial administrative seats of the central government. In the years after the breakup of the Han some were taken as capitals by one or another regional satrap or imperial aspirant. It is only with this transformation that there appear in crude or partial form some elements of the imperial cosmology of the city.

Early Nanking is illustrative of the long and varied evolution of southern cities in this period. The site of the future city was a small alluvial plain on the south bank of the Yangtze where a minor tributary enters the great river. The plain was very vulnerable to flooding and was virtually surrounded on three sides by hills and scarps. Strongpoints were built there at an early date and were repeatedly fought over during the Warring States period, when the semicivilized states of Wu, Yüeh, and Ch'u contended for control of the plain. Under the Ch'in, a small fortified town above the alluvial plain was made a *chün*—one of the 36 administrative headquarters for the new system of territorial control of the unified empire. The Han continued to recognize its strategic and economic importance and kept garrisons and officials in a walled or stockaded town toward the southern extremity of the plain.[59]

The last puppet emperor of the Han, on the recommendation of Ts'ao Ts'ao, conferred the title Marquis of Wu on Sun Ts'e, a military satrap of the Lower Yangtze area. His brother Sun Ch'üan succeeded him and in 229 set himself up as Emperor of Wu and built his capital, which he

The Cosmology of the Chinese City

called Chien-yeh, on the site. The Wu rulers, by building a series of canals, gradually made the plain less subject to flooding. The city was initially fairly primitive; but we see in the little we can learn about it certain elements of the imperial cosmology of the city. It was located in the center of the plain and oriented toward the south. The canalized tributary of the Yangtze ran to the south, and behind the city lay a range of hills. It was rectangular, some seven and a half miles in circumference (compare Han Ch'ang-an, whose circumference was some fourteen and a quarter miles), and was surrounded not by a pounded earth wall but by a bamboo stockade. The names of the southern and northern gates were in accord with the ancient directional symbolism. Some of the gates must have been topped by wooden gatetowers (presumably built on earth or brick foundations), for we hear of their destruction by fire. In 247 Sun Ch'üan built within the outer walls a palace enclosure that was a modest one and one-tenth miles in circumference.[60] Its walls were punctuated by eight gates, five of them giving to the south. The east gate was called the Azure Dragon gate, and the west, the White Tiger gate. These names were in accord with ancient directional symbolism and became part of the technical vocabulary of *feng-shui*, about which we shall have more to say below. The palace enclosure was called the T'ai-ch'u Kung, a name with referents both to the Taoist classics and to the *Book of Changes*. The market that served the area seems to have been far to the south of the city wall and was thus not a part of the city plan.[61] Imperial ceremonies were performed when the slackening of warfare permitted, but the sources do not specify where they occurred. It was not until 255 that the Temple of the Imperial Ancestors (*T'ai miao*) was built. On the disposition of this and other buildings of religious-symbolic significance, the sources have nothing to say.

Although the Wu empire was destroyed and its capital sacked and reduced again to the status of a local administrative seat, Nanking reemerged soon afterward as a capital—this time of the Eastern Chin dynasty. The Chin, in flight after their loss of the whole of North China to the steppe peoples in 317, chose this city as their capital and established in it "their ancestral temple and their altar of the spirits of the land and grain." Divinations to place the T'ai miao on its proper site were carried out by Kuo P'u, of whom more will be said below.[62]

But rather than follow the fortunes of Nanking as capital, let us consider its topography, which is not untypical of that of other southern cities. The site displays an intimate relation between a great river, tributaries, canals, and lakes, on the one hand, and hills, mountains, scarps, and ravines, on the other. This is in striking contrast to the flat city sites of the North China Plain. It is my hypothesis that it was here—and at similar sites throughout the South—and in this period that a new set of ideas became loosely appended to the imperial cosmology of the city: the system of ideas known as *feng-shui*. This system represents the only accretion to the cosmology of the city from the fall of Wang Mang to the end of the imperial order. Let us therefore consider the provenance of the system and its application to cities.

The origins of *feng-shui* are to be found in the systematic organicism that was characteristic of the Han synthesis. This organicism translated natural and human phenomena into number-symbols—the symbols of the *Book of Changes*, the Five Elements, and the two forces of *yin* and *yang*—and then used the relationships between and among the symbols to interpret phenomena. Various ingredients of the system can be traced back to the Chou, and some continued as separate traditions for many centuries. There is ample early evidence of the manipulation of the Five Elements system and of the symbols of the *Book of Changes*. There are also references from late Chou, Ch'in, and Han times to practitioners known as *wang-ch'i-che* who surveyed the ambience or emanations (*ch'i*) of a site or situation to determine its favorable or unfavorable character.[63] This subtradition persisted and, I suggest, was fused with *feng-shui* theories in the third or fourth century A.D. The earliest text that lays out *feng-shui* as a system is attributed to Kuo P'u (276–324), who applied his principles to the siting of ancestral graves in order to ensure the good fortune of the descendants.[64] The basis of the system, grounded in the distinctive Chinese view of the dynamic interaction of man and nature, was the belief that certain configurations of land—preferably those with a balance between *yang* and *yin* features—would retain the favorable life-essence (*sheng-ch'i*) that in others would be dispersed by the wind; well-located water was held to be the best block to this dispersal.

The application of the "emanation" theory and the *feng-shui* system to the siting of cities is only partially and uncertainly reflected in the sources. A story current in the third century A.D. was that Ch'in Shih Huang-ti, on a visit to the east, had been told by a *wang-ch'i-che* that the site of the future Nanking "in the configurations of its land has the ambience (*ch'i*) of a kingly capital."[65] We have noted Kuo P'u's divinations in 317 on siting the T'ai miao of the Eastern Chin. In 552 the court of Liang Yüan-ti was divided on whether or not to reoccupy the old Liang capital at Chien-k'ang (Nanking). One of those arguing against the return said, "Although Chien-yeh is the old capital, its kingly ambience (*ch'i*) is already used up."[66] In other words, the site that traditionally had been judged rich in kingly ambience had now exhausted the supply.

The Cosmology of the Chinese City

Yet in 1138, a minister tried a last-minute argument to prevent Sung Kao-tsung from moving the capital from Nanking to Hangchow. His argument was, in part, "Chien-k'ang from the Six Dynasties has been a capital for emperors and kings. Its ambience (*ch'i-hsiang*) is awesome. Using this as a capital it will be possible to control the central plain (lost to the Jurchen in 1127)."[67]

Later scholars returned to the "emanation" theory and elaborated the *feng-shui* system as it applied not only to capital cities but by extension to the whole geography of China. Chu Hsi was a particular enthusiast of *feng-shui*. In his *Recorded Sayings* (*Yü-lu*) he exclaims, "As a place for building a capital in ancient or modern times, no place surpasses Chi-chou [the North China Plain, north of the Yellow River]. It is what may be called a place where there is no wind to disperse it and there is water to contain it."[68] This is an odd statement by a native of Fukien who never saw the North and who spent much of his life at the southernmost imperial capital in China's history and the only one ever located at a coastal site. But there were skeptics among the Neo-Confucians who objected to *feng-shui* on both moral and rational grounds. Chang Tsai (1020–77) dismissed the whole system, even in its limited application to grave sites, as "utterly contrary to correct principles."[69] So did another northern Neo-Confucian, Ssu-ma Kuang.[70] Thus despite its ancient pedigree and the approval of Chu Hsi, *feng-shui* and the "emanation" theory associated with it did not become an integral part of the dominant Confucian ideology or of its subideology of the city. It was introduced into later city planning not by the scholar-officials but by their often restive masters, the emperors of China. It tended to be practiced as a profession by the subelite, and to be more prevalent in the South than in the North.[71] The ramifying influence of *feng-shui* ideas in the later dynasties no doubt introduced among the common people a consciousness of the good and bad features of a city's site and made them judge some cities to be more fortunate than others.

The experience of building in southern terrain encouraged the application of *feng-shui* to city sites and secular buildings. But for cities, it seems to figure more in the retrospective writings of later scholars than in the actual choice of a site. Once the empire was reunified in 589, the influence of the northern Chinese norms and the Han ideology of the city again became dominant.

Evidences of the Classical Cosmology in the Design of Later Cities: Sui to Ming

Sui and T'ang Ch'ang-an. The reunifying government of the Sui built Ta-hsing-ch'eng (called Ch'ang-an under the T'ang), the last Chinese capital to be built ab ovo on an unoccupied site (see Map 1). The architects and planners were of mixed Chinese and non-Chinese descent and worked under a variety of inspirations: the Sui vision of a new united empire having a capital on a grand scale; the informed knowledge of cities and capitals built in the North during the period of disunion; the knowledge (perhaps at secondhand) of the great cities of Central Asia; and the ideal of an empire that should be unmistakably Chinese in the Han manner, yet open to new influences and relatively free of constraining traditions. The city that they planned was on an unprecedented scale and accommodated at its height a population of a million.[72]

Let us consider how much of the classical cosmology and the *feng-shui* tradition was included in the plan of the new city. The founding emperor, Wen-ti, conducted divinations regarding the site and may have been the last Chinese ruler to do so. The outer walls formed a rectangle (not a square, as the *Chou li* prescribes), and excavations have shown the north-south walls to be only sixteen minutes west of true north.[73] Thus the orientation of the city was according to the ancient canons; it literally "faced south," and the central and widest north-south street served—according to *Chou li* prescriptions—as the principal axis of the city. In its siting we find no influence of *feng-shui* principles. The Wei River, with mountains beyond, lay to the north of the city, and the Chung-nan mountains lay to the south. The names of gates, streets, and wards reflect nothing of *feng-shui* theories. There are T'ang texts that maintain that the architects discovered six minor elevations on the site that symbolized the hexagram *ch'ien* in the *Book of Changes* and that they took account of this in laying out the major buildings. This is dismissed by modern researchers as post hoc theorizing.[74] When we notice the number of wards in the original city plan, we find that both the total number (108) and the number in various sectors (12 to the west of the palace and 12 to the east; 36 grouped on either side of the central avenue) are in the Han tradition of emblematic numbers. All these units and multiples are numbers symbolic of the harmonious rapport between heaven and earth. They reflect in numbers the *Chou li* passage that speaks of the capital as a place "where the four seasons come together, where the winds and the rains gather, where the forces of *yin* and *yang* are harmonized." The emperor, as cosmic pivot, saw to the harmonious operation of these natural forces, and he did so from the great main palace called T'ai-chi Tien, whose name symbolizes the astral center of the universal order.

The city did have, as the *Chou li* prescribed, three gates in the south, east, and west walls, but there were more than the prescribed nine east-west and nine north-south streets. The great north-south street was wider than the others, as the *Chou li* prescribed. The T'ang rulers had their ancestral hall to the east and their altar of the land and grain to the west, according to canonical prescriptions, but both these buildings were located in the southern part of the administrative city far from the palace, and their precincts gave onto streets lined with government offices. They were the objects of sporadic concern on the part of court ritualists and were occasionally visited by the T'ang emperors, but they seem not to have been major cult centers in a time when Buddhism and Taoism were the dominant faiths. The metropolitan temples of these faiths—the Buddhist to the east, the Taoist to the west—faced each other across the broad central north-south street of the city proper.

The *Chou li* had said, cryptically, "hall of audience in front, markets behind." Yet in Sui and T'ang Ch'ang-an, the palace was not in the middle of the city but centered against the north wall, with only the imperial Forbidden Park (*Chin-yüan*) behind. One could say that the planners took the expression audience hall to mean by extension the offices of government, for they designed an unprecedented administrative city in front of and just south of the palace enclosure. This is at best a very "stretched" interpretation of the canon, and one doubts that it was much in the planners' minds. When it came to markets, there was no question of locating them behind or north of the palace since the palace backed to the north wall. Rather, the two official markets were located, quite pragmatically, where they were convenient both for suppliers from outside the city and for consumers within, namely in the central east and central west parts of the city. When the need for other markets arose they were established for a time in various quarters of the city; when they were no longer patronized, they were closed down.

The centers for imperial cults such as the sacrifice to Heaven and the plowing of the first furrow in the spring lay south of the city and slightly to the east of the north-south axis. Several of the Sui and T'ang emperors discussed with their specialists the idea of building a *ming-t'ang*, a cosmic house, that would symbolize their pivotal position in the universe. The most interesting proposal of this sort was that of the master architect of the city, Yü-wen K'ai, to build a twelve-storied *ming-t'ang*. When challenged from all sides by Confucian scholars, he replied, "Although a twelve-storied design does not accord with the ritual texts, still one story for one month is surely not unreasonable."[75] I suspect that he wanted at least one important building associated with the imperial ideology tall enough to rival the Buddhist pagodas that increasingly dotted the skyline of the city.

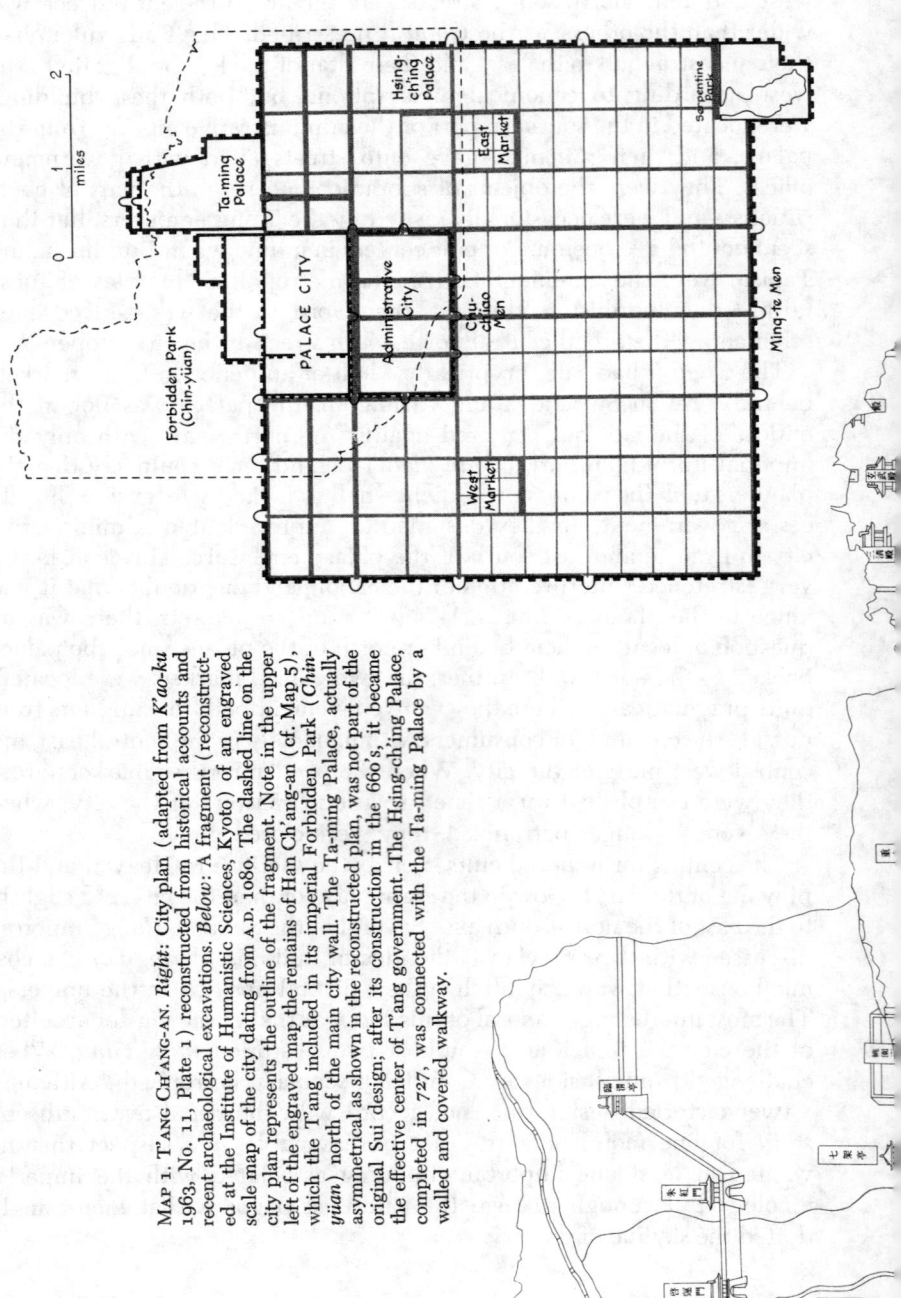

MAP 1. T'ANG CH'ANG-AN. *Right*: City plan (adapted from *K'ao-ku* 1963, No. 11, Plate 1) reconstructed from historical accounts and recent archaeological excavations. *Below*: A fragment (reconstructed at the Institute of Humanistic Sciences, Kyoto) of an engraved scale map of the city dating from A.D. 1080. The dashed line on the city plan represents the outline of the fragment. Note in the upper left of the engraved map the remains of Han Ch'ang-an (cf. Map 5), which the T'ang included in its imperial Forbidden Park (*Chin-yüan*) north of the main city wall. The Ta-ming Palace, actually asymmetrical as shown in the reconstructed plan, was not part of the original Sui design; after its construction in the 660's, it became the effective center of T'ang government. The Hsing-ch'ing Palace, completed in 727, was connected with the Ta-ming Palace by a walled and covered walkway.

Perhaps enough has been said to show that the imperial cosmology had discernible but limited authority over the planners of Ch'ang-an. Pragmatic considerations—convenience, functional zoning, ease of policing—outweighed the canonical prescriptions whenever a choice had to be made. The planners used selected elements of the classical cosmology to reiterate the claims of the Sui to be the heirs of the long-vanished Han and thus the new and rightful rulers of a reunited empire.

Northern Sung Kaifeng. Kaifeng, which had been a political and administrative center since the Warring States period, was originally walled by the military governor (*chieh-tu shih*) Li Mien in 781. By reason of its strategic location in the midst of the North China Plain and its access to convenient water transport, it grew in importance as T'ang power ebbed. Chu Wen, who administered the *coup de grace* to the T'ang, proclaimed himself emperor of the dynasty of Later Liang with his capital at Kaifeng. One of his successors in 955 built an outer wall some eighteen and three-quarter miles in circumference that no doubt took in a substantial suburban population. This was the city the Sung inherited when they came to power in 960 (see Map 2).

Kaifeng was the first Chinese capital that was basically a "natural" city. It drew rich revenues from the south and east, but it was also a bustling industrial and commercial center located at a key point in the burgeoning internal commerce of Sung times. Robert Hartwell, who has made intensive studies of the economic history of the Sung, says: "During the Northern Sung, K'ai-feng became a multi-functional urban center, quite possibly unsurpassed by any metropolis in the world before the nineteenth century."[76] Shops and ateliers invaded every corner of the city, and trading went on day and night. Huge cargo vessels and other commercial craft sailed into the heart of the city on numerous waterways. Edward Kracke says:

The unplanned and utilitarian character of the city was, in a way, not inappropriate for the capital of a China far different from early T'ang. There was no longer glory in overwhelming military power and expanded frontiers; in an old aristocracy, opulent and leisured; in omnipresent and often magnificent Buddhist shrines; in an easy sense of superiority over neighbors. Instead, within narrowed frontiers China bent her efforts to maintain nearly twice the T'ang population; life involved continuous and intense competition in every realm.[77]

As one might expect, the ancient imperial cosmology of the city received scant attention from the Sung rulers. The first ruler rebuilt the palaces he found on the model of the T'ang palaces in Loyang, and "for

The Cosmology of the Chinese City

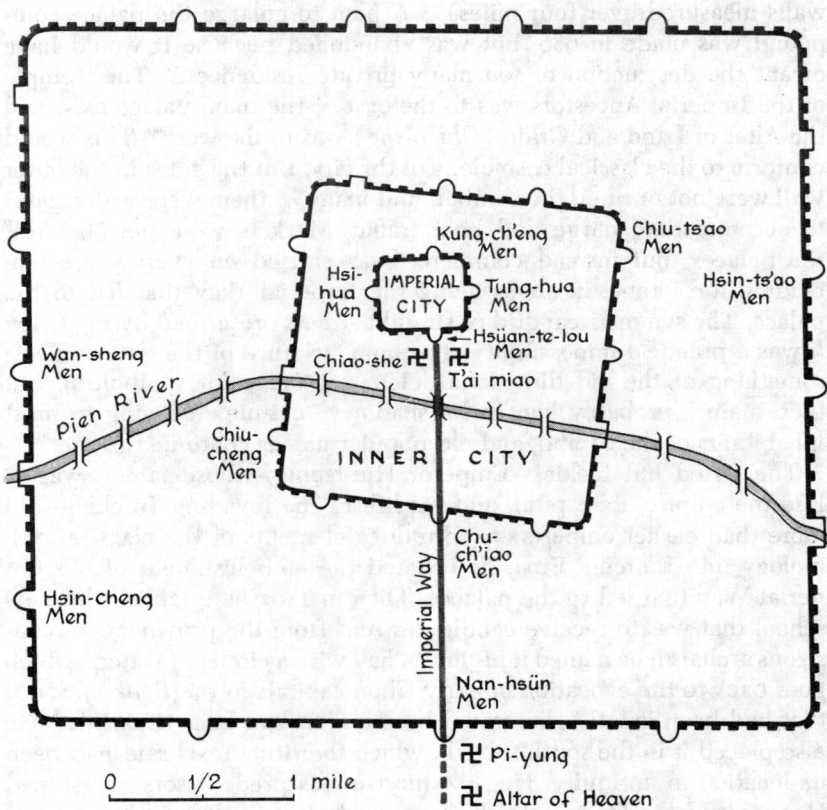

MAP. 2. NORTHERN SUNG KAIFENG. This map is a speculative reconstruction. The location of ceremonial places is approximate. Chiao-she is the Altar of Land and Grain; T'ai miao is the Temple of the Imperial Ancestors. Although the names of all gates are known, only the most frequented are labeled here. Water gates are squared off. Sources include the outline map presented by Hsü Kuang-ta on p. 2 of his essay in the pamphlet, edited by Cheng Chen-to, that accompanies the facsimile publication (Peking, 1958) of the famous *Ch'ing-Ming shang ho t'u*; and E. A. Kracke, Jr., "Sung K'ai-feng ... ," in John W. Haeger, ed., *Crisis and Prosperity in Sung China* (Tucson: University of Arizona Press, 1975), pp. 49–77, especially the schema of population distribution on p. 58.

the first time, the imperial residence had appropriate magnificence." The palaces lay southeast of an imperial park (*Hou-yüan*) that was located in the northwest sector of the city. They occupied the old walled headquarters compound built by tenth-century warlords, and the space was constricted (less than two miles in circumference; contrast this with the main palace compound—one of three—in T'ang Ch'ang-an, whose walls measured over four miles).[78] A plan to enlarge the palace compound was made in 986, but was abandoned because it would have meant the destruction of too many private residences.[79] The Temple of the Imperial Ancestors was to the east of the main palace axis, and the Altar of Land and Grain (*Chiao-she*) was to the west.[80] This would conform to the classical cosmology of the city. But the gates in the outer wall were not of the right number, and many of them were water gates to accommodate barge and boat traffic. Markets were not "behind" the palaces, but instead commerce was carried on everywhere—including for a time, in shops along the Imperial Way that led to the palace. The symmetrical grid of straight streets prescribed by the *Chou li* was a practical impossibility. The nomenclature of the gates reflects something of the old directional, element, and color symbolism, but these names probably had but a shadowy "cosmic" meaning to most inhabitants of the capital, and old popular names continued in use.

The gifted but feckless Emperor Hui-tsung—whose fate it was to lose the empire, its capital, and his life to the invading Jurchen—did more than earlier emperors to introduce elements of the classical cosmology into Kaifeng. First, he ordered the embellishment of the Imperial Way that led to the palaces. Then in 1102 he established a new school that was to receive candidates sent from the provinces. In conscious archaism he named it *pi-yung*, "hall with a circlet of water," which goes back to the evocation of early Chou capitals in the *Book of Songs* that had been greatly elaborated by the Han and later ritualists.[81] He also placed it in the south suburb, which the ritual texts said had been its location in antiquity. He, like most of his predecessors, worshiped Heaven and the God on High at a round altar in the south suburb.[82] In 1115 he ordered the building of a *ming-t'ang*.[83] In 1117, under the influence of Taoist adepts, he began the building of an immense complex of hills in the northeast part of the city; when completed they were 450 feet high and over three miles around.[84] The whole was covered with rare rocks and plants from every corner of the empire, and the names of the numerous pavilions evoked the many strands of the Taoist tradition: longevity, supernatural powers, miraculous occurrences, and the spirit of the Taoist immortals (*hsien*) with their many occult powers. The disposition of the hills in relation to various artificial lakes and watercourses strongly suggests the influence of *feng-shui* theories. In its symbolism this complex was a Taoist microcosm of the ideal world; each feature evoked a mystical or a magical formula, and in many were echoed the rich traditions of ancient folklore and folk religion. This immense project, carried out when the Northern Sung was under increasing pressure from its enemies and from internal problems, is a grandiose but literal expression of what Max Weber called the "magic garden" function of Taoism: a way of escape from harsh realities, from the austere moralism of the Confucian cult into a world of myth, of aesthetic pleasures, and of wish-fulfillment fantasies.

The personal projects of Hui-tsung aside, there are grounds for thinking that in the atmosphere of Kaifeng the canonical cosmology of the city must have been greatly attenuated; to some it must have seemed an obvious irrelevancy, an anachronism. Yet there were forces at work then, which became stronger later, that tended to perpetuate the old symbol system. Indeed, in Naba's view, in post-Sung times that system was reimposed upon the builders and planners of cities with added force. The Neo-Confucianism developed in Sung times was an attempt to create a new Chinese ideology; yet, like all such systems, it was made up of many strands of ideas and traditions. Along with rationalism and the organic-holistic view of man and the universe went what de Bary calls "fundamentalism"—a return to the classics as the basis of all norms —that shaded off into archaism and indeed into cultural chauvinism. This latter strain, I believe, was greatly strengthened in the Southern Sung, when China was the beleaguered and isolated defender of its ancient heritage; it was reasserted, after the trauma of the Mongol conquest, in the Chinese restorationism of the Ming dynasty.

Southern Sung Hangchow. The choice of Hangchow as *de facto* capital was a difficult one for the Sung ruler and his officials, who had fled south after the Jurchen conquest of the North China Plain. One writer says that the Emperor Kao-tsung divined regarding a suitable capital area,[85] but the choice seems to have been made—after a decade of hesitation and argument—at a time when invasion and disorder threatened the precarious continuity of the Sung dynasty. The negative view of the city may be represented by the comment of Wei Fu-min, who said after a visit that it was "narrow, overcrowded, and noisy, . . . a mean little place, lost in a corner of the empire and most unworthy of becoming a capital."[86] It was not until 1138, after hope had been given up of using Nanking, in its strategic position facing the North China Plain, that Hangchow (then Lin-an) was designated as temporary capital (*hsing-tsai*).

The town had begun, like others on the southeast coast, as a fort in the wars between Wu and Yüeh in the fifth century B.C. In Ch'in and Han times it was a fortified outpost in a semibarbarian region. The land was low, insalubrious, and subject to flooding by high tides until in the Later Han a dike was built to control the tides and a lake created behind the town to provide fresh water for the people and for irrigation. The assimilation of the aborigines and the development of agriculture encouraged the growth of a market town. The town grew into a thriving commercial center after it became the terminus of the southern extension of the Sui Grand Canal. The first permanent walls were built in 591. More substantial dikes were built in later dynasties, and the city was a prosperous commercial center and port by the time the Sung settled there in 1138.[87]

Hangchow as it then was offered manifold physical obstacles to the introduction of the classical cosmology of the city: first, it was crowded in a narrow plain, with the lake and mountains to the west and the Che estuary and the sea to the south and east; second, it was densely populated, and the population grew after it was chosen as capital; third, the main approach to the city was by road or canal to its northwestern corner; and fourth, the streets were not on a grid plan, and the narrowness of the city from east to west, plus its elongation from north to south, made symmetry out of the question (see Map 3).

The battered remnants of the Sung, when they decided to settle here, found a city that had recently suffered occupation, sack, and the ravages of nine fires and two epidemics.[88] The imperial government, when it arrived, was notably short of funds. Nevertheless, it began immediately to introduce elements of the classical plan and persisted in this effort for the next century and a half. D'Argencé shows that the early steps to remodel the city were taken with great caution in order not to arouse the animosity of the townspeople; condemnation of buildings was properly paid for, and in many cases the imperial government waited for the death of a major landholder or for the disgrace of a notable official before acquiring needed pieces of property.

We cannot follow all the moves in this long and complex effort, but a few steps may be noted. A palace compound was built on the site of a Buddhist temple in the hills south of the city; this was subsequently surrounded by a second enclosed space called the imperial or administrative city, later substantially enlarged and connected to the original walls of Hangchow proper. The question of orientation and appropriate nomenclature plagued the ritualists from the start. The palace city, of course, should face south, as did the Son of Heaven. Here a compromise was reached: "The Principal Gate (*Ch'eng-men*) would have to be a *Li-cheng-men* in the south when the function implied by such an appellation would in fact be performed by the *Ho-ning-men* in the north."[89] The T'ai miao was located on the narrow strip of land that connected the palace city with the old city of Hangchow, whereas the Altar of Land

The Cosmology of the Chinese City

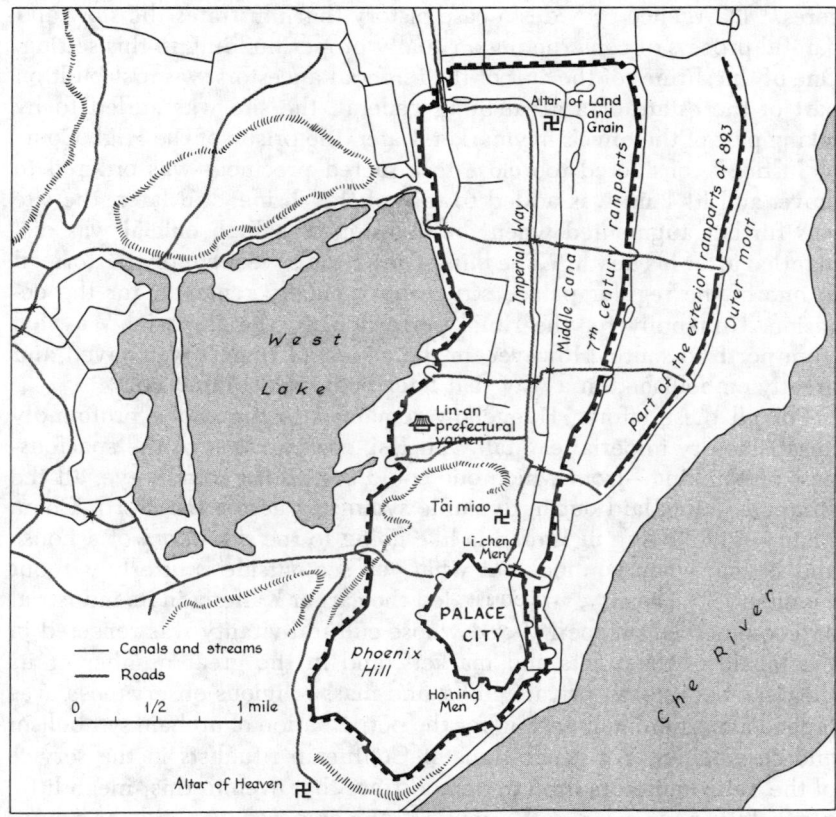

MAP 3. SOUTHERN SUNG HANGCHOW, 1274, after A. C. Moule's reconstruction from thirteenth-century plans and modern surveys. Prior to the addition of the Imperial City, the southern wall of the old city crossed the hills north of the T'ai miao (Temple of the Imperial Ancestors). The total built-up area, inclusive of extensive suburbs to the north, east, and south of the walled city, probably exceeded seven square miles.

and Grain was established near the northern end of the Imperial Way, which ran south through the city proper to the palace city. Later, an altar for the imperial sacrifice to Heaven and Earth was established in the *actual* southern suburb, i.e., to the south of the imperial city. This was a high altar whose construction reflected the numbers symbolic of the Chinese emperor's control of the universe: for example, the altar was in four tiers (= seasons), with twelve steps (= months) leading from the third tier to the top. Here, too, the emperor worshiped the 360 stars (= days of the year) and the ancient gods of the five directions, which in Han and earlier times had had their cult places outside the city gates.⁹⁰ D'Argencé provides a case history that illustrates the slow and painful process of constructing a ritually proper building in this setting. One of the shrines of the cult of the imperial ancestors was first built on part of the estate of a great Sung general; the site was added to by taking part of the town's haymarket. Later, the prison of the High Court of Justice—considered too close to a sacred precinct—was ordered to move, and its land was added to that of the shrine; still later, the site was further augmented when the mansion of a high official was dismantled after his death.⁹¹ The *ming-t'ang* rituals were simply performed in one of the regular palace structures specially renamed for the occasion. Unhappily for the ritual perfectionists, the Imperial Way led from north to south. However, in the course of time it was paved and greatly embellished in a way that later bedazzled Marco Polo.⁹²

For all these efforts, Hangchow remained to the end a profoundly unsatisfactory imperial capital. Chu Hsi, comparing it to the spaciousness of Nanking—from which one could see, in the mind's eye, all the strategic points laid out in dynamic symmetry across the North China Plain—said, "Being in Lin-an is like going to the side-room of a house and sitting; when you look out what you see outside is utterly without symmetry."⁹³ The city, which rivaled the earlier Kaifeng in its industrial and commercial prosperity, and whose cultural vitality was reflected in the bustle of its streets and markets, and in the great number of its theaters, bookstores, private clubs, and mass religious observances, was indeed a most unlikely setting for the perpetuation of archaic symbolism and ceremonies. Yet generations of Confucian ritualists in the service of the Sung emperors tried to demonstrate that even in this "mean little place, lost in a corner of the empire," the emperor was still the Son of Heaven and pivot of the cosmos, and that the Sung were the rightful heirs and perpetuators of a universal system.

Ming Peking. In the building of this city the Chinese realized, after two and a half centuries, their dream of returning to the North China Plain. The site, like those of many other cities we have discussed, had a long history as a regional administrative seat and frontier garrison post. The city attained capital status rather late and at the hands of the non-Chinese dynasties of Liao, Chin, and Yüan; it was Khubilai Khan, reigning as Yüan Shih-tsu, who made it the capital of all China. When he decided to rule as Son of Heaven as well as Khan of Khans, he adopted much of the ceremonial and symbolism of the Chinese monarchs. He entrusted the design of his city to a Chinese of wide learning but mixed cultural background, Liu Ping-chung; and he named as architect a Mohammedan and as supervisor of the work a high-ranking officer of the Mongol-Chinese army. The new city took in one of the

Chin palaces, but the design was strongly influenced by canonical prescriptions.[94] A legendary source says that Liu's design was influenced by *feng-shui* considerations.[95] But Khanbalig, or Ta-tu, remained at best a semi-Chinese city. As late as 1353, the "felt palaces" or large yurts set up for Khubilai's use were still in the city.[96]

The Yung-lo emperor, the "second founder" of the Ming, forced his way to power in 1403 and almost immediately began the long and complex process of moving the seat of power from Nanking, which his father had rebuilt on a lavish scale, to Peking. Arguments for and against Peking as a capital site had gone on from the beginning of the Ming and had centered on supply problems, construction costs, defense considerations, climate, historical precedent, and *feng-shui* principles.[97] But the Yung-lo emperor overrode all opposition and marshaled huge supplies and forces to reconstruct Khanbalig on a massive scale. What emerged at the formal inauguration of the northern capital in 1421 was Ming Peking, the first Chinese capital to dominate the subcontinent from the northern fringes of the North China Plain (see Map 4 and Figures 1 and 2).

The city was further embellished by later Ming rulers, but we might consider the city of 1421 as a reassertion—for the last time—of many elements of the classical cosmology of the city in the sort of terrain that had originally produced it. The outer walls formed a rectangle, oriented to the points of the compass, with a circumference of 14.63 miles[98] (compare Han Ch'ang-an's 14.10 and T'ang Ch'ang-an's 22.41). The walls were of earth, strengthened with layers of mortar and bricks, but it was not until later in the Ming that the walls were faced with bricks. The walls of the Mongol capital had had the canonical three gates in each of the walls save the north—where an eastern and a western gate, but no central gate, had been built. Since such a gate would have exposed the central axis of palaces to negative *ch'i*, I suspect that its elimination from the plan was on *feng-shui* grounds. The Ming moved the north wall of the city but reduced the total number of gates to nine, the number prescribed in the *Chou li*.

The streets within were a grid of north-south and east-west thoroughfares that divided the city—with notable variances for the chain of lakes through the west-central portion—into blocks. Centered within this outer rectangle was another that enclosed the imperial city, *huang-ch'eng*. Unlike the Sui and T'ang imperial city, this was not an ordered bureaucratic complex but rather included a variety of functional areas. There were the three artificial lakes running from north to south in the western part of the imperial city; around them was a variety of temples, pavilions, and pleasances. To the north was an artificial hill known in

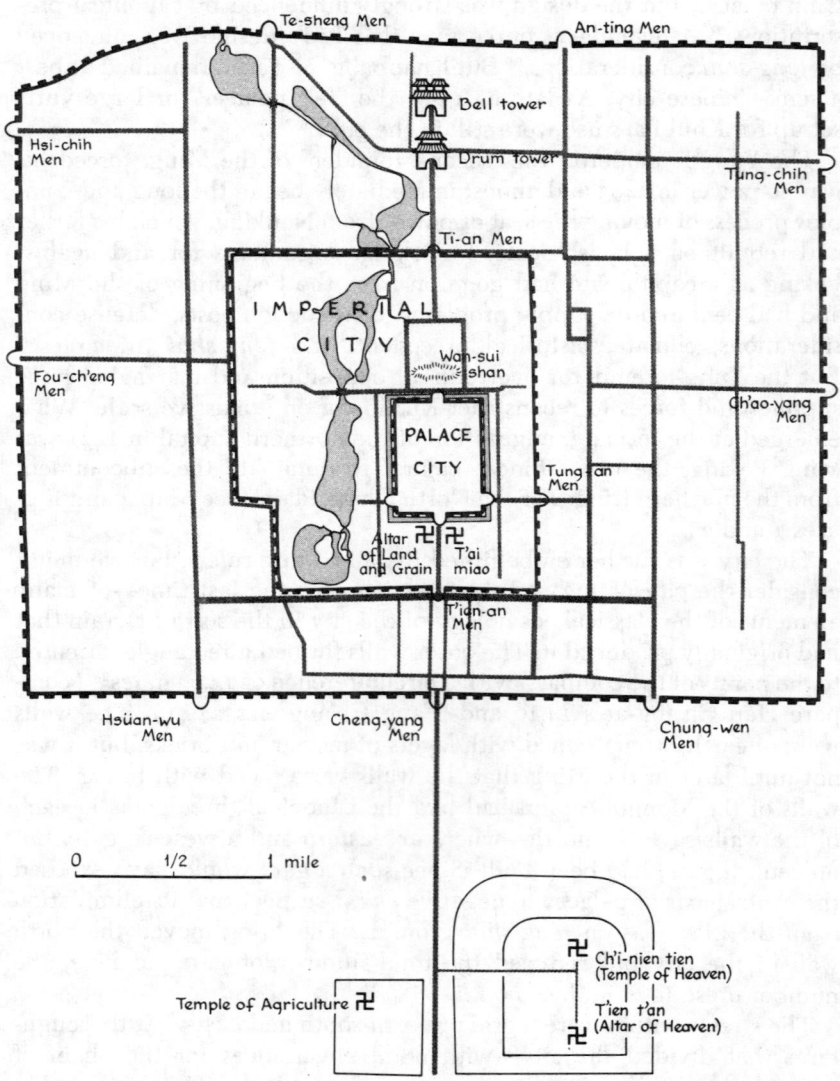

MAP 4. MING PEKING as built in the 1420's. In 1552, the southern suburbs, including the temples shown, were enclosed by an additional wall with seven external gates.

FIG. 1. THE WALLS OF PEKING. The square fortification, lower right, is at the southwest corner of the wall built in the 1420's. The moat outside the original wall is crossed by the lesser wall of 1552, which runs due west for nearly one-third of a mile before turning south (and eventually east) to form the rectangle of the Outer City. Aerial photograph from Wulf Diether Graf zu Castell, *Chinaflug* (Berlin and Zurich: Atlantis-Verlag, 1938).

Fig. 2. Hsi-chih Men, the northernmost gate in the west wall of Peking (original Ming city). From Donald Mennie, *The Pageant of Peking* (Shanghai: A. S. Watson, 1920).

The Cosmology of the Chinese City

Ming times as Wan-sui shan and later as Mei shan; its origins are uncertain, but it was at least added to, if not built, by the Yung-lo emperor in the course of dredging the moat around the imperial city and deepening the lakes. The hill's location north of the palace complex and its contours—five peaks, the central one being the highest—strongly suggest the influence of Taoism and of *feng-shui* theories, but I have found no textual evidence for this. Hou Jen-chih says that this high point in the very center of the city was meant to symbolize not only the rulers' control over the whole world (*t'ien-hsia*) but their preeminence over everything else.[99] During the Ming, it was gradually adorned with small temples, gazebos, and pavilions and provided a "mountain" outing place for residents of the imperial city. Other areas and zones were occupied by residences and stables of the guards, granaries and warehouses, houses for the palace staff, and so forth. Slightly east of center within the imperial city was a third walled rectangle, that of the palace or forbidden city. Within, the principal palaces were arranged on a north-south axis, with the Great Throne Hall (*T'ai-ho tien*) as the southernmost of the three great palaces. Just to the south of the palace city and still within the imperial city were the Temple of the Imperial Ancestors on the east and the Altar of Land and Grain (*She-chi t'an*) paired with it on the west. The altar was square with a yellow center surrounded by earth colored to correspond to the colors of the four directions, the four quarters over which the Son of Heaven ruled.

There is no evidence that the Yung-lo emperor tried to locate the "markets behind" the palace enclosure, as enjoined by the *Chou li*. But at least in his time there were no markets in front, and the parts of Peking to the east and west of the imperial city were given over, as the *Chou li* prescribed, to the residences of the people.

In the southern suburb east of the main north-south axis of the city, there was built in 1420 an Altar of Heaven (*T'ien t'an*). In its design were reiterated the Son of Heaven's claims to be the center and pivot of the cosmos: the altar was built in three terraces symbolizing the three realms given order by the Son of Heaven; ascent to the top was by three flights of nine steps each; the layout of the top was in marble slabs, moving from a round center outward in multiples of three to 81 at the outside rim; the number of balusters in the circular balustrade totaled 360, the number of days in the year or degrees in a circle; and so on. Nearby stood a porcelain furnace used to burn a bullock as an offering to Heaven.[100] This complex represents the final elaboration of the suburban sacrifice to Heaven whose beginnings we noted in the Duke of Chou's ritual sacrifice of two oxen outside the new city of Lo.

From our brief description of Ming Peking, it is clear that this city was in closer accord with the canonical cosmology than were either of the Sung capitals or, indeed, Sui and T'ang Ch'ang-an (see Map 5). A grid plan of principal streets led to the main gates. There was an emphasis on the north-south axis, and the palace enclosure occupied approximately the center of the city. The palaces themselves had the audience halls in front and the imperial residences behind. The whole city, and especially the palace and imperial enclosures, faced south. The Temple of the Imperial Ancestors and the Altar of Land and Grain were laid out on the classical plan. In details as well as in the broad outlines, every effort was made to see that the city conformed to the most ancient precedents. I have noted the Altar of Heaven as one example

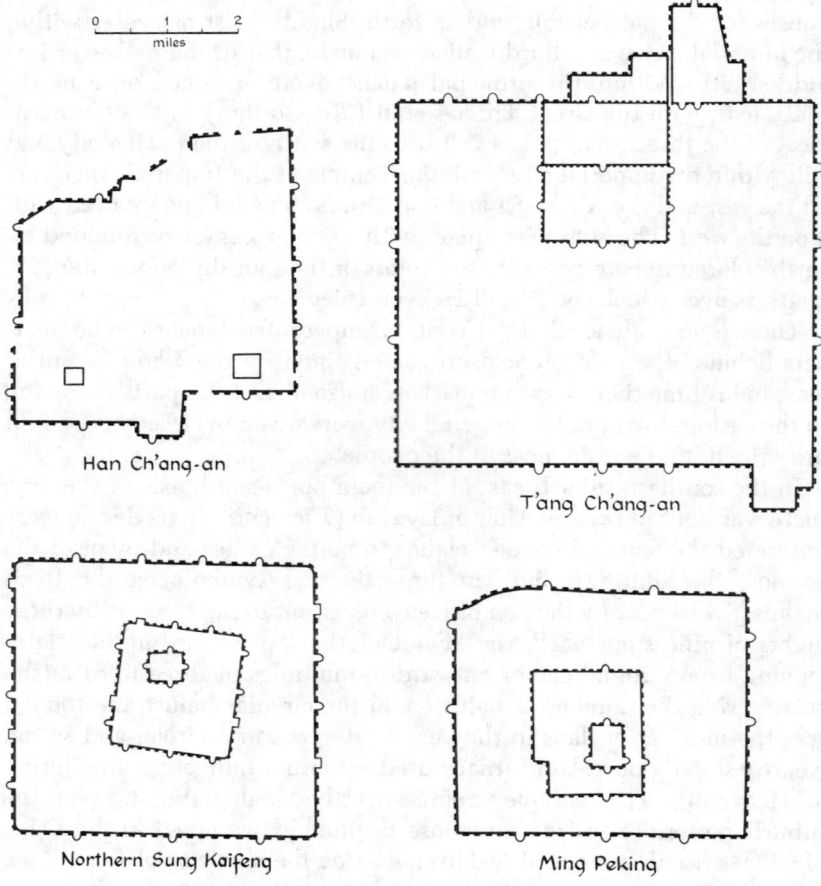

MAP 5. FOUR CAPITALS, A COMPARISON OF SIZES AND SHAPES

of this, but others could be given. The construction of the principal buildings was traditional. For example, the Great Throne Hall, with its great forecourt and its marble balustrades, has awed generations of Chinese and foreigners, yet it is largely built in wood of basic post-and-lintel construction. It stands on a raised platform of pounded earth, as did the ceremonial buildings of the Shang. The whole is magnified, but the basic principles are the same as they were in remote antiquity.

Conclusion

We have reviewed the longest tradition of city cosmology the world has ever known. We might speculate briefly on some of the reasons for its persistence. One reason is that the symbolism of Chinese cities became a part—if only a minor one—of the imperial ideology, with its emphasis on the centrality of China in the world and on the Son of Heaven as *radiator maximus* of civilization. It was, of course, the literate elite, in their long symbiotic relationship with the Chinese emperors, who insisted time and again on the importance of the ritual-symbolic acts of "their" emperor, on his role as pivot of the cosmos who should operate in a microcosm of the Chinese universe—the capital. A second reason is that the cosmology from which city symbolism derived was part of the enduring world view of the Chinese people. A third reason is that the artisans kept alive, in good times and bad, a profoundly conservative architectural tradition, so that when the time came to build anew, they resorted to traditional forms and techniques.[101]

Other forces may also help to account for the longevity of this symbol system. One was the cumulative weight of history, which became in time a formidably detailed and complex body of precedent. Historical precedent had for the Chinese something of the power of law and logic for Westerners. If this is true, the increasing weight of cumulative history was against innovation whether in city building or in any other field. Further, one may speculate that the Neo-Confucian synthesis of the tenth to the twelfth centuries drove men back to ancient models, to meticulous reexamination of classical texts. At the same time it undoubtedly discouraged innovation in many realms, including the design and the symbolism of cities. Finally, the defensive posture of the Chinese order from the Northern Sung onward, followed by the harsh century of Mongol domination, brought into being the fervent Chinese restorationism of the Ming. If this had not occurred, one could argue that—despite the other brakes we have noted—the period from 1368 to modern times might have seen a wider range of innovation in social policies, in thought, and indeed in the design of cities.

The Morphology of Walled Capitals

SEN-DOU CHANG

Walls have been so central to the Chinese idea of a city that the traditional words for city and wall are identical, the character *ch'eng* standing for both. In imperial times the great bulk of China's urban population was concentrated in walled cities; an unwalled urban center was at least in some senses not a proper city.

Archaeological evidence has revealed that the earliest city walls were simply pounded earth ramparts. These ramparts in later times were faced with bricks, ceramic blocks, or cut stones as a protection against weathering and erosion. Although some prosperous cities probably had their walls faced as early as in the T'ang period, evidence from local gazetteers makes it clear that the brick or stone walls of most nineteenth-century cities date from no earlier than the late fourteenth century. The walls of the early cities on the site of Peking were all of pounded earth, and it was not until late in the Yüan period that the city walls were faced with reed matting to prevent weathering.[1] The brick facing was added only after Peking became the Ming capital in 1421.

The Ming period and the first century of the Ch'ing witnessed the extensive construction of city walls. Few walled cities had been built under the Yüan dynasty (1280–1368), whose Mongol founders, pastoral in origin, were unsympathetic to walled city construction. In fact, at one time the Mongols had forbidden the building of city walls throughout China in order to display their power. Those walls that predated the Mongol conquest deteriorated during the thirteenth and early fourteenth centuries; as a result, hundreds were in need of repair by the time the Mongols were overthrown.[2]

The materials used to face city walls in late imperial times differed from one region to another. In the river valleys of the Middle Yangtze

Fig. 1. City Wall and Corner Tower of T'ai-ku, a county capital in T'ai-yüan *fu*, Shansi. From C. P. Fitzgerald, *China: A Short Cultural History* (London: Cresset Press, 1935).

and in the Canton delta, where clay is abundant, city walls were usually faced with large fired bricks laid in lime plaster. In the Upper Yangtze region, where easily worked red sandstone is readily available, walls were often faced with dressed stones laid in regular courses of equal thickness. The moat-encircled walls, with their bastions and towers rising over the bare surrounding countryside, acquired an appearance of antiquity in fairly short order from the weathering of the facing and the decay of the crenellations. When repairs were undertaken they did not as a rule occasion any considerable change in the architectural appearance of the walls.

Like many city walls in Europe and the Middle East, those in China were built essentially to protect palaces, temples, granaries, residences, and certain natural resources against barbarian invasion, tribal uprising, and peasant rebellion. Towers were erected at corners and over gates: the corner ones, of brick or stone, were fortified on their outer faces and loopholed for cannon; those above gates, usually fashioned in the form of three-story rectangular pagodas, were built largely of wood and normally had tiled roofs. These latter towers, typically the most striking feature of a city's architecture, served as living quarters for soldiers on duty at the gates and as posts for archers in times of siege. (For an example of a corner tower, see Figure 1.)

Before the introduction of modern artillery, Chinese city walls were almost indestructible. Their solidity made any attempt to breach them by mining or bombardment a difficult task; and their height, ranging from five to fifteen meters, made scaling difficult and hazardous, even though scaling ladders had been used as early as in the fourth century B.C. A city resolutely defended could withstand attack from the largest armies, and Chinese history includes many tales of famous sieges and heroic defenses. To break through the walls of a city was considered such an exhausting task that success was more likely than not to leave the attackers too weak to meet the fresh strength of the defenders.[3] Even in modern warfare city walls have continued to play a vital role in the Chinese concept of effective defense. In explaining why the People's Liberation Army was unable to take the city of Ta-t'ung, Shansi (see Map 1 for the layout of its walls), despite a siege of 45 days in the summer of 1946, a journalist wrote: "All you need do is to look at the outer walls, and then the inner ones. . . . In places, the masonry is at least 50 feet thick. Communist artillery shells may have been able to play havoc with the old wooden drum tower above one gate, but they could not make more than dents and scratches on the brick work."[4]

Conspicuous hills and bluffs were sometimes utilized to improve the

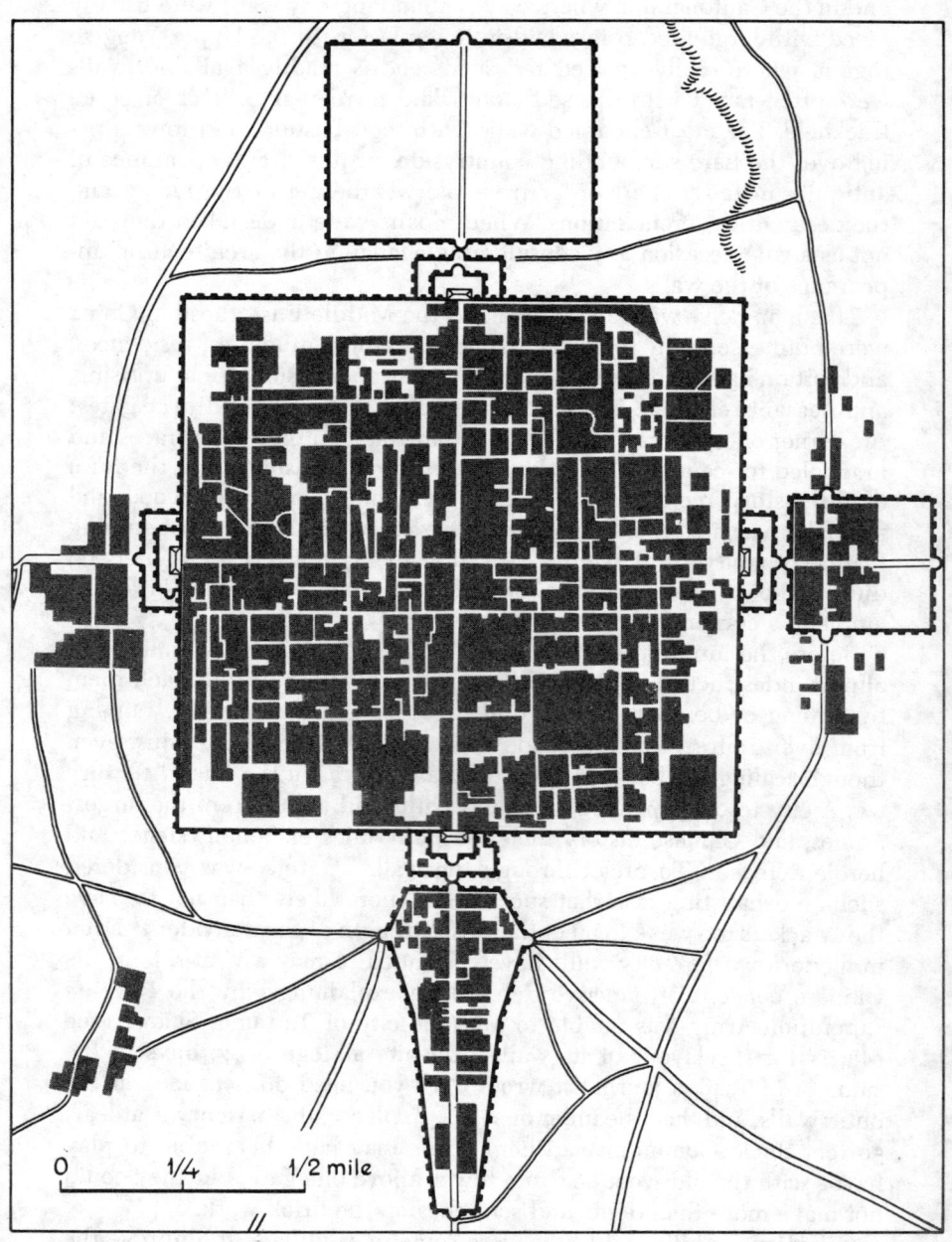

MAP 1. TA-T'UNG-FU, Shansi, showing built-up areas and details of gate enceintes and enclosed suburbs.

The Morphology of Walled Capitals

defensive function of the walls, though of course a hilly site for a city was seldom preferred to a level one. In the case of Lu-lung, a county capital in Chihli, for example, most parts of the north and east walls were built along the crest of a range of hills, and a cliff was even substituted for the central portion of the north wall (see Figure 2). The walls of some garrison towns established on the coast in Ming times also rested partly on sea cliffs.

Whereas most cities in China were surrounded by only a single wall, a few—notably Peking, Tsinan, Lanchow, and Canton—had a full or partial second wall. In most cases, this second wall was constructed to extend the city's defensive system to settlements that had grown up outside the original wall. Cities with double walls were for the most part provincial- or higher-level capitals and frontier towns of strategic importance. Other major cities without elaborate second walls often had enceinte walls forming small semicircular or rectangular enclosures around their gates, since a city's gates were the main target of attack in traditional Chinese warfare. Examples of such gate defenses may be seen in the panoramic view of Lu-lung provided by the county gazetteer (Figure 2) and in the photograph of Loyang (Figure 3).

The city wall was ordinarily surrounded by a moat, and the pair of characters for city walls and moats came to be used as a single technical term in Chinese military literature.[5] As the earth used for constructing the wall was for the most part obtained through excavating the moat, the two were built at the same time. Moats were generally narrower in North and Northwest China than in other regions. For example, the moats surrounding Peking and Taiyuan were only some thirty meters wide; those around the Lower Yangtze cities of Nanking and Soochow were approximately eighty meters wide. This disparity reflects the differences in the water supply available to fill them. Moat depth also varied from city to city, but the majority fell in the range of from three to five meters.[6] Moats were typically broadened near each city gate, access to which was normally provided by means of a stone-slab or wooden bridge. The road leading from the bridge to the gate was seldom straight. In most cases it followed a right angle and thus paralleled the city wall; in the most elaborate defense structures it followed a zigzag alignment, piercing three or four preliminary gates.

The walls around riverine cities in many cases had the additional function of defense against the floods that were a continual menace in many lowland areas. In this respect, the cities of China resemble the walled cities of the Middle East. Even though gates were often concentrated near the river to facilitate access to ferries, bridges, and wharves (see

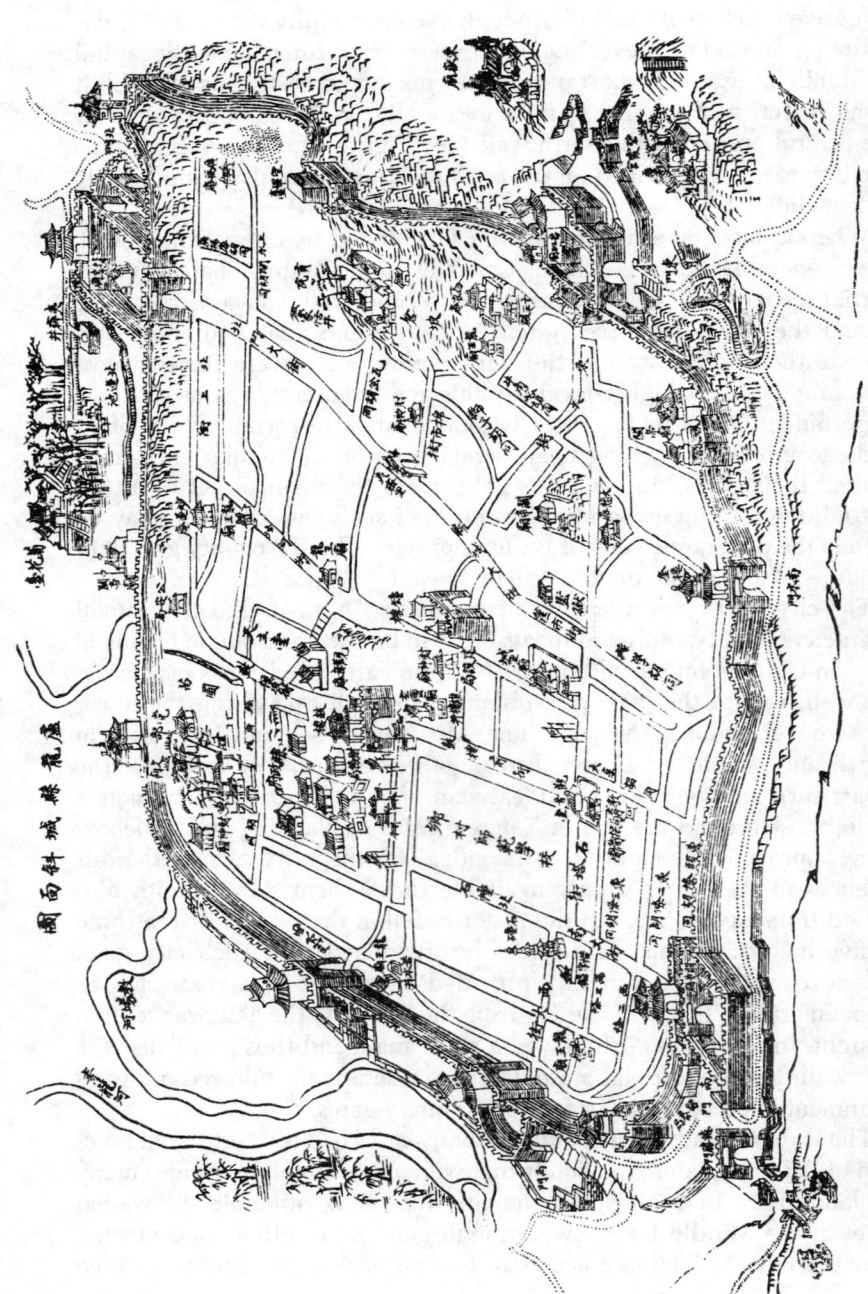

FIG. 2. LU-LUNG, a county capital in Yung-p'ing fu, Chihli. The north wall is at the top. In addition to the five gates, the city wall is punctuated by four corner towers and, on the east, a military lookout. The two arches near the city's center are the drum tower (northwest) and bell tower (southeast). The county yamen is located in the block immediately northwest of the drum tower, the City God temple just south of the bell tower. From Ho-pei Lu-lung hsien chih, 1931.

FIG. 3. LOYANG, showing enceinte wall around the west gate and suburban development. Aerial photograph from Wulf Diether Graf zu Castell, *Chinaflug* (Berlin and Zurich: Atlantis-Verlag, 1938).

Map 2 for an example), they could be effectively closed off by sandbagging in the case of a serious flood. When such a flood occurred, the walls also prevented the intrusion of silt into the city. From the outside, the walls of many riverine cities appear to be half buried under sand and gravel.

Surrounding the walls of certain cities in North China were earth ramparts of more or less circular form and (on average) twice the radius of the walls themselves. In many cities the ramparts were only partial—limited to the section facing the river. In the case of Chung-mou (Honan), for example, located only about ten miles south of the Yellow River in an area of frequent inundation, two earth ramparts were constructed to the north of the city as a permanent measure of flood prevention. Such landmarks characterized the outskirts of many cities along the lower courses of the Huai and Yellow rivers. (For an example of ramparts in another region, see the map of Hsin-chu, Taiwan, on p. 163.)

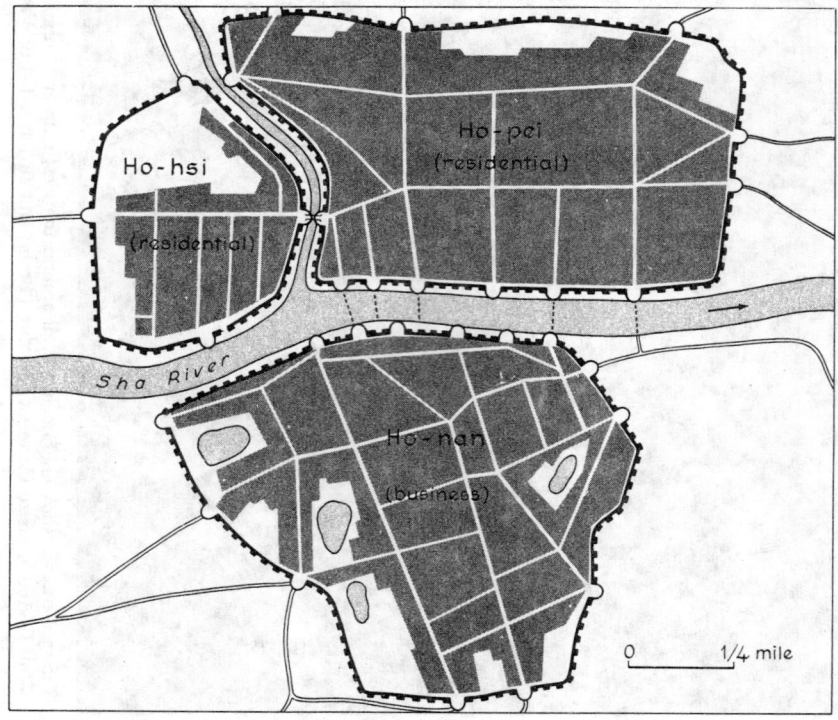

MAP 2. CHOU-CHIA-K'OU, a nonadministrative city in Huai-ning *hsien*, Ch'en-chou *fu*, Honan.

The Morphology of Walled Capitals

The Site of the Walled City

One of the characteristic features of walled cities is their sites. In contrast with the usual situation in Europe, the Middle East, and Japan, walled cities in China were located almost exclusively in lowlands—conspicuous relief being avoided to the extent permitted by local topography. Rarely is a town in the South sited on the slope of a mountain or hill; almost never is one so sited in the North. In 1890, of the 58 county capitals of Fukien, a province with rugged topography, 53 were situated at an altitude of less than 400 meters, and no less than 50 were on rivers, streams, or other bodies of water.

Among the 1,276 county capitals in the eighteen provinces of China Proper in the 1890's, 913, or well over 70 percent, were located at elevations below 400 meters (see Table 1). Even those cities situated above that level were largely concentrated in the lowest-lying portions of each province. Yet areas below 400 meters account for less than a quarter of the total territory in the eighteen provinces.

The Chinese preference for low-lying urban sites is closely associated with the heavy concentration of their predominantly agrarian popula-

TABLE 1. DISTRIBUTION OF COUNTY CAPITALS BY ALTITUDE, 1890's
(*Elevations in meters*)

Province	No. of county capitals	Elevation above mean sea level						Prevailing elevation in the province
		0–50	50–200	200–400	400–1,000	1,000–2,000	2,000–3,000	
Kiangsu	62	62	–	–	–	–	–	0–50
Shantung	96	75	18	3	–	–	–	0–200
Chekiang	75	55	15	5	–	–	–	0–200
Anhwei	51	33	12	6	–	–	–	0–200
Kwangtung	78	53	15	10	–	–	–	0–200
Chihli	123	78	29	6	10	–	–	0–200
Kiangsi	75	25	35	12	3	–	–	50–400
Honan	96	14	60	16	6	–	–	50–400
Hunan	64	10	25	24	5	–	–	50–400
Kwangsi	49	2	22	18	7	–	–	50–1,000
Hupeh	60	20	23	7	9	1	–	50–1,000
Fukien	58	24	9	20	5	–	–	200–1,000
Szechwan	112	–	–	44	42	11	15	200–2,000
Kweichow	33	–	–	1	14	18	–	400–2,000
Shansi	85	–	–	18	40	27	–	400–2,000
Shensi	73	–	–	9	52	11	1	400–2,000
Yunnan	39	–	–	–	5	32	2	1,000–3,000
Kansu	47	–	–	–	–	31	16	1,000–3,000
Total	1,276	451	263	199	198	131	34	

SOURCE: Ting Wen-chiang et al., *Chung-kuo fen sheng hsin t'u* (New atlas of China's provinces; Shanghai: Shen pao, 1933).

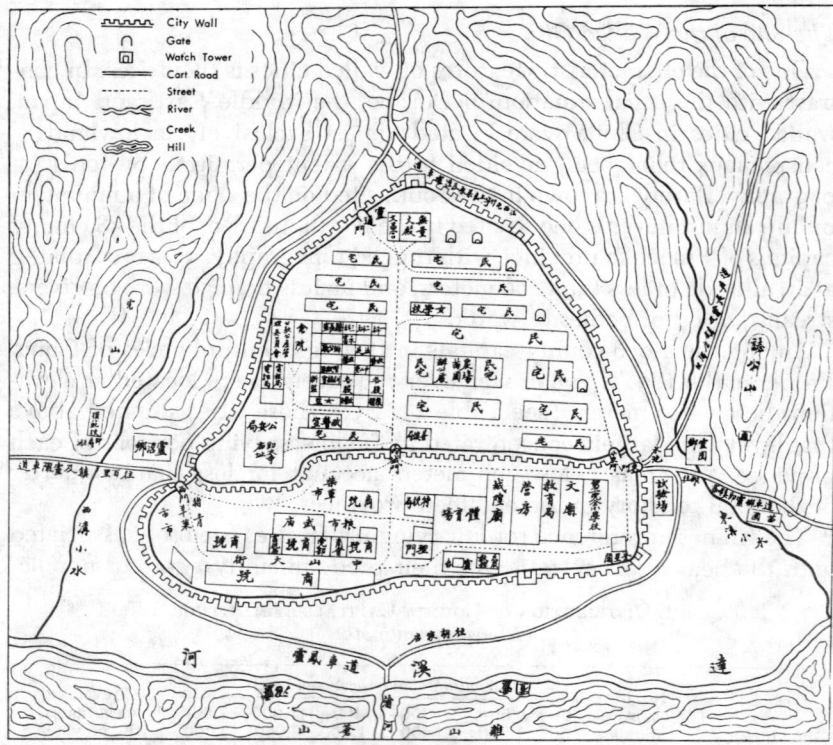

Fig. 4. Ling-t'ai, a county capital in Ching *chou*, Kansu. Note the north-bank siting. The county yamen is in the western quarter of the northern city. Business districts and markets appear only in the southern city. From *Ling-t'ai hsien chih*, 1935.

tion in the lowlands—in flood plains, river valleys, intermontane basins, and small oases along the foothills. As a result, upland areas, marginal for Chinese agriculture, remained largely unsettled and undeveloped. Since urbanization developed to serve the basic economic, political, and social needs of the rural population, it was natural for cities to grow up along the navigable waterways that were an important means for connecting them with rural communities or with other cities. Mining towns, lumbering centers, and resort towns—common features in the mountainous regions of many Western countries—were rare in China. The Chinese penchant for a level site may have been influenced by the traditional preference for square or rectangular city walls. Nonetheless, in hilly regions where the topography afforded little level land, the square or rectangular ideal was flouted in order to bring within the city walls

The Morphology of Walled Capitals

the necessary amount of flat land. The capital of Ling-t'ai *hsien* in Kansu (see Figure 4), illustrates the tendency in such cases for the wall to follow a contour line.

Water was probably the most important factor influencing the site selection of walled cities, since it figured in transportation, defense, water supply, and (indirectly, through irrigation) food supply. As can be seen from detailed maps of every region in China, the most favored place for a walled city was on a river bank. In South and Central China, where hills are numerous and level land scarce, the small pockets of flat land formed by riverine deposits on the convex bank of a meander often constituted the most favorable sites for city construction. In certain cases, the level land on the river bank was so narrow that a portion of the city wall had to be built on the slopes of a hill, with the result that the area enclosed by the wall was an inclined surface facing the river. In the far Northwest, where annual rainfall is less than ten inches, oases were the only possible locations for settlements large enough to serve as capitals. The major cities in the Kansu corridor were located near alluvial fans, which were irrigated naturally every spring by the snow-melt tumbling down from the high mountains to the southwest.

The association of walled cities with bodies of water is often reflected in their names.[7] Of several categories of such names, we may distinguish first those denoting simply a riverine site. The word *lin* means "near to" or "along." Names of walled cities that use this character include Lin-hsiang (Hunan), Lin-t'ung (Shensi), and Lin-fen (Shansi), the other character in each case specifying the name of the river near which the city is located. *P'u*, which means "the bank or reach of a river," figures in such city names as Chang-p'u (Fukien), "on the bank of the Chang River"; Hsü-p'u (Hunan), "on the bank of the Hsü river"; and Chiang-p'u (Kiangsu), "on the river bank." Other cities bear such general names as Chiang-tu (Kiangsu), "river metropolis," and Chiang-ch'eng (Yunnan), "river city."

The names of a second category of cities indicate their compass positions in relation to rivers. Examples include Kuei-tung (Hunan), "east of the Kuei River"; Fen-hsi (Shansi), "west of the Fen River"; and Wei-nan (Shensi), "south of the Wei River."

A third category of cities bears names that specify their position in relation to the entire course of a river. For example, Wei-yüan (Kansu) means "the headwaters of the Wei River," Wu-yüan (Anhwei) means "the source of the Wu River," Chung-chiang (Szechwan) means "the middle course of the river," and Chiang-k'ou (Kweichow) means "the mouth of the river."

The names of a fourth grouping denote the city's relation to two or more rivers. Examples include Ho-chien (Chihli), "between the rivers"; Shuang-liu (Szechwan), "two parallel streams"; San-shui (Kwangtung), "three waterways"; Chiao-ho (Chihli), "intertwining rivers"; Chih-chiang (Hupeh), "branching rivers"; and Wu-ho (Anhwei), "five rivers."

The physical characteristics of a city's riverine site are expressed in a category of names derived from geological or geomorphological features. Examples include Ho-ch'ü (Shansi), "river bend"; Ch'ü-chiang (Kwangtung), "meander"; Ch'uan-sha (Kiangsu), "alluvial sands"; Hsia-chiang (Kiangsi), "river gorge"; Chiang-ling (Hupeh), "river valley terrace"; Ch'ang-t'ing (Fukien), "long sand spit"; Ch'ien-chiang (Kwangsi), "migratory river"; and P'ing-ku (Chihli), "level vale."

Flood control has traditionally been an important task for the Chinese ruling classes. Cities were founded in the valleys of troublesome rivers in part as centers for managing hydraulic works, and many such cities were given suitably auspicious names. Thus Chiang-ning (Kiangsu) means "river of peace," P'ing-chiang (Hunan) means "smooth river," An-ch'i (Fukien) means "tranquil creek," Chen-chiang (Kiangsu) means "to subdue the river," and Ts'ung-chiang (Kweichow) means "obedient river."

A final category of names denotes sites near bodies of water other than rivers. Lakes and springs were attractive city sites, and many inspired poetic names. For example, T'u-ch'üan (Liaoning) means "gushing fountain," Kan-ch'üan (Shensi) means "sweet spring," Lung-ch'üan (Chekiang) means "dragon's fountain," Ho-tse (Shantung) means "lotus marsh," Shen-ch'ih (Shansi) means "sacred pond," and P'ing-hu (Chekiang) means "unruffled lake."

Studies of river towns often attempt to explain the preference for one bank over the other.* In this regard, a number of generalizations appear to hold for agrarian China as a whole. First, a factor of obvious importance is the direction from which local products enter the river traffic. This consideration goes far to account for the fact that local capitals on the Min River (Szechwan) from Hsin-ching south to its confluence with the Yangtze at Hsü-chou-fu were all sited on the west bank. Products from the Tibetan plateau such as herbs, drugs, hides, metals, minerals, and lumber usually came by land to the west bank of the Min for water transport downstream on junks or rafts. A second and closely related factor is the productivity of the basin land on either side of the river. This consideration came into play in the upper Han River basin (from the river's source down to Tzu-yang, Shensi) where the most productive

---

* I am grateful to Andrew J. Watson and G. William Skinner for data and arguments that have enabled me to revise my initial analysis of riverbank siting.

The Morphology of Walled Capitals

land, including almost all that was suitable for paddy, lay north of the river; capitals were thus sited exclusively on the north bank. Two additional factors have favored the north bank of rivers. From earliest times, the direction of Chinese migration has been predominantly southward. Thus, as the frontiers of Chinese civilization moved first to the Huai and the Han, then to the Yangtze, and finally to the West River, walled cities were in most cases built on the north banks, partly because land to the north would have been developed first by Chinese colonists and partly because the river could thereby provide a defensive barrier against the hostile or at least unfamiliar non-Han peoples farther south. This is perhaps the major factor that accounts for the north-bank location of ten of the eleven capitals that lie along the West River from Heng-chou (Kwangsi) to Canton. Finally, sites on valley slopes facing south afford more sunshine and, in most parts of China, better air circulation than sites on slopes facing north. These latter considerations, of particular importance in the northern regions where Chinese civilization began, are functionally related to the priority given the south over the other three compass directions in Chinese cosmology and ritual. (See the paper by Arthur F. Wright for evidence of this emphasis in city planning.) For these reasons, then, cities on the north banks of rivers far outnumber those on the south banks. In Chinese cosmology, sun and shade are associated with *yang* and *yin*, respectively, and it is no accident that Chinese local capitals include more than eighty with the character *yang* (e.g., Huai-yang, Fen-yang, Sung-yang, Liu-yang) but fewer than ten with the character *yin* (e.g., Huai-yin, Chiang-yin).

Other things being equal, the sites of major cities tend to alternate from one bank to the other as one proceeds along waterways that are used for transport. This holds, for instance, for central market towns and cities along most stretches of the Grand Canal and for sites along the Han River from Tzu-yang to its confluence with the Yangtze; but since some of the nonadministrative towns are unwalled, demonstration of this point falls outside the scope of this paper.

Shape and Size

Walled cities in ancient China were usually square or rectangular in shape.* Virtually all of the imperial capitals built in the regions of North

---

* In his contribution to this volume, Professor Wright has called attention to the relationship between the Han cosmological conception of the earth as a perfect square and the square or rectangular design of the capital city. As he also notes, the preference for a square or rectangle was related to the still earlier practice of aligning cities with the four directions (see pp. 47 and 37, respectively).

and Northwest China, where Chinese civilization originated, were in fact square or rectangular, the most notable exception being Han Ch'ang-an. Every one of the five cities built at the present site of Peking—from the Shang city of Ch'i to Ming Peking—was square or rectangular.[8] Cities approximating a perfect square are far more common in the North and Northwest than elsewhere in China (Ta-t'ung-fu in Shansi, Map 1, is a prime example). Departures from the rectangular are more frequent in the central and southern regions. For instance, the only cities outside the North and Northwest that have served as imperial capitals, Southern Sung Hangchow and Ming Nanking, were both characterized by highly irregular walls. Of the eighteen provincial capitals in the 1890's, the walls of five (Nanchang, Kweiyang, Kweilin, Canton, and Foochow—all located in southern regions) bore no relationship to a rectangle; the only two with perfectly rectangular walls—Sian and Taiyuan—were both located in the Northwest.

At less exalted levels of the administrative hierarchy the north-south dichotomy persisted, with rectangularity of walls more closely approximated more often in the North and Northwest than elsewhere. Moreover, in these two regions a direct correlation was evident between wall rectangularity and the city's administrative rank. For example, the prefectural cities of Kung-ch'ang-fu (Kansu), P'u-chou-fu (Shansi), and Ch'ang-te-fu (Honan), all had rectangular walls, whereas at least some of their subordinate county-level capitals were irregular in shape.[9] In most of the South, any tendency toward orthodoxy in the planning of higher-ranked cities appears to have been offset by the generally rugged topography, which made it harder to achieve regularity with a large city than with a small one. None of the nine prefectural capitals in Kwangtung, including Canton itself, was square or rectangular. One of the few square cities in Kwangtung, Shih-hsing in Nan-hsiung *chou*, had an intramural area of only 65 acres.[10] The city's small size made square walls possible even in an area of rugged terrain.

In the case of rectangular cities, the ratio between the sides varied from a true square to an extreme of 1 : 4, as in the city wall of Han-tan (Chihli). The modal ratio, however, closely approached $1 : \sqrt{2}$, which is generally considered by modern psychologists to be optimal in terms of aesthetics and visual stability. Rectangular walls were oriented with the long side running east-west more often than north-south. Departures from perfect rectangularity include one or more curving sides, one or more corners departing from a right angle (parallelograms, trapezoids, and trapeziums are legion), one or more truncated corners (the most

The Morphology of Walled Capitals

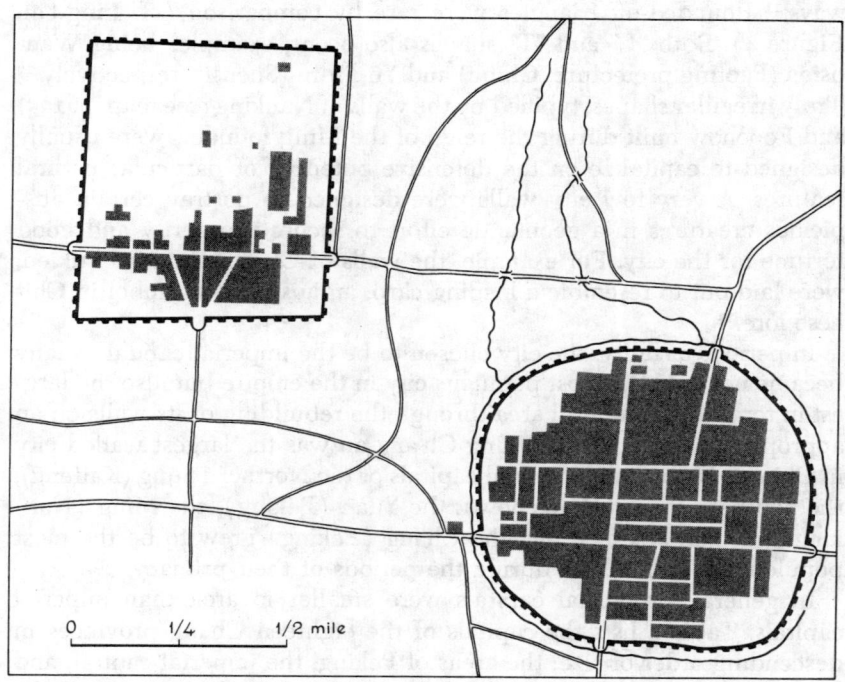

MAP 3. FENG-YANG-FU (*lower right*) AND CAPITAL OF
FENG-YANG HSIEN (*upper left*), ANHWEI

notable example being the northwest corner of Peking), and one or more corners rounded off.

City walls that were essentially circular were especially common in the peripheral areas of central and southern regions. Nineteenth-century I-lan, Taiwan (see map on p. 165), provides a typical example. Since circular walls require fewer construction materials per unit of enclosed area than rectangular walls, it may have been considerations of economy that encouraged departure from the cosmological ideal. Yet it is interesting to note that the wall of Feng-yang-fu, a city the Ming founder had built in his native area, is essentially circular (see Map 3).

After the more or less rectangular and circular shapes, perhaps the most common wall shapes in late imperial China were those ranging from ovals through egg shapes to rounded-off diamonds. Typical examples were Ningpo (see map, pp. 406–7), Wu-hsi, and Hsin-chu, Taiwan (see map, p. 163). Many cities in this category, Ningpo and Wu-hsi among them, were shaped to follow prominent features of local waterways.[11] Rounded-off triangles were rare by comparison (cf. Ling-t'ai, Figure 4). Both "L" and "T" shapes also occur, examples being Wan-hsien (Paoting prefecture, Chihli) and Yü-lin-fu (Shensi), respectively.[12] Truly irregular shapes, typified by the walls of Nanking (see map, p. 135) and Foochow built during the reign of the Ming founder, were usually designed to capitalize on the defensive potential of particular natural features. A very few city walls were designed to portray certain auspicious creatures in a geomantic effort to secure prosperity and good fortune for the city. For example, the walls of Ch'üan-chou-fu, Fukien, were laid out to resemble a leaping carp, an auspicious symbol in Chinese lore.[13]

In periods of unity, the city chosen to be the imperial capital usually became not only the most populous city in the empire but also the largest in terms of intramural area through the rebuilding of its walls on an appropriately grand scale. T'ang Ch'ang-an was the largest walled city in Chinese history; the imperial capitals of the Northern Sung (Kaifeng), the Southern Sung (Hangchow), the Yüan (Peking), the Ming (Nanking and then Peking), and the Ch'ing (Peking) grew to be the most populous cities in China during the periods of their primacy.

In general, provincial capitals were smaller in area than imperial capitals. Table 2 lists the capitals of the eighteen Ch'ing provinces in descending order of size; the areas of Peking, the imperial capital, and Nanking, the so-called "secondary" imperial capital and seat of the governor-generalship of Kiangsu, Anhwei, and Kiangsi, are given for comparison. The nineteenth-century walls of Hangchow and Nanking were essentially unchanged from the days when these cities served as imperial capitals, but those of Kaifeng and Sian were much reduced. The provincial capital was the largest city in fourteen of the eighteen provinces. Two of the exceptions were the obvious cases of Peking (larger than the Chihli capital Paoting) and Nanking (larger than the Kiangsu capital Soochow). The other two involved Anhwei, whose capital city Anking was just over half the size of Lü-chou-fu (506 hectares), and Fukien, whose capital Foochow was slightly exceeded in area by Ch'üan-chou-fu (640 hectares). Both of these exceptionally large prefectural cities had been far more prosperous in Sung times than they were in the nineteenth century: in 1077, Lü-chou-fu ranked eighth in commercial tax revenues throughout the Northern Sung empire;[14] during the Southern Sung, Ch'üan-chou-fu, known to Arab traders as Zaitun, served as China's chief seaport.[15]

Table 3 makes it clear that the correlation between a capital city's walled area and its level in the administrative hierarchy extended down

The Morphology of Walled Capitals

TABLE 2. WALLED AREA OF IMPERIAL AND PROVINCIAL CAPITALS, 1890's

City	Walled area ha.	Walled area mi.^{2}	City	Walled area ha.	Walled area mi.^{2}
Peking	6320	24.40	Tsinan	510	1.97
Nanking	4055	15.66	Foochow	505	1.95
Soochow	1480	5.71	Changsha	415	1.60
Kaifeng	1290	4.98	Nanchang	395	1.53
Hangchow	1280	4.94	Paoting	325	1.25
Sian	1200	4.63	Kunming	320	1.24
Chengtu	1150	4.44	Lanchow	270	1.04
Taiyuan	840	3.24	Anking	260	1.00
Wuchang	635	2.45	Kweilin	235	.91
Canton	520	2.01	Kweiyang	225	.87

SOURCES: Topographic sheets of U.S. Army Map Service, China 1:250,000 series (city plans at the scale of 1:25,000 on reverse sides of selected sheets) and 1:50,000 series (1944) except as follows. For Hangchow, Chengtu, Wuchang, Lanchow, Kweilin, and Kweiyang, Ting Wen-chiang, et al., *Chung-hua min kuo hsin ti t'u* (New atlas of the Republic of China; Shanghai: Shen pao kuan, 1933); for Sian, Albert Herrmann, *Atlas of China* (Cambridge: Harvard-Yenching Institute, 1935); for Kunming, *Kun-ming shih chih* (Gazetteer of Kunming; Kunming, 1924). The area for Peking includes the southern "Chinese" city, for Canton the "New City," for Tsinan and Lanchow the territory enclosed by the outer wall, and for Sian the main city enclosed by the rectangular walls.

TABLE 3. AVERAGE WALLED AREA OF SAMPLE PREFECTURAL AND COUNTY CAPITALS, SELECTED PROVINCES, 1910

Province	Prefectural capitals Number measured	Prefectural capitals Average area in ha.	County capitals Number measured	County capitals Average area in ha.
Kiangsu	5	194	12	175
Honan	4	186	7	160
Shansi	4	175	5	155
Chihli	6	154	12	125
Shantung	5	147	8	117
Chekiang	5	136	15	110
Anhwei	4	138	9	109
Fukien	5	109	18	104
Kiangsi	6	107	8	94
Hunan	3	73	5	60
Kwangtung	6	45	28	39

SOURCES: U.S. Army Map Service, 1:50,000 topographic sheets on China, 1944–45; *Kita shina chikei zu* (North China topographic maps), 1:50,000 (Japan [Rikigun], Shinkoku Chūtongun, Shireibu, Rikuchi Sokuryōbu, 1907–11); *Shina jōkaku no gaiyō* (A general description of Chinese cities; n.p., Shina Hakkengun Soshireibu, 1940).

to the prefectural and county levels. In each of eleven provinces, the average area of a sample of prefectural capitals was significantly greater than that of a comparable sample of county capitals. Table 3 also points up marked differences from one part of China to another in the average size of capitals at both levels.

Multiple Cities

Cities consisting of two or more separately walled components—though hardly commonplace in the nineteenth century—were found in all regions of the empire.*

One distinctive type of multiple city was designed to achieve ethnic segregation and thereby facilitate control by the group wielding state power. The Manchus, in the wake of their conquest of China in the seventeenth century, were concerned to preserve the ethnic identity and military prowess of their troops stationed at key central places; to this end, they appropriated for exclusive Manchu residence entire sections within the walls of many cities and in a few instances built a partial wall to create an enclosed site for a Manchu quarter. Another approach was to construct a completely separate enclosure within a short distance of an existing Chinese city. Some 34 twin cities were created by the Manchus, most of them in North and Northwest China.[16] A notable example is Ch'ing-chou-fu in Shantung, where the Manchu city was built less than a mile north of the existing prefectural capital. Other twin cities were created in the second half of the nineteenth century as Chinese control and settlement expanded in Northwest China and Sinkiang. In suppressing the Moslem rebellions that began in the 1860's, Chinese troops, Hunanese for the most part, were in several cases garrisoned alongside Uighur settlements, and these camps became the nuclei of new Chinese cities. By 1870, the city of Urumchi (Ti-hua) was composed of three separately walled components: the Chinese, the Manchu, and the original settlement, whose population was predominantly Turkic.[17] Elsewhere in Sinkiang separate "Chinese cities" were established at Kashgar, Hami, and Khotan.[18]

A second fairly common type of multiple city was the riverine conurbation with two (or in a few instances involving a confluence, with three) separately walled components on either side of a river or canal. This type may be subcategorized by administrative status according to the number and location of yamens, if any. In most cases where only one of the components contained a yamen or yamens, the conurbation was considered a single city and called by a single name. This was true of Kuang-chou (the capital of an independent department in Honan), Yü-yao (a county capital in Shao-hsing *fu*, Chekiang), Jui-chou-fu (Kiangsi), and Ch'ung-jen (a county capital in Fu-chou prefecture, Kiangsi). In the case of one important riverine conurbation where both

---

* In this section I have drawn on data compiled by Professor Skinner and have profited from his suggestions for revision.

components were walled but only one was a capital, the traditional view was that they were separate cities: Hsiang-yang-fu and Fan-ch'eng on the Han River in Hupeh. In the few cases where each of two components supported a yamen, the riverine conurbation was perceived as two separate cities. A prominent example was Chungking, a prefectural capital at the confluence of the Chia-ling and Yangtze rivers. Across from the great city, on the north bank of the Chia-ling, was the smaller walled city of Chiang-pei, capital of a *t'ing* (subprefecture) subordinate to Ch'ung-ch'ing prefecture. Another example involved Hsü-yung (Szechwan); the yamen for Hsü-yung *t'ing* (an independent subprefecture) was in the city on the west bank; that for Yung-ning *hsien* was on the east bank. A further and well-known case is the great Wuhan conurbation where the Han River flows into the Yangtze. This was traditionally considered three separate cities, since the distances among the components were relatively great and different prefectures were involved: Wu-ch'ang served as the capital of Hupeh province, of Wu-ch'ang prefecture, and of Chiang-hsia *hsien*; Han-yang was the capital of Han-yang prefecture and of Han-yang *hsien*; Hankow had no administrative status, being subordinate to Han-yang. A conurbation where none of the components supported a yamen was invariably perceived as a single city. A number of important nonadministrative cities were of this type—one being the triple city of Chou-chia-k'ou, the most important collection and distribution center of agricultural products in central Honan during the nineteenth century. As Map 2 suggests, the business firms that conducted the city's shipping, trade, and finances were concentrated in the south-bank city, the other two smaller settlements being chiefly residential.

The usual administrative pattern in imperial China was for higher-level offices to be housed in cities that also served as capitals at lower levels. Thus all provincial capitals were also prefectural and county capitals, and almost all prefectural-level capitals also served as county-level capitals. A third type of multiple city consisted of departures from this standard administrative practice whereby a prefectural-level capital was left without the yamen of its "metropolitan" *hsien*. In the preceding discussion of riverine multiple cities, I have already noted two such cases: Chungking and Hsü-yung-t'ing, each with the yamen of its subordinate county-level unit across the river in a separate walled city. Only two other such cases are known to me: Hui-chou-fu (Kwangtung), whose metropolitan *hsien* (Kuei-shan) was administered from a separate walled city to the east of the prefectural capital; and Feng-yang-fu (Anhwei), whose metropolitan *hsien* (also known as Feng-yang) was administered from a separate walled city to the northwest of the prefectural capital (see Map 3). Kuei-hua-ch'eng and Sui-yüan, twin cities on the northern frontier of Shansi, were both administrative capitals, but neither was subordinate to the other.[19] Each of the five cases mentioned has a unique history, and the category as a whole may be considered anomalous.

A fourth type of multiple city consisted of an administrative city and its commercial "outport." Whether a seaport, a river port, or a post on an imperial highway, the nonadministrative city was closely linked to the capital of the county or department of which it was a part. Hankow's relationship to Han-yang was thus a special case of this type. Another well-known example farther upstream on the Han River is the twin city of Kuang-hua, a county capital in Hsiang-yang prefecture, and Lao-ho-k'ou, its riverine port. Ch'iung-chou-fu, a prefectural capital in Hainan, and its seaport Hai-k'ou (also walled) provide another prominent example.[20]

A fifth and final type of multiple city resulted from a site change. For one reason or another—damage from floods or warfare, an epidemic or other misfortune attributed to inauspicious geomancy, the silting up of a waterway, or a change in the course of a river—a walled city was abandoned as a capital and a new wall constructed at what was taken to be a favorable site nearby. In the few cases where both settlements survived as living cities, we are left with a twin city, one "new" and one "old," one a capital and the other not. Examples are Mi-yün, capital of a county in Shun-te prefecture, Chihli; and Nan-hsiung, capital of an autonomous department in Kwangtung.

Land Use and Transport Grids

In many traditional cities, surprisingly large proportions of the total intramural area were given over to cultivation and to lakes, ponds, streams, canals, springs, and other bodies of water. A city's ability to last out a military siege or cut itself off from rural disorder was greatly enhanced by intramural agriculture and an assured water supply. At the same time, open areas within the walls could be and were devoted to parks, and lakes and ponds were landscaped for recreational purposes. It is difficult in retrospect to determine the considerations that city builders had in mind when they decided how much of the landscape to include within the walls at a given site. However, we can make a few empirical generalizations.

The intramural areas of cities were on the average larger in relation

The Morphology of Walled Capitals

to their population in the North and Northwest than in other regions of China. The proportion of cities that included lakes, ponds, and springs within the walls also was higher in these two regions than elsewhere. These facts stem from the vulnerability of cities in North and Northwest China—regions dominated by vast plains, bordering the steppes from which came periodic nomadic invasions, and subject to a semiarid climate that enhanced the importance of an assured water supply. Cities situated in the lowland cores of the Lower and Middle Yangtze regions and of the Lingnan region naturally had a large number of internal canals and other waterways within the walls.

The higher the administrative status of the city, the more likely it was that open land and surface water within the walls would be devoted to parks. These recreational areas were preserved for the most part for the use of the aristocracy, officials, and local gentry. All imperial and many provincial capitals included parks and lakes that became famous. The Ta-ming Hu, a recreational lake in Tsinan, the capital of Shantung, occupied about one-fifth of the total area enclosed by the original city wall.

As we noted earlier, the higher the rank of an administrative city, the greater the area enclosed by planners in its original walls. High-ranked cities may have been built large in part out of concern for their defensibility, but the more usual consideration was likely to have been the expectation that the natural course of urban development would lead to larger populations in prefectural capitals than in department capitals, in department capitals than in county capitals, and so on. Cities built large because of their high administrative level or rank, yet that failed to develop important commercial functions, were inevitably left with large tracts of intramural land that could be devoted to agriculture, whether or not self-sufficiency in case of siege was an initial consideration.

Since gates in the walls determined traffic flow in and out of the city, their number and placement went far to determine the internal grid of streets and canals. Gates built solely for land traffic—by far the most common—were known simply as *men* ("gates"), whereas gates that connected internal canals to the city's moat or other external bodies of water were called *shui-men* ("water gates"). In certain instances both a road and a canal passed through a single gate. Of the nine gates that pierced the walls of Shao-hsing-fu, Chekiang, three were for land traffic only, three for water traffic only, and three for both.[21]

Because intramural canals were relatively rare in the cities of North and Northwest China, many of which even lacked moats for want of an adequate supply of running water, water gates were rare. (Note in Figure 4 the absence of a moat or water gates in Ling-t'ai, Kansu; but note, too, in Figure 2 the water gates that pierced the south and west walls of Lu-lung, Chihli.) Water gates were also uncommon in cities of the Yunnan-Kweichow Plateau and generally in cities in the high-altitude peripheries of all physiographic regions. In many cities of the Lower Yangtze region, and in certain cities in the lowland cores of other southern regions, water traffic rivaled or surpassed land traffic in importance; in such cases, the number of water gates was likely to approach or equal the number of regular gates. In some cases, water gates were symmetrically arranged in relation to the north-south axis of the walls; Ju-kao, a county capital in T'ung *chou*, Kiangsu, is a case in point.[22] When the number of water and land gates was approximately equal, the usual arrangement was to position each water gate to the left of a land gate when viewed from within the city. This is exemplified by three county capitals in Kiangsu: Tan-yang in Chen-chiang prefecture, Yen-ch'eng in Huai-an prefecture, and Tung-t'ai in Yang-chou prefecture.[23] Since the left side of an axis is the more honored in traditional Chinese thought, this practice may symbolize recognition of the overwhelming importance of waterways in the Lower Yangtze region.

In general, there was a direct relationship between the level of a city in the administrative hierarchy and the number of (land) gates in its wall. In part, this is a necessary concomitant of the correlation already established between the intramural area of cities and their administrative status. But normative considerations were also at work. As Professor Wright's contribution to this volume makes clear, imperial and other important capitals were expected to have two or more gates in each wall, and in fact T'ang Ch'ang-an, Northern Sung Kaifeng, Southern Sung Hangchow, and post-1552 Peking all had twelve or more gates. On the other hand, ordinary cities at the county level were expected to have only one gate in each wall. Of the eighteen provincial capitals, thirteen had more than four gates and none fewer. According to an unpublished study by Professor Skinner, in 1820 cities with exactly four gates were a majority of all capitals in every region except the Lower Yangtze—and even there a majority of county-level capitals had exactly four gates.

In a city with exactly four gates, each was associated with one of the cardinal directions. The significance of various gates was integrated into the symbolic system associated with the Five Elements and the five directions (the fifth being central). In obvious symbolism, the east gate

The Morphology of Walled Capitals

is associated with spring, the south gate with summer, the west gate with autumn, and the north gate with winter. The south gate symbolized warmth and life, the north gate, cold and death. Civil pomp and ritual were associated with the south gate and its suburbs, whereas the north gate and the northern suburbs had military associations. In his contribution to this volume, Stephan Feuchtwang has pointed up the significance of these and related cosmological concepts for the locations of temples and altars.

Assuming four gates, we may now look at the street grids associated with them. The most regular is a Latin cross formed by two streets connecting the four gates (see Figure 5, model *a*). The city's drum tower is typically located at the central intersection. Ta-t'ung-fu, Shansi (Map 1), is a classic example, whereas Feng-yang-fu, Anhwei (Map 3), and I-lan, Taiwan (see p. 165) illustrate more characteristic slight departures from perfect symmetry. A second general pattern departs from the first in omitting the northern half of the north-south thoroughfare, so that the street running north from the south gate forms a T with the east-west thoroughfare (see Figure 5, model *b*). In most cases, this street pattern is associated with a north-central location of the yamen and other official buildings, a feature that is doubtless modeled on the layout of T'ang Ch'ang-an. In many such cases there is no north gate, and when a city has only three gates it is generally the inauspicious north gate that is left out. The capital of Feng-yang *hsien*, Anhwei (upper left, Map 3) illustrates this pattern. It is also clearly reflected in the complex layout of Ningpo (see pp. 406–7), where the drum tower marks the intersection of the street from the south gate with the main thoroughfare connecting the west gate and one of the gates in the east, and where all three yamens are in the north-central part of the city.

The majority of city plans, however, show a clear-cut preference for avoiding an uninterrupted thoroughfare running straight from one gate to another. This preference is doubtless related both to considerations of defense and to popular beliefs that *kuei*—ghosts and other evil spirits —travel only in straight lines.[24] In this regard, it is noteworthy that cities

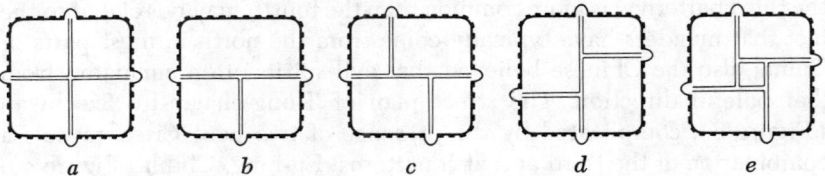

FIG. 5. MODELS OF STREET GRIDS IN CITIES WITH FOUR GATES

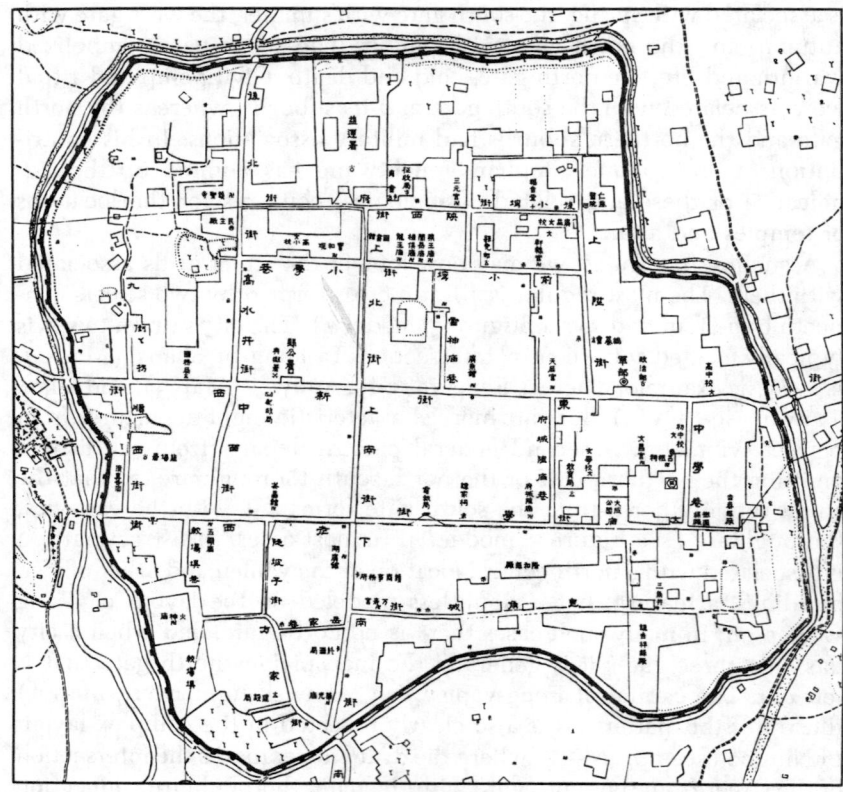

Fig. 6. T'UNG-CH'UAN-FU, Szechwan. From *San-t'ai hsien chih*, 1929.

adopting the symmetrical Latin-cross plan often have outworks at the gates (as in the case of Ta-t'ung-fu, Map 1) and/or a drum tower at the intersection in the form of a fortified four-way gateway built over the crossroads—arrangements that deflect *kuei*, invading troops, and unruly mobs alike. In any case, the concern to break up intergate thoroughfares produced the remaining three city plans (*c, d,* and *e*) in Figure 5. That the third pattern was more common than the fourth may be related to the fact that invaders have typically come from the north in most parts of China; also the Chinese believed that evil spirits often emanated from that baleful direction. The street plan of T'ung-ch'uan-fu, Szechwan (Figure 6), complicated by the presence of two west gates, reveals a combination of the third and fifth patterns. Lu-lung, Chihli (Figure 2), also illustrates the general principle, for the main street leading inward from each of the four land gates ends in a T.

The Morphology of Walled Capitals

In general, the yamen and associated buildings and compounds (including the Confucian temple, the examination hall, the temple of the City God, public offices, and residences of officials) were located near the center of an administrative city. Also located centrally, usually at a major crossroads, were the drum tower, from which the hourly watches were sounded, and the bell tower, whose chief function was to warn the populace of approaching hostile troops or bandits. Although unofficial temples—prominent features of any city—could be located anywhere inside or outside the walls, the favored sites were centrally located.[25] Population density around the official buildings and religious institutions near the city center was lower than in those areas of the city where businesses and residences were located. In addition to this lack of central density that characterized most traditional cities, in many cases the population dropped sharply near the walls.

A systematic exception relates to the development of suburbs outside city gates. The relaxation of urban control that began in the later T'ang period and the increase in urbanization during the Southern Sung led to the growth of suburbs at the gates of many cities. Since gates channeled all traffic to and from a sector of the city's hinterland, the areas immediately outside them were favored sites for markets and businesses serving the rural populace. Inns and other services catering to travelers and traders were established outside the particular gates that gave access to long-distance routes. Many of the cities whose walls were built in the Ming period or earlier could not contain the absolute growth in urban population that occurred during the Ch'ing. By the nineteenth century, few walled cities lacked suburban development outside at least one gate, and in many cities, particularly those in Kwangtung, built-up areas in the suburbs exceeded those within the walls. It should be noted explicitly that in many if not in most cities, suburbs outside the most frequented gates developed before the intramural area had been completely built up.

Concern for the security of the suburbs led to new wall construction in some of the more important cities. In certain cases, an entire concentric outer wall was built encompassing all suburbs. A more common solution was to add a partial wall enveloping only the major suburbs. Four of the twenty major capitals listed in Table 2 had such extensions: the southern suburbs of both Peking and Canton had been enclosed in the sixteenth century, but even more extensive second walls had been built around Lanchow in the fifteenth century and around Tsinan in the nineteenth, encompassing in each case suburbs on the east, south, and west. A third solution was to build an entirely separate wall around the suburb outside a particular gate. The enclosed suburbs outside the east and south gates of Ta-t'ung-fu are typical (see Map 1). In some instances, the wall around a suburb rivaled the original city wall in size. The eastern suburb of Fen-chou-fu, Shansi, is a case in point. Such cases in effect constitute a subtype of the category of multiple city that consists of an administrative center plus a commercial outpost, for the overdeveloped suburb inevitably lay in the direction of the major traffic flow on an important transport route.

Conclusion

Chinese civilization was identified with the growth and spread of walled urban centers right up to the end of the imperial era. Walled cities, with their carefully selected sites, their close association with local drainage systems and waterways, their cosmologically significant designs, their ideologically informed patterns of land use, and their role as functional nodes of largely self-sufficient regions, were perhaps the major landmarks of traditional China. Their morphology was determined above all by the layout of the city wall and the patterning of its gates. The result was a family of urban forms distinctively Chinese and, despite gradual evolution, remarkably stable in worldwide perspective.

The Transformation of Nanking, 1350–1400

F. W. MOTE

Nanking, in the period in which we shall examine it, was at once (1) in a general sense heir to all the city-building traditions and skills that Chinese civilization had developed up to that time; (2) a specific site whose importance and historical traditions went back in a continuous line to the first millennium B.C.; and (3) a great new city under construction to serve as the capital of the Chinese empire and the center of the civilized world as the Chinese knew it. Today, the physical remains of the early Ming capital are overshadowed by the transformations that have occurred since the fourteenth century. But in this paper we will try to recreate in our mind's eye the capital built by Chu Yüan-chang, founding emperor (T'ai-tsu) of the Ming dynasty, who reigned from 1368 to 1398. To do that, we must try to see what Nanking represented to him, to his assistants, and to his subjects as a site, a locus of important functions, and the potential great city of a new imperial era.

We must begin by attempting to summarize the city-building skills and the urban traditions that existed in China in the mid-fourteenth century. Next, we must examine Nanking's particular associations, its functions, and its relevance for the life of China as these aspects came to bear on the process of its transformation. Finally, we shall try to describe the transformation of the site into the great capital it became in the last quarter of the fourteenth century. These three tasks determine the form of this paper; the third accounts for most of its length.[1]

Some Characteristics of the Traditional Chinese City

Some peculiarly Chinese attitudes about the city. No single great city has either dominated Chinese civilization in the way that Rome and Constantinople dominated phases of Roman history or typified Chinese civilization in the way that Paris and London typify for us the French and the English civilizations. Rome, Constantinople, Paris, London—each has been the hub and the symbol of the history and cultural achievements of its civilization. Which city was the Chinese Rome or the Chinese Paris? There neither is nor ever has been one.

This can be explained in many ways. For one thing, China has been too vast a cultural and political area for 3,000 years or more to have been dominated by one city. Nor was it ever a congeries of cities or city-states that eventually came under the domination of one "world city" (Rome), or "national city" (Paris), or that failed to do so, as in the case of the Italian city-states in their heyday. In Europe, Lewis Mumford sees the "medieval" multiplication of urban centers ending, and the rise to supremacy of the single great metropolis beginning, as the result of the achievement of political centralization and the creation of despotic national states.[2] That observation seems to have no analogy in, or significance for, Chinese history; China achieved centralization and political despotism with the founding of the empire, but there was no corresponding influence on the development of the city.

Another line of explanation for the lack of any single great city that symbolizes China for the Chinese or for us involves a rather obvious and often-mentioned fact: Chinese civilization, for many reasons that lie beyond our focus here, has not granted the same importance to typically urban activities that other civilizations have. Thus Chinese values did not sustain a self-identifying and self-perpetuating urban elite as a component of the population. As a result, the Chinese have never felt the impulse to create one great city that would express and embody their urban ideals, nor has the urban sector in the aggregate typified or dominated the tone of Chinese life. Yet a large number of great cities have existed in China throughout the last 2,500 years. We are forced to ask, then, what the distinctive Chinese attitudes were toward the urban component of the cultural environment they had created. The Ming founder in the fourteenth century built a great city at Nanking to serve as the capital of his empire; what were his attitudes toward it and his expectations with regard to its role in the life of his dynasty? Nanking was to be the center of the world, but was it to be the epitome of Chinese culture?

Probably not. The idea that the city represents either a distinct style or, more important, a higher level of civilization than the countryside is a cliché of our Western cultural traditions. It has not been so in traditional China. In early Chou times the *kuo*, which in modern Chinese means "state," was actually the walled or stockaded town seat of the head of a fief. From the social history of the period we can gain some awareness of the *kuo* town as an island of civilization surrounded and threatened by a sea of less-civilized and often hostile peasantry. Yet that sharp division into distinct urban and rural civilizations disappeared very early in China, although it remained characteristic of much of the rest of the world until recent times and produced distinct urban attitudes in other civilizations. The conditions allowing such attitudes in China seem to have vanished by the beginning of the imperial era, so long ago that a sense of that kind of urban superiority has not remained.

Chinese civilization may be unique in that its word for "peasant" has not been a term of contempt—even though the Chinese idea of a "rustic" may be that of a humorously unsophisticated person. The disappearance of the urban-rural separateness—in social-psychological terms, though not of course in all the realities of daily living patterns—no doubt is related to the changes in social structure that accompanied the breakup of the classic Chou civilization. In that historical process ancient China achieved in theory and in actual social practice an open society; the Chinese attained the rights to own land freely and to change their place of residence and way of life. Some practical access to both geographical and social mobility — over and above the mere rights to them — was achieved very early in Chinese history. We have no parallel for the long Chinese experience within these particular defining conditions of social life. Whether large numbers actually participated in either kind of mobility is less important than the psychological fact that such mobility was possible. And this fact must be related to the existence of an urban-rural continuum, both as physical and as organizational realities, and as an aspect of Chinese psychology. It must have worked to overcome the earlier (and to our history, the characteristic) psychology of separateness of the urban and the rural sectors. We know from the researches of P. T. Ho,[3] for example, that by the second half of the imperial era an intermediate stage of urban residence and urban-based commercial activity was typical of families (or branches of families) on the upward-mobility course or aspiring to it, whereas return to rural-based elite patterns was normally affected by those who succeeded in that upward course. Downward mobility also kept persons moving from the one environment to the other. Even in some open societies, parallel and distinct mobility patterns exist apart from each other within the rural and the urban sectors; in China the two meshed in one pattern that, one must hypothesize, reinforced the organic unity of rural and urban.

When we turn from individual and family histories to the daily patterns of living, we find, too (at least in the last thousand years of Chinese history, for which the evidence is better), that there was frequent—in many cases almost daily—movement of large numbers of people into and out of cities. And as we shall note when we discuss the physical and organizational aspects of the rural-urban continuum, the people involved in this movement were not aware of crossing any definite boundary; for the one thing that might seem to qualify as a definite demarcation, the city wall, was not in fact a boundary between an urban-within and a rural-without. It could assume the character of a real boundary between protected and unprotected areas in times of real crisis, but most Chinese in most periods had never experienced that. When we think of the attitudes associated with the city in the West, especially prior to the Industrial Revolution, we may think first of the city as the symbol of safety. In China it simply was not the same. There is an old and very common saying, "In times of minor disorders, flee the countryside; in times of major disasters, flee the cities."[4] This may reflect the fact that, in Chinese history, social turbulence of the kind that could produce rebellions against the authority of the state seems never to have been urban in origin; urban populations were under better control. However, in a war or a major disorder, cities usually became the scenes of pitched battles or the objects of plunder. Thus this saying suggests that the kind of separateness of the safe bastion, the city, from a normally lawless countryside simply did not exist in China. Cities have become the most turbulent and dangerous environments of modern life in the industrial West, and it may be difficult for us to recollect that this is a very recent phenomenon. Yet Lewis Mumford graphically sums up the antagonism between town and country and the sense of safety associated with the city in medieval Europe:

As urban occupations step by step drove out the rural ones that had at first been pursued in the city with almost equal vigor, the antagonism widened between the town and country. The city was an exclusive society; and every townsman was, in relation to the country-folk, something of a snob....

Though the wall existed for military defense and the main ways of the city were usually planned to facilitate rallying to the main gates, the psychological import of the wall must not be forgotten. One was either in or out of the city; one belonged or one did not belong. When the town gates were locked at sundown, and the portcullis was drawn, the city was insulated from the outside world. As in a ship, the wall helped create a feeling of unity between the inhabitants: in a siege or a famine the morality of the shipwreck—share-and-share-alike—developed easily. But the wall also served to build up a fatal sense of insularity: all the more because of the absence of roads and quick means of communication between cities....

The protected economy of the medieval city was capable of being maintained by one fact alone: the superiority of the city over the barbarous, insecure life of the open country.[5]

There is no analogy in imperial China for the situation that these paragraphs describe.

Giovanni Botero, the writer of the famous sixteenth-century treatise *The Greatness of Cities* (1588), knew something of China from Marco Polo's book and other writings. Though suspicious of the credibility of those sources, Botero was greatly impressed by the number and size of China's cities, and by the difference between their functions and those of cities in Renaissance Italy. He concluded a lengthy comparison with an apt simile: "... for that it is not lawful for any of the Chinese to go out of their country without leave or license of the magistrates, so that, the number of persons continually increasing and abiding still at home, it is of necessity that the number of people do become inestimable, and of consequence the cities exceeding great, the towns infinite, and that China itself should rather, in a manner, be but one body and but one city."[6] "But one body and but one city" seems to indicate that Botero realized China was not an agglomeration of semiautonomous city-states, and that it was not a country in which island-cities were surrounded by seas of rude peasants. Nor does he mean that China was dominated by "but one city"; rather he means that all of China, as it were, constituted one organizational entity as though it were "one city." This strikes me as being a very perceptive observation. Despite the political centralization that was so fully realized in the later centuries of the imperial era, there was no premier city that claimed for itself the prerogatives of the great city of the realm and that drew to itself exclusively such characteristic metropolitan activities as (1) setting fashions, (2) providing the locus for intellectual, artistic, and creative developments, and (3) concentrating the cultural achievements of civilization in the form of libraries and art collections. The dispersion of these activities throughout many urban and rural settings, and the consequent lack of any single great urban center that was both the acme and the microcosm of Chinese civilization, strengthens our awareness of rural China. The rural component of Chinese civilization was more or less uniform, and it extended everywhere that Chinese civilization penetrated. It, and not the cities, defined the Chinese way of life. It was like the net in which the cities and towns of China were suspended. The fabric of this net was the stuff of Chinese civilization, sustaining it and giving it its fundamental character. To extend this metaphor, China's cities were but knots of the same material, of one piece with the net, denser in quality but not foreign bodies resting on it. Whether or not this is precisely what Giovanni Botero meant, his phrase "but one body and but one city" is very appropriate.

Yet in the millennium of late imperial China, there certainly were attitudes and characteristics associated with the city. Peasants were not despised, but they were far less mobile than town dwellers, led simpler lives, had contacts with far fewer people, and were exposed to less varied experiences. They were expected to be more simpleminded and naive than townspeople in an admirable if often humorous fashion. On the one hand, the crafty city dweller (usually a petty merchant) who takes advantage of the simple countryman is a stereotype as well known in China as in most other civilizations; on the other hand, the city represents sophistication and skills in dealing with complex situations. Even a learned gentleman who knew both city and country life well (but probably preferred the latter) might declare himself a mere "country fellow," a "rustic simpleton," as a gesture of conventional humility before the rich and the prominent, or even before his intellectual peers and old neighbors who happened to be in office. It was obvious to the townsman of traditional China that he could enjoy a more varied and exciting life, could know more of the products of faraway places, could find higher levels of craftsmanship in the things he purchased and used, could have more entertainment, and could achieve more direct contact with the administrative arm of the imperial government in the city than in the country. In some large and important ways the city stood for the same things in traditional China as in the West. Thus "urban attitudes" did exist in China; but in their specific content, in their intensity, and in their significance for the whole culture of China, they differed profoundly from those in the West.

Are urban functions uniform across civilizations? Glenn Trewartha, writing in 1952, was one of the first persons in the West to analyze the functions of Chinese cities in order to explain their formation and growth.[7] Naba Toshisada and Miyazaki Ichisada, writing in Japanese in the 1920's and 1930's, also discussed the significance of city forms in relation to the factors that led to their development.[8] T. F. Tout's famous piece on "Medieval Town Planning" (1917) is one of the first examples of this kind of analysis of Western cities. As one of the latest, L. Hilberseimer's *The Nature of Cities* (1955) is an impressive book except in its discussion of Chinese cities; the brief comments on the form and functions of Peking (p. 136) are both superficial and bizarre. But all of these writings adopt some version of the distinction between "natural" and "planned" cities (other sets of terms used include "geometric/organic" and "administrative/economic"). Trewartha concludes his evaluation of form in relation to function with this statement: "Probably in no other country has the political influence on city development operated in such a pure fashion and, at the same time, so strongly and continuously through the centuries as in China."⁹ With the recognition of the political factor as a determining element in the nature of Chinese cities, a basis exists for comparing Chinese cities with cities in other parts of the world.

The Chinese city usually and quite properly means to us the roughly 1,500 to 2,000 urban concentrations that were designated the seats of administrative arms of the central government, that is, imperial and provincial capitals plus prefectural- and county-level capitals—the *fu*, *chou*, and *hsien* cities. In Chinese they are *ch'eng* (literally "wall"), because their administrative significance gave them the right or the need to be walled. The administrative function contributed much to form: the walls, square or rectangular in shape (sometimes, though less often, curved or round), were oriented to the cardinal points of the compass; the major streets formed a similarly oriented grid whose intersections were right angles; gates were surmounted by gate towers; and a moat usually surrounded the walls. Certain expectations about form were automatically established, therefore, by the presence of a seat of local government. Yet the study of city maps preserved in local gazetteers shows that circumstances of history, topography, location of transportation routes, and the like have injected much individualism into the appearance and layout of Chinese cities.¹⁰

If we are to draw some contrast, it would seem to be between the administrative city and the natural or economic city. The latter in most cases retains some of the characteristic street patterns of the unwalled market town (*chen*). Its shape is irregular, and its streets straggle unevenly along waterways or roadways, around hillocks and important buildings (such as temples) that existed before the town grew up. Even when large towns of this characteristically unplanned pattern were taken over as administrative centers—thereupon to be enclosed within walls and adapted to the needs of government—much of the informality of the original layout would remain. Superficially observed, then, most Chinese cities fall into not two but three main types: the planned, regular city; the unplanned, sprawling large town; and the hybrid created when some degree of planning was superimposed on the natural city, but too late to be thoroughgoing. Generally speaking, the cities of North China are older and therefore further from their presumed origins as natural cities; moreover, they tend to be on land transport routes (or at intersections of land and water routes) that can be made to adjust to city planning needs. Southern cities, with some notable exceptions, are later, closer to their unplanned origins, and often on unalterable bodies of water that carry transport into them and determine some of their boundaries. The degree of irregularity in form certainly is greater in the South than in the North, and the schematization of "planned," "natural," and "hybrid" is useful to help account for obvious differences between the two regions.

Yet in fact all Chinese cities (*ch'eng*) are in some sense "hybrid," for all are multifunctional, and have been throughout imperial times. The two most clearly identifiable functions are those mentioned above: the economic and the administrative (or "dynastic," or "political-military"). But either of these functions demands the support of the other at a certain stage of development. In late imperial times the exceptions to this last statement were so rare that the four prominent, very large market towns which failed to be designated seats of local government were bulked together and referred to as the "four great towns," or *ssu ta-chen*.[11] They were spoken of as curiosities, because despite their size and importance they did not acquire political functions and remained mere "towns" instead of county-seat walled cities. Yet they, too, were at least minimally multifunctional, for in addition to their impressive marketing roles they had to have government tax collection offices; and they served educational, cultural, and religious functions in the same way that all other large urban concentrations did. Even more were the proper *ch'eng*, the walled cities with offices of government, multifunctional cities. They contained offices of military and civil government as well as official and private educational institutions. That they were almost invariably the chief market towns of their regions can be assumed; and other economic functions included both official ones (taxes, tariffs, management of granaries) and private ones, the latter enhanced by the presence of a corps of government employees. Thus we clearly cannot say of premodern China what Hauser says of premodern Europe:

The European city which survived the Dark Ages as a fortress developed various functions. Each tended to have a special function, political or economic. Medieval cities may be classified either as "towns with predominantly political or intellectual functions" or as having "a predominantly economic function." The multifunction city is seen as a recent phenomenon associated with modern industrialization, technology, transport, and administration. The multifunction city may be traced to the relationship between advancing technology and diversification of functions.[12]

The phrases in quotation marks in this passage are quoted from an article by Bert Hoselitz, and both writers are seeking some guidance on "the overall conditions and processes of economic development" from the study of Europe's past. Perhaps they have succeeded, but analogies between European and non-Western cities should not be extended without examining overall conditions of comparability. And those conditions do not appear to me to have existed in the case of China.

Such unjustified extension of general statements to include cases not adequately understood is best seen in the work of Gideon Sjoberg. His references to China consistently display faults of fact and of judgment, all in the interest of making broadly comparative statements and sweeping interpretations. He believes that urban forms were disseminated from the Fertile Crescent to all other parts of the world except Mesoamerica, and that empires were their effective disseminators. The intermediary empires that accomplished this diffusion for China are not named. And he sees the modern industrial city arising first in England because "England's social structure lacked the rigidity that characterized most of Europe and the rest of the civilized world."[13] He apparently knows nothing of Chinese social structure and assumes that a closed class system prevailed there, making the class structure of China's urban masses comparable to that of the rest of the premodern world's city dwellers. In short, it would seem safe to conclude that the knowledge available in English of the Chinese city, and of traditional China in general, is too limited to sustain the flights of overambitious synthesizers.

The cities of medieval and early modern Europe and the cities of late imperial China were alike in the sense of being historical contemporaries and the urban forms of civilizations at comparable levels of economic and technological development. This makes comparison interesting and potentially fruitful, but it does not imply general similarity. The medieval European city developed within the varying patterns of European feudalism; and Europe's many postfeudal societies, and many of their special characteristics, derived directly from the highly particular conditions that fact implies. Those conditions have few if any significant parallels in traditional China. The general levels of economic and technological development in China and Western Europe continued to be roughly comparable well into Europe's postfeudal, early modern age. Yet even when postfeudal Europe became somewhat more like China in having more highly centralized states, a more fluid social order, greater uniformity of cultural forms throughout larger areas, and the like, the careful student of history must still be dissatisfied with easy analogies. If Hauser sees the multifunctional city (not just *certain* multifunctional cities) as "a recent phenomenon associated with modern industrialization, technology, transport, and administration," we must either accept his statement for China also, or point out how it is inapplicable. An analysis of the functions of the traditional Chinese city may help us do the latter.

Chinese cities, of course, have served some of the same basic functions that cities everywhere have. Pirenne says that trade created cities in medieval Europe, and Mumford, disagreeing, says that cities made trade. This same chicken-or-egg question existed so far back in Chinese antiquity that we can assume a long-standing inseparability of cities and trade there, too. Already in prehistoric times, there is good reason to believe that China's cities were places where grain surpluses could be collected, stored, and protected, and where such highly specialized crafts as ceramics and metalworking were concentrated. Local trade has always centered in towns, and regional trade activities have been associated with the more important cities. In the imperial period—especially in T'ang and later times, when domestic commerce grew increasingly important — the movement and exchange of goods and money strongly influenced the location and growth of cities; in its way, the city of imperial China was also entrepôt, factory, bourse, and bazaar. In the broad view, the economic activities of Chinese and Western cities look very similar; it is only when we examine the manner in which the entrepreneurial functions were exercised, for instance, and look into the social and cultural consequences of those functions (as the late Etienne Balazs has done in some of his highly perceptive writings[14]), that we begin to see how sharply the Chinese situation differed from the apparently comparable situation in premodern Europe. So the functions of Chinese cities, surely embodied to some degree in their forms, were many and varied. The administrative and the economic functions were only the most obvious ones; those of the military, of transport and communication, of religion, of cultural life, of intellectual activities, and of education were also part of the Chinese urban scene. Yet these all existed within the particular dynamics of Chinese society, were ordered by Chinese government, and expressed Chinese cultural values.

Comparative study of urbanism is of course essential, and when adequately informed about the Chinese case, it will be fruitful. Abstracting the seemingly comparable elements to construct broad generalizations, however, must be done with considerable understanding of peculiarly Chinese conditions. This is the comparativist's dilemma: he can neither ignore China nor deal with it adequately at this stage in our knowledge of traditional Chinese civilization.

The element of conscious design in Chinese cities. We have suggested that once urban concentrations developed to the point of being designated *ch'eng*, the hand of government came to interfere directly with

The Transformation of Nanking

aspects of their form. There are also examples where peculiar political or strategic considerations gave rise to planned cities built virtually from nothing. Thus we must postulate the existence of a highly developed capacity to design cities in traditional Chinese civilization. Since this element of conscious design was so highly developed, the following questions arise: (1) who did the planning; (2) what were the sources of design ideas or models; and (3) what writings were the repositories of the design concepts? Unfortunately, these questions cannot be answered with any certainty.

Chinese history abounds with legends about magical elements entering into the planning and building of capitals. As an example, Arlington and Lewisohn in *In Search of Old Peking* (p. 28) say that around 1400 the astrologer (sic) Liu Po-wen gave the plan for the city of Peking to the emperor. This plan provided that the city be laid out with its central features corresponding to the parts of the human body. "Liu Po-wen" is actually the eminent statesman and thinker Liu Chi (1311–75), who is often confused in popular history with Liu Ping-chung (1216–74), an earlier figure who served several early Yüan emperors, and Yao Kuang-hsiao (1335–1418), a later personage who was indeed a chief minister to the Yung-lo emperor at the time of the building of Peking in the early fifteenth century. But Liu Chi never saw Peking. He may indeed have played an important advisory role in the designing of Nanking in the decade from about 1365 to 1375, but his collected works contain nothing that dwells on principles of city design. Liu Ping-chung is indelibly associated in legend with the design of Khubilai Khan's capital built in the 1260's and 1270's on the site of modern Peking, but again no precise or full documentation for this connection exists.[15] And if Yao Kuang-hsiao manipulated the symbolic aspects of the design of Peking, again we have no way of knowing what in fact he contributed, what his sources of symbolic knowledge might have been, or what exactly the symbolic elements of the design were.[16] To my knowledge there are no thirteenth- or fourteenth-century writings discussing the practical, the cosmological, or the symbolic aspects of city design per se.[17] This is not to ignore many general works on geomancy, some of which are apocryphally attributed to Liu Chi and other eminent scholars associated with city design.

A work that does purport to explain the explicitly symbolic aspects of Ch'in and Han city and palace design is the anonymous *San-fu huang-t'u*,[18] a book usually attributed to the Han period but now generally considered by scholars to date from the fourth or fifth centuries. It was a well-known and perhaps influential work in Sung, Yüan, and Ming times.

Throughout its interesting description of Han cities, especially the capitals and their palaces, sentences such as this one occur repeatedly: "The south gate of the city wall symbolizes (*hsiang*) the emperor's position facing to the south and assuming his imperial office." But even here no systematic presentation of the symbolism is offered, nor is it justified in terms of any body of thought or writing.

Modern Chinese writings on the history of Chinese architecture also refer to the element of conscious design, but again fail to present systematically and fully the sources of the concepts involved. Liang Ssu-ch'eng, the best-known modern authority in the field, touches on the problem in passing in his *Chung-kuo chien-chu shih* (History of Chinese Architecture). He discusses the "four characteristics of Chinese architecture." First, it neither seeks permanence nor values the use of materials assuring permanence. Second, all architectural activity is conditioned by ethical concepts (in theory this should have restricted size and splendor, but of course it did not eliminate imperial ostentation). Third, layout and ground plan are of great significance. As the influence of Confucian thought grew in the late Chou and Western Han periods, government increasingly stressed ritualized behavior and deportment; this can be seen in regulations governing layouts and arrangements of buildings, in whose descriptions much importance is attached to names and placement. For later periods, discussions of buildings usually are found in those treatises (*chih*) in the dynastic histories on the "Five Elements" or on "Rites and Deportment." Interestingly, the descriptions always stress ground plan and layout, whereas they ignore details of elevation, of appearance, and of construction. Fourth, and most important, the architectural arts were transmitted from craftsmen to apprentices; books and written records were unimportant in this process. Architectural skills were associated with workmen, not with the literati. Hence there is very little in the written record about architecture and city planning. Only two dynasties seem to have compiled official works on these subjects; these are the Sung *Ying-tsao fa-shih* of 1163 and the Ch'ing *Kung-pu kung-ch'eng tso-fa tse-li* of 1734.[19]

The Yüan capital at the site of modern Peking, called Ta-tu and built in the 1260's and 1270's, has been described as having been "[designed according to] a unitary planned conceptualization, in imitation of the Han system whereby 'the ancestral shrine is on the left, the altars of the state on the right, the imperial court to the front, and the markets at the rear,' and built up upon a flat plain,"[20] permitting full realization of the ideal plan. And another recent work on Chinese architecture claims that "the Yüan city of Ta-tu is the only city [in all Chinese history?] built in accordance with the chapter *K'ao kung chi* in the *Institutes of Chou [Chou li]*."[21] These comments hold a measure of truth, but we must not take them literally. In any event, very little city building was done in the Yüan period other than the rebuilding of Peking. The Ming period, on the other hand, was the great period of city building, and especially of city-wall building, in Chinese history. Earlier, virtually all city walls, including those of imperial capitals, had been built of pounded earth (*hang t'u*); the Ming, starting with Nanking, began building new walls of stone and brick or refacing earlier pounded earth walls with such materials. Yet it is unlikely that the Yüan example of systematically utilizing the *Chou li* in conceiving a city plan had much influence on the Ming builders. The Mongol period tended to be discredited, and the Mongol capital in particular was held up as an example of inordinate extravagance. The form of Ta-tu was changed during the first Ming reign; and when the city was thoroughly rebuilt in the third Ming reign to serve as the new capital, Nanking was ostensibly its model, particularly in the construction of the magnificent palace city, known in both Nanking and Peking as the Forbidden City (*Tzu-chin ch'eng*).

Where, then, did the plan for Nanking—the greatest of city-building projects of the fourteenth century and, indeed, of any later century—come from? For despite indications of some uncertainty regarding specific elements of design and some shifting of plan during the course of the building,[22] there is no lack of evidence of a fully worked out conceptualization of what a capital city should be, how its parts should relate to each other, and what symbolic or functional significance those parts should have. Moreover, the builders of Nanking utilized recently developed engineering techniques and incorporated the latest features of defense in the face of the rapidly changing military technology of the times.[23] Yet none of the many books and writings on Nanking known to me says anything about the sources of the ideological, practical, and technical knowledge employed by the planners and builders, or about who they were and how they worked. The capital city in China was not fixed permanently for all time but could shift, like the Mandate of Heaven, without losing any legitimacy. Existing or previous models, like Loyang,[24] no doubt were part of the consciousness of the learned elite; and the entire cumulative experience of the civilization was at hand to be drawn upon, in very general ways, as new cities were built. Nanking, like the Southern Sung capital at Hangchow, was a site peculiarly influenced by topography. But within the limitations imposed by this fact, a great capital incorporating both essentials from the whole tradition going back to Han and T'ang times as well as elements of recent technological advances was quickly put together in a manner satisfactory to the despot who had just founded the new dynasty. Yet in the most record-conscious of civilizations, the need to record the particulars of this planning and building activity did not seem to exist. This anomalous fact forces us to accept tentative and incomplete answers about what the sources of Chinese city design were and how the theoretical and practical knowledge necessary to city building was preserved and transmitted.

The physical and the organizational components of the traditional Chinese city. Hilberseimer, writing of the medieval European city, says that "cities were much like villages at first, but they soon began to show the characteristics of urban development, industrial, political and architectural. Cities had to protect themselves with fortifications. They had to have a city hall, a place of assembly where citizens could exercise their political rights. There had to be a church also, eventually perhaps a cathedral, a place of worship dominating the city both spiritually and architecturally."[25] Almost nothing in this passage holds true for the Chinese city. It is particularly striking that the organizational (and psychological) separateness of the medieval and premodern European city from the surrounding countryside was attested in physical monuments that dominated the city. The Chinese city had no "civic monuments"; further, it had no "citizens," and it possessed no corporate identity, no government distinct from that of the surrounding countryside. It had no need of a town hall as "a place of assembly where citizens could exercise their political rights." It did not defend itself; its defenses were built by authority of the central government, to which all alike were subservient, and as part of its nationwide defense system.

Nor were there physical symbols of the religious element of Chinese life comparable to those in the West. On the one hand, China had no sacred cities or holy public shrines. The state cult was the private business of the emperor; its important physical monuments were the Temple of the Imperial Ancestors and the Altar of Land and Grain (both in the palace precincts), the Altars of Heaven and Earth in the suburbs of the capital, and the tombs of the imperial ancestors, which were invariably located in rural and often quite remote settings. On the other hand, Chinese public religion was simply not comparable to Western religion in terms of its organization, its financing, or its links with the city as the place where its monuments might attest to its role in society. Both Buddhist and Taoist churches had merely nominal and rudimentary administrative hierarchies imposed by the state; neither church had a hierarchy generated from within to fulfill its own organizational needs; in fact, both religions existed in atomized structure, and each temple was an independent unit. There were no bishops or archbishops, no diocesan or synodal structures of authority, no cathedrals or chapter houses. It is true that every city and town had its important temples, many patronized by the government and its officials. Those called the Confucian temples or temples of literature were in fact state offices, important chiefly for their secular functions. The Buddhist and Taoist temples were licensed by the state, which was normally rather unsympathetic toward them and at times suppressive. They could be closed or required to move by secular authority. Although city temples were often wealthy, ornate, and not infrequently the tallest buildings on the low and sprawling profile of the Chinese city, they did not dominate it spiritually or architecturally. And temples in rural settings were often larger, richer, and more ornate than city ones. With relatively few exceptions, the great European church buildings are identified with city life. The great and enduring centers of Chinese religions, on the other hand, are not marked by permanent architectural monuments of stone and glass, and most of them are in remote rural, often mountain, settings. Most important of all in this comparison, however, is the fact that the cities of China were not keystones in an important religious institutional structure—a state within the state as in Europe, or an arm of the state as in ancient Egypt and the Classical and Islamic worlds. This deprived the Chinese city of one of the elements that contributed most conspicuously to the importance of cities elsewhere.

Religion's organizational forms and physical monuments offer us one striking point of contrast between the Chinese city and the premodern city in the West. Perhaps other characteristics of the Chinese city will suggest still further links between its physical components and the organizational basis of Chinese life. The architectural peculiarities of the Chinese city are suggestive. Chinese urban houses, business structures, temples, and government buildings remained essentially one-story structures or combination one- and two-story parts forming single units.[26] The profile of the Chinese city thus is flat. Moreover, the parts of a single unit, be it small house or large official building, are arranged to enclose, and to include the use of, open ground. Exposure to air and sun is essential to the design of buildings. In these essentials of design, in materials used, and in style and ornamentation, Chinese urban structures were indistinguishable from rural structures. There is in traditional Chinese architecture no such thing as a "town house" style, a "country church" style, or a "city office" style. The Chinese city did not force structures up into the air like the four- and six-story burghers' houses in old European cities or the tenements of ancient Rome. Nor did the pressure on space gradually remove from the city its courtyards and gardens as it tended to in Renaissance and modern Europe. The Chinese city did not totally lack public squares and public gardens, but it had less need of them because its citizens had, and probably preferred, their small, private, but open and sunny courtyards.

The continuum from city to suburbs to open countryside thus was embodied in the uniformity of building styles and layout and in the use of ground space. Neither the city wall nor the actual limits of the suburban concentration marked the city off from the countryside in architectural terms. Nor did styles of dress, patterns of eating and drinking, means of transportation, or any other obvious aspect of daily life display characteristic dichotomies between urban and rural.

Another point of contrast between the premodern cities of China and those of Europe emerges from the following observations by Mumford:

Cities are products of time. They are the molds in which men's lifetimes have cooled and congealed, giving lasting shape, by way of art, to moments that would otherwise vanish with the living and leave no means of renewal or wider participation behind them. In the city, time becomes visible: buildings and monuments and public ways, more open than the written record, more subject to the gaze of many men than the scattered artifacts of the countryside, leave an imprint upon the minds even of the ignorant or the indifferent. Through the material fact of preservation, time challenges time, time clashes with time: habits and values carry over beyond the living group, streaking with different strata of time the character of any single generation. Layer upon layer, past times preserve themselves in the city until life itself is finally threatened with suffocation: then, in sheer defense, modern man invents the museum.

By the diversity of its time-structures, the city in part escapes the tyranny of a single present, or the monotony of a future that consists in repeating only a single beat heard in the past.[27]

Much of what Mumford has so effectively observed here is true of Chinese cities and perhaps of all cities; that is, the urban concentration of physical monuments undoubtedly does leave its imprint on the viewer and helps to make him aware of his society and his cultural traditions. But in one striking way the Chinese city again is an exception to the most important point of the passage: the Chinese city did not possess visible "diversity of its time-structures." Time did not challenge time in the eyes of a wanderer in a city street in traditional China. In China there was no danger of the past not preserving itself; but neither did the architectural monuments remind one of the past, because architecturally the present was never strikingly new or different. No Chinese building was obviously datable in terms of period styles. No traditional Chinese city ever had a Romanesque or a Gothic past to be overlaid in a burst of classical renascence, of a Victorian nightmare to be scorned in an age of aggressive functionalism. In that sense, the Chinese city did not escape "the tyranny of a single present," but neither did it consider "a future that consists in repeating only a single beat heard in the past" to be monotonous. Here, though, from a description of the physical appearance of the city we have digressed to note a continuum in time, whereas the rural-urban continuum in space is more pertinent to this discussion.

It would be a mistake to exaggerate urban-rural uniformities, to be sure. Yet the cultural life of Chinese civilization, in particular from Sung times onward, did not fall into two widely divergent spheres that we can label the urban and the rural. In part this was because of the rural ideals of the upper classes, the permeation of those ideals throughout the whole society, and the tendency of the upper classes to alternate between living in town and living in the country. It is easy to concentrate on the life of the educated upper classes because it is so difficult to learn much about the masses of the people. Nonetheless, it is significant to observe that the lives and cultural activities of the elite were not confined to the cities. Among the lower ranks of society there probably were much more clearly identifiable urbanites and ruralites, and no doubt the distinction between city and country must have had greater meaning in their daily lives. As I said earlier, Chinese cities were not beleaguered islands in a sea of barbarism, and the continuity of cultural tone throughout Chinese society must reflect some aspects of its organization.

The concentration of people and wealth, and the possibilities for division of labor and specialization, enabled cities to support some cultural activities that were not possible in the countryside. Some of the arts and crafts and protosciences depended on shops and markets, goods and craftsmen, and the patronage of densely concentrated populations. This point is obvious, and it fits our expectations about the roles of cities in cultural history. Once again, however, it is the qualifications on analogies drawn with other times and places that are important. For example, Chinese schools were in cities in the case of government institutions (the exceptions being a few famous private *shu-yüan* [academies] that became recipients of government subsidies and thereafter functioned as semiofficial schools). But many of the *shu-yüan*, which in Sung and later imperial history often functioned as centers of intellectual activity, were located in villages or out-of-the-way rural settings, especially in the centuries of Sung through Ming. (Tilemann Grimm elsewhere in this book notes a mid-Ch'ing and later trend toward urban locations.) Publishing activities frequently were not in the major cities; some of the most important publishing was done at the village properties of scholar-officials. Government offices and government schools usually had small libraries, and these were located in walled cities. But the great libraries (except for those belonging to the imperial court) were private, and they were located as often as not in the rural-village or small-town properties of their gentry owners. Private art collections, too, were frequently housed in the rural villas of the rich. Scholars, poets, thinkers, writers, and artists customarily were in public service for a portion of their lives, and hence for some time necessarily resident in cities far from their native places. But their productive years were often the years of their private life, when they were widely dispersed and very apt to be residing in rural places.

These features of Chinese cultural life probably did not exist in any equivalent fashion in the cultural life of Europe or the Classical world. Perhaps we can formulate the concept of a culturally "open" situation in China. That is, Chinese cultural activities involved both the cities and the countryside, they were indistinguishably "urban" and "rural," and they reflected attitudes toward city and country that were perhaps distinct from those in premodern Europe, where a few great cities tended to monopolize a more "confined" cultural life.

Similarly, it may be that the concept of the "provincial" as opposed to the "metropolitan" did not exist in China (especially from T'ang times onward) as it did in the cultural life of Europe. True, careers in the capital were different in character and prestige from those in the provinces. But in the cultural life of the empire there was no corresponding gulf between the capital and the provinces. Some of the Chinese provinces were culturally inferior, especially those more distant or more recently sinicized, such as Kweichow and Yunnan. But the cultural life of some of the Yangtze Valley provinces was recognized as being superior to that of the capital and the provinces adjacent to it. In the Yüan period, the cultural life of China continued to center in the Lower Yangtze area even though the political capital was at Ta-tu, modern Peking. And through the Ming and Ch'ing periods, even though the dynastic capital created at Nanking in 1368 was moved to Peking after 1420, the provinces of the Yangtze area continued to rival the northern capital as centers of culture and exceeded it in overall richness of cultural life. Thus not all the provinces were provincial in a cultural sense.

The Transformation of Nanking

Were we to examine the organization of economic life, we would find that in some ways it paralleled the dispersion of cultural activities. For example, many of the most flourishing market areas and commercial concentrations were outside city walls, though adjacent to major cities. Some beginnings of "national markets," such as the Wu-hu rice market, were not located in major cities. And economic centers as such seem to have been widely dispersed.

Our case for an urban-rural continuum in traditional China thus rests upon evidence from the physical form of cities, from styles in architecture and dress, from evidence about urban and rural attitudes in elite (and perhaps in popular) psychology, from the structure and character of cultural activities, and even from some glimpses into the pattern of economic life. It suggests that cities, important concentrations of Chinese life, related to the whole of China's national existence in ways that differ from our expectations about the premodern city elsewhere. As we examine the transformation of Nanking in the fourteenth century, these distinctive features of Chinese civilization must be kept in mind.

Nanking: The Site and Its Historical Associations

The earliest historical notice concerning the general location of Nanking dates from the end of the Shang dynasty. A granduncle of the future King Wu of Chou, by name T'ai-po, fled the Shang state to the region of the Ching barbarians (*Ching man*), introduced himself and was accepted as their ruler, and is credited with having brought the refining elements of Chinese civilization to them. The Chou rulers, who succeeded the Shang, acknowledged T'ai-po's presence in the region, associated the name of Wu with his state, and confirmed the descendants of his brother Chung-yung in their tenure as regional princes. Their city of Wu is said to have been located some forty miles southwest of modern Nanking. And though cities as such are physically impermanent things in Chinese history, this set of imperishable historical associations is regarded as the beginning of Nanking's history. The "Historical Outline" sections of all the successive gazetteers of Nanking have commenced with this story. This legend reveals that the Lower Yangtze was then only on the fringes of Chinese civilization, still a barbarian area well after the first flowering of classical Chinese civilization in the Yellow River valley.

The traditions of a legitimate state of Wu in the Lower Yangtze valley, a state that gradually became involved in the politics of Chou China, are continuous if initially scanty from that time onward. Only in the fifth century B.C. do they become specific and give evidence that the region was maturing culturally and politically. The most venerable of Nanking's many names, Chin-ling ("gold tumulus"), dates from this era; early legends explaining the name have been accepted as historical though they clearly are not readily verifiable. Around 220 B.C., the victorious First Ch'in Emperor, touring the newly absorbed parts of his great empire, visited the site of Nanking and is said to have noticed its auspicious attributes. His astrologers told him that five hundred years later a mighty ruler would arise here. To break up that threat to his descendants, he had part of a mountain (a "sleeping dragon") cut away and diverted the Ch'in-huai River through the place. Of course this failed; true to the prediction, a ruler making strong claims to become emperor of all China did occupy the site five hundred years later. (That is, the Eastern Chin rulers made Nanking their capital about five hundred years later; if one's computations are adjusted slightly to a more conservative reckoning, Sun Ch'üan, ruler of the Three Kingdoms state of Wu also could be considered the prophecy's subject.)

The Ch'in emperor also ordered the auspicious name Chin-ling changed to the much more humble-sounding Mo-ling ("hay mound"). Nonetheless he retained it as one of the county seats of the new centrally administered empire, and throughout the centuries of Ch'in and Han it remained always at least that, administered under the commandery of Yangchow. That ancient city, some 50 miles away across the Yangtze to the northeast, and Soochow, almost 200 miles downriver near the coast, were the great cities of the area. As seats of provincial-level administration they dominated the Lower Yangtze region, and as centers of superior agricultural areas they were also far richer and more important than Nanking.

It was not until the end of Han that Nanking became an important political center, and that came about as regional warlords sought bases from which to challenge the authority of the crumbling Han empire and each other. One of these warlords, Sun Ts'e, began to build independent military power in the Lower Yangtze area in A.D. 195. At first he chose as his base Chen-chiang, a city on the south bank of the Yangtze opposite Yangchow; it seemed to be a strategic location from which to challenge Yangchow and move on northward while utilizing the security offered by the great river. But when he died in 200, his younger brother Sun Ch'üan succeeded him and chose as his base Nanking, the future capital of the Three Kingdoms state of Wu. Under the names Chien-yeh and Chien-k'ang, the site we call Nanking served several successors of Sun Ch'üan until 317. In that year the emperors of the state of Chin, the major power in China in this period of disunion, were defeated by invaders in the North; they fled to Nanking and made it their capital.

The Transformation of Nanking

It was thereafter continuously the capital of the "Southern Dynasties"—the Eastern Chin, the Sung, the Ch'i, the Liang, and the Ch'en—until in 589 the Sui dynasty again united all of China under one rule and, like the Han dynasty before it, made its capitals at ancient sites on the Yellow River.

The variegated history of the place is too rich in detail—stirring detail to the Chinese audiences of marketplace storytellers and opera performances. It probably would stir the contemporary Western reader less, and we must forgo most of it. But one or two large issues of importance to us emerge from this colorful era in Nanking's history.

What was it about the site of Nanking that enabled the city to become a political and military base dominating the Lower Yangtze and threatening the whole of North China? Was it really the "royal air" that successive rulers of the Southern Dynasties kept discovering there, confirming them in their imperial pretensions, that made it an appropriate site for the capital of an empire? Did accumulated legend become a major factor in realpolitik? The Sui conqueror, fearing the city as a symbol of southern power, ordered that it be destroyed, that plows overturn the earth within its former walls, and that a new, smaller administrative city be built slightly to one side of the old site. This was partially a symbolic act, for it was designed both to destroy physically the symbol about which resistance to the Sui might form and to weaken the site's geomantic features. However, the answer to the question about Nanking's importance in history probably does not lie in geomancy, despite the consistency with which the historical accounts refer to that factor. Lao Kan, a modern historian noted for his critical acumen and his knowledge of the early imperial period, provides another kind of answer. It merits summarizing:

Throughout the Han period, Soochow and Yangchow with their canal locations, being central to agricultural regions of high productivity, embodying conjunctions of political and transport significance, far outweighed Nanking in importance.

Although Nanking was not in the center of an important agricultural area, it was central to the relations among several important agricultural zones. And although it derived no significance from a canal location, it commanded one of the strategic locations on the Yangtze, a still more important transportation artery. During the four hundred years of Han, the Kiangnan (Lower Yangtze) area steadily advanced in economic development and in transportation facilities. Water transportation in particular became ever more important. A need was recognized for additional urban centers in the area, and this naturally tended to enhance the growth and economic importance of

Ching-k'ou (modern Chen-chiang), and of Nanking. But beyond this, Nanking possessed an additional and quite important factor—its military position.

The importance of Nanking is qualitatively different from that of Soochow and Yangchow. The latter represent locations at which water transport is more important than land; in the case of Nanking, both are important. From the beginning of history China's cultural hub had been within the "Yellow River Triangle," and the center of wealth also was there. The important urban centers there were Han-tan, Yeh, Ch'ü-fu, and so on, as well as nearby cities such as Loyang, Lin-tzu and P'eng-ch'eng. In terms of population density and level of commerce, these places all were superior to Soochow and Yangchow at least through the Han and Wei periods. If we speak of water transport to the North to serve these cities, Yangchow was situated where it could draw traffic from the Yangtze and pass it on via the Huai River, this giving Yangchow an adequate basis for prosperity. But when we turn to land transport from the Lower Yangtze to the important centers of the North, then Nanking, not Yangchow, lay across the shortest and most direct route. In terms of transport costs for commercial goods, it was more economical to go via Yangchow and the water route. But if one intended to draw on the grain surpluses of the Lake T'ai region and create a military base from which to move northward, then there was more at stake than mere transport costs. The time factor would demand the use of a more direct route as a primary concern. Second, the case of moving northward would demand avoiding low-lying swampy and water-channel crisscrossed areas through which to march armies. Yangchow in this light becomes an inferior choice of base; Nanking offered far greater ease of moving armies once the Yangtze had been crossed.

This point is not one that was immediately recognized; Sun Ch'üan, the first person to establish a capital at Nanking, initially selected Chen-chiang as his capital because of its location on the south bank of the Yangtze across from Yangchow. Later on he became aware of Nanking's superior qualifications and moved his capital there.

After destroying the Nanking of the Southern Dynasties, the Sui left a small administrative city and military garrison on the single most important fortified hill, and intended that the city remain insignificant. But by a century and a half later, in mid-T'ang times, it had recovered its former importance and again flourished. The great wealth and resources of Kiangnan caused its recovery, and maintained its steady growth onward from that time to the present. Note, for example, how quickly Nanking overcame the destruction suffered when it was the Taiping capital in the 1860's.[28]

Lao Kan analyzes factors of strategic importance in relation to the wealth of the Lower Yangtze region and the political and military centers of the North. These conditions were enhanced by the continued economic growth of China, but they reflect essentially unchanging relationships within its economic and political structure. In the second

The Transformation of Nanking

half of the fourteenth century, when the Ming founder sought a base at which to build a military and political movement, advisers learned in history used the "royal air" argument and other auspicious signs in support of Nanking. Such arguments also had public value in social-psychological terms. But the real reason his advisers urged him to seize and utilize Nanking was probably that they were aware of the strategic factors Lao Kan describes. Nonetheless, the historical record enlarges on Nanking's "royal air" and related favorable auspices and somewhat suppresses the strategic factors involved in the decision.

China's leaders have been as hardheaded about geopolitical factors as those in any civilization, but by the fourteenth century the rich layers of accumulated historical associations also were a "real" component of the site we call Nanking. A number of elaborate tombs of the Ch'i and Liang dynasties, some stone remnants of old fortifications, terraces on which palaces had stood—these were virtually all that had endured of the physical city that had been the capital of the Southern Dynasties. But the site was also endowed with the elements of a mystique that had the power to command the minds and the attention of the people. History had given Nanking claims to importance in other, but no less real, spheres than the geopolitical.

We must consider the scope and the depth of these claims. In the fourth through sixth centuries, Nanking was the capital of the small territory held by a succession of dynasties that considered themselves quite self-consciously the repository of Chinese cultural values in a time when aliens had invaded the old heartland in the North. The zeal with which the Chinese of the Southern Dynasties carried the transforming influences of their civilization into the frontier regions of the South was heightened by their feeling that the T'o-pa and other alien invaders in the North seemed to be threatening the very existence of their cultural values. (In fact, the hindsight of history shows that it was the other way around; civilization was threatening the very existence of the T'o-pa.) The heroic figures of the centuries of disunion—men like the imperturbable Prime Minister to the Chin, Hsieh An, and the recluse poet, T'ao Ch'ien—are among the great heroes of Chinese civilization, their significance not at all limited to this period and region.[29]

Nanking and the Southern Dynasties also were of particular importance in the history of Buddhism. Though Neo-Taoism had flourished in the fourth century, especially in the South and at the court in Nanking, it was a short-lived movement in intellectual history and was rapidly displaced by Buddhism in the same intellectual environment. It is fair to say that Buddhism made its first great strides toward complete sinicization in the fourth, fifth, and early sixth centuries, and did so most notably under the patronage of the southern court and the southern elite. In the early sixth century Nanking had dozens of famous temples; a T'ang dynasty source states that in the entire territory controlled by the Liang dynasty at that time there were 2,846 temples and 82,700 monks, the numbers of both having grown fantastically during the preceding century.[30] In popular legend some rulers and eminent Buddhist figures of the southern court were bodhisattvas, and Nanking became a revered place in vulgarized religious traditions.

In literary history, too, Nanking acquired a status that later ages revered. The great monuments of Six Dynasties literary theory are associated with Nanking; the golden age of T'ang poetry looked directly to antecedents in the Southern Dynasties; and most T'ang poets who visited Nanking wrote nostalgic verse recalling the rich associations of the place. Some of these poems were among the best known of the T'ang period, and in later ages were very widely known and were recited even by illiterate commoners. Few places in China could surpass Nanking in the depth of its literary associations, and no other kind of associations contributed more to the fame and glory of a place in the Chinese mind.

These associations all endured the physical destruction of the city in 589; in fact, that event assumed little significance in the subsequent tellings of local history, for recovery was rapid. Nanking was a flourishing city by late T'ang, and naturally again became a regional warlord base at the end of the T'ang in the tenth century. Throughout the Five Dynasties period it was the capital of the regional dynasty called the Southern T'ang, which, though not of major political importance, achieved imperishable fame in literary history. Its three emperors were literary figures, and the last, by name Li Yü, was in particular one of the great *tz'u* poets of history. After the Sung dynasty was founded in 960, the Southern T'ang lingered on for another fifteen years before the Sung emperor somewhat reluctantly decided to use force against it. The Sung troops captured the poet-emperor Li Yü but brought little destruction to city or population,[31] and throughout the Northern Sung period (960–1126), Nanking remained an important city, even though reduced in status again to a seat of provincial administration.

When the Chin Tartars conquered the Sung capital at Kaifeng in 1126, the Sung court sought safety in flight to the South, at first designating Nanking the "temporary capital"; then it was decided that Hangchow offered impressive qualifications as a city and still greater safety from Chin attacks along the Yangtze. Nonetheless, Nanking was re-

The Transformation of Nanking

garded as one of the key bastions in the Southern Sung defense system, and was a major post in the administrative structure. So throughout the Sung and on into the Yüan period, Nanking remained one of the three or four most eminent places in China both in psychological terms, with its historical associations, and in geopolitical terms, as a regional center of great strategic significance. If some qualitatively new factors were added in the Sung-Yüan period, they were ones that were transforming all of China's cities—especially those of the rich southeast. These factors were economic growth, commerce, and technological advances in agriculture and industry; they combined to present new and greatly enlarged possibilities for the size, power, and wealth of cities.

Katō Shigeshi's study of urbanism in the Sung period has established a high point in our knowledge of the city in traditional China. He has provided a wealth of information and interpretation concerning the form, size, functions, organization, and life of cities in that age. He also offers some very meaningful comparisons with the city in the preceding T'ang era, revealing trends of development in the whole civilization that are clearly mirrored in the urban scene. Anyone attempting to examine Chinese urbanism in the post-Sung era would do well to commence with a careful reading of Katō's work. In his famous 1931 monograph, "The Development of Cities During the Sung Dynasty," he discusses (1) city walls and city moats; (2) the city ward system (*fang*) and its collapse; (3) the urban subprefectural organization (*hsiang*); (4) the collapse of the controlled market system (*shih-chih*); (5) the new urban entertainment places called *wa-tzu*; and (6) taverns (*chiu-lou*). He concludes the study with the following brief summary of his findings:

The materials presented in the foregoing sections all represent principal components of the more significant phenomena making their appearance in the cities of the Sung period. Among these, some emerged for the first time only in the Sung. Examples are the collapse of the city ward system; private houses having entrances opening directly onto the main streets; the market system progressively sinking into complete collapse; shops and businesses being able to set up any place within or without the city wall and to be opened directly onto the main streets; the establishment of *wa-tzu* as places of recreation and entertainment marked by concentrations of theaters; and taverns (or wine houses) rising to two and three stories and dominating main streets. From all of these we can see that many kinds of restrictions imposed by the [previous] forms of urban organization had now been thrown off, that the life of residents had become very free and uninhibited, and that they passed lives in pursuit of pleasure. It goes without saying that these changes were the consequence of increases in the urban population, the flourishing of urban commerce and of communications, the increase in the wealth in cities, and the reinforcement of the urban dwellers' many desires and demands. However, the reasons for all of this still must be carefully studied. Moreover, the relationships of these changes with government, military affairs, literature, art, and the like must all be investigated. These questions all await some future study; for the time being one can merely describe the phenomena of change, and with that rest his pen.[32]

Fortunately, Katō Shigeshi's pen was not to rest permanently for another fifteen years, and he eventually added much further knowledge on the questions of cause that he had left unexplored in his 1931 study. His contemporary in China, Li Chien-nung, also explored many of the same economic and social issues in the history of the Sung, Yüan, and Ming periods. In discussing markets in their urban settings, he drew on many of the same materials Katō had used; and from his somewhat different point of view, he corroborated many of Katō's findings.[33]

To my knowledge, there exist no studies of these phenomena attendant upon economic growth and social change that focus specifically on Nanking in the Sung and Yüan periods. Moreover, there are no very obvious materials from that time from which to make a detailed study. There are extant a Nanking Yüan-period gazetteer of 1344 and portions of still earlier ones from Sung times, and there are informal notes and sketches of Yüan-period residents of the region. But it is not possible at this time to attempt a detailed reconstruction of the life of Nanking in the fourteenth century prior to the city's fall in 1356 to the band of rebels who a dozen years later founded there the Ming dynasty. We can only assume that this ancient city, with its particular circumstances of site, its strategic significance, and its rich accumulation of legend and historical associations, shared in the changing character of the Chinese city in that age.

From Rebel Base to Imperial Capital

The logic of the site as the Ming capital. The mid-fourteenth century was a time of breakdown for the Chinese state, foreshadowing the imminent end of the rule over China by the descendants of Chinggis and Khubilai. In some places the common people still could be coerced by fragments of the sinicized Mongol state's once all-powerful military machine. And many in the higher ranks of society, particularly the legitimists among the Confucian literati, were restrained from repudiating the collapsing regime by their sense of propriety and the demands of loyalty. But in its public aspects, society was breaking up.

In the winter of 1354–55, an ambitious young military leader named

The Transformation of Nanking

Chu Yüan-chang, nominally in the service of a senior rebel warlord but actually planning an independent rebellion of his own, observed the crumbling of Mongol rule throughout China from a small county capital he had captured during the late summer of 1354 near the north bank of the Yangtze River. Then, as now, it was called Ch'u or Ch'u-hsien. Chu Yüan-chang saw rebel bases springing up all about him in the Lower Yangtze basin during that winter, isolating pockets of the highly fragmented Mongol military power. A shrewd observer, he realized that he would need a better base than Ch'u-hsien from which to compete in the struggle ahead, for he recognized that the town did not qualify as a "central place" for even his current modest insurrection. The *Veritable Records* (*T'ai-tsu shih-lu*), a day-by-day account of his political acts, quotes him on the subject: "Ch'u is a hill town. Boats cannot reach it. Merchants and peddlers do not gather in it. It has no topographical advantages as a military bastion. It is not adequate to serve as our base."[34] So the following summer, after crossing the Yangtze just west of Nanking, he sought advice from an old Confucian literatus. In reply to the question "What about taking Nanking?"* he got the following typical scholar-official advice. "Nanking has been the capital of emperors and kings past; there 'the dragon coils and the tiger crouches.' It is bounded by the natural barrier of the Yangtze. Take it and hold it. Utilize its setting, from which to send out armies and extend yourself on all four sides. Then where shall you turn that you shall not conquer?"[35]

The subsequent Nanking of Ming imperial grandeur, the city built to match those geomantic features and historical associations, could scarcely have been in the mind of the future Ming founder when he was planning his attack on the stronghold then guarding the site. During the remainder of 1355, Chu Yüan-chang moved his small but growing army close to Nanking, capturing county capitals on all sides. He also reflected on Nanking itself: "Nanking's walls and moats are [half] encircled by the Great River on the right, and on the left rest on imposing hills.† On three sides it leans against the river. The hills serve it as walls [beyond its walls], and the river as moat [beyond its moats]. The lay of the land, thus offering natural defenses and barriers, gives no advantages to an attacker employing ground forces."[36] The *Veritable Records* goes on to discuss what stratagems had been employed on three earlier occasions when imperial rule over southern parts of China had been

---

* The original text says "Chin-ling"; Nanking is used throughout this paper in translating whatever names may have been used for the city in Chinese texts.

† Nanking is located east and south of a wide bend in the Yangtze (the river is flowing north at this point). See Map 1.

ended by the capture of Nanking. For the military conquest of Nanking by the Western Chin in A.D. 280, by the Sui in 589, and by the Sung in 975 had in each case reduced a southern power and permitted dynastic consolidation by a state based in the North.

The Chinese obsession with history was thus reflected even in this scarcely literate peasant upstart as he considered a base for rebellion. In the spring of 1356, after having studied the situation over the recent months, Chu Yüan-chang besieged and quickly took Nanking. This done, he took steps that gave evidence of the importance he attached to his conquest. He changed the city's name from then current Chi-ch'ing[37] to Ying-t'ien, meaning "in response to Heaven"—a name that announced a claim on the Mandate of Heaven. He also took for himself the title "Duke of the State of Wu," indicating that (for the time being) the Mandate was being claimed for someone else, i.e., his nominal overlord in the rebellion to which he still proclaimed his allegiance. But by establishing the offices of the rebellion's central and provincial military and civil government in Nanking—again in his overlord's name—where he could keep watch over them, Chu Yüan-chang made certain that he would be the master of the rebellion's central command post in any event. And he began to look about the city he had seized, to see what it offered and what it needed in order to serve his ambitions.

Chu Yüan-chang had no personal connections with Nanking or any of the other great cities along the Lower Yangtze, and there is a fortuitous element in his selection of Nanking as a base. To be sure, the geographic range in which his small military force had freedom of action was quite restricted, yet within that area Nanking was not the easiest city to seize. It was garrisoned and valiantly defended, of course; but in overcoming the garrison and conquering this particular place, Chu Yüan-chang had accomplished much more than the mere taking of a stoutly defended city. He had vastly propelled the rebellion of which he was a part and had achieved personal eminence for the first time. Ch'u-hsien had been a relatively meaningless site; Nanking, though, was of another order of magnitude. The small mountain city he had felt forced to abandon in his search for a base still looked in this century—perhaps still looks today—much as it looked to the fourteenth-century rebel's eyes. But Nanking, under his vast energy and ambition, was soon transformed again into one of the world's great cities, far outstripping in physical size and splendor all of its previous existences.

The Ming founder was never quite sure that he had settled on the perfect site. In 1368 he made the city the first capital of a united China ever to be located south of the Yangtze and far from the old heartland

The Transformation of Nanking

of Chinese history. All of the historical precedents for a center of political power in the South were inauspicious from a dynastic founder's point of view, suggesting division, weakness, and short duration. The urge to "return" to the North was very strong, even for this founder whose regional identity was Lower Yangtze; he had been born nearby and his family origins were to be traced to Chü-jung, one of the counties traditionally administered from the provincial seat at Nanking. Throughout the first two decades of his reign, Chu Yüan-chang asked his advisers to investigate and report on Loyang, Sian (ancient Ch'ang-an), and other northern sites, and he sent his son and heir to again consider a move to the North that would identify his Ming dynasty more directly with the past traditions of the Chinese empire. But eventually he decided that the vast new city he was building at Nanking would serve. He continued to build it, he had his own tomb erected beyond its walls, and he expected it to remain the principal political center of his dynasty; only metahistorians can solve the problem of whether the pull of the Great Wall frontier upon the politico-military center of the Chinese state is irresistible and has made inevitable the transfers of the central government to Peking in 1421, in 1912, and in 1949. In Chu Yüan-chang's lifetime, in any event, the choice of Nanking seemed reasonable and appeared to be permanent.

The Ming founder had gained by accident the opportunity to capture Nanking, but once he possessed it, its virtues as a center of empire were obvious. He was aware of the strategic significance of its location, for he had defeated major rivals based downriver at Soochow and upriver at Hankow, as well as the Mongols themselves with their military and administrative center at Peking. He had captured Hangchow and Nanchang, other important regional bases in the center of China. Thus he knew the geopolitical factors that gave advantages to Nanking, for his rise to power had benefited directly from them. Also, he learned about the site's traditions as a political center and about its fame in legend and history. From beginnings of the most humble kind and a childhood of destitution and cultural deprivation, Chu Yüan-chang became one of the most avid and accomplished adult learners in all history.[38] Though it is true that his chief advisers in political and cultural matters were all men of the region, they were more devoted to the traditions of Chinese history than to any region, and their support of the Ming founder in his creation of a new capital for China in this region cannot be ascribed to parochialism.

In fact, Nanking was so clearly in the cultural and economic heartland of China at the time that it would have been impossible to govern the country without drawing predominantly on the human and material resources of this region; the Yung-lo emperor also found this to be true after 1401 and throughout his preparations for moving the capital to Peking in 1421. Moreover, when the administrative center was moved to Peking, Nanking did not revert to the status of "secondary capitals" of earlier history. In Han and T'ang times, the secondary capitals had been important symbols but relatively unimportant administrative centers. They retained nothing more than a special garrison and offices of local administration designated by somewhat more grandiose titles than otherwise would have been the case. But Nanking, even after 1421, had an unprecedented range of significant political and administrative functions for a second capital. The late Ming writer Ku Ch'i-yüan has argued this perceptively after brushing aside an official's criticisms about the limited functions, and hence superfluous nature, of the duplicate Six Ministries in Nanking:

Alas, this [writer] fails to display awareness of the dynasty's profound calculation and far-ranging considerations! For there are palaces and imperial tombs located here. There are the affairs of the armies and the defense garrisons. This is the place where there are treasuries and where the nation's land registers and taxation records are stored. This is the hub of all the wealth and resources of the southeast. Though there have been established here the Six Ministries to carry on their separate management of all these affairs, yet one might fear that still would not be adequate. How can one slightingly refer to them as superfluous offices!

Ably stated indeed are the views of the late Ch'iu [Chün 1420–95], who observed: the wealth of the realm is all produced in the southeast and Nanking is its center; garrisoning and military affairs assume great proportions in the northwest and Peking is its key. Establishing two capitals is to dwell amidst [each] and provide for good order; food is thereby sufficient and soldiers are thereby sufficient; it is based on the strategic features of the situation and it accomplishes mastery on all sides.

Ah, that says it well!

. . .

The secondary capital's offices and bureaus were not changed [i.e., abolished when the new capital was established at Peking], thereby to maintain everlasting [domestic] security, and strength into the farthest reaches; how can the [systems of] former dynasties and previous states be considered comparable![39]

As Ku Ch'i-yüan saw so clearly, the two-capital system in Ming China was different from that of previous dynasties; the overall level of China's governmental functions was higher, and thus the supplementary activities maintained at the secondary capital were now essential and not just of formal and ritual significance. Nanking's continuing role is witness to the increased importance both of the South in the economy of the empire and of the government's hand in controlling and maintaining its managerial interests. The logic of Chu Yüan-chang's choice of capital was further evident in the new form the two-capital system achieved in the century following his death.[40]

Building the new city walls. The city that Chu Yüan-chang captured in 1356 is described in the Nanking gazetteer of 1344.[41] The walls, and the layout of the streets and markets, were those of the Southern T'ang city (the Southern T'ang had taken over the city, which had been built anew in 920 by their immediate predecessors in the Five Dynasties period, and had improved it throughout the next half century). The city walls were more or less square, roughly two miles on a side, and had eight gates. Originally, the walls were said to have been 25 feet wide at the top, 35 feet wide at the base, and 25 feet high.[42] The Southern T'ang court perhaps further heightened the walls a few feet, and certainly built massive gate towers of immense blocks of stone and added moats and outer works. Sung writers still spoke of these fortifications as some of the most formidable in the empire, unusual in their use of stone and in their imposing appearance.[43]

The inner walled area (*tzu-ch'eng*) had served as the palace city of the Southern T'ang until 975. When the Sung dynasty conquered the Southern T'ang and reduced the city to the status of a provincial capital, the former palace city continued to house the appropriate government offices. At the time of the Chin conquest of the northern part of Sung China in 1126, the Sung emperor lingered at Nanking for a time in his flight to the South and considered designating it his temporary capital. And although he ultimately selected Hangchow as a safer site, the former palace city again was called by that name and remained a "detached palace" (*hsing-kung*) throughout the Southern Sung. That meant that its buildings were kept up and even enlarged and improved; a number of Southern Sung emperors stayed there temporarily from time to time.

During the Yüan period, a number of important regional administrative offices were assigned to Nanking briefly, only to be moved to Yangchow or Hangchow. Beyond the prefectural administration, the main administrative organ of Yüan government to be located at Nanking more or less throughout the dynasty was the Southern Censorate, one of three main divisions of the Yüan Censorate (the others being the central government Censorate offices and the Northwest Censorate, whose regional offices were at Sian). The chief censor, with rank 1b, was the highest official resident there, and he headed a censorate staff of about 100 civil service appointees plus several times that number of subofficials. The prefectural administrative office (*tsung-kuan-fu*), responsible for the civil government of the prefecture (*lu*), was staffed by a Mongol chief prefect of rank 3a, a Chinese assistant prefect of rank 4a, and about 40 other officials. Five counties, two of them with seats within the walls and three with seats at other cities lying south as well as east (Chü-jung, Li-yang, and Li-shui), were administered under this prefecture. The garrison command (*wan-hu fu*) was headed by a Mongol military officer with rank 3a and was staffed with about 100 other military officers. Each of the two county governments located within the walls had its own compound with attached educational, taxation, and other offices; was headed by magistrates with rank 7a; and was staffed by seven or eight other officials, plus subofficials and clerks.[44] Such was the official community of the Yüan city in normal times; in late Yüan, though, times were not normal, and incomplete staffing of offices probably existed, giving evidence of the deterioration of Mongol rule.

We cannot be sure about the population within the walls in the 1350's. Such figures normally are not preserved since they are bulked with those for the county to which the area belongs. In this case, two counties shared the population within and lying beyond the city to the east and south to a distance of some 25 miles away from the river. Disappointingly, the gazetteer of 1344 simply repeats the generally reliable census of 1297, perhaps indicating that no proper census had been carried out in this area after that date. But those figures do include a separate figure for the population "within the walls," a rare item. That figure is 95,000, while the population of the two-county area (including those 95,000) is 300,000, and that of the five counties making up the prefecture (and again including the 300,000 given above) is 1,250,000. When the Ming founder captured the city and the prefecture in 1356, he reportedly "gained a total military and civilian population there in excess of 500,000."[45] Though these figures are difficult to interpret, we can gain some sense of the size of the city that the Ming founder made his base in 1356 and that became the new imperial capital soon thereafter. In 1356, it probably was a city of about 100,000; within two decades it was to expand tenfold.

At first Chu Yüan-chang is said to have used the home of a rich citizen both for a residence and for offices, but within a year he moved into the *tzu-ch'eng*, the former palace city, which in Yüan times had been

The Transformation of Nanking

used for various administrative offices.[46] During the next five or six years, he was too occupied with building a military and political movement and fighting off nearby rivals to devote much time or energy to city building. In the year 1360, though, the walls were slightly enlarged and repaired to permit the addition of fortifications along the river sides. Some offices of government were built, and most temples and other semipublic buildings were "borrowed," in whole or in part, to help house the expanding administrative staff. In the mid-1360's Chu Yüan-chang began to give outward evidence of his imperial ambitions. He had thrown off his allegiance to his former overlords and increasingly was building his own model of an imperial government, directly challenging the Mongols in Peking as the other regional warlords about him fell to his armies in the field. In 1365 he changed the prefectural Confucian Academy into an Imperial University, and in 1366 he began work on vastly enlarged city walls and a new inner palace city. The ancestral shrines, the altars of the state, and other shrines necessary to an imperial government were also laid out in appropriate relationship to the new imperial city.

In 1367, after defeating his last major enemy in the central part of China and launching the final attack on the Mongols in Peking, he decided to proclaim his new dynasty as of the first day of the first lunar month in the new year corresponding to 1368.

Undoubtedly certain advisers throughout these years were entrusted with the task of formulating plans for transforming the small Yüan prefectural city into a vast imperial capital. A great army of builders must have been employed to complete the Altars of Heaven and Earth by the eighth month of 1367, the Temple of the Imperial Ancestors in the ninth month, and the three main audience halls of the new palace city later in that same month. But except for notices in the *Veritable Records* announcing that this or that project was commenced (usually with some ritual act and following consultation with some adviser) or completed, we know almost nothing of the actual process of building. We do know that stone quarries were opened and that brick and tile factories were established, and we know that thousands of households of artisans and builders were moved into the city from other prefectures, but we have no descriptions of the building work or technical reports on plans, engineering, materials, or other features. These details did not command the interest of the Chinese responsible for creating the historical record.

According to most sources, the building of Nanking's new city wall was begun in the eighth lunar month of 1366, although apparently it was not conceived as one unitary project. Other accounts say that it was begun only in 1369, but most agree that the work was fundamentally concluded in the eighth month of 1373. The initial intent probably was to add a large bulge to the east of the old Southern T'ang city as it existed in 1356; this bulge would enclose the new palace city and make a "new city" side by side with, and two-thirds the size of, the old city, which was to remain substantially unchanged.[47] This plan also envisaged an extension of the city to the north and west of the tenth-century north wall. The drum tower (*ku-lou*) as we know it, lying well within the present city, was to have been the north gate of the city wall, a little to the west of the center of a new straight north wall (see Map 1). But in the course of the building a new plan was developed. A decision was made to extend the walls about three miles farther to the northwest to enclose Lion Hill (*Shih-tzu shan*), a strategic height near the river. This added another large, irregular bulge northwest of the intended new city wall, and the area was used primarily to house military units.[48] The result is probably the most irregular shape of any major Chinese city, the largest space enclosed by a city wall, and the highest, longest, widest, firmest, and most impressive city wall in China. Unlike most previous walls, it was built on a foundation of large stone blocks, was from the first faced entirely either with specially fired bricks of immense size or with cut stone, was paved on the top with further immense slabs of stone, and was topped with brick crenellations. This was the *lo-ch'eng* or main city wall of Nanking. Inside it was the new inner enclosure called the *huang-ch'eng* or imperial city wall; outside it was the *wai-kuo*, an outer line of barriers and gates set in a wall of less substantial construction but of twice the *lo-ch'eng*'s length.

How long is the main city wall of Nanking? As it stands today it is essentially the fourteenth-century wall built by the Ming founder. There should be no ambiguity about its size, but the historical records and even the modern descriptions all differ on this point. The modern *Capital Gazetteer* (*Shou-tu chih*), compiled in 1935 by a distinguished group of historians under the supervision of the Nationalist government, quotes one modern study:

Of old it has been stated that the walls of Nanking are 96 *li* in length; in fact they are only 61 *li* in length. But that length still makes them number one in the world. The walls are more than 60 feet high in places, at their lowest spot 20 feet high, and average more than 40 feet in height. The width of the top of the wall, except for one very short section, is 25 feet. At its broadest it reaches a width of 40 feet. Moreover, this has been paved with stone to make a roadway. The wall is built on a foundation of stone from the Hua-kang

The Transformation of Nanking

quarries, and the walls are made of huge bricks. The exterior surface has been additionally hardened by covering it with plaster and rice glue. So wherever you scratch off the surface and examine it, it is still pure white in color, and that is why this imposing wall has stood there so boldly for several hundred years, still solid and unchanged today.

But the same gazetteer adds the following, citing a different source: "The wall length is 57 *li* and five-tenths; it is topped by 13,616 crenellations and has 200 guard shelters."[49]

Ninety-six *li* would be approximately 32 miles; 61 *li* would be about 20 miles. A very recent semiofficial publication from mainland China

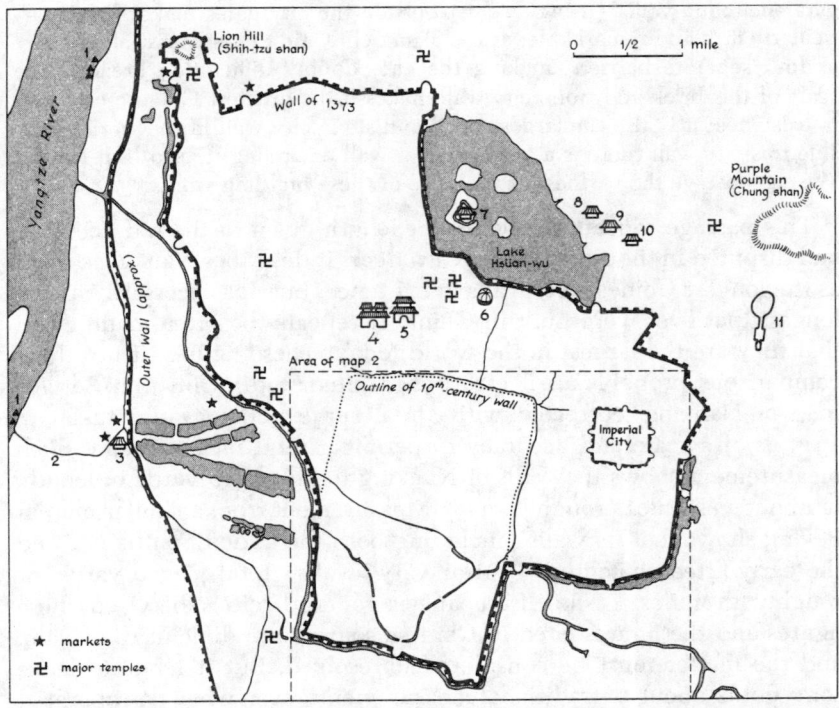

MAP 1. MING NANKING, ca. 1390. For details within dashed rectangle, see Map 2.

1. Docks and shipyards
2. New channel opened in the 1370's
3. Commercial tax office
4. Bell tower
5. Drum tower
6. Imperial University
7. Warehouses for tax and census records
8. Censorate
9. Ministry of Justice
10. Grand Court of Revision
11. Ming founder's tomb (*Ming Hsiao-ling*)

on the history of Chinese architecture describes Nanking's walls as follows:

Nanking's walls reach a length of 96 *li*, the base is between ten and eighteen meters broad, and the height is between fifteen and eighteen meters. It winds and turns according to the variations in the topography. Its top is level and flat, seven to twelve meters in width. There is a foundation of immense slabs of stone on top of which the wall is built of pounded earth, the exterior encased in huge bricks. Lime is used for the bonding mortar—or it may be that the walls are covered in a material composed of quicklime mixed with glutinous rice paste to form a grout—and the top of the wall is covered with a material composed of earth mixed with tung oil. The engineering of the extra gate-encircling walls (*weng-ch'eng*) outside the city gates makes them particularly firm and remarkable; at the T'ung-chi Gate these consist of as many as four separate barriers, making the gate doubly difficult to breach. The scale of this brick and stone city wall makes it the greatest Chinese city wall in existence; it is also the largest brick and stone city wall in the world. Outside this city wall there is a further outer wall encircling it, 180 *li* in length. We can observe the vastness of the scale of these building works.[50]

This passage repeats the figure for length given in the old accounts and disputed in the 1935 *Capital Gazetteer*. It describes Nanking's walls as the longest Chinese city walls in existence, but not necessarily as the longest that ever were built in China. It repeats the often-made claim that they are the largest in the world today. These figures, if not these comparisons, probably are in error. The United States Army Map Service map of Nanking, corrected with aerial survey photographs taken in 1945, is of a scale and accuracy to permit careful measurement. Such measurement shows the walls of Nanking to be 39,500 yards in length, or about 23.2 miles (roughly 70 *li*). Measurement from a similar map of Peking shows that its walls (including both the added South City and the early-fifteenth-century "Tartar City" walls) total 36,500 yards, or roughly 21 miles.[51] The discrepancies for both cities between these figures and the figures cited in Chinese sources are difficult to explain, and the matter must be considered unresolved. But it tends to leave some doubt about all traditional measurements, even when corroborated in very recent studies. Regardless of the ultimate outcome of such issues, the walls of Nanking built by the Ming founder are an overwhelming engineering and building achievement. The sight of them has awed countless millions of Chinese and foreigners and continues to do so, even though the walls are in disrepair, their former gate towers have been destroyed, and modern concrete and steel buildings compete with them now for dominance of the skyline.

The Transformation of Nanking

One may well ask why the Ming capital needed such walls, and what purposes they were expected to serve. We might keep in mind that the early Ming rulers, after repeated campaigns into the Mongolian steppe to defeat the prime enemy of the age on his own ground, also completely rebuilt the Great Wall using huge bricks and stone, and lined it with garrisons, communications posts, and strategic stockpiles of war matériel. In addition, most of the county capitals in China have walls that were rebuilt of firmer materials and in more imposing design during the Ming dynasty. In fact, this was the great age of Chinese wall building. All of this would seem to indicate a national, or at least dynastic, obsession with defense. That, however, is probably not the correct explanation.

The Great Wall of Ming China was not very effective in purely military terms; the dynasty relied much more on offensive operations to break the back of Mongol power on the steppe, or on diplomatic and trade activities to keep the Mongol enemy divided, complacent, and unwilling or unable to fight. The Great Wall itself had little tactical significance; rather, was its true significance not that of its psychological effect on the enemy, and conversely on the Chinese defender? It marked in truly awesome form the Chinese presence at the boundaries of Chinese government, at the limits of the Chinese way of life. These limits had been breached repeatedly in the alien invasions of the preceding centuries, but the Ming rulers at last had recovered the Chinese stance along the cultural dividing line between steppe and peasant village. They reaffirmed China's ancient position there by ostentatiously rebuilding the Great Wall, but they defended themselves by other means.

Perhaps in a larger sense the walls of Nanking and of other cities rebuilt in Ming times served the primarily psychological function of reaffirming the presence of the Chinese state rather than the purely physical function of making cities and their inhabitants secure against possible sources of danger. Walled cities were not in fact more secure than nonwalled ones insofar as the day-to-day life of the people and government officials was concerned, for the Chinese countryside was secure. The walls around administrative cities did not divide off a zone of guaranteed safety from the rest of the population. The high walls and broad moats of Nanking did not protect the shrines of Heaven and of Earth, the tombs of the imperial ancestors, or even the major government entrepôts and factories, for all of these were outside them. They did not protect a large number of the government's highest civil and military officials, who resided in government-built housing outside them. They certainly did not divide the urban concentration from the open countryside. They did not protect a large number of the most important markets or other palaces where basic economic and fiscal activities were centered. Finally, they did not divide an urban subculture from a rural one. What they did, though, above all, was to mark the presence of the government. They dignified cities; they did not bound them.

That is not to deny entirely their military function. They were reminders of military power, and they could become bastions of defense, able if necessary to withstand protracted siege and the most ingenious weaponry of assault. (But how often in Ming history was that necessary?) The Ming founder certainly had some purely military functions in mind when he decided to include readily fortifiable points within the enlarged walls of Nanking, and when he had the multiple gates built to withstand any attack. But the builder of these massive fortifications was not primarily a military man, nor was his government a military government. Despite the fact that his revenues were largely employed to maintain the expensive military component of government, he ruled primarily by civilian means, and these means included above all the ritual ordering of society and government and the reliance on a mystique of legitimacy expressed in the Mandate of Heaven. The city walls of Nanking were, like other acts of government, designed to reinforce that mystique and maintain the awesome sense of the government's presence. That, I would hypothesize, is their primary significance in Chinese cultural history and in the study of the city in traditional China.

Other physical components of the new capital. The new capital built in the Hung-wu reign period (1368–98) is described in many gazetteers and other writings, some of them dating from the Hung-wu period itself. Surprise at the accomplishment is not reflected in them, although appreciation of it is. The power of the Chinese state, and above all the effective organization that characterized Chu Yüan-chang's government, was apparent in the city's great transformation. Within two decades of the proclamation of the new dynasty late in 1367, the city grew from perhaps one hundred thousand to about one million inhabitants, most of them directly related to the new official community making up the central government of the Chinese world. The degree of change worked upon Nanking when the Ming founder declared it his capital, and the rapidity with which that change was accomplished, have perhaps no ready parallels in Western historical experience. We, at least, must be amazed.

A great and ever-evolving system of centralized government, one observing models and precedents well established throughout the pre-

The Transformation of Nanking 139

vious millennium, had collapsed under Mongol mismanagement, leaving its battered parts scattered across the landscape; under new dynastic leadership the system was rebuilt with amazing rapidity, like a jigsaw puzzle being reassembled by persons who have done it before and recognize all the pieces. This new government, however, was being brought together at a new site, and occupying a new physical structure built to match, in functional utility as well as in ideological and cosmological significance, all the parts of the political and social order that simultaneously was being reconstituted. Despite the facts that all government posts had to be created out of nothing, that all the housing and physical requirements of government had to be built from scratch, and that all procedures and operational regulations had to be formulated and established anew, this new government was from the outset conceptually complete in the minds of the men creating it. They had viable models in ideal form and in very recent experience. Moreover, potential bureaucrats were at hand, possessing ideological group coherence and technical training, educated for official careers if not always experienced. They could be assigned immediately to roles they understood and whose demands they could meet.

Within the decade from 1360 to 1370, Nanking was transformed from a rebel base that had been a small branch station of a malfunctioning government to the center of a tightly organized bureaucracy, the largest and most complex then existing and indeed that had ever existed. From being the seat of a civil service staff of about 200 officials, Nanking almost overnight became the seat of an imperial bureaucracy staffed by 10,000 civil and 12,000 military officials and by perhaps 50,000 subofficials not ranked in the civil service. Of these, most were on rotating assignment in the provinces; but still there could have been no fewer than 5,000 of the ranked civil and military officials and 10,000 of the subofficials resident and on duty in and around the capital by the end of the fourteenth century. Military garrisons (*wei*) stationed at the capital were reported to include 200,000 men in 1391.[52] Also, there were in the Imperial University (the *Kuo-tzu-chien*, in that period a kind of massive talent pool where young men who hoped to become officials engaged in study between periods of ad hoc assignment to special tasks) between 8,000 and 9,000 students, all on government stipend.

The buildings housing government were built mostly within the imperial city and in the "new city" surrounding it (see Map 2). The walls of the imperial city (*huang-ch'eng*), with their moats, bridges, and gates, followed the style of the main city walls although on a smaller scale and with more elaborate decoration and finer materials. It was about one and

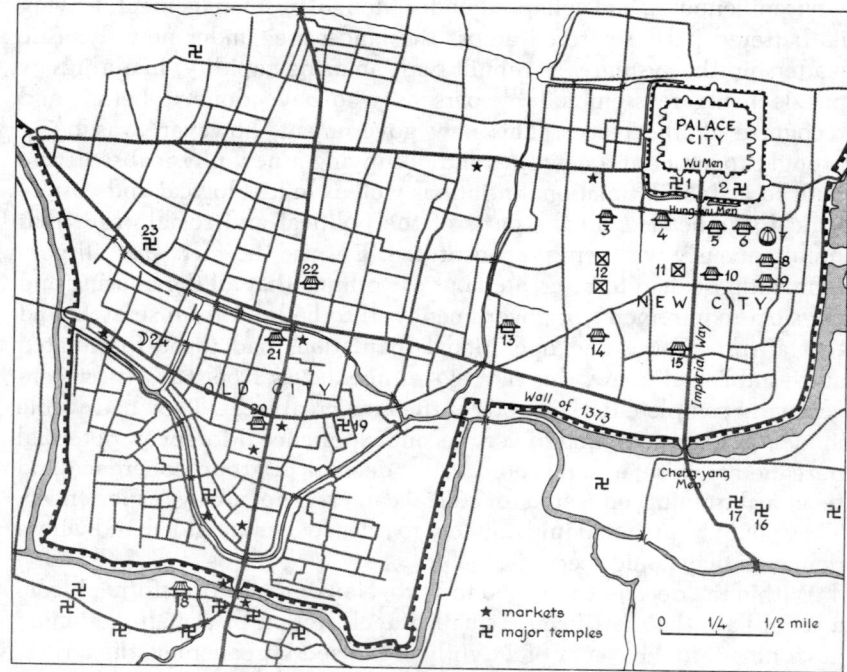

MAP 2. MING NANKING, ca. 1390, showing major built-up areas.

1. Altar of Land and Grain (*She-chi t'an*)
2. Temple of the Imperial Ancestors (*T'ai miao*)
3. Office of Transmission
4. Hui-t'ung Kuan (hostel for embassies)
5. Imperial Clan Office (*Tsung-jen fu*)
6. Bureau of Court Ceremonial (*I-li ssu*)
7. Hanlin Academy
8. Offices of the Heir Apparent
9. Imperial Medical Bureau
10. Ministries of Civil Office, Revenue, Rites, War, and Works
11. Five Military Commands
12. Imperial Palace Guard units (*Chin-i wei*)
13. Metropolitan tax offices
14. Bureau of Astronomy (Chinese)
15. Court of Sacrificial Worship
16. Altars of Heaven and Earth (*T'ien-ti t'an*)
17. Altar to Mountains and Rivers (*Shan-ch'uan t'an*)
18. Commercial tax office
19. Prefectural Confucian school-temple
20. Chiang-ning county yamen
21. Ying-t'ien prefectural yamen
22. Shang-yüan county yamen
23. Ch'ao T'ien kung (main Taoist shrine)
24. Mosque

one-half miles on a side, roughly square, oriented with its main gate to the south. Within it the court was convened, and from it emanated the ultimate authority and decision-making in government. It also contained the residence of the emperor and his household, his family shrines, and certain altars of the state. Some principle of avoidance was observed in locating any symbol of imperial power; it was not desirable simply to rebuild a site formerly occupied by the emperors of an earlier dynasty. Therefore the move to the east of the old city had some ritual significance. First, geomancers were consulted, and then a lake was filled in to make a flat terrace on which to locate the palace city; its location to the east of the old city put the highest mountain in the region, the Purple Mountain (*chung shan*), auspiciously to the rear of the whole complex. The imperial city suffered severe destruction at the close of the Taiping wars in 1864, and was almost totally obliterated at the time of the Revolution of 1911. In a generally accurate way, though, we can visualize the Nanking complex of palace city within imperial city from its approximate replica in Peking, built in the early fifteenth century on the new Nanking model, if somewhat more ostentatious than it in scale and design. Most of the names of gates and palaces and other parts duplicate those of counterparts in Nanking.

As pictured in the old gazetteers, a broad avenue called the Imperial Way led from Cheng-yang Men, the chief gate in the southern wall of the "new city," directly north to Hung-wu Men, the south gate of the imperial city, and on to Wu Men, the main south gate of the palace city. This avenue, like a number of other major streets in the government section of the city, was lined with raised covered walkways so that officials and clerks could move along protected from rain, wind, and sun. Along the Imperial Way were ranged five of the Six Ministries, the Five Military Commands (on the west side of the avenue, opposite the ministries), the Imperial Clan Office, the Court of Sacrificial Worship, and other major offices. But the government was not confined to this area. The sixth of the ministries, the Ministry of Justice, was located symbolically outside the city wall to the north of the palace city; north was the direction of winter, the season of punishments and death. The execution ground was adjacent. The Censorate also was located nearby. The Imperial University at first occupied the grounds of the former prefectural Confucian Academy in the old city, but vast new quarters for it were built in 1381 in the new north section of the city, approximately on the site later occupied in republican times by the National Central University. Many other offices of government were scattered throughout the city.

The scale of these buildings was large; most were situated within grounds that preserved open space, and most included gardens. The architecture was not distinctively "early Ming" in any specific sense; it was "imperial grand" in a traditional sense, marked by the Ming founder's preference for austerity and dignity. There may have been some

West Asian influences on early Ming architecture but only in quite superficial ways. The Mongols had brought Persians and Arabs and other West Asian craftsmen, engineers, and builders to China. Nanking's mosques, serving the Moslem fifth of its population, were West Asian in their interiors and in elements of decoration. Some historians have noted similarities to the Mogul arch in the thin line of decorative embellishment on the archways of the founder's tomb (*Ming Hsiao-ling*), built by Ming T'ai-tsu in the 1390's beyond the northeast corner of the city wall. But even in Khubilai's Ta-tu—built by a Mongol emperor with much aid from non-Chinese assistants—the influence of other cultures in the architecture and city planning was minimal; we must assume also that Nanking's great new buildings were undistinguished by architectural or engineering features that reflect period, region, or any particular school of architectural design.

All of the palaces, gates, avenues, and shrines not only were adapted ingeniously to their sites but also were located in ways that symbolized the imperial role and the proper order among men. But they were not mere blind copyings of precedents; and Nanking did acquire a highly individual character, if not in originality of architectural design, then in layout of the total ground space. It is a city of rolling ground and a few hills, with some waterways running through it; of large open spaces, some of which have always been devoted to intensive commercial gardening; and of many temples with groves and gardens. The change from provincial town to imperial capital not only vastly expanded the size of the government installations, it also created the need for hundreds of new streets, dozens of markets, parks, pleasure quarters, private residences for officials, barracks, factories, and warehouses. Nonetheless, the city remained a very open kind of urban concentration that included many activities and uses of space that we do not ordinarily associate with large cities in the premodern West. The ex-commoner founder issued a command limiting the size of gardens surrounding the city residences of officials so that space would not be denied to the common people.[53] But all of Nanking's residents, rich and commoner alike, lived on the ground floors of houses that at best boasted a main hall with a higher ceiling, or that perhaps had a partial second-floor section. Otherwise, buildings were of one story, and virtually all had some open courtyard and garden space.

The old city, the "South City" of modern Nanking, was also largely rebuilt, not by plan but just in the normal course of urban renewal under the influences of expansion, of increase in wealth, and of stimulus to change in the flourishing period of the new dynasty. The main streets,

The Transformation of Nanking

the waterways, and the locations of bridges and gates are much the same there as they have been since the old city was built in the early tenth century, but though many of the bricks and stones probably have been repeatedly reused, no building there claims to be as old as the early Ming. The physical shell of the Chinese city must be constantly renewed; enduring material elements of it have little to do with its continuity as a locus of history. Ming Nanking was suddenly new, but not novel; modern Nanking occupies the shell of an ancient city, but its awareness of that fact is not derived from omnipresent architectural reminders of its past (except for the walls), nor is it denied by recent physical changes.

Population and administrative subdivisions. The forms of administrative organization imposed at the basic level by governments in successive dynasties tended to change in fact more than in name. The term *fang* or "city ward" meant something quite specific in T'ang times,[54] but although it continued to be used on into the Ming, by then it carried quite different implications about the degree of organization and control among the urban population. The urban and suburban populations of early Ming Nanking, like those of other cities, were organized into three types of administrative units coexisting at the basic level of formal organization, in combination implying a spatial structuring of the metropolitan area. Each unit apparently maintained separate registries for census purposes and probably for corvée and taxation and mutual-security organization as well. The late Ming writer Ku Ch'i-yüan describes these as follows:

At the beginning of the dynasty persons and households from Chekiang and [Southern] Chihli (i.e. Kiangsu-Anhwei) Provinces were moved in to fill out the population of the capital. In all cases when they were located within the capital's walls they were [organized into units] called *"fang."* Those outside the city walls in the suburbs were called *"hsiang."* And those [units] originally registering the local population in the suburbs were called *"shiang"* [spelled here to make an arbitrary orthographic distinction from the preceding term, a homonym]. *Fang* and *hsiang* subdivisions had their own registry-charts (*t'u*); *shiang* also were divided into their subsidiary *li*.[55]

The next item in the same source states that the two counties making up the area including the capital and its environs and having their seats within the city walls, i.e. Shang-yüan and Chiang-ning, had the following populations: Shang-yüan, 38,900 households or 253,200 individuals; Chiang-ning, 27,000 households or 220,000 individuals. These apparently are the figures from the census of 1391. The ratio of individuals to households is somewhat suspicious. Also, the figures do not include military units and their families (as mentioned above, garrison troops were said to have numbered 200,000 in 1390) or officials and their families. But they do suggest that what was regarded as the permanent civilian resident population on the local government's registries numbered close to half a million. These half a million were divided into 24 *fang*, or urban wards for new residents; 24 *hsiang*, or suburban subdivisions for new population; and 39 *shiang*, or suburban and rural subdivisions for the original inhabitants. This would average about 5,400 individuals, or about 1,000 households, per organizational unit listed.[56]

There is a question about the original inhabitants residing within the city. Apparently, moving population from other areas to "fill out the population of the capital" was done not merely to effect a net increase but also to replace the original residents, who were forcibly moved out. Ku Ch'i-yüan wrote that the founder feared opposition on the part of the original residents of Nanking and moved them all to distant Yunnan to prevent trouble:

> When the Emperor Kao [i.e. the founder, referred to by a posthumous title] established the center of his realm at Nanking, he expelled the former residents and had them located in Yunnan. Also, beginning in 1381 and thereafter he got more than 45,000 wealthy households (*shang-hu*) from Soochow, Chekiang, and such places and had them brought to fill out the population of the capital. The adult males (*ting*) were assigned to various factories and offices to serve as craftsmen; the rest were registered in commoner households. They were located within and without the city walls in [units] called *fang* and *hsiang*.[57]

The removal of population mentioned above probably refers to the dispatching of expeditionary forces, said in the *Veritable Records* to have numbered 300,000 men, to occupy and administer Yunnan in the years 1381–89 as that province was added to the Chinese empire. Those armies were made up principally from units formed in the capital area, and most of the military personnel and their households remained in Yunnan. Some sources on Yunnan history state that the province gained tens of thousands of households from Nanking at the time. These figures probably are used loosely, and they do not in themselves account for the total lack of Nanking urban wards whose populations are described as being made up of original residents. But they suggest at least a major factor in the probable solution of the problem.

The households moved into Nanking during the reign of the founder are variously described and appear not to have been of one character. The *Capital Gazetteer* cites three items from fourteenth-century sources bearing on the forced recruitment of population for the city. First, some

The Transformation of Nanking

45,000 "wealthy households" from the richer regions to the east—around Soochow, Hu-chou, and those prefectures that had adhered to the rebel leader Chang Shih-ch'eng—were moved to Nanking in 1381 "to fill out the population" and to punish them for having resisted the founder in supporting a rival. The adult males were assigned as laborers and craftsmen in various government work projects. Using a factor of five and one-half, about standard for the population at large but perhaps too small for "wealthy households," we get a possible total of 247,500 persons drawn into the city by this single move. Moving dissident wealthy households into the capital to keep them under surveillance may seem inconsistent with sending away the total original population, whose capacity to revolt against the government was feared. But rich urbanites assigned to punitive labor may have been docile, generally speaking, and more susceptible to intimidation by the new imperial regime than the original mixed population of the city, who had known Chu Yüan-chang and his cohorts ever since they had entered the city as a ragged rebel band 25 years before. Second, another 14,000 households of "the wealthy of the realm" were conscripted to become the well-to-do of the city, to be listed on the population registries as *fu-hu* (wealthy households). Wealthy households in the early Ming system were needed to assume certain basic-level administrative functions, such as heading the *fang-hsiang* units and supervising tax collections and corvée works; they were an element of the population that was necessary to government. Third, another record refers to 20,000 craftsmen households (or about 100,000 people) moved from Chekiang to fill specialized labor and building jobs.[58]

These figures and the phenomena they represent are very difficult to interpret. There are hints in other sources that upper-class households forced to migrate as punishment often found methods of buying their way out of the labor to which they were assigned by paying for alternates and of eventually returning to their home regions, where they had in the meantime retained ownership of property and other interests. But even if many evaded forced migration, the demographic makeup of a capital city, especially at the time of the founding of an era, was subject to influences that were not typical of other cities. When the Yung-lo emperor decided to make Peking the principal capital, for example, he took 27,000 households of skilled craftsmen from Nanking to Peking to assist in its rebuilding.[59]

Fang and *hsiang* as names for organizations of new population (as opposed to *shiang*) are themselves one item of evidence that different parts of the city had different characters. They became names for quarters of the city, and each quarter acquired the special flavor of the dialect backgrounds, professional specializations, and other characteristics of its residents. These features of Nanking's demography were still apparent in late Ming times and were commented on even in the nineteenth century. Some population units merely have numbers as names, e.g. "Twelfth Fang," "Thirteenth Fang," and "Eighteenth Fang," but there is no complete sequence of numbers and the explanation of these names is difficult to reconstruct. Other *fang* names are more revealing, for in some cases they suggest groupings by occupation. There was a "Brocade Fang," a "Carpenters' Fang," a "Singers' and Artistes' Fang," a "First Craftsmen's Fang," a "Second Craftsmen's Fang" (on up to Fifth), and a "Poor People's Fang." Some had names such as "Due West Former First Fang," where the word "former" may mean that this *fang* and others with similar names were in fact for old carry-over population; but it could also mean simply that they had replaced former *fang*. In general, the *fang* names that reveal anything are descriptive of the population. The *hsiang*, on the other hand, all either have names suggestive of geographic location ("Southeast Corner Hsiang," "Purple Mountain Hsiang") or have auspicious names like "Virtue and Benevolence Hsiang." The *shiang* names are likewise descriptive neither of occupations nor of class status; they all seem to have centered on the rural villages about Nanking.

The internal organization of the *fang-hsiang-shiang* system in early Ming Nanking merits thorough investigation. However, since the functioning of these lowest levels of government did not directly involve civil-service-ranked officials (unless crises arose), materials from which to study this system are not very plentiful. It may be that fiction of the middle and late Ming will provide us with the best evidence of how the *fang, hsiang,* and *shiang* worked. But the urban society of late Ming Nanking clearly was somewhat different from that of early Ming Nanking; moreover, the *fang-hsiang-shiang* system had undergone some structural changes by late Ming times. Ku Ch'i-yüan, our best source for the local history of late Ming Nanking, notes that the transfer of the capital to Peking in 1421 took away so much of the population that afterward the system did not work as originally intended. He also discusses changes in the regulations commencing with the middle of the fifteenth century. At that time a governor of the imperial prefecture noted that the corvée exactions tended to fall heavily on the rural *shiang* units; the urban *fang* and *hsiang* commoners were exempt but paid an annual cash fee. He proposed that the three kinds of units be integrated and the burden rationalized. The details of the service and tax obligations

The Transformation of Nanking

are not clear to me, but it is obvious that the *fang-hsiang-shiang* system was intended to regulate primarily these service and tax functions. The headship of the *fang* (and *hsiang*) rotated among the heads of rich households, who were called *tsung-fang* (later *fang-chang*, and still later *fang-fu*). The difficulties that arose in the system in later Ming times all had to do with the inequitable apportionment and collection of service obligations and taxes, and with the relations between the *fang* heads and the subofficials of the county offices who oversaw them. Although local responsibility was encouraged or demanded in some matters, no local self-government was incipient in the system. But it is notable that the people could protest and effect improvements when the situation became intolerable.[60]

Other Aspects of Urban Life in Ming Nanking

Economic role. The place of Nanking, the city and the region, in the economic life of fourteenth-century China is a large and complex subject deserving a separate monograph. In the sixteenth century, the change in Ming economy sometimes referred to as the "buds of capitalism" deeply affected urban life in the city, the region, and the whole empire; that, however, is a still more difficult subject to assess at this stage of our knowledge. Some awareness of these economic factors is of course implicit in much of the foregoing. The details cannot be made explicit here, but some highly generalized conclusions may suffice to characterize aspects of Nanking's economic life in Ming times.

Nanking lies just west of the alluvial plain created by the delta of the Yangtze. Agricultural productivity in Nanking's immediate hinterland cannot compare with that in the rich prefectures farther downriver to the east and south, of which Su-chou, Sung-chiang, Ch'ang-chou, and Hu-chou are the most notable. The great "rice-bowls" of the Middle and Upper Yangtze also are more favored.[61] Nanking was a grain-shortage prefecture in Southern Sung times,[62] probably because of the large garrisons stationed there. In short, there are no agricultural surpluses locally. The city for a thousand years has depended entirely on the wealth of the larger region, and it is unusually well situated to command that unless, as in the mid-fourteenth century before Chu Yüan-chang's successful buildup, there are rival power centers in the richer areas upriver and downriver. Chu Yüan-chang's success, a triumph over economic odds, was achieved through organization and planning; he gradually attached to his movement districts providing wealth to his nearer rivals, and then he utilized his resources more efficiently than they had done.

The districts immediately adjacent to Nanking lacked the sources of wealth that characterize the Lower Yangtze generally—agriculture, sericulture, fishing, mining, salt. Nanking had some important crafts, especially weaving, but it did not acquire its fame as a center of fine silk and brocade production until later in the Ming period; and even then it was largely dependent on raw materials—silk floss and dyestuffs—produced elsewhere. Despite the word "Nankeen" for the durable brown cotton cloth that was a staple in nineteenth-century trade, Nanking's textile industry in Ming times was limited to silk; it did not yet share in the great growth of cotton textile production that was making rapid headway in the late fourteenth century at Soochow and Sungchiang. Nor did Nanking play a role in salt production and distribution like that which brought immense wealth to nearby Yangchow. In short, Nanking's economic position was based on its political and military dominance of a large area extending east and west along the Yangtze and north and south along the Grand Canal, and not on any unusual local productivity.

The same of course can be said of Peking, and of some other great capital cities of Chinese history. Like them, Nanking became a city of great wealth and ease, thanks to the regional and national integration of the economy and the centralizing influence of the political structure. In addition, however, Nanking's capacity to develop significant economic enterprise to accompany its political life was somewhat greater than that of Peking and some other capitals in the north, for the total environmental factor in the Yangtze basin was much more conducive to entrepreneurship and growth. Nanking's famous silk factories, developed especially from mid-Ming times on, are the best single illustration of that capacity. They used the raw materials and skilled labor of nearby prefectures, and supplied simultaneously the court and Central Asian markets (via the Grand Canal) and the entire Yangtze basin.[63]

Cosmopolitan character. Fourteenth-century China was less cosmopolitan than thirteenth-century China, and much less so than T'ang China. The land routes to Asia had been rather effectively diminished in significance between the time Marco Polo went overland to China in the 1270's and the time he returned, perforce by sea via India, in the 1290's. The Ming emperors did not associate the origins of their dynasty with Inner Asia or with alliances with non-Chinese people, as had been the case with the T'ang and the Yüan. The Ming was a dynasty of nativist revival; it came to power by expelling Inner Asians and associated its national responsibilities strongly with border defenses.

Yet it would be a mistake to assume that strong sentiments of antiforeignism marked the tone of life in Ming China, or that the capital of the Chinese world lacked important cosmopolitan elements. Henry Serruys has shown that, although Mongol cultural influences were not valued, the Mongols remaining in China did not suffer from discrimination or persecution and continued to make contributions to political and social life.[64] Early Ming Nanking probably was not a brilliant international crossroads in the way T'ang Ch'ang-an appears in the lively descriptions of Arthur Wright.[65] But as the capital of China, it was as cosmopolitan a place as East Asian realities could afford in the late fourteenth century. Embassies came from Southeast Asia, Japan, Korea, and some nearby Inner Asian states.

Nanking had a considerable Moslem community, and it probably still had remnants of the Nestorian, Jewish, and Central Asian communities that we know existed there in late Yüan times.[66] Schools for interpreters employed foreign nationals. The astronomy bureau continued to use Central Asians and the so-called Arab methods. Hostelries for diplomats and for their entourages, which often consisted of merchants with exotic goods, were among the first buildings erected by the new imperial government. The emperor's park had a zoo filled with strange animals brought by these ambassadors, and on some occasions the people of the city could come and look at them.

From the beginning of the fifteenth century, the famous shipyards on the Yangtze just below Nanking began building the fleets that Cheng Ho took to the South Seas, India, and Africa on his six or seven expeditions. Nanking was a seaport as well as a center of inland water transportation. Although the Ming government preferred to establish its control points for the admission of foreigners and foreign goods farther from its capital cities, the water transportation route did bring to the markets of Nanking goods that could not so easily reach all other places.

Entertainment. Nanking acquired elaborate facilities for entertainment in the sixteen great "storied buildings" (*lou*) built by the founder for official entertainment but not limited to that use. Some of these were outside the main gates of the palace city, but most were still farther away, outside the south gates of the city wall in an area of markets, inns, and brothels that since the tenth century had existed there along water transportation routes into the city.[67] The emperor's new official pleasure halls were combination hostelries, taverns, restaurants, and singsong houses. Theaters and amusement areas featuring jugglers, acrobats, storytellers, and prostitutes abounded, especially in the zone adjacent to the south city wall.

The Ming founder's own temperament kept him somewhat hostile to persons who displayed too much interest in pleasure, frivolity, and ostentation. But as a very large city thronged with a new official elite, Nanking became a bustling place of commerce and of luxury trade in particular. The emperor's personal austerities and the harsh tone of the court did not obliterate the pleasure-seeking capacities of the residents, and the city's famous pleasure quarters survived even the removal of the capital to Peking in the 1420's to become still more celebrated in late Ming times.

Intellectual life. The tone of the early Ming court was not very encouraging to intellectual and literary activity. The Ming founder was personally suspicious of the highly educated. His chief rival in the period of his rise to power, Chang Shih-ch'eng, had drawn many more of the intellectual and literary figures of the day about him at his Soochow base, and their obvious preference for him and for life in the area controlled by him was one of the factors in the Ming founder's suspicions. His reign was marked by vicious and unpredictable purges in which the literary talents of the age were prominent victims. The usurpation carried out by his fourth son against his grandson and heir, the Chien-wen emperor, was again a ruthless military suppression of a ruler sympathetic to intellectual and literary personages. The Chien-wen emperor had encouraged literary figures and had drawn intellectual leaders to his service; as a group, they represented the culturally advanced southeast region. His displacement was followed again by rigorous suppression both of those who had found his rule encouraging and of the region they represented. Therefore, the reigns of the founder and of the usurper stifled any flowering of intellectual and literary life at the early Ming court. At best, the talent was there but did not find encouragement to express itself.

Nevertheless, the cultural life of China flourished most vigorously during the early Ming in the region around Nanking—in modern Kiangsu, Anhwei, and Chekiang. Nanking came into its own as a great intellectual and literary center only in the middle and late Ming, not during its period as principal capital. Yet though no one city dominated the development of culture or drew all the leading intellectuals to it during the early Ming, that did not dampen the growth of cultural activity. Indeed, as we have seen, Chinese culture has never been dependent on any one metropolitan center for its development or continuing vitality.

Role as secondary capital. When the Yung-lo emperor moved the capital to Peking in 1421, the population of Nanking decreased considerably; most accounts say it was reduced "by one half," which is not a precise expression but a meaningful one. Between that time and the end of the century, Nanking was a city very much robbed of the major role for which it had been so recently rebuilt

In the sixteenth century great changes occurred in the life of the city. Some of these reflected the profound changes general throughout Chinese life at the time—the increase of population, of agricultural production, of commerce, and of wealth. These forms of growth were especially evident in the Lower Yangtze area, and they brought about urban recovery in Nanking along with urban growth everywhere.

Late Ming writers in Nanking and other cities were quite aware of changes in urban life-styles and social attitudes. They relate some of this change to the reform of the tax system, the "Single Whip System" that was progressively developed and applied throughout several decades.[68] Some features of the reformed fiscal system, particularly those involving commutation of labor services and special exactions, are said by writers of the time to have been conducive to ostentatious consumption in the cities. Urban commoners who had money were no longer under great pressure to conceal that fact; they could display their wealth in elegantly enlarged houses, gardens now free of restrictions on size, gaudier entertainment. A pleasure-loving elite came to be identified with the city by late Ming times.

These changes were greatly reinforced by a new role the secondary capital came to serve. A type of successful official who wanted position and emolument without the responsibilities and competitive juggling for place that characterized Peking and the court found the trappings of power in Nanking preferable to real power in Peking. It became a more glamorous official environment than it had been, now associated with low-keyed alternative patterns of success in the political sphere and more refined and sybaritic living in the private sphere.

The comparison with Peking. As we have noted, Nanking's population declined considerably during the century after the capital was moved to Peking. The gazetteer of 1521 makes this clear in a number of specific comparisons. But the 1593 gazetteer shows a great recovery in population and wealth. At the end of the Ming dynasty Nanking had acquired the character of a center of great wealth and ease, famous for concentrations of artists, writers, and rich book collectors. The second capital of the realm gradually came to take on a peculiar role in the intellectual and artistic life of the nation as its official posts became attractive to officials with cultural interests, men who would previously have preferred careers in Peking, close to the actual exercise of power. Nanking, as secondary capital, retained a full lineup of administrative posts at the highest levels that duplicated the structure of government in Peking. These were posts equal to Peking's in rank and emolument, but with very limited actual responsibility and with power over regional government only, except in fiscal administration and a few other areas (see p. 130). By late in the dynasty these posts, especially those carrying position and rank without demanding duties, came to be actively sought by officials who had no taste for the dogfights of political life. Nanking, close to the region of wealth and refinement that produced most of the nation's intellectuals, became the place where the scholar-official in office could have everything but the guts of political life.

In terms of cultural life, this was an important development in the history of Nanking; and in terms of social dynamics, it held significant potential for Chinese history. The government's ability to hold the most talented men of the nation—keeping them dependent on government service for self-realization—and to keep the needs of government first in its command of human talent, is one of the great achievements of the bureaucratic imperial system from Sung times onward. Nanking, as opposed to Peking, came to represent an attractive alternative course where previously there had existed only a single acceptable course for men of talent and ambition. The rich life of the great city came close to being politically subversive as well as morally scandalous in the late sixteenth and seventeenth centuries. The study of how this came about will help us understand the maturing of the city in traditional China.

As a final note of comparison, let us endeavor to reconstruct in our mind's eye the Nanking that existed in Ming times. Chinese architecture's stylistic immutability in time and relative uniformity throughout urban and rural space, and especially the Chinese city's characteristic of physical impermanence, have combined to deprive Nanking today of the physical magnificence we associate with great imperial capitals. Peking is the single great city whose physical presence within the lifetime of living men has been capable of communicating something of the greatness of traditional Chinese capitals to our consciousness. Peking has been the single Chinese imperial capital with all its monumental grandeur still intact in our time. Somewhat ignorantly, therefore, we tend to concentrate superlatives on it. Matteo Ricci, a cultivated traveler who arrived in Nanking in 1595, wrote about it: "In the judgment of the Chinese this city surpasses all other cities in the world in beauty and grandeur, and in this respect there are probably very few others superior or equal to it. It is literally filled with palaces and temples and towers and bridges, and these are scarcely surpassed by similar structures in Europe. In some respects, it surpasses our European cities.... This city

The Transformation of Nanking

was once the capital of the entire realm and the ancient abode of kings through many centuries, and though the king changed his residence to Pekin, ... Nankin lost none of its splendor or its reputation."[69] And after seeing Peking in 1600 Ricci wrote: "The size of the city, the planning of its houses, the structure of its public buildings and its fortifications are far inferior to those of Nankin."[70] Let those Peking chauvinists who so often think of it as the only city in the world worthy of the ultimate adjectives consider Ricci's discerning comparison, made in an age when both cities were complete, even though Nanking was no longer at its physical best.

The Formation of Cities: Initiative and Motivation in Building Three Walled Cities in Taiwan

HARRY J. LAMLEY

For well over three millennia, walled cities in China served as capitals and administrative centers symbolizing state authority and the Chinese moral order. Not surprisingly, therefore, the Chinese walled city has been identified more with the continuity evident in China's long historical tradition than with the diversity characteristic of its local society and rich cultural heritage. Neither is it extraordinary that traditional genres of Chinese literature, reflecting a bureaucratic image of imperial China, should have ascribed essentially political functions to these urban seats of government. Such standardized accounts made walled cities seem remarkably uniform in nature and constant in their pattern of development over the ages—despite differences in their sizes, layouts, and locations and variations in their actual roles.

In reality, walled cities in traditional China were neither so immutable nor so detached from everyday life as has been alleged. As seats of government, they proved susceptible to influences from the territories they administered; moreover, as centers of local commercial and cultural activity, they continued to be responsive to the needs of their hinterlands. The expansion and change that the "Middle Kingdom" experienced from Shang and early Chou times down to the late Ch'ing period affected Chinese cities as well. Walled centers multiplied, and urban life assumed new dimensions, particularly in the sphere of commerce.

Diversity among walled cities in traditional China is apparent in the Ch'ing period when administrative centers subordinate to the central and provincial levels of government are examined. Far more numerous than imperial and provincial capitals, these lesser seats of government developed under conditions that varied with the region. Differences among widely dispersed cities were inevitable, yet we can also find differences among lesser walled cities constructed in a given region within the same century, as this paper will show. The three cities that form the subject of this study—Hsin-chu, I-lan, and T'ai-pei-fu—all arose in northern Taiwan under Ch'ing rule. Founded during or shortly after periods of intensive settlement, these cities assumed permanent shape in the nineteenth century while their particular hinterlands were undergoing transition from a frontier situation to one resembling that of Fukien and Kwangtung communities on the mainland. During their formative years, these three Taiwan cities emerged as distinct entities representing different stages and patterns of settlement in northern Taiwan.

In the first part of this paper, the background and setting of each city are examined within the context of its hinterland and administrative territory. Then the process of settlement and the local society that evolved in these outlying areas are described. Finally, after a summary of city building precedents established in mid and southern Taiwan, where intensive settlement first occurred, there follows an attempt to ascertain the initiative and motivation behind the construction of each city.

City building in northern Taiwan entailed joint efforts on the part of the officials and the inhabitants. Hence in dealing with questions of initiative and motivation, we must treat these walled centers less as simple appendages of state authority than as places where the formal apparatus of government and the informal local sociopolitical structure interacted. Through such an approach we can assess the roles of both the authorities and the inhabitants in the formation of these cities; and we can also see how the authorities and gentry or other commoner spokesmen responded to local conditions and needs, particularly in respect to city wall construction. We can thus learn something about the interplay between government and society as it affected each city, and about the impetus behind urban development as a whole in a region settled comparatively late in imperial times.

This study focuses on the relatively brief periods when the three cities began to function as key administrative centers housing a normal complement of civil officials. It was during these periods that major construction projects, including the building of substantial city walls and durable public structures, were planned and carried out at each site. In the case of Hsin-chu, such massive construction was initiated almost a century after the center was established. In contrast, both I-lan and T'ai-pei-fu were built up as key administrative centers soon after their founding, even though their respective hinterlands differed markedly in **degree of settlement** and **commercial activity**.

The Formation of Cities in Taiwan

Local support was an important factor in the building of these three cities. The construction of a traditional administrative center—complete with walls and moats, gates and towers, government offices (yamens), shrines, and temples—necessitated a considerable outlay of funds and a sizable labor force. In late imperial China such large-scale public works usually drew heavily upon the resources of the localities involved.[1] This was the case in Taiwan under Ch'ing rule. On that isolated island, where public works projects normally employed hired labor rather than labor conscripted through corvée or military service, major construction projects were undertaken only when most of the required funds and services were provided by the inhabitants.[2] Thus, not only did the localities involved have to be prosperous to support projects of such magnitude, but the inhabitants also needed to be inspired to begin them and prodded sufficiently to carry them out.

In the construction of all three Taiwan cities, prominent inhabitants shared a role with officials in providing the necessary inspiration and leadership. In the case of wall construction, the close cooperation between the authorities who supervised the projects and the gentry or other influential inhabitants who managed them is evident from the records of the period. However, merely to depict city building as a joint effort between local officials and leading gentry or commoners is too simple and vague a description of the political process involved. Each case witnessed, on the one hand, an array of decisions, plans, and policies emanating from various levels of the Ch'ing civil administration and, on the other, concerted efforts by spokesmen representing diverse groups among the inhabitants to influence those decisions.

Officially, local authorities were held responsible for the actual construction. Nonetheless, direct action by authorities on higher administrative levels, in both Taiwan and Fukien, was required as well. Then, too, directives and sanctions were needed from officials in Peking, particularly from those associated with the Board of Revenue and the Board of Works. The throne also became involved, as we find from memorials and endorsements dispatched to and from the imperial court. Pronouncements by the Ch'ien-lung emperor (r. 1736–95) even had a bearing on the construction of Taiwan's walled cities during the nineteenth century.

The involvement of the inhabitants in the formation of these cities was also a complex matter. The composition of local society varied with the nature and extent of settlement at and around each site. In the cases of Hsin-chu and T'ai-pei-fu, where society had advanced well beyond the rude frontier stage, gentry leadership, aided by merchant support or direct participation, was of vital importance in bringing construction efforts to pass. At I-lan, where influential gentry and merchant classes had not yet developed, the situation was somewhat different: heads of the diverse groups of settlers who had recently migrated to the area helped effect the building of that walled administrative center. In all three cases, local leadership stemmed from representatives of the various Hoklo (*Fu-lao*) and Hakka (*K'o-chia*) communities that together composed the heterogeneous Chinese society in Taiwan during the Ch'ing period. When accounting for local Chinese support of these building projects, we must take into consideration such subethnic affiliations of outstanding leaders in each area in addition to their status and family background.

Background and Setting

The three cities discussed in this study arose independently of one another in separate areas of northern Taiwan (see Maps 1 and 2). Hsin-chu, situated on the alluvial plain skirting the northwest coast of the island, was founded in 1733 to serve as the seat of Tan-shui subprefecture (*t'ing*), which had been established ten years earlier. At the outset this new administrative center was enclosed by a hedge of thorny bamboo native to Taiwan, whence its original name Chu-ch'ien, literally, "Bamboo Moat." It retained hedges of planted bamboo, along with moats and four wooden gates with towers, for the remainder of the eighteenth century. Early in the nineteenth century earthen walls were added. Nevertheless, the name Chu-ch'ien lasted until Hsin-chu county (*hsien*) was set up in 1875. For convenience, the name Hsin-chu will be used here, even though this study will concentrate on the brief period centering around the years 1827–29 (Tao-kuang 7–9), when city walls of stone and brick were constructed and the Tan-shui subprefectural seat assumed a more enduring form.[3]

The increasingly substantial walls acquired by Hsin-chu suggest stages in that city's development over the decades. Originally, Hsin-chu functioned as a small, sparsely populated garrison town sheltering a deputy subprefect (*hsün-chien*) and a complement of military personnel. Not until the middle of the eighteenth century did the remainder of the *t'ing* officials, including the subprefect (*t'ung-chih*), move north from their temporary headquarters at Chang-hua and reside within the

MAP 1. TAIWAN, 1810–75 (*opposite*). The shaded area, encompassing the central mountain ranges and most of the east coast, was as yet beyond the reach of direct imperial rule. Based on *T'ai-wan fu yü t'u tsuan yao* (Compendium of geography and maps of T'ai-wan prefecture; Taipei: T'ai-wan yin hang, 1963 reissue).

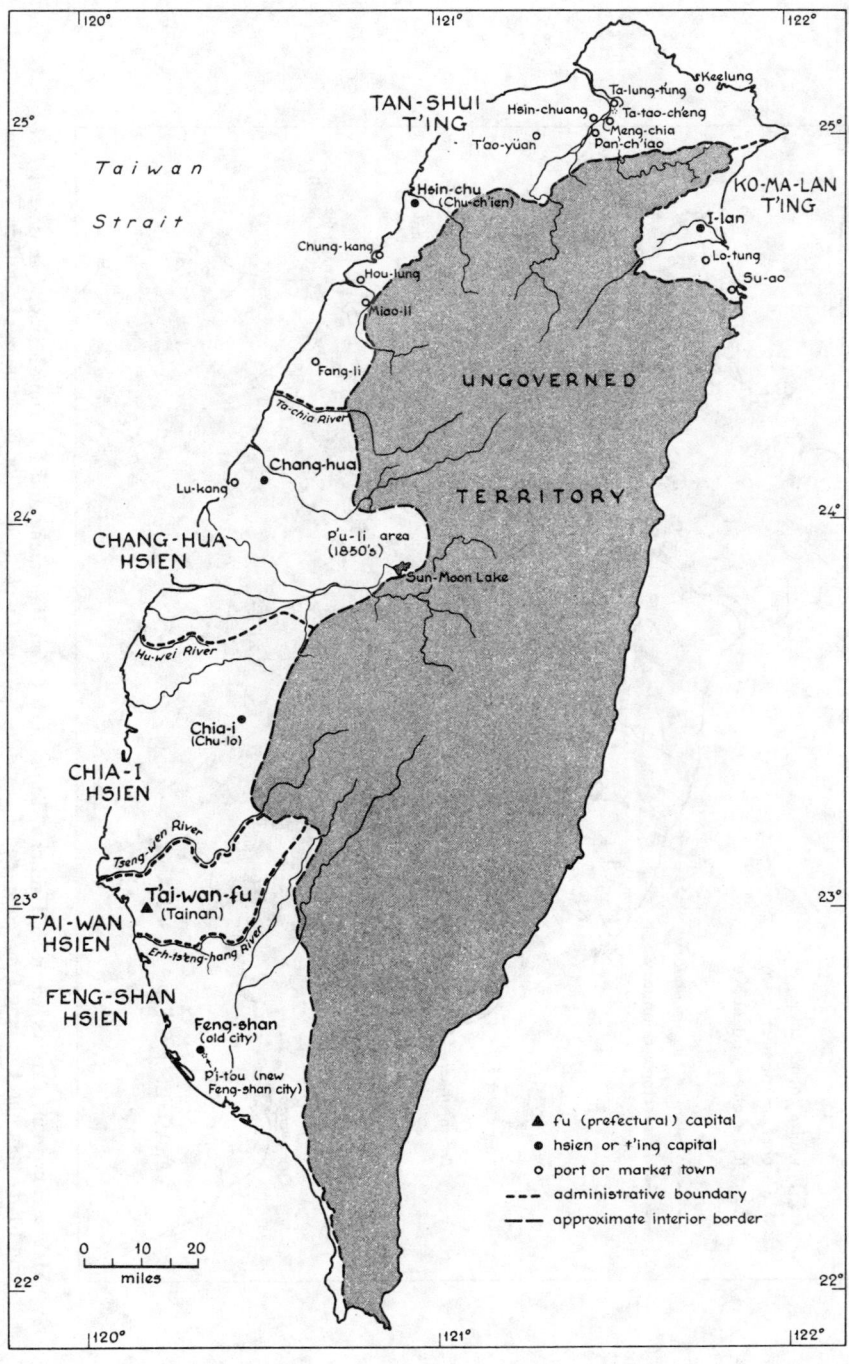

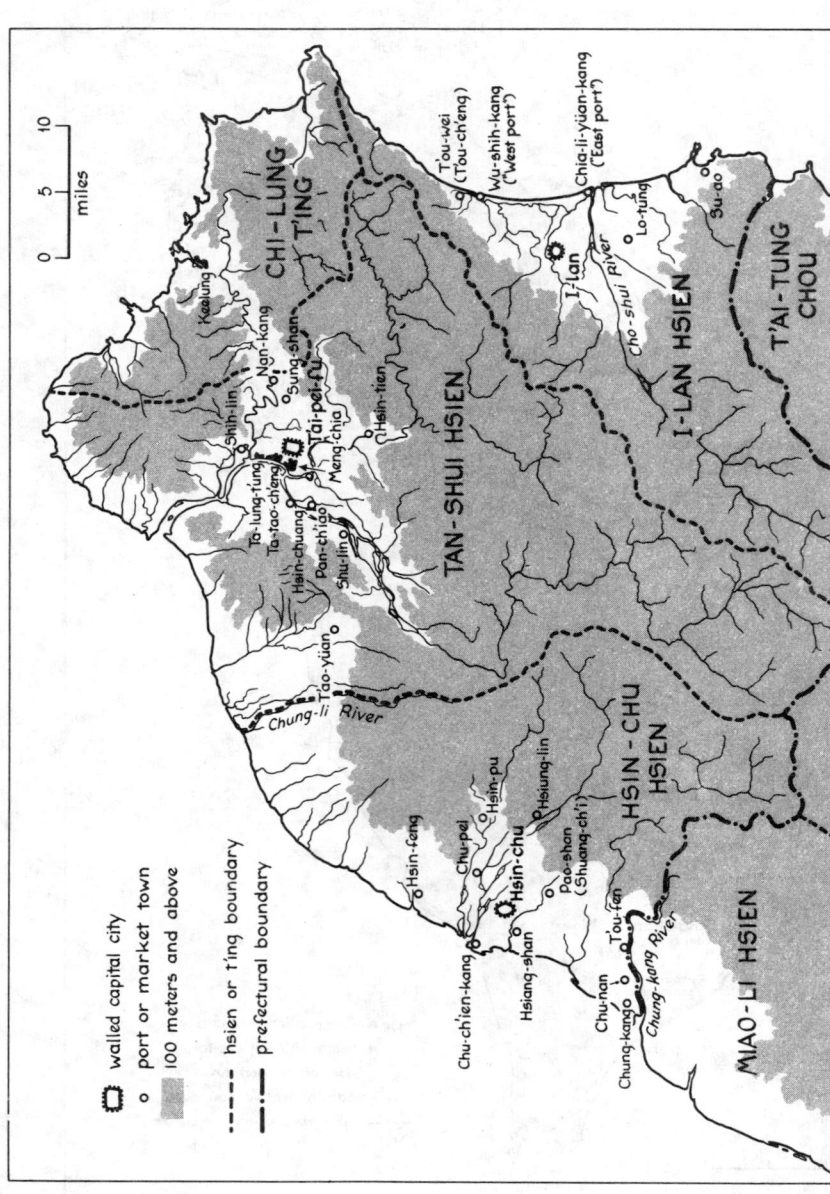

MAP 2. NORTHERN TAIWAN, ca. 1888. Hsin-chu, Tan-shui, and I-lan *hsien*, plus Chi-lung *t'ing*, composed T'ai-pei *fu*, one of four prefectural-level units the island was divided into in 1886. Based on Ch'ing-period maps reprinted in Ch'en Han-kuang and Lai Yung-hsiang, comps., *Pei-T'ai ku yü t'u chi* (Collection of old maps of northern Taiwan; Taipei: T'ai-pei shih wen hsien wei yüan hui, 1957), pp. 29–32.

bamboo enclosure. By then, the internal arrangement of Hsin-chu had assumed a highly irregular form, quite in contrast to the more symmetrical street patterns evident in I-lan and T'ai-pei-fu during the nineteenth century. (Compare the Hsin-chu street pattern [Map 3] with those of the latter two cities [Maps 4 and 6].) Hsin-chu's irregular layout may well have resulted from the absence of the ranking civil official, the subprefect, for the first 23 years of the city's existence. Without much formal supervision, temples and markets were sited more or less at random in the central portion of the city. When the subprefect finally took up permanent residence in 1756, the location of the main offices of government that then had to be built merely added to the haphazard arrangement of the city.

After 1756, Hsin-chu grew steadily and cultural activity there increased. In 1781, the rise of a local group of scholars was aided when the local academy (*shu-yüan*) was shifted from its original location close within the south city gate to a permanent site near the principal civil administrative offices situated in the central portion of the city. The subsequent growth of an influential gentry-scholar class stimulated in turn the steady cultural advances that occurred during the Chia-ch'ing period (1796–1820). Backed by wealthy commoners, prominent Hsin-chu gentry promoted education and sponsored a number of public undertakings including the construction of additional local temples, a shrine dedicated to the patron god of literature (*Wen-ch'ang tz'u*), and a Confucian temple (*Wen miao*) completed in 1824.[4] Moreover, earthen city walls were built in 1813 on extensive embankments that had been formed eight years previously by the local inhabitants as protection against a notorious Fukienese pirate, Ts'ai Ch'ien.[5]

In the late 1820's, almost a century after the founding of Hsin-chu, the city was largely reconstructed. Over roughly three years, an impressive amount of building was carried out. Government offices and installations were repaired and rebuilt, and a number of religious edifices were constructed or improved through the initiative of local officials and inhabitants. Above all, durable stone and brick city walls replaced the earthen ones. Yet neither the haphazard arrangement nor the congestion of the central portion of Hsin-chu was alleviated. In fact, the relocation of the city walls and gates led to a reduction of the total area within the walls and may have heightened the crowded conditions in the city's center.

By this time Hsin-chu had become a small but significant trading center as well as the major cultural center in northern Taiwan. Commercial streets and marketplaces existed within the city, and shops and enterprises stretched west of the city walls. Hsin-chu's importance as a cultural center had increased with the completion of the Confucian temple in 1824 and the inception, a few years earlier, of *t'ung-shih* entrance examinations for scholars of the subprefecture who sought degrees and gentry status under the imperial examination system. Irrigated fields abounded in the surrounding lowlands, except to the southeast, where the presence of hostile aborigine tribes retarded Chinese settlement.[6] In keeping with the prosperity of the general area, Hsin-chu experienced a constant population growth. By the late 1820's the number of inhabitants dwelling in the city and its five suburban divisions (*hsiang*) probably approached 8,000, for the approximate population reported in 1841 exceeded that figure.[7] In effect, the reconstruction of Hsin-chu took place at an opportune time when the city had reached its most impressive stage of development under Ch'ing rule.

Thereafter, other significant construction projects continued to be undertaken in and around the city, but at a slower rate than during the brief period of reconstruction in the late 1820's. The more important of these projects were the creation of two scholar-family gardens in 1849

MAP 3. HSIN-CHU CITY, ca. 1843 (*opposite*). Reconstructed (on a base derived from modern maps) from maps and information contained in *Tan-shui t'ing chih*, compiled 1871, and Hsin-chu hsien wen hsien wei yüan hui, comp., *T'ai-wan sheng Hsin-chu hsien chih kao* (Hsin-chu, 1957). Letters preceding numbers in the key below indicate approximate order of construction: A = first stage, prior to 1800; B = second stage, 1800–1827; C = reconstruction of 1827–29; D = to 1843.

A1. Tan-shui subprefectural yamen
A2. Office of the Chu-ch'ien deputy subprefect
A3. Outer Ma-tsu temple (*Wai T'ien-hou kung*)
A4. City God temple (*Ch'eng-huang miao*)
A5. Fu-te shrine (*Tung-ying fu-ti*)
A6. Inner Ma-tsu temple (*Nei T'ien-hou kung*)
A7. Shui-t'ien fu-ti (shrine)
A8. God of War temple (*Kuan-ti miao*)
A9. Ch'ien-chia tz'u (shrine)
A10. Ming-chih academy
B1. God of Literature shrine (*Wen-ch'ang tz'u*)
B2. Kuan-yin temple (*Fa-lien ssu*)
B3. Altar for malevolent spirits (*Li t'an*)
B4. Ta-chung temple ("South Altar")
B5. Ta-chung temple ("East Altar")
B6. Confucian temple (*Wen miao*)
B7. God of Agriculture shrine (*Shen-nung tz'u*)
B8. Kuan-yin t'ing (pavilion)
B9. Subprefectural granary
C1. Battalion headquarters
C2. Training pavilion and drill field
C3. Ti-ts'ang an (temple)
C4. Shrines for the meritorious and loyal
C5. Shrine for the chaste and filial (*Chieh-hsiao tz'u*)
C6. Dragon God shrine (*Lung-wang tz'u*)
C7. Altar to wind, clouds, thunder, and rain (*Feng-yün-lei-yü t'an*)
C8. Altar of Land and Grain (*She-chi t'an*)
C9. Agricultural deities temple (*Wu-ku miao*)
D1. Shrine for former outstanding officials (*Te-cheng tz'u*)
D2. Charity granary

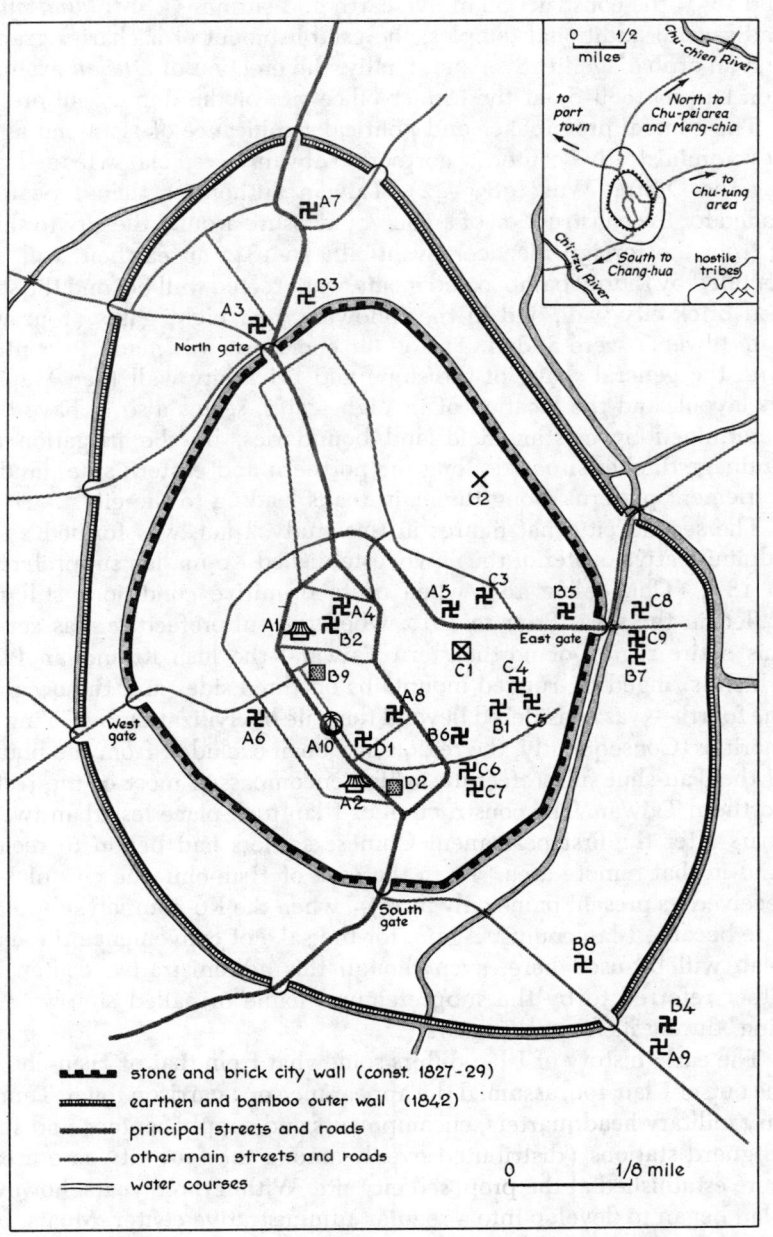

and 1851; the construction of five earth-god shrines (*T'u-ti-kung miao*) and several additional temples; the establishment of a charity granary and an orphanage in 1870; and, finally, the erection of a *hsien* examination hall in 1886–87 at the former office site of the deputy subprefect.

The general prominence and political significance of Hsin-chu as the key administrative center in northern Taiwan were acknowledged during the Opium War (1839–42). Taiwan authorities then repeatedly called for the construction of an outer enclosure around the city to shield it from the foreign menace. Eventually in 1842 an earthen wall, surrounded by thorny bamboo and moats, was erected well beyond the stone and brick city wall, and in the following year eight gates (four with gate towers) were added. This outer enclosure was made to conform with the general shape of the stone and brick city wall (see Map 3). Its layout, and the location of its eight gates, seems also to have been determined by existing field-land boundaries, by the irrigation and drainage ditches situated along the northern and eastern sides, and by settlement patterns along the main roads leading to the city.

The second city that figures in this study, I-lan, was formed as the administrative center of the newly established Ko-ma-lan subprefecture in 1813 (Chia-ch'ing 18), when quite primitive conditions still prevailed in the area. Prior to 1810, when the subprefecture was set up, this entire region of northeastern Taiwan—the lush Ko-ma-lan Plain, which is ringed by rugged mountains on three sides and the ocean on the fourth—was considered beyond the pale of civilization by Ch'ing authorities. Consequently, the region had been excluded from the bounds of the Tan-shui subprefecture, which encompassed most of the rest of northern Taiwan. The construction of I-lan took place less than twenty years after the first permanent Chinese settlers had begun to reclaim land in that remote area.[8] As in the case of Hsin-chu, the city of I-lan received its present name only in 1875, when the Ko-man-lan subprefecture became I-lan county. Again, for the sake of convenience the name I-lan will be used here, even though this administrative center was either referred to by the subprefectural name or called simply "Lan-t'ing" during its formative years.

The early history of I-lan differs somewhat from that of Hsin-chu. At the outset I-lan, too, assumed the appearance of a garrison town. Temporary military headquarters, encampments and supply centers, and some 48 guard stations (distributed evenly among the four city-gate areas) were established at the proposed city site. Within three years, however, I-lan began to develop into a regular administrative center. Moats, four wooden gates with drawbridges, and an earthen enclosure surrounded

MAP 4. I-LAN CITY, ca. 1835. Reconstructed (on a base derived from modern maps) from information in *Ko-ma-lan t'ing chih* (compiled 1831–32); *Ko-ma-lan chih lüeh* (ca. 1840); and *I-lan hsien chih* (compiled in the 1960's).

1. Ko-ma-lan subprefectural yamen: built 1813, repaired and enlarged 1819 and 1824.
2. Office of the Lo-tung deputy subprefect: built 1813, rebuilt 1819.
3. Training pavilion and drill field: built 1819.
4. Battalion headquarters: built 1813, rebuilt 1819.
5. Patrol headquarters: built 1813, rebuilt 1826.
6. Yang-shan academy: built 1810, rebuilt 1830.
7. Ever-normal granary: built 1811–12, rebuilt and enlarged 1815, repaired and expanded 1826.
8. City God temple (*Ch'eng-huang miao*): built 1813.
9. Ling-hui miao (temple established by Chang-chou natives): rebuilt 1831 at indicated site.
10. God of Literature temple (*Wen-ch'ang kung*): built 1818, rebuilt 1845.
11. Ta-chung miao (temple): built ca. 1833.
12. Ma-tsu temple (*T'ien-hou miao*): built 1808, rebuilt 1834.
13. Earth God temple (*T'u-ti-kung miao*): built ca. 1819.
14. Altar to clouds, rain, wind, and thunder (*Yün-yü-feng-lei t'an*): built 1813.
15. Altar of land and grain (*She-chi t'an*) and two other altars: built 1812, rebuilt 1823.
16. Agricultural deities temple (*Wu-ku miao*): built 1812.
17. Fire God temple (*Huo-shen miao*): built 1820.
18. Altar for malevolent spirits (*Li t'an*): built ca. 1833.
19. Ku-wang miao (temple established by Chang-chou natives): built ca. 1835.
20. Kuan-yin temple (*Mu-fo ssu*): built 1829.

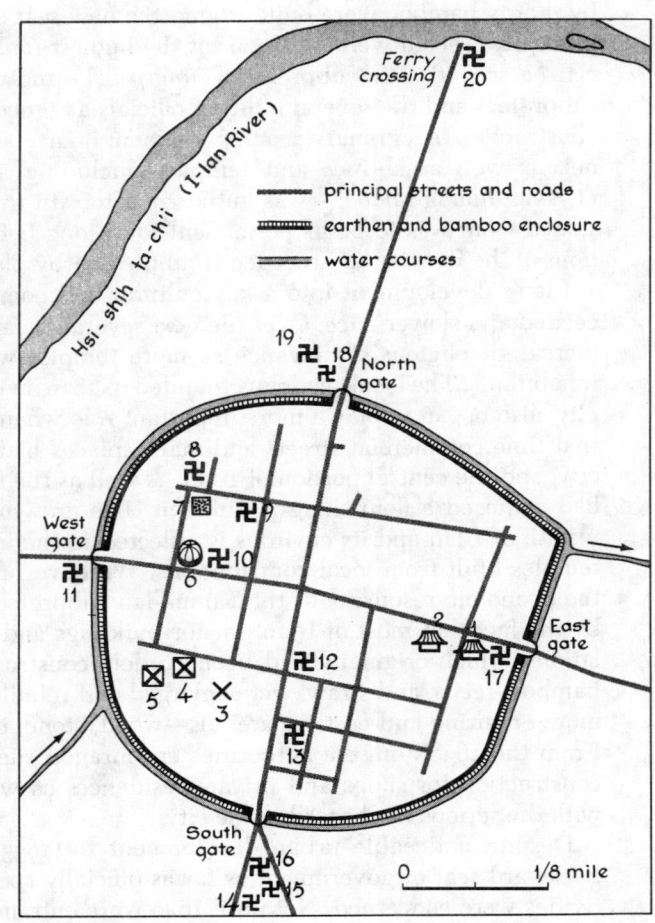

by thorny bamboo were built around the new seat of government. Also promptly erected were a yamen for the highest ranking Ko-ma-lan official (a second-class subprefect [*t'ung-p'an*]) and offices for a deputy subprefect and the several military officials assigned to the region. The construction of a granary, a jail, permanent quarters for military personnel, as well as shrines and temples—including a City God temple (*Ch'eng-huang miao*)[9]—was authorized, too. In this manner, I-lan assumed what was to be its permanent form long before the rude conditions of the frontier had receded from the nearby plain.

I-lan's development into a key cultural and commercial center proceeded at a slower pace. Over the next several decades the city took on increased religious significance as more temples were erected by the inhabitants. The local academy, founded in 1810 on the site of the future city, also began to play a more important role when rebuilt in 1830. By that time commercial streets and marketplaces had formed within the city, and the central portion of I-lan, as well as the four city-gate areas, had acquired a flourishing population. The growth in population and wealth of I-lan and its environs is reflected in the increased number of temples built from local contributions. We have further evidence that the economic resources of the Ko-ma-lan subprefecture had increased by the fact that most of I-lan's major buildings and government installations, which originally had been crudely constructed of inexpensive bamboo, reeds, and straw, were enlarged and rebuilt by the 1830's with more enduring and costly materials—wood, stone, brick, and even tile. From the 1830's on, the authorities encouraged such improvements in construction for shops and private residences as well, mainly to cope with the serious fire hazard in the city.

Despite noticeable urban development by 1835, I-lan remained a backward seat of government as far as officially sponsored cultural activities were concerned. Not until 1840 were entrance examinations for registered scholars established for Ko-ma-lan subprefecture and held in I-lan. Moreover, the city lacked a Confucian temple until 1869 and did not house an educational office (*ju-hsüeh*) until 1876, a year after it became a county seat. Even then, I-lan was still a relatively small and isolated urban center situated in one of the more remote areas of the Ch'ing empire. Nevertheless, the local scene came to resemble that of other lesser cities throughout China, as exemplified by the emergence of artisan, merchant, and gentry-scholar classes.[10]

T'ai-pei-fu, the third city treated in this paper, was formed under still different circumstances during the final quarter of the nineteenth century. In 1875, northern Taiwan was redivided into three counties and one subprefecture, and T'ai-pei prefecture (*fu*) was created to consolidate the overall administration of this entire region. None of the existing cities or towns in northern Taiwan was deemed a satisfactory location for the new prefectural center. Therefore, a fresh site was chosen in the fertile Taipei Basin adjacent to two large port towns, Meng-chia and Ta-tao-ch'eng. Between 1879 and 1884, moats, stone and brick walls, and five gates with towers were constructed, and the prefectural center, called T'ai-pei-fu, began to assume permanent form.[11]

Unlike Hsin-chu and I-lan, this walled city was founded in a settled and prosperous area. The vestiges of an earlier frontier society had almost disappeared. Moreover, the higher status of T'ai-pei-fu as a prefectural center enabled this new city to gain a certain eminence that the two subprefectural centers had not attained. These factors had an important effect on the development of T'ai-pei-fu, as did two others: (1) the decision to have the city serve concurrently as the seat of the recently established Tan-shui county; and (2) the 1886 choice of the city as the temporary site of the new Taiwan provincial government as well. Shortly before the Japanese takeover of Taiwan in 1895, T'ai-pei-fu was declared the permanent capital of the island province.[12]

T'ai-pei-fu, a traditional walled city, takes on added interest because of its establishment after the onset of Western influences. Even before the Japanese occupation, signs of Western practices were already apparent in the Taipei Basin. British and other Western firms had opened branches in nearby Ta-tao-ch'eng, where the tea trade flourished. Then after Taiwan's first governor, Liu Ming-ch'uan, took up residence in T'ai-pei-fu, he introduced such modern innovations as stone-paved streets, a small number of electric street lamps, and a narrow-gage railroad connecting the new city with the port town of Keelung (Chi-lung) to the east and the city of Hsin-chu to the south.[13] Such foreign influences, however, played only minor roles in the early development of T'ai-pei-fu, and contacts with Westerners were restricted mainly to the port towns where treaty-port regulations were in effect. The new city itself assumed the general form and functions characteristic of walled administrative centers elsewhere in late imperial China, although it remained relatively underdeveloped under Ch'ing rule. As indicated in Maps 5 and 6, the street grid and population were concentrated in the northern and northwestern portions of the walled city. The prefectural and provincial yamen, as well as the permanent *hsien* offices completed in 1893, also were located there within easy access of the north and west city gates, which guarded the only thoroughfares to the city. During the last years of Ch'ing rule, after the departure of Liu Ming-ch'uan, T'ai-pei-fu actually experienced little growth.

Although diverse in nature, these three northern Taiwan cities shared certain common features with other walled administrative centers on the island. Like most, they were situated in lowland areas not far from the seacoast or, in the case of T'ai-pei-fu, a navigable body of water (the Tan-shui River). Each was served by one or more port towns. Again, like the enclosed centers to the south, all three were irregular in layout and shape, and relatively small compared to walled cities on the mainland. T'ai-pei-fu ranked as the second-largest Taiwan city in area at the time of its construction; its almost rectangular walls were about three and a half miles (1,506 *chang*) in circumference. The north and east city gates were shielded with massive outer walls, often used to strengthen the defenses of rectangular walled cities. In contrast, Hsin-chu and I-lan were roughly circular and considerably smaller. The walls of Hsin-chu measured less than two miles in length (860 *chang*). Like those of T'ai-pei-fu, they were of a height that was standard in Taiwan for stone city walls (about 22 feet) and were topped with brick ramparts. The earth and bamboo enclosure built around Hsin-chu in 1842 measured a respectable 1,495 *chang*, but the earthen wall stood only about twelve feet high. In comparison, the more lofty enclosure of bamboo and earth maintained at I-lan was reportedly of the same height as the city walls of Hsin-chu and T'ai-pei-fu. However, this I-lan enclosure was only slightly over a mile and a quarter (640 *chang*) in circumference, making the city the smallest administrative center on the island.[14]

The outlying areas. The size and physical makeup of the three cities reflect not only their development and status as seats of government but also their relations with outlying areas in northern Taiwan. At the time these cities assumed permanent form, their resources were insufficient to provide for the large-scale public works undertaken. Support stemmed mainly from settled areas within their respective administrative territories. Particularly substantial assistance, in the form of contributions

---

MAP 5. URBAN GROWTH IN THE TAIPEI AREA TO 1894 (*opposite*). The earliest settlement, on the river in Meng-chia, was founded around 1701. Ta-lung-t'ung, founded 1805, and Ta-tao-ch'eng, founded 1851, had grown together by the time T'ai-pei-fu was built. Along the sparsely settled riverfront that still separated Ta-tao-ch'eng from Meng-chia, Governor Liu Ming-ch'uan established a number of government facilities in 1886–91. A riverfront area of Ta-tao-ch'eng was reconstructed with paved streets during the 1880's and was favored by mainland Chinese merchants, Western trading firms, and foreign consulates. See Map 6 legend for source.

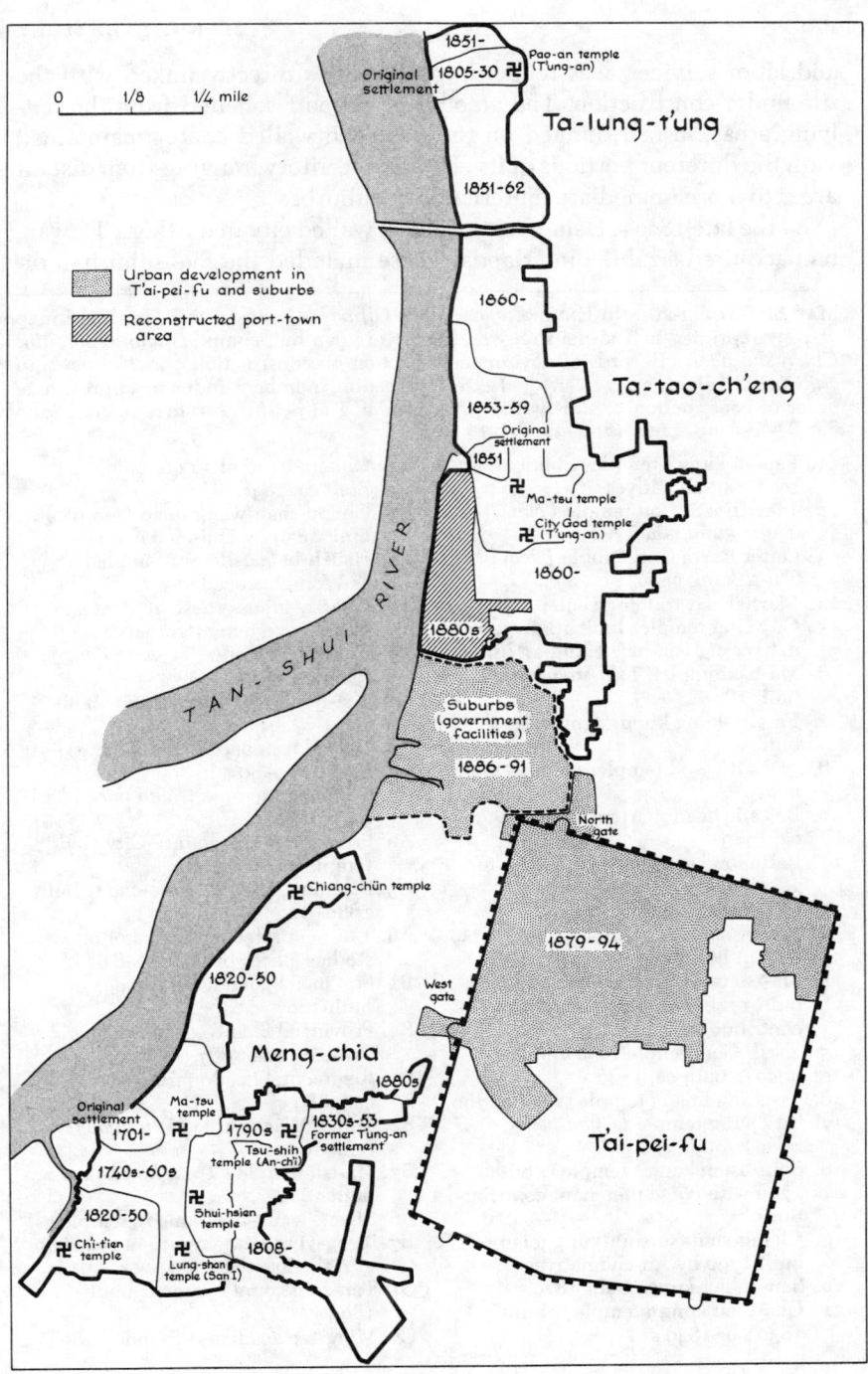

and labor services, was rendered by localities directly linked with the site under construction. The amount of support solicited from the outlying areas, in fact, hinged on the ties each walled center maintained with the different portions of its extensive territory, ranging from distant areas to more immediate hinterlands or suburbs.

By the late 1820's, Hsin-chu, the oldest walled city in northern Taiwan, had acquired sizable hinterlands. These included the five suburban di-

---

MAP 6. T'AI-PEI-FU AND ENVIRONS, ca. 1894 (*opposite*). Based on a Japanese map of 1897 reprinted in T'ai-pei shih wen hsien wei yüan hui, comp., *Cheng chih chih: Chien she p'ien* (Records of government: Section on construction), in *T'ai-pei shih chih kao* (Taipei, 1957), ch. 3. Letters preceding numbers indicate approximate order of construction of sites within the walls of T'ai-pei-fu: A = first stage, 1879–84; B = second stage, 1886–91; C = to 1894.

1. Pao-an kung (temple): built 1805 by T'ung-an natives
2. Inner Earth God temple (*Nei T'u-ti-kung miao*)
3. Outer Earth God temple (*Wai T'u-ti-kung miao*)
4. Martial arts training center
5. City God temple: built 1856–59 by natives of Hsia-hai, T'ung-an *hsien*
6. Ma-tsu temple (*Tz'u-sheng kung*): built 1869
7. Fa-chu-kung kung (temple): built 1894
8, 9. Earth God temples (*T'u-ti-kung miao*)
10. Brigade headquarters from 1825 to ca. 1889
11. Battalion headquarters: built after 1825
12. Military stores area
13. Lung-shan ssu (temple): built 1740 by San I natives
14. Ma-tsu temple (*Hsin-hsing kung*): built 1746 with *chiao* merchant contributions
15. Earth God temple (*T'u-ti-kung miao*): built ca. 1746
16. Ti-ts'ang miao (temple): built 1760
17. Ta-chung temple (*Chao-hsien miao*): built 1760
18. Shui-hsien kung (temple): built 1790 with *chiao* merchant contributions
19. Ch'ing-shui tsu-shih-kung miao: built 1790 by An-ch'i natives
20. San-ch'ing kung: built 1820's
21. Ch'i-t'ien kung (temple): built 1830's or 1840's
22. Chiang-chün miao (temple): built ca. 1841
23. Ch'ing-shan-wang miao (temple): built 1856 by Hui-an natives
24. Hsüeh-hai academy: founded 1837 as Wen-chia academy
25. Charity granary: est. 1856 at site of old government granary
26. Foundling home (*Yü-ying t'ang*): founded 1870
A1. T'ai-pei prefectural yamen: built 1879
A2. Official residence hall (old site): built 1879–80
A3. Confucian temple (*Wen miao*): built 1880
A4. Prefectural and county City Gods temple: built 1881
A5. Examination hall (*K'ao-cha*): built 1880–81
A6. T'ai-pei prefectural director of studies office: built 1880–81
B1. Provincial governor's yamen: built 1887
B2. Provincial finance commissioner's yamen: built 1887
B3. Regimental headquarters: built ca. 1889
B4. God of War temple (*Wu miao*): built 1887–89
B5. Ma-tsu temple (*T'ien-hou kung*): built 1888
B6. Sheng-wang-kung miao (temple)
B7. Teng-ying academy: founded 1880 at A5, relocated 1890
C1. Tan-shui county yamen: built 1893
C2. Ming-tao academy: founded 1893

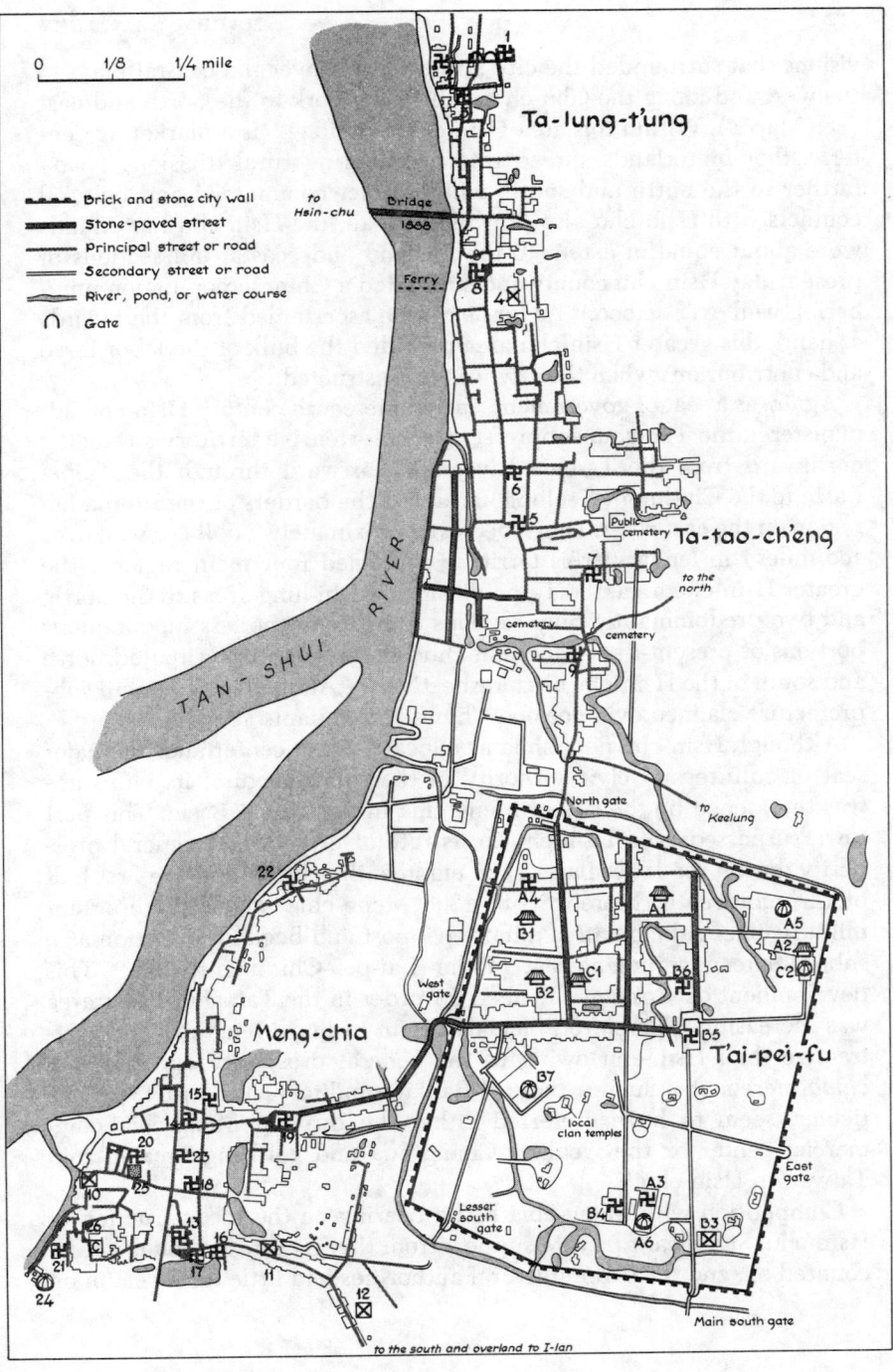

visions that surrounded the city and extended over the coastal plain to the west and along the Chu-ch'ien River network to the north and east (see Map 2). Within this area Hsin-chu functioned as a marketing center. Other hinterlands spread into neighboring rural divisions (*pao*) farther to the north and south, where direct commercial and cultural contacts with Hsin-chu also prevailed. In all, the Hsin-chu hinterlands were about equal in extent to the lowland and coastal hill sections of present-day Hsin-chu county and supported a Chinese population numbering well over 40,000.[15] As far as can be ascertained from the records at hand, this greater Hsin-chu area provided the bulk of the labor force and contributions when the city was reconstructed.

Again, as a seat of government, early-nineteenth-century Hsin-chu administered the Tan-shui subprefecture, an extensive territory stretching northward from the Ta-chia River and eastward through the Taipei Basin to the Chi-lung (Keelung) area and the borders of the Ko-ma-lan region on the east coast. Described as approximately 345 *li* (or well over 100 miles) in length,[16] this territory contained four main regions: the greater Hsin-chu area, the Taipei Basin and Chi-lung areas to the north, and two predominantly hilly sections comprising the less mountainous portions of present-day T'ao-yüan and Miao-li counties (situated north and south of the Hsin-chu area, respectively). Altogether, Tan-shui subprefecture claimed over 200,000 Chinese inhabitants at the time.[17]

Although Hsin-chu flourished as a local trading center and the major seat of culture and civil authority in the subprefecture, its eminence was threatened by the rise of Meng-chia in the Taipei Basin. This port town surpassed even Hsin-chu in its rate of growth and general prosperity during the latter part of the eighteenth century and the first half of the nineteenth. Moreover, in 1808 Meng-chia acquired important military offices along with a minor civil post and began to function as a subordinate government seat in the T'ai-pei–Chi-lung region.[18] This development occurred as the need for order in the Tan-shui River area was increasing. Thereafter, officials began to find Meng-chia more attractive than Hsin-chu owing to the general prosperity and the rich *chiao* merchant influence there.[19] Ranking military authorities, in particular, seem to have preferred either the thriving Meng-chia commercial center or the wealthy Chang-hua and Lu-kang area in mid Taiwan to Hsin-chu.[20]

Competition with Meng-chia had a bearing on the reconstruction of Hsin-chu. Significant private support from that rival town could not be counted on, and the subprefectural authorities had little direct claim on the commercial wealth there. Hence leaders planning the Hsin-chu wall-building project had to rely on contributions from elsewhere in the subprefecture. They eventually had recourse to land assessments as an additional source of funds, a source, however, that could hardly have been profuse since the registered field land in the entire subprefecture amounted at the time to only some 83,180 *mou* (12,600 acres), there being a high incidence of "hidden fields" (*yin-t'ien*) excluded from the tax records in northern Taiwan.[21] Ultimately, owing to the limitations on available funds and the high cost of stone and brick construction, the new Hsin-chu city wall was made only about two-thirds as long as the earthen enclosure it replaced.[22]

The subsequent formation of T'ai-pei-fu as the ranking administrative center in northern Taiwan reflects the continued growth in the Tan-shui River area over the next fifty years. Although Meng-chia experienced economic decline, the neighboring port town of Ta-tao-ch'eng underwent rapid development and in the 1880's replaced Meng-chia as the leading commercial center in northern Taiwan. By then, these two towns formed a densely populated riverine community of almost 100,000 inhabitants.[23] Despite the protests of local Hsin-chu gentry, Ch'ing authorities remained firm in their resolve to establish the new prefectural center in the Meng-chia vicinity rather than to adapt the old subprefectural site at Hsin-chu as the main seat of government for northern Taiwan.[24]

Accordingly, T'ai-pei-fu was laid out among paddy fields in an area that had been an extension of the Meng-chia countryside. The new walled center remained dependent on the trade and services of Meng-chia and Ta-tao-ch'eng and failed to develop an economic hinterland of its own during the remaining years of the Ch'ing period.[25] The initial support for the construction of T'ai-pei-fu came almost entirely from the two adjacent port towns and nearby settlements in the Taipei Basin. The other settled areas of the prefecture—consisting of the reorganized Hsin-chu and I-lan counties, the new Chi-lung subprefecture, and the rest of the newly established Tan-shui county (as shown in Map 2)—provided little assistance for this large-scale undertaking.

Accounts of the formation of T'ai-pei-fu imply that Taiwan authorities found it more convenient to draw on the wealthy area close by rather than seek funds and services farther afield within the prefecture. Actually, circumstances forced them to turn to the vicinity for support. The first prefect divided his time between Hsin-chu and Keelung, and failed to elicit widespread backing for the future prefectural capital near Meng-chia.²⁶ The building of T'ai-pei-fu was thus delayed for over four years until the second prefect selected the exact site. Hsin-chu's rivalry with Meng-chia over the site of the prefectural capital meant that sizable donations from major areas to the south would not be forthcoming. Moreover, this second prefect lacked special funds for city building. He consequently had to rely on contributions from wealthy inhabitants of the T'ai-pei-fu area. A few years later, as discussed below, the Taiwan intendant sought in vain to help this prefect gain additional funds through assessments on field lands in the three northern counties. Later on, Liu Ming-ch'uan also was beset by similar fund-raising difficulties when he undertook to initiate further construction projects at T'ai-pei-fu.

Earlier in the century, I-lan had also been founded with the inception of government, this time on the subprefectural level. This new administrative center served a relatively small and compact territory remote enough to avoid competition from outside port towns and other government seats. Owing to its isolation, the Ko-ma-lan subprefecture received little assistance from other regions. Support for the construction of I-lan stemmed almost entirely from labor services provided by nearby settlements and funds secured from the subprefectural land tax. By such means this administrative center was built rapidly, but in the least costly manner possible. Even so, its construction placed a severe strain on the limited resources available to the local authorities. The Ko-ma-lan population, including some 5,500 aborigines, totaled only about 43,000 at the time, and the registered field land under cultivation was estimated to be merely one-fifth that in Tan-shui subprefecture.²⁷

The fact that I-lan so quickly assumed permanent form may be attributed in part to its ideal location in the approximate center of the Ko-ma-lan Plain. This proved to be a strategic site. From here the surrounding lowland areas could be kept under surveillance and close check maintained over both the coastal defenses to the east and the string of mountain guard stations that encircled the plain on the other three sides.²⁸ Defense and the preservation of order in that troubled and hitherto poorly guarded region were vital services, as the local authorities and inhabitants well knew. Moreover, I-lan's central location helped it develop economic and cultural ties with Chinese settlements in the plain. Clusters of villages continued to spring up around its enclosure and spread outward into the neighboring rural divisions.²⁹ I-lan, like Hsin-chu, became a multifunctional city with a distinct hinterland of its own.

The Formation of Cities in Taiwan

Local Society and the Settlement Process

The heterogeneity of local Chinese society was another factor that affected city building in northern Taiwan. The Hoklo and Hakka inhabitants mainly lived apart from one another and were further separated into diverse groups based on distinctions of provenance and ethnicity. Generally, members of these groups claimed a particular county in Fukien or Kwangtung as their place of origin. In Taiwan such aggregates formed subethnic communities distinguished principally by differences in speech and religious observance. These subethnic communities were territorial in nature, forming separate localities with definite boundaries in the countryside. The type and location of the various Chinese communities existing in any one area, as well as the relative size of each group and extent of the members' landholdings, reflected the settlement process that had evolved there over the decades.

Characteristic of the settlement of Taiwan was the opening of new areas for cultivation by bands of immigrants from southern Fukien and eastern Kwangtung. These bands formed in-groups among their own kind and proceeded to reclaim lands, lay out villages, and establish separate communities. In northern Taiwan, settlement along these lines took place gradually and, on the whole, later than in most mid-island and southern areas.[30] Settlers migrated to northern Taiwan not only directly from the mainland but from other areas of the island as well. Nonetheless, each new in-group retained a strong consciousness of mainland provenance regardless of the immediate origins of its members.

These in-groups at first consisted mainly of family and lineage fragments. Oftentimes common-surname (*t'ung-hsing*) linkages were devised as a means of organizing the settlers and their descendants along more functional lines. This type of association continued to operate among segments of subethnic communities in northern Taiwan during the nineteenth century.[31] Descriptions of the early settlement of the Ko-ma-lan region indicate that the "heads" of newly formed Chinese settlements were either senior members of powerful households and common-surname groups, or else the original leaders of armed settler bands that had entered the region and remained intact as village units.[32] When I-lan was built, support was solicited from nearby villages through such local Hoklo and Hakka "heads."

By the time Hsin-chu was reconstructed, local subethnic communities with formalized kinship and class systems had developed throughout the older established areas in the north. Accordingly, the officials in charge took pains to consult and elicit support from prominent gentry, wealthy merchants, and powerful family or lineage members who represented their communities at large. By this time, too, some of these leaders had gained renown outside their own communities and served as spokesmen for higher-level Hoklo and Hakka groupings. Among the Hoklo inhabitants, at least, such higher-level groupings were again based on distinctions of mainland provenance—usually at the Fukien prefectural level, though, rather than at the county level on which their subethnic communities normally were grouped. Higher-level groupings enabled communities stemming from counties in the Chang-chou and Ch'üan-chou prefectures to cope with matters beyond their immediate localities. When massive construction projects were undertaken at Hsin-chu and T'ai-pei-fu, spokesmen for local Chang-chou and Ch'üan-chou groupings succeeded in gaining inter-community support from among their own people. Moreover, at Hsin-chu several Hakka gentry leaders secured widespread backing from extended Hakka community groupings.

All three cases of city building we are discussing reveal instances when disparate Chinese in-groups participated in common undertakings. However, in nineteenth-century Taiwan joint enterprises of such a constructive nature were uncommon among various Chang-chou and Ch'üan-chou communities, and cooperation of any type was rare between Hoklo and Hakka people. Since strife was so prevalent during most of the Ch'ing period, local self-contained communities normally operated apart from one another for the preservation and aggrandizement of their own particular group.

The lack of positive migration and settlement policies for Taiwan until late in the nineteenth century helped foster this intense subethnic rivalry as well as perpetuate other conditions causing unrest. Even after Taiwan came under the sway of imperial China in 1683, the early Manchu rulers considered the island to be a remote frontier useful only as a shield to protect the southern coastal provinces from sea attack. Consequently, Ch'ing authorities issued regulations of a decidedly negative cast to prevent Taiwan from again becoming a rendezvous of pirates and rebels. Strict prohibitions were enforced to limit Chinese migration to Taiwan, and rigid restrictions were imposed to control all major access from the mainland. Moreover, the island was not fully opened for settlement. Instead, boundaries were fixed from time to time in order to keep the Chinese from encroaching upon lands reserved for various indigenous tribes, which were categorized either as "domesticated aborigines" (*shu-fan*) or as "wild aborigines" (*sheng-fan*). These prohibitions and restrictions were occasionally revised and their negative influence was gradually mitigated, yet they were not rescinded until 1875, only twenty years before Taiwan fell into Japanese hands.[33]

Such negative policies had an adverse effect on the settlement process. Boundaries demarcating what were officially considered aborigine lands created dissension. Immigration and shipping restrictions failed to regulate the often surreptitious crossings of immigrants from the southern Fukien and eastern Kwangtung regions. Bands of Hoklo settlers (mainly from Ch'üan-chou and Chang-chou prefectures in Fukien) and, beginning somewhat later, bands of Hakkas (primarily from Chia-ying *chou* and the prefectures of Ch'ao-chou and Hui-chou in Kwangtung) still migrated to Taiwan. During the remainder of the Ch'ing period these peoples continued to open up new areas for themselves and dwell in close-knit village settlements. Even market and port towns in Taiwan tended to be inhabited almost exclusively by one group or another.[34]

The habitable areas of Taiwan soon proved inadequate to enable this heterogeneous type of society to flourish without serious friction. During the eighteenth century, as a dense Chinese population formed in the lowlands along the west coast and in the Taipei Basin, new in-migrants had no choice but to settle in close proximity to other exclusive subethnic enclaves. Conditions then developed that led to continuous tension among sizable bodies of settlers or their descendants. Friction arose from land and water shortages, grudges, and long-standing prejudices, and acts of lawlessness and violence occurred with increasing frequency.[35]

Disorders among the Chinese inhabitants of Taiwan assumed several major forms. Popular uprisings broke out frequently and occasionally swelled to the proportions of large-scale rebellions. Invariably one or another community would become embroiled on the insurgent side, whereas rival groups in each affected area would remain neutral or else would rise to the defense of their communities and the support of the government. Another form of disturbance, feud strife termed "armed conflicts" (*hsieh-tou*), also occurred with increasing frequency during the nineteenth century. These conflicts ranged from limited encounters between common-surname groups to pitched battles involving whole communities. Whenever two or more subethnic communities were the belligerents, the situation was regarded as serious. Such disturbances could readily spread to neighboring areas and distant regions where similar community groupings existed. As larger portions of the population—including bandit gangs, vagrant (*liu-min*) bands, and sometimes even vengeful aborigine tribes—joined the fray, "armed conflicts" brought about not only widespread pillaging and destruction of property but also formidable internecine strife that threatened society and government alike.[36]

One recent work estimates that during the 212 years of Ch'ing rule in Taiwan there were 70 serious disturbances (42 uprisings and 28 "armed conflicts"), or an average of one every three years. Fifty-nine of these disturbances occurred from 1782 to 1867, during the peak period of city building on the island.[37] According to these figures, an uprising or sizable "armed conflict" flared up on the average of once every eighteen months over this 86-year span.

Settlement and strife in northern Taiwan. This latter turbulent period was one of intensive settlement in northern Taiwan. The growth of a dense heterogeneous population and the increase of local strife in turn stimulated the construction of city walls in that part of the island during the nineteenth century.

When Hsin-chu was reconstructed, a discordant Hoklo-Hakka population had already grown up in the surrounding suburban divisions, and relations between these two main bodies of inhabitants were not good. Hoklo settlers from T'ung-an county in Ch'üan-chou opened the area to cultivation shortly after the inception of Ch'ing control in 1683. Some 30 years later Hakka people from counties of Hui-chou in eastern Kwangtung began to engage in separate land reclamation projects upriver from the T'ung-an settlers. For most of the remainder of the eighteenth century more Hoklo and Hakka settlers stemming from the same areas arrived upon the scene, as did other groups whose origins were mainly San I (the three counties of Chin-chiang, Hui-an, and Nan-an) in Ch'üan-chou *fu* (on the Hoklo side), and counties in Ch'ao-chou *fu* and Chia-ying *chou* (on the Hakka side).[38]

Conditions of settlement in the Hsin-chu area changed significantly following the widespread Lin Shuang-wen rebellion in 1788. In return for the help of local "tamed" aborigine bands in quelling that rebellion, the authorities registered them as frontier guards and then turned over much of the remaining uncultivated land in the area to them under a military colonization plan. The aborigines proved poor farmers, however, and depended on Hakka settlers to clear and till their lands. Under the large and small rentholder arrangements prevailing in Taiwan, Hakka people were eventually able to secure permanent rights to till and sublet much of this reclaimed land. Meanwhile, Hoklo immigrants who had settled in the area, including some of Chang-chou origin, were deprived of additional arable lands to cultivate. The Ch'üan-chou people increasingly turned to commercial activities in Hsin-chu city and the nearby market and port towns. Even in an urban environment they continued to regard the area as theirs and to look down upon the Hakkas as intruders.[39]

By this time, however, the Hakkas were too numerous to be driven out of the Hsin-chu localities where they had settled. Moreover, the Ch'üan-chou people remained split into separate communities based on their T'ung-an or "three counties" origins. Hence the armed bands they were able to muster against the Hakkas were seldom overwhelming in size. Furthermore, Taiwan officials had come to accept the Hakkas as one more bellicose group in the turbulent island society. Although Hakkas from Kwangtung were considered outsiders because they were not of Fukien registry, the authorities found them useful in helping to stem Hoklo disturbances. During the Lin Shuang-wen rebellion, for instance, Hakka militia bands aided the government forces in recovering Hsin-chu after it had been overrun by local Hoklo insurgents.[40]

By the 1820's relatively permanent patterns of settlement had formed in the Hsin-chu area. These patterns indicate the close proximity of Hoklo and Hakka localities and suggest how vulnerable their communities were to destructive "armed conflicts" between the two peoples.[41] Altogether, the Hakkas formed a sizable minority in the greater Hsin-chu area. Moreover, they formed an even larger proportion of the Chinese population in the T'ao-yüan and Miao-li regions to the north and to the south. The extensive Hoklo-Hakka disturbances that continued to break out intermittently in the outlying areas between 1826 and 1853 thus menaced not only Hsin-chu city, but much of Tan-shui subprefecture as well.

Again, the growth of a heterogeneous Chinese population in the Taipei Basin resulted in serious strife during the nineteenth century—this time mainly among Hoklo communities. Early in the previous century Ch'üan-chou and Chang-chou settlers had begun to reclaim lands along navigable portions of the Tan-shui River. Then during the 1730's other Ch'üan-chou settlers moved north from the Hsin-chu region, opening up the Hsin-chuang area and more of the Meng-chia vicinity downstream. Hakka arrivals, as well as additional Chang-chou settlers, also reclaimed nearby localities in the western portion of the Taipei Basin. In the nineteenth century Hoklo-Hakka friction developed there; but around 1844, the local Hakka groups sold their lands and businesses to Chang-chou and Ch'üan-chou interests and moved south into the T'ao-yüan region.[42] Their departure apparently increased the tension among the Chang-chou and Ch'üan-chou riverine communities.

Subsequently, two particularly destructive "armed conflicts" occurred in the Taipei Basin. The first flared up during 1853 in Meng-chia, where the inhabitants were of Ch'üan-chou origin. This struggle pitted the local T'ung-an community against "three counties" groups. It ended when another group, originating from An-ch'i county in Ch'üan-chou, permitted "three counties" armed bands to gain access to the T'ung-an neighborhood and drive the inhabitants from Meng-chia. These T'ung-an people then moved northward and joined with Chang-chou communities to form the port town of Ta-tao-ch'eng. The second conflict broke out five years later and featured extensive skirmishes between the Ch'üan-chou and Chang-chou peoples throughout the Tan-shui River area. Lasting for two years, this strife was largely instigated by Ch'üan-chou leaders of Meng-chia and powerful Chang-chou families from Pan-ch'iao to the southwest.[43] Memories of these two severe "armed conflicts" were still vivid in the minds of those Hoklo leaders who supported the construction of T'ai-pei-fu some twenty years after the second disturbance had subsided.

Elsewhere, the initial settlement of the Ko-ma-lan Plain resulted in dire struggles in that region at the outset of the nineteenth century. The first band of permanent Chinese settlers had entered the plain from mountainous areas to the northwest in 1796. Although this band included a few Ch'üan-chou and Hakka people, about 90 percent were of Chang-chou origin, as was the main leader.[44] Subsequent migrant bands also were composed mainly of Chang-chou settlers. During the first years of settlement, attempts were made to keep peace among these mixed bands by allotting the Chang-chou people lands north of the Cho-shui River, which divides the plain. The Ch'üan-chou and Hakka settlers reclaimed areas to the south. Despite such precautions, "armed conflicts" broke out. Such struggles became especially severe when the outnumbered Ch'üan-chou people enlisted the services of aborigine bands to offset the numerical superiority of the Chang-chou settlers.

The presence of large numbers of aborigine tribes still dwelling in the Ko-ma-lan Plain contributed in other ways to the turbulence in that region. These tribes naturally resisted each new intrusion by Chinese settlers into their areas. In 1804, when over a thousand "tamed" aborigines fled across the mountains into the Ko-ma-lan Plain from Chang-hua county, problems involving aborigine boundaries and relations were further complicated. Nevertheless, the numerical superiority of the Chang-chou people enabled them to persevere against these aborigines as well as all other tribes and Chinese subethnic groups in the region. By the time Ko-ma-lan subprefecture was established in 1810, groups of

Chang-chou settlers had pushed south of the Cho-shui River as far as the Lo-tung area.⁴⁵

The "armed conflicts" that broke out soon after the Ko-ma-lan Plain was opened to Chinese settlement were reportedly more intense and destructive than those in other parts of Taiwan. They commenced before civil and military authority prevailed in the region, and they tended to be renewed upon the least provocation. Authorities familiar with the chaotic situation there were wise in selecting the village site of Wu-wei, situated to the north of the Cho-shui River, as the location for the subprefectural center. This area had become something of a neutral zone between the Chang-chou people and the concentrations of Ch'üan-chou and Hakka settlers to the south. When I-lan was laid out, the area remained one of the few settled spots on the plain where members of the heterogeneous Chinese population dared to mingle.⁴⁶

The strife prevalent throughout northern Taiwan during the nineteenth century suggests that the erection of walled administrative centers there was carried out for protective purposes. However, merely to equate city building with an immediate need for protection is too simple a generalization in each of the three cases dealt with here. To the inhabitants, such joint undertakings on the part of diverse groups in the area represented a stake in their future security with the possibility of less strife and a more peaceful environment. Again, incentives that led to their support of large-scale construction projects depended on how these centers fit into the pattern of local society.

In general, Taiwan's walled centers took on added significance as settlers and their descendants turned from farming and essentially rural activities to trade and scholarly pursuits. The shortage of land and the likelihood of economic gain and social advancement were factors that encouraged Chinese inhabitants to make this change.⁴⁷ Hsin-chu and I-lan thus developed into commercial centers and, along with T'ai-pei-fu later in the century, became seats of culture for an emerging local gentry-scholar class. In turn, these urban activities attracted influential and wealthy members of various subethnic communities from the outlying areas. At Hsin-chu, even Hakka inhabitants were drawn to Hoklo city life.

These walled centers also fulfilled certain needs of local society. Hsin-chu and I-lan, for example, maintained through their heterogeneous populations commercial and other beneficial ties with disparate hinterland communities that remained shut off from one another. Moreover, all three centers administered to the religious needs of the general population. Each, in effect, completed the local cosmology. Illustrative of the integrative nature of their religious role was the I-lan City God ceremony conducted by an early Ko-ma-lan subprefect. Acting to appease the spirits of inhabitants slain during the past "armed conflicts" in the subprefecture, this official summoned local "heads" from the Chang-chou, Ch'üan-chou, and Hakka communities, along with representatives of "tamed" and "submissive" aborigine tribes in the region, to the "altar for malevolent spirits" (*Li t'an*) situated outside the I-lan north gate. There these Chinese and aborigines worshiped, each according to his own custom, before the City God, who was supposed to govern the spirits of the subprefecture's dead.[48]

City-Building Precedents in Taiwan

The Ch'ing officials assigned to Taiwan also had a vested interest in the construction of walled cities. Since early in the Ch'ing period, the turbulent conditions on the island had led local authorities to call for the building of enclosed seats of government to safeguard civil and military rule.[49] Despite the concern expressed by resident officials, the formation of walled centers on Taiwan proved to be a slow process. However, the eventual construction of such walled centers in the mid and southern portions of the island set precedents that subsequently affected city building in northern Taiwan.

At first, the negligent attitude of the early Ch'ing rulers delayed the building of even temporary enclosures. In 1684, when Taiwan was declared a prefecture of Fukien province comprising three counties, no attempt was made to construct walls and moats around the new seats of government. Twenty years passed before the first enclosure—a wooden palisade—was built around an administrative center on the island. This crude structure was erected at the secluded county capital of Chu-lo rather than at the higher-level prefectural center of T'ai-wan-fu, located at present-day Tainan.[50]

After Taiwan's first major uprising, the Chu I-kuei rebellion of 1721, Ch'ing authorities in Fukien and Peking began to take more interest in the island's needs. Over the next decade or so, enclosures of thorny bamboo, wood, or earth were erected at the existing administrative centers as well as at that of the new Chang-hua county. We have already noted that the capital of Tan-shui subprefecture (established to the north in 1723) was enclosed by a hedge of thorny bamboo when it was built in 1733. Even then, however, the stock argument at court continued to be that walls and moats should not be constructed on Taiwan. If sturdy walled cities existed on the island and chanced to fall into the hands of pirates or rebel-bandits, it was reasoned, large and costly military operations would be needed to regain these easily defended places. The rationale behind this argument found expression in the complacent adage "easily lost, easily recovered" (*i-shih i-fu*).⁵¹

A 1734 decree by the Yung-cheng emperor still expressed this negligent attitude in regard to Taiwan city building, for it merely approved of protective enclosures around the administrative centers. This was in accord with what was loosely termed "appropriate measures according to the locality" (*yin-ti chih-i*).⁵² The Yung-cheng emperor's decree was frequently cited, and it indicated the general policy that guided city wall construction in Taiwan throughout most of the eighteenth century. The main idea behind this policy was that whereas cities might have enclosures for protection, they should not have walls built solidly enough to afford a haven for insurgent forces. In practice, this meant that brick and stone were not to be used to construct city walls in Taiwan, even though such materials were commonly used in southern China during Ming and Ch'ing times. On the other hand, the building of formidable city defenses consisting of earthen walls ringed by moats and outer enclosures of thorny bamboo was permitted and even encouraged by the authorities. Such projects were undertaken initially at the county capitals of Chu-lo and Feng-shan.⁵³

The general Ch'ing policy in regard to city building in Taiwan was revised in 1788, after the island's second major uprising, the Lin Shuang-wen rebellion, had been quelled. The Ch'ien-lung emperor decreed that since it was difficult to maintain order in Taiwan, more forethought and planning were necessary. He directed that an investigation be made at each administrative center to determine whether city walls and enclosures should be reconstructed, heightened, or even shifted to more defensible sites. Moreover, during the rebellion dramatic events had occurred at the county capital of Chu-lo that attracted the emperor's attention. Impressed by the fact that a Taiwan city had been able to hold out against insurgent forces, he bestowed the propitious name of Chia-i, "commendable loyalty," on the city and county. He also recommended that the walls of Chia-i and T'ai-wan-fu be strengthened by the use of stone and brick, materials not previously allowed for wall construction on the island.⁵⁴

At that time the wealth and other resources available in southern Taiwan were deemed inadequate to support such costly construction.⁵⁵ Nonetheless, these pronouncements by the Ch'ien-lung emperor ushered in a more positive policy toward city building on the island. No longer were cities in Taiwan regarded merely as expendable sites that might be lost to pirate or rebel bands, then easily recovered and rebuilt at the convenience of the authorities. More substantial walls were erected and, as a rule, consideration for the security of the local inhabitants was evidenced whenever administrative centers were planned or reconstructed.

Over the first several decades of the nineteenth century the walls of most Taiwan administrative centers were reconstructed with stone and brick. Although costly and not always more easily defended than earthen ones, stone and brick walls were held to be stronger and more durable. Such walls, surrounded by deep moats, intervaled with wooden gates and towers, and topped with impressive ramparts and gun emplacements, signified that the local economy had advanced to the point of parity with the economies of older established communities on the mainland.

Viewed in this perspective, it is evident that city building eventually formed part of the Chinese endeavor to settle and civilize habitable areas of Taiwan. Land reclamation and irrigation projects were initiated, villages and towns were built, and then territorial administrative centers were established as local government followed the flow of settlers into each region. Five enclosed centers existed in Taiwan by 1734. During the nineteenth century the number more than doubled.[56]

After 1788, registered inhabitants in the densely settled lowlands of the mid-island and southern regions began to muster effective support for the construction of substantial city walls. They did so as the incidence of serious disturbances rose on the island. The Taiwan authorities, for their part, sought to make good use of the local enthusiasm and support for city-building ventures. They worked closely with spokesmen of various subethnic communities, encouraged these leaders to take increased initiative in financing and planning such undertakings, and often assigned influential gentry and wealthy inhabitants important duties as managers. The local officials supervised the operations and were held accountable for the outcome of all public works. Meanwhile, in keeping with the Ch'ing government's more positive approach to city building in Taiwan, the prefectural authorities at T'ai-wan-fu, the provincial officials at Foochow, and ranking members of the central government and imperial court in Peking generally approved of plans for urban construction after careful investigations had first been carried out. Various ways in which government authorities might cooperate with local leaders when undertaking city-building projects became evident in the cases of Chang-hua and Feng-shan. Both of these county capitals underwent major reconstruction during the early nineteenth century.

In Chang-hua a group of prominent gentry and commoners initiated the reconstruction effort by petitioning that new city walls be built. These petitioners, representing Chang-chou, Ch'üan-chou, and Hakka communities of the area, reported that sixteen wealthy inhabitants already had pledged 25,000 silver dollars for this project. They also promised that rich landholders, merchants, and influential families would supply the remainder of the funds needed without the assistance of government revenues. This group of spokesmen submitted their petition to the Fukien-Chekiang governor-general when he inspected the county in 1809. Pleased by their request and their assurances of support, that high official readily accepted the petition and helped the project get under way.[57]

In the following year, while the matter was still under investigation, a group of wealthy Chang-hua contributors submitted several more petitions to the governor-general. These contained new proposals as well as changes in the requests previously made.[58] After plans for the Chang-hua project were amended and approved, the county magistrate proceeded to solicit additional contributions. Over the years 1811 to 1815, brick and stone walls, moats, city gates, and some essential government structures, including a granary, were built at a total cost of somewhat over 190,000 silver dollars, which sum was in large part contributed by the local populace.[59]

The reconstruction of Chang-hua was the largest and most costly city-building venture yet attempted in Taiwan. The support of the county's inhabitants was essential for this undertaking, as was continuous cooperation among the community leaders. The authorities apparently realized the importance of encouraging these local spokesmen to take the initiative and work together in harmony. The governor-general specifically recommended that influential gentry and commoner representatives be allowed to manage the construction work, and he also stipulated that the local officials should provide close supervision but should not allow their yamen underlings to control the operations.[60]

The reconstruction of Feng-shan also involved close cooperation between the authorities and local leaders. This county seat had long been subject to devastating attacks by bandit and rebel forces. After the Lin Shuang-wen rebellion the city was shifted to a new site, only to be destroyed again in 1806 during the Ts'ai Ch'ien disturbances. Eventually the governor of Fukien, on an inspection tour of the area in 1824, recommended that the Feng-shan county capital be moved to a more defensible location near the old site. The county magistrate then assigned to selected local gentry the task of laying out the new boundaries for the relocated city. During the period of major construction, which lasted from August 1825 to September 1826, these gentry managed the project while the magistrate supervised the operations.[61]

In the case of the Feng-shan undertaking, more initiative seems to have stemmed from the authorities than was the case in Chang-hua. Financial support, totaling over 150,000 silver dollars, was derived in part from sources outside the county. On the other hand, during the major construction effort (which involved the building of stone city walls) the local gentry managers apparently exercised tighter control over affairs than had their counterparts in Chang-hua. The Feng-shan managers kept close account of all expenditures and of all contributions and services rendered by the local inhabitants. It was probably owing to their careful management that surplus funds remained after construction had been completed.[62]

The Reconstruction of Hsin-chu

The manner in which Chang-hua and Feng-shan were reconstructed set precedents for similar efforts in northern Taiwan during the nineteenth century. This was evident at Hsin-chu, where a massive reconstruction project was undertaken in 1827–29. Shortly before construction work began there, a group of Hsin-chu gentry visited Chang-hua to inspect that city's new walls and layout. Some of the same officials who had been instrumental in promoting the Feng-shan project also became involved in the Hsin-chu undertaking: for example, the Fukien financial commissioner and the Taiwan intendant backed both projects. More important, the Fukien-Chekiang governor-general, Sun Erh-chun, lent his support just as he had previously in the case of Feng-shan while serving as governor of Fukien. In fact, Sun personally visited each city prior to its reconstruction during official tours of the island. The procedures by which Hsin-chu was reconstructed came to resemble those followed during the Chang-hua and Feng-shan undertakings. The same arrangement of gentry and commoner management under official supervision was adopted, although procedures were tightened to ensure a more efficient use of materials and an even stricter accounting of expenditures.[63]

On the other hand, conditions in the north differed somewhat from those that had prevailed earlier at Chang-hua and Feng-shan. The reconstruction of Hsin-chu came about as a direct response to a destructive Hoklo-Hakka disturbance in 1826. When Governor-General Sun visited Hsin-chu late in the year, he was petitioned to allow more substantial walls and defenses to be erected there. The petition bore the names of 26 gentry and the designations of 21 merchants of the area. Appended to it was a statement by the subprefect, Li Shen-wei, urging that the request be acted upon without delay so that peace and order might prevail.[64]

The Formation of Cities in Taiwan

The walls and defensive installations so urgently sought by the Hsin-chu inhabitants and authorities marked a somewhat different approach to city building in Taiwan. Formerly, all such major construction projects had been initiated after uprisings or bandit attacks had either devastated or at least threatened particular administrative centers. As a consequence, city building in Taiwan had centered around efforts to create self-sufficient bastions of defense.[65] Hsin-chu, however, was reconstructed after local Hoklo-Hakka strife had been quelled but by no means eradicated. It was recognized that walls and moats alone were no defense against recurring "armed conflicts." Unlike uprisings and bandit attacks, such disturbances often involved even "law-abiding" inhabitants (*liang-min*) in both the city and the countryside.

Understanding the peculiar nature of these disturbances, Governor-General Sun readily endorsed the Hsin-chu petition for protective walls, but included this project in a more general rehabilitation plan designed primarily to curb "armed conflicts" and banditry in northern Taiwan.[66] Sun's plan, which was favorably received at court, called for the redeployment of military commanders and troops in the Tan-shui subprefecture and the selection of responsible inhabitants to oversee matters in their localities. Sun fit Hsin-chu rather neatly into these designs. A higher-ranking military official was stationed there, along with several additional subordinate officers, but almost half of the soldiers formerly garrisoned in the city were shifted to strengthen outlying posts in the subprefecture south of the Taipei Basin. Meanwhile, as preparations to reconstruct Hsin-chu proceeded, local overseers and project managers were appointed to direct the project. These influential leaders exercised considerable vigilance over the local population, in keeping with Sun's plan.

The inception of the Hsin-chu wall-construction project marked a positive effort by the authorities to lessen tension among the local Hoklo and Hakka communities. Instead of playing off one group against another, as was usually done in the countryside during times of strife, the officials sought to induce responsible leaders representing the discordant communities to work harmoniously together. The type of overseers (*tsung-li*) and managers (*tung-shih*) that the Taiwan intendant and Subprefect Li selected to direct the wall construction indicates the care they exercised to make this project a genuinely cooperative endeavor.

The three gentry named to oversee the entire project were young or middle-aged scholars from the most prominent Hoklo families in Tan-shui subprefecture. Cheng Yung-hsi and Lin Hsiang-lin were of T'ung-an (Ch'üan-chou) extraction and resided in or near Hsin-chu city.

Cheng, who held a *chin-shih* degree, was a well-known figure and a member of the foremost local scholar family. Lin stemmed from a powerful household and had numerous kinsmen in the vicinity.⁶⁷ The other general overseer, Lin Kuo-hua, came from a wealthy family of Lung-ch'i (Chang-chou) origin that had settled in the Hsin-chuang area to the north. Owing to the wealth and prominence of his father, P'ing-hou, Lin had connections with both Chang-chou and Ch'üan-chou inhabitants of the Hsin-chu vicinity as well as with the Chang-chou communities of his own area. His association with the younger Lin Hsiang-lin in this project undoubtedly impressed the local populace, for their fathers had jointly managed the Taiwan salt industry and were among the island's most eminent inhabitants.⁶⁸

Three less prominent men were selected as assistant overseers, two of them being Hakka gentry of Kwangtung registry. Of the two, Liu Hsien-t'ing was known as an outstanding scholar from the Miao-li region to the south of Hsin-chu. The Hakka representatives were active in support of the wall-building project. Together they solicited 19,000 silver dollars, presumably from their fellow Hakkas.⁶⁹ In addition, twelve managers were selected to direct the construction of sections of the city wall. These managers hailed from Hoklo communities in the Hsin-chu area, and apparently were chosen on the basis of their wealth and local influence. Five were rich commoners, whereas the rest had purchased titles giving them gentry status.⁷⁰

In all, these overseers and project managers formed an outstanding group in northern Taiwan. They were esteemed members of local society and represented the major subethnic groupings in the subprefecture. Moreover, as a result of their interests and activities the overseers, at least, had come to transcend local community bounds. Through their wide connections and gentry status they or their fathers before them had gained renown as island notables. Their reputations were enhanced by the many public-spirited activities in which they participated. Virtually all of them had sponsored important local undertakings, and Liu Hsien-t'ing and eventually Cheng Yung-hsi won acclaim by helping to quell serious subethnic strife in their areas.⁷¹ The construction of city walls at Hsin-chu was yet another way these overseers bettered their standing among the authorities and inhabitants while helping to relieve tension and improve conditions within the subprefecture.

Furthermore, both the overseers and the managers had to some degree become involved in urban affairs. Thus they shared a vested interest in the fortune of Hsin-chu. Two-thirds of them had expressed concern for the city by signing the petition submitted to Governor-General Sun—

The Formation of Cities in Taiwan

or else their more prominent fathers had done so. Subsequently they all contributed substantial sums to help finance the construction work there. In their efforts on behalf of Hsin-chu they evidenced a dedicated spirit tantamount to civic pride.

At this juncture Hsin-chu must have seemed well worth protecting and improving. The gentry and merchants who signed the 1826 petition certainly implied that this was so. In effect, they urged reconstruction in order that Hsin-chu might be on a par with the walled administrative centers to the south. The local scholars appear to have exhibited particular concern on this point, for they had already done much to enhance the reputation of Hsin-chu. The dedication of a Confucian temple there in 1824 had been one of their achievements. Local pride had also been aroused the previous year when Cheng Yung-hsi had gained the first civil *chin-shih* degree ever awarded to a northern Taiwan scholar. From the time of these two events Hsin-chu began to be rated one of the island's leading cultural centers.[72]

The reconstruction of Hsin-chu also figured in that city's cultural development. While the wall-building project was still under way, Subprefect Li and prominent inhabitants set about erecting and repairing public edifices in the city and its environs. Although Li was able to allocate only a small portion of the reconstruction funds for this purpose,[73] he nonetheless managed to have the offices of the subprefect and deputy subprefect renovated, seven separate altars and shrines erected, two government temples repaired or rebuilt, and the city's academy restored to full operation. Meanwhile, local leaders secured private funds and continued to build and repair temples over the next few years as part of the general reconstruction effort.[74] In 1842, Hsin-chu gentry members solicited additional funds and, under official supervision, erected the earthen and bamboo enclosure around their city.

In terms of total funds spent and amount of building carried out, the reconstruction of Hsin-chu ranked second only to that of Chang-hua as the most costly city-building venture yet attempted in Taiwan. Such a large-scale undertaking required considerable enterprise on the part of both the authorities and the local leaders. On the side of the government, the initiative was taken by officials actually on the scene, as had been the case in Chang-hua and Feng-shan. Governor-General Sun, after his 1826 visit to Hsin-chu, played a key role: not only was he instrumental in gaining the approval of the Ch'ing court for his rehabilitation plan, but he also lent support to city building by contributing 1,000 taels from his own salary and by encouraging other Fukien and Taiwan officials to make sizable donations.[75] Again, the efforts of Subprefect Li and his deputy in Hsin-chu enabled the reconstruction program to get under way. Li assisted with the surveys and estimates, helped appoint the local overseers and managers, arranged for the requisite building materials and skilled craftsmen, and selected an auspicious date for construction to commence. The deputy subprefect supervised the day-to-day work as directed by the overseers and managers.[76] The prefect at T'ai-wan-fu and the Taiwan intendant stationed there also lent their support to the project.

At the provincial level, arrangements for the Hsin-chu undertaking also involved the governor, the provincial judge, and the finance commissioner at Foochow. Under the cumbersome Ch'ing administrative system, both the governor and the governor-general submitted separate evaluations, necessitating reports on the part of the provincial judge and the finance commissioner. The Fukien officials also called for independent evaluations by the Taiwan intendant and the prefect of T'ai-wan-fu. In due course, the Taiwan intendant and the Fukien finance commissioner personally inspected the Hsin-chu site. Their separate reports, together with the petitions submitted by Subprefect Li, furnished the bulk of the information transmitted to all levels of government concerning the reconstruction project.[77]

Initiative on the part of local leaders, no less essential to the Hsin-chu undertaking, may be divided into three phases. First, the 47 signatories of the 1826 petition provided inspiration for the project at the outset. The list of petitioners constituted a particularly influential group that managed to gain the backing of authorities and populace alike. Heading the list were the *chin-shih* Cheng Yung-hsi; the wealthy Hsin-chuang notable Lin P'ing-hou, who formerly had served as a Kwangsi subprefect; and three local gentry holding the civil *chü-jen* degree. The names of other important gentry figures possessing lesser degrees and titles also appeared, followed by the designations of local merchants.

Some of the gentry signatories already had discussed the possibility of reconstructing Hsin-chu with the authorities prior to submitting the petition. Apparently they gained the impression that they, rather than the government, would have to accept full responsibility for financing the undertaking. In their petition these spokesmen, like those of Changhua, pledged to contribute and solicit funds on their own. The second phase of local initiative concerned developing ways and means of carrying out this pledge of support. Several local leaders requested that the costs of labor and materials for wall construction be kept proportionate to the total amount of arable land in the subprefecture. Their suggestion was followed to the extent that the circumference of the new city wall was calculated on the basis of the registered field acreage.[78] Meanwhile, other gentry members devised a plan to revamp land-tax procedures in order to secure sufficient revenue for the project. Their plan called for what amounted to an 11-percent levy on the grain payments that tenants made to small-rentholder households (*hsiao-tsu hu*). This plan was unique in that such assessments were to be collected by the project overseers from small rentholders rather than by the local officials from large-rentholder households (*ta-tsu hu*), as was done under the regular Taiwan land-tax system.[79] Accordingly, the tax burden was shared directly by a greater number of inhabitants than would otherwise have been the case. Since the overseers kept strict accounts of such assessments under the close supervision of Subprefect Li, there also was less opportunity for corruption and avoidance of payment than in the established land-tax arrangements, which enabled powerful large rentholders to conspire with local officials or their underlings.

The third phase of local initiative began when the Hsin-chu reconstruction effort actually got under way. The overseers and managers involved in the wall-building project exercised control over the funds and materials allocated as well as over the labor forces employed. Their duties required considerable managerial skill, which many of them had already gained through previous participation in local public works.[80] The important role played by these overseers and managers in the reconstruction of Hsin-chu is well documented in the detailed records of local contributions rendered. These records indicate that the six overseers donated 32,440 silver dollars, and the twelve managers another 8,940 dollars. And through their auspices another 37 wealthy gentry and commoner households in the subprefecture contributed 40,050 dollars. Thus, 55 prominent households provided a total of 81,430 dollars, or more than one-third of the entire amount (217,560 dollars) collected for the undertaking.[81]

In addition, the overseers and managers collected 68,184 dollars from other sources. Since few merchant designations appear in the lists of contributors, one may assume that much of this amount was raised through canvassing the business community.[82] Moreover, the records include a long list of gentry, shopkeeper, large-rentholder, and commoner households whose contributions ranged from 35 to 500 dollars. Altogether, 384 such households, mainly from the Hsin-chu area, are listed as having contributed 34,104 dollars.[83] Added to the 55 contributors noted above, a total of 439 households, families, and individuals provided well over half of the financial support. The records further state that numerous other inhabitants made contributions of less than 35 dollars upon the entreaty of gentry members.[84] Thus, the overseers and managers appear to have been successful in gaining substantial local backing. Contributions formed the bulk of the funds for the entire project, and revenue from assessments on small rentholders apparently made up most of the remaining funds expended. Outside help, such as donations by officials, proved relatively insignificant. Local initiative and leadership thus provided the means whereby a sizable number of inhabitants from separate subethnic communities were urged, or else compelled through assessments, to support the reconstruction of Hsin-chu.

The Formation of I-lan

The formation of I-lan in 1813 was carried out in conjunction with the inception of formal Ch'ing rule over the recently opened Ko-ma-lan region. By this time the need for regular civil and military authority permanently established in a local seat of government had become apparent to both Taiwan and mainland officials. Unless peace and order could be maintained in the new subprefecture, they held, the region would soon fall into the hands of rebel-bandits. Such outlaws might then organize local discontented elements into armed bands and use the region as a base from which to prey upon the settled communities of western Taiwan and the coastal areas of the mainland. Already in 1805-6, the Fukienese pirate Ts'ai Ch'ien had attempted to seize control of Ko-ma-lan ports with such a scheme in mind. The following year another band of sea robbers from southern Fukien, led by Chu Fen, also had stirred up trouble at the local seaports with the same objective.[85] In 1810, the Ko-ma-lan subprefecture had been established for fear of the consequences should the region be left outside the Chinese "pale of civilization" any longer.

Leaders among the Chinese settlers scattered over the Ko-ma-lan Plain also were anxious to have an administrative center built and government instituted in the region. The rise of a walled city representing imperial authority promised security from internal strife and external attacks that their enclosed villages were unable to provide. No one settlement or group, they realized, could offer its members adequate protection or curtail the destructive "armed conflicts" rampant among the local Chinese in-groups.

The chaotic situation in the Ko-ma-lan region lent a sense of urgency to the building of I-lan. Early in 1813, the occupants of the Wu-wei village site were moved elsewhere and work on the moats and enclosures was promptly begun. This construction was divided into five sections. The predominant Chang-chou settlers provided the labor for three of the sections, and the smaller Ch'üan-chou and Hakka communities were each held responsible for building one section. Local heads from various groups were placed in charge of the work undertaken in their respective sections. According to an official account, the inhabitants labored diligently under this arrangement without thought of material reward.[86] Within nine months the moats had been dug and an earthen and bamboo enclosure erected.

Although support was rendered by the inhabitants, the pressing need for an administrative center in the region forced the authorities to assume most of the initiative in building I-lan. Official interest in such a project arose after Governor-General Fang Wei-tien paid a visit to Meng-chia in 1810. Fang, who had backed the proposed reconstruction of Chang-hua the previous year, met with Chinese headmen and aborigine chiefs from the Ko-ma-lan Plain. Having learned of the turbulent conditions there, he dispatched Yang T'ing-li, a former Taiwan intendant, to inspect the region.[87] The construction of I-lan some three years later came about mainly through Yang's determined efforts to bring the region under direct Ch'ing rule.

In 1807, Yang had led a force into the region and had quelled the Chu Fen disturbance. Through this exploit he had gained the respect and confidence of the local Chinese settlers. When he appeared there again in 1810, Yang devised a plan whereby government could be introduced to the region. He chose the Wu-wei site and planted a ring of willow trees to serve as an enclosure for the future administrative center. The eighteen-point program he then submitted was eventually followed when I-lan was built and regular government initiated in 1813.[88]

Yang proved a bold and resourceful leader. He relied on his own reputation among the inhabitants, as well as on their desire for order and security, to gain backing for the I-lan project and other public works in the region. The major problem he faced was how to finance such undertakings. The Ko-ma-lan region was smaller, less densely populated, and less productive than Tan-shui subprefecture, yet funds would have to come from the region itself. In order to solve this dilemma Yang demanded that the entire large-rentholder yield be remitted as land-tax revenue to the Ko-ma-lan government. He incorporated this radical tax proposal in the program he devised in 1810. Subsequently, when he stayed on for a time in 1812–13 to implement his program, Yang prevented the double-rent system that had become customary in western Taiwan from being officially sanctioned in the region. He thereby deprived many headmen of anticipated profits as large rentholders. In later years the outcry against his tax measure was considerable,[89] but at the time he managed to secure sufficient revenue in his capacity as acting prefect to build I-lan and finance other vital undertakings elsewhere in the subprefecture.

The resourceful nature of Yang T'ing-li is also apparent in his selection of the Wu-wei site. The relative peace among settler in-groups there enabled Yang and the first subprefect, Ch'ai Kan, to enlist local support in a cooperative city-building venture. The belief that the diverse inhabitants of the vicinity would continue to act in accord may also explain why Yang did not erect stouter defenses for the new administrative center. He initially built an inexpensive enclosure of a type that offered less protection than the earthen walls erected around villages in the region. In 1813, Subprefect Ch'ai replaced Yang's 1810 willow enclosure with a more substantial earthen and bamboo one.[90] Nevertheless, I-lan was still by no means a defensive bastion. Local protection continued to stem mainly from the small military force stationed within the city, whereas defense against outside attack was provided by coastal garrisons and distant mountain guard posts, as Yang had envisioned.

The building of I-lan and the inception of regular government were noteworthy accomplishments acclaimed by all concerned. Yet alternative proposals, along with the cumbersome Ch'ing system of government, brought delay and uncertainty to the whole endeavor. Four years of deliberation had passed before Ko-ma-lan subprefecture was established in 1810,[91] and it was another two years before construction of the administrative center commenced. During the latter interval local opposition to Yang's land-tax scheme proved a major hindrance. Aroused Chang-chou headmen of the region proposed that they be allowed to undertake the construction of the enclosure and government installations of I-lan on their own.[92] Although their proposal was a pretext to have large-rentholder rights endorsed in the subprefecture, their petition cast doubt on the program and estimates that had been submitted a few months earlier by Yang.

There then ensued a drawn-out series of deliberations between provincial officials in Foochow and the prefectural authorities in T'ai-wan-fu. Governor-General Fang's replacement feared that Yang's reports were faulty and called for the Taiwan intendant, brigade-general, and prefect to confer together in council with Yang. Then in 1811, a new appointee as governor-general felt that the Taiwan authorities lacked sufficient data. Therefore, he ordered the intendant to travel to the Ko-ma-lan region to investigate. On the basis of the intendant's report, the prefectural council and its provincial counterpart in Foochow, which included the governor-general, the governor, the finance commissioner,

The Formation of Cities in Taiwan

the provincial judge, and the salt intendant, approved the basic program Yang had submitted the previous year. The project was subsequently reviewed by the grand secretaries in Peking before receiving provisional imperial approval. In 1812 the court referred the case back to the Fukien authorities for further clarification of details.[93] More months passed before Yang and Subprefect Ch'ai began to put Yang's program into effect.

Despite some local resentment over Yang's land-tax measure, the building of I-lan apparently was carried on without undue friction. Accounts suggest that Yang and Ch'ai exercised care in selecting managers and assigning duties. An influential commoner of Chang-chou origin was chosen to supervise the other headmen assigned to the wall construction project. This man had apparently been on close terms with Yang since 1807, when he had prevailed upon the latter to quell the Chu Fen disturbance.[94] Yang and Ch'ai enlisted the active help of other inhabitants in addition to the headmen. Local shopkeepers, for example, subscribed to and managed the building of drawbridges leading to the four city gates. Various inhabitants helped erect temples and other public edifices. In the case of important temples of special interest to the government such as the one housing the City God, local managers were appointed to solicit funds and direct the construction work. When government offices and shrines were built, labor was hired, the wages being paid from tax revenues.[95]

The construction of a number of officially sponsored temples and shrines at the outset indicates that this new seat of government was expected to play a civilizing role in the Ko-ma-lan region. Yang T'ing-li had always been anxious to advance Chinese culture there. When he first entered the region in 1807, he found that the settlers lacked temples or even major Chinese deities to worship. Accordingly, he requested that images of Kuan-ti, T'ien-hou, and Kuan-yin be obtained.[96] Subsequently, Subprefect Ch'ai sponsored the construction of temples in I-lan for each of these deities, as well as for the City God. In addition, Ch'ai undertook to introduce orthodox rituals and learning there by erecting government altars and shrines, a temple dedicated to the patron god of literature, and a hall for the academy that Yang had founded at the I-lan site.[97]

However, all such religious and cultural edifices, with the exception of the T'ien-hou temple and small altars and shrines devoted to agricultural deities, were built after the I-lan enclosure and subprefectural offices had been constructed. Clearly, the need for permanent government was uppermost in the minds of the officials who had sanctioned the formation of this administrative center. In order to make sure that the enclosure, moats, and government yamen would be completed with the limited resources available, the Fukien authorities in council had stipulated that government altars and shrines were to be constructed with funds left over from these other projects. The council also specified that religious temples of a popular nature could be financed only through personal contributions on the part of the authorities and inhabitants. Government revenues were not to be used for such purposes.[98] This regulation further delayed the construction of most religious edifices in I-lan. Apart from land-tax receipts, there were as yet few local sources of funds for such costly undertakings.

The Rise of T'ai-pei-fu

The rise of T'ai-pei-fu reflected improved conditions in northern Taiwan and throughout the island. In 1875, the cumbersome regulations that had adversely affected Chinese settlement were rescinded, and from that time until the end of Ch'ing rule in 1895 Taiwan experienced more internal stability. The Taipei Basin, in particular, underwent significant development during this period as the north came to surpass the middle and southern portions of the island in wealth and rate of population growth. The establishment of a northern prefecture in 1875 was advocated by officials who recognized the prosperity and strategic importance of the basin area. The elevation of T'ai-pei-fu, the new prefectural center, to the status of a temporary provincial capital in 1886 was a further recognition of accelerating development in the north as well as of the island's new status as an integral part of the empire.

T'ai-pei-fu underwent two early stages of development. During the first stage city walls and moats were built, and prefectural offices, a Confucian temple, and several other public edifices were erected within the enclosed area. As this construction work proceeded, efforts were made by the prefect to lay out streets, lanes, and lots in order to induce inhabitants from the outlying areas to set up shops and residences in the new city. By 1884, the year the Sino-French War broke out and the French launched their attack on northern Taiwan, T'ai-pei-fu had begun to assume the appearance of a traditional Chinese walled city, complete with its own City God temple. The second stage commenced after Taiwan achieved provincial status in 1886. Then Governor Liu Ming-ch'uan, who had taken up residence in T'ai-pei-fu two years earlier to command operations against the French, initiated a number of major construction projects in the new city. Under his vigorous rule provincial offices and separate facilities for the Tan-shui county capital were added, more public temples erected, and paved streets introduced. Liu also shifted the northern military headquarters from Meng-chia to a new location inside the city wall. Altogether, he proposed major building projects costing over 124,386 taels (141,800 silver dollars), according to his estimate.[99] Moreover, Liu made determined efforts to promote further commercial enterprise in the still thinly populated city. His departure in 1891 brought this second stage of development to an end only four years before Taiwan fell to the Japanese.

During the first stage, the formation of T'ai-pei-fu proceeded in a manner resembling the way Hsin-chu and other centers to the south had been reconstructed earlier in the century. Most of the funds and labor were expended on construction of a stone and brick city wall. This massive undertaking was carried out as a cooperative venture between the authorities, headed by Prefect Ch'en Hsing-chü, and leaders representing various subethnic communities in the Taipei Basin. The prefect sought the support of these influential gentry and merchants, and selected fourteen managers from among them for the wall-building project. The managers solicited funds and directed the construction of sections of the city wall and moat. Some managers, along with other wealthy inhabitants, made special contributions toward the building of the five city gates and the first temples erected within the city.[100] However, this familiar manner of city building was motivated by somewhat different needs and circumstances in the case of T'ai-pei-fu. In the first place, T'ai-pei-fu was founded as a prefectural center rather than as a subprefectural or county capital at the lowest level of administration. Normally, decisions concerning the location and function of a new prefectural center could be expected to reflect primarily political considerations, and this proved true in respect to T'ai-pei-fu. Early in 1875, Imperial Commissioner Shen Pao-chen had called for the establishment of an additional Taiwan prefecture as part of his plan to revamp the administrative setup in the northern portion of the island. He recommended the Meng-chia area as the most suitable site for a new prefectural center.[101] When local Hsin-chu gentry protested against his proposal and requested that the major seat of northern Taiwan government be retained in their city, the T'ai-pei prefect defended Shen's recommendation by elaborating upon the strategic importance of Meng-chia.[102]

Moreover, T'ai-pei-fu was founded during a relatively peaceful period in an area where flourishing towns already provided an urbanlike environment. Hence, there was not the critical need for the inception of order and the civilizing influence of a walled government seat as there had been in the case of I-lan. In fact, the new city of T'ai-pei-fu that arose in the paddy fields adjoining Meng-chia and Ta-tao-ch'eng remained something of an upstart among these older established port towns during the remainder of the Ch'ing period.

Although there was not such a sense of urgency about the building of T'ai-pei-fu, the local support rendered during the first stage was substantial. Altogether, over 200,000 taels (228,000 silver dollars) were eventually solicited to cover the costs of constructing the stone and brick city wall.[103] Wealthy households of the nearby port towns and lesser settlements in the Tan-shui River area contributed the bulk of these funds. The degree of local backing is impressive when one considers that the island's first prefectural center, T'ai-wan-fu, had been reconstructed with earthen walls in 1788–91 because the cost of stone and brick construction was deemed prohibitive in southern Taiwan at the time.[104]

There are various reasons why the construction of T'ai-pei-fu received such substantial local support at the outset. Local pride was an important factor, further stimulated by the authorities with the promise that the governor of Fukien would reside there for half of each year.[105] Then, too, wealthy inhabitants welcomed the rise of a new city in their area, realizing that this would increase local land values and open up additional commercial opportunities. Hence large-rentholder rights to substantial tracts of field land in the vicinity changed hands while the site of T'ai-pei-fu was being laid out. Several enterprising inhabitants of Meng-chia and Ta-tao-ch'eng acquired rights to land close to their respective towns but within the designated bounds of the city. There they proceeded to develop new market centers even before the construction of city walls commenced in 1879.[106]

Moreover, the rise of T'ai-pei-fu meant that local scholars might more readily compete in the prefectural examinations leading to the *sheng-yüan* degree. While wall building was still in progress, certain influential inhabitants took steps to improve local educational facilities and ensure the prompt inauguration of examinations. Funds were raised for a new T'ai-pei-fu academy, founded in 1881. During the same year, a wealthy resident of Meng-chia donated land and paid for the construction of an examination hall large enough to accommodate 2,000 candidates.[107]

Once again, local support for the construction of a walled capital also stemmed from a craving for security. Even though relatively peaceful conditions prevailed in the basin area by this time, the enmity stemming from the two destructive "armed conflicts" that had erupted there several decades earlier still lingered. The presence of a walled seat of government headed by a prefect seemed a safeguard against such strife in the future. However, the cooperative wall-building venture undertaken at T'ai-pei-fu apparently did not reduce the tension between the two

The Formation of Cities in Taiwan

major Hoklo groups in the area. Without the imminent threat of violence and disorder, Chang-chou and Ch'üan-chou spokesmen wrangled and prolonged the project, particularly after the costs of wall building proved higher than anticipated.

The main argument between the two groups centered around the issue of how much money the Chang-chou leader, Lin Wei-yüan, was to contribute. The son of Lin Kuo-hua and head of the richest family in Taiwan,[108] Lin had already contributed the huge sum of 500,000 silver dollars to the government in 1878 for relief efforts in Shansi province and dike work elsewhere, as well as for city wall building. The Fukien governor had exempted him from the obligation of making further public contributions. Backed by other Chang-chou spokesmen, Lin refused to render additional support to the T'ai-pei-fu wall project, even when the Taiwan intendant and Prefect Ch'en personally called on him to do so in 1883. The Ch'üan-chou spokesmen backed the intendant and prefect on this occasion. They demanded that "equal subscriptions" (*yün-chüan*) be exacted from all who could afford to contribute, regardless of previous payments.

The matter was settled only after the intendant had petitioned to have "equal subscriptions" imposed on those households in Tan-shui, Hsin-chu, and I-lan counties holding rights to the best grades of land there. Both the governor-general and the governor objected to the "equal subscription" idea and supported Lin Wei-yüan in his refusal to make further contributions.[109] Consequently, Prefect Ch'en continued to rely on local contributions, and the burden of the first stage of city building fell primarily on the fourteen local managers and ultimately on the communities of the Taipei Basin.

Despite their disagreements, the fourteen managers of the wall-building project were influential personages who by and large were able to rise above the immediate interests of their own communities. In the past some had helped to mitigate local subethnic strife. Lin Wei-yüan, for example, had functioned as a moderate spokesman of the Chang-chou people both in his native Pan-ch'iao and in Ta-tao-ch'eng, where he maintained business connections. Ch'en Hsia-lin, a gentry-scholar of repute, often acted as a public-spirited leader of the Ch'üan-chou people in the area at large as well as of his own T'ung-an community in Ta-tao-ch'eng. The Meng-chia merchant Pai Ch'i-hsiang performed a similar role on behalf of the local An-ch'i people.[110] Other managers representing various Chang-chou and Ch'üan-chou communities of the river ports as well as towns to the north of T'ai-pei-fu also exerted a positive influence in localities still afflicted by strong subethnic rivalries.

Besides supporting the construction of T'ai-pei-fu, these powerful managers helped arrange for the city's internal development. A major problem that confronted Prefect Ch'en was how to form plots for commercial and residential use that would attract permanent urban dwellers. The problem was partially solved when the managers, in consultation with Ch'en, proposed that city lots of uniform dimensions be leased at a fixed rate. Under this plan payments would be made to the managers, who would then turn over the funds to households possessing large-rentholder rights to the land. Soon it was found that this procedure did not protect the urban tenants from further assessments exacted by the large rentholders. Therefore, these local leaders petitioned the prefect to abolish the large-rent system within the city. In spite of protests from the rentholders, Prefect Ch'en endorsed this proposal.[111] Once again Taiwan's double-rent system was adversely affected—this time through the initiative of public-spirited local leaders.

When T'ai-pei-fu underwent the first stage of construction, Prefect Ch'en was in direct charge. However, his decisions and actions were sanctioned by his superiors, including the Taiwan intendant in the south and the ranking provincial authorities at Foochow. This arrangement changed during the second stage. Then the Taiwan governor served as the ranking official on the island instead of the Taiwan intendant, overseeing matters relating to civil administration and reform. Moreover, after Taiwan was designated a province in 1886, the Taiwan governor residing at T'ai-pei-fu held the concurrent title of Fukien governor, whereas the Fukien-Chekiang governor-general assumed the duties of the Foochow governor's office on the mainland. Thus the Taiwan governor functioned on a par with the ranking Fukien officials, yet operated with minimal control and supervision from Foochow.[112] This new arrangement allowed Governor Liu Ming-ch'uan considerably more leeway than Prefect Ch'en or any previous Taiwan official had enjoyed with respect to local urban construction.

When Governor Liu initiated additional building, however, he faced a number of problems. T'ai-pei-fu was neither prosperous nor particularly attractive. Only the northern and western sections were partially built-up, but even there the streets were nearly impassable. Then, too, the officials serving under Liu were preoccupied with the host of reforms and improvements he was launching elsewhere in Taiwan. These included the work on a new provincial capital carried on for a time at a previously selected site in the mid-island region. This other city-building project, which was officially abandoned only after Liu's departure,

The Formation of Cities in Taiwan

served to distract official attention from the needs of the unfinished walled center of T'ai-pei-fu, then regarded as the temporary provincial capital.[113]

Furthermore, local support for the completion of T'ai-pei-fu had fallen off during the French attack on northern Taiwan in 1884–85. Afterwards, Liu attempted to rekindle interest in the city's development. In doing so, he apparently depended largely on the services of Lin Wei-yüan, just as he did for other major undertakings he sponsored in northern Taiwan. Lin helped form a company for the purpose of carrying on construction work in T'ai-pei-fu and its environs.[114] Yet this arrangement tied Governor Liu even closer to Ta-tao-ch'eng interests and may have lessened his chances of securing substantial support from Meng-chia and other places dominated by Ch'üan-chou people.

Eventually, Liu Ming-ch'uan came to realize that he could not gain sufficient local support or adequate funds from regular sources of government revenue to carry on major undertakings at T'ai-pei-fu. Funds from customs, salt, and the likin taxes were already budgeted for other uses. Moreover, the inhabitants had previously contributed so heavily to the T'ai-pei-fu wall-construction project and the defenses built to withstand the French that Liu was not inclined to press them for further contributions. He also was reluctant to follow what he termed the "corrupt custom" of levying additional assessments on registered landholdings while his land registration and survey project was still under way.[115] Consequently, he turned to more distant sources for support of his city development efforts at T'ai-pei-fu.

Liu succeeded in gaining funds and other forms of help from wealthy merchant and gentry elements in the Lower Yangtze region and southeast China. He persuaded one group of wealthy persons in Shanghai, Soochow, and northern Chekiang to form a joint enterprise called the City Promotion Company (*Hsing-shih kung-ssu*). Starting with 50,000 taels as capital, this company set up shops and financed many of the modern installations and improvements Liu introduced to T'ai-pei-fu. This mainland enterprise also attracted merchants and shopkeepers to the new city from urban centers in the coastal regions.[116]

The influx of an outside commercial class was accompanied by a growth in the number of mainland officials and scholars serving at the various seats of government housed in T'ai-pei-fu. These outsiders (*wai-sheng-jen*), mainly from Anhwei, Kiangsu, and Fukien, were joined by clerks and underlings from areas of northern Taiwan in taking up residence within the walled city.[117] This assortment of commercial types and government personnel formed the nucleus of an urban population that might have turned T'ai-pei-fu into a bustling Chinese metropolis had Taiwan remained longer under Ch'ing rule.

The reason Liu Ming-ch'uan exerted such effort to build up T'ai-pei-fu was that, like Shen Pao-chen and many other officials of the period, he felt the Taipei Basin was the natural location for a key administrative center. As he sponsored various construction projects there, Liu came to favor T'ai-pei-fu over the mid-island site for the provincial capital.[118] Hence he eventually allowed work on this other city-building project to lapse. Owing to Liu's foresight in constructing provincial offices at T'ai-pei-fu, that city eventually was designated the permanent capital in 1894. Yet when Liu departed in 1891, well over half of the city's enclosed area remained paddy fields. Moreover, T'ai-pei-fu still had not developed into a prosperous trading center even though the city served as the established seat of government on three levels.[119]

Conclusions: Lesser Walled Centers and City Building

This study of the formation of three seats of government suggests how diverse in character lesser walled centers in traditional China could be. Although all were formed in northern Taiwan during the Ch'ing period, varying needs of government and local society caused them to undergo different rates and stages of development. Hsin-chu gradually assumed in the course of many decades the functions of a subprefectural capital and economic center. In contrast, I-lan quickly became a multifunctional center in a backward and turbulent region. T'ai-pei-fu was founded as a prefectural seat of government amid more orderly and prosperous conditions. Even so, Hsin-chu and I-lan came to flourish as major commercial centers in their respective areas, whereas T'ai-pei-fu did not, owing to competition from the existing river-port towns nearby. These varied origins and roles affected city-building efforts at each of the three centers and led to physical differences among them.

Distinct as they were during their formative stages, all three centers shared certain common features. None was an outgrowth of the frontier, not even the small and remote I-lan center in the newly settled Ko-ma-lan region. Neither did these seats of government evolve from villages: where a village existed at a chosen site, as at Hsin-chu and I-lan, the occupants were removed and resettled elsewhere.[120] At T'ai-pei-fu, even though a sizable portion of the area within the city walls remained in paddy fields, plans already had been devised to redivide these lands into lots for urban development.

On the other hand, these walled centers were not isolated from the surrounding countryside. Hsin-chu and I-lan functioned as commercial hubs for their respective hinterlands, and all three government seats administered extensive territories. Moreover, regional settlement patterns influenced their formation and growth. Eventually, close contacts with local subethnic communities were formed as influential and wealthy members were drawn to the city and elements of the heterogeneous Chinese population gravitated from rural to urban locales. After T'ai-pei-fu became the temporary provincial capital, direct commercial links with the mainland were established there. Thereafter the city's economic transactions included a significant long-distance component paralleling the extension somewhat earlier of its political influence beyond the jurisdiction of T'ai-pei prefecture. Nevertheless, on the whole the three walled centers functioned mainly through networks and systems developed locally. Since support for city building came in large part from the centers' hinterlands, this study has dwelt upon the interaction between the capitals and local society beyond their walls.

The political influence of the three centers proved more extensive than their commercial or informal sociocultural ties in the outlying areas. Within each administrative unit in Taiwan, as elsewhere in late imperial China, government service on the lowest levels emphasized the maintenance of order along with the collection of taxes. These vital functions influenced city building in northern Taiwan in several noteworthy respects. First, the defenses of each walled center were designed to fit in with the peripheral military garrisons, coastal defenses, and mountain guard posts established to safeguard the center and the region in general. This differed from the policy of constructing solitary defensive bastions that had stimulated city building to the south and had led to the erection of an outer enclosure around Hsin-chu in 1842, but it accorded with the strategy commonly employed on the mainland.[121] Second, in conjunction with their tax-collecting duties, the Taiwan authorities imposed special assessments on field-land in Tan-shui subprefecture to help finance the reconstruction of Hsin-chu. Furthermore, early officials of Ko-ma-lan subprefecture and T'ai-pei prefecture adopted tax or landholding measures that adversely affected Taiwan's double-rent system in their efforts to launch proper administrative centers.

The ties that existed between the walled centers and the territories more or less dependent on them were complex, and they are only partially described in local records. Functional relationships of a commercial and cultural nature may be envisioned in terms of a spatial system embracing the central city, towns, and villages in a naturally bounded subregion. Within such a system the multifunctional capital cities shared urban roles with local port and market towns. Also, both cities and towns maintained direct contact with villages in rural hinterlands. Since the subregional setting at the time of city building varied from one case to another, so too did the locus of support. I-lan, founded in a backward region amid village settlements, drew mostly upon rural support by way of the land tax and labor services. T'ai-pei-fu, by contrast, arose close to flourishing port towns, and construction there during the first stage was financed mainly by contributions from these neighboring urban centers. Hsin-chu, by the time of its reconstruction, was in a position to gain both rural and urban backing from its own general area as well as from other subregions in Tan-shui subprefecture, prosperous Meng-chia excepted.

In Taiwan a few major port towns, like Meng-chia and Ta-tao-ch'eng, grew so prosperous that they exercised commercial dominance over nearby administrative centers. Meng-chia even developed into a subordinate government seat and competed with Hsin-chu before the rise of T'ai-pei-fu.[122] With their large urban populations these bustling port towns resembled cities, whereas in comparison the capitals appeared more like towns. Nonetheless, in traditional China capitals were distinguished from towns on the basis of their politico-administrative functions alone. Towns failed to acquire the offices and trappings of capitals, although they sometimes housed large garrisons and headquartered minor officials. Hence they were deemed inferior in the imperial order and not accorded the status of *ch'eng*, or walled cities.

In the highly segmented society of northern Taiwan this formal distinction between town and city proved to be of more than conventional significance. As capitals and multifunctional urban locales, the three centers were able to serve diverse subethnic communities in the outlying areas and to attract migrants from most of them. Hsin-chu and I-lan even drew local Hakka inhabitants; and when T'ai-pei-fu became a provincial capital, a large number of "outsiders" took up residence there. The towns, on the other hand, tended to be populated more exclusively by specific Hoklo or Hakka subgroups, and they normally catered to the needs of the predominant subethnic community or higher-order ethnic grouping in the vicinity. Whereas administrative centers became the symbols of cross-ethnic regional unity, nonadministrative towns, like villages, remained enclaves of one or another particularistic group.

These differences between towns and cities were reflected in dissimilar modes of town and city building throughout northern Taiwan. When the incidence of serious disturbances rose during the latter part of the eighteenth century and the first half of the nineteenth, a number of towns there acquired enclosures of thorny bamboo and earth, or even of brick and stone. Certain market towns, most notably T'ao-yüan, came to resemble miniature *ch'eng* with their walls and ditches, temples and marketplaces, City Gods, and oftentimes government installations, including granaries, garrisons, and headquarters for minor officials.[123] Yet town-building ventures were normally carried out by a single dominant subethnic group. City building, by contrast, featured public works involving official supervision together with mutual support by rival communities within the wider bounds of a region or administrative territory.

Moreover, unlike town construction, city building required the sanction of an array of officials and government bodies. Surveillance by the imperial government assured that administrative centers, when founded or reconstructed, would assume the standardized attributes of walled cities appropriate to their administrative functions. Furthermore, the need to have official authorization for each undertaking meant that extant city-building policies would be followed. The three walled centers in northern Taiwan were built in accordance with precedents set in the southern and mid-island regions after early Ch'ing policies unfavorable to city-wall construction had been modified. Construction at I-lan was carried out under the flexible *yin-ti chih-i* arrangement that had been resorted to during the Yung-cheng reign.[124] The more massive city-building projects at Hsin-chu and T'ai-pei-fu, involving the use of stone and brick, conformed with standard mainland practice, adopted in Taiwan after the Ch'ien-lung pronouncements of 1788.

The initiative behind city-building efforts reveals complex interaction between government sponsorship and local support. Officials on the scene, along with local spokesmen representing various subethnic groups, provided the initial impetus. Visits paid to northern Taiwan by governors-general or other important mainland dignitaries, before plans for each city-building venture began to materialize, also had a stimulating effect locally and paved the way for serious consideration of that particular undertaking within official circles. Thereafter, officials on different levels investigated the location, layout, and construction costs while Taiwan and Fukien authorities, together with local leaders, devised ways and means to carry out each project. When city-building plans were formally approved, responsibility for overseeing the entire undertaking was assigned to the ranking civil official on hand.

The initiative displayed by local spokesmen at the outset continued in evidence throughout each undertaking. At Hsin-chu and T'ai-pei-fu, overseers and managers performed services that were essential to the actual construction of both walls and other public works. Headmen fulfilled similar though more limited functions at I-lan. In all three cases the local leaders gave advice and proved indispensable in encouraging diverse subethnic groups from different localities to respond and work together on a common undertaking. Essential to this leadership was the influence such spokesmen wielded within their respective Hoklo and Hakka groups through family connections as well as through common lineage and surname ties. On the whole, those spokesmen who displayed initiative and assumed responsible duties proved to be powerful figures in their own communities. They proceeded to mobilize local support for wall construction in much the same particularistic manner as was customary for exclusive community enterprises of the period, including destructive "armed conflicts" waged against rival subethnic groups.

Wealth and social status were important prerequisites for this local leadership. These qualities enabled spokesmen both to exert influence in their communities and to form connections outside their immediate localities. Officials on the scene selected such wealthy and socially prominent leaders for responsible managerial roles precisely because of their influence and connections as well as their evident concern for peace and order within the area. Liu Ming-ch'uan, too, attempted to utilize this leadership when he revived city-building activities at T'ai-pei-fu. However, his endeavor to make that center a grand and flourishing seat of higher government proved overambitious for its time. Subsequently, he turned more to moneyed interests on the mainland as a source of wealth and inspiration for further city development.

Governor Liu's attempt to secure backing and even civic leadership from "outsiders" may have been appropriate for a prefectural seat destined to become a provincial capital. At lower levels of the administrative hierarchy in Taiwan, however, city building continued to depend mainly on the joint efforts of government officials and an elite body of local leaders. The reconstruction of Hsin-chu indicates that even after a lesser walled center had flourished for decades, this pattern of joint responsibility still prevailed. Since cities in traditional China lacked specifically municipal institutions of government, the urban political process was informal and oftentimes appeared ad hoc. At Hsin-chu the local elite managed city affairs when a specific need arose; otherwise, the resident officials supervised urban matters. Moreover, since that center was relatively small and had only slender resources of its own, projects of any magnitude required not only the efforts of the authorities and elite members living in the city and its immediate environs, but also the cooperation of spokesmen hailing from the surrounding areas. During the reconstruction of Hsin-chu, several prominent persons from the more distant areas of Tan-shui subprefecture served as overseers.

The authorities and local headmen who initiated city-building undertakings in northern Taiwan were generally motivated by the need to cope with disorder. Intensive settlement and rapid population growth had led to further turbulence, which in turn resulted in mounting tension among subethnic communities and settler in-groups. In particular, large "armed conflicts," which menaced government and society alike during the nineteenth century, caused officials and spokesmen to attend to the construction of walled centers as means of providing security and fostering more effective government control. All three cities were built or reconstructed with these objectives in mind.

Nevertheless, considerations varied with the conditions and specific needs of the local area. I-lan, for example, arose when the Ko-ma-lan region was threatened by pirate attacks from the sea, aborigine disturbances on the inland peripheries, and severe subethnic strife at its very core. Under these circumstances the need for a proper walled city was strongly felt, as illustrated by the determined efforts of Yang T'ing-li. Local headmen of rival groups promptly cooperated with the early officials in constructing I-lan, despite disgruntlement over Yang's actions to thwart the double-rent system in that region. In T'ai-pei-fu, by contrast, where external constraints were less pressing, the local managers became embroiled in intergroup dissension that delayed completion of the city wall. Moreover, the fact that government administrators were functioning at Hsin-chu and I-lan, as well as at the newly established Keelung subprefectural post, made a difference. Continuity in local rule allowed the early T'ai-pei prefects to proceed more cautiously in forming a higher-level center for northern Taiwan than Yang and the first Ko-ma-lan subprefect had been able to do when they initiated city building along with formal government on the basic level.

Considerations of local culture and local pride played a role in city building at each of the three centers. Early officials in the backward Ko-ma-lan region regarded the founding of I-lan as a civilizing influence. Local spokesmen at Hsin-chu heralded the reconstruction of that city as another step in its emergence as a major cultural center. During the initial stage of construction at T'ai-pei-fu, certain managers and other ambitious notables helped found temples, schools, and academies, the last with an eye to the advantages to be gained from the examination system. Motives reflecting local commercial interests also were evident in accordance with the trade patterns and level of economic development in each general area.

The founding of I-lan and T'ai-pei-fu shows, however, that the needs of government invariably received prime attention whenever walled administrative centers were to be built from scratch. Local motives of a commercial and cultural nature, though deemed important by the authorities, were accorded less weight than immediate political and strategic concerns. When an established center like Hsin-chu was reconstructed, the situation was somewhat different. Although political and military considerations were still important, motivation was multifaceted and much of the initiative behind city building stemmed from local leaders.

There are other factors related to the problems of initiative and motivation that have not been examined in this study. In all likelihood religion and geomancy played some role in either encouraging or discouraging local support for each undertaking.[125] Another factor was the labor supply. Northern Taiwan was troubled by a large vagrant population during the nineteenth century. Thus the authorities and managers at Hsin-chu and T'ai-pei-fu may have favored city building in part as a means to employ the indigent people in their areas. Unfortunately, available sources give little indication of the type of labor used at these two centers, where massive wall construction projects required considerable manpower.[126] Still another factor that cannot be adequately dealt with here relates to the system of awards utilized by the Ch'ing authorities to encourage private support of city-building undertakings. At all three centers, those who contributed substantial sums or performed outstanding services were recommended for decorations and honors, or even for academic titles and official rank, as under the purchase system for gentry status. It was partly for this reason that managers of the Hsin-chu wall-construction project kept careful accounts of contributions and services.[127]

Despite my efforts to elucidate the motivations behind the northern Taiwan undertakings, an element of irrationality remains. The erection of stone and brick walls at Hsin-chu and T'ai-pei-fu, in particular, required such heavy expenditures that one may question the wisdom of the decision to proceed with such elaborate plans. Neither center was designed to be a self-sufficient bastion of defense. Moreover, critics of earthen enclosures, as well as of stone and brick walls in Taiwan, complained of the difficulties and heavy expenses involved in their upkeep.[128] Despite these recognized disadvantages, most local Chinese seemed to want substantial city walls. Not only did walls and moats provide local protection and betoken increased security, they also testified to the cultural level and general affluence of a region. In northern Taiwan the form and dimensions of city walls also became a matter of local pride. Village enclosures had long been in evidence there,[129] and during the nineteenth century some towns, too, acquired walls. For an administrative center not to have impressive walls and moats appeared a sign of negligence on the part of both the government and the local inhabitants. Judging from the Hsin-chu petitioners, the desire to emulate Chang-hua and other centers to the south clearly figured in the choice of stone and brick materials for northern city walls.

Here one may discern the spread of long-standing Chinese attitudes concerning city walls to a more recently settled region of the empire. Wall construction was indeed a strongly ingrained practice in traditional China. During the nineteenth century, even critics of earthen and stone wall construction in Taiwan did not condemn wall building per se, but merely pointed out the disadvantages of such elaborate construction. One astute critic writing early in the century asserted that problems of disorder in Taiwan would not be solved by building massive city walls. Instead, he claimed, simple bamboo enclosures were adequate to achieve what was needed—literally, "walled cities representing a unanimity of purpose."[130]

The conclusions reached here about city building in Taiwan, of course, may not apply in toto to city formation elsewhere in China. Nonetheless, the case of northern Taiwan does underscore the persistence of the tradition of constructing walled cities. Moreover, the three instances of city building treated here indicate the nature of the variation possible within this long tradition, even as the imperial era drew to a close.

Regional Urbanization in Nineteenth-Century China

G. WILLIAM SKINNER

What proportion of China's population was urban in late imperial times? The attempt made in this paper to provide an answer starts with the assumption that the question must be specified rather precisely in both time and space. On the temporal side, my concern is with the nineteenth century, and the specific objective is to develop estimates for two dates fifty years apart—1843 and 1893. On the spatial side, the position taken here is that in premodern times urbanization rates for China as a whole are very nearly meaningless and that the question should be reformulated in terms of regions.

The Regional Approach

Fairly early in my research on Chinese cities it became clear that in late imperial times they formed not a single integrated urban system but several regional systems, each only tenuously connected with its neighbors. In tracing out the overlapping hinterlands of the cities in each one of these regional systems, I came to the realization that the region they jointly defined coincided with minor exceptions to a physiographic unit. In short, it appears that each system of cities developed within a physiographic region. I eventually came to conceive of urban development—the formation of cities and the growth of their central functions—as a critical element in regional development—the processes whereby regional resources of all kinds, social and cultural as well as economic and political, were multiplied, deployed with greater effectiveness, and exploited with increased efficiency.

In imperial times regions differed from one another not only in resource endowment or potential, but also in the timing and nature of the development process. And just as each developing region was distinctive, so was the system of cities that provided its skeletal structure. Thus it is that one would expect the degree of urbanization and the very characteristics of urbanism to have varied systematically from one region to another. Accordingly, I have ordered my data on cities regionally, approached urban history in the context of regional development, and analyzed urbanization separately for each physiographic region.

First-order regional units are depicted on Maps 1 and 2. Without exception they are defined in terms of drainage basins. All regional boundaries follow watersheds (except in the few places where they cross rivers) and more often than not follow the crests of mountain ranges. There were two critical questions that had to be answered in setting regional boundaries. First, in the case of great river systems spanning two or more regions, precisely where along the trunk river's course was the critical cut to be made? And second, with which regions were self-contained interior drainage basins and small river systems along the coast to be aligned? The criteria for answering these questions had to do with transport efficiency and trade flows as well as with physiography per se.

Together the nine regions include virtually all of agrarian China, i.e., that part of the empire where sedentary agriculture as traditionally practiced by the Chinese was feasible. In the west, regional boundaries were defined to exclude the arid and otherwise inhospitable basins of six rivers upstream from the cutting points shown on Map 1.[1] The Yun-Kwei region, a plateau in which virtually no rivers are navigable and all official and commercial transport moved by land, was defined to include the upper reaches of the Hung-shui (a tributary of the West River), of the Wu (a tributary of the Yangtze), and of the Chin-sha (as the Yangtze is known along its upper course) from approximately the point where each becomes unnavigable even for small junks.

For the rest, regional definitions presented few problems.[2] Lingnan is the drainage basin that includes the West, North, and East rivers. The Southeast Coast includes the basins of the myriad rivers that flow from the Wu-i mountains to the sea. The Lower Yangtze, whose core is the fertile Kiangnan area that figures so prominently in the literature on imperial China, includes the basins of the Ch'ien-t'ang and other rivers that flow into Hangchow Bay. The Middle Yangtze region includes the great basins of four major tributaries—the Han, Kan, Hsiang, and Yüan rivers. The Upper Yangtze region has as its core the fertile Red Basin of Szechwan. Northwest China, consisting in large part of the upper basin of the Yellow River, has been extended, as is customary, to include the internal drainage systems in which the chief oases of the Kansu corridor are situated. North China includes the lower basin of the Yellow River plus the drainage areas of the Huai, the Wei, and the host of smaller rivers that cross the North China Plain.

Manchuria, the ninth region of agrarian China, is excluded entirely from my analysis, as it is also from the coverage of the book as a whole. The chief reason is that settlement of the region by Han Chinese got under way on a large scale only in the last decade of the Ch'ing period. Thus Manchuria was little developed by the 1890's, and its urban system was embryonic or at best emergent; the rapid changes that were to transform Manchuria into China's most highly urbanized region were all twentieth-century developments. Moreover, it was only in the first decade of this century that the regular Chinese system of civil field administration was extended to Manchuria, so that classification of cities according to administrative rank as of 1893 is not possible for Manchuria as it is for the other eight regions. My analysis, then, covers agrarian China minus Manchuria, a total territory that is roughly equivalent (see Map 2) to the traditional "eighteen provinces" of Ch'ing China.[3]

Though the eight regions treated here are equivalent in physiographic terms, they are by no means commensurate. Table 1 shows for each the approximate area, the estimated population, and the population density as of 1843 and 1893 (1953 data are given for comparison).[4] Regional differences in area and population were reflected in the number of cities at any given level in the urban hierarchy that were "supported" by the

TABLE 1. THE MACROREGIONS OF AGRARIAN CHINA, EXCLUDING MANCHURIA: AREAS, ESTIMATED POPULATIONS, AND POPULATION DENSITIES, 1843, 1893, and 1953[a]

Macroregion	Area (sq. km.)	1843		1893		1953	
		Population in millions	Density	Population in millions	Density	Population in millions	Density
North China	746,470	112	150	122	163	174	233
Northwest China	771,300	29	38	24	31	32	42
Upper Yangtze	423,950	47	111	53	125	68	160
Middle Yangtze	699,700	84	120	75	107	92	131
Lower Yangtze	192,740	67	348	45	233	61	316
Southeast Coast[b]	226,670	27	119	29	128	36	159
Lingnan[c]	424,900	29	68	33	78	47	111
Yun-Kwei	470,570	11	23	16	34	26	55
Total	3,956,300	406	103	397	100	536	135

[a] See note 4, p. 708, for the procedures followed in constructing the estimates in this table.
[b] Includes Taiwan. The corresponding figures for the Southeast Coast region excluding Taiwan are area, 190,710 sq. km.; 1843 population, 26 million; 1843 density, 136; 1893 population, 26 million; 1893 density, 136; 1953 population, 29 million; 1953 density, 152.
[c] Includes Hainan.

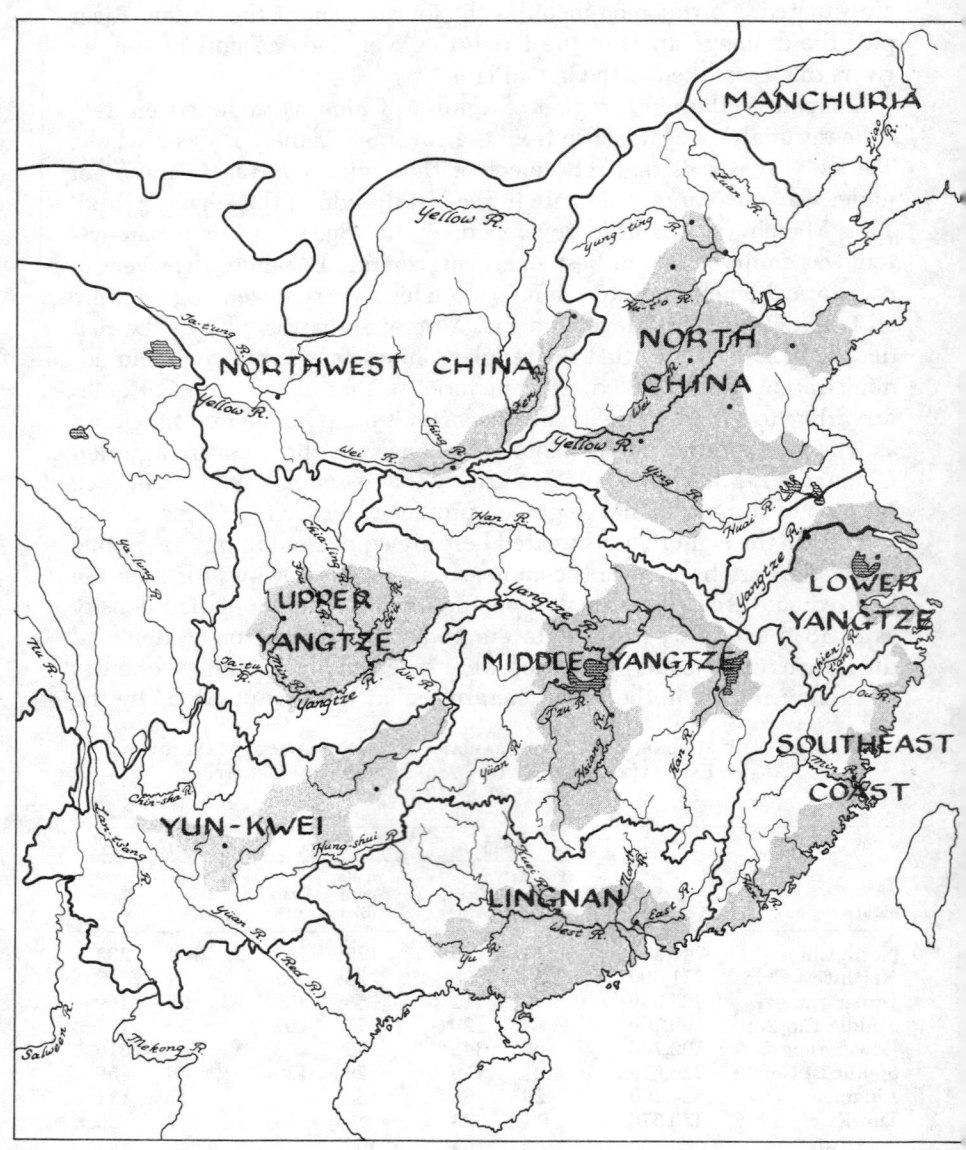

Map 1. Physiographic Macroregions of Agrarian China in Relation to Major Rivers, with Regional Cores Indicated by Shading

MAP 2. PHYSIOGRAPHIC MACROREGIONS IN RELATION TO PROVINCES, AND SHOWING METROPOLITAN CITIES, 1843

region's resources or, to turn it around, the number required to perform the region's central functions at a given level. For instance, from Map 2, which plots all metropolitan cities as of 1843, it may be seen that the Southeast Coast had only one such city, whereas at the other extreme North China had seven. (For the significance of this category of city, which performed high-order central functions, see my Part Two paper.)

In human geography, the term region refers to any partition of activity-space made according to one of two criteria: (1) the homogeneity of things to be considered, producing a set of *formal* or *uniform* regions; or (2) the interrelatedness of things to be considered, producing a set of *functional* or *nodal* regions. The regions just defined are of the second type, and if Map 1 appears novel to most readers it is because we are used to regionalizing China according to the homogeneity criterion, producing uniform regions about which generalizations can be made, whether the subject be soils, climate, agriculture, or ethnicity. In contrast to uniform regions, functional regions are internally differentiated and constitute systems in which activities of many kinds are functionally interrelated. In the regions of China under discussion here, cities are the nodes of the systems, the "command posts" that serve to articulate and integrate human activity in space and time.

We are now in a position to account in general terms for the fact that in each of the major physiographic regions there developed a reasonably discrete urban system, i.e., a cluster of cities within which interurban transactions were concentrated and whose rural-urban transactions were largely confined within the region. We start with the key fact that each region was characterized by the concentration in a central area of resources of all kinds—above all, in an agrarian society, arable land; but also, of course, population and capital investments—and by the thinning out of resources toward the periphery. As will be described in my paper in Part Two, ecological processes, natural as well as technological (e.g., the transfer of fertility through erosion, on the one hand, and the use of irrigation and of fertilizer, on the other), boosted agricultural productivity in the lowland cores. An indication of where regional resources were concentrated, Manchuria aside, is given on Map 1, where each region's area of highest population density is shaded.

It will be noted that, with the exception of Yun-Kwei, these regional "cores" are river-valley lowlands, which almost by definition had major transport advantages vis-à-vis peripheral areas. Because of the low unit cost of water as against land transport, navigable waterways dominated traffic flows in all regions except Yun-Kwei and the Northwest; and even where rivers were unnavigable their valleys typically afforded the most efficient overland routes. Thus the transport network of each region climaxed in the lowland cores, where most of the transport nodes were situated. River systems aside, the less rugged terrain of the core areas made it relatively inexpensive to build roads and canals.

For these reasons it is hardly surprising that the major cities of each region grew up in the core areas or on major transport routes leading into them, and that all cities within a physiographic region developed hierarchical transaction patterns culminating in one or more cities in the regional core.

Transactions between the centrally located cities of one region and those of another were minimized by the high cost of unmechanized transport and the great distances involved. It cost as much to transport grain 200 miles on the back of a pack animal as it did to produce it in the first place, and the corresponding figure for coal was less than 25 miles.[5] Transport costs of this order of magnitude effectively eliminated low-priced bulky goods from interregional trade. Moreover, we have to take into account the increased expense of transport in the more rugged terrain that characterized most portions of the regional peripheries; even the most advantageous routes between adjacent regions often traversed mountain passes or hazardous gorges.* It should be emphasized that systematic differences in transport efficiency affected politico-administrative and social transactions no less than commerce: interregional intercourse was depressed in all spheres.

Insofar as these general arguments can be sustained, it follows that physiographic macroregions† are the proper units for analyzing urbanization. To consider units that cover only part of a macroregion is to wrench out of context a more or less arbitrary portion of a systemic whole. This would be true even if the part were a regional subsystem of the macroregional system, for the core-periphery structure is a function of the whole rather than of its parts. For instance, the Middle Yangtze may be further regionalized into the Yangtze corridor and the basins of four major tributaries, but most of the regional core falls in the corridor and the Hsiang basin, whereas other subregions are largely or entirely peripheral. Wuhan served as the central metropolis for the entire region, not just for the corridor it dominated; and the centrality of two other major cities in the corridor, Chiu-chiang-fu and Sha-shih, also extended into one or more of the adjacent subregions. Thus the low

---

* The exceptions, navigable water routes linking macroregions, are of course crucial to an understanding of the extent and nature of interregional integration. Their effect on regional city systems is discussed below.

† When necessary to distinguish them from regional subsystems, the nine great regions of agrarian China are referred to here as "macroregions."

urbanization rate of the Han River basin, say, and the high urbanization rate of the Yangtze corridor are systemic statements about the macroregion's structure. Not one of the five regions of the Middle Yangtze is properly comparable to the Southeast Coast region, a systemic whole, despite their similarities in size. To take as units for analyzing urbanization territories that include parts of two or more macroregions is ipso facto even less defensible than to take subunits in isolation.

These principles may be illustrated with reference to provinces. Map 2 shows nineteenth-century provinces in relation to physiographic regions. Though provincial boundaries run fairly close to regional boundaries in several important stretches, even the closest fits—Szechwan with the Upper Yangtze region, Kwangsi and Kwangtung with the Lingnan region—are grossly imperfect. Several provinces lie directly athwart regional boundaries, the most striking cases being Shensi, Shansi, Anhwei, Kiangsu, Chekiang, and Kweichow. Thus, it is methodologically indefensible and generally misleading to compare provincial urbanization rates, for the explanation of differences found is a function not of what the characteristics of the provinces as systems were but simply of how the boundaries happened to be drawn. For instance, whereas a comparison of Chihli, Honan, and Shantung would probably show urbanization rates declining in that order, the differences would be in large part a simple reflection of the relative proportion of each province that lies in the core of the North China region. The inappropriateness of such a comparison is further illustrated by the fact that the hinterland of Kaifeng, the leading city of Honan in the nineteenth century, extended into southern Chihli and western Shantung, while the hinterland of Chi-ning-chou, the major city of western Shantung, included parts of Honan (not to mention Kiangsu and Anhwei.)* Urbanization aside, it is simply inefficient to describe spatial variation in China's urbanism in terms of provinces. The only way to go about making an accurate description of cities in Chekiang, or Anhwei, or Kiangsu would be to start with the basic regional dichotomy within the province and to repeat the ways in which one part of the province more closely resembles the adjacent portions of

---

* There is, of course, a very real sense in which the *administrative* cities of a province constitute an urban system. However, as I shall be at pains to point out in Part Two, the structure and functioning of field administration in a province was so strongly conditioned *in late imperial times* by the physiographic structure of macroregions and their component regions that regularities in the field-administrative system itself appear in sharpest relief when analyzed in regional terms. Nor should it be automatically assumed that the arenas of politics "in the provinces" were limited to provinces and their administrative subdivisions; physiographic regions and their subdivisions, as we shall see, were important units for political as well as economic and social transactions.

Regional Urbanization in Nineteenth-Century China

neighboring provinces than it does the other part. One can specify in the descriptions of Honan, Shensi, Kweichow, Kwangsi, and so on that a certain portion of each province falls within the maximal hinterland of the Wuhan conurbation, but the ultimate significance of these facts is lost when they are presented separately in provincial context.

Let me adduce, finally, two important reasons why a dynamic approach to urbanization and urbanism requires separate analysis by regions rather than aggregate treatment by the empire as a whole. One is that the major catastrophies that have punctuated Chinese history, the late imperial era included, were almost always limited in scope. Disastrous floods were particularly frequent in the lowland cores of North China and the Middle Yangtze. Disastrous droughts affected Northwest and North China more severely than other regions. Invasions from Inner Asia repeatedly laid waste North and Northwest China, whereas regions in the Yangtze Valley and farther south rarely suffered comparable depredations. Internal disturbances seldom wreaked havoc in more than one or two regions at a time. Chang Hsien-chung's rebellion in the 1640's, which had only minor repercussions in the Northwest and the Middle Yangtze, seriously disrupted the Upper Yangtze region and precipitated a sharp population decline there. The Taiping Rebellion in the 1850's and 1860's affected primarily the Lower Yangtze region and the Kan basin in the Middle Yangtze region. The Moslem rebellions in the 1860's and 1870's were limited to Yun-Kwei and the Northwest. Other uprisings during late imperial times were for the most part even more narrowly localized.

The second reason for eschewing an empirewide approach to urbanization, ironically enough, is that critical decisions by the *imperial* court typically induced or retarded cycles of *regional* rather than empirewide development. The shift of the imperial capital from Ch'ang-an to Kaifeng at the beginning of Northern Sung marked the onset of devolutionary decline in the Northwest even as it accelerated the regional development of North China. The selection of Hangchow as the Southern Sung capital affected development primarily within the Lower Yangtze region. The monopoly of overseas trade granted Canton in 1757, which accelerated development in the Lingnan region, doomed the economy of the Southeast Coast to nearly a century of stagnation.

Thus, despite a general tendency for the upswing phases of regional development to coincide with the dynastic heyday and for the downswing phases to coincide with dynastic decline and interdynastic disruption, the developmental cycles of the various regions had their own distinctive rhythms.[6] The relevant point here is that cycles of economic development and decline, of urban development and devolution, and of population growth and reversal within each region were closely interrelated. We can define a more developed regional economy as one in which areal specialization in production, a differentiated occupational structure, and a hierarchical system of credit supported a coordinated network of intraregional trade, and in which prevailing levels of technology were translated through myriad cumulative investment decisions into region-wide social-overhead construction (roads, bridges, canals, dikes, and irrigation works).[7] Such achievements were inseparably intertwined during the upswing of regional cycles with population growth and urban development—i.e., with growth in the size of particular cities, with the rise of new central places, with the development of hierarchical patterns in intercity transactions, and with increased centrality at all levels. Whereas the upswing of a regional cycle invariable saw progress toward a more integrated urban system, the effects of the downswing on the urban system were of variable severity, ranging from a mere slowing of growth as intercity transactions were restructured to the physical destruction of the cities and of the transport infrastructure on which their integration depended. Thus the history of each region was marked by distinctive cycles that affected both the total population and the urban population, i.e., the numerator as well as the denominator of the urbanization formula.

Urbanization in the 1890's

In general, the quality and quantity of data on the population of particular cities improves with the passage of time from the early 1840's, when the first treaties gave foreign observers access to selected Chinese cities, to the early 1950's, when China's first modern census was undertaken. Thus, the soundest procedure is to work backward in time, extrapolating better, more recent data to somewhat earlier dates, and building up a consistent time series culminating with the fairly hard data for 1953.

The first set of estimates presented are for the early 1890's. The Treaty of Shimonoseki in 1895 may be seen as something of a turning point in China's urban development, for its terms encouraged the development of modern mechanized industry in an expanded number of treaty ports and initiated an era of railroad construction. Thus the modern transformation of several regional urban systems in China effectively commenced in the late 1890's. For this reason, and also because Taiwan was lost to the empire by the terms of the same momentous treaty, it was considered desirable to select a year prior to 1895. On the other hand, the relatively abundant and reliable urban data of the 1895–1915 period commended a later rather than an earlier year for the standardization of estimates. In the end 1893 was selected, partly because it predated administrative changes made in 1894 that created certain discrepancies between the de jure and de facto administrative status of several cities, and partly because estimates for 1893 could be fitted into a decennial series culminating in 1953, the year of China's first census.

For the purpose of analyzing China's cities in 1893, I created a comprehensive file of over 2,500 data cards designed to cover every city and town that (1) served as a county- or higher-level capital or was designated a municipality at any time during the 60 years 1893–1953, (2) attained during any part of the same 60-year period the type of economic central functions symptomatic of "local" and higher-level cities in the economic hierarchy of central places, (3) reached a population of 4,000 or more during the last two decades of the Ch'ing period, and/or (4) had a population of 50,000 or more in 1953. Without doubt, the first and fourth objectives were more reliably achieved than the second and third; but the systematic inclusion of every central place—1,190 in all— where a post office of any grade (as opposed to a mere postal agency) had been opened by 1915 probably served to bring into the file the great majority of the smaller nonadministrative towns of any economic importance.

For the cities and towns in this file, population estimates and other data indicative of central functions were systematically collected from a wide variety of sources. The level and rank of every capital and the official categorizations of the top bureaucratic posts in its major yamen(s) were recorded as of 1893.[8] The circumference of the city wall was ascertained for the majority of capital cities.[9] The postal status of every city and town in the file was recorded as of 1915, including the level of the post office or agency, if any, and the specific services offered.[10] Population estimates as of about 1915 were recorded for each of the 800-odd cities and towns described in a comprehensive series of provincial gazetteers compiled by Tōa Dōbunkai.[11] Over 200 nineteenth- and early-twentieth-century gazetteers for prefectures and counties were consulted for data indicative of the size and functions of particular cities,[12] and the more important travel accounts of reliable Western observers were consulted for the period 1840–1910.[13] Trade statistics up to 1920 were compiled as available, and an effort was made to ascertain the number of merchant *hui-kuan* (native-place associations of outsiders) in cities and towns of commercial importance.[14] In order to avoid anachronistic extrapolations of population and economic functions, the date when a place was opened to steamship or rail traffic was recorded for all cities and towns that had obtained such service prior to 1912.

On the basis of these data, each central place in the file was classified on a number of dimensions, only three of which need be mentioned here, all estimated or standardized for the year 1893: population class, administrative status, and level in the economic hierarchy. The population estimates assigned particular cities and towns are, except for the largest cities, ranges rather than specific figures. To simplify estimation procedures and to facilitate mathematical manipulation, class intervals were defined so that the upper boundary of each class is twice the lower boundary;[15] and in order to avoid the coincidence of class boundaries with the round figures that are frequently encountered in population estimates (10,000, 20,000, 25,000, 50,000, 100,000, and so on), the following series was used: 1,000, 2,000, 4,000, 8,000, 16,000, 32,000, and so on.

The administrative status of cities in Ch'ing China is analyzed in some detail in my paper in Part Two; it suffices here to use a simple three-way classification that distinguishes high-level capitals, low-level capitals, and nonadministrative centers. The first category includes capitals of prefectures (*fu*) and autonomous departments (*chih-li chou*)—and, ipso facto, provincial and imperial capitals as well, since all of the latter were also prefectural capitals. The second includes capitals of counties (*hsien*), ordinary departments (*san chou*), and subprefectures (*t'ing*), autonomous as well as ordinary.

The economic hierarchy of central places in late Ch'ing times is also analyzed in my paper in Part Two; here it is necessary only to distinguish central market towns from the various levels of cities higher in the hierarchy and from other market towns lower in the hierarchy.[16] Levels in the economic hierarchy of central places are distinguished by functions such that centers at a given level supply a set of goods and services not available at lower-level places while also supplying the less specialized set of goods and services available in centers at the next lower level. Thus we may characterize the two cutting points used here by specifying a few of the services and facilities that tended to be found in the late nineteenth century in central market towns but not in intermediate market towns, and in "local cities" but not in central market towns. The list of "incremental" goods at each level was not everywhere identical (see pp. 347–51). The examples given here relate specifically to the core of the Upper Yangtze region. The first catgory, symptomatic of central market towns, included bathhouses, dyers, shops dealing solely in firecrackers and fireworks, organized prostitution, money shops, and licensed brokers. Services and facilities usually found in "local cities" (the level in the hierarchy immediately above central market towns) but not in market towns at any level included shops renting sedan chairs, tinsmiths, seal cutters, paper shops, leather-goods shops, loan and deposit banks, and commercial guilds.

We are now in a position to discuss the significance for late imperial China of different definitions of urban, and to present urbanization data by region. The term "central place" as used here may be characterized as a settlement that performs significant central functions (politico-administrative, cultural, and social, as well as economic) not only for its own population but also for a hinterland including minimally a group of nearby villages. In the context of late imperial China, all administrative capitals were central places, as were all towns that supported a periodic market. (Small settlements that supported a market are often referred to in the literature as "market villages," but in the terminology used here "village" is reserved for settlements without markets). Following this usage, I estimate that in addition to approximately 800,000 villages, the eight regions of agrarian China, excluding Manchuria and Taiwan, supported in 1893 some 39,000 central places.[17] The great majority of the latter, however, were small towns with sharply circumscribed central functions, and the problem at hand is where to draw the line between urban and nonurban central places. The distinction is normally made in terms either of population or of function.

The issues may be specified by reference to Tables 2A, 2B, and 2C. The columns of all three tables show two sets of data: figures indicating the number of central places defined by the stub and column headings; and figures indicating the combined populations of those central places. Thus, looking at the left-hand column of Table 2A, we find that the combined population of the 224 high-level capitals whose population exceeded 4,000 was 12,184,000; that the combined populations of the 442 low-level capitals whose population exceeded 4,000 was 5,801,000; and so on. Totals aside, each table has three columns (doubled in the sense already described) and three rows, and hence nine cells. Grand totals (far lower right) are the same in all tables, for they depict different tabulations of a single cumulative model whereby some 35,314,000 persons lived in the estimated 39,000 central places. The breakdowns for all cities (in the economic hierarchy), all capitals, and all central places with a population of 4,000 or more are derived from a direct count of the data cards already described. Thus, in Tables 2A and 2C the seven cells in the first column and/or the first two rows are filled by a count of particular cities and towns; figures in the remaining two cells, by con-

TABLE 2A. CENTRAL PLACES BY ADMINISTRATIVE STATUS AND POPULATION CLASS, AGRARIAN CHINA EXCEPT MANCHURIA AND TAIWAN, 1893

Administrative status	Population class							
	4,000+		2,000–3,999		Under 2,000		Totals	
	No.	Pop. (000)	No.	Pop. (000)	No.	Pop. (000)	No.	Pop. (000)
High-level capitals	224	12,184	21	63	4	7	249	12,254
Low-level capitals	442	5,801	384	1,152	471	532	1,297	7,485
Nonadm. centers	211	2,822	497	1,491	36,746	11,262	37,454	15,575
Totals	877	20,807	902	2,706	37,221	11,801	39,000	35,314

TABLE 2B. CENTRAL PLACES BY LEVEL IN THE ECONOMIC HIERARCHY AND POPULATION CLASS, AGRARIAN CHINA EXCEPT MANCHURIA AND TAIWAN, 1893

Level in the economic hierarchy	Population class							
	4,000+		2,000–3,999		Under 2,000		Totals	
	No.	Pop. (000)	No.	Pop. (000)	No.	Pop. (000)	No.	Pop. (000)
Cities	729	19,823	197	591	32	49	958	20,463
CMT's[a]	148	984	650	1,950	1,521	2,005	2,319	4,939
IMT's+SMT's[a]	0	0	55	165	35,668	9,747	35,723	9,912
Totals	877	20,807	902	2,706	37,221	11,801	39,000	35,314

[a] CMT, IMT, and SMT stand for central, intermediate, and standard market towns, respectively.

TABLE 2C. CENTRAL PLACES BY ADMINISTRATIVE STATUS AND LEVEL IN THE ECONOMIC HIERARCHY, AGRARIAN CHINA EXCEPT MANCHURIA AND TAIWAN, 1893

Administrative status	Level in the economic hierarchy							
	Cities		CMT's		IMT's and SMT's		Totals	
	No.	Pop. (000)	No.	Pop. (000)	No.	Pop. (000)	No.	Pop. (000)
High-level capitals	232	12,186	17	68	0	0	249	12,254
Low-level capitals	595	6,067	580	1,287	122	131	1,297	7,485
Nonadm. centers	131	2,210	1,722	3,584	35,601	9,781	37,454	15,575
Totals	958	20,463	2,319	4,939	35,723	9,912	39,000	35,314

trast, are the cumulation of regional estimates. The tables are constructed so that the unambiguously urban cell is at the upper left, whereas the least urban category of central places is the lower right cell.

It should be apparent that a great variety of more or less inclusive definitions of urban central places are possible. A strictly demographic definition yields 877 urban central places if the threshold of 4,000 is adopted, or 1,779 (877+902) if the line is drawn at 2,000. Functional definitions that encompass both administration and economic activities (see Table 2C) could range from the extremely exclusive "high-level capitals that are also cities in the economic hierarchy" (232 cases) to the extremely inclusive "all administrative capitals and, in the economic hierarchy, all central market towns and cities" (39,000 − 35,601 = 3,399 cases; i.e., all but the single cell defined as nonadministrative centers that were only standard or intermediate market towns in the economic hierarchy). The implications of these various definitions for the size of the urban population may be seen by reference to the figures for combined populations shown in each case to the right of the number of central places.

Five definitions of urban central places are applied to regional data in Table 3. They range from the most exclusive of the reasonable possibilities (all places with a population of 4,000 or more) to the most inclusive (all central places except those nonadministrative intermediate and standard market towns that had an estimated population below 2,000). The first thing to note is that although increasingly inclusive definitions yield a sharp growth in the number of urban central places (compare the total of 877 under the first definition with the 3,445 under the fifth), they yield much more modest increments in the total urban population (compare the 20,807,000 under the first definition with the 25,673,000 under the last). This follows directly from the obvious fact that the central places added by increasingly inclusive definitions are smaller, less populous towns. On the basis of these models, then, which exhaust the range of reasonable definitions, one can place the urban population of agrarian China in 1893 between 20.8 and 25.7 million persons, and the urbanization rate between 5.3 percent and 6.6 percent. The third and fourth definitions strike me as optimal on several counts, and thus I prefer as round estimates 23.5 million for the urban population and 6 percent for the urbanization rate.

Before turning to regional differences, a word should perhaps be said about the general level of these estimates. They are likely to seem low to most students of China, especially when juxtaposed with the markedly higher estimates for the 1920's and 1930's. Although there can be

TABLE 3. URBANIZATION BY REGION, AGRARIAN CHINA EXCEPT MANCHURIA
AND TAIWAN, 1893: FIVE DEFINITIONS[a]

Region	Estimated total pop. (in millions)	1. Demographic: 4,000+			2. Strictly functional			3. Demographic: 2,000+			4. Eclectic: Elaborate			5. Eclectic: Maximum		
		No.	Population (000)	Percent of total	No.	Population (000)	Percent of total	No.	Population (000)	Percent of total	No.	Population (000)	Percent of total	No.	Population (000)	Percent of total
Lower Yangtze	45	135	4,345	9.7%	147	4,239	9.4%	270	4,750	10.6%	261	4,710	10.5%	388	4,915	10.9%
Lingnan	33	95	2,569	7.8	162	2,635	8.0	193	2,863	8.7	213	2,888	8.8	382	3,113	9.4
Southeast Coast	26	71	1,467	5.6	100	1,493	5.7	138	1,668	6.4	143	1,663	6.4	224	1,783	6.9
Northwest China	24	57	1,130	4.7	164	1,362	5.7	114	1,301	5.4	148	1,352	5.6	293	1,506	6.3
Middle Yangtze	75	143	3,455	4.6	275	3,705	4.9	293	3,905	5.2	320	3,937	5.2	582	4,301	5.7
North China	122	236	5,053	4.1	439	5,357	4.4	488	5,809	4.8	549	5,885	4.8	975	6,454	5.3
Upper Yangtze	53	102	2,203	4.2	156	2,289	4.3	202	2,503	4.7	211	2,508	4.7	426	2,772	5.2
Yun-Kwei	16	38	585	3.7	112	738	4.6	81	714	4.5	104	747	4.7	175	829	5.2
Total	394	877	20,807	5.3%	1,555	21,818	5.5%	1,779	23,513	6.0%	1,949	23,690	6.0%	3,445	25,673	6.5%

[a] The five definitions are specified as follows.
1. All central places with estimated populations of 4,000 or more.
2. All higher-level capitals; all low-level capitals that were central market towns or cities; and all nonadministrative centers that were cities.
3. All central places with estimated populations of 2,000 or more.
4. All cities and all higher-level capitals; all low-level capitals with estimated populations of 1,000 or more if central market towns and of 2,000 or more if intermediate or standard market towns; nonadministrative centers with estimated populations of 2,000 or more if central market towns and of 4,000 or more if intermediate or standard market towns.
5. All central places except those nonadministrative intermediate and standard market towns that had estimated populations below 2,000.

little doubt that China's urbanization rate was substantially higher in 1923 and 1933 than in 1893, I consider the majority of contemporary assessments of urbanization in Republican China to err on the high side. With the hindsight provided by the 1953 census, it is clear that the populations of particular cities were overestimated far more often than underestimated[18] and that the rural population (and hence the total population) was consistently underestimated. Moreover, some of the most authoritative sources of conventional wisdom on the subject of China's urbanization are badly flawed. Two examples may be mentioned. The Hsien Survey completed in the early 1930's under the direction of J. Lossing Buck yielded an estimate for China as a whole showing 21 percent of all families resident in cities and market towns.[19] But Buck's sample was seriously biased in the direction of more urbanized *hsien*. For instance, counties situated in regional cores were disproportionately represented, and there was a consistent overrepresentation of more accessible (and hence more urbanized) counties in the peripheries of regions. A different kind of error inflates the total urban population yielded by the Trewartha and Shie series of city populations for 1949: a considerable number of duplications, the same city appearing under both its *hsien* name and its traditional *fu* name.[20] The chief difficulty with the Trewartha and Shie series, however—as with the estimates of Stauffer, Torgesheff, and the other authorities Trewartha quotes—is that the figures for particular cities are almost invariably overlarge. In general, an urbanization rate of 6 percent for 1893 appears consistent with the census data of 1953 and with what is known about urban development and demographic processes during the intervening 60 years.[21]

Turning to regional differences, we might take note from Table 3 first that four of the five definitions essentially agree in showing declining urbanization rates for the eight regions in the order in which they are listed in the table. (For reasons stemming basically from the overall sparse distribution of their populations, the strictly functional definition yields exceptionally high urbanization rates for Northwest China and Yun-Kwei.) Three regions were significantly more urbanized in 1893 than agrarian China as a whole: the Lower Yangtze, Lingnan, and the Southeast Coast, in that order. Next came Northwest China and the Middle Yangtze, with rates somewhat below the China-wide average; though the difference is minor, all five models are consistent in showing Northwest China more urbanized than the Middle Yangtze. The least urbanized regions were North China, the Upper Yangtze, and Yun-Kwei; though four of the five models give a distinct edge to North

China, there is little basis for distinguishing between the Upper Yangtze and Yun-Kwei. Note the geographical distribution of these findings (see Map 1): the three coastal regions of Central and South China were the most urbanized; next came the adjacent interior regions of the Middle Yangtze and Northwest China; third, North China; and last, the two regions in Southwest China.

Urbanization in the 1840's

There are at least two important reasons why urbanization in the late nineteenth century cannot be considered representative of late traditional patterns. One follows from the contrast between the peace and prosperity that generally prevailed in most regions of agrarian China from the 1680's through the 1840's and the violent devastation that swept six of the eight regions during the decades 1850–90. The Taiping, Nien, and Moslem Rebellions together laid waste vast areas in all regions except Lingnan and the Upper Yangtze, reduced China's total population by tens of millions, and destroyed hundreds of cities and towns. The regional urban system was shattered in the Lower Yangtze region; badly disrupted in the Northwest and in two of the five regions of the Middle Yangtze macroregion; and partially disrupted in Yun-Kwei, the Southeast Coast, and North China. Recovery in many areas was only very partial by 1893.

The second difficulty with taking urbanization in the 1890's as indicative of traditional patterns relates to the increase in foreign trade and the introduction of mechanized transport during the immediately preceding half century. The levels of overseas trade attained by 1893 were unprecedented in late imperial times (though by no means in the medieval period), and mechanized transport, which prior to 1893 was essentially limited to steamships and steam launches, was of course a wholly novel factor. As a consequence, the half century from the early 1840's to the early 1890's saw the rise of completely new port cities (e.g., Hong Kong and Swatow) and the spectacular growth of others, most notably Shanghai and Tientsin. The urban system was substantially restructured in the Lower Yangtze and significantly altered in the other three coastal regions.

For these reasons, then, it is desirable to carry the analysis back to the time of the Opium War. This I have done within the limits of available data and within the framework of a greatly simplified model.[22] It goes without saying that the estimates presented for the 1840's are less reliable than those already presented for the 1890's. Table 4 sets out the necessary figures for computing the percentage of the total

TABLE 4. URBANIZATION BY REGION, AGRARIAN CHINA EXCEPT MANCHURIA AND TAIWAN: 1843 COMPARED WITH 1893[a]

Region	Estimates for 1843				Estimates for 1893			
	No. of urban central places	Urban pop. (000)	Estimated total pop. (in millions)	Urban pop. as pct. of total	No. of urban central places	Urban pop. (000)	Estimated total pop. (in millions)	Urban pop. as pct. of total
Lower Yangtze	330	4,930	67	7.4%	270	4,750	45	10.6%
Lingnan	138	2,044	29	7.0	193	2,863	33	8.7
Southeast Coast	125	1,515	26	5.8	138	1,668	26	6.4
Northwest China	119	1,408	29	4.9	114	1,301	24	5.4
Middle Yangtze	303	3,777	84	4.5	293	3,905	75	5.2
North China	416	4,651	112	4.2	488	5,809	122	4.8
Upper Yangtze	170	1,950	47	4.1	202	2,503	53	4.7
Yun-Kwei	52	445	11	4.0	81	714	16	4.5
Total	1,653	20,720	405	5.1%	1,779	23,513	394	6.0%

[a] Urban central places are here defined as those with an estimated population of 2,000 or more.

population in each region estimated to have resided in central places of 2,000 or more in 1843, together with comparable figures for 1893. It will be noted that for the three regions hardest hit by the nineteenth-century rebellions (Lower Yangtze, Middle Yangtze, and Northwest China) the total regional population was larger in 1843 than in 1893, and that in two of those regions (Lower Yangtze and Northwest China) so too was the urban population. However, in these regions, as in all others, the proportion of the population that was urban was lower in 1843 than it was fifty years later. For agrarian China as a whole, the urban population was larger in 1893 than in 1843, perhaps by as much as three million, whereas the total population was somewhat smaller, yielding a significant increase in urbanization during the half century in question.[23] Most of the growth in the urban population must be attributed to increased commercialization, associated in the coastal regions at least with more extensive overseas trade and steam transport. However, by no means should all of this growth be attributed to exogenous factors—data on the establishment of new market towns during the Tao-kuang reign (1821–50) suggest that commercialization may have been proceeding more rapidly than population growth in many regions—and the growth that occurred during 1843–93 in the Upper Yangtze and Yun-Kwei regions had nothing to do with mechanized transport but instead must have rested almost entirely on endogenous processes.

Despite their historic significance, the momentous events of 1843–93 did not alter the relative ranking of the regions according to degree of urbanization. The three most highly urbanized regions in 1843, as in 1893, were the Lower Yangtze, Lingnan, and the Southeast Coast, in that order, and in both years the three least urbanized regions were North China, the Upper Yangtze, and Yun-Kwei.

Explaining Regional Differences

What accounts for regional differences in the urbanization rate? The sinological literature tends to emphasize the special importance of the administrative factor in China's urbanization.[24] The argument starts with the fact that most urban places in China above any reasonable size threshold were capitals, and that the population of a capital was in large part a function of the number, size, and rank of its yamens. Higher-ranking capitals had more yamens, larger yamen staffs,[25] and more official families of higher rank; and the direct effect of these factors on city size was multiplied by the presence in the city of service, commercial, and artisan personnel to meet the needs of this administrative component.

We may test this proposition by assigning population-generating values to capitals of different rank, applying these to the actual distribution of types of capitals in each region as of 1843, and comparing the predicted rates with those shown at the top of Table 4. The ratio of the values assigned to capitals of different levels and ranks roughly parallels the population averages of such capitals as computed from my numerical models: 800,000 for the imperial capital, 200,000 for a provincial capital, 30,000 for a prefectural capital, 15,000 for the capital of an autonomous department, 8,000 for the capital of an ordinary department, 7,000 for the capital of an autonomous subprefecture or of a county in a prefecture, and 5,000 for the capital of an ordinary subprefecture or of a county in an autonomous department. The results are as follows, with regions ordered according to the urbanization rate predicted by the administrative component alone.

Region	Population density, 1843 (see Table 1)	Urbanization rate predicted by adm. component, 1843	Empirically estimated urbanization rate, 1843 (see Table 4)
Yun-Kwei	23	10.7	4.1
Northwest China	35	6.0	4.9
Lingnan	67	5.1	7.0
North China	151	3.8	4.2
Southeast Coast	119	3.6	5.9
Middle Yangtze	116	3.1	4.6
Upper Yangtze	116	2.8	4.2
Lower Yangtze	322	2.1	7.9

Regional Urbanization in Nineteenth-Century China

It is immediately apparent that the proposition lacks merit. The administrative component alone predicts that Yun-Kwei would have the highest urbanization rate and the Lower Yangtze the lowest, whereas the reverse was true.

In fact, these results are less than astonishing. On first principles, we would expect the administrative component of urbanization in any area to be related inversely to the average population of the basic administrative unit (at the county level, in this case) and to the span of control within the field-administrative hierarchy. Large county populations mean fewer county-level capitals per unit of population. A broader span of control (i.e., many rather than few county-level capitals subordinate to one prefectural-level capital) means fewer higher-level capitals. In general, the average population of basic-level units is a function of population density—in sparsely populated areas administrative units tend to be relatively large in area and to have small total populations, in densely populated areas they tend to be relatively small in area and to have large total populations. And, as will be shown for late imperial China in Part Two below, span of control in the field-administrative system grew narrower with distance from the provincial capital and, within a region, was narrower by far in the low-density periphery than in the high-density core. So on both counts, one expects the administrative contribution to urbanization to be proportionately more important in areas of low population density. That this was generally so in mid-nineteenth-century China is apparent in the tabulation above, where the estimated population density of each region as of 1843 is included in order to call attention to the inverse relation between regional urbanization rates as predicted by the administrative component and the region's population density. Only North China, the region with the imperial capital, is seriously out of order in a rank correlation.

Any attempt to account for interregional differences in urbanization must cover, it seems to me, in addition to the administrative component five closely interrelated factors: population density; division of labor, as evidenced by territorial specialization within the region and between the region and territories outside it, and by occupational diversity; level of technology, with special reference to its application to transportation; degree of commercialization, as evidenced in particular by levels of intraregional trade and the relative dependence of rural households on the market; and finally levels of extraregional trade, which term is meant to include both interregional and foreign trade. Reliable measures for most of these variables are wanting, which makes it impossible to assess with any rigor what portion of the total variance is accounted for by each variable. It is even possible, given the degree of interaction among them, that one or two of these variables might prove to be wholly subsumed by the others and thus could be omitted entirely from a parsimonious explanation. Despite the redundancy, however, a qualitative discussion of these variables plus recourse to some approximate weighting can at least demonstrate that in all likelihood these are the most important factors affecting the level of urbanization in late imperial China.

Population density. In the absence of mechanized transport, a dispersed population places severe limitations on feasible levels of commercialization and revenue extraction. By increasing the costs of delivering administrative and economic services, population dispersion depresses both administrative and economic central functions. Great distances relative to the total magnitude of productivity discourage areal specialization and the division of labor. By contrast, a dense population concentrates demands for products to the point where it pays to supply many of them and concentrates sources of revenue to the point where it pays to extract them efficiently. Large accessible markets make possible good returns for investment in land, encourage cash cropping, and foster areal specification. It goes without saying that population density is itself a function of productive potential in relation to prevailing technology. Sociopolitical arrangements for extracting rents and taxes, when optimal, help in realizing the full productive and full demographic potential of an area; so also does the spread of technological innovation. Migration, the process whereby each area approaches its population potential in the long run, is of course not unrelated to transport efficiency. Weighting for population density for the various regions can be derived directly from the estimates for 1843 given in Table 1.

Division of labor. Occupational specialization has a close empirical relation to territorial specialization within a region. It requires minimal levels of technology for processing raw materials and overcoming the friction of distance. The very fact of exchange among different geographic areas means that different items are being produced, and this in turn is a basic factor in occupational differentiation. Trade requires the establishment of commercial institutions and related occupations, and the flow of raw materials in particular encourages processing to reduce bulk and enhance preservation; all of these activities stimulate industrial and commercial specialization. The division of labor is encouraged by complementary diversity within a region. In an agrarian society, it is also encouraged by a long growing season, which fosters peasant reliance on the market for nonagricultural products. The many items typically manufactured by each household for its own consumption in North and Northwest China, where the agricultural slack season averaged six months or more, were far more likely to be produced for the rural market by full-time specialists in the more southerly regions. This factor is important in accounting for the remarkably low levels of rural commercialization in North China and for the high levels found in the double-cropping areas of the more southerly regions. Weighting for the division of labor has been assigned on an impressionistic basis as follows: 5 for Lingnan, 4 for the Southeast Coast, 3.5 for the Lower Yangtze, 3 for the Upper Yangtze, 2.5 for the Middle Yangtze and Yun-Kwei, 2 for Northwest China, and 1.5 for North China.

Application of technology. Indications are that regional differentials in technological knowledge were fairly minor in the nineteenth century. In part, this follows from the fact that the most important technological innovations affecting agriculture, industry, and transport were made in the medieval rather than in the late imperial period.[26] The printing press, official encouragement of agricultural activity, the practice of rotating bureaucratic officials from one province to another, and interregional movements of merchants together sufficed to ensure diffusion throughout the empire of any useful innovation within a century or two.[27] The important differentials here relate to the extent to which the natural endowments of the various regions provided scope for particular technologies and to the availability of capital. The single most important application of technology in China, in terms of its effect on urbanization, was that to water transport. The scope for the elaborate Chinese technical repertoire as it related to shipbuilding, navigation, canals, locks, and waterworks of all kinds[28] is in the first instance a function of physiographic givens within a region, especially the structure of the river system and prevailing terrain characteristics. But this potential can be realized only through capital investment, which points to a feedback loop between transport efficiency and all the factors that tend to concentrate capital in more urbanized areas. Efficient transport acts as a booster to every other factor in this multivariate analysis: it encourages population growth, territorial specialization, rural commercialization, and both intra- and extraregional trade. Weightings for technological application have been assigned impressionistically as follows: 6 for the Lower Yangtze, 5 for Lingnan, 3.5 for the Southeast Coast, 3 for the Middle Yangtze and Northwest China, 2.5 for the Upper Yangtze and North China, and 1.5 for Yun-Kwei.

Commercialization and intraregional trade. Rural commercialization, i.e., the extent to which farm households are self-sufficient or dependent on the market, is so closely intertwined with the amount and structure of intraregional trade as to render separate treatment bootless. Given certain thresholds of population density and technological level, rural commercialization increases in direct response to population growth and investment in more efficient transport, for the former increases demand density whereas the latter enlarges the demand cone for particular goods. Patterns of commercialization, however, are by no means a simple function of transport efficiency, for they depend on the absolute distances over which different types of transport prevail (i.e., to accessibility) and on the comparative advantages of climate, soil, and other givens which together create a potential for territorial specialization. Moreover, there is clear evidence for China that increased extraregional trade directly stimulated commercialization within the hinterland of the regional trading center.[29] Weightings for this factor must be estimated on a per capita basis: the proportion of households more or less dependent on the market, or the absolute amount of interregional trade divided by the total population. I have assigned weightings as follows: 6 for the Lower Yangtze, 5 for the Southeast Coast, 4.5 for Lingnan, 3 for Northwest China, 2.5 for North China and the Middle and Upper Yangtze regions, and 1 for Yun-Kwei.

Extraregional trade. We start here with geographic givens. Because of the overwhelming importance of water transport in interregional trade, its spatial structure was dominated by the great sideways T that tied together five of China's eight regions. The Lower Yangtze was the cross of the T whose leg to the west was the Yangtze, whose arm to the north was the Grand Canal, and whose arm to the south was the sea route to the major ports of the Southeast Coast and Lingnan. Along these routes flowed the bulk of China's interregional trade.[30] The Yangtze gorges, the San-men Gorge, and high mountain barriers minimized the trade of the Upper Yangtze, Yun-Kwei, and the Northwest with the other five regions.[31] On the side of foreign trade, the Northwest dominated overland routes and in all probability supported more overland trade with areas outside agrarian China than the other three regions fronting on Inner Asia combined. Prior to the 1830's, Lingnan had a strong lead in China's overseas trade, owing in part to its southerly location somewhat closer to ports in Southeast Asia and the Indian Ocean but more importantly to the deliberate imperial policy favoring Canton. Data assembled by Dwight H. Perkins permit a rough estimation of the volume of extraregional trade by region as of the 1890's, but these must be adjusted in certain instances for application to the 1840's.[32] The weightings adopted for 1843, once again conceived in per capita terms, are as follows: 8 for the Lower Yangtze and Lingnan, 6 for the Southeast Coast, 5.5 for the Middle Yangtze, 5 for Northwest China, 4 for North China, 3.5 for the Upper Yangtze, and 1.5 for Yun-Kwei.

Administration. This variable has already been treated. The weightings used are a direct translation of the "urbanization rates" that would be expected if the administrative component were the sole determinant. (The putative rates and the basis for their calculation were set out on p. 230 above.) It remains only to note that, as measured, this variable takes into account the average size of county-level units in each region, which factor in turn relates importantly not only to population density but also to the rate of population growth between the 1720's, when the Ch'ing system of field administration was essentially stabilized, and the 1840's. For instance, in the Upper Yangtze, which experienced a veritable population explosion during the period specified, county-level units were markedly larger in 1843 than predicted by population density.

This discussion has emphasized the interaction of each variable with at least some of the others, and pointed to probable redundancies.[33] Nonetheless, it is not wholly egregious simply to add together the

TABLE 5. DETERMINANTS OF REGIONAL LEVELS OF URBANIZATION, 1843: A MODEL USING RELATIVE WEIGHTS

Weightings for determinants	Lower Yangtze	Lingnan	Southeast Coast	Northwest China	Middle Yangtze	North China	Upper Yangtze	Yun-Kwei
Population density	7.0	1.5	2.6	0.8	2.5	3.3	2.5	0.5
Division of labor	3.5	5.0	4.0	2.0	2.5	1.5	3.0	2.5
Application of technology	6.0	5.0	3.5	3.0	3.0	2.5	2.5	1.5
Intraregional commercialization	6.0	4.5	5.0	3.0	2.5	2.5	2.5	1.0
Extraregional trade	8.0	8.0	6.0	5.0	5.5	4.0	3.5	1.5
Administrative component	1.8	4.3	3.0	5.0	2.6	3.1	2.4	9.0
Sum of six weightings	32.3	28.3	24.1	18.8	18.6	16.9	16.4	16.0
Index (sum x .248)	8.0	7.0	6.0	4.7	4.6	4.2	4.1	4.0
Urbanization rates for 1843 (%)	7.9	7.0	5.9	4.9	4.6	4.2	4.2	4.1

assigned weightings and take note of how well they account for regional variation in urbanization rates. From Table 5, where the sums of the six weightings are uniformly reduced by the factor needed to bring them into the range of estimated urbanization rates, it can be seen that the fit is quite good. Without exception, the sum of the weightings predicts the ranking of the eight regions according to urbanization in 1843.[34] This suggests that the major determinants of urbanization levels in late imperial China may in fact have been isolated and points the way toward an interaction model of premodern urbanization in which the relative importance of particular causal flows can be more precisely identified.

It is of some interest to note the ease with which the theoretical framework developed by Jack P. Gibbs and Walter J. Martin for the analysis of variation in urbanization levels between modern nations[35] can be respecified for the analysis of variation among regions in a large premodern society. The major variables in Gibbs's and Martin's analysis are technological development, division of labor, and "the dispersion of objects of consumption." This last variable, characterized elsewhere as "organization to requisition dispersed materials," is defined as "the average distance between the points of origin of raw materials and the points at which the materials are consumed."[36] Two types are distinguished, "internal dispersion" when both points are within the society's border and "external dispersion" when one point lies outside the society. These two variables, then, are but an abstracted version of my "intraregional commercialization" and "extraregional trade" applied to nations rather than to regions. Gibbs's and Martin's paradigm might well be extended to include population density, which has been shown empirically to be a partially independent determinant of urbanization rates within such large modern nations as the Soviet Union,[37] and on first principles ought to relate with equal force to international differences. It is possible that what I have isolated here as the "administrative component" is to a considerable extent subsumed in Gibbs's and Martin's more inclusive and generic version of the division of labor.

Rank-Size Relationships by Region

Additional insight into regional urbanization in late imperial China may be obtained from a comparison of rank-size distributions of the eight urban systems that have been identified. Over thirty years ago, G. K. Zipf observed a statistical regularity in city-size distributions: if the cities of a country or region are arranged in order of size, the second largest city is likely to have about half the population of the largest city, the third city about one-third the population of the largest city, and so on.[38] If the population of cities in a group are plotted on one axis of double-log graph paper and their rank on the other, Zipf's empirical rule amounts to the prediction that the distribution will approximate a straight line at an angle of 45°, i.e., a slope of −1.00. If the cities of various regions are so plotted, departures from "normal" distributions are graphically revealed.

Figure 1 shows rank-size distributions of urban central places for each of the eight regions, city population estimates for 1843 having been plotted on identical double-log grids. The most populous 25 cities are separately plotted on each chart, and cities with a population over 50,000 as of 1843 are labeled. Below rank 25, plottings are limited to places at set intervals: every fifth city to rank 50, every tenth to rank 150, and every fiftieth thereafter. Needless to say, the distributions at the lower end of the scale are no more than estimates derived from the numerical models already introduced. Each chart theoretically plots all central places with a population of 1,000 or more. In the eight regions treated, their number ranges from a low of 110 for Yun-Kwei, the least populous region, to a high of 830 for North China, the most populous region. For consistent reference, a −1.00 slope line is shown on each chart crossing the horizontal x axis (which in the format adopted here is the 1,000 population line) at the rank of the smallest central place shown. Double-log graph paper is so constructed that a slope line drawn from the intersection of rank 110 with the 1,000-population line, as on the Yun-Kwei chart, intersects the vertical y axis at population 110,000. Similarly, on the chart for North China, which has 830 central places with a population of 1,000 or more, the slope line runs from rank 830 on the x axis to population 830,000 on the y axis. Zipf's empirical rule, then, leads us to expect that the largest city in Yun-Kwei would have a population of 110,000, the second largest 55,000, etc., and that the largest city in North China would have a population of 830,000, the second largest 415,000, and so on down the line.

Let us first examine these distributions for primacy, a feature of urban systems that is said to obtain when the largest city contains a disproportionate share of the urban population.[39] A survey of the eight charts reveals two clear-cut cases of primacy, namely in Lingnan and North China. If we adopt as a primacy index the ratio of the population of the largest city to the combined population of the nine next largest cities,[40] then the index number is 1.02 for Canton in Lingnan and .86 for Peking in North China. The next largest index number, .64 for Sian in North-

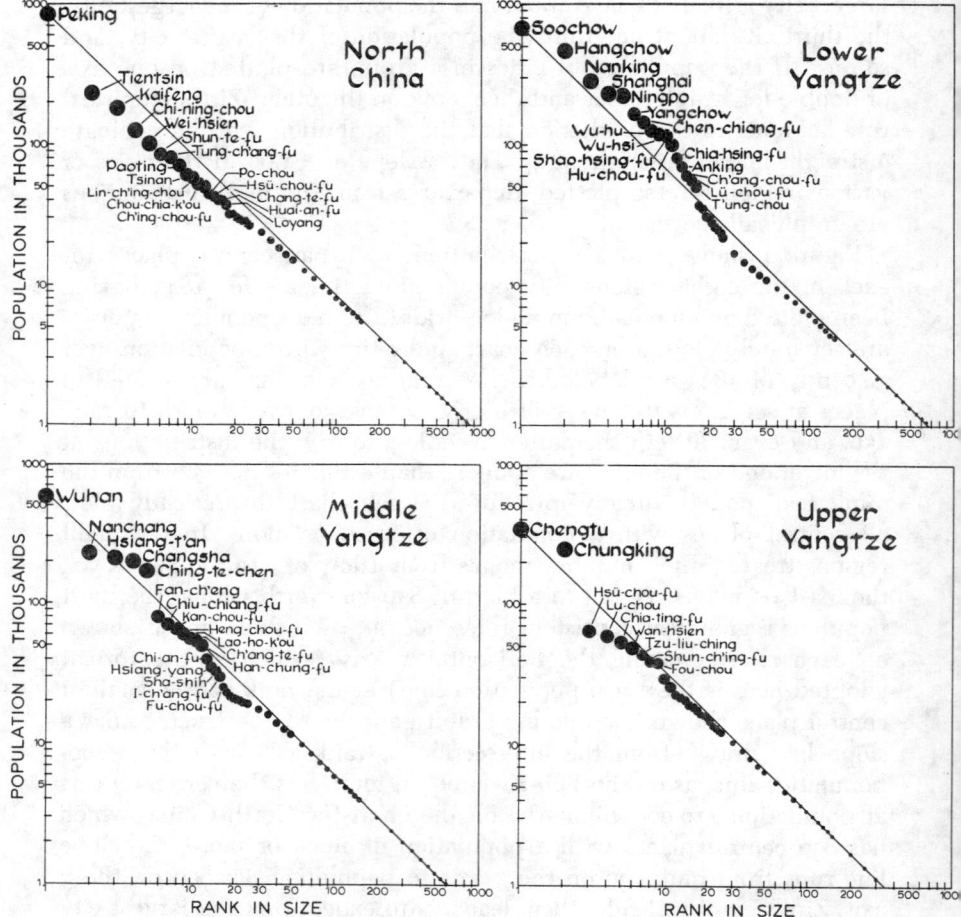

FIG. 1. RANK-SIZE DISTRIBUTION OF URBAN CENTRAL PLACES, BY REGION, 1843

east China, somewhat above the theoretical threshold of primacy, cannot be accepted as a reliable indication of primacy since Sian's "excess" population comes close to the likely margin of error in estimating city populations.

On the face of it, primacy indicates an excess of centrality and suggests either an extraordinary centralization of regional services or a role for the primate city that extends beyond its regional hinterland.[41] Peking's regional primacy as of 1843 obviously stemmed from its status as imperial capital. In civil and military administration, it performed

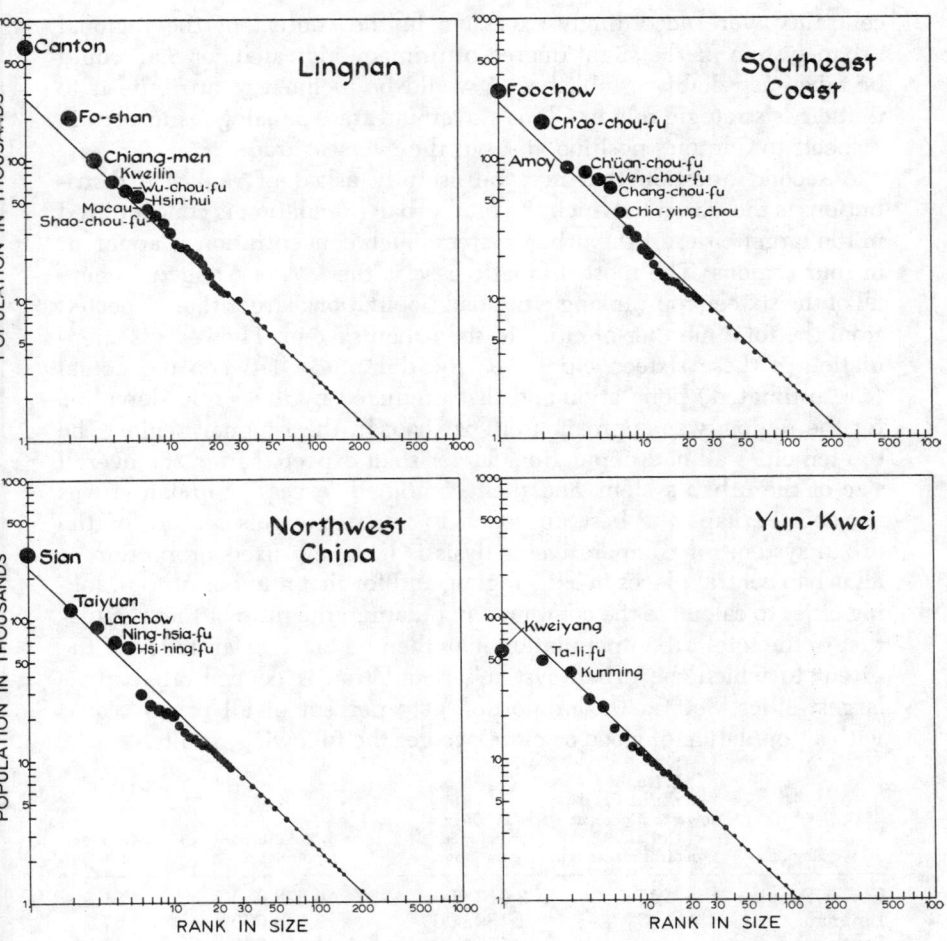

FIG. 1. (CONTINUED)

central functions for the empire as a whole. Moreover, it requisitioned from regions beyond North China resources in the form of cash revenue, tribute grain, and luxury goods for the court and capital bureaucrats. The cause of Canton's primacy in the 1840's is scarcely less obvious. During most of the preceding century, the imperial court had reserved for Canton a virtual monopoly of the empire's overseas trade and designated that city as the port of entry for several important tribute missions.[42] In these respects, then, Canton performed functions for the entire empire, not simply for the Lingnan region, and its population and centrality were accordingly excessive in the context of the regional urban system. If the slight degree of primacy indicated for Sian could be taken as reliably established, I would be inclined to attribute it to that city's strategic role in China's overland trade, analogous in certain respects to Canton's position vis-à-vis the overseas trade.

A second question that may be usefully asked of rank-size distributions is the extent to which the total urban population is concentrated in the larger cities of the urban system. Such concentration is apparent in four regions. The most dramatic case is the Lower Yangtze, where all of the sixteen top-ranking cities had populations larger than expected from the total number of cities in the urban system. The "excess" population in these sixteen cities, i.e., the difference between the actual (i.e., estimated) population and that predicted by the -1.00 slope line for the region, was approximately 620,000. In the Lingnan region, the top ten cities all had populations larger than expected from the overall size of the urban system, and their combined "excess" population was 460,000. Perhaps the best approach to measuring this feature of the urban system for comparative analysis is to take a fixed proportion of all urban central places in each region, and for that number of top-ranking cities to calculate the combined population; the ratio of that population to the total urban population may then be taken as an index of the extent to which the urban system's population is concentrated in its largest cities. Setting the proportion at 5 percent of all urban places with a population of 2,000 or more, we get the following results.

Region	1. No. of largest cities down to 5 percent of all central places	2. Their combined population	3. Total urban population	4. Index (2 ÷ 3)
Lower Yangtze	17	3,013,000	4,878,000	61.8
Lingnan	7	1,180,000	2,044,000	57.7
Southeast Coast	6	775,000	1,513,000	51.2
Middle Yangtze	15	1,928,000	3,776,000	51.1
Upper Yangtze	9	954,000	1,949,000	48.9
North China	21	2,250,000	4,648,000	48.4
Northwest China	6	675,000	1,407,000	48.0
Yun-Kwei	3	125,000	420,000	29.8

In respect to this feature, then, the regions fall into four groups. In the Lower Yangtze and Lingnan regions, the urban population is heavily concentrated in the regions' largest cities. In the Southeast Coast and Middle Yangtze there is a moderate concentration. Yun-Kwei falls at the other extreme, its urban population being concentrated in small cities and towns, with the largest cities smaller than expected. The remaining three regions show a fairly even distribution of the urban population between the largest cities and smaller cities and towns.

This feature of regional urban systems appears to be closely linked to extraregional trade.[43] The weightings assigned each region on this variable in Table 5, based in large part on the data assembled by Dwight H. Perkins, are in general agreement with these index figures; they show the same ordering for the top four regions, with a break between the first and second pairs, and they show Yun-Kwei sharply differentiated from the others at the bottom of the list. Thus, we may tentatively hypothesize that the increment to the population of cities within a region that may be attributed to extraregional trade disproportionately accrued to the top-ranking cities. Turning the proposition around, when a region's largest cities were exceptionally large, their excess centrality may in all probability be attributed to relatively heavy participation in the region's external trade. Our reasoning concerning Canton's regional primacy accords with this proposition, as does the fact that large industrial cities whose population in 1843 was overlarge for their rank (e.g., Ching-te-chen, Fo-shan, Wu-hsi) all specialized in the production of export items.

The most important of the clues offered by a comparative analysis of rank-size distributions concerns the relative integration of the various regional systems. A distribution showing a low slope among the larger cities is indicative of very imperfect integration at the level in question.[44] A "flattop" distribution of this kind appears in only one of the eight macroregions, namely Yun-Kwei, where the leading cities all show a deficit of centrality. As of the 1840's, in fact, Yun-Kwei might best be seen as a congeries of five small, fairly autonomous central-place systems whose centers were widely dispersed in terms of travel time and only very tenuously interrelated. By the 1890's, the dominance of Kweiyang and Kunming was more pronounced and their deficit of centrality less marked, but a fully integrated urban system was achieved in this plateau only after the close of the imperial era. The rank-size distribution for Yun-Kwei, then, suggests an urban system that was at best emergent in 1843.

Greater but still markedly imperfect functional integration is indicated by a "layered" distribution in which one or two leading cities of "expected" centrality form the top layer. Such a distribution points to strong regionalization within the urban system.[45] The distribution shown in Figure 1 for the Southeast Coast is prototypical. There the two top-ranking cities, Foochow and Ch'ao-chou-fu, constitute one layer, while the next four form another, each with a slope more gentle than 45°. Similar layering characterizes the Upper Yangtze, where Chengtu and Chungking form a top layer and the seven cities ranking below them form a second. As Chauncy D. Harris notes with respect to countries, "The existence of two or several large cities of more nearly the same size than might be expected by the rank-size rule ... is suggestive of residual regionalization," and he cites contemporary Spain with Madrid and Barcelona, Australia with Sydney and Melbourne, and Brazil with Rio de Janeiro and São Paulo.[46] This principle clearly applies to China's regional systems in the 1840's. Strong subregionalization characterized the Southeast Coast, where each major river basin is fairly well isolated by mountains from its neighbors. Moreover, the location of Foochow, the region's metropolitan city, somewhat to the north of the region's center, enhanced the centrality of Ch'ao-chou-fu, the most southerly regional city. Similarly, the Upper Yangtze region was fairly sharply divided between the economic spheres of influence of its two largest cities (see Map 1, p. 289, for a demarcation), and the structure of the river system fostered subregionalization within those great subregions.

Layering is also readily apparent in the chart for the Middle Yangtze, where, however, the top "layer" consists of a single city, the metropolitan center of Wuhan. This is exactly what might be expected from the internal structure of that region. The lowland Yangtze corridor is flanked by four regions, each dominated by a major river system and rimmed by mountains except where the tributary rivers flow into the corridor. Thus, though Wuhan, which dominates the corridor, is unique in having ready access to all of the region's other major cities, and though the corridor cannot be considered an autonomous region in its own right, rather sharp regionalization characterized each of the four tributary basins.

The rank-size distributions for the remaining four macroregions, each rather distinctive, nonetheless reveal little residual subregionalization. The relatively steep slope of the Lingnan urban system as a whole, and the relatively gentle slope of the North China urban system as a whole, may reflect a particularly sharp contrast between these two regions in the pervasiveness of commercialization. Imperial policies were designed to minimize commercialization within the region of most direct imperial control, and in fact the means whereby Peking was provisioned did more to stimulate commercial activity within the Lower Yangtze and Lingnan regions than in North China itself.[47] I have no consistent explanation for the peculiar outline of the overall rank-size distribution for the Lower Yangtze, which, as it happens, closely resembles that for Poland in 1960.[48] The slight tendency toward layering that may be detected in the chart for Northwest China suggests an urban system that was somewhat less well integrated than those of Lingnan, the Lower Yangtze, and North China.

The Lower Yangtze and North China Compared

It should be apparent from the brief analysis of rank-size distribution just concluded that urbanization rates alone do not begin to suggest the basic nature of variation among China's regional urban systems. Regions with identical urbanization rates may differ with respect to degree of primacy in the urban system, the distribution of the urban population in the size range from large cities to small towns, and the level of integration achieved by their respective urban systems. But even rank-size analysis cannot speak directly to functional differentiation within an urban system. I want now to extend our analysis in that direction in a comparison of the Lower Yangtze, the most urbanized region, with North China, one of the least. For these two regions only, I have endeavored to gather the data needed to flesh out in full for 1843 numerical models comparable to those constructed for all regions as of 1893.

Tables 6A and 6B bring urban functions into the analysis of regional differences by showing for the urban central places in each region their administrative status and level in the economic hierarchy. Table 6A directly compares in three cross-tabulations the 432 urban central places in the Lower Yangtze region with the 875 urban central places in North China. Table 6B presents in identical format cross-tabulations for the more nearly equal urban populations of the two regions, approximately 5.1 million for the Lower Yangtze and 5.3 million for North China. That we are dealing with urban populations of similar size, even though North China's total population in 1843 was nearly twice that of the Lower Yangtze, dramatizes the sharp contrast between the two regions in the extent of urbanization. Just what that difference implies for distribution of urban places by size may be seen in the right marginals (totals column) of the upper-tier cross-tabulations of both tables. Note in Table 6A, for instance, that the proportion of all urban places that had a population under 2,000 was less than a quarter in the Lower Yangtze but more than a half in North China; and in Table 6B that the proportion of the urban population resident in urban places of less than 4,000 was only thirteen percent for the Lower Yangtze as against 26 percent for North China. The marginals of the upper tier in Table 6B also serve to underline one of the points revealed by rank-size analysis,

TABLE 6A. COMPARATIVE URBANIZATION OF THE LOWER YANGTZE AND NORTH CHINA REGIONS, 1843: URBAN CENTRAL PLACES BY POPULATION CLASS, ADMINISTRATIVE STATUS, AND LEVEL IN THE ECONOMIC HIERARCHY[a]

Lower Yangtze

Population class	Administrative status							Totals	
	High-level capitals		Low-level capitals		Nonadm. centers				
	No.	Pct.	No.	Pct.	No.	Pct.		No.	Pct.
Over 16,000	17	68	12	11	2	1		31	7
8,000–15,999	7	28	24	22	12	4		43	10
4,000–7,999	0	0	37	34	48	16		85	20
2,000–3,999	1	4	25	23	145	48		171	40
Under 1,999	0	0	10	9	92	31		102	24
Totals	25	100	108	100	299	100		432	100

Population class	Level in the economic hierarchy							Totals	
	Cities		Market towns		Nonadm. centers				
	No.	Pct.	No.	Pct.	No.	Pct.		No.	Pct.
Over 16,000	31	26	0	0	0	0		31	7
8,000–15,999	36	31	7	2	2	1		43	10
4,000–7,999	43	36	42	13	13	4		85	20
2,000–3,999	8	7	163	52	52	17		171	40
Under 1,999	0	0	102	32	32	11		102	24
Totals	118	100	314	100	299	100		432	100

Level in the economic hierarchy	Administrative status							Totals	
	High-level capitals		Low-level capitals		Nonadm. centers				
	No.	Pct.	No.	Pct.	No.	Pct.		No.	Pct.
Cities	24	96	72	67	22	7		118	27
Market towns	1	4	36	33	277	93		314	73
Totals	25	100	108	100	299	100		432	100

North China

Population class	Administrative status							Totals	
	High-level capitals		Low-level capitals		Nonadm. centers				
	No.	Pct.	No.	Pct.	No.	Pct.		No.	Pct.
Over 16,000	29	51	9	2	4	1		42	5
8,000–15,999	14	25	31	8	8	2		53	6
4,000–7,999	10	18	71	19	27	6		108	12
2,000–3,999	3	5	115	31	95	21		213	24
Under 1,999	1	2	144	39	314	70		459	52
Totals	57	100	370	100	448	100		875	100

Population class	Level in the economic hierarchy							Totals	
	Cities		Market towns		Nonadm. centers				
	No.	Pct.	No.	Pct.	No.	Pct.		No.	Pct.
Over 16,000	42	17	0	0	0	0		42	5
8,000–15,999	51	20	2	—	—	—		53	6
4,000–7,999	81	32	27	4	4	1		108	12
2,000–3,999	66	26	147	24	24	5		213	24
Under 1,999	10	4	449	72	72	16		459	52
Totals	250	100	625	100	448	100		875	100

Level in the economic hierarchy	Administrative status							Totals	
	High-level capitals		Low-level capitals		Nonadm. centers				
	No.	Pct.	No.	Pct.	No.	Pct.		No.	Pct.
Cities	51	89	179	48	20	4		250	29
Market towns	6	11	191	52	428	96		625	71
Totals	57	100	370	100	448	100		875	100

[a] The definition of urban central place followed here is the "Eclectic: Maximum" of Table 3, i.e., all central places except those nonadministrative intermediate and standard market towns that had estimated populations below 2,000.

TABLE 6B. COMPARATIVE URBANIZATION OF THE LOWER YANGTZE AND NORTH CHINA REGIONS, 1843: URBAN POPULATION (IN THOUSANDS) BY POPULATION CLASS, ADMINISTRATIVE STATUS, AND LEVEL IN THE ECONOMIC HIERARCHY[a]

Lower Yangtze

Population class	High-level capitals		Low-level capitals		Nonadm. centers		Totals	
	Pop.	Pct.	Pop.	Pct.	Pop.	Pct.	Pop.	Pct.
Over 16,000	2,628	97	715	54	48	5	3,391	67
8,000–15,999	84	3	288	22	144	14	516	10
4,000–7,999	0	0	222	17	288	28	510	10
2,000–3,999	3	–	75	6	435	42	513	10
Under 1,999	0	0	14	1	130	12	144	3
Totals	2,715	100	1,314	100	1,045	100	5,074	100

Administrative status

Population class	Cities		Market towns		Nonadm. centers		Totals	
	Pop.	Pct.	Pop.	Pct.	Pop.	Pct.	Pop.	Pct.
Over 16,000	3,391	83	0	0	0	0	3,391	67
8,000–15,999	432	11	84	9	216	21	516	10
4,000–7,999	258	6	252	26	829	79	510	10
2,000–3,999	24	1	489	50	—	—	513	10
Under 1,999	0	0	144	15	—	—	144	3
Totals	4,105	100	969	100	1,045	100	5,074	100

Level in the economic hierarchy (Lower Yangtze)

Level in the economic hierarchy	High-level capitals		Low-level capitals		Nonadm. centers		Totals	
	Pop.	Pct.	Pop.	Pct.	Pop.	Pct.	Pop.	Pct.
Cities	2,712	100	1,177	90	216	21	4,105	81
Market towns	3	–	137	10	829	79	969	19
Totals	2,715	100	1,314	100	1,045	100	5,074	100

North China

Population class	High-level capitals		Low-level capitals		Nonadm. centers		Totals	
	Pop.	Pct.	Pop.	Pct.	Pop.	Pct.	Pop.	Pct.
Over 16,000	2,293	91	313	19	122	11	2,728	52
8,000–15,999	168	7	372	23	96	9	636	12
4,000–7,999	60	2	426	26	162	15	648	12
2,000–3,999	9	–	345	21	285	26	639	12
Under 1,999	2	–	169	10	430	39	601	11
Totals	2,532	100	1,625	100	1,095	100	5,252	100

Level in the economic hierarchy

Population class	Cities		Market towns		Nonadm. centers		Totals	
	Pop.	Pct.	Pop.	Pct.	Pop.	Pct.	Pop.	Pct.
Over 16,000	2,728	68	0	0	0	0	2,728	52
8,000–15,999	612	15	24	2	2	2	636	12
4,000–7,999	486	12	162	13	13	13	648	12
2,000–3,999	198	5	441	36	36	36	639	12
Under 1,999	15	–	586	48	48	48	601	11
Totals	4,039	100	1,213	100	1,095	100	5,252	100

Administrative status (North China)

Level in the economic hierarchy	High-level capitals		Low-level capitals		Nonadm. centers		Totals	
	Pop.	Pct.	Pop.	Pct.	Pop.	Pct.	Pop.	Pct.
Cities	2,506	99	1,282	79	251	23	4,039	77
Market towns	26	1	343	21	844	77	1,213	23
Totals	2,532	100	1,625	100	1,095	100	5,252	100

[a] By urban population is meant the combined population of the urban central places as defined in Table 6A.

namely that the Lower Yangtze's urban population was heavily concentrated in large cities whereas North China's was not: two-thirds of all urbanites in the Lower Yangtze as of 1843 resided in cities with populations larger than 16,000, whereas the corresponding proportion for North China was only slightly more than half.

It follows from the urbanization differential that capitals at all levels would tend to be more populous in the Lower Yangtze than in North China. The top tier of Table 6A reveals a sharp difference in this regard; note, for instance, that county-level capitals of North China tended to be much smaller than those of the Lower Yangtze: 70 percent under 4,000 as against only 32 percent. The mean population of county-level capitals in the Lower Yangtze was approximately 12,200, whereas for North China it was only 4,400. And for high-level capitals, the difference in means was only slightly less marked: 109,000 for the Lower Yangtze versus 44,000 for North China. These differences, in fact, are sharper than anticipated in terms of urbanization levels alone. A fuller explanation must take into account the proportion of urban places that served as capitals—and this ratio was markedly higher in North China than in the Lower Yangtze (49 percent as against 31 percent). The explanation for this difference, as might be expected from the earlier discussion of the administrative component of urbanization, is that county-level units were less populous in North China (an average population of 303,000 versus 574,000 for the Lower Yangtze) and the span of control broader (on the average seven county-level units in each prefectural-level unit versus five for the Lower Yangtze). County-level units were smaller in North China in part because the population density was lower (151 in 1843 versus 322 for the Lower Yangtze) and in part because of administrative lag in readjusting field administration to changing circumstances, the basic arrangement of counties and capitals having been laid down in North China at an earlier historical period than in the Lower Yangtze. The span of control was broad in North China precisely because it was the metropolitan region. As we shall see in some detail in Part Two, where the Ch'ing government found the logistics of administrative control difficult, the span of control was narrowed in compensation. Holding other factors constant, then, the span of control narrowed with distance from Peking, and we ought therefore to expect a smaller ratio in the Lower Yangtze than in North China. Thus it is that with proportionately fewer of its central places large and proportionately more of them capitals, North China necessarily saw far more of its county-level capitals located in small towns than did the Lower Yangtze.

When we turn from the administrative to the economic hierarchy of central places (see the second tier of tabulations in Table 6A and 6B), a comparison of the two regions reveals a similar displacement of functions down the population scale in North China. Whereas in the Lower Yangtze only 7 percent of cities (as contrasted with market towns in the economic hierarchy) had populations of 4,000 or less, the comparable figure for North China was 30 percent. There was, however, no counterpart on the side of economic functions to the sharp contrast between the two regions in the proportion of urban places that performed administrative functions. If anything, the proportion of urban places that ranked as cities in the economic hierarchy was higher in the Lower Yangtze than in North China. (Note the right-hand marginals in the third tier of Table 6A.) The paradoxical consequence of the overabundance of administrative centers in North China coupled with the slight preponderance of high-level economic centers in the Lower Yangtze is that the proportion of capitals that also served as cities in the economic hierarchy was far higher in the Lower Yangtze than in North China, as shown in the third-tier tabulations in Table 6A.

The systematic differences among China's regional urban systems that have been pointed up in this and the two preceding sections raise a thorny methodological issue. The simple fact is that the quantity and quality of our sources about traditional Chinese cities are a function of characteristics of the urban systems themselves. It can be readily demonstrated that more urbanized prefectures had better developed educational systems, produced proportionately more scholars, and diverted more resources per capita to scholarship. In such areas the quality of local gazetteers was generally higher, and editions tended to appear more frequently and with greater regularity. Moreover, in regional cores, which were richer in resources and more commercialized than their peripheries, scholarship was more heavily subsidized from private sources, and the reduced reliance on bureaucratic support meant that gazetteers and other relevant sources were less biased in the direction of official stereotypes. Modern scholars have quite naturally concentrated on those areas for which local sources are more abundant, more detailed, and more objective—which under the circumstances has meant the more urbanized as against the less urbanized regions, and regional cores as against regional peripheries. Thus the secondary literature on Chinese urbanism and urbanization is itself strongly biased. The Canton delta is not Lingnan, nor is the Wei-Fen crescent representative of the Northwest. Above all, Kiangnan is not China.[49] Attention to regions, to

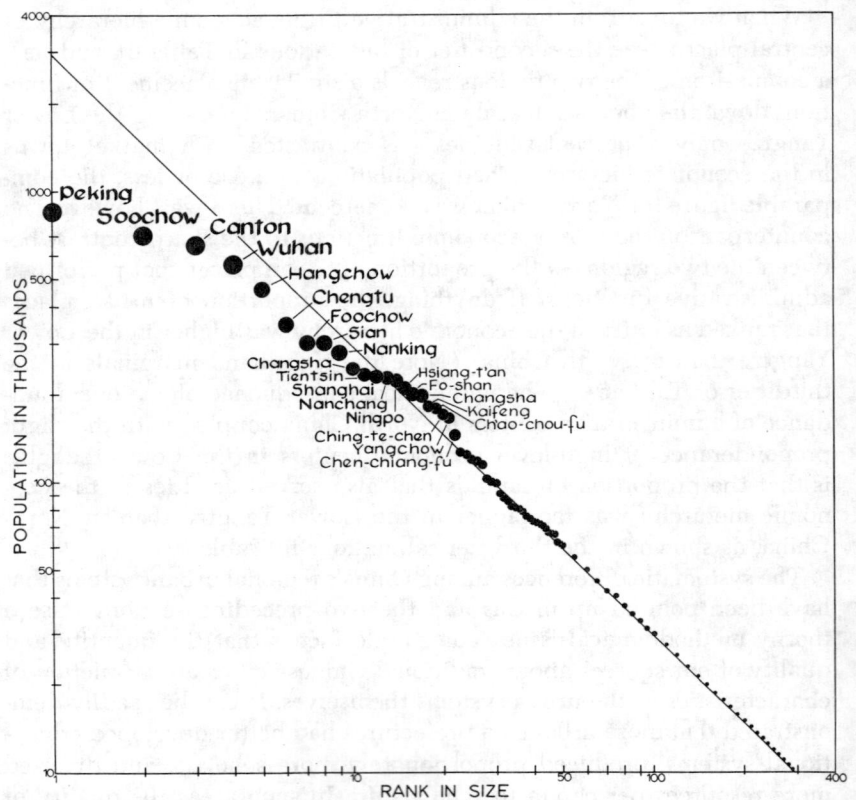

Fig. 2. Rank-Size Distribution of Cities with a Population of 10,000 or More, Agrarian China Except Manchuria and Taiwan, 1843

their internal structure and their systemic processes, is essential if we are to put Chinese urban phenomena in balanced perspective. Generalization must be informed by considerations of spatial and temporal structure.

Rank-Size and the Integration of Regions

Finally, let us return to the rank-size distribution of cities, this time in the context of agrarian China as a whole. As of 1843, the eight regions of agrarian China combined included some 292 cities with an estimated population of 10,000 or more.[50] The empirewide rank and estimated population of these cities are plotted on Figure 2, individually for the 50 largest cities, then at intervals of five to rank 100, and thereafter at intervals of ten. Cities from number 17 (Changsha) down to number 292 have a slope near the normal −1.00, which is to say that they follow closely the rank-size formula, but for the cities from Peking to Changsha the prevailing slope is more gentle, approximately one-third less than expected. Here we have graphic evidence of the point with which the paper began: the cities of China did not form a single integrated urban system. Peking's population, scarcely larger than would be expected for the metropolitan city of North China alone, was less than a third of what it would have to have been if it formed the apex of an integrated empirewide system of cities. Scale aside, the rank-size distribution for China as a whole resembles that for Yun-Kwei, except that the departures from Zipf normality are much sharper. If the gentle slope of Yun-Kwei's largest cities and their modest "deficit" of centrality are indicative of an urban system so poorly integrated in 1843 as to be properly characterized as emergent, then the still gentler slope that characterized the largest cities of the empire as a whole and their massive "deficit" of centrality indicates no more than negligible integration of the various regional urban systems. Peking, Soochow, Canton, and Wuhan each in its way performed important extraregional functions in the mid-nineteenth century, but none exhibited the centrality needed to integrate a Chinese system of cities. A unified urban system on such a scale was most likely simply infeasible in an agrarian society prior to the extension of mechanized transport.

Part Two
THE CITY IN SPACE

Introduction: Urban and Rural in Chinese Society

G. WILLIAM SKINNER

Part Two is focused on the external relations of cities, that is, on the transactions linking them to other central places and to the countryside. Here we are concerned with the embeddedness of cities in essentially agrarian regional systems, with the ways in which cities served and exploited their hinterlands, and with the nature of rural-urban differentiation in Chinese society. Most of the papers in Part Two have something to say about the historical development of cities (the theme of Part One); in addition, they all address, directly or indirectly, aspects of urban social structure (the focus of Part Three). They are grouped together here because of the importance of their subject matter for understanding cities in the context of China's spatial structure. Of the six contributions that follow, the first two are analytical studies of broad scope, the second two are detailed case studies of Lower Yangtze cities, and the last two support their arguments with data drawn largely from Kwangtung. Following a brief characterization of each paper, I take up some of the themes they jointly illuminate.

My own paper is given pride of place because of the overview it provides of the spatial distribution of different types of cities. In it I distinguish cities as commercial centers from cities as administrative capitals. Economic central places are shown to have formed regional systems of cities, each system a multilevel hierarchy internally differentiated by the degree of economic centrality of its components and their position in the core-periphery structure of the region. The commercial hinterlands of economic central places were hierarchically stacked in a manner that involved systematic overlap from one level to the next—a structural arrangement that conditioned politics and social structure as well as economic activity. Administrative capitals, a subset of economic central places, also formed spatial hierarchies, each culminating in the capital of a province or governor-generalship; but in this case the associated hierarchy of territorial units was discretely stacked. The contrastive structure of administrative and commercial hinterlands and their very imperfect alignment are shown to have had important consequences for the intersection of bureaucratic government with informal governance and societal management at the local level. The chief argument of the paper is that the formal administrative attributes of capital cities stemmed in large part from their place in the relevant regional system of economic central places. A secondary thesis is that the size and strength of informal political systems varied inversely with the intensity of bureaucratic government—a covariation that expressed the structure of "natural" economic regions at least as much as the arrangement of provinces.

In his provocative analysis of the county-level yamen, Professor Watt illuminates the institution that was seen by the Chinese as the quintessence of urbanism. His primary concern is the interaction of a predominantly urban administration with a predominantly rural society, and in seeking to understand the nature of this interaction he reviews the transformation of field administrative practice during the late Ming and early Ch'ing—the centralization of control within and between yamens through the proliferation of minutely detailed regulations, the abasement of clerical status, the attrition of bureaucratic posts subordinate to the magistrate, the increased fiscal self-sufficiency of the yamen, the localization of administrative procedures through the Single Whip reforms, and the emergence of private secretaries. Using concepts drawn from organization theory, Watt shows how some of these changes brought the yamen closer to the ideal model of a modern bureaucracy whereas others caused it to diverge from that model. Among the features of the Ch'ing yamen, three stand out as paradoxical in their consequences for rural-urban relations. One was the curious isolation of yamen personnel from the common people, the sole exception being the despised yamen runners. Another was the tendency for the yamen to function as a business, selling administrative services to the highest bidder. And the third was the ironic development whereby official government employees—clerks and runners—came to represent local interests within the yamen, whereas nonofficial personnel—private secretaries and personal servants of the magistrate—came to represent the interests of the state. Watt also takes a fresh look at the recurrent attempts of yamen officials to impose institutions of administrative control in the countryside and shows how their successes and failures reflected the divergent interests both of the functionaries within the yamen and of the various

Introduction: Urban and Rural in Chinese Society

social groups using its services. He concludes that the yamen was above all an institution that mediated these divergent interests.

Professor Shiba's paper, concerned chiefly with economic centrality, provides a neat foil for Watt's concern with administrative centrality. Watt treats county-level capitals in general, whereas Shiba is concerned with a particular prefectural capital. Ningpo, the subject of this extraordinarily comprehensive case study, has been the economic center of its region (in northeastern Chekiang) since the T'ang period, when it was first designated a prefectural-level capital. Shiba traces the regional development of the Yung Basin from the first large-scale waterworks undertaken by the T'ang government to the last of the drainage canals constructed under private auspices in the nineteenth century—a development that saw the insalubrious or saline marshes of the central plain transformed into fertile paddy fields, and cash-crop agriculture and commercial fishing extended to the farthest reaches of Ningpo's economic hinterland. Shiba's description of Ningpo's urban economy may well be the most complete account we have in English of any traditional Chinese city, and the analysis is all the more remarkable for relating the city's internal structure to the structure of its hinterland. His treatment of Ningpo's regional-city trading system adds flesh and blood to the bare-bones model set out in my paper; and in emphasizing the local-system specializations on which the regional economy rested, he complements my own account in a theoretically important way. Throughout most of its history Ningpo was an entrepôt for overseas trade as well as a regional center, and in the final section of his paper Shiba discusses the interplay between these two roles and relates it to the remarkable expansion of Ningpo merchants and financiers first to Shanghai and then to commercial centers throughout the empire.

Cotton, the local specialty of two diked coastal areas within Ningpo's commercial hinterland, was the dominant crop throughout the coastal area of southern Kiangsu that is the subject of Dr. Elvin's study. Shanghai was already that area's major cotton emporium in the early fifteenth century, when Elvin picks up the story, and the next five centuries saw it grow from a small but prosperous unwalled county seat to the central metropolis of the Lower Yangtze region and China's largest city. The numerous waterways on which the area's cotton cultivation depended for irrigation, drainage, and flood control gained importance as commercial routes during the sixteenth century, when cotton spinning and weaving expanded throughout most of the countryside as subsidiary industries. Subsequent centuries saw a secular trend in which the significance of waterways for commerce steadily increased relative to their significance for agriculture. Elvin's study focuses on institutional arrangements for managing and maintaining the elaborate network of waterways in Shang-hai *hsien* and vicinity, and one of his many theses is that these arrangements—most notably the dike administrators of late Ming and the gentry directors in middle and late Ch'ing—were unusual precisely because of the exceptional importance of waterborne commerce.

From Elvin's richly contextual institutional analysis, I seize here on only a few points relating to urbanization. First, he calls attention to the gradual exodus of landholding gentry from villages to market towns and capital cities, a process under way already in the late sixteenth century and continuing into the twentieth. If it was not unique to the regional core of the Lower Yangtze, this development was certainly most pronounced there; together with the tendency for wealthy urbanites to invest in agricultural land, it helps account for the rather special nature of rural-urban relations in the Lower Yangtze region and for the region's exceptionally high urbanization rate. Second, Elvin documents the proliferation and growth of market towns in the Shanghai area, linking this aspect of urbanization not only to the market dependency of rural households and the changing residential preferences of landlords, but also to Shanghai's growing importance as a center of long-distance trade. Third, he identifies the gentry directors who came to dominate the maintenance of waterways in the course of the eighteenth century not as interested landowners but as professional organizers drawn from the degree-holding gentry. The rise to prominence of such men, residing (as most of them did) in cities and towns and positioned (as most of them presumably were) to encompass if not transcend the special interests of landlords and merchants, constituted yet another facet of the urbanization process. Finally, he shows that by the mid-nineteenth century, the costs of hydraulic maintenance were largely borne by businessmen in the towns directly concerned.

The last two papers in Part Two take us to a different region of China and introduce urban topics that on the face of it are cultural and social rather than political or economic. The findings of Professor Grimm concerning educational institutions, and those of Dr. Baker concerning kin groups, though based primarily on data from Kwangtung, ought to hold on first principles wherever academies and extrafamilial kin groups were found in significant numbers.* As we shall see, the topical shift is also

---

* In this regard, however, one should keep in mind that academies were least common in the interior of China—i.e., in Northwest China, the Upper Yangtze, and Yun-Kwei—and that lineages and clans were weak in North and Northwest China by comparison with the more southerly regions.

Introduction: Urban and Rural in Chinese Society

less than abrupt, for neither the institutional arrangements nor the geographic distribution of academies and kin groups can be understood without reference to economic and political considerations.

Grimm treats a subject that would have had no place in a book on Chinese cities prior to the sixteenth century. Early academies were for the most part rural institutions, supported from agrarian trust funds and wedded to an antiurban "mountain-recluse" philosophy. The major objective of his paper is to describe, document, and account for their subsequent urbanization. Critical developments were the atrophy of education per se within the official school-temples, the growing importance of the imperial examination system, and the increasing role of bureaucratic officials in founding academies. By the nineteenth century, advanced academies situated in capital cities had achieved semiofficial status; moreover, the areas from which students were recruited to such academies tended to reflect the administrative jurisdiction of the capitals in which the academies were located. Yet not the least interesting of Grimm's findings concern the development during the Ch'ing period of an educational hierarchy that reflected not only field administration but also the structure of the regional economy. Cities whose position was high in both the administrative and the economic hierarchy (together with their immediate hinterlands) came to enjoy clear-cut academic advantages. Thus, the urbanization of academies meant that the most urbanized local systems were increasingly favored in the examination system.

Baker's paper explores rural-urban differences in the nature and distribution of extrafamilial kin groups. He demonstrates that although localized lineages may be found throughout the settlement hierarchy in China, their numbers and strength varied inversely with level. He accounts for the weakness of lineage organization in high-level cities (but fortunately does not leave the subject before providing a detailed description of an urban lineage in Canton). Higher-order or multiplex lineages (those with genealogically linked branches in different settlements) had a broad geographic spread, and Baker argues that they were normally contained within standard and intermediate (sometimes central) marketing systems, with the ancestral hall located in the relevant market town. As for the federations of lineages (both localized and higher-order) that sinological anthropologists call clans, Baker finds these to be organized within the hinterlands of cities and considers the clan hall to be an essentially urban institution. His analysis of several Canton-based clans makes an important contribution to the limited literature on this aspect of extended kinship; of particular interest here is his suggestion that the catchment areas of clans (that is, the area within which member lineages were distributed) may typically have been one of the commercial hinterlands of the central city even when that area was specified in terms of more inclusive administrative units. Finally, after a careful consideration of the evidence, he concludes that true surname associations were rare and anomalous in premodern China, at best an insignificant element in urban social structure.

Regional Systems and the Urban-Rural Continuum

All the papers in this part (and several elsewhere in the volume) wrestle with some manifestation of an urban-rural continuum whose subtlety and complexity mock the simple image of it often found in the sociological literature. One tends to think of a landscape in which degree of centrality, settlement size, nonagricultural character of occupations, and accessibility all decline steadily with distance from a central city. But no earthly landscape is so neat. For one thing, settlements of small size and low centrality are everywhere positioned between larger centers of greater centrality—a feature predicted and explained by location theorists, whose shorthand phrase for it is the "interstitial placement of centers." But if one were to discard the spatial element and conceive the urban-rural dimension as a continuum of settlement size, or of occupational structure, or of degree of centrality, the notion of a functionally differentiated system with both rural and urban components would be lost. And it simply will not do to fall back on the native Chinese trichotomy of city (equals walled capital), market town (equals unwalled nonadministrative commercial center), and village—a scheme that is not exhaustive, whose elements are not mutually exclusive, and that is far too undiscriminating for scholarly analysis.

One purpose of introducing the concept of regional systems in my paper below is to bring the various dimensions of the urban-rural continuum into an integrated framework. The scheme may be restated in terms of four elements. First, central places are classified according to their level of centrality in particular functional hierarchies. Thus, in the administrative hierarchy, provincial capitals are more urban than prefectural capitals, which in turn are more urban than county capitals; and in the economic hierarchy, greater cities are more urban than local cities, which in turn are more urban than central market towns, and so forth.*
Second, central places at the same level are taken to be more or less urban according to their relative remoteness from higher-level centers. A county capital with direct access to its prefectural capital (that is,

---

* For many purposes, of course, a generalized composite classification is useful (see Table 20, p. 340).

Introduction: Urban and Rural in Chinese Society

a capital whose county adjoined the metropolitan county so that one could travel to the prefectural capital without passing through any other county capitals) is considered to be more urban than a county capital with only indirect access (that is, where one or more counties intervened). Thus a county capital with direct access to a prefectural capital that also served as the provincial capital was even more urban in this sense than a county capital that was twice removed from its prefectural capital, which in turn was twice removed from the provincial capital. A comparable continuum could, of course, be defined for the economic hierarchy alone. Third, central places per se are contrasted with the hinterlands dependent on them. If one adheres strictly to comparable levels in the system hierarchy (e.g., either metropolitan counties or ordinary counties, either central marketing systems whose nodes were local cities or central marketing systems whose nodes were central market towns), then one can in straightforward fashion contrast the nodal central place (urban) with the remainder of its relevant system (rural). Fourth, total systems (node *plus* hinterland) at the same level are taken to vary in their relative "urbanness" in accordance with the logic illustrated by the following classification of central marketing systems (CMS): (1) CMS's whose node is a central market town that has only indirect access to any higher-level economic center; (2) CMS's whose node is a central market town that has direct access to a local city or other higher-level center; (3) CMS's whose node is a local city that has only indirect access to any higher-level center; (4) CMS's whose node is a local city that has direct access to a greater city or other higher-level centers; (5) CMS's whose node is a greater city that has only indirect access to any higher-level center; and so on. A continuum of this kind is related empirically to the regional economic systems analyzed in my paper below, and the range covered by it is wide. CMS's of the first type would be situated at the rims of economic macroregions, those at the other extreme at their most urbanized cores. It is possible, of course, to develop similar typologies based on the administrative hierarchy alone or to derive a more complex continuum from a synthetic typology of central places. In any case, the essential point is far simpler than its multifarious applications: total systems as such varied in degree of urbanization.

The virtues of a more rigorous conception of the urban-rural continuum may be pointed up by reference to three of the papers that follow. In his analysis of kin groups, Baker argues that "the strongest lineages would have been found at the lower end of the rural-urban continuum"; and indeed, there is no reason to doubt that lineages were most common in villages and low-level market towns. But a realization that local systems at the same formal level in the hierarchy varied in degree of urbanness points up a countervailing specification—for the evidence is fairly extensive that lineages were stronger in more urbanized local systems (that is, in counties or central marketing systems with relatively direct access to high-level cities).[1] Baker's rationale is sound enough— "the more rural the situation, the greater the homogeneity of interest and the ease of keeping the lineage united"—but it is less than the full picture, for the more urbanized the local system the more favorably it was situated to pursue advantageous mobility strategies and maximize profits from its corporate holdings.[2] A similar point is deftly made by Grimm in explaining the paradoxical finding that Kwangtung's most urbanized counties (the four that included and surrounded Canton) had an exceptionally *rural* distribution of academies. In fact, the counties in question also had more urban academies on the average than other counties did; what distinguished these four was the large number of academies they also supported outside the cities. Grimm sees the explanation for this distribution in the high levels of wealth and aspiration even in the countryside of such highly urbanized counties, where local systems centered on major market towns founded their own academies to enhance their success rate in the examinations.

Grimm is also concerned to demonstrate that the greater the economic centrality of a capital city, the more likely its academies were to be dependent on commercial capital for their support and to have been founded without substantial official initiative or funding. The data he musters suggest that his arguments are sound, but to clinch them it would be desirable to hold administrative level constant while comparing local cities with greater cities with regional cities. A similar point could be made concerning the kind of analysis Dr. Feuchtwang introduces near the beginning of his paper in Part Three on the official religion. He shows that not all of the altars and shrines prescribed by the official statutes were in fact present in every capital city, and that in many instances official cults were not exclusively sponsored by officials. Implicit hypotheses are that the complement of prescribed institutions (1) would be fuller for prefectural capitals than for county capitals, holding the cities' level in the economic hierarchy constant, and (2) would be fuller for cities ranking high in the economic hierarchy than for those ranking low, holding level in the administrative hierarchy constant. One might also hypothesize that in county-level capitals a fuller complement of official altars and temples would be associated with a higher degree of gentry and merchant participation in sponsorship. These propositions can be given a rigorous test once the cities are classified according to a differentiated conceptualization of urbanness.

Baker's treatment of clans is also relevant in this regard. No one would dispute his general conclusion that clans were urban-centered kin groups, and it may well be that his data do not permit greater specificity. But a rigorous categorization of cities raises some interesting questions. If the major raison d'être of clans was the pursuit of political advantage, would one expect them to be concentrated in the *most* urban centers, that is, in a city like Canton that was at once a central metropolis in the economic hierarchy and the capital of a governor-generalship? There are several reasons for supposing that clan headquarters might have been more viable in less exalted cities. First, if the clan's area extended beyond the metropolitan prefecture, then maintaining a hostel for examination candidates in the provincial capital would discriminate against member lineages in other prefectures, whose only use of it would be for their very occasional entrant in the provincial examinations. Second, the political objectives that even the most powerful clan might entertain were likely to be more feasibly pursued at a prefectural yamen than at the level of a province or governor-generalship. Third, given the suspicion with which large clans were viewed by the state apparatus,[3] clan halls might prove to be particularly vulnerable in the highest-level capitals. And fourth, investment by a large clan in the enterprises of one of the empire's greatest commercial metropolises might be expected to intensify official suspicion that the state was witnessing a dangerous concentration of power.

How Central Were Urban Functions?

Any attempt to assess the central functions of cities in late imperial China must address the extent to which the services provided by cities were actually consumed or used throughout their hinterlands. Two separate questions are involved. In what respects, if any, was there institutional differentiation within a territorial nodal system in terms of the availability of services—differentiation of the node from its hinterland, or between different sectors or concentric zones within the hinterland? And to what extent in practice did the availability of services decline with distance from the central place?

With respect to administrative units, the cognitive norm was unambiguous in traditional times. A capital city had no corporate existence apart from the total administrative territory of which it was the node and the symbol. Capitals were known by the names of their administrative units, the generic included; sinologists conventionally distinguish the prefecture from the prefectural capital by an arbitrary orthographic difference—Ch'ao-chou *fu* versus Ch'ao-chou-fu—but no distinction was made in either written or spoken Chinese. The word for province, *sheng*, was also used to mean provincial capital. It is entirely in keeping with Chinese cognition in general that the geomantic fate of a county was held to derive from the siting of its capital city.[4]

It can be safely said, I think, that the Chinese ideal of a spatially undifferentiated central function was realized only in the ritual realm. As Feuchtwang points out, the official rites for Confucius conducted in the *hsüeh-kung* within the walls of the capital were held to maintain the basis of civilization throughout the administrative unit, just as those conducted at the suburban altars were held to secure food and shelter for everyone within the capital's jurisdiction. The ritual benefits of these and other official sacrifices were in no sense limited to urbanites. True, few of the common people ever witnessed—much less participated in—these rites; but the basic view of the cosmos on which they were predicated was common to popular as well as to elite religion,[5] and they may have been among the most widely appreciated functions of government.

The case of the City God brings us closer to the ambiguities of administrative reality. Was he the tutelary deity of the city per se, as a literal rendering of his name implies (God of Walls and Moats: *Ch'eng-huang-yeh*), or of the entire administrative unit of which the city was the capital? In most parts of China, rural folk considered their T'u-ti-kung (local territorial deities) to be subordinate functionaries in an otherworldly territorial hierarchy; and in some instances that hierarchy was seen as culminating in the "yamen" of the City God in the county capital. On the other hand, Ch'eng-huang-yeh was seldom worshiped by the rural populace, and his annual birthday festival was organized by and for residents of the capital. When he was taken out in procession, his sedan chair was normally carried to every quarter of the city; but if there was any indication of his jurisdiction over the countryside, it was no more than a gesture at the city gates.[6]

It is only fitting, then, that Ch'eng-huang-yeh was commonly seen as the otherworldly equivalent of the magistrate or prefect, for the latter's administrative role, too, was in practice much attenuated outside the capital. He was enjoined to visit the countryside but, in the face of pressing business at the yamen, seldom did. As Watt points out below, "the yamen showed a strong propensity for dealing with urbanites." The extreme view is that capitals served only their own populations, their extramural hinterlands being essentially zones of theoretical but unrealized urban influence. One of the first sociological works on China

Introduction: Urban and Rural in Chinese Society

asserted that "the administration of a district [county] means that of a city and not more."[7] Though this is clearly an overstatement, there can be little doubt that the effectiveness of government within any administrative unit was at a peak in the capital and diminished with distance from it. Such security as the government provided was most nearly adequate in the capital, and those who sought legal or administrative action had to travel there. For the most part, those who traveled to their county capital on government business were elite leaders of local systems seeking the assistance of ranked bureaucrats or their personal staffs, whereas those who moved from the capital to the countryside were yamen runners or troops, low-status personnel whose points of contact in the villages were the despised *ti-pao*, a kind of constable. Either way, the intensity of transactions was lower for the more remote communities by reason of the high cost and inconvenience of unmechanized travel.

In this respect, one must take note of the tendency for areas close to prefectural-level capitals to be favored by a concentration of productive resources and of efficient transport facilities. The reasons, some of which are spelled out in my paper below, need not detain us here, but the consequences are germane to the subject at hand. In many cases, it meant that only the county-level unit within which the high-level capital was located, or only the cluster of administrative units immediately surrounding the capital, were able to take advantage of a particular "service" at the capital. The disadvantage of counties situated away from the metropolitan area was, of course, augmented by the friction of distance. Thus, as Grimm points out, the effective catchment area of the head academy of a prefecture was likely to exclude peripheral counties, and metropolitan counties were exceptionally successful in the imperial examinations. In another context I have estimated that in Chekiang the metropolitan counties whose capitals were greater cities or higher in the economic hierarchy (fourteen out of a total of 79 county-level units) accounted for approximately two-thirds of the entire province's production of *chin-shih* degree-holders during the Ch'ing period.[8] The point is a general one that applies with equal force, say, to the legal services available at the prefectural yamen or to the ritual services at popular temples (to Wen-ch'ang or Kuan-ti, for instance) sponsored by the prefectural government. It is less than surprising that the metropolitan county was given administrative pride of place within the prefecture, its magistrate being styled *shou-hsien* ("head county [magistrate]").[9]

Institutional arrangements serving the urban population alone became apparent only at a fairly high level in the urban hierarchy. The periodic market serving a central marketing system catered to the townspeople as well, and the markets typically found at the gates of a local city that was also a county-level capital served those within as well as without the walls. In greater and higher-level cities, however, one typically found specialized markets attuned specifically to the tastes and needs of city folk. In the realm of popular religion, the catchment areas of the more important market-town temples almost always included at least the standard marketing community, whereas most local cities boasted at least one communal temple whose parish was the town alone. And in higher-level cities—e.g., Tainan as described by Professor Schipper in Part Three, or Ningpo as described by Shiba—most communal temples served only one quarter or even a single ward within the city. Finally, one can glimpse informal city "governments" in capitals as low in the economic hierarchy as local cities, and virtually all cities at higher levels were characterized by a structure of urban leadership that was clearly differentiated from the government of the official administrative unit. As a rule, the internal administrative subdivisions of local and higher-level cities were of a different order from those imposed on the countryside. The hierarchical system followed in the city of Ningpo is described by Shiba. Occasionally, three types of ward-level units were employed, one for the intramural area, another for the built-up suburbs and peri-urban fringe, and a third for the remainder of the county; a system of this sort in Ming Nanking is mentioned in Mote's paper. The distinctive aspects of urban wards and the nature of specifically urban political structures, unfortunately very imperfectly understood, are treated in Part Three.

Class and Culture in Chinese Urbanism

To broach the interrelation of class and culture in a traditional agrarian society is to enter what the late Maurice Freedman called "the rather tired intellectual world of the Great and Little Traditions."[10] To do so in the context of urban-rural distinctions is to raise the hackles of sinological anthropologists and historians alike. Why do most students of imperial China find the Redfieldian approach uncongenial, if not pernicious? A brief answer will help set the stage for two problems confronted, if not resolved, in the present volume: the extent to which (and the senses in which) (1) the Chinese elite were urban, and (2) a distinctive urban culture existed in imperial China.

One is hard put to distinguish a specifically peasant Little Tradition in imperial China. It is not only that cultural variation from one local system to another was marked; more critical is the fact that nonpeasants were an integral part of the major culture-bearing units to which peas-

Introduction: Urban and Rural in Chinese Society

ants belonged. The families of the local elite residing in villages and standard marketing communities partook of their little-local traditions just as much as did the peasantry—though it is true, of course, that they gave certain elements a more cosmopolitan or sophisticated twist. Nor can one overlook the wide range of occupational specialists (traders, artisans, religious specialists, scribes, pettifoggers, geomancers, and so forth), many of them literate, who were neither of the peasantry nor yet of the elite. The point is that the little-local tradition of the standard marketing community was essentially the only culture of the peasant, whereas others developed greater cultural versatility—a versatility acquired not only through class-specific experiences within the local system (e.g., tutorial instruction for sons in local-elite families), but also through more extensive mobility to and sojourning in higher-level central places. Other difficulties relate to differentiation within Chinese high culture. Casting Confucianism in the role of the Great Tradition has the effect of obscuring or downplaying the high cultures associated with the Buddhist and Taoist institutional complexes. Moreover, regional variants within the dominant Confucian tradition were alive and well in late imperial China, for even as the examination system tended to homogenize elite culture, the development of hierarchical networks of academies within regions fostered differentiation—especially during the Ch'ing period, when, as Grimm's analysis of Kwangtung suggests, they became increasingly self-sufficient and inbred. Finally, the assertion by synthesizing comparativists that the Great Tradition was nourished and transmitted by an *urban* elite is the last straw for most sinological scholars, for it equates an unacceptable cultural dichotomy with an unacceptable urban-rural dichotomy in a static formulation that flouts the basic dynamics of Chinese society.[11]

How urban were the Chinese elite? We can begin with the superficially obvious but profoundly tricky statement that all social categories other than peasants were, at least in some senses, more urban than were the peasantry. One of the pitfalls here concerns the distinction between residence and abode. Residence was maintained in one's native place, and one's native place was in the short run of generations virtually an ascribed characteristic; abode, by contrast, was an exigency of the moment, though the moment could easily stretch to decades.[12] The point, then, is that nonpeasant social groupings were more urban in their abode than in their residence. The contrast with which I began is therefore sharper in the case of abodes of *persons* than it is in the case of residences of *families*—and the latter, after all, were the ultimate units in stratificational analysis. This distinction holds with greatest force for those who staffed yamens: they were almost exclusively urban in their abode, but their residences were more evenly distributed between settlements in relatively urban and relatively rural systems. The distinction between abodes and residences was least marked in the case of yamen runners and most pronounced in the case of ranked bureaucrats. With respect to the intellectual elite, Mote puts it this way. "Scholars, poets, thinkers, writers, and artists customarily were in public life for a portion of their lives, and hence in these years necessarily residents of cities and away from their native places. But their productive years often were the years of their private life when ... they not only were not concentrated in one or two great cities of the realm, but were widely dispersed and very apt to be residing in rural places." Comparable mobility patterns were characteristic of the peddler-trader-merchant order and the artisan-industrialist order. The simple fact is that aside from the peasantry large numbers of men in traditional China pursued their occupational calling away from home; they were sojourners, and the local systems and central places where they sojourned were typically more urban than the native places where they still maintained their residence.

Mote's remark just cited was made in the context of his paper on the early Ming period. In his article below, Elvin stresses the exodus of the rural elite to towns and cities beginning in the sixteenth century, a movement that involved not sojourning but a change of residence. Thus the question arises of whether differential mobility during the last centuries of imperial China had the effect of urbanizing the Chinese elite. On this point a study published in 1947 by P'an Kuang-tan and Fei Hsiao-t'ung throws important light.[13] They analyzed the social background of over 900 *chin-shih* degree-holders, most of whom (approximately three-quarters) had passed the metropolitan examination during the T'ung-chih and Kuang-hsü reign periods (1862–1908). Data on native places were available for 758 men, of whom 52.5 percent were from capital cities, 6.3 percent from market towns, and 41.2 percent from more rural settlements. Since the authors collected their source materials in Peking, residents of Shun-t'ien *fu*, the imperial prefecture, and of Chihli (not distinguished in the published data) were greatly overrepresented and, not surprisingly, disproportionately urban (65 percent from capital cities). For the rest, *chin-shih* from the two Lower Yangtze provinces of Kiangsu and Chekiang were the most urban in background, with 75 and 47 percent hailing from capital cities, respectively, a finding that appears to confirm Elvin's observation that the Kiangnan elite had urbanized to a substantial degree during the period from the sixteenth to the nineteenth century. However, a more representative picture is provided by

Introduction: Urban and Rural in Chinese Society

chin-shih from Shantung, Anhwei, Honan, and Shansi—provinces that fell in the middle range in terms of overall urbanization and that included portions of both regional cores and regional peripheries. Of the 238 *chin-shih* from these four provinces, 36.6 percent were from capital cities, 7.6 percent from market towns, and 55.9 percent from more rural settlements. These figures, too, are doubtless biased in favor of urban provenance because of tendencies in the original sources to mute humble origins and to let the county capital stand for the county as a whole; moreover, the cases excluded from the analysis because only the county was specified (17 percent of the total) were more likely than not to have involved a nonurban origin. We must also keep in mind that *chin-shih* degree-holders were the topmost stratum of the bureaucratic elite, and that the urban bias of academies and of the examination system affected this group far more strongly than the gentry elite as a whole.

My own projection from the P'an and Fei study and from other analyses based on elite biographies[14] is that China-wide at most a quarter of all elite families maintained an urban residence, when urban is defined in terms of both administrative and economic centrality (as in column 2 of Table 3 on p. 226).* Whatever the precise facts in this regard, it is clear that China stands out among traditional agrarian societies in having an elite that was by no means predominantly urban.

Was there a distinctively urban culture in traditional China? The problems addressed here primarily concern the culture of the literati, and they may be summarized in the form of two questions. Did elite culture exhibit either a rural or an urban bias? And were there significant differences in the culture of the literati that can safely be attributed to the rural/urban location of their residences?

On the first question, there is an apparent disagreement among contributors to this volume. The view enunciated in Watt's paper is that the proper function of *chün-tzu* (men of virtue and elite status) was to govern, that government was ipso facto urban, and that the purpose of government was to civilize the countryside. "In the Confucian view," Watt argues, "the natural order appeared chaotic and destructive, and people who lived close to nature were seen as vulnerable to disasters and prone to brutality. The function of government was to lift men out of this precarious condition and provide them with livelihood and order,

---

* Counting in sojourners, as we must for comparison with the de facto populations derived in my Part One paper, this figure implies that in the 1890's the elite constituted somewhat over one-fifth of China's total urban population of 23.5 million, a proportion that appears from the literature on nineteenth-century cities to be reasonable and certainly not too low.

i.e., to humanize them." Feuchtwang echoes this position in recounting the reasons why officials saw particular urban institutions as essential to civil governance. A county that lacked a Ming-lun T'ang, one of the components of the school-temple, would risk "the obscuring of human relationships, the destruction of human principles, and the darkening of the human mind." Official rituals were also justified in terms of their efficacy in maintaining civilized norms. It is in keeping with this hoary Confucian ideal that Watt at one point refers to gentry in the countryside as "those elements of the rural population attracted to city culture." Against this view Mote emphasizes "the rural ideals of the upper classes" and explicitly denies that Chinese cities were "beleaguered islands in a sea of barbarism." Some of the flavor of those "rural ideals" (and an indication of their Taoist and Buddhist origins) is conveyed by Grimm's discussion of the antiurban bias of early academies. It may be added that homiletic family and lineage instructions often inveighed against the comforts, extravagance, conspicuous consumption, and dissipation of urban life, and that sojourners normally sent their children back to the family residence for their upbringing rather than risk the specifically urban dangers to successful socialization.[15]

I do not doubt that all of the contributors cited would recognize the validity and persistence of both themes in traditional Chinese thought. There was an urban jungle and a rural jungle in the mind of the literati, as well as a rural idyll and an urban utopia; and this very dualism helps us understand why the elite were disproportionately urban despite the dangers of urban life and why a majority of them lived in the countryside despite the attractions of the city. One might expect urban gentry (and officials-in-office) to have emphasized the one theme and rural gentry (and officials-out-of-office) to have emphasized the other.

Was there then no distinction to be drawn between the urban and rural versions of elite culture? Mote argues persuasively in his paper that such differences as could be identified were inconsequential. Although I am not disposed to take serious issue with this, I should like to note a few points that Mote overlooked in his eagerness to dissociate the Chinese case from the hasty generalizations of synthesizers. To begin with, there is the merchant influence. I do not wish to suggest that a peculiarly merchant culture developed in imperial Chinese cities; to the contrary, a cultural development comparable to that of the bourgeoisie in late medieval Europe or of the *chōnin* in Tokugawa Japan was forestalled by the absence of effective barriers to the eventual translation of commercial wealth into gentry status. But the continual incorporation of assimilat*ing* (and hence only partially assimilat*ed*) merchants into the urban elite—vide Elvin's conclusion that by the early nineteenth century

Introduction: Urban and Rural in Chinese Society

"the more important merchants and gentry of Shanghai had become, to a substantial extent, members of the same class"—inevitably affected its cultural tone.[16] It might be possible, for instance, to demonstrate a connection between this assimilative process and the conspicuous consumption in connoisseurship, the diversified investment strategies of charitable organizations, the shrewd Dickensian realism that became evident in the popular novel, and certain innovations in poetry and painting. Rather more important is the great subcultural variety that characterized Chinese cities. Larger central places drew migrants from larger regional hinterlands, and the more important centers of interregional trade attracted subethnic trader colonies. Organization on the basis of subcultural origin, and intergroup competition and confrontation, together heightened cultural awareness and, in the case of many intellectuals, fostered a kind of reintegrating cosmopolitanism. One senses an intensity in the cultural life of Chinese cities that was absent among the rural elite.

On the more prosaic level of architectural forms, Chinese cities did have their distinctive edifices: the drum tower and bell tower, the great examination hall, and the elaborate towers at the corners and gates of the city wall. As for consumption patterns, how much do we really know? In Chengtu as of 1949, apprentices in traditional Chinese shops could expect meat with their noon meal every market day—nine times each lunar month. Their counterparts in the surrounding market towns ate meat once a month and on the days of major festivals. Were differences of this kind any less likely in an earlier era?

But Mote's essential point holds. The basic cultural cleavages in China were those of class and occupation (complexly interrelated) and of region (an elaborate nested hierarchy), not those between cities and their hinterlands. This conclusion, however, by no means implies a negligible cultural role for China's cities. For the exchange of cultural material that perpetuated the distinctiveness of each nodal territorial system while at the same time keeping cultural differentiation in check occurred primarily in market towns and cities; and the mechanisms for the refinement and universalization of local-cum-rustic forms and their incorporation in literate traditions (and, conversely, for the coarsening and parochialization of elite forms and their incorporation into little-local traditions) were, once again, concentrated in the hierarchically ordered central places of China's regional systems.

The Integration of Urban Systems

The final theme warranting comment here concerns the mechanisms by which systems of cities were integrated. The formal features integrating capitals within the field administration are fairly well understood. The chain of command that linked subordinate yamens to their superiors in the bureaucratic hierarchy rested on a complex communications network among capital cities. An elaborate system of postal and courier routes linked every county-level capital to its prefectural capital, every prefectural capital to both its circuit and its provincial capitals, every circuit capital to its provincial capital, and every provincial capital to Peking.[17] And the procedures for dispatching and receiving administrative documents within yamens and for transmitting them along the official routes connecting them were formalized and regulated to a point verging on baroque ritual and bureaucratic overkill.[18] Yet the system was capable of moving important messages between distant capitals at a rate of from 100 to 175 miles a day.[19] In his paper, Watt describes how the performance of county magistrates was reviewed and supervised by prefects in a different city; in mine, I analyze the significance of broader or narrower spans of control for different kinds of supervision. It should be noted that field administration in the nineteenth century, which I show to be closely attuned to the realities of regional structure, was little changed from the system as reorganized by the Yung-cheng emperor in the 1720's and 1730's. A critical feature of that radical overhaul was the creation of new prefectural-level units outside the regional cores, thereby reducing the span of control in peripheral areas and facilitating supervision of remote county-level units. The Yung-cheng reorganization markedly tightened the integration of cities as administrative capitals.

Informal links among yamen functionaries in different cities were doubtless of greater importance for interurban integration than our present level of knowledge suggests. Some of these derived from official institutions. Watt's analysis of preferment and transfer posts makes it clear that appointment by the provincial government of key officials at the county and prefectural levels had the effect of establishing within the official hierarchy of capital cities a structure of clientage focused on the governor or governor-general as patron. The particularistic bonds forged among those who passed the provincial or metropolitan examinations at the same sitting under the same examiner were often the basis for the development of cliques within the field administration as well as the central government. Same-native-place ties, too, were important in facilitating interurban transactions among yamens. The specialization of Shao-hsing *fu* in producing private secretaries is well known; one source commented that Shao-hsing secretaries "are ensconced in all yamens, from those of governors-general down to those of county magistrates. They work with one another, communicating readily among themselves. ... The reason why officials must use them is their ability to deal effectively with higher-level yamens."[20] The natives of particular localities not infrequently dominated the clerkships within the yamens of a prefecture, thereby opening up informal channels of interurban communication that paralleled the formal ones linking the prefect with his subordinate magistrates.

However important subsequent research may show same-native-place ties to have been for interurban transactions within the field administration, they played a still more critical role in the economic integration of cities. If the Upper Yangtze constituted a regional economy, it was in no small part a function of the flow of information, goods and services, money and credit, and economic specialists among the region's principal cities. It was these flows above all that enable us to identify Chungking, Chengtu, Hsü-chou-fu, Lu-chou, Shun-ch'ing-fu, and Wan-hsien, together with the many lesser cities in their hinterlands, as a *system* of cities. Moreover, the prime indicators of an emergent empirewide economy in late imperial times were, of course, the trade and other economic transactions between commercial cities in one region and those in others. To the extent that these transactions and the institutions on which they rested have been examined, it appears that a high proportion involved entrepreneurs who shared a common origin. A Hokkien firm in one city exported goods to a Hokkien firm in another. The purchasing agent sent to Chungking by a Shensi firm in Chengtu was typically a Shensi native. Shao-hsing breweries shipped their products to Shao-hsing wholesalers in Hangchow. Couriers carried market and price information from the Hui-chou guild in Nanking to the Hui-chou guild in Hankow. Remittances went from a Shansi bank in Foochow to another Shansi bank in Tientsin.

There are many reasons for expecting long-distance economic transactions to make use of *t'ung-hsiang* ("same-native-place") bonds whenever possible, but in the last analysis it comes down to a matter of trust and accountability,[21] on the one hand, and of reliable business competence, on the other. On the one hand, fellow natives could trust one another because both were socially grounded in, and would eventually return to, the same local system, in which the reputations of their families, lineages, and particular native places were at stake. On the other hand, the skills and knowledge specific to particular lines of business were developed through experience, cumulated within local systems, and perpetuated through established practices of business recruitment, selection, and socialization. On both counts, then, the risks of long-distance business transactions were minimized by keeping within *t'ung-hsiang* alignments.

I have elsewhere analyzed the "export" of specialized human talent as a maximization strategy pursued by local systems favorably located with respect to urban opportunity structures, institutional resources, and transport routes.[22] The specialities involved ranged from lowly and even despised crafts and services to high-status commercial and financial occupations. Interurban transactions within subregions rested on scores of local-system specializations, those within macroregions on hundreds. Yet a certain few of these were of special importance to the integration of regional urban systems in that multibranch enterprises, organizational and business affiliations, and the sheer weight of business transactions within a single "common origin" group linked together all the major commercial cities within the region. Interurban business transactions between macroregions, the riskiest of all, were dominated by entrepreneurs from a very few regional systems, and theirs was a vital role in the articulation of China's semiclosed regional economies. Not the least of the virtues of Shiba's paper are its keen perception of the significance of these regional merchant groups and its detailed account of the Ningpo merchants, the last of these groups to rise to prominence in traditional times.

I want to give notice, finally, to some of the arrangements that served to integrate systems of cities containing both capitals and nonadministrative centers. In this regard the examination system was of critical importance, for as I argue in my paper below, the upward mobility of scholars it fostered forged an effective link between the leadership of local parapolitical systems and the imperial bureaucracy. Of particular relevance here are two points. On the one hand, the central foci of informal local politics at each level were market towns, and the headquarters of leadership councils tended to form a hierarchy that corresponded to the spatial structure of standard, intermediate, and central market towns. On the other hand, ascent up the regular academic ladder recapitulated the hierarchy of administrative capitals. In the orthodox route, an aspiring scholar sat for an examination in the capital of his native county and, if successful there, was eligible to sit for subsequent examinations in the capital of his native prefecture, and so on. Thus in dispensing only from capital cities the status symbols that were of critical importance to local elites throughout the central-place hierarchy, the government forced a kind of integration between market towns and the capitals of the county and prefecture in which they were located. It also fostered the kind of development described by Grimm, whereby the educational institutions managed by lineages and communities at the local level served as feeder schools for academies in the county-level capital, which in turn fed their best "graduates" to more advanced academies in the prefectural-level capital.

Other factors include the obvious but important point that roads and canals built and maintained by the government as courier and postal routes also facilitated trade between the capitals involved and between cities and the market towns through which the official routes passed. Watt discerns in official policies "an urban strategy designed to bring strong administrative influence to bear at nodal points of economic development." At least for the long run, my own analysis confirms Watt's view that government policy aimed to incorporate higher-level economic centers into the field administration as capitals.[23] Of greater importance in the short run was the tendency to post subofficials to major market towns. The role of subcounty posts in integrating market towns with their county-level capitals has not been systematically investigated. It is clear that several hundred *hsün-chien* and other categories of deputy and assistant magistrates and subprefects were posted in otherwise nonadministrative central places. Professor DeGlopper's study of nineteenth-century Lu-kang (see his paper in Part Three) illustrates how the presence of subofficials in commercial towns gave such places the aspect of minor seats of government. Although Lu-kang lacked a wall, other subcounty "capitals" could even boast that emblem of urban status. (Chiu-lung [Kowloon] and Wei-hai-wei are instances that became well known by virtue of coming under British control at the end of the nineteenth century.) The nature of subcounty administrative divisions, the degree of alignment between their headquarters and the lower levels of the economic central-place hierarchy, and the relation of both to informal local governance are subjects whose potential significance is only now becoming apparent. They are among the topics whose importance for future research can readily be grasped by anthropologists, sociologists, and institutional historians alike.

Cities and the Hierarchy of Local Systems

G. WILLIAM SKINNER

This paper considers the place of cities in imperial China's spatial structure.[1] Two hierarchies of central places and of associated territorial systems are distinguished, one created and regulated by the imperial bureaucracy for purposes of field administration, the other given shape in the first instance by economic transactions. The first reflected the bureaucratic structure of "official" China—a world of yamens and ranked officials arrayed in a formal hierarchy of graded administrative posts. The second reflected the "natural" structure of Chinese society—a world of marketing and trading systems, informal politics, and nested subcultures dominated by officials-out-of-office, nonofficial gentry, and important merchants.

In this paper I attempt to model these two structures and their interaction. It should be noted at the outset that administrative capitals were but a subset of economic central places, for all capitals performed significant economic functions for their hinterlands. In the eighteen provinces of China proper in the 1890's, there were some 39,000 economic central places, only 1,546 of which served as capitals in the imperial field administration.[2]

Despite the role of capitals as both administrative and economic central places, the distinction drawn between the two hierarchies is by no means simply a heuristic device. The boundaries of administrative units seldom coincided with those of marketing or trading systems. Thus, a given capital city fitted into two empirically distinct spatial structures. It is this feature that enables us to view low-level capitals as the locus of articulation between the official structure of field administration and the nonofficial structure of societal management.

My approach here gives some analytical precedence to commercial as against other central functions. In taking this stance I mean neither to imply that commercial functions outweighed all others nor to suggest that all or even most cities and towns originated as primarily economic centers.[3] But there are three senses in which economic central functions may be seen as basic. First, market towns and commercial cities were central nodes in the flow of goods and services, money and credit, and persons pursuing their livelihood and other economic interests. This meant that trading centers at all levels were logical sites for such public institutions as communal temples, schools, and benevolent institutions as well as for headquarters of the nonofficial structures exercising political, administrative, and even military control. In this sense, commercial centers attracted other types of central functions; thus there was a distinct tendency for religious "parishes," the catchment areas of schools, and the jurisdictions of parapolitical structures to coincide at local levels with the economic hinterlands of trade centers and to reflect their nodal structure.[4] Second, since the extraction of economic surplus is everywhere a critical enabling mechanism of politics, it was efficient for political institutions to focus on commercial centers in their efforts to control and regulate the means of exchange and (indirectly) production, and to tap the wealth of any given local system. Thus the headquarters of secret-society lodges and of other parapolitical institutions were normally located in market towns and cities in part because control of markets and of other key economic institutions figured prominently among the prizes of political competition.[5] Thus, too, a regular feature of the periodic adjustments and reorganizations of the imperial field administration was the incorporation as capitals of newly prominent trading centers.[6] Third, trade appears to have been far more potent than administrative transactions—or, for that matter, any other form of interurban linkages—in shaping *systems* of cities within China. This followed in part from the low intensity of bureaucratic field administration but more importantly from the fact that commerce, ever sensitive to cost distance, was more sharply constrained by physiographic givens than administration was. Thus, geographic constraints and trading patterns tended to reinforce one another in shaping urban systems.

For reasons implicit in these remarks, I begin with an analysis of China's cities and towns as commercial centers and take up field administration only after placing economic central places in the context of physiographic regions.

Modeling the Economic Hierarchy

The general economic importance of a settlement in late imperial China, as in most traditional agrarian societies, was in large part a function of three factors: (1) its role in providing retail goods and services for a surrounding tributary area or hinterland; (2) its position in the structure of distribution channels connecting economic centers; and (3) its place in the transport network.* In what follows I start with a theoretical discussion of the first factor, presenting an idealized model that I subsequently modify to incorporate elements of the other two factors.

Central-place theory in the strict sense is concerned solely with retailing.[7] The basic notion is that higher-level centers purvey more specialized goods and consequently have more extensive maximal hinterlands than lower-level centers do. The two key concepts here are the *demand threshold* of the supplier and the *range* of a good. Demand threshold may be defined as the area containing sufficient consumer demand to enable the supplier to earn normal profits. It reflects economies of scale in the provision of certain services and agglomeration advantages accruing from locating centralized retailers near to one another. The chief determinant of threshold is purchasing power per unit of area, itself a function of population density and the extent to which household economies are dependent on the market. Range may be defined as the circumscribed area beyond which buyers would not be willing to travel to purchase the good in question. The main determinants of the range of central goods are economic distance (i.e., geographic distance converted into transport costs) and production costs. If transport costs and demand density do not vary by direction from the central place, then the areas of both demand threshold and range will be roughly circular, with the radius of the circle varying for different goods and services.

Using the concepts of threshold and range and hewing to a number of stringent assumptions,† central-place theory predicts hierarchical patterns of trading centers on the landscape. Common goods in heavy demand are available in all centers at whatever level, whereas more specialized goods are available only at higher-order centers in accordance with the extent of their range. Thus, the set of goods supplied by a more complex center includes all goods supplied by simpler centers plus an increment of different higher-order goods. The result is a system in

---

* In a traditional agrarian society, industrial production tends to be relatively atomized and dispersed, and the location of handicraft industry closely reflects the three factors specified. Thus industrial location has not been incorporated in the models developed here.

† Most notably, full knowledge of market conditions on the part of both suppliers and consumers, full rationality on the part of suppliers in seeking to maximize profits and on the part of consumers in seeking to minimize costs, perfect competition, and a sufficient number of suppliers to meet all "threshold" demand.

which marketing centrality is discretely stratified, yielding functionally distinct levels of centers. A consequent feature of every regular central-place system is that the number of centers steadily decreases and the average size of hinterlands steadily increases as one moves up the hierarchy.

On the assumption of uniform demand density, centers at any given level will be spaced according to an isometric grid, as if at the apexes of space-filling equilateral triangles; since the size of threshold areas is affected by distance from competing suppliers in neighboring centers, hinterlands tend to be hexagonal rather than circular in shape. Thus, a honeycomb of hexagonal hinterlands develops, each in contact with six others at the same level. Finally, centers at one level are interdependent with their neighbors at adjacent levels in the sense that increased development of one higher-order town will result in the lesser development of the low-order centers in its immediate hinterland. The tributary nature of the system means that larger centers draw trade from nearby smaller centers and thus restrict their commercial growth.

One of the more common central-place patterns is diagramed in Figure 1, where four levels of centers are shown. Although this kind of model is derived from a theoretical analysis of the behavior of retailers and consumers, the geography of wholesale trade is at least as important as that of retailing in accounting for the location of cities and the structure of urban systems.* I shall argue briefly that, in a preindustrial economy lacking mechanized transport and communication, regular central-place hierarchies of the kind modeled in Figure 1 are optimal not only for retail marketing but also for the collection and export of local products, for the import and distribution of exogenous products, and for the wholesaling, transport, and credit functions essential for these activities.

Let us assume that the major transport routes on the hypothetical landscape of Figure 1 are those connecting A centers (each route passing through one B center and two C centers), that the next most important routes are those connecting B centers (each passing through one C center and two D centers), and so on. Efficiency alone dictates that the importance of particular centers as transport nodes should decline as the number and variety of suppliers and the size of the market decline. Given this pattern of nodes and links, and assuming uniform transport costs (i.e., that the fraction of distance does not vary), the collection

* The convention within location theory is to define "central place" narrowly as a retail center. In this paper, however, the term has reference to all kinds of central functions, including but not limited to retailing.

Cities and the Hierarchy of Local Systems

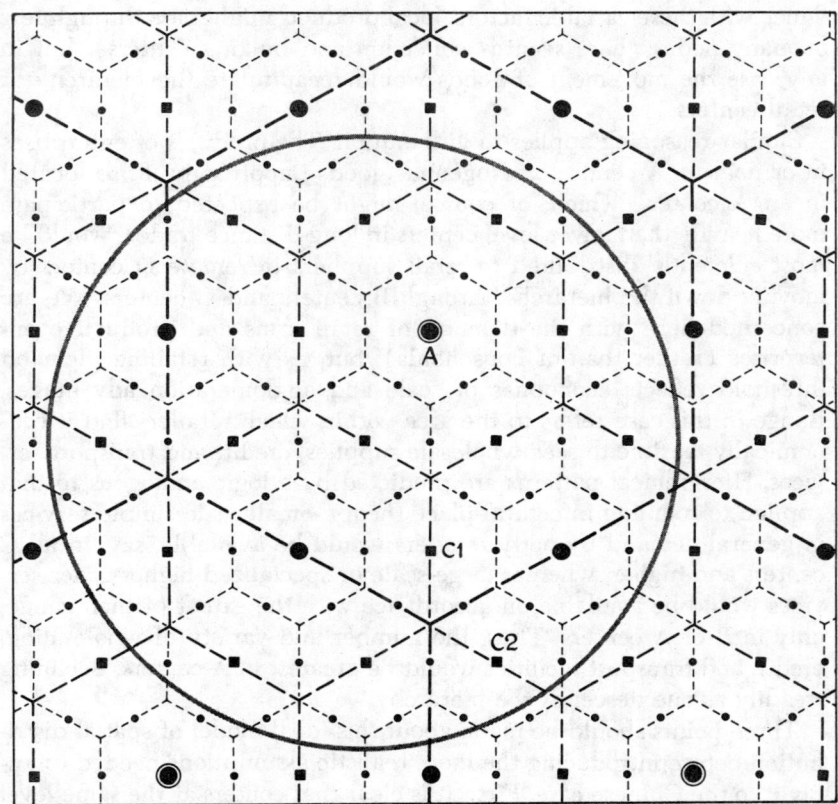

FIG. 1. A REGULAR CENTRAL-PLACE HIERARCHY, BOUNDLESS AND BOUNDED. The limits of D-level hinterlands are not shown.

◉ A centers   ● B centers   ■ C centers   • D centers

points for rural goods would normally be the nodes of the lowest-level (i.e., D-level) systems. How far up the hierarchy goods move is a function not only of such factors as their range (in the case of consumer goods) and of the location of processing and manufacturing industry (in the case of commercial crops and other raw materials), but also of the level of the nodes of systems that are themselves at the same level. For instance, the nodes of some D-level systems are C and B centers, and in these cases collection and bulking of goods of relatively high demand might cease at the center of first collection; there goods would be processed and distributed to lower-level centers throughout the C-level or B-level system whose node was the original collection point. In accordance with these variable factors, local products might pass through few or many nodes (here seen as collection and bulking centers), but in any case the movement of goods would recapitulate the hierarchy of retail centers.

Similar reasoning applies to distribution. The products of enterprises in or near an A center, or exogenous goods imported by firms located in an A center (which, of course, might be expected to participate more heavily than lower-level centers in long-distance trade), would be most efficiently distributed to retail suppliers in remote D centers by moving down the hierarchy through B centers and C centers. We are concerned here with the demand of retail firms and productive enterprises (rather than of households), but, as with retailing, demand threshold reflects economies of scale and agglomeration advantages. Range in this case refers to the area within which retailers find it economically feasible to seek wholesale supplies, credit, and transport services. Hierarchical patterns are predicted by a logic analogous to that applied to retailing in central-place theory. Small-scale simple services in general demand by petty retailers would be available, say, in all C centers and higher, whereas large-scale or specialized higher-order services would be available, in accordance with the extent of their range, only in B or A centers. Thus, the number and variety of wholesaling, credit, and transport facilities would be greatest in A centers, declining steadily as one descends the hierarchy.

Three points should be made about this ideal model of spatial distribution before introducing the more realistic assumptions needed to apply it to the Chinese case. First, it is clear that centers at the same level in the hierarchy are differently favored in terms of location in relation to higher-level centers. Suppliers in the ring of D centers immediately surrounding an A center are better off in terms of transport, credit facilities, wholesale prices, and goods selection than suppliers in the D centers immediately surrounding a B center; D centers lying on the roads connecting C centers are still less favorably situated. Even in a regular central-place hierarchy, then, the selling prices of retail goods and the purchase prices for local products at a D center may be expected to vary systematically according to that center's position in the overall structure. Second, the regular model ensures spatial competition because a center at any level is oriented to two (in the particular system modeled in Figure 1) or more higher-level centers. Thus, in Figure 1, retailers in every D center may choose between wholesalers in two higher-level centers; this means that wholesalers in a given higher-level center are competing with wholesalers in another higher-level center to supply each intervening D center. Third, the two-way trade and transport linking higher-level towns with their dependent lower-level centers strongly reinforce the systemic integrity of central-place subsystems. This is another facet of the interdependence described above in terms of the diversion of trade from lower-order centers to their higher-order neighbors.

The model developed so far assumes an idealized landscape characterized by (1) a flat and featureless topography, (2) an even distribution of demand or purchasing power, (3) equal transport facility in all directions, and (4) an indefinite extension of the same invariant pattern in all directions. In order to proceed to an analysis of the Chinese landscape, we must deal systematically with departures from these unrealistic assumptions.

The Structure of Regional Systems

In conceptualizing regional systems in agrarian China, I have drawn on four different approaches. The first equates regions with the maximal hinterlands of high-level central places.[8] As applied to nineteenth-century China, this approach would distinguish as first-order regions the trade areas of the highest-order goods and services supplied by such major metropolises as Sian, Wuhan, and Canton. Alternatively, a region might be defined as the maximal extent of the network of wholesale credit transactions centered on a given metropolis. One difficulty with this "metropolitan-dominance" approach is that the outer limits of the metropolitan region may give way to rural areas that consume none of the diagnostic higher-order goods or services. And in fact, China in the nineteenth century provided several instances of rural borderland areas that were not linked with any nodal region we could define using the above approach.

A closely related approach focuses on functionally integrated urban systems.[9] If we connected all the central places on a landscape by lines whose thicknesses were proportional to the magnitude of the trade between any given points, then the cores of economic regions would appear as a concentration of heavy lines connecting clusters of higher-level cities. The network of lines would thin toward the peripheries, and small market towns on regional frontiers would be assigned to one region or another on the basis of the direction of the greater trade flow.

The third approach is concerned with the differential distribution of economic resources. The concentration of critical resources may be indexed by such data as per capita income, demand density (purchasing power per unit of area), and (in an agrarian society) the value of agricultural production per unit of land or even the proportion of land that is arable or cultivated. In following this approach, I take population density as the major indicator of resource concentration on the grounds that it is a major component of demand density and correlates strongly with agricultural productivity both as cause (labor inputs) and as effect (the carrying capacity of the land).[10] As applied to China, this involves plotting county-level population densities, from which contours are derived showing density gradients. Extensive pockets of high population density are taken as the cores of economic regions, and regional boundaries are assumed to pass through the areas of lowest density between cores.

The fourth approach of concern here begins with physiographic features. The particular tradition on which I draw dates back to the eighteenth century, when Philippe Buache visualized the earth's land surface as consisting of river basins separated by mountain chains that provided convenient boundaries.[11] Taking the river basin as the essential regional determinant is particularly appropriate in the case of agrarian China, where crop inventories and productive techniques were specifically adapted to a plains-and-valley ecology and where water transport was of the greatest importance. In most Chinese physiographic regions, the river system provided the skeleton of the transport network that underlay the region's functional integration.[12] Although the definition of river-basin units involves a number of operational problems (see p. 212 above for their resolution in the Chinese case), watersheds are readily identified and taking them as regional boundaries leaves no areas unaccounted for.

When these four approaches are followed in regionalizing nineteenth-century China, the results are in large part mutually reinforcing and/or complementary. Nine major "islands" of relatively dense population were identified, each surrounded by concentric gradients of declining densities. Each high-density "core" was wholly contained within one of the nine physiographic macroregions as defined in my Part One paper above (see Map 1, p. 214),* and with minor exceptions the watersheds that constituted regional boundaries passed through areas that were sparsely populated, at least in relation to the populations of the cores.

With the exception of Yun-Kwei and Manchuria, the maximal commercial hinterland of each region's major metropolis was wholly contained in, but did not exhaust, that physiographic region. (As of 1893,

* The map on p. 214 shows a single undifferentiated core within each macroregion; obviously, the distribution of population densities within most of these cores would permit further delimitation of concentric density zones.

the metropolises and their regions were Peking in North China, Sian in Northwest China, Chungking in the Upper Yangtze, Wuhan in the Middle Yangtze, Shanghai in the Lower Yangtze, Foochow in the Southeast Coast, and Canton in Lingnan.) In each case, the major commercial cities of the region had stronger economic links with one another than any had with cities outside the region,[13] and the densest interurban trade was almost wholly contained within the regional core. Moreover, the densely populated and urbanized core areas were closely associated with riverine lowlands.

Since it is virtually axiomatic that in a traditional agrarian society population density is a close function of agricultural productivity per unit of area, I will not document the assertions that a higher proportion of land was arable in the cores of regions than in the peripheries, that arable land in the former was generally more fertile than it was in the latter, and that the proportion of irrigated acreage in the cores was generally greater than that in the peripheries. The level of capital investment in drainage, reclamation, irrigation, and flood control was far higher per unit of arable land (and in some cases per capita) in cores than in peripheries, and in fact the very extent of a core was in many instances shaped by decisions to invest or not to invest in such waterworks. For reasons suggested earlier, investment in transport—roads and bridges, canals and locks—was also comparatively heavy in core areas. Finally, because of the relatively low cost of transport in cores and their denser transport net, the local economies of core areas were consistently more commercialized than those of peripheral areas, both in the sense that more commercial crops and handicrafts were produced for the market and in the sense that households were more dependent on the market for consumer goods.

We are now in a position to modify the idealized model of central-place systems discussed in the previous section to accord with the structure of China's major regional systems. We may begin by abandoning the assumption that the same invariant pattern extends indefinitely in all directions. Suppose a landscape is bounded by high mountains along the circumference of the shaded circle in Figure 1. The system of central places within the circle now includes one A center, three B centers, fifteen C centers, and 62 D centers. All four of the B-level hinterlands (three whose nodes are B centers and one whose node is A) are contained in A's hinterland and dependent on the A center. All 19 of the C-level hinterlands (15 whose nodes are C centers, three whose nodes are B centers, and one whose node is A) are contained in one or more B-level hinterlands and dependent on one or more of the higher-level centers. And all 81 of the D-level hinterlands (62 whose nodes are D centers, 15 whose nodes are C centers, etc.) are contained in one or more C-level hinterlands and dependent on one or more of the higher-level centers. Thus the whole constitutes a single system of centers whose hinterlands form nested subsystems at four levels.

Adding boundedness to the model has two other consequences that deserve mention. First, spatial competition is generally reduced, and for many centers near the newly introduced system-limits it is eliminated entirely. Note that the three B centers are now oriented to only one A center, that several of the C centers near the periphery are now oriented to a single B center, and that many D centers around the rim are oriented to only one C center. Second, an additional element of differentiation among centers at the same level is introduced through truncation of the transport network around the rim of the system. For instance, in the unbounded model the locations of centers C_1 and C_2 were equally favorable in terms of transport to the nearest B and A centers, but in the bounded model C_2 is doubly disadvantaged: it is no longer on a road connecting B centers, and it is more distant than C_1 from the sole A center. Thus, boundedness alone creates a core-periphery structure within the central-place system.

If we now equate the bounded model just delimited with the upper reaches of the central-place system of one of the seven major macro-regions in agrarian China, we are constrained to modify the three other major assumptions of classical central-place theory. The notion of a uniformly flat and featureless topography must be replaced by one of systematic variation ranging from a productive level plain in the vicinity of the central metropolis (the A center) to relatively nonproductive and impenetrable terrain at the regional periphery. (In most of China, the rim of regional peripheries was marked by rugged mountains; by swampy saline marshes, as along much of the littoral of North China; or by desert, as along most of the Inner Asian peripheries of North and Northwest China.) The assumption of uniform demand density must be replaced by one of variable distribution whereby population density and the degree of market dependency both diminish toward the periphery. And finally, the notion of uniform transport facility must be replaced by one of systematic variation in transport costs from low values in the generally low-lying and well-watered core areas to high values in the relatively rugged periphery.

Given these modifications of the central-place model, we can postulate, first, that the average distance between centers at each level will be smaller in the core than in peripheral areas. Thus, moving from the

Cities and the Hierarchy of Local Systems

core toward the periphery, the average area of trading systems increases. (One can imagine Figure 1 printed on a rubber sheet and then stretched so that distortion increases with distance from center A.) The rationale for this expectation is less simple than might appear at first glance, for transport efficiency has an effect on the spacing of centers (and hence on the size of hinterlands) that countervails the effect of demand density. Regional cores tend to couple high demand density with efficient transport; the former favors a close spacing of centers (small trading systems), whereas the latter favors a dispersed spacing of centers (large trading systems). The reverse is true in regional peripheries, where low demand density has the effect of increasing the distance between centers and inefficient transport has the effect of decreasing it. In practice, however, the effects of transport efficiency were strong enough to counteract those of demand density in only a few areas, such as the core of the Lower Yangtze region, characterized by a dense network of navigable waterways.

Second, we can postulate that within each class of central places the size of the market (that is, the volume of business transacted per unit of time) will be relatively large for centers near metropolis A and will decline steadily as we approach the periphery. At any given level of the central-place hierarchy, then, peripheral cities will be likely to have fewer firms in the same line of business than core cities, and thus less competition.

Third, within each class of central places, peripheral cities will tend to have fewer *types* of firms purveying high-order goods and services than will their counterparts in regional cores. We have seen that a center's level (A, B, C, or D in Figure 1) is determined by the availability in it of specialized goods not obtainable at a lower level. But certain of the goods that are diagnostic of C centers in the core may be available in the periphery not in C centers but only in B centers. This upward displacement may occur at any and all levels of a central-place system, and it has the important consequence that subsystems occurring at the same level but differently situated with respect to the structure of the region may be characterized by somewhat different schedules of diagnostic incremental goods.[14]

Let me now characterize economic central places and their hinterlands in China with respect to the expectations derived from central-place and regional-systems models. On my analysis the economic hierarchy in the late nineteenth century consisted of eight levels.* In ac-

---

* See the appendix (pp. 347–51) for an account of the procedures followed and criteria used in classifying central places by level in the economic hierarchy.

cordance with the expectations of central-place theory, the number of centers decreased sharply with each step up the hierarchy. In ascending order, I have classified the economic centers of agrarian China in 1893 as follows: standard market towns (27,000–28,000), intermediate market towns (ca. 8,000), central market towns (ca. 2,300), local cities (669), greater cities (200), regional cities (63), regional metropolises (20), and central metropolises (6).*

The standard market town, which typically serviced a hinterland of fifteen to 30 villages, met the week-to-week marketing needs of peasant households. (I have discussed elsewhere the essential characteristics of this basic town-plus-hinterland as an economic system: transport, trade, industry, and credit were all structured within it spatially according to the principle of centrality and temporally by the periodicity of its market days.[15]) Standard marketing systems were nested within intermediate systems, and so on in the manner suggested by central-place models, but always subject to the constraints of topography and the distorting effects of the transport grid. According to my analysis, this structure ultimately culminated in 26 metropolitan trading systems, which in turn formed eight great economic systems, each essentially coterminous with one of the physiographic macroregions described in my Part One paper. The spatial characteristics of the full hierarchy will be illustrated below by reference to the Upper Yangtze region.

Macroregional cores were, of course, more urbanized than their surrounding peripheries, but the models now before us make it possible to specify two distinct ways in which this was true. Table 1 shows that at each ascending level of the economic hierarchy a higher proportion of central places were situated in cores as against peripheries, the difference being greatest at the two highest levels. The table also shows that for each level in the hierarchy city size was significantly larger in regional cores than in peripheries. It would be wrong, however, to interpret these population differentials as a simple consequence of the primordial physiographic aspects of regional structure. On the contrary, it was Chinese patterns of occupance that transformed physiographic regions into city-centered functional systems whose very "natural" features were to a considerable degree man-made. Urbanization itself contributed to core-periphery differentiation, and large cities have had the effect of intensifying the core-like character of their environs. The ecological consequences of Chinese urbanization may be illustrated with respect to deforestation and the disposal of human waste.

* The shift in terminology from market "town" to "city" between the third and fourth orders is not meant to imply a critical distinction; it appears to me that the orders constituted an integrated and evenly graded hierarchy.

TABLE 1. LOCATION OF CENTRAL PLACES IN REGIONAL CORES OR
PERIPHERIES BY LEVEL IN THE ECONOMIC HIERARCHY,
SHOWING MEAN POPULATIONS, 1893

Level in the economic hierarchy	Cores		Peripheries	Total	Mean population of cities/towns in class	
	No.	Pct.			Cores	Peripheries
Central metropolis	6	100 %		6	667,000	
Regional metropolis	18	90.0	2	20	217,000	80,000
Regional city	38	60.3	25	63	73,500	39,400
Greater city	108	54.0	92	200	25,500	17,200
Local city	360	53.8	309	669	7,800	5,800
CMT[a]	1,163	50.2	1,156	2,319	2,330	1,800
IMT[a]	3,905	48.7	4,106	8,011	690	450
SMT[a]	13,242	47.8	14,470	27,712	210	100
Total	18,840	48.3%	20,160	39,000		

[a] CMT, IMT, and SMT stand for central, intermediate, and standard market towns, respectively.

From time immemorial Chinese architecture has relied on timber as the basic structural material. Wooden pillars and beams provided the framework not only of houses and shops but also of urban public buildings: palaces and yamens, academies and examination sheds, gate houses and drum towers, guildhalls and covered markets. Thus, an enormous amount of timber was required for the construction of a Chinese city, more than was needed for urban construction in most other civilizations, which placed a greater emphasis on stone and brick. These cities of wood with their narrow streets were subject to continual fires that were difficult to contain. Between the burning of cities in wars or rebellions and the burning of them in accidental conflagrations, much timber was reduced to ashes. Additional inroads on China's forest cover were made to supply charcoal for urban industry (including the firing of roof tiles), fuel for urban residences, and paper and black ink (made of soot from burnt pine) for administrative records, scholarly essays, and merchant account books.[16] Since the forest cover of regional cores was depleted fairly early, by late imperial times forest products for urban consumption came largely from mountainous areas in the peripheries. These developments had two important consequences: there was a direct transfer of fertility through the conversion of peripheral timber to peri-urban ash, and there was an indirect fertility "migration" as a result of erosion caused by deforestation in peripheral highlands. The river systems that formed the skeletal structure of most Chinese macroregions removed a great deal of soil by erosion from the peripheral highlands and deposited it as silt in the lowlands of the core. Part of this silt was further redistributed in the alluvial plains by the canal systems, irrigation works, and dikes that were also concentrated in lowland cores.[17] The mud that collected in canals, ditches, and other lowland waterways was, of course, periodically removed, if only to avoid obstruction; if the sludge was not applied directly to adjacent fields, it was dried for transport and sale to enrich the soil of nearby farms.[18] In the process, ash and silt whose ultimate origin was in the regional periphery enhanced the fertility of peri-urban agricultural areas in lowland cores.

The zones of high soil fertility that surrounded all of the larger cities in China's regional cores owed even more to the characteristically Chinese practice of husbanding night soil for use as fertilizer. Buchanan refers to the relevant process as the "continuous transfer of fertility from often distant hinterlands to supply urban populations with food."[19]

The organic and nutrient content of this food, in the form of human excreta, is eventually returned to the soils of the peri-urban area and these soils show a high humus, nitrogen, and base content which makes possible very high and stable yields. This use of night soil diminishes sharply with increasing distance from the cities, [which are consequently] surrounded by concentric zones of diminishing fertility; as a corollary ... it is evident that the remoter food-supplying regions must be undergoing a continuous depletion of fertility as a result of this outflow of nutrients (including the phosphorus loss due to export of animal products).

Thus, urbanization in lowland areas helped bring about the higher fertility and dense rural populations characteristic of regional cores. And the very process of urbanization in regional cores proceeded at the expense of urbanization potential in the surrounding peripheries. In this sense, urban development in the core areas caused urban underdevelopment in the peripheries.

The Economic Hierarchy in the Upper Yangtze Region

I want now to focus on a single macroregion, the Upper Yangtze, in order to analyze the structure of its regional urban system. This section aims to present the contextual significance of cities at each level and to suggest the ways in which level in the hierarchy of economic central places necessarily implies position in a regional urban system.[20]

Map 1 presents an overview of the upper levels of the regional economy of the Upper Yangtze. The regional core, defined in terms of population density, included the major navigable stretches of the region's river system and, as one might expect, coincided rather closely with the Red Basin. As of 1893, the population density of the core was approximately 294 persons per sq. km., and that of the periphery about 47. Note

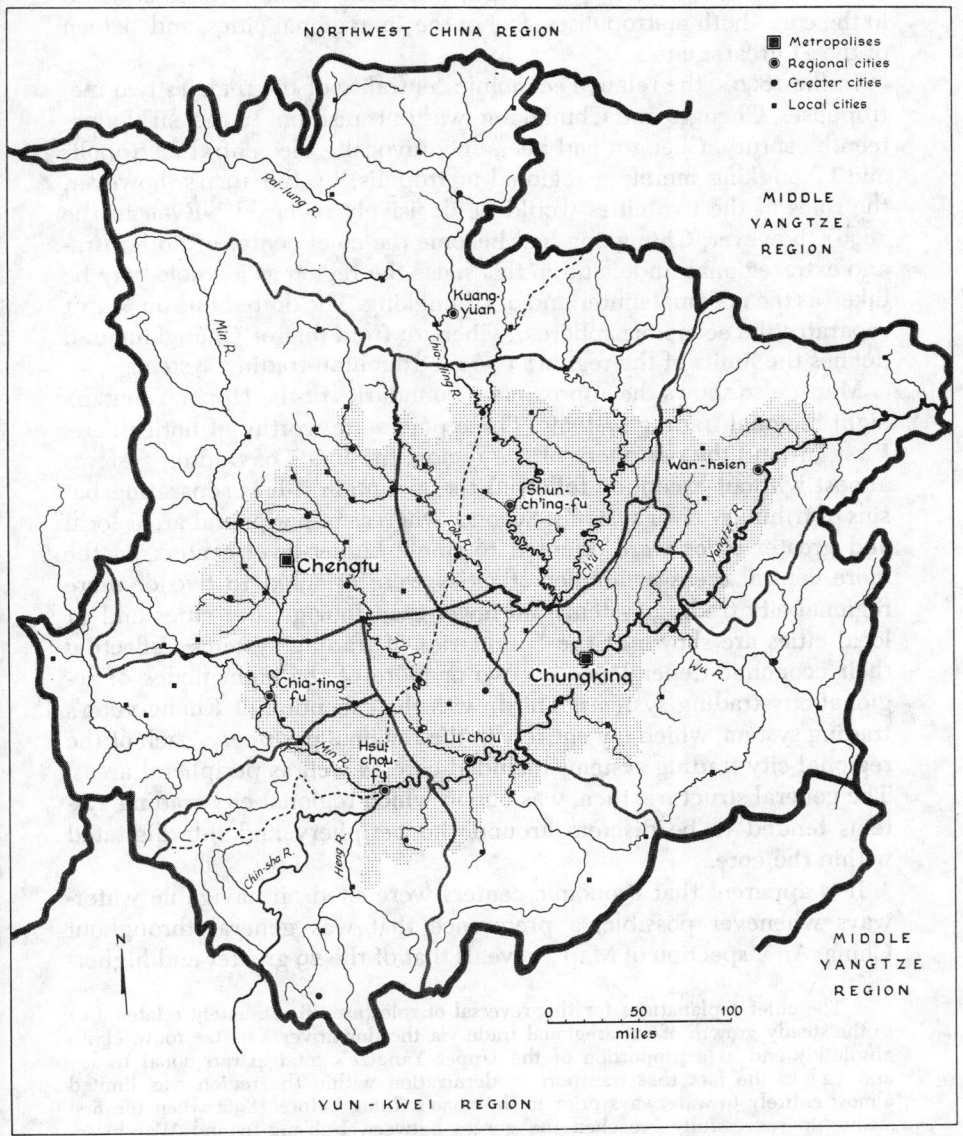

MAP 1. THE UPPER YANGTZE REGION, 1893, showing the extent of the regional core, rivers, central places down to the level of local cities, and the approximate extent of regional-city trading systems. The dotted line bisecting the region separates the economic sphere of Chengtu from that of Chungking.

that most of the region's high-ranking economic centers were situated in the core: both metropolises, five of the six regional cities, and sixteen of the 21 greater cities.

In the 1890's, the relative economic centrality of the region's two metropolises, Chengtu and Chungking, was in transition. In the early nineteenth century, Chengtu had been unequivocally the central metropolis and Chungking merely a regional metropolis; by the 1920's, however, the roles of the two cities would be decisively reversed.* Even in the 1890's, however, Chungking had become the chief center of both intra- and extraregional trade, and in this sense the region as a whole may be taken as the maximal hinterland of Chungking. The dotted line on Map 1 separates the economic sphere of Chengtu from that of Chungking and defines the limits of the region's two metropolitan trading systems.

Map 1 also shows the approximate boundaries of the Upper Yangtze's eight regional trading systems. Three points are worthy of notice here. First, around the periphery of the region, the limits of trading systems almost without exception followed the mountain ridges separating basins of tributary river systems. Second, whereas in peripheral areas local and greater cities were oriented to single higher-level centers, in the more central areas a number of cities were oriented to two or more regional-city trading systems; no fewer than four greater cities and 21 local cities are shown at the boundaries of trading systems, reflecting their economic dependence on two or more of the eight nodes of regional-city trading systems. Third, with the exception of Kuang-yüan's trading system, which lay entirely in the regional periphery, each of the regional-city trading systems included core as well as peripheral areas. The general structure, then, was one in which regional-city trading systems tended to be discrete around the periphery and interdigitated within the core.

It is apparent that economic centers were sited on navigable waterways whenever possible, a preference that was general throughout China. An inspection of Map 1 reveals that of the 29 greater and higher-

---

* The chief explanations for this reversal of roles are all ultimately related (1) to the steady growth of extraregional trade via the downriver Yangtze route (both absolutely and as a proportion of the Upper Yangtze's total extraregional trade) and (2) to the fact that transport modernization within the region was limited almost entirely to waterways prior to the 1950's. Long before 1896, when the first steamship successfully breached the gorges between I-ch'ang-fu and Wan-hsien, Chungking had benefited from the increased economic activity in the Lower and Middle Yangtze regions that had followed the opening of Shanghai and Hankow as treaty ports and the introduction of mechanized transport in those regions. As of 1893, Chengtu was still the more populous of the two cities, although Chungking probably surpassed it in the number of shopkeeper households.

Cities and the Hierarchy of Local Systems

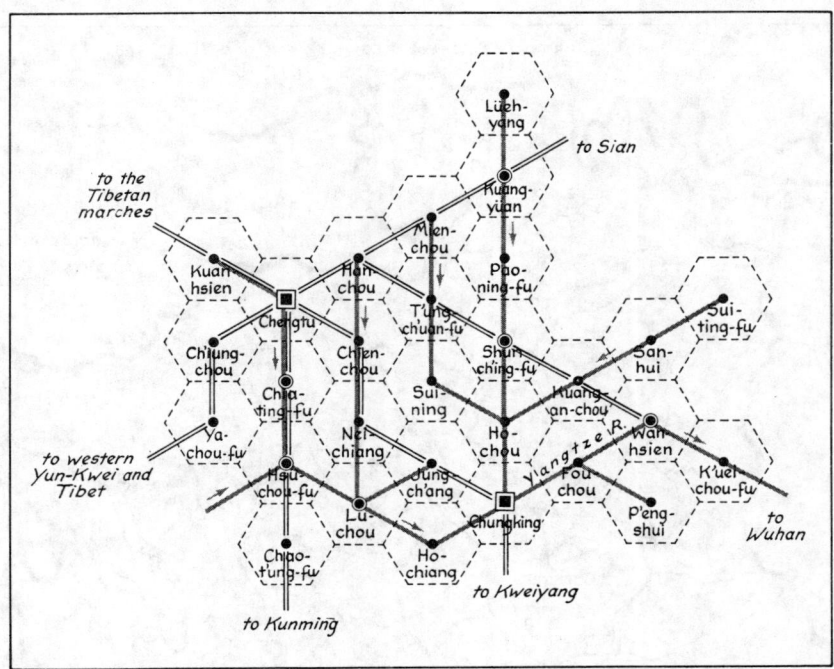

FIG. 2. GREATER-CITY TRADING SYSTEMS IN RELATION TO RIVERS AND MAJOR ROADS (SCHEMATIZED), UPPER YANGTZE REGION, 1893. Arrows show direction of flow of rivers.

level cities in the Upper Yangtze region, only one (Chao-t'ung-fu) was not sited on a river. (The Ch'ing-i River, on which Ya-chou-fu was situated, was unnavigable for certain downstream stretches.) This means that 27 cities of this class were served for at least part of the year by at least small craft.[21]

The essential structure of the region's transport network is schematized in Figure 2. It shows not only those portions of the Yangtze River and its tributaries that linked higher-level cities, but also the most important of the official roads (*kung-lu*), all of which radiated from Chengtu, the provincial capital of Szechwan.[22] In many respects, the highway that ran from Ya-chou-fu through Chengtu to Kuang-yüan (continuing on to Sian and eventually to Peking) was the functional equivalent in Chengtu's metropolitan trading system of the Yangtze River in Chungking's metropolitan trading system. It is apparent that the structure of the river system virtually determined the siting of the region's higher-level economic centers and that major roads had the

MAP 2. THE UPPER YANGTZE REGION, 1893, showing rivers, central places down to the level of local cities, and the approximate extent of greater-city trading systems.

effect of compensating for deficiencies of the river system in linking those cities.*

Map 2 shows greater-city trading systems, the next level below the regional-city trading systems shown in Map 1. In general, the pattern noted in Map 1 is recapitulated for the hinterlands of greater cities. System boundaries in the periphery were relatively impermeable, following mountain ridges that limited intercourse between cities in the various drainage basins, whereas those in the core passed through numerous local cities that were members of two or more greater-city trading systems.

Two of the most important ways in which transport systematically distorts the regularity of the central-place hierarchy were apparent in the Upper Yangtze, as in most other regions of late imperial China. First, major transport routes of all types foster linearity by attracting (as it were) central places that would otherwise be sited on a triangular lattice. This effect is evident in the siting of two local cities (rather than one) between higher-level cities along major rivers. On Map 2, note the placement of local cities between Wan-hsien and Fou-chou on the Yangtze, between Pao-ning-fu and Shun-ch'ing-fu on the Chia-ling River, between T'ung-ch'uan-fu and Sui-ning on the Fou River, between Chienchou and Nei-chiang on the T'o River, and between Chia-ting-fu and Hsü-chou-fu on the Min River. A second distorting effect, wholly expectable in a regional system whose basic transport network is a river system, is the tendency for cities to be situated within their hinterlands off-center in the downstream direction. Examples apparent on Map 2 are the greater-city trading systems of Lüeh-yang, Kuang-yüan, Mienchou and Kuan-hsien in the northwest, of Ho-chiang and P'eng-shui in the southeast, and of Sui-ting-fu and San-hui in the northeast.

It is dramatically evident in Map 2 that the areas of greater-city trading systems at or near the periphery were larger than those in the regional core. This pattern illustrates the expected effect of sparse population and low commercialization in fostering large trading systems. Another feature of the Upper Yangtze system that has general significance is the contrast between relative irregularity in the spatial patterning of regional cities (and higher-level centers) vis-à-vis greater cities,

* In general the importance of navigable waterways in structuring regional urban systems was comparable in four other macroregions—the Middle Yangtze, the Lower Yangtze, the Southeast Coast, and Lingnan—to what we have seen for the Upper Yangtze. The importance of roads and overland transport was relatively greater in North China, absolutely greater in Northwest China, and overwhelmingly greater in Yun-Kwei.

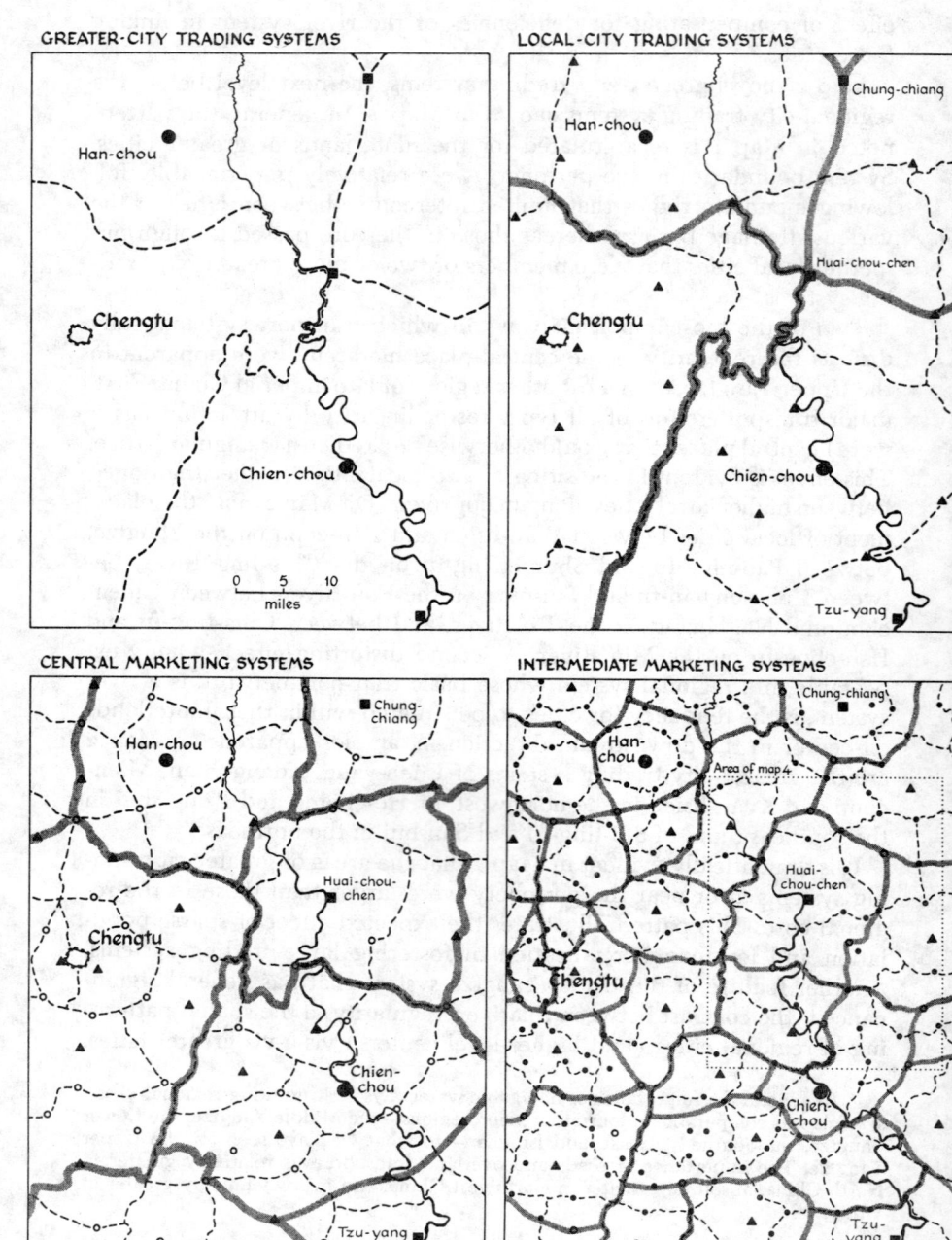

MAP 3 (*opposite*). A SMALL PORTION OF THE UPPER YANGTZE REGION, 1893, showing the approximate extent of greater-city and local-city trading systems and of central and intermediate marketing systems. The wide shaded boundaries show the next higher system level in each case: the limits of greater-city trading systems upper right, of local-city trading systems lower left, and of central marketing systems lower right. Greater cities are shown as large solid circles, local cities as solid squares, central market towns as solid triangles, and intermediate market towns as open circles.

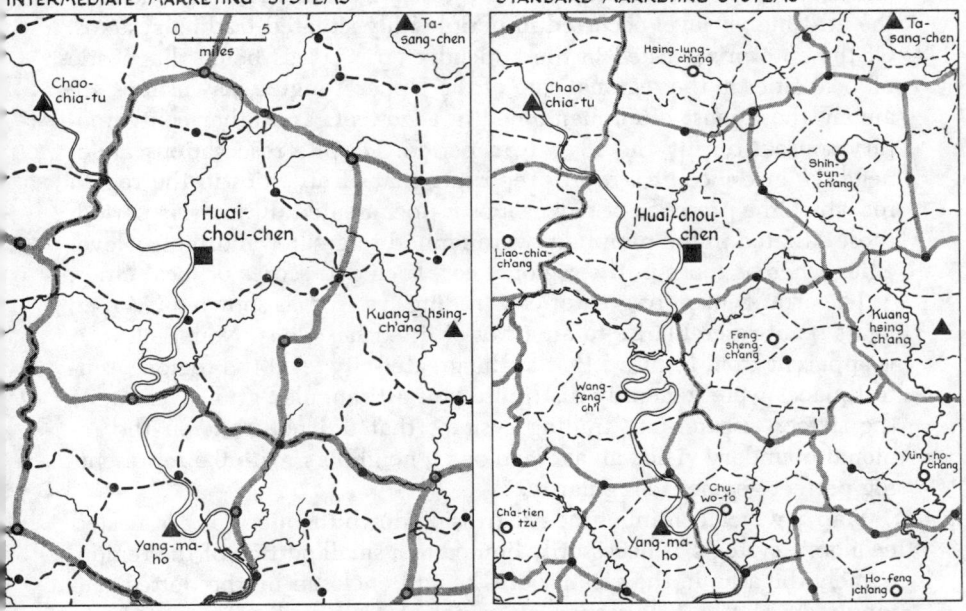

MAP 4. A STILL SMALLER PORTION OF THE UPPER YANGTZE REGION, 1893, showing the approximate extent of intermediate and standard marketing systems. The wide shaded boundaries show the next higher system level in each case: the limits of central marketing systems on the left and of intermediate marketing systems on the right. Local cities are shown as solid squares, central market towns as solid triangles, intermediate market towns as small open circles, and standard market towns as dots.

as against fairly regular patterning at lower steps of the economic hierarchy. Note in Figure 2 that the pattern established by the siting of Kuang-yüan, Shun-ch'ing-fu, Wan-hsien, Chungking, and Lu-chou vis-à-vis their dependent greater cities was broken in the western portion of the region, a function in part of "irregularities" in the structure of the river system, whereby the major river confluences at the sites of Lu-chou and Hsü-chou-fu are exceptionally close together, and in part of the "clumping" of resources in the Chengtu Plain, along the Yangtze between Hsü-chou-fu and Lu-chou, and northwest of Lu-chou along the T'o River. Such "coarse-grained" variations took their toll of regularity in the siting of regional and higher-level cities in most macroregions.

In general, within the same subsystem of centers I find that discrete stratification prevailed and that upward shift of functions to centers of the next higher level occurred in peripherally situated trading systems. Of the enterprises listed in the appendix (p. 351) as being diagnostic of local cities in the regional core of the Upper Yangtze, pawnshops are among those most often mentioned in gazetteers and other contemporary sources during the 1875–1912 period. Despite reservations about negative evidence, it is worth reporting that of all cities in the region for which the presence of pawnshops is documented during this period, those situated in the periphery were limited to greater and higher-level cities whereas those in the regional core included scores of local cities.

The arrangement of greater-city trading systems, as shown on Map 2, bears scant resemblance to an array of fitted hexagons. Nonetheless, it is apparent from Figure 2 that at the greater-city level the region's central places were generally distributed on a triangular grid. A count of the sixteen greater-city trading systems that did not abut on the regional boundary yields an average of 5.3 neighbors, with 6.0 representing perfect geometric regularity.

Map 3, which continues the progression down the hierarchy of nested economic systems, is necessarily limited to a small portion of the region, namely the area in the vicinity of Chengtu enclosed by the dotted rectangle on Map 2. The upper-left panel of Map 3, like Map 2, shows greater-city trading systems, thereby conveying a feel for the sharp increase in scale. Each of the other three panels of Map 3 takes us a step lower in the economic hierarchy. The upper-right panel shows local-city trading systems and central places down to the central market town; the lower-left panel shows central marketing systems and central places down to the intermediate market town; and the lower-right panel shows intermediate marketing systems and central places

Cities and the Hierarchy of Local Systems

down to the standard market town. In each case, system boundaries at the next higher level are indicated by wide shaded lines, thereby dramatizing the manner in which economic centers and hinterlands at each level were related spatially to those at adjacent levels in the hierarchy. In conjunction, they illustrate a general feature of the hierarchy of local economic systems, namely that whereas higher-level systems completely enveloped only one system at the next lower level (the one with the same node), they enveloped several systems at the level below that. We also see at each level the interstitial placement of orders that is characteristic of a regular central-place hierarchy: note in particular that the great majority of intermediate market towns fell at the borders of central marketing systems, i.e., were oriented economically to two or more central market towns, and that the great majority of standard market towns were similarly situated with respect to intermediate marketing systems.

The effect of topography may be seen in the coincidence of systemic boundaries at each level along the crest of the Lung-ch'üan Mountains, which range is penetrated by the T'o River just northwest of Huai-chou-chen. This feature illustrates the general principle, already noted with respect to higher-level systems in the regional periphery, that topographic barriers impede the usual overlapping of systems at adjacent levels of the hierarchy. The tendency for higher-level centers (in this case central market towns on up) to favor through transport routes is apparent along the course of the T'o River.

Map 4 completes the progression down the hierarchy of local economic systems. It is limited to a still smaller portion of the landscape, namely that enclosed by the dotted rectangle shown in the lower-right panel of Map 3. To ensure visual continuity, the left panel of Map 4 repeats at the larger scale what is shown within the dotted rectangle of Map 3. The right panel of Map 4 makes clear that nodes of standard marketing systems were not limited to standard market towns, but also included intermediate market towns, central market towns, and local cities. It shows that standard market towns were normally situated interstitially between higher-level towns and that standard marketing systems were invariably split between intermediate marketing systems. It was these spatial features, all predicted by central-place theory, which, through replication at successively higher levels, integrated local economic systems into the complex interlocking network of higher-order trading systems.

There is no space here to present a schematization of the landscapes shown in Maps 3 and 4. However, the chief point that might thereby be conveyed visually can be suggested quantitatively by neighbor counts at the various levels. It was noted above that inspection of sixteen greater-city trading systems in the central area of the Upper Yangtze region indicated an average of 5.3 neighbors per system. The corresponding figures for lower-level systems wholly or partly included in Map 3 are 5.7 for the nine local-city trading systems, 5.8 for the 31 central marketing systems, 5.9 for the 75 intermediate marketing systems, and 6.0 for the 230 standard marketing systems. Such progressions were characteristic of core areas throughout agrarian China. We may conclude that within regional economic systems the arrangement of central places conformed most closely to the regular central-place model at lower levels of the hierarchy and in core areas as against regional peripheries.

A Comparison of Regional Urban Systems

Because of the unique physiographic configurations of China's macroregions and the semi-independent nature of their various economic histories, no two urban systems were alike. The Middle Yangtze and the Southeast Coast are sharply subregionalized by physiographic features, whereas North China and the Lower Yangtze are not. Great variation obtained in the relative size and shape of the core and in the centrality of its location within the region, which factors strongly conditioned the characteristics of the various urban systems. Nonetheless, systematic comparison across all regions reveals regularities of some interest.

Table 2 sets out for each of the eight macroregional systems the num-

TABLE 2. NUMBER OF CENTRAL PLACES BY REGION AND BY LEVEL IN THE ECONOMIC HIERARCHY, 1893
(*Down to Central Market Towns*)

Region	Central metropolis	Regional metropolis	Regional city	Greater city	Local city	Central market town	Total
Northwest China	1	2	7	18	55	178	261
Yun-Kwei	—	2	3	13	36	112	166
Lingnan	1	2	7	24	71	223	328
Middle Yangtze	1	3	10	25	115	403	557
Upper Yangtze	1	1	6	21	87	292	408
Southeast Coast	—	1	4	11	42	147	205
North China	1	6	18	64	189	697	975
Lower Yangtze	1	3	8	24	74	267	377
Total	6	20	63	200	669	2,319	3,277

ber of central places at each level of the economic hierarchy down to and including central market towns. (Note that the urban system of the Upper Yangtze was about average in terms of number of central places.) The implications of these regional data are brought out in Table 3, which displays the average areas and populations of trading systems at five levels of the hierarchy. In relating Table 3 to the figures of Table 2, it should be remembered that high-level cities have multiple concentric hinterlands. A regional city is the node not only of a regional-city trading system but also of a greater-city trading system, of a local-city trading system, and of a central marketing system. Thus, the numbers of trading systems in Table 3 are cumulations of the numbers of centers shown in Table 2. Regional cities, for instance, were nodes of only 63 of the 89 regional-city trading systems, the others being accounted for by the twenty regional metropolises and the six central metropolises. As expected, the size of hinterlands, whether measured by area or population, decreased decisively in each region from one order to the next lower order in the hierarchy.

Rather more interesting are the comparative size regularities to which attention has been called by ordering the regions according to their average population densities. The pattern that holds in general for trading systems at all levels appears most clearly in the case of central marketing systems: whereas the average area of hinterlands at a given level is related linearly to population density (with area declining steadily as density increases), the average hinterland population shows a curvilinear relationship, increasing along with density up to a point and thereafter decreasing with still higher densities. The overall dynamics of these interrelationships can be captured by comparing four groupings of regions without reference to within-group differences. Demand density (purchasing power per unit of area) was highest in the Lower Yangtze, relatively high in the Southeast Coast and in North China, middling in the Upper and Middle Yangtze regions and Lingnan, and low in Yun-Kwei and Northwest China. It is apparent that as demand density decreases (moving up the table), hinterland area increases by way of compensation. It does not keep pace, however, because a declining population density is related not only to the decrease in demand density but also to an increase in the distance from the center in question to the limits of its hinterland. If the area of hinterlands were to be enlarged in proportion to the decline in demand density, then purchasing power in the more remote areas would be lost to *any* center by reason of excessive transport costs. Thus, in that portion of the regional continuum with relatively sparse populations, one sees a trade-

TABLE 3. CITY-CENTERED ECONOMIC SYSTEMS, BY REGION, 1893

Region[a]	Area (sq. km.)	Pop. (000)	Density (persons per sq. km.)	Metropolitan trading systems			Regional-city trading systems		
				No.	Ave. area (000)	Ave. pop. (000)	No.	Ave. area (000)	Ave. pop. (000)
Northwest China	746,470	24,000	32	3	248.8	8,000	10	74.6	2,400
Yun-Kwei	470,570	16,000	34	2	235.3	8,000	5	94.1	3,200
Lingnan	424,900	33,000	78	3	141.6	11,000	10	42.5	3,300
Middle Yangtze	699,700	75,000	107	4	174.9	18,750	14	50.0	5,357
Upper Yangtze	423,950	53,000	125	2	212.0	26,500	8	53.0	6,625
Southeast Coast	190,710	26,000	136	1	190.7	26,000	5	38.1	5,200
North China	771,300	122,000	158	7	110.2	17,429	25	30.9	4,880
Lower Yangtze	192,740	45,000	233	4	48.2	11,250	12	16.1	3,750
Total	3,920,340	394,000	101	26	150.8	15,154	89	44.0	4,427

[a] Regions are ordered according to population density, low to high from top to bottom.

Region	Greater-city trading systems			Local-city trading systems			Central marketing systems		
	No.	Ave. area	Ave. pop. (000)	No.	Ave. area	Ave. pop. (000)	No.	Ave. area	Ave. pop. (000)
Northwest China	28	26,660	857	83	8,994	289	261	2,860	92
Yun-Kwei	18	26,140	889	54	8,714	296	166	2,834	96
Lingnan	34	12,500	970	105	4,047	314	328	1,295	101
Middle Yangtze	39	17,940	1,923	154	4,543	487	557	1,256	135
Upper Yangtze	29	14,620	1,828	116	3,654	457	408	1,039	130
Southeast Coast	16	11,920	1,625	58	3,288	448	205	930	127
North China	89	8,670	1,370	278	2,774	439	975	791	125
Lower Yangtze	36	5,350	1,250	110	1,752	409	377	511	119
Total	289	13,570	1,363	958	4,092	411	3,277	1,196	120

off whereby the average area increases (with declining demand density) at so gradual a rate that the average hinterland population declines. In Northwest China and Yun-Kwei, goods appropriate to centers at a given level had ranges that were, in a manner of speaking, unduly restricted for the ecological environment, whereas firms appropriate to such centers had thresholds that were unduly extended; the result of this "squeeze" was that hinterlands were at once overlarge in area and not large enough in population.

In that portion of the regional continuum with relatively dense populations, purchasing power becomes critical in understanding the relationships revealed in Table 3. The Lower Yangtze as a whole was far more commercialized than the Southeast Coast, which in turn was more commercialized than the Middle Yangtze. The implication is that 1.2 million people in the Lower Yangtze (the average population of a greater-city trading system) generated at least as much demand as 1.6 million in the Southeast Coast and 1.9 million in the Middle Yangtze. And there is no reason to doubt it; one would, in fact, expect the *total* purchasing power of a greater-city trading system, say, to be smaller in the Middle than in the Lower Yangtze (rather than the same) owing to the effect of higher transport costs in limiting hinterland size. In short, the curvilinear relationship of population density with average hinterland population is but a manifestation of a more basic linear relationship with the total purchasing power of the various regions.

Note the following irony. The Upper Yangtze was chosen as the region for detailed analysis in part because of its typicality: an internal physiography that fell midway between the extremes, an urban system of average size, and an overall population density that put it closer than any other region to the empirewide average. Yet its city-centered trading systems were among the most populous in all of China.

The Official Administrative Hierarchy

Most of China's central places that ranked as local cities or higher in the economic hierarchy also served as administrative capitals. For instance, in the Upper Yangtze as of 1893, all eight of the regional cities and metropolises were capitals, as were twenty of the 21 greater cities, 68 of the 87 local cities, and 43 of the 292 central market towns. I now turn to a description of field administration in order to explore the ways in which the administrative central functions of cities and their place in the administrative hierarchy interacted with their economic central functions and place in regional economic systems.

The Ch'ing field administration[23] may be conveniently described as having four levels below the imperial capital.* At the highest level, the eight governor-generalships and eighteen provinces were interdigitated to constitute in effect nineteen governments in as many capital cities. Only three of the eight capitals with a governor-general's yamen (Canton, Wu-ch'ang-fu, and Kunming) also housed a governor's yamen. Three provinces (Shansi, Honan, and Shantung) belonged to no governor-generalship, and two governor-generalships consisted of a single province each (Chihli and Szechwan). Nanking, capital of the Liang-chiang governor-generalship, was situated in Kiangsu, whose provincial government was at Soochow; nonetheless, the Nanking government included several high officials (e.g., a lieutenant governor and a provincial director of education) otherwise found exclusively in provincial capitals.[24] In any case, the present analysis ignores the administrative distinctions among the nineteen cities that served as capitals of provinces and/or governor-generalships.

The eighteen provinces were subdivided into 77 circuits (tao), some of which were classified as military circuits. In some respects, circuit yamens resembled specialized offices of the provincial government more than administrative offices at a separate level of the territorial hierarchy. For instance, circuit intendants were primarily responsible for diplomatic relations with foreigners even within the circuit that contained the provincial capital. The official educational hierarchy concerned with supervising and accrediting scholars and administering imperial examinations bypassed circuits altogether. Nor were official temples and altars prescribed for the circuit level, as they were for the other three levels of field administration. Nonetheless, the circuit intendant maintained a yamen in a city within the territorial area of his circuit, and prefects and other officials at the next lower level were directly accountable to him for a wide range of civil and military affairs. And despite anomalies, circuit yamens were traditionally located in cities that were capitals by virtue of having yamens for other levels of the administrative hierarchy.

* This analysis is limited to agrarian China minus Manchuria and Taiwan, specifically to the eight macroregions defined in my Part One paper (see Maps 1 and 2, pp. 214–15). As of 1893, the combined territory of these regions contained 1,576 county-level units, inclusive of areas directly administered from prefectural-level capitals. At that time the empire as a whole contained approximately 80 additional county-level units, not treated here; most of the excluded units were in Sinkiang, Manchuria, and Taiwan, but several were located in the arid and/or mountainous periphery of China proper, most notably northern Chihli, western Szechwan, and northwestern Yunnan (see Map 2). The 1,576 county-level units under consideration contained only 1,549 capitals because yamens of adjacent county-level units were occasionally located in the same city.

The next lower level included three types of administrative units: prefectures (*fu*), by far the most numerous; autonomous *chou*, also called independent departments (*chih-li chou*); and autonomous *t'ing*, also called independent subprefectures (*chih-li t'ing*). The relative importance of these prefectural-level units is suggested by the bureaucratic rank of the superior incumbent official, normally 4b for a prefecture, 5a for an autonomous *chou*, and 5a or 6a for an autonomous *t'ing*.* This rank order was reflected in the relative population of prefectural-level capitals. On the average, the capitals of prefectures were more populous than those of autonomous *chou*, which in turn were more populous than those of autonomous *t'ing*.[25] The classic contemporary description of Ch'ing administration tells us that autonomous *t'ing* "represent a lower form of local government," having been "made independent of the prefectural government because of their importance or territorial magnitude." Moreover, autonomous *chou* and *t'ing* "represent intermediate stages in the transformation of ordinary [*chou* and *t'ing*] into prefectures. For this reason they are observed to be most numerous on the borders of the Empire."[26] We shall have reason below to modify and elaborate this interpretation, but for the moment it may serve to signal the status of autonomous *chou* and *t'ing* as at once lower ranking than prefectures and somehow special.

Three different types of units were also found at the fourth and lowest level of bureaucratic administration, namely, counties (*hsien*), by far the most numerous; ordinary *chou*, also known as dependent departments (*san-chou* or *shu-chou*); and ordinary *t'ing*, also known as dependent subprefectures (*san-t'ing* or *shu-t'ing*).† All three types of county-level units could be subordinate to prefectures, whereas with one exception ordinary *chou* and *t'ing* were never subordinate to autonomous *chou* or *t'ing*.[27] By contrast with the prefectural level, where autonomous *chou* and *t'ing* were outranked by prefectures, at the county

* There were nine bureaucratic ranks, each divided into an upper (a) and lower (b) subrank. Rank 1a was highest, 9b lowest.

† Arguably a still lower level of administration existed in embryonic form. Certain county-level units contained subdistricts (*ssu*) whose "capitals" were towns where a special category of deputy magistrate (*hsün-chien*) served. Since such towns typically ranked among the most important within their counties, there would be good reason for keeping them distinct in analysis. On the other hand, subdistricts were never considered a regular administrative unit at the subcounty level—on the contrary, *hsün-chien* were considered an integral part of the county-level government—and their number was repeatedly reduced during late imperial times. At any event, in the present analysis I have reluctantly merged this small class of subadministrative towns with nonadministrative centers—a decision that greatly simplifies presentation without materially altering the results.

level ordinary *chou* and *t'ing* officially outranked counties. The chief bureaucrat of an ordinary *chou* was normally of rank 5b and that of an ordinary *t'ing* of rank 6a (occasionally 5a), whereas the rank of a county magistrate was normally only 7b. City size, however, suggests a different ordering. True enough, *chou* capitals tended to be larger than either *hsien* or *t'ing* capitals, but *t'ing* capitals were smaller on the average than *hsien* capitals, not larger—as might be expected from the official ranking.[28] This discrepancy will be explained when the regional distribution of types of capital cities is considered below.

The hierarchical ordering that ran from province to prefecture to county was seen as the standard administrative arrangement. Prefectures and counties, as we have seen, greatly outnumbered other administrative units at their respective levels. Moreover, provincial capitals were invariably capitals of prefectures (never of autonomous *chou* or *t'ing*), and prefectural capitals were invariably capitals of counties (never of ordinary *chou* or *t'ing*). The standard hierarchy of province-prefecture-county was structured in the manner familiar to us from most modern administrative arrangements. The territory of a province was exhausted by prefectural-level units, and the capital of one of these, termed hereafter the metropolitan prefecture, also served as the provincial capital. Similarly, the territory of a prefecture was exhausted by county-level units, and the capital of one of these, termed hereafter the metropolitan county, also served as the prefectural capital. Thus, every provincial capital had minimally three yamens, one each for the provincial governor, the prefect, and the county magistrate, and every prefectural capital had minimally two yamens, one each for the prefect and the county magistrate.

The arrangement was quite different in the case of an autonomous *chou*, whose territory was not exhausted by its subordinate counties. Rather, what would otherwise be considered the metropolitan county-level unit had no government of its own. Known as the *pen-chou* (the "root" *chou*, or *chou* proper), it was administered directly by the government of the autonomous *chou*, whose capital thus lacked a county-level yamen. The entire category of *pen-chou* tends to be lost in administrative records and to be overlooked in analyses of Ch'ing administration since *pen-chou* do not appear as administrative units in official compendia such as the *Hui-tien* or the *Chin-shen ch'üan-shu*. Autonomous *t'ing* were more anomalous still in that, with two exceptions, they lacked subordinate county-level units altogether. Thus, the county-level "*pen-t'ing*" (the term was not used) exhausted the territory of the prefectural-

TABLE 4. SPAN OF CONTROL BY TYPE OF ADMINISTRATIVE CENTER, 1893
(*Prefectural and Higher-level Capitals Only*)

Span of control[a]	Capitals of								Total	
	Metropolitan prefectures		Ordinary prefectures[b]		Autonomous *chou*		Autonomous *t'ing*			
	No.	Pct.	No.	Pct.	No.	Pct.	No.	Pct.	No.	Pct.
1			4	13%		0%	28	88%	32	100%
2			4	27	9	60	2	13	15	100
3			8	25	24	75		0	32	100
4			21	53	19	48			40	100
5		0%	22	71	9	29			31	100
6	2	6	22	71	7	23			31	100
7–8	3	6	48	94		0			51	100
9–10	4	16	21	84					25	100
11–13	4	29	10	71					14	100
14+	7	78	2	22					9	100
Total	20	7%	162	58%	68	24%	30	11%	280	100%

[a] I.e., the number of county-level yamens supervised by a given prefectural-level yamen.
[b] Includes the two sectoral capitals in the imperial prefecture that served as circuit capitals.

level autonomous *t'ing*, and there was of course only a single administrative yamen in the capital city.*

This last distinction draws our attention to span of control, a formal feature of field administration that sharply differentiated the three types of prefectural-level units. The analysis pursued here refers solely to control of county-level yamens by their superior prefectural-level yamens. Span is said to be narrow when the superordinate office has only a few subordinate offices to supervise, and broad when the subordinate offices are many. In Ch'ing China, the number of county-level units per prefectural-level unit ranged from one to eighteen, not counting the exceptional imperial prefecture, which had 24; the mean fell between five and six. Table 4 shows the span of control of all prefectural-level units

---

* In fact some "rectification of names" would have been in order in the field administrative system of late Ch'ing. Two autonomous *t'ing* (Pai-se in Kwangsi and Hsü-yung in Szechwan) and six prefectures (Hsing-i, Shih-ch'ien, Ssu-chou, Ssu-nan, and Ta-ting, all in Kweichow, and Ssu-en in Kwangsi) were structurally identical to autonomous *chou*, and I have been unable to ascertain any reason why they were not so designated. The anomalous *t'ing* each contained one county in addition to the directly ruled area, and in the anomalous prefectures what would have been the metropolitan county was a directly ruled area analogous to a *pen-chou*. The six prefectures thus constitute an exception to the general rule given in the text that every prefectural capital contained at least one county yamen. Where appropriate in subsequent statistical analyses, these anomalous cases are classed with the capitals of autonomous *chou*.

TABLE 5. SPAN OF CONTROL BY TYPE OF CAPITAL, 1893
(*County-level Capitals Subordinate to Prefectures Only*)

County-level capital	Span of control[a]							
	−6		7–8		9+		Total	
	No.	Pct.	No.	Pct.	No.	Pct.	No.	Pct.
Hsien	225	25%	242	27%	421	47%	888	100%
Chou[b]	37	27	48	35	51	38	136	100
T'ing	26	43	10	17	24	40	60	100
Total	288	27%	300	28%	496	46%	1,084	100%

[a] Span of control refers here to the number of units in the prefecture to which the county-level unit in question belonged.
[b] Excludes sectoral capitals in the imperial prefecture.

by type of prefectural-level capital. We have already noted that the span of control of autonomous *t'ing* was normally only one, and it is clear from the table that autonomous *chou* had relatively narrow spans; they ranged from two to six with a mean of 3.7. Ordinary prefectures had spans clustered in the range from four to ten, with a mean of 6.6, whereas metropolitan prefectures (i.e., those whose capitals were provincial or higher capitals) had still broader spans, ranging from six to 24, with a mean of 11.9.

At the county level, too, units were distinguished by span of control. It follows from what has already been said that counties in autonomous *chou* would be more closely supervised (in the sense of belonging to superordinate units with relatively narrow spans of control) than counties in prefectures. However, there is no a priori reason for expecting differences among the three types of units within prefectures. Nonetheless, as shown in Table 5, ordinary *t'ing* were disproportionately found in prefectures with narrow spans (six or less), ordinary *chou* in prefectures with intermediate spans (seven to eight), and *hsien* in prefectures with broad spans (nine or more).

The key to span variations at both levels of the administrative hierarchy lies in the distinctive locational patterns of different types of capitals within regional urban systems, a subject I take up in the following section. But first a summary of the various types of capital cities is in order. Details are presented in Table 6, where the numerical preponderance of prefectural and county capitals at their respective levels is immediately apparent. Table 6 also points up the peculiar distribution of circuit yamens. If circuits had fitted "properly" into the field-administrative system, then all higher-level capitals would also have been circuit capitals and all circuit capitals would also have been prefectural-level capitals. However, exceptions to both expectations are apparent

Cities and the Hierarchy of Local Systems

TABLE 6. CAPITALS BY ADMINISTRATIVE LEVEL AND RANK, 1893

Capitals of	Also circuit capitals No.	Also circuit capitals Pct.	Not also circuit capitals	Total
Provinces and/or governor-generalships	16	84%	3	19
Sectors of the imperial prefecture[a]	2	50	2	4
Prefectures[b]	41	26	119	160
Autonomous *chou*	6	9	62	68
Autonomous *t'ing*[c]	2	7	28	30
Chou in prefectures	2	2	134	136
T'ing in prefectures[d]	3	5	57	60
Nonmetropolitan *hsien* in prefectures	5	1	883	888
Hsien in autonomous *chou*	0	0	184	184
Total	77	5%	1,472	1,549

[a] Of the four sectors into which Shun-t'ien *fu*, the imperial prefecture, was divided, three formed one circuit whose capital was at Ch'ang-p'ing-chou, which also served as capital of the North sector. The East sector, together with Yung-p'ing *fu*, formed a separate circuit whose capital was at T'ung-chou, which also served as capital of the East sector. Thus, the capitals of the South and West sectors, Pa-chou and Wan-p'ing (the latter one of Peking's two metropolitan counties) did not serve as circuit capitals, and Peking (which does not appear elsewhere in this table) was not itself a circuit capital.

[b] The Wuhan conurbation, which in this analysis is counted as a single economic center, appears in this row as two prefectural capitals, Wu-ch'ang-fu and Han-yang-fu, both also circuit capitals. This was not strictly true in the latter case, for the circuit yamen was located in Hankow, an otherwise nonadministrative center in the metropolian county of Han-yang *fu*.

[c] Kuei-sui, which in this analysis is counted as a single economic center, appears in this row as two *t'ing* capitals. Sui-yüan also served as a circuit capital, whereas Kuei-hua-ch'eng did not.

[d] Chiang-pei-t'ing, situated directly across the Chia-ling River from Chungking, is in this analysis considered together with that prefectural capital as a single economic center. However, it appears in this row as a separate capital.

from the table. Peking and three provincial capitals (Soochow, Hangchow, and Canton) did not serve as circuit capitals, whereas ten county-level capitals did. These administrative irregularities, together with the functional anomalies of circuits mentioned previously, can best be understood when related to China's spatial structure, to which we now return.

The Regional Basis of Field Administration

In late imperial China, field administration was designed not only to promote social order and foster the well-being of the populace, but also—and more importantly—to ensure the regular flow of revenue, to defend the various parts of the realm against internal and external enemies, and to prevent the concentration or consolidation of local power that might pose a threat to imperial control. It is my thesis that all of these administrative concerns varied in rough correspondence with the structure of physiographic regions, and that in consequence so did administrative arrangements and the character of capital cities.

In a word, I argue that revenue and defense were inversely related in regional space such that in the central areas of regional cores local government was preoccupied with taxation to the virtual exclusion of military affairs, whereas along regional frontiers local government was preoccupied with defense and security to the virtual exclusion of fiscal affairs. As for the potential threat of local power, I would suggest that in core areas the chief danger lay in concerted action by the leading elements of society, whereas in peripheral areas it lay in the mobilization of heterodox elements. Finally, I believe it can be shown that the political structure, and above all the leadership of local social systems, varied according to place in the overall regional structure in such a way that the burden of societal management to be shouldered by local government was relatively lighter in cores than in peripheral areas. If, as these propositions suggest, the mix of administrative priorities and tasks varied systematically through the spatial structure of regions, then the central functions of administrative capitals would have been differentiated accordingly.

Let us begin with the distribution of the various types of capitals as between regional cores and peripheries. Table 7 summarizes the relevant data for the eight macroregions combined. We see in the upper portion, which focuses solely on administrative centers within prefectures, that the capitals of metropolitan prefectures (i.e., provincial and higher-level capitals) were far more often located in regional cores than were nonmetropolitan prefectural capitals. Moreover, county-level units

TABLE 7. CAPITALS OF DIFFERENT LEVELS AND TYPES BY LOCATION IN REGIONAL CORES OR PERIPHERIES

Capitals of	Cores		Peripheries	Total
	No.	Pct.		
Metropolitan prefectures	17	85%	3	20
Ordinary prefectures	80	53	70	150
Other counties in prefectures	468	53	420	888
Chou in prefectures[a]	63	45	76	139
T'ing in prefectures	13	22	47	60
Autonomous *chou*[b]	31	41	45	76
Hsien in autonomous *chou*	72	39	112	184
Autonomous *t'ing*[c]	6	19	26	32
Total	750	48%	799	1,549

[a] Includes T'ung-chou, Ch'ang-p'ing-chou, and Pa-chou, sectoral capitals in the imperial prefecture.
[b] Includes capitals of the two autonomous *t'ing* and six prefectures that were structurally analogous to autonomous *chou*.
[c] Includes capitals of the four prefectures with only a single subordinate *hsien*.

within prefectures were sharply differentiated in this respect by administrative type. Ordinary *chou* were more likely to be peripherally situated than nonmetropolitan counties, and ordinary *t'ing* were still more strongly concentrated in regional peripheries. This reflects two systematic biases: (1) only the more peripherally situated prefectures were likely to contain any *chou* or *t'ing* at all; and (2) within such prefectures, the *chou* and/or *t'ing* were situated more peripherally than were counties. In the lower part of the table we see that capitals of autonomous *chou* and their component counties were somewhat more peripheral in their distribution than were ordinary *chou*, and that autonomous *t'ing* were concentrated no less heavily in the peripheries than were ordinary *t'ing*. As one might suspect, the rough dichotomization of regions into cores and peripheries obscures another regularity that in fact obtained: within regional peripheries, *t'ing* tended to be more peripherally located than *chou*.

The next question concerns the extent to which the differences in span of control that were found above to be associated with level and type of administrative capital were themselves simply a reflection of place in the core-periphery structure of regions. We see in Table 8 that for higher-level capitals of each type the span of control was relatively broad in the regional cores and relatively narrow in regional peripheries. Once again, there obtained a fairly regular progression that is partially obscured in Table 8 by the simple dichotomization of the core-periphery variable: the broadest spans tended to occur in the centers of regional cores, and the narrowest ones toward the rim of the regional peripheries. This resulted not only from a concentration of autonomous *t'ing* (typically with a span of one) in the far periphery and of autonomous *chou* (with spans of two to six) in the intermediate range, but also from systematic variation in the number of county-level units within both prefectures and autonomous *chou* according to their specific location within the region's core-periphery structure. Note, however, that span of control is not simply a function of the prefectural-level unit's position in the core-periphery structure; that is, type of capital has an independent effect, a point that can be readily grasped by focusing on units with the same span. Of those with a span of six, for instance, the proportion situated in the cores declined from 71 percent of the autonomous *chou* to 39 percent of the prefectures to none of the provincial and higher-level capitals.

As for the different types of units at the county level, we have already established that peripherally located prefectures were more likely to

TABLE 8. SPAN OF CONTROL BY LOCATION IN REGIONAL CORES OR PERIPHERIES, 1893
(*Prefectural and Higher-level Capitals Only*[a])

Provincial and higher-level capitals					Prefectural capitals					Capitals of autonomous *chou* and autonomous *t'ing*				
Span of control	Cores		Periph- eries	Total	Span of control	Cores		Periph- eries	Total	Span of control	Cores		Periph- eries	Total
	No.	Pct.				No.	Pct.				No.	Pct.		
6	0	0%	2	2	–3	4	24%	13	17	1–2	6	15%	33	39
7–10	6	86	1	7	4–5	14	34	27	41	3	7	29	17	24
11+	11	100	1	11	6	9	39	14	23	4	7	37	12	19
					7	11	44	14	25	5	5	56	4	9
					8+	32	59	22	54	6	5	71	2	7
Total	17	85%	3	20	Total	70	44%	90	160	Total	30	31%	68	98

[a] Span of control in this table refers to the number of county-level units subordinate to the prefectural-level yamen in the capital in question. Sectoral capitals in the imperial prefecture are not included. Han-yang-fu is counted separately from Wu-ch'ang-fu, and Kuei-hua-ch'eng is counted separately from Sui-yüan. Status as circuit capitals is not taken into account in the classification of capitals. The core/periphery classification relates here to the prefectural-level capital per se, not to the prefecture as a whole; cf. Table 10.

TABLE 9. SPAN OF CONTROL BY LOCATION IN REGIONAL CORES OR PERIPHERIES, 1893
(*County-level Capitals Subordinate to Prefectures Only*[a])

	Hsien in prefectures[b]				Ordinary chou[c]				Ordinary t'ing			
Span of control	Cores No.	Cores Pct.	Peripheries	Total	Span of control	Cores No.	Cores Pct.	Peripheries	Total	Span of control	Cores No.	Cores Pct.	Peripheries	Total

Span of control	Cores No.	Pct.	Peripheries	Total	Span of control	Cores No.	Pct.	Peripheries	Total	Span of control	Cores No.	Pct.	Peripheries	Total
–6	64	27%	168	232	2–3	0	0%	3	3	–5	0	0%	16	16
7	46	36	82	128	4–7	14	25	42	56	6–8	4	25	16	20
8–10	144	46	168	312	8–10	16	36	28	44	9	8	30	16	24
11–13	69	57	53	122	11+	18	50	18	36					
14+	93	78	26	119										
Total	416	46%	497	913	Total	48	35%	91	139	Total	12	20%	48	60

[a] Span of control in this table refers to the number of units in the prefectural-level unit to which the county-level unit in question belonged. Chiang-pei-t'ing is counted separately from Chungking. Status as circuit capitals is not taken into account in the classification of capitals. Reconciliation: from Table 8: 20 + 160 + 98 = 278; from this table, 913 + 139 + 60 = 1112. In addition, there were 186 hsien in autonomous chou, not shown here. The total number of county-level units covered by this analysis is 278 + 1112 + 186 = 1576.

[b] Includes 25 "extra" *hsien* whose capital was shared.

[c] Includes T'ung-chou, Ch'ang-p'ing-chou, and Pa-chou, which also served as sectoral capitals within the imperial prefecture.

include ordinary *chou* and *t'ing* among their subordinate units and that *t'ing* in particular were concentrated in the most peripheral prefectures. As shown in Table 9, this finding is also closely associated with differences in span of control. One could conclude either that prefectures had been made smaller in areas where proportionately many of the county-level units were *chou* and *t'ing* (which areas were empirically concentrated in regional peripheries) or that prefectures had been made smaller in regional peripheries (where *chou* and *t'ing* happened to be concentrated); but either way, *t'ing* yamens were likely to be more closely supervised than *chou* yamens, which in turn were likely to be more closely supervised than *hsien* yamens.

We are now in a position to demonstrate that the span of control of prefectural-level units varied systematically not only with position in the regional core-periphery structure but also with the level of their capitals in the economic central-place hierarchy. Since the spans of prefectural-level units at any given level tended to be narrower in the periphery than in the core, it is parsimonious to present the data by grouping peripheral capitals at one level of the economic hierarchy with core capitals at the next lower level of the economic hierarchy, as in Table 10. This arrangement in effect shows the span of control of all capitals at the prefectural level or higher arranged by position in their respective economic systems. The message of the table is unmistakable. Cities whose economic centrality was exceptionally high tended to be capitals of extra-large prefectures with extraordinarily broad spans of control (upper-right corner of the table). Span declined steadily and regularly with the capital's economic centrality until, in the lower-left corner of the table, cities of exceptionally low economic centrality are seen to have been capitals of very small prefectural-level units with extraordinarily narrow spans of control.

A part of the explanation for this relationship undoubtedly relates to the effective distance between the prefectural-level yamen and the yamens of its subordinate counties. In the prefectures at the upper-right of Table 10, counties on the average were relatively small in area (though large in population), and transport costs were relatively low. County-level units in the diagonally opposite corner, however, were on the average much larger in area (though small in population), and transport costs were relatively high. Thus, in terms of the friction of distance to be overcome in reaching subordinate capitals from the prefectural-level capital, the most distant county capital in a fourteen-county prefecture (upper right) might well be closer than the closest subordinate capital in a two-county autonomous *chou* (lower left).

TABLE 10. SPAN OF CONTROL BY POSITION IN REGIONAL ECONOMIC SYSTEMS, 1893
(I.e. by a Classification Combining Level in the Economic Hierarchy with Location in Regional Cores and Peripheries, Prefectural and Higher-level Capitals Only)

Level in the economic hierarchy	Regional cores (C) or peripheries (P)[a]	Span of control[b]												Total	
		1–2		3–4		5–7		8–9		10–13		14+			
		No.	Pct.	No.	Pct.	No.	Pct.	No.	Pct.	No.	Pct.	No.	Pct.	No.	Pct.
Central metropolis	C		0%		0%		0%		0%	1	20%	4	80%	5	100%
Regional metropolis	C		0%	2	12	3	18	3	18	5	29	4	24	17	100
Regional metropolis Regional city	P C	1	4	2	7	10	36	7	25	7	25	1	4	28	100
Regional city Greater city	P C	2	3	9	13	33	49	13	19	10	15	0	0	67	100
Greater city Local city	P C	12	15	24	30	33	41	5	6	6	8			80	100
Local city Central market town	P C	12	22	27	49	12	22	3	5	1	2			55	100
Central market town	P	20	71	8	29		0		0		0			28	100
Total		47	17%	72	26%	91	33%	31	11%	30	11%	9	3%	280	100%

Pct. of county-level units in core	Prefectural-level capital in core or periphery?	Classification of prefectural-level unit
51–100	C	C
	P	C
30–50	C	C
	P	P
–29	C	P
	P	

[a] In analyses of span of control within prefectural-level units, the core-periphery distribution of all capitals within the prefecture is taken into account in assigning the prefecture to either the core or periphery:

[b] I.e., the number of county-level units subordinate to the prefectural-level yamen in the capital in question.

Although this factor is helpful in understanding the feasibility of the arrangements indicated by Table 10, it does not speak to their underlying rationale. My argument, to be developed below, is that the critical factors were fiscal strategy and defense policy. A broad span of control and the standard administrative arrangement of counties in prefectures appear to have been optimal for revenue collection in the hinterlands of cities with high economic centrality, whereas a narrow span of control and the peculiar administrative arrangement of *chou* and *t'ing* appear to have been optimal for defense and security, which were particularly salient in regional peripheries.

Post designations. Support for this line of interpretation may be drawn from an important feature of Ch'ing field administration not yet introduced. The superior bureaucratic post in every county- and prefectural-level yamen was officially characterized according to the presence or absence of four stereotyped attributes.* These post designations, as I shall refer to them, consisted of the various combinations of four binary variables, each indicated by the presence or absence of a Chinese character. Altogether there were sixteen possible designations, one consisting of all four characters, four consisting of combinations of three characters, six consisting of combinations of two characters, four consisting of a single character, and one without any characters. The four elements of these post designations may be briefly described as follows. *Fan* ("troublesome, abundant") was conventionally taken to signify a great deal of official business at the yamen in question. *Ch'ung* ("thoroughfare, frequented") was held to indicate a center of communications; more closely than any of the other three characters, it indicated a capital's commercial importance. *Nan* ("difficult, vexatious") purportedly referred to a post that had to cope with an unruly, crime-prone populace. *P'i* ("fatiguing, wearisome") referred to the difficulty of collecting taxes.[29]

The sixteen possible post designations were assigned with quite different frequencies. Capitals boasting a four-character post were fairly rare, numbering only 59 altogether; they were strongly concentrated (59 percent) in regional cores. By contrast, capitals with a no-character designation were the most numerous (424 altogether) and were poorly represented in regional cores (only 30 percent). For the rest, the four characters occurred in post designations as follows: *nan* (hereafter N), "insecure locale," 697; *fan* (hereafter F), "busy yamen," 637; *ch'ung* (hereafter C), "trade center," 526; and *p'i* (hereafter P), "unremunera-

---

* The posts of circuit intendants were similarly designated, but post designations at the circuit level are excluded from the present analysis.

Cities and the Hierarchy of Local Systems

tive post," 258. A frequency analysis of the two- and three-character designations reveals patterning that may be diagrammed as follows:

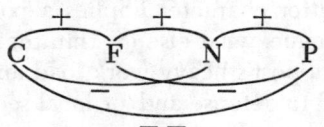

When arranged in this sequence, the affinity of any character for another is a function of proximity. Each has a positive affinity only for its immediate neighbor(s), and C and P constitute the least compatible pair.

The internal logic of this symbolic system is fairly straightforward. That C and P should be incompatible makes eminent sense if—as my previous analysis suggests is reasonable—we assume that an important transport node–cum–trade center was likely to be the center of an extensive high-level trading system. A yamen situated in such an economic central place would hardly be expected to experience revenue problems or to be considered an unremunerative post. As shown in Table 11, CP was by far the least common of the six character pairs, and the two three-character designations containing both C and P were rare indeed by comparison with the other two combinations. The lesser incompatibilities of C with N and of F with P become more readily understandable if the connotation of F is expanded slightly to include the idea of a politically sensitive or important post. If a city was important as a trade center and hence as a source of revenue (C), *and* located in an area with problems of security or social control (N), then its yamen was almost by definition a politically sensitive post, so that one would ex-

TABLE 11. FREQUENCIES OF TWO- AND THREE-CHARACTER POST DESIGNATIONS AND THEIR DISTRIBUTION AMONG CAPITALS IN REGIONAL CORES AND PERIPHERIES

Character designations		Actual	Expected	Ratio	Cores		Peripheries	Total
					No.	Pct.		
CFN	FNP	280	196	143 ▲	173	62% ▲	107	280
CFP	CNP	22	106	21	8	36	14	22
Total		302	302		181	60%	121	302
CF	FN NP	357	275	130 ▲	181	51% ▲	176	357
CN	FP	85	144	59	33	39	52	85
CP		12	35	34	3	25	9	12
Total		454	454		217	48%	237	454

pect C plus N to occur only rarely without F. Hence the underoccurrence of CN and the overoccurrence of CFN. As for the combination of F with P, since the latter character implies a post that was unimportant as a source of revenue, what else (within the limits of the scheme) could be the cause of a post's heavy work load and political sensitivity if not activities related to defense and/or local security? Thus F plus P should occur only rarely without N.

Simply taking the three-character designations at their face value, one would expect CFN, rather than FNP, to have been assigned to capitals whose political importance rested heavily on high revenue potential and the problems of controlling transient traders and a large merchant population. In fact, on my analysis, nearly half of the CFN posts were in greater cities or higher-level economic central places as against less than a third of the FNP posts. Taking the two-character posts at face value, one would expect CF and FN to have been assigned to capitals that were less important overall than CFN or FNP capitals but more important overall than NP capitals, and one would further expect that a comparison of CF and FN cities would show the former to have had greater economic centrality. In general, these expectations are borne out by tabulations of cities with the post designations in question. CFN and FNP designations were overrepresented among cities that ranked high in both the economic and the administrative hierarchies, CF was overrepresented among cities whose economic level was higher than their administrative rank, FN was overrepresented among cities whose administrative rank was higher than their economic level, and NP was overrepresented among cities that ranked low in both hierarchies.[30]

Table 11 also makes the interesting point that the uncommon, internally inconsistent post designations were seldom assigned to cities in regional cores. I attribute the concentration of anomalous post designations in peripheral areas (1) to the irregularities that, as we have already noted, were frequently encountered around the periphery of regional central-place systems, and (2) to the greater diversity of administrative problems posed by peripheral as against core cities.

The system of post designations was rather less straightforward (and more informative) than the above description suggests because it was also designed to serve as a general importance rating. The importance of posts was held to be indicated by the number of characters in their designation. The official importance rating (four categories ranging from very to least important) was printed in the *Chin-shen ch'üan-shu* directly adjacent to the CFNP post designations, and among bureaucrats assignments were known colloquially as "four-character posts," "three-character posts," etc. Nothing in the Chinese or the Western literature suggests that the importance rating was anything other than a direct translation of the number of characters, but in fact I found that for 170 posts (11 percent of the total) the assigned importance rating was higher than indicated by the post designation. It was as though each such post designation included an unspecified or invisible character that served to raise its importance rating. I have dubbed this invisible character the "secret" strategic component on the grounds that everything about the geographical location of the posts so designated and their administrative characteristics suggests that it flagged capitals strategically situated for the defense of regional cores and their principal cities.

Before pursuing this lead for what it can tell us about the defense functions of late imperial cities, let us briefly consider its implications for the system of post designations. That the military component of local administration should be indicated by an invisible code is, after all, not particularly surprising in a sophisticated bureaucracy that was dominated by Confucian values (which exalted normative over coercive power) and that subordinated specialized military officials in both form and symbol to their civil counterparts. But if the coding were to have validity, it would obviously have been necessary to bring the designations of nonstrategic posts into perfect agreement with their importance rating. I suggest that the usual procedure in such cases was to add or subtract P as necessary to bring the designation into alignment with the rating. P was unquestionably the most protean of the four characters. In some contexts it was a foil for C, indicating the unremunerative nature of the post. In other contexts, it was a foil for F, indicating a low-pressure post of no particular political importance or sensitivity. Clearly it had neither connotation when used with all three other characters, for CFNP was the designation of the most important capitals in the realm, e.g., Peking, Soochow, Nanking, Canton, Sian, Chengtu, and Kunming. CFNP cities were themselves military prizes and often the centers of military command, to be sharply differentiated from cities whose significance stemmed from a strategic site on a single approach to the center of a macroregion. Thus, it appears that P also functioned as a foil for the secret strategic component of post designations. When necessary to up the importance rating of a "nonstrategic" city beyond the number of characters yielded by the appropriate assignment of C, F, and N, the character P was added, thereby salvaging the significance of the secret component.

Defense. We are now in a position to muster all relevant evidence concerning the distribution within regions of capitals with a significant

TABLE 12. THE "SECRET" STRATEGIC POST
DESIGNATION IN RELATION TO CHARACTER DESIGNATIONS, 1893
(*All Capitals Except Those Whose Designations Included
All or None of the Four Characters*)

Character designations	"Deficit" of designation characters?			Total
	No	Yes No.	Pct.	
FN	97	39	29%	136
F	46	6	12	52
N	112	13	10	125
F and/or N with C or P	547	38	7	585
F or N with C and P	21	1	5	22
P	22	1	4	23
CP	12	0	0	12
C	111	0	0	111
Total	968	98	9%	1,066[a]

[a] By definition, capitals (59 in all) with the FCNP designation cannot show a deficit of designation characters. Of the 424 capitals with a no-character designation, 17 percent show a "deficit." Reconciliation: 59 + 1066 + 424 = 1549, the total number of capitals.

defense function. We may begin by scrutinizing the character portion of post designations that included the "secret" strategic component. As shown in Table 12, the latter occurred most frequently with FN, the combination whose face value pointed to politically sensitive security problems, and least frequently, which is to say not at all or only very rarely, with CP, C, and P, components unrelated to, or even negating, the notion of strategic importance. These findings and the logic of the intermediate gradations provide circumstantial support for the interpretation offered here for a deficit of designation characters. A mapping of the cities in question offers still firmer support. With few exceptions, cities whose post designations included the "secret" component were sited at the approaches to strategic passes, in mountainous areas subject to attack by non-Han peoples, on roads breaching a regional frontier, on islands or rivers commanding the approach to seaports or major inland waterways, at strategic sites along major rivers, and on roads approaching high-level capitals.

On the assumption that strategically important cities would be distributed in accordance with the strategic significance of different types of frontiers, I classified all administrative cities into seven categories according to whether the county-level units of which they were the capital lay on or near external or internal frontiers. The external categories were three: (1) China's international borders to the south and south-

TABLE 13. THE "SECRET" STRATEGIC POST DESIGNATION IN RELATION TO THE FRONTIER SITUATION OF CAPITAL CITIES, 1893

Location of capitals in relation to frontiers	"Deficit" of designation characters?			Total
	No	Yes No.	Pct.	
External frontiers				
1. South and southwest	15	23	60.5%	38
2. Inner Asian	68	21	23.6	89
3. Maritime	182	24	11.7	206
Internal frontiers				
4. Regional only	94	12	11.3	106
5 + 6. Provincial[a]	672	72	9.7	744
Removed from any frontier	348	18	4.9	366
Total	1,379	170	11.0%	1,549

[a] Two categories are here combined, capitals situated near provincial boundaries but not regional frontiers and capitals situated near both, there being no difference between them in the proportion of "secret" post designations.

west; (2) the Inner Asian regional frontiers, that is, those regional boundaries of Yun-Kwei, the Upper Yangtze, Northwest China, and North China that abutted on Inner Asian territories rather than other regions of agrarian China; and (3) the coastal or maritime frontier. Internal frontiers were classified as (4) regional only (that is, lying on the boundaries of my physiographic regions but not on provincial boundaries); (5) both regional and provincial; and (6) provincial only. The seventh category included county-level units removed from frontiers of any kind. Table 13 shows the distribution according to this scheme of cities with the "secret" strategic post designation. The heavy use of the "secret" component for cities along the empire's more sensitive frontiers is telling, as is its negligible use for posts removed from any frontier.

Table 14 displays span of control in relation to the same categorization of frontiers. It is notable that apart from maritime frontiers (of which more below), the distribution of narrow control spans closely parallels that of the "secret" strategic component. These data strongly support the notion that a narrow span of control was held to be advantageous in the case of militarily vulnerable capitals.

Finally, let us contrast the different types of capitals. With respect to the telltale deficit of characters in post designations, the differences were stark. The "secret" strategic component was present in the post designations of 75 percent of ordinary *t'ing* capitals and 65 percent of autonomous *t'ing* capitals (the difference reflecting not the lesser strategic

TABLE 14. SPAN OF CONTROL IN RELATION TO THE
FRONTIER SITUATION OF CAPITAL CITIES, 1893

Location of capitals in relation to frontiers	Span of control						Total	
	1–5		6–8		9+			
	No.	Pct.	No.	Pct.	No.	Pct.	No.	Pct.
1. South and SW international frontiers	27	71%	11	29%		0%	38	100%
2. Inner Asian frontiers	44	49	27	30	19	21	90	100
4. Internal frontiers: Regional only	44	41	38	35	26	24	108	100
5. Internal frontiers: Reg. *and* prov.	167	36	176	38	116	25	459	100
6. Internal frontiers: Provincial only	89	31	88	30	114	39	291	100
3. Maritime frontiers	35	16	83	38	101	46	219	100
7. Removed from any frontier	60	16	134	36	177	48	371	100
Total	466	29%	557	35%	553	35%	1,576	100%

importance of the latter but rather their greater general importance, whence post designations with more characters on the average). The corresponding figures for capitals of prefectures and of *chou*, both autonomous and ordinary, clustered around 17 percent. As for ordinary *hsien*, whether in prefectures or autonomous *chou*, the incidence of the "secret" component was less than 4 percent; for provincial and higher-level capitals it was nil. We may also discern a distinct tendency toward spatial specialization in the defense function. At the borders of the empire—the international boundaries to the south and southwest, the Inner Asian frontier, and the seacoast—the main burden of defense was carried by the capitals of autonomous and ordinary *t'ing*. As for internal frontiers, the major burden was borne by ordinary *t'ing* capitals along regional frontiers that were distinct from provincial boundaries; by *chou* capitals along regional frontiers that coincided with provincial boundaries; and by both autonomous and ordinary *chou* capitals along provincial boundaries within regions. In the areas away from any frontier, the defense function devolved largely on ordinary *chou* capitals.[31] From the perspective of the major cities at the heart of regional cores, then, the first and second lines of defense were associated primarily with the capitals of ordinary and autonomous *chou*, respectively, whereas more distant defense perimeters were marked largely by *t'ing* capitals. It will be recalled that of these four types of capitals (all characterized by relatively narrow control spans), the narrowest spans were associated with autonomous *t'ing*, concentrated at the outermost periphery, and the broadest with ordinary *chou*, concentrated at the innermost defense perimeter. It is scarcely necessary to add that when the "secret" component was used for prefectural-level capitals other than those of autonomous *t'ing*, it was heavily concentrated among units with exceptionally narrow spans of control.

The thrust of my first argument should by now be apparent. A narrow span of control, entailing as it does close supervision and minimal competition for channels of communications, was highly desirable for centers vulnerable to military invasions, uprisings, or other violent disruptions. In military terms the odd arrangement of the autonomous *t'ing* was ideal, for the subprefect in charge of the strategically important town reported directly to a military circuit intendant or to provincial-level officials rather than indirectly through a prefectural-level yamen. The peculiar administrative arrangement of the *pen-chou* also made military sense in that the *chou* city itself (as opposed to the entire area of the autonomous *chou*) was normally the strategic prize; direct control of the *pen-chou* by the prefectural-level official had the effect of putting the man in charge of the *chou* city's defense under the direct command of high-level military officers. The fewer the counties supervised by the magistrate of an autonomous *chou*, the less distraction there would be in times of military emergency. Similarly, the narrower the span of a prefecture to which an ordinary *chou* or *t'ing* belonged, the less disruptive it would be in times of crisis to monopolize the communication channels from the prefect to higher-level authorities with orders and reports relating to the emergency.

It is notable that all autonomous *chou* and *t'ing* (but not all prefectures) fell into the category of administrative units whose ranking posts were filled through nomination by the governor or governor-general from among acting or probationary officials under his own control. Such appointments were restricted by statute to men with at least three years of prior experience.[32] As a result, the official in supreme command of a province could be certain that subordinates in the most strategic of local posts would be experienced officials who had earned his confidence. Moreover, unlike *hsien* posts, most of which were available for a first appointment, all ordinary *chou* and *t'ing* posts, whether controlled by the Board of Civil Office or by the governor, could be filled only by men with previous administrative experience.[33]

This analysis calls into question Brunnert and Hagelstrom's contention that autonomous *chou* and *t'ing* should be viewed as traditional forms eventuating in prefectural status. It is true that the capitals of ordinary *chou* were normally selected as the capitals of newly formed autonomous *chou*, but not more than twenty autonomous *chou* were ever converted to prefectures, and against these must be set an even greater number of contravening changes. The history of Ch'ing field administration provides no support whatsoever for a developmental sequence from ordinary *t'ing* to autonomous *t'ing* to prefecture. One response to the growing threat of British power off the Chekiang coast in the 1840's was to change the status from *hsien* to *t'ing* of Ting-hai, an administrative unit encompassing the archipelago that commanded the approach to Ningpo and Hangchow.

A certain congruence may be noted between the defense function of many frontier cities and the special character of other administrative functions in the more remote portions of regional peripheries. It was along China's regional frontiers that local society assumed its most heterodox and variegated guise: there one found tribes of non-Han aborigines and pockets of incompletely sinicized groups; autonomous kongsis pursuing illicit productive activities beyond the reach of the law and of tax collectors; heterodox sodalities ranging from religious sects to seditious secret societies; and bands of bandits, many imbued with romantic-rebel ideologies.[34] The populace at large included disproportionate numbers of smugglers, outcasts, political exiles, sorcerers, and other deviants. In dealing with such elements, normative strategies of administration were largely ineffective, and frontier administrators necessarily relied on repression, containment, and divide-and-rule strategies. Thus the military posture and coercive power needed for defense around the rim of regional peripheries were also appropriate to the other objectives of field administration in such areas—the maintenance of social order and the prevention of local concentrations of power that might pose a threat to imperial control.

Revenue collection. Let me now turn to fiscal strategy. We start with the proposition that revenue collection, both of land tax and of commercial levies, was most efficient (in the sense of greater tax take per unit of administrative effort) in regional cores, particularly in the environs of cities high in the economic hierarchy. Among the myriad reasons are the high levels of productivity and per capita income, the high density of taxable units (households, farms, business firms, periodic markets, etc.) per unit of area, the comparatively strong leadership of local social systems, and a local populace with relatively firm community roots and relatively high aspirations. In general, the efficiency of tax collection may be seen to decline as one moves outward from the center toward the periphery of the economic region and downward through the hierarchy of trading and marketing systems.³⁵ The continuum in question may be conceptualized as in the row labels of Table 10. Somewhere along this continuum, a break-even point was reached where the tax take was barely covered by the costs of collecting it, and below that point county-level units were dependent for part of their operational budget on subsidies from higher-level yamens.³⁶

It is widely recognized that provincial governments, and above all the imperial government, looked to a limited number of populous, commercialized, and relatively rich areas for the great bulk of their revenue. My point here is that these areas may be specified with some precision in terms of (1) the relative urbanization of the eight great regional economies (with the Lower Yangtze at the head of the list and Yun-Kwei at the tail), and (2) position within each of these regional economic systems as specified in Table 10.

The strategy followed, or so I infer, was to extend the area under the jurisdiction of key tax yamens (i.e., those in high-level capitals that were at once regional cities and metropolises in the economic hierarchy) so as to include within their boundaries as much as feasible of the high-revenue areas, and to concentrate in this small number of supervisory posts the ablest and most trustworthy personnel in the imperial bureaucracy.³⁷ Thus, the optimal administrative arrangement for areas of highest revenue potential was very nearly the reverse of that for areas of greatest strategic importance. In the latter, it was desirable to make both county-level and prefectural-level units as small as possible, the former in terms of area and the latter in terms of component units. In areas of highest revenue potential, by contrast, it was desirable to make both county-level and prefectural-level units as large as possible, the former in terms of population and the latter in terms of component units.

I wish now to show that the gradation of capitals by revenue potential was precisely indicated by the system of post designations already described. I begin by establishing the significance of these designations for city population size. As demonstrated in Table 15, F tended to be assigned to the most populous cities (which makes sense if one assumes volume of official business to be a function of urban population),³⁸ and P to the least populous cities (which also makes intuitive sense on the assumption that relatively small capitals were disproportionately located in sparsely populated counties with poor transport where tax returns were likely to be low in proportion to bureaucratic effort). C and N were intermediate with respect to city population, but on the average C was assigned to more populous cities than was N. Table 15 also makes it clear that the *number* of characters in the post designation was positively associated with city population.

TABLE 15. POST DESIGNATIONS IN RELATION TO CITY SIZE OF THE CAPITALS INVOLVED, 1893[a]

A. Cities whose yamen posts received 3- and 4-character designations

	Population classes							
	Over 16,000		4,000– 16,000		Under 4,000		Total	
	No.	Pct.	No.	Pct.	No.	Pct.	No.	Pct.
FCNP	37	63% ▲	18	31% ↓	4	7%	59	100%
FCN	61	37	92	56 ▲	12	7	165	100
FNP CNP FCP	21	15	67	49 ↑	48	35 ▼	136	100
Total	119	33%	177	49%	64	18%	360	100%

B. Cities whose yamen posts received 2-character designations[b]

	Population classes							
	Over 8,000		2,000– 8,000		Under 2,000		Total	
	No.	Pct.	No.	Pct.	No.	Pct.	No.	Pct.
FC FN FP	86	29% ▲	197	67% ▲	11	4%	294	100%
CF CN CP	53	23	150	66	26	11	229	100
NF NC NP	60	21	184	65	39	14	283	100
PF PC PN	11	11	57	57	32	32 ▼	100	100
Total number of characters	(210)		(588)		(108)		(906)	
Total number of capitals	105	23%	294	65%	54	12%	453	100%

C. Cities whose yamen posts received single-character designations

	Population classes								
	Over 4,000		2,000– 4,000		1,000– 2,000		Under 1,000		Total	
	No.	Pct.	No.	Pct.	No.	Pct.	No.	Pct.	No.	Pct.
F	23	45% ▲	23	45% ▲	6	10%		0%	52	100%
C	29	26	36	32	40	36 ↓	6	5	111	100
N	19	15	29	23	54	43 ▲	23	18	125	100
P	2	9	5	22	9	39 ↑	7	30 ▼	23	100
Total	73	24%	93	30%	109	35%	36	12%	311	100%

[a] For purposes of this table, the following multiple-nuclei conurbations are counted as single cities and classified according to the population of the whole. First we have Wuhan, Kuei-sui, and Chungking (together with its satellite Chiang-pei), even though each contains two capitals. Second are the two anomalous cases of Hui-chou-fu (Kwangtung) and Feng-yang-fu (Anhwei), each with a separate walled city in which the yamen of the metropolitan county was located. Third are three twin cities involving one capital and one nonadministrative center: Lao-ho-k'ou and Kuang-hua, a *hsien* capital (Hupeh); Fan-ch'eng and Hsiang-yang-fu (Hupeh); and Ch'ing-chiang-p'u and Ch'ing-ho, a *hsien* capital (Kiangsu). The 422 capitals with no-character designations, not shown, have a size distribution between that of N-designated cities and P-designated cities. Reconciliation: 360 + 453 + 311 + 422 = 1546, the number of cities involving capitals.

[b] Each city covered by Subtable B appears twice, i.e., in the rows for each of its designation characters. FC posts are, of course, the same as CF posts, and so forth; the order of each pair is reversed so as to point up the significance of the groupings in each row.

The pecking order established by the population significance of the four components establishes a rank-order of the sixteen designations. On the basis of their correlations with several other urban variables, three significant "breaks" were established in this series, yielding four groupings here designated High (FCNP and FCN), Medium (FCP, FNP, CNP, FC, and FN), Low (FP, CN, CP, NP, F, C, N, and P), and No-character.[39] When post designations, so grouped, are cross-tabulated with the level and type of capital city, as in Table 16, it is apparent that, apart from the two types of *t'ing*, the rank-order of post designations closely parallels the official ordering of capital types. (The "exceptionally" high frequency of Medium post designations for autonomous and ordinary *t'ing* results, as we might expect, entirely from an excess of the FN designations that signaled their strategic importance.)

If my overall argument is correct, rank-ordered post designations should have indexed not only the population and the ranking of capitals but also span of control. Table 17 demonstrates that they did just that for prefectural-level capitals. The remarkable fact is that rank-ordered post designations served to differentiate prefectural capitals and the capitals of autonomous *chou* into three grades each, so related that the bottom grade of prefectural capitals was still distinguished from the top grade of *chou* capitals. The net result was that, in conjunction with type of capital, post designations marked out eight graded types of prefectural-level capitals, the entire series being correlated with the span of control.

It remains to show that rank-ordered post designations in fact differentiated cities according not only to span of control but also to the position of capitals in regional economic systems. We have already observed (see Table 10) the pervasive tendency to match the size of prefectural-level units (i.e., the number of component county-level units) to the revenue potential of the economic system centered on the prefectural-level capital. Table 18 is designed to test the proposition that the post designations of prefectural-level capitals varied according to all the factors built into Table 10—that is, according to a complex calculus that took into account the city's level in the economic hierarchy, its location in the regional core-periphery structure, and the span of control of the administrative unit of which it was the capital. The grid of the upper diagram recapitulates the structure of Table 10, and the data in tabulations A and B relate to the five diagonal groupings of cells defined on that grid. Diagonal 1 includes prefectural-level capitals that ranked at the top of the hierarchy of economic central places, that were centrally located in their regional economies, and whose administrative jurisdiction encompassed an extraordinarily large number of counties with

TABLE 16. POST DESIGNATIONS IN RELATION TO LEVEL AND TYPE OF
ADMINISTRATIVE CENTER, ALL CAPITAL CITIES, 1893

	Post designations[a]									
	High		Medium		Low		No-character		Total	
Capitals of	No.	Pct.	No.	Pct.	No.	Pct.	No.	Pct.	No.	Pct.
Provinces, etc.	20	100%		0%		0%		0%	20	100%
Circuits[b]	38	63	17	28	2	3	3	5	60	100
Prefectures	51	46	40	36	19	17		0	110	100
Autonomous chou[c]	17	24	36	51	8	11	9	13	70	100
Ordinary chou	16	12	40	30	53	39	26	19	135	100
Hsien in prefectures	71	8	224	25	323	37	265	30	883	100
Hsien in autonomous chou	7	4	39	21	71	39	67	36	184	100
Autonomous t'ing[d]	2	7	10	33	4	13	14	47	30	100
Ordinary t'ing	3	5	11	19	3	5	40	70	57	100
Total	225	15%	417	27%	483	31%	424	27%	1,549	100%

[a] This classification of the sixteen possible post designations is based on a generalized pecking order, established empirically, of F, C, N, P. High includes FCP, FNP, CNP, FC, and FN. Medium includes FCP, FNP, FCN and FCN. Low includes the other eight character designations.
[b] Capitals of provinces and governor-generalships that are also circuit capitals are not included. The total includes 40 capitals of prefectures, six of autonomous chou, two of autonomous t'ing, two of sectors in the imperial prefecture, two of ordinary chou, five of hsien, and three of ordinary t'ing.
[c] Includes capitals of the two autonomous t'ing and six prefectures that were structurally analogous to autonomous chou.
[d] Includes the four prefectures with only a single component hsien.

TABLE 17. SPAN OF CONTROL BY TYPE OF ADMINISTRATIVE CENTER AND BY POST DESIGNATIONS, 1893
(Prefectural and Higher-level Capitals Only)

Capitals of	Post designations[b]	Span of control[a]													Total	
		1		2–3		4		5–8		9–10		11–13		14+			
		No.	Pct.	No.	Pct.	No.	Pct.	No.	Pct.	No.	Pct.	No.	Pct.	No.	Pct.	No.	Pct.
Provinces, etc.	High		0%		0%		0%	5	25%	4	20%	4	20%	7	35%	20	100%
Prefectures[c]	High			2	2	5	6	51	62	15	18	7	9	2	2	82	100
	Medium			5	10	7	14	30	60	5	10	3	6		0	50	100
	Low			3	15	8	40	8	40	1	4		0			20	100
Autonomous *chou*[d]	High			9	43	6	29	6	29							21	100
	Medium			18	47	10	26	10	26							38	100
	Low			10	59	4	24	3	18							17	100
Autonomous *t'ing*[e]	—	32	100		0		0		0							32	100
Total		32	11%	47	17%	40	14%	113	40%	25	9%	14	5%	9	3%	280	100%

[a] I.e., the number of county-level units supervised by a given prefectural-level yamen.
[b] The few No-character designations are grouped here with Low designations.
[c] Includes the two sectoral capitals in the imperial prefecture that served as circuit capitals.
[d] Includes capitals of the two autonomous *t'ing* and six prefectures that were structurally analogous to autonomous *chou*.
[e] Includes capitals of the four prefectures containing only a single *hsien*.

TABLE 18. POST DESIGNATIONS IN RELATION TO LEVEL IN THE ECONOMIC HIERARCHY, LOCATION IN REGIONAL CORES OR PERIPHERIES, AND SPAN OF CONTROL, PREFECTURAL-LEVEL CAPITALS ONLY, 1893

Definition of "diagonal classes" simultaneously indicating level in the economic hierarchy, location in regional cores or peripheries, and span of control

Level in the economic hierarchy	Regional cores (C) or peripheries (P)[a]	Span of control[b]										Total
		1	2	3	4	5	6	7	8	9–10	11–13	14+	
Central metropolis	C											5	5
Regional metropolis	C										1		17
Regional metropolis	P												28
Regional city	C												
Regional city	P									2			67
Greater city	C												80
Greater city	P						3						
Local city	C												55
Local city	P				4								
Central market town	C												28
Central market town	P	5											
Total		32	15	32	40	31	31	29	22	25	14	9	280

Table 18, continued

A. Post designations classed in terms of High, Medium, Low, and No-character

Diagonal class	Post designation[c]						Total	
	High		Medium		Low and no-character			
	No.	Pct.	No.	Pct.	No.	Pct.	No.	Pct.
1	32	100%		0%		0%	32	100%
2	27	64	15	36			42	100
3	45	51	32	36	11	13	88	100
4	20	24	41	48	24	28	85	100
5	1	3	11	33	21	64	33	100
Total	125	45%	99	35%	56	20%	280	100%

B. Post designations classed in terms of C and F components

Diagonal class	Post designation[d]						Total	
	C and F[e]		C or F		Neither C nor F			
	No.	Pct.	No.	Pct.	No.	Pct.	No.	Pct.
1	32	100%		0%		0%	32	100%
2	34	81	8	19			42	100
3	55	63	31	35	2	2	88	100
4	37	44	33	39	15	18	85	100
5	3	9	14	42	16	48	33	100
Total	161	58%	86	31%	33	12%	280	100%

[a] In analyses of span of control within prefectural-level units, the core-periphery distribution of all capitals within the prefecture is taken into account in assigning the prefecture to either the core or periphery. See Table 10 for operational definitions.

[b] I.e., the number of county-level units supervised by a given prefectural-level yamen.

[c] For the classification of post designations into High, Medium, and Low, see Table 16.

[d] C stands for *ch'ung*, F for *fan*.

[e] Includes three cases in which the post designation of the prefectural yamen shows one character and that of the county yamen the other.

above-average populations. In all these respects, successive diagonals 2, 3, and 4 grade cities from that extreme to its opposite, diagonal 5, which includes capitals that ranked exceptionally low in the economic hierarchy, were situated peripherally with respect to their regional economies, and whose jurisdiction encompassed at most three sparsely populated county-level units.

Tabulation A of Table 18 shows that post designations did indeed closely reflect the factors encompassed in the definition of the diagonals. Note in particular that every one of the 32 cities in diagonal 1 had a high post designation. (It is not unlikely that in the late nineteenth century the 31 prefectures and one autonomous *chou* involved supplied nearly half of all revenues received at Peking.) Tabulation B indicates the particular diagnostic value of the F and C components of the post designations. Finally, the data presented in Table 19 show that at *all* levels of the administrative hierarchy, and in regional peripheries as well as cores, the post designation of a capital closely reflected its place in the hierarchy of economic central places.

One beauty of the post designations was their value for posting officials of varying competence, experience, and trustworthiness in accordance with the posts' importance for sustaining the flow of imperial revenues. Positions in the field administration were filled either through direct appointment by the Board of Civil Office in Peking or through nomination by the governor (or governor-general), subject to the Board's approval. Whereas the Board's appointments could be made from the pool of expectant officials who had never before served in office, the governor's nominations were by statute limited to men who had served under him for a minimum of three years (five in certain categories). Posts classified as "most important" or "important" (that is, all three- and four-character posts plus others containing the "secret" strategic component) were controlled by the province,[40] thereby establishing a floor of experience and trustworthiness for the most critical assignments. For all incumbents, no matter how appointed, there were elaborate procedures for the periodic evaluation of performance. Post assignments, as well as promotion or demotion within the bureaucratic ranks, depended on the results. In the triennial "great reckoning" (*ta-chi*), which assessed the achievements of each local official, "by far the most important criterion was his ability to collect taxes. Thus a magistrate was not eligible for recommendation if he had been unable to collect the land tax according to the quota."[41] The data presented in Tables 18 and 19 imply that so long as bureaucratic "promotions" involved transfers to posts with higher designations (e.g., from No-character to

TABLE 19. THE RELATIONSHIP BETWEEN THE POST DESIGNATION OF CAPITALS AND THEIR LEVEL IN THE ECONOMIC HIERARCHY, 1893
(Showing Tabulations Separately for High-level as Against Low-level Capitals and for Regional Cores as Against Regional Peripheries)

	HIGH-LEVEL CAPITALS/REGIONAL CORES Post designations										HIGH-LEVEL CAPITALS/REGIONAL PERIPHERIES Post designations									
	High		Medium		Low		Low and no-char.		Total		High		Medium		Low		Low and no-char.		Total	
	No.	Pct.	No.	Pct.	No.	Pct.	No.	Pct.	No.	Pct.	No.	Pct.	No.	Pct.	No.	Pct.	No.	Pct.	No.	Pct.
Regional cities & higher	43	81%	9	17%			1	2%	53	100%	14	74%	3	16%			2	11%	19	100%
Greater cities	24	50	19	40			5	10	48	100	18	37	24	49			7	14	49	100
Local cities	12	39	14	45			5	16	31	100	13	30	21	48			10	23	44	100
CMT's		0		0			3	100	3	100	1	8	3	25			8	67	12	100
Total	79	59%	42	31%			14	10%	135	100%	46	37%	51	41%			27	22%	124	100%

	LOW-LEVEL CAPITALS/REGIONAL CORES Post designations										LOW-LEVEL CAPITALS/REGIONAL PERIPHERIES Post designations									
	High		Medium		Low		No-char.		Total		High		Medium		Low		No-char.		Total	
	No.	Pct.	No.	Pct.	No.	Pct.	No.	Pct.	No.	Pct.	No.	Pct.	No.	Pct.	No.	Pct.	No.	Pct.	No.	Pct.
Greater cities & higher	16	30%	24	45%	9	17%	4	8%	53	100%	9	22%	16	39%	4	10%	12	29%	41	100%
Local cities	48	18	101	39	79	30	34	13	262	100	15	6	73	32	91	39	52	23	231	100
CMT's	6	2	49	19	114	44	89	34	258	100	5	2	60	19	132	41	125	39	322	100
IMT's & SMT's	0		0		12	30	28	70	40	100	0		1	1	13	16	66	83	80	100
Total	70	11%	174	28%	214	35%	155	25%	613	100%	29	4%	150	22%	240	36%	255	38%	674	100%

C, from FP to FC, or from CNP to FCN), they were likely to entail a step up the economic central-place hierarchy and/or a move to a city whose prefectural-level unit had a broader span of control—i.e., to a post of greater fiscal importance.

Special cases. It is, of course, an oversimplification to portray the administrative salience of security as everywhere inversely related to the administrative salience of revenue. We have already pointed to a possible departure from this generalization in the case of cities along China's maritime frontiers. The incidence of the "secret" component of post designations (Table 13) suggests that the proportion of cities with an important defense function was somewhat higher along the coast than near internal frontiers; the distribution of control spans (Table 14) suggests that the same was true of cities important for revenue. This anomaly resulted from the fact that the maritime "frontiers" of several regional cores lacked the peripheral zone that everywhere buffered cores along their internal regional frontiers. The critical question concerns the extent to which the two functions were conjoined in the same coastal cities. Many seaports in core areas were indeed the nodes of high-revenue trading systems, whence the high incidence of broad control spans along the maritime frontier as a whole. However, prior to the rise of ocean ports in the late nineteenth century, the typical pattern was for important seaports to be sited upriver from the immediate coastline, with their seaward approaches being guarded by fortresses or smaller defense-oriented capitals. Canton, Foochow, Ningpo, and Tientsin are classic cases.* Nonetheless, by its very nature, the maritime frontier did have an exceptionally high proportion of cities for which commerce and defense were both important. A prominent example was Amoy, a deepwater port located on an offshore island and hence highly vulnerable to attack. Not surprisingly, its administrative status was that of a *t'ing* capital and its post designation included the "secret" strategic component. At the same time, it was the most important commercial city in its highly commercialized subregion and ranked as a regional city in the economic hierarchy.

Significantly enough, Amoy was also a circuit capital, a fact that points us toward resolution of the anomalies surrounding circuits in the Ch'ing field administration. After its recapture from Koxinga, Amoy was seen by the Ch'ing as essentially a military outpost, and in the 1680's

* On the map of the Ningpo area at p. 402, note the location of Chen-hai, a county capital with the "secret" strategic component in its post designation, in relation to Ningpo. The map also shows three fortresses (Kuan-hai-wei, Lung-shan, and Ta-sung-so) built in early Ming times for purposes of maritime defense.

it was incorporated into the administrative system as an ordinary *t'ing*. Meanwhile, the unwonted security brought to the Taiwan Strait by the Ch'ing after their annexation of Taiwan enabled Amoy, despite its vulnerability, to thrive as never before, taking full advantage of its excellent harbor. In 1727, by which time Ch'üan-chou-fu had lost the bulk of its maritime trade to Amoy, the circuit yamen was moved to the *t'ing* capital.[42] From a garrison town, Amoy had developed into a city from which the defense and trade of the entire subregion could be controlled and coordinated.

It was the special character of the circuit intendant's role that caused the court to favor as capitals cities, like Amoy, that were strategically situated for both defense and trade. We noted above that the intendant was responsible for dealing with foreigners who penetrated his circuit, and it may be added here that he normally also served as the superintendant of customs.[43] As a preliminary formulation, then, we might say that the circuit intendant's primary mission was the conduct of "local" foreign relations—trade, diplomacy, and war—and that his local administrative role concerned the coordination and control of activities within the circuit only insofar as they affected these larger concerns of the court. The departures from a regular administrative chain of command to which I earlier called attention make sense in these terms. Of the four high-level capitals that lacked circuit yamens, Peking, the imperial capital, and Canton, the open port to which the Ch'ing directed foreigners from overseas, both had specialized alternative institutions for handling foreign relations. Hangchow and Soochow, the other two capitals involved, provide examples of "forward" siting, whereby circuit yamens were situated within their territories off-center in the direction of foreign pressure. The circuit in which Hangchow fell was headquartered in Chia-hsing-fu to the northeast, whereas the eastern approach to Hangchow Bay was under the supervision of the circuit intendant at Ningpo. Soochow had been the capital of Su-Sung-T'ai circuit until 1730, when the yamen was transferred to Shanghai,[44] a growing but much smaller city that had, however, come to dominate the Lower Yangtze's coastal trade with both northern and southern ports and that had emerged as the focal link between these two branches of the coastal trade and the commercial network of the Lower and Middle Yangtze regions.

The other kind of administrative anomaly—circuit yamens located in cities that were not even prefectural-level capitals—may also be attributed to the court's overriding concern to locate intendants in whatever city within the circuit was most strategically situated for their mission. The pragmatic responsiveness to external developments that caused circuits to be established during the eighteenth century in Amoy and Shanghai, both county-level capitals, was no less evident during the subsequent era of Western encroachment. In 1861, the court transferred the yamen of Han-Huang-Te circuit (Hupeh) from Huang-chou-fu to Hankow, the commercially dominant nonadministrative component of the Wuhan conurbation.[45] Later in the century, in response to French aggressiveness and the growth of the Tonkin trade, the government established circuit yamens in Meng-tzu (an ordinary county capital in Yunnan), by then a regional city in the economic hierarchy, and in Lung-chou (an ordinary *t'ing* capital in Kwangsi), by then a greater city.[46]

As of 1893, the Chinese ecumene was ringed by 25 circuit capitals: eight along the northern Inner Asian frontier, four on the western frontier facing Tibet, three on the southern frontier facing Tonkin, and ten along the coast. Though many of these were, in fact, the largest and most important prefectural-level capitals within their circuits, others were lower-ranking or smaller capitals whose more peripheral position was strategic for the coordination of trade with, and defense against, the relevant "barbarians."

Still, circuits at the periphery of the imperial domain accounted for fewer than a third of all circuits, and the preoccupation of their intendants with foreign relations in the strict sense should perhaps be seen as a peculiarly intensified manifestation of the intendant's role. A more generic formulation of it might be phrased as responsibility to see that the external affairs of his circuit conformed to the strategic policies of the court. Here we have a rationale for the intendant's peculiar mixture of concerns—regional defense, long-distance trade, revenue from commerce, and control of outsiders—and for his peripheral role with respect to education, justice, the land tax, and other matters primarily affecting the local populace.

The variable guise of the circuit intendant—here primarily occupied with military affairs, there with customs, elsewhere with negotiations with non-Han border peoples—is only to be expected from our survey of inter- and intraregional differentiation. If one asks why the seat of T'ung-Shang circuit (Shensi) was situated at the southeastern border of its territory in an ordinary *t'ing* capital of no particular commercial importance, the answer lies in the great strategic value of the San-men Gorge, through which the Yellow River flows from the Northwest physiographic region into North China. It is notable that T'ung-Shang's neighboring circuits in adjacent provinces—in this area the river constituted the boundary separating Shansi province from Shensi and Honan (see

Cities and the Hierarchy of Local Systems

Map 2, p. 215)—were also headquartered in small cities sited directly on the Yellow River, namely P'u-chou-fu (Shansi) at a strategic site above the gorge, and Shan-chou (Honan) at a comparable site below it. Other anomalies may be accounted for primarily in terms of the hierarchy of economic central places. Why was it not always the most important trade center among the prefectural-level capitals in a circuit that was made the capital? The answer in several cases is that the circuit's most important economic center was a nonadministrative city, in which case the capital of the county-level unit in question was made the circuit capital. Feng-yang-fu (Anhwei) and Ching-chou-fu (Hupeh), for instance, both merely local cities in their own right, were nonetheless circuit capitals, and their prefect posts carried four-character designations; each owed its administrative preeminence to the presence within the metropolitan county of a nonadministrative center ranking as a regional city in the economic hierarchy—Lin-huai-kuan and Sha-shih, respectively. Hsiang-yang-fu (Hupeh) and Li-chou (Hunan) are comparable cases, their status as circuit capitals and their FCN post designations reflecting in each case close proximity to nonadministrative greater cities—Fan-ch'eng and Ching-shih, respectively. Hsin-yang (an ordinary *chou* capital in Honan) and Wu-hu (an ordinary *hsien* capital in Anhwei), both circuit capitals of long standing, were regional cities in the economic hierarchy.

These examples suffice to account for the logic of anomalies in the administrative status of circuit capitals and to make the point that the flexibility and responsiveness peculiar to the circuit level of administration often served to bring a city's place in the administrative hierarchy into closer alignment with its level in the economic hierarchy. It should also be clear why so many circuit capitals were exceptions to the general rule that military and fiscal salience did not go together in the same urban posts.

Finally, a word about ordinary *chou* capitals, whose role in defense, as we have seen, was often to guard the immediate approaches to high-level capitals. Being situated on major roads in regional cores, many *chou* capitals were also commercial centers of some importance. A number of them, interestingly enough, carried the anomalous post designation of CN, signifying their modest importance for both trade and security. It should now be clear why the official ranking of county-level units within prefectures (declining from *chou* to *t'ing* to *hsien*) differed from their ordering by population size—from *chou* to *hsien* to *t'ing*. The official elevation of ordinary *chou* and *t'ing* above counties reflected their strategic importance, but the distinctive strategic role of each meant that *chou* capitals were likely to have greater economic centrality than county capitals whereas *t'ing* capitals normally had less.

Informal governance. In an earlier analysis of marketing in rural China, I argued that in most respects the organization of informal politics paralleled the structure of marketing systems found at the lower reaches of the economic hierarchy as described in this paper.[47] At a level that was one or two steps removed from villages, the arenas of politics and the units of informal administration were standard marketing systems, and politico-administrative action, like economic activity, was centered in the market town and reflected the periodicity of the marketing week.[48] In most parts of China, such informal power structures extended up the hierarchy at least to central marketing systems and often to local-city trading systems or higher.[49] It should be emphasized that the leadership bodies involved were not town councils, even though they usually met in the central place; leaders were drawn from throughout the relevant territorial system, and hinterland and town were "administered" as an undifferentiated unit. Naturally the more powerful leaders were involved at more than one level, and the considerable degree of such vertical overlap in the corps of leaders was accompanied by some horizontal overlap, as when a resident of an intermediate market town played a role in the power structures of both central marketing systems to which his native place was oriented.

In relating the arrangements for informal governance to the formal administrative hierarchy, two points are of particular significance. Since political arenas and marketing systems were spatially coterminous, and since the interrelations of parapolitical systems recapitulated the hierarchy of economic systems, the interests of local traders coincided with those of local gentry leaders more closely than might otherwise have been the case; in any event, gentry control of leading merchants was facilitated. In the usual case, the leading merchants of the market town or local city were brought into leadership councils by the gentry "establishment," and in intersystem conflicts economic and political issues were closely intertwined. Second, the element of spatial competition inherent in the overlapping hierarchical mode that we have shown to characterize the natural economic hierarchy rendered local-level politics particularly flexible and adaptive. The parapolitical system centered in a standard market town might align with higher-level systems centered on any of the neighboring higher-level market towns or, if power were roughly balanced, find itself in a position to play one off against another. By the same token, neighboring high-level political systems were in competition for the allegiance of intervening low-level systems.

Cities and the Hierarchy of Local Systems

The nature of the hierarchy also permitted a kind of territorial aggrandizement that was not possible in political systems contained within administrative boundaries. An exceptionally powerful political structure at the local-city level might dominate all of the systems centered in the surrounding ring of central market towns and even extend its sway to the intermediate systems on the far side of those central market towns, thereby truncating the political structures centered on neighboring local cities.

We have already established the point that the population of economic systems at the same level of the hierarchy (say, central marketing systems) varied according to position in the regional structure: populations were smaller in such poorly endowed and underdeveloped regions as Yun-Kwei and larger in richer, better developed regions such as the Lower Yangtze; smaller in peripheral areas and larger in regional cores; smaller in the case of systems whose nodes were central market towns and larger in the case of systems centered on local or higher-ranking cities. The same pattern held for the total economic demand within the system and for the total volume of business transactions. On first principles, we would expect comparable patterning in the strength of the informal political structures that inhered in these economic systems. In particular, of course, elites were disproportionately concentrated in more favorably situated, richly endowed, "urbanized" marketing systems, so that the nonofficial elite and, a fortiori, the bureaucratic elite would be far more numerous in a central marketing system whose node was a greater city in the regional core than in a central marketing system whose node was a central market town situated in the far periphery. Consequently, leadership councils would be more selective in systems of the former type, with comparatively heavy representation of officials-out-of-office and powerful merchants. Finally we would expect territorial aggrandizement (of the kind described above) by a strong parapolitical system within a regional core at the expense of more peripherally situated neighboring systems. Thus, we would have every reason to believe that the relative power of informal politico-administrative systems and the standing of their leaders varied systematically in accordance with the model developed above of regional economic systems.

The first point of contact between the hierarchy of local parapolitical systems and the hierarchy of bureaucratic administrative units was normally the county-level capital. That critical intersection was, in most cases, in a local city or central market town, but in this respect, too, there was sharp variation in accordance with place in the regional structure. Over 60 percent of the high-level economic centers (greater cities or above) that housed county-level yamens were situated in regional cores. The corresponding figures are 49 percent for local cities, 40 percent for central market towns, and 32 percent for intermediate market towns; the handful of standard market towns that served as capitals were all located in regional peripheries. Thus, the range of variation was great on two counts. The local leaders who dealt with the magistrate of a peripheral county were likely to have headed the unusually weak power structure of a relatively small central marketing system, encompassing, say, a population of 50,000; few among them would have been graduate degree-holders or former officials of any importance. By contrast, local leaders who confronted the magistrate of a metropolitan county in a core city were likely to have headed the exceptionally strong power structure of a relatively large local-city trading system, encompassing a population that most likely exceeded half a million; few among them would not have been graduate degree-holders or former officials of great power. In the one case the scope for informal governance below the intersection with the bureaucratic government was fairly restricted, in the other case extremely broad.

It would appear, then, that the strength and resources of informal parapolitical systems varied through regional space in an approximation of complementary distribution with the capacity of bureaucratic government to attend to those aspects of governance not focused on the court's overriding concern with revenue and defense. We may conceive of the matter in terms of a variable division of labor. The "services" at issue included resolving civil disputes and maintaining local order; apprehending and punishing criminals; dispensing famine and disaster relief and other welfare services; promoting education and supervising institutions related to imperial examinations; constructing and maintaining public works; and licensing and regulating certain semiprofessionals and businessmen. For simplicity's sake, let me lump these activities together as societal management and social control and point to the obvious fact that the extent to which formal government could shoulder responsibility for them was a function of administrative intensity.

It was possible, I argue, to make a go of giant prefectures at the heart of great economic systems—that is, bureaucrats could concentrate on revenue collection in such prefectures—only by allowing much of the responsibility for societal management to devolve on informal parapolitical structures. And it was in just such areas that local parapolitical structures were largest and strongest. In the rich core areas where counties were populous and span of control broad, nonofficial societal

Cities and the Hierarchy of Local Systems

management was institutionalized under the leadership of urban elites, merchants as well as gentry, whose "governmental" activities so reduced the routine of county-level yamens that control by the prefectural yamen was not necessarily perfunctory despite the broad span of control;[50] it was even possible for overburdened prefects to rely on native officials-out-of-office to help keep tabs on county magistrates. In less favorably situated areas near the transition between core and periphery, where both county populations and spans of control were closer to the empirewide average, local parapolitical structures tended to be weaker, less effective, and controlled by less exalted leaders; and there county-level yamens were in a position to shoulder more of the responsibilities of governance, and prefectural-level yamens were able to spread their attention more evenly over the whole range of governmental functions.

If one asks how the government induced leaders throughout the nested hierarchy of local systems to serve as its informal agents, the answer appears to rest heavily on the state's control of the status symbols that defined and graded elites, namely the "academic" degrees associated with the imperial examination system. The manifest function of that system was to cultivate and identify talented men for recruitment to government service, but it also enabled the state to monopolize the most important status symbols in the society at large and to control their significance and distribution by setting quotas, fixing the academic content of the examinations, canceling or adding examinations, and (of particular importance in this context) denying certain groups access to the examination sheds.[51] It is hardly accidental that the local systems most strongly caught up in the government-sponsored academic competition were found in those very areas where field administration was least intensive. Academically successful localities in Ch'ing China were heavily concentrated in the local-city trading systems of cities that were at once greater or higher-level cities in the economic hierarchy *and* prefectural or higher-level capitals in the administrative hierarchy.[52] These corresponded in large part to the metropolitan counties of the prefectural-level units whose capitals are shown in the first and second diagonals of Table 18.

It all fits together. Areas of high revenue potential had the resources to invest heavily in grooming young men for academic success, producing in the process degree-holding elites that were dependent on bureaucrats and particularly susceptible to their normative controls. And these were the elites whose leaders would man the extensive and elaborated parapolitical structures on which so much of local governance necessarily devolved by virtue of the highly extensive form of field admin-

TABLE 20. DISTRIBUTION OF CENTRAL PLACES BY LEVEL IN THE ADMINISTRATIVE AND ECONOMIC HIERARCHIES, 1893

Level in the economic hierarchy	Level in the administrative hierarchy[a]						Total
	Imperial	Provincial	Circuit[b]	Prefectural and aut. chou[c]	Low-level[d]	Non-adm.	
Central metropolis	1	3	2				6
Regional metropolis		15	1	3	1		20
Regional city		1	26	20	8	8	63
Greater city			19	77	85	19	200
Local city			12	62	494	101	669
CMT				17	581	1,721	2,319
IMT					106	7,905	8,011
SMT					12	27,700	27,712
Total	1	19	60	179	1,287	37,454	39,000

[a] Wuhan and Kuei-sui are counted as single cities, and Chiang-pei-t'ing is counted as part of Chungking. See notes to Table 6.

[b] Excludes the sixteen provincial capitals that were also circuit capitals. The table appears to lack one circuit capital, since the yamens of two circuits are housed in Wuhan, which is counted here as a single city.

[c] Includes the two autonomous *t'ing* that were structurally analogous to autonomous *chou*.

[d] Includes capitals of prefectural-level units (25 autonomous *t'ing* and four prefectures) that contained but a single county-level unit.

istration favored in areas with a high revenue potential. Where obverse conditions produced local leaders who were less reliable agents of local yamens, more intensive administrative arrangements reduced the state's reliance on informal governance.

An obvious problem with the basic strategy of Ch'ing field administration was how to enlist the services of local gentry and merchants as informal agents of bureaucratic government without so strengthening them and the parapolitical structures they controlled that their power could pose a threat to bureaucratic control. As suggested above, institutional arrangements that tied the interests of local elites to those of the state were doubtless the chief means of coping with this problem. They did not preclude additional precautions, however. It appears likely to me, for instance, that where the potential danger from concentrated local power was greatest, administrative boundaries were deliberately drawn with an eye to their divisive consequences.

The kind of entrenched power that involved illicit connivance between officials-in-office and local elites was effectively contained in Ch'ing China by such bureaucratic devices as rules of avoidance and rapid turnover of incumbents. Thus, the greatest danger lay in collusion between powerful gentry and wealthy merchants in areas where both were concentrated. From evidence available to me, it appears that within the informal political systems discussed above, cooperation between gentry and merchants was less than exceptional,[53] and as one source of a community of interests I pointed to the fact that for gentryman and trader alike the field of operations at each level was identical, namely the commercial hinterland of a given central place. Above the level of intersection between the "natural" economic hierarchy and the formal administrative hierarchy, however, the relevant arenas of the two leading social groups tended to diverge, as the interests of the gentry were pulled inexorably toward the hierarchy of official administrative units. If for no other reason than that the regular academic ladder recapitulated the structure of field administration, the concerns of the higher gentry were largely contained within and focused on the hierarchy of counties, prefectures, and provinces, whereas those of merchants related to the hierarchy of trading systems centered on greater cities, regional cities, and metropolises.

To what extent did the two hierarchies coincide? Part of the answer may be seen in Table 20, which shows the distribution of cities by level in the administrative and economic hierarchies. It is evident that there was considerable divergence between the maximal administrative and economic hinterlands of particular cities, especially those in the middle range. The leading gentry of a given prefecture, for instance, might find their political action focused at a city whose leading merchants were concerned either with a local-city trading system that was much less extensive than the prefecture or with a regional-city trading system that extended well beyond the prefectural boundaries. Cities classified in the upper-right cells of Table 20 all point to more or less extreme cases of misalignment whereby extensive trading systems climaxed in cities that were not even capitals of the smaller prefectural-level administrative units wholly contained within them. Chou-chia-k'ou, for instance, one of eight nonadministrative regional cities, was the base of great merchants whose area of operations extended far beyond the prefecture (Ch'en-chou) in which it was located, a prefecture whose capital was a city of relative insignificance. Focusing on the column of Table 20 showing low-level capitals, we may note that the one county-level capital that served as a regional metropolis (Wei-hsien in Shantung), the eight county-level capitals that served as regional cities (including Te-chou in Shantung, Wu-hsi in Kiangsu, and Wan-hsien in Szechwan), and most of the 85 county-level capitals that served as greater cities were all centers of commercial systems that extended beyond the prefectural-level administrative units to which the counties in question belonged. In these instances, not only were the commercial systems to which great merchants were oriented and the administrative systems to which leading gentry were oriented of different territorial magnitude; they were also differently structured in space, being centered on quite separate nodal cities.

It should be clear, moreover, that the data in Table 20, showing the alignment of *centers*, seriously understate the amount of misalignment between *systems*. By the very nature of the two structures of territorial systems—the uniform discreteness of the one, the indiscrete overlapping of the other—the alignment of systems was necessarily grossly imperfect. And, to focus on the point at hand, they could be made to diverge radically by deliberately drawing administrative boundaries to minimize convergence.

Limiting examples to the exalted level that can be illustrated by reference to Maps 1 and 2 (pp. 214–15), we may focus our attention on the cores of the Lower Yangtze and North China regions. Had the former been included in a single province—and the Lower Yangtze as a whole would have made a smaller-than-average province in terms of area—the hierarchy of administrative units would have coincided all too closely with the hierarchy of commercial systems within the region.

Cities and the Hierarchy of Local Systems

In an area that included the strongest concentrations of rich merchants *and* of powerful gentry in the entire realm, potential collusion between the two groups at all levels extending up to the central metropolitan trading system would have posed a very real threat to imperial power. By drawing provincial boundaries so that the core of the region was divided among three provinces *and* so that the metropolitan trading systems were split between administrative units (the entire portion of the regional core in Anhwei province, for instance, was oriented economically to Nanking in Kiangsu province), the region's powerful gentry were fractionated into competing elites, and the hierarchy of administrative systems within which each provincial gentry group was focused was sharply differentiated from the commercial territorial hierarchy that shaped the interests of Lower Yangtze merchants. It will be noted, moreover, that of the three provinces involved, Kiangsu and Anhwei each included a portion of the North China regional core, while Chekiang incorporated the northern portion of the Southeast Coast regional core. Thus, in interprovincial competition, the Lower Yangtze gentry within each province allied with gentry in the core of different regional economies.

In that part of the North China core farthest from the imperial capital, provincial boundaries strongly suggest high-level gerrymandering. One effect of extending a leg of Chihli deep into the southern portion of the regional core was to split the metropolitan and the regional-city trading systems of both Kaifeng and Tung-ch'ang-fu between two provinces and to tie the interests of the powerful gentry of Ta-ming *fu* (the prefecture forming the southern leg of Chihli) to the metropolitan province rather than to Honan or Shantung, the provinces on which the interests of Ta-ming merchants were focused.

I am inclined to interpret in similar terms a fairly rare and highly peculiar administrative arrangement at the local level. If the concentrated power of merchants and gentry within local parapolitical structures reached dangerous proportions anywhere, it would have been in the local-city trading systems centered on cities ranking high in both hierarchies—such Lower Yangtze cities as Soochow, Nanking, Hangchow, Yangchow, Ch'ang-chou-fu, Hu-chou-fu, and Shao-hsing-fu; and such metropolises elsewhere as Peking, Sian, Chengtu, Changsha, Hengyang-fu, Nanchang, Foochow, and Canton. The administrative peculiarity in question was common to all of these cities, and it resulted from the fact that each served as the capital of more than one county, three in one instance (Soochow), two in all others. In such cases, the county boundary ran through the city, and the yamen of each county was located in the appropriate sector.* This administrative sectoralization of the city's immediate hinterland meant that there was no county-level yamen to which the extraordinarily strong power structure of the local-city trading system as a whole could relate. As a result, their political focus would have been directed upward to the prefectural yamen. In all probability, this escalation served to weaken the informal political system in two ways. Lesser merchant and gentry leaders whose interests did not extend beyond the local-city trading system and whose standing was uncomfortably low for negotiations with the bureaucrats posted to such high-ranking prefectural yamens may well have declined to participate, focusing their political activities at the next lower level. As for the more exalted leaders of the system, escalation would have brought out the divergent interests of gentry and merchants, whose respective systems of reference at the higher level—the prefecture and the greater-city trading system—were spatially differentiated.

Conclusions

In this paper I have described how regional urban systems were shaped by physiography and how they in turn structured the economy of different physiographic regions. The economic centrality of cities was shown to vary from one region to another and systematically within each region in accordance with its core-periphery structure and transport grid. Although the details of this analysis provide what I believe to be a useful framework for investigating the economy and society of late imperial China, the close correspondence found between central-place systems and physiographic regions, on the one hand, and the relative autonomy of those regional economies, on the other, might well be expected in the case of an agrarian society of subcontinental magnitude lacking mechanized transport.

* Altogether 24 cities throughout China served as the capitals of more than one county. All but two of these cities were located in regional cores, and thirteen were found in the Lower Yangtze region. They included ten of the twenty provincial and higher-level capitals, ten prefectural capitals, and only four county capitals. In addition, *chou* and *t'ing* capitals provide examples—only two to my knowledge—of cities that were administratively divided. T'ai-ts'ang, the capital of an autonomous *chou* in Kiangsu, housed not only the *chou* yamen but also the yamen of Chen-yang, a subordinate county, and the boundary running through the city separated the county from T'ai-ts'ang *pen-chou*. Hsü-yung, the capital of an autonomous *t'ing* in Szechwan, consisted of two separately walled components on either side of a river, with the yamen for the *t'ing* on the west bank and that for its subordinate county, Yung-ming, on the east bank; the boundary between the county and the directly ruled area followed the course of the river.

Cities and the Hierarchy of Local Systems 345

My findings concerning the regional basis of field administration, however, are less than intuitively obvious. I am led to conclude that Ch'ing field administration was marvelously adapted to the realities of regional structure within the empire. On the one hand, the revenue potential of different localities was largely a function of their place in the hierarchy of nodal economic systems that culminated in eight regional economies, each with a core-periphery structure. On the other hand, defense requirements varied in conformity with the structure of physiographic regions; critical defense perimeters were closely associated with regional frontiers, and other strategic sites guarded the major approaches to the heartland of physiographic regions, whose rich resources and great cities constituted the ultimate military objectives. The basic strategy underlying the design of field administration was to adjust the size of county-level units in accordance with position in the macroregional structure—maximizing county populations in the high-revenue portions of the core and minimizing county areas in the insecure and vulnerable areas along the regional frontiers—and then to form prefectural-level units that contained many county-level units at the core (so as to incorporate in as few prefectures as possible the key economic areas on which the empire depended for the bulk of its revenue) but few at the periphery (so as to simplify the chain of command and achieve closer supervision of local officials in times of crisis). The capstone of the system was the meticulous classification of capitals that faithfully reflected the core-periphery structure of regions, the capital's level in the hierarchy of economic central places, span of control, and the relative salience of distinctive administrative tasks. This complex scheme, involving post designations as well as administrative level and rank, enabled the central government to deploy its bureaucratic cadre to maximum advantage. Finally, the specialized functions of circuits introduced some critical differentiation into the administrative chain of command and modified the basic design as necessary to serve broader geopolitical goals.

These findings effectively dispose of the notion that cities in imperial China were but microcosms of empire, more or less uniform creations of an omnipotent state. Rather, they give evidence of skilled husbanding and deployment of the limited bureaucratic power that a premodern court could effectively control. Bureaucratic government may have imposed elements of formal uniformity on Chinese cities, but in practice field administration expressed rather than suppressed functional differentiation within the urban system.

Our investigation of urban networks in relation to regional structure has underlined the remarkable degree to which cities were at once embedded in society and essential to its overall structure. The point can be phrased in terms of hinterlands. That cities shape their hinterlands is axiomatic. This analysis points to the probable virtues of turning the matter around and examining cities in terms of the number, size, and characteristics of their various hinterlands, and of the degree of coincidence and overlap among them. For in a manner of speaking, these determined variation in urban social structure. The relative strength of gentry and merchants in a given city and their propensity to cooperate in urban governance were functions not only of its position with respect to the two hierarchies of central places (as tabulated in Table 20) but of the degree of fit between the city's economic and administrative hinterlands. Similarly, the relative importance of the bureaucratic element in the governance of cities depended not on administrative level alone but rather on the entire interrelated structure of commercial hinterlands and administrative units. We have also found it useful to relate local parapolitical systems to the hinterlands of economic centers, and to examine their intersection with bureaucratic governance in terms of the superposition of two contrastive modes for stacking hinterlands.

The overall fit, throughout the core-periphery structure of a region, between administrative intensity and the political strength of local systems, together with the complex interaction between economic and political power within regional systems of cities, directs our attention to the mechanisms of dominance and dependency that expressed and reinforced the structure as a whole. The present analysis virtually requires us to ask in what ways the exceptional development of such regions as the Lower Yangtze was dependent on underdevelopment in interior regions, and to what extent development in the cores of regions *caused* underdevelopment in their peripheries. Those who pursue these questions are likely to find differentiation among cities and interurban relations close to the heart of the matter.

Cities and the Hierarchy of Local Systems 347

Appendix: Criteria and Procedures for Classifying Central Places by Level in the Economic Hierarchy

This appendix characterizes and illustrates the nature of the data used as indicators of economic centrality and specifies the procedures followed in classifying Chinese cities and towns according to level in the economic hierarchy as of 1893.

Central-place systems are spatial systems in which the commercial centrality of any one center is very much a function of its cost-distance from all neighbors at the same and adjacent levels. For this reason it is essential that all relevant data concerning central places and the links between them be related to the major features of their spatial setting. To this end, large-scale work maps were prepared for each of the eight macroregions, using the most accurate of recent map sources as a base for such physical features as altitude contours, watersheds, and river systems. Major transport and trade routes as of the 1890's, both roads and navigable waterways, were plotted from sources produced in the period 1885–1915; these included Chinese manuals and treatises on waterways and merchants' routes, accounts of Western and Japanese travelers and trade missions, and above all a series of detailed reports on inland transport solicited in 1890 by the Council of the China Branch of the Royal Asiatic Society from nearly 50 locally resident experts.[54] The regional core, as described in the text, was also delimited on each map.

The next step was to plot on these regional maps all central places that stood any chance, as of 1893, of having commercial functions at the local-city level or higher. This involved a selection from the approximately 2,500 central places for which data had been prepared, as described on pages 221–22. The following criteria delimited the subset to be mapped: (1) all centers in which a post office of any grade had been established by 1915 (820 capital cities and 370 nonadministrative centers); (2) every place considered important enough as a trade center to warrant a descriptive sketch in *Shina shōbetsu zenshi*, a comprehensive series of provincial gazetteers compiled by Tōa Dōbunkai and reflecting data as of 1911–15 (659 capital cities and 234 nonadministrative centers); (3) all capitals any one of whose top bureaucratic posts had been officially designated by the character *ch'ung* ("thoroughfare; frequented"), indicative of an important transport node (585 cities in all); and (4) all central places above a specified size threshold, set for most regions at 4,000 for the core and 2,000 for the periphery. Since city size is a function of many factors in addition to economic centrality, its use in this regard was primarily as a failsafe—to avoid leaving out towns whose appreciable size might have been due largely to economic centrality. City population estimates and indicators had been culled from a wide variety of sources, including local gazetteers and the more reliable accounts of Western and Japanese travelers. Since the four variables used as selection criteria were strongly intercorrelated, the number of central places to be plotted was less than 1,500—approximately 1,000 of the 1,546 capital cities, plus 400-odd nonadministrative centers.

The single indicator on which I relied most heavily in developing comparative profiles of economic centrality was the postal status of the center as of 1915.[55] The Imperial Postal Service was established in 1896, and during the next fifteen years service was rapidly extended throughout the empire. Branches were of four grades: first-class, second-class, and third-class post offices, and postal agencies. Branches were further distinguished by the number and type of special services offered. Of particular interest here, because of their significance for business activity, are express delivery and the availability of money orders, whose upper limits were specified as 50 or 100 yüan. Available special services provide little basis for discriminating within the category of first-class post offices (all of which offered most) or third-class post offices (most of which offered none); but in the case of second-class offices, the number and configuration of special services turned out to correlate rather closely with other indicators of economic central functions. Thus, central places were classified according to available postal facilities as follows: (1) first-class PO; (2) second-class PO offering three or more special services including express delivery and money orders up to 100 yüan; (3) second-class PO offering two or more special services including express delivery and money orders up to at least 50 yüan; (4) second-class PO offering two or more special services that did not include express delivery; (5) second-class PO whose only special service was the availability of money orders not exceeding 50 yüan; (6) second-class PO offering no special services; (7) third-class PO; (8) agency only; (9) no postal facilities of any kind.

There are three obvious sources of error in using the postal hierarchy of 1915 as an indicator of the economic hierarchy as of 1893. First, although businessmen were clearly the heaviest users of postal services overall—for correspondence as well as for parcel post and money orders—government use was also significant in central places that served as administrative capitals. Second, to some unspecified degree the extension of postal services was biased in favor of long-distance trade routes and the modernizing sector of the business community, and at any point in time (though less so in 1915 than in 1910 or 1905) postal services were more fully developed (holding degree of commercialization constant) in coastal regions than in the interior. Third, despite the lag between the level of postal facilities provided and local demand for them, the inherent anachronism meant that the level of postal services reflected the reordering of economic centrality that had occurred in certain areas as a consequence of transport modernization, particularly the introduction of railroads and steamships, during the twenty years after 1893.

The first of these difficulties was minimized by also coding central places according to administrative status, so that the governmental portion of postal demand could be systematically discounted. The second difficulty was largely circumvented by analyzing the central-place hierarchy of each region separately. Since postal codes were compared only within regional systems and subsystems, there was no operational assumption of cross-systemic equivalence of codes. The third difficulty was confronted by adding to the postal code the subscripts r (for railroad) and s (for steamship) when the center in question had acquired such service prior to 1912, so that the interim effect of modern transport could be systematically discounted. With these biases partially controlled, the postal facilities code was found to be closely related to all of the more direct, but less comprehensive, indicators of commercial central functions in the 1890's.

When the postal-facilities codes of each plotted central place were added

Cities and the Hierarchy of Local Systems 349

to the regional maps, the general outlines of the central-place hierarchy became apparent. Centers sited at major transport nodes, with postal-facilities codes higher than those of any other cities within a radius of 20–30 miles, could only be high-level commercial cities, whereas those poorly served by transport routes, and whose postal-status codes were lower than those of all their immediate neighbors, could only be low in the economic hierarchy. On the basis of the postal data and spatial configuration alone, each of the 1,400-odd mapped central places was assigned to one of six tentative categories, namely (1) putatively a central or regional metropolis, (2) putatively a regional metropolis or regional city, (3) putatively a regional city or greater city, and so on down to (6) putatively no higher than a central market town. The purpose of this preliminary classification was to identify the groupings of central places within a region for which comparable data would be sought in order to make reasonably valid final assignments to functional levels.

For this purpose, a variety of specific data were collected as available. Trade statistics were compiled for the period from 1880 to 1920 and used in conjunction with contemporary accounts of the nature and extent of the trade at particular cities. Particularly useful in this regard were the surveys, travel accounts, and assessments made by Western and Japanese trade missions, businessmen, and consular agents, together with the reports, already mentioned, that were collected in the early 1890's by the China Branch of the Royal Asiatic Society. Revenues from the taxation of commercial activities are reported in many county gazetteers, sometimes specific to the various central places within the county, more often than not aggregated for the whole; even the latter were helpful when the county contained a single city of overwhelming commercial importance. The number of merchant *hui-kuan* (same native-place associations), together with the geographic spread of the native places involved, provided important clues to the city's place in interurban trade. The number of shopkeeper households, at least in the capital city, is recorded in many local gazetteers, and in due course I developed a working table of diagnostic ranges for core and peripheral areas (e.g., for local cities, 280–900 shopkeeper households in core areas, 165–525 in peripheral areas; for greater cities, 900–2,700 in core areas, 525–1,600 in peripheral areas). For certain cities, an estimate of the size of the built-up area exclusive of yamens, examination halls, and other official buildings (in the case of capitals), but inclusive of commercial suburbs, could often be made using contemporary gazetteer maps in conjunction with recent, more accurate city plans.

With all relevant data at hand, I proceeded with the classification of centers, beginning at the top of the hierarchy. After deciding which cities ranked as central and regional metropolises in the empire as a whole, I then pursued decisions at lower levels one region at a time, moving down the hierarchy. In cases where the level of an entire subsystem was debatable—was central place X with its satellites a local city surrounded by central market towns or a central market town surrounded by intermediate market towns?—I sought specific evidence in relevant gazetteers. More than half of all county-level gazetteers for the Kuang-hsü period (1875–1908) provide some economic indicators for all central places in the county, which typically included central as well as intermediate and standard market towns and often one or more higher-level centers as well. Center-by-center data supplied by particular gazetteers include number of firms by line of business, number of brokers by type, commodities sold and/or local products purchased (sometimes with an indication of the volume of transactions), revenue from sales taxes by commodity, number of shopkeeper households and/or total households, market schedules, and folk classifications of markets by "size" or "bustle."[56]

An example may illustrate the manner in which gazetteer data enabled me to fix the level of the highest-ranking central place in a county. The 1911 gazetteer for Ch'ing-p'ing, a county in Tung-ch'ang *fu* (Chihli), lists for each of fourteen central places the number of dealers in five classes of taxable goods, together with the annual tax revenue from each.[57] Ten of the towns, which I tentatively identified as standard market towns, had only one or two dealers and tax revenues under four taels. In the county capital and two other towns, which three places appeared to be intermediate market towns, the number of dealers ranged from twelve to sixteen and tax revenues from eighteen to 23 taels. The remaining market town had twenty dealers and provided nearly 33 taels of tax revenue. The spatial relations of these towns to one another confirmed the supposition that the highest-ranking center was a central market town; this in turn helped establish level alignments within the regional-city trading system centered on Tung-ch'uan-fu.

The distribution of market schedules among central places was a reliable indicator of level in the economic hierarchy within many, if not most, local-city trading systems. I have demonstrated elsewhere[58] that when new markets were established in rural China, local leaders were normally careful to select market days that avoided or minimized scheduling conflicts with neighboring higher-level market towns. As a result, neighboring towns with the same market schedule were both almost certain to be merely standard market towns; and the monopolization of particular market days by a town may be taken as strong evidence that the town in question performed higher-level commercial functions for its neighbors. The principle is illustrated in Professor Shiba's paper in this volume (pp. 428–29), where he shows that three central market towns monopolized certain market days throughout the western sector of Ningpo's greater-city trading system. Perhaps the most common local pattern was this: intermediate market towns were distinguished from dependent standard market towns by dovetailed scheduling rather than by frequency of market days; central market towns were distinguished by a doubled schedule (say, four market days rather than two in each ten-day segment of the lunar month); and local cities were characterized by multiple markets whose combined schedules often added up to a daily market. Whatever the local pattern, the mapping of market schedules normally enables one to ascertain the economic level of the highest-ranking central places with reasonable assurance.

Finally, I should mention incremental goods and services diagnostic of level in the economic hierarchy—the type of evidence on which classic central-place analysis places greatest emphasis. The chief complication here is that the precise schedules of such goods varied from one trading system to another in accordance with different levels of population density and commercialization and also with distinctive regional preferences. Thus, I illustrate functional differentiation by reference to a single relatively homogeneous area: the core of the Upper Yangtze region. My examples of "incremental"

Cities and the Hierarchy of Local Systems

retail goods are limited to those sold in shops that were open for business daily, as opposed to those offered only periodically or occasionally in marketplaces and roadside stalls—largely because the former are better documented in gazetteers. Shops distinguishing intermediate market towns from standard market towns included those specializing in hardware or miscellaneous tools, caps, wine, and religious supplies (notably incense, candles, and money paper). Shops diagnostic of central market towns included those dealing solely in iron utensils, firecrackers and fireworks, bambooware, cloth, salt, and tea leaves. Specialist shops making their first appearance in local cities included those selling paper and stationery, leather goods, lanterns, altar carvings, flour, and lard. Diagnostic of the greater-city level were shops dealing exclusively in silk and satin fabrics, playing cards and mahjong sets, musical instruments, garlic, and ginger. Specialized retail shops normally found only in regional cities and metropolises included those selling embroidered insignia panels for officials, buttons for officials' caps, animal furs, goldfish, and birds' nests.

A briefer list of diagnostic artisan services (again with reference to firms established in shops) includes, for intermediate market towns, coffinmakers, blacksmiths, tailors, and noodle makers; for central market towns, dyers, shoemakers, and beancurd makers; for local cities, tinsmiths, seal cutters, and lacquerware makers; for greater cities, scroll makers, printers, and glue manufacturers; and for regional and higher-level cities, lapidaries, cloisonné makers, printing-block carvers, and manufacturers of silk cord for fastening Chinese gowns. Other diagnostic incremental services include winehouses for the intermediate market town (teahouses being present in the average standard market town), bathhouses and inns for the central market town, pawnshops and shops renting sedan chairs for the local city, and laundries and transport firms for the greater city. Organized prostitution (usually in connection with inns) first appeared in central market towns; ordinary brothels first appeared in local cities; and graded brothels (first-class, second-class, etc.) first appeared in greater cities. In regional cities and metropolises one found brothels differentiated not only by grade but also by type (e.g., those limited to girls of a particular provenance, specializing in certain kinds of sex, or combining sexual services with particular forms of musical or dramatic entertainment).

As argued in the text, one also expects economic functions associated with interurban trade to be discretely stratified by level in the central-place hierarchy. In core areas of the Upper Yangtze region, wholesaling and brokerage, at least for the staple grains, were nearly universal in intermediate market towns. Specialized (and usually licensed) brokers were typically found in central market towns, where many retail shops sold supplies at wholesale prices to itinerant traders circuiting lower-level market towns. At the local-city level, one typically found brokers in the same line specialized by clientele—some would deal with small buyers from the surrounding market towns, and others with large buyers from nearby higher-level cities. Greater cities usually supported godowns, large-scale wholesalers, and commission houses. As for financial institutions, money shops ("money-exchange" banks, usually *ch'ing-p'u*) were incremental at the level of central market towns, loan and deposit ("money-lending") banks (including *yin-hao* and *ch'ien-chuang*) at the local-city level, and remittance banks (usually *p'iao-hao*) at the regional-city level.

The Yamen and Urban Administration

JOHN R. WATT

The Ch'ing yamen remains one of the most conspicuous institutions in Ch'ing society, for it was the principal vehicle of political administration in a civilization that placed great emphasis on administration. Of the many public offices at the various levels of the Ch'ing government, the county-level yamen had greatest impact on the lives of the people because it was the most immediate and frequently encountered form of imperial authority. The county yamen served also as the main center for negotiation between bureaucratic government and informal local authority. This *sub rosa* activity was as important a function of the county yamen as its more visible public undertakings. In short, the county-level yamen served both as the leading instrument of public authority and as the primary arena of political exchange. Because of the diversity and significance of these functions, the county yamen was an exceptionally busy institution, astir "from sunrise to sunset."[1]

The Urbanization of Local Administration

As a major political institution, the county yamen relates closely to the process of urbanization in Chinese society. It was situated in the *ch'eng*, or walled administrative city. Several of the more important administrative cities housed more than one county yamen. (See Figure 1 for an example.) Many yamen functionaries, from the magistrate on down, lived as well as worked inside the yamen. Apart from the runners sent out to harass taxpayers or arrest suspects, yamen functionaries were no longer directly engaged in rural life. During their terms of service (which were in some cases considerable), they tended to stay inside the yamen and were discouraged from going outside it.[2] Thus, the

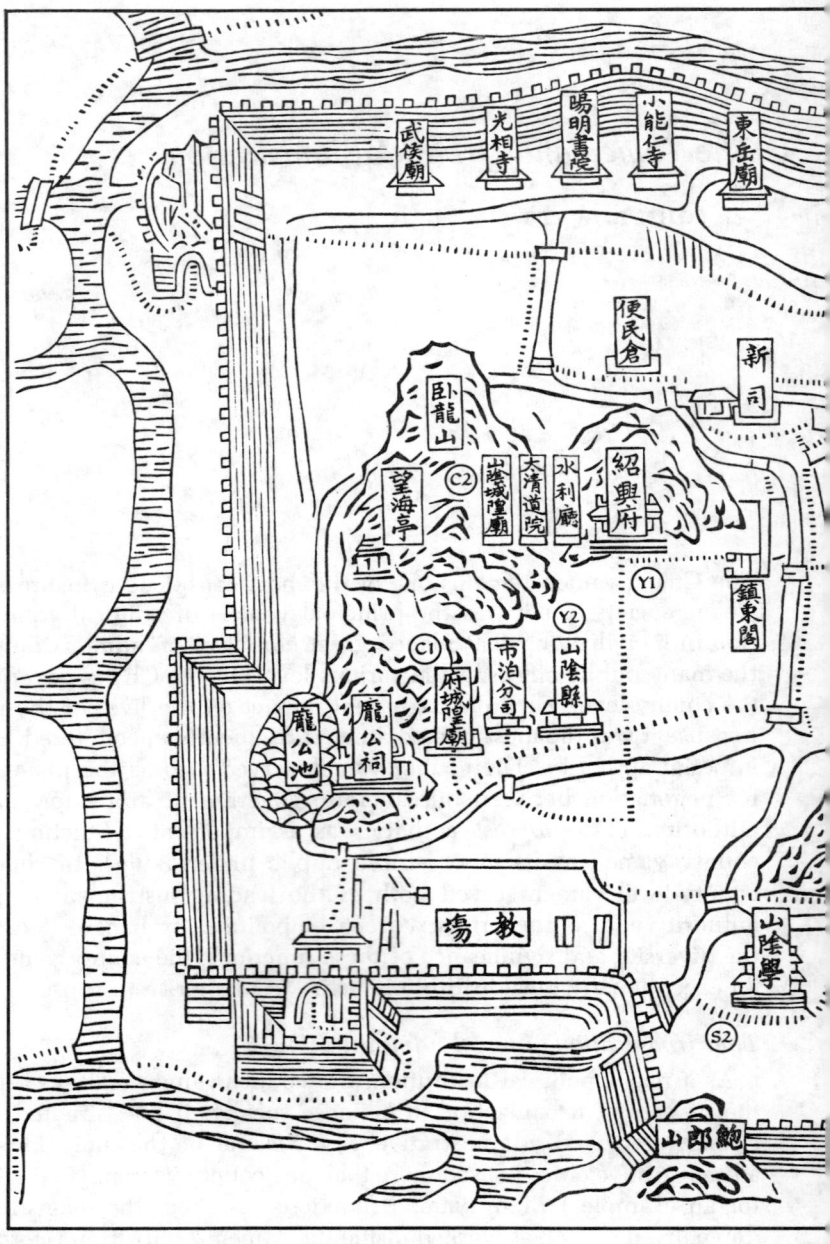

Fig. 1. Shao-hsing-fu, Chekiang, as depicted in a map of 1683. The open ribbons snaking through the city represent major canals; they are connected to two lakes (indicated by fish scales) within the walls, one in the far northeast corner and one in the southwest, and to the moat via water gates. The bands crossing canals are bridges, and the routes indicated by dotted lines are streets. The city housed governments of two counties as well as of Shao-hsing prefecture. The boundary between Shan-yin *hsien* to the west and K'uei-chi *hsien* to the east ran from Chih-li Men (the water gate east of the center of the south wall) north along the city's main canal as far as the T, where it turned east, following canals to Ch'ang-an Men (the sole gate in the north wall). Circled emblems have been added to key

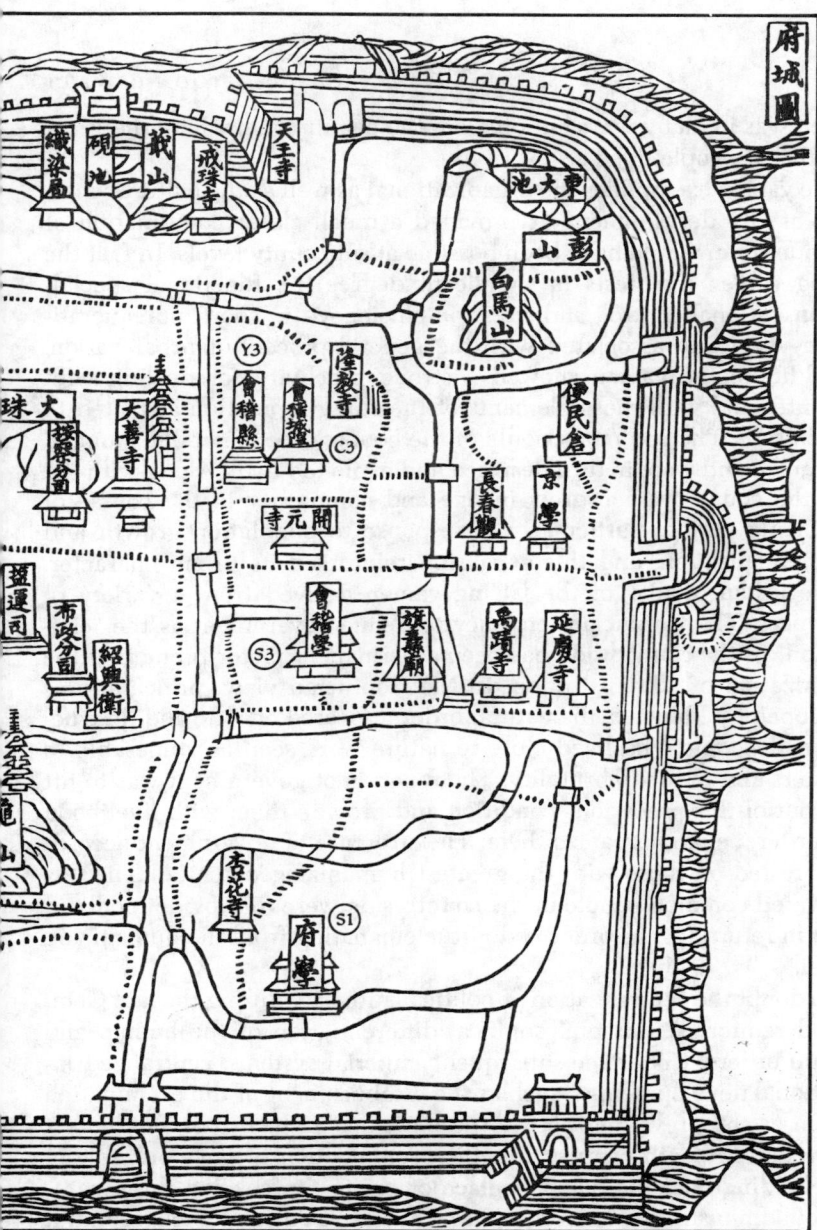

the three civil yamens, the three Confucian school-temples (*hsüeh-kung*), and the three City God temples. Y1 is the prefectural yamen, Y2 and Y3 the county yamens of Shan-yin and K'uei-chi, respectively. S1 is the *fu-hsüeh*, S2 and S3 the *hsien-hsüeh* of Shan-yin and K'uei-chi, respectively. C1 is the City God temple for the prefecture, C2 and C3 the City God temples for Shan-yin and K'uei-chi, respectively. The examination sheds are against the south wall next to the southwesternmost gate. Most of the remaining institutions depicted on this typical city plan are temples, military offices, lesser offices of the civil government, academies, and public granaries. From *K'ang-hsi K'uei-chi hsien chih* (1683), ch. shou, 1b–2a.

yamen was in many ways cut off from the countryside, where the great majority of people lived.

The yamen exemplifies the organizational as well as the cultural character of city development. It provided a much closer coordination of functions than would have been possible at subcounty levels. In fact the Ch'ing yamen manifests in significant degree the functional specialization, rational control, and stress on efficiency—in short, bureaucratization—typically associated with the general process of urbanization. In addition, the yamen showed a strong proclivity for dealing with urbanites and with those elements of the rural population attracted to city culture. The common people of the countryside generally shunned the yamen and were in turn despised and exploited by it. Along with the city, the county yamen grew in size and complexity in the course of the Ch'ing period, particularly in response to population growth and commercialization, and this expansion reinforced its urban character.

The urban quality of the Ch'ing yamen derived from a variety of influences. The Confucian tendency to define government as the "civilization" of the countryside has been a permanent factor promoting the urbanization of administration. In the Confucian view, principally as developed by Mencius, the natural order appeared chaotic and destructive, and people who lived close to nature were seen as vulnerable to disasters and prone to brutality. The function of government was to lift men out of this precarious condition and provide them with livelihood and order, i.e., to humanize them. The structure of government accordingly rested on those with the greatest humanizing potential. The less cultivated common people in the countryside were to provide food and labor in return for the order and virtue emanating from the humanizing nuclei.[3]

No doubt the centralization of political authority during the late Chou period reinforced this philosophical differentiation of the human and natural orders. Under the subsequent imperial systems, centralized institutional developments—such as the establishment of the examination system as the prevailing path to public office (which took final effect in the mid-fifteenth century), or the promulgation of laws prohibiting officeholding near the official's place of origin—intensified the separation of administration from rural life. Given this cultural background, it is not surprising that Ch'ing administrators should have continued to regard rural society as ignorant and disorderly.

The exclusiveness of the imperial state also substantially influenced the urbanization of administration. Throughout the ages, Confucian commentators never ceased to point out that the imperial system, far from belonging to the social order, was imposed on it by outside force and denied local society any separate legitimation. Instead, the imperial state brought the entire domain under centers of authority, which were gradually consolidated as extensions of imperial authority. Ch'ing administration reinforced the dichotomy between the state, whose loci were in cities, and society, whose center of gravity was in the countryside. As foreigners who seized power by military conquest, the Manchus were in no position to identify with rural Chinese society. Instead, they allied themselves with the literate and urban classes, extended their power through garrison cities, and attempted to bring rural society under centralized control.

Another factor in the urbanization of administration was the trend toward concentration of landownership, which tended to undermine the success of rural-based administrative institutions. Despite the political factors mentioned above, there were determined efforts throughout the imperial era to develop effective rural administrative institutions. In the Ming period, outstanding examples were the *li-chia* and *li-lao* systems of the founding emperor and the *hsiang-yüeh* system revived by Wang Yang-ming. However, these institutions of local control and administration were all crippled by the endemic competitiveness of rural economic life and by the reluctance of successful families to associate with unrelated commoners. Moreover, the growing concentration of landownership during late imperial times was part of a broader trend toward economic differentiation that manifested itself in the monetization of political administration. On the one hand, economic success tended to be associated with movement from the countryside toward the towns and cities; on the other hand, monetization both decreased the need of the government to tax the people in physical labor (an essentially rural product) and promoted specialization within the humbler service roles of local administration.

The chief question pursued in this study is, How did a predominantly urban administrative system interact with a predominantly rural society? In attempting an answer, this paper examines the functions and organizational character of the yamen in order to estimate the extent of its urbanization and differentiation from rural society. It also explores further the local administrative conditions from which the Ch'ing yamen emerged, and considers what forces promoted the concentration of administrative functions within the yamen and with what effect on urban-rural relations. It argues that the significant changes in local administration during late imperial times created tensions in the definition and pursuit of societal goals, and asks to what extent such tension promoted social and administrative differentiation.

Before these questions are reviewed, it should be emphasized that what follows is of necessity a general analysis of the county yamen rather than a comparative analysis of differences. Yet in the empire as a whole, county-level units varied substantially in size, locational advantage, and wealth, and these variables affected the size of the yamen and the degree of internal differentiation. This has bearing on the Skinnerian model for interrelating administrative and economic centers, for whereas administrative units at the same level were comparable in terms of official functions, they differed significantly in the organization of political control. This point may be illustrated by looking at variations in the relationship of yamen organization to central government control (also variations in the organization of informal political alignments). Subprovincial yamens were administratively classified as "most important," "important," "medium," and "easy." "Most important" jurisdictions were those to which all four of the following characterizations applied: "frequented" (centers of communications), "troublesome" (much official business), "wearisome" (many overdue taxes), and "difficult" (an unruly populace). "Important" jurisdictions were defined as including any three of the above four characteristics; "medium," any two; and "easy," any one or none. In general, it appears that population size, level of public revenue, and extent of the legal case load were the primary determinants of jurisdictional importance.

These differences in classification, which applied to all jurisdictions at the prefectural and county levels, determined influence over, and qualifications for, appointment to the office of chief administrator. In the case of counties (*hsien*), the roughly 350 characterized as important or most important were assigned to magistrates nominated by the provincial governor or governor-general from officials under his authority with at least three to five years (depending on appointment procedure) of prior administrative experience. These nominations had to be ratified by the Board of Civil Office. The remaining 950 or so were staffed by Board-appointed officials who were not required to have prior administrative experience. In addition, differences in importance affected the number of offices within a yamen and the size of its staff. Although there are as yet no clear findings on this matter, by the early nineteenth century some 350 counties (many but not all of which were most important or important) had an assistant magistrate, who was located either in the yamen or in a separate office situated generally in a market town. There were also over 900 subcounty magistrates divided among prefectures, departments, and counties and posted near passes, fords, and other strategic places. As we shall see later, however, the really significant variations among jurisdictions were in the numbers of

The Yamen and Urban Administration

subordinate yamen personnel, whose appointments were determined at the regional or local level.

The Ch'ing government was sufficiently aware of socioeconomic changes to adjust from time to time the classifications of, and appointment procedures for, jurisdictions where significant change could be substantiated. To protect its control, the government would not raise the classification of one county to important, thereby adding its magistrate to the provincially selected list, without lowering the classification of another, thereby bringing it onto the Board-selected list. Over the years the Ch'ing also abolished some county jurisdictions and created others, changed departments and subprefectures into counties and (less often) vice versa, demoted counties to subcounties, and reassigned counties to different prefectures. Despite the long-term attrition of subordinate official positions, the central government also juggled their overall distribution; the abolition of a position in one county would often be coupled with the creation of a similar position in another, thus temporarily maintaining overall numbers.

These variations and alterations in the classification, size, and organization of county-level jurisdictions need to be borne in mind in considering the interrelationship of the administrative and economic hierarchies of central places in late imperial China. On the face of it, central government policy was intended to maintain an alignment of administrative centers with economic centers in order to prevent the usurpation of political control by those whose power rested on economic control in commercial centers. Provincial officials, for their part, were interested in placing administrators of their own choosing in important local capitals. In short, Ch'ing administration appears consciously geared to an urban strategy designed to bring strong administrative influence to bear at nodal points of economic development. By no means did this strategy work out solely in favor of the central government; however, as suggested below, it did increase the power of city-based social groups who had a mutual interest in living off the countryside.

All this is to suggest that the system of administrative central places was more complex and flexible than it may appear on the surface. Below the provincial and circuit level it included (1) important prefectures (the majority, for which appointment was controlled by imperial edict); (2) regular prefectures (with Board-appointed magistrates); (3) autonomous departments (*chih-li chou*, which were functionally at the same level as prefectures but fewer in number and inferior in official salary and status, and whose magistrates were nominated by provincial governors); (4) ordinary departments (*san-chou*, approximately 150 in all, functionally at the same level as counties but superior in salary and status, though not necessarily in economic productivity, and whose magistrates were fairly evenly divided between the Board-appointed and the provincially selected); (5) important or "busy" counties; (6) Board-appointed "easy" counties; and (7) a small number of subprefectures (*t'ing*) and commanderies. Below the county level were city wards, suburban districts, and rural districts, exhibiting great variety in size and nomenclature, all for the most part denied effective formal administration. Below them came the *pao-chia* ("watch-group") system for organizing population surveillance and accountability, which despite its unpopularity became a significant element in Ch'ing rural control.

Of the various levels in this administrative hierarchy, the county-level unit was operationally the more important, and clearly the more efficient, agency for achieving the extractive and normative objectives of the various power groups represented in both state and society. We must now turn to an analysis of how and why this was so.[4]

Functions of the County Yamen

The Ch'ing county yamen was a collectivity of differentiated personnel that pursued a variety of social and political objectives. As the instrument of a centralized dynastic house that came to power through invasion and conquest, it was first and foremost under orders to carry out imperial policies. For the administrative elite, it was a necessary means for the pursuit of related but rather different political objectives. The yamen also played a role in resolving local power struggles and was under pressure to serve objectives arising from the structural development of local society.

For the central government the county yamen was the principal office for carrying out administrative policies. Within the state apparatus as a whole, the metropolitan administration formulated imperial policies and supervised their execution. The provincial, circuit, and prefectural administrations acted as intermediaries between the central government and the county level. But it was up to the roughly 1,500 county-level yamens, and in particular to their magistrates, to apply these policies to the populace and see that they were respected. Thus, although county officials were low in the administrative hierarchy, the effectiveness of the entire apparatus was dependent on their administrative conduct.[5]

The main responsibilities of county magistrates were to maintain public security and to collect taxes. As chief administrator, the magistrate was officially charged with superintending the government of a county, regulating its taxes and labor services, hearing and adjudicating legal suits, promoting education, raising the cultural level, and controlling customs. He was also to take responsibility for helping the aged, for sacrificing to the spirits, and for supporting scholars and regulating their study.[6] The Ch'ing emperors themselves, however, put security and taxation foremost and reinforced this emphasis with an elaborate system of disciplinary regulations designed to spur official activity in these areas.[7] An annual review, known as k'ao-ch'eng ("examination of accomplishment") and carried out by metropolitan and provincial officials, scrutinized the magistrate's performance in collecting taxes and arresting robbers. It provided a series of rewards and penalties backed up by time limits and closely graduated by magnitude.[8] In the Shun-chih and K'ang-hsi reigns (1644–1722), triennial reviews designed to assess official integrity and competence were linked to success in clearing tax records and robbery cases.[9] In addition to these specific reviews, a compendium of disciplinary regulations defined the conduct of local officials in every aspect of their administrative duties. As in the k'ao-ch'eng review, these regulations operated on the principle of rewards and penalties, with the latter heavily predominating.[10] Because the responsibility of surveillance of local magistrates fell to senior officials, managing this complex system of administrative controls became one of the principal functions of high provincial officials.[11]

Though it emphasized political power, the Ch'ing government did not neglect the promotion of cultural values. It saw this as a means of furthering Confucian principles and of inhibiting the development of political heterodoxy. Ch'ing cultural policy was expressed in the well-known Sacred Edict, which was drawn up by the K'ang-hsi emperor and greatly amplified by his son the Yung-cheng emperor. Its basic purpose was to explain the need for public security and urge the public to "eschew disorderly conduct." Specifically, it propounded such control values as obedience and resignation. It urged the people to pay their taxes on time and to join the pao-chia rural control institution; it also urged them to desist from litigation.[12] The significance of the Edict for county-level administration was threefold. First, it was the county magistrate who was responsible for implementing the Edict. It was his duty to lead the twice-monthly recitations in the capital and to select the personnel to do likewise in the towns and villages within his jurisdiction. Second, the Edict specifically reinforced values that eased the magistrate's administrative tasks and that it was his duty to propagate. Third, by exhorting against social conflict, it countered an activity that was vital to the livelihood of yamen personnel, as I explain below. Intended to diminish tensions among the people, the Sacred Edict actually increased them within the local administration.

The functions that the central government assigned to administration at the county level were almost exclusively the responsibility of the county magistrate. Subordinate officials had specified roles to play, but they were of minor importance. The magistrate in person had to see to it that specific and mandatory imperial instructions were properly discharged. To do this, he needed a highly articulate and coordinated organization, capable of meeting deadlines and avoiding administrative or physical sanctions. This need, together with the focus of responsibility on the magistrate, effectively promoted the centralization of local administration.

For Ch'ing writers on administration, the dissemination of Confucian values formed a vital part of the magistrate's function. They held that these values contributed both to popular welfare and to the fulfillment of the administrative role. Among such values, Ch'ing writers particularly stressed *yang* (nurture) and *chiao* (education). They saw the common people as culturally immature and argued that administrators must be responsible for protecting their physical and mental welfare. Here again, it was on the county magistrate as the official "close to the people," the "shepherd," the "father and mother" of the "newborn children" that this responsibility rested. No other office had the combination of closeness and authority necessary to perform this cultural role.[13]

Their own education, the exhortations of senior officials, and some degree of general social expectation combined to put magistrates under some pressure to carry out their cultural responsibilities. Ideally, they were expected to visit the countryside (with as few attendants as possible) and there encourage the virtuous and warn the obstinate. It was also their task to promote scholarship (i.e., study for the examinations) and to attend certain ceremonies at Confucian and other temples. In practice, however, Ch'ing magistrates preferred to direct their cultural influence to the administration of justice, which took up much of their time anyway. In this way they did not have to leave the yamen, and they had a ready audience in the large crowds that gathered for the public trials. Even the most Confucian-minded officials recognized how suitable the law court was as a cultural forum, for there the magistrate could play the role of *chün*, or Confucian moral exemplar, combining benevolent education with heavy punishment.[14]

So far this account has dealt with public functions defined by imperial and ideological objectives. The county yamen also served a variety of

The Yamen and Urban Administration

unstated but well-recognized goals arising from its local administrative authority.

For the local gentry, the yamen was a critical arena for articulating local interests, resolving power struggles, and influencing administrative decision-making. Few political systems barred local elites from holding administrative office more deliberately than the Ch'ing. Appointment procedures prevented gentry from holding office in or near their native county and made it difficult for any but the top metropolitan degree-holders to gain office elsewhere. Provincial degree-holders, though eligible to become county magistrates, usually had to wait twenty or more years for an appointment. Assistant administrative and local educational posts were more easily had but were politically ineffectual and unattractive to ambitious degree-holders. Ordinary licentiates were normally barred from holding official appointments or from serving as clerks; positions as private secretaries were available in nonnative areas, but the prestigious secretarial positions demanded technical skills uncongenial to gentry both as Confucianists and as examination candidates. The expenditure of large sums could qualify degree- or status-holders for appointment to local administrative offices, but the elaborate appointment procedure required purchasers to wait in turn with degree-holders for nomination to office. All these restrictions were part of a deliberate state policy to prevent local interests from taking control of county administration.[15]

In the face of these barriers, the gentry pursued their political objectives through personal liaisons with yamen officials. By means of such connections, they obtained preferential treatment in tax collection and were able to negotiate tax-farming arrangements, and they also obtained support in litigation against commoners. Yamen personnel drummed up lucrative business for the gentry by delaying the processing of suits, which forced rural litigants to put up in town at hostels owned by gentry. Officials directed litigants to notaries, many of whom were down-at-heel gentry scholars. Generally, the gentry used the county yamen to enhance their local prestige and to gain information about the attitudes of senior provincial officials.[16] They traded a measure of their local social and economic power, which was denied to the nonnative yamen officials, for a measure of the political authority that was denied to the gentry class by statute. Each side gained something from the exchange: the gentry, political leverage; the yamen, social authority.

For the people at large, the county yamen served as the court of first instance in civil disputes. Despite widespread popular distrust of the yamen because of the rapacity and severity of its personnel, litigation seems to have been a prevalent phenomenon in Ch'ing society and regulations existed requiring officials to hear suits within certain time limits.[17] Efforts by social institutions such as lineages to keep their members from taking cases to the public courts seem to have been ineffective, and could not have affected the millions of families who lacked institutional connections.[18] Though the Ch'ing emperors discouraged litigation, they could not prohibit it because it arose from civil dispute, which it was the duty of the administration to adjudicate.[19] Some magistrates did try to follow the imperial lead and urged the people to cease their suits, but the income generated by litigation was generally too important to the yamen to give up.[20]

The Ch'ing central government refused to put administration on a fully salaried basis, so an important function of the county yamen was to provide a livelihood for its personnel. The government paid nominal salaries—based on official rank, not duties, and unrelated to expenses— to the regular establishment of officials, clerks, and workers, and paid supplementary salaries to administrative officials. Introduced in the Yung-cheng period (1723–35), these supplementary official salaries were intended to reflect current expenses, but failed to do so either then or later. Moreover, the majority of yamen personnel were not a part of the government establishment and so drew no official stipend. Among these, only private secretaries could obtain viable salaries from officials.[21] In consequence, the county yamen was under considerable pressure to produce substantial income for all levels and categories of administrative personnel. Many officials came to office only after years of waiting for an appointment. The appointment procedure itself involved a long and costly visit to Peking and for some a further costly delay at the provincial capital.[22] Officials came to posts with a retinue of relatives, family retainers, and personal servants, all financially reliant on a term of service that could well be cut short by disciplinary sanctions. In addition, county-level governments had to finance many of the activities of higher administrations.[23]

To meet these pressures, yamen personnel charged a variety of fees for public services and practiced extortion on a widespread scale. This enabled county officials to amass substantial incomes for themselves as well as for others. In this respect, the advantage of the county-level yamen lay in its strategic control over tax collection and the administration of justice. On the other hand, the financial pressures on the local yamen forced its officials both to devote a disproportionate amount of attention to fund-raising and to judge administrative business by criteria of profitability. In fact, the county yamen could well be characterized as in business to sell administration at the highest marketable rates.[24]

As part of their effort to prevent localization of administrative authority, the Ch'ing imposed time limits on service in established posts. Magistrates were normally entitled to serve three years in one post. Clerks holding established positions were limited to a total service of five years.[25] In fact, magistrates usually served for less than three years, in some cases much less, whereas informal subordinates served at the will of the resident official. Both groups were under pressure to make as much money as possible in the time available and if possible to stay clear of troublesome business and concentrate on pleasing senior administrators and influential gentry.[26] On the other hand, the regular clerks and runners were able to stay in office for long periods and then hand their posts over to relatives or sell them. Because of their familiarity with local conditions and administrative procedures, they provided a continuity useful if not essential to the nonnative officials.[27]

These unstated yamen functions both clashed and correlated with the imperially specified functions. On the one hand, they contravened the fiscal restraint practiced by all early Ch'ing rulers except the Ch'ien-lung emperor, negated the imperial desire to discourage litigation, and counteracted the effort to prevent localization of authority. On the other hand, they reflected the full acceptance of the primacy of imperial authority, operated within the centralized structure of imperial control, and were grafted onto public fiscal and security functions. Locally, yamen functions conflicted with the general popular desire to keep as far away as possible from local administration but combined with the desire of local gentry to derive political and economic advantage from local administration. Within the yamen itself, the financial objectives of administrative subordinates conflicted both with the political and ideological considerations that influenced official conduct and, to some extent, with the financial objectives of the official establishment and the personnel of higher provincial offices. But there was an almost universal desire on the part of officials to make a profitable venture of administration. In fact, there was a complex interplay between these two kinds of functions that the structure of the yamen duly reflects.

The Structure of the County Yamen

The structure of the county yamen has been extensively described by Ch'ü in his study of local government in China under the Ch'ing. Here we will consider chiefly the relationship of that structure to the functions described above.

The Ch'ing yamen combined formal and informal structures. The formal structure consisted of a hierarchy of officials charged with carrying out the political and ideological objectives of the state. The magistrate held the pivotal position: he was the central government's representative in the county, the seal-holding official, as much the "father and mother" of the county as the emperor was of the empire. He had authority over all administrative functions and was directly responsible for the conduct of his subordinates.

Magistrates were supposedly impartial outsiders. Three-quarters of them were senior examination graduates steeped in Confucian ideology and members of the established gentry order (i.e., *shen-chin*). They came to office through an appointment system strongly favoring metropolitan and provincial graduates. Because of the backlog of available candidates, the system tended to bring in men well on in age. A little under half had held previous civil service appointments or had had experience as private secretaries, teachers, or temporary officeholders. But those for whom the post was a first appointment were both generally ignorant of administrative procedures and regulations and specifically ignorant of the area to which they were appointed. For men responsible for a vital executive post this was a very serious disadvantage. Handbooks urged such men to study the local fiscal records in the metropolitan and provincial capitals and to locate native gentry and merchants with whom to discuss local conditions. Even so, magistrates were said to be out of touch with those conditions for at least their first year in office.[28]

If they survived the disciplinary system, magistrates holding substantive (*pu*) appointments might serve for several years. Magistrates could not be promoted directly to the position of prefect (their immediate administrative superior), and a bottleneck in the promotion system blocked off the vast majority of magistrates from any hope of climbing the administrative ladder. Therefore, we find some magistrates serving in a variety of different county-level posts and others remaining in the same post for several terms of service. These situations generally reflect the confidence of provincial officials in these men and the great need for experienced officials in important county positions. On the other hand, county rosters were inflated with a great many officials holding acting (*shu*) appointments for a few months or even a few days, so that the rate of turnover for officials tended to be well in excess of once every three years.

The subordinate county officials consisted of assistant magistrates, registrars, jail wardens, subcounty magistrates, and a number of miscellaneous positions. Except for the jail wardens, these men generally held office in market towns or at sites strategically located with respect to fords and passes. Therefore they were not normally part of the county yamen establishment. Only jail wardens were to be found throughout the empire.

The centralization and attrition of subordinate officials was already a prominent feature of Sung dynasty policy. The Sung rulers inherited a local administration whose subordinate officials had been appointed and paid by their immediate superiors. They responded by cutting back the number of secondary offices, by limiting the appointment of assistant magistrates to important counties, and by confining the pool of candidates to metropolitan graduates with prior administrative experience. The Ming dynasty, by abolishing the long-standing method of appointment to the post of magistrate by recommendation, dealt a further blow to the role of subordinate official. The abolition of secondary positions continued in late imperial times, and those who held such offices were allegedly despised even by menial underlings. The Shun-chih and K'ang-hsi emperors abolished many assistant magistracies. In 1646 the office of registrar was abolished entirely, although subsequently some 40 posts were reestablished. Later rulers continued to cut the number of assistant magistracies and miscellaneous positions. When new counties were established, jail wardens were the only subordinate officials appointed. In some cases, a subordinate position was abolished in one county and established in another. Furthermore, such positions went to officials with low degrees; county jail wardens were unranked and usually held no degree at all. Subordinate officials received small salaries and had negligible prospects of promotion. County rosters suggest that they tended to stay in office for long periods, but it is clear that they could exert little influence over the conduct of administration. This meant that in most counties, and in virtually all yamens, the Ch'ing county magistrate was the only ranking and degree-holding official and the only one with any substantial administrative authority. He could not count on administrative support from his subordinates.[29]

The rest of the formal yamen structure consisted of specified quotas of clerks and runners. The clerks were in charge of routine documentation and were divided into six sections corresponding in function to the central government boards. Those in the administrative office kept records on all officials and clerks serving in the county administration, all county natives holding established appointments elsewhere, and all local metropolitan and provincial graduates and senior licentiates awaiting selection for office. The clerks in the revenue office kept records on the collection and delivery of taxes. Those in the office of ritual kept lists of temples and sacrificial places, and records of praiseworthy people such as virtuous wives, filial children, obedient grandchildren, and meritorious former officials. They also kept records on persons serving in the *hsiang-yüeh* lecture system, on those holding academic degrees or statuses, and on Buddhist and Taoist priests. Clerks in the military office kept records on guards and runners, with details of where they were stationed. Those in the punishment office kept records on prisoners and prison guards, on suits in hand and criminal cases, and on the administration of the *pao-chia* rural surveillance system. Those in the public works office kept records on military allocations and on public buildings and bridges and their state of repair. There were also usually a number of miscellaneous clerical offices dealing with the distribution of documents, the collection and storage of grain and money, and any other requisite documentation. Subordinate officials and educational officials had their own small quotas of clerks and runners.[30]

The clerks who performed these public functions were men of commoner status who had little hope of obtaining examination degrees or of rising in the administrative service. Degraded well before the Ch'ing period, clerical service originally had been open to scholars. Paradoxically, even as the state was degrading the status of the clerical service it was increasing the significance of local administration. In part, this arose from the efforts by late Ming and early Ch'ing local officials to compensate for the breakdown of the *li-chia* system by relating fiscal procedures more directly to local economic conditions. This process, known collectively as the Single Whip reforms, put a premium on knowledge of local economic and fiscal conditions, and the clerks, as local inhabitants, were quick to exploit the situation. By the end of the Ming dynasty, Ku Yen-wu (1613–82), who made an intensive study of local administration, found clerks entrenched in office. He complained that they were handing their offices down to younger relatives and taking over all the authority of officials.[31]

During the first two centuries of Ch'ing rule the scale of clerical business continued to increase. This was owing partly to the relentless increase in population and partly to the centralized Ch'ing administration, with its burgeoning load of documents. County quotas of regular clerks generally remained in the 10 to 30 range; but even by the late seventeenth century, the addition of copyists and unofficial or nominal clerks sometimes brought the total number of these functionaries up to several hundred or even a thousand, depending on the size of the county. Undoubtedly *sub rosa* yamen functions contributed largely to this increase. Nevertheless, officials held that even imperial business required the services of around 100 clerks, so that as a result the central government was unable to keep the number of clerks down to the nominal quotas.

The Yamen and Urban Administration

The government abolished clerical wages, which made clerks dependent on fees and bribes, and it also made officials responsible for clerical conduct and established specific sanctions for abuse of that responsibility.[32]

The lowest members of the formal yamen structure were the so-called runners. As direct agents of the yamen they served as court attendants, prison guards, policemen, and tax collectors. In connection with imperial objectives, runners were charged with arresting and detaining suspects and executing punishments. It was also their task to pressure people into paying taxes, to bring in delinquents for punitive hearings, and to arrest parties to civil suits. In connection with informal objectives, runners acted as the key link between government representatives and those with local power—from gangs of robbers and village thugs to members of the gentry. In return for fees, they were able to protect rural gangs from criminal punishment or aid gentry in obtaining extensions of tax deadlines or in profiting as tax farmers or notaries. These fees formed an important element in the informal revenue that higher administrative levels siphoned off to support their own public and private operations. As Ch'ü points out, clerks and runners collaborated in extracting revenue in order to protect themselves from the all-pervasive administrative sanctions.

Unlike the clerks, most categories of runners were classified as "mean people" and barred from access to the examinations or to administrative office. Originally, their functions had been carried out by conscripted labor. With the monetization of administration in the late Ming and early Ch'ing, though, taxpayers were able to replace labor service with monetary contributions and administrations to replace conscripts with paid professionals. The Ch'ing administration continued to pay nominal wages to runners while retaining their menial status and demanding strict surveillance of their conduct. It also limited county quotas to between 50 and 100 men. But the unstated functions of the runners were sufficiently significant to defy these restrictions. Actual numbers of runners varied from several hundred to well over a thousand per county, and the runners themselves proved powerful functionaries, able to intimidate the countryside with their coercive capabilities.[33]

Alongside this formal structure of strictly government personnel, Ch'ing local administration developed an informal structure of private aides. Consisting of secretaries, personal servants, and family retainers, these aides functioned specifically to assist the presiding magistrate and performed their services mainly within the yamen enclosure.

The secretaries were much the most important group. They came to office as administrative specialists and took charge of the management and supervision of all administrative procedures. In particular, it was their function to represent the principles of *li* (reason) and *fa* (law or method), and to protect the magistrate from falling foul of the administrative sanctions. County yamens usually had from five to ten secretaries, each in charge of a specific aspect of administrative business. The secretaries of law and taxation held the most influential positions, because of the complexity and urgency of fiscal and legal functions. Within the yamen they enjoyed a prestige comparable to that of the seal-holding official.[34]

The emergence of the private secretaries is one of the more remarkable and intriguing developments in Chinese imperial administration. Once again, it is bound up with the transformation of administration and society that gradually took effect during the late Ming and early Ch'ing. All the changes within local administration we have just discussed—the degradation of clerical status, the attrition of subordinate official posts, the increasing subjection of local administration to control by regulations, and the localization of administrative procedures through the Single Whip reforms—created among officials an intense need for proficient and personally dependable assistance. On the other hand, the supremacy of the examination system as the road to office drew ambitious men away from subordinate posts and committed them to examination careers. Yet the double exclusiveness of the examination and the appointment procedures left a reservoir of literate talent available for office. Though changes in land use probably enabled the late Ming and early Ch'ing economy to sustain a widespread social commitment to these expensive and time-consuming procedures, many who failed to rise within a certain period of time were undoubtedly forced to look for work capable of utilizing their talents and fulfilling (at least in part) their professional, social, and economic expectations. The fact that in the early Ch'ing period magistrates were often Manchus unfamiliar both with the local situation and with Chinese administrative and documentary practices was an additional circumstance leading to the emergence of private secretaries as informal but integral parts of both provincial and local administration.[35]

The secretaries were for the most part degree-holding gentry: some were senior degree-holders either awaiting office or in retirement; most seem to have been students or licentiates. Like the magistrate, secretaries always came from other counties or provinces and did not represent any local community interest. Though usually hired and paid by the local magistrate, they were often recommended by officials or secretaries of higher provincial offices; in that case they also served to represent the interests of the upper administration. As administrative specialists, secretaries tended to be career men able to move from job to job as officials entered and left office. As such they provided a continuity of experience often lacking in official careers. They were hardly subject at all to central government control. Their dependence on the official and their self-respect as professionals and gentry seem to have provided the main restraint on their public conduct. The careerists among them sacrificed the role of Confucian exemplar for that of Legalist technician, and this involved self-denial and in some cases embitterment. They lived by themselves in the yamen, working and sleeping in individual rooms. But their social prestige and mastery of the political functions gave them authority to demand high salaries and polite treatment, and enabled them to share in making administrative decisions.[36]

The personal servants functioned as watchdogs and emissaries for the seal-holding officials. They stood in somewhat the same relationship to the secretaries as did the runners to the clerks. Whereas the secretaries principally supported the public functions of the official, the personal servants mainly served his informal interests. In particular the chief of them, as Meadows accurately noted, were "the negotiators of all the special bribes, and the channels through which the other illegal gains of a mandarin are conveyed to his purse." The gate porter and the document-endorsement attendant were the most important of the personal servants. They supervised the flow of personnel and documents, respectively, in and out of the yamen. The office of gate porter required experienced and authoritative persons able to restrain crowds, control the movements of yamen personnel, and ascertain the names, titles, and business of visiting gentry. In particular, it was their function to prevent the formal and informal subordinates from getting together to spy out the activities of the magistrate and the private secretaries. The gate porters were in a position to exert considerable control over the interaction of formal and informal personnel and the interpenetration of public and private functions. The dependence of Ch'ing administration on documentation put the document and seal attendants in similarly strategic positions. The public reputation of officials was said to be dependent on the conduct of the gate porters and document attendants.

Like the private secretaries, personal servants were outsiders and quite often professionals. They obtained their positions from incoming magistrates and held them at his pleasure. Legally they held the low status of "mean people," but the successful among them were able to accumulate considerable wealth and prestige. Personal servants were not necessarily part of the magistrate's personal following; many obtained their positions by waiting at the provincial capital for the arrival of new and often impecunious officials. Some then found posts by advancing loans at high interest, which bound the official to keep them until the loan was paid off. Others were recommended by relatives and friends of the magistrate or by other officials in the provincial administration. Those who obtained office in this way were under little obligation to the appointing magistrate and, like many private secretaries, went wherever positions were available. For this reason some officials employed relatives or family retainers in these key posts; but even the latter found that the pressures and prerequisites of the job conflicted strongly with personal loyalties. In general, personal servants led risky but colorful lives, often consorting with gamblers and prostitutes and getting into fights. Numbering in the tens or twenties per yamen, they played a vital role in manipulating the informal revenue by which local government supported itself.[37]

Finally, we must mention briefly the family retainers and servants. Provincial officials were allowed to bring specific quotas of retainers into office. County-level magistrates, if Chinese, were permitted twenty, Manchus could have double that number. This entourage ran from close relatives to slaves, from trusted personal servants to cooks and waiters. All seem to have participated in the endless circulation of information and perquisites that kept local government going. In common with all informal aides, the retainers and servants lived in the yamen and were restricted from communicating with clerks and runners or from moving freely in or out.[38]

Thus the yamen performed a variety of formal and informal functions for which it evolved parallel formal and informal structures. Yet the formal structure of officials, clerks, and runners was intensely interested in informal functions, that is, in serving local and personal interests. Furthermore, the state's insistence on increasing centralized control and on diminishing or degrading the formal structure seems only to have fostered this localization of interest. Yet because taxation and the administration of justice demanded knowledge of local economic and social conditions, the state could not afford to do without local representation in county administration. By contrast, the informal structure performed functions demanding skills rather than knowledge. It emerged both to support the formal administrative functions and to relate the centralized official establishment to its localized yet formal subordinate structure.

The Yamen and Urban Administration

This complex interplay of function and structure developed basically in response to an underlying political contest between central and local forces. Specifically it turned on a deadly serious struggle for control of the country's substantial and growing economic resources. On the one hand, the informal structure produced a nucleus of mobile and city-centered administrative specialists, largely free of either local or central control and motivated by personal interest. On the other hand, the formal structure proliferated into an unwieldy nexus of relatively static but comparably specialized functionaries, centered on each capital city and representing both personal and local interest. The yamen was the place where these two groups of local and interregional administrators, and the social forces they represented, confronted each other. How far did this functional specialization proceed? To answer this question we shall examine the organizational character of the yamen and its historical relationship to systems of rural administration.

The Yamen as a Formal Organization

This section offers a preliminary appraisal of the yamen's organizational and bureaucratic character so that we can assess the extent of organizational differentiation in Ch'ing local administration.

Organizations have been generically described as including three characteristics: a division of labor designed to promote specific goals; power centers directing the pursuit of these goals; and turnover of personnel to protect the impersonality of the organization and to improve its functional efficiency.[39] All of these characteristics were present in the county-level yamen, though all were inhibited by countervailing pressures.

Division of labor. In assessing division of labor, one must distinguish between the functions defined by the objectives of the organization itself, and those defined by the objectives of the body politic. The former we may call institutional or operational functions; the latter, societal functions. In the case of the operational functions it is clear that a substantial division of labor existed and increased during the late Ming and early Ch'ing. Furthermore, functional differentiation developed within as well as between specific categories of personnel. Thus there was little overlap between subordinates in the formal structure (clerks and runners) and those in the informal structure (private secretaries and personal servants). Rules handed down by metropolitan and provincial authorities increasingly defined the duties of the formal personnel, and the record of experience—whether written in reports, essays, and handbooks or handed down by word of mouth—increasingly clarified the duties of the informal personnel. In the case of the societal functions the division of labor is much less clear. All public and private societal objectives focused on the magistrate, who was committed to the role of Confucian exemplar. The magistrate was to be the emperor in microcosm, exemplifying the imperial style of government within each county. As a result, his role lacked functional specialization.[40] Subordinate personnel did develop a certain degree of specialization, though conflicts between state and private interests retarded and in fact created contradictions in it. We have noted the paradoxical developments whereby official government employees—clerks and runners—came to represent local interests, whereas nonofficial personnel—secretaries and personal servants—came to represent the interests of the state, the provincial administration, and the county magistrate himself. For example, the private secretaries were as a whole more committed to the maintenance of the formal and public fiscal and security functions than were the clerks. Conversely, clerks were much more dependent on private fund raising than were secretaries. Senior secretaries received from officials substantial salaries that relieved them of the necessity of (if not the desire for) private fund raising.

In terms of the urban-rural paradigm posited in this paper, these distinctions in functional specialization suggest the following comments. First, the policies of the state promoted organizational differentiation in local administration. On the one hand, they indirectly brought into being a body of mobile and urban-oriented administrative specialists. On the other, they forced (both directly and indirectly) increasingly precise definitions of the functions of all administrative groups. The duties of the magistrate and other formal personnel were defined minutely by the disciplinary regulations and by provincial regulations promulgated by officials responsible for administrative surveillance. Magistrates in turn drew up rules defining and controlling the behavior of their subordinates, both formal and informal. These rules and regulations indicate a degree of formalization for which there are few parallels in premodern administration. They represent a massive effort to differentiate administration from its social environment.

Second, the emergence of the private secretaries marked the breakthrough of rationalization into local administration. The principles of *li* and *fa* had always been present in imperial central administration and had been attacked by Confucian analysts for their obstruction of *ch'ing* and *shih*, the human factors not susceptible to generalized regulation. With the emergence of private secretaries, these conflicting principles could now be structurally separated. This major division of labor helped

The Yamen and Urban Administration 375

to lift local administration above the tangle of human relations intrinsic to a rural society and put its operation on a rational basis. Moreover, the private secretaries, by consciously training in *li* and *fa*, had broken themselves from Confucianism, although sometimes at serious emotional cost. This mental switch helped to inject the rationalization that the state alone, for all its sanctions, had so much difficulty in introducing.

Undoubtedly the prevalence of state regulations assisted this development. In addition, the diversification and intensification of the agrarian economy encouraged social and geographic mobility, which in turn provided a social context more favorable to the promotion of rational criteria in local administration. Local administrations were no longer able to "know" the vast majority of the people, and this put a greater premium on bureaucratic efficiency in training for, and management of, local administration.

These systematizing trends should not, however, be overemphasized. The vast numerical domination of the clerks and runners is a reminder that local administration was still local in functional orientation. Though men representing the interests of the central government occupied strategic positions in the yamen organization, local interests undoubtedly predominated.

Power centers and turnover of personnel. An examination of the yamen's power centers and of the turnover of yamen personnel can help to clarify why local interests were more influential than what I shall call "external" interests—those of higher administrations and of the relatives and friends of nonnative yamen personnel. The representatives of external interests within the yamen were the magistrate and subordinate officials and the private secretaries and personal servants, especially if the latter were nominees of provincial authorities. They had control over the authorized use of physical sanctions and, if experienced and if enjoying the confidence of their superiors, they were well placed to promote external objectives.

The local forces, consisting of power groups among the inhabitants of the county, had a much broader base of representation. The gentry could expect the good will of the magistrate because, as someone holding examination degree or status, he was of their class. They also had their contacts with the masses of formal subordinates. In addition, members of the gentry could hope to establish relationships with degree- or status-holding functionaries in provincial or metropolitan administration through which to bring indirect pressure on local officials.[41] At the other end of the social ladder, local gangs had arrangements with clerks and runners, whom they helped to finance in return for protection. These gangs, too, were able indirectly to sway the impartiality of the yamen by threatening physical reprisals against individuals or groups insufficiently well represented within the yamen power structure.[42]

The strength of the local power-holders lay in their control over (1) the all-important economic resources and (2) the incidence of crime. Because of the operation of the *k'ao-ch'eng* system, local power groups had merely to hold back public and private payments or protect criminals to place the magistrate's career in jeopardy. Clerks and runners also knew that superiors would face impeachment within predetermined time limits and could simply refuse to press the people for tax payments; or through their control of the records and proximity to the populace they could manipulate fiscal and judicial administration to favor local power-holders.[43] But the chief significance of local economic control lay in its relationship not to public taxation but to the much larger informal financing of administration. The ubiquitous dependence of administration on informal financing put local power groups in a position to control the conduct of local administrative policy.[44]

Turnover in yamen personnel gives further evidence of the measure of local influence—and the limits to organizational differentiation—in Ch'ing administration. As we have seen, the external functionaries, both formal and informal, were kept regularly on the move. Few were able to develop prolonged associations with any one county; and for the informal functionaries (secretaries and personal servants) such stability was not essential to professional advancement. By contrast, the clerks and runners, at the bottom of the formal hierarchy, were able through such simple expedients as changing their names to defy the law and stay in office. The lack of continuity in external personnel made it difficult, if not impossible, for the state to control this "malpractice." This suggests the growing power of the unprivileged groups who took these offices. More generally, it shows how local forces were able to continue defying the state's attempts to differentiate local administration from its environment.[45]

So far this account has suggested that the degree of organizational differentiation in the Ch'ing county yamen depended on whether the objectives of external or of local forces were in the ascendant. We should now see to what extent this judgment applies to the yamen as a specifically governmental institution. Inasmuch as the yamen represented a form of political organization influenced by powerful long-range centralizing and rationalizing tendencies, we should expect to find in it increasing evidence of bureaucratic development, at least in the organization of its internal functions. To what extent was this the case?

At first sight the yamen appears to display many of the marks of bureaucratization.[46] It was certainly an organization of official functions bound by rules. Moreover, during the Ch'ing era local yamen offices and functions were increasingly bound by the rules proliferating at all higher echelons. In the yamen itself, a chain of command extended down from the magistrate through the secretaries and personal servants to the clerks and runners. The magistrate enjoyed summary powers over nonranking subordinates and could have them beaten or dismissed for infractions. The documentary character of Ch'ing administration is perhaps its most outstanding bureaucratic feature. Though this documentation applied only to official or formal business, it developed sufficient volume and complexity to require expert management. It reveals clearly the impersonal and methodical character of local administration under the Ch'ing. This record-keeping is an index also of the technical character of local administration. It was the complexity of the penal and administrative regulations, the variety and complexity of the systems of fiscal assessment, and the documentary sophistication demanded in the administration of these regulations and systems that necessitated the emergence of the informal but influential secretarial specialists.

The offices of the yamen functionaries also show many bureaucratic features. All offices show signs of becoming vocational. This does not mean that the majority of subordinate yamen personnel, or even the majority of magistrates, were pursuing a bureaucratically vocational career. Rather, the systemization of local administration effected both by the Single Whip reforms and by central and provincial government regulations promoted the growth of vocations in the key secretarial, clerical, and personal-servant offices controlling the management of local government. The apprehensive respect enjoyed by yamen functionaries (if we omit the assistant officials) is another conspicuous feature of Ch'ing society. This respect was a product not of social status but of functional significance.

Two other aspects of Ch'ing bureaucratization deserve special mention. In many respects the management of yamen business was as confidential and secretive as that of central government business. Much, though not all, of the communication between magistrates and their superiors was conducted through confidential documents. Furthermore, the yamen was built to restrict communication between formal and informal subordinates and to prevent the majority of formal subordinates (clerks and runners) from gaining advance knowledge of the decisions arrived at by the magistrate and his informal advisers. The division worked the other way as well, though; clerks kept close control over their records and were reluctant to show them to the magistrates. Finally, yamen officials in general went to considerable lengths to control the information about local conditions that reached higher administrations. Much of this secrecy was inspired by the fear of administrative sanctions. But it also stemmed from the conflicting goals of local and external forces and the desire of the one to undercut the other. The evolving dualistic structure of the Ch'ing yamen facilitated the growth of secrecy between local and external power interests in their attempts to exert control over each other as well as over the general public.[47]

Ch'ing administration is also noteworthy for its emphasis on the distinction between public and private. This distinction developed from long-standing antecedents based on Legalist ideology, a discussion of which is beyond the scope of this paper. In the Ch'ing period it took the form of a systematic attempt to demarcate public responsibility and to prevent private influence from intruding on it. The central government, which was the main force behind the imposition of "public" and the repudiation of "private" goals, used the disciplinary regulations as a means to this end. These regulations characterized every administrative offense in terms of these two categories, the difference essentially turning on whether or not the offense involved deliberate intent to harm the public interest. The punishments the regulations imposed applied directly to the county magistrate and secondarily to his administrative superiors; but the offenses themselves were in large part those committed by yamen subordinates. In this connection it is worth noting that the disciplinary regulations represented a reinforcement of the penal code, which also in effect punished private infractions of public responsibility. However, though the disciplinary regulations systematized the accountability of officials for the conduct of their subordinates, the articulation of public offenses in the regulations actually constituted a form of exoneration of officialdom.[48]

The distinction between public and private carried over into the physical layout of the yamen (see Figure 2). Yamens were generally divided into four sequential divisions, two outer and two inner, with intercommunication limited to main gateways. The clerks and runners were confined to the outer divisions. The magistrate also conducted his public business in the great hall, situated in the second outer division.

The Yamen and Urban Administration

The first inner division normally contained the offices of the informal subordinates as well as rooms in which the magistrate conducted his personal correspondence and informal entertaining. The last division held the private residence of the official and was confined to his immediate family and domestic employees. Clerks and runners were not admitted into the inner divisions. Private secretaries, in return, were not allowed to be present at hearings in the main hall. This division separated the personal and informal roles of the magistrate from his public role as seal-holding official. More generally, the physical barriers between formal and informal subordinates restricted their opportunities to conspire to support private interests.[49]

Despite all these efforts to differentiate administration from local society, the county yamen was both unable and unwilling to maintain the dichotomy. The importance of informal revenue to all employees was perhaps the chief reason.[50] We have seen that basic administrative salaries during the Ch'ing period were nominal and grossly inadequate, forcing yamen personnel to depend on informal sources of income.[51] Yet it is clear that office-holding could be a very profitable venture. Chang Chung-li, on somewhat sketchy evidence, estimated the annual income of magistrates at an average of 30,000 taels. There seems to be little evidence on the actual income of clerks and runners. Although officials invariably accused them of devoting their efforts to the accumulation of profit, they seldom mention specific figures. Private secretaries obtained fixed salaries, paid by the magistrate and varying with the cost of living. In the early nineteenth century, legal secretaries in busy counties were said to command annual salaries of around 2,000 taels; fiscal secretaries received half this amount; and the remainder received substantially less. In addition, secretaries could supplement these salaries by taking pupils or by accepting fees and bribes. Personal servants, as private revenue-collecting agents of the official, were perhaps the most deeply involved in the accumulation of informal income. Meadows reported that the Chinese "frequently speak" of senior personal servants getting as much as 10,000 to 30,000 taels a year. Others did not get more than a few hundred taels annually.[52]

This remarkable lack of bureaucratic control over the income of Ch'ing administrative personnel actually represented a loss of control dating from the early Ming period. In his reorganization of local administration, the Hung-wu emperor established viable official salaries under an overall policy that gave the county-level yamen less involvement in local administration than under almost any other dynasty. The decline in these official salaries began in the fifteenth century and

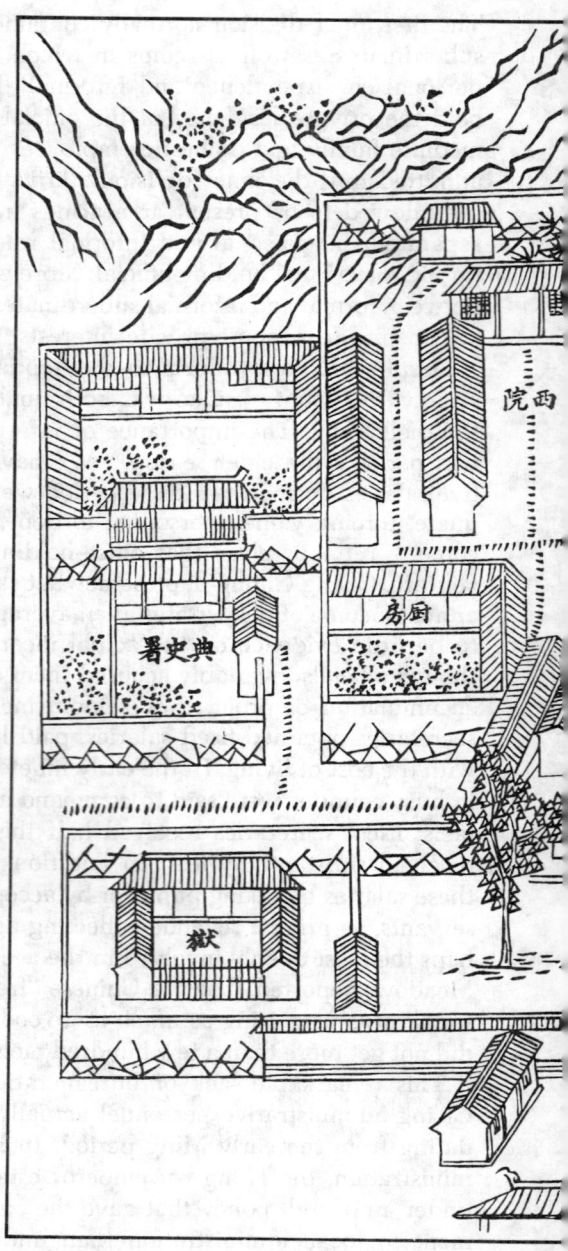

FIG. 2. THE SHAN-YIN COUNTY YAMEN in the city of Shao-hsing-fu, Chekiang. Inside the main gate to the immediate right (east) is the local T'u-ti-kung (Earth God) shrine. To the far right is a granary; at the far left (west) is a prison for detaining suspects. The courtyard beyond the second gate (labeled I Men) is flanked on either side by unlabeled buildings housing clerks' offices; facing that courtyard on the north side is the Hall of Administration (Chih-t'ang), in which the magistrate conducted formal business. This is backed by a wall (labeled Chao-ch'iang) separating the inner from the outer divisions. The central building north of the wall (labeled Erh-ssu-t'ang) housed the business offices of the magistrate, and the innermost buildings along the central axis are the magistrate's private quarters (labeled Nei-shih). East of the Nei-shih are the magistrate's personal offices, where he examined and signed documents, and at the extreme upper right is the eastern archive. Also on the east is the guest hall facing north onto an inner courtyard. West of the Nei-shih is the western archive, and south of that is the kitchen. The detached office of the jail warden is at the far left, north of the jail. The separately walled offices of the assistant magistrate are at the far right in the center. From *Chia-ch'ing Shan-yin hsien chih* (1803), ch. 5, 8a–9b.

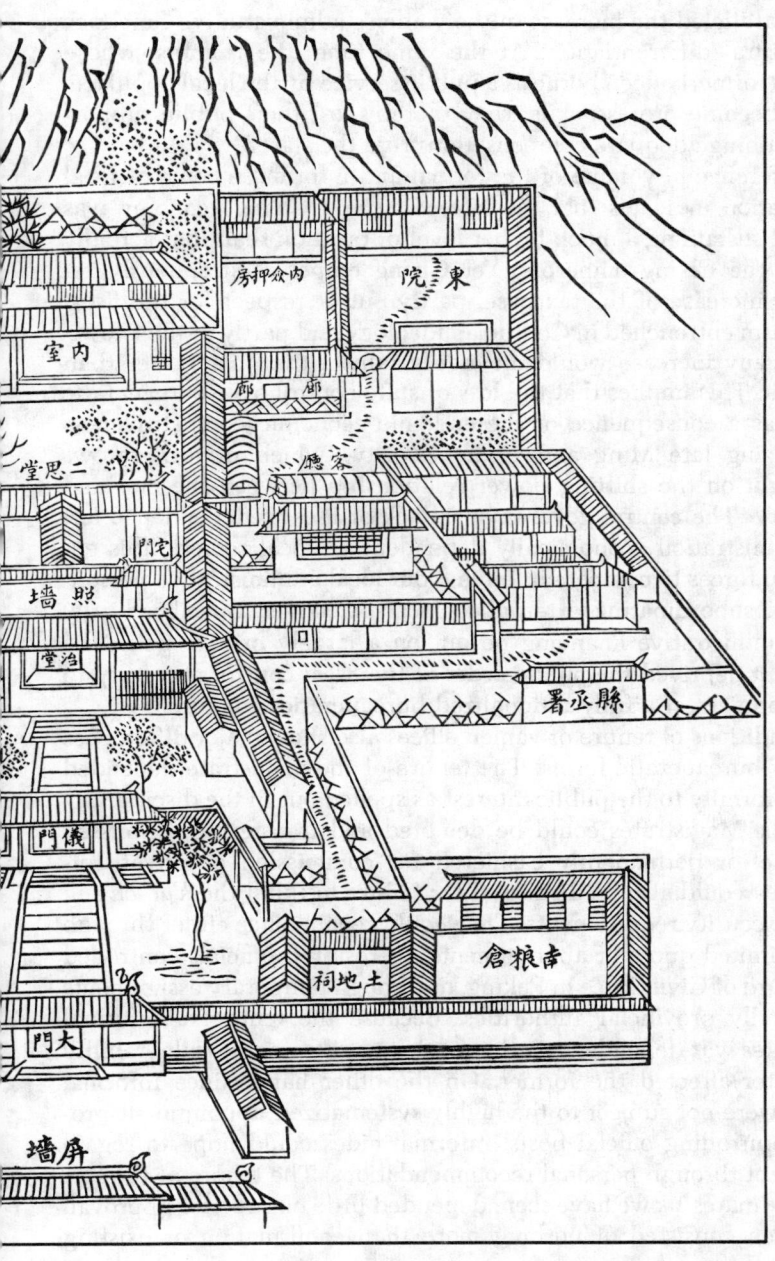

actually paralleled the increase in the yamen's administrative functions and structural differentiation. At the same time, the runners, whose duties had formerly been borne as a public service by the local populace, began to become professionals; they thereby lost their public support without gaining adequate compensation from the state.[53]

The difference in volume of the formal and informal income of local administration indicates that the late Ming and Ch'ing economy was capable of sustaining a much higher level of taxation than that actually levied by the Ch'ing emperors. Yet Ch'ing emperors strenuously resisted any increase of the tax base, partly out of respect for the fiscal conservatism entrenched in Confucian ideology and partly in the knowledge that any increase would inevitably fall on the poor rather than on the rich. This implies that the loss of state control over bureaucratic income was a consequence of the endemic economic competitiveness characterizing late Ming and Ch'ing society—which in turn throws further light on the shifting power relationship between the city and the country. The central government's lack of fiscal independence left local administration economically dependent on local society; this enabled local forces to compete in buying out local administrative personnel and in subordinating external to local objectives. Specifically, by letting administrative financing be put on a largely private basis, the government deprived the public order of the fiscal control necessary to the development of a fully rationalized bureaucratic structure.[54]

The conditions of tenure of yamen offices also show major differences from fully bureaucratic forms. The tenure of the magistrate depended on his conformity to the public interest as spelled out in the disciplinary regulations. Magistrates could be demoted and transferred, dismissed from office, or permanently cashiered for commission of private offenses; they could also be dismissed for failure to fulfill the *k'ao-ch'eng* fiscal and security requirements. They could regain office either through the very limited quota of appointments for restored officials controlled by the Board of Civil Office in Peking, or through temporary assignments from friendly provincial authorities. Because the tenure of informal subordinates was dependent on that of the magistrate, the vulnerability of the latter affected the former. On the other hand, since informal positions were not subject to the highly systematized appointment procedures controlling official posts, informal aides could hope to regain employment through personal recommendations. The tenure of the formal subordinates, as we have seen, depended little on superior approval, which often consisted of nothing more than confirmation of existing arrangements.

The Yamen and Urban Administration

Another striking feature of yamen office-holding was its lack of upward mobility. Yamen functionaries could hope to rise within their general functional category, but not from one category or rank to the next. Upward mobility in rank depended on external criteria closely controlled by the central government. Commoner or gentry subordinates could only move into official positions by obtaining the requisite examination degree or status and one of the closely controlled appointments. Legislation barred runners and personal servants from upward mobility. This stratification of rank increased during the Ming and Ch'ing eras as the central government strove to externalize local administrative authority.

The ideological and social basis of legitimation is perhaps the non-bureaucratic attribute of Ch'ing office-holding most frequently noted. Here it should be said that this basis of legitimation applied only to the performance of societal functions; the operational functions required a technical legitimation. The role of magistrate called for both forms. To be a Confucian exemplar the official had to demonstrate parental solicitude. In the prevailing axioms, he should "promote the beneficial and get rid of the harmful" and conduct his fiscal and judicial administration with "sincerity" and "closeness." Officials who succeeded in this effort were rewarded with popular accolades, pressed to remain in office, and ceremoniously honored on retirement by the populace. Conversely, there were instances in which the people prevented officials with reputations as oppressors from taking office, or upbraided those in office in scurrilous placards. In other instances, inhabitants of county seats punished unjust officials after they had left office by barring the city gates, beating up the official's servants, and stripping the clothes off his female relatives.[55] On the other hand, the central government's objectives required substantial fiscal, judicial, and documentary skills; and Ch'ing systems of investigation judged officials more by their technical capability in these areas than by their ideological purity.[56] In consequence, though officials utilized private secretaries to shore up their technical competence, handbooks also urged them to be self-dependent in this vital area, especially if they wished to retain office. Furthermore, as we have seen, important county posts were restricted to officials with at least three to five years of prior experience in local administrative office. Although this does not mean that county officials as a whole acquired fiscal and judicial skills, such skills became a distinct advantage for those seeking better posts, and some skill in conforming to regulations became essential for retaining office.

Finally, one may note that the Ch'ing government's obsessive insistence on the segregation of official activities from private life is an index to the interrelation between them in actuality. Here again it seems that the central government's efforts to promote bureaucratization foundered on its inability to come to terms with local power.

This account of the Ch'ing yamen has suggested that strong external trends toward rationalization and bureaucratization were thwarted by the dominance of local interest groups over particular aspects of administration. In particular, the yamen was dependent on local economic and social power. Here one must distinguish between the inability of the central government to fully bureaucratize the public order and the power of the yamen as a local agency to dominate and oppress the local populace. The vast majority of the Ch'ing populace lacked social and economic power. These masses stood in a weaker relationship to the local yamen than to the central state. For the local power-holders, though, the opposite was true. This implies that the differentiation of the yamen from local society may have been a product of changes in social organization as much as in central state policy. Otherwise it is questionable why local society should have accepted the degree of administrative centralization that did take place under late Ming and Ch'ing rule.

County Administration and Rural Society

The development of the county yamen as the nucleus of Ch'ing local administration took place in connection with the breakdown of Ming systems of rural administration. These systems had been introduced by the founding emperor, Ming T'ai-tsu, in a deliberate attempt to reduce the power of local officialdom and gentry over rural society. Because he had had personal experience of rural life, the Ming founder knew that local authority had betrayed its commitment to the people's welfare and instead had indulged in rapaciousness and cruelty. Consequently, he took the responsibility for fiscal and judicial administration out of the hands of local officials and gave it to newly formed rural organizations, the *li-chia* and *li-lao* systems. In addition he provided these systems with forms of rotational leadership and gave them the right to bypass local officialdom and communicate directly with the capital. Finally, he established the most stringent penalties for the punishment of officials attempting to exploit or oppress the rural leadership.

With the death of the Ming founder, the rural administrative systems began a protracted but inevitable decline. Economic and social expansion and loss of continued central government support both contributed to this decline. More specifically, the Ming fiscal policies, originally designed to uphold fiscal equity, undermined it in the context of an increasing pressure of population on land, which these policies helped to stimulate. They encouraged the economically and socially successful to maneuver out of the tax system, leaving local administration to collect more from the less successful. A combination of economic competitiveness and fiscal oppression led to an unprecedented flight of the poor from the land, ruining those responsible for tax collection and leaving the rural systems hopelessly undermanned and impoverished. Moreover, a combination of economic revival and monetary incentives in the Ming fiscal system set in motion a prolonged inflation of the economy. This increased administrative pressure for fiscal resources, and made the solvency of taxpayers more than ever dependent on success in the market. More generally, it promoted the long-term monetization of the fiscal system and undercut the role of the *li-chia* in providing and equalizing labor service.[57]

By the late sixteenth century, the breakdown in rural fiscal machinery, and increasing central government pressure for funds, forced local administrations to begin to reform the whole procedure of tax collection. These Single Whip reforms, introduced in the economically advanced southeast, spread throughout the country over about two hundred years. Essentially, they abolished the household as the primary unit of taxation, placed the tax burden on the land, and monetized the tax collection.

These changes systematized trends already in progress. Nevertheless, they profoundly affected the administrative relationship between the government and the people. The *li-chia* system had unified the responsibilities for collecting and paying and systematically graded them according to economic means. In so doing, it had established an organizational buffer between the individual household and the state manned not by officials but by citizen taxpayers. Henceforth there would be no such buffer. The responsibility for paying was placed on each primary landowning cultivator and that of collecting on the county magistrate and the yamen. No formal intermediary system would combine households or afford any popular control over assessment and collection. Second, the transference of the levy from the household to the land depersonalized the fiscal system. Administrations henceforth would be interested preeminently in the economic solvency of landowners. The survival of the household would no longer be of direct fiscal significance. Third, the monetization of collection played into the hands of landowners favorably related to marketing systems and to yamen agents controlling assessment and collection rates. Henceforth the possession of land would no longer suffice, unless it was accompanied by these all-important urban connections.[58]

The Single Whip reforms confirmed a number of other changes of administrative significance. We have seen that their localization of rates of assessment and collection put outside magistrates in a position of dependence on local subordinates controlling the fiscal records, even though the magistrates bore responsibility for the success of the annual collection. On the side of the taxpayers, the unification of the levies and their transference to the land neutralized many of the forms of evasion that had been available under the previous system and increased the pressure to obtain favorable land assessments. Quite apart from these fiscal consequences, the decline of the *li-chia* system also ensured the breakdown of the *li-lao* system and left the rural populace without public control over judicial and security administration.

The Ch'ing government accepted the breakdown of the *li-chia* system and made no attempt to provide any alternative form of rural fiscal organization. It approved of the "simplicity" and "convenience" of the Single Whip reforms and preferred to maintain solvency by decreasing the levies and increasing their yield. This does not mean that it sacrificed the social policies inherent in the *li-chia* system for the sake of administrative efficiency. Rather, it replaced a social policy stressing equalization and participation with one stressing authoritarian beneficence. Social and economic conditions virtually necessitated such a change. But its effect on the relations between the individual and the government was to demote the political significance of the individual and increase that of administration.[59]

Concurrent with the decline of the *li-chia* and the *li-lao* systems, late Ming and Ch'ing administrators reintroduced rural security systems that were firmly subordinated to administrative control. Ironically, it was the Confucian idealist Wang Yang-ming who played a leading part in this reform. Ordered to suppress widespread banditry and rebellion in southeastern China, Wang based his policy on a major effort to restore organization to rural life. To this end he revived the *pao-chia* ("watch-group") and *hsiang-yüeh* ("rural pledge-group") systems, which had previously appeared during the Sung dynasty. The purpose of his watch-group system was to check the whereabouts of people and to provide mutual aid in case of attack. Group members were made responsible to local administrations for the cooperation of their associates and for reporting offenders to officials for heavy punishment. The purpose of the *hsiang-yüeh*, by contrast, was to promote social rehabilitation and conciliation. As a moral agency it was conceived on a largely self-regulating basis to encourage cooperation in public and private affairs. Wang emphasized that the necessity for the *pao-chia* reflected governmental rather than popular inadequacy. He hoped that the *hsiang-yüeh* would restore social self-control to the countryside and reduce the need for administrative interference.[60]

Other late Ming *hsiang-yüeh* systems also reflected Wang's concern over the growing economic and social stratification of society. But they accepted this trend and were set up to protect property and reinforce the prestige of the wealthy. The Ch'ing government expanded on these objectives. It used the *pao-chia* to expose robbers and bandits and report on population movement, and ordered local administrators to enforce the system throughout the empire. Conversely, it used the *hsiang-yüeh* as a counterweight to economic oppression of the weak and well-intentioned. Both systems were set up under local government control, and magistrates were made responsible for their implementation.[61]

Local officials, for their part, utilized the *pao-chia* as an adjunct of local administration. Since counties were becoming too populous for a single person to "know," some administrators urged that the *pao-chia* be used as an intelligence agency, supplying under threat of punishment the information necessary for administrative control. Other administrators used the *pao-chia* to help enforce the *k'ao-ch'eng* fiscal and robbery deadlines. On the other hand, they neglected the *hsiang-yüeh* or saw it at best as a means of encouraging submissiveness to the public order. Consequently the *pao-chia* became the chief instrument of rural control, while the *hsiang-yüeh* contracted into a formal lecturing system.[62]

The significance of Ch'ing rural control lies in its subordination of rural organization to local government objectives. Despite specious efforts to give administrative stature to *pao-chia* leaders, these leaders were put in the most menial relationship to local government. They were bound by monthly guarantees, made responsible for local security, and exposed to corporal punishment or exploitation by yamen subordinates. Significantly, the gentry were exempt from participation in this oppressive institution, which was used largely to reinforce the position of political and social power-holders against the powerless or subversive. On the other hand, many magistrates, despite continual state pressure, neglected to enforce the *pao-chia* rather than risk trouble by perverting its functions. Instead they made use of personal village agents. These *ti-pao* or *ti-fang* began appearing in the late seventeenth and early eighteenth centuries. They were appointed in conjunction with the *pao-chia* system but assigned to natural villages, city blocks, and suburban quarters. Unlike the *pao-chia* heads, they did not represent any popular organization. Therefore, administrators could exploit them to spread government authority throughout the villages without directly oppressing the rural populace.[63]

From this viewpoint, the scope of the magistrate and yamen personnel appears larger than might be expected, in view of the governmental and societal pressures indicated earlier. Although caught between expansion and polarization of society from below and expansion and bureaucratization of administration from above, late Ming and Ch'ing local government evolved a structure that continued to provide it with administrative maneuverability. At the same time, these pressures necessitated an urban alignment, which challenged the ideological groundwork of local administration.

In the first place, this alignment continued the trend towards depersonalization of local government. The failure of Ming reformers to establish rural institutions able to reconcile social and political interests placed this burden back on the shoulders of the county magistrate, where it had traditionally been. But Ch'ing magistrates as a whole were unable to develop a direct relationship between the official and the people. Instead, this relationship began to institutionalize around the yamen and the *pao-chia*. The yamen and the village agents or constables took over the authority of the official; the *pao-chia* assumed the responsibility of the people.

This institutionalization of administrative relations did not proceed without active resistance from both officials and common people. The officials, besides stalling the local control systems, developed a profound antipathy for their subordinate yamen functionaries. Administrative writers inveighed against the untrustworthiness of all yamen subordinates, condemning their interest in profit and propensity for corruption. They particularly denounced those who, like notaries, participated indirectly in the administrative process. Some of this rancor must be attributed to the financial muscle of the subordinate functionaries and to their encroachment on official authority. Officials complained that their subordinates purveyed false information, deceived and manipulated officials, and attempted to "entangle" the lives of the people. More generally, they charged that the subordinates came between the magistrate and the people, blocking communications between "above and below." More neutral observers simply noted that the subordinate yamen functionaries were assuming effective control of local authority, eroding the public role of the officials, and encouraging their pursuit of private interest. All this would suggest that the vituperation of the officials genuinely reflected their failure to prevent official authority from slipping into the hands of the nonranking yamen subordinates.[64]

For social and economic support, Ch'ing magistrates inevitably leaned on the local gentry. In their view the gentry possessed both the local knowledge that the officials lacked and the identification with officialdom that the yamen subordinates and rural watch-group leaders lacked. As local residents, the gentry were closer to the people than the magistrate was; they were more "trusted" by the people; consequently, they could serve as intermediaries between the officials and the people. Given the deceitfulness of yamen subordinates, gentry were an essential source of information for the local official; as his "eyes and ears," they could provide knowledge about local economic conditions and intelligence on subversive elements in each county. They were a vital help in financing public works and public assistance. More generally, as the first of the four social orders they were culturally equipped to assist the magistrate in the task of spreading civilization. They had education and self-respect, and they shared a stake in the maintenance of order. With all these qualifications, it is not surprising to find Ch'ing administrative writers urging magistrates to treat the gentry with great respect and to turn to them for administrative assistance. As a concomitant to this liaison, most officials were willing to denounce the gangs of village "thugs" and subversives from whom the gentry had most to fear, and to punish them brutally whenever they were caught.[65]

No doubt this alliance was heavily influenced by the economic and political power of the gentry, by their extensive interference in rural tax collection, and by their connections with higher authority. It also reflects a more general cultural differentiation developing in late Ming and Ch'ing society based on control of property and education, which became the keys to the assumption of both local and metropolitan power. In this power structure, at least three distinct yet interrelated strata emerged, of which only the top two constituted the gentry proper: first, those who were able to use their control of property and education to gain the higher examination degrees or statuses on which access to metropolitan culture and jurisdictional office depended; second, those who gained a foothold in the examination system and so entered the path toward attainment of office; third, those who were prevented by law or ill fortune from entering the examination system and who used what property and education they had to gain influence over local administration. County magistrates and their superiors had gained admittance to metropolitan culture. They shared both the general propertied background of the gentry and their cultural aspirations. Behind their talk of what "we *chün*" must do for the "child people" existed a barely concealed distaste for the "stupid" people and the "rapacious" and "verminous" local subordinates, and a preference for the polite and profitable company of the metropolitan-directed gentry class.

Nevertheless, this official-gentry alliance remained far from solidified. Higher gentry were not necessarily in the running for office. Lower gentry licentiates were not yet qualified for office and were vulnerable to disqualification from the examination system. These groups, especially the latter, were more dependent on local ties and more prone to try to gain local power. In the eyes of officials, such gentry could be as untrustworthy as yamen subordinates. They were as liable to entice officials with presents and undermine their public loyalty; they were more liable to disparage official prestige through their abuse of scholarly status.[66]

In this context of disparate and fluctuating power alignments, the yamen served as a structure capable of providing mediation and adjustment. Within the administrative system it struck a balance between the forces of local and external power. It enabled these forces to coordinate their common interests and regulate their conflicts. For the body politic as a whole, it provided all groups with some access to administrative power, whether legitimate or otherwise. Its impersonal structure and urban setting aided this mediatory role. The magistrate was in a position to act as impartial arbitrator in intrasocial conflicts. The yamen was in a position to minimize local responsibility toward the differing objectives of state and society. More specifically, it avoided the direct social and political confrontations that rural control systems provoked. In the long run, the urbanization of the yamen broke down the vital Confucian relationship between the official and the people and signaled the eventual divorce of administration from rural life. But for the time being it maintained a localized framework for the interaction of the traditional state and society.

Ningpo and Its Hinterland

YOSHINOBU SHIBA

The city we know as Ningpo is first mentioned in the records of the Former Han period. After it was moved to its present site in the eighth century, it developed into an outport of the Lower Yangtze region and flourished for the next thousand years as a center both of the coastal trade and of the longer-range trade with other regions of China, with Japan, and with Korea.[1] In late 1843 the city was opened to Westerners as a treaty port with great anticipation of international trade, but even at the end of the Ch'ing period its traditional junk trade remained little changed. The stability and persistence of this traditional commerce in Ningpo profoundly affected the development of the regional economy the city dominated. In this paper I describe Ningpo and its commercial hinterland and provide a tentative analysis of how the city functioned in the nineteenth century.*

Historical Development in the Ningpo Region

Taming the regional landscape. Chekiang province can be divided roughly into two zones. The fertile alluvial plains around Hangchow Bay in the north account for about three-tenths of the province's land, whereas the mountainous or hilly districts in the south account for some seven-tenths. Despite a slowly growing coastal trade and recurring waves of Han Chinese migrants from the north, Chekiang remained a backward region until the Six Dynasties period.[2] The Yung River drainage basin, the immediate hinterland of what was to be Ningpo, lay in the easternmost portion of the province along the south shore of Hang-

---

* This paper owes much to Professor G. William Skinner's helping hand. I wish to acknowledge with thanks the advice and aid I have received from him through the entire process of writing it.

chow Bay, and was thus rather isolated; it also suffered from floods, droughts, and tidal waves, elements hardly conducive to the development of a large city. Fishing along the offshore bank around the Chusan archipelago (later a productive sector within Ningpo's commercial hinterland) and along the south coast of Hangchow Bay was as yet underdeveloped.

Under the Sui and T'ang dynasties the situation changed greatly. Above all, the construction of the Grand Canal effectively extended the main overland trading route to the east coast. It not only linked the producing South with the consuming North, but also stimulated specialization and economic development in the areas it served, most notably the Lower Yangtze region. Coincidentally, the maritime trade that linked the Yangtze delta with ports along the China coast, in East Asia, and on the Indian Ocean flourished in the wake of improvements in navigation (notably the steering compass).[3] By virtue of waterways linking it to Hangchow via Yü-yao, Ts'ao-o, and the Che-tung Canal, Ningpo in effect became the southern terminus of the Grand Canal. Furthermore, owing to shallows and tidal currents in Hangchow Bay and at the mouth of the Yangtze, large ocean-going junks from southeastern China were forced to transfer their cargoes at Ningpo either to smaller boats capable of negotiating the canals and other inland waterways or to small luggers, which sailed in turn for Hangchow, the Yangtze River ports, and the north coast of China.[4] Conversely, products from the Lower Yangtze region were gathered and shipped to Ningpo for export. Ningpo's advantages were not shared by the two other Chekiang ports, Wen-chou and T'ai-chou, which were separated from the rest of the province by a chain of high mountains. An Office of Overseas Trade (*Shih-po ssu*) was accordingly stationed at Ningpo in 992, and from there it supervised the coastal trade and controlled the maritime tribute of Korea and Japan almost without interruption until 1523.[5] By Southern Sung times, China's interregional trade was centered in "the key economic area" of the Yangtze delta.[6]

In response to growing commercial opportunities, the city of Ningpo had been moved in 738 from a more easterly site to its present location at the heart of the drainage basin of the Yung River. The Yü-yao and Feng-hua rivers, which join to form the Yung River some 13 miles inland from the coast of Hangchow Bay, formed the northeastern and southeastern flanks of the city, respectively. The city was further protected, especially on the northwest and southwest, by walls and moats built at the end of the T'ang period. A large plain surrounded the city,

Ningpo and Its Hinterland

separating it from the hills to the east, south, and west and from the sea to the north and northeast.

During the T'ang period, the northeastern portion of what is now Chekiang was subdivided into three prefectural-level units, which, names aside, remained virtually unchanged until the end of the imperial era. Administrative arrangements at the county level, too, have been remarkably stable, being fixed by the eleventh century in the form that was to persist until the twentieth century.[7] It should be noted explicitly that these administrative boundaries probably never did correspond very closely to the limits of the commercial hinterlands of the capital cities. Ningpo's "natural" economic hinterland was considerably more extensive than the territory under its administrative jurisdiction. The six counties in Ming *chou* (Ning-po *fu* in Ming-Ch'ing times) were Yin *hsien* (the metropolitan county of which Ningpo was the capital), Tz'u-ch'i, Ting-hai (after 1687 known as Chen-hai), Feng-hua, Hsiang-shan, and Ch'ang-kuo (after 1687 known as Ting-hai). Of the counties to the west in Yüeh *chou* (Shao-hsing *fu* in Ming-Ch'ing times), four were partly within Ningpo's economic sphere—most of Yü-yao, and certain eastern sections of Shang-yü, Ch'eng *hsien*, and Hsin-ch'ang. Of the counties to the south in T'ai *chou* (T'ai-chou *fu* in Ming-Ch'ing times), two were partly within Ningpo's economic sphere—most of Ning-hai and the northern strip of T'ien-t'ai.

The establishment of Ming *chou* as an autonomous unit of field administration in the T'ang period brought with it conditions needed for the development of the Yung River basin—a measure of law and order, water conservancy projects, and improved communications—as illustrated by the construction of canals and highways, and by the establishment of official postal stations along them. The construction of T'a-shan dam upstream on the Feng-hua River by the T'ang prefect Wang Yüan-hui was a notable water-control project that had important consequences for the drainage and irrigation of the Ningpo plain and for the city's water supply.[8] Fresh water from the western hills flowed eastward through the plain via two canals (the Hsi-t'ang and the Nan-t'ang) and into the city through the sluices near the west and south gates (see Map 1). Small canals carried the water through the city to two small lakes, and water from the lakes flowed out through sluices near the two east gates. The two streams joined outside the walls in a single canal that carried the water to the Yung River.

That the water supply was adequate for the city is evidenced by an episode from the Pao-ch'ing period (1225–27). Provincial governor Wu

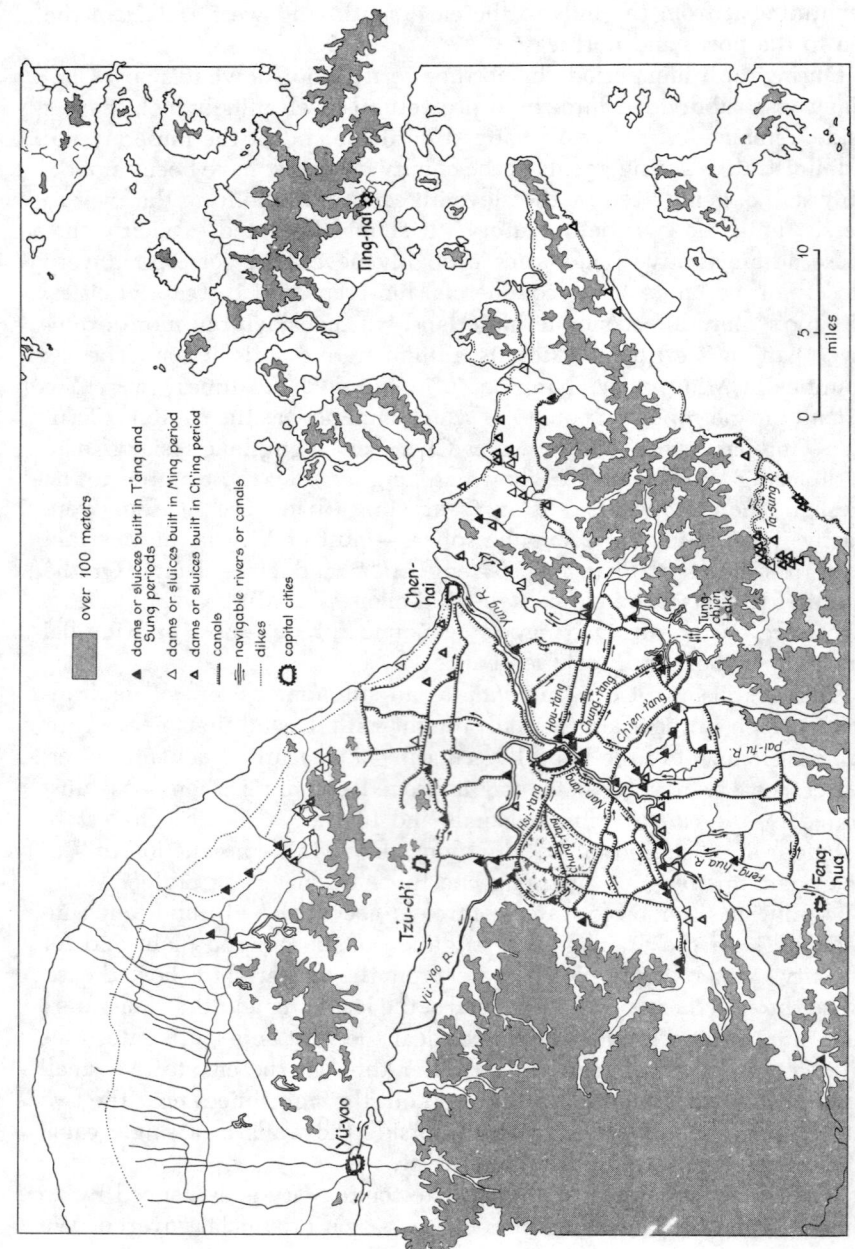

MAP 1. WATERWORKS ON THE NINGPO PLAIN. The enclosed area due west of Ningpo indicates the approximate extent of Kuang-te Lake as of late T'ang; its drainage and reclamation were completed during the Northern Sung.

Ch'ien, who had done much to improve the water-control system of Yin *hsien*, took a boat trip from the city to the headwaters of the Feng-hua River in the west to inspect the water-supply system. On his return he had a stone slab erected in the canal at the center of the city with the character *p'ing* ("equitable level") carved on it to show the level appropriate for the city's water supply as well as for irrigation in the western plain. From this episode we also learn that the city was freely accessible to plains-dwellers by boat via the canals.[9]

From T'ang times on, dams and floodgates were constructed throughout the Ningpo Plain (see Map 1) by local officials, sometimes in collaboration with powerful local lineages. Several major canals promoted agricultural production and rural settlement. In the western plain, Kuang-te Lake was reclaimed and converted into paddy fields during the Five Dynasties and Northern Sung periods. The problem to the southeast of the city was how to control the water in Tung-ch'ien Lake, guiding it into the Feng-hua and Yung rivers through the fertile fields to the south and east of the city or directly into the sea by a northerly route. Dams and floodgates were built around this lake, and canals led fresh water from it to the central plain; however, the land there was so low-lying that further dams and sluices were needed to protect the plain against the inflow of sea water.[10]

Farther south, the scarcity of water and the hilly country made irrigation more difficult. The runoff from the southern hills to the Feng-hua and Pai-tu rivers was diverted by dams and sluices into a network of canals that irrigated the southern plain and eventually drained again into the Feng-hua River. The plain to the north of Ningpo, in which the county capitals of Chen-hai, Tz'u-ch'i, and Yü-yao were located, was well watered by the runoff from the nearby hills. However, the areas to the northeast of Tz'u-ch'i were somewhat hilly and, what was worse, close to the sea. A system of canals and floodgates was constructed here as well to protect the area from drought and tidal waves. These improvements, which were made during the T'ang and Sung periods, greatly facilitated the development of agriculture in the area, for in earlier times crops had been dependent on small irrigation ponds for water. Most of the coastal region along Hangchow Bay (from north of Yü-yao to east of Chen-hai) was originally unfit for production owing to the sandiness of the soil and the prevalence of tidal waves. Only limited rice culture was possible around the small lakes at the foot of the hills above Tz'u-ch'i. Fishing and salt production were important along the shore, but it was not until the construction in Sung times of a long stone dike along Hangchow Bay that the salt farms and fields were protected from tidal water. This area eventually became the center of cotton production for the Ningpo region.[11]

By the thirteenth century the basic structure of canals and dikes needed to tame the landscape and exploit its productive potential had been laid down. Although vast tracts of the Ningpo Plain had yet to be converted to paddy fields through the construction of small-scale drainage and irrigation canals, by early in the Southern Sung the region was very nearly self-sufficient in rice. Imports were required only in years of bad harvest, when shortages were exacerbated through speculation by powerful families.[12]

Economic development since the twelfth century. By Southern Sung times, shipping flourished in Ningpo, and both domestic and foreign markets had expanded. The cosmopolitan character of the city's merchant community is suggested by the origins of those involved in the Korean trade. Of 27 voyages by Chinese merchants from Ningpo to Korea during 1015–1138, twelve were made by Ch'üan-chou merchants, five by Ningpo merchants, three each by Kwangtung and T'ai-chou merchants, and two each by Foochow and Kiangnan merchants.[13] At this time Ningpo was the key collection and distribution point along the entire coast between Ch'üan-chou and the Shantung peninsula, importing iron, lumber, sugar, dyestuffs, hemp, pepper, incense, and ivory from the South; silk from the North; and lumber, sulfur, mercury, gold, and pearls from Japan. Exports included silk, porcelain, lacquer ware, medicines, incense, printed matter, stationery, straw mats, and silver and copper coins.[14] The concentration of shipping and of the shipbuilding business in Ningpo accelerated the economic specialization of the city's hinterland, stimulating the production and marketing of materials necessary for the transport industry. In 1259, there were nearly 8,000 junks, luggers, and fishing boats along the region's coast, of which 624 were recorded as belonging to natives of Yin *hsien*, 1,191 to natives of Ting-hai (i.e., the Chen-hai of a later period), 776 to natives of Hsiang-shan, 1,699 to natives of Feng-hua, 282 to natives of Tz'u-ch'i, and 3,324 to natives of the Chusan archipelago (then Ch'ang-kuo *hsien*). Other industries in and around the city were mat-weaving, shoemaking, fishing, and the processing of iron and copper utensils. Inside the city there were at least two general markets, in addition to shopping areas specializing in lumber, coffin boards, bamboo, slate, leather goods, flowers, vegetables, fruits, dried fish, medicines, incense, and oils. There were also two amusement centers, a foreign merchants' residence, and various hotels. Outside the walls were ironworks and copperworks, shipyards,

Ningpo and Its Hinterland 397

wholesale rice markets, and places where daily early-morning markets were held.¹⁵

A temple fair held in Shao-hsing city annually on the fourteenth day of the first lunar month attracted people from all over the Lower Yangtze region, as well as marine traders, to buy and sell such luxury items as silks, embroidered goods, incense, pearls, jade, lacquer ware, ceramics, furniture, and curios. Thanks in good part to such attractions nearby, people crowded into Ningpo. For the years 1165–73, of 41,617 taxable households in Yin *hsien*, 5,321 (about one-eighth) were recorded as residing within the city walls, and an unspecified portion of the remainder lived in extramural suburbs. Business districts had grown up just outside the main gates—one each in the west and south and two in the east—and city officials were forced to create new suburban wards (*hsiang*) to assimilate these newly settled areas.¹⁶

If we turn our attention from the bustling city to the surrounding countryside, we find a rather different picture. Map 2 shows the distribution of rural markets in Ningpo's hinterland as of 1227. Apart from those in Ningpo's immediate suburbs, there were no markets in the Ningpo Plain, much of which had not yet been brought under cultivation owing to problems of drainage. Of the markets depicted, nos. 2 and 14 served to link Ningpo's immediate trading area with neighboring dependent economic regions, whereas nos. 13, 19, and 20 (by inference from Ming data) were break points in the transportation system—i.e., towns with inns and entertainment facilities for the relaxation of merchants and transport coolies. Almost all the others were situated where the plains gave way to hills. Apparently, then, rural trade was mainly a matter of exchanging hill products for products of the plain. We know that goods for exchange in nos. 5, 6, 7, 8, 9, 18, and 21 included firewood, charcoal, bamboo, and bamboo shoots; and that nos. 4, 15, and 18 were the locations of rice-purchasing offices for government breweries. Wholesalers carried away great quantities of these goods, most probably destined for Ningpo.¹⁷

During the transition from Yüan to Ming, Ningpo's development was hindered by riots and rebellions in the Lower Yangtze region that disrupted the Grand Canal route and paralyzed the economy of the areas dependent upon it. To make matters worse, heavy land taxes were levied on the peasantry, and the xenophobic Ming imposed severe restrictions on foreign relations. These developments, together with harsh regulation of the private coastal trade, caused an extensive decline in maritime commerce and fostered smuggling and piracy. Ningpo became at once

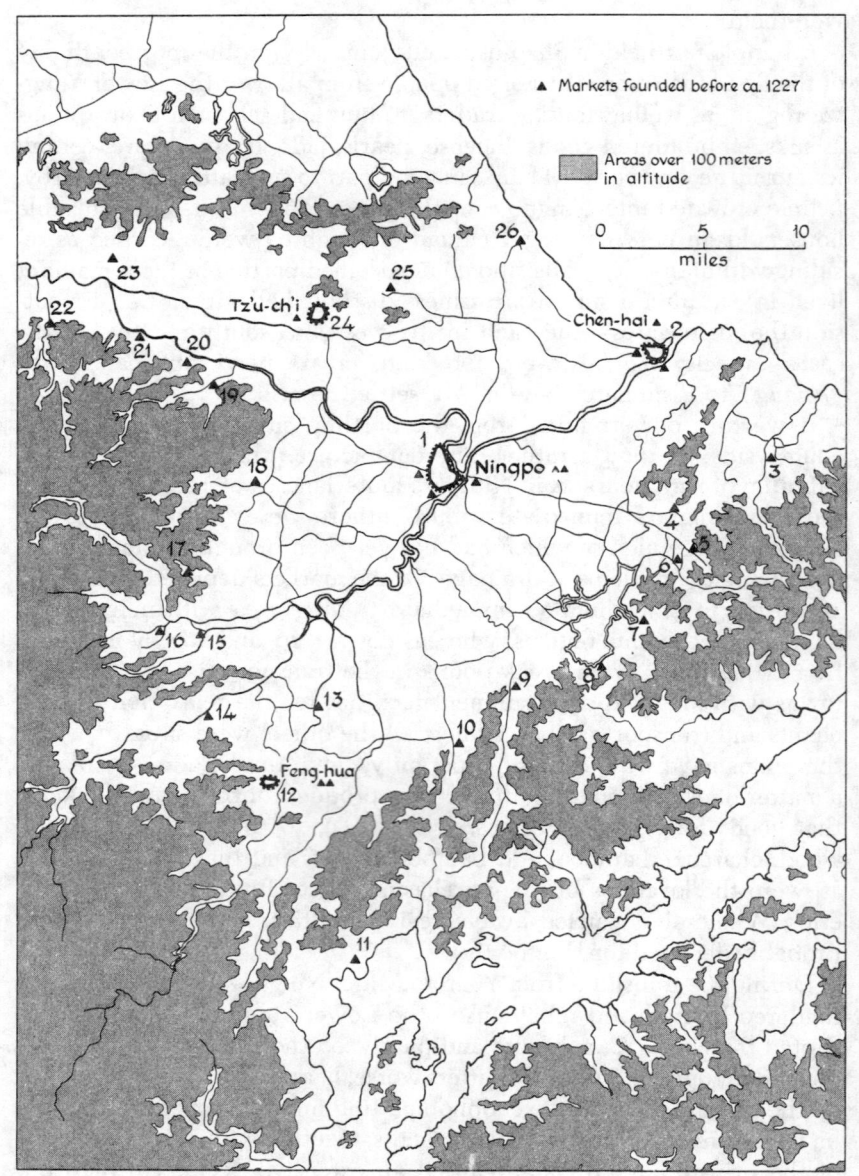

MAP 2. MARKET TOWNS IN THE NINGPO AREA, CA. 1227

a target for attacks by Japanese pirates and a center of the illegal coastal trade.[18]

Although the population count of 1391 indicates that the population in Yin *hsien* may have doubled since the Southern Sung period—in other words, even though the number of peasants in the county should have been able to provision a considerably enlarged Ningpo—the population of the city appears to have declined during the first century of the Ming period. Economic life in both Ningpo and its hinterland stagnated. As shown on Map 3, only two new rural markets were established between 1227 and the Ch'eng-hua reign (1465–87), whereas during the same 250-odd years two of the pre-1227 markets closed down.

During the middle of the Ming, however, the pace of commerce began to quicken. Agricultural recovery and industrial diversification moved ahead in tandem with the resurgence of the coastal trade. Since Yüan times maritime shipping agents in the Lower Yangtze ports specialized in trade either with ports in the Southeast Coast and Lingnan regions or with ports to the north. Specialists in the southern trade, known in Ningpo as *nan-pang* or *nan-hao*, imported lumber, exotic woods, iron, copper, hemp cloth, dyestuffs, medicines, pepper, sugar, dried fruits, incense, and sundries and exported to southern ports silk, cotton, textiles, ceramics, and marine products originating in the Middle and Lower Yangtze regions. Specialists in the northern trade, known as *pei-pang* or *pei-hao*, imported beans, beancakes (in growing demand as a fertilizer in cotton cultivation), oxbone, lard, medicines, dyestuffs, dried fish, and dried fruits and exported rice, sugar, marine products, medicines, cotton textiles, paper, bamboo, lumber, and sundries (commodities that originated in the Lower and Middle Yangtze as well as farther south). Ningpo shippers participated in both groups, though they dominated neither. Their chief competitors were Cantonese and Fukienese merchants among the *nan-hao* and merchants from Kiangnan and Shantung among the *pei-hao*.[19] The role of Ningpo as a regional transshipping center for both northern and southern goods became increasingly important in the sixteenth century. The diffusion of silver currency in rural areas accompanied the revival of native commerce, and when restrictions on overseas trade were lifted in 1567, silver from Japan, Portugal, and Spain poured into inland China via Ningpo.[20] The economic recovery during mid-Ming was reflected in the structure of marketing in Ningpo's hinterland. As shown on Map 3, the period from ca. 1487 to ca. 1560 saw the establishment of seven new periodic markets and the extinction of none.

We have some interesting data on repairs, dredgings, and reorganiza-

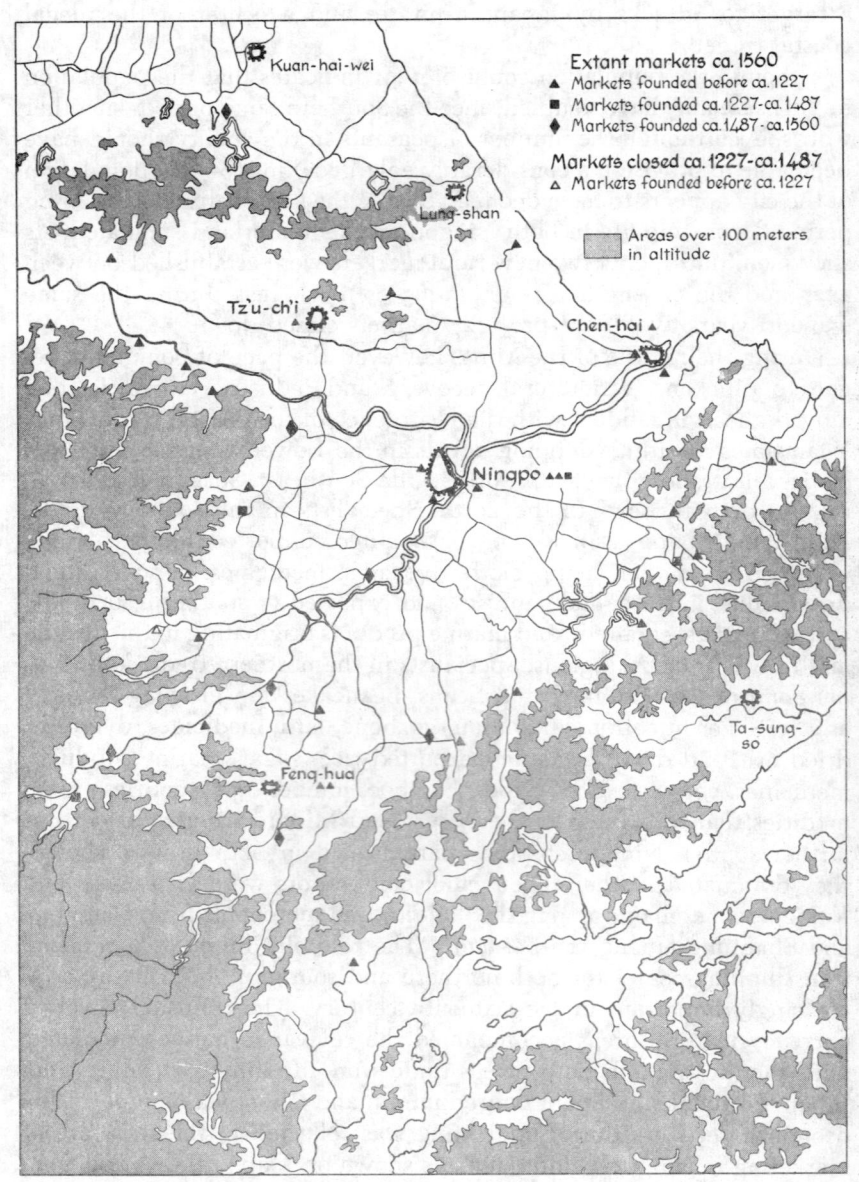

MAP 3. GROWTH OF MARKET TOWNS IN THE NINGPO AREA, CA. 1227–CA. 1560

tions of the water system of the Ningpo Plain in the Wan-li, K'ang-hsi, Ch'ien-lung, and Hsien-feng periods.[21] It seems that most of this work was carried out on the initiative of prominent gentry and rich merchants. For example, during the K'ang-hsi period (1662–1722) Lin Meng-ch'i, a magistrate of Tz'u-ch'i county, presented a memorial to the government proposing means by which the entire canal system of the Yü-yao River valley in the county could be dredged. He stressed that the funds needed should be raised pro rata from landlords who owned more than fifty *mou* of land, from pawnbrokers, and from the owners of large shops, and not from the great majority of petty landowners. He further suggested that labor for the dredging should be recruited throughout the county—excluding the impoverished, the disabled, the aged, and juveniles. Lin also argued against using the *pao-chang* (headmen of the superordinate unit in the *pao-chia* surveillance system) to direct the work, since most were reputed to be villains; he favored instead the selection of two able and impartial men, either gentry or commoner, for each *t'u* ("rural district").[22]

Map 4 shows the development of the marketing network in the Ningpo area during the century and a half from the late Chia-ching period (ca. 1560) to the Yung-cheng period (1723–35). It seems that the peasant economy in the plain lying north of the Yü-yao and Yung rivers attained its classical form during this period as a network of rural markets spread over the whole area. Significant growth in rural markets is also apparent west of Ningpo and in the plain northeast of Feng-hua. Considerable progress in the construction of waterworks, particularly dikes and drainage canals, facilitated the gradual settlement of the plains east and south of Ningpo and the northern littoral of Hsiang-shan Bay. The embankment of the Ta-sung River early in the Ch'ing was a particularly notable achievement. But local productivity in these areas had not yet developed to the point where more than a few rural markets could be supported.[23]

Settlers of the Ningpo Plain faced some difficult problems. Where the water level varied from place to place, farmers had to expend much of their labor on irrigation works. Landholdings tended to become smaller and smaller, and overcrowding became characteristic of land tenure in certain areas, particularly around Chen-hai and Tung-ch'ien Lake.[24] To supplement their income from rice cultivation, many farmers developed sideline specializations. Mat-weaving (in the plain west of Ningpo) and the growing of *pei-mu* (a cough medicine) had become local specialties by the Ch'ing period. Unfortunately, the soil was suitable for growing cotton only along the northern sandy reaches of Yü-yao and Chen-hai

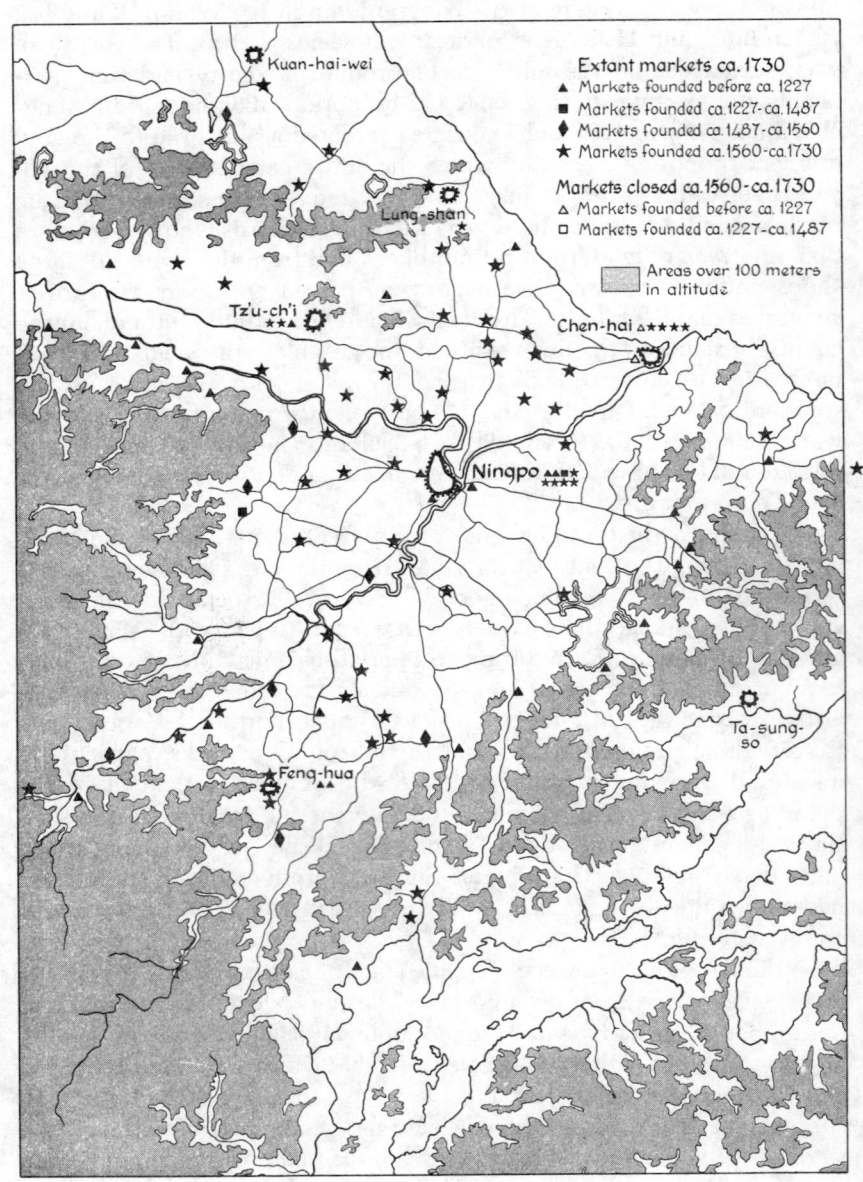

MAP 4. MARKET TOWNS IN THE NINGPO AREA, CA. 1730

counties and along the lower reaches of the Ta-sung River valley. In Yü-yao county, cotton culture had been introduced during the Yüan period, and it developed to such an extent that by late Ch'ing times about 70 percent of the farmers there were engaged in it; the corresponding figure for Chen-hai county was about 17 percent.[25]

Above all, though, the people of the Ningpo region specialized in and monopolized fishing and water transport. By the nineteenth century, perhaps as many as one-fifth of the gainfully employed were engaged in these occupations. Villages near Chen-hai and along the shore of Hsiang-shan Bay, in particular, made a specialty of fishing.[26]

By the early eighteenth century, native trade in all but the isolated interior regions of China was dominated by three groups of prominent traders, the Hui-chou merchants of Anhwei, Shansi merchants, and Fukienese merchants from the Ch'üan-chou–Chang-chou region. Hui-chou merchants had gained control of the salt monopoly in most regions of the empire; Shansi merchants had developed a remittance banking system vital to the government's fiscal operations as well as to long-distance trade; and Fukienese merchants had long dominated interregional water-borne trade. Merchants from Shantung ports, Foochow, and Canton were also important in the coastal trade. During the first half of the nineteenth century, Hui-chou merchants consolidated their control of the salt trade in Ningpo, whence they also conducted a vigorous import-export business. It was in this situation that Ningpo merchants gradually rose to prominence. Inevitably they were on guard against their competitors, but it is likely that much of their manifest commercial skill and financial acumen was learned from their rivals, particularly those from Hui-chou and Ch'üan-chou.[27] Trade expansion during most of the eighteenth century stimulated the development of a sophisticated banking system in Ningpo.[28] Most of the city's influential *ch'ien-chuang* were founded during the century after 1750. This type of bank, which issued notes and used a clearinghouse, almost certainly originated in Ningpo and was introduced to Shanghai by Ningpo emigrants.[29]

Paradoxically enough, the expansion of Ningpo merchants throughout the Lower Yangtze region was stimulated by Ningpo's commercial decline in favor of Shanghai. As a center for trade with the interior, Ningpo could not compete with Shanghai because of the costly haul-overs and portages along the waterways linking the city with Hangchow and the Grand Canal. The advent of the steamship deprived Ningpo of its transshipment functions, and the limited extent of Ningpo's regional hinterland did not provide a sizable market for foreign manufactures. Thus

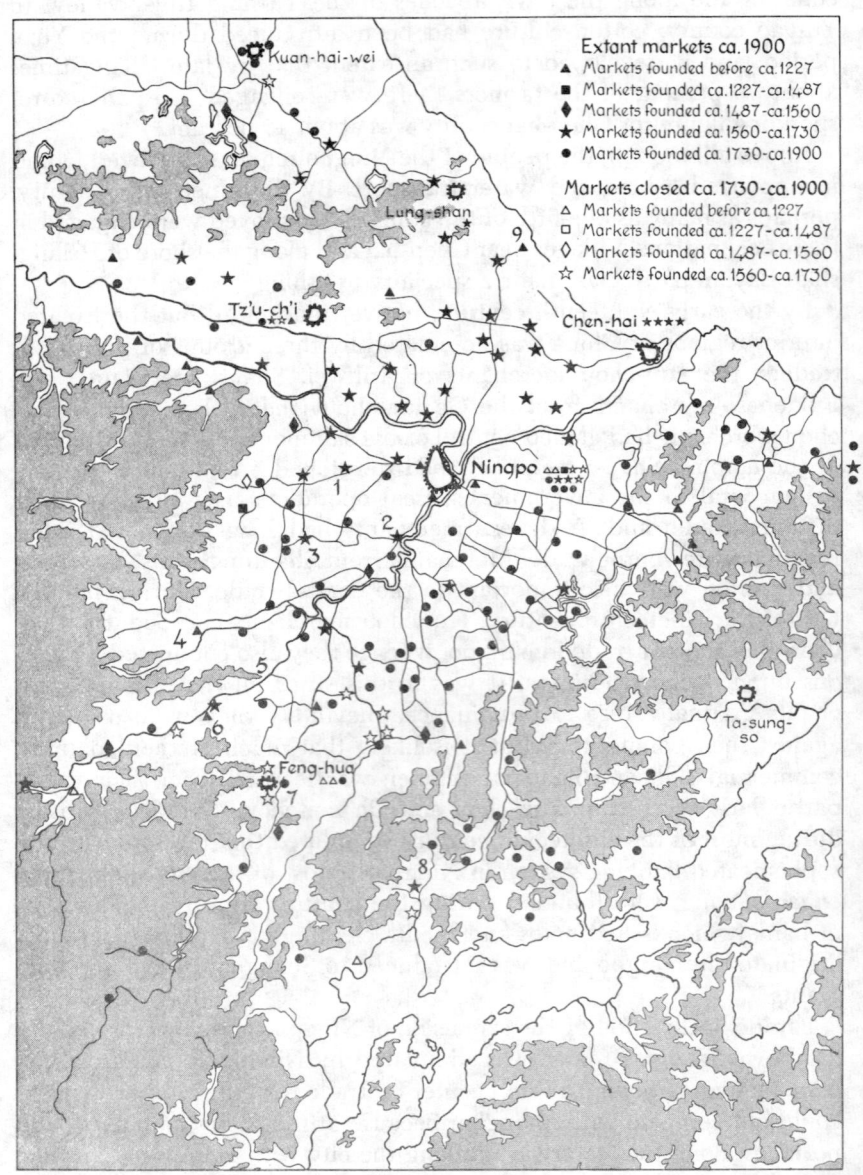

MAP 5. MARKET TOWNS IN THE NINGPO AREA, CA. 1900. Numbered market towns are discussed in the section headed *The Trading System Centered on Ningpo* (pp. 424-32): (1) Mai-mien-ch'iao, (2) Shih-ch'i, (3) Huang-kung-lin, (4) Hsiao-ch'i, (5) Chiang-k'ou, (6) Ch'üan-k'ou, (7) Ta-ch'iao, (8) Shun-hu, and (9) Hsieh-p'u.

Ningpo never developed a sizable foreign trade after it became a treaty port in 1843, and its stature as an entrepôt declined still further after Hangchow was opened to trade in 1896. Meanwhile, Ningpo merchants had long since responded to commercial shifts within the region, and their migration to the rapidly rising port of Shanghai was already under way in the eighteenth century.

Although Ningpo's importance as a center of long-distance trade declined, it prospered as a regional center. It is said that Ningpo's traditional junk trade had its heyday during the Hsien-feng and T'ung-chih periods (1851–74),[30] and as Ningpo settled into its new functional position as the center of a region economically dependent on Shanghai, it enjoyed sufficient trade to support a brisk regional development. During the second half of the nineteenth century, such cottage industries as hatmaking, embroidery, weaving cotton fabrics, making fishnets, and tailoring expanded. The advent of regular steamer traffic with Shanghai and modest improvements in the efficiency of local transport increased the range of imported goods within Ningpo's hinterland and fostered the commercialization of agriculture. Scores of new periodic markets were established throughout the city's hinterland. From Map 5 it is apparent that only during mid-Ch'ing did the rural economy in the plains southeast of the Feng-hua and Yung rivers attain mature development. A dense network of market towns now spread throughout the Ningpo Plain, and rural marketing was also well developed in such peripheral areas as the plains near the coast north of Tz'u-ch'i, southeast of Chenhai, and north of Hsiang-shan Bay.

The City of Ningpo as an Urban System

We have already noted the physical characteristics of Ningpo's site—the confluence of the Yü-yao and Feng-hua rivers along the east side of the city, the canal-cum-moat along the west side (see Map 6). Within the city a network of canals reached almost every section. The major road of the city, and the broadest, linked the west gate with the Tung-tu Men in the east. It was crossed by two important north-south streets. One, paralleled by a major canal, ran from the southern commercial districts to the Ho-i Men in the northeastern section of the wall. Küan Ch'iao, the bridge over which the main east-west street crossed this canal, was seen as the directional center of the city, for the boulevards radiating from it (Pei Ta-lu, Tung Ta-lu, Nan Ta-lu, and Hsi Ta-lu) bore the names of the principal points of the compass. The second major north-south street led from the yamen of the circuit intendant in the northern part of the city to the Ta miao, a major temple in the south,

MAP 6. NINGPO, 1877

Civil offices
1. Ning-po prefectural yamen
2. Ning-Shao-T'ai circuit yamen
3. Yin *hsien* yamen

Religious institutions
4. Prefectural City God temple
5. Prefectural Confucian school-temple (*fu-hsüeh*)
6. County City God temple
7. County Confucian school-temple (*hsien-hsüeh*)
8. Temple of Literature (*Wen-ch'ang ko*)
9. Temple of the Queen of Heaven (*T'ien-hou kung*)
10. Medicine God temple (*Yao-huang tien*)
11. Great temple (*Ta miao*)
12. New temple of the Water Immortal (*Hsin Shui-hsien miao*)

Academic institutions
13. Yüeh-hu Shu-yüan (academy)
14. T'ien-i Ko (library)

Guilds and native-place associations
15. Nan-hao Hui-kuan (Southern Trade Guild)
16. Pei-hao Hui-kuan (Northern Trade Guild)
17. Ch'ien-yeh Kung-so (Money Trade Guild)
18. Ling-nan Hui-kuan (Kwangtung Guild)
19. Min-shang Hui-kuan (Fukien Guild)
20. Hsin-an Hui-kuan (Hui-chou Guild)
21. Lien-shan Hui-kuan (Shantung Guild)

Markets extant as of 1877
▲ Founded prior to 1487
■ Founded 1487–1788
● Founded 1788–1877

Markets defunct as of 1877
⊗ Extant 1465–87 but defunct by 1788
◻ Extant 1465–87, still extant 1788, but defunct by 1877
○ Founded by 1788 but defunct by 1877

Other
⊞ Warehouses
▲ Moorings

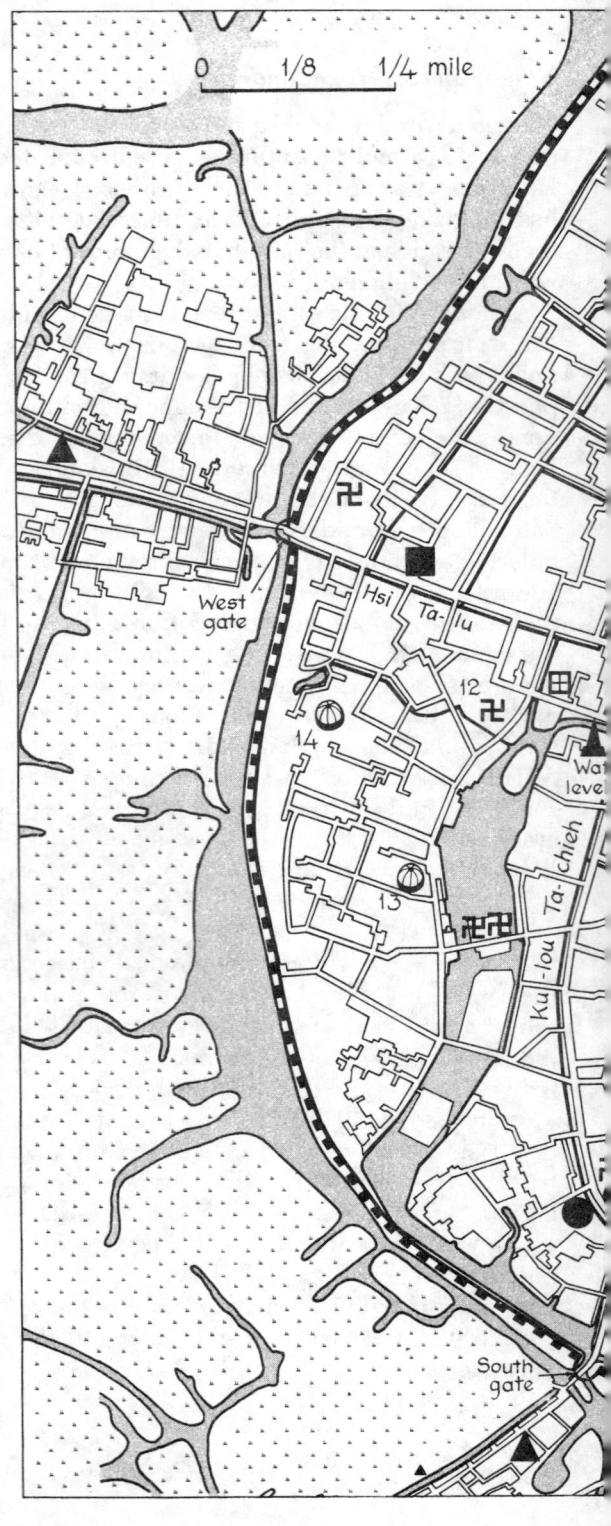

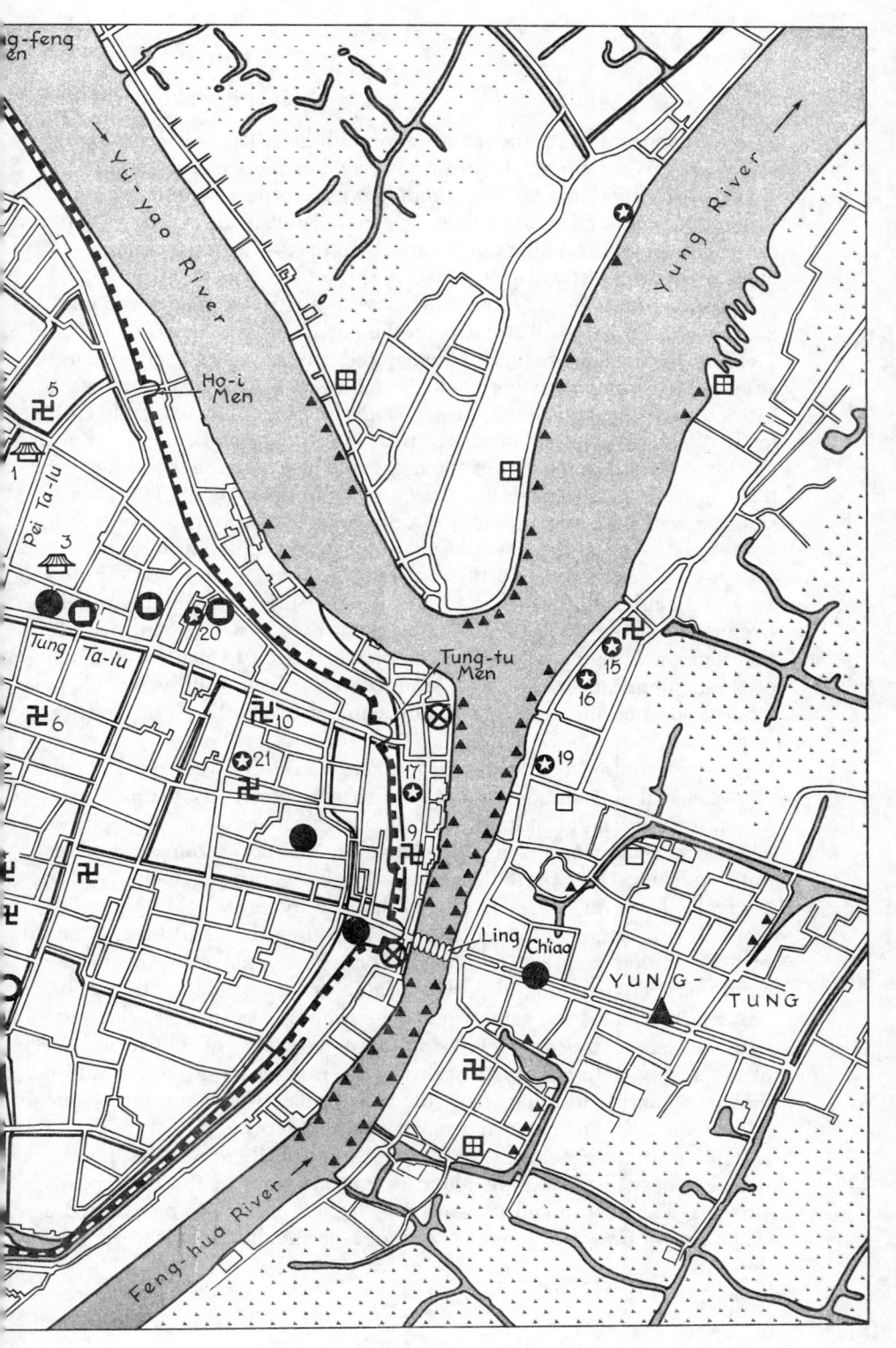

where it connected with the road to the south gate. Its intersection with Hsi Ta-lu was the site of the drum tower, whence its name Ku-lou Ta-chieh. Most other streets, lanes, and alleys were narrow and tortuous. In general, civil and military offices were located in the northern part of the city and official altars in the southern part—a pattern common to many other administrative cities.

Urban markets. In the fifteenth century the city had only three markets within the walls, all situated on the north side of Tung Ta-lu. The Ta Shih was held in the plaza between the county yamen and the main street; the Chung Shih was held two blocks to the east, somewhat further back from the main street; and the Hou Shih was held still farther east, close to the northeast wall. Additional markets were held outside each of the city's four main gates. These markets convened on a once-per-*hsün* schedule (i.e., three times per lunar month): that outside the west gate was on an 8–18–28 schedule, that outside the south gate was on a 7–17–27 schedule, that outside the Ling-ch'iao Men was on a 4–14–24 schedule, and that outside the Tung-tu Men was on a 9–19–29 schedule. A fifth suburban market, the Yung-tung Shih, was held irregularly in the Yung-tung district about five *li* east of Ling Ch'iao, the pontoon bridge serving the gate that had been named for it. Each of these suburban markets was situated on or near waterways where wharves or moorings served sampans coming from villages around the city.[31]

Some time after 1566, the two markets outside the east gates were closed, and their functions and schedules were assumed by a new market, the Tung-ching Shih, situated about two *li* east of Ling Ch'iao. Thereafter there was virtually no change in Ningpo's suburban markets until well into the twentieth century. Marketing arrangements within the walls, however, were far less stable. The three early Ming markets were all still extant in the 1780's, by which time they had been joined by five additional markets within the city. By 1877, however, six of these eight markets, including all of the original trio, were defunct, and five new markets had been established (see Map 6). As of 1877, then, the city was served by seven markets within the walls, of which one lay near the west gate and one just inside the Ling-ch'iao Men. As Map 6 indicates, market locations have tended to reflect the transport system as structured by the gates and major thoroughfares.

Aside from these periodic markets dealing in daily necessities, permanent business districts were found in various parts of the city and its suburbs. Tung Ta-lu and its western extension Hsi Ta-lu constituted a major axis of business. Segments of it or lanes feeding into it were lined by shops dealing in cloth, food, bags, hats, furniture, lumber, bamboo, silk thread, and medicines; pawnshops and restaurants were also found here. For the most part these shops were localized by trade, as indicated by such street names as Chu-hang Hsiang (Bamboo-dealers Alley), Yao-chü T'ung (Medicine-shops Lane), Ping-tien T'ung (Pastry-shops Lane), and Nan-fan Hsiang (Southern-style Food Alley). Inside the Tung-tu Men was one of the busiest business districts, dominated by dealers in wooden articles and bamboo ware, and by printers. Inside the Ling-ch'iao Men was another major business district, in which medicine dealers and shops selling wooden articles, bamboo ware, and lacquer ware predominated. Nearby, Yao-hang Chieh, of course, was the street where medicine dealers were concentrated. Chiang-hsia, the district between the east gates and the river, was the busiest suburb of the city. Along the shore were wharves for junks, lorchas, and sampans. *Ch'ien-chuang* banks were concentrated in this district, as were shops selling marine products, sugar, lumber, hemp, and cereals; here, too, were centered the firms (*pei-hao* and *nan-hao*) specializing in the staples of the coastal trade, northern and southern, respectively. A shipyard, the Fukienese guildhall, the T'ien-hou kung (temple), and the Ch'ing-an Hui-kuan (the guidhall of shipping agents) were all located here. Names like Yü-chan T'ung (Fish-wholesalers Lane), T'ang-hang Chieh (Sugar-wholesalers Street), and Ch'ien-hang Chieh (Money-shops Street) indicate where specialized shops were concentrated. Yung-tung was another busy suburb just east of the city across the river. Here, too, were found *pei-hao* and *nan-hao*, and dealers in marine products, lumber, and cereals. Other businesses were more exclusive to Yung-tung, namely dealers in slate, ironware, fuel and candles, paper, dyestuffs, sundries, cattle, vegetables, fruit, and other foods. This district was particularly noted for its warehouses and ricemills. The shipyards were located at the downriver end of this suburb, whereas the wharves for sampans were at the upriver end. Localization of particular trades is indicated by such names as Rice-wholesalers Street, Lumber-wholesalers Street, Mat-dealers Bridge, Mutton-shops Street, and Food-dealers Bridge. Other names attest to the localization of artisan industry: Cast-iron Street, Blacksmiths Lane, Pan-factories Lane, Anchor-works Lane, and Scow-builders Lane. Chiang-pei, across the Yü-yao River to the northeast of the city, developed into an active commercial suburb only after Ningpo was opened as a treaty port.[32]

Enterprises and occupational specialization. In the absence of reliable data on Ningpo's labor force, we must fall back on gross estimates indicative of occupational differentiation. According to George Smith in

1857, an "intelligent native scholar" estimated that four-fifths of the gainfully employed living within the city walls were laborers or businessmen, the remainder being of the literary class; in the suburbs, 60 percent were said to be peasants, 30 percent artisans, and 10 percent fishermen and boatmen.[33] This last estimate is partially corroborated by the Kuang-hsü gazetteer, which states that 60 to 70 percent of the suburban population were peasants and 20 to 30 percent fishermen and boatmen. The figures for the city proper given above, however, appear to be called into question by the analysis of Dr. Nyok-Ching Tsur, who cites figures compiled by a water-supply company in the early 1900's. On his telling, of 300,000 people inside the walls, 120,000 were gainfully employed—60 percent in business, 30 percent in agriculture, and 10 percent in miscellaneous professions (scholars, monks, fortune-tellers, doctors, slaves, and cooks). The business sector of the population was further analyzed as follows: 40 percent were involved in commercial firms, 35 percent were independent handicraftsmen or employed by artisan firms, and 25 percent were laborers of one sort or another.[34]

In describing Ningpo's business establishment, it is often difficult to distinguish producer from dealer, or industry from commerce. Enterprises producing handicrafts, however, can be considered primarily "industrial" whether or not they also marketed their product. Lacquer ware, wood carvings, inlaid furniture, and both precious and nonprecious metalwork were handicrafts for which Ningpo had a well-deserved reputation and a wide market. Much of the best work was done to order. The metal industry was so well known, for example, that customers from all over China, and even from Singapore and Vladivostok, eagerly sought the skilled chasing of Ningpo. Scarcely less famous were the city's distinctive furniture, fine lacquer ware (*chu-hung-ch'i, ts'a-ch'i,* and *tsao-kuang*), and Buddhist altar-fittings.[35] According to Nyok-Ching Tsur, the artisans in Ningpo produced on special demand personal effects, luxuries, and items farmers could not provide for themselves.[36] Since in general exports were rather limited in volume and orders fluctuated with the season, the number of handicraftsmen could not but be limited. Those whose customers were officials or rich people lived comfortably in the ward near the official residences in the city, but those whose customers were farmers or ordinary citizens had a more precarious existence. As artisans often suffered from the irregularity of demand, they were eager to organize and to form guilds. As a rule, an apprentice was recruited from among the master's kinsmen at the age of thirteen or fourteen. After three years' training without pay, he became a journeyman, and after another three years of assisting in his master's workshop he could choose either to remain there or to set up on his own. These customs were much the same throughout the region.

Craft shops were of two kinds—the individual master's enterprise, and the *ho-ku* or partnership of two or more masters. In general, small industries providing everyday necessities were of the former type. For example, makers of cloth shoes, toys, paper lanterns, and small items of bamboo, as well as those who collected rags and used articles and reworked them into new goods, had limited capitalization and membership; typically, the personnel of such enterprises was limited to one master and two apprentices. Likewise, makers of goods for daily use or for local consumption (e.g., furniture, shoes, straw products, bags, trunks, chopping boards, and wooden ladles) required little capital and were organized simply: one master, one to four journeymen, and two apprentices. Naturally, in such cases specialization was limited, work was uncomplicated, and the whole manufacturing process was under the master's direction. The master of a furniture shop, for instance, might purchase wood from the timber traders or at the market, and his sons might deliver finished goods to the customers' homes.

On the other hand, the makers of expensive luxury articles had to have enough funds to cope with sharp seasonal fluctuations in gross income. At the lunar new year, demand increased as debts were paid and people shopped for gifts; whereas in the summer and toward the end of the lunar year, credit grew so tight that business was sometimes suspended. Thus the great majority of producers of luxury goods formed *ho-ku* partnerships, pooling their funds, materials, tools, workshops, and labor. Furthermore, such industries as inlaying furniture, carving wood, making lacquer ware, and working precious and nonprecious metals were so specialized, not only in manufacturing but also in selling, that masters must have felt it more profitable to form partnerships. The personnel of two such *ho-ku* together consisted of twelve masters, twenty journeymen, four apprentices, and some miscellaneous employees. Their operation involved 20 to 25 separate manufacturing processes, each under the general supervision of one of the masters. Finished goods were inventoried for later sale. In precious metal firms the production department was likely to include about ten masters, each directing a specialized group of assistants, journeymen, and apprentices; the sales department might consist of eight to ten persons (one cashier, two accountants, and five or more salesmen).

The "putting-out" system was another form of enterprise prevalent in Ningpo, and it, like the handicrafts enterprises just discussed, can also be considered primarily industrial rather than commercial.[37] This system involved a factor (called *chan, chuang,* or *hang*) who organized and financed the collection and distribution of goods produced by cottage industry. The factors were large-scale entrepreneurs with warehouses and with agents or wholesale-retail shops in other cities. They financed and acted through itinerant merchants, collectors, and middlemen, who undertook (1) to supply materials to, or to order articles from, the cottagers, and (2) to collect, appraise, and pack the finished goods and send them on to the factors. Since demand differed from one locality to another, only large-scale entrepreneurs had the information about interurban market conditions needed to avail themselves of a good opportunity in advance of individual demands.

Businesses of this kind can be divided into those in which the home-produced items are components of a finished product and those in which they *are* the finished product. The manufacture of latticework, beds, and bamboo umbrellas illustrates the first type. A number of *ho-ku* furniture-making enterprises were organized by factors, who put out work to specialized artisans whose workplaces dominated city streets totaling over one mile in length. In the case of umbrella making, the manufacture of bamboo ribs was a specialty of villagers in the hills who owned their own bamboo fields. Men cut the bamboo ribs and women polished them. On each market day they sold them to the umbrella dealer (the factor), who in turn sorted them into two quality grades. After that the factor had oiled paper or hemp pasted on the ribs. The oil used for the paper was obtained from a dealer in Hangchow or from a middleman in Ningpo on three months' credit.

The second type of putting-out system is illustrated by the manufacture of straw mats, straw hats, embroidered silk cloth, and cotton cloth. In the case of straw mats, the factor commissioned the items from peasants in the suburbs, ordering lots of specific widths and sizes. The mats were produced as follows: after peasants mowed their fields in the fifth lunar month, they collected the straw, soaked it in mud, dried it, and wove it into mats. The finished goods were sold to the factor in packs of a hundred, and he in turn disposed of them through his commission agents stationed in other cities. In the case of the manufacture of straw hats, the entrepreneur purchased in advance a large amount of straw from private or corporate landowners (including urban clans and lineages with trusts of agricultural land) and had it distributed, along with sample hats, to small cottage artisans by his agents. Sometimes he had as many as twenty agents, each of whom in turn dealt with 30 to 50 families who actually made the hats. Most of the entrepreneurs needed extensive capital, because they had to pay for the straw in advance, deal in cash with their agents, and store the finished goods for several weeks.

As if to confirm the words of the Kuang-hsü gazetteer that Ningpo was *pai-huo hsien-pei*, "provided with a hundred kinds of goods," some 80 commercial specialties were recorded in the 1935 county gazetteer.

Specialization within the medicine trade was more or less typical of commercial specialization generally. Four different roles were well defined. *Shan-huo hang* were itinerant middlemen who collected their medicines exclusively in Chekiang province, whereas *li-hao* (*k'o-pang*) were itinerant middlemen who ranged widely in collecting their medicines, going in particular to Szechwan, Yunnan, Shansi, Fukien, and Kwangtung. Both *shan-huo hang* and *li-hao* sold their products to *ch'ang-lu hang*, "wholesalers," who in turn supplied *yao-p'u*, "retailers."[38]

Following Himeda's article on the salt-water fishing industry in Ningpo during the Ch'ing period,[39] specialization in the region can be summarized as follows. *Yü-tung* were the entrepreneurs who operated the fishing boats, hiring and overseeing the crew (*yü-huo*) and making the critical production decisions. Normally the *yü-tung* rented his boat and gear (or was buying them on credit) from the wholesaler with whom he dealt or sometimes from independent shipowners. The *yü-tung* sold his catch to middlemen (*hsien-k'o*), stationed offshore near the fishing grounds, receiving a sealed receipt (*mai-hsien-che*) rather than cash. The middleman then shipped the catches of several boats to wholesalers (*hsien*[fresh]-*yü hang* and *hsien*[salted]-*yü hang*) in Ningpo, from whom he received a commission. The wholesaler bulked, processed, and graded the fish and either shipped them to importers in other cities, or delivered them to local or nearby retailers (*hsien*[fresh]-*huo p'u* and *hsien*[salted]-*huo p'u*) on twenty days' credit. Itinerant retailers (*hsing-fan*) normally got their supplies from retail shopkeepers but occasionally got them directly from a wholesale firm. The *yü-tung* entrepreneurs periodically took their sealed receipts to their wholesaler in Ningpo, either collecting cash or receiving a bill of exchange (*hsien-tan*), which they converted to cash at the *ch'ien-chuang* bank that financed the wholesaler. Payments both ways were such that middlemen in effect received a commission from the *yü-tung* as well as the wholesaler. It goes without saying that the wholesaler exercised decisive control over *yü-tung* through setting prices, renting out the factors of production, and issuing bills. Wholesalers in turn were dependent for credit on the *kuo-chang* system of the *ch'ien-chuang* banks.

In the nineteenth century, examples were legion of functional specialization between wholesalers or factors and retailers within the same line. Rice firms were either *hang-chan* (alternatively *mi-chan*) or *ch'ang-tien* (alternatively *mi-tien*); wine firms were either *chiu-fang* (brewer and wholesaler), *chiu-hang* (wholesaler only), or *chiu-tien* (retailer); paper dealers were either *chih-hang* or *chih-tien*; foil dealers were either *po-chuang* or *po-p'u*; cotton dealers were either *hua-hang hua-chuang* or *hua-tien*. Wholesalers were often differentiated according to the nature of the goods they sold. For example, timber wholesalers dealt either in imported high-quality lumber or in lumber from the region, and within the latter group were those dealing solely in pine or fir. Finally, retailers were also differentiated according to the nature of the goods they sold. They could be roughly divided according to whether they were shopkeepers or had small stalls; the latter were further divided into *t'an-fan*, whose stalls were located in covered vegetable markets, and *chien-fu*, whose stalls were in open-air markets.[40]

Wholesaling and retailing were not always sharply differentiated. A 1942 report discusses two Ningpo firms, Yüan-k'ang and Lung-ch'ang, both established in the last years of the Ch'ing, that engaged in both wholesaling and retailing, one dealing in textiles, the other in clothing and linens. Other firms, however, were strictly retailers. Two of these discussed in the report had been founded prior to the Opium War: Yün-chang dealt in cotton, silk, and woolen textiles; and Ta-yu-feng dealt in cotton, dyes for silks and woolens, kettles, and wash basins.[41]

Finance was a well-developed specialty of Ningpo people. The institutions involved were basically of two types, the first limited to *ch'ien-chuang* and the second comprising *tang-p'u*, *t'i-chuang*, and *ch'ai-i-chuang*.[42]

A *ch'ien-chuang* was a native bank using the credit system called *kuo-chang*.* Banks were distinguished into those with more than a specified amount of liquid capital (*ta-t'ung hang*—over 30,000 taels as of 1858) and those with less (*hsiao-t'ung hang*—under 30,000 taels). The latter were not permitted to extend credit or make loans independently of a *ta-t'ung hang*.

* The workings of the *kuo-chang* "transfer-tael" system are described in Susan Mann Jones's article cited in note 29. In its simplest form it may be described as follows (p. 60): "Traders, merchants, and gentry or officials who kept accounts with ... *ch'ien-chuang* were issued passbooks in which they recorded the date and amount of, and the parties to, each transaction. No cash passed from hand to hand. Passbooks were handed in for auditing at the end of every day, at which time representatives of the various *ch'ien-chuang* met and settled up their accounts with such cash payments as might be necessary. Accounts were reckoned in terms of the *Chiang p'ing* tael, an imaginary unit of account unique to Ningpo."

The internal organization of *ch'ien-chuang* reflected a high degree of specialization. The partner-owners, who were seldom directly involved in management, employed a *ching-shou*, "manager," who was responsible solely to the partner-owners and served as liaison between them and the staff. The manager, who served as the firm's external representative and public relations officer, was assisted by one or two *fu-shou*, "deputy managers," who were primarily responsible for day-to-day management. The top echelon also included at least one *san-chien*, "assistant deputy manager," a sinecure assumed by a shareholder or a shareholder's kinsman. The staff below the top management were organized into an inner office, responsible for internal accounting and general operations, and an outer office, responsible for public relations and external accounts. The inner office included the *fang-chang*, "chief accountant"; the *yin-fang*, "shroff," in charge of the assay of bullion; and *hsin-fang*, "clerks," responsible for record keeping, general correspondence, and orders transferring funds. The outer office was headed by the *fang-chang p'ao-chieh*, "loan teller and canvasser," who was very nearly on a par with the assistant manager in status. He solicited deposits and negotiated loans, and it was his responsibility to ascertain the credit rating of prospective clients and to check on the use made by clients of the bank's loans. Also in the outer office was the *chang-t'ou*, "market representative," who participated in the guild discussions that established interest and exchange rates. *Hsüeh-t'u*, "apprentices," who normally served for three years, could be assigned to either office. They typically moved up from performing menial tasks to serving as errand boys, delivering passbooks, and keeping accounts. The bank's personnel roster was completed by a *chan-ssu*, "warehouseman," responsible for guarding the bank's reserves and transporting bullion or cash.

Tang-p'u, ti-chuang, and *ch'ai-i-chuang* were pawnshops or small moneylending shops. Their business personnel were broken down as follows: (1) *tsung-shang*, "managing director"; (2) *cheng-k'an, fu-k'an*, and *ping-k'an* (ranked in the order given), "assistant managers" who examined and appraised pawned articles; (3) *chang-fang*, "accountant"; (4) *ch'ü-fang*, "inspector of articles prior to redemption"; (5) *p'iao-fang*, "keeper of pawn tickets"; (6) *p'ai-fang*, "classifier of pawned articles"; (7) *i-fang*, "supervisor of pawned clothing"; (8) *lou-t'ou, lou-erh*, and *lou-san* (ranked in that order), "warehousemen" who performed such services as drying leather clothes; and (9) *yin-fang*, "shroff" or "cashier."

Occupational associations. We find evidence of protoguilds in Ningpo as early as the Sung period. Of course, the terms *hang* and *t'uan* used to describe these associations were rather ambiguous, referring sometimes to a category of shops, sometimes to a street or a row of shops of the same occupation even when cooperation was wholly informal, and sometimes to a guild proper. Merchants and craftsmen engaged in the same economic activity typically established themselves next to one another in order to promote their common interests.[43] In mid-Ch'ing, for example, the city's ten dealers in imported indigo (*tien-ch'ing-hang*) had shops side by side along the east bank of the river near the Ling Ch'iao.[44] Similarly, medicine dealers lined a street near the east gates, and dealers in sugar and dried fish, as well as banking firms, were concentrated in the Chiang-hsia district. Moreover, as stated above, the great majority of craft firms tended to congregate by specialty. All these groupings or associations were traditionally called *hang* in the case of stores and *tso* in the case of craft shops.

According to Katō Shigeshi, the native-place associations found in Chinese cities had normally been established in connection with long-distance trade; the merchant *hui-kuan* emerged as a type in the sixteenth century.[45] In Ningpo, however, we find a clear prototype as early as 1191. In that year, one Shen Fa-hsün, a sea captain serving a Fukienese shipping agency in Ningpo, established there a shrine to T'ien-hou, the patron deity of Fukienese traders.[46] Believers presumably consisted of members of the shipping agents guild. Similarly, a temple to T'ien-hou was established at the mouth of the Yung River in Chen-hai in 1279 and rebuilt outside the south gate of the town in 1734 by merchants not only from Fukien but also from those parts of Chekiang in the Southeast Coast region.[47] Common economic interests must have been the chief integrating factor. As Ningpo people increasingly came to participate in the coastal trade, however, the cult-cum-guild subdivided. In the Chia-ch'ing period (1796–1820), when the guild of Ningpo shipping agents engaged in the northern trade established the Che-ning Hui-kuan in Shanghai, they enshrined T'ien-hou in their guildhall.[48]

In Ningpo itself, the T'ien-hou kung established in 1850 together with the Ch'ing-an Hui-kuan came to be considered the main shrine or mother temple. D. G. MacGowan mistakenly thought it a Shantung guild, but it was in fact established by nine powerful *pei-hao* shipping agents from Tz'u-ch'i, Chen-hai, and Yin *hsien*. Another T'ien-hou temple served Fukienese shipping agents, and yet another served other *nan-hao* shipping agents. Subsequently, two more branch temples were established, one in Ta-sung-so, a walled garrison town situated north of Hsiang-shan Bay, and the other in the San-chiang-k'ou district of Ningpo in connection with Nan-pei Hai-shang Kung-so, a guildhall established by shipping agents specializing in both *pei-hao* and *nan-hao*. In the meantime,

Ningpo and Its Hinterland

Fukienese merchants had established a new guildhall in Chiang-hsia.[49] As of 1854, there were several thousand Fukienese emigrants in Ningpo, most of them engaged in shipping. Although Fukienese merchants were united in an inclusive native-place association (known as *Min pang* or *Chien pang*), they were divided into subassociations according to their native counties and prefectures. There were nine component *pang* altogether, one of which was defined strictly in terms of the product dealt with: opium. Among the others were the *Ch'üan pang* (Ch'üan-chou subguild) and the *Hsia pang* (Amoy subguild), both of which specialized in the import of sugar, grain, lumber, rattan, sundries, and dried fruits; and the *Hsing-hua pang* (representing the prefecture immediately north of Ch'üan-chou *fu*), which dealt exclusively in fresh and dried *lung-yen*.[50] By the end of the nineteenth century the major native-place associations in Ningpo were those for natives of Fukien (*Min-shang hui-kuan*), Kwangtung (*Ling-nan hui-kuan*), Shantung (*Lien-shan hui-kuan*), and Hui-chou *fu* in Anhwei (*Hsin-an hui-kuan*).[51]

Membership in the various guilds in Ningpo seems to have been open to all of the same profession, in the case of merchant or craft guilds, or to all of the same local origin, in the case of native-place associations. Any journeyman who had been personally acquainted with a guildsman for three years could be admitted to a craft guild. In general, firms were not forced to join. As a rule, guild regulations treated the following business matters. First, credit transactions: For example, the preamble of the Shantung Guild (*Lien-shan hui-kuan*) of Ningpo reads "All purchases and sales are to be in dollars. Payment for grain is due forty days after purchase, for oil and beancake fifty days after purchase, and for commodities sold in bundles sixty days from the date of the bill of sale. Infringements of this rule impose on seller and buyer alike the costs of a restitutive theatrical performance and banquet." Second, storage: The above-cited preamble reads "At the expiration of seventy days, storage is to be charged. Ten days is the limit allowed for removal of goods from on board junks. Up to five days after a sale, the buyer is not liable for goods consumed by fire in godowns; thereafter the seller is no longer responsible." Third, weights and measures: In this area each guild established its own standards. For example, in the Shantung Guild the ordinary "sixteen-taels-to-carry" steelyard was the standard to be employed by every firm connected with the guild. Weighing was to be done in the presence of all concerned, with subsequent discussion disallowed. Fourth, transgressions: For example, fictitious buying and selling were forbidden to members of the guild; offenders were to be reported to the magistrate for punishment. Fifth, exceptional transactions: Since business was normally suspended during the first fifteen days of the first lunar month, urgent business was transacted during this period under the "public" purview of the guild to avoid suspicion of irregularity. Finally, many guilds managed cemeteries and temples and provided forms of social security and charitable services.

The revenue of guilds was of five types: (1) contributions from corporately owned land and houses, (2) rental income, (3) interest from bank deposits, (4) fines, and (5) dues and impositions. In this last regard, each member or shop was liable for dues imposed on net profits at a rate that was usually 1 : 1,000 or more. In Wen-chou-fu, for instance, dues were levied at a rate of 8 : 1,000 by the Ningpo Druggists Guild and at a rate of 2 : 1,000 by the Ningpo Beancake Dealers Guild. Another common mode of collecting fees is illustrated by the Ningpo Guild in Shanghai, which levied a fee of two taels on every ship arriving from Ningpo.[52]

Urban real estate. In the conventions of Chinese realty the "building lot" had come to be included in the category *ti*, in contradistinction to *t'ien*, "farmland." With the development of commerce, lots on which shops and other business enterprises had been built were distinguished as a special type of *ti* and designated as *chi-ti* or *kai-ti-chi*, and in the city as *tsai-ch'eng kai-ti*. In due time, the ownership of urban business property was differentiated into *p'u-ti* (surface usufruct including the buildings) and *chi-ti* (the "substratum," i.e., basic ownership of the lot per se), a distinction that paralleled the surface and substratum rights in agricultural land: *t'ien-mien* vs. *t'ien-ti*. Rentals, leases, and transfers of urban property were made in accordance with these distinctions. It goes without saying that in Ningpo *tsai-ch'eng kai-ti* occupied far more of the urban area than any of the following: *t'ien*, "farmland," *yüan*, "vegetable gardens," *chieh-hsiang*, "lanes," *tao-lu*, "streets," *ho-ch'uan*, "canals and rivers," *ma-t'ou*, "wharves," etc.

The owner of a house (*fang-chu*) might own the lot on which it was built, but he might also be renting the lot from its owner (*chi-ti-chu*). In either case he could rent or sublet his house to a tenant (*fang-k'o*) for either a fixed period or indefinitely. Both owner and tenant had to exchange a written contract at the outset, and the tenant was required to give a deposit (*ya-tsu* or *hsiao-tsu*) or to pay a rental advance (*t'an-tsu*), and sometimes also to pay key money (*hsiao-fei* or *wo-fei*) to his landlord. When the tenant moved, the landlord would return to him the deposit or rental advance, discounting some part of it in proportion to the term of occupancy. Rental was to be paid monthly or quarterly. Not infrequently the tenant sublet rooms or the house itself with the consent of the owner. This was called *fen-tsu, chuan-t'ien*, or *tui-t'ien*, and in this situation the right of *p'u-ti* devolved on the original tenant. So the transfer of both the building and of its usufruct was possible.

During the T'ang and Sung periods, most of the lucrative and important urban real estate was owned by the government and leased to the people through an official real-estate office, the Lou-tien Wu. During the late imperial period, however, official lands came to be distributed among the citizens, and the tenants of official lands or buildings often sublet in turn to third persons. By the Ch'ing period, the only city in Ning-po *fu* in which the Lou-tien Wu still functioned was Hsiang-shan.[53]

Government taxation and control. Before the Taiping Rebellion the revenue of the Ch'ing government came from three main sources: the land tax, profits from monopolies (especially the salt monopoly), and customs duties. The land tax accounted for about two-thirds of the total revenue.[54]

In terms of urban revenue, the building lot was the main object of taxation, buildings per se being exempted. In addition, there were the following miscellaneous taxes on commerce: (1) taxes on such major items as cattle, horses, lumber, rafts, iron, gypsum, mercury, wine, tea, tobacco, dyestuffs, cocoons, and cotton; (2) *kuo-shui*, "customs duties," which were divided between *hai-kuan*, "foreign customs," and *ch'ang-kuan*, "inland customs," the latter including duties levied by the Ministry of Finance on cloth, food, and sundries, and those levied by the Ministry of Works on lumber and ships; (3) *lo-ti-shui*, import taxes on goods arriving at certain cities or towns; (4) *ya-shui*, taxes and license fees levied on middlemen; (5) *tang-shui*, the profit tax on pawnshops; (6) *ch'i-shui*, taxes on bonds and contracts; and (7) *hang-shui*, taxes on guilds.[55] Moreover, an occasional *ch'üan-chuan*, "special subscription," was levied on wealthy merchants or guilds. But on the whole, owing to the lack of reliable data on urban land use, the taxes levied in the city and on commerce were insignificant in comparison with those levied in the countryside. Of course, the situation changed after 1862, when likin taxes were introduced in Chekiang, but that is a chapter of modern history with which we are not concerned here.

Apart from taxation, some further business restrictions remain to be considered: market regulations, rules governing middlemen, and security regulations. The strict regulations on urban commerce characteristic of the early T'ang period—e.g., evening curfews, officials stationed in the market, prohibitions on transactions outside the officially demarcated market area, and a government imposed fixed-price system—had been gradually relaxed, and by the end of the Northern Sung period they had largely disappeared.[56] According to Nyok-Ching Tsur, the market in Ningpo was open to all: "In Ningpo, and so far as I know in China as a whole, ... whoever wants to attend a market and offer goods for sale can do so without applying to the officials for permission."[57] Nonetheless, the government reserved the right of direct control over such important enterprises as salt, tea, alum, native banks, and pawnshops.

The middleman was likewise subject to government control. It was prescribed by law that important transactions (those involving real estate and certain major categories of movable property) be conducted only through licensed middlemen. In 1863 the number of licensed middlemen in Chekiang as a whole was fixed at 9,962. Every applicant had to obtain a guarantee of liability from another middleman and his neighbors prior to his application to the local government. Once granted, the *ya-tieh*, "broker's license," could be revoked if the holder was found guilty of making unfair appraisals, embezzling, exacting unreasonable commissions, or misappropriating funds.

Security measures remained strict throughout late imperial times. Every innkeeper or middleman was required to keep a book for recording the names of visiting itinerant merchants, the number in each party, and their dates of departure; he was to submit this to the local officials at the end of the month. In addition, every immigrant merchant who maintained a permanent establishment in the business quarter was to be entered in special registers analogous to those of the *pao-chia* system and subjected to supervision by a *k'o-chang*, "headman for outsiders."

Administration and municipal services. Ningpo was more important as a center of government than the usual prefectural capital. In addition to the yamen of Yin *hsien*, the metropolitan county, and the yamen of Ning-po *fu*, it also housed the yamen of the circuit intendant for Ning-Shao-T'ai, one of the four circuits into which the prefectures of Chekiang were grouped. In this respect, then, Ningpo's administrative centrality extended into the two neighboring prefectures of Shao-hsing and T'ai-chou, and its rank as an administrative city was more exalted than that of either Shao-hsing-fu or T'ai-chou-fu. The city's long-standing importance in foreign trade and its official role as port of entry for tribute missions from certain overseas "dependencies" meant that throughout late imperial times it supported special offices that were not found in the usual prefectural capital. We have already mentioned the Office of Overseas Trade (*Shih-po ssu*) first established in 992; in the nineteenth century, Ningpo was the site of major offices of the Imperial Maritime Customs (*Hai-kuan*).

Ningpo and Its Hinterland

Because of its strategic location with respect to the exposed coastline of northeastern Chekiang, Ningpo was also important as a center of military power. From the Sung period on, large naval forces were stationed there to defend the city against possible attack and to maintain security along the coast. In the Ming period, several fortresses (*wei-so*) were built near the coast of Hangchow Bay and Hsiang-shan Bay, primarily to protect the region from marauding Japanese pirates, and the various garrisons stationed there were commanded from military offices in Ningpo. Early in the Ch'ing period, the office of the Commander-in-Chief of Chekiang was established at Ningpo, which thereby became the command post of naval forces as well as of army garrisons throughout the province.

This extraordinary concentration of civil and military offices had important consequences for the city. The officials stationed in the various yamens and their extensive staffs created a considerable demand for luxury goods, and the large number of sailors and soldiers billeted in the city swelled the city's population and increased its need for provisions. In peacetime the military personnel were not infrequently assigned to work on water-control and reclamation projects that directly benefited the city.

For purposes of fire-fighting and police services, the metropolitan area as a whole was subdivided during the Sung period into six *hsiang*, one for each quadrant of the intramural area (northeast, southeast, etc.), one for the eastern and northern suburbs, and one for the western and southern suburbs. By the Yüan period the *hsiang* had been renamed *yü*, but the basic division into six major quarters persisted throughout late imperial times. Each of the quarters was subdivided into wards, known during the Ming and Ch'ing as *pi*. The Southeast Quarter (Tung-nan yü), for instance, contained ten *pi* in the Ming and eight in the Ch'ing. *Pi* in turn were made up of neighborhoods or "streets" (*chieh*), the minimal territorial unit for purposes of security.[58]

In the Southern Sung period, fire-fighting was seen as a responsibility of bureaucratic government. Official regulations specified that every city of average size should be equipped with water tanks, watchtowers, and other fire-fighting facilities in each quadrant of the city and/or in the vicinity of major government buildings. Fire-fighting and police services were initially undertaken by army personnel commanded by a military official. But by the thirteenth century these responsibilities had passed from the army to the city's militia, recruited through the *pao-chia* system and commanded by an officer recruited from among the principal families of the city.[59] The system was markedly improved in the mid-nineteenth century when twelve fire stations were established in Ningpo through private initiative, Hui-chou merchants playing a leading role. Each station, equipped with a watchtower and an alarm drum, had as its responsibility a particular quarter of the city. Costs were covered by levies on those renting out houses and apartments at a rate of three percent of rental income, and a station's management was in the hands of houseowners resident in the area of its responsibility.

The long-term secular trend from official to private responsibility that appears to characterize fire-fighting is also apparent in other domains of public works and public welfare. In general, prior to the seventeenth century, maintenance of the city's water supply, repair of the dikes and floodgates that protected the city's suburbs, and the dredging of its shipping lanes and internal canals were the responsibility of officials, whether civil or military. Soldiers and sailors provided most of the manpower. Officials also played the leading role in establishing emergency granaries, orphanages, and homes for the aged. Toward the end of the Ming period, however, responsibility for municipal services came to be shared in ever larger part by the city's gentry and wealthy merchants. For example, when four emergency granaries were built in 1639, contributions were made by commercial houses, pawnshops, and gentry families as well as by civil officials, and the management of each granary was in the hands of a gentleman assisted by two commoner citizens. By the nineteenth century, wealthy merchant and gentry families regularly contributed to dredging works and to maintaining the night watch, and the actual work was done by hired workers rather than by military personnel or corvée labor. Private initiative was also more frequent in the realm of education. The Huang-yüeh Charitable School, for instance, was established in 1831 solely on the initiative of the Salt Merchants Guild.

In Ningpo, as in most other Chinese cities of moderate size, sewage and garbage disposal presented a relatively minor problem because of efficient recycling. Night soil was removed from the city by private entrepreneurs, who sold it as fertilizer to vegetable gardens in peri-urban areas and to farmers along the canals radiating from the city's gates. Other liquid waste was drained into the internal canal system, and most solid waste that was not recycled was burned.

Religion and urban life. In traditional Chinese society, group interests were almost always given religious expression. Thus, the variety of temples in a city reflected the principles of organization on which its social structure rested. In Ningpo, resident bureaucrats were closely associated with the official temples of the state cult, most notably the two Confucian "school-temples," the *fu-hsüeh* and the *hsien-hsüeh*, connected respectively with the governments of Ning-po *fu* and Yin *hsien*. The city's gentry supported temples to famous local men and patronized temples associated with bureaucratic career lines such as the Wen-ch'ang ko and the Kuan-ti miao. Immigrant groups established temples to the deities associated with their native places, and occupational groups dedicated temples to the patron deities of their callings. The goddess T'ien-hou, whose origins were in Fukien and who began her supernatural career as the patroness of Fukienese seafarers, was appropriately enough first honored in Ningpo with a temple established by Fukienese traders. In time, however, her functions became more generic, and temples to T'ien-hou were founded in the Lower Yangtze region by shipping agents of whatever provenance. The Yao-huang tien, a temple built by medicine dealers in 1708 near the streets where their shops were located, was still the home temple for that calling in the nineteenth century. The Tsao-chia miao, the shrine of a special cult popular among medicine dealers, also served as a warehouse for their drugs. A prominent Ningpo example of a temple serving craftsmen was the Kung-shu hsien-shih miao, whose ten deities included the patrons of carpenters, masons, plasterers, and shipwrights.[60]

Though many temples in Ningpo were patronized primarily by those of a particular class, subethnic group, or occupational calling, most were essentially communal in nature, serving residents in their immediate vicinity or within a specific territory defined in terms of the deity's jurisdiction. Important temples of this kind were distributed fairly evenly throughout the city. The households supporting a given temple were organized into religious associations called *she-huo*. One of the largest communal temples, the Hsin-shui-hsien miao (no. 12 on Map 6) boasted a *she-huo* of some 1,400 households. Small ones, such as Hua-lou miao, were supported by *she-huo* of scarcely one-tenth that size. Each communal temple had at least one major festival, financed and organized by its *she-huo*, and characterized by a procession through the streets and a theatrical performance in honor of the deity. The larger *she-huo* were subdivided into up to five *ching* or *pao*, defined territorially in terms of streets and blocks, among whom religious duties rotated.[61]

It is likely that the "streets" already described as the basic units in the city's security system were conventional neighborhoods, each defined by and focused on a particular *t'u-ti* or other locality god. Further research will be necessary to establish the manner in which neighborhood cults related to Ningpo's larger communal temples, and the extent to which the jurisdiction of the latter coincided with the wards (*pi*) into which the six quarters of the city were formally divided.

It remains to mention the City Gods. There were two Ch'eng-huang miao, one each for Ningpo as prefectural capital and as county capital. Annual processions and plays indicate that these were perceived as communal temples whose "community" was the city as a whole. In this respect they capped the city's hierarchically structured religious geography. At the same time, they provided a ritual link between the popular religion of the city people and the official state cult, for the City Gods were considered the supernatural counterparts of the magistrate and the prefect, respectively; and these men, who officiated at the state rites, were enjoined to pay ritual visits to the appropriate City God temple.

The Trading System Centered on Ningpo

Apart from its role in interurban coastal trade, Ningpo served as the central city of a regional trading system where division of labor, specialization of local products, and differentiation of demand and consumption were articulated through a network of collection and distribution. Ningpo's commercial hinterland included the entire drainage basin of the Yung River, plus peripheral areas to the east and south—most notably the Chusan archipelago, the area draining into Hsiang-shan Bay, and the peninsula farther south with its two towns of Shih-p'u and Nan-t'ien.

Local-system specialization. In the metropolitan area itself the following specialties were produced: iron and copper utensils, lacquer ware, metalwork, wood carvings, inlaid furniture, oil, printed matter, native cotton cloth, wooden or rattan utensils, and bamboo umbrellas.[62] (See Map 7.) Shipbuilding went on in the northern suburb of the city and at Tuan-t'ang to the southwest of the city. Marine products such as fresh fish, dried fish, salted fish, fish glue, and salt were specialties of the Chusan archipelago, the southern shore of Hangchow Bay, and the seacoast along Hsiang-shan Bay. Products from Hsiang-shan Bay were either shipped to Ningpo directly or collected at the market at Ta-ch'iao just east of Feng-hua city for redistribution locally or to Ningpo.[63] Among the marine products, salt was a government monopoly. It was produced under government control in salt farms along the southern shore of Hangchow Bay, along Hsiang-shan Bay, along the eastern coast of Hsiang-shan county, and in the Chusan archipelago. The salt was distributed in the cities by licensed salt merchants and in the countryside by petty itinerant traders known as *chien-fan*. The latter were in most cases fishermen.[64]

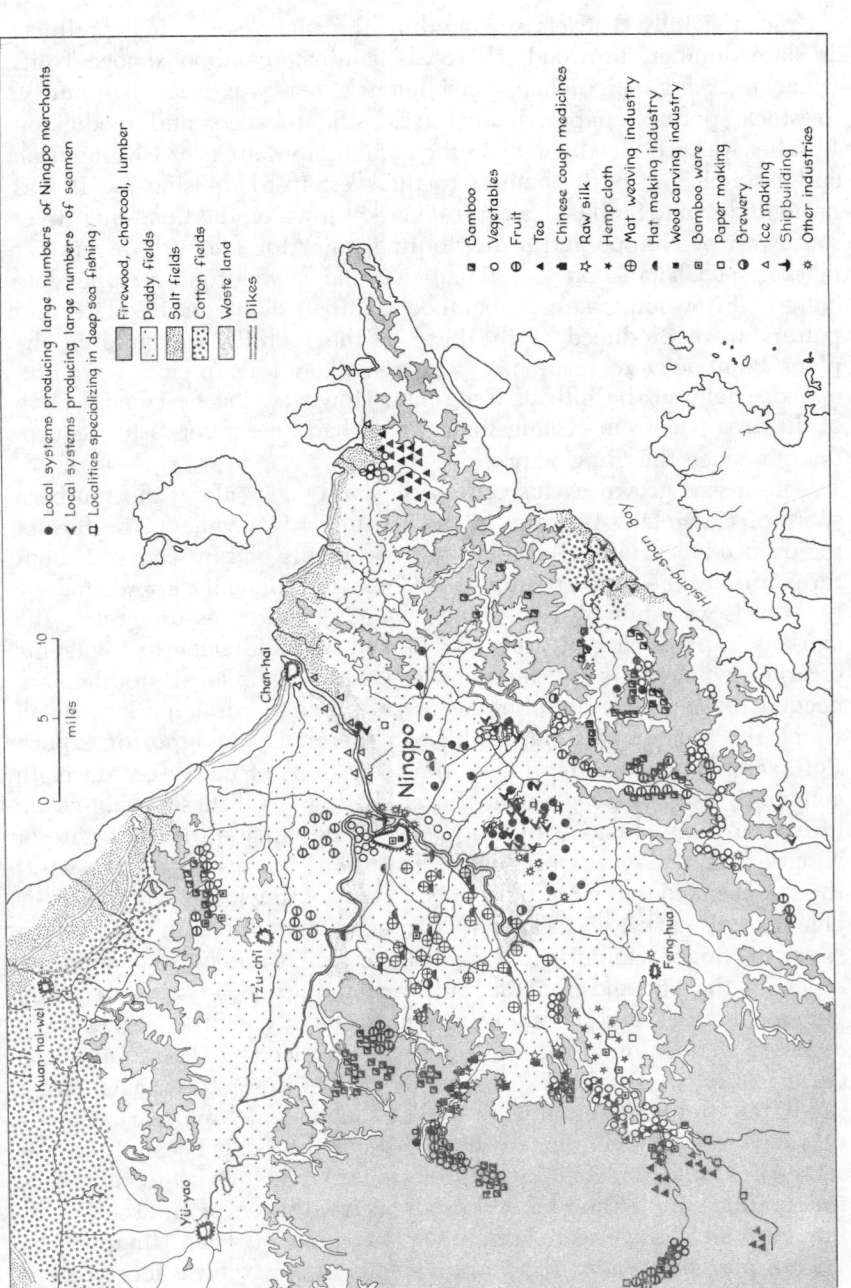

MAP 7. LOCAL SPECIALIZATION IN THE NINGPO AREA, LATE NINETEENTH CENTURY

From the hilly districts surrounding the plain came such products as slate, lumber, firewood, charcoal, bamboo, bamboo shoots, fruits (peaches, *yang-mei*, lichee, persimmons), tea, wax-tree oil, poultry, livestock, pottery, paper, hemp cloth, silk, tobacco, and medicines. Lumber was produced chiefly in the mountainous areas of Ch'eng *hsien* and Hsin-ch'ang, both counties to the west in Shao-hsing *fu*. It was brought down to Shih-ch'i, a central market town on the Feng-hua River southwest of Ningpo and a distributing point for lumber, via upriver markets at Ch'üan-k'ou and Hsiao-ch'i, and it was then reshipped to Ningpo. Firewood, charcoal, bamboo, bamboo shoots, fruits, slate, and pottery were produced at the base of the foothills surrounding the plain. Bamboo ware, tea, paper, wax-tree oil, and hemp cloth were produced chiefly in the hills of Feng-hua. However, the best hemp cloth of the area was from Hsiang-shan, which had been famous for its production since the Sung period.[65]

Cotton was grown exclusively in the sandy soils along the southern shore of Hangchow Bay and in the Ta-sung River valley. The former region produced annually about 500,000 piculs of raw cotton (about three-fifths of the cotton produced in Chekiang), of which approximately two-thirds was spun locally.[66] The remaining third was brought to the markets in producing districts and bulked by middlemen or by agents of urban wholesalers for shipment to Ningpo. Thus local products not needed for local consumption were collected in rural markets, from which the greater part was sent on to the city of Ningpo for export. For example, in 1886 there were fourteen kinds of native cotton cloth commonly used by people in and around Ningpo. Of these, *p'eng-ch'iao* (from Yü-yao), *wang-ch'un-ch'iao* (produced outside the west gate of Ningpo), and *t'u-pu* (a product of Yin *hsien*) were sold by dealers at the market held every ten days outside the south gate of Ningpo; their chief export market was Taiwan.[67] Straw mats produced in the western sector of Ningpo's hinterland were collected at Huang-kung-lin and then sent on to the city; and from the southwestern part of Yin *hsien*, rice, silk, bamboo, lumber, and *pei-mu* were sent to the city via the market town of Hsiao-ch'i. In Feng-hua, hill products produced in Hsin-ch'ang and Ch'eng *hsien* were sold in a market at Ch'üan-k'ou; straw mats, straw shoes, tea, and hemp cloth were sold at Chiang-k'ou; and marine products were sold at Shun-hu. In the middle of the Yung Basin, Ta-ch'iao served as a collection and distribution center for such local goods as marine products from Shun-hu, hill products from the west and south, and iron farm tools; these were largely sold to merchants from Ningpo.[68]

Transport and commodity flows. The city of Ningpo was located centrally and was open to communication from all directions. Needless to say, water transportation assumed great importance in this area (see Map 1). The Yung River was deep enough to let large ocean-going junks sail upstream to the wharves along Chiang-hsia (see Map 6). In the Yü-yao River there were constant streams of lorchas plying between Chiang-hsia and Ts'ao-o. From the western plains, sampans sailed to the wharves near the west gate via two canals—Hsi-t'ang and Chung-t'ang. Small boats could enter the city freely through a sluice near the west gate. In similar fashion, sampans from the southwestern plains sailed to the south gate via the Nan-t'ang, and small boats went into the city through a sluice near the south gate. Sampans and rafts from farther south in Feng-hua county came to the wharves outside the east gates via the Feng-hua River and its tributaries. As these were shallow rivers that tended to dry up, however, boats often preferred to break their journey and switch to canals, especially the Nan-t'ang, which ran parallel to the Feng-hua River. From the eastern plain, sampans plied to the wharves near the east gates via three canals—Ch'ien-t'ang, Chung-t'ang, and Hou-t'ang.[69]

Thus, waterways extended out from Ningpo like the spokes of a wheel. Along them, flowing toward the hub, came the major commercial products of the region and transit goods destined for export. From the northwest came cotton, P'ing-shui green tea, Shao-hsing wine, medicinal *mai-tung*, tobacco, livestock, and silk cocoons; from the west came straw mats, fuel, bamboo, rice, and vegetables; from the southwest, south, and southeast came silk cocoons, silk, medicinal *pei-mu*, lumber, tea, fruits, oil, bamboo products, marine products, paper, and livestock; from the east came rice, fuel, fishnets, embroidery, and fruits; finally, from the northeast came marine products from the Chusan archipelago and Hsiang-shan, livestock from Hsiang-shan and farther south in T'ai-chou *fu*, cotton from Chen-hai, and various imported goods from the coastal provinces as well as from overseas.[70] The commodities moving from Ningpo out toward the peripheries of its trading area flowed along the same spokelike waterways. For the greater part they consisted of agricultural and craft specialties of one directional sector of the region (e.g., mountain products from the southwest, marine products from the northeast, or straw mats, wine, and tea from the west) being redistributed to other sectors of the trading system, or of goods processed or manufactured in Ningpo and its suburbs. Apart from rice, wholly exogenous products—those imported into Ningpo from outside its hinterland in a form suitable for retailing—formed a small part of the commodities shipped from Ningpo for sale within its trading area.

Temporal aspects of integration. In terms of its economic functions, Ningpo in the nineteenth century counted as a regional city in the hierarchical model outlined elsewhere by Professor Skinner. It was ringed, at a distance along waterways of 20–25 kilometers, by six or seven local cities, three of which (Chen-hai; Tz'u-ch'i; and Feng-hua, together with its outlying commercial center Ta-ch'iao) were administrative cities, the remainder being large *chen*. Markets were held daily in most of these local cities, including at least one of the *chen* (Hsieh-p'u, situated due north of Ningpo).

All of the central places that were economically oriented to one of these local cities, or to Ningpo directly, counted as central, intermediate, or standard market towns, as defined by Skinner. In market towns at all three levels as of ca. 1875, the market convened only every few days, according to fixed schedules specified in terms of the *hsün*, the 10-day segments into which the lunar month was divided. The most common periodicity of these rural markets was twice per *hsün*, e.g., 1–6, which amounted to six times per lunar month (i.e., on the 1st, 6th, 11th, 16th, 21st, and 26th). However, all frequencies from once per *hsün* to five times per *hsün* (i.e., every other day) occurred in Ningpo's hinterland.

As Skinner has demonstrated for China generally, these schedules were not simply distributed among markets in such a way that each shared the same schedule with as few of its neighbors as possible. Rather, the schedules of lower-level markets were set to minimize conflict with the higher-level markets with which they had economic transactions. We may illustrate this synchronization with reference to the plains west of Ningpo in 1877. At that time three central market towns coordinated the collection and distribution of commercial goods within this sector. One, Mai-mien-ch'iao on the Chung-t'ang, dominated the direct route to Ningpo's west gate. Another, Shih-ch'i on the Nan-t'ang, held the corresponding position vis-à-vis the city's south gate. The third, Huang-kung-lin, lay equidistant from the other two on canals linking it with both. All other market towns between the city and the western hills held standard or intermediate markets commercially oriented to one or more of these three central markets. The notable fact is that every one of the lower-level markets within each of those three central marketing systems maintained a schedule that dovetailed with that of the central market in question. Thus, the ten markets oriented wholly or in part to Huang-kung-lin, whose schedule was 3–7–10, had the following schedules (in approximate clockwise order of the towns around Huang-kung-lin): 2–8, 2–8, 4–8, 1–5, 4–8, 4–8, 5–9, 2–5–8, 1–6, and 4–9. Mai-mien-ch'iao, like Huang-kung-lin, had a 3–7–10 schedule, whereas

Shih-ch'i had a 3–5–9 schedule; and as expected, the only lower-level markets that included 7 or 10 in their schedules were oriented to Shih-ch'i and not to the other two central markets. Moreover, since all three central market towns convened on the 3d, not a single lower-level market on the western plains was held on that date.

Coordinated scheduling of this kind, whereby the central market town monopolized three of the possible ten market days per *hsün*, made it possible for economic specialists to carry out hierarchically ordered transactions in the desired sequence without costly delays and with no need to be in more than one place on any given day. Purchasing agents, itinerant traders, and even shopkeepers ordering stock from wholesalers in the central market town benefited from this intrasystemic synchronization. For that matter, so did such professionals of the marketplace as brokers, measurers, and weighers, and even revenue agents. Central-marketing systems of the kind described overlapped with one another in the sense that most intermediate markets were oriented to more than one central market town. Similarly, most standard markets received commodities from and shipped commodities to two or three intermediate markets. Even central market towns that were only indirectly linked to Ningpo often had a choice in transactions. Traders in Huang-kung-lin, for instance, could obtain supplies from Ningpo via the south gate and Shih-ch'i market, or via the west gate and Mai-mien-ch'iao market. The spatial and temporal dovetailing of market systems enhanced competition and facilitated price integration throughout Ningpo's trading system.

For the peasant, the basic rhythm of life was set by the schedule of the market town where he shopped and sold his products—typically a five-day week. The more complex activities of traders and other economic specialists were normally shaped within the ten-day cycle of the lunar *hsün*. The annual cycle of agricultural production inevitably had repercussions for traders and artisans as well as agriculturalists. Quite apart from annual fairs, special markets were held on a seasonal basis. For instance, at the beginning of each harvest season a mowers' labor market was held at Tung-ching Shih in Ningpo's eastern suburbs. The Nan-kuo Shih outside the south gate was only one of several markets that added an extra market day each *hsün* during the harvest season. During the fifth month, a special straw-mat market was held in Huang-kung-lin on a two-per-*hsün* schedule.

The terms of credit, too, were fixed according to the lunar calendar. Short-term credit was usually calculated in multiples of ten days or months. Particular dates were customary in different businesses. For example, the accounts of medicine collectors with wholesalers were traditionally settled on the 14th day of the lunar month; *shan-huo-hang*, those who collected only in Chekiang, settled accounts every month, whereas *li-hao*, who ranged more widely, settled accounts every three months. Longer-term credit was almost always set in terms of the three segments into which the fiscal year was divided, marked off by the festivals of Tuan-wu (5th day of the fifth month), Chung-ch'iu (15th day of the eighth month), and the New Year (1st day of the first month). As a general rule, customers were expected to make payments on their debts with retail shops before each of these festivals, and most retailers settled their accounts with wholesalers at these three times of the lunar year. This was true, for instance, in the medicine business and was specified in the regulations of the Wen-chou Druggists Guild in Ningpo. These conventions meant that the money market followed a characteristic rhythm, growing tight before each of the three festivals. One of these festivals always counted as most important for credit purposes; in most parts of the region it was the New Year, but in Yü-yao business circles it was Chung-ch'iu.[71] To meet the needs of debtors, the *ch'ien-chuang* banks offered a special type of short-term loan known as *chin-lung-chi*, issued only on the 20th day of the twelfth month, a few days before debts had to be settled.

The structure of credit throughout Ningpo's trading system culminated in the guildhall of the city's *ch'ien-chuang* banks. There two meetings were held daily, one at 9 A.M. to set exchange and interest rates for the day, the other at 4 P.M. to clear accounts and settle differences in cash. This daily cycle within the city was matched by a monthly cycle in which money orders drawn on Ningpo banks by bankers and traders in other cities and towns were paid up with interest.

The regional economy. As a total system, Ningpo and its regional hinterland were far from self-sufficient. Although more than half of the Ningpo Plain was subject to sporadic water shortages, its paddy fields yielded in an average year one million piculs of rice (15 piculs = 1 ton). This amount, however, was far from sufficient to feed the overcrowded city and its maximal hinterland. In fact, most of the locally produced rice was distributed by Ningpo wholesalers to outlying, non-self-sufficient areas in Ting-hai, Feng-hua, Ch'eng *hsien*, and Hsin-ch'ang, and the local population was supplied with imported rice, most often from the Middle Yangtze region via Soochow, but also from the southern coastal regions, Cochin-China, and Siam. Such goods as lumber, iron, copper, dyestuffs, and livestock were also imported in large quantities from outside the region. Indeed, most of Ningpo's well-known specialties—ships, inlaid furniture, wood carvings, lacquer ware, paper, Chin-

Ningpo and Its Hinterland

hua cured hams, Shao-hsing wine, and P'ing-shui green tea—were either the processed products of imported raw materials or transit goods. The chief exceptions were the marine products produced around the Chusan archipelago. Even in Sung times, Ningpo fish glue circulated far away in Hupeh, and in Hangchow there were 200-odd fishmongers who dealt in dried or salted fish from Chusan.[72] In the Ch'ing period, marine products from Chusan found good markets throughout the Middle and Lower Yangtze regions and as far afield as Kwangtung.[73]

In a previous section treating the division of labor within particular industries, we described the complex arrangements whereby deep-sea fishing was organized and financed and the fish brought to Ningpo for processing and marketing. Let us conclude this section with another example of economic arrangements within an industry concentrated in one directional sector of Ningpo's hinterland, namely cotton.[74] In the early twentieth century, some 4.2 to 4.3 million piculs of cotton were marketed annually throughout the empire, of which approximately 2.9 million piculs were produced in the Lower Yangtze region. The major collection points in the region were Shanghai, including P'u-tung (1,300,000 piculs); T'ung-chou (1,000,000); and Ningpo (600,000). Most of the 600,000 piculs collected annually at Ningpo was exported, including 170,000 to 180,000 to Shanghai. As stated earlier, this cotton was produced chiefly along the southern shore of Hangchow Bay. In the eighth lunar month, the busiest month for farmers and also the time when cotton was harvested, farmers took this cotton in small lots to a nearby market in the early morning and sold it to small local middlemen (*hsiao hua-hang* or *hua-fang*). Since the harvest season was short and peasants were eager for cash, it was a buyers' market. Middlemen occasionally went directly to farmsteads to purchase the cotton. In either case, the cotton was weighed, appraised by the merchants, and packed. Then some of the middlemen sent these goods on commission to Shanghai through members of their profession in Ningpo. Others, however, notably those whose loans had to be repaid by the Chung-ch'iu festival, would sell to the *hua-hang* (commission merchants) in Ningpo, charging a slight commission and bearing the freight costs themselves. Sometimes the commission merchants in Ningpo sent agents to the cotton-producing districts and purchased directly from the farmers. Some of them dealt in futures, but these were a small minority. When the cotton arrived at Ningpo, the commission merchants might put it on the market immediately, but if market conditions were not then favorable, they preferred to store the cotton in warehouses to wait for a later rise in price. The commission merchants had their own *chiao-i-so* (commodity exchange), which operated its own warehouses. This exchange and its branches throughout the southeastern coastal area acted as commission agents for the cotton trade centered on Ningpo. In addition, many of the commission merchants had their own branch shops in Shanghai and made full use of the information on market conditions they gathered there to engage in speculation.

The situation was much the same in the case of the marketing of native cotton cloth. According to Nyok-Ching Tsur,[75] rural householders on market days took the cloth they had woven to middlemen's shops situated in one of the suburban marketplaces. The middlemen sold the accumulated goods to commission merchants in the city, who exported them to the textile merchants of Soochow and Shanghai.

In general, wholesalers and commission agents in Ningpo effectively controlled prices of both cotton and cotton textiles. In the last analysis, however, they were dependent for credit on loans from the *ch'ien-chuang* banks, which exercised ultimate financial control over the whole marketing system of Ningpo.[76] (In this connection, see also the case of dealers in marine products discussed earlier.)

Ningpo and China's Economic Integration

I have already called attention to the fact that in the early eighteenth century, interurban business transactions among macroregional economies were dominated by entrepreneurs from a very few regional systems—most notably three or four coastal subregions in Fukien and Kwangtung, Hui-chou prefecture in Anhwei, and a restricted area of Shansi. *Intra*group business dealings among Fukienese traders, among Hui-chou merchants, and among Shansi bankers were essential strands in the articulation of China's semiclosed regional economies. Ningpo merchants and financiers joined this select company toward the end of the imperial era—the last historical example of an intriguing traditional phenomenon. In this final section I explore some of the reasons for their extraregional success as entrepreneurs and relate it to the preceding description of Ningpo's development as an entrepôt and as a regional city. Why Ningpo? And why did the breakthrough of Ningpo entrepreneurs come when it did, during the century beginning around 1780?

As I emphasized above, the development of Ningpo's hinterland into a closely articulated and commercialized regional economy was a long-term, gradual process. The first large-scale waterworks were constructed in the T'ang period, and the last of the drainage canals that converted the swamps south of the city into paddy fields were built in the nineteenth century. Though the region's administrative cities all existed by the Sung period, a mature central-place hierarchy developed only during the Ch'ing, and new market towns were springing up even as the nineteenth century dawned. It would appear to be crucial that throughout this millennium of regional development Ningpo was an important port of trade. That is, regional development was conditioned throughout by the fact that the regional city was also an entrepôt. As a result, the economic institutions that evolved and the dynamics that developed differed from what they might otherwise have been. What was distinctive about them and how did they facilitate the extraregional expansion of Ningpo entrepreneurs?

To begin with, Ningpo's longstanding ties with exogenous markets encouraged territorial specialization as its regional economy evolved. The early development of navigable waterways centered on a city with far-flung overseas and coastal trade routes reduced to a minimum the transport costs that did so much to inhibit commercial specialization in premodern agrarian societies. As a result, the comparative advantages of climate, soil, topography, natural flora and fauna, and simply location with respect to the city-centered transport grid could be translated with exceptional efficiency into local specializations geared to demand in the central city. As the regional economy matured, then, it emerged as one that was extraordinarily commercialized, internally differentiated in a complex yet integrated manner, and exceptionally centralized. These characteristics imply a relatively high proportion of economic specialists in other than extractive industries, and within their ranks a well-developed division of labor and an entrepreneurial orientation.

Whereas Ningpo's entrepôt functions were dominated during the formative centuries by alien specialists, the development of its regional economy was in the hands of local people. That developing economy was an exceptional training ground for entrepreneurs and a breeding ground for institutional innovation, I suggest, precisely because it was conditioned by the entrepôt role of its regional city. To be specific, business developments within Ningpo's trading system witnessed extraordinary entrepreneurial corporate activity by lineages, the emergence of firms with branches in different cities and towns, widespread recourse to partnerships, an institutionalized differentiation between investors and managers, internal diversification of firms, the founding of private letter agencies, and, of course, the development of sophisticated credit and banking institutions. All these features stood Ningpo entrepreneurs in good stead when they extended their operations abroad.

The Ningpo region was one of the few in China where most of the countryside was dominated by strong lineages. Single-lineage villages were not uncommon, and marketing communities and other intervillage systems were often dominated by one or two powerful lineages. The precise nature of the interrelation between lineage strength and the fact that the region developed in the shadow of Ningpo qua entrepôt is obscure, but one may conjecture that lineages benefiting from commercial opportunities were enabled to mobilize the capital and manpower needed to build irrigation works and reclaim land. At any rate, well-endowed lineages in the Ningpo region early mobilized their resources to educate their brightest young men to compete in the imperial examinations. However, since fewer than one in twenty passed any given quota examination, successful lineages inevitably had to contend with many failures. In a developing economy such as that in the immediate hinterland of Ningpo, many thwarted scholars turned to business. One of the first successful Ningpo merchants outside the region was Sun Ch'un-yang, who left Ningpo for Soochow around 1600 after failing the provincial examination. There he established a prosperous business that eventually had six departments devoted to particular kinds of imported goods.[77] In any case, by the eighteenth century many lineages had developed strategies for setting up their talented young men in business in towns and local cities within the region, or in Ningpo itself. As the land filled up, lineages increasingly invested their corporate capital as well as their manpower in business enterprises. Jones (1972, pp. 84–85) underlines the subsequent importance of these patterns in her account of the Ningpo success story in Shanghai. Dominant economic power within the large Ningpo community in Shanghai lay with members of two localized branches of the Fang lineage in Chen-hai county. The financial backing of the home lineage was vital to their reputation and success in Shanghai. And the expanding Fang business empire in Shanghai and other cities could recruit personnel from among lineage mates who had already been tested and tempered in Fang enterprises in the cities and towns of the Ningpo region.

It is notable that the Fang lineage of Chen-hai had invested much of its corporate funds in urban enterprises, both commercial and financial, and that individual families within it owned other businesses in Ningpo, Chen-hai, and various towns within the region. Such urban investment was by no means exceptional within Ningpo's trading system. A prominent example of another form of investment is that of Feng Hsiao-lien, the head of a wealthy family in Tz'u-ch'i county, who owned most of the firms and shops on several riverside business streets in Ningpo's east-

Ningpo and Its Hinterland

ern suburbs.[78] Supervision of these lucrative properties was entrusted to managers, a pattern that was commonplace in this highly differential economic system.[79] We have already noted the tendency within the *ch'ien-chuang* banking business for owners to be inactive, relying on the integrity and skill of their managers. The latter were selected according to relevant merit from among those who had shown their mettle in more lowly positions within that line of business, and for reasons of accountability they were normally chosen from among the owners' *t'ung-hsiang* fellows.

These and other special features of business organization attest to the impressive scale of many enterprises. Partnerships were common among Ningpo merchants and bankers because the optimal scale in many lines of business required more capital than the average wealthy family could muster. The establishment of branches by successful firms was closely related to the fleshing out of the central-place hierarchy during the eighteenth and nineteenth centuries. As scores of new standard markets were founded, there developed a need for expanded services and higher-order functions in the towns already extant, and this need was at least partially filled through the establishment of branches by enterprising wholesalers, pawnshops, and money shops in Ningpo and some of the local cities. Many of the better capitalized firms experimented with diversification to secure either their supply of stocks or regular outlets for their products. As the *ch'ien-chuang* banking network developed in the late eighteenth century, a number of trading firms established their own banks.

Large-scale enterprises also increased in the late eighteenth and early nineteenth centuries as Ningpo entrepreneurs began to establish firms directly related to the port's overseas trade. In long-distance shipping, for instance, Ningpo men got their start crewing on ships owned and operated by Fukienese and Soochow merchants. Not until the late eighteenth century did some experienced Ningpo crewmen branch out on their own with capital put up by investors; but thereafter Ningpo merchants rapidly expanded their stake in the growing shipping business. Ningpo-owned ships were wholly manned by natives of the region; though wages were low, officers and crews were allowed to carry their own cargo in the hold and dispose of it as they wished.

The first private letter agencies were said to have originated in Ningpo. Possibly commercial firms that delivered their clients' letters along with their own eventually developed the service into a sideline. Routes were most likely initiated along the waterways linking Ningpo to its local cities, but in any case interurban postal service was extended to

Shanghai and other extraregional cities as Ningpo entrepreneurs captured a larger share of Ningpo's coastal trade.[80]

Doubtless the most important asset of the Ningpo entrepreneurs who established themselves in cities outside the region was the *ch'ien-chuang* form of banking, with its sophisticated transfer-tael system and clearinghouse procedures. The precise antecedents of the various elements of this institution are moot and need not concern us here, but it seems reasonably certain that the *ch'ien-chuang* system was developed in Ningpo by Ningpo natives during the very decades (1760's–1820's) when (1) the regional economy was approaching maturity with a full-fledged hierarchy of functionally differentiated economic central places, and (2) Ningpo entrepreneurs began seriously to break into the city's entrepôt trade as shippers, shipping agents, importers, and exporters. It could be said that Ningpo entrepreneurs as a class, having completed the economic exploitation of their region, were now turning their surplus energy, capital, and manpower to the city's extraregional trade.[81] Was it the new needs and demands of this group during a fresh phase of Ningpo's double role as entrepôt and regional center that stimulated the refinement, extension, and consolidation of the *ch'ien-chuang* banking system?

Whatever the cause, the last piece in the success formula of the Ningpo entrepreneur fell into place just as the departure of native sons to try their hand at business elsewhere began to change from a trickle to nearby cities into a systematic exodus directed to cities of the Lower Yangtze region in seemingly direct proportion to those cities' economic potential. As the coastal trade expanded during the half century prior to 1842, Shanghai captured an increasing proportion of the growing volume at the expense of other Lower Yangtze ports, Ningpo included. And it was to Shanghai that the largest and most systematically organized stream of Ningpo migrants flowed.

It is said that by the end of the eighteenth century several thousand Ningpo merchants had settled in Shanghai; and in 1797 the Ningpo Guild (*Ssu-ming kung-so*) was established there as a native-place association for all immigrants from Ningpo's commercial hinterland. A decade or so later, the Che-Ning Hui-kuan was established in Shanghai as a guild for Ningpo shipping agents engaged in the northern coastal trade. By the time Shanghai was opened as a treaty port, Ningpo natives had gained control of the Shanghai Money Trade Guild (*Shanghai ch'ien-yeh kung-so*). The success story of the Ningpo *pang* "clique" in treaty-port Shanghai has been well told by Susan Mann Jones.[82] Suffice it to say here that, as Shanghai rose to become the central metropolis of the entire Lower Yangtze region and the leading entrepôt of the empire, Ningpo merchants consolidated their control of the city's economy.

The financial power and commercial control exercised by natives of Ningpo at Shanghai facilitated their expansion not only to other cities of the Lower Yangtze—as of the third quarter of the nineteenth century, major Ningpo "colonies" were to be found in Shao-hsing-fu, Hangchow, Hu-chou-fu, Soochow, Chen-chiang-fu, and Nanking—but also to wherever Shanghai's growing commercial importance was directly felt. Within China, Ningpo people settled in major commercial cities in the Middle and Upper Yangtze (e.g., Hankow, Sha-shih, I-ch'ang-fu, and Chungking), in seaports to the south (Canton, Swatow, Amoy, Taipei, Tan-shui, Foochow, Wen-chou-fu, and T'ai-chou-fu), and in the North (Chiao-chou, Chefoo, Tientsin, and Mukden).[83] Overseas they went as far as Japan, the Philippines, Cochin-China, Singapore, Sumatra, and Ceylon.[84]

In the nineteenth century, Ningpo businessmen abroad were noted for their "clannishness" and fierce regional loyalty. In a characteristic phrase of the local patois, they referred to themselves as *a-la t'ung-hsiang-che*, "we fellows of common origin."[85] It was said that a Ningpo man of power—whether a comprador, a bank manager, a shipping magnate, or simply a shopkeeper or ship's officer—never failed to employ fellow natives. In fact, preferences followed the usual concentric circles of particularistic loyalties that prevailed in Chinese society. Recruitment to Ningpo enterprises outside the region displayed a preference first for kinsmen (sons and nephews first, then other lineage mates), then for others from the same native place narrowly defined, then for those from the same county, and finally for persons native to other parts of the Ningpo region. Jones notes that the base of recruitment tended to broaden in the course of the nineteenth century, with the most successful entrepreneurs in the early period strongly favoring close kinsmen. One of the functions of native-place associations was job placement for immigrants from Ningpo. In time, "prominent businessmen from Ningpo ... established themselves as [guarantors] who could contract with an apprentice from Ningpo seeking employment in any trade, and serve as bondsmen responsible for financial losses in his behalf. Where this kind of bonding (*pao*) was deemed unnecessary, a simple introduction (*chien*) was readily provided."[86] It is noteworthy that when the number of Ningpo entrepreneurs in a city was insufficient to warrant separate organization, still wider circles in the *t'ung-hsiang* hierarchy were resorted to. Strictly Ningpo guilds were organized as far afield as

Peking, Hankow, and Canton, but in many cities (e.g., Chungking and Foochow) Ningpo traders joined with those from other parts of Chekiang to form Che-Ning Hui-kuan or Che-chiang Hui-kuan; moreover, in a few cities in Chihli and Manchuria the level at which Ningpo merchants organized was expanded to include the four adjacent provinces of Kiangsu, Anhwei, Chekiang, and Kiangsi (known as San-chiang Hui-kuan, Anhwei and Kiangsu being counted together as Kiangnan, the former province that included them both).

Successful emigrants were expected to expand their family estates back home, to endow their lineages, and to invest in community property in their native places. A high proportion appear to have done so, and many of the successful also retired to their native places, having ensured the continuity of their businesses abroad by grooming kinsmen or fellow natives for management. These normative arrangements sharpened the aspirations of other young men in the emigrant's lineage and hometown and, in fact, strengthened both the local systems and the extraregional business. Family and lineage estates back home were "often the key to remaining solvent during crises in the business world."[87] Many of the most successful early emigrants were from Chenhai (most notably from the Fang, Li, and Yeh lineages) and Tz'u-ch'i, and other successful emigrant lineages were also found in Feng-hua and even Yü-yao. But as the Ningpo diaspora became a flood during the nineteenth century, it was particularly in Yin *hsien* that local systems came to specialize in the cultivation of commercial and financial talent for export. Their location is indicated on Map 1, and a comparison with Map 7 shows that these emigrant communities were heavily concentrated in that portion of the southern plain that was last to be drained and brought under cultivation and last to be integrated into the regional economy, as evidenced by the late introduction of markets. To the very end, local-system specialization developed in relation to the timing of opportunities in the interrelated sequence of internal and external development.

In their nineteenth-century expansion outside their native region, Ningpo entrepreneurs put to good use all the institutions and business practices that had proved advantageous in their consolidation of economic control within the region during the eighteenth century. *Ch'ien-chuang* banks spread wherever Ningpo merchants settled, and the transfer-tael system was adapted to meet the needs of a vastly expanded urban system. Procedures for recruitment, socialization, and selection of employees that had been developed by firms in Ningpo were simply extended to another level by Ningpo firms in Shanghai. The establish-

Ningpo and Its Hinterland

ment of branches was favored as a means of firm expansion. For instance, Tung Yung-fu, great-grandson of a man by the name of Tung Ti-lin who had migrated from Tz'u-ch'i to Shanghai around 1800, opened branches of his successful bank in Hangchow and Hankow as well as in Shanghai and Ningpo.[88] Diversification was almost universally practiced by successful Ningpo entrepreneurs. Li Yeh-t'ing of Chen-hai, a prominent pioneer in the shipping business, made his fortune in the coastal trade based in Shanghai, importing beans and oils from northern ports in exchange for lumber from the Southeast Coast. He then invested part of these profits in banking.[89] The private letter agencies that originated in Ningpo also played an important role in the expansion of Ningpo business. Ningpo people were heavy investors in agencies of this sort as new branches or new firms were established in commercial cities elsewhere in the Lower Yangtze region and farther afield.[90] By the 1870's, networks of private letter agencies linked all cities within each regional urban system, and long-distance service paralleled the major routes of interregional trade.

Although later chapters in the saga of the Ningpo entrepreneurs involve their adaptation to steamships, modern banks (*yin-hang*), the telegraph, and a national postal system, it is clear that their role in forging stronger economic links among the cities of the Lower Yangtze region and between that regional economy and its neighbors was being carried out in classic traditional form prior to the onset of the modern era. I have tried to suggest that this expansion rested on institutions and dynamics peculiar to Ningpo's regional trading system and that it occurred just as that system's internal economic frontier was exhausted and just as the system of cities in the Lower Yangtze region was undergoing a profound realignment.

Market Towns and Waterways: The County of Shang-hai from 1480 to 1910

MARK ELVIN

> Wheeled transport is not used in South Kiangsu, and the roads and bridges are quite unfitted for it.
> —British Naval Staff Intelligence Division, *A Handbook of China Proper* (1917)

The peninsula that juts out into the sea south of the Yangtze River, north of the Ch'ien-t'ang River, and east of Lake T'ai was originally a swamp. It was only as a result of extensive hydraulic engineering and the building of a seawall along its eastern edge that it was made habitable and productive. Once this had been achieved, it rapidly became one of the richest areas in China.*

Economic progress in the region was directly connected with the intricate network of waterways that covered it. By the Southern Sung, if not somewhat earlier, these waterways supplied irrigation water for a high-yield agriculture and served as the means of communication for a flourishing waterborne commerce.[1] The silting up of a river could seal the fate of a great city. Thus Ch'ing-lung (which lay near present-day Ch'ing-p'u) was a center of international trade in Sung times, but as the Wu-sung and Ch'ing-lung rivers shrank, and with them its access to the sea, it had to yield preeminence to Shanghai on the bank of the widening Huang-p'u. By Ming times Ch'ing-lung had sunk to a mere market town.[2]

---

* Comments by Professor G. William Skinner on some of the materials I had collected were the starting point of this essay and, though he should not be held responsible for what I have done with his ideas, it is fair to say that without the stimulus of his insights it would never have been written. I am also grateful to the participants in the Wentworth conference for the kindly and constructive way in which they criticized my preliminary draft. For a number of specific suggestions and corrections I am much indebted to Professors F. W. Mote, Arthur F. Wright, Lien-sheng Yang, and Shiba Yoshinobu.

Thanks are due to Cambridge University Library for permission to reproduce part of a Chinese manuscript map in their possession, to Dr. Eugene Wu of the Harvard-Yenching Institute for copying material unavailable in Britain for me, to my former colleague Bill Forsyth for advice on the maps, and to Dr. Greta Scott of Cambridge University Library for constant help.

This shifting landscape was characteristic of the area. In the words of the British naval handbook for Kiangsu, "there is not a seasonal flood but brings about modifications to the existing topography."[3] It is not easy, therefore, to reconstruct a detailed picture of this delta land in past centuries. Old maps that survive suggest a substantially, even startlingly, different pattern from the present one.[4]

We may be confident, however, that the general nature of the region has not changed much since late Sung times. An idea of the main features may be had from Figure 1, which reproduces part of a mid-nineteenth-century manuscript map of the county capitals and military posts in Kiangnan. Shanghai city is in the upper left and Ch'uan-sha and Nan-hui are in the upper and lower right, respectively. It is obvious to what

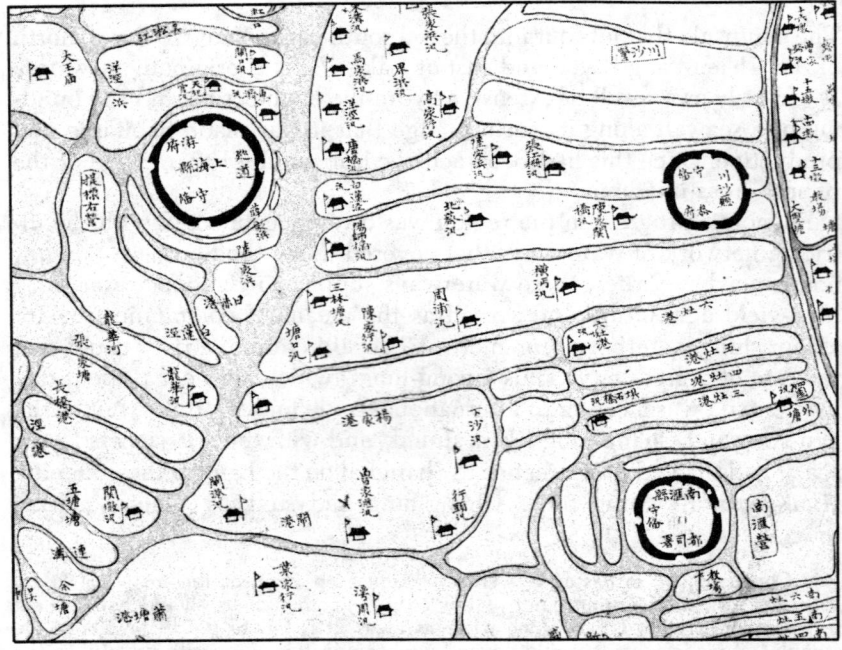

FIG. 1. WATERWAYS, WALLED CITIES, AND MILITARY STATIONS IN NORTHEASTERN SUNG-CHIANG PREFECTURE. Part of a mid-nineteenth-century manuscript map in the Cambridge University Library, MS Plans 636 (R). The main north-south river is the Huang-p'u. The unbroken dike at the right is the inner seawall that lies about a mile and a half inland from the coast. Market towns are not marked; but in more than half the cases shown here the military stations bear the same names as the towns in or near which they were situated.

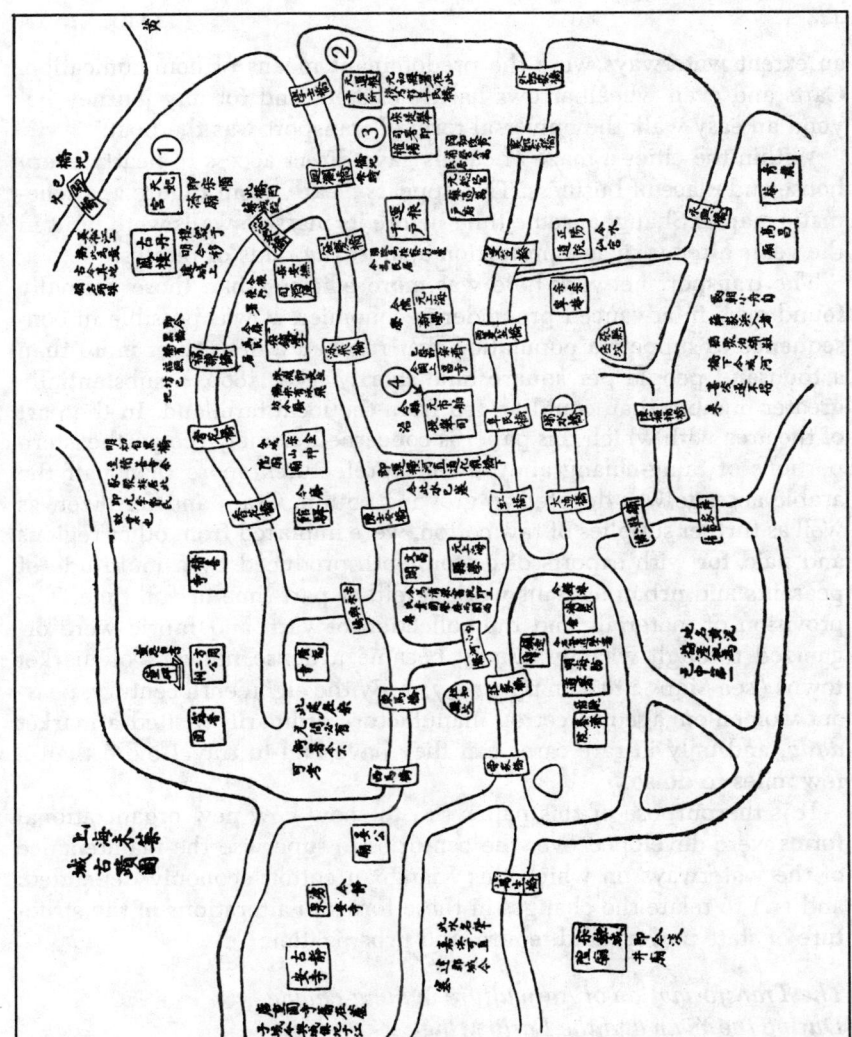

FIG. 2. SHANGHAI BEFORE THE BUILDING OF ITS WALLS. A map in *Hu-ch'eng pei-k'ao* (Notes on the city of Shanghai) by Chu Hua (late eighteenth century). The oblong cartouches contain the names of the principal bridges; the square ones, those of important temples and public buildings. Worthy of note in connection with the theme of this essay are (1) the Temple of the Queen of Heaven (*T'ien-fei kung*), (2) the Headquarters of the Grain Transport Battalion (*Yün-liang ch'ien-hu so*) of Yüan times, (3) the office of the Superintendent of Foreign Trade (*T'i-chü-ssu*) of Sung times, and (4) its counterpart (*Shih-po t'i-chü-ssu*) of Yüan times.

an extent waterways were the predominant means of communication. Carts and even wheelbarrows hardly existed, and for any journey beyond an easy walk the universal form of transport was the boat.[5]

Within the cities a maze of canals gave direct access to nearly every house and place of business. This appears clearly from Figure 2, a schematic map of Shanghai some time before its massive walls were built in the years after 1553 as a protection against the raids of pirates.[6]

The transport network here was more efficient than those normally found even in advanced premodern economies. It was possible in consequence to support a population that reached a density of more than a thousand people per square mile shortly after 1800, a substantially greater number than could be fed from the local farmland. In the part of the area with which this paper is concerned, namely the northeastern portions of Sung-chiang and Su-chou prefectures, more than half the arable acreage was devoted to growing cotton. Grain and fertilizer, as well as further supplies of raw cotton, were imported from other regions and paid for with exports of cotton cloth produced by a multitude of peasants and urban artisans working either part-time or full-time. The provision of materials and the collection of yarn and fabric were organized through what gradually became a dense network of market towns (see Maps 2 to 6 on pp. 470–71). By the eighteenth century, peasant women engaged in cotton manufacture ordinarily visited a market *daily*, and only in rare cases can they have had to travel more than a few miles to do so.

It is the purpose of this paper (1) to show how new organizational forms were developed over the centuries to supervise the maintenance of the waterways on which this Kiangnan cotton economy depended, and (2) to relate the changes in these forms to alterations in the structure of state power, land tenure, and urbanization.

The Transformation of Agriculture in Sung-chiang During the Yüan and the Early Ming

There were local variations in the character of agriculture in Sung-chiang. The western section, which lay on the border of the smaller lakes east of Lake T'ai, was low-lying and so easy to irrigate that a man and his wife could cultivate from 25 to 30 *mou* in a year. The eastern section, in which Shang-hai was situated and which extended topographically into the northeastern part of Su-chou, was relatively hilly; there a couple had to exert themselves to tend five *mou* of paddy.[7] The reason for this discrepancy was the varying ease of access to water, as is explained by a passage cited in Ku Yen-wu's *Documents Relating to the Advantageous*

Market Towns and Waterways

and Disadvantageous Characteristics of the Commanderies and Principates of the Empire.

Fields that have no access to creeks cannot be drained if flooded, and cannot be watered if dry. It is hard to bring manure to them and to remove the harvest. These fields are mostly owned by poor people in distressed circumstances who should be treated with compassion. Fields which abut on a creek, or lie along its length, are easy to irrigate when dry and easy to drain when flooded. Manure can easily be brought to them and the harvest can be easily taken away. These fields are mostly owned by rich and powerful persons.[8]

Where the land was difficult to water, or where proximity to the sea made it somewhat salty, it was more profitable to grow cotton than rice. After cotton was introduced late in the Sung period, it soon became the dominant crop throughout a belt that stretched from Ch'ang-shu and Chia-ting to Shang-hai. By the beginning of the Ch'ing dynasty, about 70 percent of the arable land in Shang-hai county was under cotton, as was about 90 percent of the land in Chia-ting.[9]

This change had implications for irrigation, as was indicated by the Chia-ting county gazetteer for the Wan-li reign period (1573–1619).

Our ancestors considered that water control was a major administrative concern. During the Cheng-te and Chia-ching reigns (1506–66) the effects of their efforts were still in evidence. At the present time 80 or 90 percent of the channels have silted up and disappeared. Those that remain are like the belts on clothing. People's lives therefore depend on cotton. The nature of cotton is such that it is best if its cultivation can be alternated with that of wet-field paddy, but in Chia-ting it is grown for several decades on end with no possibility of a change.[10]

There was thus a region of some size in which the problems of water conservancy were significantly different from those in the rest of southeastern China. It was in this general region and nowhere else (with one exception) that the late Ming institution of the dike administrator (*t'ang chang*) was found (see Map 1)[11]—a geographical correlation to whose possible significance we shall return later.

The Growth of a Commercial Rural-Urban Nexus

The development of cotton cultivation in Sung-chiang and Su-chou prefectures in the Ming period was accompanied by the expansion of both a rural and an urban textile industry. One reason for this growth was the combination of good natural conditions for the production of raw cotton with the availability of the sophisticated techniques of spinning and weaving perfected in the Su-chou silk industry. Another reason

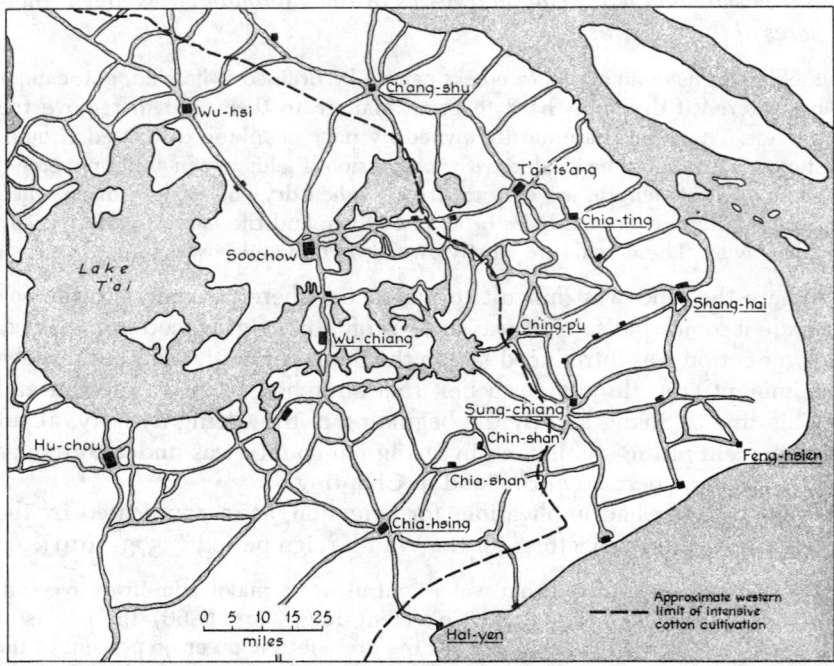

MAP 1. SOUTHEASTERN KIANGNAN, CA. 1600. Underlining indicates centers of administrative units in which the dike administrator system is known to have been in operation around 1600 (only Hsing-hua, off the map to the north, is not shown). The distribution of these centers suggests that both the need to drain Lake T'ai and the particular circumstances of the cotton belt may have played a part in the creation of the system.

was that the abnormally heavy burden of rents and taxes inflicted on the peasantry in this area made it hard for them to make ends meet from agriculture alone. Fiscal pressures drove them to supplement their incomes through the practice of subsidiary handicrafts.[12] The outcome was a commercialized rural society that depended for its existence on merchants and market towns where raw cotton, ginned cotton, cotton yarn, and cotton cloth, as well as basic foodstuffs, could be bought and sold.

The dependence of peasants who grew only cash crops upon the marketing system is illustrated by a passage in a late Ming gazetteer for Chia-ting: "Our county does not produce rice, but relies for its food upon other areas. When the summer wheat is reaching ripeness and the autumn crops are already rising, the boats of the merchants that come loaded with rice form an unbroken line.... If by any chance there were to be an outbreak of hostilities ... such that the city gates did not open

Market Towns and Waterways

for ten days, and the hungry people raised their voices in clamor, how could there fail to be riot and disorder?"[13] By the end of the Ming period, Kiangsu could only obtain enough food by relying on regular imports from the Middle Yangtze provinces.[14]

In similar fashion, farmers and their wives, pathetically short of working capital, could only spin and weave as a subsidiary occupation (unless they grew adequate cotton on their own fields) if there were merchants to buy the cotton crop when it came on the market in the autumn and then release it to them in small quantities throughout the year, buying their finished products in return. These merchants operated what were referred to as the "cotton cloth shops in the rural market towns" (*hsiang-chen chih pu-chuang*), and in some places there were also "farmer-merchants" (*nung-ku*) who "specialized in gathering cotton and cotton cloth and going as traders to sell it."[15] Probably the commonest system was that described by a late Ming gazetteer for Sung-chiang: "The old ladies of the countryside go to the market in the morning with their thread, exchange it there for raw cotton and come home. The next morning they go forth again with their thread, never wasting a moment."[16] The demand of the Sung-chiang textile industry for raw cotton was so great that extra supplies had to be shipped down the Grand Canal from Shantung, and down the Yangtze from Hupeh.[17]

A large part of the cotton cloth woven in Sung-chiang was sold in other parts of the empire, and the welfare of the prefecture was immediately affected by any drop in demand from distant provinces. Yeh Meng-chu, a Shang-hai scholar, spoke of this when writing of the terrible year 1641: "Half the profits which the people of Sung-chiang earn from trade depend upon weaving and spinning. Thus, with Shantung smitten by famine and rebellion, and Honan even more severely disrupted, the people in our region had to exchange their children to eat, or break up corpses and steam them. Since the cotton cloth merchants failed to come, the inhabitants of Sung-chiang could only stand and wait for death."[18] Each of the rich merchants who came to buy cloth or ginned cotton disposed of working capital that might amount to tens of thousands of taels. Shang-hai cotton cloth brokers treated them "as though they were princes or marquises."[19] A considerable network of local transport must have been needed to support the county capital as the hub of this interprovincial traffic.

The density of the local waterborne commerce concerned with the cotton trade may be inferred from a passage in the late Ming work *Routes by Water and Land*. Discussing how best to go from Chia-hsing to Sung-chiang, it says: "If you have no goods with you, do not hire a small boat. Go from Tung-shan-k'ou in a small vessel to Chia-shan, and there embark on a cotton yarn boat (*mien-sha ch'uan*) for Sung-chiang. One never thinks of taking a large boat."[20] Shanghai merchants who "went to other places in search of a sale" were called "waterborne traders" (*shui-k'o*).[21] Traffic with Shantung, Fukien, and Kwangtung was of course all by means of ships.

Wang T'ao, writing in 1875, thought that the native Shang-hai merchants had made their fortunes above all by shipping food to neighboring counties.[22] Water-conservancy projects must have been undertaken sometimes with the object of facilitating either this shipping or the cotton trade, though I have so far found no record that explicitly says so. One passage that is indirectly relevant is perhaps worth citing. It is from an early-sixteenth-century document quoted in the Shang-hai county gazetteer for the T'ung-chih reign period (1862–74).

> Hsin-ch'ang [in present day Nan-hui county] is a great market town near the seacoast. To the east lies Five Dragon Salt Mound; further east still are the various northern and southern Salt-boilers' creeks and the Lung-yu creek. The market town is placed about midway between them in a north-south direction. To its west is the Ma-lu creek, and the tidal flow comes in by it from the Huang-p'u and the Ch'ing-lung-p'u and reaches all these creeks. The latter irrigate a large number of farmers' fields, and merchants use them for the passage of salt boats, making a limitless profit. They are of great benefit to the southeast. Toward the end of the Cheng-te reign (1506–21) they had become silted up; only their outlines could be made out, and the tides were reduced to the barest trickle. Both merchants and commoners suffered from this for many a day. . . . In 1518 . . . the local man Ni Yung . . . was entrusted with the direction of this [dredging] project . . . and the work was finished in no more than a month. He [opened channels] for several tens of *li*. As a result, all was rich farmland as far as the eye could see. Merchant boats gathered in great numbers, and the peasants were happy in their livelihood, both relying on them [the creeks].[23]

Yeh Meng-chu's description of Shang-hai water conservancy in the seventeenth century makes it clear how important the waterways were as a means of transportation. He recalls, for instance, how as a boy he had seen "the seagoing vessels with their flapping sails" plying back and forth along a river that later silted up, and speaks of the difficulties faced by local boatmen in finding alternative routes when several of the waterways east of the Huang-p'u became choked with sand and overgrown with reeds.[24] It seems reasonable to conclude that the maintenance of the commercialized rural economy and of the vital connections between country and city, and between city and city, depended to a high degree upon the maintenance of the water routes.

The Late Ming System of Water Control in Shang-hai County

It seems that water control in Shang-hai county and the surrounding area went through three main phases. During the fifteenth century and part of the sixteenth, general direction was given by agricultural officials (*chih-nung kuan*), sometimes termed "water officials" (*shui-kuan*). They commanded the conscripted administrators who ran the tax-collection organization known as the "cantons and tithings" (*li-chia*). In the late fifteenth century a specialized water-control version of the *li-chia* began to develop, displacing the regular system in the sixteenth. At the same time the role of the agricultural officials in hydraulic works diminished, and most such officials had their posts abolished in 1559. In the first half of the seventeenth century the weaknesses of the new conscript administrator system were exploited by a semicriminal group called "mud men" (*ni-t'ou*), who set up a contracting system under which most of the actual work was done. Throughout the period various forms of ad hoc organization also appeared, and several officials suggested setting up a permanent professional force of maintenance workers (though this was never realized). Table 1 offers a simplified guide to the complexities of the more detailed discussion that follows.

Special agricultural officials at the prefectural and county level were first appointed for Sung-chiang and six adjacent prefectures in 1404, following the severe floods of the preceding year. According to the *Documents on Water Conservancy in Wu*, "every year, in the agricultural

TABLE 1. WATER CONTROL IN SHANG-HAI DURING THE FIFTEENTH AND SIXTEENTH CENTURIES

Administrative level	System			
	Agricultural officials	Conscripted administrators		Selected specialists
		General *li-chia*	Special *li-chia*	
Prefecture	Assistant prefect	—	—	—
County	Vice-magistrate	—	—	—
Division	—	Grain tax administrator	Dike administrator	Administrator of a thousand
District/Canton	—	Canton administrator	Annual overseer	Administrator of a hundred
Polder	—	Off-duty administrator	Polder administrator	—

off-season, the officials in charge of agriculture led the landowners and tenants in repairing the polders with earth."[25] In Su-chou, "the ditches and banks of a polder were the responsibility of the off-duty administrators (*p'ai-nien*), those of a district (*t'u*) of the canton administrators (*li-chang*). This was the warp of this system. Waterways requiring a hundred workers were the responsibility of the elders (*lao-jen*), those requiring a thousand workers of the grain tax administrators (*liang-chang*). This was the woof of this system."[26] The agricultural officials at the top were responsible for making regular inspections, for initiating projects where necessary and assisting with their organization, and for checking on results. Sometimes they selected the lower-level administrators, and rewarded the energetic and punished the lazy. Their planning powers included control over the erection of bridges, the planting of reeds (for fuel), the installation of bamboo fishtraps, the building of houses on piles driven into the streambed, and the mooring of boats, all of which might cause silting and obstruction.

The need for a specialized lower-level system for water-control administration soon made itself felt, and various experiments were tried. The institutional instability prevailing at this time is conveyed in an account of Wu-chiang county in Su-chou written by Su Chien toward the end of the fifteenth century.

During the Yung-lo reign (1403–24) all matters of water control were entrusted to the grain tax administrators, with supervisory control exercised by the officials. Now the duties of a grain tax administrator are confined to [promoting] successful farming and the collection of taxes. His attention has to be concentrated on these. In recent years dike administrators (*t'ang-chang*) have been established in addition, and also elders (*ch'i-lao*); but the dike administrators have been abolished again, and district administrators (*t'u-chang*) established. Subordinate officials have also been deputed to coordinate the grain tax administrators and the elders. There is confusion and there are numerous systems—"one state with three rulers" and "nine shepherds for every ten sheep." The common people lack any fixed purpose and have no idea whom to follow. . . . What is more, the selecting and guaranteeing of the elders and district administrators is all done by the grain tax administrators, from which one can tell what sort of people they are. They rely on the law to act as criminals, and grievously afflict the common folk. In my humble opinion we ought to abolish completely all these various systems, and issue special orders that the grain tax administrators and polder administrators (*yü-chang*) should be in charge, the grain tax administrators of their boroughs (*tu*) [= divisions], and the polder administrators of their polders.[27]

It was, however, the dike administrator system that emerged from this confusion in the sixteenth century to become the usual method of or-

Market Towns and Waterways

ganizing all but the largest and smallest works. In the words of a document of the year 1595 in the Wan-li reign gazetteer for Hsiu-shui county in Chia-hsing prefecture: "The State established quotas of dike administrators and polder administrators especially to deal with the banks of the polders."[28] The late Ming gazetteer for Sung-chiang prefecture describes the resulting structure in detail.

The present system makes use of canton administrators and elders to manage the affairs of a canton. They resemble the canton chiefs (*li-cheng*) and seniors (*ch'i-chang*) of Sung times. Grain tax administrators (*liang-chang*) direct the taxes of a division (*ch'ü*), and dike administrators have the boundary walls of the fields repaired and the waterways dredged....

There are 14,350 canton administrators enrolled in the Yellow Registers. Each year some 1,435 of them perform the duties in rotation. The remainder are off-duty administrators. There are 1,435 elders, old men of good conduct being picked to fill this post. There are 209 grain tax administrators, men of good conduct and liable for both labor service and grain tax being chosen for this post. There are also 209 dike administrators.

Each county has jurisdiction over a certain number of wards (*pao*). Each ward controls a certain number of divisions. Each division controls a certain number of districts. The numbers differ from case to case.

Each district shares out a ten-year period among its ten tithings (*chia*), and for each of these a tax prompter (*ching-ts'ui*) is enrolled, though the post may either be filled by a single household, or by two or three together.... Each year it is the turn of one of the tithings to have special responsibility for managing the tax payments of the households in its district. Suppose, by way of example, that the first tithing, assigned to the first year of the cycle, is filling the post of tax prompter. Then the tenth tithing, assigned to the tenth year, [that] is to say the year before, will fill the post of annual overseer (*kai-nien*), and the ninth tithing, assigned to the year before that, will fill the post of tithing-general (*tsung-chia*). The annual overseer has to undertake such chores as gathering together laborers, having the waterways dredged, and having mud and undergrowth removed. Each district changes its annual overseer each year. It is he who takes the initiative in leading out the laborers to join forces in dredging and in building the dikes.

In some cases there are six or seven districts in a division, in others more than ten. Out of the annual overseers in a given division it is the one who has served as general divisional tax prompter (*ling-ch'ü tsung-ts'ui*) who becomes dike administrator. His special duty is to direct the laborers from the various districts in undertaking the water conservancy works of the division.[29]

The polder administrators (*yü-chang* or *wei-chang*) probably originated earlier than the dike administrators. In Hai-yen county they appear as the subordinates of the grain tax administrators in the late fourteenth century. In Su-chou in the 1430's, each division had polder generals (*tsung yü-chang*) and polder elders (*yü-lao*) appointed from the ranks of former or of off-duty grain tax administrators, who were heads of "great households" and in charge of the lesser polder administrators (*hsiao yü-chang*). The Sung-chiang gazetteer for the Ch'ung-chen reign (1628–44) also describes the polder administrators there as "persons of good quality" and "great households," helped in their tasks with gifts of official grain or official loans, and rewarded with the "cap and sash" of official rank or a tablet of official commendation if they did well.[30] The system depended on landowners of the middle rank, as is made clear by regulations issued in 1577 by Lin Ying-shun, Regional Inspector of South Chihli.

The polder tithings (*yü-chia*) [= polder administrators] are established to ensure an equal distribution of activity and rest. A dike administrator is established with respect to a division, but within this division there will be several polders. Without a tithing how can they be led and matters coordinated? Wealthy families ought to be selected to fill the position. . . . Even if it is not possible to determine what their wealth is, if they own the most agricultural land in the polder, then they are fit to serve as the administrator of that polder. . . . If there are landowners who do not obey their leadership, they may report their names to the authorities. If a polder tithing does not do the job in person, or finds someone else to undertake it in his stead, then once this has been discovered he shall be punished with the cangue for all to see.[31]

Thus conscripted administrators were not members of the official gentry class but wealthy landowning commoners. Yeh Meng-chu makes this extremely clear.

[In Ming times] these services were all performed by persons who possessed land, but the gentry (*chin-shen*) had by law a privileged exemption and did not participate in them. Senior licentiates (*kung-sheng*), Imperial University students (*chien-sheng*), and licentiates (*sheng-yüan*) only had a privileged exemption for a hundred *mou*. It was the rich families, with numerous fields but no privileged exemption, who had together to fulfill these obligations. By and large the rural gentry (*hsiang-shen*) who held the metropolitan doctorate (*liang-pang*) were not liable for any labor service at all, regardless of what official rank they held and how extensive their lands might be. For those with the provincial doctorate (*i-pang*), official rank was taken into account. Those with a high rank could be exempt of obligation for two or three thousand *mou*. If a senior licentiate had had an official career his rank might also be taken into consideration. If he had a high one he might be exempted of tax for a thousand *mou*; if a low one, for not more than three to five hundred *mou*. Imperial University students who had had no official career were on a par with the licentiates, which meant that they benefited but little from their promotion.[32]

Market Towns and Waterways

Freedom from the duties of water-conservancy administration was a privilege that the official gentry must have relished, for their untitled landlord neighbors were held personally responsible for any failure. As the Governor of the Southern Metropolitan Area wrote in 1608: "If a division does not do all the work that has been assigned to it, then the dike administrator shall bear the blame. If a district does not do all the work that has been assigned to it, then the annual overseer shall bear the blame."[33]

This picture of Sung-chiang water control in the fifteenth and sixteenth centuries needs to be completed with an account of the ad hoc organizations created to handle really big projects. Here is Regional Inspector Lu Kuang-hsun planning the dredging of the Wu-sung, one of the arterial rivers of the cotton area, in 1544.

If the laborers are to be enlisted on the basis of the acreage, then those who have much land will have difficulty in meeting the requirements and those who have little land will suffer from being interfered with. If corvée laborers (*i-ting*) are to be enrolled household by household, the whole family of well-to-do households may be taken without there being any way to summon poor persons to fill up the vacancies. The best method would be to follow the system of hiring and recruiting used for famine relief. . . .

Before the appointed date a clear proclamation should be issued to each borough (*tu*) and district (*t'u*) to report their quota of names to the officials in charge of recruiting. Those who come to labor on account of their poverty shall also be enrolled by the boroughs and districts, regardless of their number. The soldiers of the guards and battalions (*wei-so*) shall be sent under strict orders by their commanders to be employed on the same terms as the commoners. . . .

Honest and capable persons should be chosen to be administrators of a thousand (*ch'ien-chang*) and administrators of a hundred (*pai-chang*); and able vice-magistrates, registrars, jail wardens, and controllers [of salt, excise, or granaries] should be deputed to supervise them. . . .

About the long-term arrangements: we ought to copy the system of dredging and clearing used by former dynasties, and institute waterway workers (*tao-ho chih-fu*). Every year local people who are liable for labor service shall be especially sought out for this task, and exempted from other corvées. Lodging houses for them will be set up in advance at the critical points along the waterways, like the lodges at the shallow parts of the Grand Canal. . . .

The vice-prefect will give silver and rice to the vice-magistrates and registrars, who will give them to the administrators of a thousand, who will in turn give them to the administrators of a hundred, who will distribute them to the various laborers.[34]

By the later sixteenth century the dike administrator system was breaking down. The financial burden, both on the administrators and on those under them, was too great. The Governor of the Southern Metropolitan Area explained why in 1608.

Evil government clerks have burrowed in. The flesh and fat of the common people have been spent, not on the waterways, but on fees. ... The method these sly rascals use to profit from the arbitrary allocation of tasks to the dike administrators is called "adapting and adjusting in the context of the whole county." In practice it amounts to ...disorder and inequity. If the dike administrators and the annual overseers are obliged to go somewhere far away they will be able to do their work there without great difficulty, but there will be under their leadership at least a hundred persons from every district and at least a thousand from every division—humble people who have to toil morning and night to wrest a living from their threshing floors. How can such as they go several tens of *li* away for labor service? Inevitably they have to contract with the "mud men" for the work, ... and this type of market bully (*shih-kun*) ... has formed the habit of conspiring with the government clerks. ... The latter will have dike administrators from high areas sent to low ones, and vice versa, with the result that, suffering unbearably from being driven this way and then the other, they are forced to have the mud men contract for the work. Once the mud men have laid their hands on the silver they share it with the clerks and runners, and pay no attention to their duties.[35]

By the end of the dynasty, "assignations to help elsewhere" (*ch'ai-chu*) were routine. Bankruptcies among dike administrators were common, and we also read of common folk selling their children or even themselves to raise the money for contractors to do the work. Another source of corruption was the commutation of labor service known as "payment for idleness" (*na-k'uang*) or "idle work" (*k'uang-kung*), which might amount to thirty or forty taels a year per district. Powerful families also acquired the habit of treating the dike administrators "as if they were their private servants."[36] By the early Ch'ing period the bankruptcy of the conscript administrators, and the irresponsible greed of the clerks, had so disrupted the system that it sometimes became necessary to "dismiss the labor service workers and undertake private action" if a project was to be successfully completed.[37] The system of contracting practiced by the mud men was not just a pretext for corruption, however; it had positive virtues, too. The proposals submitted in 1629 by Cheng Yu-hsuan of Hua-t'ing county (adjacent to Shang-hai), and later officially accepted, are quite complimentary toward them.

The canton administrators and off-duty administrators have on successive occasions made suggestions about a system that might stand the test of time. According to them, if the mud men are given a contract, once the fees are paid the work is done, and this is of very real help to water-conservancy. The

Market Towns and Waterways

[duties of the] dike administrators are popularly referred to as "small-scale banishment for military service." This is because they always have to do their work in the winter when the weather is cold and raw. They take their spades and shoulder their burdens to somewhere twenty or thirty miles away. . . . Given such human conditions, there would be no progress even if they were strictly led and worked hard, merely a wasting of time. Would it not be much more convenient to entrust the whole business to mud men, and sit at our ease to watch them finish it off? . . . Every year the yardage of waterway to be dredged should be calculated, along with the sum to be paid to the mud men for this work. Apart from the repairs that the dike administrators ought to carry out in their own divisions . . . it is desirable in all cases to pay silver. Let the water-control officials call the mud men together and sanction their doing of the work at the standard rate of 0.3 taels for every 100 cubic feet of mud. At the beginning of winter the dike administrators shall help them with the silver [levied] according to acreage. In this way the mud men will not dare make great demands, the government runners will not be able to extort or cheat, the clerks will be unable to perform their manipulations, the officials will be spared the bother of going into the countryside to take charge of operations, and commoners will no longer be burdened with having to go and do the work.[38]

These mud men, who were "market bullies" and so not unlike the "bullies living in the county capitals" who did much of the tax collecting,[39] were a symptom of the growing urbanization of local government and water control. The need for their services also reflected the problems raised by the geographical separation between the place where drainage work had to be done and the place where those who benefited from it lived.

In 1667 the late Ming water-conservancy system was abolished in conjunction with the introduction of the new method of taxation (which gradually became general in the country) known as "equal fields and equal labor services" (*chün-t'ien chün-i chih-fa*). The agricultural land in Shang-hai county was reregistered, "everyone paid in their own taxes, and there was no need for others to act as prompters."[40] The dike administrators were abolished on the assumption that "when waterways become choked with silt the landowners of the districts affected will do the dredging themselves, . . . and if sometimes there are [large-scale] tasks that must be undertaken, these too will be suitably assigned according to the acreage [held by each landowner]." This apparently applied with equal force to the members of the official gentry, for they are said to have been "aggrieved at the lack of distinction made between the honorable and the mean, . . . and to have wanted to restore the canton labor services."[41]

The use of commoners as lower-level administrators persisted for a few years longer. In 1671, when the Wu-sung had to be dredged, "each division selected one elder (*ch'i-lao*), and every ten elders set up a tithing administrator (*chia-chang*), every ten of whom in turn set up an administrator of a hundred (*pai-chang*)." In 1677, for the dredging of the Ma-chia creek, which linked the town of Kao-chia-hang (in the northeast corner of the county) with the Huang-p'u some two and a half miles away, the following arrangements were made: "Since the dike administrators had been abolished at this time, workers were recruited from the fields near the waterway. Landowners contributed rations and tenants their labor. The burden was equitably shared, each *mou* having to supply three pints of rice. Elderly commoners (*ch'i-min*) were selected to direct the labor service."[42] This was the end of a chapter, however, not the beginning. During the decades that followed the first sprouts of a new system began to emerge, that of gentry administration.

The institutional changes summarized above present a problem: were they merely surface phenomena, or can they be related to the changing social and economic structure of the Kiangnan countryside? I argue in the section that follows that there was indeed such a relationship, and I try to show its nature. Here we may usefully conclude by making some general points to set this argument in its proper context.

First, Sung-chiang prefecture was of critical importance for the drainage of the sunken basin around Lake T'ai farther inland.[43] This meant that from time to time the state had to mount a massive operation to dredge the Wu-sung or the Huang-p'u, an undertaking beyond the reach of the local inhabitants.[44] Second, the area was of concern to the government as a major source of taxes. This was particularly true in the earliest part of the dynasty, when confiscations of private estates had turned more than four-fifths of the prefecture into state land farmed by state tenants.[45] The changes in the duties of the agricultural officials at the start of the 1430's[46] from an emphasis on water control to one on tax collection, and the rise of new systems of the dike-administrator type slightly later, correspond in time with the reemergence of private estates as the dominant form of property. Third, the dike administrators were concerned with hydraulic projects of intermediate size. In Shang-hai county, at least, these were as much for the sake of transport as for irrigation. According to the gazetteer for the Ch'ien-lung reign (1736–95):

Sung-chiang is a region of waters. Low-lying fields have to have dikes built around them to prevent flooding, and upland fields need to have [their channels] cleared and dredged to prevent drought. Under these circumstances it was necessary to use dike administrators. Furthermore, in those places affected by the rise and fall of the tides "the turbid enters and the clear flows out," so that as the days and months go by the waterways become choked with mud. *If they are not dredged in good time it causes great difficulty for communications between the towns and the country villages.* It was for this reason that our forebears made use of dike administrators and general prompters (*tsung-ts'ui*) who held office in rotation.[47]

This may explain the high element of coercion. Where negligence presents no threat to life (as with a seawall) and diligence offers no great immediate rewards (as it might with irrigation elsewhere), it does not pay landowners or tenants to clear waterways for the sake of other people's transport. Fourth, the downfall of the dike administrators was obviously part of a larger story—the collapse of the *li-chia* system of tax collection and rural organization. This compels us to look at the wider question of what was happening to rural society in the seventeenth century; and to this we now turn.

Landlord and Tenant, Town and Countryside: The Changing Pattern of Relationships

With the failure of the early Ming agricultural command economy in the state land region around Lake T'ai,[48] a form of manorialism reasserted itself. Early in the sixteenth century, Mao K'un wrote a description of his maternal grandfather that may serve as an illustration of this sort of social order.

When I was a boy, I . . . was accustomed to seeing my maternal grandfather personally lead off the serfs to cultivate the land to the West of Lin-hsü [in Hu-chou]. The stars would be in the sky when he went out and up once again when he returned. Even in wind or rain, in great heat or in cold, he never missed a day. When I resigned from official position . . . my maternal grandfather was over seventy and his hair was white, but he invariably acted in the same way. I was also accustomed to seeing my maternal grandmother personally direct the women serfs at weaving in their own houses, starting by lamplight and finishing by lamplight. Even in wind or rain, in great heat or great cold, she never missed a day. When she was old she invariably acted in the same way, Thus the income from the fields was twice that of other people's, and purchasers in competition offered high prices to buy what they had woven.[49]

The typical estate had a home farm surrounded by fields let out to tenants. As an anonymous author put it: "If you own a hundred *mou*, make your serfs (*p'u-ts'ung*) cultivate thirty of them themselves; and have tenants (*tien-jen*) till the rest."[50]

The distinction between serfs and tenants was real, but should not be pressed too hard. As Ch'in Chün observed in the fifteenth century, "south of the Yangtze ... the inhabitants who rent the fields of the great families are their slaves (*nu-li*)"; and other writers echoed these sentiments while noting local variations.[51] These powerful landowners often acquired poor people's land by physical or legal pressures, and enserfed debtors as a means of "making good" (*chun-che*) their unpaid debts.

This manorial system, based on direct management by a master or his representatives and on powerful noneconomic as well as economic controls over the labor force, began to break down in the middle of the sixteenth century. The trend may be illustrated by a passage in a letter from Hsu Chieh to Regional Inspector Lu Kuang-hsun written around 1546.

It has been the custom in Sung-chiang for the great families to own land that they cannot farm themselves and to use dependent tenants. The tenants desire to do the farmwork but do not have enough food; so they must rely for it upon the great households. The feelings and circumstances involved are not only those of *the mutual assistance of master and serf*, and of the mutual nourishing of the older and younger members of a family. Even if the great households cannot avoid all harshness toward their tenants, they do not dare to be very harsh, for fear that they will have no one to farm for them. Before the Cheng-te reign (1506–21) the common people were well-off and the countryside uncorrupted by evil practices. . . . In recent years, the authorities on several occasions issued a ban on pursuing [tenants] for their debts, and made it worse by punishing arrangements for repayment by installments [?]. As a result the tenants gave vent in clamorous fashion to their dishonorable and untrustworthy impulses. The great households were terrified, fearing that they might be caught in the nets of the authorities. It was at this point that what in times past was called "mutual aid and sustenance" changed into *mutual suspicion and enmity*. Not only did it become impossible to recover debts; rents too often went unpaid. At first it seemed that only the great households would be hurt by their inability to get their loans paid back. It was not realized that if the tenants had no one to rely on for support, they could hardly avoid dying where they stood. When many rents went by default, all those in authority were delighted. They congratulated themselves on the blend of firmness and softness in their policies, convinced that the ancients were not their equal. They did not realize that if no rents were paid, there was nowhere for taxes to come from. . . . Concerning a policy for the present, I would request that the new regulations be abolished, and that the great households be told in a decree to show compassion to their tenants. If we could reunite *the feelings of alienation in the villages*, and make honest the corrupted habits of a degenerate age, then there would be no need for the state to be bankrupt and the officials troubled, and the people would lack nothing.[52]

The unwillingness of landowners to help their tenants in times of famine surprised other observers, but it was part of a pattern of increasing hostility between the two sides marked by rent resistance and violent uprisings.[53]

Water control was neglected because in the words of Chou Feng-ming, a mid-sixteenth-century official from Su-chou, "the property does not belong to the humble folk and the great households are only interested in receiving rents."[54] Ch'en Hu, who was active in hydraulic works around Su-chou at the end of the Ming period, created an organization in which the landowners merely supplied a rice ration; the polder administrators took direct charge of the tenants, and it is probable that some of the administrators were tenants themselves.[55]

What were the underlying causes of these changes? There seem to have been three: the rise of rural subsidiary industries, the urbanization of all but the smallest landowners, and a state policy hostile to serfdom. Together these three factors transformed the life of the Kiangnan countryside.

The extensive practice of spinning and weaving made the peasants much less dependent upon the land, and thus upon the landlords, for their economic survival. This is illustrated by an eighteenth-century account of the counties of Wu-hsi and Chin-kuei.

There are five counties in Ch'ang-chou prefecture, and only in ours is cotton not cultivated. Yet we make a greater profit from cotton cloth than do the other counties. The country folk only live off their fields for the three winter months. When they have paid their rent they pound the husks off the rice that remains and deposit it in the bins of the pawnshops, taking back the clothes they had there in pawn. During the spring months they close their doors and spin or weave, eating by exchanging their cloth for rice. There is not a grain to spare in their houses. In the fifth moon, when the demands of farming become pressing, they once again pawn their winter clothes.... The autumn is somewhat rainy, and the noise of the shuttles of the looms is once again to be heard everywhere in the villages. They trade the cloth in order to have rice to eat. Thus, even if there is a bad harvest in our counties, our country people are not in distress so long as the other counties have a crop of cotton.[56]

At the same time, most of the rural landlords, many of whom were also merchants,[57] moved out of the villages and into the towns, while well-to-do city-dwellers began to invest in agricultural land. According to an eighteenth-century work on the town of Fu-li in Wu *hsien* (Su-chou *fu*): "Half of the fields of the highest quality belong to rich families in the prefectural capital."[58] The prefectural gazetteer for the Tao-kuang reign (1821–50) quotes a passage to much the same effect: "There are many landowners in Kiangnan, but forty to fifty percent of them live in the county capitals or their suburbs, and some thirty to forty percent in the market towns. Ten to twenty percent live dispersed in the country villages."[59] This urbanization of the landlord class may first have become important in the late sixteenth century, for it was said of Shan-yüan county (near Nanking) that only after the introduction of the Single Whip system of taxation "were the rich families in the county capital willing to purchase land."[60]

As most landowners moved to the cities, individual landholdings became increasingly fragmented and scattered. The Su-chou prefectural gazetteer for the Tao-kuang reign (1821–50) says, "Boats can row everywhere in the watery land of Kiangnan. Therefore many of those who live in one district also have land in another district. Many of those who live in the county capitals or their suburbs also have property in various districts. Even if their fields do not exceed several tens of *mou* they will still be scattered all over the place."[61] Keng Chü, magistrate of Ch'ang-shu county in 1605, thought this pattern of land tenure was an obstacle to water conservancy: "Why is it that so many of the embankments are ruined and not repaired? I asked the elders, and it appears that there are five reasons.... The fields of the great households and of the humble folk are laid out in an intermingled fashion; when one small flaw impairs a thousand feet of good dike, the great households are therefore irresolute, look this way and that, and do not do the repairs."[62] Under these circumstances coordinated management and the maintenance of discipline over the labor force were all but impossible.

State opposition to serfdom and servile tenancy also played its part. Under the Ming it was illegal for nonofficial families to own serfs, though the practice was widespread under a variety of disguises. State intervention on the tenants' behalf in their financial relations with their landlords has been indicated by the letter of Hsü Chieh quoted above. The Ch'ing dynasty, perhaps fearful of a repetition at some point of the serf and tenant rebellions of the 1640's, also tried to limit the powers of the landlords. In 1681, for example, the K'ang-hsi emperor approved a memorial from the governor of Anhwei to the effect that "henceforth, when landlords are buying and selling land they must allow their tenants to do as they please. They may not sell them along with the fields, or compel them to perform services."[63]

The tenants benefited from their newfound freedom to organize themselves to resist the payment of their rents, and the landlords reacted by using to an increasing degree the apparatus of the county government to enforce their claims. Often the clerks and runners of the permanent subbureaucracy were simply their dependents or creatures, who were given additional employment and pickings as agents of the powerful rent-collecting agencies or "bursaries" (*tsu-chan*) that the landlords formed to handle the incomes from their scattered properties.[64]

Under these changed conditions the locus of social and economic power shifted decisively to the towns and cities. The *li-chia* system, of which the dike administrators had been a part, had depended on landowners living in the countryside to man its ranks. Now it was no longer viable. The larger proprietors were urban absentees. The "middle and small households with several tens of *mou* or only a few *mou*" described by an official report on Shang-hai county in 1675 had "their fields in several polders and these polders in different divisions."[65] It was no longer easy to assign landowners in definitive fashion to duties in one specific district or division.

A variety of new systems emerged in late Ming and early Ch'ing to deal with these problems. Their characteristic features were the levy of labor, provisions, and money on an acreage basis, and the bypassing of the landowners to organize their tenants directly. An example is the system created by Ch'en Hu in a village in K'un-shan county in the middle of the seventeenth century.[66] Three registers were compiled, covering eighteen polders. One copy went to the county magistrate, one went to the "great households," and one was "kept in the village." Each polder was under the orders of a field-tithing (*t'ien-chia*), equivalent to a polder administrator. He led an average of ten tenant households "in the way that squads of five and ten soldiers are controlled." Landowners "provided rice according to the acreage of the fields that they had under cultivation," and two honest men were publicly selected (*kung-chü*) by the village to take charge of the work. Presumably they were landowners, since they were exempted from payment for a certain number of *mou*. Their work was said to be burdensome and to give rise to resentment. They were told "not to fear powerful opponents." Tenants who failed to do their allotted tasks properly were made to provide wine for the other workers; if the failure was serious they were reported to the officials for punishment with the cangue. According to Ch'en, the method used to levy labor was "not to ask the landowners but to ask the tenants, putting the responsibility on the polder administrators," and to "give every worker a warrant entitling him to deduct two pecks per *mou* from his rent to serve as his wages." For the conservancy of Lake Lien, also in Kiangsu, it was laid down that "if the landowners do not come to do the repair work, their [tenant] households must do it in their stead, a deduction being made when the rent is collected. If anyone relies on his strength not to obey, the men of the ten tithings shall gather together and send him to the officials for investigation and punishment."[67] The "public selection" of leaders (whatever exactly that meant in practice) and public discussions were new features and suggest an increased role for the rural community in water control.

Nonetheless, the removal of the more important landowners from the countryside left a leadership gap. To some extent it could be filled by deputies (*wei-yüan*), expectant officials assigned to a province and gaining administrative experience through this sort of work,[68] or by canton clerks (*li-hsü*);[69] but neither of these seems to have proved entirely satisfactory. As a result a new institution began to develop.

The Gentry Directors

In 1678, Chang Hsi-i, a native of Shang-hai who was a metropolitan graduate and held official rank, proposed that an assistant county magistrate should "be deputed in conjunction with the rural gentry (*hsiang-shen*)" to manage the county's dredging.[70] The first record of the actual participation of "the gentry and scholars" (*shen-shih*) in a hydraulic project comes in a gazetteer entry dated 1684 but referring to an event some years before.[71] This was an isolated incident that should not be construed as evidence of a regular system, but it was a portent of things to come.

In 1720 it was proposed that the official in charge of a conservancy project "should select several upright and capable members of the gentry, or scholars from the cantons, who will help him to spread his influence downward."[72] In 1753 we find another instance of such leadership being provided by the rural gentry,[73] and in 1763 the new system seems to have begun to take definitive shape with the proposals of Chang Shih-yu, an official deputy, for a scheme he himself described as "seasonable, sweeping, and bold."

The method is threefold. . . . When it is necessary to request government funds, the local officials shall be ordered to undertake the repairs. The prefects, department magistrates, and independent subprefects will have the responsibility for directing these projects. In this way the response will be brisk and the management specifically allocated, rendering large works easy to accomplish. In those cases [of somewhat smaller undertakings] where the acreage has to be estimated district by district [in order to determine the landlords' obligations for the provision of labor], the order shall be given for the gentry and scholars of the county involved to gather for discussions and publicly select leaders (*chi-i kung-chü ling-pan*). The local officials will be used to supervise them. In this fashion the network of personal obligations will work in its accustomed way and neither public nor private interests will be thrown into confusion (*jen-ch'ing hsi erh kung-ssu pu-jao*). When there are repairs that need to be done in rotation year by year, the landlords of the various districts shall be ordered to carry out this maintenance dredging themselves. Regulations for them will be drawn up by the local officials.[74]

Shortly after this the gentry emerged as the accepted directors of all large hydraulic projects that were yet not so large as to demand special organization by the government. In 1775, according to the county gazetteer for the T'ung-chih reign (1862–74), for a clearance of the major and minor waterways of the county capital ordered by the intendant and supervised by the county magistrate, "this year *for the first time* the levying of funds and the dredging were done by the gentry and scholars, and hereafter all the work done on the 'market rivers' (*shih-ho*) of the county capital followed the proposal first made [on this occasion]."[75] In this and the following year, members of the gentry took charge of two projects in the countryside. By the early part of the nineteenth century, members of the gentry who administered hydraulic projects, either on their own or in conjunction with official deputies, were being referred to as "gentry directors" (*shen-tung*) or "directors" (*tung-shih*) in recognition of their services as professional organizers rather than as interested landowners.[76]

The precise social and political status of these directors is not entirely clear. They seem to have been thought of as a distinct category of person, for the gazetteers implicitly contrast their work with that of rank-holding Imperial University students (*chih chien-sheng*), stipendholders of the first degree (*lin-sheng*), village gentry (*li-shen*), elderly gentry (*ch'i-shen*), titled landowners (*chin-yeh*), farming landowners (*t'ien-yeh*), elderly landowners (*ch'i-yeh*), elderly students (*wen-sheng*), military students (*wu-sheng*), elderly commoners (*ch'i-min*), merchant commoners (*shang-min*), villagers (*li-jen*), and so forth. There were a limited number, too, whom we can say with certainty possessed academic degrees or official titles.[77] This would suggest that the directors were senior members of the local gentry—holders of the higher degrees or official rank—though there is one consideration that weighs against accepting this view. The sources refer not only to gentry directors but also to district directors (*t'u-tung*), ward directors (*pao tung-shih*), and town directors (*chen-tung*). Considering that Shang-hai in the nineteenth century had 214 districts, 13 wards, and over 30 important market towns, it is rather unlikely that all of the foregoing were invariably titled persons, though it is not necessarily impossible.[78]

In neighboring Pao-shan there were sector directors (*tuan-tung*), each in charge of a mere 500 feet of seawall. There seems to have been a distinction between them and the "elected" gentry directors, "enjoying everyone's trust," who had general control.[79] In the Lake Lien area there were even directors from individual villages.[80] Any meaningful conception of the late traditional managerial gentry will therefore have to extend some way below the formal demarcation line provided by the possession of a degree or title.

The directors' powers were considerable. Once they had obtained the sanction of the county magistrate they were entitled to levy a variety of supplementary taxes, to determine (within the limits of certain established conventions and popular tolerance) the allocation of labor, and to manage the conservancy funds. We may take as typical cases of gentry management the dredging of the Sha-kang in 1873 and that of the Hsien-t'ang in 1879.

(1) Chang Chen and the other directors decided, after a discussion, that the primary responsibility for the dredging would fall upon the 41st, 48th, 13th, 12th, 11th, 10th, 57th, 9th, 78th, and upper 36th districts of the 16th ward. [The owner of] each one of the estimated 36,299 *mou* of land would have to remove 183.6 cubic feed of mud. A secondary responsibility would rest upon the western halves of the 42d, 39th, 47th, and 49th districts of the 16th ward and the lower 36th district of the 18th ward. Each of the estimated 6,401 *mou* of land would have to do half the amount of dredging incumbent upon those with the primary responsibility, namely some 91.9 cubic feet [*sic*]. The total cost of pumps, embankments, and administration came to 3,395,475 *cash*. County Magistrate Yeh T'ing-ch'üan contributed 300,000 "from his salary."* Chang San-yü and other landowners gave 305,000. Some 2,295,038 *cash* were temporarily advanced from the Huang-p'u and Ch'ao-chia creek dredging fund. This was still not enough, and so Director Chang provisionally lent 495,437 *cash*, and the next year, when the regular land tax was collected, the parishes with a primary responsibility for the dredging paid a surcharge of 64 *cash* per *mou*, which yielded an estimated 2,323,136 *cash*. After the Huang-p'u and Ch'ao-chia cheek fund had been repaid, there was a surplus of 28,098 *cash*, which was set off against miscellaneous items and used to pay for the clerks.[81]

(2) Since there was no provision for the cost of pumps, embankments, and administration at this time, Director Chu Ch'i-ch'un proposed to follow the precedent set in 1868 and levy 60 *cash* per *mou* from the fields of the districts that adjoined the waterway. He exempted from the dredging the 2,976 *mou* from which he had taken workers to pump out the water.... The rest did the work according to acreage. He collected a levy on the land along the waterway

---

* A customary phrase often used to describe a magistrate's contribution.

Market Towns and Waterways

that yielded 386,000 *cash,* and a levy on gentry, merchants, and shopkeepers that yielded 1,198,000 *cash.* The Yü-yüan pawnshop contributed a monthly levy throughout the year and this totaled 2,463,000 *cash.*[82]

These passages illustrate the main features of the administration of water conservancy in nineteenth-century Shang-hai. The county government clerks, and to a great extent the official deputies, have disappeared as organizers. There is a financial symbiosis between the imperial government and the gentry directors, based on the interest-free loan of government moneys and the use of the regular tax-collecting machinery to gather conservancy surcharges. It is not only landlords now who pay for dredging but pawnbrokers, shopkeepers, and merchants as well; and the directors themselves seem sometimes to be called upon to make a financial contribution.*

The two projects just described were of the kind to be undertaken on an irregular basis as need arose. Where there were permanent installations to be looked after, there were probably regular employees, also under gentry supervision. This was certainly the case for the locks of the north Chekiang silk district and those of Lake Lien.[83]

The gentry directors, unlike the dike administrators, were of course not compelled *nolentes volentes* to administer hydraulic projects, and their power to do so, although it enjoyed the formal backing of the state, depended in fact upon that "network of personal obligations" of which Chang Shih-yu had spoken. For this reason, whenever there was any difficulty over conservancy policy, or a departure from commonly accepted routine, they worked through a mechanism of consultations either with the magistrate or with each other, or else with the landowners, merchants, and common people.

A representative example of the kind of collective advice that the gentry directors, and others, might be called upon to give to the authorities is provided by the case of the Ch'ao-chia creek in 1870.

Chu Feng-t'i, the acting county magistrate, called together the directors and wardens of the county, city and countryside (*ch'eng-hsiang tung-pao*). It was concluded after a discussion that in 1836 the whole county had provided laborers on the basis of acreage, no wages being given for the quantity dredged and administrative expenses being provided by the officials. In 1858 a payment had been made for the amount dredged and administrative charges had all been met from unallocated levies and fines, no money being taken from the landowners and tenants of the county. In recent years the officials had become poor and the commoners rich; the latter had had ample resources since the

---

* There is no record of whether Director Chang Chen was ever repaid his 495,437 *cash.* Even if he was, it was almost certainly without any interest.

reduction of taxes.... They requested that, on the precedent of Hua-t'ing county's levy for its seawall, a levy on acreage should be imposed.... Each *mou* ought to pay 66 *cash*, which would be collected together with the tribute grain.... Where the "market river" (*shih-ho*) was twisty or turbulent, or encumbered with sandbanks, reeds, or irrigation channels, places in the past designated as being tedious and difficult, and such that the normal payment per hundred cubic feet of mud was insufficient, it had been the practice of the group directors (*k'un-tung*)* who were in charge of the dredging to advance the difference. Usually the work had been finished off carelessly, the waterway hardly being dredged before it silted up again. The gentry directors suggested that on this occasion the best thing to do would be to make an additional payment for the difficult parts.... In addition, the miscellaneous expenses for pumps, for embankments, for salaries of deputies, for retinues and sedan chairs for the directors, and for the clerks and constables should all be reported to the county magistrate.[84]

There are several other instances of this use by a magistrate of an assembly of gentry for advice; and the proposals made seem invariably to have been accepted.[85]

Disputes between different groups of gentry would often be settled in the same way. Thus, in 1880, "Li Ts'eng-yü, a town director of Fa-hua town, and other persons requested the authorities that the Li-ts'ung creek should be dredged at the same time as the Huang-p'u and the Ch'ao-chia creeks.... [But] Wang Ts'ui-fen, a district director, and others later asked that the project be postponed on the grounds that the people could not manage two dredgings in one year. County Magistrate Mo thereupon asked them all to a public discussion."[86] Sometimes a project failed when the interests of those who had to bear the burden were not carefully enough consulted in advance. Thus, in 1868,

the first-degree-holder Chiang Chung-jen and the Imperial University student Chiang Hsi-jung petitioned the prefect to the effect that the Hsing drain had been silted up for a long time since its last dredging in the K'ang-hsi reign, and that although they had repeatedly begged the county magistrate to come and look at it and to express an opinion, nothing had been done. They had therefore invited the landowners of groups concerned (*k'un-yeh*) in the various districts to a public discussion. [It had been settled that] workers would be sent out on the basis of acreage in accordance with the regulations.... All of a sudden Wang Shih-ying and other commoners from the western half of the 1st district expressed the desire to dredge Temple creek instead, on the grounds that they would not benefit from the [other] conservancy work. Subsequently commoners from the 54th and 55th districts asked to dredge Fresh-

---

* The group (*k'un*), subdivided into ten bundles (*shu*), and covering a district, was merely Shang-hai's peculiar version of the ward and tithing (*pao-chia*) system.

water conduit, and those of the 42d district to clear Wu-heng creek. There were numerous conflicting proposals ... and the original petitioners resigned from the undertaking.[87]

Sometimes the leading persons in an area would publicly select (*kung-chü*) directors to carry out a project they wished to see accomplished. More frequently, the magistrate would select them; but most commonly of all, they in effect selected themselves on the basis of social position and accepted competence.

These quasi-democratic features were far from being unique to Shang-hai county. By comparison with the Sang-yüan-wei polderlands in Kwangtung, for example, where regular annual meetings of publicly selected representatives and the systematic public selection of hydraulic managers were well established practices,[88] Shang-hai consultative institutions had an intermittent and ill-defined character.

This new gentry system of hydraulic administration was of course only one manifestation of the general evolution of Chinese society toward the end of the premodern period; but that the gentry directors should have had what was essentially a monopoly of all but very large-scale or very small-scale water conservancy was the product of special circumstances, and was not repeated in most other parts of China. When water is a scarce resource used primarily for irrigation, there has to be a permanent organization, either collective or commercial, to handle its allocation; when the safety of polderlands is at stake, a permanent organization, though of a rather different kind, is equally necessary; but when water is mainly used for transport, conservancy is sporadic and carried out only as required. In the last situation, water is also a relatively diffuse general concern rather than an indispensable part of agriculture or of the physical security of a community. Gentry administration (of a kind) was found in some other areas but it was a form that was particularly well-suited to a region where transport was the most important concern. It is here that there appears the underlying continuity between the two Sung-chiang conservancy systems, that of the Ming conscript administrators* and that of the Ch'ing gentry, both of them in a rather exceptional context empirewide.

"Market Rivers"

After the Ch'ing government lifted its restrictions on the transport of goods by sea in 1684, the demands of the Sung-chiang cotton economy

---

* Before corruption among the clerks became serious, it was quite common for a dike administrator to pass through his year of office without being called upon to do anything.

for Manchurian beancake as fertilizer led to an upsurge in the coastal junk trade. This was especially so after 1749, when the last legal restraints on beans as a commodity of maritime commerce (long ignored by the bolder merchants) were finally removed.[89] This new development was based upon the "sand boats" (*sha-ch'uan*), junks of relatively shallow draft whose name may perhaps have derived from the sandy coasts of North Kiangsu and Shantung,[90] and was centered upon Shanghai. According to Pao Shih-ch'en, an early-nineteenth-century official who was much interested in the problems of practical statecraft,

> about 3,500 to 3,600 sand boats gather at Shanghai. The larger ones can carry 3,000 piculs of the official standard measure, and the smaller ones 500 or 600 piculs. The owners of these boats are all wealthy persons who are natives of Ch'ung-ming, T'ung-chou, Hai-men, Nan-hui, Pao-shan, and Shang-hai. It costs 7,000 to 8,000 taels to build one of these boats, and the largest owners have up to 40 or 50 of them. They are therefore called "shipping merchants" (*ch'uan-shang*). After the lifting of the maritime interdict in 1685 [1684], over ten million piculs of beans and wheat came every year to Shanghai from Kuan-tung, and the sand boats also took north with them such southern products as cotton and tea to Shantung, Chihli, and Kuan-tung.[91]

These merchants were remarkable for their honest dealing. They also enjoyed a much greater measure of safety on the seas than had their Ming predecessors.[92] Possessed of ships that could make up to four round trips a year to Manchuria, they undoubtedly made enormous profits.

Their social position was of commensurate importance. When in 1826 the temporary blocking of the Grand Canal forced the Ch'ing government to transport more than a million and a half piculs of its annual supply of rice by sea, it entrusted the task to 46 merchants based on Shanghai; and the records show that 26 of them were either provincial graduates, Imperial University students, senior licentiates, or holders of purchased official rank.[93] Thus by this time, if not much earlier, the more important merchants and gentry of Shanghai had become, to a substantial extent, members of the same class. This and the increase in local shipping that must have accompanied the expansion of the coastal trade help to explain the growing preoccupation of the gentry directors of the county with "market rivers" (*shih-ho*) in the latter half of the Ch'ing dynasty.

Strictly speaking, the term "market river" only applied to a waterway inside a market town or city, but it was sometimes extended to the commercial arteries linking towns. This is apparent from the passage referring to the Ch'ao-chia creek quoted on page 465 above, in which "sandbanks," "reeds," and "irrigation channels" are described as causing

Market Towns and Waterways

difficulties for the dredgers. Most of this "market river" was in the countryside, as can be seen from the fact that it was about 52,000 Chinese feet in length.[94] It is therefore not stretching the Chinese usage more than slightly to speak of a growing network of market towns linked by market rivers.

Maps 2 to 6 show the increase across time of market towns in Shanghai and the surrounding areas. The coverage of the gazetteer sources on which they are based is probably not complete,[95] but the message they convey of a relatively late and swift growth in numbers seems plausible. According to *A Record of the Customs of Wu*, a work dating from the middle of the fifteenth century: "The large villages and famous towns all developed shops that sold every kind of commodity, so as to monopolize the profits; and those who carried goods on their backs between the towns and villages were all in distress."[96] Nonetheless, there are places that can be shown to have had markets some considerable time before they were listed as "towns,"[97] and a certain caution is therefore in order.

The origins of these market towns have, in the main, been made familiar already through previous research.[98] They grew up around temples, around the manors of wealthy landlords and the country residences of important merchants, and around industrial undertakings such as pottery works. They appeared at nodes in the transport system, at bridges, at the intersections of waterways, at resting-spots along main water routes, and at customshouses in "places through which merchants have to pass." They were the by-products of the location of official salt stores, military stations, and arsenals. Sometimes they were set up by influential persons as a deliberate act of will. In other instances they were the outcome of accident, as when bad harvests in a region forced the inhabitants into commerce, or rebels overlooked a village in their otherwise wholesale plunder of the countryside.[99] Some of them straddled county borders.

Incomplete evidence makes it impossible to differentiate the towns on the maps in terms of size, but there were enormous variations. The British Naval Intelligence *Handbook of China Proper* lists market towns in this area with as many as 800 houses and with as few as 25. The Chinese gazetteers speak of some where there were "only ten families" or "a few lonely shops." Dramatic reversals of fortune were not uncommon. Some towns, like Kao-chia-hang and Tung-kou, in the extreme northeast of the county, seem to have disappeared (in this case probably as the result of the inroads of the "Japanese" pirates) and then to have revived later (see Maps 2, 3, and 4). Others, like Wu-ni-ching, the first home of the Kiangnan cotton industry (and shown about nine miles due west of Shanghai in Map 2), vanished permanently (Maps 4, 5, and 6).

By the middle of the nineteenth century there were over a thousand people per square mile in the Shang-hai area.[100] Many of them depended on handicrafts, and in particular on the manufacture of cotton yarn and cloth, for a living. In consequence, during the last 50 or 60 years of the premodern period the market towns acquired a previously unprecedented importance as nodes in the network of commodity exchange. A large portion, possibly even the predominant portion, of water conservancy work undertaken hereafter was in the direct service of urban mercantile interests. Dredging had long been done with a lively awareness of its significance for the movement of shipping between cities, but it was not until 1843 that the townspeople of Shang-hai county began regularly to pay for the maintenance of the waterways that served them. In 1856, most of the twenty million *cash* needed for dredging the Wu-sung and nearby rivers were provided by "the merchants of the various trades of Shanghai."[101] In the years that followed, comparable examples may be found with a monotonous frequency. Thus in 1872 the inhabitants of Fa-hua town financed the dredging of the Li-ts'ung creek "to be a market river, and had bricks and stones laid on the

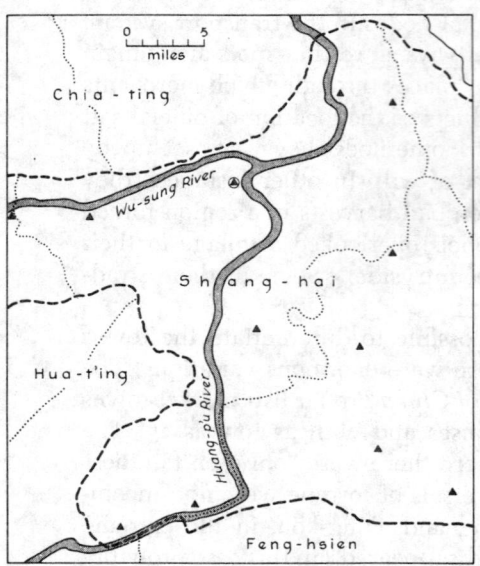

MAP 2. MARKET TOWNS IN THE VICINITY OF SHANGHAI, CA. 1470

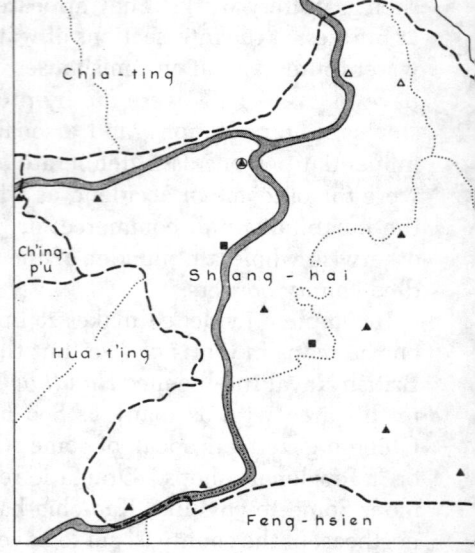

MAP 3. MARKET TOWNS IN THE VICINITY OF SHANGHAI, CA. 1600

MAP 4. MARKET TOWNS IN THE VICINITY OF SHANGHAI, CA. 1750

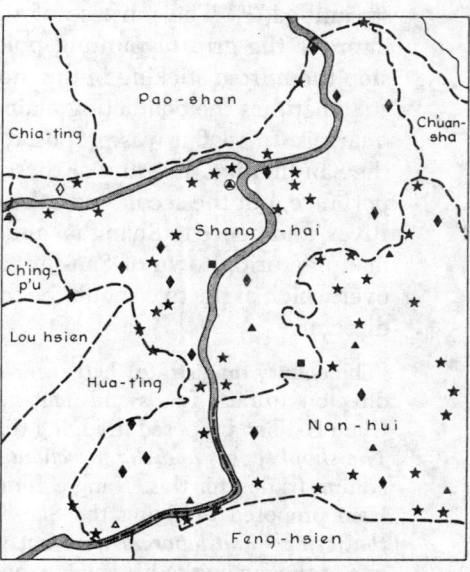

MAP 5. MARKET TOWNS IN THE VICINITY OF SHANGHAI, CA. 1870

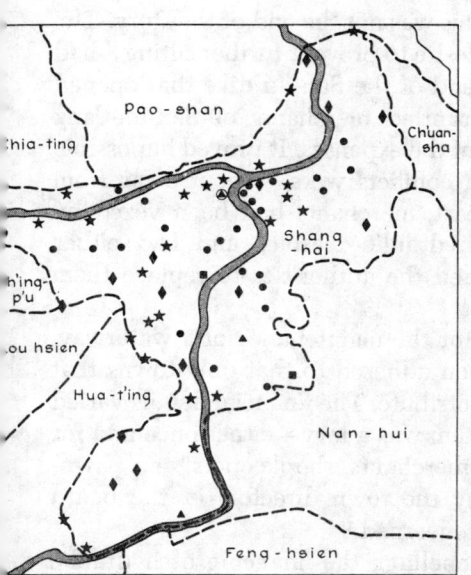

MAP 6. MARKET TOWNS IN THE VICINITY OF SHANGHAI, CA. 1910

KEY FOR MAPS 2–6

- ▲ *Hsien* capital with market
- ▲ Towns with markets founded before ca. 1470
- ■ Towns with markets founded ca. 1470–ca. 1600
- ♦ Towns with markets founded ca. 1600–ca. 1750
- ★ Towns with markets founded ca. 1750–ca. 1870
- ● Towns with markets founded ca. 1870–ca. 1910

Open symbols represent sites of markets that had closed since the time of the preceding map.

- ------ *Hsien* boundaries
- .... *Hsien* boundaries as of 1900, for comparison

streambed."[102] The purpose of the latter measure was presumably to improve the grip of punting poles or quants on the riverbed, and to stop them from sticking in the mud.

Sometimes the conflicting claims of transport and agriculture caused quarrels. In 1896 it was proposed to clear both the Yang-tz'u sluice and the San-lin dike. The first of these apparently had some agricultural importance, but the second was the main route of access to the Huang-p'u River, and hence to Shanghai and to the Yangtze, for the famous cotton-manufacturing town of San-lin-t'ang. The following dispute took place over which of the two should be dredged, as reported by the chief gentry director.

[The county magistrate] had received the order from the prefect to instruct directors to raise funds and manage this work. [But] Chou Hsiao-chen and Chou Hsi-lien proposed dredging the Yang-tz'u and leaving the San-lin alone. *The shopkeepers and the merchants* would not agree to provide the costs of administration for this. T'ang Ssu-ma, Hsüeh Ch'ao, Chao Chih-tz'u, and Lü Hsin proposed dredging the San-lin and leaving the Yang-tz'u alone, but *the farmers and laborers* were not willing to do the work in this case. Each one of them clung to his opinion, and they came to me to decide what would be equitable. I proposed that they should cooperate in dredging both waterways.[103]

Although the work was then done, this was not the end of the story. The directors—no doubt moved by the desire to prevent further silting—had placed an embankment across the end of the San-lin dike that opened into the Huang-p'u, and the disgruntled merchants of San-lin-t'ang therefore refused to pay their share of the expenses. It proved impossible to shake their determination. Such conflicts were of course far from new. Since the Ming dynasty at least, merchants had been vexed by dams put across waterways for hydraulic reasons, and had either breached them illegally or persuaded the authorities to replace them by locks.[104]

Often, several towns would pay for the maintenance of a waterway, but the principle seems to have been adhered to that only towns that benefited from it were obliged to contribute. The financial details varied from case to case, but the usual system was a levy—either once and for all or in monthly installments—on merchants, shopkeepers, and pawnbrokers. The work was handled by the town directors or the board directors (*chü-tung*) of the towns concerned.[105]

During and after the Taiping Rebellion, the financing of hydraulic works by merchants, usually through levies on trade, seems to have become common in the central areas of both the Middle and Lower Yangtze regions.[106] Developments in Sung-chiang were thus part of a more widespread pattern.

Conclusions

The organization of water control was not uniquely determined by ecological and technological conditions. It was also the product of the prevailing economic and social structures, and of state policies, and usually changed when they did. Comparative analysis of different regions, based in the first place on the now quite extensive materials made available by Japanese scholars, is desirable to clarify the complex causal patterns at work. The geographical structure of water-control systems, whether for irrigation, transport, drainage, or defense against floods, imposed a spatial pattern on social action that was distinct from that of the marketing system, though obviously not unrelated to it. Local studies of small areas are needed to establish the details of this divergence, and the influences of the two systems on each other.

Academies and Urban Systems in Kwangtung

TILEMANN GRIMM

This paper investigates the extent to which, and the ways in which, academies were urban institutions in late imperial China. The major empirical focus is on Kwangtung during the Ch'ing period, but other provinces are occasionally brought into the analysis for comparison and an effort is made to relate Ch'ing developments to the earlier history of academies. The generic term for the institution in question is *shu-yüan*, "study hall," but certain academies were known by another name, *ching-she*, "house of refinement." Though the latter term came out of a distinctive tradition, by the Ch'ing period (if not before) academies known as *ching-she* were indistinguishable from those called *shu-yüan*.[1]

Early Development of Academies

Although both terms predate the tenth century, it was only during the Sung period that the academy became a recognized institution. Academies were founded in substantial numbers during the Southern Sung (1127–1280), particularly in the provinces of the Middle and Lower Yangtze regions and along the southeast coast. In subsequent centuries, academies spread to all regions of China Proper and their numbers increased. Growth was slow until the sixteenth century, when the rate accelerated appreciably. Drawing on the provincial gazetteers for five provinces, three from the North (Shansi, Shantung, and Honan) and two from the Middle Yangtze (Hunan and Kiangsi), we can glimpse the general trend (see Table 1). It would appear that the first wave of academy foundings peaked before the Ming period, during the Southern Sung in some provinces and during the Yüan in most others. Despite the rather large number of Ming *shu-yüan* that are not specifically dated for some of these provinces, it seems clear that the rate at which *shu-*

TABLE 1. SHU-YÜAN BY PERIOD OF REGISTRATION, SELECTED PROVINCES, SUNG THROUGH MING

Period	Shansi	Shantung	Honan	Hunan	Kiangsi	Five-province total No.	Foundings per decade
Sung (960–1280)	1	8	4	47	150	210	6.6
Yüan (1280–1368)	17	14	7	14	48	100	11.4
Ming, 1st half (1368–1505)	2	13	7	3	26	51	3.7
Ming, 2d half (1506–1644)	10	29	29	63	93	224	16.2
Ming (undated)	22	7	24	—	63	116	
Total	52	71	71	127	380	701	

SOURCES: *Shan-hsi t'ung chih* (Gazetteer of Shansi; 1898), ch. 76; *Shan-tung t'ung chih* (Gazetteer of Shantung; 1729), ch. 14; *Ho-nan t'ung chih* (Gazetteer of Honan; 1730), ch. 43; *Hu-nan t'ung chih* (Gazetteer of Hunan; 1885), ch. 70; *Chiang-hsi t'ung chih* (Gazetteer of Kiangsi; 1880), ch. 81 and 82.

yüan were founded was everywhere substantially higher during the second half of the Ming than during the first. Data to be presented below suggest that this contrast actually reflects a second wave of foundings that began to accelerate late in the fifteenth century and peaked in the decade or so prior to 1567, declining thereafter to the end of the dynastic period in 1644.

It is ironic that the origins of academies reflect traditions that carried a distinctly antiurban bias. The mountain-recluse ideal was dominant in the *shu-yüan* founded during the first wave.[2] The inspiration came from medieval sources both Taoist and Buddhist. The Taoist emphasis on scenic rural settings for meditation and study may be traced to references in the *Hou Han shu*;[3] the Buddhist emphasis, to the Jetavana Garden where monks assembled for meditation and discussion.[4] The Ch'an (Zen) movement, a special school of Buddhist instruction that contributed elements to Neo-Confucianism, was particularly influential in the development of Sung academies. Many of the early *shu-yüan* were direct heirs or successors of Ch'an and other Buddhist places of study: the Pai-lu-tung (White Deer's Cave) Academy in northern Kiangsi is one of the more renowned examples.[5]

It was Neo-Confucianism, above all, that informed the academies founded from Sung through Ming.[6] And the Neo-Confucian founders of the *shu-yüan* were inspired not only by the mountain-recluse ideal but also by the wandering scholars of Eastern Chou and the confraternities they formed. Instruction in Ming-period *shu-yüan* echoed the pedagogical techniques favored by Confucius, and discussion seemed to resume dialogues that had been interrupted 1,700 years earlier. Academies sought to embody the simpler life of Eastern Chou, when scholars made do without certain amenities. The relaxed atmosphere of an academy situated on a hillside or lakeshore was deemed appropriate for recreating the intellectual give and take of the idealized ancient era.

Most of the early *shu-yüan* were in fact situated in scenic surroundings outside cities, often at secluded sites. The headmasters of Sung academies were normally called *shan-chang*, "mountain masters," a title that persisted in many instances into the Ch'ing period. In Ming times almost all *shu-yüan* were supported largely by rental income from agricultural land. The ground swell of local enthusiasm for academies that developed in the sixteenth century was for the most part underwritten by an essentially agrarian economy. Nevertheless, an urbanizing trend became apparent in the development of Chinese academies at least by the sixteenth century. Increasingly, new *shu-yüan* were being established in cities, and *shu-yüan* generally were becoming more closely oriented to and integrated with official urban institutions. Let us briefly review the institutional changes that underlay this trend.

The growth and expansion of *shu-yüan* were not unrelated to the changing functions of an older institution, the *hsüeh-kung*, "school-temple." Under the names *fu-*, *chou-*, and *hsien-hsüeh*, these were the official government schools of the prefectures, departments, and counties. An alternative name for them was *ju-hsüeh*, "literati school," and in late imperial times the building that housed the ceremonial halls came to be called colloquially the *wen miao*, "temple for civil rites." By late Sung a school-temple was attached to virtually every civil yamen in the field administrative system, and like the yamen it was invariably situated within the walls of an administrative city.

Originally a school as well as a ritual and administrative center, the school-temple eventually lost its teaching function altogether. Even as the system of government schools was being fleshed out during the Sung period, the shift in function was under way. By late Ming, school-temples were primarily concerned with the annual official Confucian rites and with administrative tasks related to the examination system. As the government schools were articulated to form a system of loci for Confucian activities through which central control could be exercised, the need developed for places of genuine teaching and study. In broad perspective, it was the academies that came to fill this need.

The growth of *shu-yüan* in late imperial times also reflected the steadily increasing prominence of the examination system. With the government's growing reliance on examinations as the chief means of recruiting bureaucrats, and with the construction of examination sheds in virtually every capital throughout the empire, higher education inevitably focused more sharply on preparation for the imperial examinations. *Shu-yüan*, originally places of free discussion among literati and local officials, and in some respects centers of learning for learning's sake despite their de facto role in training schoolteachers, began to place increasing emphasis on training students to pass the examinations. Classical education, formerly an end in itself in terms of social standing, now became a means toward the ultimate status symbols—the graduate degrees of *chü-jen* and *chin-shih*, attainable only through the imperial examinations. Once society (i.e., local elites) had embraced the government-controlled markers of relative eliteness, there was all the more reason for cooperation between the resident gentry and locally posted officials in preparing scholars for the hierarchically graded examinations.

It is seldom easy to disentangle the precise roles of gentry and officials in the foundation of particular academies. From the very beginning of the process, official approval and recognition were required; and it is clear that by late Ming, credit for founding an academy added to the reputation of an aspiring bureaucrat and furthered his career. But since the local social unit invariably stood to gain by a new *shu-yüan*, through enhanced reputation and improved chances in the competition for the coveted degrees, its leading gentry were consistently and strongly motivated to found and sustain one. More often than not, the gentry provided most of the funds, looked after the appointment of teachers, and attended to the recruitment of students. Thus one can seldom be certain in the case of a founding recorded as "official" whether it was the magistrate (using his bureaucratic power as necessary to extract contributions) or the local gentry (manipulating the magistrate as a convenient figurehead) who took the initiative and played the leading role.

Despite these ambiguities, available data suggest a growing interest in academies on the part of state authorities and an increasingly active role on the part of magistrates in their founding. Kiangsi may serve as an example. As shown in Table 2, the number of academies sponsored by officials in the Ming period marked an enormous absolute increase over the number of official foundations for the Yüan period. Moreover, the percentage of official sponsorship in the Ming shows a significant relative increase over those of Yüan and Sung (37 percent, as compared with 27 percent and 20 percent, respectively). This trend toward in-

TABLE 2. OFFICIAL VERSUS PRIVATE SPONSORSHIP OF NEWLY ESTABLISHED ACADEMIES, KIANGSI, SUNG THROUGH CH'ING

Period	Private sponsorship		Official sponsorship		Total
	No.	Pct.	No.	Pct.	
Sung	120	80%	30	20%	150
Yüan	35	73	13	27	48
Ming	114	63	68	37	182
Ch'ing	37	32	80	68	117

SOURCE: *Chiang-hsi t'ung chih* (1880), ch. 81 and 82; see Grimm 1960, p. 119f.

creased official sponsorship continued into the Ch'ing—the importance of official initiative being heightened by a sharp decline in private foundations.

In sum, the development of academies during the centuries from Sung through Ming was clearly in the direction of semiofficial status. *Shu-yüan* were ever more closely tied to the examination system; they were increasingly founded if not on official initiative then with official blessings and encouragement; and their activities came to be closely supervised by government officials. This integrated set of changes underlay a shift in emphasis from rural to urban. *Shu-yüan* in close touch with the city-based official director of studies were at a distinct advantage; and it was beneficial, too, to maintain an ongoing familiarity with examination procedures. Urban *shu-yüan* were also more visible to two categories of potential donors—officials and merchants. In any case, a growing proportion of new foundings were in capital cities or in the suburbs immediately outside their walls. Moreover, of established academies, those located in cities were more likely than their rural counterparts to grow in importance and take on higher-order functions. A tendency was already apparent in late Ming for the more important *shu-yüan*—the ones that specifically prepared students for the provincial and metropolitan examinations—to be located in or near cities, especially cities high in the administrative hierarchy. Even Wang Yang-ming, whose influence was so important in the spread of "free" academies, once proposed that a *shu-yüan* be established in every prefectural capital to facilitate preparation for higher-level examinations.[7] By the end of the eighteenth century, his proposal had virtually been realized.

Mention should be made in this regard of two other types of educational institutions, the *i-hsüeh*, "charity school," and the *she-hsüeh*, "community school." *I-hsüeh* were normally sponsored and endowed solely by local gentry, ostensibly to serve the children of families not wealthy enough to pay for private tutors. The best of them were functionally quite close to the less exalted of the *shu-yüan*, providing advanced training in the classics and preparing students for the county-level examinations.[8] *She-hsüeh*, first established during the reign of the Ming founder, were designed to bring some basic education to the common people. Ch'ing sources make it clear that they had been founded not only in rural towns and villages but also in cities, typically one in each of the four quadrants. Not enough research has been done on *she-hsüeh* to ascertain to what extent they provided genuine schooling as against simply serving as staging points for admonishing the local populace to behave.[9] *She-hsüeh* appear in any case to have been highly transitory—those listed in gazetteers more often than not carry the laconic remark *chiu-fei*, "long defunct"—and it is probably wise to resist as a general proposition the view that *she-hsüeh* served as feeder schools for more advanced *i-hsüeh* and *shu-yüan*.

Official Versus Private Foundings in Time and Space

Turning now to Kwangtung, let us first examine temporal patterning in the establishment of academies. Table 3 establishes the overall secular increase that characterized the late imperial era as a whole. Although data are of dubious reliability for the first half of the Ming period, we may be sure that the rate at which new academies were founded was markedly lower than the 10.8 per decade shown for the second half.* Rates for the first century and a half of the Ch'ing period are significantly higher (13.7 per decade) than the late Ming rates, and those for the 110 years ending with the abolition of the examination system are higher still.

As suggested earlier, however, this secular trend by no means implies a sustained increase from one decade to the next over the centuries. Rather, its temporal shape is wavelike. The first wave of *shu-yüan* foundings, as noted above, appears to have peaked in the Southern Sung for the Yangtze provinces and southeastern China, and in the Yüan for most of North and Northwest China. The second peaked in most regions of China during the Chia-ching reign (1522–66) of the Ming period. The contours of the second wave are clearly apparent in the data for Kwangtung, as shown in Table 4, where a peak rate of 17.3 foundings per decade is shown for the Chia-ching reign, followed by a steady decline through the remainder of the Ming period. The Kwangtung data reveal

---

* The division of the Ming period into a first half (1368–1505) and a second half (1506–1644) is not arbitrary, for the beginning of the Cheng-te reign period has often been considered a watershed by historians of the Ming. The validity of that division is corroborated by the data in Table 1.

TABLE 3. ACADEMIES ESTABLISHED OR REVIVED, KWANGTUNG, 1368–1905

Period	No. of years	No. of academies	No. per decade
1368–1505	138	18[a]	1.3
1506–1644	138	150	10.8
1644–1795	152	208	13.7
1796–1905	110	207	18.8
Total	400	565	

SOURCE: Liu Po-chi, *Kuang-tung shu yüan chih tu* (The academy system in Kwangtung; Canton: Shang wu yin shu kuan, 1938), pp. 46–53.
[a] This figure is undoubtedly an undercount.

TABLE 4. OFFICIAL VERSUS PRIVATE SPONSORSHIP OF NEWLY ESTABLISHED AND REVIVED ACADEMIES, KWANGTUNG, 1506–1905

| | | Newly established and revived academies | | | | | | |
| | | Private sponsorship | | Official sponsorship | | Total | | Official foundings as a pct. of total |
Period	No. of years	No.	Per decade	No.	Per decade	No.	Per decade	
1506–21	16	4	2.5	4	2.5	8	5.0	50
1522–66	45	27	6.0	51	11.3	78	17.3	65
1567–1619	53	6	1.1	41	7.7	47	8.9	87
1620–43	24	3	1.3	14	5.8	17	7.1	82
1644–61	18	1	0.6	3	1.7	4	2.2	75
1662–1722	61	12	2.0	69	11.3	81	13.3	85
1723–35	13	0	0.0	20	15.4	20	15.4	100
1736–95	60	21	3.5	82	13.7	103	17.2	80
1796–1820	25	20	8.0	31	12.4	51	20.4	61
1821–50	30	22	7.3	24	8.0	46	15.3	52
1851–61	11	24	21.8	4	3.6	28	25.5	14
1862–74	13	17	13.1	14	10.8	31	23.8	45
1875–1905	31	37	11.9	14	4.5	51	16.5	27
Total	400	194	4.9	371	9.3	565	14.1	66

SOURCE: Same as for Table 3.

a third wave during the Ch'ing period, dramatic in its contrasts and rising to unprecedented heights. From a low of 2.2 foundings per decade during the first Ch'ing reign period, the rate steadily rose to a high of 20.4 foundings per decade during the Chia-ch'ing reign (1796–1820). Though the rate dropped off during the Tao-kuang reign, it showed a resurgence during the third quarter of the nineteenth century, when academies were established at an unprecedented rate. This period of growth was followed by one of marked decline during the 31 years of the Kuang-hsü reign prior to the end of the examination system.

We may better understand these trends by distinguishing academies according to whether they were founded privately or with official sponsorship. (See the middle columns of Table 4.) The terms used in most sources are *kuan-li*, "founded by officials," and *ssu-li*, "founded by private parties." The latter usually referred to members of the resident gentry, often termed *i-shen*, "county gentry," in the sources, but sometimes simply *li-jen* or *hsiang-jen*, "local people."[10] In many cases such private parties collected funds before approaching the magistrate to urge him to take the lead in founding an academy. In other cases the magistrate took the initiative and called in leading gentry to discuss plans. Given the bias of protocol, however, we may assume that the *kuan-li* category is overinclusive and that *ssu-li* refers only to cases in which the official did little more than bestow formal blessing and approval. Thus the 371 foundings listed in Table 4 under official sponsorship probably included most of the genuinely joint foundings, whereas the 194 foundings listed under private sponsorship probably excluded most cases where the official role was more than perfunctory. Since there is no reason to expect any change in bias over time, the trends shown in Table 4 most likely provide a faithful reflection of the relative importance of officials in establishing academies.

The decennial rates shown in the official sponsorship column align in remarkably precise fashion with accepted indicators of dynastic strength and administrative vigor. The low rates of 1620–61 may be seen as the almost inevitable response to governmental concern with internal rebellion and foreign invasion during the last Ming reign period and with pacification during the first Ch'ing reign period. Official foundings were most frequent during High Ch'ing (the Yung-cheng and Ch'ien-lung reigns, 1723–95, by all counts the dynasty's heyday). The low rate during the Hsien-feng reign (1851–61) reflects preoccupation with the Taiping Rebellion; and the sharp resurgence during the T'ung-chih reign (1862–74) coincides with the renewed vigor of the post-Rebellion restoration. Official foundings as a percentage of all foundings shows a pattern identical to the one just reviewed, at least for the Ch'ing period.

The chief surprise in the column showing privately sponsored foundings is the tremendous increase in private activity from the mid-nineteenth century to the end of the examination system—a change that runs counter to the long-term secular rise in the proportion of official foundings, already documented in Table 2. In all probability this increase is related (1) to the acceleration of foreign trade that followed the establishment of Hong Kong and the opening of Canton as a treaty port, and (2) to the consequent spurt in the commercialization of the hinterlands of these two ports. Two other localities within Kwangtung received

TABLE 5. OFFICIAL VERSUS PRIVATE SPONSORSHIP OF ACADEMIES, TO CA. 1875 ONLY, KUANG-CHOU, HUI-CHOU, AND SHAO-CHOU PREFECTURES

	Nature of sponsorship						Subtotal		Data inadequate to classify	Total
	Private		Mixed		Official					
Prefecture	No.	Pct.	No.	Pct.	No.	Pct.	No.	Pct.		
Kuang-chou	20	30%	13	20%	33	50%	66	100%	6	72
Hui-chou	4	20	5	25	11	55	20	100	1	21
Shao-chou	2	17	2	17	8	67	12	100	4	16
Total	26	27%	20	20%	52	53%	98	100%	11	109

SOURCES: *Kuang-chou fu chih* (Prefectural gazetteer of Kuang-chou; 1879), ch. 72, 12a ff; *Hui-chou fu chih* (Prefectural gazetteer of Hui-chou; 1881), ch. 10, 1a ff; *Shao-chou fu chih* (Prefectural gazetteer of Shao-chou; 1874), ch. 18, 1a ff.

similar external stimulus prior to the 1880's—Swatow, the new ocean port for Ch'ao-chou *fu*, and Pei-hai (Pakhoi), the ocean port for Lien-chou *fu*, which were opened as treaty ports in 1858 and 1876, respectively. The assumption is that the wealth generated by rising foreign and domestic trade was in part invested in *shu-yüan* in order to strengthen the competitive position of particular local systems in the examination game. If this interpretation is correct, we should expect to see an enhanced role for commercial capital in *shu-yüan* foundings during the second half of the nineteenth century and a geographic concentration of privately funded academies in the hinterlands of the major ocean ports.

In this regard, a comparison of academies in three prefectures within Kwangtung is instructive. For this purpose I collected from the relevant prefectural gazetteers all information concerning gentry participation in the establishment or revival of *shu-yüan*.[11] With the detailed data available in these gazetteers, it was possible to distinguish "mixed" foundings—those in which a significant role for both gentry and officials is specifically documented. The results are shown in Table 5. Kuang-chou prefecture incorporated the entire Canton delta and most of the core area of the West River basin. Hui-chou prefecture, directly east of Kuang-chou, included most of the East River basin. Shao-chou prefecture, directly north of Kuang-chou, included the upper reaches of the North River basin. Differences in the absolute number of academies shown for the three prefectures are in large part accounted for by relative size: Kuang-chou included fourteen county-level units, Hui-chou ten, and Shao-chou six. Moreover, the population differentials were even sharper than the numbers of administrative subdivisions imply. When size factors are held constant, however, there is little doubt that the prefectures differed in general wealth and productivity in the order shown from Kuang-chou, which led the whole province in per capita agricultural productivity, industrial output, and volume of trade (extraregional, including foreign, as well as intraregional), to Shao-chou, which was inferior to Hui-chou in all these respects. For example, there had been a long-standing differential among the three prefectures in the extent to which agriculture had been commercialized. In addition, post-1842 spurs to economic activity had been most effective in Kuang-chou, whose capital was Canton itself, next most effective in Hui-chou, the southern portion of which had by the 1870's been reoriented commercially to Hong Kong, and least effective in Shao-chou, whose role in extraregional trade probably declined after the opening of treaty ports in the Lower Yangtze region and in Fukien. These factors are doubtless all significant in assessing the relative importance of the official and private roles in establishing academies. The data in Table 5 suggest that private parties were more active where disposable wealth in private hands was proportionately greater. Specifically, one may note that Canton, capital of Kuang-chou *fu*, was in economic terms the central metropolis of a vast region including most of Kwangtung and Kwangsi, whereas the capitals of the other two prefectures were merely regional cities with relatively restricted hinterlands. One would expect this difference to have consequences for capabilities of mobilizing private capital for collective goals. Another perspective on these data comes from the realization that the absolute numbers of *shu-yüan* founded with full official sponsorship (33, 11, and 8) were a fairly faithful reflection of the relative populations of the three prefectures. Thus the official role fostered a relatively egalitarian distribution of academies, and the more favorable opportunity structures in particular local systems appear to have resulted primarily from greater private initiative, activity, and funding. This interpretation fits well with what we know of the philosophy of government in late imperial times and the dynamics of competition among prefectures aimed at winning a larger share of the province's fixed quota of imperial degrees.

Brief notice of comparable data for Anhwei may be useful.[12] First, the total number of *shu-yüan* is smaller than in Kwangtung; and, in accordance with the argument above, the relative role of private sponsorship is less. Second, the temporal patterning of academy foundings was similar to that shown for Kwangtung. For instance, the peak rates for official foundings came during the High Ch'ing and the T'ung-chih Restoration, with the nadir in the Hsien-feng reign, the era of Taiping disruption. Third, the spatial patterning of private versus official sponsorship appears to reflect the interrelationships that seemed plausible for Kwangtung: for instance, the four southernmost prefectures of

Academies and Urban Systems in Kwangtung

Anhwei, relatively rich and commercialized,[13] show a rate of strictly private foundations (34 percent) comparable to that for Kuang-chou *fu* (30 percent), whereas the corresponding figure for the remainder of Anhwei (12 percent) is even lower than that for Shao-chou *fu* (17 percent).

Urban Versus Rural Location

The extent to which *shu-yüan* were in fact urban may be explored for the three Kwangtung prefectures discussed above. I have classified *shu-yüan* (together with the few *i-hsüeh, she-hsüeh,* and similar schools treated with them in the same *chüan* of the gazetteers) according to whether they were situated (1) within the walls of the capital city, (2) in the immediate suburbs of the capital city, (3) in a market town (as indicated by *chen, shih, hsü,* or related terms in the place name), or (4) putatively in a rural area. Since the fourth category includes locations indicated not only by such unambiguous terms as *ts'un* (village) or *pao* (walled village) but also by *hsiang* (rural township, usually including a market town as well as villages) and *tu* (subdivision of a county, usually including market towns as well as villages), this classification errs on the side of overstating the number of *shu-yüan* in strictly rural locations. Nonetheless, as shown in Table 6, fewer than 35 percent of all academies in each of the prefectures could have been strictly rural, and well over half were located within the administrative cities and their immediate suburbs.[14]

TABLE 6. URBAN-RURAL LOCATION OF ACADEMIES, CA. 1875, KUANG-CHOU, HUI-CHOU, AND SHAO-CHOU PREFECTURES

Administrative unit	Urban-rural location									
	City proper		Suburban		Market town		Other		Total	
	No.	Pct.	No.	Pct.	No.	Pct.	No.	Pct.	No.	Pct.
Kuang-chou *fu*	30	33%	19	21%	12	13%	31	34%	92	100%
Hui-chou *fu*	9	32	13	46	1	4	5	18	28[a]	100
Shao-chou *fu*	8	50	5	31	0	–	3	19	16	100
Kuang-chou *fu* 4 urbanized delta counties[b]	10	20	10	20	10	20	19	39	49	100
10 other counties[c]	20	47	9	21	2	5	12	28	43	100

SOURCE: Same as for Table 5.
[a] No location data were given for two additional academies in Hui-chou *fu*.
[b] Namely, P'an-yü, Nan-hai, Shun-te, and Hsiang-shan. Of the twenty "academies" listed for Hsiang-shan, five were specified as *i-hsüeh* or other types.
[c] Of the 43 academies in these counties, all were designated *shu-yüan* except for six *i-hsüeh* (all in Tseng-ch'eng) and three *she-hsüeh* (two in San-shui and one in Hsin-hui).

The data shown in Table 6 are somewhat anomalous, however, in that academy location was more urban in the less urbanized prefectures of Hui-chou and Shao-chou than in the comparatively highly urbanized prefecture of Kuang-chou, where nearly half of all academies were located in market towns or "rural areas." This paradox can be understood, I believe, in terms of Professor Skinner's regional-systems model, which holds that local systems per se (nodes *plus* hinterlands) at the same level of analysis tend to be more urbanized the closer they are to the regional metropolis at the center of macroregional cores. It may be noted in the lower part of Table 6 that, when the four most urbanized counties (including Canton and the most productive tracts of the Canton delta) are distinguished from the remaining ten counties in Kuang-chou prefecture, it is the former that exhibit the abnormally "rural" distribution of academies. In fact, however, those four counties had more urban *shu-yüan* on the average than any of the other counties (5.0 per administrative city as against 2.9 for the other ten Kuang-chou counties and 2.2 for both Hui-chou and Shao-chou prefectures); what is distinctive about them is that they also had many academies outside the cities. The explanation almost certainly lies in the high levels of wealth and aspiration even in the countryside of counties in the immediate vicinity of Canton. Here the competition was intense at the subcounty level, and subcounty local systems such as those centered on Fo-shan and Hsiao-lan founded their own academies to enhance the local success rate in the examinations. We may be glimpsing here another facet of a general pattern. In the peripheries of regions, where local resources were fewer, most *shu-yüan* were founded by officials and situated in or near the local capitals; but in the rich, urbanized cores of regions, private foundings swelled the total number of academies, not only in the cities but also in the countryside, where the official role was negligible.

Other evidence suggests that it was the larger, more important, and academically more advanced *shu-yüan* that were most likely to have an urban location. A simple but telling index is the number of lines devoted to each *shu-yüan* in the prefectural gazetteer. When the academies in Kuang-chou *fu* are classified in this fashion and cross-tabulated by urban-rural location (see Table 7), the correlation is striking. Over three-fifths of the academies receiving four or more lines of description were located within the walls of administrative cities; and nearly two-thirds of those receiving only a one-line notice were putatively rural. Even if we discount a tendency toward urban bias on the part of gazetteer compilers, we find the data indicating what common sense sug-

Table 7. Urban-Rural Location of Academies by Lines of Description in the Gazetteer Text, Kuang-chou Prefecture, 1879

Lines of text in gazetteer	Urban-rural location									
	City proper		Suburban		Market town		Other		Total	
	No.	Pct.	No.	Pct.	No.	Pct.	No.	Pct.	No.	Pct.
1	8	20%	4	10%	7	18%	21	53%	40	100%
2	8	33	5	21	2	8	9	38	24	100
3	4	33	5	42	2	17	1	8	12	100
4	10	63	5	31	1	6	–	0	16	100
Total	30	33%	19	21%	12	13%	31	34%	92	100%

Source: *Kuang-chou fu chih* (Prefectural gazetteer of Kuang-chou; 1879) ch. 66.

gests, namely that the more important academies were located in more strictly urban centers.

The Educational Hierarchy

There are some grounds, in fact, for positing a rural-urban hierarchy of educational institutions in the nineteenth century, with respect not only to prestige and educational standing, but also (1) to extent and type of official recognition, (2) to flow of students from elementary to more advanced levels, and (3) to size of catchment area. The gazetteers imply, though they are by no means explicit, that each administrative unit had its "head" *shu-yüan*. Almost invariably what I call the head *shu-yüan* was given pride of place in the list of educational institutions described in the gazetteer, was described at greater length and in more elaborate detail, and had the largest "official" endowment of all academies within the administrative unit—which does not mean that private endowments were thereby any smaller, the contrary being more often the case. In addition, the description of the head *shu-yüan* often indicated in one way or another that its catchment area was the county or prefecture in question.

As identified in this fashion, head *shu-yüan* turn out to have been overwhelmingly urban in location. Of the fifteen in Kuang-chou *fu* (one for the prefecture and fourteen for the component counties), twelve were situated within the walls of their capital and two in the immediate suburbs, the data for the remaining case being unclear.[15] Of the seven head *shu-yüan* in Shao-chou *fu*, four were situated within the walls and three in the immediate suburbs. In this case, the prefectural academy, the Hsiang-chiang Shu-yüan, one of the few in Kwangtung dating back to the Sung period, lay close to the northern wall of the city, just across the river.¹⁶ In Hui-chou prefecture, of the ten county-level head *shu-yüan*, six were situated within the walls and four in the immediate suburbs.¹⁷ The head academy for the prefecture, Feng-hu Shu-yüan, famed for its scenic beauty and explicit in its "nature mystique," was in fact sited at the shore of the lake that lay outside the east wall of the prefectural capital.¹⁸

It is notable that the great majority of head *shu-yüan* were founded no earlier than in the Ch'ing, which is what might be expected if in fact the development of a clear-cut hierarchy was a late development. Of the seven head *shu-yüan* of Shao-chou *fu*, one dated from the Sung, one from the Ming, and the remaining five from the Ch'ing. Of the eleven head *shu-yüan* of Hui-chou *fu*, all but one (the prefectural *shu-yüan*, dating from the Sung) were founded in the Ch'ing period. In Ch'ao-chou *fu*, in the northeastern corner of the province, the head *shu-yüan* stand out for their ancient vintage: of the ten identifiable cases, one dates from the Sung, five from the Ming, and four from the Ch'ing, all of the last having been founded prior to 1770. By contrast, Kuang-chou *fu*, the metropolitan prefecture, stands out in that none of its head *shu-yüan* predate the Ch'ing, and eleven of the fifteen were founded after 1770. This suggests that the pinnacle of the provincial hierarchy was stabilized rather late; and in fact, as we shall see in a moment, keen competition and shifting power alignments led to rather frequent changes at the very top—in the provincial capital of Canton.

What are the outlines of the hierarchy as a whole? At the base, of course, were the elementary institutions that introduced students to the classics—tutorials for gentry children; *ssu-shu* (the private schools typically operated by a single teacher); lineage schools, which were sometimes known as *i-hsüeh*; and perhaps some of the *she-hsüeh* that actually functioned as community schools. These institutions were found in settlements of all types and levels, from villages up to great cities. Next were the more advanced *i-hsüeh*, some of the *she-hsüeh*, and the smaller *shu-yüan*, all of which were typically located in or near market towns as well as cities, and whose "graduates" fed into the head county-level *shu-yüan*. An atypically neat case is that of Lo-ch'ang *hsien* in Shao-chou *fu*, where the single *shu-yüan* in the county capital was fed by fourteen *she-hsüeh*, one in the capital "to the right of the county yamen" and one each in the thirteen *tu* into which the county was subdivided.¹⁹ In twelve of the sixteen county-level units in Hui-chou and Shao-chou prefectures, a second institution in the county capital appeared to serve as the second choice for students who failed to win a place in the head *shu-yüan*; two of these institutions were known as *she-hsüeh*, the remainder as *i-hsüeh* or *shu-yüan*. Similarly, the prefectural capitals of Hui-chou and Shao-chou each boasted a second school that appeared to serve as a backup for the prefectural head *shu-yüan* and as a feeder to it.[20] The manner in which lower-level schools fed the prefectural head *shu-yüan* is indicated by a regulation for Shao-chou dated 1852. Annually around the New Year, the *shu-yüan* supervisor (*chien-yüan*) petitioned the prefect for permission to send examiners to the various counties for the purpose of selecting the brightest students. "When all [candidates] are assembled at the appointed date, the graduates (*sheng*) and undergraduates (*t'ung*) are examined and re-examined on two different days behind closed doors, and only those who show genuine talent on both occasions obtain permission [to enter the head *shu-yüan*]."[21]

Inevitably the richer counties, with greater per capita investment in education and more elaborate feeder schools, fared better in the competition for places in the head *shu-yüan* of the prefecture than did the poorer counties. And it was the head *shu-yüan* of the prefecture above all that groomed advanced students for success in the provincial examinations. The metropolitan county of Hui-chou *fu*, Kuei-shan *hsien*, and its immediate neighbor, Po-lo, held the lead in graduate degrees won during the period 1851–79, with 111 and 89, respectively.[22] In the case of Shao-chou *fu*, the metropolitan county (Ch'ü-chiang *hsien*) also took the lead with 76 graduate degrees, followed closely by two adjacent counties, Weng-yüan with 68 and Ying-te with 67.[23] In both cases the leading counties encompassed the productive, commercialized, and urbanized core of the subregions in question.[24] Peripheral counties in some prefectures did so poorly that one suspects the de facto catchment area of the prefectural *shu-yüan* to have been only the better endowed portion of its theoretical area, i.e., of the prefecture as a whole. In any case, it is apparent that the patterning both of recruitment to prefectural head *shu-yüan* and of examination results expressed rather faithfully the economic structure of the subregion the prefecture dominated.

At the pinnacle of the whole system were the six or seven outstanding *shu-yüan* located in Canton itself. Until the late 1820's, the Yüeh-hsiu Shu-yüan led the pack, serving as the de facto head *shu-yüan* for all of central Kwangtung. It had the right to call in for further training the top performers in the intermediate *sui* and *k'o* provincial examinations from four major prefectures (Kuang-chou, Shao-chou, Chao-ch'ing, and Kao-chou). Its large student body of 150 included 120 graduates (*sheng* and *chien*), most of whom were preparing for the provincial and metropolitan examinations. The headmasters of Yüeh-hsiu were far more likely than others to receive mention in the gazetteers.[25] The Hsüeh-hai

T'ang, which was founded in 1820 and began operation in 1824, very quickly became the most prestigious *shu-yüan* in Canton. It began under the auspices of Juan Yüan, then Governor-General of Kwangtung and Kwangsi, and it counted a number of renowned scholars among its early directors and lecturers, including Lin Po-t'ung (1775–1845), Chang Wei-p'ing (1780–1859), Liang T'ing-nan (1796–1861), T'an Ying (1800–1871), and Ch'en Li (1810–82)—all born in or near Canton.[26] Its intellectual tradition favored the Ch'ing school of pragmatic Confucianism.[27] The Hsüeh-hai T'ang enrolled only 40 very carefully selected students, drawn largely from major academies in Canton and its suburbs; most were preparing for the metropolitan examination. Situated on the slope of Yüeh-hsiu hill just outside the city wall, it was financed by official subsidies and rental income from a handsome endowment of landed property. Later in the century two other newly established academies rose to challenge the Hsüeh-hai T'ang's supremacy in training scholars for the metropolitan examination. The Ying-yüan Shu-yüan, founded in 1869, enrolled some 65 *chü-jen* recruited from throughout Kwangtung,[28] and the Kuang-ya Shu-yüan, founded in 1887 by no less a figure than Chang Chih-tung, enrolled about 100 *chü-jen* selected from both Kwangsi and Kwangtung.[29]

Not far behind these four leading academies were three others of high academic standing: the Yüeh-hua Shu-yüan, which recruited primarily from prominent merchant families; the Yang-ch'eng Shu-yüan, formed through consolidating three *i-hsüeh* and two earlier *shu-yüan*; and the Chü-po Ching-she, which according to the P'an-yü county gazetteer of 1871 "selected students from three *shu-yüan*—Yüeh-hsiu, Yüeh-hua, and Yang-ch'eng—for monthly examinations on poetics, literary exposition, and ancient classics," topics geared in particular to the provincial examination.[30] Other academies in Canton were less selective, were sustained by a less elaborate feeder system, and drew on a more restricted catchment area.

Funding and Control

Budgetary data for academies are occasionally provided by gazetteers, but normally only for head *shu-yüan*. As might be expected, the annual incomes of the leading Canton academies were exceptionally large. In the 1870's, the annual budget of Ying-yüan Shu-yüan was 2,760 taels, of Hsüeh-hai T'ang 2,071 taels, and of Yüeh-hua Shu-yüan 2,052 taels.[31] The budget was normally increased by one-twelfth in the case of years with an intercalary month. The major expenditures of Ying-yüan Shu-yüan were specified as (1) salary of the headmaster, (2) salary of the supervisor, (3) expenses of the gentry elder, (4) "oil and firewood money" for students, and (5) expenses of students participating in provincial and metropolitan examinations.[32] Of Hsüeh-hai T'ang's total budget, no less than 38 percent was allocated to various modes of supporting and motivating students.[33] Data for the head *shu-yüan* of two prefectures show budgets about half those of the leading Canton academies. Hsiang-chiang Shu-yüan in Shao-chou-fu had an annual income of 1,014 taels around 1870, of which 300 went to the headmaster as salary, 300 to the students as stipends, and 24 to the supervisor as a food allowance.[34] Feng-hu Shu-yüan in Hui-chou-fu during the 1870's had an annual income of between 800 and 1,000 taels, of which 400 covered the headmaster's salary and 400 the stipends for 130 students, nonresident as well as resident; in this case the supervisor's annual allowance was 40 piculs of rice.[35] In general, the headmaster's salary appears to have been fixed at a level equal to the total of student stipends, with each item accounting for 30 to 40 percent of the total budget. Student stipends normally varied with academic achievement (the monthly allowance of those who did poorly in examinations was typically cut by half or discontinued) and with residential status (nonresidents received less than residents, often only half as much).[36] Extrapolating from these data, we may assume that annual budgets of head *shu-yüan* at the county level were significantly below 1,000 taels and that those of ordinary academies amounted to no more than a few hundred taels.

Support for *shu-yüan* came largely from three sources—officials (i.e., donations and subsidies made by imperial bureaucrats from government monies or unofficial income), the local gentry, and local merchants. Income normally took the form of rents from agricultural land, rents from urban real estate, interest from trust funds (often with provisions for regular augmentation), and operating capital given in the form of regular subsidies. Official support could take all forms—arable land, urban property, and trust funds, as well as regular subsidies. Gentry support was disproportionately in the form of trusts of agricultural land, whereas merchant support was disproportionately in the form of trust funds. Exceptions nonetheless occurred. One academy drew income from gentry investments in local pawnshops and commercial firms as well as in overseas Chinese enterprises.[37]

Land rental remained important to the end of the imperial era, even for strictly urban *shu-yüan*. Whereas the usual government school-temples (*hsüeh-kung*) had landholdings of perhaps a hundred *mou*, the average *shu-yüan* held several hundred *mou* of agricultural land. The Hsüeh-hai T'ang in Canton started off in the 1820's with rural landholdings in excess of 3,000 *mou*. Of twenty leading academies in Kuang-chou *fu* (the top six in Canton plus the head *shu-yüan* of the fourteen component counties), eleven were financed entirely from land rents, and another three obtained half or more of their income from land rents.[38] Thus only 30 percent of these important and unambiguously urban academies relied primarily on what might be considered strictly urban funding. On the other hand, since a majority of these same leading *shu-yüan* (and for that matter a majority of head *shu-yüan* elsewhere in Kwangtung) had been funded at least partially through official donations, it is apparent that many landed trusts had been purchased with government funds. The traditional view persisted that investment in land was "proper" for long-term endowments, and in any case more secure.[39]

Nonetheless, a trend toward greater reliance on income from capitalist investment became evident in the nineteenth century. The records of Canton's Yüeh-hsiu Shu-yüan show 21 separate endowments from 1667 to 1887, the initial donations all being endowments of agricultural land. Six of the 21 were investment trusts in business firms and urban real estate, and of these four were established only in the nineteenth century, accounting in fact for all new donations after 1829. In the case of 67 Kwangtung *shu-yüan* for which data are available, I find 131 entries of donations involving capital property between 1732 and 1900. Of these, only 26 predated the nineteenth century.[40]

As might be expected, there was also a tendency for academies funded in whole or in part through urban property and commercial capital to be those situated in or near the most important commercial cities.[41] An interesting if atypical case is that of the Hsiang-chiang Shu-yüan in Shao-chou-fu, which was supported solely by the income from five pawnshops, four transport firms, and one coal dealer; interest from these holdings was sufficient to pay all expenses, including the headmaster's salary and student stipends.[42]

If we limit ourselves to urban academies during the nineteenth century, the prevailing picture is one of joint or cooperative funding that involved officials, merchants, and/or gentry. A case in point is the Kao-wen Shu-yüan in Kao-chou-fu, which was supported by income from thirteen different trust funds, seven official (accounting for 40 percent of total income) and six private.[43] In the case of the Yüeh-hua Shu-yüan, founded to meet the demand from salt-merchant families, the basic endowment was provided by the Salt Commission, a government agency; the salt merchants together put up subsidies for 30 students.[44] In the usual nineteenth-century case, the nonofficial portion of the funding came from both gentry and merchants.

Surprisingly, there is nothing in the available source material to suggest that government control was weaker or less effective in the case of academies that relied heavily on private funding. A telling case is that of the Hsiang-chiang Shu-yüan in Shao-chou-fu, which, as we have seen, was supported entirely by commercial capital. Its regulations specified that the supervisor was to be appointed by the prefect and that the headmaster could be appointed only with the prefect's approval. The supervisor petitioned the prefect with respect to such important matters as sending examiners to the county capitals to select students.[45] Those admitted were graded into three classes according to their examination results, with a quota of twenty for each of the top two classes. It is notable that examinations administered by officials counted more heavily than those administered by the *shu-yüan*'s teachers. Once admitted to the academy, students were tested at regular intervals by the prefect or the circuit intendant.[46] And the academy's regulations had been fixed by the prefect.[47]

In general this level of control obtained throughout the hierarchy of *shu-yüan*. Not only the prefect, but the education intendant and the provincial governor each had at least one *shu-yüan* to supervise. In the county capitals, the larger numbers of students were controlled by the *hsien-kuan*, "surveillance staff."[48] The number of students was fixed by the government throughout the province in accordance with the three-class system that originated with Wang An-shih in the eleventh century.[49] Periods of study, from one to three years, were geared to the schedules of imperial examinations. And the government provided uniform travel grants to those participating in the metropolitan examinations: 50 taels for first-class students, 40 taels for second-class students, and 30 taels for third-class students.[50] Finally, it is clear that texts, teaching, and exercises were closely attuned to the content and form of the various imperial examinations. Since the private parties who funded academies wanted to maximize students' success in the examinations, they were no less interested than the officials in hewing closely to the prescribed curriculum.

Thus the nineteenth-century resurgence of private funding for *shu-yüan* was not accompanied by any departure from the officially defined orthodoxy or by any lessening of government control. By late Ch'ing, academies were too closely geared to the imperial examination system to escape the rigidities of official educational prescriptions.

Academy Headmasters

A brief analysis of headmasters of Kwangtung academies at once illustrates and helps explain the strong orientation of *shu-yüan* toward the imperial bureaucracy.[51] Of 515 headmasters active in the province during the Ch'ing period, we know the highest degree attained for all but 27; the breakdown in descending order is as follows.

Degree	No.	Pct.
Han-lin	33	6.8%
chin-shih	150	30.7
chü-jen	198	40.6
kung-sheng	76	15.6
fu-pang	18	3.7
sheng-yüan	13	2.7
	488	100.0%

An impressive 78 percent held regular graduate degrees that had to be earned via the provincial and metropolitan examinations. *Han-lin* scholars were, of course, the academically superior subset of *chin-shih* degree-holders, so that the number of the latter very nearly matched the number of *chü-jen* degree-holders. Though it is hardly surprising, one might note the total absence of degrees obtained through purchase; all the headmasters had experienced the "examination life." It goes without saying that headmasters holding the less prestigious degrees were more likely to have served in the less advanced and more remote academies. The reverse was also true, of course, as illustrated by the case of Canton's top-seeded Yüeh-hsiu Shu-yüan. Of the 45 headmasters employed through the years by this academy, only three were not holders of the *chin-shih* degree, and no fewer than eight were *Han-lin* scholars.[52]

Moreover, within each category of degree-holders the proportion that had actually held bureaucratic office was higher among these Kwangtung headmasters than within the degree-holding group at large. We have records of the highest office held by 288 of the 515 headmasters (i.e., 56 percent), a total that probably understates the number who were former officials. The breakdown of this subset by highest office held is as follows.

Highest post held	No.	Pct.
Metropolitan posts	75	26.0%
Prefects, or provincial-level deputy examiners	25	8.7
County-level magistrates	52	18.1
Local directors of study	104	36.1
Other posts in the field administration	32	11.1
	288	100.0%

Academies and Urban Systems in Kwangtung

We should take note of the exceptionally high proportion of scholars who had served as local directors of study or who had otherwise held field positions where the duties normally involved supervision of academies and/or of local examinations. These figures suggest that at least 70 percent of the headmasters who had served in office (equivalent to approximately 40 percent of the total of 515) had previously dealt with academies in an official capacity.

No less than 90 percent of the 515 Kwangtung headmasters were natives of the province. It appears that most of the outsiders served in higher-ranking *shu-yüan* that prepared students for the provincial and metropolitan examinations and paid high salaries. This meant, of course, a concentration of outsiders in academies situated in high-level capitals and in more urbanized subregions. Thus, of the 53 Kwangtung headmasters from outside the province, nearly two-thirds (34) served in Kuang-chou *fu*—and fifteen of those served in Canton itself.[53]

However, even as the centralizing trends already described for the latter part of the Ch'ing period were strengthening the academic standing and performance of the *shu-yüan* in the metropolitan prefecture, the academies' reliance on scholars from outside the province was steadily declining. As shown in Table 8, nearly half of the headmasters appointed between 1662 and 1820 were outsiders, whereas for the period after 1820 the proportion dropped to about one in ten. Moreover, as indicated in the first column, natives of Canton steadily improved their position in the academic leadership within the metropolitan prefecture during late Ch'ing. These data suggest that the nineteenth-century trend toward academic "self-sufficiency" characterized not only the provincial level but also the prefectural level and probably the county level as well. It is likely that this reflects heightened competition among local systems in the production of degree-holders, for local leaders preferred native

TABLE 8. ACADEMY HEADMASTERS IN KUANG-CHOU PREFECTURE BY NATIVE PLACE AND YEAR OF APPOINTMENT

Years of appointment	Native place									
	Canton		Elsewhere in Kuang-chou *fu*		Elsewhere in Kwang-tung		Outside Kwangtung		Subtotal		Native place unknown	Total
	No.	Pct.	No.	Pct.	No.	Pct.	No.	Pct.	No.	Pct.		
1662–1795	3	10%	7	23%	7	23%	13	43%	30	100%	3	33
1796–1820	3	15	0	–	6	30	11	55	20	100	–	20
1821–50	16	52	5	16	7	23	3	10	31	100	1	32
1851–1905	45	70	9	14	3	5	7	11	64	100	–	64
Total	67	46%	21	14%	23	16%	34	23%	145	100%	4	149

SOURCE: Liu Po-chi 1938, pp. 222–90.

sons on whose chauvinistic loyalty they could count. The spectacular success of Canton natives during the nineteenth century is doubtless related to the establishment in that city of several new top-seeded *shu-yüan* during the century. By mid-century the pool of topflight academic talent among the local-born had grown to the point where it could meet expanding local needs.

Another factor may also have been at work. We have already noted the importance during the nineteenth century of capital investment in academy endowments. In Canton at least, this was associated with the increased activity of merchants in academy affairs. As Cantonese merchants upped their contributions to *shu-yüan* and diverted more of their sons to orthodox academic careers, it may be that their support was thrown behind those favoring native sons rather than outsiders as headmasters. Since their business competitors were typically organized according to provincial origin, the major Cantonese merchants in Canton may well have been more ardent local chauvinists than their gentry counterparts.

At any rate, the ranks of headmasters of Canton academies included several scholars of merchant origin. Ch'en Li (1810–82), headmaster of at least three *shu-yüan*, including Hsüeh-hai T'ang, and a *chü-jen* of 1832, was the son of a Canton merchant. Li Wen-t'ien (1834–95), a sometime official and renowned writer who headed the Ying-yüan Shu-yüan for seven years, was born into a Fo-shan business family. The names of other nineteenth-century scholars attest to the academic interests of Cantonese merchants. Wu Jung-kuang (1773–1843), for instance, a *Han-lin* scholar and governor, came from a Nan-hai salt-merchant family; and Wu Ch'ung-yueh (1810–63), a bibliophile and literary patron, was one of the Howqua hong merchants.

Conclusions

Our data on Kwangtung academies indicate institutional changes that we take to reflect general trends in late imperial China. Early *shu-yüan* tended to be situated outside cities, to depend solely on trusts of agricultural land, and to espouse an antiurban "mountain-recluse" ideal. The gradual transformation of official school-temples into strictly ritual and administrative institutions, coupled with the growing importance of the official examination system, set the stage for the gradual urbanization of academies. *Shu-yüan* that were centrally located found themselves increasingly advantaged in terms of access to funds and to the official apparatus associated with the imperial examination. During the second wave of academy foundings in the Ming period, the trend toward location in capital cities was already apparent, and a clear majority of *shu-yüan* established during the Ch'ing expansion were sited in capital cities and their immediate suburbs. Official initiative in the founding of academies tended to increase up to the nineteenth century, and *shu-yüan* activities, ever more sharply focused on preparation for official examinations, were by High Ch'ing closely supervised by government officials. Thus advanced *shü-yuan* situated in capitals came to acquire a semiofficial status that involved educational functions for a catchment area corresponding in theory to the relevant administrative unit—county, prefecture, or province.

Nineteenth-century trends reflect the growing economic importance of cities favored by commercial expansion. In Canton and its immediate hinterland, the role of commercial and other forms of urban capital became increasingly significant in the funding of *shu-yüan*, and merchants became increasingly active in academy affairs. New high-level *shu-yüan* were established at Canton in unprecedented numbers specifically to train advanced scholars for the provincial and metropolitan examinations; and new commercial wealth enabled subcounty local systems to establish academies that might strengthen their competitive position in the examinations. These changes in the Canton area, paralleled to a lesser degree in and around other commercial centers, capped the development of an educational hierarchy that reflected not only the official administrative system but also the hierarchy of economic centers. By the nineteenth century, academies that rated high in terms of academic function and official standing tended to be located in high-level cities; and the entire structure whereby lower-ranking academies fed students to academies further up in the hierarchy and whereby the better academies provided headmasters and lecturers to less exalted institutions culminated in Canton.

One important consequence was that Canton—regional metropolis as well as provincial capital—and its immediate administrative and commercial hinterland enjoyed an advantaged academic opportunity structure. This was clear enough already in the eighteenth century: the number of those earning the *chü-jen* degree (through success in the provincial examination) during the Ch'ien-lung reign (1736–95) was 830 for Kuang-chou *fu*, as against 166 for Hui-chou *fu* and only 25 for Shao-chou *fu*. During the nineteenth century the position of the metropolitan prefecture improved still further. Its share of the province's *chü-jen* was never less than 40 percent and rose in certain years as high as 70 percent. The absolute number of the prefecture's successful candidates rose above 50 per examination early in the nineteenth century and exceeded

100 twice in the 1860's. Within the prefecture, the three most urbanized counties—Nan-hai, P'an-yü, and Shun-te, collectively known as Sam Yap—consistently made the best showing. Kuang-chou prefecture also improved its performance in the metropolitan examinations, having eleven or more winners of the *chin-shih* degree on four separate occasions in the T'ung-chih period (1862–74).[54] The urbanization of *shu-yüan* inevitably meant that academic selection increasingly favored the most urbanized local and regional systems.

Extended Kinship in the Traditional City

HUGH D. R. BAKER

In dealing with Chinese society we are faced with a plethora of kin groupings that range from "simple family" to amorphous "common surname." Although attempts to reduce the entire complex to order may result in much unwieldy terminology, it is not too difficult to pick out the major forms of kin grouping while ignoring the subforms that bedevil more sophisticated analysis. Family (*chia* or *chia-t'ing*), various manifestations of the lineage (*tsung-tsu*), clan (*t'ung-tsung*), common surname (*t'ung-hsing*), and phratry are the major ripples in an ever-widening circle of kin, although no one person is necessarily involved in all these forms. It is important that we should have a clear idea of the differences between them.

Olga Lang has distinguished three main types of family—the conjugal, the stem, and two forms of joint family. With the conjugal and stem families we need not be concerned here, merely remarking that they accounted for the majority of Chinese families. The joint family "consists of parents, their unmarried children, their married sons (more than one) and sons' wives and children, and sometimes a fourth or fifth generation."[1] As the "five-generation family" (*wu-shih t'ung-chü*), the joint family has long been idealized by the Chinese, though in practice it has not been as common as its received value would lead us to anticipate. Where the normal pattern of family development involved either (1) the setting up of a separate residence and separate economy by each married couple with or without unmarried children (i.e., the conjugal family) or (2) the setting up of a separate residence and economy by each married son other than one who lived with his parents (i.e., the stem family), the joint family continued to expand without domestic fission or economic division. With few exceptions, daughters moved out on marriage—for the general pattern of residence was virilocal—but sons brought their wives into the family. As generations were born, the family tended to grow larger, subject of course to fluctuations in birth and death rates. Economically it remained a unit, individual members partaking of the profits of the joint estate ("Every male born or fully adopted into the family is, from the moment of his existence as a son, a coparcener"[2]) and contributing to the common fund according to ability and income. The whole was subject to the authority of the family head (*chia-chang*), who might be either a senior male or a senior female. Expansion of this kind could not continue indefinitely, and the "five generations" of the Chinese term for the joint family no doubt marks the very limit of undivided growth.[3] The problems involved in holding together a large joint family were enormous. Conflicts between father and son, mother and daughter-in-law, brothers, and the wives of different brothers were latent in even the smallest joint family. By the time such a family had built up to as many as five generations, the most distantly related of its members might be almost outside the pale of the *wu-fu*, the recognized mourning grades, at their greatest extent.[4] Where such a family, in the face of the strong pressures for fission, was held together largely by an idealistic cleaving to Confucian values, the spilling of its members over the edge of the *wu-fu*—resulting in the co-residence of people who may be said to be only informally related—was probably enough to bring about its collapse. In any event, the joint family was very much a phenomenon of the wealthy, poor families being unable to expand in this way for a variety of reasons.[5]

The lineage (*tsu*), like the joint family, consists of a group of agnates, their wives, and their unmarried daughters. But unlike the joint family, where all property is held in common and no economic division has taken place, the lineage embraces any number of economically independent kin groups, all linked by more or less vestigial common economic ties (for all members of a lineage have shares in lineage property); in other words, whereas the joint family is totally undivided, the lineage is only partially undivided. The joint family lives together as one unit, and the lineage lives in one locality—in a settlement or group of proximate settlements. The joint family tends to be finite in its lineal and lateral expansion, but the lineage may continue to expand for an indefinite number of generations without regard to mourning grades or family division. Both the joint family and the lineage reinforce the sense of kin and economic unity by means of the ritual unity fostered by ancestor worship. The lineage may be highly segmented internally;[6] in addition, it may itself be a segment of another, geographically discrete but not too distant lineage. A group of lineages in this kind of relationship has been called by Freedman the "higher-order lineage,"[7] and this higher-order lineage also owns and maintains common property.

For the purpose of this analysis, I will define the clan (*t'ung-tsung*) as an aggregate of lineages of the same surname that have deliberately organized for some specific purpose. We can distinguish the clan from the higher-order lineage by the fact that in the former the component lineages are separate lines of descent that are not interrelated. These component lineages are likely to trace their origins back to an ancestor who is common to all, but this need not necessarily be done; moreover, the fact that another lineage can prove its common kinship with a component lineage does not necessarily entitle it to membership of the clan. This concept of the clan I am labeling with the term *t'ung-tsung*, though I am aware that the terms *tsung* and *tsu* are commonly used as synonyms.[8] My usage of *tsung* is not without precedent, however. "In a few cases, *tsung* has the additional connotation that the clan group branched out over a wide geographic area and the branches no longer remained in one single organization, though each branch still recognised the others as being loosely connected through a remote ancestor."[9] More specifically, Amyot talks of "the lineage as a whole (*tsu*) or ... the whole surname group or clan (*tsung*)."[10] The clan may hold a certain amount of property in common, shares belonging to component lineages on a *per stirpes* basis (that is, individual members of the component lineages would not have shares). In the case of the lineage, common property is theoretically indivisible[11] and membership in the owning group is permanent, inclusive, and inalienable; but with the clan, not only is the membership exclusive, but the property is likely to be held in common for a specific purpose and possibly for a comparatively short time only. A component lineage could withdraw from the clan by selling its share to other member lineages or perhaps to a previously excluded lineage. The clan may recruit new member lineages.

Common surname (*t'ung-hsing*) is a term applied to all bearers of a surname regardless of membership or nonmembership in lineages. A common origin for all those having one surname is assumed, though the absurdity of this is patent—the T'ang emperors, for example, bestowed their surname (Li) on subjects as an honor.

A form of what might be termed quasi-extended kinship is the phratry. Here there is recognition of a bond of "sworn clanship" or "sworn common surnameship," and it is on this basis that people of different surnames unite—the association of names deriving from particular instances of sworn blood brotherhood. Probably the most notable example of this is the alliance between the surnames of the major heroes of the Three Kingdoms period, Liu, Kuan, Chang, and Chao.

Urban Kin Groupings

If these types of extended kin groupings are considered the major forms, we must examine their claims to consideration in the urban context.

The joint family. The joint family was dependent upon and largely consequent upon wealth. The rural joint family tended to be founded on large holdings of agricultural land. In the city the joint family was more likely to depend on income from trade, moneylending, and urban real estate, though not a few also held agricultural land in the city's hinterland. The following quotation, for instance, refers to one of the Co-hong merchant families of Canton: "we saw the large town residence of the 'Ng,' or Howqua family. This mansion consists, in short, of three or four houses.... In this large family residence, not less than five hundred souls reside."[12]

Given the concentration of wealth in cities, it seems likely that the joint family might have been rather more common there than in the countryside. However, nothing about the structure of an urban joint family appeared to distinguish it from its rural counterpart. Since the joint family was not dependent upon a particular kind of environment, occurred everywhere, and was discrete in that it did not "link" spatially separated groups, it is of minor interest for present purposes.

The lineage. In the *Kuang-tung hsin yü* it says: "The famous surnames and prominent lineages [*tsu*] of Ling-nan are most numerous in Kuang-chou prefecture, and [within the prefecture] most numerous in the villages [*hsiang*]."[13] Hu Hsien-chin echoes this point. "The *tsu* is of the greatest importance in rural neighborhoods, in large villages and small towns, although at times its main ancestral hall is located at the county seat or even in the provincial capital."[14] Miss Lang says that "clans [lineages] exist only in villages or small towns. There are practically no clan ancestor temples and no clan heads in the cities."[15] And more recently Fried has said of Taiwan: "While some lineages are totally rural, few (if any) have been strictly urban."[16]

There is general agreement, then, that lineages were seldom found in cities. The reasons for this were diverse, but probably the most important were economic ones. In the first place, it seems clear that the basis of the rural lineage's strength was its command of land-based wealth. All members of a lineage retained an interest in the communal landholdings, but in order to participate in the benefits of that lineage trust they had to be physically present. That is, since lineage trust land was theoretically, and for the most part practically, indivisible, the individual stood to gain economically only from the return on the capital land investment, this return often being in the form of feasts, local public works, or perhaps small share-outs in kind, all of which were available to the man on the spot but not to those absent. The economic benefit of lineage trust membership was thus a long-term cumulative one, and only the geographically stable really stood to gain.

But if we look at the city in this context, several points emerge. First, there is the perhaps minor point that, because of the continuing interest in the land which ownership or coparcenary gave, there was much incentive for the person moving into the city to remain rural-based. Indeed, he might well have left behind on the land a wife or family in order to keep up his participation in the benefits from his land. Examples of this same pattern are those men who went overseas to Southeast Asia leaving families behind to continue their interests, and, more recently, the restaurant workers who migrated to Britain from Hong Kong's countryside. It follows that the newly urbanized person would have been unlikely to try to form a lineage in the city when his orientation was still to the countryside.

Second, there is the much more important factor of the economic difference between city and countryside. In rural lineages, segments that had established trusts were faced at a certain early point in their development with the choice of either breaking up that trust and dividing it into sizable individual shares or continuing the trust in the knowledge that the increasing numbers of members would gradually bring the returns to each of them down to negligible size.[17] In such cases it was not uncommon for the first alternative of fission to occur. How much more probable, then, that a similar move to fission should prevail in the urban context, where the members of such a trust were likely to be socially much more highly differentiated and lacking the homogeneity of interest found in the agricultural situation. As Hu has said, "in the large cities, with their sharp differentiation of the professions and of social classes, it [the *tsu*] becomes lost."[18] Furthermore, in the urban context there were wider opportunities for investment, and therefore greater incentives for a person to put his wealth into undertakings of short-term profitability. In the face of opportunities for comparatively rapid individual economic advancement, the drive to a group unity of the kind afforded by the lineage seems to have been much less strong.[19] City-based ancestral trust groups of the type found in the rural lineage were probably rare and, owing to their tendency to fission, would tend not to develop far enough to qualify for the status of lineage.

Third, geographic mobility in cities was probably much higher than in villages, and the resultant lack of stability would tend to militate against settled and enduring kin ties.[20] Where benefit from lineage trusts depended upon presence in the lineage environment, individuals might well not have been interested in running the risk that they or their descendants would lose contact with their investment.

The nature of urban investment may itself have been inimical to the setting up of enduring trusts. Far greater risk attached to investing in city activities than to investing in agricultural land. Of course, an urban lineage could have bought land in the countryside, but then it would have been divorced physically from its investment and would have stood to lose control over it.

Differences in urban and rural living may also have been important in setting the pattern of lineage development. The lineage in the countryside was important to its members as a protection against the hazards of a dog-eat-dog society that was underadministered by the central government. Heavily backed by a universally accepted ethic, kinship was an excellent basis for organization; and the larger the organized group, the safer it was. In the city, on the other hand, law and order were a less pressing problem. Again, in the countryside a fair degree of economic homogeneity gave rise to fewer divisive tendencies than was the case in the more stratified cities; there the solid citizen probably gained more from emphasizing his connection with other men of equivalent social status than from associating with kin of lower status. Since lineages were inclusive groups of agnates that denied membership to no male born to them, all members ran the potential risk of being "saddled" with less fortunate fellow lineage members. This risk would have influenced the tendency to fission on the part of the more advantaged.

Despite the foregoing, urban lineages did exist. I would suggest, however, that they were much more limited than rural lineages both in development and in social significance. In the first place, there was likely to be little economic differentiation among the membership, for as soon as differences arose they would have tended to result in fission. Second, urban lineages were unlikely to be of great generational depth, because the passing of generations would probably see unequal development of different sections of the lineage, and again the fission factor would operate. Third, they were unlikely to be affluent, because for the urban wealthy there was little to be gained from lineage organization. Fourth, they were likely to exhibit occupational homogeneity, although there were limiting factors involved in this, too, particularly with regard to the necessity to employ and perhaps "carry" unsuitable lineage members, and with regard to problems of organizational control where kinship and not competence was important in leadership selection. Another

Extended Kinship in the Traditional City

danger of the "occupation-based lineage" is evident from the material of Hsü and Hu, who point to the economic plight of the butchers of West Town caused by monopolistic expansion within kin groups.[21]

The clan. The clan was centered on the city. Hsiao, who several times makes the point that cities and clans (he generally uses the term to cover what I have defined as a lineage) did not go together, says the following. "However, the cities, being centers of social and political influence, were often chosen by clans of relatively large size and strong organization as sites for their *ta tsung-tz'u*, that is, common or central clan temples shared and supported by branch halls located in the surrounding countryside."[22] He goes on to translate a section from the *Chia-ying chou chih* of 1898: "The local custom attaches importance to the kinship tie. All clans, large and small, have ancestral halls. Inhabitants of villages who dwell together by clans invariably have *chia-miao* [family shrines], which are really ancestral halls. In addition to these halls, there are *ta tsung-tz'u* in the prefectural city. These are built jointly by [the branches of] the clans that dwell in the several districts that compose the prefecture." Clearly the spread of the kin groups that are described here is enormous, and the likelihood of their being lineages recedes as distance grows. It is interesting that Hsiao should refer to cities as being "chosen" as sites for temples, for it underlines the point that clans tended to be "deliberate" organizations. And of course it is probably in the cities that causes large enough to require the joint efforts of clans would exist. An excellent example of this point is adduced by Freedman:

The Chu lineage, descended from an ancestor who lived some 300 years ago, are the sole occupants of X Village, which is one of six villages making up "the Chang River clan of Chus." Besides this group of Chu lineages there is "the South River clan of Chus with nine villages and the Stone River clan of Chus with fifteen villages. . . . The Chu county clan has no definite organization." They combine only in some extraordinary circumstance. Some fifty years ago a Chu with a grievance against the magistrate of a neighbouring county complained to the members of the Chang River Chu "and they decided to take revenge." Chu men from two "districts" of the county came together and about a thousand people marched to seize the offending magistrate and haul him off to the prefect, who consented to the demand that the magistrate be dismissed.[23]

This example also brings out the latent unity of clanship, such that an ad hoc organization may quickly be formed at any time. The connection between clans and cities is further illustrated by two passages quoted by Hsiao:

Some persons who perhaps originally inhabited rural areas as clans gathered together other persons who bore identical surnames but did not belong to the same clans and built [ancestral] halls in the city, pretending that they were clansmen. The purpose of joining such [ancestral] halls was to obtain illicit gains and to create a power [group] upon which they might rely.

Another governor ... found the custom of "combining clans and building temples" as rampant as ever. He memorialized the Ch'ien-lung emperor in 1764 that persons who bore identical surnames but did not necessarily belong to the same clans and who lived in different villages, towns, or cities organized themselves into "clans." Funds were collected from those who were interested and "ancestral halls" built (in the prefectural or provincial city), often endowed with a certain amount of ritual land. Ancient emperors, kings, or high officials were usually chosen as the "first ancestors."[24]

The common surname. Common-surname organizations are legion among the overseas Chinese, and we have data on them from the United States and from many parts of Southeast Asia. It is commonly assumed that the emigrants developed social structures after a traditional Chinese urban pattern. Thus "although most of the Chinese who went overseas were from rural areas, they were able to re-create traditional urban forms wherever they went, out of the common stock of Chinese culture they took with them."[25] The corollary to this assumption is that any form found among the overseas Chinese must probably have a mother form in the Chinese city; and so we may read that "the overseas clan association (in which men of a common surname are grouped together for limited purposes) is a development of a form of grouping found in the large towns and cities of China itself."[26] And yet the bonds of common surname seem in some cases to have taken a long while to assert themselves as a unifying factor among the overseas Chinese. To take the Philippine case, Wickberg tells us that "common surname associations, like those now existing among the Philippine Chinese, were apparently not formed until after 1898."[27] And Amyot, seemingly a little puzzled at the dilatory appearance of these associations, says this: "Although the principle they are based on dates back many centuries, most of these associations in their present form are relatively recent, extending back to the twenties or thirties. The oldest were founded in Manila in the first decade of the century."[28] In Madagascar, surname associations apparently have not developed at all.[29]

It would seem, then, that surname associations were not a grouping that sprang readily to the minds of early Chinese emigrants, and for this reason alone we might suspect that they did not occupy the position of importance in the Chinese city that they came to occupy from time to time and from place to place overseas.

Extended Kinship in the Traditional City

Fried has given us some details of such organizations in present-day Taiwan; however, not only do the associations he describes apparently date back merely to the last decade of the nineteenth century,[30] but it might also be argued that the Taiwanese case more closely resembles that of the overseas Chinese than that of traditional China. To take another "doubtful" area, Hong Kong, a work devoted to the organizations of the Chinese in the Colony in 1947 gives details of only three *tsung-ch'in hui* (the usual term for the surname association), and at least two of those certainly do not cater to all of the same surname and may even concern groupings as narrow as the lineage or clan.[31] The earliest founded of the three dates back to 1918.

Indeed, there seems to be only scant evidence that surname associations existed at all in the Chinese city. According to Parker, Canton in the 1870's boasted "ancestral shrines open to all persons in the Province who bear the same surname, and have contributed to the general fund, irrespective of race or origin (i.e., *Hakka, Punti,* etc.). Tls. 200 are frequently paid for the privilege of placing a tablet therein, and grand sacrifices and feasts are held in the spring and autumn of each year."[32] Yet forty years later, a *Guide to Canton* that listed organizations in the city failed to identify a single *tsung-ch'in hui* or other recognizable common-surname organization.[33] Similarly, a later guide does not list any such organizations, despite a small section devoted to overseas Chinese associations.[34]

Fried has given us an interesting picture of two types of organization in Taiwan.

One, the *tz'u-t'ang*, tends to be a tightly structured corporate unit with carefully apportioned rights, duties, and privileges. The other, known as *t'ung-ch'in hui*, is loosely organized, with a theoretically unbounded membership that comprises all people of the same surname, including those from different parts of China, of different languages, and even of different ethnic origins.

The former grouping ... may exist side by side, in the same shared quarters, with the less restrictive type of group. What this amounts to is a throwing open of the temple, on the great ritual occasions, to all those of common surname who wish to come.[35]

Here is an example that could be construed as a clan (or a Taiwan form of clan) with an attached surname association. It is possible that such a phenomenon might form the subject of the above quotation from Parker. But the slowness of overseas Chinese to adopt the mere common surname as an organizational focus seems to point to the rarity and insignificance of surname associations as such in the homeland.[36]

A description of "common-surname temples" in Canton has been given above. I have further hinted that perhaps Parker may have been describing something closer to the associations described by Fried than to those "genuine" surname associations commonly found among the overseas Chinese. Such data as I have been able to uncover tend to confirm this. Thus in 1866, when in return for entering tablets contributions toward restoration were being sought by one hall (of the Liang surname) in Canton, it was stated that both lineages (*fang-tsu*) and individuals (*ssu-ch'in*) might apply. However, it is clear from another context that membership was confined to natives of the two prefectures of Kuang-chou and Chao-ch'ing; and indeed, entry seems to have been restricted to those persons who were in any case qualified through their membership in the shareholding lineages.[37]

In general, it is perhaps true to say that the common surname was a relationship so weak that it was less likely to be recognized by formally constituted groups than on an ad hoc basis by people who for some particular reason felt constrained to do so or expected profit by doing so. Similarly weak was the relationship between linked surnames that could lead to the formation of the phratry.

Extended kinship. The various forms of extended kinship with which we have been dealing have so far been viewed only in the light of the likelihood of their existence in cities. But we may also see them as forming a progression of complexity and importance from family up to common surname; and by so doing, we may consider the possibility of there being a correlation between the degree of kin-group complexity and the point on the socioeconomic landscape at which each form operated.

Clearly, the simple and stem families were universally viable and would be found as much in the city as in the countryside. The joint family was less common than either of these forms and was very much associated with wealth; but, allowing that greater wealth in the cities might have resulted in a higher proportion of joint families there than in the countryside, there remains the fact that the joint family could exist at any point on the rural-urban continuum where sufficient wealth could accumulate.

It is at the next level of kinship complexity, the lineage, that significant rural-urban differences begin to emerge. Whereas the joint family was heavily biased toward the wealthy, the lineage had a membership inclusive of all agnatic descendants of its founder, regardless of whether they were rich or poor. In the city, as we have said, greater possibilities of personal advancement brought the temptation to the individual of seceding from and breaking up the lineage (or, of course, of not founding a lineage), so that there was less likelihood of lineages existing in

Extended Kinship in the Traditional City

the urban context. The greater the degree of urbanization, the less likely was the lineage to hold together; by the same token, the more rural the situation, the greater the homogeneity of interest and the ease of keeping the lineage united. Therefore, we should expect that the strongest lineages would have been found at the lower end of the rural-urban continuum, that is, at the level of the village and the standard marketing community.

But we may surely take it as a given for Chinese society that organization of groups on the basis of agnatic kinship was both ethically satisfying and effective. One of the great strengths of the lineage lay in its ability to keep large numbers welded together in one unit, but there was the bar to carrying lineage organization into the urban sphere. The application of the principle of extended kinship at higher levels of the rural-urban continuum, therefore, must have taken a different turn. It is above the level of the standard marketing community that we are likely to find the higher-order lineage and the clan.

The higher-order lineage, being an amalgamation of segmented simple lineages, is bound to be spread over a wider geographical area. It may still be contained within the standard marketing community, or it may be the intermediate or even the central marketing system that harbors it. We have sufficient knowledge of lineage organization to know that lineages were controlled by their wealthy and their gentry members, and we know also that the relations of a lineage with the outside world were largely carried on by these same men. The cooperation of the lineages bound together in this way would thus probably be arranged by these men operating in the market town that served the total group. The concern of the higher-order lineage was likely to be with local problems—that is, the lineage elite would be working to manipulate local conditions for their own and the lineage's benefit.

But to become involved in more general affairs, and particularly to try to make capital out of the administrative system, it was necessary to operate at higher levels. It is at the centers of government that we might expect the clan to appear. By and large, the basis of group action in the clan was no longer the "natural" kin group that the lineage or even the higher-order lineage may be said to have been, for the "natural" group was probably too limited in extent, but an "artificial" kin group that was formed deliberately with probably only the flimsiest of known or ascribed genealogical ties. The larger the membership, the greater the potential power of the organization; therefore a clan set up in a given city was likely to try to muster as full and representative support as possible from the lineages existing within the area dependent upon that center. At the level of the clan, it was again the elites of the lineages that were principally involved.

The various forms of extended kinship thus tended to be associated with different levels of the rural-urban continuum. The joint family was common to all levels, the lineage tended to occur at the rural end of the continuum, the higher-order lineage was found in the upper reaches of the rural end, and the clan in the urban sphere. The common-surname tie per se, it has been suggested, was probably not of importance as an organizational force in Chinese society. It might be hypothesized that if and where common-surname associations did exist they would be mutual-aid groups for the poor in the largest cities, for it would only be there that sufficient numbers of men of a given surname would be gathered together and cut off from a (rural) home base.

The Pattern of Urban Extended Kinship

In an attempt to elucidate the pattern of urban extended kinship, material on the city of Canton during the Ch'ing period was examined. Sited in an area of China where lineage organization was strong, and being both a provincial and a prefectural capital, the capital of two counties, and an important economic center, Canton should have been the locus of several different manifestations of the extended kinship group.

The existence of joint families in Canton may be taken for granted, though a particular instance has been mentioned above. The presence there of the common-surname organization was not proved by the material found, though we might point to the element of doubt raised above in connection with the quotation from Parker and the evidence of the Liang hall.

The factual evidence, then, was bound to concentrate upon lineages and clans. Among other works consulted were a large number of genealogies in the collections in Tokyo, and relevant data from these have been used below. It should be emphasized that the relevant material was not plentiful, although it does throw some light upon the workings of extended kinship groups, and clans in particular, in the city.

Lineages. Only one Canton lineage genealogy was found. Fortunately it is a very detailed work that gives a clear picture of the lineage structure.

The founding ancestor, Liang I-lung, moved in pursuit of trade from Shun-te *hsien* to nearby Canton during the K'ang-hsi reign (1662–1722), but the lineage really seems to date only from an ancestor who bought a building site and improved it in 1851. In 1877 a man of the seventh generation from I-lung purchased 152.8 *mou* of land in the P'an-yü *hsien* countryside.³⁸ When in 1909–11 an ancestral hall was built on the original 1851 site, the P'an-yü land came to the lineage as ancestral trust land. It was leased to farmers of another surname. Besides the agricultural land and the hall, the lineage owned three shops in Canton and a hall, two house plots, a mulberry plot, and a fish pond in Shun-te (about 100 *li* from Canton). All descendants of I-lung lived in the area around the ancestral hall. Management of the trust property and the lineage ceremonies rotated annually among the five major segments (*fang*) of the lineage, who "were born here, grew up here, and grew into a lineage [*chia-tsu*] here." The proximate residence pattern fulfills one of the requirements for the lineage label, and the genealogy makes it quite clear that this was in fact a lineage. For instance, the rules for worship in the hall laid down that all male members of every branch should be notified of the time fixed for the Spring and Autumn Rites, and that all male members should receive a share of meat at these ceremonies (with graduated extra shares for the aged, for graduates, etc.) and at Ch'ing Ming. All members should be consulted before any important matter was decided upon, though the managers had certain powers of urgent decision. For the peace of the ancestral spirits, the occasions on which the hall was to be used were limited to such things as the above ceremonies, lineage meetings, wedding feasts, birthday celebrations, and school-teaching. There was to be financial help to insure the proper burial of poor members; lump sums for every son born, for every child starting school, for those getting married for the first time, and for those graduating from schools; an annual payment as a clothes allowance to the managers of the estate; and so on.

There were clear statements about adoption rules and personal conduct for lineage members, including a pithy set of general principles entitled "The Liang lineage's six warnings" and "The Liang lineage's four teachings." There was the requirement that once in ten years (on the *chia* year of the cycle) an especially large ceremony should be held in the hall on the birthday of the ancestor who had donated the land; but there seems no reason to suppose that it was the urban context that led to the stipulation that both males and females should attend.³⁹ In short, the genealogy is concerned with the day-to-day life of an entire lineage community, unlike a clan genealogy, which could not deal with its vast membership in this way.

It is interesting that a land base outside the city was established, though something of the mystery of the countryside to the city-dwellers shows through in their marveling at the honesty of the tenant, who always brought the rent to them himself on the right day. It is even more interesting that the land and buildings in Shun-te were bought in 1900 from an ancestral trust of the home lineage from which the first ancestor had come in the K'ang-hsi period.[40] The genealogy states that this was done in remembrance of the lineage founder. There is no indication that this reconnection of a segment to its stock resulted at this stage in any form of higher-order lineage, but certainly a potential basis for cooperation was established.

From the founding of the lineage organization in 1851 to the publication of the genealogy was a mere 60 years. Although we are clearly dealing here with an urban lineage, and a successful one, it is true that generationally the lineage was still very shallow; and it was still very wealthy, which in itself would tend to offset the disruptive effect of urban life.

Clans. The evidence for the existence of clan organizations in Canton is overwhelming. Many of the clans had a membership so wide that in order to find a ritual first ancestor they had to go back in some cases to mythical times. One clan named the Yellow Emperor as its first ancestor, tracing the line through two surname changes until the surname Ho finally emerged in the Ch'in dynasty.[41] Another went back to the famous Su Tung-p'o of the Sung dynasty.[42] A third claimed to be genealogically united in an ancestor who lived in approximately A.D. 400, during the Eastern Chin dynasty.[43] Yet another was said to descend from a first-generation disciple of Confucius.[44]

Membership of the clan was by lineage or lineage segment, these being known as *fang*. One genealogy goes into some detail about the naming procedure for the *fang*: "Why use the *hsien* names as *fang* names—e.g., Hsin-hui *fang*, Hsin-hsing *fang*, Ssu-hui *fang*—when there are separate *fang* in these *hsien*?" The answer is that the first lineage to settle in any county takes the county name to itself, and all others in the county respectfully subordinate themselves to it, taking for themselves the name of their village or ancestral trust.[45]

In some cases false *fang* were created in order to tidy up a large number of separate lineages. Thus the Su clan, with a membership of 123 *fang*, amalgamated them into six "great *fang*" (*ta-fang*) and used these as administrative units.

Membership in a clan was exclusive. The Su clan prohibited from using its hall in Canton all non-Su and all Su who were not members of its component *fang*, and it further insisted that members should identify themselves by carrying a genealogy with them (*tai shih-p'u*).[46] The Ho clan also excluded Ho who were not members of its component

Extended Kinship in the Traditional City

fang, and the Liang clan did not recognize those with the Liang surname unless they came from Kuang-chou or Chao-ch'ing.[47]

Membership involved taking a financial share in the clan. These shares were not necessarily equal, so that we find the nine *fang* of the K'ung clan with shares of 10, 20, 6, 6, 6, 21, 15, 7, and 9 percent.[48] The shares were represented by ancestral tablets placed in the halls—the more shares, the more tablets their purchasers might enter. Recruitment generally occurred when clan property needed restoring. The clearest picture of this is given in the Ho clan genealogy. Their library was first built between 1808 and 1813, when 86 *fang* shared the cost. At the first restoration, in 1839, nine more *fang* joined in; at the second restoration, in 1863, another three were recruited; and at the last restoration noted (combined with the building of an annex), in 1891–94, 101 new *fang* were admitted, making a total of 199 *fang* in all.[49] The member *fang* of the Hsien clan numbered 28 when they decided in 1622 to build a clan temple (*tsung-tz'u*) to house the tablet of the remote ancestor who was recognized as the founder of the Ling-nan clan. Most of the *fang* had built their own lineage temples (*tsu-tz'u*) during the Ming Chia-ching reign. The *tsung-tz'u* was restored in 1690 and again in 1825. On the former occasion one more lineage was admitted, the last to join the clan (*lien-tsung*). It had not been established near Canton until after the original building had been completed, and it was the only lineage to lack an ancestral hall of its own.[50]

Shareholders in a clan had rights proportionate to the number of shares they held, but it was not necessarily true that all *fang* were equivalent units outside the clan. Thus, whereas some *fang* were lineage segments, others were full lineages, and yet others might be higher-order lineages. The Ho clan *fang* were clearly heterogeneous in that some were whole lineages, known by the name of the village or town occupied by the lineage, and others were segments, known by the name of the ancestral trust (*tsu* or *t'ang*) on which the segment focused. In a number of cases one such group had purchased more than one share.[51] Among the Hsien clan *fang* were five small groups of *fang* that were probably higher-order lineages, the component lineages being labeled *fen-fang* and listed below the lineage from which they segmented. However, the *fen-fang* each took shares in the clan, so that in relation to the clan they were full *fang*. Contrasted with such presumably large *fang*, we know that the last *fang* to join the clan consisted of only 47 *ting* (males).[52]

All the clans with which I am dealing owned halls in the city, and all had ancestral tablets in them. The halls were in many cases very large and well planned. The tortured prose of the Rev. Gray has described one of them for us.

> We proceeded to a street . . . in which stands the . . . ancestral hall of the clan, Tam. This ancestral hall is, without exception, the finest edifice of the kind, which the city of Canton contains. Above the altar, there are arranged on shelves, three, or four thousand ancestral tablets. The court, or quadrangle of the hall, is spacious. It is paved with slabs of granite. On each side of the quadrangle, there is a narrow passage, or lane consisting of several apartments. In these rooms, previous to the examinations, which for literary degrees, are, periodically, held at Canton, the students of the Tam family, or clan, reside and study. There, stands, also, in close proximity to these apartments, a lofty brick tower. It is in honour of the gods of learning, and to it, the students have recourse to pray.[53]

The hall of the Ho clan cannot have been much inferior to this, for when it was restored in 1894 it had, in addition to the main ritual hall (*cheng-tz'u*), a banquet and meeting hall and 39 separate apartments for examination candidates, each with its own kitchen and separate entrance to the main building. These apartments were carefully planned, and each member *fang* was allotted its own share of one. The genealogy notes that 200 *fang* were allowed for, but that there were only 199. The Su clan hall provided accommodation for all its members who were taking the provincial examination in Canton, for members from Nan-hai and P'an-yü (the two counties that shared the city) taking the county examinations, and so on. In addition to the hall, some clans had property that they rented out in order to have an income for ritual and other purposes. The Su clan had many properties of this kind, as did the Ho clan, whereas the Hsien genealogy laments that clan's lack of income-producing property.[54]

The Hsien clan hall originally housed the tablet of the remote clan ancestor and a tablet for the first ancestor of each component *fang*. There was always a charge for placing tablets in the halls. The Hsien clan charged individuals 10 taels for entering tablets (*ju chu*) in the hall, as did the Liang clan. The Su clan had a system of more and less favored tablet sites, with charges of 20 taels and 10 taels, respectively. Many halls were bursting with tablets. Gray's three or four thousand apparently was not unusual. The Su clan had several thousand tablets in its hall, and the Liang clan had nearly two thousand.[55]

The halls were usually governed by strict rules that forbade gambling, the presence of women, the making of tea in the main halls, the entry of outsiders, the use by members of one *fang* of the rooms allotted to other *fang*, etc.[56] The halls and their properties, as well as the major ritual ceremonies, were managed on a rotating basis, the *fang* (or in some cases, as we have seen, the false *fang*) taking turns. In the case of the six *ta-fang* of the Su clan, each was allotted two characters of the twelve-branch series, the estate was divided into six portions, and each of the *ta-fang* acted as managers of a portion twice in the twelve-year cycle. In the Ho clan, sixteen or seventeen *fang* shared the managership each year. The K'ung clan's ten *fang* divided into five paired *fang* to rotate managership.[57] Managers were frequently given emoluments.[58] Caretakers were often required to be nonmembers of the clan in order to avoid difficult relationships of superiority/inferiority within the clan.[59]

Ritual occasions were carefully controlled by detailed rules. The Ho genealogy had very strict regulations on ritual and specified many details, from the amount, nature, and cost of the offerings down to the exact duration of time officiants should devote to preparations before the ceremony. The Su clan insisted that all members be dressed in hats and robes for the ceremonies, and the Liang clan stipulated that at the Spring and Autumn Rites only members wearing ceremonial hats and robes were to be allowed to receive a share of the sacrificial meats.[60] The Spring and Autumn Rites were the most commonly favored ceremonies of the clans, but the Chien clan stressed one major ceremony a year, to be held on an auspicious day in the first *hsün* of the eighth month.[61] The Liang urban lineage ensured that *all* male members were notified of imminent ceremonies, but the clans had to be content with lesser measures. Thus the Ho clan managers were required to post a notice on the gates of the hall ten days before each of the Spring and Autumn Rites; it was then up to the members of the constituent *fang* to observe the notice and attend the ceremony.[62] Similarly indicative of the clans' nonconcern with the individual is the Su clan's warning that anyone going to the ceremony "whether from near or far is responsible for his own food, ferry dues, sedan-chair fares, and all such items," and that members should be early, because the ceremony would not be held up for late arrivals.[63]

Each of the clans produced a genealogy. The Ho clan built their clan hall in 1812, and then set about compiling a genealogy. Of their 60-odd *fang*, more than twenty produced manuscript genealogies, and from these it was worked out that all member *fang* were connected at a point 106 generations from the Yellow Emperor. The final version retained what was common to all the originals and disregarded all that was not. The Hsien genealogists were less fussy. They recorded that all the *fang* genealogies had mistakes, but that it did not matter; in any case, all could trace descent from the Eastern Chin dynasty ancestor.[64]

The geographical spread of those clans centered on Canton differed so much from case to case that it is hardly possible to find a clear pattern in it. The K'ung clan was confined to the three counties of Nan-hai, P'an-yü and Shun-te,[65] and was thus clustered very tightly around the city of Canton. The Ho clan, as we have noted, was set up to amalgamate the lineages from the two prefectures of Kuang-chou and Chao-ch'ing, and it kept to this principle despite its later massive expansion. In fact, though, whereas every county of Kuang-chou prefecture is represented in the list of member *fang*, the remoter counties of Chao-ch'ing (i.e., Feng-ch'uan, K'ai-chien, Te-ch'ing, Kuang-ning, Ssu-hui, Hsin-hsing, Yang-ch'un, and Yang-chiang) do not figure,[66] so that there is again a clustering around Canton as a center. The Liang clan membership also came from these two prefectures, and the clan's rules laid it down that no members from other prefectures would be permitted. The Hsien clan drew its members from eleven districts, but although there was a central core around Canton sited in Nan-hai, P'an-yü, and Shun-te, the distribution of the other *fang* was both far-flung and erratic. Thus there were *fang* in En-p'ing, Ho-shan, Kao-yao, Kuang-ning, and Te-ch'ing (all in Chao-ch'ing prefecture), in Ch'ing-yüan and Hsin-an (Kuang-chou prefecture), and in Yung-an (Hui-chou prefecture). The Su clan was found in 25 counties, 21 of which form a fairly solid cluster around Canton; the outlying *fang* were found in Mou-ming (Kao-chou prefecture), Lo-ting (*chih-li chou*), Yang-ch'un (Chao-ch'ing prefecture), and Hai-yang (Ch'ao-chou prefecture). The Chien clan had member *fang* in 35 county-level units scattered through nearly every part of Kwangtung province, and in addition member *fang* were found in Heng *chou* and Kuei-p'ing *hsien*, both situated on the West River in Kwangsi.[67]

The area from which a clan drew its membership seems always to have been defined in administrative terms, that is, with reference to county, prefectural, or provincial boundaries; and the heavy stress on library buildings and on accommodation for those taking examinations seems to point clearly to the preoccupation of the clans with the administrative sphere. In one case, even, a rural lineage was found to maintain a library in Canton for the use of its members when taking examinations there. Known as the Shu-te Shu-she, it was built in 1873,[68] but there is no indication of any urban segment of the lineage connected with it.

Yet the geographic patterns of clan membership suggest that factors other than administrative divisions might have been of some significance. The Ho clan's neat, solid cluster of *fang* surrounding Canton, with none

Extended Kinship in the Traditional City

from the remoter counties of Chao-ch'ing prefecture, indicates that its catchment area may coincide closely with Canton's regional-city trading system. And the smaller number of *fang* of the K'ung clan may well have included all eligible lineages within Canton's local-city trading system, which encompassed most of the three specified counties. The administratively inexplicable inclusion of Kwangsi *fang* in the Chien clan headquartered in Canton could relate to settlement patterns shaped by the West River transport route.

The Function of the Clan

The clans themselves projected a very fuzzy image of their purpose. The Hsien clan was formed in order that it might worship Hsien Chung-yi as founding ancestor of Ling-nan. The Chien wanted a hall and a genealogy so that all descendants might know their origins. The Ho wanted to amalgamate the lineages of Kuang-chou and Chao-ch'ing.[69] Genealogies were compiled, halls were built, and ancestors were worshiped. Encouragement to scholars was given by building examination study rooms (most clans seem to have done this), by paying expenses in some cases to those taking the higher examinations, by giving rewards (*hua-hung*) for passing examinations, by hanging up honors boards,[70] etc.

The common factor in the activities of all the clans seems to have been elite participation. Clans were for gentry, for the leaders of the component lineages—note the Liang clan's insistence on formal dress for ceremonies, a wealth-biased rule. This point perhaps explains why an urban Liang lineage and a Liang clan could both exist in Canton without cooperation or connection. Lineages had inclusive membership and catered to rich and poor alike. An elitist clan organization might have found it embarrassing to be in association with poor members of the same surname—we have already seen that clan members were often excluded from holding such menial positions as gatekeeper or caretaker. The Chien clan had a *fang* apparently in Canton, but this *fang* does not seem to have been swallowed up by the clan, nor is there evidence that it had any other than normal elite contact with the clan.

Clans brought the elite together and provided the personal contacts on which so much social action was based. They did not always do this by bringing people face to face. Clan genealogies were a method almost as effective, for as Freedman has said, "the 'great houses' and their subdivisions are not groupings for action (although they may in some circumstances come to be); they presuppose common origin and not joint interest; they explain 'history' and not 'sociology.' "[71] Clans were indeed not kinetic but potential. They concerned themselves not with "doing" but with providing a framework by means of which things could be done. In one of the genealogies there is what seems to be an attempt to make an active unit of a clan—the Chien clan set up a "self-government society" in 1909. But it is clear that the activities of the society were almost entirely confined to sorting out the genealogical problems of component lineages.[72]

In talking of lineages, Freedman has said: "The Chinese of Kwangtung and Fukien were notorious for their turbulence. In part this reputation rested on their opposition to the state; trying to collect taxes and suppress seditious organizations, the government often found itself face to face with people whose bellicosity earned them a name for barbarism. But the distaste with which officialdom often looked upon the villagers of the south-east was also caused by the frequency and intensity with which local groups took up arms against one another."[73] Since clans were bolstered by much the same ethos as lineages, they were also a potential menace to the social order. They created groups that could apply pressure to government officials: indeed, I have quoted an example where a clan did take such action. One attempt to put an end to clans failed in the Ch'ien-lung reign. Noting that their hall, the Ch'ü-chiang Shu-yüan, used to be called the Hsien-shih Ta Tsung-tz'u, the Hsien genealogy says that in Ch'ien-lung 37 (1772) the provincial governor took steps to outlaw ancestral temples and memorialized that they should be proscribed. To counter this, ancestral temples of all surnames changed their titles to *shu-yüan*, and it is from that time that the Hsien temple bears this name.[74]

Clans probably did little to make the task of governing easier, so it is hardly surprising that the central government should have looked on them with disfavor.

Part Three
THE CITY AS A SOCIAL SYSTEM

Introduction: Urban Social Structure in Ch'ing China

G. WILLIAM SKINNER

We know surprisingly little about urban structure in late imperial China —despite the existence of abundant data for hundreds of cities—because few scholars have done the kind of detailed microstudies on this subject that exist for so many other areas of Chinese studies. As a result, generalizations have been insufficiently grounded in hard data, and plausible assertions have become received wisdom through repetition. Into this vacuum social anthropologists have brought models from research on urban Chinese communities overseas, and the assumption was sometimes too quickly made that what was common to Chinese social structure in various overseas cities necessarily derived from a common heritage of premodern Chinese urbanism. It is hardly surprising, then, that the papers on urban social structure in this book represent a movement back to the relevant sources and reflect a preoccupation with accurate contextual description. Although it is not possible in this introduction to attempt a wide-ranging synthesis, I would like to review what this book has to say about the internal structure of traditional cities and relate its contributions to several themes that hold interest for sinologists and urbanists alike.

The papers of Part One, my own excepted, all treat in one way or another the effect of ideology on urban forms: the manifestation of cosmological notions and ideological norms in planning imperial capitals is central among the topics treated by Wright and Mote; and the studies of Lamley and Chang make it clear that peculiarly Chinese ideas about the city affected urban ecology at all levels in the hierarchy of administrative centers in late imperial times. In addition, Chang's treatment of urban geography serves to define the spatial setting of urban social structure, and raises questions about ecological variation within and between cities. Lamley's case studies have important implications for the structure of urban leadership. Was the effective cooperation they document among officials, merchants, and gentry in getting a capital city properly launched a first step in developing an informally instituted mode of "municipal" governance? Or, with their immediate objective achieved, would the various elites of the new city once again pursue narrower objectives within parochial sectors of urban society? One is led to wonder if citywide leadership structures might not be intermittent in nature, with city formation merely the first of the crises—periods of heightened activity and mobilization in response to exceptional threats or opportunities—that would periodically breathe life into otherwise latent political forms? My paper on regional urbanization, in pointing up the systematic nature of variation in city sizes (and the wide range of that variation) poses anew the classic question of how size and population density condition social structure. Can the Chinese case tell us anything about the sociological consequences of population concentration per se?

Most of the papers in Part Two speak even more directly to issues of internal urban structure. My paper points to differences in the social structure of cities that stemmed from particular combinations of economic and administrative central functions; it raises the question of how the migrations shaped by regional systems were reflected in the social composition, residential patterns, and organizational structure of cities. Watt analyzes the yamen as an urban institution; Shiba devotes a long section of his paper to Ningpo as an urban system; Elvin alerts us both to the intense interest of many townspeople in keeping open the vital transport routes on which their livelihood and their city's survival depended and to the political significance of the institutional arrangements for managing waterworks; Grimm shows us the importance of academies for the urban elite and points to the role of academies as yet another focus of competition and cooperation among the differentiated constituencies of a large city; and Baker is primarily concerned with the forms of kinship organization in urban settings.

In the first of the five papers in Part Three, Professor Golas discusses the development and nature of guilds from late Ming to the 1850's, when many declined or dissolved in the face of mid-century rebellions and when Western manufactures and manufacturing techniques had their initial impact on guild organization. He sees the "modern" origins of guilds in the organizational activity whereby urban sojourners of all kinds, scholar-officials as well as merchants, formed fraternal organizations on same-native-place lines. Golas naturally takes common economic activity as the touchstone of a guild, and of the two features that were

Introduction: Urban Social Structure in Ch'ing China

virtually universal among the earliest guilds—religious corporation and native-place particularism—he finds the former more resistant to change. He concludes that, contrary to the impression conveyed by some twentieth-century treatments, as an indigenous institution the Chinese guild had reached its full development prior to 1850.

Golas sees the major goal of guilds as "the preservation of a stable economic environment where each member could carry on his activity free from competition by outsiders and undercutting by fellow members," and he provides a searching analysis of just what guilds did and how their activities served that objective. The external relations of guilds—recruiting apprentices, handling encroachment on the guild's specialty or territory, dealing with officials, building a reputation—are shown to be closely interrelated with techniques for maintaining internal discipline. Golas carefully considers how class interacted with guild structure and, while recognizing the ubiquity of exploitation within the Ch'ing business world, concludes that guilds per se were seldom an instrument of that exploitation. In terms of organization theory, Golas finds Ch'ing guilds remarkably nonpervasive, surprisingly effective given their "rudimentary" organizational structure, and reliant on coercive sanctions as well as on normative appeals.

It was from deities of the popular religion that guilds and other urban associations drew their patrons; and since this was no less true for territorially based associations, popular temples were critical elements in the social structure of all Chinese cities and towns. In the first half of his chapter in *The Chinese City Between Two Worlds*, Dr. Feuchtwang provided a penetrating analysis of the role of popular temples in one Ch'ing city—Taipei prior to 1895. In his chapter for this volume he treats the official religion of Ch'ing China with special emphasis on its confrontation in capital cities with the popular religion. The official religion was an integral part of the state apparatus that recapitulated throughout the empire the hierarchical structure of field administration. The two official religious institutions emblematic of capital cities were the Confucian school-temple and the City God temple, and almost without exception one of each was associated with every yamen in the regular administrative hierarchy. (For example, see the woodcut of Shao-hsing-fu, Chekiang, reproduced on pp. 354–55.) Feuchtwang also discusses the suburban altars prescribed for all capitals and the official temples to popular deities that had been canonized by the imperial court. With this administrative form of official religious subdivision Feuchtwang contrasts the popular religion's *fen-hsiang*, "division of the incense," whereby a daughter temple was founded by transferring to its new incense burner ashes from the burner in the mother temple. Feuchtwang finds that tablets, memorialism, officials, and kin ritual went together in the official religion, forming a contrasting set to the images, magic, priests, and god ritual of the popular religion. At the same time, he emphasizes the cosmological elements on which both drew, the complex ways in which the one shaded into the other, and the senses in which elements of one can be seen as transformations of counterparts in the other. These subtleties are explored by comparing one of the major official sacrifices with the Taoist rite of cosmic renewal and community purification, and by exploring the dual role of the City God. The latter was represented by a tablet in the austere official rites held at a suburban altar, but was worshiped by the urban masses as an image in his own yamenlike temple, where his seal, the other-worldly counterpart of the magistrate's, was considered an instrument of magic.

By incorporating superior gods from the popular pantheon and specifying the limits of orthodoxy, the official religion exercised a form of control over both lower gods and people. As such it was an element in the mechanisms of social control treated by Dr. van der Sprenkel in her paper. She distinguishes enacted law, administered by the yamen, from the customary law and practices centered in guilds, native-place associations, neighborhood *hui*, and temples. Van der Sprenkel's focus is on matters relating to commerce and industry. She first accounts for the relative insignificance of enacted law for business: on the one hand, yamen courts were not designed to adjust business disputes or capable of doing so; and on the other, the government only rarely had recourse to court action in enforcing its economic policies. The government's toleration of guilds and native-place associations was probably related not only to their competence to resolve altercations between guild members that might otherwise have overburdened the criminal dockets in the magistrate's court, but also to their wholly complementary function of adjudicating commercial disputes arising from conflicts of interest or claims for loss or damages. Van der Sprenkel stresses the importance of establishing a personal relationship as a precondition of any important commercial transaction; though this tended to concentrate business relations within particularistic channels, it also accounts for the great importance of the institutionalized middleman in the Chinese business world. Her sophisticated treatment of this role illuminates the customary law of contract and agency, makes it clear why professional guarantors were required by law to be guaranteed by another, and helps account for the scale and complexity of commercial and financial transactions in Chinese urban markets. In the final section of her paper, van der Spren-

Introduction: Urban Social Structure in Ch'ing China 525

kel suggests ways in which control mechanisms might be expected to vary from one city to another in accordance with position in the economic and administrative hierarchies.

The last two papers in the volume are case studies of two Taiwanese cities, Tainan and Lu-kang. As T'ai-wan-fu, Tainan had been the island's chief political and economic center ever since the Ch'ing conquest in the late seventeenth century. Lu-kang, also a port city on the west coast, became important only in the eighteenth century as the Changhua Plain, its immediate hinterland, was brought under cultivation by mainland settlers. From the 1780's to the 1880's, Lu-kang was a flourishing center of trade, the backbone of its overseas commerce being the export of rice to the ports of Ch'üan-chou *fu*, directly across the Strait. According to my analysis of economic central places as of 1843, Tainan [T'ai-wan-fu] ranked as a regional city, the only one on the island, whereas Lu-kang ranked as one of Taiwan's two greater cities, the other being Meng-chia, the port city in northern Taiwan that figured heavily in Lamley's account of the rise of Taipei. Like many large regional cities on the mainland, Tainan was the capital of both a circuit and a prefecture; by contrast, Lu-kang's administrative status was lower than might be expected from its commercial importance, being not even a county capital but rather the seat of subofficials posted there to regulate and tax the trade. With this much background, let us turn to the not unremarkable findings of these two quite different case studies—first Professor DeGlopper's analysis of social structure in Lu-kang and then Professor Schipper's analysis of religious organization in Tainan.

In reconstructing nineteenth-century Lu-kang, DeGlopper paints a fascinating picture of a city in which native-place ties counted not at all (the entire population considering itself to be of Ch'üan-chou origin), of overlapping groups recruited on different principles and defined in different ways, and of balanced oppositions and exchanges. One set of segments into which the city's population was divided were surname groups, whose interrelations were marked by a pervasive low-keyed hostility. A second set of segments were neighborhoods, each focused on the incense burner of a deity and hosting at least one annual festival on the occasion of that deity's birthday. In some instances, several neighborhoods cooperated in the support of a single "higher-order" temple. Festivals during the seventh month linked all neighborhoods in ritual exchange, competition, and emulation, and a moiety structure became evident every few years when competitive street processions were staged between Uptown and Downtown.

Although neighborhoods and surname groups provided significant categories for the social intercourse of all townspeople, they were mobilized as effective groups only intermittently. By contrast, guilds were enduring corporate groups; and the eight guilds of Lu-kang together dominated the city's economic and political life. DeGlopper's wry description of the growing pressures in Lu-kang to acquire the full complement of capital-city emblems and to be designated the capital of its county is reminiscent of the developments in cities farther north already described by Lamley; with its ambitions in that regard thwarted to the very end, Lu-kang stands as something of a foil for Lamley's three success stories. DeGlopper concludes by comparing and contrasting Lu-kang's guilds with lineages, and Lu-kang's urban structure with that of overseas Chinese communities.

Schipper's study of the larger and older city of Tainan is closely focused on religious organizations—neighborhood cult associations in particular. He shows that in the 1870's Tainan was subdivided into over 70 neighborhoods (streets and combinations of streets rather than blocks), each organized as the *lu-hsia* (those "under the incense burner") of a particular T'u-ti-kung (Earth God). Like other communal associations in Chinese society, the T'u-ti-kung *hui* was formally organized, with a charter, a defined set of members, clearly designated officers, and explicit finances; and as with other associations, the rationality of the arrangements was embedded in religious idiom. The annual festive banquet that cemented group solidarity was held to honor the deity, and the theatrical performances that accompanied it were for the deity's entertainment. Officers were selected by the deity, by means of throwing lots before his image, and fees, dues, and levies were all given euphemistic religious designations. Schipper shows that these associations were concerned with keeping the neighborhood clean and peaceful, with controlling unseemly behavior, and with preventing construction that might upset the neighborhood's *feng-shui*, but even these policing activities were carried out in order to avoid offense to the deity. The essential autonomy of urban neighborhoods was underlined by a feature distinctive to T'u-ti-kung: whereas other cults were usually related by *fen-hsiang* to mother temples elsewhere, T'u-ti-kung was unaffiliated, his burner typically being filled with rice. Schipper explores the mythological origins and symbolic associations of T'u-ti-kung and discusses the other religious associations that were often organized within the neighborhoods defined in the first instance as the *lu-hsia* of that deity. Schipper then shows that conventional groupings of adjacent T'u-ti-kung *hui*, normally clustered around certain deity temples, served to define another, more inclusive level of urban community; it was for

Introduction: Urban Social Structure in Ch'ing China

wards at this level, for instance, that the *ta chiao* (the great Taoist rite of community purification) was held every twenty years or so. The effective territories of guilds, which also took the form of religious confraternities, cut across the territorial hierarchy already described. Finally, Schipper mentions the San-i T'ang, a federation of the three guilds that encompassed the city's major overseas traders. When the T'ang was established early in the nineteenth century, it took as its headquarters the Temple of the Water Immortal in the western suburb; the temple was rebuilt and refinanced on a greatly enlarged scale, and with the income from its endowments the San-i T'ang not only organized several of the largest citywide religious festivals but provided most of Tainan's "municipal" services.

Urban Ecology

The first of the issues I wish to raise in the remainder of this introduction concerns the nature of social differentiation within traditional Chinese cities, and in particular its relation to the partitioning of urban space. I sense a tension among, first, descriptive analyses of particular Chinese cities (including the case studies of this volume), second, the generalizations frequently encountered in the sinological literature, and third, the theoretical predictions of urban geographers and sociologists. Take the location of business enterprises. Sen-dou Chang has called attention to the "dispersed distribution of shops and markets" within cities,[1] and C. K. Yang has argued that the Chinese city had "no counterpart to the central business district of a Western city."[2] The disciplinary literature, on the other hand, leads one to expect that in premodern cities a central business district would normally develop at "the point of most convenient access from all parts of the city," at which point land would have its highest value.[3] The impression one gets from the studies in this book is different still. Business activity appears to climax in a district that is never central but instead sharply skewed in the direction of the city's main commercial trade routes. In nineteenth-century Ningpo (see the map on pp. 406–7), the business district was focused on the two eastern gates, with land values and commercial activity if anything higher in the extramural Chiang-hsia and Yung-tung districts than within the walls. In nineteenth-century Tainan, the business center of gravity was far off center in the direction of the port. The map of Tainan on p. 658 shows most of the west wall torn down, but when it still stood in the 1870's the Great West Gate was by far the most important for commercial traffic, and the largest wholesalers and major guilds were located in the western suburb.[4] The aerial photograph of Soochow on p. 15 proclaims to the practiced eye that the "central" business district of that great city was focused on the northernmost gate in the west wall. We need hardly be told that "the commercial and banking concentration" extended along the Grand Canal in the suburbs west of that gate.[5] In Chou-chia-k'ou (see the map on p. 82), the great merchant houses and their guildhalls were concentrated along the river in the southeastern of the three walled settlements. In his paper for *The Chinese City Between Two Worlds*, Winston Hsieh has shown that during the Ch'ing period urban development in Shih-ch'i (a county capital in the Canton Delta) was heavily concentrated in the western suburb between the wall and the nearby navigable river, and the map accompanying his article (p. 128) is as telling in this regard as any in this book.[6]

A second area of discrepancy concerns socioeconomic differentiation. "It is rare," we are told by C. P. Fitzgerald, "to find Chinese cities divided into a rich and a poor quarter. The large houses of the well-to-do, with their many courtyards and gardens, jostle the small single-courtyard houses of the poor in the same lane."[7] Mote echoes the point in his study of Soochow, insisting that traditional Chinese cities lacked "fashionable quarters, or slum quarters, as those have existed in the West. All residential streets looked the same, more or less, masking the life of individual homes behind uniform walls."[8] C. K. Yang once modeled the traditional Chinese city as a congeries of essentially similar, internally differentiated "neighborhood units," each containing both business firms and residences, both rich and poor, and a minimal complement of production enterprises, markets, temples, and schools. "Under this spatial arrangement," he argued, it was possible "to work and live in one neighborhood with minimum contact with other parts of the town."[9] For the most part, these views are greeted with skepticism by the comparative urban sociologist, for whom the question is not so much the existence of residential concentration by social class as the way in which it was patterned. The consensus is that in premodern cities social class is inversely related to distance from the center. "The preindustrial city's central area is notable . . . as the chief residence of the elite. . . . The disadvantaged members of the city fan out toward the periphery, with the very poorest and the outcastes living in the suburbs."[10] Is this pattern (which appears to hold for an impressive number of preindustrial cities in Europe, Latin America, and India[11]) wholly invalid for late imperial Chinese cities?

A third area of discrepancy concerns population gradients. In this respect, too, generalizations about Chinese cities tend to minimize differentiation, the usual view being that echoed in Chang's Part One paper, where he posits a relatively uniform population density within the walls.

Introduction: Urban Social Structure in Ch'ing China

On the other hand, Mote (in his Part One paper) notes that even as densely populated suburbs expanded outside the gates of such cities as Yangchow and Soochow, some of the land within the walls was devoted to agriculture; and in another context Chang argues that many capitals were designed to contain "within their walls large stretches of cultivated land" in order "to produce food for the population in case of siege."[12] On this point, comparative urban geographers generally consider the tendency for density to decline with distance from the city's central area to be virtually universal, but they argue that the gradient was particularly steep in premodern cities because of their less efficient and less flexible transport and (once again) the prevailing preference of the elite for centrally located residence.[13]

Although I can hardly resolve all these issues here, I should like to clarify them with some additional examples and suggest a few hypotheses to guide future research. Let us begin with Peking, hardly a typical Chinese city, to be sure, but one whose very size and multifunctional importance can be made to strengthen part of the argument. Figures 1 and 2 show two districts of the city as depicted on an incredibly detailed large-scale map of the city prepared ca. 1750.[14] We see clearly every *chien*, the basic architectural module of both shops and residences; and the enclosed compounds and interior courtyards to which Mote has already called our attention are everywhere apparent. Although the spatial arrangements are unmistakably Chinese in both districts, they nonetheless suggest strikingly different cityscapes. In Figure 1, buildings and compounds are small, the street pattern compact, and a high proportion of the buildings are shop-homes fronting alleyways. In Figure 2, the layout is more spacious in all respects, and fewer buildings front the street. I submit that we are looking at wards that were sociologically quite distinct, and I should like to tease out of data from a much later period what those differences might have been. The locations of the two districts within the city are shown upper left in Figure 3. The ward in Figure 1 was situated in the southern or Outer City near the heart of what was (in the 1910's as in the 1750's) Peking's "central" business district; the ward in Figure 2 was located east of the Imperial City in what was (in the 1910's as in the 1750's) an area favored by aristocratic and gentry families. Data collected by Gamble in 1917–18 put these wards in ecological context.[15]

Figure 3 reveals (upper right) sharp differentiation in population density within the walls, varying from 6,200 persons per square mile in the southeastern corner of the Outer City (where cultivated fields were still to be found in 1917) to a high of over 80,000 persons per square

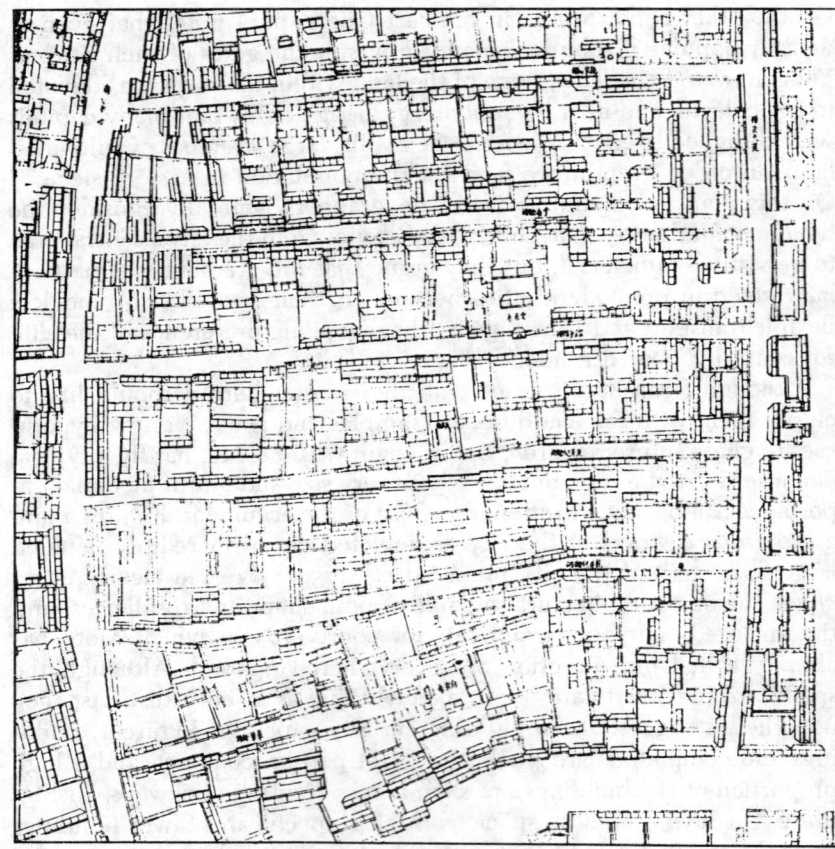

Fig. 1. Ward in the Major Business District of Peking, ca. 1750. This tract lay in the Outer City west of the axial avenue running south from Cheng-yang Men, the central gate in the south wall of the Inner City. The north-south street on the left is Mei-shih Chieh. Source: see note 14; this is a portion of the 6th leaf in the 13th row.

mile in the heart of the business district. In 1917, the density of the ward shown in Figure 2 was approximately half that of the Figure 1 ward, and if anything one would have expected the discrepancy to have been greater during High Ch'ing. From the plotting of sex ratios (lower left in Figure 3), we see that in general the most densely populated areas showed the greatest disproportion of males. In the ward of Figure 1 there would have been only one female for every three males, whereas in the Figure 2 ward the ratio must have been much more favorable: at least three females for every four males. At the lower right in Figure 3 yet a

Introduction: Urban Social Structure in Ch'ing China

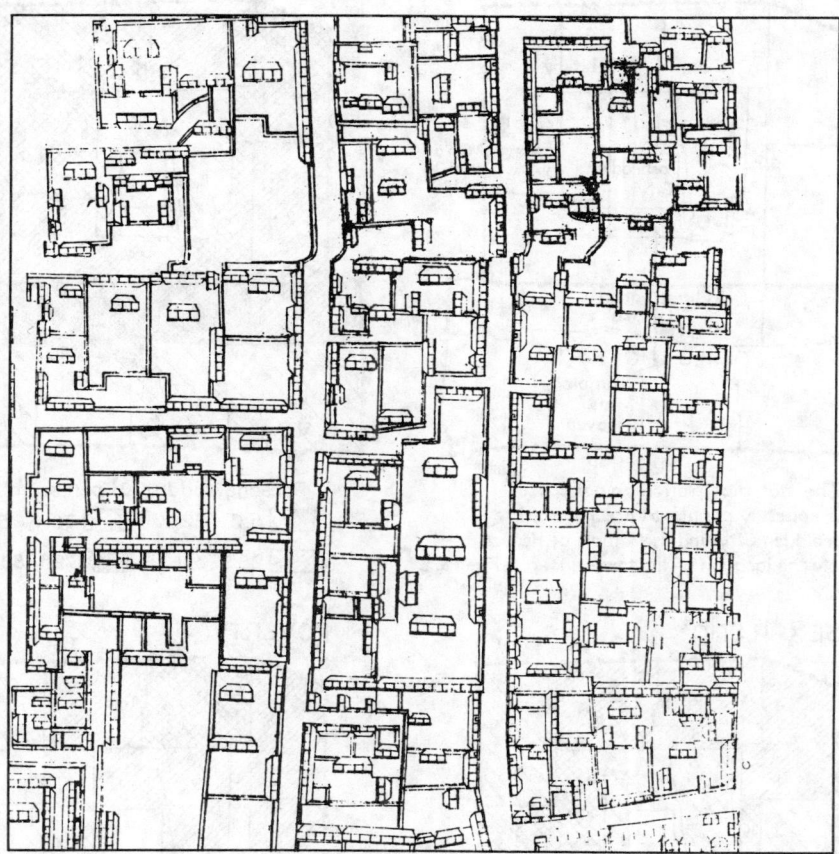

FIG. 2. WARD IN AN UPPER-CLASS DISTRICT OF PEKING, CA. 1750. This tract lay near the east wall of the Inner City just north of the street called Tung Shao-chiu Hu-t'ung. The wide north-south avenue at the right runs along the wall north of Ch'ao-yang Men. Source: same as for Figure 1; this is a portion of the 1st leaf in the 6th row.

third variable is plotted, the proportion of households classified by the police in 1918 as "very poor." Here we see that both the business districts of the Outer City (illustrated by Figure 1) and the areas south and east of the Imperial City (illustrated by Figure 2) were characterized by an absence of extreme poverty. Impoverished households were concentrated most heavily in the southeastern bulge of the Outer City walls, and they were relatively numerous along the north and west walls of the Inner City and the west wall of the Outer City. The relatively high level of poverty as of 1918 in the Imperial City itself (the two central

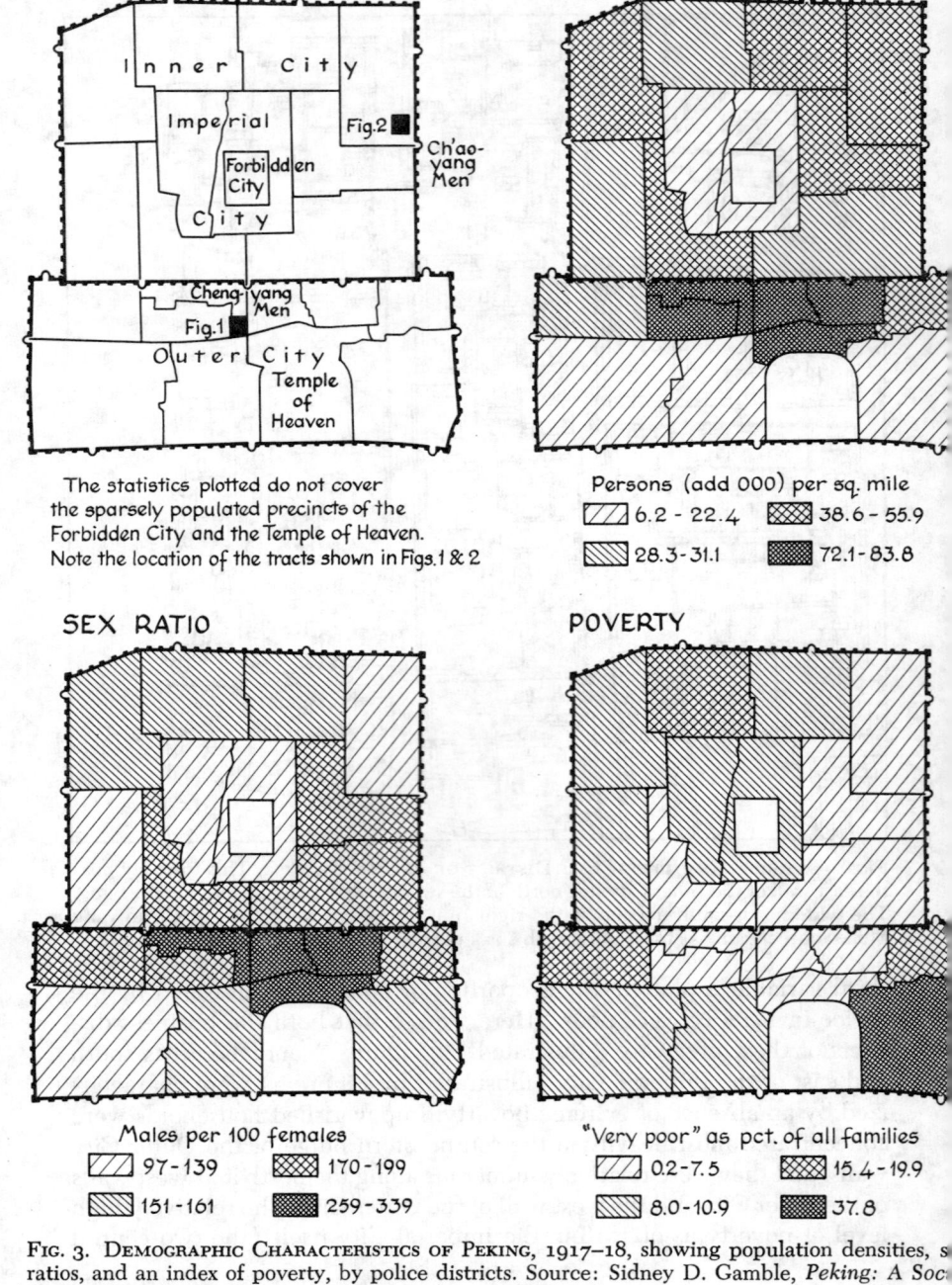

FIG. 3. DEMOGRAPHIC CHARACTERISTICS OF PEKING, 1917–18, showing population densities, s ratios, and an index of poverty, by police districts. Source: Sidney D. Gamble, *Peking: A Soc Survey* (New York: Doran, 1921), pp. 100, 412–13, 486.

police districts) and to some extent in the districts to the north and west of it doubtless reflects the impoverishment of Manchu stipendiaries that had been accelerating throughout the second half of the Ch'ing period, so that this feature of the distribution would not have obtained in 1750.

The situation in Ch'ing Peking illustrates a model of urban ecology that may have held generally for late imperial Chinese cities. It was characterized by two nuclei, one the center of merchant activity, the other the center of gentry and official activity. The business district was dominated by shop-houses (in large cities these were normally two-story buildings) in which the salesrooms of stores and the workrooms of craft-shops doubled as dining rooms and sleeping rooms for the largely male employees. Quarters were cramped because of high land values, the normal desire of businessmen to keep nonessential overhead down, and the frugality of sojourners out to save as much as possible of their income. The sex ratio was sharply skewed because of the high proportion of sojourners who had left their families behind in their native places and the large number of young unmarried apprentices. In the "central" business district the guilds and other mutual-aid associations led by merchants were at peak effectiveness, and the indigent unemployed were either dispatched to their native places at "public" expense, adequately cared for by benevolent institutions, or denied lodging in the area. The location of the business nucleus appears to have been determined more by transport costs of the merchants than by convenience of access for consumers, and it was typically displaced from the geographic center of the walled city toward (or to or even beyond) the gate or gates affording direct access to the major interurban transport route. (Peking's business district had grown up outside the three gates in the south wall of the original Ming city long before 1552, when the Outer City wall was built to enclose it and the official southern altars.)

Residences of the urban gentry tended to cluster near the official institutions of greatest interest to them. Sen-dou Chang has called attention to the pattern whereby academies, bookstores, stationery shops, and used-book stands favored locations near the Confucian school-temple (*hsüeh-kung*) and examination hall,[16] and in general the gentry nucleus of the city tended to be on the school-temple side of the yamen. In the special case of Peking, the gentry-official nucleus lay in the eastern third of the Inner City, between the T'ai-hsüeh (the imperial school-temple) in the north and the great examination hall in the south. The gentry district was characterized by a high proportion of residences with spacious compounds, by relatively many complex families (those with more than one conjugal unit) and relatively many complete conjugal units

FIG. 4. CHIANG-LAN CHIEH, a business street in the southwestern suburb of Canton, in the 1890's. The first store on the left (Ch'ien Chi Hao) sold ink and other writing materials; the second (Chang Chi T'ang), wax-cased pills. The first on the right (T'ien I) sold table covers and cushions; the second (Yung Chi), imported swallows' nests. The photographer noted that each shop on the street had a small shrine like the one at lower left "dedicated to the god who presides over the tradesman and his craft." John Thomson, *Through China with a Camera* (Westminster, Eng.: Constable, 1898), pp. 67–70.

Introduction: Urban Social Structure in Ch'ing China

(those with husband, wife, and children all present), and by a female population swelled by the concubines and maidservants of gentry households. Sex ratios, though far less extreme than in the business nucleus, were still unbalanced because many of the yamen clerks were sojourners and because of the concentration in this area of sojourning (male) students and, in high-level capitals, of expectant officials. It was in this part of the city that the charitable institutions and mutual-aid associations typically under official sponsorship and gentry management were most effective in providing for the deserving poor; and in general the police, together with the sentries of official buildings, kept the district clear of beggars and other undesirable elements.

Data for Canton in the late nineteenth century lend support to the binuclear concept. A general description is provided by Edward J. M. Rhoads: "In Canton, the division between merchants and gentry could virtually be drawn on a city map. Most of the commerce and handicrafts, and most of the merchants, were concentrated in the western half of the city, especially the Western Suburb.... The eastern half of the city, on the other hand, was the stronghold of the gentry. The old examination hall, the prefectural Confucian temple,... and many of the old-style academies (*shu-yüan*)... were located there."[17] Though the geographical focus of each nucleus could be specified with greater precision, there is little point in doing so here—for the 1895 statistics[18] that I wish now to pin to Professor Rhoads's description are already overaggregated for the purpose at hand, the entire Old City and the entire New (southern) City being undifferentiated. Even so, when the Old City and Eastern Suburb (which together encompassed the gentry nucleus) are compared with the New City and its adjoining Southern and Western Suburbs (which together encompassed most of the business nucleus), they present significantly different profiles. The sex ratio in 1895 was 168 males per 100 females for the northeastern "gentry" districts of the city, and 224 males per 100 females for the southwestern "merchant" districts. Moreover, the proportion of "multiple-family households," i.e., complex families, was significantly higher in the gentry-dominated portion of the city (.13.8 percent) than in the merchant-dominated portion (7.7 percent). (See Figure 4 for a glimpse of a street near the heart of Canton's business district as it appeared in the 1890's.)

Apropos of the contrast being made here, we might recall the clear distinction drawn by Shiba between the "ward near the official residences" in Ningpo and the "centers of business activity," and we might note the remark made in passing by Lien-sheng Yang in a paper on urban merchants[19] that in late imperial times one of the few restrictions on the location of shops was that they should not be "too near the yamen to spoil its dignity."

This model differs from that initially enunciated by Gideon Sjoberg (and recently restated with some rigor by Walter F. Abbott[20]) in having two nuclei, at least one of which was off-center geographically, instead of a single nucleus that ipso facto defined *the* city center. It also differs in that the urban periphery bears no spatial relation to wider concentric circles. Rather, the sociological periphery in Chinese cities was to be found in "purest" form at those corners of the intramural area that were least accessible from the more important gates.[21] Moving from the twin nuclei toward the isolated corners of the walled city, one found in ever greater numbers the hovels and shacks of the urban poor—porters, sedan-chair carriers, transport coolies, and dockworkers;[22] hawkers, peddlers, and such other itinerants as cooks with portable kitchens and craftsmen with portable repair shops;[23] medicine men, fortune-tellers, sorcerers, storytellers, musicians, and acrobats; prostitutes ejected from the lowest-class houses; "mean" people peculiar to particular cities (such as the To-min of Ningpo and Shao-hsing-fu); lepers; and, above all, beggars. Those who grew vegetables on vacant land in the remotest corners were often squatters. In many cities the dwellings of the poor were built up against the wall—or even in it, by scooping out "caves."[24]

This formulation retains some vestige of the general proposition that in premodern cities social status declined with distance from the center, but it would clearly be misleading to assert for Chinese cities that the poorest elements were "in the suburbs," for, as we have seen, certain suburbs lay squarely within the business nucleus. I would venture two additional propositions that appear to have some validity for late imperial cities of any appreciable size. First, we have already noted the pattern whereby wholesalers in the same line, retail specialty shops, and craftsmen of the same type were concentrated along one or more streets. I suggest that spatial differentiation within the business district was such that capital-intensive lines—including banks and trading companies specializing in low-bulk, high-value products—tended to lie at the center of the business nucleus, whereas labor- and land-intensive lines were at a greater remove from the center. The lowly crafts requiring heavy labor (e.g., tin-beating in connection with the manufacture of religious money-paper) or open space (e.g., dyers and furniture makers) were often located in quite peripheral neighborhoods. Second, the area between the two nuclei (no more than a narrow strip in some cities) tended to be heterogeneous as between gentry and merchants and as between shophouses and residences in the strict sense, but rather more homogeneous

Introduction: Urban Social Structure in Ch'ing China

in terms of per capita wealth than the business district per se. It was in this zone that one was likely to find the temples and other public institutions that were jointly sponsored by merchants and literati.

Having emphasized what I take to have been the overall ecological structure of late imperial cities, we may now place in perspective the within-block diversity that Western observers generally considered exceptional. The several statements by sinologists quoted at the beginning of this section largely reflect a preoccupation with distinguishing Chinese from Western cities. Shops *were* more widely dispersed in traditional Chinese cities than in modern Western cities, and it is doubtless true that the kind of social homogeneity found in an upper middle-class suburb or a central-city slum in the United States had no counterpart in traditional China. In one Peking district that covered some 80 acres, the population along eight business streets was over 82 percent male, whereas that along two interior residential streets had a balanced sex ratio.[25] Mote conveys the correct flavor when he writes: "One might not know, before stepping through a gate and around a screen wall to look into the courtyard beyond, whether he would find a mansion or a soy sauce factory, or a mansion being used as a factory."[26] But he would surely agree that the probabilities of finding a factory would be high in certain districts and low in others—and that the likelihood of being surprised would be greatest in districts lying between the city's two nuclear areas. As for the intermingling of rich and poor residences, the range was undoubtedly great in certain urban neighborhoods, with many a courtyard occupied by families that would be poor by present-day Western standards. But the majority of the urban poor to which I addressed myself above—numbering, most likely, between a tenth and a fifth of the entire urban population—did not live in "residential neighborhoods"; few had gates to be stepped through.

Naturally, one expects the relative importance of the two nuclei to reflect a city's position in the administrative and economic hierarchies. This is not the place to ring the changes in this regard or to muster evidence, but it is worth recording my general impression that the gentry nucleus was by no means absent from the urban ecology of nonadministrative central places. The papers in this book make it clear that the more important nonadministrative cities were likely to support a subofficial yamen (Watt), an academy (Grimm), and/or a Wen-wu miao (Feuchtwang); the gentry nucleus was likely to have been focused on one or more of these institutions. Even in the standard market town I studied in Szechwan, a gentry nucleus could be identified in the neighborhood of the local benevolent society, a *ju-yüan* ("Confucian hall") located on a quiet side street at a decent remove from the business center, whose central focus was the bustling courtyard of the town's major temple.

Sojourning and Urban Associations

It is easy to get the impression that in late imperial times most urbanites were sojourners. From the sixteenth century on, Chinese writers on particular cities have emphasized the numerical importance of natives with characteristic hyperbole. One Ming source claimed that nine out of ten persons in Lin-ch'ing, a flourishing port on the Grand Canal, were merchants from Hui-chou.[27] Another asserted that in Yangchow "natives are outnumbered by immigrants one to twenty."[28] In the nineteenth century, Western travelers picked up the refrain. Of Hangchow, Frederick Cloud wrote that only a tenth of the population were natives, "the remainder being made up of sojourners from every province of the empire."[29] In the early 1870's Richthofen, an experienced and judicious observer, wrote of Kalgan in northern Chihli: "Of the resident population, the greater part consider themselves as visitors on a long term, and have their families in some other place or province."[30] Guild regulations often provided for sending indigent members back to their native places, and a favorite recourse of yamen officials was to deport troublemakers to their places of origin;[31] it seemed to be taken for granted that every guildsman or every unruly urbanite had a native place somewhere else.

In fact, of course, every city had its permanent residents—those whose native place was the city in question—and their numerical strength vis-à-vis sojourners varied within a wide range. Why some cities attracted sojourners and others did not, and why sojourners dominated some cities but not others are questions to which I shall return below. But for the moment let us grant that a sizable proportion of the population of most cities were nonnatives and focus on their place in urban society. Three related points are often made about the sojourner component of city populations: (1) that they were occupationally specialized by place of origin, (2) that they typically organized themselves along native-place lines, and (3) that their native-place identities were slow to erode.

On the first point, Cloud's characterization of Hangchow may stand for hundreds like it concerning a wide range of cities. "Practically all the carpenters, wood-carvers, decorators, cabinetmakers, and medicine dealers are from Ningpo. The tea and cloth merchants, salt dealers, and innkeepers are from Anhwei. The porcelain dealers are from Kiangsi, the opium traders from Canton, and the wine merchants from Shaohsing. Many of the bankers and money-changers are also from Shaohsing, as well as many of the blacksmiths; ... Soochow furnishes a large number of the official class, the 'sing-song' girls, and restaurant keepers."[32] The second point is dramatically illustrated by reference to Peking, where the number and diversity of *Landsmannschaften* (associations based on common place of origin) were truly phenomenal. In his classic 1966 study,[33] Ping-ti Ho identified 391 such associations in nineteenth-century Peking; but a manuscript acquired by Niida Noboru that has recently come to light in Tokyo[34] lists for Peking no fewer than 598 native-place associations of various types, including *hsiang-tz'u* (compatriots' temples). Almost all served the natives of particular counties, prefectures, and provinces, or conventional combinations of contiguous units at each of these administrative levels. Ho's analysis called attention to the fact that many of these associations limited their membership to scholars, and he emphasized the role of most of them as hostels for examination candidates. By contrast, Niida's research emphasized their commercial aspects, showing inter alia that merchants and artisans also used many of the *hui-kuan* that catered primarily to scholars and that the membership of scores of native-place associations was limited to those pursuing a particular line of business (such as the Yen-Shao Hui-kuan, limited to paper merchants from the adjacent prefectures of Yen-p'ing and Shao-wu in Fukien, and the Che-Tz'u Hui-kuan, limited to tailors from Tz'u-ch'i *hsien*, Ning-po *fu*, Chekiang).[35]

The third point is really a cultural matter: native place was an essential component of a person's identity in traditional Chinese society. Strangers thrown into contact would in their initial conversational exchange invariably ascertain one another's native place as well as surname. A person's native county commonly appeared on doorplates (and invariably appeared on tombstones) and was used in correspondence and belles lettres as a surrogate given name for prominent figures. The normative pattern was clear: a young man who left to seek his fortune elsewhere was expected to return home for marriage, to spend there an extended period of mourning on the death of either parent, and eventually to retire in the locality where his ancestors were buried. Even when these expectations were not realized, the son born to a sojourner inherited his father's native place along with his surname. Residences were not immutable, as we shall see, but within the span of a few generations native place must be seen as an ascribed characteristic.[36]

Sojourning was seldom an individual matter. The man who left to try his luck in the city normally did so as a "representative" of his family, his lineage, and his native place. He was "selected" to go. For reasons that are obvious to students of Chinese society, "only sons" almost never emigrated; sojourners were selected from sets of sons, and relevant criteria—ambition, venturesomeness, intelligence—played a role in deciding who should go. There was often a period of testing and tempering in local schools or small-town enterprises operated by kinsmen or others from his native place. A promising young man received help and support at every step of the way from kinsmen and native-place fellows, and such assistance was conceived not only as a moral obligation but also as an investment calculated to yield benefits for corporate groups of variable inclusiveness. I have elsewhere analyzed sojourning in terms of mobility strategies—that is, as a form of maximization by families, lineages, villages, marketing communities, counties, and even prefectures.[37] Particular localities cultivated specific occupational skills for "export" to the cities where opportunities were concentrated. The men who climbed the central-place hierarchy to take advantage of those opportunities for the most part followed one of two tracks—they went either to exploit business opportunities in *economic* central places, or to take advantage of the opportunities for education and bureaucratic service in *administrative* central places.

Success in the latter track was the more prestigious, and the preferred mobility strategy was to groom young men for academic success. In the paradigmatic case a local system selected the brightest of its boys and provided the resources to support them through the early years of study in a bid for academic degrees and bureaucratic office. The odds were long, but the rewards of success—placing a native son in office—were overwhelming and comprehensive. The benefits returned included power with which to protect the local system and further its interests, wealth to enhance its living standards and productivity, and, above all, prestige, which by enhancing the community's reputation yielded specific payoffs for families throughout the local system. Despite the lower prestige of business in comparison with academic achievement, the cultivation of specialized business talent for export was also a widespread maximization strategy. The importance of regionally based merchant and financial entrepreneurs was discussed in Part Two, where Shiba addressed many of the relevant factors in analyzing the case of Ningpo merchants. Even more widespread than strategies involving the scholar-official or the merchant-financier tracks were local-system specializations in the export of craftsmen, semiprofessionals, and the purveyors of services. The potential for spectacular success was, of course, more limited, and most such specializations were focused on opportunities within a particular city or the market towns and cities of a circumscribed subregion. The low respectability of a calling was no necessary barrier to local-system specialization: the security of an occupational niche in the city was an important consideration for a village or marketing community with limited resources; and in any case, the techniques for converting wealth to respectability were well understood. Though this is not the place to pursue the matter, it goes without saying that the importance and type of sojourner strategies were strongly conditioned by the local system's place in the overall structure of territorial systems—particularly with respect to cities at different hierarchical levels and to the transport routes linking the cities within an urban system.

Sojourning strategies, predicated on native-place loyalties, were furthered by the organization of urban sojourners on the basis of common origin. Native-place associations in Peking and the various provincial capitals improved the competitive position of local systems with respect to the imperial examinations and official appointments, and the native-place associations in economic centers were a manifestation of the struggle to monopolize or control an occupational niche. These instrumental objectives should, however, be seen in the context of the particular advantages of the *t'ung-hsiang* (same-native-place) bond as a principle of organization. One of these is that it encompassed a large proportion of the other types of particularistic relationships (*kuan-hsi*) that were considered by the Chinese to be potential bases for the development of trust. As Baker points out, the number of kinsmen in a city was seldom large enough to afford an organization of any appreciable size or power, but in practice both affinal and consanguineal relationships were subsumed by and reinforced *t'ung-hsiang* ties. Many if not most of the experiential *kuan-hsi* of potential importance in Chinese society—being students of the same teacher, taking the county examinations at the same time, going together on a religious pilgrimage, crossing the Strait in the same junk, and so on—were likely to have been shared with those whose residences were fairly nearby. Thus, these too were encompassed by native-place ties and served to strengthen them.

A second advantage stemmed from the hierarchically cumulative nature of the *t'ung-hsiang* bond. Community membership necessarily entailed membership in the higher-order local and regional systems in which that community was located. This gave *t'ung-hsiang* remarkable flexibility as a principle of urban organization. The relevant units for cumulating native-place ties ranged from subcounty townships-cum-marketing communities up to conventional groupings of provinces. The inclusiveness of membership was, of course, a function of the relative numbers of sojourners from various local systems as well as of the competitive situation. Time and again, sojourners from local systems within a trading system or an administrative unit joined forces at whatever level in the hierarchy was necessary to claim a prize in a distant city and to deny it to similar alliances elsewhere. We have seen the principle in operation repeatedly in the case studies of this volume. Natives of Nan-hui *hsien* (Fukien) were variously organized (1) at the county level, (2) at the level of San I, a conventional grouping of three counties, (3) at the level of Ch'üan-chou prefecture, or (4) at the provincial level. Ningpo merchants were variously organized in associations limited to those from Ning-po prefecture, to those from the two adjacent prefectures of Ning-po and Shao-hsing, to those from Chekiang province as a whole, or to natives of the four adjacent provinces covered by the designation San-chiang.

A third advantage of *t'ung-hsiang* as an organizing principle is that it cut across class and other vertical bonds (including those of many experiential *kuan-hsi*, which tended to be class-specific). This commended it in particular to the rich and powerful, who were able to utilize an ostensibly egalitarian principle to institute within the organization a division of labor that left the "dirty work" to lower-class members, and who were able to define association objectives in terms that served the interests of their own enterprises. At the same time, the context of *t'ung-hsiang* solidarity was ideal for socializing and supporting the upwardly mobile greenhorn.

Golas's paper points up the difficulties in disentangling guilds from native-place associations in Ch'ing cities. The generic terms used for "association" or "hall" (*kung-so, hui-kuan, tien, kung*, and so forth) are wholly unreliable indicators, and we know from both Ch'ing and Republican materials that an association whose name specified only a place might function as a guild (e.g., the Shang-yüan Hui-kuan in Hankow, named for one of the metropolitan counties of Nanking, which in fact served as a guild for traders from that city specializing in dry goods and groceries[38]), and that an association whose name specified only an economic specialization might in fact be limited to natives of a particular locality (e.g., the Gold-beaters Guild in Wen-chou-fu, which was monopolized by natives of Ning-po *fu*[39]). The extent of economic specialization by native place is likely to be underestimated on two other counts. First, when sojourners from a given local system pursued more than one economic specialization in a particular city, they might organize as a native-place association with specialized subdivisions acting as guilds. We have seen in Shiba's paper a rather special instance of this arrangement: one subdivision of Ningpo's overarching Fukien provincial asso-

Introduction: Urban Social Structure in Ch'ing China

ciation, the Hsing-hua Pang, was limited to merchants dealing in fresh and dried *lung-yen* fruit. In several cities the native-place associations of sojourners from Ning-po *fu* had separate guild-like subdivisions for *ch'ien-chuang* bankers and for shipping agents.[40] Second, economic specialization by native place was by no means limited to cases of monopolization. Niida identified several trades in Peking that were shared by two or more guilds, each organized on the basis of native place, and in some cases competing native-place guilds joined forces to protect their shared monopoly. Thus the Sugar-cake Bakers Association was formed of two component units, Pei-an and Nan-an (literally northern and southern "tables"), limited to natives of Peking and Nanking, respectively.[41]

Landsmannschaften-cum-guilds almost invariably specified their areas of common origin in terms of administrative units. Nonetheless, available evidence suggests that the relevant catchment areas were typically marketing or trading systems at one level or another in the economic hierarchy I described in my Part Two paper—administrative terminology being used out of deference to the official bureaucratic view and for the very practical reason that few people in a given city could be expected to be familiar with the economic geography of distant regions. We get a strong hint of the precedence of commercial systems from cases where the specified administrative units constitute a combination that flouts the hierarchy of field administration. The P'ing-Li Kung-so in Hankow, for instance, was an association of traders from adjacent counties in different provinces, P'ing-hsiang (Kiangsi) and Li-ling (Hunan);[42] in fact, the catchment area was a trading system within the drainage basin of a tributary of the Hsiang River. The guild of bathhouse operators in Peking was generally thought to be monopolized by natives of I-chou, an autonomous department some 65 miles southwest of the city, but in fact its members were from the greater-city trading system that included Ting-hsing *hsien* in Pao-ting *fu* as well as two county-level units within I-chou itself.[43] The Su-Hu Kung-so in Hankow was a comparable example at a higher-level of the administrative hierarchy, its membership being limited to natives of Su-chou *fu* in Kiangsu and Hu-chou *fu* in Chekiang, adjacent prefectures at the economic core of the Lower Yangtze region.[44] Three levels at which "Cantonese" merchants were organized in various cities may serve to illustrate the general principle. Those known as Liang-Kuang Hui-kuan (associations for natives of Kwangtung and Kwangsi) were, I suggest, limited to traders from Canton's metropolitan trading system, that is, the Lingnan region as a whole; those known as Kuang-Chao Hui-kuan (associations for natives of Kuang-chou *fu* and Chao-ch'ing *fu*) were limited to traders from Canton's regional-city trading system; and those known as San I Kung-so (associations for the three contiguous counties of Nan-hai, P'an-yü, and Shun-te, known in Cantonese as Sam Yap) were limited to traders from Canton's local-city trading system.

The pattern of economic specialization by native place that prevailed in late imperial cities can be profitably analyzed in terms of an ethnic division of labor. There is no difficulty whatsoever in viewing the "colonies" of extraregional traders in Chinese cities as ethnic minorities. "The Cantonese is as much an alien in Shanghai," Morse pointed out, "as the Portuguese was in Spain when Philip II was sovereign over both countries."[45] Anhwei merchants in Chungking, Ningpo merchants in Peking, Hokkien merchants in Hankow, Ningpo merchants in Canton, Shansi merchants in Foochow—all spoke languages unintelligible to the natives and practiced customs that appeared outlandish at best. But if recent studies of ethnicity have taught us anything, it is that ethnic solidarity is no simple function of cultural distinctiveness;[46] slight accents and even minor mannerisms may serve as ethnic markers if either side finds it advantageous to maintain or erect ethnic boundaries. There is no want of examples in Chinese cities of economic specializations by local systems in their near vicinity. The pig brokers in Peking were natives of an area 15–30 miles to the northeast (Mi-yün and Shun-i counties);[47] and in Hankow the specialists in the manufacture and trade of tobacco pouches were natives of Huang-p'o, less than twenty miles north of the city.[48] Was the difference between Hui-chou and Huang-p'o traders, both of whom found it worthwhile to maintain a guildhall in Hankow, one of kind or of degree? Were the mechanisms for keeping a grip on their respective economic niches basically different? Did Huang-p'o traders, too, find it advantageous to emphasize their cultural distinctiveness? Future research may find it useful to consider these questions in the framework of a hierarchy of regionally based ethnicity and subethnicity.

This brings us to the matter of assimilation, to which Golas rightly calls our attention in accounting for the trend he discerns during the Ch'ing period away from economic specialization by native place. The maintenance of ethnic boundaries *and* of economic specializations was naturally easiest when the sojourning community maintained continuing close relations with its native area. So long as Hsing-hua retained a comparative advantage in the production of *lung-yen* for the Ningpo market, one would expect the Hsing-hua community to be ethnically renewed from one generation to the next and its monopoly of *lung-yen* wholesaling to persist. But China's regional economies were subject to

Introduction: Urban Social Structure in Ch'ing China

continual flux, and local systems were everywhere poised to respond to opportunities created by changed circumstances. If Hsing-hua lost its comparative advantage to another region, or if Hsing-hua merchants in Ningpo found it advantageous to diversify into lines unrelated to their native prefecture, then in time one would expect the Hsing-hua community to assimilate and the Hsing-hua Pang either to atrophy or to change its character. The life expectancy of a *Landmannschaft*-cum-guild was apparently not long in late imperial China; few lasted for more than two or three generations without reorganization. And the historical record is clear that in particular cases hyphenated associations became guilds *tout court*. What is less clear to me than to Golas, however, is that such cases added up to a secular trend away from economic specialization by native place. It is just possible that the reverse may have been true prior to the onset of modernizing change: that increased competition for occupational niches in Chinese cities led to more frequent displacement of one territorially based "ethnic" group by another, speeded up the developmental cycle of urban associations, and accelerated the assimilation of urban ethnics. The evidence for any trend appears inconclusive.

I have in passing directed attention to the likelihood that many urban natives were the residuum of successive waves of sojourners. From our knowledge of overseas Chinese communities, we may assume that the wholly unsuccessful—those unable to keep up remittances, to afford return visits, to repay the loans of *t'ung-hsiang* benefactors—often failed to return; in many cases they had, out of considerations of face, cut themselves off from their native-place compatriots in the city and died an anonymous and ignominious urban death. Traveling in North China in the 1870's, Williamson noted that "one can form an idea of the size of a city by the number of graves that lie immediately outside its walls. These will be graves of the poor and of strangers."[49] Failed sojourners were among those buried in such paupers' graves. Since few would have had offspring in the city, their contribution to the urban population cannot have been great. The many cemeteries maintained by *Landsmannschaften*, however, tell a rather different story. In an ideal Chinese world, sojourners would have returned to their native places by the onset of old age, and those unfortunate enough to die in the city would have been sent back in coffins. According to Morse, *Landsmannschaften* "invariably have a mortuary, in which may be deposited the coffined bodies of ... members, waiting ... for the accomplishment of the desire of all Chinese, that their bones may be taken back for burial in their ancestral home."[50] For sojourner communities that did not maintain their own mortuaries, public institutions of the same type were to be found in all major cities.[51] Morse accounts for same-native-place cemeteries in terms of poverty: provincial clubs, to use his term, "invariably have their own cemetery, in which they grant graves for their poorer members, in order that their bones may lie in ground which is a substitute for their native soil."[52] We may also surmise that such cemeteries, some of which date back to Ming times,[53] were used by the assimilating descendants of sojourners, regardless of socioeconomic status.

The very dynamics of sojourning, then, account for part of the variation in the relative size of the native urban population. Commercial cities whose trade was expanding attracted many sojourners, those whose trade was contracting attracted few. The most dramatic contrast should be provided by cities whose economic centrality changed so radically that they moved up or slipped down a notch in the economic hierarchy. During the nineteenth century, Shanghai's trade and population more than quadrupled and its status changed from a regional metropolis—one of several in the Lower Yangtze—to that region's dominant central metropolis. Little wonder that in the late nineteenth century natives were swamped by sojourners.[54] Kalgan in Chihli was growing rapidly at the time of Richthofen's visit in the 1870's; it was a greater city in the process of acquiring the additional economic centrality of a regional city. Hangchow, whose domination by outsiders at the turn of the century was so graphically described by Cloud, had for the preceding forty years afforded exceptional opportunities for sojourners, as it recovered from the devastation wrought during the Taiping Rebellion. On the other hand, both Lin-ch'ing and Yangchow, noted in late Ming as cities dominated by sojourners, were in decline by the late nineteenth century. Both had slipped a notch in the economic hierarchy, and in both urban natives—largely the residuum of past sojourners—had become numerically dominant. An even more extreme case is Lu-kang, whose decline as a port during the nineteenth century left it a city devoid of sojourners.[55]

Of course, not all urban natives were the descendants of sojourners in any strict sense. The native gentry of cities consisted of the descendants not only of successful sojourners but also of landlords who had gradually changed their residence from more rural settlements in the city's immediate hinterland. And the urban poor included not only unsuccessful sojourners but migrants from the countryside who lacked community roots in any village or town. With no native place, they were the ultimate "expendables"[56] of society, and their only hope for security in an urban setting was acceptance into the ranks of beggars.

Introduction: Urban Social Structure in Ch'ing China

Urban Associations and "Municipal" Governance

I raise as a final issue perhaps the most important question posed by the papers of Part Three: How was urban society managed? We know only enough to be certain that the answer varied from one city to another and that for most cities the Ch'ing period was one of marked institutional change in this regard. The papers below help define an area where additional research would be richly rewarded. To what extent was the late imperial city an integrated sociopolitical entity? What municipal services were provided and through what institutional arrangements? How was the political power of officials, gentry, and merchants exercised and mediated? In what senses could it be said that the city was governed at all?

We might start with an organizing principle not previously mentioned in this introduction, namely place of urban residence. It appears to have been generally true that in cities of any appreciable size the population was organized into neighborhoods, normally defined in terms of streets rather than blocks. This was so in every city treated in any detail in this volume—Ningpo, Canton, Nanking, Peking, Taipei, Tainan, and Lukang. From Schipper's article, it is apparent that neighborhood associations took responsibility not only for the ritual purity of the area but also for its general order, harmony, and cleanliness. C. K. Yang, generalizing from his study of nineteenth-century Fo-shan, holds that "normal collective operations of urban life such as fire prevention, garbage removal, ... maintenance of ... order in the street neighborhood, certain types of ... charity and religious celebrations, were all traditional parts of the neighborhood associations, which were self-governing bodies entirely independent of ... the *li-chia* system."[57] He also points out that disputes between residents of the same neighborhood were normally mediated within the association.

It would be rather surprising if sociologically marginal elements of the city population were in fact incorporated in organized neighborhoods— the beggars who slept under bridges, for instance, or the squatters whose shacks were built against the city wall—but there is no reason for doubting that the "households" (i.e., shop-houses and residences) of sojourners were included. Schipper's Tainan data reveal fairly rapid turnover in the composition of a neighborhood, and the mechanisms he describes for incorporating newcomers into the neighborhood corporation must have been important in the adjustment of sojourners to urban life. Although we know that shops and stores in the same line of business were concentrated along particular streets and that particular lines of business were often dominated by regional ethnics, the implications of these facts for neighborhood organization appear to be unexplored.

As Shiba points out, and as Schipper's article dramatizes, group interests were normally given religious expression in traditional cities. There is no reason to doubt that urban neighborhoods throughout China took the form of religious corporations along the lines described by Schipper for old Tainan. The neighborhood cult of T'u-ti-kung (or Fu-te Cheng-shen) appears to have been ubiquitous in both the cities and the countryside of China; and John Kerr's remark that in nineteenth-century Canton every street had its Fu-te Tz'u[58] might, with an appropriate discount for its sweeping character, have been made about almost any other city. The great virtue of Schipper's analysis is that we now have a basis for surmising what those shrines in Chinese cities implied about urban social order.

It is also a safe generalization, I believe, that in all late imperial cities certain temples were the focus of territorial units uniting several neighborhoods. Whereas T'u-ti-kung *hui* were inward looking, with the annual feast limited to association members, the sectors or wards of the city centered on deity temples were outward looking, their festivals designed to attract visitors from other wards and to provide occasions for hosting kinsmen, *t'ung-hsiang* fellows, business associates, and friends residing elsewhere. DeGlopper's case study emphasizes the integrative effects of competition and exchange among sections of the city defined as the *lu-hsia* of particular temple deities, and it is clear that in all but the largest cities particular temples (sometimes only the Ch'eng-huang miao) were seen as servicing the entire city and certain religious festivals as expressing the distinctive spirit of the city as a whole. Many of the cults that appealed to particular subsets of the population had adherents residing throughout the city, and when it is realized that both guilds and native-place associations were normally organized as religious corporations, it is clear that DeGlopper's image of a hierarchy of crosscutting allegiances has much to commend it in terms of religious organization alone.

The various case studies of this volume indicate that at least by the nineteenth century many if not most urban services were provided by nongovernmental corporate groups and financed through assessments and dues or the income from corporate property. Whether the same pattern held during the earlier centuries of the late imperial period I must leave to the historians, but the example of the San-i T'ang in Tainan suggests that relatively undifferentiated religious corporations had the capability of providing a wide range of municipal services even in the absence of guilds and *Landsmannschaften*. In the extreme long run, of course, we see a sharp retrenchment of the yamen's role in the governance of cities, but it is unclear to me how closely it was synchronized with the rise of guilds and native-place associations, which became characteristic features of the institutional landscape only in the eighteenth century.

One can, I think, discern two lines of development toward citywide leadership structures that coordinated urban services. One grew out of merchant associations, the other out of gentry institutions (though, as we shall see, the two were never wholly independent and became increasingly intertwined during the nineteenth century). On the merchant side, the first significant development was the extension into the public realm of services initially provided by guilds and native-place associations for their members alone. The significance of this development is underscored by Niida Noboru in his study of Hung-chiang, a regional city in Hunan dominating the upper Yüan Basin, where ten *hui-kuan* were established.[59] In the case of certain functions taken on by particular guilds—fire fighting and policing, for instance—the benefits that may have been designed primarily for members were inevitably enjoyed by others within the quarter. It made no sense for a guild's fire brigade to ignore a conflagration just because it began in a non-member's shop. De-Glopper makes it clear that the militia operated by the Ch'üan-chou guild in Lu-kang was designed to protect the city as a whole. In all probability competition for prestige and power was a major factor in the extension of services to the general public. When the Hsin-an Hui-kuan took the initiative in establishing a citywide system of fire stations in Ningpo, it was at once a demonstration of financial power, a declaration of public-spirited concern for the native population, a means of placing the entire business community in its debt, and an assertion of supremacy among the various business associations of the city. Guilds that operated charity schools, infirmaries, and dispensaries for their members alone could easily gain a reputation for stinginess, especially when others following a more open policy were able to pose as exemplars of Confucian virtue. It was a short step to cooperation among guilds in these matters, or at least to a division of labor among them. A case in point is the Ai-yü Shan-t'ang, founded in Canton in 1871 jointly by the leading guilds: it was a charitable institution that "provided free outpatient care to the indigent sick, financial support for destitute widows, and free coffins for the poor; it also supported several free primary schools for the children of the poor."[60]

Institutional historians of the Ch'ing period have emphasized the significance of the federations of merchant associations that in certain cities took on the aspect of a municipal government. Two of the best documented cases are those of Chungking and Hung-chiang. The Chungking federation, later known as the Eight Provincial Associations (*Pa-sheng hui-kuan*) began in the K'ang-hsi period (1662–1722) as an informal meeting of the heads of the several associations to settle disputes between their respective members—primarily commercial disputes of the kind that van der Sprenkel shows to have been beyond the competence of magistrates' courts, but also altercations of a criminal nature.[61] It was also concerned to keep the city's wharves in good repair and standardize regulations of the various merchants' associations. A joint office was eventually established, and by the mid-nineteenth century the federation had assumed responsibility for a wide range of charities and public works. It operated an orphanage, an old-people's home, and a granary, and organized disaster relief and charitable work among the poor. It also maintained fire-fighting brigades and a militia, and during the Taiping era it was pressured by the yamen to assume responsibilities for regional defense.[62] A similar federation of ten *hui-kuan* was formed in Hung-chiang probably in the 1850's, and by 1880 it operated an orphanage and granary, maintained a militia, and was responsible for fire fighting, the maintenance of roads and bridges, and disaster relief.[63] In addition to these two cases, we know of similar federations in Ch'iung-chou-fu, Hainan, where five *hui-kuan* were involved; in Chia-ting, a county capital in Ts'ang *chou*, an autonomous department in Kiangsu; and in Sha-shih, a nonadministrative port near Ching-chou-fu in Hupeh.[64]

The federation in Swatow known as Wan-nien-feng was rather special, for its six component *hui-kuan* represented the counties of Ch'ao-chou *fu* immediately surrounding the city that were dominated by Teochiu speakers. Hakkas from the prefecture were organized together with all other Hakka traders from the upper Han Basin in a separate association known as the Pa-shu Hui-kuan, and Cantonese and other outlanders were likewise excluded from the dominant Teochiu federation.[65] A similar ethnic element was probably present in Tainan, where the San-i T'ang, described by Schipper as a federation of three guilds, was probably limited to natives of Ch'üan-chou *fu*, who were predominant among Tainan's overseas traders generally and especially in the western suburb where the T'ang's headquarters was located. Both the Swatow and the Tainan federations assumed a range of governmental functions similar to those described for Chungking and Hung-chiang.

We would do well, I think, to question the sharp distinction drawn

Introduction: Urban Social Structure in Ch'ing China

by some historians between cities with formally constituted merchant federations and those without. Effective cooperation among associations does not require a separate office or a formal charter. The need for standardizing weights and measures within a city, for mediating disputes between members of different guilds or native-place associations, for repairing the wharves and dredging the channels on which the entire trading community depended, and for avoiding costly duplication and injustice in charitable activities must have been felt in scores of other commercial cities for which we have no record of merchant federations. The political structure of overseas Chinese urban communities is instructive in this regard. In many Southeast Asian cities, Chinese merchant leaders of different guilds and associations joined forces to establish and manage temples, schools, hospitals, cemeteries, and charitable foundations.[66] Even when no single association was dominant, formal federation was not a precondition of joint action. Leaders of the seven Chinese *hui-kuan* of Bangkok (whose constituencies theoretically encompassed all regions of origin in China) came together whenever a crisis arose affecting the interests of the community as a whole (or its dominant mercantile segment), but there was no joint office and no written charter—not even a name for the informal institution.[67] I do not find it surprising that the guilds of Canton jointly founded a comprehensive charitable foundation 28 years before we have any record of formalized cooperation (namely the "formation" of the Seventy-two Guilds in 1899); nor can the absence of such formalization be taken as prima facie evidence of "little or no cooperation among guilds, even for economic purposes."[68]

Lawrence Crissman has argued that urban Chinese in China and overseas faced a similar situation in that both had to "govern themselves without having noticeable governmental institutions."[69] If it was generally true that "noticeable governmental institutions" would have been regarded with suspicion by bureaucratic officials in the yamens of late imperial cities, then one would expect formal confederation to have occurred only in the exceptional circumstances where it served the interests of the yamen and was specifically encouraged by the officials. It is notable in this regard that Hung-chiang, Sha-shih, Lu-kang (if we may legitimately include it in this context: the degree of formalization of the Eight Guilds is not apparent from available data), and Swatow were all major commercial centers whose economic centrality far outweighed their administrative status. All were "governed" from another city, although a *hsün-chien* was posted to each to oversee the trade. In these circumstances, harried officials might be expected to have welcomed the convenience of dealing with an overarching federation that could assume responsibility beyond the capacity of bureaucratic government. That this was true in Lu-kang is implicit in DeGlopper's account, and Niida explicitly argues that the Ten Guilds of Hung-chiang were requested by officials to assume particular governmental functions and that the federation cooperated closely with the yamens in both Hui-tung and Ching-chou, the capitals of the county and the autonomous department to which it was administratively subordinate.[70] Chungking, the capital of a circuit and a prefecture, was a very different case, but even here its emergence in the nineteenth century as the central metropolis of the Upper Yangtze region meant that its economic centrality surpassed that of most provincial capitals elsewhere in China. In this case, too, our authority is explicit that officials pressured the confederation to assume governmental responsibilities during the hectic years of the Taiping Rebellion.[71] Guild confederations, then, may have appeared in China only when they were specifically encouraged by bureaucratic officials, but this does not mean that informal arrangements amounting in effect to a sub-rosa municipal government were necessarily absent from commercial cities where officials saw no necessity for risking the potential threat of formally consolidated merchant power.

Comparable developments involving the consolidation of gentry power have been ably analyzed by Mark Elvin in his paper in *The Chinese City Between Two Worlds*.[72] The three relevant trends he discerns all involved a measure of official-gentry cooperation. One was the establishment of specialized local boards partly run by "gentry directors"; the first such case in Shanghai was the Shanghai Board for the Sea Transport of Kiangsu Tribute Grain, founded in 1825. The second innovation was the assembly of local gentry called together by the magistrate; the first documented instance in Shanghai was an assembly called in 1864 to advise the county magistrate on water conservancy. In this regard, K'ang Yu-wei called attention to "public boards" in capital cities "where the gentry and scholars meet for discussions. If there are important matters [to be discussed] the Hall of Human Relationships in the Confucian Temple is opened for a public debate, and the authorities usually send a deputy to attend it."[73] The third trend was the proliferation of gentry-run charities, of which the first in Shanghai was the Hall of Infant Care, established in 1710. "What was distinctive about the new gentry-run charities . . . was that they represented a modest form of institutionalized gentry power in the domain of public affairs. They were endowed with considerable grants of land, and often received official subventions." Certain of their functions "were of a kind that one would not normally have expected of a charity": fire fighting, policing, street cleaning, and the lighting of thoroughfares.[74] From C. K. Yang we learn that even in Fo-shan, a nonadministrative industrial city, there existed in the nineteenth century a "semiformal" gentry association known as the Ta-k'uei T'ang, which provided leadership for public events, trusteeship for nonofficial public property, and advice to officials on request.[75]

Finally, we must note the interpenetration in many cities of merchant and gentry leadership structures. Guild leaders and local gentry not infrequently served together on the managing committees of temples and the organizing committees of major festivals. In Canton "the gentry and officials gave assistance" to the merchant organizers of charities,[76] and in Shanghai the gentry-run charities were supported by merchant contributions as well as official subventions. In Chungking, the leaders of most *hui-kuan* included degree-holders, the Fukien Association in particular being noted for the number of former officials on its managing committee.[77] A text of 1888 refers to the "gentry and merchants of the Ten Guilds" in Hung-chiang,[78] and we learn from DeGlopper that in Lukang the Eight Guilds and a group of local degree-holders cooperated with the subprefect in establishing an academy. Can one speak of the consolidation of a new urban elite that transcended the hoary social distinctions between gentry and merchant? Probably not. But future research might well verify a widespread social process that would eventually have transformed the sociopolitical structure of Chinese cities quite apart from any Western influence. What a strictly Chinese municipality might have looked like is one of the intriguing what if's of history.

Early Ch'ing Guilds

PETER J. GOLAS

The vigorous guild activity that marked the first two centuries of the Ch'ing had its origins in the flourishing economy of the late Ming. There is little evidence to support the suggestions of some authors that these Ch'ing guilds had a continuous history stretching back to the well-known merchant *hang* and craftsman *tso* associations of the Sung,[1] but careful combing of Yüan and early Ming sources may yet turn up more than the few ambiguous texts now available to testify to the persistence of active guilds throughout this period. Until then, however, the benefit of the doubt must lie with the traditions of the early Ch'ing guilds themselves, which never claimed an origin earlier than the second half of the Ming.

From that time onward, the expansion of domestic and foreign trade gave a powerful impetus to handicraft and industrial production. Luxury products (such as the fine silks and cottons of Soochow, Sung-chiang-fu, and Hangchow; the pottery of Ching-te-chen and Li-ling [Hunan]; the silk thread of Hu-chou-fu) as well as more mundane items (such as the iron pans and hemp products of Kwangtung, the farming implements of the cities and villages of Kiangnan, and the bean oil and straw products of Kiangsu) entered into what was becoming an empirewide trading system. Soaring demand led not only to bigger and more sophisticated enterprises but also to a sharp increase in the number of merchants needed to move the ever greater quantities of commodities to their markets.

At first, this transport was largely in the hands of traveling merchants, or *k'o-shang*, who picked up commodities at their point of production and delivered them to brokers or warehousemen at the markets. While the brokers and warehousemen handled further distribution and sale, the merchant returned for another shipment. In time, some of these merchants, and often fairly large numbers of them, succeeded in bypassing the middlemen and establishing their own permanent shops in the cities to which they had been making deliveries. For instance, during the Ming, much of the population of Lin-ch'ing in Shantung consisted of merchants from Hui-chou in Anhwei.[2] These Hui-chou or Hsin-an merchants, together with the Shansi merchants from the north,[3] spearheaded the expansion of commerce until few important trading centers were without their merchants from one or the other group.

Business may have been lucrative, but life was often difficult for those first small groups of entrepreneurs who settled in a strange city. Without the intricate web of long-established family and personal ties that trapped the Chinese but at the same time gave them strength and comfort, such merchants were outsiders to a degree difficult for us to imagine. In many cases, even their dialect and customs differed radically from those of the natives. As strangers and outsiders, they often met with discrimination at the hands of the local populace and naturally preferred to associate with others who shared the same hardships.

Out of this desire there gradually emerged in trading centers across the empire associations of alien merchants intended to promote friendship and mutual aid among their members. The spirit behind them appears succinctly in the 1721 regulations of the Peking silver shop owners, natives of the Shao-hsing–Ningpo region in Chekiang. They called their association the Cheng-i Tz'u, after Cheng-i Hsüan-t'an Ts'ai-shen, one of the deities they worshiped. "The good people from our area who carry on business at the capital are scattered like men on a chessboard or stars in the sky. If they are not able to assemble regularly, how will they be able to know each other well and be unified as fellow-countrymen? In this changing, unpredictable life, if one suffers misfortune, how will the others be able to come to his aid? We have therefore established the Cheng-i Tz'u to show gratitude to the gods for their protection and to strengthen our cohesion."[4] The desire to present a common front against discrimination by natives is vividly emphasized in the preamble to the rules of the Ningpo merchants' association at Wen-chou-fu: "Here at Wênchow we find ourselves isolated; mountains and sea separate us from Ningpo, and when in trade we excite envy on the part of Wênchowese, and suffer insult and injury, we have no adequate redress. Mercantile firms, each caring only for itself, experience disgrace and loss—the natural outcome of isolated and individual resistance. It is this which imposes on us the duty of establishing a Guild."[5]

Early Ch'ing Guilds

The sense of alienation prompted by life in a strange city affected not only merchants but also officials. The latter, too, responded by forming fraternal associations. As early as the Ming Yung-lo period (1403–24), clubs whose membership consisted of officials originally from a single region had begun to appear at Peking. Furthermore, Ho Ping-ti has shown that from a very early period these merchant and official associations were by no means mutually exclusive.[6] In Peking, with its multitude of government offices, officials founded most of the early *hui-kuan* (the most common term at this time for both official and merchant associations as well as for the buildings that housed them) or *Landsmannschaften*.[7] But many of these Peking *hui-kuan* also included merchants, and some even owed their halls to merchant contributions.[8] In other cities it was typically merchants and craftsmen—the two roles often met in the same person—from a particular area who organized the *hui-kuan*, though officials often took part.[9]

From the Wan-li period (1573–1619) on, and especially during and after the K'ang-hsi period (1662–1722), *hui-kuan* of both kinds began to proliferate. At the same time, the character of those *hui-kuan* in which merchants made up the major element was slowly changing. Katō Shigeshi pointed out in his study of Peking merchant *hui-kuan* that he often found it impossible to sort out the motivations behind the founding of early *hui-kuan*.[10] Economic and fraternal concerns were mutually reinforcing, and it is difficult to assign a priority to one or the other. Eventually, however, from an emphasis on serving social needs, *hui-kuan* increasingly turned to promoting the one or more economic activities in which their members engaged. The permanent meeting places they established proved very useful as centers of business activity, as hostels for merchants coming in from the road, and as secure storehouses. A 1772 tablet inscribed by the famous scholar Hang Shih-chün to commemorate the establishment of the Ch'ien-chiang Hui-kuan for cloth merchants at Soochow illustrates this trend. It emphasizes that *hui-kuan* founded by merchants in cities and towns throughout the empire differed from those in Peking that existed for officials. The latter were social, whereas merchant *hui-kuan*, like this Ch'ien-chiang one, were primarily places of business. In 1774, the same Ch'ien-chiang merchants found themselves seriously inconvenienced when a new official arrived with his family and took over more than 30 rooms of the *hui-kuan* for what appeared to be an indefinite stay. The merchants protested to the authorities, claiming not only that the residence of their deity had been defiled by the birth of a baby there but also that they had been deprived of the only available place for storing their wares.

They won a decision prohibiting officials from using the *hui-kuan*, since it was "absolutely essential for the carrying on of the [cloth] trade."[11]

With the accent on economic activities, interest in restricting membership to people from a single geographical area declined. From the Yung-cheng period (1723–35) on, merchant associations tended to bring under their wings all the people in a single trade, regardless of their origins.[12] Some, like the traveling pig traders of Wu-yang and surrounding districts (Su-chou *fu*, Kiangsu), went so far as to forbid the use of their hall by fellow countrymen in other trades.[13] These changing attitudes were reflected even in the names given to those *hui-kuan* that served mainly economic purposes. Less and less did they contain geographical references (the *hui-kuan* of tobacco merchants from Ho-tung, the *hui-kuan* for natives of Lin-fen and Hsiang-ling [Shansi]); instead, they tended to use the name of the trade or craft of their members (the hatmakers *hui-kuan*, the paper trade *hui-kuan*). Furthermore, in some areas at least, the term *kung-so* was increasingly used instead of *hui-kuan* for those associations, with or without special geographical ties, that were primarily economic.[14] Even established *hui-kuan* sometimes changed their names to reflect the growing importance of their economic function. Thus in Soochow, for example, the Tung-yüeh Hui-kuan became the La-chu Kung-so (the candle dealers *kung-so*).[15]

In China as in Europe,[16] the emergence of associations limited to workers lagged behind the development of merchant associations. In the more advanced sectors of the economy, such as cloth production in the Soochow area, workers had to wage a long and bitter battle against the combined power of merchants and officials before winning the right to organize and act together to obtain higher wages and improved working conditions. At the same time, probably in response to increasing economic differentiation, many of those *hui-kuan* and *kung-so* that had included both producers and sellers began to split apart, with merchants and shopowners forming their own associations and, not long afterward, workers doing the same. The end of the eighteenth and the beginning of the nineteenth centuries saw this process occurring in such widely separated and economically disparate areas as Soochow[17] and Kuei-sui,[18] suggesting that this was an empirewide phenomenon. Meanwhile, other groups—such as brokers, transport workers, cooks, barbers, actors, and even those engaged in such marginal economic activities as gambling—began to form associations to protect their interests.

Thus far I have avoided designating *hui-kuan*, *kung-so*, and similar associations as "guilds" in order to be able to construct a definition of the Chinese guild based on its real functions rather than on the terminological tangles that often screen those functions. The foregoing capsule history has described, first, the emergence in late Ming and early Ch'ing cities of various fraternal associations of nonnative officials, merchants, and craftsmen, and, second, how these were followed by similar associations of natives and nonnatives or, sometimes, associations reserved for natives only. For purposes of the definition, we can range these associations along a continuum. At one end are the *hui-kuan* and, in some cases, *kung-so* that primarily served officials, scholars, and examination candidates who shared a common geographical origin. These associations had little or no economic function. As one moves along this continuum, economic functions become increasingly prominent; the importance of common geographical origin, on the other hand, tends to diminish. I prefer to reserve the term "guild" for those associations where economic goals play a major role[19] and to define a Ch'ing guild as "an urban fraternal association[20] whose members usually engaged in a single economic activity; often, but not necessarily, shared a common geographical origin that was not the city in which the guild was located; and joined together under the protection of one or more patron deities to promote their common economic and other interests."*

The decision to limit this discussion to the first two centuries of the Ch'ing is not entirely arbitrary.[21] I believe that, judging from their frequent statements on the subject, guildsmen in the second half of the nineteenth century often found it necessary to reconstitute their guild and update its practices.[22] In part, this was owing to the Taiping Rebellion, which brought about the temporary decline or dissolution of many guilds, especially in the economic heartland areas of central China that had been occupied by the rebels. To this was added the disruption brought about by the introduction of foreign techniques and competition.[23] Although these two factors explain in large part the need for changes in the guilds at this time, they tell us nothing of the extent and

---

* I am not unaware of the objection that may be raised against the use of the term "guild." It *does* tend to carry certain connotations from European history that do not apply in the Chinese context. Against this objection, however, is the weight of a tradition in which all non-Chinese scholars have used the term "guild" (Japanese *girudo*) when referring to these associations. This unanimity makes one hesitate before doing battle for a more neutral term, especially when it would have to be something unwieldy like "urban economic associations." Furthermore, one should not harp excessively on the dissimilarities with European guilds. There is no reason to expect that Chinese guilds were any closer to their European counterparts than Chinese "feudalism" was to French "feudalism," or the Chinese "gentry" to the English "gentry." There were, however, many important similarities. The term "guild" can therefore serve as a reminder that our grasp of either Chinese or European guilds will likely be stronger for having kept in mind both the similarities and the differences between them.

significance of those changes. Earlier studies, drawing heavily on the far more abundant documentation available for the guilds of the late Ch'ing and Republican periods, have generally avoided this question. This paper takes the opposite approach and relies especially on pre-1850 materials. In this way it becomes clear that, contrary to the impression left by later documents, all the major indigenous elements in guild organization had appeared, often in highly developed form, before 1850. The changes that occurred after this time were either elaborations and minor modifications of earlier practices or, more significantly, innovations prompted by Western models.

The remainder of this paper will consider (1) the structure of the guilds, including the recruitment of members, the role of the leadership, meetings, and finances; (2) the economic and mutual-aid activities undertaken by the guilds; and (3) the nature and relative importance of cohesive and coercive forces in the guilds' actual functioning.

Before turning to these questions, however, it may be useful to consider the kinds of materials available on early guilds. By far the most valuable sources are the many surviving stone tablets commemorating the building or repairing of a guildhall, listing the regulations adopted by a guild at a certain point in its history, or recording an official decree on behalf of a guild. Many of these materials were collected before and during the Second World War by indefatigable Japanese scholars such as Katō Shigeshi, Niida Noboru, and Imahori Seiji, and have made their way into their writings, unfortunately usually in bits and pieces. A happy exception is the final section of Professor Imahori's book on the guilds of the Kuei-sui region, which includes 136 pages of primary materials.[24] By far the richest collection of materials yet to appear, however, is the volume of Ming and Ch'ing stone inscriptions from Kiangsu that was published in China in 1959;[25] it is especially useful for the study of early guilds because the inscriptions record conditions in the most economically advanced region of the empire, where guild organization was correspondingly well developed.

The commemorative tablets usually provide relatively little concrete information except a reaffirmation of the guild's devotion to its patron deity or deities, perhaps a thumbnail summary of the early fortunes of the guild, and a list of those whose contributions made the present construction possible. Many of the earlier guild regulations are hardly more informative, for an obvious reason: early guild rules were never meant to stand as the only, or even the major, precepts governing guild members. In China's cities as in its villages, oral traditions passed on by elders played a dominant role in the daily life and actions of the people.

Guilds therefore did not feel the need of modern organizations to begin their existence with a set of bylaws. Instead, most of them functioned for many years without written regulations and many even built their own guild halls before adopting any formal written rules. During this time, an ever more elaborate oral tradition determined the actions of the guild and its members. This reliance on tradition also helps account for an increased emphasis during the early Ch'ing on age as a qualification for guild office.[26] Greater age presumably meant not only greater general wisdom but also, and perhaps even more importantly, greater familiarity with the traditions, customs, and precedents of the guild. When the writing down of detailed regulations became increasingly frequent, age as a qualification for holding office declined in importance.

It is only with difficulty that we can piece together even a tentative and incomplete picture of the traditional practices of the guilds, especially those practices that never made their way into written regulations. The 1721 regulations of the southern silver shops in Peking illustrate the problem: the guild threatens to "drum out" any member who engages in improper business practices but neglects to define these offenses in any but very general terms, such as activities that cause the guild to lose face.[27] Of course, many later regulations surely embody long-standing customs, but even here we encounter the same problem pointed out by Sylvia Thrupp for European guild rules: "Statutes may claim to state ancient custom, but there is a fair presumption that the transition from oral to written rules forced a clear and hence a novel definition of many customs that had previously been left ambiguous."[28]

Until it became a regular practice for all guilds to establish fairly detailed, written rules (not until well into the nineteenth century), it was usually the need to solve one or more fresh problems that prompted a guild's decision to commit its regulations to writing and perhaps to have them inscribed on stone. Often the motivation is given only in very general terms: the observance of earlier customs and rules has become lax, the people of today do not measure up to the standards of our predecessors, we are afraid that the younger generation may not uphold the customs of the guild if they are not written down. Without other evidence, it is often difficult or impossible to assess what these phrases really meant. Sometimes the content of the rules themselves will suggest either (1) that the guild was in or just emerging from a period of relatively low interest on the part of its members, and that this had resulted in widespread neglect of earlier customs; or (2) that all or part of the membership of a flourishing guild had decided on a new tightening-up of guild practices and, in good Chinese fashion, was appealing to earlier precedents, real or imagined, to support the change. On the other hand, the very frequency with which certain phrases appear has the ring of cliché and suggests that they were sometimes nothing more than custom-hallowed verbal icing.

Sometimes the purpose in formulating a set of rules was merely to make explicit an established but complicated practice. This seems to have been the case in 1793 when the Soochow paper shops defined the complex piecework system, complete with incentive payments, used for calculating workers' salaries.[29] Or the guild might be attempting to counter a specific problem that had arisen. In 1828, for example, the Peking Dyestuffs Guild adopted its regulations to deal with controversies that had arisen about weighing practices in the trade.[30] The 1829 regulations of the Guild of Building Craftsmen of Kuei-sui allowed non-members of the guild to work in the trade provided they came to the guild to get a bamboo permit slip; this practice assured that they would make a payment to the guild. The practice had existed in theory before the posting of the rules, but the guild was afraid that some outside workers had in fact found employment without picking up their permits.[31]

This emphasis on solving particular problems accounts for the fragmentary and varied character of guild regulations before the late nineteenth century. Problems that were obviously of the keenest concern to one guild receive no mention in the regulations of another. In the absence of a statistical study of all the regulations extant from this period, it appears that the major problems to which the guild regulations addressed themselves were the standards for carrying on the trade or craft, the time and manner of worshiping the guild's patron deity or deities, and the means of financing the guild's operations. Treated less often or in more general terms were the obligations of the members to help one another, and the charitable activities of the guild as a whole (e.g., maintaining a cemetery for indigent members); the holding of guild meetings; and the management of the guildhall, if there was one. The activities of guild officers are often spelled out but, in contrast to the regulations of European guilds, their manner of selection is usually passed over in silence. Finally, even regulations that are quite explicit about what was expected of guild members usually provide little information on enforcement procedures.

Guild Structure

The "members" of a guild might be either individuals or shops. In merchant guilds and in guilds of both merchants and craftsmen, each

Early Ch'ing Guilds

shop in the trade often held a single membership regardless of how many people it contained. In craft and service guilds, as well as in some commercial guilds, membership was individual. These two systems of membership continued to exist side by side throughout the later history of the guilds. Even in Peking in the 1920's, as Burgess pointed out, craft guilds tended to include both managers and workmen whereas shop managers alone tended to represent their entire shop in the commercial guilds.[32]

Guilds usually sought to draw their membership from the people engaged in a single economic activity, or what the Chinese texts frequently refer to as *t'ung-yeh*. To attempt a precise definition of this term would be both frustrating and pointless, for it was broad and flexible. Usually, however, it meant those people producing and/or selling a certain product—e.g., cloth, paper, tea, pork, silver, leather and furs, tobacco, leather boxes, lacquer, dyes—or those engaged in providing a single service—e.g., carpenters or barbers. Sometimes not all the groups dealing with a single product belonged to the guild. A merchant guild, for example, might include brokers, wholesalers, and retailers, but brokers increasingly came to have guilds of their own. Moreover, some merchant guilds limited membership to resident merchants (*tso-ku*), excluding traveling merchants (*k'o-shang*). In the crafts, too, various combinations were possible. A carpenters' guild, for instance, might include only those engaged in carpentry and woodworking; at other times, masons and plasterers also joined.

Where membership was by shop, shops that were sold or that were passed on through inheritance carried guild membership with them, either automatically or by the payment of a reduced entrance fee.[33] Otherwise, the two major criteria for guild entry were that new members come from a particular native area (some guilds only) and that they pass through a period of apprenticeship (most guilds).

The requirement in many guilds that members be natives of a single area other than the city in which the guild was located provides one of the most striking contrasts between European and Chinese guilds.[34] The size and makeup of this native area varied greatly from guild to guild, conforming not to any ideal concept of what constituted a native area but rather to an existing reality. If the guild had developed from a *Landsmannschaft*, it would ordinarily continue to draw members from the same area originally represented. If, on the other hand, the guild originated in a trade or craft that happened to be dominated by nonnatives who came from a single, fairly well-defined region, it might continue to reflect this existing geographical base. In either case, the native area might be as small as a single *hsien* or might consist of two or more neighboring *hsien* or even one or more provinces.

As we have already noted, the interest of the guilds in geographical homogeneity gradually declined. Nevertheless, there are many examples of guilds that very successfully resisted this trend. In his research in Peking during the Second World War, Niida Noboru found that the Leather Box Guild, which had been founded in 1689, still consisted exclusively of people who had originated in Shantung.[35] This is only one among many examples, not only in Peking but in other cities as well.[36] Why then did geographical homogeneity decline in most guilds but survive in some?

Ho Ping-ti has discussed some of the reasons for the strength of the concept of "geographical origin" among the Chinese, especially among the elite of scholar-officials. The strong customary and even legal emphasis on *hsiao*—the filial love and respect due to parents and ancestors, requiring a man to care for parents in life, bury and mourn them properly in death, and see that their graves and the graves of his ancestors are kept up—reinforced the ties to one's place of origin. The geographically based examination system, the law of avoidance that kept officials from serving in their native provinces, and the empirewide system of local schools (from the Ming and Ch'ing on) also served as periodic reminders that a man's anchor remained firmly embedded in the place where he was born.[37] There were other reasons, too, why not only the elite of scholar-officials but other Chinese as well retained a strong attachment to their native area, even after having lived away from it for long years. The alien often found considerable discrepancies between the life-style of his native area and that of his adopted city. Differences in language, food, clothing, customs, and religious beliefs served to remind him constantly that he was away from "home." Moreover, the scholar-officials were not the only group with special reasons for a strong attachment to their place of birth. Merchants and craftsmen in an alien city often had a clear economic stake in limiting a trade to natives of their particular region. Against these tendencies to preserve geographical homogeneity, however, must be balanced a variety of forces, growing stronger with time, that tended to erode and often destroy a guild's links with a particular area. Economic considerations were perhaps the most corrosive. Particularly when several geographically based guilds divided a single craft or trade among them, they might well decide that their interest in gaining greater control over the trade and in securing everyone's livelihood dictated a merger into a single guild. This happened, for instance, in the Soochow cloth and printing trades.[38] In particular, traveling merchants, accustomed to a high degree of mutual cooperation on the road, were prone to submerge concern with geographical origin in order to promote their common economic interests. This was the case with the Kiangsi and Fukien merchants at Hankow.[39]

Sometimes a guild's control over an occupation had to give way to determined competition from outsiders. If these competitors were capable of establishing themselves independently, as happened with the influx of Peking and Tientsin merchants into Kuei-sui, the result was either a new guild lacking a well-defined geographical base or a division of the trade among several geographically based guilds. Indeed, in any trade that was lucrative enough to tempt outsiders to compete,[40] a geographically based guild could preserve its monopoly only if it enjoyed special economic advantages. If, for instance, substantial capital investment was necessary to open a new shop, the guild members might control enough of the available capital to make it impossible for anyone to begin business without their approval.[41] Or natives of a particular region might have a skill that enabled them to monopolize an occupation, as in the case of the Ningpo sailors.[42] Where a single region dominated production of a given product or its raw materials, people from that region or traveling merchants who could establish firm contacts there had a particularly good chance of maintaining a monopoly.[43]

But economic considerations do not tell the whole story. If outside competition was a threat, so too was the possibility that a guild's geographical consistency might break down from within. Immigrants tend to be assimilated, in China as elsewhere. Frequent association with natives over the years and intermarriage could not but weaken the attachment of many merchants and craftsmen to their home area, especially where this attachment had not been hardened by a particularly strong animosity against the natives.[44] Furthermore, if guild members did not rigidly limit *all* jobs in the trade to people from their area of origin and instead hired natives to fill some positions, the inevitable result would be the gradual infiltration of the more outstanding natives into higher positions and even partnerships, causing a breakdown of the geographical character of the trade.

The apprenticeship system was often used to maintain geographical exclusion, though it served other equally important or more important purposes. Some sort of apprenticeship seems to have been present in almost all the early Ch'ing crafts. Many merchants also required new workers to serve an apprenticeship. Beyond this, however, the paucity of information in pre–Tao-kuang (1821–50) materials makes it difficult to generalize with confidence about the system. Imahori, who has done the most significant work on apprenticeship during the Ch'ing, feels that it underwent little change throughout the dynasty.[45] The increasingly frequent regulations after the mid-nineteenth century were, according to him, an attempt to shore up long-established customary practices that were beginning to disintegrate. The sources do provide some evidence for this view, especially in their references to attempts by workers to eliminate the apprenticeship system.[46] On the other hand, it is also possible that we have more rules on apprenticeship from the mid-nineteenth century on primarily because guild rules in general became more numerous and more detailed at this time. In any case, what evidence there is from the earlier period suggests that many basic elements of the apprenticeship system did in fact remain largely unchanged through the Ch'ing.

One point seems beyond dispute. The existence of an apprenticeship period and its length had usually only a very remote connection with the time required for a novice to learn a given trade. Notwithstanding the varying complexity of different trades, there was a high degree of standardization in the length of the apprenticeship period: the great majority of guilds fixed it at approximately three years.[47] This arbitrary period, together with the extremely low status of apprentices and the fact that they ordinarily received no wages,[48] indicates that apprenticeship represented primarily a custom-sanctioned initiation, as it were, before one could enter a trade.

Some guilds made efforts to limit the exploitation of apprentices. In 1793, the Paper Shops Guild of Soochow specifically forbade shop managers or foremen from taking advantage of apprentices by demanding banquets or monetary contributions from them.[49] But in general, the ideal held out to the apprentice was total submission to those above him. He was locked into a fictitious family relationship that required him, in house and shop, to address associates with kin terms appropriate to their status and seniority.[50] His work was to leave nothing to be desired. When his period of apprenticeship was over, he still carried the same obligations toward his master as a son toward his father.[51]

Thus, the apprenticeship system did not serve as a means of determining who had the requisite ability to enter a trade. Most of the tasks in this relatively uncomplex economy could be performed by anyone with the will to do so. I know of no case where a worker who had completed his apprenticeship was required to present evidence of his ability to carry on his craft satisfactorily; entry into the guild was automatic on the payment of the required fee.⁵² From another point of view, however, the apprenticeship system insured that most of those who survived it possessed the requisite character traits to fit smoothly into the paternalistic structure that prevailed in shop and guild.

Leadership in both Ch'ing and Republican guilds was usually vested in a group rather than in a single person.⁵³ The group might consist of anywhere from two to thirty members,⁵⁴ but three or four officers serving simultaneously was especially common. Guild officers regularly filled a one-year term, reflected in early guild rules by such modifiers of *hui-shou* (guild head) as *tang-nien* (current year), *hsien-nien* (present year), and *chih-nien* (annually rotating).⁵⁵ It is not at all certain, however, that these positions were always rotated and that one year's officers stepped down automatically at the end of their term. Sometimes, and perhaps often, the yearly selection must have resembled a simple expression of confidence in the existing leaders and a request that they continue for another year. (Martin C. Yang has described this procedure in a modern Chinese village.⁵⁶) There were also guilds where the fixed term was longer than a year and others where leaders were chosen to serve for their lifetime.⁵⁷ In some cases, the term was not specified.

The qualifications sought in guild leaders varied from guild to guild and even in the same guild often changed over the years. In the early Ch'ing, age, as we have seen, and moral prestige (the latter often synonymous with economic and social standing) were the most important qualifications. Later, as guild organization and activities became increasingly complex, ability to handle the job grew in importance.⁵⁸ In the Peking craft, commercial, and professional guilds studied by Burgess in the 1920's, "capability" had become overwhelmingly the quality most looked for in guild leaders.⁵⁹

Apart from these general qualifications, a number of guilds established, either formally or by custom, specific requirements for their officers. Occasionally these might be based on kinship. Among the Peking oil merchants from the early Ch'ing on, ten families monopolized the privilege of providing guild leaders.⁶⁰ The Dyestuffs Guild restricted its leadership on a geographical basis, requiring that its eight officers be members of families that had originated in P'ing-yao *hsien* in Shansi.⁶¹ Furthermore, in guilds consisting of both shopowners and workers, it was not uncommon, especially toward the later Ch'ing, for offices to be restricted to shopowners only. In many cases, too, shopowners monopolized the privilege of selecting leaders.⁶²

Leadership of a guild was not always synonymous with the holding of an office, however. The right to carry on guild business was sometimes a source of personal advantage for guild officers, but the offices were often primarily a burden and probably were assiduously avoided by those who exercised real power in the guild. Most of the normal business was mainly routine chores: seeing that the guildhall was kept in repair; keeping check on the watchmen, making sure they did not drink and gamble; limiting use of the guildhall to members; handling minor disbursements of guild funds and having them properly recorded in the account books.[63] The guild officers were also sometimes charged with collecting dues at regular intervals and with other supervision of the trade,[64] as well as with resolving minor disputes among members.[65] Some guilds created two or more levels of offices, reserving the higher ones for the real leaders and assigning the lower ones to their "aides," i.e., the people who really did the work.[66] Nevertheless, assuring that officers carried out their tasks was a major problem for the guilds, and it required them to resort to fines and other sanctions for neglect of duty.[67]

Many guilds also had provisions to prevent their leaders from assuming too much authority. For instance, in the southern silver shops at Peking, any serious matter that concerned the common good, a breach of the law, or a large contribution by the members required a meeting of the full guild for open discussion.[68]

Regular guild meetings were usually held once a year—although prosperous guilds that could afford the banquet and theatrical performance that ordinarily accompanied the meeting might meet more often.[69] The meeting opened with sacrifices to the patron deity or deities of the guild, either by the officers on behalf of the whole guild or by officers and members alike. Then followed the banquet and the performance of a play in honor of the guild god or gods. These plays, unlike those of European guilds, did not have religious themes but were merely chosen from the standard repertory of the actors' companies, probably on the assumption that the gods would enjoy the same fare that pleased the members.

Between the acts of the play and the courses of the banquet came reports on guild affairs and discussions of important matters, including the selection of the next year's officers (if that were the practice of the guild), contributions for guild expenses, and revision of rules governing the trade. Disputes might be arbitrated, if necessary, or sanctions imposed on those members who had violated the rules. Some guilds also had more frequent regular assemblies of members to offer sacrifices on religious festivals. The 1835 regulations of the Peking Dyestuffs Guild fixed six days in the course of the year on which all members were to assemble by 9 A.M. in order to offer sacrifice in common. Each member was to contribute one thousand *cash* for the cost of the ceremony, with the entire expense to be borne by anyone who came late or not at all.[70]

Because normal expenses were ordinarily small, obtaining sufficient funds does not seem to have been a major problem for the guilds, although many of them took great pains to see that everyone contributed his share. The largest expenses of any guild usually came in building or buying a guildhall and in providing for its upkeep afterward. Only a lucky few had a hall donated by a wealthy member.[71] Otherwise, collecting the money to establish a guildhall usually required many years. Even in the prosperous Soochow cloth trade, ten years of contributions were necessary before the guild had amassed the money to establish the Ch'ien-chiang Hui-kuan.[72]

The most frequently mentioned regular expenses were the sacrifices and yearly play and banquet "to honor the spirits."[73] Where there was no great difference of wealth among members, or where the amount asked of members was small in proportion to their wealth, members might be asked to contribute equally.[74] In other cases, contributions were often scaled to the member's financial status, for instance by assessing shops according to their size[75] or by collecting a percentage on all sales.[76] In guilds of craftsmen and workers, occupational status and salary determined the fees. For instance, in the 1857 rules of the Kuei-sui Fine Hides Guild, tanners were assessed 250 *cash* yearly, sewers 400 *cash*, and masters 500 *cash*. A boy or man accepted for apprenticeship had to contribute 400 *cash* initially and another 3,000 *cash* when he became a master. Those who completed their apprenticeship elsewhere and came to work in Kuei-sui were charged 5,000 *cash*.[77]

Economic and Mutual Aid Activities

The ultimate economic goal of the guilds was the preservation of a stable economic environment where each member could carry on his activity free from competition by outsiders and undercutting by fellow members. Ho Ping-ti, speaking of the wealthy merchant princes of the Ch'ing, has noted: "These immensely rich individuals not only failed to develop a capitalistic system; they seldom if ever acquired that acquisitive and competitive spirit which is the very soul of the capitalist system."[78] If this was true for the wealthiest Ch'ing merchants, the economic activities of the guilds show that it was equally true for less wealthy merchants and for craftsmen. In rules designed not only to keep outsiders out but also to inhibit competition among members, the unspoken law of the guilds was that each member had a right to at least a small piece of the cake and that no one was entitled to nibble on his neighbor's portion.[79]

The success of the guilds in establishing and preserving monopolies against outsiders differed from trade to trade. Various tactics were used with varying effectiveness. Although a firmly established guild could usually count on custom to induce most of those eligible to join, few guilds relied on custom alone. Especially in craftsman and worker guilds, checks to see that no unauthorized workers were employed and fines on those shops violating the rule appear frequently. For instance, the Kuei-sui Fine Hides Guild, in its regulations of 1857, stated specifically that it was the responsibility of all members and not just of the officers to check that all workers belonged to the guild. Only in this way could it continue to maintain its perfect monopoly. The fine set for any shop that employed nonguild workers was 3,000 *cash*.[80]

Of course, a guild's ability to preserve a monopoly was that much stronger if peculiar economic circumstances hindered outside competition. Special craft secrets, such as those of the southerners making cakes and beancurd in Peking,[81] enabled a guild to maintain its monopoly by limiting this knowledge to guild members. In the same way, those crafts that required complex skills could and did demand that all new workers serve an apprenticeship with a guild member, who would then be responsible to see that the apprentice joined the guild at the end of his training period.[82] If a guild dealt in a product that came from some distance, it might effectively preserve its monopoly by controlling either the source of supply or the transport network necessary for delivery, secure in the knowledge that no individual or group would have the resources to arrange for a competing supply. In this way, the dyestuff merchants in Peking and the Hupeh tea merchants in Kuei-sui maintained very effective monopolies.[83] Obviously, many of the same conditions also helped guilds preserve the geographical homogeneity that often went hand in hand with economic monopoly.

Merchants had to be prepared to counteract the efforts of various kinds of middlemen or brokers to carve out a part of the trade for themselves. Around 1735, the tung-oil merchants of Peking faced the problem of brokers from T'ung-chou-fu in Shensi who relied on forged documents to try to insert themselves as middlemen between the T'ung-chou-fu and Peking merchants. The Peking merchants appealed to the authorities and won a decision excluding the brokers from the trade.[84] Sometimes the collective strength of the guilds enabled them to win this kind of battle without government help. For instance, in 1780, the Peking Ho-tung Tobacco Guild won a long-standing dispute with the tobacco brokers at I-chou (Chihli) by carrying out a year-long boycott.[85]

A wide variety of measures restricted competition among members. Here, too, customary rules played an important part. Each occupation had a number of generally observed practices that posed no particular problem of enforcement and therefore never came to be written down in guild regulations. For instance, standard working hours, varying according to the season, must have prevailed in most trades, but they are seldom the subject of specific regulation by the guilds.[86] Rules on the setting up of new shops, too, were often customary.[87]

Controlling prices was one potentially effective way of minimizing competition among members. Mention of guild-enforced prices occurs less often than one might expect, however. Apart from the fact that customary rules were probably particularly strong in this area, the silence on prices may result from the fact that so much of our information on guilds comes from stone inscriptions. Fixed prices inscribed on stone would ordinarily be incompatible with the need to react to fluctuating market conditions, though there are examples of guilds that tried to give their price scales this permanence.[88] A procedure for setting prices and modifying them at regular intervals might or might not be described in the written regulations. One mention, from the second half of the nineteenth century, is found in the rules of the Wen-chou dyers: "Owing to the fluctuating price in indigo, it is to the interest of all concerned that charges for dyeing should be fixed twice a year; that during the semestral period, the tariff should undergo no change whatsoever."[89]

The guilds sometimes sought to minimize competition among members by regulating the quality of their service or product. A Western observer described with a dash of satire the very specific rules governing barbers: "Barbers ... are in many parts of the country forbidden to add the art of shampooing to their ordinary craft, it having been determined by the union that to shampoo was beneath the dignity of the knights of the razor. During the last six days of the year, when the heads of the whole male portion of the empire are shaved, barbers are forbidden to clean the ears of their customers, as it is their wont to do during the rest of the months. Anyone found breaking this rule is liable to be mobbed, and to have his tools and furniture thrown into the street."[90] Money shops often led the field in the regulation of products, with controls on the content and weight of metals and currency, conversion rates, and the like.[91] The standardization of products, together with the emphasis on moderate profits, accomplished a dual purpose: it not only made it easier to limit competition among members but also created a "good image" for the guilds, both among the people, who wanted honest goods at fair prices, and among the officials, who might step in at any time that the guild's practices threatened the common good or public order. Many guilds, in their regulations, stressed that members should take only a just profit and inveighed against those who would violate this rule and stain the guild's reputation.[92]

The same concerns, together with the further desire to facilitate business transactions, lay behind the frequent efforts of the guilds to standardize weights and measures. Niida Noboru has argued against putting too much emphasis on the variety of weights and measures in traditional China and underestimating the standardization that lay behind the apparent confusion. For instance, there was a Soochow "foot" used for measuring Soochow silk; guild rules saw to it that this measure and none other was *always* used for Soochow silk.[93] Many guilds had official steelyards and sometimes issued one to each member who joined the guild.[94] Guild regulations even fixed the tare, or weight of different containers, that was to be deducted in determining the price of goods sold by weight.[95] Guild efforts at standardization extended even to complex business practices. Shansi and southern bankers had different procedures for the issuance of drafts, but all Shansi and southern banks used the methods of their respective regions exclusively.[96]

The varying size of the shops represented in any guild effectively precluded attempts to limit expansion by imposing a ceiling on the number of workers who could be employed, although there were often either customary or written rules against luring away the workers or apprentices of a fellow member. Moreover, some trades (such as the Wuhan Weighing Scales Guild and the Leather Box Makers of Kanchou-fu, Kiangsi) limited, very often to one, the number of apprentices that could be taken on at any one time.[97]

Finally, many guilds even forbade their members to entice away each other's customers. The most common measures were strict limitations on the opening of new shops and surcharges to be levied on customers who transferred their patronage. The Peking Barbers Guild, for instance, required that any customer of one shop who went to another be charged an extra ten percent for a haircut or shave.[98]

Apart from unrestrained competition, the greatest potential threat to the stability of a trade or craft was the conflicting interests of employers and workers. Both MacGowan in the 1880's[99] and Burgess in the 1920's[100] felt that relatively little strife occurred between employers and workers in China. However true this may have been for the post-

1850 period, serious clashes were certainly not uncommon in the seventeenth and eighteenth centuries, especially in Soochow, where invective-laden documents record long and bitter struggles by workers to better their wages and working conditions.[101] More work will have to be done on the economic and social history of the early Ch'ing before we can be certain, but it appears that the most severe conflicts arose in a few relatively advanced industries, such as cloth and papermaking, that were marked by sizable factories employing large numbers of workers, many of them brought in from other areas. The government played a prominent role in these struggles. Ever alert to the dangers inherent in organization by the lowest elements in society, it viewed with suspicion what it considered the similarities between workers' organizations and secret societies.[102] As a result, employers and officials often formed de facto coalitions against workers; this is testified to by frequent official decrees forbidding them to organize or to strike and setting a ceiling on their wages.[103]

The kind of control that shopowners sought over their workers and undoubtedly sometimes achieved is vividly described in the rules for the Soochow paper trade, approved by the authorities in 1793. First, all workers had to be registered. In theory, no worker was to be hired until it was established that he had a clean past. In order to guard against workers who got into trouble and were fired only to change their names and go to work in another shop, the workers themselves were held responsible for checking on their fellow workers. Second, the shops were to appoint inspectors who would regularly check stirrings of unrest among the workers. Third, the workers were to have periodic indoctrination to make sure that they understood the rules of the trade and to encourage them to work diligently, confine themselves to their own business, and not associate with bad elements. Fourth, if a worker contracted a debt at his shop and then stayed away from work or went to work for another shop, his guarantor was to be punished and the worker returned to his shop in order to pay off the debt. Fifth, shop managers were to see that all workers slept in the shops every night in order to keep them from gambling, whoring, and robbery. Workers who stayed away from their shops overnight were to be flogged and fired. Managers who did not report their absence were also to be punished.[104]

Despite the efforts of shopowners and officials, in Soochow and elsewhere, workers did gradually win the right to bargain over their wages and working conditions. In time, too, many of them formed guilds limited exclusively to workers, although guilds of this type remained relatively few compared to merchant, merchant-craftsman, and professional guilds. Where the workers did succeed in creating their own guilds, they usually considered the ability to obtain decent wages as the main benefit of the guild.[105]

While struggling to organize, workers often downplayed their desire for better wages and stressed instead their interest in creating an association to look after those members who, through no fault of their own, had fallen on bad times.[106] In this way, they identified their efforts with one of the most widely practiced and irreproachable guild activities, mutual aid among guild members. We have seen the importance of mutual aid among the early alien merchant associations, and it is possible that this spirit of helping one's fellows was never again as strong as among those early groups of entrepreneurs who found themselves left to their own resources in a "foreign" city. Nonetheless, mutual aid became a regular component of all guilds—merchant, craftsman, and worker, alien and native.

Some authors have professed to see a greater emphasis on mutual aid in craft than in merchant guilds.[107] This contrast may be more apparent than real, depending on what one views as mutual aid. Those craftsmen and workers who lived close to the subsistence level naturally were very much concerned with how they and their families would survive if they became sick or unemployed. Even more important, could they look forward to a proper burial when they died?[108] To help meet this latter need, many guilds even had their own cemeteries, reserved for the burial of members.[109] The more prosperous merchant guilds, however, would have fewer destitute members requiring a subsistence dole or having to rely on the contributions of their fellow members for a proper burial. In these guilds, helping out members who had run afoul of the officials or who had become involved in legal disputes was of far greater concern; this kind of mutual aid is frequently mentioned in the regulations of merchant guilds.

A characteristic of the mutual-aid activities of guilds for nonnatives was the provision to send destitute members back to their native area where, presumably, they would have family ties to fall back on. The main point was not to allow a fellow member to become a drifter.[110] These same guilds also often had a room reserved for the storage of coffins awaiting shipment home for burial.[111]

Though mutual aid is one of the most frequently mentioned subjects in the guild inscriptions, it is difficult to say how effective it was in practice. Many references to it have a seemingly perfunctory character. Even more significant, penalties are not usually outlined for those who fail to render aid when they should. Nevertheless, it is difficult to ac-

Early Ch'ing Guilds

count for the frequency of references to the obligation of guildsmen to help one another if this was a mere cliché. Moreover, in some cases the rules become considerably more explicit, outlining precisely what members are required to do in given circumstances and fixing penalties for those who fail to do so.[112] Here at least, it is reasonable to suppose that the agreement by the members to institute such specific provisions must have led to at least some action.

Of considerably greater importance to the general life of the cities where the guilds were located was the sporadic assumption of responsibility by the guilds for fire-fighting, policing, and other municipal functions. We have only scanty evidence for this kind of guild activity before the late nineteenth century, which suggests that the practice developed rather late. What is clear from the evidence we do have, though, is that even in an earlier period it would be more likely to be a federation of several guilds rather than an individual guild that took on these functions. Writing in 1909, Morse could cite only three well-confirmed guild federations in all of China.[113] More recent studies have turned up a good many more, especially in smaller central places, which suggests that merchants were to a large extent the local government in those economically vigorous towns that were nevertheless too small to be presided over by an official from the central government.[114]

Cohesion and Coercion in Ch'ing Guilds

One of the most striking characteristics of early Ch'ing guilds was their attempt to achieve a wide range of goals with only very rudimentary organizational structures. What this meant in practice—i.e., when actual measures were taken to implement the goals—was that the large number of general goals were narrowed to a small number assigned high priority. In the long run, the attempt to resolve the incongruity between ambitious goals and limited means available to achieve them brought about what was probably one of the key trends in the history of Ch'ing and early Republican guilds: the parallel shift from simple to more complex organization and from general to more limited goals.

One should perhaps not underestimate the ability of the guilds to achieve their goals merely because of the poor organizational means available. To begin with, most of the goals were of a kind that could well be accomplished, at least in part, with a low level of organization. Few of them required an intensive and continuous effort over a period of time. One sacrifice each year, or at most a few, satisfied the guild's obligation to its patron deities. Mutual aid, too, was viewed as a sporadic obligation. Where achievement of the guild's goals required a more sustained effort, as in standardizing trade practices, the guild's role was still usually intermittent. It established standards and only periodically took measures against those who did not conform. Finally, the very variety of goals at which the guilds aimed probably aided the achievement of each individual goal. Even among modern organizations, "it appears that many multi-purpose organizations tend to serve each of their goals separately and all of them together more effectively and efficiently than single-purpose organizations of the same category."[115] This was probably also true of the guilds, since their various goals were ordinarily compatible and mutually reinforcing. For instance, ties of friendship promoted by the guild made common action for economic goals easier.

In any discussion of how effectively the guilds achieved their goals, the question inevitably arises: whose goals? Some authors, especially those of a Marxist bent, have assumed that the stated goals of the guilds, looking to the interests of all the members, were merely a smoke screen to disguise the real goal of furthering the interests of the richest and most powerful members. Although this interpretation usually results from arbitrarily forcing the data on guilds into a wholly inapplicable, a priori class analysis, the question is nevertheless valid and important. It is also extremely difficult to answer. In frustration, the historian asks what really happened, and his materials insist on telling him what was supposed to have happened or what someone wanted others to believe happened. Nevertheless, the right questions and a willingness to settle for less than absolute certainty make it possible to hazard a few answers.

A distinction must be made at the outset between a group's domination of decision-making power and the misuse of that power to further the group's own aims at the expense of others. We shall never be in a position to study in any detail the actual allocation of power in the guilds; that would require a great deal more documentation, and much of it of a different kind than we possess. We can assume, of course, that the more prosperous and prominent members tended to dominate guild decisions. Nevertheless, we find little evidence that they used this power to promote their own interests at the expense of the other members. Even in those guilds that included employers and workers, there is little indication of specific measures designed to exploit the workers, such as limits on wages, restrictions on the freedom of the workers to change jobs, penalties that applied only to workers, and the like. In general, guild regulations and their enforcement seem to have been directed to the general good of all the guildsmen, in opposition to outsiders. This is not to say, of course, that there was no exploitation of the weaker by the stronger. Rather, the point is that the guilds themselves do not seem to have been notably an instrument of this exploitation.

To assess the ability of guilds to realize their goals, one must also appreciate the complex mixture of cohesive and coercive forces acting to secure the allegiance of members to the guild and its goals. By cohesive I mean those forces that prompted a largely voluntary, unconstrained acceptance of the guild and its rules by the members. This occurred when there was a high coincidence between the goals of the guild and the personal goals of the members. Coercive forces operated in those cases where the guild found it necessary to devise sanctions to assure compliance by the members. Coercion was especially necessary where a member might be tempted to violate the guild rules out of a feeling that his personal interests ran counter to the interests of the guild. This distinction will become clear as we look at the simultaneously cohesive and coercive role of religion.

Religion was very important in the life of the guilds. Probably most of the guilds arranged for their first meeting place by renting a temple or a room in a temple. Since only a small minority eventually succeeded in building their own guildhall,[116] many never knew another meeting place. At best, they might succeed in reserving all or part of the temple for their exclusive use. This practice accounts for the frequent occurrence in guild names of various words meaning "temple," especially in North China.[117] Furthermore, no guild ever built its own guildhall without providing a place for its patron deity or, usually, deities. Just as the guilds described themselves as associations for carrying on religious worship, so too the most common characterization of the guildhall was as a home for its deities. Misuse of the guildhall was usually condemned as profanity. The southern silver shops in Peking, in their rules of 1721, made this clear: "This temple was built as a place for honoring the spirits. It is not a place for amusement and feasting. No people from outside the guild may borrow or rent it to present plays." These same rules also prevent women from entering the guildhall, since that would dishonor the spirits.[118]

Guild meetings were regularly timed to coincide with the birthday of one of the patron deities and, as we have seen, usually included a simple sacrifice, a banquet, and a play in honor of that deity and the others. Sometimes sacrifices were held more often,[119] and a special ceremony before the gods was often an integral part of the acceptance of new members into the guild. Even standard fees, such as the three or five *cash* that had to be paid to the Peking Dyestuffs Guild for each basket of tung oil that came from outside, were frequently referred to as "incense money" to provide for sacrifices to the spirits.[120] Guilds also contributed in times of plague and other catastrophes to special sacrifices for appeasing the relevant gods; this was one of their very few "philanthropic" activities on behalf of nonmembers.[121] All of this seems to add up to a recognition by the guildsmen that they had a certain obligation to propitiate the heavenly powers, especially those responsible for the establishment and protection of their own trade or craft.[122] To those for whom this was a genuine conviction, the guild provided a welcome opportunity to fulfill their responsibilities.

The sources are not without their plaints that members have not taken their religious duties seriously.[123] These must be weighed, however, against a good deal of evidence suggesting very real devotion on the part of some members. Niida, for example, describes the fourth month pilgrimage to the shrine of the goddess Pi-hsia-yüan-chün at the Miao-feng Shan west of Peking, during which those believers who were shoemakers repaired the shoes of pilgrims free of charge, tinkers repaired pots at the roadside inns, and paper workers put new paper in the windows of the temple's halls.[124] Guilds also looked to their patron deities to help them in times of difficulty. In the 1779–80 dispute between the Peking tobacco merchants and the I-chou brokers, the tobacco merchants finally "relied on the efficacy of the Three Sages" to help their boycott. When the dispute was won, they contributed for the renovation of the "shelter for the spirits," i.e., the guildhall.[125] Religion could also bolster, and be bolstered by, the geographical solidarity in those alien guilds that maintained religious beliefs and customs brought by the members from their home area.[126] Even in the twentieth century, not a high point in Chinese religious fervor, many guildsmen still considered religious worship an integral part of guild life and felt that the guilds might not have endured had it not been for religious bonds.[127]

To the extent that members took their religion seriously, it could also be used as a coercive force against them. Ch'ü T'ung-tsu has described how a magistrate arriving at a new post gained "a measure of supernatural sanction" by sacrificing at the temple of the City God, taking an oath that he would be honest and just in his administration and asking that he be punished by the god if he violated his oath. The magistrate later often asked the aid of the City God in deciding legal cases, in "the belief that a man's crime could escape the eyes of human beings but not of the gods."[128] The same kind of attitude prevailed in the guilds. For instance, the 1828 rules of the Peking Dyestuffs Guild warned the members: "Be cautious. Take care. If our investigations do not reveal those who, with evil heart, have violated the guild regulations,

Early Ch'ing Guilds

then the gods will find them out and cease to aid them."[129] Moreover, the punishments levied on members, such as the obligation to pay incense money or provide for the performance of a play, were often described as expiatory offerings to the gods as well as to the guild and fellow members.[130]

Among other predominantly cohesive forces in the guilds, we have already discussed the feeling of common geographical origin. Common ethnic grouping was also a cohesive force in those areas where two or more ethnic groups, each having its own guild, engaged in the same trade or craft.[131] Tradition and custom not only encouraged entry into the guild but also promoted conformity to its practices.[132] Finally, the stress on consensus that prevailed in the guilds, together with the high value placed on respect for authority in China, was also a strong cohesive force. It must be remembered that most guilds were small associations, seldom with more than 30 members. Under these conditions, each member was personally acquainted with all the others.[133] Face thus played an important role in the guilds. Given the loss of face that would result from clear disagreements requiring a decision against one of the parties, the Chinese deployed a great deal of skill to avoid such confrontations. This, together with the real interests that the guildsmen had in common, suggests that most guild decisions did arise out of a genuine consensus.[134] This stress on consensus occurs again and again in the guild documents. Even if we agree with Imahori's contention that, in practice, this meant that a handful of people initiated policies with which the rest of the members usually went along,[135] it must still be noted that this procedure did usually include an open discussion that continued until some sort of genuine agreement was achieved. If such agreement proved impossible, the guild might even specify different courses of action among which the members could choose.[136] The decision-making process of the guilds was therefore probably more of a cohesive than a coercive force.

In few guilds, however, did the interests of the members coincide so completely that the guild was able to forgo coercion entirely. The most common means of coercing recalcitrant members was to levy fines on those who violated a specific tenet of the regulations. These fines might be either money for the general use of the guild or an offering in the form of incense money, a play, or a banquet in honor of the gods. MacGowan pointed out the suitability of the latter forms of punishment to the purposes and spirit of the guild. "Although these compulsory entertainments and feast [sic] involve a certain degree of discredit to the host, yet he has the satisfaction as host of being treated with decorous politeness, a thing so dear to this ceremonious people."[137] Only in rare cases and for the severest offenses did the guilds envision application of the most extreme punishment available to them: expulsion from the guild, which deprived a man of his livelihood.[138]

Various other measures were used from time to time to enforce observance of the guild's rules. Government approval of the goals and regulations of the guild and cooperation in enforcing them were sometimes sought and obtained, but this means was resorted to rather seldom, the guilds preferring to settle their problems internally and with their own resources. Carving regulations on stone tablets and setting them up in public view was also a means of providing an extra aura of authority for guild decisions.[139] These and other measures, however, remained clearly of secondary importance as means of coercion.[140]

Finally, a note on the overall importance of guilds in the lives of their members. Most members probably had little connection with the guild outside of special occasions. General meetings, as we have seen, were usually held only once a year. Even in the minority of guilds that had their own halls, the hall does not seem to have served as a social center in the sense of, say, the hyphenated "national homes" of immigrant groups or the V.F.W. halls in the United States. With the exception of occasional references to guild members using the hall for a party and, in certain merchant guilds, references to its serving as a center of business activity, the guildhall seems to have been relatively unused between meetings.[141] One should probably not assess very highly, then, the importance of guilds in the daily life of the cities during the early Ch'ing. They did introduce a principle of cohesion among the members that would otherwise have been absent, but they did not replace or even greatly affect the more basic ties of home and shop.

School-Temple and City God

STEPHAN FEUCHTWANG

When I started to research the "state cult" I had very little idea what it might have been. I knew that it was centered in the administrative capitals of China, i.e., in cities. Now that I have done some research,* I find it difficult to make my report of it directly relevant to the quality of urban life in traditional China, although it is entirely relevant to the relations between rulers and ruled in traditional China and therefore in some degree to the power structure within cities and to urban-rural relations. The state cult was of course closely related to sociopolitical control, but the objects of control were not so much the populace at large as the bureaucracy and local elites. The use of religion to control the common people may have been legitimated by the state cult, but in manipulating the masses, the managers of society necessarily looked to religious arenas outside the strict confines of official religion.

A second source of difficulty lies in the number of gross misconceptions of Chinese religion that have grown up over the years as a result in part of overcategorization, by which (for example) we have too easily identified Confucianism with state orthodoxy. The official religion as I found it in my research is not the same as the Confucianism we associate with the Confucian classics or with the schools in which they were studied. Faced with the problem of how to describe the state orthodoxy, I decided to focus on documenting the religious attitudes of officials and on discussing the place of the official religion in Chinese religion as a whole. This is not, therefore, a strict account of the rites, deities, and edifices of the official religion, although these are all mentioned in the course of the discussion.

I have translated and studied as the official religion (1) what is written

* The research on which I based this paper was conducted in March and April of 1968, thanks to the generosity of the Subcommittee on Research on Chinese Society.

in the *Ta Ch'ing hui-tien* under the headings "Tz'u-chi" (shrines and sacrifices), "Ch'i-ssu" (sacrifices and offerings), or the combined term "Tz'u-chi-su," and (2) what is contained in local gazetteers in the sections entitled "Ssu-tien" (sacrificial statutes), where official temples are listed before or apart from those of the popular religion and from those specifically Buddhist or Taoist. Official temples were also specified as *t'an-miao*, "altars and temples," whereas all others were called *tz'u-miao*, "shrines and temples"; but it must be remembered that all temples given in gazetteers were listed by their scholarly, not their popular, nomenclature, and that a great many popular temples were not listed in the gazetteers at all. *Ssu-tien*, the official religion, was also the term for rites addressed to deities, and I have of course included them; but the many other official rites not directed to deities have not been considered. The *Hui-tien* was a collection of statutes that was revised several times during the Ch'ing dynasty; I have used the one issued in the K'ang-hsi reign. In the section devoted to the affairs of the Board of Rites (*Li pu*), the whole range of *li* includes not only the official religion but also mourning rites, court etiquette, the protocol of dress at court, enfeoffment, reception of foreign dignitaries, the making and receiving of presentations, and propaganda such as *hsiang-yüeh* (the recital of the Imperial Edict in rural districts). The scope of the Board of Rites follows the example of the *Li-chi* (Record of Rites), only two sections of which—the "Chi-fa" and "Chi-i"—concern the official religion. I mention this here merely as a reminder before I narrow my sights that the official religion was only part of what we would call etiquette, protocol, ceremonial, and propriety.

"Religion" is here confined to communal, not individual, worship. "Worship" may be taken as avowed communication with beings who are not subject to the physical conditions of the known world. There are those who will count Chinese religions as three: Confucian, Taoist, and Buddhist. Others feel unable to include Confucianism as a religion, because the Confucian classics contain passages expressing scepticism over, or dismissing the issue of, the existence of "gods," and drawing attention rather to "spirits": the examples, names, and reputations of men and women who have lived and died. "Spirits," then, are heroes—historical figures whose examples are to be emulated, or one's own ancestors whose reputations are to be maintained, enhanced, or created. To make the contrast clear, we may say that such "spirits" *exist* only as names, whereas "gods" are believed to be agents.*

---

* "Agent," according to the Shorter Oxford English Dictionary, is "The efficient cause, . . . any natural force or substance which produces phenomena."

I do not want to prejudge the question of the religion of the scholar-officials of China, nor do I want to start with undefined categories that may be misleading. I want to offer a view of certain Chinese institutions of symbolic action as they were distributed throughout Chinese society. This view is logically anterior to the labeling of these institutions as Buddhist or Taoist or Confucian, which we may do either according to philological analysis and the history of the texts used in these institutions or according to the way the participants labeled the institutions and themselves. In other words, on principle, I am making a distinction between action (and institution) and interpretation (recording, philosophizing, and labeling). I am aware of the dangers of such an enterprise when it is itself based on documents checked with direct observation only in a much later period (Taiwan, 1966–68). But I have done my best to be sure that what I am reporting was real and not just paper action.

The Confrontation in the City

The establishment of an administrative city was marked by the building of city walls. Other emblems were a temple to the City God (*Ch'eng-huang miao*) and a school-temple (*hsüeh-kung*) within the walls, and at least one of the prescribed open altars outside the walls. This would seem to have been a minimum at the lowest level of administration, the county.[1]

In only very rare cases would a city have been purely administrative. It would have been founded at or next to an already existing economic center, or else it would itself have become the basis for the development of economic functions. Among the institutions almost invariably found in economic central places were temples of the popular religion, some of them centers of cults that were shared by or adopted into the religion of the state. Two such that I will draw attention to were the cults of Kuan-ti, god of trustworthiness and loyalty in war and trade, and T'ien-hou (or, to give her equivalent popular name, Ma-tsu), goddess of seafarers. Both deities were very popular as patrons for merchant associations in the Ch'ing period, T'ien-hou more so in coastal than in inland regions.

In instances where government funds officially raised were sufficient, officials could afford to build separate temples to these gods for their exclusive use, as was the case for example in the administrative walled city of T'ai-pei-fu, built late in the nineteenth century next to the flourishing port of Meng-chia. But even in such instances exclusion of the non-official populace could not last long in the life of the city as it developed its own markets and nonofficial institutions. In the case of T'ai-pei-fu, repair funds for temples came from the pockets of nonofficials. In at least one of the city temples to T'ien-hou or to Kuan-ti—there were often several to each even within the city—officials and nonofficials would mix.

Merchants desirous of converting their wealth into status and moving into the literati class would contribute to the building of official temples. In the absence of official temples, they would sponsor the building of temples to gods or spirits included in the official cults. An example of this face-improving enterprise—an even better one than the building of temples to Kuan-ti and Ma-tsu, who were popular in all classes of the population—was the building of temples dedicated to both Confucius and Kuan-ti, often called Wen-wu miao and often founded in conjunction with the establishment of a private school.*

I hope to show that there was also a counterprocess in which popular cults were incorporated into the official religion (*ssu-tien*). Kuan-ti and T'ien-hou are only two examples of popular cults thus adopted, and in their cases the adoption went so far that temples to them were built by officials throughout China. The scholar's equivalent to the merchant's T'ien-hou cult was the cult of Wen-ch'ang, which also had temples within and without the official religion throughout China. There were other cults that were less widespread, or that were honored by officials but not yet formally incorporated into the *ssu-tien*. These borderline temples were often the largest and most frequented in a city. A case in point seems to have been the Ling-ying miao, in Ningpo, cult center of a deity honored since the twelfth century by tablets with the imperial seal for various acts of protection of officials traveling at sea but not accepted into the *ssu-tien*.

Although the most crowded and striking to look at, these temples were below or at the bottom of the official religious hierarchy, which was organized into ceremonial divisions. Tables 1, 2, and 3 chart this ceremonial hierarchy. All the open, suburban altars (Table 2), except for the altar to the local unworshiped dead, are superior to the mass of the temples in the lowest level. When we move up from this point, we find a sharp distinction from popular religion. It is possible to detect the gradations of exclusion by noting from the relevant sections of the gazetteers who sponsored the building of and repairs to the several shrines. Since in at least half the cases this had not been recorded, our findings must be crude. But it appears that the altars to the land and grain and to wind-rain-thunder-clouds, as well as certain shrines to Hsien-nung (god of

---

* In Taiwan, Hsin-chu, Tainan, Kao-hsiung, and Lu-kang all had Wen-wu miao; and so did Taipo in the New Territories of Hong Kong. All of them were nonofficial temples. Both merchants and local scholars would have joined in such enterprises.

TABLE 1. THE THREE LEVELS OF SACRIFICE IN LATE CH'ING OFFICIAL RELIGION

Level	Description
1. Great Sacrifice (*ta-ssu*)	Rites at this level were conducted at the imperial capital only, either at the open suburban altars or at the temples within the walls. Sacrificial animals were washed three lunar months in advance; there was a three-day fast before the rite; and the emperor in person was the leading participant.
2. Middle Sacrifice (*chung-ssu*)	Rites at this level were conducted at the imperial capital and at lower-level capitals. Sacrificial animals were washed 30 days in advance; there was a two-day fast before the rite; and either the emperor in person (at the imperial capital) or a delegated official of the appropriate administrative rank (at lower-level capitals) was the leading participant.
3. Common Sacrifice (*ch'ün-ssu*)	Rites at this level were conducted at all capitals. Sacrificial animals were washed 10 days in advance; there was a one-day fast before the rite; and an official of the appropriate administrative rank was the leading participant.

agriculture) and Huo-shen (god of fire), were, in the two prefectures I investigated (Ning-po and T'ai-wan), the only ones sponsored exclusively by officials.* In the case of Hsien-nung and Huo-shen, however, there were other temples, not officially sponsored. This leaves the two open altars as the only exclusively official cults.

Other cults occurring in seven or more of the eleven counties are, in order of the increasing involvement of nonofficials, the altar for unworshiped dead (officials and gentry); the school-temple and Wen-ch'ang (officials, gentry, and commoners, with gentry outnumbering commoners); the City God; and T'ien-hou and Kuan-ti (officials, gentry, and commoners, with commoners outnumbering gentry).[2]

Since the *Li-chi* was written, every dynasty has had its version of the official religion, and the changes it underwent as dynasty succeeded dynasty, and reign succeeded reign, were substantial. Even the several open altars (to the land and grain, to wind-rain-thunder-clouds, to mountains and rivers, and to unworshiped dead—all cults directly sanc-

---

* I have put under the general heading "officials" all persons referred to by office above and including the rank of magistrate. "Gentry" are all those given only examination-degree title or referred to merely as *shih* or *shen-shih*. And "people" are those referred to as *min*, plus merchants, monks, priests, and men named but without degree or title. It is, of course, more than likely that common people contributed either through special taxes or through a special fund in cases where only officials and gentry were actually named.

TABLE 2. MAJOR OFFICIAL TEMPLES WITHIN THE WALLS, CH'ING CHINA

Great Sacrifice (ta-ssu) Level

Rites at this level were held in the imperial capital only, at the T'ai miao (Great Temple).

The objects of worship were the ancestors of the reigning emperor; great imperial predecessors; and great statesmen and warriors.

Worship was held on auspicious days in the 1st month of each of the four seasons; on Ch'ing Ming; and on the birthdays and deathdays of the objects of worship.

The color of the silk offerings and notices (petitions) was white with yellow borders.

Middle Sacrifice (chung-ssu) Level

Emperors of previous dynasties were worshiped at the imperial capital only, at the Li-tai Ti-wang miao (Temple of All Former Emperors).

The rite was held on an auspicious day in the 8th lunar month.

The color of the silk offerings and notices was white with yellow borders.

Confucius and his disciples, their respective fathers and most noted followers; famous officials; wise men; and virtuous women were worshiped at the imperial and lower-level capitals, at the Wen miao (Temple of Civil Culture) or the Hsüeh-kung (School-Temple).

Rites were held on the 4th stem day of the 1st *hsün* of the 2d and 10th lunar months.

The color of the silk offerings and notices was white with yellow borders.

Common Sacrifice (ch'ün-ssu) Level
Rites at this level were held at all capitals

1. Kuan-ti (Imperial Ruler of the Passes, or God of War) was worshiped at the Wu miao (Temple of Military Culture) on the 13th day of the 5th lunar month.

2. Hsien-i (Former Physicians) or Huang-ti, Fu-hsi, and Shen-nung (the Three Emperors of Man, Heaven, and Earth) were worshiped at the San-huang miao (Temple of Three Emperors) on the 1st stem day of the 1st *hsün* in the 2d and 11th lunar months.

3. Huo-shen (the Fire God) was worshiped at the Huo-shen miao on the 23d day of the 6th lunar month.

4. Lung-shen (the Dragon God) and/or other gods of water, rain, and sea travel were worshiped at the Lung-shen tz'u.

5. Ch'eng-huang (the City God), often in association with military gods and the gods of the North and of the Sacred Eastern Peak, was worshiped at the Ch'eng-huang miao on an auspicious day in the 8th lunar month and on the emperor's birthday.

TABLE 3. RITES HELD AT OPEN SUBURBAN ALTARS, CH'ING CHINA

Sacrificial level and location of altar	Object of worship	Shape of altar	Date of worship	Color of offerings
Great sacrifice, Imperial cap, S suburb	T'ien (Heaven); plus the tablets of WRTC* and of the heavenly bodies (from the agriculture complex)	Round mound	Winter solstice, and (from 1742) New Year's morning (harvest prayer)	Green-blue
Great sacrifice, Imperial cap, N suburb	Ti (Earth); plus tablets of the 5 mountains and of the 4 seas (from the agriculture complex)	Square with a pit	Summer solstice	Yellow
Great sacrifice, Imperial cap, N suburb	She-chi (Land and Grain)	Square with a pit	5th stem day of the 1st *hsün* of middle months of Spring and Autumn	The 5 colors of the 5 elements
Middle sacrifice, Imperial cap, E suburb	Chao-jih (Sun)	Round mound	Vernal equinox of odd-numbered stem years	Red
Middle sacrifice, Imperial cap, W suburb	Hsi-yüeh (Moon)	Square with a pit	Autumnal equinox of certain branch years	—
Middle sacrifice (after 1726), Imp, and lower-level caps, S suburb	Hsien-nung (patron deity of agriculture); plus, at the Imperial capital only, tablets of WRTC and MR,* and the Great Year Calendar	Round mound	*Hsien-nung*, 12th branch day of the 1st *hsün* of the middle month of Spring; *WRTC and MR*, 6th branch day of the *Great Year Calendar*, the New Year	White with yellow borders
Middle sacrifice, provincial and lower-level caps, N or E suburb	Local Land and Grain; and, on separate altars, WRTC and local MR	Square	*Land and Grain*, 5th stem day of the 1st *hsün* of the middle months of Spring and Autumn; *WRTC and MR*, 6th branch day of the 1st *hsün* of the middle months of Spring and Autumn	*Land and Grain*, black; *WRTC and MR*, white
Common sacrifice, provincial and lower-level caps, N suburb	Li (the local unworshiped dead, overseen by the City God)	Square	Ch'ing Ming, Chung-yüan (the 15th day of the 7th month), and Meng-tung (the 1st day of the 10th month)	White

SOURCES: *Ta Ch'ing hui tien*, K'ang-hsi edition (1690), and contemporary local gazetteers.
* WRTC = Wind-Rain-Thunder-Clouds. MR = Mountains and Rivers.

tioned in the *Li-chi*—have been changed in their position around the city, merged, separated, neglected, or rehabilitated, both in the ritual statutes and in practice. The official cults that occurred with greater regularity in county capitals, including those to Confucius and the City God, were only indirectly sanctioned by the *Li-chi* and its criteria for the Five Sacrifices (the *wu chi-ssu*). They all had histories of entitlement as gods and promotion through feudal ranks of nobility, and they were all popular as well as official. Judging from the Ning-po gazetteers, which are continuous from the Sung to the Ch'ing, the cults that survived most steadily and for the longest time were those of the schools (to Confucius) and of Kuan-ti and the City God. Cults to other gods derived from the popular religion were subject to the vagaries of imperial favor; canonization might last only as long as a dynasty.

People without degrees or aspirations to join the scholar-official class did not generally frequent the school-temple for the official worship of Confucius and worthy Confucians, much less the open altars. But even where commoners and officials shared temples, official rituals were distinctive in their ceremonial, in the absence of priests, and in the strict order of participation by official rank and degree.

The county capital was the lowest level of the hierarchy both of yamens and of official temples and altars. In nonadministrative cities and towns, and in all lower places in the central-place hierarchy, temples of popular cults proliferated. It was in administrative capitals that popular religion met with and contrasted with official religion: the theater, noise, color, urgency, and bustle (in short, *je-nao*) of the popular temple contrasted with the dignified and ascetic seclusion of the official shrine; the market contrasted with the yamen.

There were several ways in which popular temples and markets were associated. A temple might have housed the figure of the patron deity of a guild and have been the meeting place for guild members for both secular and sacred business—that is to say, annual worship, feasts, and theatrical entertainment. The open space in front of the temple, the temple yard, might have been the site for regular markets or fairs, as well as for theater; temple dues would then have been collected from the traders. In other cases a popular temple might have produced its own commerce on festival days in ritual goods (incense, spirit money, candles), food, snacks, fortune-telling and so on. The official altars and the school-temple had none of these associations.

City God temples, on the other hand, as much as if not more than any other shrines, were the sites of markets and all other kinds of *je-nao*. The cult of the City God was only partially incorporated in the Ch'ing *ssu-*

School-Temple and City God

tien. Yet because such temples existed only in cities (unlike the temples of other popular cults), they were closely associated with the idea of official government—so much so that officials had to perform certain ritual duties at them. City God temples were linked according to the organizational principle characteristic of the altars of the official religion.

Various aspects of the position of the City God cult as a point of transformation between the official and the popular religions will be developed throughout this paper. Here I want to dwell briefly on some of the marks of distinction between the two, including the organizational principle I just mentioned. Gods in the top and middle ranges of official ritual were represented by narrow upright blocks of wood called *shen-wei* (deity position) or *shen-p'ai* (deity board) or just *chu* (roughly, "host"). These blocks were inscribed with the full title of the being to be worshiped at them, and they resembled in all ways the tablets for ancestors on domestic altars and in ancestral halls. As far as I know there was no special ceremony for the consecration of a tablet, not even the dotting that was done to inject the spirit of the deceased into an ancestral tablet. This contrasts strongly with the elaborate rite for the consecration of images in the popular religion, which was an elaborate version of the dotting rite.

The eyes of a properly made and consecrated image, I have heard it said, should light up when incense is burned in front of them. Such an image is said to contain *ling* (numen, or uncanny intelligence and power). In the ceremony of consecration, the priest inscribes a mirror or an incense pot in front of the image with a charm headed by the character *ling*; he then performs *fa* (magic ritual), in which all the parts of the body, which are a microcosm of the universe, are invoked and an oath written in the air for each. A crude form of consecration involves the killing of a chicken and the dotting of the image's ears (by which the god hears prayers) with its blood. Also dotted with blood are the mouth (by which the *ling* of the god responds to prayer), the eyes (*yin* and *yang*), and the nose (human society), as an expert told me in Taiwan. Into the back of the image are placed the five precious metals, the five viscera, plaited threads in the colors of the Five Elements, and a piece of bread or a living thing—for instance, a bee. To purify the image, Huo-shen is then invoked in some cases, a stretch of burning coals or burning spirit money laid out and the image carried over it.

Ideally, in the regulations of the *Hui-tien*, the official cults celebrated at the open altars and the City God cults were set in a ranked hierarchy that exactly paralleled the administrative one, i.e., the county-level cults were subdivisions of the prefectural-level cults, and so on up to the imperial capital. The regulations were not often put into practice exactly, but their principle was followed. For instance, the tablet at the altar of the land and grain would have inscribed on it *"hsien* land and grain" at a county-capital altar, *"fu* land and grain" at a prefectural-capital altar, and so on. The school-temples were also subdivided. They were ranked according to administrative level and there were rules specifying the rank and position of the chief celebrants—prefect for prefecture, magistrate for county. It is not surprising that the official religion should have been organized in this way parallel to, and indeed dovetailed with, the imperial bureaucracy. In contrast is the principle of organization that was peculiar to popular religion. A temple that had grown up around a peculiarly powerful manifestation of a deity became a center of that deity's cult from which shrines subdivided by a process known, in southeastern China at least, as "division of incense" (*fen-hsiang*) or "division of power" (*fen-ling*). There were, for instance, according to the Republican *Yin hsien t'ung chih*, in the first urban district of Yin hsien twelve branch temples of the cult whose center was the above-mentioned Ling-ying miao in Ningpo.[3]

The most important ideological difference between the two principles of organization was that the popular division was of a specific *shen-ming* (god) and his power, or of the *place* where *ling* had been remarkably manifest; official division, in the case of City Gods and official altars, was based on administrative level, independent of the *shen-ming*. The structure of official cults was not subject to the vagaries of supernatural power and its manifestations. As for such borderline cults as that of T'ien-hou (Ma-tsu) on the popular side, continued worship of a *shen-ming* depended on repeated miracles—response to prayers. Once a deity was adopted by the *ssu-tien*, however, worship of it was a remembrance and became a regular spring and autumn duty.

The bureaucratic division of areas into lesser areas of supernatural administration continued down into the countryside below the county level. But the division of power was peculiar to the popular religion; and, in Taiwan at least (and I see no reason in this case why Taiwan should be exceptional), many city temples were and are the centers of networks of local village temples—networks established by the ritual of the division of incense from the city temple's incense burner. At the popular level, the social jurisdiction of a temple—whether that temple is a bureaucratic subdivision of another, a center of a network, a branch temple, or an independent temple—is known as *lu-hsia* (those beneath its incense burner). As far as I know, this expression was never used for official temples. It signifies the absence of the discrimination by rank and class that characterized the official cults. A popular temple's area is defined purely territorially—all those within a given territory, whatever their rank or class, are expected to participate in its major festivals, at least by paying the ritual maintenance tax.

A point I shall develop later is that village temples had the character of being for the village area what the City God temple was for the capital. But it was not these local village temples (very often centers or divisions of *fen-hsiang* networks) that the officials who wrote the gazetteers considered to be subdivisions of their own cults and therefore the only proper temples for the people of the county. The only ceremonies they encouraged for the people were spring and autumn rites at the temples they called *she* or *t'u-ku shen*, or at the altars for *li*. Virtuous local elders, not officials, were supposed to officiate at them. The *she* temples were obviously considered to be subdivisions of the capital's *she-chi* (land and grain) altar, and the *li* a subdivision of the capital's *i* or *hsien-li* (unworshiped dead) altar. What they were calling *she* temples were in fact what the people generally call *t'u-ti* (local territory) temples. What they would have liked to think of as local *li* shrines I think must have been what in northern Taiwan are usually called Yu-ying-kung (Responsive Gentlemen)—a euphemism for those dead that have become malicious, that have to be calmed with offerings of food and money, and that in some cases may reverse their negative power into a positive beneficial one in order to pass out of purgatory.*

The official interpretations were attempts at controlling popular religion. It would appear from a passage in the gazetteer of Fo-shan *chen* in Kwangtung, quoted by C. K. Yang,[4] that this nominalistic control was sometimes converted into practice. It is there described how the rites of the "earth and grain god" in every neighborhood of one hundred households were (or should be?) used for "the reading of the law and the elucidation of the agreements" to help the poor and aged, and for feasting in order of seniority and rank. In this way "officials who are skilled in government use the gods to assemble the people, and use the congregation to demonstrate the rules. This may be a good way to improve the customs and traditions."

Kung-chuan Hsiao in his *Rural China* considered the state religion to be a form of ideological control in nineteenth-century China, putting it after the *hsiang-yüeh* (Imperial Edict) lecture system. I want now to

---

* There are a number of other names for similar types of shrines. Common in other parts of Taiwan is Wan-hsi T'ung-kuei (Ten Thousand Joys for Those Returned [or Gathered] Together), another euphemistic title for shrines containing the bones of those found dead—for example, the bones of the unknown soldier and the unidentified stranger.

sketch out the attitude of officials to the rites as a form of control—how rites were to be used, and what they were meant to encourage and discourage.

Ideological Control

Performing the rites correctly was believed to have lasting effect, to exemplify the order of the universe, and to maintain the correct distinctions. Mencius, whose work (as part of the Confucian classics) was chanted in the school-temples much as sutras were in Buddhist shrines, excoriated as heretics the epicurean Yang Chu and the undiscriminating humanitarian Mo Ti. Lack of discrimination and egalitarianism would lead to cannibalism and bestiality, he wrote.[5] The school-temple, or more colloquially, the Temple of Civil Culture (*Wen miao*), was as its name implies both school and shrine. It was in two parts. One was centered on the main shrine, in which stood the tablets for Confucius and his peers. The other half was centered on the Ming-lun T'ang (the hall in which human relationships are illuminated). Next to it was a small pagoda mainly for Wen-ch'ang, the patron of learning, but often also for tablets in memory of renowned local officials and scholars. Magistrate Chou of Chu-lo *hsien* in Taiwan rebuilt the school-temple in the capital of his county in 1715 and added a Ming-lun T'ang, which to his expressed regret it had lacked. Since the school's establishment, he wrote, the county had had to wait thirty years for a place of ritual, music, and instruction in the teaching of the three ancient dynasties (Hsia, Shang, and Chou), which illuminate the human relationships (ruler-official, father-son, husband-wife, elder brother–younger brother, friend-friend). As the provincial governor of Fukien had written in his memorial for the completion of the Ming-lun T'ang in the capital of Taiwan (present-day Tainan), "Since there have been humans there have been human minds and human principles. Since heaven creates and earth forms, there is a Ming-lun T'ang [to make creation and formation intelligible (*ming*) is the function of man (*jen*) in the San Ts'ai—the Three Powers of Heaven, Earth, and Man]. If the hall is not established then the children of gentlemen have no place to discuss and recite [*chiang-sung*, the process of learning and rehearsing the classics by heart]. This would inevitably lead to the obscuring of human relationships, the destruction of human principles, and the darkening of the human mind. Men would no longer be human."[6]

The rites "are really the responsibility of the guardians of the land [i.e., the county magistrates]," says one of the prefaces to a handbook on ceremonial.[7] "The ritual of all matters of worship [*ssu*] has one root in rever-

School-Temple and City God 593

ence [*ching*]." "The rites and music and sacrificial vessels are means of reverence and of communication [*t'ung*] with the gods [*shen-ming*]. But now the rites have fallen into disarray and neglect. How can worship be serious or the keeping of the law illuminated?" This preface was written in 1835, shortly before the Opium War and the Taiping Rebellion, the beginnings of the end of the dynasty. An attempt to maintain order ritually was made by distributing the handbook to all administrative capitals so that the official religion should not be neglected. Another preface of the same handbook says that "incense and vessels [that is to say, ritual offerings] can control [keep in place, *ko*] the lower gods and spirits [*kuei-shen*]. Jade, silk, bells, and drums [other offerings and instruments of worship] can reveal the rites and music.... Awe of virtue and the passing on of merit [through worship] civilize the people and form customs."

And in the 1788 gazetteer for Yin *hsien* it is written that the *li* (rites) came down to us from the golden age of Yao and Shun. "*Ssu-tien* rituals are composed on an altar... in order to grasp the hidden virtue of unostentatious good and spread the transforming influence of the ruler [*yüan-hua*, which also means the beginning of creation]."

There follows a passage on how the people are ruled if they respect the gods. "Gentlemen [*chün-tzu*, the literate and enlightened men] assist government well if they perform the rites and thus illuminate tradition. Prosperity results. Thus it is meritorious and scholarly. Through the secret, pure, and profound ceremony of the *shen*, the universe [*T'ien-ti*, heaven and earth] is aided and benefited and the people protected. Whereas if the altars and rites are allowed to go to rack and ruin, disaster follows."

It is evident that in the ideology of Chinese officials—who wrote the gazetteers and the handbooks on ceremonial, and who set up the shrines of the official cults—the performance of correct ritual was a vital part of man's function in the universe, which was to order what heaven had created and earth completed.* If order was correctly maintained, there would be universal harmony and prosperity. This was government by example, the culture of nature and society. More specifically, the rites of the official religion were a form of control, control of both the people and the lower gods.

The *Li-chi* supports the idea of social and spiritual hierarchies, which

---

* The gazetteers were organized and introduced by officials, who of course were never posted to their native areas. That they were outsiders writing in their official capacity undoubtedly influenced their work; in their home areas they would have been more bound to local traditions.

are, as it were, the two sides of the same ladder. Its "Chi-fa" section specifies the depth of ancestry to be worshiped for each rank in the feudal hierarchy, shortening in the climb down from the emperor until in the last rank no ancestral shrines at all are permitted. As a worshiped ancestor, the deceased is a *shen*. But the dead of the lowest feudal class "become *kuei* as soon as they die." A full discussion of this pair of concepts *shen* and *kuei* is impossible here, but a brief outline is necessary. They are variously used in the sense of spirit and of god (or demon). Any dead human is a *kuei*, unless he is worshiped as an ancestor or as having lived a life worthy of commemoration, in which cases he is a *shen*. An exalted *shen*, one whose life and works are highly respected and have been for many generations, is called a *shen-ming*. *Kuei-shen* I take to be a usage that developed after the time when all classes were known to worship their ancestors; it refers to the spirits of the lowest class, of the common people whose lives had not shone with any officially noteworthy merit. The lowest class of spirit given credence in official religion is formally called *li*, the unworshiped dead, otherwise known as *kuei*.

But the institutions of the official religion did not of themselves restrict interpretation of the category *shen* to the memory of ancestors and exemplars. If anything, the substantial offerings, even to Confucius, of cooked and uncooked food and of wine, and the burning of a eulogy written on silk and addressing him directly, would seem already to imply a being more active than a mere exemplar. The passage from the handbook, with its talk of communication with *shen-ming* and the control of *kuei-shen*, would also seem to imply something more active.

Magistrate Chou in the gazetteer of Chu-lo *hsien* takes an agnostic position. He recommends, in a detailed guide to the Confucian rites, the text of a eulogy almost identical with the text given in the 1875 handbook. The one line he omits, however, is the most openly pragmatic line of all: "You maintain the constancy of the sun and moon." The rest is confined to praise of Confucius's virtue and wisdom. Chou's position meant discomfort in some of his religious duties as an official: "As to the establishment of the shrine to Wen-ch'ang, former people, considering the securing of salary and office to be scholar's luck, put the absurd god of Taoism [i.e., Wen-ch'ang] beside the former master [Confucius]. Most of the Confucian schools in the empire have borrowed in secret the blessings of the god in order to encourage students. Nor was any of this abolished by the sage men and sage ways of those who set up instruction. I record its establishment." The K'ang-hsi emperor had instituted the cult of Wen-ch'ang as part of the official religion.

The phrase "borrowed in secret" would seem to indicate not a denial of the existence of "the absurd god of Taoism" and other luck-influencing gods, as one would perhaps expect, but rather a sentiment that it is wrong to have truck with them. We shall see later how this ambiguity was acted out in the official religion when the need to apply to gods for pragmatic results in the here and now became urgent, typically in times of flood and drought. The official did not then deny the existence of supernatural agencies, but he avoided dealing with such categories by employing Taoist priests to do the magic for him—thus withholding recognition, as it were.

The official religion, an institution of government, was subject to the wide range of interpretations put on it by the officials who ran it. But as a product of a ruling class and its history, it did set limits of orthodoxy.

Individual officials came to it with various ideological commitments and manipulated it accordingly. There would be officials like Magistrate Chou who would concentrate on the Confucian cult, deemphasize belief in the existence of demonic and supernatural agencies, and stress the enlightening function of ritual. Performance of the correct ritual for them was an exercise in the revelation of immanent reason in the universe, a process of self-enlightenment at the same time as a demonstration of that reason, dispelling confusion from the common people and hence part of the practice of good government.

The officials could believe in a *t'ien* (Heaven) that was the moral nature of the universe,[8] a metaphysical category that was dominant over all other categories, being the arbiter of their and the world's destiny (*ming*). This *t'ien* was not substantial. As Lien, the historian of Taiwan, wrote: "Good and evil depend on *t'ien*. What is *t'ien*? *Ti'en* is something that has no voice and no smell, that you can see and yet cannot see, can hear and yet cannot hear. . . . Its meaning is naturalness [*tzu-jan*]. . . . This cannot be comprehended by the common people, who therefore resort to Shang-ti [supreme emperor]."[9] Shang-ti is the personification of Heaven. But in many texts, despite Lien and those like him, Shang-ti and Heaven are used interchangeably where the sense is "moral arbiter,"[10] and are so used by the emperor himself in worship at the Altar of Heaven as part of the official religion.

The emperor was, after all, *t'ien-tzu*, "son of Heaven," and it was his prerogative alone to worship Heaven directly. There was only one altar to Heaven officially, and that was the one in the imperial capital. Its lower-level equivalent was the land and grain altar, one in every administrative capital. There is thus another side to the ideology of Lien and that is its support for this imperial prerogative—the maintenance of the idea of supreme power in the hands of the sage ruler. On the grounds that the lower orders in their illiteracy and ignorance cannot understand *t'ien*, this ideology provides for the prosecution of heterodox worship of Heaven. Alternative interpretations, or challenges to the possession of the right to the cult of Heaven, were also challenges to the ruler.

Along with Lien's strictures against popular worship of Heaven went equally strong disapproval of the use of charms and magic by Taoists, who in Lien's words, "confused the world and cheated the people like snakes and scorpions." An Imperial Edict of 1724 had made the point that Taoism was strictly for the cultivation of essence, Buddhism for the nonmaterial, and Confucianism alone for social relations. Taoism and Buddhism were corrupt (i.e., heterodox) when they were used to affect, or worse to organize, social relations.

To refer directly to *kuei* and *shen* for material benefits instead of to law and order under enlightened government was corrupt. If gods or spirits were to be worshiped, it was only in recompense for past benefits, not in hope of future blessings. Yet government funds were spent on astronomers, geomancers, doctors, herbalists, musicians, dancers, Buddhist monks, and Taoist priests—a nice enumeration of occupations filled by literates who were nevertheless not part of the official literate class.[11] Such people constituted a subclass in possession of dangerous alternative ideologies, interpretations, and religious practices.

Practice

In order to show the limits of the official religion in action, I want now to take up a number of contrasting pairs of religious practices as indexes of transformations between the official and popular religions. For the basis of my comparison I shall take for the official religion the annual or biannual ceremony of recompense (*pao*) called *shih-tien*, performed as I saw it in Taiwan for Confucius and prescribed, also for Confucius, in the 1875 handbook already cited. For the popular religion a comparable ceremony is the *chiao*, which is performed in local temples at intervals of a year or more.*

In both ceremonies there are ritual experts who guide the rest of the participants. And in both there are among the participants some who take leading parts and others who are generally passive. In the *shih-tien*, the ritual experts are members of the local directorate of education and teachers at the school. Their role is to stand on either side of the chief

---

* The following comparison is tentative. My knowledge of the *chiao* and the Taoist priesthood has been substantially enlarged by discussion with Kristofer Schipper. Use of the present tense in the following comparison for convenience and clarity should not be taken to indicate that the official ceremonies occur in Taiwan today exactly as they did in imperial times.

celebrants and guide them from their appointed places to wherever the rites demand they be—at an altar for instance—there handing them the proper offerings and announcing the proper number of kneels and kowtows they are to undergo. In the *chiao*, the ritual experts are Taoist religious practitioners—priests. They perform all the rites themselves, the leading participants delegating to them even the presentation of offerings and merely standing behind them, holding incense, and bowing and kneeling when signaled by the priests to do so.

The knowledge that the experts in the official religion have is qualitatively no different from that of the rest of the participants. They are set apart from the other participants only to the extent that specialists in one branch of government are from specialists in another. Neither does the ceremony itself remove them from the other participants. The leading participants lead by virtue of their rank, which has been established outside the ceremony. The knowledge of the Taoists, on the other hand, is gained only after a rite of passage that initiates them to a more sacred status than that of the rest of the population. Their knowledge is esoteric, and at points in the ceremony they propitiate those patron deities through whom they have their knowledge—deities whose worship is not shared by the other participants. And the ceremony itself gives the leading participants a more protected and more sanctified status than it gives the rest.

In both ceremonies, then, there is status differentiation; but in the *shih-tien* the statuses are extrinsic, whereas for the *chiao* they are intrinsic, created for and by the religious ceremonies themselves. The final selection of leading participants in the *chiao* is not by code, decree, or law of the land but by the authority of the chief deity of the temple concerned, before whom the candidates are announced and his approval tested for each by divination blocks. For the duration of the *chiao* the temple takes on the character of a government office, its *lu-hsia* area being its administrative region; but its leaders are representatives of its population, not delegated to it as the officials of the official religion are.

All women, and all men without degrees, are entirely excluded from the *shih-tien*, whereas the *chiao* always includes the entire population of the area in the last part of its rites. For the *chiao* everyone in the temple's region has to be ritually clean, whereas for the *shih-tien* only the leading participants need be. Only the leading participants have anything to do with the offerings to the gods in the official religion. In the *chiao* everyone makes offerings outside the temple and in their homes, and the leading participants witness the presentation of offerings in the temple itself.

The precautions for the *shih-tien* fast are read out in ceremony to the leading participants and guides three days before the main ritual: "There will be one communal fast when they [the leading participants] will lodge together in the fasting house thinking of the *shen* [in this case Confucius]. They will think of the *shen*'s eating and drinking, the *shen*'s residence, the *shen*'s laughter and talk, the *shen*'s will, whatever the *shen* enjoyed, the *shen*'s occupations and tastes. Each will purify his own mind and be the more reverent and discreet and care for the precautions." The climax to this meditation comes on the main day of the ceremony, when the great gate of the temple is opened and the *shen* welcomed to the august rites and the munificent offerings. And this is the nearest there is to a physical presence of a *shen* in the *shih-tien* or, for that matter, in all the official cults where gods are represented only by tablets.

Both the *shih-tien* and the *chiao* are believed by their respective participants to have a generalized good effect. In the case of the *shih-tien* for Confucius and his associates, it is the spread of learning and the maintenance of civilization; and in the case of the spirits of Wind-Rain-Thunder-Clouds and Mountains-and-Rivers, for whom the *shih-tien* is also performed, it is the maintenance of food and shelter for all in the administrative region. But where the official would explain that disaster and confusion are avoided by respect for the proper relationships and the performance of the proper rites to glorify those that exemplified and illuminated them, the people (though not necessarily the priest) would explain that prevention of calamity and assurance of a good harvest are brought about by the protection of a god who is to be propitiated by the proper rites. To the people, then, temple ritual is performed either by officials or by priests, both of whom have ritual knowledge that they, the people, lack. There is a sense in which the god of popular religion is imperial: he sanctions statuses that in the official religion are those of the imperial government. And there is a sense in which priests are the equivalents of officials in relation to these gods.

There is a core ceremony of showing respect that is common to both *shih-tien* and *chiao*, just as the kowtow and other gestures of deference are common to all Chinese culture, and that is the *san-chüeh li*—the triple offering of wine. But the *shih-tien* and the *chiao* differ in their elaborations of this rite, in the contexts in which they set it, in the beings respected, in the wording of the eulogies and texts read and played, and in the fact that the *chiao* is a manipulation of the forces of the universe (magic, if you like) involving a great number of other rites, all of them absent from the *shih-tien*.

Within the official religion itself, elaboration of the *san-chüeh li* dif-

School-Temple and City God

fered according to the being addressed. There were minutely specified differences in the amount of offerings, music, and obeisance required and, of course, in who constituted the proper worshipers. The official pantheon was divided largely into three levels of ritual importance, which I have charted in Tables 1, 2, and 3, indicating a few of the ritual distinctions between them. Within these levels the gods were again kept distinct by finer ritual prescriptions, such as those for the measurements of their altars, the positions of their tablets on the altars, and the number of steps up to the altar. When there was more than one god in a single temple or ceremony, the gods were ritually ranked by whether they were housed in the back or front shrines, or by whether they received as animal offerings *shao-lao* (which was without an ox) or *t'ai-lao* (with an ox). These and many other kinds of prescription were what constituted the *ssu-tien*. They defined which gods were to be worshiped by whom and at what time and place.

The *chiao*, in contrast, means the setting up at the center of the temple region of a ritual area that is movable and the same wherever the priests take it. It consists of the Taoist pantheon of cosmic forces and deities superimposed on whatever the *shen-ming* and *kuei* of the local temples happen to be. In other words, it is the whole structure every time and not an exclusive part of it. The *chiao* is a purification of the region: the gods are called upon to protect it and to act as mediators to greater powers, and the ghosts are fed to keep them away from it. *Shih-tien* is rank-specific, whereas *chiao* is place-specific. Both evoke a universe, but that of the *shih-tien* is of rank in a hierarchy; that of the *chiao* is of a place as microcosm of the macrocosm.

A lesser form of *shih-tien*, called *shih-ts'ai*, was performed on the 1st and 15th of the month at the school-temple. According to the handbook, it was also performed in weddings at the visit to the bride's family, and in funerals at the viewing of the dressed corpse. Worship in ancestral temples is also, as I have observed it, a lesser form of *shih-tien*. There appear, then, to be two sets. The one is kin ritual, memorialism, officials, and tablets. The other is god ritual, magic, priests, and images. Nevertheless, they share a cosmology and interpenetrate in several ways, some of which we shall now examine.

The emperor's birthday was celebrated with rites very similar to those for Confucius, rehearsed, as were Confucius's rites, in the Ming-lun T'ang and performed in a Longevity Hall that was in all respects like a temple. On New Year's Day (lunar) and at the winter solstice the emperor himself in the imperial capital worshiped *t'ien* and his own ancestors, while simultaneously in the provinces the same rites as those for the emperor's birthday were performed in the Ming-lun T'ang. Receiving the orders of the emperor in the provinces involved going out into the eastern suburb to welcome them much as spring was welcomed in the same suburb at the vernal equinox. "We must welcome the spring in the eastern suburb because the people rely on it, and present the military banners in the west drillyard so that confusion and evil can be suppressed before it rises. It cannot be said that the rites [*li*] were invented today. We are following ancient practices," says the introduction to the "Chi-ssu" in the T'ai-wan *hsien* gazetteer of 1721.

At the Altar of Heaven, as the gods and spirits were welcomed, the tablets of the gods and the imperial ancestors were brought from the temples where they were stored to the open altar where they were to be worshiped.[12] The tablet of Huang-t'ien Shang-ti, God of Heaven, was put on the top terrace of the circular altar, flanked by those of the imperial ancestors. At the emperor's own flanks but on the second terrace were put, to the left and superior side the Sun and then all together the Northern Dipper, Five Planets, the Twenty-eight Lunar Mansions, and the Three-hundred-and-sixty Stars of the Heavenly Circumference. These astrological bodies were common to all Chinese religious institutions. They were used by the Directorate of Astrology for making up the ritual calendar, and by diviners for making up the annual almanac of the days propitious for weddings, opening shops, or visiting the sick, or dangerous because of monsters and *kuei*. And they were part of the cosmology used by Taoists in the *chiao*. To the emperor's right on the second terrace was the Moon and Wind-Rain-Thunder-Clouds—the latter worshiped in spring and autumn throughout the capitals of the land together with local mountains and rivers and the City God. The emperor himself sat on the second terrace, opposite and facing Huang-t'ien Shang-ti. He, like the gods, had been preceded to his place by his own tablet carried by his ceremonial guides to mark where he should stand for every movement in the rites. On the third terrace, behind the emperor, sat princes of the first, second, and third ranks, plus dukes. The gods' and ancestors' tablets had been taken up the sacred way—the time was predawn and the way was lighted by red lanterns—through the central opening of the gates leading to the altar, while the emperor, princes, and dukes passed through their side openings. They were guided by the presidents and officials of the Boards of Rites and Music and of the Censorate. All other officials were excluded, just as the common people were excluded from the provincial rites. The imperial progress through the city from the palace to the altar area was masked from all those not taking part. The street was cleared and the side alleys screened at their entrances by green-blue (the color of Heaven) cloth hangings. During the rites only the emperor and his guides moved. He was the sole leading participant.

As the officials claimed, the rites ordered both natural and social classes. As we move down the ranks of the *ssu-tien* from altars to temples, and from the highest to the lowest levels of ceremonial (see Tables 1, 2, and 3), there is an increasing personification of natural bodies and forces, and an increasing tendency to attribute to the spirits of those who have had a personal existence the power to effect events in the here and now. The lower the deities the more they conform to a bureaucratic image of the universe, namely the filling of its parts as offices with the spirits of the worthy dead as officials. At the top level, Land and Grain, Heaven, and Earth have no title but their very names. On the second level, Wind-Rain-Thunder-Clouds each have titles; the first Earl (*po*), the others Master (*shih*). At the lowest level, Ch'eng-huang (literally "walls and moats," the City God) is clearly a spiritual office. It is noteworthy that Ch'eng-huang was represented by a tablet when worshiped at the open altar and by an image when worshiped in his own temple.[13]

The City God temple was within the walls. But the tablets of the Land and Grain were kept in his temple and taken out to their altar—with the City God's own tablet—on days of worship. Similarly the tablets of Wind-Rain-Thunder-Clouds were kept in the Hsien-nung temple when one was built. In the many cases where the prescriptions for the directional position of the altars were not kept, the altars for the Land and Grain, Wind-Rain-Thunder-Clouds and Hsien-nung (plus his temple) were often built all in the same place.

The City God had another side. He was thought to be the otherworld (*yin*) equivalent of the chief of the administrative capital, the this-worldly (*yang*) ruler. It was the rule that an incoming magistrate, before taking up office, first seclude himself in the City God temple and report himself to the god, swearing an oath: "If I govern disrespectfully, am crafty, avaricious, get my colleagues into trouble, or oppress the people, may the *shen* [you] send down retribution upon me for three years."[14] As *yin* administrator, the City God was welcomed as chief deity at the official rites for the unworshiped dead at their altar. He was believed to be in charge of all the spirits of the local dead, but the *li* were his special responsibility and were his underlings in the detection of good and evil among the living (the magistrate resorted to him in cases that he could not decide) and in the discovery of injustices in the lives of those already dead.[15]

When it came to officially still lesser rituals, the populace joined the officials and the City God's image was used. For instance, worship of the City God for himself was not part of the statutory official religion. His annual birthday celebration was largely a popular ceremony. Yet Gray[16] reported that in Canton on the City God's birthday the prefect in the name of the government presented for the image a new suit of silk with which wealthy families had vied to supply him, and he produced the god's jade seal which had been in his keeping for the year. This jade seal was the mark of rank by administrative level ordained by imperial decree in the Ming dynasty. It was turned by the populace into a magic implement, the stamp of which, on a charm or the garment of a sick person, could cure.

The local administrator was the emperor's delegate to the people. The City God, as his *yin* complement, was Heaven's delegate to the people and to their dead. Here the official either pandered to or really subscribed to the beliefs of the people. We can see how close official religion and popular beliefs are when it comes to an occasional rite such as a rain ceremony, as the following account from the 1788 gazetteer for Yin *hsien* shows.

> The ceremony is abundant and the power of the god [*shen-ling*] magnificently manifest. Pray and he responds throughout the year or when it rains too much and the people grieve to him. The *shen* [i.e., the City God] blesses the people munificently. Now, the year after Prefect Lu [of Ning-po] took up office there was drought. He prayed to the *shen* and *t'ien* rained. Again there was drought and again he prayed to the *shen* and *t'ien* rained. He [the prefect] illuminated the people of the prefecture. From the *chin-shih* [degree-holder] to the head of a Board, when they had virtue toward men shrines were built for them. How, too, can the officials for whose virtue the fathers of Yin *hsien* were grateful be forgotten for even one day? The official takes benevolence to govern the people and the *shen* takes sincerity. So the *shen* controls [*ko*] and the people have good faith [*hsin*]. Therefore the people of the whole prefecture asked for an image [*shen-hsiang*] to be made for the temple and they bought it gowns and a crown. The temple's appearance was suddenly new and awesome, uncannily [*ling*] brilliant. The civil and military offered congratulations. Gentry all looked upon it with reverence. That was in 1445, on the tenth day of the eleventh month. The next year Prefect Lu went to make presentations at the Imperial Court and the magistrate of Yin *hsien* asked [him to relay a request to] Marquis Yang to compose a memorial to be engraved for the beautification of the temple in the name of gentry and people.

The order of the provincial rain ceremony, as detailed for Taiwan in the *Fu-chien t'ung chih, T'ai-wan fu*, 1830–69, was that there should be worship first at the altar of Mountains and Streams, and then at the altar of the Land and Grain. The ceremony was to be the same as

School-Temple and City God

that of the regular rites, with the addition of a petition prayer for rain. All officials were to take part. Next, all were to go to read the prayer and burn incense to the City God and then to the Dragon God, in their respective temples. The Dragon God was included in the official rites only for rain ceremonies, not for the regular ones.

The officials wore court dress to the altars, but after the plea for rain had been read they changed into plain linen, as for mourning, which they continued to wear as they went to the two temples every day until rain came. In addition to the usual fast, there was a general taboo on the slaughter of animals, and thus the common people were involved. They were even more involved if sufficient rain did not come within seven days. In such a case a committee of officials was formed that went again—after a repeat of the rites at the two altars—to pray and burn incense in the City God and the Dragon God temples. If the drought was severe, the officials had to burn incense and pray in public as they walked, without parasols in the blazing sun, to the temples through the streets. In Tan-shui *t'ing*, Taiwan, there was a shrine to a virtuous magistrate who had died of exposure while praying for rain.

The wearing of mourning and the exposure to the elements were a penitence and an effort to move heaven; the fast was a purification. If the plea was still not successful, Taoist and Buddhist priests were ordered to plead in their ways, which for the Taoists was the *chiao* in the City God temple. The gazetteer qualifies this by saying that it used to be done thus in the old days, but de Groot[17] at the end of the nineteenth century observed this stage of officials and priests praying for rain. If rain still did not come, then the image of the City God was taken out into the sun, stripped of his headgear, and sometimes chained to experience the drought himself and to move Heaven to rain. Similar events were reported for Canton by Gray on personal observation at the Dragon God temple. When rain came, the officials retreated to the exclusive altars and tablets to give thanks, dressed now in embroidered robes.

It was common practice for degree-holding scholars of literary repute to write the preliminary address to the deity for rain read in the *chiao*. After the address came the more esoteric Taoist rites. A Taoist handbook of the 1870's listing documents to be prepared for a number of ceremonies includes such an address (called *su-i*) written by a *chin-shih* degree-holder. Both the address and the document that follows it—an announcement text (*piao-wen*) that we may attribute to the Taoist compiler of the book—appeal to Heaven and all the spirits (*chu shen*) to put an end to the misery of drought. But the *chin-shih* leaves the relationship between the supernatural and the living vague. He goes so far as to call

Heaven "imperial Heaven" (*Hao-t'ien*) and to say that it would not order living things to be lost and that the spirits who protect the people would not leave them with no support. In the Taoist's document the relationship is much more specific. Heaven has strength, earth has achievements; Heaven and earth have virtue, and the empyrean (*shang-tsang*) has mercy. The spirits have love for the people and have power (*ling*). Appeal is made to a list of entitled deities in this order: Hao-t'ien Chin-kuan Yü-huang Shang-ti (the full Taoist name of Yü-huang Shang-ti—the supreme *shen-ming*); Duke of Thunder; Mother Lightning; Earl Wind; Master Rain; the forces of the five quarters; the rain Dragon God and the spirits of the dragon kings of the five lakes; the four seas; the spirits of the mountains and streams and of the land and grain. They are all besought to use their power (*ling*) to drive out the drought demon (or star influence—*k'uei*). The *chin-shih* never mentions the drought as a demon or as star influence, nor does he mention *ling* once in his prayer.

Another *chin-shih*'s prayer for rain[18] addressed to the City God does, however, go further than the above *su-i*. This prayer refers to the *ling* of the City God, to his virtue as guardian of the territory, and to the *shen* of rain and the *ling* of such broad natural categories as the ocean. He implores the City God to take his appeal to the gates of Heaven. But the *ling* categories all occur in couplets paired with references to Buddhist concepts.

The Taoist priest who lent me the handbook wrote out another plea for rain for one of his pupils to learn. It is a combination of the *su-i* and the announcement text. Features not found in either of the *chin-shih*'s prayers are references to the cause of the drought as a *k'uei* and to the *ling* of the sage strength of the spirits of Heaven and earth, of empyrean Heaven, and of the thunder god, who is to open the gates of Heaven with his peals. Most importantly, this plea states the intention to establish communication with Heaven by means of a *fu*, a document that is a cross between a memorial and an order (and is usually translated as charm) and that is held by the Taoist during the prayer.

With the concept of malignant influences to be expelled by the use of charms we have moved completely out of the realm of official religion, for only Taoists use charms. A glimpse at some of the oaths, or commands, and the movements prescribed to accompany the burning and brandishing of the charms takes us beyond the bureaucratic universe of the announcement text mentioned earlier. For these more esoteric rites refer to less anthropomorphic forces of the universe, such as the spirits (*ch'i*) of the four quarters, of the Five Elements, and of *yin* and *yang*. A new imagery of cosmic forces and of alchemy is here introduced into the rain ceremony, and into all occasions when the *chiao* is performed. The Taoist priest seeks to concentrate in himself as a microcosm forces of the universe sufficient for him to realign things that have gone out of balance and to counter malignant forces that have come into play.

One can move from popular religion into the Taoist as well as into the official religious traditions. The two shared a common ground of metaphysical speculation. But it is in Taoism and not in the official religion that the metaphysical categories of this cosmology are applied as real forces. In the official religion, the notion of a hierarchical structure in the moral universe is consistently displayed. This notion is anthropomorphized as it approaches popular religion, for the metaphor of bureaucracy becomes increasingly elaborate as the spirits of men who have died take on greater and greater powers and the representations of gods are themselves treated as having power.[19] The distribution of this power is through a hierarchy, that is to say by *delegation* through ranks from the top. The image of bureaucracy is applied to the universe in Taoist religion, too, and with it the attribution of substantial powers to the spirits of the dead—again as Taoism approaches popular usage. But between Taoist religion and popular religion—the former in its application of transcendental metaphysical categories; the latter in the use of the concept *ling*, in particular—an alternative relationship is added to that of delegation. It is the diffusion and concentration of power from a center. In Chinese metaphysical tradition this is the concentration of power in any spot of time or space as a center appropriately oriented to the greater arrangement of power on a transcendent plane. The ultimate center at the most transcendent plane is known as the great unique (*t'ai-i* and its synonyms). One may call this a process of *identification*, and it is common to Taoist religion, alchemy, and geomancy.

Popular religion is pragmatic religion; metaphysical categories are latent in concrete phenomena. Power is immanent, manifested in extraordinary phenomena and events, and tapped from them. At the same time *shen* and *kuei* can become gods and demons of this immanent power and can be brought under control through the officials of a supernatural bureaucracy. Taoist priests perform rites in the name of these gods and demons; officials do not.

Bureaucratic Control

By a regulation promulgated in the first year of the Ch'ing period, the state sponsored the building of shrines to celebrated officials and local worthies. Candidates for canonization were to be recommended to the emperor, who would authorize their enshrinement. The criteria for canonization were contained in five statutes of the *Li-chi*. Now it is true that almost all popular temples were also dedicated to former humans, many of whom had lived in or administered the localities where they were enshrined. In Ningpo, a number of popular temples not included in the *ssu-tien* or else crossing the line between official and popular (having been built by officials but having no official rites performed in them) were dedicated to past officials posted to Ningpo—many of whom had relieved the people by reducing taxes in times of hardship.

There was certainly an overlap between the official and the popular religions, and there was an exchange of gods, or rather a transformation of each other's gods, between them. It was characteristic of the popular and not of the official religion that the former official had to manifest his power as a god if he were to continue being worshiped. To be worshiped officially, a candidate must have been worthy by official standards of virtue—loyalty to the emperor, and so forth—and recommended by the appropriate officials. Like the degree system, this was open to corruption. Hsiao has shown how local gentry bribed the appropriate officials to recommend their ancestors for canonization.[20]

The principle of judging a *shen* by his life as a human was often abandoned, however, especially where the *shen* had become very popular. Canonization of the latter into the official religion was a form of control. More direct means of control have been documented by others,[21] but we can mention here the bureaus in every administrative capital for the registration of Taoists and Buddhists, and for the commissioning of one of their number for such official services as the rain ceremony. This had the effect of creating an orthodoxy under official control. At its highest point was the head of the Cheng-i sect, the so-called Taoist pope, who was given the task of appointing jointly with the emperor former officials and worthies who should fill the posts of the City Gods of the empire.

There are many examples of popular cults that were adopted into the *ssu-tien* because the *shen* had been officially recommended for saving emperors' or officers' lives (e.g., Ningpo's Hsieh-chung miao to the six generals who died defending Sui-yang city against the forces of An Lu-shan), or for producing rain (e.g., Ningpo's Pai-lung-wang miao, a Dragon God temple to two Sung-period brothers who lived in the mountains). Kuan-ti, the various gods of Wen-ch'ang, and T'ien-hou are examples of the most thoroughgoing adoption, for they were recommended so many times from so many different places that in the Ch'ing period it was ordered that official temples to them be built—in all capitals for Kuan-ti and Wen-ch'ang, and in all coastal capitals for T'ien-hou.

It was characteristic of this class of beings that they were reputed to have led unorthodox lives, or not to have fulfilled their allotted span, or to have met violent death. Kuan-ti was supposed to have died in battle without blood descendents. T'ien-hou to have died a virgin. It was this extraordinary aspect about them that manifested *ling*. As *kuei* their unspent force was dangerous. They chose to use it positively, to bring prosperity to those who prayed to them. With their incorporation in the *ssu-tien*, an official interpretation of their deeds and function was imposed and an orthodoxy dictated by the Board of Rites.[22]

The school-temple and the City God are both the oldest and the most constant features of the county-level cities I have investigated. There is a case to be made for their being the two most essential features of the official religion: the City God was the focus of a religion based on natural forces and ghosts, and thus was the god for the control of the peasantry, as it were; the school-temple was the center for the worship of sages and exemplars of official virtues, for the spirits of bureaucracy. The school-temple was the center of the cult of literacy. For Confucians the spirit was in the written word, not in any object or image or natural body. The written word was enough: it was the vehicle of tradition, the trace of the sages and of the golden age. In most Wen-ch'ang temples there was an incinerator for the respect of the written word. It was, in theory, the only place where scraps of paper containing writing could be destroyed, since it was a shrine to the inventor of writing.

To scholars, skill in writing was the way up the official ladder. Worship of Wen-ch'ang was only one of many ritual observances by which members of the scholar-official class "borrowed in secret" blessings for scholars' luck. To the illiterate people, writing meant statutes and decrees, on the one hand, the means by which their rulers governed them, and secret charms, on the other, known only to the initiated and effective as cures for sickness or ill-luck.

There was a dialectic in which officials adopted deities from popular religion and bureaucratized them, while the people worshiped gods that were like magic officials or that were magic official deities. Gods that in popular religion were fluid, whose identities flowed into one another, whose functions were potentially universal, and who were magic in their ability to metamorphose and to fuse man and nature in themselves, were in the official religion standardized and classed, minute distinctions and the separation of rites and cults keeping them apart.

Taoism offered confirmation of an alternative to the official type of power structure. To place the official religion in a completed context it would be necessary to show how Buddhism offered a third tradition out of popular religion.

As a last point, let me make it clear that what I have described as the official religion did not constitute the religion of all those who were, or who aspired to be, officials. In his home county before he became an official, in his nonofficial capacity while he was an official, and when he retired, a scholar-official might well sponsor nonofficial temples and take part in nonofficial rites. At the very pinnacle of the hierarchy, the Ch'ing emperors had their nonofficial religion in the inner palace.[23] The official religion with the office of emperor at its head was an institution of government; and, like the examinations, possession of it and the content of it could be disputed and changed. On either side of the official religion, so to speak, were on the one hand the *shu-yüan* and on the other the secret societies. Outside the city were the places of Buddhist and Taoist retreat. All of them were places where the institutions of government and the official religion could be disputed. The walled cities of administration stood for official power. The power of nonofficial religious institutions and the governed lay beyond the walls in the countryside and in unwalled central places.

Urban Social Control

SYBILLE VAN DER SPRENKEL

In most societies the law and legal institutions have been concerned with the resolution of conflicts and disputes: "The pervasive problems of conflict and conflict resolution are central in legal studies," to quote a recent writer.[1] Can the same be said of China? And were there differences between urban and rural communities in this respect? And again, although modern sociologists tend to think of the various norms and mechanisms that arise out of social interaction rather than of a generalized entity, social control, may this concept still have usefulness when one is thinking of a premodern society? Perhaps these questions may serve as a starting point for our inquiry.

It must be stressed at the outset that in traditional China "urban" was not a category to be sharply distinguished from "rural." Consequently, we are dealing here with a sector that is part of the general spectrum of social behavior, not a sharply differentiated and localized category. The idea that the degree of urbanization varies along a continuum is applicable also in this field: no Chinese communities ever established themselves as municipalities possessing defined powers of independent jurisdiction. Town and country were alike governed by a blend of two different kinds of organization: the first, the territorial network of the centralized imperial authority reaching from the top downward to the family or household at the base, the seat of whose administration was merely located within one city in the *hsien*; and the second, the customary unofficial organization of overlapping groups and associations, which arose not by design or by explicitly established right but spontaneously wherever and whenever groups of people associated regularly and shared neighborhood, activities, cult practices, common interests, or general interdependence. It will be the purpose of this paper to describe how these different systems of official and customary jurisdiction operated; how their spheres were delimited in practice, or at what points they merged or overlapped; and what relevance the hierarchy of local systems may have had for them.

There are grounds for thinking of the urban central place generally as the locus of dispute settlement, both formal and informal, for the area around it; and whether the disputes had arisen in the town itself or in the surrounding countryside, the town teahouse, frequented regularly by influential leisured persons and on market days by others, is often referred to as the venue for village mediation.[2] To ensure, therefore, that what are being considered are predominantly urban phenomena, the major emphasis in this paper will be on matters related to commerce and industry (at least at the artisan level), since these activities may be assumed to have been relatively more significant in towns and cities.

The choice of a starting point for our exposition is to some extent arbitrary—official and unofficial organization each being influenced, though in different ways, by the other. Official organization undoubtedly owed something to forms and beliefs that had their roots in custom; the form "spontaneous" organization took was just as certainly affected by, and in some ways a response to, the actual character of the official administration.

Let us deal first, then, with the control and jurisdiction that were exercised by statute law and the courts of the imperial administration. The intention behind these (if we may ignore for present purposes the question of whose intention and for whose advantage) may be said to have been to reinforce Confucian morality—to govern in such a way that people would choose to obey their moral nature, and to provide additional sanctions for those people, whether populace or officials, who would not be obedient without them.*

Although each successive dynasty enacted its own administrative and penal statutes and amended them at intervals, the models were ancient and both form and content reflected the thinking of earlier times. The headings of Ming and Ch'ing penal codes were virtually unchanged

---

* Law was, of course, only the extreme pole of the attempt to impose orthodoxy. No opportunity was lost of propagating orthodoxy both directly through education and indirectly through other inducements—such as rewards of honor for filial sons and chaste widows. Moreover, the entrance examinations for the bureaucracy were structured to direct the attention of each generation to Confucian ethical texts. This of course went on in towns (see the paper by Tilemann Grimm elsewhere in this volume), and we know that the sons of successful merchants were drawn into the system. It may be doubted, however, whether Confucian ideals really made much appeal to the commercial community as such; in this connection a content analysis of urban literature and drama might be revealing.

from those of T'ang, and their arrangement reflected the structure of the imperial administration. The purpose of laws (as proclaimed in the Sacred Edict, for example) was twofold: to prohibit people from doing evil and to encourage them to do good.³ Since rulers were responsible, according to Confucian political philosophy, for creating conditions in which their subjects could behave properly, the pursuit of this objective led incidentally to the attempt on the part of government to regulate much of people's lives.* Thus the penal code not only covered matters commonly regarded as crimes everywhere (e.g., killing and stealing), matters of significance from the point of view of Confucian values (e.g., ritual, and family and sumptuary laws—including the style of life permitted to persons of different ranks), and offences against state power and orthodoxy (e.g., heresy and rebellion); but it also included provisions that reinforced Confucian economic thinking—punishments for a range of actions in the economic sphere that were held to be contrary to the public interest.

The early Confucian thinkers on whose ideas the provisions were based believed that the amount of wealth a community possessed was determined by the amount of primary production; beyond that, a larger share of wealth could only be enjoyed by some at the expense of others. So they held that essential occupations (*pen-yeh*) should be encouraged and inessential ones suppressed (*chung-pen i-mo*). In the orthodox view, therefore, trade, commerce, and financial operations for private gain were accorded little prestige and were controlled by the government in the interest of its subjects. From Han times on, Chinese governments operated a system of economic controls, issuing licenses for the production of certain commodities, such as salt and iron, and requiring that important business transactions be conducted through a government-recognized agent.†

Through the centuries both the volume and the real significance of

* It would be an oversimplification to describe this as the ethic of a simple agrarian community. The Confucian Han empire incorporated elements of universalistic Legalist thinking (which itself reflected a growth in the scale of society), but perhaps these elements may be said to have affected the *method* of enforcement—the use of punishment and coercion for those whose commitment to norms could not be gained by education (i.e., a shift in the power mix)—more than the *content* of the moral norms they were aimed at enforcing.

† This system of control in China (unlike that in Muslim cities, according to Ira Marvin Lapidus, *Muslim Cities of the Middle Ages* [Cambridge: Harvard University Press, 1967], p. 67) extended also to magistrates, who were not allowed to be connected with local families by marriage or to involve themselves in local business affairs in the county where they held office. Subordinate yamen staff were more difficult to control; sometimes subordinate posts were held hereditarily by local families whose rapaciousness was a byword and formed an obstacle to communication between the administration and other local residents.

trade grew. Specialized products became associated with particular localities, and interregional trade developed on a considerable scale. Life in towns and cities pulsated with the rhythm of commerce, which was recognized as an important source of official revenue. In practice, the social and legal position of merchants consequently improved: in the Ch'ing period, for example, the taxation to which they were subject was relatively light; and the salt merchants in particular actually enjoyed certain privileges, for example the provision that their sons could enter the official examinations in the center where their family was "sojourning." But these were relatively minor modifications, and the basic ideas remained too fundamental to the structure of government to permit the adaptation of official procedures so that they could actually be of *use* to those engaged in commerce: this would have required a complete and explicit reversal in official thinking. The substance of the laws continued to support the notion of trade as nonproductive.

The "Hu pu" section of the penal code (that is, the section on the revenue department, which was concerned with family and marriage law, registration of population, and registration and taxation of land) included statutes designed to deal with commercial and financial affairs: penalties were provided for evasion of duties; for usury (including a rather weak section treating nonpayment of a debt as a failure to return borrowed property*); for neglect or misuse of property entrusted for safe custody; for offenses against the official licensing system; and, in particular, for attempts to monopolize the market in a commodity.[4] The system thus provided that cases concerning economic affairs would come into court as offenses against government economic regulations; that is, that the courts should form part of the apparatus of government economic control. The courts, associated primarily with the punishment of offenses,† never developed the techniques introduced in other societies to handle the adjudication of interpersonal or interhouse disputes arising from conflicts of interest or from claims for loss or damage.[5] Persons with a grievance could denounce others, but the yamen court offered neither adequate recourse for the hearing and adjustment of claims nor machinery for assessing compensation or awarding other

---

* In another part of the code, in the section on driving another to commit suicide (under the general heading of homicide), owing money is given as one in a list of reasons why this might occur. The penalty was raised to strangulation if it was the local magistrate who was driven to commit suicide for this reason.

† A certain procedural distinction was made between matters dealt with under the "Hu pu" (family and commerce) section and those under "Hsing pu" (crimes). Cases were forwarded to different offices of the provincial government (which had competence to conclude all but capital cases).

remedies. In short, the magistrate's court was not the venue for the adjustment of commercial disputes. Furthermore, it is evident that the government resorted to court action only to a very limited extent in forcing its economic policies on those engaged in industry and commerce.

We must be on our guard, as Ch'ü T'ung-tsu cautions, against exaggerating the extent to which the yamen courts were bypassed.[6] However, in the best known of the Ch'ing collections of cases (which one presumes must have been to some extent representative, since they were intended as models for the guidance of magistrates), there are very few references to merchants at all, and the fact of the persons mentioned being connected with trade appears (with the exception of the salt merchants[7]) as a largely incidental circumstance.*

Imperial law on these topics never having developed beyond the concern to enforce ethical norms and safeguard the public interest, people were left to pursue their activities locally with a minimum of interference—so long as they did not flagrantly contravene the statutes—and without benefit of court adjudication. In other words, much was left to unofficial social organization.

This organizing of activities locally went on mainly in the particularistic groups and ad hoc associations for which Chinese everywhere have shown such outstanding talent. (One sees that the need for them originated in imperial China, and that Chinese abroad have simply been drawing on the experience of a long tradition.) The structure, membership, and leadership of these associations were quite formal, and they

---

* According to Bodde and Morris 1967, p. 205, the *Hsing-an hui-lan* and its two supplements together contain only two cases under "Stabilization of Commodity Prices by Market Supervisors," though there are 53 cases under the section on the salt laws. The cases translated in Bodde and Morris 1967 are admittedly a selection from what is already a selection. However, consultation of the full Chinese text of some relevant sections of HAHL bears out the assertions made in the text above. Examination of the section on usury (HAHL, ch. 10, "Wei chin chü li," 19a–20a) is revealing: of the cases included, *none* relate to what might be described as normal commerce. They involve such matters as nonpayment of debts being made the excuse for rape or kidnapping; felling of a debtor's trees as self-help for nonpayment of rent (assimilated to the prohibition on seizure of cattle for this purpose); loans to expectant magistrates followed by the lender's accompanying the magistrate to his post (in itself an improper act); and, in one case, threats leading to the suicide of the magistrate. Of three cases selected in Bodde and Morris (out of nine in HAHL) from the section treating restraint of market operations, two turn out to be about transport workers demanding higher wages (on grounds of higher "productivity" and higher cost of living, respectively); the third, a case of purchase of grain from a government granary on false pretenses, was brought under the section on "restraint of market operations in order to acquire monopolistic profits," by analogy, as there was no statute exactly covering this offense. See Bodde and Morris 1967, pp. 266–71.

had their own rules and sanctions that were well known to their members. (The unorganized or unincluded, it will be seen later, were at a certain practical disadvantage, so the implicit sanctions of expulsion or loss of reputation were always in reserve if no particular sanctions were specified.)

The extent to which the imperial administration exercised real control locally depended on how much power it could command. It is commonly asserted that its power was felt more in towns than in the countryside and of course in the capitals and garrison cities more than in other towns. In the countryside, where land was the chief means of production, the landowning function of the kinship group gave it significant power to control members' lives. In towns and cities, the lineage was less significant in this respect. Though business at both the merchant and the artisan level was organized on family lines (and of course within the family discipline was exercised by senior family members over their juniors, as was general in China), kinship organization was not the machinery by which business was regulated.[8]

A large part of what went on in towns and cities had to do either with temples or with trading, and other contributors to this volume describe urban neighborhood religious associations and the guilds in which craftsmen and merchants were organized. Apart from family occasions, i.e., weddings, funerals, and private ancestor worship (and guilds also served as proxy family in the case of funerals and burials of deceased sojourners), temples and guilds probably covered the activities that were most significant in the lives of urban residents: neighborhood temples were associated with street markets, festivals, and processions; guilds with the practice of crafts and trade; and both with such recreations as theatricals, jugglers, and feasts.

A good many towns, perhaps most, possessed religious foundations—Confucian temples, lama temples, Buddhist monasteries, mosques, and so on—more important than those based on purely local cults, and the rituals associated with them punctuated the year and enhanced the lives of the area residents. Temples located in towns were sometimes also connected with secret societies, which, by their nature, tended to overlap with heterodox sects. Leong and Tao mention temples built by ephemeral societies through public subscription led by someone well-to-do. "When the work is completed, nothing but the temple with the monks remains. Yet the utility of these temples, which are found everywhere in China, is manifold, as the site of festivals, the warehouse of goods, the classroom of private tutors, the meeting-place of poor artisans, the dining-room of feasting parties, etc."[9] These indications of overlap of clientele and ambiguity of function—at times religious, political, economic, and social, perhaps changing cyclically—warn against making too sharp a distinction between temples and other types of organization.

Neighborhood religious associations formed the focus of a sort of local self-government. The pervasive beliefs in spirits associated with places, and the consequent needs that premodern Chinese, urban as well as rural, seem to have felt, gave rise to practices which, as they were shared by people in the neighborhood, had somehow to be organized and financed; and presumably the association took on other functions by accretion, like the parish in Western cities. Elsewhere in this volume, Professor Schipper discusses the entrance subscriptions paid by members of the neighborhood association (a virtually compulsory levy) that were then invested in property to provide a continuing income for the support of the cult, and of a rotating leadership to manage association affairs and allocate duties. Shared supernatural beliefs would no doubt serve to reinforce the authority of leaders if there were disputes about obligations or disagreement about the conduct of association business. And if other interpersonal disputes arose in which adherents were involved, the same leaders would be available to arbitrate. This seems to be a recognizably Chinese pattern.

The organization of townsmen's workaday lives was in the hands of guilds. The purposes for which these existed, their manner of organization, and the means by which they maintained control over their members are fully dealt with in another paper in this volume. Suffice it here to recapitulate. They varied in their structure—some were relatively democratic and others hierarchical—but they were alike in adopting rules or standards appropriate to the particular business of their members and in providing effective machinery for intragroup adjudication and sanctioning. They were both inclusive and exclusive. Membership offered benefits without which the individual trader could not hope to survive (protection against official demands that went beyond what was usually exacted, against unfair or improper practices on the part of fellow members or competitors, and against the hostility experienced by sojourners at the hands of the host community), but these were bought at a cost. The cost was obedience to the guild's own authority, which rested on its indispensability to members. Guilds also offered their members certain other attractions such as conviviality, assistance in time of need, and the opportunity to participate in the most immediate political processes and to share in the exercise of some authority. They were of course particularistic and sectional in their interests and not directly concerned with the welfare of the general public, though insofar as they kept up the quality of goods and the standards of work and helped to maintain order they could be said to have served the public interest also. Their existence was recognized by the authorities, with whom guilds were in regular communication—merchant guilds through their secretaries, craft guilds through their leaders—and magistrates were frequently called on to approve guild rules, in the hope perhaps of avoiding charges under the statute on monopolies or under other government regulations.* The context in which they operated, we must remember, included not only the imperial administration (concerned as described above with controlling the economy) but also the prevailing intellectual climate in which the economic philosophy of the limited good was generally accepted, and the actual existence in the Chinese countryside of a permanent reservoir of surplus labor, among whom many would have been ready to leave the hardships and insecurity of the rural scene for work in the towns unless some deterrent had been placed in their way. The premise on which guilds were based (or perhaps one should say on which most of them were based) was the belief in trade as a stagnant pool.[10] Each group watched jealously to preserve its position and to maintain the status quo between its members through such methods as putting barriers in the way of alienating another member's customers and restricting the numbers who might be taken on for training. For porters within a city, for example, additional rules delimited areas within which members might operate. The regulations of various guilds dealt directly or indirectly with the subject of debt—stipulating how and when accounts were to be settled, or setting out measures to prevent anyone who did not pay up from continuing in the trade. Guilds were concerned to avoid friction between members because group solidarity was indispensable to the pursuit of their primary objectives; and, no doubt for this reason and also in order to preserve both their strength and their "public image," the rules of some guilds ordered members not to take disputes to the yamen without first bringing them before the guild for a hearing.[11] Some guilds, if they were convinced of the justice of a member's cause, would then undertake to prosecute on his behalf.[12] The disciplining of members and the arbitration of disputes may be regarded as secondary or derived functions of the guild, as in another context they may be of the lineage.†

* Analogously, beggars had their own association rules, as did the blind. These associations would not have owned their own hall but would have met in a temple.

† Note that although there are recorded instances of yamen courts referring commercial cases back to guild courts for settlement (and endorsing their decisions),

Differences were adjusted, erring members were disciplined, and decisions were given in accordance with norms that were either formally adopted or customary, the latter being a sort of customary law of the trade, akin to customary land tenures. It is perhaps worth observing that careful "legislation," that is, specification of norms, by guilds (and other bodies) could obviate or reduce the scale of disputes, and no doubt this was a motive for their reformulation. If the rules specified clearly, for example, the period for which the seller was responsible for the safe custody of a consignment and at what point the purchaser had to assume responsibility, how long the purchaser was allowed before payment had to be made,[13] the conditions under which the work had to be done, or criteria for judging the quality of the product, and if these rules were clearly understood by all concerned, then the incidence of disputes about such matters was likely to be reduced. Explicit specification would also have made policing of the norms, by mutual observation, a simpler matter. But cases could still arise—through bad faith, falsification of fact, or simple mistakes—that would make adjudication necessary. It is easy to see the advantage a guild would have over the imperial authorities in the specification of norms appropriate for each particular branch of business; and, as adjudication was partly a matter of interpreting and applying norms so specified and understood, we can also see the headstart over the official courts given to guild machinery of adjudication by the norm-specification function.

Adjudication is said to have been informal, and the sanctions the guilds imposed, ranging from small fines to expulsion or worse, were practical.[14] Presumably on account of both the rotation of duties that was the practice in many guilds and the personal familiarity that existed in most, it seems likely that there may have been a "there but for the grace of God . . ." atmosphere about the proceedings. The fact that the guild premises were the scene of the occasional ritual to the patron deity no doubt added strength to any reprimand received there. Perhaps it is worth noting that whereas the diffuse character of the functions of the imperial administration militated against the usefulness of the yamen for judicial purposes (the magistrate being responsible for tax collection, the census, and land registration besides legal work), the reverse was true of the guild. The diffuseness of its activities made it more

---

this was not the *intention* of the law. Unlike Tokugawa Japan, for example, where mediation procedures were the rule, Ch'ing China prohibited private settlement once a dispute had been brought to the attention of the magistrate. However, in the actual context of Chinese life resort to mediation was frequently no more voluntary than it was in Japan. On this point see Jerome Alan Cohen, "Chinese Mediation on the Eve of Modernization," in *California Law Review*, 54, no. 3(Aug. 1966): 1223.

effective for purposes both of control and of adjudication: continuing personal familiarity opened up many opportunities for exerting pressure or influence, on which the effectiveness of informal adjudication rests.

Although the guild and the neighborhood temple association both existed to serve the interests of their members and exercised a high degree of autonomy, it will be seen that they in fact exercised a control that the sociologist would regard as being of essentially the same type as that of the imperial administration—namely a blend of normative and coercive power. Though to the outside observer there appears to be a great difference between the yamen court and a hearing by an autonomous group in terms both of the point of view of the person with the grievance or involved in the dispute and of the type of power structure involved, perhaps there was not too much difference in the kind of treatment the plaintiff and defendant would receive. In one case judgment would be by his peers, and in the other by the administrative authorities: the former might be less terrible than the latter, but it was probably still very unwelcome, and it left the individual equally unfree. Both represented authoritative adjudication in terms of norms that the individual had very little power to affect—i.e., the application of normative/coercive power, felt as slightly less oppressive perhaps when exercised by the guild because of the latter's diffuse functions and the range of the members' needs it met. Authority would be tempered on account of judges and judged having at other times shared in common struggles or common enjoyments, whereas the county magistrate remained always a distant figure. The member might have some part (more nominal than real for some, for, as in the lineage, some members were more powerful than others) in shaping or amending the norms, but, that done, compliance was expected and sanctions would be enforced for nonobservance. When disputes between members were mediated, appeals would be made to the norms and the solution offered would have to be in terms of what conformed best to them; amends would have to be made then by the party in the wrong. The requirement that an offender provide a feast was a subtle punishment, as MacGowan has pointed out. For though a man suffered financial loss thereby, he could regain face by playing the host; but the occasion also served to teach the deference due to seniority and subordination to authority.[15] Perhaps this kind of control can be thought of in some cases as representing the enforcement of a code of professional conduct—a kind of status ethic of an occupation organized to defend and promote its interests against both government and public. In other cases it might even be thought of as representing an ethic adopted by a group of sojourners on the defensive against native residents, i.e., sets of norms controlling the behavior of incoming townsmen during a period of urbanization, the norms gradually undergoing change in response to other social changes.[16] Furthermore, though the guild may have come into existence as the trade's response to government exactions, it is clear that the government attempted to exercise control over guild members through it by recognizing one member as responsible for the trade. And, to individual merchants or craftsmen, the guild and official administration together seem to have represented a two-tiered system of normative/coercive control.

The control guilds exercised over their members gave them strength in conducting their external power struggles with the public, their competitors, and the imperial administration. The stance they adopted toward administrative authority varied at different times and in different instances: at some times complying with yamen demands, at others resisting, and sometimes one guild petitioning against others for a decision or action in its favor, i.e., manipulating the power of the administration for its own ends. The precise position depended no doubt on the local power relations at the time.[17] Oscillations of this kind were probably among the factors that determined the exact form guild organization took, and this subject deserves study. However, considered solely under the aspect of adjudication of disputes, it seems clear that the absence of a clearly articulated power structure linking the different elements of the situation was another factor that made the yamen court ineffective as an impartial judicial organ of appeals. It might be aligned with or opposed to the guild. In neither case had an individual anything to gain by appeal to it, and one presumes that the guild only referred cases for decision where the local situation was such that a verdict in its favor could be expected; i.e., administrative power was thus used to reinforce the guild's own power.*

In contrast with this, machinery of another type existed for the conduct of transactions on the basis of mutuality or complementarity of interests that did allow the parties some power in the determination of the obligations into which they entered and did provide for settlement

---

* There is one other form of the exercise of arbitrary power that should perhaps be mentioned, if only to show the limitations of the regime's control or of any other control—namely, the set of supernatural beliefs associated with *feng-shui*, "geomancy." These were a means of coercing the credulous to act or refrain from acting (usually in the matter of siting buildings or graveyards) in accordance with the spirits of the locality. This was no doubt operated by natives against newcomers. See Stephan Feuchtwang, *An Anthropological Analysis of Chinese Geomancy* (Vientiane: Editions Vithagna, 1974).

of ensuing disputes by negotiation rather than by authoritative normative pronouncement; in other words, this machinery functioned as a kind of embryonic form of contract.*

There were of course customary procedures according to which these transactions were conducted and there were recognized institutionalized roles associated with them.

Probably few commercial transactions of any consequence in traditional China were either impersonal or casual. At their heart, as a necessary condition, was the prior establishment of a personal relationship. In the case of routine purchases of any commodity, purchaser and vendor usually maintained a continuing relationship (though the purchaser did not necessarily do so exclusively with one vendor, of course). For articles or services to be supplied to order (whether the particular item were a gown from a tailor or a coffin from a coffin-maker), for a service to be performed for another, or for any deal involving trust and credit, the parties to the transaction entered it as *persons in relationship*, normally using an intermediary to arrange the terms of the agreement. And the same would apply to taking on staff or apprentices and to borrowing a sum of money. One got nowhere until a relationship of trust had been established. The intermediary served two purposes: first, he forged a circle of acquaintance, testifying to the good faith of the parties; and later, if difficulty arose, he served as a witness to the terms agreed on, a channel of communication and, if necessary, perhaps even an arbitrator.

There were recognized rituals to be gone through: references to common acquaintances or to friends who had been customers to the satisfaction of both sides; the negotiation of the particular deal and the specification of the terms agreed on (such as date of delivery, quality, and price), all of which would have to be in conformity with local custom or guild practice. Often these terms were specified in writing, or an entry might simply be made in an order book; but written or not, the terms agreed on were clearly specified. For some types of transaction samples would be inspected and accepted, and then the supplier was under an obligation to produce similar goods and the purchaser to accept goods similar to the sample seen, even if they contained faults. Thus the principle of *caveat emptor* applied. No contract of sale, written or unwritten, was considered binding unless a deposit had been paid

---

* This was not an exclusively urban development, for a similar form of organization is observable in rural compacts for exchange of labor or hire of work animals, but the expansion of trade must have increased the number of occasions for its employment.

as bargain money or earnest money.[18] "Once bargain money has been paid, there is no going back by either of the principals."[19]

Could this be the Chinese version of what Durkheim called the noncontractual elements of contract (more correctly perhaps, of quasi contract)? The precise details of a specific transaction had to be spelled out, but the negotiations were conducted and the compact was concluded according to customary forms that helped to ensure that the transaction *would* be regarded as an obligation and honored in due time. If not, further customary actions would be taken to uphold the terms agreed on, to redress the infraction of the newly extended normative order (for this is what results from the process of "contracting"), or to "adjust" the situation to the satisfaction of all concerned.

What our nineteenth-century writer called the law with regard to Broker and Principal reflects the key role of the middleman-guarantor, referred to above as the intermediary.* A case heard in the Shanghai Supreme Court in 1867 established the principle (established it, that is, for the benefit of ignorant foreigners; it was not invented then, of course) that Chinese sellers looked in the first instance to the middleman, and as long as they trusted him, the name of the principal (i.e., the purchaser) did not appear; but if they could not obtain payment from the middleman, they held to their right to fall back on the principal.[20] We have here what looks like a specific extension for commercial purposes of a basic principle in all Chinese dealings—the responsibility of the guarantor.

Two consequences followed from this: first, the middleman was involved in the detailed terms of the specified transaction; and second, he was also taking a certain risk on the deal since, however carefully it was arranged, changes might occur outside the control of his client or himself that might make it impossible for the bargain to be honored. And as there was risk, commission was payable as a percentage charge on his agency.[21] This would seem to be in line with the institution of the government-licensed brokers at markets, who took fees for their services as agents, and it seems therefore to mesh with accepted traditional forms.[22] (It is also in line with the principles on which Chinese banking was conducted.)

Let us revert to the theme of the mediation of disputes, bearing in mind particularly the commercial transactions just discussed. Reference

---

* Authorities differ on whether this was one role or two separate roles. There seem to be two possible explanations: either that custom varied according to place or conditions of business, or that the role was in process of evolution at the time it was being observed.

was made above—in the section about the guilds—to the guild's function of norm-specification being thought of as a preliminary factor in conflict settlement. I will now suggest that the processes of negotiation —of both agreements and subsequent disagreements—should likewise be regarded as a continuity. It can be thought of perhaps as divided into stages, with the attainment of the later stages contingent upon some hitch having arisen in the earlier ones (see Table 1). Compare this with the sort of dispute that might come up for hearing in an artisan or occupational guild—say between two barbers, where one accuses the other of stealing his customers; or where coffin-maker A accuses B of taking too many apprentices; or where a master silk-weaver accuses an employee of moving to another employer and taking some of his raw materials. The sequence of actions might go as shown in Table 2 (slightly amplifying information given by Burgess.[23]

It is clear that the sequence shown in Table 1 represents a more dynamic process than that in Table 2, though it is likely that, over time, cases of the second type might also result in shifts in the normative order by rule revision.

No simple or necessary historical succession from one form of mediation/arbitration to the other is suggested. Both forms must have existed

TABLE 1. STAGES OF A SAMPLE NEGOTIATION

Stages	Actions
1.	An intermediary is approached by one or both potential parties to a transaction; he investigates the circumstances surrounding the contemplated deal.
2.	Negotiations and adjustments between the intermediary and both parties lead to a specification of terms satisfactory to all concerned.
3.	The parties signify their acceptance of the terms, and the intermediary guarantees that the terms will be honored.
4.	The failure of one party to fulfill its obligations creates a potential rift.
5.	The intermediary is called on to mediate; he investigates to see how circumstances have changed and what would now be a reasonable or practicable settlement.
6.	The intermediary suggests a compromise.
7.	The parties either accept the compromise and fulfill the obligations as adjusted (in which case the negotiation process is concluded) or refuse to accept it.
8.	Where mediation by the original intermediary has failed, the parties seek mediation by more influential persons—each party bringing to bear all the strength it can muster. This will probably produce a settlement, if the parties wish to continue in business or even to live in the same locality.
9.	Where mediation and negotiation have failed completely, one party might invoke the support of its guild, which would apply pressure to the other party by making life difficult in whatever ways were open to it—by withdrawing supplies, by physical action, or by denunciation in yamen court and official trial.

TABLE 2. STAGES OF A DISPUTE WITHIN A GUILD

Stages	Actions
1.	Fellow guild members try to conciliate the disputants but fail.
2.	Guild officials or guild members sitting as a court hear the parties to the dispute.
3.	The "court" determines which rules apply and attempts to interpret them to fit the case.
4.	The guild "court" suggests a solution to the parties. If the parties accept, the dispute is settled.
5.	Where the parties do not accept the guild's solution, further argument or sanctions follow until peace is restored.

side by side to meet different needs, though it seems at least probable that the volume of cases of the negotiated-compromise type must have increased over time as trade expanded and as the quickening tempo of social change made it more difficult for terms agreed on to be fulfilled.

Could it be said that we have here an embryonic or customary law of contract and of agency? Jamieson agreed with this conclusion. He also pointed to the treatment of guarantors as *vestiges* (perhaps therefore a transition stage) of the principle that a person's responsibilities were governed by his status.

The idea however that a middleman is somehow responsible for the contracts which he has been the means of bringing about still survives, but it may be assumed that as legal ideas become more definite it will disappear. Throughout Chinese law a man's responsibilities are largely governed by status, that is, the condition of life in which he was born or in which he has voluntarily placed himself. The march of events throughout the world has been to replace status by contract, and China cannot but follow the same path. The responsibility of a middleman has been implied from his position, but in future the question will be more frequently asked whether or not he has expressly contracted a responsibility, and if not he will be discharged.[24]

Another piece of evidence that might indicate that this was a form lying closer to contract than to status is the fact that, unlike most other personal responsibilities in China, the responsibility of the guarantor died with him—it was not passed on to his heirs.[25]

Leaving aside the question of the development and succession of the forms institutions took to return to the matter of mediation, it seems to me that the area of commercial transactions was the place of mediation and compromise settlement par excellence in Chinese society. This has not perhaps been sufficiently noticed in studies up to now, when we have stressed the readiness to accept compromise settlement as characteristic of Chinese law. It may be true that there was considerable incentive to keep disputes regarding family matters out of court and to settle them within and between lineages (or smaller kinship units) or otherwise by private mediation; but it is clear from recent work[26] that there was no reluctance on the part of yamen courts to pronounce (that is, to lay down the law unequivocally) on the rights and wrongs of cases arising in that field. These were not matters for compromise; in disputes arising from commercial transactions, however, informal settlement appears to have been the method chosen and permitted. The courts never developed machinery for dealing with the negotiation of claims and counterclaims; nor *could* they so long as they were burdened with the function of enforcing Confucian ethical norms. In matters of commerce, the logic of the whole situation drove people to rely on personal relationships (though they might be institutionalized with the support of custom and mediation) rather than on official law, and to aim at equitable settlement in the light of various considerations: the entitlement previously and specifically agreed on, the changes in circumstances that might make fulfillment impossible or inequitable, and the resources and other commitments of the parties. No wonder, then, that there was confusion about the role of the guarantor and whether he was guaranteeing man or money. He could only do the one through the other.[27]

Moreover, in a society of inveterate traders depending for their security and the expansion of their business largely on a mechanism that involved another person who negotiated on their behalf and underwrote part of their risk for a fee, one would expect to find this mechanism institutionalized and the people involved of some substance and standing in the community. A parallel was suggested above with the government-licensed brokers; and the hypothesis that this was indeed the model from which the role was developed occurred also to Jamieson.[28] If this is correct, an interesting and significant development must have occurred: an agent originally acting in the government's interest has been transformed into a private agent acting in the interests of his client (and himself, of course). He framed an agreement and guaranteed the terms, thus providing as a private person a security the imperial government failed to give. Could the explanation be that the superiority of unofficial organization for purposes of mediation resulted in more use being made of this private role, and its having become, through use, more specialized? And could this be a specialist role that, in the commercial field, provided a sort of substitute for the Western lawyer comparable to the "magistrate's law secretary" (*mu-yu*) in the criminal field?

Yet it was not completely private, for whereas the magistrate's adviser remained outside the official legal/judicial system, the guarantor was brought under administrative control by the license system. One who acted as guarantor was obliged himself to have the guarantee of another, so the role appears to have been semiprivate, semiofficial. As the intermediary/guarantor assumed a part in the role system and himself took on an obligation, namely the liability for the execution of the terms of the agreement, we seem to have here a form of relationship intermediate between status and contract. This probably goes a long way toward explaining why Chinese traders were preoccupied with keeping the widest possible range of personal contacts—a latent function of membership in ascriptive groups—for purposes of introduction, guarantee, and mediation.[29]

The pressures the guarantor/mediator could bring to bear would be a complex of intangibles—concern for his reputation and "face," for his self-interest and that of his clients, and for prospects of further trading—but their result would be quantifiable and negotiable, as distinct from adjudication in terms of right and wrong. Both parties and the guarantor had something to gain from the successful conclusion of a deal, and the interest of all concerned, for present and future, must generally have exercised the most powerful influence on the process of arriving at an acceptable compromise. Moreover, traders were likely to realize that they had much to gain by early settlement; involvement of others as mediators would only mean further expense and waste of time. The facts that the guarantor himself had to have a guarantor behind him, and that brokers (presumably specialists in the role) had their own guild in important trading centers, meant that other means of "persuasion" were available if difficulty was experienced in reaching a settlement. It seems that instead of developing an impersonal money market that would have required an impersonal system of law through which claims could be asserted, the Chinese improvised a chain of personal guarantors. Gentry connections might be utilized for mediation in case of dispute, and official connections would obviously have been useful in conferring immunity from official exactions.[30]

Besides the obligations arising from status in ascriptive groups and this type of contractual relationships between two parties, there were certain other ways of entering into relationship and undertaking ad hoc obligations by agreement. One was partnership—without limited liability, and therefore restricted in size because of the risks incurred. Another that was common all over China was the customary loan society based on mutuality. This was a form of enterprise in which a number of participants agreed to subscribe a sum of money at regular intervals for a specified period (fixed according to the number of those taking part): the initiator took the pool first and then the others followed in rotation, usually with a slight addition to allow for an element of interest. The transactions were regularly recorded in writing. These associations were called into being whenever someone was in need of money (or saw an opportunity for making good use of a little capital) and could find others with money to lend.[31] One can see that there must also have been practical limits on the scale to which such operations could be extended.

In the Chinese system of dispute settlement and enforcement of social obligation, the allocation of functions between institutions differed from that found in other advanced commercial communities. These differences resulted in developments that strike the Western readers as curious: for example, the custody of articles by pawnshops was subject to legal safeguards (i.e., preventing improper use of existing wealth) whereas the conduct of banks—apart from some ancient prohibitions against counterfeiting—was left almost entirely to guild regulation.[32] Since the registration and sale of land were matters over which the government exercised control, it might be thought that disputes between landlord and tenant would have come before the yamen court. Yet Doolittle reports as follows:

Chinese landlords oftentimes experience trouble in regard to the collection of rent for houses or land leased to tenants. The latter seem frequently to act on the principle that possession is nine points in law, and, after a few regular payments of rent-money according to contract, begin to offer less than the sum agreed upon. If this sum is received, the amount tendered is often lessened the next time, or the day of payment is delayed. Unkind words follow; and as litigation is proverbially dubious in regard to the justness and the promptness of the magistrate, very much depending on the amount of bribe-money presented to his honour and his satellites, landlords usually shrink from invoking the law, and resort to the established custom of ordering the obnoxious or dilatory incumbent away, giving him the privilege of remaining three months without rent from the date of the notification. Landlords who serve this notice are content to have the premises vacated at the time intimated, not demanding the arrearage of rent, however great it may be.[33]

It seems likely that the intended reference here is to an urban setting (the mention of land would not preclude this in China, as cities usually included some agricultural land within the walls), since knowledge of the demand for land might be supposed to have encouraged rural tenants to meet their obligations, and since the system of paying a share of the crop as rent would have made those obligations difficult to avoid. It sounds as though a money rent payable to an unfamiliar landlord formed the subject of Doolittle's passage. If the city were large, it might have been more difficult for landlords to form a ring than it would have been for suppliers of other commodities. This passage thus indicates a flaw in the system of guaranteeing agreements and compromise settlements from at least one point of view.

It should not be thought, of course, that no traders ever defaulted on their obligations. The underworld of crime and banditry testifies to the contrary, though how far such roles were filled by specifically urban recruitment is difficult to assess. At least one may say that traders had reason to abide by the rules so as to continue in business, and one can find reports of good faith being respected. Any who were drummed out of the trade by their guilds no doubt added to the numbers of vagrants, some of whom may have become lawless. Viewed as a whole, the system of social control appears in the main to have worked effectively to promote the orderly conduct of business and to permit a measure of expansion (though from the point of view of many, especially the most enterprising, it must always have been felt as restrictive). Jernigan and most other writers on the subject of commerce in the nineteenth century give a favorable overall impression of the way things worked generally.[34] Interestingly, some well worked out ideas, almost parallel to some of those advanced above, have been put forward by Donald R. DeGlopper in a thesis on the general subject of conflict resolution in China.[35] He contrasts two models. The first was based on Confucianism, which, by refusing to recognize the legitimacy of conflict at all, treated all conflict as reprehensible; this was applied within the state and within bounded ascriptive groups such as the lineage, especially where solidarity was required, as in circumstances of interlineage rivalry and feuding (and, one might add, commercial rivalries). In the second type, conflict developed between people who were not related in the ways just mentioned; here the parties appealed to whatever influential people they could call on among the crosscutting groups and segments around them, and neither the issues nor the settlement could be clear-cut. Beyond the range of acquaintance within which appeal to "face" operated, a relationship had to be established by means of a third party who would introduce, guarantee, and mediate if necessary for the contracting parties; this third party would then represent society in general.

It is not possible here to do justice to DeGlopper's thinking, nor is this the place to comment on it beyond suggesting perhaps that, though the Confucian refusal to admit the legitimacy of conflict is undoubtedly an important element in the situation, other institutional factors also have to be taken into account: other societies have invented new doctrines to suit new circumstances.

The mix of the different kinds of power that supported norms and enforced decisions clearly varied in different situations. It seems correct to make a distinction between the model that operated in the main according to normative/coercive power in varying blends and that operated by normative/remunerative power—i.e., by appeal to "face" and self-interest. Let us look, for example, at the mutual loan society referred to above. Its members would have known one another well and would have seen to it that none among them evaded his responsibilities (mainly normative/coercive, with a trace of remunerative, since they might want to repeat the process in the future). Compare that situation with a credit transaction, probably between a rural borrower and an urban lender. Here there would assuredly have been a third party involved to introduce the parties and, since he shared liability, to bring pressure to bear to see that the debt was cleared (mainly remunerative/coercive with overtones of normative).

One can hypothesize that wherever possible the attempt would have been made to shift a normative/coercive situation toward a remunerative one in which bargaining was possible, and that even within ascriptive groups there might have been an attempt to submit a matter to prestigious mediators rather than to authoritative seniors by a sort of feedback effect from one model to the other.

Yet reliance on unspecified mediators, though no doubt acceptable if not inevitable in many other spheres where disagreements were unpredictable, would not have produced sufficiently clear-cut or predictable solutions for purposes of commerce, perhaps for the reasons that De-Glopper suggests (namely, that disputes were not always disposed of but were sometimes transformed into more lasting and large-scale conflicts). Hence the choice before the transaction was entered into of a negotiator acceptable to both parties would have had an extra advantage in commercial dealings.

Did the mediator represent society or the public? His involvement would certainly have prevented the matter from being entirely a private one between two parties striving to assert their own interests as perceived subjectively. His engagement was private, in the sense that he was chosen by the parties as someone trusted and acceptable to both, but the formalities were not of their invention and for all important transactions his role was technically brought within the ambit of administrative control. Mediation, it is perhaps worth saying, is to some extent always a moral process;* there must be some standards to which to appeal, even if only in terms of respectability and reputation for the sake of future prospects, so an element of social control is inevitably involved, for how else is reputation to be maintained?[36] The relevant question to be asked is "Of what range of generality are the standards that are being applied?" Even an argument in terms of the mediator's reputation—"face"—implies a degree of generality.

It remains to consider the relevance of the hierarchy of central places to matters discussed in this paper. I shall refer first to "legislative" functions—that is, the formulation of norms—and then to jurisdiction.

First, it might be hypothesized that, in general, with ascent in the scale of central places, the work of formulating norms was undertaken by agencies of increasing functional specificity, or, in associations of the *Landsmannschaft* type, probably of increasingly specific local origin. However, besides the increase in scale and volume of activities and in numbers of persons involved, other random factors may have been at work (e.g., special features of geographical location), so the trend may not have corresponded exactly to the hierarchy of central places.

Second, as the quest for improved social status drew upwardly mobile persons toward centers progressively higher in the urban hierarchy, the norms of the groups the new townsmen or sojourners were obliged by their own necessities to form or join provided them with a code of conduct to be observed—if they were to be accepted and to profit from the wider opportunities offered in the town or city. Thus, in toto, such codes may be said to have served as an ethic of mobility and a factor facilitating the process of increasing urbanization.

Third, it seems likely that the proportion of activities governed by obligations of the contractual type and subject to third-party negotiations would have increased *pari passu* with ascent in the scale of trading centers and, by implication, in the degree of urbanization (provided, of course, that this urbanization happened as the result of spontaneous growth and not of administrative convenience).

Fourth, role specialization connected with contractual relationships would have followed the same ladder, the intermediary role found in

---

* In the International Sociological Association's *The Nature of Conflicts* (Paris: UNESCO, 1957), there is a statement of the preconditions for effective mediation that can be summarized as follows: (1) the issues should be clear; (2) the parties involved must be self-conscious; (3) a decision must be necessary for the functioning of the social system; that is, a crisis of some kind is involved (as contrasted with more diffuse accommodation in reduction of prejudices, intercultural education, and so forth); (4) parties must have faith in the integrity of the mediator; (5) they must inhabit the same moral universe; (6) they must want a solution.

small market centers becoming that of the broker, with a separate guild and more specialized line of business, in larger trading centers.

As regards jurisdiction specifically, transfer of cases upward through the ascending levels of the hierarchy of places would have been most significant for those cases—however they originated—that did reach the yamen to be dealt with by the coercive authority of the administration; and then, according to the seriousness with which matters were officially regarded, cases would have been transferred to higher authorities according to the measure of their competence. This would obviously have routed them by the administrative significance of places, which was not necessarily the same thing as progress up the ladder of economic central places as seen from a Skinnerian point of view.

At an earlier stage, transfer from ascriptive group to yamen probably happened in a number of different circumstances. Among them the following are suggested as examples: instances where some extra power of coercion was needed against an offender who did not prove amenable to other forms of group pressure; where conflict developed between two rival ascriptive groups of the same type; where a guild was fairly evenly divided in its counsels and one faction could not prevail against another (though one would think that fairly strenuous efforts would have been made to avoid this); and perhaps where the local magistrate was strong—whether through personal qualities or factors in the local situation—relative to the guild.

In cases that required mediation, when the chosen mediator was not successful in offering an acceptable solution, other more influential persons would have been called on to try to produce one; and in the nature of things it is likely that the chain of persons so brought in would have owed their persuasive power to experience or position in progressively wider circles, circles likely to be correlated with the Skinnerian hierarchy of economic centers and systems. But because mediation depended on essentially personal factors—acquaintance and connections to establish communication, and persuasion of and acceptance by the parties involved—there must have been practical limits to the possibility of extension in this manner. It seems certain that a point must soon have been reached at which remoteness and unfamiliarity with the persons concerned would have reduced the usefulness of a potential mediator; so, for the best chance of successful mediation it is likely that ascent would have halted just before that level. Moreover, as the process of third-party mediation became more remote from the original disputants, there must, one assumes, have been a gradual shift toward more authoritative pronouncements on the case (i.e., arbitration), however much coercion may have been disguised by a show of prestige or

Urban Social Control

by argument on principle. And in cases where the arbitrator owed his influence to bureaucratic connections, this factor might have been another reason for deviation from the economic hierarchy. Of course, if mediation failed completely and rupture of relations led to violence and then criminal trial, this would have constituted a linkage between the two modes, and such cases would of course have followed the yamen court hierarchy as described above.

We have discussed the different modes of control governing the lives of people in Chinese towns and cities in late imperial times, with particular attention to the areas of commerce and artisan-level industry.

As happened generally in China, people's lives were subject to control by organization of two kinds, with some overlap existing between the two: on the one hand, local and particularistic groups and associations, in which most of life was lived, that devised their own rules and procedures and enforced them by customary mechanisms; on the other hand, the official state administration governing by statute, courts and bureaucracy, which was normally somewhat remote unless stirred to action by specific appeals or disturbances. Together, and to some extent in conjunction, the two types of organization attempted to enforce the normative order—made up of morality, rules, and statutes—and in practice they no doubt did so to the extent that their real power allowed, for such a comprehensive system of control naturally stimulated techniques of evasion.

Though there was a long tradition of government intervention in economic affairs in China—with the exceptions noted of salt and iron, whose production and trade were always subject to government control—we find the detailed regulation of much of commerce and industry and the adjustment of disputes in this sphere left mainly to guilds, occasionally in consultation with the administration. In some other of their activities, town and city dwellers came within the scope of local temple organizations.

Traditionally in China a person's obligations depended mainly on status—as subject, as subordinate, or as member of this or that group—and were enforced by the group or association concerned, or occasionally by yamen courts. From the viewpoint of a person subject to (1) the discipline of seniors within the family, (2) the authority of whatever groups he belonged to, and (more remotely) (3) the authority of the imperial administration, it must have appeared that both official and unofficial systems exercised an authoritative type of control over him (depending, we can see, on a blend of normative and coercive power, though this might have been disguised as prestige or influence).

However, obligations of another kind could be entered into by means of agreements concluded according to customary forms. This variant represented a more dynamic and flexible means of control than authoritative regulation, something more akin to contractual than to status obligations. Terms could be negotiated according to the interests of the parties, and conditions of performance, the liability of each party, and penalties for nonfulfillment could be specified ad hoc. In cases of this type, negotiations were conducted through an intermediary, who himself guaranteed the agreed terms for a fee and who could later be called in as mediator if difficulty or dispute arose. It can be seen that adjustment of claims in this way by negotiation involved a power mix including a remunerative element and lesser (and variable) amounts of normative and coercive power.

Since the official legal system never developed mechanisms to provide security against business risks, such assurance had to depend on a system of personal (but not arbitrary) guarantees and negotiation. The state was involved only to the extent that it required the guarantor of an agreement himself to have a guarantor. The importance of the intermediary/guarantor function—the culmination of an interesting historical development and still probably in a transitional stage in late imperial times—suggests a specialist role in the commercial sphere comparable to the functions performed in the West by professional lawyers. A parallel development in the field of criminal law was the position of the *mu-yu*, the magistrate's adviser.

Finally some tentative correlations were suggested between the modes of social control employed and the hierarchy of central places established by Skinner. Matters of concern to the Confucian state—family affairs (particularly succession and inheritance), crimes of violence and crimes against the state, and ritual offenses—were subject to control by authority, and jurisdiction over them followed the administrative hierarchy. However, commercial matters (apart from the salt trade and the production of iron) tended to be left in practice to control by unofficial organization, whose dependence on local and personal connections set limits to its expansion. Variations that might be demonstrated, it has been suggested, were the increasing proportion of obligations of the negotiable type (relative to those dealt with by authoritative regulation) and the increasing specialization in the norm-specification function with ascent in the hierarchy of central places.

Social Structure in a Nineteenth-Century Taiwanese Port City

DONALD R. DEGLOPPER

> The Chinese urban dweller legally belonged to his family and native village in which the temple of his ancestors stood, and to which he conscientiously maintained affiliation—*Max Weber*, THE CITY, p. 81

Max Weber, working with inadequate data, was wrong about the social structure of the Chinese city. In *The City* he argued that there was in China no urban community, for the lineage and the ancestor cult ("the magical closure of the clans") precluded the formation of civic confederations.[1] Since Weber wrote, however, practically every study of urban overseas Chinese settlements has discussed the urban community and its civic confederations.[2] Still, the questions Weber raised—essentially about the character of urban corporate groups and about the relations of such groups to each other and to the occupants of political offices—provided the stimulus for this account of the social structure of a nineteenth-century Taiwanese port city.

My account is imperfect. It is based on eighteen months' residence in Lu-kang and on subsequent research in the Cornell University Library.[3] It relies on the projection of some contemporary patterns into the past, on old men's tales of the days of their fathers, on my acquaintance with the physical structure of the city, which has changed but little, and on my interpretation of the scanty documentary material on Lu-kang's past—material that consists largely of Ch'ing local gazetteers and histories, Japanese statistical compilations, and contemporary memoirs and brief notes on folklore.[4] The primary justification for this exercise is the absence in the literature of accounts of the internal structure of particular Chinese cities. Only when we know something about the internal order of a number of cities and about the kinds of variations in their structures may we proceed beyond the delusively simple picture of "the Chinese city" that trapped Weber.

Lu-kang lies halfway down the west coast of Taiwan. First settled in the late seventeenth century, it was from the 1770's to the 1880's the second largest city in Taiwan. The proverbial expression "First T'ai-nan, second Lu-kang, third Meng-chia [Taipei]" refers to this period. The city's growth in the mid-eighteenth century, and its precipitous decline in the late nineteenth and early twentieth centuries were consequences of its location and its function as a node of the large-scale trading system that exchanged the rice and other agricultural produce of central Taiwan for the cloth and other manufactured goods of southern Fukien. Nearly all the trade was funneled through Lu-kang. The city was built on the mouth of a small river; and as ports go, it was not a good one. The river mouth tended to silt up and could only be approached by a shifting channel that wound through the offshore shoals and sandbanks. Through most of the nineteenth century, the river could only be entered by small junks at high tide with a favorable wind. There are no natural harbors on the west coast of central Taiwan, and during the period from about 1725 to 1775, when Chinese settlers brought the rich Chang-hua Plain under cultivation and trade with Fukien burgeoned, Lu-kang was the best of the many river-mouth anchorages along the coast. Furthermore, the Ch'ing government was much concerned to regulate and tax the junk trade in the Taiwan Strait. It recognized only a few legal routes across the Strait, and ships could only sail from designated ports, each the seat of an official who inspected and taxed the cargo. In 1785, Lu-kang and Han-chiang on Ch'üan-chou Bay were established as legal ports for direct trade, the others being T'ai-wan-fu [Tainan], linked with Amoy, and Tan-shui, linked with Foochow.[5]

Although it was the largest city and the unquestioned commercial center of its region, Lu-kang was not an administrative seat and never had a wall. When Chang-hua *hsien* was established in 1723, its capital, Chang-hua, was built seven miles inland from Lu-kang. Chang-hua remained the capital, although several high civil and military officials suggested at various times that the county seat be moved to Lu-kang. Lu-kang, however, was not bereft of officials, and at one point it had three, two civil and one military. In 1731 the authorities of Fukien declared Lu-kang a port legally open for trade along the coast of Taiwan (Taiwan was until 1885 a prefecture of Fukien) and posted a deputy subprefect (*hsün-chien*, civil rank 9b) to the city to supervise trade. In 1811 this office was transferred up the coast to Ta-chia. In 1785 a subprefect (*t'ung-chih*, civil rank 5a) was posted to Lu-kang to oversee the trade with Ch'üan-chou. He outranked the county magistrate and was a direct subordinate of the prefect of T'ai-wan *fu*, the island's highest official. There had been a minor coast-guard station at Lu-kang since the Ch'ing conquest of the island in 1683, but in 1789 a battalion (*ying*) of 708 troops, commanded by a major (*yu-chi*, military rank 3b), was installed in a mud-walled fort overlooking the harbor.

There are few detailed descriptions of Lu-kang in its prime. In 1774 Chu Ching-ying's *Record of the Eastern Sea* observed: "Lu-kang is a port where many small ships come and go to trade. It has several thousand households; sails and masts crowd together; brokers and wholesalers are settled there."[6] The *Chang-hua hsien chih*, compiled in 1831, says that "At Lu-kang streets and lanes meet and cross like hairbands. The main street extends for three *li* (about a mile), and there are many businesses of the Ch'üan-chou and Amoy guilds. It is a place where ships and carts come together like spokes converging at the hub of a wheel, and all sorts of goods can be had in abundance. Apart from T'ai-wan-fu [Tainan] it is the most important market of the island."[7]

Economic stagnation during the Japanese period (1895–1945) and the benign neglect of the U.S. Air Force during 1945 have meant that Lu-kang today preserves its nineteenth-century street pattern and a good many of the buildings of that time. Shaped like a leaf, or perhaps a fish, the city lies along the old river channel, now filled in, with its head at the northwest, facing the Taiwan Strait, and its tail to the southeast, where the main street becomes the road to Chang-hua. The main street runs the length of the city like a backbone. Before the Japanese colonial government's "urban renewal" in 1934, which widened the street by cutting off the front segments of all the houses on the south side, the main street was eight feet wide, covered with a permanent wooden roof, and punctuated with three internal gates that were closed at night. Smaller lanes, also with gates, cut across or paralleled the main street. Substantial two- or three-story brick and tile houses—narrow and very long, with two or three internal courtyards—still line the main street and some of the smaller lanes. The houses of the great merchants are built like fortresses; there are no windows on the ground floor, which was used for storage and shops, and there are small windows directly above the front door from which rocks and boiling water could be hurled at thieves or bandits attempting to break in. The city was, and to a large extent still is, a compact huddle of red-brick buildings; the only open spaces are the small squares and paved plazas in front of the many temples. The houses face inward, away from the flat and windswept countryside, and the city as a whole is a labyrinth of foregrounds, walls, facades, and enclosures. A good Occidental analogy would be Venice without the water.

There are no reliable figures on the size of the city's population in the mid-nineteenth century. A figure of 100,000 people is often cited in today's publications, and some natives of the city, who may well have read these articles and essays, use the same number. I consider it an overestimate. The first Japanese count in 1896 put Lu-kang's population at 20,420.[8] Though there was substantial outmigration from the city in the last quarter of the nineteenth century, it is hard to imagine where 80,000 Lu-kang people might have gone when Taipei, the island's largest city, had but 69,000 people in 1900. I would estimate Lu-kang's population in the mid-1800's at around 20,000, and consider it most unlikely to have been less than 10,000 or more than 30,000.

In Lu-kang's prime, the city people did not have very close ties with the immediate hinterland. The city is located in that littoral zone that receives less rain and more wind than anywhere else on Taiwan—a sparsely populated area of poverty-stricken sweet-potato farmers and fishermen. In the past, as now, the richest farmland lay inland at the foot of the hills, where there was more rain, less wind, and better soil, and where small streams could be tapped easily for irrigation. The produce from these areas was transported to Lu-kang by porters, oxcarts, and bamboo rafts and small coasting vessels. Lu-kang employed thousands of porters and longshoremen, at least some of whom were permanent residents of the city rather than seasonal rural migrants. As the trade with Fukien developed in the eighteenth century, well-to-do merchants came over from Ch'üan-chou and to a lesser extent from Amoy, and these men had no ties with the farming villages of the Changhua Plain. Their native places were urban, and they brought with them the mercantile culture of the coastal cities of southern Fukien. Lu-kang developed quickly during the Ch'ien-lung period (1736–95), and the bulk of its population came to consist of immigrants or descendants of immigrants from Fukien. They traded with the rustics, but they did not worship with them or marry them. If they identified themselves with some ancestral village, that village was on the other side of the Strait, not in the Taiwanese countryside.

In the eighteenth century, Lu-kang's population was divided into groups defined by place of origin on the mainland, and each such group had its own temple and patron god. It is claimed that the first settlers at Lu-kang were from the Fukien coastal prefecture of Hsing-hua. Today there still exists the small Hsing-hua Ma-tsu temple, which according to oral tradition was founded in the 1680's or 1690's. Other settlers came from the Fukien prefectures of Ch'üan-chou and Chang-chou, and from Ch'ao-chou in northeastern Kwangtung. The Ch'ao-chou men appear to have been Hakka, for their temple, which still exists, is dedicated to San-shan Kuo-wang, a deity peculiar to Ch'ao-chou Hakka.

The temple contains a stone inscribed with a 1791 edict assuring Kwangtung people resident in Taiwan that they may return to their native places without penalty, and informing them that they may obtain the necessary documents, at a set fee, from the Lu-kang subprefect.[9] At some unrecorded date early in the eighteenth century, the Ch'üan-chou settlers founded a temple dedicated to Ma-tsu. Today it is claimed that the image in this temple was presented to the Ch'üan-chou settlers by Admiral Shih Liang, who conquered Taiwan for the Ch'ing dynasty in 1683. Then in 1783 the merchants from Chang-chou built the Nan-ching Kuan-ti temple (Nan-ching was a county in Chang-chou *fu*).

The eighteenth-century division of the populace by place of origin did not long endure. By the end of the century Lu-kang was considered a predominately Ch'üan-chou city, whereas most of the inhabitants of Chang-hua were Chang-chou men. The Hsing-hua, Hakka, and Chang-chou people had either left the city or been assimilated to the dominant Ch'üan-chou group, speaking with their accent, marrying with them, and joining with them in the armed conflicts between Hokkien and Hakka, Ch'üan-chou and Chang-chou, which were so frequent in nineteenth-century Taiwan. The non–Ch'üan-chou peoples' temples still exist but today function as neighborhood temples, and the people who live around them are either ignorant of or quite uninterested in the original ethnicity or provenance of their neighborhood gods. In the nineteenth century, groups defined by common place of origin played no part in Lu-kang's social structure.

This brings me to the topic of this essay—social structure in nineteenth-century Lu-kang. I use the term social structure to refer to the major, enduring corporate groups and to the patterned relations among them. I thus exclude families, kinship, particularistic business relations, personal networks, sworn brotherhoods, factions, and many other elements that were doubtless to be found in old Lu-kang. I do this because there does not exist enough information to say anything worthwhile about them. With a past made simple by the loss of detail, an account of corporate groups and formal rituals is the best I can offer from available materials.

The settlers of Lu-kang came from a part of China well known for its large corporate lineages, and descent groups were an important element in the city's social structure. As was often the case in Taiwan, though, Lu-kang's descent groups were not replicas or segments of the lineages of Fukien. The groups in Lu-kang held no common property, had no ancestral halls, lacked complete written genealogies, and were apparently less "corporate"—however that term may be defined—than the classic southeastern Chinese lineages. Today they are usually referred to simply as *hsing*, "surnames," and they are probably best labeled as clans or surname groups. Three major surnames, Shih, Huang, and Hsü, account for at least half of the city's present population. Other names, such as Lin, Ch'en, Wu, Li, and Ts'ai, are quite common. In speaking of the past, people refer to the three big surnames, Shih, Huang, and Hsü, and these are the only ones to which some degree of solidarity and corporate character are ascribed. Each surname is associated with a particular quarter of the city. In the past the great surnames fought with each other, and this is the activity for which they are best remembered. A proverb current in Lu-kang says: "Shihs, Huangs, and Hsüs; the women all are shrews." This is explained as meaning that women from the three major surnames made bad, quarrelsome wives, for they were proud and unwilling to accept the authority of their husbands' families. The internal organization of each major group differed, and it is best to begin by briefly describing each in turn.

The largest group, the Shihs, most closely resemble the classic lineage. All Shihs claim descent from a common ancestor, one Shih Lin-pu, a man of Honan who was an official in the last years of the T'ang dynasty. Men today know which generation of the lineage they belong to. All Lu-kang Shihs stem from Ya-k'ou *hsiang*, in Chin-chiang, the metropolitan *hsien* of Ch'üan-chou prefecture. They are divided internally into two main segments (usually referred to as *p'ai*), each of which has a name. They are the Ch'ien-chiang and the Hsin-hai, also known as the Ch'ien-kang and Hou-kang, "Front and Rear Harbors." Today these two segments are said to descend from two brothers who lived three hundred years ago in Fukien. These segments in turn are further divided into branches (*fang*). The smallest, lowest-level groups are called *thiau* in Taiwanese Hokkien. This term, whose Mandarin reading is *chu*, has the primary meaning of a pillar or post, and is commonly used in central Taiwan to refer to a small, shallow, agnatic group, such as the descendants of a common grandfather or great-grandfather. There are in Lu-kang between twenty and thirty Shih *thiau*, each named after a street or neighborhood. Thus one speaks of the Ch'ien-chiang Shihs of Ax Street or of the Hsin-hai Shihs of Behind the Temple. It is significant that for the smallest subunit, the *thiau*, residence rather than descent is used as a criterion for membership, for a *thiau* has no genealogical charter. When asked, some older men said that if a man moved to a different neighborhood, once he got to know his new neighbors he would become a member of that vicinity's *thiau*. With reference to this seeming ambiguity of criteria for membership, we must keep in mind that *thiau* never held any common property and that their most common joint activity seems to have been fighting with equivalent small groups of Huangs or Hsüs. There is thus no pressing need for strict rules to determine just who is eligible for membership and who is not.

The Huangs, the second most numerous surname, recognize no common ancestor. They are subdivided into five groups, each said to have come from a different place in Fukien. Each group is said to occupy its own neighborhood and is usually known by the name of that neighborhood, so that one speaks of the Ch'üan-chou Street Huangs. The third of the great surnames, the Hsüs, are most easily described, for they are said to have no formal organization whatsoever. They came from different places on the mainland, have no genealogy or ritual focus, and have never had any common property. Most of the Hsüs live in one neighborhood of Lu-kang.

Here it must be understood that the association between surnames and neighborhoods is not absolute, and that the city is not segregated residentially by surname. In a neighborhood identified with a given surname often no more than half the residents will bear that name. There are Ch'ens, Lins, Kuos, Wangs, and Wus living all over the city, sometimes in small clusters of their own, and it is quite likely that any family's next-door neighbors will bear a different surname. Except for the Kuos, who live in a neighborhood called Kuo Village, only the three big surnames are associated with specific named neighborhoods, in which they may constitute from 40 to 80 percent of the inhabitants.

Today the surname groups are best remembered for their battles with one another. In 1891, T'ang Tsan-kun wrote in his *Record of Things Seen in Taiwan* that "[In Lu-kang] there are three big surnames, with some 40,000 to 50,000 adult males in all. Each, because of its great strength, goes so far as to start fights."[10] The fighting seems to have resembled that between the lineages of Ch'üan-chou, which was described by Amyot as being "about everything and about nothing.... The use of a water passage, field boundaries, or personal insults."[11] In Lu-kang today the usual explanation for fighting between surname groups is that since they did not like each other they fought, and the more they fought the less they liked each other. Members of the big surname groups were said to have been very touchy, and to have gone around elbowing members of minor surname groups out of their way and looking for confrontations with men of other major groups. A chance insult in the market could result in an appointment to fight the next morning at a certain place. From twenty up to a hundred or so men might take part in such affrays, which usually resulted in nothing worse than bruises, lost teeth, or an occasional broken bone. Battles between surname groups seem to have been a common feature of life in nineteenth-century cities in central Taiwan, for in 1867 the British merchant and linguist W. A. Pickering found himself in the middle of a fight between the Ch'ens and the Ts'ais in Wu-ch'i, a minor port seventeen miles north of Lu-kang.[12]

In Lu-kang the battles between surname groups seem to have resulted in few deaths, for the conflicts were limited in many ways. The relations between the city's major surname groups appear to have been marked by pervasive but low-keyed hostility, by gossip, rude stories, and occasional brawls. But there was never any concerted effort to decisively defeat another surname group or drive it out of the city, as the Ch'üan-chou men from San I (the three counties of Chin-chiang, Hui-an, and Nan-an) drove those from T'ung-an *hsien* from Meng-chia in the 1860's. The parties to any single brawl or fight were the neighborhood surname groups, the *thiau*, rather than the entire body of people bearing particular surnames. For example, there are many stories of the Shihs from the area around the vegetable market fighting with the Huangs from the area around the New Ma-tsu Temple, but never were these groups joined by others of the same surname.

Of course, since surname groups were not property-holding units, as were guilds, temples, and charitable foundations, there was less reason to decisively defeat a rival group—for nothing material was at stake. Furthermore, the surname groups of Lu-kang were not the equivalents of the lineages of Fukien and Kwangtung. Mainland lineages were often entire villages or communities, whereas the surname groups of Lu-kang were categories that cut across class, occupation, and neighborhood boundaries. A serious and protracted contest between surname groups would have pitted against each other members of the same guild, the managing committees of temples and schools, in-laws, and the rich, and would presumably have disrupted the life and commerce of the city. Even had the merchants been willing to put up with some loss of livelihood for the honor of their surname group, the resident officials who depended on the taxes and extralegal fees they levied on Lu-kang's commerce would presumably have intervened against large-scale violence between surname groups.

If the matter is seen in this light, it is not surprising that the only occasion on which the entire body of Shihs, Huangs, and Hsüs came together was in a very well defined and circumscribed, near-ritual, combat. This was the famous Lu-kang rock fight, which went on until the beginning of World War II. Each year on a certain day in the early spring members of all the major surname groups would gather on a field at the edge of the city to fight. According to elderly men who took part in it in their youth, the men would form up around the edges of the field, facing inward and toward each other. Although the three big surnames provided the bulk of the combatants, members of less populous groups like the Wangs and the Lis also took part. There was no fixed arrangement, save that men of the same surname stood together; and where any particular group stood, or whom they stood next to or opposite from, does not seem to have made any difference. Rather than taking the form of two matched sides, the annual battle was one of each surname group against all. The participants began by throwing rocks at each other and then eventually moved in and fought with fists and sticks. Most of the participants were young, but anyone who wanted to could take part, and some old men carefully prepared slings and throwing sticks to compensate for their loss of strength.

I was assured that no one was ever killed in the melee, and that those injured were healed by using water from the ponds in front of certain temples. "People were tougher then than they are now. If somebody got cut or bruised, or lost some teeth, he would drop out, wash his injury off, apply a plaster made of tobacco leaves and water buffalo dung, and then go back and fight some more." The day of the rock fight is described as having been a festive holiday, very exciting. Thousands of spectators turned out to watch; hawkers sold snacks; beggars did well; and a good time was apparently had by all.

The most common reply to questions about why the men of Lu-kang lined up by surname once a year to throw rocks at their fellow citizens is that "It was an old Lu-kang custom." A satisfactory explanation of this most peculiar local custom is beyond the scope of this essay, and here I will simply point out that the vernal brawl may be interpreted as a ritual, since it had no victors, was an annual event, and was restricted by time, place, and intent to do serious or lethal harm to the other participants. Participation was also limited, for only inhabitants of the city took part; residents of nearby villages were excluded, as they still are excluded from Lu-kang's public, collective rituals. As ritual, the battle defined both the limits of the community and one of the sets of segments into which the community was seen as divided. The only common activity of surname groups was gathering once a year to throw rocks at each other.

This tells us two important things about the surname groups of Lu-kang. First, their solidarity was low and their members had few interests in common. The surname groups were arbitrarily defined segments of the population of a commercial city—a population marked by a high degree of division of labor and by distinctions of wealth and education. Fighting, or just feeling antagonistic toward each other, was one of the few means available to bolster their dubious internal solidarity. Second, the surname groups were defined primarily by opposition to each other, and this mutual opposition was more important than their internal organization. The Hsüs, with nothing but their name in common, were the social and functional equals of the Shihs, with their numbered generations, internal segmentation, and links to a real and immense lineage (40,000 people in 30 villages, according to Amyot[13]). If this is the case, then the profound lack of interest I found in 1968 in such matters as genealogical reckoning, segmentation, and ways that *thiau* fit into *fang* becomes more understandable. In the context of Lu-kang, what mattered about the surname groups was that they were associated with certain neighborhoods and fought each other. In anthropological terms, alliance theory, which focuses on groups as parts of systems and on the exchanges that define the relations of the groups to each other, seems more relevant here than descent theory, which focuses on the internal structure and continuity over generations of groups like lineages.

The theme of limited opposition between equivalent groups within the city, which was most crudely expressed in the ritual (though not mock) battle between surname groups, characterized the relations between neighborhoods and guilds as well. Neighborhoods expressed their competition primarily in rituals and festivities, whereas guilds were involved in more straightforward commercial and political rivalry.

Lu-kang is divided into an indefinite number of named neighborhoods —indefinite because of the possibility of making ever-finer territorial distinctions, especially in the vicinity of a person's own home.[14] Physically the city was one compact mass of houses, and any internal subdivisions were arbitrary. In the last century the streets were closed off at night by internal gates, which may or may not have served to define neighborhoods or wards. Sometimes, at least, the gates did serve to demarcate sociologically meaningful units. The main street had a gate at each end, and three along its three-*li* length, thus forming four segments. Every household along the street participated in the cult of San-shan Kuo-wang, the onetime Hakka temple halfway along the street. Each year one of the segments defined by the gates took responsibility for the temple's annual festival, thus forming a four-year cycle.

Today neighborhoods are not segregated by class, and there is no reason to assume that they were one hundred years ago, either. And although some are associated with certain surnames, the identification has never been complete, and the major surnames do not form compact residential blocs but are scattered throughout the city like islands. Besides having names, some neighborhoods are considered to have special characteristics. One is where the woodworkers live, another is the home of the oystermen, another has a distinctive accent. There are local proverbs such as "End of the Street for opera; Market Garden for pigs." This means that the people of the first neighborhood are especially fond of opera and always have one or more in their festivals, whereas festivals in the second are marked by the slaughter and display of large pigs. One can identify someone as "a man of An-p'ing Street," and people today have a strong sense of neighborhood identity.

In the past most natives of Lu-kang married other Lu-kang people, though marriages with people from the villages around Lu-kang were not totally unknown. The wealthy were more likely to take their brides from, or marry their daughters off to, equally wealthy families in the other market towns and minor cities of central Taiwan. But on the whole, most marriages were within the city and between people of different neighborhoods. In abstract terms one can speak of a tendency toward endogamy for Lu-kang and toward neighborhood exogamy. Neighborhoods would thus be linked by exchange of women, and a person's network of matrilateral and affinal kin was likely to be confined to Lu-kang but to extend to several other neighborhoods.

Neighborhoods were ritually focused on temples, or on incense burners that circulated from house to house.[15] Every household contributed to the cost of the annual festival and to periodic fund drives to rebuild or refurbish the local temple. At least once a year the patron deity was carried on a tour of his district, expelling evil influences and being greeted by each householder with incense. On the day of the annual festival, every household hosted a banquet to which guests from other neighborhoods came; and the gods of other neighborhood temples could be invited as "guests." Apart from this activity, two distinct sets of festivals linked all the neighborhoods of Lu-kang in ritual exchange, competition, and emulation. Each demonstrated the solidarity of neighborhoods and their ritual interdependence, and underlined the limitation of that interdependence to the city itself.

The first of these was the great festival of the hungry ghosts in the seventh lunar month. In Lu-kang the festival lasted for the entire month. On the first, seventh, fifteenth, and thirtieth days, all of Lu-kang, every household, feted the hungry ghosts. On the other days a different neighborhood put on a festival each day. Thus every day in the seventh month one or another neighborhood was the scene of opera performances, rituals by Taoists, and elaborate domestic banquets to which guests from other neighborhoods were invited. The rotating festival, an orgy of hospitality and food exchange among townspeople—the living and the hungry ghosts—was confined to Lu-kang and its natives, and the inhabitants of the surrounding villages played no part in it. During the seventh month the guilds sponsored temple celebrations and processions, and on the fifteenth the eight guilds cooperated in a huge ceremony at the Lung-shan Ssu, a Buddhist temple founded in 1785 by the men of the Ch'üan-chou Guild. Beggars did well during the seventh month, as it was their habit or right to take the food set out for the hungry ghosts. On the first day of the eighth month, they had their own celebration, a riotous occasion of license and clowning, eagerly watched by the respectable citizens of Lu-kang.

The internal differentiation of Lu-kang and the solidarity of its neighborhoods and larger territorial units was demonstrated every few years with competitive street processions. For the purposes of this event the city was divided into two halves, the Uptown and the Downtown, the line bisecting the city midway along the main street. On any major ritual occasion, such as the renovation of an old temple or the installation of a new image in one of the several temples common to all Lu-kang, the Uptown and Downtown moieties, subdivided into neighborhood groups, would arrange parades with floats, marching bands, and acrobatic–cum–martial-arts troupes each night for up to a month.

On the first night the Uptown people might provide three floats, escorted by bands and drill teams and representing scenes from the "Journey to the West," the "Three Kingdoms," or some other story or episode from Chinese folklore. If the Downtown people had but two floats, they would consider themselves bested, so they might prepare five for the following night. In this way the contest quickly escalated until there were as many as 60 or 70 floats lit by torches and elaborate paper lanterns moving through the narrow streets, accompanied by the din of gongs, pipes, drums, and flute-playing troupes of children (a Lu-kang specialty). The topics of the floats played off against each other in subtle counterpoint and folkloristic one-upmanship, and the occasion was used to make fun of the other half of the city and its prominent men. As one man put it, "One side would do something and the other would immediately respond, like a shout and an echo."

Of course, the nightly processions pitted Shihs against Shihs, Huangs against Huangs, men of the Amoy Guild against their fellows, some men against their mother's brothers, and so on. The cost of this nightly exercise in local emulation and competition is said to have been borne primarily by the wealthy merchants, although as in a temple festival every household was expected to contribute something, if only labor. The processions might be interpreted as serving to redistribute some wealth from the merchants to their poorer fellow-citizens who pulled the floats and carried the torches. Since the reputation and the face of half the town and its wealthy men were at stake, neither side wanted to give up before the other. As with other demonstrations of group solidarity in Lu-kang, the excitement generated in the nightly display often spilled over into brawls, and the affair often ended with a pitched battle. I was assured that the wounds incurred, like those sustained in the annual rock fight, were never lethal, injured people leaping into pools in front of the major temples of their quarters and so being healed.

Neighborhoods and surname groups provided significant categories for the daily life and social relations of individuals, and on a few days of the year were mobilized as effective groups. The enduring corporate groups that dominated the city's economic and political life and that handled its relations with the outside world were the guilds. The Eight Guilds of Lu-kang were famous throughout Taiwan. According to a stone tablet commemorating the reconstruction of the Ma-tsu Temple in 1817, the Eight Guilds were the Ch'üan-chou Guild, the Amoy Guild, the South Guild, the Oil Guild, the Sugar Guild, the Cloth Guild, the Dyers Guild, and the "Sundries" Guild. Old men today sometimes speak of the Ship Guild, the Opium Guild, and the Rice Guild, although there is no record of such associations and they may well be referring to trade associations of the early Japanese period. The guilds were not organized on comparable principles. Four were organized around trade in a commodity, two by the place of origin of the ancestors, one by an occupation, and one by the area its members traded to (South of Amoy). Although the primary export of Lu-kang was rice, there was no Rice Guild.

The unit of membership in a guild was a shop, or *hang. Hang* had titles (*hao*), some of which seem to have persisted over the generations, the names of now defunct *hang* still being visible carved in the stone over the front doors of Lu-kang's old mansions. According to Chou Hsien-wen's *An Economic History of Taiwan During the Ch'ing Period*, the commercial establishments called *hang* were wholesalers rather than exclusive retailers.[16] The guilds of Lu-kang represented large-scale, wealthy merchants rather than petty retailers, and so brought the city's upper class together in associations that cut across surname and neighborhood lines. It is not difficult to understand the purpose of the Oil Guild or the Dyers Guild, but that of the Ch'üan-chou and Amoy Guilds is less clear: that is, a guild was an association of wholesalers, and a *hang* had to deal in something, yet Ch'üan-chou and Amoy were not commodities or services but places. From everything I could discover on the matter, it seems that a *hang* could belong to more than one guild, so that a merchant whose grandfather had come from Ch'üan-chou and who sold sugar to Swatow could belong to three guilds—the Ch'üan-chou Guild, the Sugar Guild, and the South Guild. The Ch'üan-chou and Amoy guilds thus cut across the other six, and since the great majority of Lu-kang people stemmed from Ch'üan-chou or claimed to, the Ch'üan-chou Guild was the largest, richest, and most powerful of the guilds. Most of the rice-exporting firms belonged to the Ch'üan-chou Guild, which itself played some part in the rice trade, sending agents abroad to report on the state of the harvest and of prices in other parts of Taiwan and of the mainland. The Ch'üan-chou Guild seems to have functioned as an overarching association or a nascent chamber of commerce.

From the recollections of old men whose fathers played active roles in the Ch'üan-chou Guild, and from its revised constitution, which the Japanese published in their 1905 compilation of Taiwanese customs, it is possible to get some notion of the guild's internal structure. Like all the guilds of Lu-kang, it was organized as a religious confraternity, dedicated to the goddess Ma-tsu, patroness of seafarers. It sponsored three great festivals each year: on the twenty-third day of the third lunar month, Ma-tsu's "birthday"; on the fifteenth day of the seventh month, the hungry ghost festival; and on the ninth day of the ninth month, the "Double Yang" or mountain-climbing festival. The guild also sponsored occasional pilgrimages to the Ma-tsu temple on Mei-chou Island, the original Ma-tsu shrine and center of the cult. Such groups usually stopped off in Ch'üan-chou as well. Each year the members of the guild met at the Ma-tsu Temple for a banquet on the evening of the twenty-second of the third lunar month. There they chose men to occupy the ritual posts of *lu-chu* (Hokkien *lo-cu*), master of the incense burner, and *t'ou-chia* (Hokkien *thau-ke*), the common term in Taiwan for "boss" or owner of a business. These were the usual terms for the men who arranged festivals, and the incumbents were responsible for the guild's celebration of the three great festivals. In addition, the *lu-chu* seems to have served as the formal, titular head of the guild, and held a seal of office. The guild also engaged a man to serve as "manager." He had to hold at least the lowest official degree, that of *sheng-yüan*, and if he held a higher one so much the better. As a scholar and a gentleman, he was able to deal with the resident subprefect as more of a status equal. Some old men described the "manager" as a hired lawyer; others said that the title was an empty honorific given to respected local degree-holders. The daily and more mundane affairs of the guild were managed by two men called "tally men" or "lot masters," the title apparently referring to record-keeping and receipts. Each received a fixed salary and served for only one month, being chosen from each member *hang* in strict rotation.

The Ch'üan-chou Guild constitution, which differs little from other nineteenth-century Chinese guild constitutions, indicates that the structure and functions of Lu-kang's guilds probably resembled those of guilds in other parts of China more closely than did those of the surname groups or perhaps the neighborhoods. This is not surprising, since the guild members regularly dealt with their counterparts in the ports of the mainland and were in close contact with the imperial administration. What is perhaps most interesting about the constitution are the hints of internal dissension and reluctance to hold the office of *lu-chu*, and the frequency with which the threat of official investigation and punishment is invoked against those members who break the rules. One is left with the strong impression that the subprefect was willing to back up the authority of the guild officers.

The officials needed the Ch'üan-chou Guild. They could not collect their taxes and supervise the city's trade without its cooperation. The guild merchants presumably provided the officials with the unofficial extra funds they needed to supplement their inadequate salaries and make their tenure of office worthwhile. It was thus in the interest of the officials to support the authority of the guild's officers. On the other side, the officials seem to have guaranteed the merchants a monopoly on the lucrative trade across the Taiwan Strait. One can thus see the wealthy merchants and the imperial officials—who in one sense were antagonists, contending for the profits of the trade—as bound together in a relation of mutual dependence and convenience.

The guilds and the officials cooperated in other ways as well. The guilds of Lu-kang owned land, both farmland and urban real estate. The rents were used to pay for the annual festivals and rituals. The guilds, or at least the Ch'üan-chou Guild, supported or contributed to the support of the Ch'üan-chou Militia, the dominant military force in northwestern Chang-hua. This force defended Lu-kang against bandits, pirates, and militant Chang-chou men from farther inland. It helped imperial troops put down rebellious peasants and Chang-chou men, and seems to have been at the service of the Lu-kang subprefect. Here it helps to keep in mind the corruption and ineffectiveness of imperial troops, especially those stationed on Taiwan, by the mid-nineteenth century. Pickering's visit to Wu-ch'i in 1867 to buy camphor led to a confrontation with the Lu-kang subprefect, for the prefect in T'ai-wan-fu claimed a monopoly over the trade in camphor. "On arriving we found our warehouse besieged by the clan Tan [Ch'en]; but, with the help of our seven-shooter rifle and two boat guns, we and our agents, the clan Ch'oa [Ts'ai] succeeded in routing the enemy for the moment.... When I had been up there a week, the Tao-tai's [i.e., circuit intendant's] troops, composed of militia under the district magistrate of Lok-kang [the Lu-kang subprefect] came in sight.... Very soon a crowd of the rabble militia collected round our enclosure."[17]

When a former Lu-kang rice merchant called Shih Chiu-tuan responded to a cadastral survey in 1888 by starting a rebellion that had to be put down by imperial troops from the Pescadores and Quemoy, the Chang-hua county magistrate accused the Lu-kang guilds of being behind the rising, and claimed that they had subverted the commander of the garrison at Lu-kang, who had stayed in his fort and done nothing to combat the rebels. Governor Liu Ming-ch'uan dismissed the garrison commander and the heads of the Ch'üan-chou Militia, and fined Lu-kang's Eight Guilds 30,000 taels.[18] If they really did back Shih Chiu-tuan in 1888, the guilds of Lu-kang went too far; but ordinarily their control of the militia constituted a major resource in their ambivalent relations with the imperial officials.

The guild merchants and the resident officials collaborated in regulating and taxing the city's trade, and they also acted together to found and manage the city's public institutions. The stone tablets that commemorate the foundation and periodic renovation of the major temples list the imperial officials and the Eight Guilds as responsible for raising the funds and supervising the work. In 1774, according to the *Chang-hua hsien chih*, the deputy magistrate founded the two public cemeteries of Lu-kang. In 1778 he acted together with the guild merchants to found a benevolent society, which managed the cemeteries, buried the bodies of the homeless dead, and constructed and maintained bridges and roads. The benevolent society's estate consisted of shops and houses in Lu-kang and farmland in the countryside. In 1825 the subprefect, acting with the guilds and a group of 24 local degree-holders (one *chü-jen*, two *kung-sheng*, and 21 *sheng-yüan*) raised funds to establish an academy (*shu-yüan*). There were already two academies in or near the county capital. The academy was built on the grounds of the Wen-wu miao, a "quasi-official" temple founded by the Eight Guilds and the subprefect in 1814 and dedicated to Confucius and Kuan-ti. The estate of the academy consisted of shops in Lu-kang and farmland throughout central Taiwan, held under various forms of tenure. From all of this one gets a picture of the resident officials going along with the drive of the merchants and gentry (whoever exactly they were) of Lu-kang for the prestige-carrying symbols of administrative centers. By 1825 Lu-kang had a yamen, a Ch'eng-huang temple, a Wen-wu temple, and an academy. All it lacked was a wall. The *Chang-hua hsien chih*, compiled in 1831, includes a proposal by an unknown official for the construction of a wall around Lu-kang. Imperial approval was not received and Lu-kang never got a wall, but the proposal may be regarded as evidence of official collaboration with the ambitions of the guilds, the informal centers of political power in the city.

The individual firms that made up the guilds competed with each other for profits and commercial success, but such competition was muted by overlapping guild membership, by cooperation in neighborhood and temple affairs and in the management of public charitable and educational trusts, and by the merchants' need to maintain a united front against the officials. The guilds competed with each other in the splendor of their ceremonies and in the size of the contributions they made to charity and to fund drives. In many ways the guilds may be seen as analogues to the corporate lineages of rural southeastern China. The guilds owned a common estate of land and shops; they were united by common worship; they controlled armed forces; they collected taxes and passed them on to the officials; they were centers of economic and political power. They differed from lineages in that they did not include poor men and so lacked the internal segmentation that marked Chinese lineages, and in their relatively close and continuous relations with imperial officials.

In some ways the political structure of Lu-kang can be seen as analogous to that of urban overseas Chinese communities. The city's elite consisted of merchants, who were organized in trade and native-place associations, and who cooperated in the supervision of public institutions. The managing committees of the major temples, the academy, and the charitable foundation brought together representatives of all the major groups, and so seem to have functioned in much the same way as school and hospital boards of directors did in overseas communities, where such bodies formed the apex of the informal power structure.[19]

At this point the reader may notice that I have largely avoided using the term "gentry." This is because I do not know who exactly the gentry of Lu-kang were, where they lived, or how they earned their living. The term *shen* is used in documents and inscriptions from nineteenth-century Lu-kang, and there certainly were degree-holders in or around

Lu-kang, but they remain shadowy figures to me, and I have avoided speculating on their identity and role.

In summary, the social structure of Lu-kang consisted of overlapping groups, each recruited on a different principle and each acting in a different sphere. On different occasions people defined themselves as members of different groups, and within each sphere the groups were opposed to each other. Within the city groups cut across each other, and both the limited opposition of the groups and the ultimate solidarity of the city were expressed in periodic public rituals. Relations with groups outside the city were restricted to economic exchange, political negotiation, or to open and unrestrained conflict.

In this essay I have presented the social structure of old Lu-kang as a symmetrical set of balanced oppositions and exchanges. One may certainly raise the question of whether it really was all that tidy. I myself am suspicious. The equilibrium model is in part a consequence of a deliberately ahistorical, synchronic approach, which I have employed primarily in the interests of brevity and clarity of exposition. As Edmund Leach puts it, what I have set out is a model of social reality, and to the extent that the parts of such a model form a coherent whole they necessarily imply equilibrium.[20] Were I writing a history of Lu-kang, a different picture would emerge. The discerning reader may have noticed the implicit use of a theoretical approach derived primarily from Georg Simmel, but also from Max Gluckman and Edmund Leach.[21] I have adopted this approach because it proved useful in helping to illuminate what was really going on in Lu-kang and in allowing me to squeeze the most information out of limited and refractory sources. This essay is a spare and skeletal account, but skeletons have their uses, especially for those interested in comparison, and I hope that those concerned with other, perhaps more fully documented, Chinese cities may find this useful.

Neighborhood Cult Associations in Traditional Tainan*

KRISTOFER M. SCHIPPER

The Temples of Tainan

Old Tainan is said to have been a city of a hundred temples. At the end of the nineteenth century the city boasted at least 115 temples, miniature sanctuaries not included. At that time Tainan had about 10,000 *hu*, or "households" (equivalent to approximately 40,000 inhabitants). This gives us an average of about one temple for 90 households—a ratio by no means extraordinary for premodern Taiwan.[1]

Only a few temples were official. Among them, the Confucian temple with its school and examination buildings had been founded on official initiative and was maintained almost entirely with state moneys. It had vast grounds, but the building itself was of poor quality and was often in need of repair. Another temple, for the official cult of the military hero and protector of the dynasty Kuan-ti, had been built on official initiative but through private subscriptions. The great temple dedicated to Ma-tsu—the holy protectress of seamen and, by extension, of the entire island—enjoyed official recognition. (Ma-tsu is the popular name in Taiwan for T'ien-hou Sheng-mu, "Queen of Heaven.") A representative of the administration would visit the temple to present offerings on the first and the fifteenth of each lunar month. But the care of the building was entirely the responsibility of the merchants of the town. There were a few Buddhist sanctuaries, too. These were inhabited by monks, and most were situated on the outskirts of the city.

All other temples, over 90 percent of the total, were situated inside the city and belonged to what is called by sinological convention the "popular religion." But the term must not be taken to suggest anything

* The author wishes to express his gratitude to Professor G. William Skinner for the many corrections and helpful suggestions for the amelioration of the original draft.

humble or crude. Unlike the Confucian temple, these popular sanctuaries were magnificent buildings, though usually not very large; they were decorated with carved beams and gilded panels, and furnished with precious tables, embroidered curtains, and bronze vessels. These temples were built by communities, neighborhoods, guilds, or other associations of which they were the center, the emblem, and the pride. Every member would contribute to the temple's construction and upkeep through voluntary donations or through taxes imposed by the community. If a person made special contributions for a part of the building, such as a column, a fresco, or a sculpted window screen, his name would be engraved on that part. Moreover, a commemorative stone stele would be erected in the temple with the names of all the donors.

Without exception, temples were dedicated to specific patron saints, of whom there were a great many. The temple building, its furnishings, and the endowment on which its upkeep depended were all considered to belong to the patron saint. Cults of the same saint were often interrelated by means of affiliation. This affiliation took the form of *fen-hsiang*, "divided or distributed incense." A new cult (i.e., a new community) would take an incense pot (*hsiang-lu*) full of ashes from the incense burner in the temple of an established cult (community). The new cult was founded on this new incense burner. A family emigrating from the mainland to Taiwan, for instance, might take with it an incense pot filled with the ashes from the *hsiang-lu* of its home temple. Groups of emigrants would do the same. They would then create a "branch" cult in their new surroundings. *Fen-hsiang* also made them tributaries to the senior temple. Money was expected from the tributaries on certain occasions, and periodically a pilgrimage had to be made to the senior temple. If the new cult grew, these contacts could become important.

Tributary relationships were also subject to change. To take an example, the great Ma-tsu temple that gave its name to the capital of the Pescadores was, through several intermediaries, affiliated with the original cult of this holy virgin in her native place in Mei-chou, a small island on the coast of Fukien. It was from the temple on the Pescadores that the Tainan cult of the Great Temple of the Queen of Heaven had originated. As trade expanded along the west coast of Taiwan, merchants established offshoots of the Tainan cult in other ports, including Pei-kang, situated a hundred miles north of the capital. As it happened, the cult in Pei-kang became extremely popular and localities all over the island founded affiliated cults and made yearly pilgrimages to the Pei-kang shrine. The influx of money from the many devotees in turn enabled the people of Pei-kang to make pilgrimages, not only to the mother temple in Tainan, but from there on to the Pescadores and, following the genealogical tree, all the way to Mei-chou.

The majority of temples in Tainan had been founded as affiliates of cults elsewhere—for the most part small places—in the two mainland prefectures of Ch'üan-chou and Chang-chou, whence the inhabitants had come originally. A certain number of temples were founded by tradespeople from Fu-chou *fu* (central Fukien) and Ch'ao-chou *fu* (northeastern Kwangtung). Two and even three hundred years after its founding, a temple's place of origin and mother temple would still be remembered. Only a few temples owed their existence to a cult that originated in Tainan itself.[2]

Types of Religious Associations

The social embodiment of a cult was known as a *hui*, "association." When a temple came to harbor more than one cult, a *hui* corresponding to each would be organized within the community. Other *hui* were unaffiliated with any temple, either because they felt no need for a temple dedicated to their patron saint or because their financial circumstances did not permit them to build one. In Tainan, religious associations outnumbered temples. A census of 1937 revealed that there were approximately three associations for every two temples, not counting ancestral cults and temples.

Japanese ethnographers of Taiwan have distinguished several types of religious associations and given them generic names.[3] First, *shen-ming hui*, literally associations for the worship of a patron saint, brought together people of the same occupation, profession, or status group. These may be characterized in English as "common-interest" associations. Second, *tsu-kung hui*, literally associations for the worship of a common forebear, brought together persons of the same surname (*t'ung-hsing hui*) or of common origin in some territorial unit on the mainland (*t'ung-hsiang hui*). These may be characterized in English as "common-origin" associations. Third, *kung-chi hui*, literally associations for communal worship, brought together inhabitants of the same street or quarter of the city. These may be characterized in English as "residential" associations. Fourth, *chi-ssu kung-yeh*, literally sacrificial trusts, brought together members of the same lineage or clan for ancestor worship.[4] Normally they established a trust fund and used the income from it to finance sacrificial offerings to the ancestors and subsidize the schooling of promising young boys. These may be characterized in English as "kin-group" associations. Fifth, *fu-mu hui*, literally associations for the care of parents, were in effect mutual-aid clubs to help families meet the costs of funerals.

It will be noted that the last two types diverge markedly from the other three. Lacking the attributes of saint cults, they fall outside our purview here. By contrast, the first three types are very much alike: their organization and function served a cultic purpose; and all were associations of communal solidarity that celebrated festivals in honor of the patron saint. Indeed, many associations had multiple functions from the beginning, so it is difficult to categorize them as belonging to one or another of the three types. The druggists of Tainan, for instance, were all located within a restricted area of the western district, and the *hui* dedicated to their patron saint was as much a residential as a common-interest association. Henceforth we shall refer to *hui* of these three types—common-interest, common-origin, and residential—as "liturgical associations" and seek lines of differentiation within the class from an internal rather than from an external point of view.

Organization of Liturgical Associations

Although liturgical associations comprehended a diverse array, as we shall see, their basic anatomy was essentially the same. Like temples, liturgical associations were always founded on an incense pot (*hsiang-lu*). This was the essential possession of the congregation, its symbolic focus and representation, passed on each year from one member household to another. The traditional incense burner of a Tainan association was an octagonal vessel with four feet and two handles, a *ting*. It was commonly made of pewter, stood about one foot high, and normally had the name and the foundation date of the association engraved on it.

The incense pot was kept in the house of the head of the association, who was invariably known as *lu-chu*, "master of the incense burner." The term of office was a calendar year, and consecutive terms were disallowed. The new officeholder was selected at an assembly of association members during the annual festival honoring the saint. The association members were called *lu-hsia*, "servants of the incense burner." The method of selection involved the throwing of divining blocks; the member who obtained the highest number of correct throws was proclaimed the next *lu-chu*.[5] The next best two or four were appointed managers, *t'ou-chia*, whose duties were to assist the *lu-chu* in the exercise of his office. After these procedures, the incense burner was transferred to the home of the new chief. This was done in style with a small procession and music. At the house of the new *lu-chu* a short rite "to install the incense burner," *an-lu*, was performed. The new *lu-chu* also acquired two lanterns on which his new title, the name of the association, and the name of the patron saint were inscribed in large red characters. These were to be hung in front of his house altar, and might be kept as an enduring token of his dignity.

The main responsibility of the *lu-chu* was to manage the funds of the association and organize the annual festival. Stable funding was of prime importance because the recurring festivals were expensive. Probably a majority of the *hui* in Tainan were endowed with holdings of agricultural land or urban real estate. However, many associations had no such property, and in these cases yearly contributions were made by members to meet the costs of the celebrations. It seems that the chief motive for establishing an endowment was to escape the hazards of a yearly collection of money and to protect the continuity of the cult from possible economic depression or defection of members. To this end, each of the members was to donate an identical fixed sum, and the total was then invested in property or loaned out to earn interest. This corporate property was ritually conceived as the community's gift to the cult. A share could never be withdrawn, not even if a member left the street or profession or whatever defined the boundaries of the *hui*, although any defector would lose his right to participate. On the other hand, on joining the association a new member had to put up a sum at least equal to the amount contributed by the charter members. This was called *ch'a-lu-chin*, "money stuck in the incense burner"—a reference to the procedure whereby a newcomer literally placed money wrapped in red paper in the incense burner of the *hui*. The *ch'a-lu-chin* of associations with important holdings could be onerous, but even associations with little or no property observed this custom, though the sum involved might be very small. All *hui* owned at least some movable property: the incense burner, a statue of the patron saint, altar trappings, and sometimes musical instruments and the paraphernalia needed for processions.

As of 1933, the combined property of temples and associations in Tainan amounted to 231 apartment houses (i.e., multiple rental units) and some seven *chia*[6] of construction land inside the town. It is difficult to estimate the percentage of urban real estate owned by liturgical organizations because of methodological problems in determining the total built-up area at any point during the nineteenth century. Moreover, one could make a case for including in "religious" holdings the property of business associations (the three *chiao*, of which more below, and other guilds), which, although not strictly religious associations of the common-interest type, closely resembled them and spent a great deal of money for religious observances. At the very least, we can say that real estate whose rental income supported religious activities amounted to a substantial portion of the total. Of property owned by religious organizations, almost all the land was held by temples, whereas nearly all the houses were owned by associations.[7]

The accounts of the year were kept by the *lu-chu*. At the end of his term, which coincided with the saint's birthday or festival, as we have noted, the balance was neatly written up—stating in detail all income and outlays—on a sheet of red paper that was posted in a conspicuous place in the street for everyone to see. Some associations also kept special cash records that were transferred together with the incense burner. Any deficit had to be covered by the *lu-chu* responsible for that year. Any surplus was transferred to the next *lu-chu* to cover the expenses of the following year. There was no remuneration for the *lu-chu* other than the pair of lanterns and the prestige of the office, with the honor of hosting the annual banquet in his own house. Also, it was considered an auspicious omen to have obtained the incense burner and a sign of divine protection to have it in one's home during the year. At the same time, the possibility of financial loss was very real.

The main and in some instances virtually the only activity of liturgical associations was the organization of "anniversary" festivals at least once a year. Such festivals involved worship, with offerings by the members and religious services performed by hired priests. In addition, there were theater performances in the open air for the enjoyment of both saints and humans, and the celebration closed with a festive meal. These banquets, which as we shall see from an account book absorbed a major part of the association's revenues, were strictly limited to cult members; they were not occasions for inviting people from other communities. Each member had the right to one plate, so to speak, and if a member was unable to come he could send a replacement. The banquet was not limited to men, for women who were household heads were expected to attend, and wives as well as sons could take the place of a household head who was out of town or otherwise occupied.

T'u-ti-kung Hui: The Basic Neighborhood Association

One kind of liturgical association stands out not only as more prevalent but also as more fundamental than others in the life of "urban" communities. These were the associations for the worship of T'u-ti-kung, (Lord of the Earth). Each *chieh* ("street" or neighborhood) was supposed to have its T'u-ti-kung cult, and people in Tainan affirmed that this was actually the case in former times. Let us try to check the validity of this statement. At the turn of the century, only about twenty of the city's temples were dedicated to T'u-ti-kung. They were typically small, though not miniature, shrines. In addition to these, however, there were a far larger number of T'u-ti-kung *hui* without temples of their own.

A Taoist manuscript dating from 1876 sheds some light on our problem.[8] This manuscript describes a ritual (*jang-tu chieh-lien*) for securing remission of sins in order to avert disaster and gain salvation. To this end, one had to ask pardon from all the agents of divine retribution inside the city. In this connection the manuscript provides a list of 138 cults in Tainan, thereby affording a rare glimpse into the religious geography of the city. It should be noted that performance of this ritual, coupled to a service to the stars of fate—the Dipper—used to be very common in traditional Tainan.

The list enumerates cults in geographical order, starting in the eastern part of the town.[9] The first listed is the Lord of T'ai-shan (the Eastern Peak); the second is the T'u-ti-kung of the neighborhood adjoining that temple. Third comes the City God for Tainan prefecture (Fu Ch'eng-huang).[10] Number four is a temple deity, the "Pure Water Patriarch," a saint from Ch'üan-chou who enjoyed a large following in Taiwan. There follows a whole string of T'u-ti-kung before we come to the east gate of the city. This gate, like all the others, also lodged a T'u-ti-kung. In short, of the 138 cults listed, 45, or roughly one third, are to T'u-ti-kung. (See Map 1.) It is notable that all saints other than T'u-ti-kung are mentioned in connection with their temples—e.g., Ma-tsu of the Great Temple of the Queen of Heaven, or Lady Ma-tsu of the Mango Yard Street—whereas the T'u-ti-kung are listed without exception in relation to their street or neighborhood, whether they are enshrined in temples or not. For instance, the manuscript mentions the T'u-ti-kung of Look West Street (*K'an-hsi chieh*), which we shall examine more closely later on. We know for sure that this street never had a T'u-ti-kung shrine, though an association for this cult had been in existence since 1765. Apart from T'u-ti-kung, cult saints not enshrined in temples are not included in the list, from which we may infer that only T'u-ti-kung *hui* were considered important enough to list along with temple-based cults. It would appear that not all T'u-ti-kung were included in the roster, for most of those listed were located in neighborhoods that had no large temple. We know that every temple building normally lodges, in addition to its tutelary saint, a T'u-ti-kung, whose jurisdiction may extend beyond the temple precincts to the immediate neighborhood. Thus associations centered on a T'u-ti-kung housed in a temple dedicated to another saint may not be reflected in this list. In any case, it becomes apparent from our list that the religious geography of the city consisted not only of its tem-

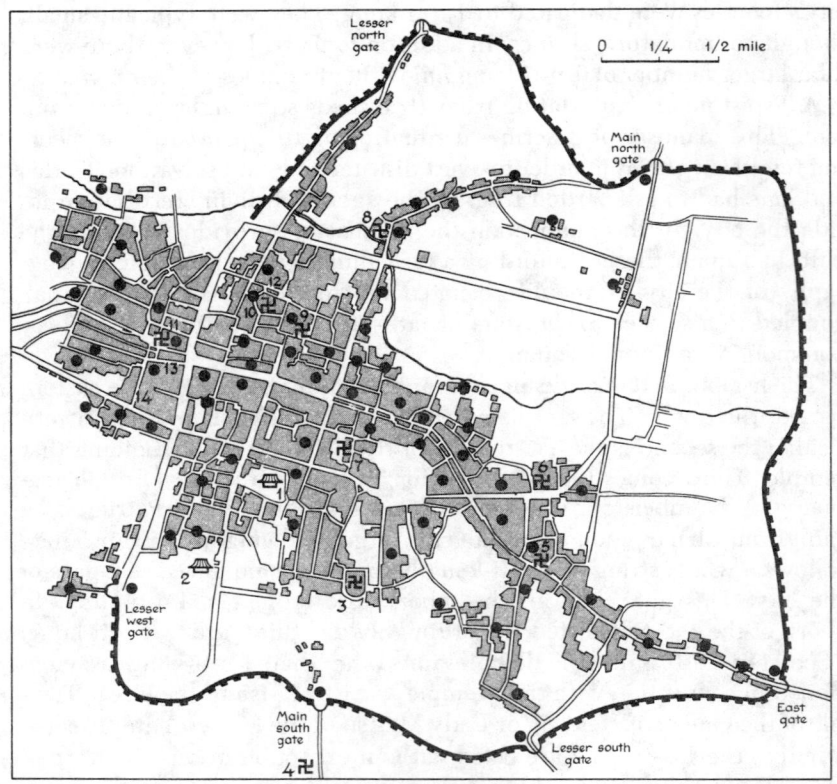

MAP 1. TAINAN IN 1907. Dots represent sites of T'u-ti-kung *hui*. Key: (1) T'ai-wan (later T'ai-nan) prefectural yamen; (2) T'ai-wan (later An-p'ing) county yamen; (3) prefectural Confucian temple; (4) Fa-hua ssu (Buddhist temple); (5) Temple of the Lord of the Eastern Peak (*Tung-yüeh miao*); (6) prefectural City God temple; (7) Temple of the Lord of Heaven (*T'ien t'an*); (8) county City God temple; (9) Great Temple of Kuan-ti (*Ta Wu miao*); (10) Great Temple of the Queen of Heaven (*Ta T'ien-hou kung*); (11) Temple of the Water Immortal (*Shui-hsien kung*); (12) Lesser Ma-tsu Street (*Hsiao Ma-tsu chieh*); (13) South River Street (*Nan-ho chieh*); (14) Look West Street (*K'an-hsi chieh*).

ples and shrines, but also of neighborhood associations for the worship of T'u-ti-kung. Other *hui* not associated with temples were not considered important in delineating the overall religious organization of the city.

Our list of 1876 gives only names, and the roster of T'u-ti-kung *hui* is almost certainly incomplete. But our knowledge on this subject is greatly advanced by another compendium based on a Japanese survey of 1930. The *Tainan shū shikyō myōkan* was published in 1933, a few years be-

Neighborhood Cult Associations in Traditional Tainan

fore massive Japanese repression brought an end to virtually all Chinese religious activity on the island.[11] For Tainan, this compendium lists 125 temples and 165 liturgical associations that lacked sanctuaries of their own. For each temple or association it gives the location, the saints worshiped, the number of members (of the temple committee or of the association), the founding date, the festival days, the names of those responsible to the government,[12] the financial resources, and a short historical note.

Among the temples listed, we find nineteen shrines devoted exclusively to T'u-ti-kung. The oldest dates from 1679. (In evaluating this date one must bear in mind that Tainan [Saccam] was founded as a Dutch possession in the middle of the seventeenth century and became part of the Ch'ing empire in 1683.) The most recent shrine dates from 1866, still well before the date of our Taoist manuscript (1876). Of the associations listed, 26 were devoted to T'u-ti-kung, the oldest having been founded in 1687 and only three dating from after 1876. As expected, the Japanese compendium lists a number of associations that do not figure in the 1876 manuscript. The two sources together yield 73 separate T'u-ti-kung shrines (*miao*) and associations (*hui*) in existence around 1870.[13] This number must be compared with the number of streets (neighborhoods) in Tainan at the time. A census of 1830 gives 83 *chieh*,[14] whereas a map of 1908 shows 104. If one considers that a certain number of *hui* functioning in the 1870's had doubtless disappeared by 1930, and also that several associations included more than one street (as we shall see from the example immediately below), the common assertion that at one time every neighborhood in Tainan had its T'u-ti-kung cult might well be true.

According to the 1930 survey, the several T'u-ti-kung *hui*, though accounting for only 15 percent of all religious associations in Tainan, owned 61 houses, or about 27 percent of all houses owned by such associations. The proportion may have been still higher in the nineteenth century, for the "house of T'u-ti-kung" had become a popular generic term for apartment houses owned and rented out by liturgical associations.[15] This meaning of the "house of T'u-ti-kung" was explained to the author several times in the following way: "Whenever a new neighborhood was established, the people set aside a piece of land for the T'u-ti-kung. On this land a house was built and then rented out, and the revenue thus obtained was used to meet the expenses of the cult. If more than the necessary money came in, it was applied to other cults supported by the same neighborhood, e.g., those for the Lord of Heaven, or for the Fire King."[16] Although this account is informative concerning popular conceptions of T'u-ti-kung foundations, the procedure described was probably seldom followed. As we have seen, houses were usually bought with money collected in equal shares from each member, and these houses were not necessarily situated within the neighborhood. The original holdings were increased by each additional new member, whereas no departing one could withdraw his share. If the common investment was insufficient, the members had to pay an additional yearly contribution.

Another indication of T'u-ti-kung's distinctiveness comes from the generic names of the cults. Professional common-interest associations were often called *t'ang*, "halls," although few of them could boast of a headquarters building. (The rest of the name was usually a flowery literary allusion, as in the case of the two associations of goldsmiths: "Auspicious Happiness" and "Golden Scepter.") *T'ang* also appeared in the names of neighborhood communal associations *other* than those devoted to T'u-ti-kung. The latter without exception were called *hui*: if not T'u-ti-kung *hui*, then Fu-te-yeh *hui*, an appellation derived from the canonical title Fu-te cheng-shen, "Orthodox Spirit of Good Merit." T'u-ti-kung *hui* stood apart from other communal associations in yet another respect. They were almost never affiliated through *fen-hsiang* with other, senior cults. With what was the incense burner filled, then, if not with the ashes from another burner? Tradition has it that in the countryside the pot was filled with earth from the locality, whereas in the city of Tainan it was filled with rice grains. In any case the symbolism is clear: T'u-ti-kung *hui* were in principle autonomous.

T'u-ti-kung: Myth and Symbol

Let us now ask how the symbolic associations of T'u-ti-kung elucidate the functions of neighborhood associations in Tainan. What do beliefs about T'u-ti-kung tell us about his role as a neighborhood cult figure? His statues show him as an old gentleman with a long flowing beard. He is always seated, wearing a "dragon robe." More important is his cap. Most often he wears the *yüan-wai-mao* of the wealthy country gentleman, one who carries no official rank but great local influence.[17] In one hand he invariably holds an ingot, in the other sometimes the long walking stick of a country patriarch. The T'u-ti-kung in Tainan, however, lack this attribute, for the walking stick is considered fit only for rural T'u-ti-kung "who must do a lot of walking," urban T'u-ti-kung being more sedentary. The following stories and opinions about him are those most frequently heard.

(1) T'u-ti-kung keeps out the *kuei*, "ghosts" or "demons." In ancient

times a courageous county official drove out the *kuei* from one locality after another with such vigor that they dared not return. He was deified.[18]

(2) T'u-ti-kung keeps out the snakes. An old gentleman who kept a general store found what he thought was a duck egg. He took it home. It hatched and out came a snake, which the old man reared. When he was absent, the snake ate the chickens and the ducks of other people. Thereupon the old gentleman turned the snake loose. But it grew and attacked people and cattle. The emperor heard of it and ordered the snake to be subdued. As no one else answered the emperor's call, the old gentleman went himself and killed the snake. He was canonized as T'u-ti-kung.[19]

(3) T'u-ti-kung epitomizes dedicated virtue. As Chang Ming-te (cf. the *Ta-hsüeh!*), he was the servant of a Chou official who served for long periods away from home. The official's daughter bewailed her loneliness, and the servant Chang agreed to accompany her as she set out in search of her father. On the road they were overtaken by a snowstorm. The girl was in danger of freezing to death. The servant stripped off his clothes and gave them to the girl to put on. When he himself died of exposure, the characters "Orthodox Spirit of Good Merit" appeared in the sky. A temple was erected and he was canonized as T'u-ti-kung and as Hou-t'u.[20]

(4) T'u-ti-kung prevents the loss of wealth. A variant of the preceding story casts T'u-ti-kung as a slave who zealously guarded the money of his wealthy master—as Shou-ts'ai-nu (see note 39).

(5) T'u-ti-kung exemplifies the tension between a utopian equity and the social distinctions that undergird civilization. Because of his outstanding virtue and wisdom, T'u-ti-kung was mandated by Heaven to divide the riches of the earth among the people. He planned to give everyone an equal share. His wife remonstrated with him, saying "This will lead to a world without servants. If all men are equal, who would be willing to carry the sedan chair of the bride to her new home?" T'u-ti-kung gave in. Since the wife of T'u-ti-kung is responsible for inequality in society, only rich people worship her.[21]

(6) T'u-ti-kung is Hou-t'u, the earth spirit of tombs. The legendary heroine Meng Chiang-nü, having lost her father, longed in vain for a husband. As Ch'in Shih-huang-ti was then building the Great Wall, he called up all young men. Han Chi-lang did not want to go and hid away from his home. On the fifth day of the fifth month (Tuan-wu festival) he was in the garden of Meng Chiang-nü's house. When she came out of the house, the lad hid in a tree above a pond. Meng Chiang-nü pro-

ceeded to bathe in the pond, whereupon she saw the image of the boy reflected in the water. She told him that, having seen her nude, he had to marry her. A wedding feast was held, but the old man who ran the general store was not invited. He reported Han Chi-lang to the authorities. The young man died while doing forced labor at the Wall, and his corpse was incorporated into the structure. Meng Chiang-nü went to look for her husband. Her tears made the wall collapse and many skeletons were uncovered. An old man told her that the bones that would absorb her blood were those of her husband. She thus found the skeleton and as her tears fell upon them flesh grew anew on the bones. The old man told her that if she put the body in a bag, it would be easier to carry. She did so and it became a skeleton once again. Out of spite, Meng Chiang-nü transformed the old man into the guardian of her husband's grave.[22]

It is not possible to deal here in detail with all the themes brought forward in these stories. The belief that T'u-ti-kung keeps the *kuei* out is the reason most often heard for organizing T'u-ti-kung associations. Snakes are *ti-ching*, demoniac spirits of the earth.[23] To pick up things found in the street and take them home contravenes public morals. The old gentleman who recognizes his monstrous error and corrects it brings to mind the Taoist ritual for the absolution of sins, accompanied as it were by a confession of one's errors. Such confessions were also prominent in the liturgy of the politicoreligious mass movements that arose during the Han period and so profoundly influenced modern religion.[24] The loyal servant brings in another ritual element from the same milieu: the exercise of will power in a sexual challenge. He not only does not abuse the lonely daughter of his master when he is alone with her in the wilderness; he freezes while standing naked by her side. This reminds us of the famous sexual rituals of the Taoists, in which adepts were to remain calm and unflustered, not even changing color, while engaging in sexual activities.[25] Such control contrasts with the free alliances of boys and girls in the spring known to us through the studies of Granet—a theme that is echoed in the story of Meng Chiang-nü, who bathed nude under the open sky and concluded a matrilocal marriage without a proper matchmaker. The story pitches natural disorder against cultural order—the young man refuses to work at the Great Wall that separates the civilized world from the barbarians, and T'u-ti-kung, as Hou-t'u, prevents the intermingling of the living with the dead. The same themes recur in the story of T'u-ti-kung's wife: agnatic marriage customs are the hallmark of civilization, contrasting with the free alliances of the barbarians and of the uncivilized past. But this same past is the subject of another projection: the ideal of *t'ai-p'ing*, the Great Equality, manifested by T'u-ti-kung when he distributes wealth to all in equal parts. This too evokes the politicoreligious movements of Han and later times that tried to realize the ideal society of the past in a new world order based on the principle of Great Equality.[26]

Still other elements link T'u-ti-kung with the utopian mass movements of early Taoism. The saint's "official" title begins with the term *fu-te*, "good merit," which appears to be of Buddhist origin. One of its earliest uses was in connection with the so-called *fu-te she*, "abodes of good merit." These were a kind of hostel operated by monks in Central Asia and described by the pilgrim Fa-hsien on his travels to India in the fifth century. These hostels, which provided food and lodging without charge, were thought to yield good merit for both monks and guests. A closely similar institution was found in China at the same period in connection with the Taoist movements already mentioned, namely the *i-she*, "equity abodes," which also offered free food and lodging to travelers. If anyone abused this hospitality by taking more than he needed, he had to confess his guilt and atone for it by working at the repair of roads, thus furthering communication and exchange among the different parts of the macrocosm. The whole atmosphere of these institutions and movements echoed the ideal of the Great Equality: "no thieves at night and people did not pick up objects lost on the roads."[27] *I-she* were associated with the so-called "pure or calm houses," *ch'ing-shih* or *ching-shih*, which served as religious centers of the Taoist movements, the places where the sacred community assembled. We know of community feasts, *ch'u*, that took place there, as well as public confessions and ceremonies of the *chiao* type. The heads of these institutions were the *ch'i-lao* and *san-lao*, the wise patriarchs of the countryside, including those of great integrity who as *kung-ts'ao* were entitled to propose officials for advancement or punishment and who, by virtue of their incorruptibility, were the fear of the local officials. The "pure houses" of the early Taoists were precursors of today's *t'ing*, the village temple and community house of South China and Vietnam. More generally, there is some evidence that the communal temples in today's "popular religion" evolved from the community houses of the politicoreligious mass movements that date back to Han times.[28]

There is still another element that points to an intimate relationship between T'u-ti-kung and these Taoist movements and their institutions. The name of T'u-ti, conspicuously absent from classical and official literary works, does figure in the liturgy of the early Taoist church. In the rite for the consecration of the incense burner, already practiced in the sixth century and still used today by Taiwanese priests, the spirit of the holy place where the ritual is enacted is called upon to serve as the intermediary between the community, on the one hand, and Heaven and the other spheres of the universe, on the other. In the rite this spirit is called *tz'u-chien T'u-ti cheng-shen*, "T'u-ti, the orthodox spirit of this place." The T'u-ti cheng-shen or Fu-te cheng-shen (see p. 660) was the spirit that ruled over the holy place, the sacred area, the center of the community. This authority is expressed by one of the derivative meanings of the word *cheng*: "to rule, to govern as an appointed official." But the primary meaning of this word is "orthodox, correct," distinguishing the T'u-ti, a *yang* force, from the spirits of the soil that are inherently *yin* and *hsieh*, obscure and vicious.

The general term for a holy place or auspicious locale is *fu-ti*. In the religious geography of Taoism, the world has precisely 72 such *fu-ti* where salvation can be obtained. But in modern religion, the application of this concept has been extended and every temple, every tomb, and, it would appear, every neighborhood is such a *fu-ti*, which makes us understand why they are invariably placed under the guardianship of a T'u-ti-kung. In Taiwan even today, the heads of traditional communities are preferably elderly gentlemen whose virtue and experience have earned them the respect of all. One calls them *lao-ta* or *ch'i-lao*, and the community that includes a man worthy of the name is considered fortunate indeed. T'u-ti-kung is the perfect *ch'i-lao*. He personifies the communal spirit that ultimately derives from the politicoreligious mass movements of early China.

Other Neighborhood Cult Associations and Their Relation to T'u-ti-kung Hui

Neighborhood cult associations in Tainan were by no means limited to T'u-ti-kung *hui*. But in this regard two facts stand out. No such association is known to have been formed in a neighborhood that did not support a T'u-ti-kung *hui*, and the neighborhood or street as ritually defined by a cult other than that of T'u-ti-kung was always coterminous with the T'u-ti-kung's community.

The range of neighborhood cults is well illustrated by Small Ma-tsu Street (*Hsiao Ma-tsu chieh*), which boasted three liturgical associations in addition to its T'u-ti-kung *hui*. One was devoted to the Lord of Heaven (*Yü-huang shang-ti*), whose festival was celebrated on the ninth day of the first lunar month. Another was devoted to the Fire King (*Huo-wang*), whose propitiation was of course held to avert conflagrations, and whose "birthday" fell on the twenty-third day of the sixth month.

The third was devoted to Li No-ch'a, a youthful exorcizing saint who was famous for the exploits related in *Feng-shen yen-i*, and who was the usual patron of local militias; his *hui* on Small Ma-tsu Street was organized among the young males of the community for reasons of protection.

Four associations were probably exceptional for a single neighborhood; but then this particular street is reputed to have been quite affluent in the old days. Having been spared by Japanese urban planners and by Allied bombardiers in World War II, Small Ma-tsu Street persists today in essentially its traditional form. It is a short street, not much more than 500 yards long, and it is lined by shops on each side with living quarters, some quite spacious, behind them. It is located at what must have been a strategic place—namely, where the road leading from the central and western sectors of the city to the harbor was joined by the main street from the north. As was typical of the four religious associations, the one for T'u-ti-kung was the oldest and the most heavily endowed. As of 1930, the T'u-ti-kung *hui* owned four apartment houses that yielded in annual rent a sum more than sufficient to cover the costs of the annual festival. By contrast, the Fire King association had two houses, the association for the Lord of Heaven had one house, and the association for Li No-ch'a had none, being supported by interest from some commercial capital. In this case the subsidiary associations were founded in the following order: Li No-ch'a (1822), Fire King (1882), and Lord of Heaven (1886).

In Tainan as a whole the situation was somewhat different. After T'u-ti-kung *hui*, associations for the cult of the Lord of Heaven were most numerous, and Fire King associations were third. The average of the founding dates for all Lord of Heaven neighborhood associations in Tainan is 1847, as against 1843 for the Fire King and 1830 for all other satellite cults. The average of the founding dates for T'u-ti-kung *hui* was, of course, the earliest of all: 1822. The average founding date for liturgical neighborhood associations that were not T'u-ti-kung *hui* was 1835.

In many cases, the residents of a certain neighborhood (given definition in the first instance by a T'u-ti-kung *hui*) would establish a *hui* directed specifically to participation—with offerings and theater—in the festivals of nearby temples. In the streets surrounding the Temple of the Five Emperors (*Wu-ti miao*), five associations had been organized, one for each of the emperors, in order to support and promote festivities on their respective birthdays. In the case of the Great Temple of the Queen of Heaven, the premier Ma-tsu temple in Tainan, a much wider circle of neighborhood associations participated in its major festivals with offerings and theater.

Common-surname associations also transcended streets and neighborhoods, but here, too, localization of potential members tended to restrict the "catchment area" to a quarter or sector of the city. The Kuos are a case in point. A family of that surname had migrated to Tainan in 1718 from Nan-an, a county in Ch'üan-chou *fu*, and had brought with them an incense burner of King Kuo, a deified servant. (Once, lacking firewood to boil water for his master's tea, this transcendent servant used his own leg as fuel.) In due time, a Kuo surname association was set up around the incense burner, and by the end of the eighteenth century the Kuos had grown in numbers and affluence to the point where they were able to build a temple to their totemic deity. By the late nineteenth century, the temple functioned not only as the headquarters of the Kuo surname association but also as a communal temple for the quarter in which the Kuos were concentrated. In the case of the Ts'ai's, there were three different surname associations in Tainan, one in the central quarter of the city, one in the north, and one in the west.

Although the whole city participated in several temple festivals, few were organized by a citywide association. The major exception in Tainan was the Temple of the Lord of Heaven, T'ien t'an, the goal of many pilgrims from outside the city.

Quite apart from the ordinary temple "committee" consisting of the *lu-chu* and his assistants, a citywide association had been created to assist in organizing and funding this temple's major festivals and related religious services. Then there were a number of *hui*—the Japanese survey of 1930 listed eight—that were devoted to various saints of literature and learning. Their membership was largely limited to officials and the local gentry—drawn in some instances, no doubt, from throughout the city. Occupational *hui* also drew their members from throughout the city, but since the shops of a certain trade or line were often concentrated in a particular quarter, the actual "catchment area" of many occupational *hui* must have corresponded to a single quarter or sector of the city. Occupational associations (i.e., guilds), like other *hui*, took the form of congregations of devotees of a saint. The Japanese survey of 1930 listed 30 such "guilds" in Tainan, specifying the patron saint of each. It is notable that very nearly half—ranging from weavers and blacksmiths to fish dealers—had taken as their patron saint Ma-tsu, the most popular deity throughout Taiwan. As has been said before, these professional common-interest associations were often called *t'ang*, "halls."

Though these forms of religious integration were not without significance for urban social structure, the more important, and in many respects more basic, forms of hierarchical buildup of street-level neighborhood associations were those involving T'u-ti-kung *hui*. Throughout the city there were conventional clusters of four to ten T'u-ti-kung *hui* in one quarter, generally centered around some major landmark such as a large temple. Thus one spoke of the "Five T'u-ti-kung of the Temple of the Water Immortal" (*Shui-hsien kung*), or of the "Six T'u-ti-kung of the Great Temple of Kuan-ti" (*Ta Wu miao*). From the viewpoint of the temples, these T'u-ti-kung *hui* represented the subdivisions of the territorial unit surrounding the temple, the so-called *chüeh-t'ou*, "corner heads." The *chüeh-t'ou* had no say at all in the management of the temple; they came into action only for the occasions that involved the quarter as such (and not only the temple). Thus, for the "birthday" of the tutelary deity of the landmark temple the T'u-ti-kung *hui* would do nothing at all; but they would participate at the yearly *p'u-tu*, the ritual Festival of the Hungry Ghosts during the seventh lunar month,[29] and also at the occasional celebration of a *ta-chiao*. This was a festival of enormous proportions held generally about once a generation after the restoration of a temple. It aimed at purification of the community in question and renewal of the life spirit within it, and was coupled with a kind of religious retreat.[30] For these festivals a special committee was formed outside the regular temple organization. The *chüeh-t'ou* played an active role in these committees, shouldering their share of the costs and of the offerings. The money for them to do this was provided either directly from the funds of the *hui* or through a special levy on their members. In such cases the committee specified the share for each street-level neighborhood, and the *lu-chu* of each T'u-ti-kung *hui* was held accountable.

The Neighborhood Associations of Look West Street

Most written sources on the T'u-ti-kung *hui* and other neighborhood associations prior to the twentieth century have been lost, and it is of course hazardous to project back to traditional times forms of organizational activity observed since the Second World War.[31] But we are fortunate to have a few surviving records on the T'u-ti-kung and Fire King associations of one particular *chieh*: the Look West Street (*K'an-hsi chieh*). This gives us the opportunity to examine in some depth the functioning of the neighborhood as a collectivity, inside of the larger social structure of its quarter and the whole city. In order to do this, a few words must be said about the quarter where the neighborhood of Look West Street was situated.

The T'u-ti-kung *hui* of Look West Street, established in 1765, was one of the five T'u-ti-kung associations surrounding the Temple of the Water Immortal (*Shui-hsien kung*) outside the west wall of the city. In the eighteenth century this quarter faced the main waterfront of Tainan; and as the Bay of Tainan silted up, great warehouses were built there.[32] But in the second half of the nineteenth century, the quarter had become the city's chief commercial center.

The San-i T'ang. The original Temple of the Water Immortal, built in 1703, was modest enough, but it was rebuilt early in the nineteenth century as the headquarters of the San-i T'ang, the overarching guild for import-export merchants. Tainan's overseas traders were organized into three major *chiao*: the T'ang Chiao for the sugar trade, the Pei Chiao for trade with mainland China, and the Nan Chiao for the trade with Southeast Asia. Tradition has it that these *chiao* were founded in 1725 by three great merchants of legendary fame.[33] Lesser *chiao*, presumably established after the dominant three, have always been subordinate to them.[34] The chiefs of the *chiao* were called *lu-chu*, as in other communal associations, and they were chosen anew each year in the manner already described for religious *hui*. In 1808, the three *chiao* gave vital assistance to the government in repelling an invasion of pirates by putting their volunteer militia, *i-min*, at the disposal of local officials. As a reward, the three *chiao* were collectively given official rank, together with a seal of office.[35] It would appear that this was the occasion for institutionalizing the informal cooperation among the three *chiao*, and the San-i T'ang was born. Through the enlarged Temple of the Water Immortal, the San-i T'ang achieved religious hegemony not only over its quarter but over the entire city, thereby solidifying its economic control.

When the temple was rebuilt, all firms in its immediate quarter took part along with the San-i T'ang and its affiliated organizations and firms. The initial contributions of the participants were invested in the usual way. The extent of the holdings is unknown to me,[36] but the annual revenue derived from them in the middle of the nineteenth century amounted to 3,000 yüan. Moreover, the San-i T'ang levied a tax of ten *wen*, "coppers," on each parcel or piece of goods imported or exported. This tax was called *yüan-chin*, "good retribution money," just what the money for temple festivals or other religious occasions was called when collected outside the community. The annual income from this source was 5,000 yüan. With these funds, the San-i T'ang operated a pilot service, dredged the harbor, controlled weights and measures, gave presents to the government officials, kept a police force (the *lu-chu* had the right to arrest and judge people), trained a voluntary militia, and established a medical dispensary. It also provided for theater performances in front of the Temple of the Water Immortal during the two weeks before the Chinese New Year to divert the debtors who sought sanctuary in the temple in order to escape their creditors at that time.

Still, less money was spent on this impressive array of public services than on strictly religious activities. For instance, the celebrated annual festival for Ma-tsu in the Great Temple of the Queen of Heaven was organized by the San-i T'ang. It cost 1,200 yüan. It was in connection with this festival that Tainan's greatest religious procession occurred. The San-i T'ang also took the lead in organizing the annual *p'u-tu* held before the Temple of the Water Immortal. Closely associated with it was a five-day Taoist service for the repose of dead sailors and the pacification of the sea. At the exhibition of foodstuffs for the nourishment of "hungry ghosts," the members of the time-hallowed three *chiao* vied with each other to see which *chiao* could build the tallest pillar of glutinous sweetened rice. The pillars are said to have been taller than the temple itself. The inscription of each pillar listed as the donor the legendary founder of the *chiao*.

It was on the occasion of the annual *p'u-tu* that the five T'u-ti-kung *hui* surrounding the temple acted in concert. Each contributed to the celebration and participated in its organization. Their roles were expressed ritually by the fact that the incense burners, together with the statues of the saint (in cases where such statues existed), were invited to the site of the celebration. The organizing committee provided sedan chairs to fetch each T'u-ti-kung and a band of musicians to accompany him from his street. The several T'u-ti-kung were placed on a high seat at the south end of the ceremonial area so that they might "inspect the offering," *chien-chiao*. They themselves were not given any special offerings. They were there to represent the different segments of the community.

The T'u-ti-kung of Look West Street. The neighborhood of Look West Street was composed not only of the *chieh* of that name but also of another that crossed it, the South River Street (*Nan-ho chieh*). I do not know of any particular reason why these two streets should have shared a single T'u-ti-kung, but it was an established convention that the position of *lu-chu* should alternate between the residents of the two streets. The two streets together also supported a *hui* for the Fire King, of which more below. The activities of the T'u-ti-kung *hui*, which had proceeded without break since 1765, were interrupted in 1887. In 1907 a general meeting of the neighborhood was called in the Temple of the Water Immortal, at which it was decided to reactivate the association. There follows a translation of the revised charter drawn up in that year.[37]

Record of the Statutes of the Fu-te-yeh (Father of Good Merit) Association

Considering that the prosperity of commerce verily rests on factors that surpass human comprehension and that the fortune of streets surely depends on divine protection, our [two] street[s] from ancient times [have] maintained the precious inscribed [incense burner] of our Fu-te-yeh. Abiding by this worship, each year we used to pass on the incense burner one to another, provide theater performances, and perform religious services;[38] and on each annual occasion with merry feasting we pledged to do even better the following year. Could there be anything more excellent than this? But in the year 1887, when the incense burner was held on South River Street, a fire happened to break out in that street and the holy image of the T'u-ti-kung was temporarily moved [from the house of the *lu-chu*] to the house of the *lu-hsia* Li Tung. Thereupon this man happened to move away, whence it came about that for the last twenty years the incense burner has not been passed on. Now, however, the more zealous among us—deploring the ruinous decline of the cult of our Fu-te-yeh and the drawnout, long procrastination of its onetime members—have invited us all to a public meeting in the San-i T'ang [Temple of the Water Immortal] to discuss the matter. This meeting has now decided to arrange for the renewed passing-on of the incense burner on the day of Mid-Autumn [fifteenth of the eighth lunar month], and also to organize the offerings and the worship that are proper for the occasion entirely as was done before, as a shining example of our sincerest reverence. This reactivation of our ancient custom must be seen as a manifestation of the divine power of our Fu-te-yeh and as an expression of the devout intentions of our community. With this we enunciate our profound hope that all of us will cooperate in heart and in deed, that those who are responsible will promote community well-being by improving the worship of Fu-te-yeh and making it more festive from one year to the next, and that the continuity will never again be broken. All this so that henceforth we shall no longer be laughed at behind our backs by people from other streets.[39]

[Here follow the rules of the association.]

The members of our association now number 31 "shops," ten former and 21 new members.[40]

Former members have already contributed the *ch'a-lu-chin*. For new members this initial contribution is hereby fixed at four pieces of silver. Hereafter, if someone wishes to join the association, he must contribute this sum before he can become a member.

All those who wish to become members of the association for the sixth-month worship of the Fire King must also join this [T'u-ti-kung] association.

The fifteenth day of the eighth month has been established as the proper day for the transmission of the incense burner. This day should not be altered, nor should there be any delay.[41]

Whenever important matters of common interest are to be decided, the association officers should convene a general meeting at the meeting place. They should not make decisions on their own.

The property [in support of] worship consists of two houses that our Fu-te-yeh [association] had built in former times. One of these houses, situated at No. 30 Look West Street, earns a rent of 100 pieces of silver per annum. The other house, situated on South River Street, brings in a rent of 84 pieces of silver per annum. The superintendent of the houses is obliged to furnish these sums in toto; and under no circumstances will there be any reductions or extras.

Adopted on a certain day of the eighth month, 1907.

As customary, the T'u-ti-kung association kept a yearly record of its accounts. This has now been lost, and only a simplified statement distributed to the members in the year 1937 has come down to us. It records that during that year the association had 48 members, of whom two had moved elsewhere during the preceding year, five had temporarily excused themselves, and two were in mourning and could not participate. The financial statement showed a balance of 553.02 Japanese yen, of which 73 yen represented a surplus from the preceding year. Major income was still from the same two houses, now producing an annual rent of 364 yen. A guaranteed loan, presumably of capital belonging to the association, brought in another 74 yen. On the debit side, the costs of worship (including theater) amounted to 89 yen. The banquet for members was still more expensive: 104 yen. The association had also sent 24.20 yen as cash gifts to members on the occasion of marriages or funerals. It used 26.60 yen to assist the Temple of the Water Immortal in the celebration of the annual *p'u-tu*. The costs of maintenance (123 yen), taxes (25 yen), and legal expenses (52.25 yen) for the houses were also included.

Some idea of the turnover rate that might be expected in such a neighborhood association over the years is indicated by the fact that slightly less than one-third of the membership of the association as revived in 1907 had been members twenty years earlier. We have more detailed data on turnover for the neighborhood's Huo-wang *hui* (Fire King association), whose membership must have paralleled that of the T'u-ti-kung *hui* very closely, as those wishing to join the Huo-wang *hui* of Look West Street had to belong to the neighborhood's T'u-ti-kung *hui*, though the reverse was not true.

The Huo-wang *hui* had 28 members in 1907, as against 31 for the T'u-ti-kung *hui*. Membership fluctuated from year to year, but the five-year averages grew steadily larger and the peak membership of 45 was reached in 1933. It is notable that only five of the 1907 members still belonged 31 years later. The average duration of membership was only eight years. The detailed records of the Fire King association provide a glimpse of the kinds of shops found in the Look West Street neighborhood. Several of the city's most important wholesalers were located there, including some well-known firms importing dry goods and other commodities from Japan. There were two drugstores (which, incidentally, had a professional communal association centered in a temple of their own not far away), a drug wholesaler, a tea merchant, a rice store, a grocery store, several bakeries, a shop selling preserved meat, a cooper, and so on.

The Fire King Association. Despite the heavy overlap in membership with the T'u-ti-kung *hui*, other neighborhood associations (such as that of the Fire King) were quite distinct. For one thing, their activities and expenditures were much more closely restricted to religious ritual. And unlike T'u-ti-kung *hui*, which were autonomous in principle and almost always so in practice, other neighborhood associations were more often than not affiliated with a mother temple.

We may illustrate these differences by looking more closely at the Fire King association of Look West Street. It will be recalled that the T'u-ti-kung *hui* of this neighborhood (South River Street as well as Look West Street) had been allowed to lapse in 1887 and was revived in 1907. The Fire King association was the only other *hui* organized by the neighborhood. It is not certain when this association was founded, but an account book that has survived starts with 1907 and continues without break until 1938.[42] A comparison of these records with the statement of the T'u-ti-kung *hui* for the year 1937 shows that all members of the Fire King cult belong to the T'u-ti-kung *hui*.

The Fire King association had no capital endowment but relied solely on dues fixed anew each year at the same rate for all. In 1907, dues were 3.71 yüan.[43] During the same period, a day's work for a coolie brought him 0.30, and a *tou* (bushel) of rice cost about the same. During the next fourteen years, the annual levy oscillated between 3.60 and 4.60. Then it rose to 5 in 1923, when total income was 155 Japanese yen, only 3.76 above expenditures. The next two years saw a decline in dues income and a growing deficit. Then in 1926 the T'u-ti-kung *hui* provided a subsidy of 40 yen, and dues were reduced to 3.50 yen. A subsidy was paid each year until 1931, and during this period annual income remained steady at around 180 yen. From 1932 on, though, there was no subsidy, nor were dues raised. Income in 1932 was only 117.20 yen, but through a drastic cut in spending, especially for the offerings, there was a surplus for the year of 8.95 yen. From then until the association was dissolved in 1938, both income and expenditures were low. In 1937, the contribution was set at 2 yen, and the T'u-ti-kung *hui* provided a loan of 36 yen, which was promptly repaid. The next year the association managed to raise only 60 yen, the lowest total ever; it ended its existence with a deficit of 5.85, to be paid, as duly stated in the account book, by the *lu-chu*.

A translation of the detailed expenditures for one year is reproduced in the notes.[44] What follows is a descriptive summary for the whole period. Expenditures were largely for three activities: theater, religious offerings and services, and the banquet. The only other expense of any significance was the small annual gift made to the shrine from which the association had obtained its cult and where its celebrations took place.

Let me explain: an old Buddhist monastery outside the south gate of Tainan had within its precincts a small sanctuary for the worship of the Fire King.[45] All Fire King associations in the city were affiliated through *fen-hsiang* with this sanctuary. The proper anniversary was the twenty-third day of the sixth month, but in practice any auspicious day of that month could be used by the various associations for their yearly pilgrimage. The annual excursion to the sanctuary by the Look West Street association was made by all the members. The association provided a sedan chair for the *lu-chu*, who carried the incense burner, and sedan chairs or rickshas for the others. There was a small band of musicians. The offerings were also carried along. In this way the pilgrims set out in procession on the morning of the festival day. The celebrations started at the monastery at noon. A gift of two yen, "oil and incense money," was made to the monastery, but there was no interaction whatsoever with the Buddhist monks who inhabited the place; on the contrary, Taoist priests were invited from the city to conduct the service, and the festive banquet was anything but vegetarian. The monastery had nice gardens and grounds covered with large trees—a pleasant place for a picnic. The night was devoted to dining and theater; and only when the city gates reopened the next morning did the burghers return to their streets from their very enjoyable pilgrimage.

The theater performed was invariably of the *luan-t'an* variety, generally considered the only genre fitting for such a religious occasion. This form of theater, now practically extinct, consisted in large part of "military theater," *wu-hsi*, and thus contrasted with *nan-kuan*, a form of purely "civil" theater, *wen-hsi*, from southern Fukien. The *luan-t'an* plays were performed in Mandarin, *kuan-hua*, as specified in the account books. This was quite unintelligible to the average spectator, a matter of little import since the stories were well known. The troupe of 30 to 40 actors and musicians, generally from Tainan City, got eight to nine yen for their performance, which started in the late afternoon and lasted until daybreak; the expense of putting up the stage was extra. Marionette (*k'uei-lei*) theater was performed during the afternoon hours, when offerings were made and the religious service performed. The choice of marionette plays was made by throwing divining blocks before the Fire King. The marionette troupe consisted of only a few persons, who got a total of 1.80 to 2.50 yen for the performance. In the early years of the association's existence, the actors of the *luan-t'an* play and the puppeteers were given a small tip at the start of the performance. This was later discontinued, and during the association's last years the marionette performance was dispensed with altogether. Calculated over the whole period, expenses for theater came to 8.5 percent of total expenditures, ranging from 12 percent in the early years to a low of 7 percent in 1937.

Offerings and religious services accounted for 28.5 percent of expenditures during the total period. Apart from incense, candles, and offering paper, none of which was very expensive, the association offered to the Fire King a whole hog and a whole goat. These were more or less expensive, according to their weight. The hog regularly cost more than 20 yen. It was the custom either to give these animals to the *lu-chu* or to divide them among the members. When the subsidy from the T'u-ti-kung *hui* ceased in 1932, these offerings were dispensed with. Eight times over the thirty-odd years of its existence the association invited Taoist priests to conduct a small *chiao* of one day. These were held at intervals of three or four years, and the last one was in 1933. A head priest, four assistants, and a few musicians together earned a fee of 10 yen for the day. The ritual, of general communal significance, bore no particular relationship to the Fire King. Special offerings for the service amounted to about 1.50 yen. The *lu-chu* took part in this ritual as the representative of the community.

As with other communal associations, the Huo-wang *hui*'s banquet was of utmost importance. Year after year, this feast accounted for more than three-fifths of all expenditures. It was prepared by a restaurant chef, who came with his helpers, a portable kitchen, and foodstuffs to cook on the premises. He was paid a lump sum to prepare dishes for three to five tables of ten persons, according to the number of participants. The account book specified each year that it was a *Man-Han ta-hsi*, a Peking-style Manchu-Chinese banquet, with a roast suckling pig, pigeon eggs, and birds' nests. Wine was separately provided for, as were bowls and chopsticks, towels, tablecloths, and so on. At the close of the banquet, each participant got a red-colored piece of pastry in the form of a turtle and a bunch of bananas to take home. This feasting was done on an even grander scale by the T'u-ti-kung *hui*. For the year 1937, the association of Look West Street spent, for the same number of participants, almost twice the sum spent by the Fire King association. By contrast, the religious services were essentially the same for the two associations. It is typical that the T'u-ti-kung *hui*, but not the Fire King association, offered small gifts of cash to its member households on the occasion of certain life-crisis ceremonies. And this brings us to our final point.

The Socioreligious Functions of the T'u-ti-kung Associations

Apart from their functions already mentioned, T'u-ti-kung associations were also involved, within limits, in policing the streets. Some light is thrown on this matter by stone inscriptions found in the quarter of the Temple of the Water Immortal. It will be recalled that the T'u-ti-kung *hui* of Look West Street was one of five organizations in the neighborhood of this quarter. Two of the others possessed T'u-ti-kung shrines, and it is to the stone inscriptions made at the time of their restoration that we now turn. One of these, erected in 1812, specifies the exact amount of money contributed by each member. The shrine must have been a rather modest structure, for the inscription states that embellishments were to be left to future generations. It continues:

The T'u-ti-kung of our street formerly had no temple but was worshiped in the houses of the people. Only in the K'ang-hsi reign period [in this case, early in the eighteenth century] did we build a temple at the west end of the street. [This was right at the waterfront; according to the text of the inscription, the shrine was surrounded on three sides by water and offered an interesting sight.] ... Since, as in any temple, there is worship of holy beings, both the interior and the exterior should be kept scrupulously clean. No garbage may be dumped here. Now that we have restored the place, it must also be kept quiet. We have fixed the following rules in public assembly to be kept forever.

(1) It is forbidden to loiter or squat in the temple and also to gamble there. Those who do not observe this rule shall be restrained by the *lu-chu* of the year. Those who persist in their wrongdoings shall be reported to the officials for prosecution.

(2) It is forbidden to dump garbage within the temple precincts or in the street or harbor [in front of the temple], even though these are public places. Those who fail to conform shall pay a fine of one day of theater.[46]

The second inscription enumerates similar rules: "The exterior of our neighborhood and of our newly restored temple—that is to say, the street before our shrine—must be kept clean and peaceful. By common consent, we prohibit the use of this area as a public place. Let there be no gambling, brawling, disposal or dumping of goods, building of high structures, extension of wide awnings [over the street], or other evil practices. In case of infractions, the *lu-chu* of the year shall do what he can to stop them. If they continue, the perpetrators shall be reported to the officials for prosecution."[47]

On the prohibition of high structures, an earlier inscription from the same temple gives an interesting account:

The cult of the Fu-te-yeh in our street already has a long history. In the spring of the year 1778, a shop on the left side was rebuilt to an extreme height, after which the faithful of our street all experienced disaster. We then collected money along the street and through collective effort dismantled the building and made it lower. The contributions made throughout the previous years now suffice for the expenses of the anniversary festival. Contributors whose names are engraved on this stela henceforth need not pay Good Retribution money [*yüan-yin*] for theater performances in the spring and in the autumn. Others should continue to contribute periodically as of old that we may all celebrate together. It is our collective decision that shops and houses along the street on which the temple fronts may not be made taller, thereby harming the temple and bringing disaster to the inhabitants. Should anyone add to the top of his shop, the *lu-chu* of the year must inform everybody and endeavor to stop him. If the culprit does not abide by our collective decision, then he shall be reported to the authorities for prosecution.[48]

Interdictions aimed at keeping the temple clean and calm may also be found in other instances.[49] Regulations concerning cleanliness, order, and decorum throughout the neighborhood appear to be a standard feature of T'u-ti-kung associations. The same is true of geomantic proscriptions. Yet even these regulations, imposed by the community, are of a cultic nature and are cast in religious terms.

Notes

Notes

Introduction: Urban Development in Imperial China

1. A longer manuscript that included most of this introduction was given a critical reading by Mark Elvin, Robert A. Kapp, Harry J. Lamley, F. W. Mote, Carol A. Smith, and Arthur F. Wright. I have been able to take into account only a fraction of their suggestions and comments, and in recording my gratitude I absolve them all of any responsibility for the many remaining shortcomings.

2. Louis Wirth, "Urbanism as a Way of Life," *American Journal of Sociology*, 44 (1938): 1–24. Robert Redfield, *The Folk Culture of Yucatán* (Chicago: University of Chicago Press, 1941); and "The Folk Society," *American Journal of Sociology*, 41 (Jan. 1947): 293–308.

3. Gideon Sjoberg, *The Preindustrial City: Past and Present* (Glencoe, Ill.: Free Press, 1960).

4. Weber's relevant writings are scattered throughout his oeuvre. A useful collection is Don Martindale and Gertrud Neuwirth, trans., *The City* (Glencoe, Ill.: Free Press, 1958). See also Hans A. Gerth, trans. and ed., *The Religion of China* (Glencoe, Ill.: Free Press, 1951), pp. 13–20. For an appreciation of Webers' typology, see Vatro Murvar, "Some Tentative Modifications of Weber's Typology: Occidental versus Oriental City," *Social Forces*, 44 (Mar. 1966): 381–89.

5. See Philip M. Hauser, "Observations on the Urban-Folk and Urban-Rural Dichotomies as Forms of Western Ethnocentrism," in Philip M. Hauser and Leo F. Schnore, eds., *The Study of Urbanization* (New York: Wiley, 1965), pp. 503–17, and the literature cited therein.

6. See, e.g., Oliver C. Cox, "The Preindustrial City Reconsidered," *Sociological Quarterly*, 5 (Spring 1964): 133–44.

7. Hauser 1965, pp. 511–13.

8. For instance, Gerhard E. Lenski (*Power and Privilege: A Theory of Social Stratification* [New York: McGraw-Hill, 1966]) distinguishes "agrarian societies" from "advanced horticultural societies," and S. N. Eisenstadt (*The Political Systems of Empires* [New York: Free Press, 1963], pp. 351–52) distinguishes bureaucratic societies from patrimonial, aristocratic, and feudal societies.

9. The *locus classicus* is Robert Hartwell, "A Cycle of Economic Change in Imperial China: Coal and Iron in Northeast China, 750–1350," *Journal of the Economic and Social History of the Orient*, 10, part 1 (1967): 107–59.

10. The regional population estimates in this paragraph are my own, based on provincial breakdowns. Provincial-level data for A.D. 742 are provided in Hans Bielenstein, "The Census of China During the Period 2–742 A.D.," *Bulletin of the Museum of Far Eastern Antiquities* (Stockholm), no. 19 (1947). Bielenstein's provincial population estimates are incorporated with others for later centuries and published in comprehensive tables presented in the Appendix to John D. Durand, "The Population Statistics of China, A.D. 2–1953," *Population Studies*, 8, no. 3 (Mar. 1960): 250–55. The estimate of Kaifeng's population increase refers specifically to the period from 742 to 1078. See Hartwell 1967: 151.

11. The figure of 90,000 is based on the Yüan census of 1330 (Hartwell 1967: 151), Hartwell estimates that as of 1200 Kaifeng's population may well have approached a million; I incline toward a peak population of 850,000.

12. I base the following summary on clues provided in the following sources: Denis Twitchett, "The T'ang Market System," *Asia Major*, n.s. 12, no. 2 (1966): 202–43; Denis Twitchett, "Merchant, Trade and Government in Late T'ang," *Asia Major*, n.s. 14, part 1 (1968), 63–95; Shiba Yoshinobu, *Sōdai shōgyōshi kenkyū* (Tokyo: Kazama shobō, 1968), trans. by Mark Elvin as *Commerce and Society in Sung China* (Ann Arbor: University of Michigan, Center for Chinese Studies, 1970; hereafter cited as Shiba/Elvin 1970), p. 42; F. W. Mote's paper below; and F. W. Mote, "A Millennium of Chinese Urban History: Form, Time, and Space Concepts in Soochow," *Rice University Studies*, 59, no. 4 (Fall 1973): 35–65.

13. The map and photograph reproduced here as Figures 1 and 2 are courtesy of F. W. Mote, who was the first to publish them in juxtaposition. Most of the data in this paragraph are drawn from Mote 1973: 38–39, 53.

14. The first full statement of this development is provided in Owen Lattimore, *Inner Asian Frontiers of China* (Boston: Beacon Press, 1940), pp. 39–41, 394–95. See also the restatement in Glenn T. Trewartha, "Chinese Cities: Origins and Functions," *Annals of the Association of American Geographers*, 42, no. 1 (1952): 70–71.

15. See Herold J. Wiens, *China's March toward the Tropics* (Hamden, Conn.: Shoe String Press, 1954), pp. 187–200, 277–87.

16. G. Edward Stephan, "Variation in County Size: A Theory of Segmental Growth," *American Sociological Review*, 36, no. 3 (June 1971): 451–61. Stephan's treatment builds on theoretical formulations by Kenneth E. Boulding and Arthur L. Stinchcombe.

17. Joseph B. R. Whitney, *China: Area, Administration, and Nation Building* (Chicago: University of Chicago, Department of Geography, 1970), chap. 4.

18. The pre-Ch'ing figures are taken from Whitney 1970, pp. 75–78. The Ch'ing figure, for the Yung-cheng reign, is taken from T'ung-tsu Ch'ü, *Local Government in China under the Ch'ing* (Cambridge: Harvard University Press, 1962), p. 2.

19. The maxima are taken from a series of consistent estimates based on my interpretation of data drawn primarily from Bielenstein 1947; Durand

1960; Ping-ti Ho, "An Estimate of the Total Population of Sung-Chin China," in *Études Song in Memoriam Etienne Balazs* (The Hague: Mouton, 1970), pp. 34–53; Ping-ti Ho, *Studies on the Population of China, 1368–1953* (Cambridge: Harvard University Press, 1959); and John S. Aird, "Population Growth," in Alexander Eckstein et al., eds., *Economic Trends in Communist China* (Chicago: Aldine, 1968), pp. 261–72.

20. The figures for Han and T'ang are from Whitney 1970, pp. 75–76. The figures for Ch'ing are from T'ung-tsu Ch'ü 1962, p. 2.

21. The breakdown was ca. 600 for Ch'en, 1,124 for Northern Chou, and 579 for Northern Ch'i. Yang Yü-liu, *Chung-kuo li tai ti fang hsing cheng ch'ü hua* (History of China's local administrative demarcations; Taipei: Chung-hua wen hua ch'u pan shih yeh wei yüan hui, 1957), pp. 124, 141, and 150.

22. Characteristically, each new dynasty started out with approximately as many county-level units as its predecessor ended up with. Within a few decades the number was reduced by the consolidation of counties in densely settled areas, after which it rose again as new counties were added, mostly along the expanding frontier. The typical addition of frontier counties late in the dynastic cycle, by exacerbating problems of governmental control and coordination, may have hastened some dynasties' decline and fall.

23. It is simply ridiculous to characterize capital cities as being "never . . . more than a day's walk" from one another "in the more fertile parts of the country" (Lattimore 1940, p. 41).

24. Twitchett 1966: 218–25.

25. *Ibid.*: 225.

26. This paragraph paraphrases Twitchett 1966: 226.

27. *Ibid.*: 205, 207ff.

28. *Ibid.*: 227–30.

29. *Ibid.*; Twitchett 1968; Shiba/Elvin 1970; Mark Elvin, *The Pattern of the Chinese Past* (Stanford: Stanford University Press, 1973), chap. 12.

30. See Shiba/Elvin 1970, pp. 126–80; Elvin 1973, chap. 12; Twitchett 1966: 230–43.

31. Twitchett 1966: 231.

32. *Ibid.*: 203.

33. Twitchett 1968: 74–95.

34. *Ibid.*: 80.

35. Twitchett 1966: 241.

36. See the summary provided in Elvin 1973, pp. 215–25.

37. Elvin 1973, p. 203: "Between about 1300 and 1500, for reasons which are still largely inexplicable, the Chinese economy fell into a decline from which it only recovered slowly." Elvin's own account, it should be noted, goes far to explain the inexplicable.

38. These characterizations of urban systems in the late imperial era are given empirical support in my paper in Part Two.

39. It would have been exactly 3 percent if the population of Kaifeng were 900,000 and that of the North China region 30 million.

40. Population estimates for the top ten cities of North China are graphed in Figure 1, p. 238.

41. Elvin 1973, esp. chap. 14.

42. I shall make no attempt here to document this sweeping assertion. It is

based as much on first principles as on my reading of the literature on the Chinese fiscal system in the medieval and late imperial eras.

43. Mote 1973: p. 39.

44. This holds only if we take 1895 as the end of the era. It is likely that the populations of Peking, Shanghai, and Wuhan rose above one million during the 1895–1911 period.

45. In his exuberant historical survey of China's changing landscape, Yi-fu Tuan tells us that the population of T'ang Ch'ang-an reached "nearly two million, one million within the city walls and another in the suburbs," that T'ang Loyang had "more than a million people within its walls," that in 1100 Kaifeng was only one of five cities whose population "exceeded one million," and that Hangchow's population rose to 1.5 million during the Southern Sung. He also quotes Arthur Waley ("Life Under the Han Dynasty," *History Today*, 3 [1953]: 24) to the effect that in A.D. 111 Chengtu had "at least a million people within its walls and some 350,000 in the suburbs." Yi-fu Tuan, *China* (Chicago: Aldine, 1969), pp. 99, 103, 105, 132, and 134.

46. For Kaifeng, see Hartwell 1967. For Hangchow, see Jacques Gernet, *Daily Life in China on the Eve of the Mongol Invasion, 1250–1276* (trans. H. M. Wright; London: George Allen and Unwin, 1962), esp. chap. 1.

47. Tertius Chandler and Gerald Fox, *3000 Years of Urban Growth* (New York: Academic Press, 1974), pp. 314–23.

48. Chandler and Fox 1974, p. 364.

The Cosmology of the Chinese City

1. Joseph Needham, *Science and Civilisation in China, Vol. 4, Physics and Physical Technology, Part 2: Mechanical Engineering* (Cambridge: Cambridge University Press, 1965), pp. 10–50, has made a preliminary but important effort to sketch the history of the artisanate.

2. James Legge, *The Chinese Classics, Vol. 4, The She King* (London: Trübner, 1871), p. 2. Cf. also Arthur Waley, *The Book of Songs* (London: Allen and Unwin, 1937), pp. 247–49.

3. Legge 1871, pp. 460–64.

4. *Ibid.*, p. 456.

5. Waley 1937, pp. 259–60.

6. Legge 1871, p. 458.

7. Waley 1937, p. 259, note 1, citing Bernhard Karlgren, "Yin and Chou Researches," *Bulletin of the Museum of Far Eastern Antiquities* (hereafter BMFEA), 8 (1935): inscription no. 14.

8. The translation is slightly adapted from Bernhard Karlgren, "The Book of Documents," BMFEA, 22 (1950): 51. Cf. also Karlgren's "Glosses on the Book of Documents," BMFEA, 20–21 (1948–49): 74–75.

9. Karlgren, 1950: 51; James Legge, *The Chinese Classics, Vol. 3, The Shoo King* (London: Trübner, 1865), pp. 420–52.

10. Legge 1865, p. 423, cites one of the standard commentaries—which I favor—to the effect that this was a sacrifice to Heaven, with which was associated the high ancestor of the Chou, Hou Chi; hence the two oxen.

11. Kwang-chih Chang, *The Archeology of Ancient China*, rev. ed. (New Haven: Yale University Press, 1968), pp. 280–311.

12. Gods of the four directions and of the center, called *fang-ti*, were a

part of the Shang pantheon. This is attested by an inscription of Shang times found in *Tseng ting Yin hsü shu ho'i k'ao shih*, ch. 3, as cited in Henri Maspero, *La Chine antique*, rev. ed. (Paris: Imprimerie nationale, 1955), p. 138, note 1.

13. See the studies of Shih Chang-ju as summarized in Te-k'un Cheng, *Archeology in China, Vol. 2, Shang China* (Cambridge, Eng.: Heffer, 1960), pp. 53–55.
14. Chang 1968, pp. 307–8.
15. Waley 1937, p. 281.
16. Chang 1968, pp. 308–11.
17. Maspero 1955, pp. 156–68.
18. Cf. Maspero 1955, pp. 138–43, and Édouard Chavannes, "Le Dieu du sol dans la Chine antique," appendix to *Le T'ai Chan: Essai de monographie d'un culte chinois* (Paris: E. Leroux, 1910), pp. 437–525.
19. James Legge, *The Chinese Classics, Vol. 5, The Ch'un Ts'ew with the Tso Chuen* (London: Trübner, 1872), p. 115.
20. *Ibid.*, p. 515; Chavannes 1910, p. 516.
21. Ssu-ma Ch'ien, *Shih chi*; ch. 6 (I am citing standard histories from the photolith edition of T'ung wen shu chü, Shanghai, 1884); for a French version, see Édouard Chavannes, trans. and ed., *Les Mémoires historiques de Se-ma Ts'ien* (Paris: E. Leroux, 1895–1905), vol. 2, p. 137.
22. Legge 1872, p. 514.
23. Cf. Maspero 1955, pp. 134–39, 169–70.
24. Te-k'un Cheng, *Archeology in China, Vol. 3, Chou China* (Cambridge, Eng.: Heffer, 1963), pp. 34–35.
25. See the outlines of the excavated city walls in Chang 1968, pp. 282–304.
26. Chavannes 1895–1905, vol. 2, pp. 164–66.
27. *Shih chi*, ch. 8, pp. 31a–b. For location of the arsenal see *Shih chi*, ch. 99; for an English version, see Burton Watson, trans., *Records of the Grand Historian of China* (New York: Columbia University Press, 1961), vol. 1, p. 297. The idea that Hsiao Ho's layout was governed by considerations of the system of compensatory magic known as *ya-sheng* is the product of later scholastic theorists.
28. *Han shu*, ch. 2; for an English version, see Homer H. Dubs, trans. and ed., *The History of the Former Han Dynasty, Vol. 1* (Baltimore, Md.: Waverly Press, 1938), pp. 181–83.
29. Satō Taketoshi, "Kandai Chōan no ichi" (The markets of Han Dynasty Ch'ang-an), *Chūgoku kōdaishi kenkyū*, 2 (1965): 233.
30. Wang Chung-shu, "Han Ch'ang an ch'eng k'ao ku kung tso ti ch'u pu shou hu" (Preliminary results from archaeological work on the walls of Han Ch'ang-an), *K'ao ku t'ung hsün*, no. 5 (1957): 102–10.
31. Satō Taketoshi, "Kandai no toshi, toku ni Chōan o chūshin ni" (Han cities, with special reference to Ch'ang-an), *Rekishi kyōiku*, 14, no. 12 (1966): 33–35.
32. Cheng Ch'iao, *T'ung chih* (Wan yu wen k'u, ed.; Shanghai: Shang wu, 1937), ch. 43, p. 571a.
33. Cf. Satō 1965: 288–331; and Chavannes 1895–1905, vol. 2, p. 139.
34. *Han shu*, ch. IB; Dubs 1938, p. 109.
35. *Han shu*, ch. 22, pp. 7a–b. The full story of his collection of old texts

by offering rewards for their presentation is told in the biography of the Prince of Ho-chien, *Han shu*, ch. 53, pp. 1b–2a, and is summarized in Bernhard Karlgren, "The Early History of the Chou li and Tso chuan Texts," BMFEA, 3 (1931): 3.

36. Karlgren 1931: 1–59. On the "K'ao-kung chi," which is said to have been substituted for a section on "Winter Offices" that neither the Prince of Ho-chien nor his contemporaries could recover, Karlgren, pp. 6–7, comes to the conclusion that "There is no . . . doubt that the *K'ao kung ki* was inserted into the *Chou li* at least not later than the time of Liu Hsin." Liu Hsin died in 23 B.C.

37. Bernhard Karlgren, "Legends and Cults in Ancient China," BMFEA, 18 (1946): 201. Italics mine.

38. *Chou li*, ch. 1, pp. 1a–2a (I am citing Classics from *Sung pen shih san ching chu su fu chiao k'an chi*, Shanghai, 1887); for a French version, see Edouard Constant Biot, *Le Tcheou-li; ou, Rites de Tcheou* (Paris: Imprimerie nationale, 1851), vol. 1, p. 1. This standard opening is missing for the last part of the *Chou li*.

39. *Chou li*, ch. 24, p. 10b; Biot 1851, vol. 2, p. 74.
40. *Chou li*, ch. 26, p. 21b; Biot 1851, vol. 2, p. 109.
41. *Chou li*, ch. 41, p. 20a; Biot 1851, vol. 2, p. 553.
42. *Chou li*, ch. 41, p. 20a; Biot 1851, vol. 2, pp. 554–55.
43. See above, notes 2 and 15.
44. For a discussion of the technical procedures of orientation before and after the use of the magnetic compass, see Joseph Needham, *Science and Civilisation in China, Vol. 4, Physics and Physical Technology, Part 1: Physics* (Cambridge: Cambridge University Press, 1962), pp. 311–13.
45. *Chou li*, ch. 10, p. 8a; Biot 1851, vol. 1, p. 201.
46. *Ibid.*
47. Marcel Granet, "Les Nombres," in *La Pensée chinoise* (Paris: Renaissance du livre, 1934), chap. 3, esp. pp. 173–74.
48. *Chou li*, ch. 41, p. 20a; Biot 1851, vol. 2, p. 556.
49. *Chou li*, ch. 14, pp.. 10b–14b; Biot 1851, vol. 1, pp. 309–30. See also Nancy Lee Swann, *Food and Money in Ancient China* (Princeton, N.J.: Princeton University Press, 1950), pp. 341–42 and *passim*; and Satō 1965: 233–35.
50. *Chou li*, ch. 7, p. 16b; Biot 1851, vol. 1, p. 145.
51. *Chou li*, ch. 41, pp. 20b–21a; Biot 1851, vol. 2, pp. 556–61. For general discussions of the *ming-t'ang*, see Granet 1934, pp. 102–4, 178–82, and *passim*. An uncritical monograph is William E. Soothill, *The Hall of Light: A Study of Early Chinese Kingship* (London: Lutterworth Press, 1951).
52. *Han shu*, ch. 25B, pp. 2a–b; for an English version, see Homer H. Dubs, trans. and ed., *The History of the Former Han Dynasty, Vol. 2* (Baltimore, Md.: Waverly Press, 1944), pp. 30, 87, 91–92.
53. *Chou li*, ch. 19, p. 13b; Biot 1851, vol. 1, p. 441. In elaborated models of the *ming-t'ang*, the altars of the directional gods are worked into the plan.
54. *Han shu*, ch. 99B; for an English version, see Homer H. Dubs, trans. and ed., *The History of the Former Han Dynasty, Vol. 3* (Baltimore, Md.: Waverly Press, 1955), p. 353.
55. *Han shu*, ch. 99C; Dubs 1955, pp. 395–96.
56. *Han shu*, ch. 99C; Dubs 1955, p. 397.

57. The excavations are briefly summarized in Hsia Nai, *K'ao ku hsüeh lun wen chi* (Peking: K'o hsüeh ch'u pan she, 1961), pp. 153–54. A ground plan of the excavated site appears in Chung-kuo k'o hsüeh yüan, T'u mu chien chu yen chiu so *with* Ch'ing-hua ta hsüeh, Chien chu hsi, joint eds., *Chung-kuo chien chu* (Chinese architecture; Peking: Wen wu ch'u pan she, 1957), p. 3.

58. For general remarks on the difference between northern and southern cities, see Yüeh Chia-tsao, *Chung-kuo chien chu shih* (History of Chinese architecture; Hang-hsien, 1933), section 2, part b.

59. For details on the history of the city under the Wu, I rely on the 1880 reprint of the *Chiang-ning fu chih* by Lü Yen-chao and Yao Nai, especially ch. 8–10 on ancient remains. I also rely on Louis Gaillard, *Nankin d'alors et d'aujourd'hui: Aperçu historique et géographique* (Shanghai: Imprimerie de la Mission Catholique, 1903).

60. The palace enclosure, which apparently replaced a modest and decaying structure, was constructed of tiles and timbers from Sun Ch'üan's old palace at Wu-ch'ang; the materials were presumably rafted down the Yangtze. Cf. *San kuo chih*, Wu-chih, ch. 2, pp. 30b–31a, and the early sources quoted in the commentary.

61. This is only noted in the outline map for the period from the *Chin-ling ku chin t'u k'ao* of 1516, as reproduced opposite p. 44 in Gaillard 1903.

62. Commentary by Wu Shih-chien and Liu Ch'eng-kan in *Chin shu chiao chu* (Peiping, 1928), ch. 6, p. 4b. The divinations of Kuo P'u are described in the commentary, which quotes from the early T'ang work *Pei t'ang shu ch'ao*, ch. 158, which in turn quotes from the *Chien k'ang chi* (Narrative of Chien-k'ang), now lost.

63. Cf., for example, *Shih chi* ch. 7, 10, 28; Chavannes 1895–1905, vol. 2, pp. 274–75, 481, and vol. 3, p. 457.

64. Cf. Andrew L. March, "An Appreciation of Chinese Geomancy," *Journal of Asian Studies*, 27, no. 2 (Feb. 1968): 253–67, esp. p. 260 for sources cited. See also Morohashi Tetsuji, *Daikanwa jiten* (Tokyo: Taishū kan shoten, 1955–60, 13 vols.), p. 12931a. Maurice Freedman, *Chinese Lineage and Society* (London: Athlone, 1966), pp. 118–43, has some very perceptive remarks on contemporary beliefs and practices related to *feng-shui* and ancestor worship in southeastern China.

65. The incident is recounted in the *Chiang piao chuan* by the third-century author Yü P'u, as quoted in the commentary to *San kuo chih*, "Wu-chih," ch. 8, p. 8a.

66. *Chou shu*, ch. 41, p. 2a. Another version of the story is found in the *San kuo tien lüeh*, as quoted in *T'u shu chi ch'eng* (hereafter TSCC; Shanghai: Chung-hua, 1934), ch. 110, p. 28b.

67. *Sung shih chi shih pen mo*, as quoted in TSCC, ch. 111, p. 6b.

68. Quoted in Morohashi 1955–60; p. 12931a. Elaborated on in the section on geography of the *Chu tzu ch'uan shu*, as quoted in TSCC, ch. 102, p. 35a.

69. *Chang tzu ch'uan shu*, as quoted in Morohashi 1955–60, p. 12931a.

70. His "Tsang-lun," or discussion of grave sites, as quoted in Morohashi 1955–60, p. 12931a.

71. Evidence on the southern origins of *feng-shui* and its far greater prevalence in the South than in the North is abundant. See, for example, the Ming writer Wang Wei, as quoted in March 1968: 261. All the later schools of *feng-shui* are named for southern provinces.

72. For further details, the reader is referred to Arthur F. Wright, "Symbolism and Function: Reflections on Ch'ang-an and Other Great Cities," *Journal of Asian Studies*, 24, no. 4 (Aug. 1965): 667–79, and Wright's chapter on Ch'ang-an in Arnold Toynbee, ed., *Cities of Destiny* (New York: McGraw-Hill, 1967), pp. 143–49.

73. See "T'ang Ch'ang-an ch'eng ti chi ch'u pu t'an tse" (Preliminary survey of the site of T'ang Ch'ang-an), *K'ao ku hsüeh pao*, 3 (1958): 79–94; and Hiraoka Takeo's critique of the survey, "Tō Chōan jō no iseki chōsa to Ka Shōju shi no Kyaku kō chi kō ni tsuite" (A study of the remains of the walls of T'ang Ch'ang-an and comments on the *Ch'ü chiang ch'ih k'ao* of Hsia Ch'eng-shou), *Tōhō Gakuhō*, 29 (1959): 373–80.

74. Cf. *T'ang hui yao* (Peking, 1955), ch. 50, p. 876; Naba Toshisada, "Shina shuto keikakushijō yori kōsatsushitaru to no Chōanjō (T'ang Ch'ang-an considered in the light of Chinese metropolitan planning, in Kuwabara hakushi kanreki kinen shukugakukai, ed., *Kuwabara hakushi kanreki kinen tōyōshi ronsō* (Essays on East Asian history in honor of the sixtieth birthday of Kuwabara Jitsuzō; Kyoto: Kōbundō, 1931), pp. 1268–69; and Hiraoka Takeo, *Chōan to Rakuyō: Chizu* (Ch'ang-an and Loyang: Maps; Kyoto: Kyōto daigaku, Jimbun kagaku kenkyūjo, 1956), pp. 25–26.

75. *Tzu chih t'ung chien* (Peking: Ku chi ch'u pan she, 1956), ch. 178, pp. 5540–42. The usurping Empress Wu, like Wang Mang, was avid for the symbols of legitimacy. In 687 she built a three-storied *ming-t'ang* in Loyang but placed a Buddhist monk in charge of the project! It was duly completed and had a circular moat in the manner of the ancient *pi-yung*. Cf. *T'ang hui yao*, ch. 11. p. 277.

76. See Robert Hartwell's richly documented article "A Cycle of Economic Change in Imperial China: Coal and Iron in Northeast China, 750–1350," *Journal of the Economic and Social History of the Orient*, 10, part 1 (1967): 125.

77. Edward A. Kracke, Jr., "Kaifeng as Capital of China, 907–1127," paper read at the 1967 Annual Meeting of the American Historical Association. I am indebted to Professor Kracke for a wealth of data and insights on Kaifeng.

78. The T'ang figures are from Hiraoka 1956, p. 12.

79. *Sung shih*, ch. 85, p. 4b.

80. *Pien ku kung chi*, by the Ming author Yang Huan, as quoted in Naba 1931, p. 1230. I disagree with Naba's conclusions regarding Kaifeng and the classical prescriptions for city plans.

81. *Wen hsien t'ung k'ao* (Shanghai: Shang wu, 1935), ch. 42, pp. 396–397a.

82. *Sung shih*, ch. 21, p. 3b. In 1101 the emperor worshiped "Heaven and Earth" at the same site. *Sung shih*, ch. 19, p. 6b.

83. *Sung shih*, ch. 21, p. 5b. Throughout the Sung there had been serious arguments on the proper relation among (1) the worship of Heaven, (2) the sacrifices to the imperial ancestors, and (3) the *ming-t'ang*. Cf. Liu Tzu-chien, "Feng shan wen hua yü sung tai ming t'ang chi t'ien" (Two forms of worshiping Heaven in Sung China, *Bulletin of the Institute of Ethnology, Academia Sinica*, 18 (1964): 45–49.

84. Data provided by Professor Kracke. See also *Sung shih*, ch. 85, pp. 8a–9a.

85. *T'u shu pien*, by the Ming author Chang Huang, as quoted in TSCC, ch. 102, p. 39b. In the same passage Chang Huang analyzes the *feng-shui* of this site.

86. Quoted from René-Yvon Lefebvre d'Argencé's introduction to his magnificent series of functional maps of Hangchow, part 3, p. 20. Mr. d'Argencé has kindly allowed me to see this introduction, a manuscript that has a wealth of precise detail on the development of Hangchow as a capital.

87. Henri Maspero, "Rapport sommaire sur une mission archéologique au Tchö-Kiang," *Bulletin de l'École française d'Extrême-Orient*, 14 (1914): 2–5. His historical sketch is based mainly on the standard local histories.

88. D'Argencé manuscript, p. 27.

89. D'Argencé manuscript, p. 33.

90. Passage from the *Wu lin chiu shih* paraphrased in Jacques Gernet, *Daily Life in China on the Eve of the Mongol Invasion, 1250–1276* (trans. H. M. Wright; London: George Allen and Unwin, 1962), pp. 201–3.

91. D'Argencé manuscript, pp. 36–73.

92. Gernet 1962, p. 41.

93. *Chu tzu ch'uan shu*, as quoted in TSCC, ch. 112, p. 35a. One should recall that in a Chinese house the symmetrical view may be got only from the ends of the north-south axis.

94. Hok-lam Chan, "Liu Ping-chung: A Buddhist-Taoist Statesman at the Court of Khubilai Khan," *T'oung Pao*, 53, no. 1–3 (1967): 134.

95. *Ibid.*, note 73.

96. *Yuan shih*, ch. 43, as cited by G. N. Kates, "A New Date for the Origins of the Forbidden City," *Harvard Journal of Asiatic Studies*, 7 (1942–43): 200.

97. See the admirable dissertation of Edward L. Farmer, "The Dual Capital System of the Early Ming Dynasty" (Harvard University, 1968). I am indebted to Dr. Farmer for many suggestions and much helpful criticism.

98. Osvald Sirén, *The Walls and Gates of Peking: Researches and Impressions* (London: John Lane, 1924), p. 43.

99. Hou Jen-chih, *Li shih shang ti Pei-ching* (Peking in history; Peking: Chung-kuo ch'ing nien ch'u pan she, 1962), p. 33.

100. L. C. Arlington and William Lewisohn, *In Search of Old Peking* (Peiping: Henry Vetch, 1935), pp. 105–8.

101. Recently, my former student Dr. Thomas H. C. Li met in Hong Kong an elderly civil engineer who recalled that the painters employed in the imperial palaces in Peking knew as many as 400 songs containing paint formulas and painting techniques. Such songs would ensure the perpetuation of the traditional ways from one generation of painters to the next; analogues no doubt existed in other building crafts.

The Morphology of Walled Capitals

1. Osvald Sirén, *The Walls and Gates of Peking: Researches and Impressions* (London: John Lane, 1924), pp. 22–24.

2. For the decreasing importance of city walls during the Yüan period, see Arthur Christopher Moule, *Quinsai, with Other Notes on Marco Polo* (Cambridge: Cambridge University Press, 1957), p. 13.

3. See J. J. L. Duyvendak, trans., *The Book of Lord Shang* [*Shang chü shu*] (London: A. Probsthani, 1928), pp. 249–51.

4. Ronald Stead, "Walls 50 Feet Thick Defend Major City in North China," *Christian Science Monitor*, Feb. 19, 1947, p. 13.

5. *Ch'eng-chi* (wall and moat) is a common term for the general defensive measures of an area.

6. *Shina jōkaku no gaiyō* (A general description of Chinese cities; n.p.: Shina hakkengun soshireibu, 1940), p. 28.

7. City names that do not allude to the city's site often commemorate historical events, famous local products, or the memory of a local celebrity. See Chin Tsu-meng, "Chung-kuo cheng chu ming ming chih fen lei yen chiu" (A toponymic study of Chinese administrative divisions), *Ti li hsüeh pao*, 10 (1943): 1–23.

8. For a diagram showing the relative location and sizes of all cities built at or near Peking, see Sidney D. Gamble, *Peking: A Social Survey* (New York: Doran, 1921), p. 47.

9. *Ch'ang-te fu chih*, 1787, ch. 1, pp. 4–10; *Kung-ch'ang fu chih*, 1687, ch. 2, pp. 1–49; *P'u-chou fu chih*, 1755, ch. 1, pp. 1–7.

10. U.S. Army Map Service, 1:50,000 series, Sheet 7829-IV, 1944.

11. See Wang I-yai, "Wu-hsi tu shih ti li chih yen chiu" (The urban geography of Wu-hsi), *Ti li hsüeh pao*, 2, no. 3 (Sept. 1935): 23–63; *Yin hsien chih*, 1856, ch. 1, p. 3.

12. *Wan hsien hsin chih*, 1934, ch. 1, p. 1; *Yü-lin fu chih*, 1841, ch. 1, pp. 8–13.

13. For the shape of the walled area of Ch'üan-chou, see an illustration in *Ch'üan-chou fu chih*, 1763, ch. 11, p. 1, or *Chin-chiang, China*, U.S. Army Map Service, 1:50,000 Series, Sheet 8729-IV, 1944.

14. Lawrence J. C. Ma, *Commercial Development and Urban Change in Sung China* (Ann Arbor: University of Michigan, Dept. of Geography, 1971), p. 165.

15. As of 1945, only about 75 percent of the walled area of Chin-chiang, the former Ch'üan-chou-fu, was settled, but the unusually large size of the elaborated city walls attests to the city's earlier importance as a port of trade. Cf. U.S. Army Map Service, 1:50,000 series, Sheet 8729-IV, 1944.

16. *Shina jōkaku no gaiyō* 1940, p. 20. The cities are not named by this source, and it is not clear whether all 34 cases were completely separated twin cities.

17. A map showing the locations of these three cities can be found in Harold J. Wiens, "The Historical and Geographical Role of Urumchi, Capital of Chinese Central Asia," *Annals of the Association of American Geographers*, 53, no. 4 (1963): 451.

18. See Shinzo Kiuchi, *Toshi chirikaku kenkyū* (Studies of urban geography; Tokyo: Kokon-shoin, 1951), p. 189.

19. Kuei-hua-ch'eng was named and rebuilt in late Ming as a frontier garrison town. The city of Sui-yüan was constructed by the Manchus in 1735. See *Kuei-sui hsien chih*, 1934, vol. 1, ch. 2, p. 1.

20. Useful reference maps of several multiple cities, including not only Ch'iung-chou-fu but also Chungking and Wuhan, are to be found in Ting Wen-chiang, *Chung-hua min kuo hsin ti t'u* (New atlas of the Republic of China; Shanghai: Shen pao kuan, 1933), Plate 53.

21. *Shan-yin hsien chih*, 1803, ch. 5, pp. 7–8.

22. *Ju-kao hsien chih*, 1808, ch. 3, pp. 8–9.

23. *Tan-yang hsien chih*, 1885, ch. 1, p. 1; *Yen-ch'eng hsien chih*, 1895, ch. 1, pp. 7–8; *Tung-t'ai hsien chih*, 1817, ch. 1, pp. 2–3.

24. This belief is related to the use of screens at the doors of houses and the portals of palaces, as well as at some city gates. See J. O. de Meira Penna, *Psychology and City-Planning: Peking and Brasilia* (Zurich, 1961), pp. 1–19.

25. For a nice example of the plethora of public buildings and temples in the central areas of a city, see the map in *Ning-hai hsien chih* (Chekiang), 1678, ch. 1, p. 5.

The Transformation of Nanking, 1350–1400

1. Part 1 of this study contains many ideas that I originally formulated in a paper entitled "The City in Chinese History" for use in a seminar in 1961. That paper was circulated among some friends and students, and I have benefited from their reactions. Although I have retained some sentences and paragraphs from the 1961 paper, the first part of this study has been considerably revised to meet their criticisms (for which I acknowledge my gratitude) and to incorporate my own recent thinking (to 1970).

2. Lewis Mumford, *The Culture of Cities* (New York: Harcourt, Brace, 1938), pp. 80–82.

3. P. T. Ho, *The Ladder of Success in Imperial China* (New York: Columbia University Press, 1962).

4. "Hsiao nan pi hsiang; ta nan pi ch'eng," I have forgotten where I first encountered this in Chinese discussions of the city, but it is widely used.

5. Mumford 1938, pp. 27, 55, 65. Robert S. Lopez, "The Crossroad within the Wall," in Oscar Handlin and John Burchard, eds., *The Historian and the City* (Cambridge, Mass.: M.I.T. Press, 1963), pp. 27–43, stresses the function of the wall in keeping the city physically and psychologically distinct: "This need not be materially erected so long as it is morally present, to keep the citizens together, sheltered from the cold, wide world, conscious of belonging to a unique team, proud of being different from the open country and germane to one another" (pp. 27–28). In his introduction to the same volume, Oscar Handlin stresses the same idea: "The towns of the Middle Ages and the Renaissance, even those of the eighteenth century, were self-contained entities walled off from their surroundings, with which they had only precisely defined contacts" (p. 2).

6. Giovanni Botero, *The Greatness of Cities: A Treatise Concerning the Causes and Magnificency and Greatness of Cities* (1588; trans. Robert Peterson, 1606), appended to his *The Reason of State*, trans. P. S. and D. P. Waley (New Haven, Conn.: Yale University Press, 1956), p. 269.

7. Glenn T. Trewartha, "Chinese Cities: Origins and Functions," *Annals of the Association of American Geographers*, 42, No. 1 (Mar. 1952): 69–93. In writing about pre-imperial times, Trewartha is too heavily dependent on Granet and on generally inadequate descriptions of ancient China; some of his conceptions of early Chinese society and government are questionable. For later periods he provides useful views.

8. Of many articles, two may be mentioned as the most pertinent to this

issue: (1) Naba Toshisada, "Shina toyu no jokaku to sono kigen" (Chinese walls and their origins), *Shirin*, 10, no. 1 (Jan. 1925); (2) Miyazaki Ichisada, "Shina jokaku no kigen isetsu" (A different view on the origin of Chinese walls), *Rekishi to chiri*, 32, no. 3 (1933).

9. Trewartha 1952: 83–84.

10. For a convenient reference to some typical city plans, see Chung-kuo chien chu shih pien chi wei yüan hui, comp., *Chung-kuo chien chu chien shih* (hereafter CKCCCS; Short history of Chinese architecture; Peking: Chung-kuo kung yeh ch'u pan she, 1962), especially pp. 100–107, 173–85.

11. These are usually listed as Fo-shan (Fatsan) in Kwangtung, Ching-te-chen in Kiangsi, Hankow in Hupei, and Chu-hsien in Honan.

12. Philip M. Hauser, "World and Asian Urbanization in Relation to Economic Development and Social Change," in Philip M. Hauser, ed., *Urbanization in Asia and the Far East* (Calcutta: UNESCO, 1967), pp. 53–93. The passage quoted (on p. 55) includes citations in quotation marks from an article by Bert F. Hoselitz entitled "The Role of Cities in the Economic Growth of Underdeveloped Countries," *Journal of Political Economy*, 51, no. 3 (June 1953): 201ff. Hauser's cultural parochialism is evident from the following sentence, found on pp. 54–55 of the same article: "Rome was probably the largest city in the history of man until nineteenth-century London or Paris, with the possible exception of Constantinople, which continued to thrive during the Dark Ages when European cities stagnated and decayed." Note that this appears in a book on urbanism in Asia!

13. I refer to Gideon Sjoberg's article "The Origin and Evolution of Cities," in *Cities, a Scientific American Book* (New York: Alfred A. Knopf, 1967), pp. 25–39. His book *The Preindustrial City: Past and Present* (Glencoe, Ill.: Free Press, 1960) could also be cited for the same qualities.

14. Etienne Balazs, "The Birth of Capitalism in China," trans. Hope M. Wright, in E. Balazs, *Chinese Civilization and Bureaucracy*, ed. Arthur F. Wright (New Haven, Conn.: Yale University Press, 1964), pp. 34–54.

15. There are many references to Liu Ping-chung's role as an adviser to Khubilai Khan in the design of Ta-tu in the writings of fourteenth-century scholars—e.g., Yeh Tzu-ch'i, *Ts'ao-mu tzu* (1378; new edition, Peking: Chung-hua shu-chü, 1949), p. 41—but they sound somewhat fanciful. Hok-lam Chan, in his recent study of Liu's life, concludes that he probably was responsible for much of the planning of the new capital. See his article "Liu Ping-chung (1216–74), A Buddhist-Taoist Statesman at the Court of Khubilai Khan," *T'oung Pao*, 53, nos. 1–3 (1967): 98–146, especially pp. 133–34 and note 73. See also pp. 110–13 for a discussion of vulgarized legends confusing Liu with Liu Chi and Yao Kuang-hsiao. In Dr. Chan's fuller study of Liu Chi (unpublished doctoral dissertation, Princeton, 1966) and in his brief biography of Liu Chi prepared for the Ming Biographical History project, he states that Liu submitted plans for Nanking to the Ming founder in 1366.

16. Popular legend equates the axial design of the city, common to most Chinese capitals, with the backbone of the human form, suggesting the correlative microcosmic-macrocosmic thinking typical of the Five Elements school and dating from the Han period, but no sophisticated discussion of this as

appropriate symbolism in the design of cities is known to me; to my knowledge none exists in the writings of Yao or of either Liu.

17. There are, of course, elaborate descriptions of Sung, Yüan, and later capitals, and awareness of their design and architectural features was probably very widespread among literati of the times. T'ao Tsung-i (ca. 1315–ca. 1403) in his *Cho keng lu* (1366; new edition in *Ts'ung shu chi ch'eng*, Shanghai: Shang-wu, 1936) includes long descriptions of the Sung capitals at Kaifeng and Hangchow (the latter he had visited personally in late Yüan times) and commends the antique propriety and modesty of their designs (ch. 18); these probably were intended to contrast with the layout of Ta-tu, elaborately described (ch. 21), which is found to be excessive and inappropriate. Although in these descriptions of the cities the acceptance of symbolism in forms and names is implicit, no explicit discussion of this is offered.

18. I am indebted to Mr. Ma Ching-hsien, formerly of the Princeton Chinese library staff for calling my attention to this work. T'ao Tsung-i (see note 17 above) included a redaction of the work in his *Shuo fu*, indicating that it was current in the fourteenth century.

19. I am paraphrasing Liang Ssu-ch'eng, *Chung-kuo chien chu shih* (History of Chinese architecture; photocopy in Princeton Library, n.p., n.d.), pp. 7–10.

20. Translated from CKCCCS, p. 106. The same work (p. 107) calls attention to the engineering contributions to the building of the city made by Chinese and Arab scholars, especially the eminent Chinese figure Kuo Shou-ching (fl. 1279), who was noted particularly as an astronomer; see Joseph Needham, *Science and Civilisation in China, Vol. 3, Mathematics and the Sciences of the Heavens and the Earth* (Cambridge: Cambridge University Press, 1959), p. 299, and *Vol. 4, Physics and Physical Technology, Part 1: Physics* (Cambridge: Cambridge University Press, 1962), p. 51.

21. Translated from Liu Chih-p'ing, *Chung-kuo chien chu lei hsing chi chieh kou* (Form types and structure in Chinese architecture; Peking: Chien chu kung ch'eng ch'u pan she, 1957), p. 29.

22. Lao Kan discusses the problems of adjusting the plans for Nanking to the realities of topography and the changing views of the emperor and his advisers in a very perceptive article, "Tui yü Nan-ching ch'eng shih ti chi tien jen shih" (Several issues with regard to the city of Nanking), *Hsüeh yüan*, 2, no. 9 (Jan. 1949): 62–67.

23. The walls of Nanking, for example, were built specifically with recent developments in naval technology in mind; Chu Yüan-chang himself had participated in naval engagements which saw the successful use of ships specially designed to approach city walls via the water channels connecting them to the Yangtze or other major waterways and to launch an escalade under the protection of naval firepower. Moreover, Nanking's walls may have been the first built on stone foundations, an innovation developed perhaps as a defense against recent advances in the use of black powder to breach walls. Unfortunately these aspects of the city's design emerge only obliquely from the incidental remarks preserved in gazetteers and other sources.

24. Lao Kan 1949 suggests that the plan of Loyang, characterized by a

square palace city located at the center of a square or rectangular city wall, may have influenced the layout of third-century Nanking and Chengtu.

25. L. Hilberseimer, *The Nature of Cities* (Chicago: P. Theobald, 1955), p. 90.

26. For an excellent discussion of Chinese house styles, see Liu Chih-p'ing 1957, pp. 30–35, and plates 37–50. Note also CKCCCS, pp. 185 (for drawings of street and house layouts in eighteenth-century Peking) and 219–38 (for various recent examples of traditional house styles). Andrew Boyd, *Chinese Architecture and Town Planning, 1500 B.C.–A.D. 1911* (Chicago: University of Chicago Press, 1962), also has some useful illustrations, many of which draw on Liu Chih-p'ing 1957 (cited in Boyd's bibliography as "Liu Hsiao-p'ing"). See also Liu Tun-chen, *Chung-kuo chu chai kai shuo* (General description of Chinese residences; Peking: Chien chu kung ch'eng ch'u pan she, 1957).

27. Mumford 1938, p. 4.

28. Freely summarized and paraphrased from Lao Kan 1949: 62–64.

29. On the role of Nanking (Chien-k'ang) as a "second Rome" and the part played by Hsieh An in developing a mystique of legitimacy and of cultural centrality in Kiangnan, see the illuminating article by Michael C. Rogers, "The Myth of the Battle of the Fei River (A.D. 383)," *T'oung Pao*, 54, nos. 1–3 (1968): 50–72, especially 57–63.

30. The figures are cited in Kenneth K. S. Ch'en, *Buddhism in China: A Historical Survey* (Princeton, N.J.: Princeton University Press, 1964), p. 136. Buddhism in the Southern Dynasties is discussed in chapters 3, 4, and 5, with many references to Nanking and to developments centered there.

31. *Die Lieder des Li Yü, 937–978*, Alfred Hoffmann, trans. and ed. (Cologne: Greven Verlag, ca. 1950), contains both an excellent study of this poet-emperor's life and work and superb translations of his poetry. It is a coincidence, perhaps, that the unfortunate last ruler of the Ch'en dynasty, captured by Sui troops in embarrassing circumstances when they stormed his palace in 589, also was a noted poet. But to many Chinese it has not seemed coincidental, since romantic and not very competent poet-emperors exemplify the spirit of the rich and cultivated South.

32. Katō Shigeshi's most important writings were collected in two volumes and published posthumously under the title *Shina keizaishi kōshō* (Researches in Chinese economic history; Tokyo: Tōyō bunko, 1952–53). In 1959 there appeared a complete and quite scholarly translation of these two volumes into Chinese, by Wu Chieh, under the same title (i.e., *Chung-kuo ching chi shih k'ao cheng*); this translation has been reprinted in one volume (Hong Kong: Lung Men Bookstore, n.d.). The Chinese version, referred to hereafter as Katō/Wu 1959, is in some ways superior to the 1952–53 Japanese edition, since the scholarly translator has inserted some corrections. The passage translated here is from Katō's 1931 article "Sōdai ni okeru toshi no hattatsu ni tsuite," republished in *Shina keizaishi kōshō* (1952), vol. 1, pp. 299–346; or "Sung tai tu shih ti fa chan" (The development of cities during the Sung dynasty), Katō/Wu 1959, vol. 1, p. 277ff.

33. Li Chien-nung, *Sung, Yüan, Ming ching chi shih kao* (Draft history of the economy in Sung, Yüan, and Ming; Peking: San lien shu tien, 1957),

especially chap. 5, on domestic commerce. Another work that offers a very informative view of Yüan city life is Yoshikawa Kojiro, *Gen zatsugeki kenkyū* (Researches on Yüan drama; Tokyo: Iwanami shoten, 1943), especially Part 1, chap. 1, on the Yüan drama. This work, which has been given an excellent Chinese translation by Cheng Ch'ing-mao (Taipei: I wen, 1960), indirectly corroborates some of Katō Shigeshi's views about the changes in city life during the Sung period, and demonstrates that those changes were further intensified in the Yüan.

34. *T'ai-tsu shih lu* (Veritable records of the T'ai-tsu emperor), in *Ming shih lu* (Veritable records of the Ming dynasty; Nan-kang: Chung yang yen chiu so, 1962 reprint), ch. 1, p. 0017. All further references are to this edition, which will be cited as MSL: T. Compare Morton Fried's 1948 description of Ch'u-hsien in *The Fabric of Chinese Society* (New York: Praeger, 1953).

35. MSL: T, ch. 1, p. 0033. "Coiling dragon and crouching tiger," or *lung p'an hu chü*, is a famous metaphor describing in auspicious geomantic terms the topography of river and mountains at Nanking. It is said in legend to have been coined by Chu-ko Liang, a Confucian-Taoist geomancer and statesman of the time of the Three Kingdoms. However, in the Yüan period it was not used exclusively to describe Nanking, despite the possessive attitude toward it of modern Nanking's residents; it appears, for example, in reference to Ta-tu (Peking) in the congratulatory essay by Yen Fu on the construction of new government offices there (see *Yüan wen lei*, original title *Kuo ch'ao wen lei* [ca. 1350; Classified anthology of Yüan dynasty literature; comp. Su T'ien-chüeh (1294–1352)], new ed., Commercial Press, Shanghai: 1936), "Shang shu sheng shang liang wen" (Congratulatory essay on the construction of the Central Secretariat Buildings), ch. 47, and it had probably become a stereotyped description of imperial capitals.

36. MSL: T, ch. 1, p. 0036.

37. Nanking had been the residence of the Yüan Emperor Wen-tsung before he ascended the throne (r. 1328–33). In 1329 he ordered his former residence there transformed into a Buddhist temple to be called Ta lung hsiang chi-ch'ing ssu, meaning loosely "the great dragon soars as felicitations assemble." At the same time he commanded that the city and the circuit administered from it be renamed "felicitations assemble," or Chi-ch'ing. Chu Yüan-chang, of course, had no interest in retaining names associated with auspicious events of Yüan history; neither did the local population.

38. Wu Han's noteworthy biography, *Chu Yüan-chang chuan* (Biography of Chu Yüan-chang; Peking: San lien shu tien, 1948), dwells at length on the emperor's personality, capacity for learning, and change of attitudes as he achieved power and success. It also cites most of the traditional materials bearing on the Ming founder's life and reign. See also brief discussions of this subject in F. W. Mote, "The Growth of Chinese Despotism," *Oriens Extremus*, no. 8/1 (1961): 1–41; and *idem*, *The Poet Kao Ch'i, 1336–1374* (Princeton, N.J.: Princeton University Press, 1962), chap. 1.

39. Translated from Ku Ch'i-yüan (1565–1628), *K'o tso chui yü* (Random talk of a visitor; n.p.: copy in the Library of Congress Rare Books Collection, postface dated 1618), ch. 2, first item, "Liang tu" (The two capitals). Ku's book is the most valuable source known to me for Nanking history in the

middle and late Ming; it deserves fuller exploitation by students of Chinese urbanism as well as by general students of Chinese cultural history. See W. Franke, *An Introduction to the Sources of Ming History* (Kuala Lumpur: University of Malaya Press, 1968), p. 117.

40. After writing this paper I was able to read the valuable dissertation submitted at Harvard in 1968 by Edward L. Farmer on the dual-capital system of the early Ming. It deals primarily with the innovations of the Yung-lo emperor (r. 1403–24) in creating a dual system during his reign.

41. Chang Hsüan, *Chih-cheng Chin-ling hsin chih* (New gazetteer of Nanking from the Chih-cheng reign period; 15 *chüan*, prefaces dated 1344). I have used the typeset edition reprinted in *Nan-ching wen hsien*, nos. 10–20 (1947–48), which unfortunately was not carefully edited for typesetting errors. The Library of Congress Rare Books Collection contains two incomplete copies of the original edition and a late-Ming Japanese reprint. The book is reported to have been reprinted in Nanking in the 1920's.

42. Liu I-cheng and Wang Huan-piao, comps., *Shou tu chih* (hereafter STC; Capital gazetteer; Nanking: Cheng chung shu chü, 1935), pp. 71–73; Lao Kan 1949: 65.

43. Ku Ch'i-yüan 1618, ch. 9, pp. 22a–b.

44. Chang Hsüan 1344, ch. 6; note that in discussing the staffing of the prefectural office in the Yüan period (*Nan-ching wen hsien*, no. 17, p. 600 ff.) he comments on lacunae in the record: "In many cases we have no information; it is not that we are carelessly omitting it." This and other comments in this section of the gazetteer testify to irregularities in Yüan government.

45. MSL: T, ch. 1, p. 0042.

46. Ku Ch'i-yüan 1618, ch. 8, pp. 13a–b.

47. The "new city" had many precedents in Chinese city building. The Northern Sung capital at Kaifeng offered a prominent one; my information is based on an unpublished paper by E. A. Kracke, Jr., on "Kaifeng as Capital of China, 907–1127," presented at the Annual Meeting of the American Historical Association, Toronto, Dec. 1967.

Another example of a "new city," and one Chu Yüan-chang may have seen, was at Yangchow. In the Sung period, a "new city" was built alongside the old one—roughly duplicating it in size and layout, but separated from it by a wall, a moat, and bridges—that contained mostly government offices. It has been called the "new city" ever since. The Nanking plan, before the decision was made to add the large area to the north, would almost have matched the size and shape of the tenth-century walls, creating a "new city" to the east of the old, very much like the Yangchow model.

48. On changes in the rebuilding plans during the progress of the work, and on the decision to incorporate the northern section, I follow Lao Kan 1949.

49. STC, pp. 74–75, citing the modern geographer Chang Ch'i-yün and a late Ch'ing source. The authors of STC give no opinion of their own, and in other places rather mechanically repeat the figures that are here contradicted. Despite minor discrepancies of this kind, this *Capital Gazetteer* is an excellent work, combining modern scholarship with the best traditions of Chinese historical scholarship. Its distinguished principal editor was Liu I-cheng, director of the Kiangsu Provincial Library and an eminent historian. The bibliographic

section (pp. 1352–1408) is very complete and stands as the basic bibliography on Nanking's history; unfortunately it lacks critical annotation.

50. CKCCCS, p. 180.

51. Maps: (1) Nanking 1:25,000, N3200–E11840/8 x 13 (100 yd. world polyconic grid), Geographic Section, General Staff, no. 3831, 1927, revised (AMS 2), 1945; (2) Peking, N3949–E11610/11 x 21, Eastern China 1:50,000, revised (AMS 3), 1944. These excellent maps, and others in the same series, are no longer in print and therefore are not now available through the Army Map Service. I have used copies in the Princeton Library, with the assistance of the Map Room Curator, Mr. Lawrence E. Spellman.

52. The basic works in English on the system of Ming government are those of Charles O. Hucker, especially his definitive article "Government Organization of the Ming Dynasty," *Harvard Journal of Asiatic Studies*, 21 (Dec. 1958): 1–61, and his book *The Traditional Chinese State in Ming Times (1368–1644)* (Tucson: University of Arizona Press, 1961). The figures given here for numbers of civil and military officials and subofficials in Nanking in the early Ming period are rough estimates based on the material offered by Hucker, but he is not responsible for my estimates. The figure on numbers of troops stationed at Nanking in 1391 comes from Wu Han 1948, p. 161.

53. Ku Ch'i-yüan 1618, ch. 5, p. 30a.

54. Katō/Wu 1959; see especially Katō's conclusions to his study on markets in the Sung period, translated above.

55. Ku Ch'i-yüan 1618, ch. 2, p. 28b ff. The use of the terms *fang*, *hsiang*, and *shiang* was not limited to the capital, but was general throughout the empire; elsewhere, however, it did not imply the displacement of original residents. For a general description see *Hsü wen hsien t'ung k'ao*, ch. 16.

56. Ku Ch'i-yüan 1618, ch. 2, p. 36b. Note, however, that Ku Ch'i-yüan, writing in the late Ming about the system from early Ming times on, states that a *fang* had ten *chia* and a *chia* ten households. By that reckoning a *fang* should have had only one-tenth the number of households that our average figure has produced. The discrepancy probably is to be explained by the fact that the rural *hsiang* were larger units; they had parallel *li-chia* systems of tens and hundreds of households under them.

57. *Ibid.*, ch. 2, p. 36a ff. Ku Yen-wu, the seventeenth-century Ming loyalist and student of Ming government, probably based his comments about the removal of Nanking's population to Yunnan in the reign of the founder on this passage in Ku Ch'i-yüan. Ku Yen-wu's comments, appearing in his *T'ien hsia chün kuo li ping shu*, ch. 13, are quoted in STC, p. 497; I have not checked the original, but the wording as quoted there is very similar to Ku Ch'i-yüan's.

58. STC, p. 497.

59. *Ibid.*, again citing Ku Yen-wu (see note 57 above); here again Ku Yen-wu seems to be drawing on Ku Ch'i-yüan 1618, ch. 2, p. 36b.

60. Ku Ch'i-yüan 1618, ch. 2, pp. 36a–39b, has a relatively long piece entitled "Fang hsiang shih mo" in which the system is reviewed and a crisis that developed in its workings in late Ming times is described. Much of the information about the system presented here draws on this work.

61. The evidence for this comparison is very complex, but it is based on

my unpublished study of the economic resources of the Ming founder and his principal rivals in the third quarter of the fourteenth century.

62. See Shiba Yoshinobu, *Sōdai shōgyōshi kenkyū* (Studies in the history of Sung dynasty commerce; Tokyo: Kazama shobō, 1968), p. 157. I am grateful to Professor Shiba for calling my attention to this and other passages in his recent work (pp. 166, 333) that bear on the economic position of Nanking in the Southern Sung period.

63. For a recent study of the imperial silk factories at Nanking in the early Ch'ing period, see Jonathan Spence, *Ts'ao Yin and the K'ang-hsi Emperor, Bondservant and Master* (New Haven, Conn.: Yale University Press, 1966), especially chap. 3.

64. Henry Serruys has contributed a series of magnificent studies of this problem; particularly pertinent to the point at hand is "Remains of Mongol Customs During the Early Ming," *Monumenta Serica*, 16 (1957): 137–90.

65. See Arthur F. Wright, "Changan," in Arnold Toynbee, ed., *Cities of Destiny* (New York: McGraw-Hill, 1967), pp. 138–49; and his paper elsewhere in the present volume.

66. The Nanking gazetteer of 1344 lists a breakdown of 33 categories of non-Han residents reported within the walls at the time of the census; many are racial (Uighur, etc.) or religious.

67. The number of the "storied buildings" erected in the early Ming varies in different accounts, some saying twelve, some fourteen, some sixteen. Ku Ch'i-yüan discusses the various accounts; see Ku Ch'i-yüan 1618, ch. 6, pp. 34a–b, and items cited in STC, p. 1090ff.

68. Ku Ch'i-yüan comments on this in a number of places and quotes others at length on the same subject; see, for example, Ku Ch'i-yüan 1618, ch. 5, pp. 38b–40a, and items cited in STC, pp. 1084–87.

69. Matteo Ricci/N. Trigault, *China in the Sixteenth Century*, trans. Louis J. Gallagher (New York: Random House, 1953), pp. 268–70. See also a different comparison quoted by A. Chan in "Peking at the Time of the Wan-li Emperor," in *Proceedings of the Second Biennial Conference*, International Association of Historians of Asia, 1962 (Taipei, 1963), pp. 119–47.

70. Matteo Ricci/N. Trigault 1953, p. 309.

The Formation of Cities: Initiative and Motivation in Building Three Walled Cities in Taiwan

1. Lien-sheng Yang has pointed out that from the Sung period on the prefectural and county governments seldom had enough funds on hand to carry out construction work on any great scale. He also indicates that funds for local projects in Ming and Ch'ing times generally were raised by "a joint effort of the local officials, gentry, and people." See the English version of his four lectures originally delivered in French entitled "Economic Aspects of Public Works in Imperial China," in Lien-sheng Yang, *Excursions in Sinology* (Cambridge, Mass.: Harvard University Press, 1969), pp. 18, 44.

2. A number of Taiwan local gazetteers mention that hired labor was common and conscripted labor uncommon in their areas. For instance, see Ch'en P'ei-kuei, comp., *Tan-shui t'ing chih* (hereafter TSTC; Tan-shui subprefecture

gazetteer; Taipei: T'ai-wan yin hang, 1963 reprint), p. 298. In at least one case of city building, involving the mid-island provincial capital site mentioned below, the labor of local *t'uan-lien* forces was used. Chiang Tao-chang, "T'ai-wan ti ku ch'eng: I ko li shih ti li hsüeh ti yen chiu" (Walled cities of Taiwan: A study in historical geography), *Ti li hsüeh yen chiu*, no. 1 (June 1966): 77. A description of large-scale construction projects in northern Taiwan during the Ch'ing period, and the local support rendered, is contained in Chu Wan-li, comp., *T'ai-pei shih tu shih chien she shih kao* (Draft history of municipal construction in Taipei; Taipei: T'ai-pei shih cheng fu, Kung wu chü, 1954), pp. 29–50.

3. A concise history of Hsin-chu is to be found in the following publication: Hsin-chu hsien wen hsien wei yüan hui (Hsin-chu County Historical Commission), comp., *Hsin-chu wen hsien hui t'ung hsün* (hereafter HCTH; The commission's report), no. 17 (Dec. 1952), pp. 5–12. For general details on the formation of Hsin-chu see also Inō Kanori (Yoshinori), *Taiwan bunka shi* (Taiwan cultural history; Tokyo: Tōkō shoin, 1928), vol. 1, pp. 630–33; and Lien Heng, *T'ai-wan t'ung shih* (General history of Taiwan; Taipei: T'ai-wan t'ung shih she, 1920–21, 3 vols.). Page references to Lien's work are to the single-volume reissue of 1955 (Taipei: Chung-hua ts'ung shu wei yüan hui), pp. 363–64.

4. HCTH, pp. 6–7, 40–41.

5. For an account of Ts'ai Ch'ien and the raids this pirate leader launched on Taiwan, see Lien Heng 1920–21 (1955), pp. 638–41. Ts'ai's appearance in Taiwan and elsewhere is also mentioned in Arthur W. Hummel, ed., *Eminent Chinese of the Ch'ing Period* (Washington: U.S. Government Printing Office, 1943), pp. 447–48.

6. HCTH, pp. 7–9; TSTC, p. 57; Huang Chung-sheng, *Hsin-chu feng wu chih* (Record of Hsin-chu folkways; Hsin-chu: Lien ho pan she, 1960), pp. 12, 14.

7. The total figure reported in 1841 was 8,523. This census count apparently included both adult males and females, as well as children, in keeping with the previous Tan-shui subprefectural census report of 1811, based on *pao-chia* household figures. TSTC, p. 89.

8. A handy account of the early settlement of the Ko-ma-lan region and the founding of I-lan is contained in a gazetteer recently published by the I-lan County Historical Commission: I-lan hsien wen hsien wei yüan hui, comp., "Shih lüeh" (Historical summary), *I-lan hsien chih* (hereafter ILHC; I-lan county gazetteer), ch. shou, hsia (I-lan: I-lan hsien wen hsien wei yüan hui, 1960), pp. 9–19. Also, Inō 1928, vol. 1, pp. 633–35; and Lien Heng 1920–21 (1955), p. 364. Map 1 of this study shows the administrative boundaries and approximate interior borders of Ko-ma-lan subprefecture, Tan-shui subprefecture, and the four *hsien* to the south from the time the Ko-ma-lan subprefecture was established in 1810 until 1875, when new administrative boundaries were created in Taiwan. During this period the prefectural center at T'ai-wan-fu (Tainan) continued to serve as the highest seat of government for Taiwan and the Pescadores.

9. "Shih lüeh," ILHC, pp. 17–20. See also K'o P'ei-yüan, comp., *Ko-ma-lan chih lüeh* (hereafter KCL; Summary gazetteer of Ko-ma-lan; Taipei: T'ai-wan yin hang, 1961 reprint), pp. 45–46, 59–62.

10. For a brief account of the cultural development of I-lan see "Shih lüeh," ILHC, pp. 27–29. This source also alludes to labor troubles involving coolies engaged in the local carrying trade. *Ibid.*, pp. 30–32. Information about the commercial streets and markets, as well as an account of the examination system as it pertained to the Ko-ma-lan subprefecture, may be found in the nineteenth-century gazetteer: Ch'en Shu-chün, comp., *Ko-ma-lan t'ing chih* (hereafter KTC; Gazetteer of the Ko-ma-lan subprefecture; Taipei: T'ai-wan yin hang, 1963 reprint), pp. 25–26, 153–59.

11. Huang Te-shih, "Ch'eng nai ti yen ko ho T'ai-pei ch'eng" (Taipei city and successive changes within its walls), *T'ai-pei wen wu*, 2, no. 4 (Jan. 1954): 17–22. Also, Inō 1928, vol. 1, pp. 636–38; and Lien Heng 1920–21 (1955), p. 363.

12. Huang Te-shih 1954: 28. Taiwan was governed as a separate province of China from 1886 to 1895.

13. Inō Kanori (Yoshinori), *Taiwan jumbu to shite no Ryu Meiden* (Liu Ming-ch'uan as Taiwan governor; Taipei: Niitakadō shoten, 1905), pp. 27–34, 37–38, 88–90.

14. The irregular shapes of Taiwan's administrative centers and the dimensions of their walls are dealt with in Chiang Tao-chang 1966: 65–68. See esp. p. 68, table 3, for a listing of the circumference of each city wall. The Ch'ing period gazetteers vary somewhat in their reports of wall lengths. For a comment on an erroneous estimate of the reconstructed Hsin-chu wall, see T'ai-wan yin hang, Ching chi yen chiu shih, comp., *Hsin-chu hsien ts'ai fang ts'e* (Guidebook for Hsin-chu county; Taipei: T'ai-wan yin hang, 1962 reprint), p. 13. A brief account of the construction of the outer enclosure around Hsin-chu is contained in TSTC, pp. 44–45. The shapes of the city walls and enclosures constructed around each of the three administrative centers dealt with in this study are clearly shown in maps 3, 4, and 5, respectively.

15. This population figure is a rough estimate based on the more sizeable count recorded a decade or so later in the 1841 census for Tan-shui subprefecture. The area covered in this estimate includes the walled Hsin-chu center, its five suburban divisions, and two rural divisions (the Chu-tung and Chu-pei areas). By 1841, this entire region, to which a sixth suburban division had been added, supported a Chinese population of approximately 55,000. For the population count and breakdown see TSTC, p. 89.

16. TSTC, p. 24. This distance was reckoned on courses extending northeasterly from the Ta-chia River boundary to roughly the Chi-lung area.

17. TSTC, p. 89. The subprefecture's Chinese population totaled 214,833 in 1811, and 283,063 in 1841, according to the census records.

18. In that year the nearby Hsin-chuang assistant magistrate (*hsien-ch'eng*) office was shifted to Meng-chia and a battalion, headed by a *yu-chi* (major), assigned there. This military official was also placed in charge of water forces, and his post was subsequently upgraded in rank. The jurisdiction of the assistant magistrate was confined primarily to the Tan-shui River area. The military post, on the other hand, made Meng-chia the headquarters for land forces in the Taipei–Chi-lung region and water forces operating around the entire perimeter of northern Taiwan from the Ta-chia River outlet on the west coast to Su-ao, the southernmost Ko-ma-lan port on the east coast of the island (see Map 1 for these locations). Chang Ku-ch'eng, comp., *Hsin-chu ts'ung chih*

(Collected records of Hsin-chu; Hsin-chu: Hsin-chu ts'ung chih pien i wei yüan hui, 1952), p. 59; and Liao Han-ch'en, "Meng-chia yen ko chih" (Record of successive changes at Meng-chia), *T'ai-pei wen wu*, 2, no. 1 (Apr. 1953): 15.

19. The remarks of a Taiwan official who traveled in northern Taiwan around 1820, for example, were much more favorable to Meng-chia than to the small and crowded Hsin-chu administrative center. Yao Ying, "T'ai-pei tao li chi" (Record of overland distances in northern Taiwan), in *Tung-ch'a chi lüeh* (Sketch of my assignment to Taiwan [1832]; reissued Taipei: T'aiwan yin hang, 1957), pp. 89–90. For an account of the Taiwan *chiao* merchants see: Murakami Tamakichi, comp., *Nambu Taiwan shi* (Record of southern Taiwan; Tainan: Tainan-shū kyōei kai, 1934), pp. 381–87; and for their rise in northern Taiwan, Wang I-kang, "T'ai-pei san chiao yü T'ai-wan ti chiao hang" (The three *chiao* of Taipei and Taiwan's *chiao* associations), *T'ai-pei wen wu*, 6, no. 1 (Sept. 1957): 11–28.

20. In 1823, for instance, a proposal by the governor-general to shift a high military post to Hsin-chu from Chang-hua was not approved partly owing to the resistance of the incumbent holding that post. This military official wished to remain in the more flourishing Chang-hua area. Yao Ying, "Kai she T'ai-pei ying chih" (Reconstructing the military system of northern Taiwan), in *Tung ch'a chi lüeh* (1832), p. 8.

21. TSTC, p. 93.

22. HCTH, p. 7.

23. Ch'en Shao-hsing, et al., comp., *Jen min chih; jen kou p'ien* (hereafter JKP; Civil records, section on population; Taipei, 1964), p. 254: a separate volume of part two (ch. 2, entitled *Jen min chih*) in T'ai-wan sheng wen hsien wei yüan hui, comp., *T'ai-wan sheng t'ung chih kao* (Draft gazetteer of Taiwan province; Taipei, 1951–).

24. The rebuttal the first T'ai-pei prefect made to the petition submitted by Hsin-chu gentry members is cited in Huang Te-shih 1954: 20.

25. However, T'ai-pei-fu did acquire dependent suburbs: small commercial areas outside the north and west city gates, and a larger river-front area situated between Meng-chia and Ta-tao-ch'eng. See Map 5 of this study. In contrast, the areas outside the south and east gates lacked markets and even thoroughfares connecting T'ai-pei-fu with the countryside. Huang Te-shih 1954: 27–28; and Taiwan tsūshinsha, comp., *Taihoku shi shi* (hereafter TSS; History of Taipei; Taipei, 1931), pp. 55–58.

26. The first T'ai-pei prefect apparently had little time to devote to city building. Plagued by many difficulties in establishing the new prefectural government, he reportedly was unable even to handle litigation and other matters stemming from the southern portion of the prefecture. T'ai-wan yin hang, Ching chi yen chiu shih, comp., *Ch'ing chi Shen pao T'ai-wan chi shih chi lu* (hereafter CCSP; Collected records of reported affairs in Taiwan contained in *Shen-pao* during late Ch'ing times; Taipei: T'ai-wan yin hang, 1968), p. 851.

27. The population figure and the registered land estimate, based on reports submitted by Yang T'ing-li (mentioned below) during his efforts to establish formal government in the Ko-ma-lan region, were not very accurate. See his land estimate contained in KCL, p. 179.

28. See the map showing early Ko-ma-lan coastal defense installations and mountain guard posts in KCL, pp. 6–7.

29. A list of these village settlements and their approximate locations with respect to I-lan is contained in KTC, pp. 25–28.

30. A graphic view of the general Chinese settlement of Taiwan from late Ming times through the Ch'ing period is to be found in Cheng-siang Chen, *Atlas of Land Utilization in Taiwan* (Taipei: Fu-min Geographical Institute of Economic Development, 1950), p. 9, map 15.

31. Common surname and common ancestral (*t'ung-tsung*) linkages, formed in northern Taiwan when few extended lineages existed there, are treated in Tai Yen-hui, "Ch'ing tai T'ai-wan hsiang chuang chih she hui ti k'ao ch'ao" (Investigation of Taiwan rural society in the Ch'ing period), *T'ai-wan yin hang chi k'an*, 14, no. 4 (Dec. 1963): 224.

32. Yang T'ing-li had selected so-called "clan heads" (*tsu-cheng*), representing various surname groups, in order to control the more numerous Chang-chou settlers. KCL, p. 148. On the other hand, some leaders were listed simply as "*chieh-shou*," or heads of the original "*chieh*" bands of adult male settlers. KTC, p. 23.

33. Tai Yen-hui 1963: 199.

34. Taiwan market towns of exclusively one group are discussed in *Ibid*.: 216. Most Taiwan port towns were populated almost entirely by one subethnic group, generally of Ch'üan-chou origin. See references to Meng-chia elsewhere in this study.

35. *Ibid*.: 205–10.

36. References to such "armed conflicts" are numerous in the literature on Taiwan in the Ch'ing period. The best secondary account of this form of strife is to be found in Inō 1928, vol. 3, pp. 929–53.

37. JKP, pp. 193–95.

38. Accounts of the settlement process and patterns in the Hsin-chu area are summarized in two recent works: Huang Chung-sheng 1960: 10–15; and Chang Ku-ch'eng 1952, pp. 75–78.

39. The worsening Hoklo-Hakka conditions around Hsin-chu at that time are described in Huang Chung-sheng 1960, pp. 13–14.

40. Kuo Hui, "Li shih ti li" (Historical geography), in Pi Ch'ing-ch'ang et al., comp., *Hsin-chu hsin chih* (New gazetteer of Hsin-chu; Taipei: Chung-hua ts'ung shu wei yüan hui, 1958), p. 282.

41. San I ("three counties") groups were predominant in Hsin-chu city, and their communities spread over the coastal plains to the west and southwest. T'ung-an and other Hoklo communities occupied hinterland areas north of the city stretching along the Chu-ch'ien River to the sea. Elsewhere, numerous Hakka villages, peopled by settlers from Hui-chou *fu* (Kwangtung), formed an outer semicircle of settlements extending from the north to the southeast around Hsin-chu and its environs. Other Hakka communities were situated in more distant hinterlands to the north and near the Chu-ch'ien River to the east. Huang Chung-sheng 1960, pp. 14–15.

42. Yang Yün-p'ing, "Kuan yü pei pu T'ai-wan k'ai fa ti i tzu liao" (One source concerning the development of northern Taiwan), in *T'ai-pei hsien wen hsien ts'ung chi, ti erh chi* (1956), p. 439. Most sources dealing with the

settlement of the Taipei Basin fail to mention the Hakka settlers who helped to open up localities in that region.

43. A brief account of these two "armed conflicts" is contained in the article by Huang Ch'i-mu, "Fen lei hsieh tou yü Meng-chia" (Armed conflicts among diverse groups and Meng-chia), *T'ai-pei wen wu*, 2, no. 1 (Apr. 1953): 55–58.

44. This Chang-chou leader was Wu Sha. His biography appears in Lien Heng 1920–21 (1955), pp. 646–48. The estimate that nine-tenths of Wu's settler band was composed of Chang-chou people is Yang T'ing-li's. KCL, p. 174.

45. "Shih lüeh," ILHC, p. 11.

46. *Ibid.* Yang T'ing-li had earlier noted that the Cho-shui River, located south of I-lan, formed a boundary that the various subethnic groups feared to cross. Tai Yen-hui 1963: 216.

47. Huang Chung-sheng points out that this is why the Hoklo people in the Hsin-chu area were attracted to the city. He also indicates that local Hakka inhabitants had dealings with centers like Hsin-chu through commercial and scholarly activities and in time acquired fluency in the southern Fukien (Min-nan) spoken language. Huang Chung-sheng 1960, pp. 12, 16.

48. This resourceful subprefect was Yao Ying. His description of the *li-t'an* ceremony is contained in KTC, pp. 384–85.

49. An advocate of city wall construction during the 1720's was the scholar Lan Ting-yüan. His views on the subject were insightful and influenced later officials who continued to ponder the problems of city building in Taiwan. See especially the following portions of his writings: *Tung cheng chi* (Collection on the eastern expedition; Taipei: T'ai-wan yin hang, 1958 reprint), pp. 27–30; and *P'ing T'ai chi lüeh* (Summary of the pacification of Taiwan; Taipei: T'ai-wan yin hang, 1958 reprint), p. 53.

50. Lien Heng 1920–21 (1955), p. 358. The three seats of county administration at that time were Feng-shan, Chu-lo, and T'ai-wan. The offices of the last were located at T'ai-wan-fu.

51. Reference to this casual attitude is made in the Ch'ien-lung emperor's edict, dated CL 53/1/25 (Mar. 2, 1788). T'ai-wan yin hang, Ching chi yen chiu shih, comp., *Ch'ing Kao-tsung shih lu hsüan chi* (hereafter CKSL; Selections from the veritable records of Ch'ing Kao-tsung; Taipei: T'ai-wan yin hang, 1964), p. 544.

52. Edict of the Yung-cheng emperor, dated YC 11/12/11 (Jan. 15, 1734). T'ai-wan yin hang, Ching chi yen chiu shih, comp., *Ch'ing Shih-tsung shih lu hsüan chi* (Selections from the veritable records of Ch'ing Shih-tsung; Taipei: T'ai-wan yin hang, 1963), p. 46. This phrase was frequently employed by Ch'ing officials. Later on, it was used in reference to the initial construction of both I-lan and T'ai-pei-fu. However, in the case of I-lan "*yin-ti chih-i*" also had a more general connotation signifying that the early Ko-ma-lan authorities had to depend on that region's wealth and resources to establish the facilities of government, including the I-lan administrative center. KCL, p. 150. The phrase was used in this broader sense by the governor-general when T'ai-pei prefecture was set up and T'ai-pei-fu was about to be constructed. CCSP, p. 850.

53. Earthen and bamboo walls were authorized at the two centers in 1734, soon after the emperor's decree. However, earthen enclosures had apparently been erected already at both centers. Lien Heng 1920–21 (1955), pp. 360–61. A positive response in regard to Taiwan city-wall building on the part of ranking Fukien and Taiwan officials is apparent in a Board of Works memorial, dated CL 5/2/23 (Mar. 20, 1740), contained in T'ai-wan yin hang, Ching chi yen chiu shih, comp., *T'ai an hui lu ping chi* (hereafter TAHL; Third collection of a series of Taiwan archival records; Taipei: T'aiwan yin hang, 1963), pp. 148–53.

54. Edict dated CL 53/1/25 (Mar. 2, 1788). CKSL, p. 545.

55. CKSL, pp. 587, 600–601; and TAHL, pp. 159–61.

56. Altogether, twelve walled administrative centers were built in Taiwan, seven of them during the nineteenth century (including Ma-kung in the Pescadores and both Feng-shan sites). Lien Heng 1920–21 (1955), pp. 359–65. Chiang Tao-chang (1966: 63–64) identifies fourteen such centers, which figure includes the nonadministrative town of T'ao-yüan and the uncompleted mid-island provincial capital near T'ai-chung.

57. That official's subsequent memorial concerning the Chang-hua undertaking is contained in Chou Hsi, comp., *Chang-hua hsien chih* (hereafter CHHC; Chang-hua county gazetteer; Taipei: T'ai-wan yin hang, 1962 reprint), pp. 396–97.

58. CHHC, pp. 398–99. Basically, these inhabitants wanted to reduce the circumference of the city wall and have a more costly brick and stone wall constructed.

59. CHHC, p. 36; Chiang Tao-chiang 1966: 76–77. See also *T'ai-wan ts'ai fang ts'e* (A guidebook for Taiwan; Taipei: T'ai-wan yin hang, 1959 reprint), pp. 15–16.

60. CHHC, p. 397.

61. TAHL, pp. 162–63.

62. TAHL, pp. 163–64. The Tan-shui subprefect wished to use the Feng-shan surplus funds for the reconstruction of Hsin-chu. His petition is included in the following collection: Liu Chi-wan, comp., "Tan-shui t'ing chu ch'eng an chüan" (hereafter TSAC; Records of city building at the Tan-shui subprefectural center), *T'ai-pei wen hsien*, no. 1 (June 1962): 143.

63. The careful accounting procedures carried on by the Hsin-chu managers are apparent in the detailed listing of the materials used and costs involved in constructing the city wall, gates, gate towers, and ramparts. TSAC: 154–72.

64. The petition and Subprefect Li's endorsement are included in TSAC: 141. The petition was dated TK 6/11/4 (Dec. 2, 1826).

65. The authorities and local leaders in both Chang-hua and Feng-shan, for example, had taken considerable pains in resolving problems related to the strategic layout of the city walls. Their behavior reflected the desire for more protection of the walled administrative center itself, a sentiment expressed earlier, for instance, by officials cited in the above-mentioned 1740 Board of Works memorial. TAHL, pp. 148–53.

66. Sun's rehabilitation plan is cited in an edict by the Tao-kuang emperor, dated TK 6/12/12 (Jan. 9, 1827). T'ai-wan yin hang, Ching chi yen chiu shih, comp., *Ch'ing Hsüan-tsung shih lu hsüan chi* (Selections from the ver-

itable records of Ch'ing Hsüan-tsung; Taipei: T'ai-wan yin hang, 1964), pp. 54–55.

67. A biography of Cheng Yung-hsi is contained in Lien Heng 1920–21 (1955), pp. 726–28. A brief account of Lin Hsiang-lin's father, Shao-hsien, appears in TSTC, p. 272.

68. Lien Heng 1920–21 (1955), p. 699. Biographies of Lin Kuo-hua and his father appear on pp. 699–700.

69. TSAC: 155, 175. The other Hakka overseer was an old gentryman, Lin Kuo-pao. A biography of Liu Hsien-t'ing is found in Wu Tzu-kuang, *T'ai-wan chi shih* (Recorded events of Taiwan; Taipei: T'ai-wan yin hang, 1959 selected reprint), pp. 60–61.

70. The names of the twelve local managers, along with brief accounts of their family backgrounds and activities in regard to the Hsin-chu wall construction project, are contained in TSAC: 175–76.

71. Both took measures against local "armed conflicts." Liu's efforts are alluded to in Wu Tzu-kuang 1959, p. 61. Cheng's attempts to restore order to areas near Hsin-chu are well known, and a literary piece he composed on the occasion of a serious "armed conflict," entitled "Ch'üan ho lun" (An essay exhorting peace), became famous as an example of prose literature. This essay is cited in full in Lien Heng 1920–21 (1955), p. 727.

72. HCTH, pp. 7, 40–41, 57.

73. Li reported that 7,246 silver dollars were spent on such lesser projects, as against 147,490 taels used for the construction of the city wall, moats, gates, and gate towers. TSAC: 174.

74. See the list of Hsin-chu temples and their main sponsors in HCTH, pp. 41–47. Moreover, a new battalion headquarters was constructed in 1827. Map 3 indicates the major repair and construction projects undertaken in and around Hsin-chu during this period of reconstruction.

75. HCTH, p. 7. The governor-general and the governor each contributed 1,000 taels, and various Taiwan officials gave another 14,285 taels. TSAC: 173.

76. TSAC: 140.

77. The reports of the intendant and finance commissioner are contained in TSAC: 144–45.

78. TSAC: 145.

79. TSAC: 144–45. For a study of Taiwan's double-rent system, including both small and large rentholders, see Shirō Kawada, "The Tenant System of Formosa," *Kyoto University Economic Review*, 3, no. 2 (Dec. 1928): 86–146; and Tai Yen-hui, "Ch'ing tai T'ai-wan chih ta hsiao tsu yeh" (Large and small leaseholds in Taiwan during the Ch'ing period), *T'ai-pei wen hsien*, 4 (June 1963): 1–45.

80. Lists of the managers who directed these projects are found in HCTH, p. 7.

81. TSAC: 174–78.

82. In Taiwan the relationship between local merchants and gentry tended to be close. Prominent families sometimes aspired to place members in both classes. The number of managers who were wealthy enough to purchase degrees or titles alloting gentry status suggests that they, like Lin Kuo-hua's family members, had business connections. Eberhard has pointed out that popular opinion in Taiwan supported a "division of labor" ideal among family

members, giving rise to what he terms "gentleman-merchants." Wolfram Eberhard, *Social Mobility in Traditional China* (Leiden: E. J. Brill, 1962), p. 217.

83. TSAC: 178–81.
84. TSAC: 181.
85. A brief account of the Chu Fen raids in the Ko-ma-lan region is to be found in "Shih lüeh," ILHC, p. 16.
86. KCL, p. 22.
87. Fang's memorial, drafted in 1810, requested that civil and military authority be established in the Ko-ma-lan region (KTC, pp. 332–33). Biographies of Yang T'ing-li appear in Lien Heng 1920–21 (1955), pp. 633–34; and "Jen wu chih" (Record of personages), ILHC, ch. 8, pp. 4–6.
88. Yang's program, containing his policies and recommendations for the Ko-ma-lan subprefecture, is included in a memorial submitted by a council of ranking Fukien officials. KCL, pp. 131–50.
89. A subsequent appraisal of Yang's tax measure by a Taiwan official, Yao Ying, reflects this criticism. KTC, pp. 335–38.
90. KTC, pp. 21, 23. A summary of Subprefect Ch'ai's many other accomplishments is to be found in his biography. "Jen wu chih," ILHC, ch. 8, pp. 6–7.
91. During this four-year period, officials proposed various means to defend and strengthen control over the Ko-ma-lan region. City-building plans were formalized only after the decision to introduce civil government was acted upon. A résumé of the prolonged deliberations concerning the establishment of the Ko-ma-lan subprefecture was drafted by Yang T'ing-li. See KCL, pp. 173–79.
92. KCL, p. 178.
93. KCL, pp. 178–79. The investigations and deliberations carried out by the Fukien and Taiwan authorities are also described in the report by the governor-general, dated CC 16/9 (Oct./Nov., 1811). KTC, pp. 334–35.
94. This prominent headman was Ch'en Tien-pang. His biography is contained in "Jen wu chih," ILHC, ch. 8, pp. 13–14, as well as in both Ko-ma-lan gazetteers.
95. KCL, pp. 22, 137–38; KTC, pp. 116–18, 350–51.
96. KCL, p. 60. The religious roles of Kuan-ti (god of war and righteousness), T'ien-hou or Ma-tsu (patron goddess of seafarers), and Kuan-yin (goddess of mercy) are briefly noted in C. K. Yang, *Religion in Chinese Society* (Berkeley: University of California Press, 1967), esp. pp. 11, 71–73, 159–61. For a detailed historical account of these three deities in Taiwan see Inō 1928, vol. 2, pp. 395–414, 463–66.
97. KCL, pp. 61–65.
98. KCL, pp. 137–38.
99. This information comes from a recently discovered memorial drafted by Liu in 1889. Feng Yung, comp., "Liu Ming-ch'uan fu T'ai tang an cheng chi lu" (hereafter LMCL, Records compiled and rearranged from archives of Liu Ming-ch'uan's governorship in Taiwan), *T'ai-wan wen hsien*, 8, no. 1 (Mar. 1957): 67.
100. For example, Pai Ch'i-hsiang, a Meng-chia merchant mentioned below, contributed to the building of the east gate. Wen-ch'iao, "Pai Ch'i-hsiang ti shih chi" (Traces of the affairs of Pai Ch'i-hsiang), *T'ai-pei wen wu*, 5, nos. 2/3 (Jan. 1957): 73.

101. Shen proposed that three counties, as well as a prefecture, be established in northern Taiwan. His memorial is contained in Shen Pao-chen, *Fu-chien T'ai-wan tsou che* (Fukien-Taiwan memorials; Taipei: T'ai-wan yin hang, 1959 selected reprint), pp. 55–59. For his recommendation concerning the Meng-chia area see esp. p. 58.

102. This was the first T'ai-pei prefect. See note 24 above.

103. Huang Te-shih 1954: 21–22.

104. CKSL, p. 600.

105. Huang Te-shih 1954: 21–22.

106. Huang Ch'i-jui et al., "Ch'eng nei chi fu chiao ch'i su tso t'an hui" (Symposium of elderly residents from the city and its environs), *T'ai-pei wen wu*, 2, no. 4 (Jan. 1954): 10.

107. Huang Te-shih 1954: 23.

108. A biography of Lin Wei-yüan is contained in Lien Heng 1920–21 (1955), pp. 700–701.

109. This matter of Lin Wei-yüan and "equal subscriptions" is set forth in a petition by the Taiwan intendant, followed by replies by the governor-general and governor, preserved in Liu Ao, *Hsün T'ai t'ui ssu lu* (Recorded considerations of a retired Taiwan intendant; Tainan: Hai tung shan fang, 1957), pp. 133–35. References to Lin's huge 1878 contribution are to be found in the Chinese newspaper *Shen pao* (CCSP, pp. 854, 878).

110. A short biography of Ch'en Hsia-lin is contained in T'ai-pei shih wen hsien wei yüan hui, comp., "Jen wu chih" (Records of personages), in *T'ai-pei shih chih kao* (Draft gazetteer of Taipei; Taipei: T'ai-pei shih wen hsien wei yüan hui, 1962), ch. 9, p. 53. For an account of Pai's career see Wen-ch'iao 1957: 71–74.

111. Huang Te-shih 1954: 22.

112. The changes in Taiwan-Fukien administrative ties that came about after Taiwan became a province—ties modeled after those between Kansu and the recently formed Sinkiang province in Northwest China—are briefly discussed in Chou Yin-t'ang, *T'ai-wan chün hsien chien chih chih* (Record of the establishment of Taiwan's prefectures and counties; Shanghai: Cheng chung shu chü, 1945, first Shanghai printing), p. 10.

113. LMCL: 66.

114. This company, named Chien-ch'ang kung-ssu, is briefly mentioned in "Cheng chih chih; chien she p'ien" (Records of political institutions; section on construction), in *T'ai-pei shih chih kao* (Draft gazetteer of Taipei; Taipei, 1962), ch. 3, pp. 8, 32; and Chu Wan-li 1954, p. 70.

115. LMCL: 67.

116. Huang Te-shih 1954: 23; Chu Wan-li 1954, pp. 70–71.

117. Huang Ch'i-jui 1954: 13.

118. Liu's preference for T'ai-pei-fu is disclosed in his memorial of 1889, cited in note 99 above. LMCL: 66.

119. Huang Te-shih 1954: 27–28; TSS, p. 57. See also Map 5 of this study.

120. When the Hsin-chu site was laid out during the Yung-cheng period, aboriginal villages in the vicinity were moved to another area (HCTH, p. 6). At I-lan the Chinese settlers received other lands in exchange for the plots they held at the site of construction; for details see KCL, p. 21. Another initial aspect of "city planning" at these new walled-city sites involved land drainage. For example, Map 4 shows that two irrigation ditches adjoining the I-lan city

site on the eastern and western sides were utilized to regulate the water flow in the moats encircling the city after I-lan had been laid out and the land drained and leveled.

121. Regional defenses protecting mainland walled cities are treated in Sen-dou Chang, "Some Aspects of the Urban Geography of the Chinese Hsien Capital," *Annals of the Association of American Geographers*, 51, no. 1 (Mar. 1961): 33.

122. Meng-chia's importance as a government seat increased as the Tan-shui subprefect came to spend about half of each year there. Yao Ying, "T'ai-pei tao li chi," in *Tung ch'a chi lüeh* (1832), p. 90.

123. For a brief account of the circumstances which caused earthen, then eventually stone, walls to be built around T'ao-yüan, see: T'ao-yüan hsien wen hsien wei yüan hui (T'ao-yüan County Historical Commission), comp., *T'ao-yüan hsien chih* (T'ao-yüan county gazetteer), ch. shou (T'ao-yüan: T'ao-yüan hsien wen hsien wei yüan hui, 1962), pp. 35–36. An account of the port town of Chung-kang (south of Hsin-chu), which had stone and brick walls, is contained in an unpublished manuscript by Tomita Yoshirō, translated into Chinese by Hsü Shih-chen et al., "T'ai-wan hsiang chen ti li hsüeh ti yen chiu" (A geographic study of townships in Taiwan), *T'ai-wan feng-wu*, 4, no. 10 (Oct. 1954): 1–16; 5, no. 1 (Jan. 1955): 23–45; 5, no. 6 (June 1955): 9–43. Information concerning still other walled towns in northern Taiwan, such as Hou-lung, Fang-li, and Pan-ch'iao, is to be found in Chiang Tao-chang, "Shih pa shih chi chi shih chiu shih chi T'ai-wan ying chien ti ku ch'eng" (Taiwan's walled towns built during the eighteenth and nineteenth centuries), *Nan-yang ta hsüeh hsüeh pao*, no. 1 (1967): 190–95.

124. Here the phrase *"yin-ti chih-i"* denotes the restrictive idea of not using stone and brick materials for wall construction as well as the more general connotation discussed in note 52 above.

125. References to divination and geomancy appear in accounts of wall construction at all three northern Taiwan cities. Geomantic (*feng-shui*) considerations proved particularly important when I-lan was laid out. In this instance someone was able to prevail upon the authorities to build I-lan facing south instead of east (as Yang T'ing-li had intended), after submitting his topographical reckonings. KCL, pp. 197–98. The connection between superstition and city building was an important one, as illustrated by the reconstruction of Feng-shan in 1825–26: the local authorities and inhabitants abandoned this new site when the magistrate in charge of the construction work happened to die there. Lien Heng 1920–21 (1955), p. 361.

126. One early-nineteenth-century writer indicates that there was no need to provide relief work through massive wall-construction projects since plenty of job opportunities existed in the cities, towns, villages, and guard stations. Yet according to his account, the erection of buildings and temples within these walled centers may have created temporary employment for the needy. Cheng Kuang-ts'e, "T'ai-wan ch'eng kung k'o huan i" (An argument that Taiwan's city wall construction may be delayed), in Ho Ch'ang-ling, comp., *Huang ch'ao ching shih wen pien* (hereafter CSWP; Compilation of Ch'ing essays on statecraft; Taipei: Kuo fang ch'u pan she, 1963 reprint), p. 2161.

127. The records of the awards bestowed for support of the Hsin-chu undertaking have been preserved (TSAC: 182). By the time the three northern

Taiwan walled centers were built or reconstructed in the nineteenth century, awards were regularly allotted to local inhabitants who rendered appreciable support, at least for wall-construction projects. See a reference to the Board of Works instructions, issued in 1807, stipulating that each province was to encourage city-wall building by making wards based on carefully kept project registers (TAHL, p. 163).

128. Such critics ranged from Lan T'ing-yüan, who thought wooden and earthen walls impractical (*Tung cheng chi*, pp. 27–29), to Cheng Kuang-ts'e, who questioned the feasibility of massive walls of any type in an area subject to floods and earthquakes (CSWP, p. 2161). Earthen enclosures deteriorated rapidly in Taiwan. The one built around Hsin-chu in 1842 eroded within ten years or so, though the bamboo hedge surrounding it still provided dense protective foliage for some decades thereafter. See Cheng P'eng-yün and Tseng Feng-ch'en, comps., *Hsin-chu hsien chih ch'u kao* (Preliminary draft of a gazetteer for Hsin-chu county; Taipei: T'ai-wan yin hang, 1959 reprint), p. 12.

129. In fact, the early practice of forming walled villages, called "*pao*," was so prevalent that this word came to denote rural divisions in the northern and middle portions of Taiwan. Lien Heng, 1920–21 (1955), p. 461.

130. This critic was Cheng Kuang-ts'e. See his piece "T'ai-wan ch'eng kung k'o huan i," in CSWP, p. 2161.

Regional Urbanization in Nineteenth-Century China

1. These six rivers are the Yellow River west of Kuei-te-t'ing, Kansu (now in Tsinghai); the Ta-tu River north of Ta-ch'ien-lu, Szechwan; the Ya-lung River west of Mien-ning, Szechwan; the Chin-sha (Yangtze) River northeast of Li-chiang-fu, Yunnan; the Lan-ts'ang (Mekong) River north of Wei-hsi-t'ing, Yunnan; and the Nu (Salween) River northwest of Yung-ch'ang-fu (Pao-shan), Yunnan.

2. The cutting point on the Yellow River that divides its drainage area between the Northwest and North China regions is the San-men Gorge, near the point where the boundaries of Shensi, Shansi, and Honan converge. The cutting points on the Yangtze are (1) between Tso shan, an outlier of the Ta-pieh mountains in Su-sung *hsien*, Anhwei, and Mei-ling, an outlier of the Huang-shan range in P'eng-tse *hsien*, Kiangsi (separating the Lower from the Middle Yangtze region); (2) the narrowest point in the famous Yangtze Gorges near the Hupeh-Szechwan border (separating the Middle from the Upper Yangtze region); and (3) the narrow defile between Yün-feng shan in the southern foothills of the Ta-liang range in what is today Chao-chiao *hsien* (but in the 1890's was part of Hsi-ch'ang *hsien*), Szechwan, and Mao-mao shan in Lu-tien *t'ing*, Yunnan (separating the Upper Yangtze from the Yun-Kwei region). The drainage area of the Wu River is divided between the Upper Yangtze and Yun-Kwei regions by cutting the river about 30 km due north of the county capital of Yin-chiang, Kweichow. The drainage area of the Hung-shui, a tributary of the West River, is divided between Lingnan and Yun-Kwei by cutting the river immediately north of T'ien-o, now a county capital (but in the 1890's a nonadministrative center in Tung-lan *chou*) in Kwangsi.

3. There were precisely eighteen provinces in China between 1662, when Kiangnan was divided into Anhwei and Kiangsu, and 1884, when Sinkiang

was made a province. Taiwan was separated from Fukien to form a separate province in 1886.

4. Regional areas were computed from the county-level data in Kuan Wei-lan, comp., *Chung-hua min kuo hsing cheng ch'ü hua chi t'u ti jen k'ou tsung chi piao* (Taipei, 1955). When a county was bisected by a regional boundary, its area was split between the regions involved in accordance with estimates derived from maps, except that a county more than 90 percent of whose area fell in a single region was assigned to it in toto. Population figures were divided proportionally except when there was good reason for doing otherwise. The proportions of the population of each province falling into the relevant regions, as computed from Kuan Wei-lan's compilation, were applied to the provincial totals from the 1953 census to obtain the regional population estimates for 1953. A similar procedure was followed using provincial data from the 1851 "census," except that the figure for Fukien (then including Taiwan) was discarded as unauthentic and invalid. (On this point, cf. Ping-ti Ho, *Studies on the Population of China, 1368–1953* [Cambridge: Harvard University Press, 1959], p. 54.) The combined population for the eight regions as of 1851 came to 421,000,000. Consistent regional population series for each decade from 1843 on were then generated from the 1851 and 1953 base-line data, taking into account major developments of demographic significance during the century in question. In this regard I relied heavily on John S. Aird's treatment of the 1851–1953 period at pp. 261–72 of his "Population Growth," in Alexander Eckstein et al., eds., *Economic Trends in Communist China* (Chicago: Aldine, 1968).

5. These are average estimates that do not take terrain into account. See Dwight H. Perkins, *Agricultural Development in China, 1368–1968* (Chicago: Aldine, 1969), p. 120.

6. In his important article on the medieval developmental cycle in North China, Robert Hartwell calls attention to "periods of marked material progress as well as times of stagnation and decline in different historical eras, geographic regions, or sectors of the economy" ("A Cycle of Economic Change in Imperial China: Coal and Iron in Northeast China, 750–1350," *Journal of the Economic and Social History of the Orient*, 10, Part 1 [1967]: 102).

7. "Social-overhead capital," to be distinguished from "directly productive activity," includes those basic services without which primary, secondary, and tertiary productive activities cannot function. In its narrower meaning it covers transportation, communications, water supply, and such agricultural overhead as irrigation and drainage systems. See Albert O. Hirschman, *The Strategy of Economic Development* (New Haven, Conn.: Yale University Press, 1968), p. 83.

8. These data were published quarterly in *Ta Ch'ing chin shen ch'üan shu*; I used the issue for Autumn 1893. Discrepancies with the listing in the Kuang-hsü edition of *Ta Ch'ing hui tien* (1899) were checked out to detect errors in the poorly printed and inadequately proofed original source.

9. Data on the circumferences of city walls were culled in the first instance from *Chia-ch'ing ch'ung hsiu i t'ung chih* (1820), corrected (a few of the largest cities only) and supplemented to some extent from later sources on particular cities.

10. For a succinct and authoritative history of the Imperial Post Office,

founded in 1896, see China [Republic], Chiao t'ung pu, Yu cheng kuan li chü (Ministry of Communications, Directorate General of Posts), *Report on the Chinese Post Office for the Tenth Year of Chung-hua min-kuo, 1921, with which is Incorporated an Historical Survey of the Quarter-Century, 1896–1921* (Shanghai: Yu cheng kuan li chü, 1922). See also Ying-wan Cheng, *Postal Communication in China and Its Modernization, 1860–1896* (Cambridge: Harvard University, East Asian Research Center, 1970), chaps. 7–8. The Imperial Post Office came to be relied on very quickly by government offices as well as by business enterprises, and in the early years carried a relatively small volume of private mail. Thus the postal hierarchy (three grades of post offices, plus postal agencies) tended to reflect the prevailing level of administrative and commercial activity in the various cities and towns. Data for 1915, then, provide a fairly good index of the combined importance of administrative and economic central functions as of the end of the imperial era. Approximately 7,000 cities and towns had post offices or agencies in 1915; these are listed together with rank and available postal services in the eighteen volumes of *Shina shōbetsu zenshi* (Provincial gazetteer of China; Tokyo: Tōa dōbunkai, 1917–20). The list of services specifies whether the post office in question sent and received mail by steamship or rail.

11. See *Shina shōbetsu zenshi*, cited in note 10 above.

12. It is not feasible to reproduce the list here. Gazetteers from all eighteen provinces were consulted, but comprehensive coverage was sought for only two subregions: the area encompassing Ning-po and Shao-hsing prefectures and the regional-city trading systems of their capital cities (Chekiang); and the regional-city trading system of Chengtu, including all of Ch'eng-tu *fu* and parts of Sui-ting *fu*, T'ung-ch'uan *fu*, Ya-chou *fu*, Ch'iung *chou*, Mei *chou*, Mien *chou*, and Tzu *chou* (all of the last four being autonomous departments). In addition, I have drawn freely on the urban data culled by Gilbert Rozman from a sizable sample of Ch'ing gazetteers. See his *Urban Networks in Ch'ing China and Tokugawa Japan* (Princeton, N.J.: Princeton University Press, 1973), chaps. 4–5. Prior to the twentieth century, local gazetteers seldom gave population figures for cities per se; however, many provided such helpful indicators of city size as the number of streets or wards within the walls and in the various extramural suburbs, and all provided at least some indicators of the relative importance of central functions (cultural as well as economic and administrative) in the capital(s) and oftentimes in other central places as well.

13. The secondary works consulted in this regard are cited in G. William Skinner, ed., *Modern Chinese Society: An Analytical Bibliography, Vol. 1, Publications in Western Languages, 1644–1972* (Stanford, Calif.: Stanford University Press, 1973) under Historical-period subheading 1644–1911 and the following Subject main headings: 10, Chinese Society in General; 11.3, Macroecology and Settlement Patterns; 14.2, Transport and Communications; 14.3, Commerce and Services; 20, Local Communities as Total Systems; 21, Regional and Local Population; 21.1, Regional Urbanization and City Population; 21.3, Microecology and Particular Settlements; 24, Local Economic Systems; 24.2, Local Transport and Communications; and 24.3, Local Commerce and Services.

14. Data were drawn primarily from the two relevant works by Ping-ti Ho: *Chung-kuo hui kuan shih lun* (An historical study of *hui-kuan* in China; Tai-

pei: Hsüeh sheng shu chü, 1966) and "The Geographical Distribution of Hui-kuan (Landsmannschaften) in Central and Upper Yangtze Provinces," *Tsing Hua Journal of Chinese Studies*, n.s. 5, no. 2 (Dec. 1966).

15. Apparently the rationale for arranging city-size classes in this fashion originated with Mark H. Skolnick. For an authoritative treatment of the issues, see Kingsley Davis, *World Urbanization 1950–1970, Vol. II: Analysis of Trends, Relationships, and Development* (Berkeley: University of California, Institute of International Studies, 1972), pp. 17–24.

16. The terms used here for central places at the lower levels of the economic hierarchy in China—standard market town, intermediate market town, central market town, and local city—were introduced in my article "Marketing and Social Structure in Rural China, Part I," *Journal of Asian Studies*, 24, no. 1 (Nov. 1964): 6–9.

17. Estimates for the total number of central places were made separately for each region by three different procedures. First, detailed contemporary data on market towns were collected from over 200 local gazetteers and from the Japanese secondary literature that has drawn on gazetteers, notably Katō Shigeshi, "Shindai ni okeru sonchin no teiki ichi" (Rural periodic markets during the Ch'ing period), *Tōyō gakuhō*, 23, no. 2 (Feb. 1936): 1–52; Masui Tsuneo, "Kanton no kyoshi" (Periodic markets in Kwangtung), *Tōa ronsō* (Tokyo: Bunkyūdō), 4 (May 1941): 263–83; Kuramochi Tokuichirō, "Shisen no jōshi" (The local markets of Szechwan), *Nihon daigaku shigakkai kenkyū ihō*, 1 (Dec. 1957): 2–32; Yamane Yukio, "Min Shin jidai Kahoku ni okeru teiki ichi," *Tōkyō joshi daigaku shiron*, 8 (Nov. 1960): 493–504 [trans. by Matsuda Mitsugui as "Periodic Markets in North China During the Ming and Ch'ing Periods," in *Markets in China during the Sung, Ming, and Ch'ing Periods* (Honolulu: East-West Center, Institute of Advanced Projects, Research Publications and Translations, 1967), pp. 109–42]; and Ishihara Hiroshi, "Kahoku shō ni okeru Min Shin minkoku jidai no teiki ichi" (Periodic markets in Hopei during the Ming, Ch'ing, and Republican periods), *Chirigaku hyōron*, 46, no. 4 (1973): 245–63. In separate research projects, I have analyzed central places down to standard market towns in the areas of Chekiang and Szechwan already described in note 12. The county-level units for which the number of market towns in 1893 had been ascertained from the sources listed above were then classified by macroregion and by location within the regional core or periphery. With due attention to the precise location of the sampled counties in relation to the overall structure of the region, the average number of market towns per county-level unit in a particular regional core or regional periphery was applied to all county-level units in that core or periphery.

Second, in my earlier study of marketing systems in China ("Marketing and Social Structure in Rural China, Part II," *Journal of Asian Studies*, 64, no. 2 [Feb. 1965]: 226–27), I arrived at the following regression equation for the size of standard marketing areas:

$$y = ax + b + \frac{c}{x}$$

where y is the size of the marketing area, x is population density, a is an index of average transport efficiency, b is a factor measuring the ruggedness of the prevailing topography, and c is a measure of household self-sufficiency or reliance on the market. Values for each variable were separately computed or estimated for each of the eight regional cores and the eight regional peripheries. The sixteen equations were then solved for y, which was divided by total area to yield estimates of the number of standard marketing systems.

Third, in general, when population class intervals are selected so that the upper boundary of each class is equal to twice the lower boundary (cf. Davis 1972, pp. 20–24), as in this study, the number of central places in each class tends empirically to be twice the number of the next higher class. On the assumption that this empirical regularity obtained in late imperial China, I extrapolated downward from the known distribution of central places in the top population classes (8,000 or more) of each region, thereby yielding an estimate of all central places with a population of 500 or more.

Where the three modes of estimation yielded significantly different results for a region, the manner in which hard data had been extrapolated, the values assigned variables in the regression equation, and the modular figures selected for extrapolation downward in the third method were all reexamined and revised. In the end, a series of values that were consistent across regions on the input side yielded closely similar results for each region by all three methods. The figure of 39,000 central places is probably correct within a 10 percent margin of error either way.

18. In 1951, Trewartha assembled earlier estimates for particular cities compiled by Stauffer for 1922, Torgasheff for 1930, Shen for 1937, and Fu and Sun for 1948, and added a series for 1949 compiled by himself in collaboration with I. Yuan Shie. See Glenn T. Trewartha, "Chinese Cities: Numbers and Distribution," *Annals of the Association of American Geographers*, 41, no. 4 (Dec. 1951). When these myriad estimates are compared with census data for 1953 and with the estimates for 1938 compiled in 1961 by Ullman, the earlier tendency toward overestimation is immediately apparent. See Morris B. Ullman, *Cities of Mainland China 1953–1958* (Washington, D.C.: U.S. Bureau of the Census, Foreign Manpower Research Office, 1961). The population data for China's largest cities presented in Perkins 1969, Appendix E, show estimates for ca. 1900–1910 that for many cities are out of line with the figures for later years: e.g., Kuei-sui, 200,000; Shao-hsing, 500,000; Chungking, 600,000; Canton, 900,000. It is also instructive to compare the careful comparative estimates of city populations provided in the eighteen volumes of *Shina shōbetsu zenshi* with contemporary estimates by Western observers; the latter are almost invariably larger, sometimes by a factor of two or three.

19. Frank W. Notestein and C. M. Chiao, "Population," in J. Lossing Buck, *Land Utilization in China* (Nanking: University of Nanking, 1937), vol. 1, p. 365.

20. Double listings include An-yang and Chang-te (i.e., Chang-te-fu), Shang-ch'ü (i.e., Shang-ch'iu) and Kweiteh (i.e., Kuei-te-fu), Ta-li and T'ung-chou (i.e., T'ung-chou-fu), Ho-p'o (i.e., Ho-p'u) and Limchow (i.e., Lien-chou-fu), Nan-ch'eng and Kienchang (i.e., Chien-ch'ang-fu), Kuei-sui and Kweihwating (i.e., Kuei-hua-t'ing).

21. Of course, it should not be imagined that what is "known" has been adequately codified. The series for 1938 published in Ullman 1961 is doubtless

the most reliable and comprehensive of those available, and the present figures may be seriously flawed through underestimating the extent to which wartime disruption, 1937–49, slowed the growth of some cities and accelerated that of others. The listing in Perkins 1969, Appendix E, yields a total urban population for ca. 1900–1910 of 16.2 million for China less Manchuria, Sinkiang, and Taiwan. This figure applies only to those cities whose population in 1958 exceeded 100,000; but when obvious overestimations of the kind mentioned above in note 16 are adjusted, Perkins's figures for the turn of the century would be compatible with an inclusively defined urban population as of 1893 in the 22 to 25 million range.

22. For the Ning-Shao subregion of Chekiang and for Chengtu's regional-city trading system in Szechwan (both described in note 12), I have analyzed the development of the central-place hierarchy in detail and thus was able to make rather precise comparisons of 1843 with 1893. For 40-odd counties outside these subregions, mostly in North China and the Lower Yangtze, I compared market towns as enumerated by a Tao-kuang gazetteer (1821–50) with those enumerated by a Kuang-hsü gazetteer (1875–1908), thereby obtaining additional empirical data of use in estimating the rates at which the number of central places increased between 1843 and 1893. For each of the large cities, data from travel accounts (see note 13) and from local gazetteers were collated in dated series and the estimates for 1843 compared (and wherever possible reconciled) with the classifications in Rozman 1973, chaps. 4–5. For North China and the Lower Yangtze regions as of 1843, I approximated in crude fashion all three modes of estimation described in note 17. For other regions I made no attempt to muster the 1840's data needed to estimate the values of variables in the regression equation, and the second procedure was omitted.

23. A comparison of 1893 with 1843 blurs the massive fluctuation that occurred. The population of agrarian China continued to rise after 1843 until some time in the early 1850's. The absolute decline of several tens of millions that followed probably bottomed out in the 1870's, allowing nearly two decades for recovery before 1893.

24. "Probably in no other country has political influence in city development operated in such pure fashion, and, at the same time, so strongly and so continuously through the centuries, as in China" (Glenn T. Trewartha, "Chinese Cities: Origins and Functions," *Annals of the Association of American Geographers*, 42, no. 1 [Mar. 1952]: 82–83). "The distribution of cities was inextricably tied to the administrative divisions of the country" (Rozman 1973, p. 63).

25. The number of ranked bureaucrats and private secretaries varied considerably from one capital to another, but their total number was never large. The number of clerks in a county-level government is said to have varied from 100 to 3,000, the number of yamen runners from 250 to 7,000. See T'ung-tsu Ch'ü, *Local Government in China under the Ch'ing* (Cambridge: Harvard University Press, 1962), pp. 39, 59.

26. Mark Elvin argues that the vigorous economic growth during the medieval period in China was accompanied by revolutionary advances in agriculture, water transport, science, and technology, but that when economic growth was resumed in the fifteenth century in the wake of two centuries of

stagnation, technological innovation was almost wholly absent. *The Pattern of the Chinese Past* (Stanford, Calif.: Stanford University Press, 1973), esp. chaps. 9, 10, 13, 14, and 17.

27. For numerous examples of technological diffusion, see Elvin 1973, Part 2. On the diffusion of new crops, see Ping-ti Ho, *Studies on the Population of China, 1368–1953* (Cambridge: Harvard University Press, 1959), chap. 8.

28. For the classic treatment of this impressive technology, see Joseph Needham, *Science and Civilization in China, Vol. 4, Physics and Physical Technology, Part 3, Civil Engineering and Nautics* (Cambridge: Cambridge University Press, 1971). See also Elvin 1973, chap. 10.

29. For examples, see Evelyn Sakakida Rawski, *Agricultural Change and the Peasant Economy of South China* (Cambridge: Harvard University Press, 1972), esp. chap. 4; and Skinner 1965: 211–27.

30. In their exemplary study *Mid-Ch'ing Rice Markets and Trade: An Essay in Price History* (Cambridge: Harvard University, East Asian Research Center, 1975), Han-sheng Chuan and Richard A. Kraus convincingly demonstrate the existence of large-scale interregional trade in rice during the Yung-cheng reign (1723–35). They estimate that the annual flow of rice downriver to the Lower Yangtze region averaged from 8 to 13 million *shih*, of which somewhat less than 2 million *shih* were sent on to ports in the Southeast Coast region—all this in addition to the average annual shipment of approximately 3.5 million *shih* of tribute grain from the Lower Yangtze to Peking. Their findings suggest (pp. 77–78) a decline in the volume of the interregional rice trade in the Yangtze Valley between the 1730's and the 1840's, a development that seems probable in light of the exceptionally high rates of population growth during the century in question in the Upper Yangtze region and in the Hsiang and Kan basins of the Middle Yangtze. However, there is no reason to believe that the mid-Ch'ing period witnessed a comparable decline in the interregional wholesale trade in commodities other than grain. It seems probable to me that as a whole this trade increased—at least through the eighteenth century, and at least as rapidly as the population grew.

31. The Yangtze Gorges were, of course, far less of an obstacle to downriver than to upriver trade. Chuan and Kraus 1975 demonstrate (p. 70) that in the early eighteenth century there was a considerable movement of rice from production centers in the Upper Yangtze to the Middle and Lower Yangtze in years when demand was high in the latter regions. They call attention to the total disappearance of this outflow by the twentieth century.

32. Perkins 1969, pp. 116–24 and Appendix I. Perkins downplays the magnitude of interregional trade, possibly egregiously; cf. Chuan and Kraus 1975, pp. 77–78. In any case, it is likely that in the 1840's absolute levels of interregional trade were higher, and those of foreign trade lower, than in the 1890's. In general, I quarrel with Perkins's conclusion (p. 124) that "for nearly one thousand years [to 1910], China's long-distance trade changed little. The absolute amounts rose, but more or less along with the increase in population." Important fluctuations in extraregional trade seem to me explicit in the historical record of medieval and late imperial China; and they appear to me crucial in understanding the course of development.

33. The division of labor and the application of technology have both been given relatively low weightings because of the near certainty that each is to

some extent redundant with respect to the other as well as with respect to the two trade variables.

34. Since only two of the six dimensions were "scored blind," as it were, it must be admitted that the numerical model as a whole is rigged. Nothing is demonstrated other than the plausibility of the arguments made in qualitative terms.

35. Jack P. Gibbs and Walter T. Martin, "Urbanization, Technology, and the Division of Labor: International Patterns," *American Sociological Review*, 27, no. 5 (Oct. 1962): 667–77.

36. *Ibid.*: 668.

37. Chauncy D. Harris, *Cities of the Soviet Union: Studies in Their Functions, Size, Destiny, and Growth* (Chicago: Rand McNally, 1970), p. 159, and chaps. 4 and 6.

38. G. K. Zipf, *National Unity and Disunity: The Nation as a Bio-Social Organism* (Bloomington, Ind.: Principia Press, 1941). In interpreting the characteristics of regional rank-size distributions, I follow closely the treatment in Harris 1970, chap. 5.

39. The concept of primacy may be extended to cover cases where the largest two or three cities contain a disproportionate share of the urban population. Cf. Brian J. L. Berry and Frank E. Horton, *Geographic Perspectives on Urban Systems* (Englewood Cliffs, N.J.: Prentice-Hall, 1970), p. 70. Recourse to the extended concept is obviated here by the two other features of rank-size distributions that are analyzed in the text.

40. This index differs from that adopted by Norton Ginsburg, ed., *Atlas of Economic Development* (Chicago: University of Chicago Press, 1961), p. 36: namely, the ratio of the population of the largest city to the combined population of the four largest cities.

41. Cf. the treatment of the Soviet cities of Baku and Riga in Harris 1970, p. 135. The conclusions concerning primacy reached by Berry and Horton 1970, p. 73, are not stated in sufficiently generic terms for direct application to premodern China.

42. For a general treatment of the development of the trading monopoly at Canton and of the "Canton system," see John K. Fairbank, Edwin O. Reischauer, and Albert M. Craig, *East Asia: The Modern Transformation* (Boston: Houghton Mifflin, 1965), pp. 71–78, 128–36. By the late eighteenth century, Canton "had been drawn into a world-wide process of commercial development, which spread from England to India, Southeast Asia and beyond" (p. 76).

43. In accounting for differences in this regard among provinces of North China, Rozman (1973, p. 212) hypothesizes that "the greater the amount of long-distance commerce imported into a province, the higher the proportion of urban residents in large cities."

44. Cf. Harris 1970, pp. 135–36.

45. *Ibid.*, pp. 131–32.

46. *Ibid.*, p. 138.

47. After outlining the economics of the tribute grain shipments to Peking, Perkins (1970, p. 150) notes that it is "no surprise that the North China Plain was not sprinkled with large cities."

48. Kazimierz Dziewonski, "Urbanization in Contemporary Poland," *Geo-*

graphia Polonica, 3, no. 1 (Jan. 1964): 37–56. A plotting of the rank-size distribution for 1960 is reproduced in Berry and Horton 1970, p. 78.

49. Japanese institutional historians, who have an excellent eye for good data, have devoted a disproportionate number of their prodigious monographic studies to the Lower Yangtze region and to the core areas of two or three others. Writing on the basis of a corpus of monographic works that is regionally skewed in this fashion, a synthesizer finds it well-nigh impossible to make generalizations about China as a whole that are not misleading.

50. The distribution shown in Figure 2 is slightly distorted by the omission of Manchuria, which in 1843 could boast at least one city (Sheng-ching, i.e., Mukden) with a population of over 10,000.

Introduction: Urban and Rural in Chinese Society

1. Cases in point are K'uei-chi and Shan-yin, the metropolitan counties of Shao-hsing *fu*, Chekiang; and Hui-an *hsien*, Ch'üan-chou *fu*, Fukien. See James H. Cole, "Shaohsing: Studies in Ch'ing Social History," Ph.D. dissertation, Stanford University, 1975, chap. 3; and Jacques Amyot, *The Manila Chinese: Familism in the Philippine Environment* (Quezon City: Ateneo de Manila University, Institute of Philippine Culture, 1973), pp. 32–34 and the map facing p. 80. Also compare the remarks on the importance for relative lineage strength of commercial development and agricultural productivity in Jack M. Potter, "Land and Lineage in Traditional China," in Maurice Freedman, ed., *Family and Kinship in Chinese Society* (Stanford, Calif.: Stanford University Press, 1970), pp. 121–38. One of the sources Baker cites notes that the most prominent lineages of Kwangtung were located in Kuang-chou *fu*, the metropolitan (and most urbanized) prefecture. In fact, lineages appear to have been stronger in the four counties that included and surrounded Canton than elsewhere in the prefecture. It is doubtless no coincidence that these were the very counties shown by Grimm to have had a high proportion of academies outside capital cities.

2. Cf. G. William Skinner, "Mobility Strategies in Late Imperial China: A Regional-Systems Analysis," in Carol A. Smith, ed., *Regional Analysis, Vol. 1, Economic Systems* (New York: Academic Press, 1976), esp. pp. 55–57.

3. The point is emphasized in the last paragraph of Baker's paper. Cf. Maurice Freedman, *Chinese Lineage and Society: Fukien and Kwangtung* (London: Athlone Press, 1966), chap. 3; and Kung-chuan Hsiao, *Rural China: Imperial Control in the Nineteenth Century* (Seattle: University of Washington Press, 1960), pp. 348–57.

4. Maurice Freedman, "Geomancy," in *Proceedings of the Royal Anthropological Institute of Great Britain and Ireland 1958* (1959): 7.

5. Cf. Maurice Freedman, "On the Sociological Study of Chinese Religion," in Arthur P. Wolf, ed., *Religion and Ritual in Chinese Society* (Stanford, Calif.: Stanford University Press, 1974), pp. 34–41.

6. The situation is complicated by the fact that City God temples were occasionally established in nonadministrative centers. The Hsia-hai City God temple in Ta-tao-ch'eng (a nonadministrative center now absorbed by the city of Taipei) originally served as a compatriot's temple for migrants from T'ung-an *hsien*, who founded it, but later became the communal temple of the town per se; it appears never to have had any territorial jurisdiction out-

side Ta-tao-ch'eng. Stephan Feuchtwang, "City Temples in Taipei Under Three Regimes," in Mark Elvin and G. William Skinner, eds., *The Chinese City Between Two Worlds* (Stanford, Calif.: Stanford University Press, 1974), pp. 269–76 *passim*.

7. Y. K. Leong and L. K. Tao, *Village and Town Life in China* (London: Allen and Unwin, 1915), p. 46.

8. Skinner 1976, p. 343, n. 17.

9. H. S. Brunnert and V. V. Hagelstrom, *Present Day Political Organization of China* (Shanghai: Kelly and Walsh, 1912), p. 434.

10. Freedman 1974, p. 37.

11. An entirely different criticism of the Great and Little Tradition approach is that it dichotomizes what is in fact a cultural whole in which the cultivated and the popular were inextricably interpenetrated. See Freedman 1974; Maurice Freedman, "Sinology and the Social Sciences: Some Reflections on the Social Anthropology of China," *Ethnos* (Stockholm, Etnografiska Museet) 40; and S. J. Tambiah, *Buddhism and the Spirit Cults in North-east Thailand* (Cambridge: Cambridge University Press, 1970), pp. 367–77.

12. This distinction was introduced in my "Chinese Peasants and the Closed Community: An Open and Shut Case," *Comparative Studies in Society and History*, 13, no. 3 (July 1971): 275.

13. P'an Kuang-tan and Fei Hsiao-t'ung, "K'o chü yü she hui liu tung" (The examination system and social mobility), *She hui k'o hsüeh*, 4, no. 1 (Oct. 1947): 1–21. For a partial translation see "City and Village: The Inequality of Opportunity," in Johanna M. Menzel, ed., *The Chinese Civil Service: Career Open to Talent?* (Boston: Heath, 1963), pp. 9–21.

14. In particular, Ping-ti Ho, *The Ladder of Success in Imperial China: Aspects of Social Mobility, 1368–1911* (New York: Columbia University Press, 1962). See also Chung-li Chang, *The Chinese Gentry: Studies on Their Role in Nineteenth Century Chinese Society* (Seattle: University of Washington Press, 1955).

15. Skinner 1976, p. 353–54. Ping-ti Ho (1962, p. 143) quotes Wang Ch'i, a sixteenth-century Ch'ing official, as follows: "It is a good thing if they [one's sons and grandsons] are content with coarse clothes and straw shoes and refrain from going to the cities.... Fortunately, [my brothers and I] were sent back to our ancestral home, thus avoiding ... bad environmental influences." A major element of the "rural is good" theme among the gentry was that the safest form of investment is land, the only form of property that never depreciates, can be neither stolen nor destroyed, and can be preserved in the family for generations. A classic expression of this position is contained in Chang Ying, *Heng ch'an so yen* (ca. 1697). For an annotated translation, see Hilary Jane Beattie, "Land and Lineage in China: A Study of T'ung-ch'eng County, Anhwei, in the Ming and Ch'ing Dynasties," Ph.D. dissertation, Cambridge University, 1973.

16. Cf. the section in Cole 1975 entitled "Gentry or Merchant?" (pp. 89–97).

17. See Ying-wan Cheng, *Postal Communication in China and its Modernization, 1860–1896* (Cambridge: Harvard University, East Asian Research Center, 1970), chap. 2; John K. Fairbank and Ssu-yü Teng, "On the Transmission of Ch'ing Documents," *Harvard Journal of Asiatic Studies*, 4, no. 1 (May 1939): 12–46.

18. Silas H. L. Wu, *Communication and Imperial Control in China: Evolution of the Palace Memorial System, 1693–1735* (Cambridge: Harvard University Press, 1970), chaps. 7–9. See also Fairbank and Teng 1939.
19. Cheng 1970, Table 4; Fairbank and Teng 1939: Tables 3 and 4.
20. Hsü K'o, comp., *Ch'ing pai lei ch'ao* (1917). Quoted and translated in Cole 1975, p. 70.
21. For anthropological analyses of trust in the context of Chinese business, see Robert H. Silin, "Marketing and Credit in a Hong Kong Wholesale Market," in W. E. Willmott, ed., *Economic Organization in Chinese Society* (Stanford, Calif.: Stanford University Press, 1972), pp. 327–52; and John A. Young, "Interpersonal Networks and Economic Behavior in a Chinese Market Town," Ph.D. dissertation, Stanford University, 1971 (Ann Arbor, Mich.: University Microfilms, Publ. 71-23,574).
22. Skinner 1976.
23. A case in point is Hsüan-hua-fu, Chihli, which had been a large market town prior to its designation as a prefectural capital in 1693. Most changes of this kind, however, appear to have been made as part of the initial reorganization of field administration in each dynasty. The early years of the Republic also witnessed the designation of many nonadministrative local cities as county capitals.

Cities and the Hierarchy of Local Systems

1. I am grateful to Sophie Laden La and John R. Ziemer for their able research assistance and to J. G. Bell for a critical reading of an earlier draft.
2. See Table 2, p. 224, for a summary of my numerical model of central places in agrarian China as of 1893.
3. It does appear to be the case that however Chinese settlements originated—whether as administrative capitals, garrison towns, religious centers, mining towns, or manufacturing centers—in the course of time they almost invariably acquired commercial central functions for a surrounding hinterland.
4. For market towns, see my "Marketing and Social Structure in Rural China, Part I," *Journal of Asian Studies*, 24, no. 1 (1964): 32–43.
5. *Ibid.*: 37–38.
6. Cf. John R. Watt's discussion of Ch'ing urban strategy at p. 359 of this volume.
7. The classic studies are Walter Christaller, *Zie zentralen Orte in Süddeutschland* (Jena: Gustav Fischer, 1933), trans. by C. W. Baskin as *Central Places in Southern Germany* (Englewood Cliffs, N.J.: Prentice-Hall, 1966); and August Lösch, *Die räumliche Ordnung der Wirtschaft* (Jena: Gustav Fischer, 1940), trans. by W. H. Woglom and W. F. Stolper as *The Economics of Location* (New Haven, Conn.: Yale University Press, 1954). Among the most accessible general treatments of central-place theory are Brian J. L. Berry, *Geography of Market Centers and Retail Distribution* (Englewood Cliffs, N.J.: Prentice-Hall, 1967); John U. Marshall, *The Location of Service Towns: An Approach to the Analysis of Central Place Systems* (Toronto: University of Toronto, Department of Geography, 1969), chaps. 2 and 3; and Carol A. Smith, "Economics of Marketing Systems: Models from Economic Geography," in Bernard J. Siegel, ed., *Annual Review of Anthropology, Vol. 3*

(Palo Alto, Calif.: Annual Reviews, 1974), pp. 167–201. As Smith points out (p. 169), the basic assumptions and simple models of central-place theory require "less modification for the analysis of agrarian marketing systems than they do for industrial economies complicated by modern transport and localized production."

8. See in particular R. D. McKenzie, *The Metropolitan Community* (New York: McGraw-Hill, 1933); and R. E. Dickinson, *City Region and Regionalism* (London: Kegan, Paul, 1947).

9. This approach as well as the first are variants of what has been called the human-ecological theory of regionalization. See Harry W. Richardson, *Regional Economics: Location Theory, Urban Structure, and Regional Change* (New York: Praeger, 1969), pp. 170–76, 227–29. The functional interconnections of cities are most often studied as the movements of commodities (trade), persons (migration and labor recruitment), or messages (news, postal service, and in modern times telegraph and telephone service). A relevant and theoretically interesting study of interurban communications in a preindustrial society is Allan R. Pred, *Urban Growth and the Circulation of Information: The United States System of Cities, 1790–1840* (Cambridge: Harvard University Press, 1973).

10. As Minshull points out, it is quite possible to "start a regional description with the facts of population," and this approach in fact follows the lead of Vidal de la Blache, the founder of modern regional geography. Roger Minshull, *Regional Geography: Theory and Practice* (Chicago: Aldine, 1967), p. 24.

11. Philippe Buache, *Essai de géographie physique* (1752). See the discussion in Minshull 1967, pp. 21–22.

12. See E. L. Ullman, "Rivers as Regional Bonds," *Geographical Review*, 41 (1951).

13. Yun-Kwei was a notable exception. The Kunming-Kweiyang trade was most likely exceeded both by Kunming's trade with Hsü-chou-fu and by Kweiyang's trade with Chungking.

14. The upward shift of functions to centers at the next higher level of the hierarchy appears to be a general concomitant of declining population densities. For examples and rationale, see Berry 1967, pp. 32–35, and Marshall 1969, pp. 152–61.

15. Skinner 1964: 17–31.

16. For a lively discussion of the causes of deforestation in China, see Yi-fu Tuan, *China* (Chicago: Aldine, 1969), pp. 37–41.

17. In his account of the soils of China, Kovda estimates that the river system that dominates the Lingnan region transports some 28 million tons of silt annually. V. A. Kovda, *Soils and Natural Environments of China* (Washington, U.S. Joint Publications Research Service, 1960), p. 63.

18. See Franklin H. King, *Farmers of Forty Centuries*, 2d ed. (New York: Harcourt Brace, 1927), p. 75.

19. Keith Buchanan, *The Transformation of the Chinese Earth* (New York: Praeger, 1970), p. 90.

20. This analysis of the Upper Yangtze region rests primarily on data culled from 60-odd county and prefectural-level gazetteers spanning the century from the 1830's to the 1930's. The more important of the Western

sources used include *Baron Richthofen's Letters, 1870–1872* (Shanghai: North-China Herald, 1872); Ferdinand Paul Wilhelm von Richthofen, "Das Südwestliche China (Provinzen Sz'tshwan und Kwéitshou)," in *China: Ergebnisse eigener Reisen und darauf gegründeter Studien* (China: Results of my travels and studies based on them; Berlin: Reimer, 1912), vol. 3, 1–286; Chambre de commerce de Lyons, comp., *La Mission lyonnaise d'exploration commerciale en Chine, 1895–1897* (Lyons: Rey, 1898); G. J. L. Litton, *China: Report of a Journey to North Ssu-Ch'uan* (London: Her Majesty's Stationery Office, 1898; Gt. Brit., Foreign Office, Diplomatic and consular reports, misc. series, 457); Alexander Hosie, *Three Years in Western China: A Narrative of Three Journeys in Ssu-ch'uan, Kuei-chou, and Yün-nan*, 2d ed. (London: George Philip, 1897); Alexander Hosie, *Szechwan: Its Products, Industries, and Resources* (Shanghai: Kelly and Walsh, 1922); S. C. Haines Watson, "Journey to Sungp'an," *Journal of the China Branch of the Royal Asiatic Society*, 36 (1905): 51–102; and Edwin J. Dingle, *Across China on Foot: Life in the Interior and the Reform Movement* (New York: Holt, 1911).

21. The following passage from *Baron Richthofen's Letters* (1872, p. 162) catches the flavor of water transport in the Upper Yangtze region: "All the affluents [of the Yangtze] below Ping-shan can be navigated by small boats as far as the limits of the Red Basin extend.... All rivers of Sz'chwan have a strong current, even at low water, and are beset with rapids. Downstream, vessels travel at a quick rate; upstream they are dragged slowly and at great expense. Either way more hands are required than is usually the case in Chinese waters.... The expense of freight increases with the distance from the great rivers. Not one artificial canal for navigation exists in the province, the country being totally unfit for their construction."

22. "Communication by land," Baron Richthofen tells us (*ibid.*, p. 163), "is difficult everywhere, with the exception of the plain of Ch'eng-tu-fu [Chengtu]. The Peking road ... is the greatest highroad in the country. Another much travelled road connects Ch'eng-tu-fu with Ch'ung-ch'ing-fu [Chungking] by way of Tzu-chou; a third goes from Ch'eng-tu-fu to Tungch'uan-fu and Pao-ning-fu; another to Ya-chou-fu, where the roads to Tibet and Ning-yüan-fu commence.... All these highroads ... are well paved with flagstones, wide enough for the packtrains to pass each other, and kept in excellent repair. But little care is bestowed upon the grading. At steep places, flights of stairs are made, sometimes of a few hundred steps at a time, with little interruption.... In general, animals are not much employed in Sz'-chwan. Usually, travellers go in chairs, and the transportation of goods is done by coolies. Away from the highroads, these are the only modes of traffic." [In this quotation city names have been converted to Wade-Giles transcriptions.]

23. The standard guide to the formal structure of administration in the late Ch'ing is H. S. Brunnert and V. V. Hagelstrom, *Present-Day Political Organization of China*, translated from the Russian by A. Beltchenko and E. E. Moren (Shanghai: Kelly and Walsh, 1912). The two most important monographic studies are T'ung-tsu Ch'ü, *Local Government in China under the Ch'ing* (Cambridge: Harvard University Press, 1962; reissued Stanford, Calif.: Stanford University Press, 1969); and John R. Watt, *The District Magistrate in Late Imperial China* (New York: Columbia University Press, 1972). Most of the data used here were culled directly from the Kuang-hsü

edition (1899) of *Ta-Ch'ing hui-tien* and from the Autumn 1893 issue of *Chin-shen ch'üan-shu*. Data are standardized throughout to 1893.

24. The exceptional nature of governmental arrangements at Nanking derived in part from its one-time role as secondary imperial capital. See F. W. Mote's paper in this volume.

25. The tabulations (of 1893 data) on which this assertion rests cannot be reproduced here for want of space. The differences noted are statistically significant at the .05 level or better.

26. Brunnert and Hagelstrom 1912, p. 426.

27. The exception was Li-fan *t'ing* in Mao autonomous *chou*, Szechwan. Ch'ü 1962 (Chart 1, p. 5) errs in indicating that ordinary *chou* could be subordinate to autonomous *t'ing* as well as to prefectures.

28. The differences cited are statistically significant at the .05 level or better.

29. See Brunnert and Hagelstrom 1912, pp. 426–27; Ch'ü 1962, p. 15; and Rozman 1973, p. 155.

30. The differences reported in this paragraph are all statistically significant at the .05 level or better.

31. Rozman (1973, p. 154 and chap. 5) cites several instances of *chou* cities situated at the gateways to major capitals.

32. Watt 1972, p. 47.

33. *Ibid.*, p. 48.

34. It goes without saying that the geography of rebellion throughout Chinese history would be clarified by systematic attention to the structure of regional systems.

35. I am in no position to broach the enormous complexities of taxation and fiscal management in late imperial China. The most detailed monographic study is Ray Huang, *Taxation and Governmental Finance in Sixteenth-Century Ming China* (Cambridge: Cambridge University Press, 1974). For a guide to the relevant literature on Ch'ing fiscal management, see the first three temporal subheadings under the main headings "14.5 State Revenue and Expenditure" and "24.5 Local Revenue and Expenditure" in each of the three volumes of G. W. Skinner et al., eds., *Modern Chinese Society: An Analytical Bibliography* (Stanford, Calif.: Stanford University Press, 1973). An analysis of the political geography of revenue collection in China may be found in Joseph B. R. Whitney, *China: Area, Administration, and Nation Building* (Chicago: University of Chicago, Department of Geography, 1970), chap. 4.

36. All county-level units were expected to be self-sufficient in fiscal terms, but there was a wide range in the ratio of retained to transferred revenue. When all transfers, remittances, and grants-in-aid are taken into account, deficit county-level units are identifiable; it would appear that ordinary *t'ing* were prominent among them. See Hosea Ballou Morse, *The Trade and Administration of China*, 3d rev. ed. (Shanghai: Kelly and Walsh, 1921), pp. 92–135; E-tu Zen Sun, *Ch'ing Administrative Terms* (Cambridge: Harvard University Press, 1961), pp. 76–186; and Huang 1974, pp. 21–29.

37. Cf. Huang 1974, p. 21: "The primary consideration behind the organization of the provincial and local governments was that of fiscal management."

In this regard, however, Huang makes nothing of the differences in the size of counties or prefectures; see pp. 21 and 27.

38. Rozman (1973, p. 155) considers F to be primarily an indicator of population size.

39. Cf. the categorization suggested by Rozman 1973, p. 155.

40. For further details, see the paper in this volume by John R. Watt. Ch'ing appointment procedures are treated in full in Watt 1972, chap. 3.

41. Ch'ü 1962, pp. 32–35; quotation at p. 34.

42. *Hsia-men chih* (Gazetteer of Amoy), 1839, ch. 2, p. 2b.

43. Brunnert and Hagelstrom 1912, p. 424.

44. *Sung-chiang fu chih* (Gazetteer of Sung-chiang prefecture), 1817, ch. 37, pp. 1a–1b.

45. *Hu-pei t'ung chih* (Hupeh provincial gazetteer), 1921, ch. 115.

46. *Hsü Yün-nan t'ung chih kao* (Draft continuation of Yunnan provincial gazetteer), 1901, ch. 5, p. 3b.

47. Skinner 1964: 40–41.

48. Local organization above the level of the village is a vastly complex subject. It is clear from work published in the last decade that the internal structure of the standard marketing system was more variegated and interesting than my 1964 article began to suggest. Extravillage local systems below the level of the standard marketing community were variously structured by higher-order lineages, irrigation societies, crop-watching societies, politico-ritual "alliances" (under a variety of terms including *yüeh*, *she*, and *hsiang*), and the jurisdictions of particular deities and temples; many if not most were multipurpose sodalities manifesting more than one organizing principle. It would appear that, in some instances at least, these local systems—for which Maurice Freedman has suggested the generic term "vicinages"—were not wholly contained within marketing systems but rather continued the overlapping mode of hierarchical stacking that I have shown to be characteristic of the "natural" economic hierarchy. The general importance of standard marketing communities as informal political systems, however, is generally supported by new research. See in particular Maurice Freedman, *Chinese Lineage and Society: Fukien and Kwangtung* (London: Athlone Press, 1966), pp. 23–25, 79–96; Philip A. Kuhn, *Rebellion and Its Enemies in Late Imperial China: Militarization and Social Structure, 1796–1864* (Cambridge: Harvard University Press, 1970), pp. 76–104; Sidney D. Gamble, *North China Villages: Social, Political and Economic Activities Before 1933* (Berkeley: University of California Press, 1963), chaps. 3–5; Wang Shih-ch'ing, "Religious Organization in the History of a Taiwanese Town," in Arthur P. Wolf, ed., *Religion and Ritual in Chinese Society* (Stanford, Calif.: Stanford University Press, 1974), pp. 71–92; John A. Brim, "Village Alliance Temples in Hong Kong," in Wolf, ed., 1974, pp. 93–103; and Arthur P. Wolf, "Introduction," in Wolf, ed., 1974, pp. 5–6.

49. Most of the relevant scholarship has focused on paramilitary organization rather than on politico-administrative organization per se, and most pertains to the nineteenth century. For the relationship between militia and the marketing hierarchy, see Robert G. Groves, "Militia, Market, and Lineage: Chinese Resistance to the Occupation of Hong Kong's New Territories in

1899," *Journal of the Hong Kong Branch of the Royal Asiatic Society* 9 (1969); Kuhn 1970, pp. 82–87; Winston Hsieh, "Peasant Insurrection and the Marketing Hierarchy in the Canton Delta, 1911," in Mark Elvin and G. William Skinner, eds., *The Chinese City Between Two Worlds* (Stanford, Calif.: Stanford University Press, 1974), pp. 119–41; and Maurice Freedman, "The Politics of an Old State: A View from the Chinese Lineage," in John H. R. Davis, ed., *Choice and Change: Essays in Honour of Lucy Mair* (London: Athlone Press, 1974), pp. 82–88.

50. "The prefect's fiscal responsibility was largely supervisory. [He] saw to it that all the scheduled tax deliveries were properly carried out [by county-level magistrates] and the reserves were kept in good order. He also operated a number of revenue and service agencies...." Huang 1974, p. 26.

51. Chung-li Chang, *The Chinese Gentry: Studies on Their Role in Nineteenth Century Chinese Society* (Seattle: University of Washington Press, 1955), pp. 197–202. On the significance of the last mentioned sanction, see Maurice Freedman, "Shifts of Power in the Hong Kong New Territories," *Journal of Asian and African Studies*, 1, no. 1 (Jan. 1966): 6.

52. For details and evidence on this point, see my "Mobility Strategies in Late Imperial China: A Regional-Systems Analysis," in Carol A. Smith, ed., *Regional Analysis, Vol. 1, Economic Systems* (New York: Academic Press, 1976), pp. 327–64.

53. In late imperial times Ch'u-chou, Anhwei, was the capital of an autonomous *chou* and a local city in the economic hierarchy. When Morton H. Fried studied the town and its environs in the republican period, he found that "successful landlords, merchants, artisans, and officials tend to associate socially on a basis of approximate equality. Wealthy landlords associate with wealthy merchants rather than with poor landlords; successful artisans prefer the company of wealthy merchants to that of indigent co-specialists.... The leadership of the various guilds is often vested in a gentleman of the town, the leadership of the combined guilds is always so vested." Ping-ti Ho's discussion of the relations between merchants and gentry in the Ch'ing period suggests that the situation portrayed by Fried can hardly be dismissed as a modern aberration. Ping-ti Ho, *The Ladder of Success in Imperial China: Aspects of Social Mobility, 1368–1911* (New York: Columbia University Press, 1962), chap. 2.

54. "Inland Communications in China," *Journal of the China Branch of the Royal Asiatic Society*, 28 (1893–94): 1–213.

55. See n. 10 to my Part One paper.

56. For a sophisticated analysis of gazetteer data on markets, see Ishihara Hiroshi, "Kahoku shō ni okeru Min Shin minkoku jidai no teiki ichi" (Periodic markets in Hopei during the Ming, Ch'ing, and Republican periods), *Chirigaku hyōron*, 46, no. 4 (1973): 245–63.

57. *Ch'ing-p'ing hsien chih*, 1911, ch. 5, pp. 11–13.

58. Skinner 1964: 21–24.

The Yamen and Urban Administration

1. Cf. Thomas Taylor Meadows, "The yamen of a district magistrate ... is the most busy of any; and the two which are situated in Canton ... form, I am told, a very striking spectacle, from the great stir that pervades them from sun-

rise to sunset," *Desultory Notes on the Government and People of China . . .* (London: W. H. Allen, 1847), pp. 114–15. Wang Hui-tsu (1730–1807), who spent most of his career in local administration, wrote that in a frequented and busy place the official's energies were drained by continuous crowds of visitors. He needed the capacities of two men to preserve himself intact. Wang Hui-tsu, *Hsüeh chih i shuo* (hereafter HCIS; Advice to administrators; Ts'ung shu chi ch'eng ed., reissued; Shanghai: Shang wu yin shu kuan, 1939), A/9. The Yung-cheng emperor (r. 1723–35), recognizing that "county business was really very complex and manifold," suggested that an assistant official be added to take charge of business outside the office. A censor had previously recommended that officials be appointed to each of the four *hsiang*, or rural townships, to aid in administration. Senior ministers opposed these proposals. Ho Ch'ang-ling, ed., *Huang ch'ao ching shih wen pien* (hereafter HCCSWP; Ch'ing essays on improving the world, 1896 ed.), ch. 18, 15b. For the classification of county-level units, cf. T'ung-tsu Ch'ü, *Local Government in China Under the Ch'ing* (Cambridge, Mass.: Harvard University Press, 1962), p. 5.

2. A regulation of 1740 ordered local officials to control the movement of their private secretaries and not to give secretarial appointments to men having relatives or dependents living in the same county seat or province. Another of 1757 ordered provincial chiefs to prevent their secretaries from coming and going at will and ordered provincial treasurers and judges to be responsible for investigating secretaries of subordinate officials. *Ta Ch'ing hui tien shih li* (hereafter TCHTSL; Institutes of the Ch'ing empire; Chia-ch'ing ed. of 1818), ch. 76, 13a and 14b. [The 1899 edition is also cited below.] See also *Li pu* or *Liu pu ch'u fen ts'e li* (hereafter LPCFTL; Disciplinary regulations of the Six Boards *or* of the Board of Civil Office; rev. ed., 1827), ch. 15, 30a–b. [The 1887 edition is also cited below.] Gate porters were appointed to prevent all dependents of officials from leaving their quarters at will and to record the movements of all who did. Ting Jih-ch'ang, ed. and rev., *Mu ling shu chi yao* (hereafter MLSCY; Essentials of works on governance; 1868 ed.), ch. 1, 42b–43a; ch. 2, 21b–22a. Regulations for Chekiang forbade magistrates to visit the provincial capital (except in an emergency) or to maintain personal representatives there. *Chih Che ch'eng kuei* (1824), ch. 2, 27b–28b. Central government regulations provided dismissal for prefectural and county officials who paid nonbusiness calls on senior officials with the intention of "seeking to please them," or who went to the provincial capital to offer birthday congratulations or bribes. *Ta Ch'ing hui tien* (hereafter TCHT; Institutes of the Ch'ing empire; K'ang-hsi edition of 1690), ch. 12, 9b–10a. [Yung-cheng (1732), Ch'ien-lung (1767), Chia-ch'ing (1818), and Kuang-hsü (1899) editions of this work are cited below.] TCHTSL 1818, ch. 75, 1b. Another central government regulation ordered local officials to prohibit clerks who maintained private residences from taking public documents to their homes. LPCFTL 1827, ch. 16, 5a.

3. Mencius distinguishes between the *kuo*, capitals of feudal principalities and centers of government, and *yeh*, the country or countryside. *Mencius* 3A3.15 and 5B7.1. He also distinguishes *yeh* from the *ch'eng*—inner city walls demarcating the stronghold of the ruler from the nongovernmental and substantially agricultural suburbs. *Ibid.*, 4A1.9, 4A14.2. See also 6B10.4 where the absence of fortified cities (*ch'eng-kuo*, inner and outer walls) is equated

with a lack of humanizing government. According to Miyazaki, by the beginning of the Warring States period outer walls were greatly strengthened for defense and inner walls disappeared. All walls were now variously called *ch'eng* or *kuo*. Miyazaki Ichisada, "Cities in China during the Han era (?)," *T'oung Pao*, 48 (1960): 376 ff.

For Mencius the vital political distinction is between producers of food and producers of order (3A3.14, 3A4.6). *Yeh* stands for land and cultivation (1A7.18, 2A5.4, 5A7.2, 6B7.2). As cultivated land, it supported the central governing establishment (3A3.15-19). *Yeh* was also the domain of tigers and other wild beasts (7A16, 7B23.2), and could be the scene of dearth, even when rulers were eating well and when their domesticated animals were fat (1A4.4). Country people, *yeh-jen*, were feeders of *chün-tzu*, who in turn were needed to bring order to the country people (3A3.14). The term *yeh-jen* was associated with remote hills and wild animals (7A16), or with barbarians ignorant of the principles of government (5B14).

In the passage on great men and small men (3A14.6), which parallels the distinction of *chün-tzu* from *yeh-jen* in terms of political function (3A3.14 and also 5B4), the author goes on to emphasize the nearness of ordinary men to brutality and natural chaos. The well-field system brought *yeh-jen* into institutionalized association with the central governing order, and at the same time differentiated them (*pieh*) from it (3A3.18-19). In the Analects, *yeh* is also associated with an imbalance of natural disposition over culture (*wen*), whereas the reverse is associated with *shih* (clerks) (Analects 6/16). In both sources, it is their functional distinction that separated *chün-tzu* and *yeh-jen*. *Chün-tzu*, as persons who understand and manifest humanity, may live in the countryside amongst *yeh-jen*; but as governors they congregate in the ruler's capital.

4. For investigating the relative importance of regional and local administrative centers, cf. the *Chin shen ch'üan shu* and *Man Han chüeh chih ch'üan shu*, or seasonal official lists. Arranged by province and prefecture, these provide information on the location of each jurisdiction and its classification and characteristics, tax base, official salaries, and number and names of officials (along with place of origin, degree, and date of appointment). For an example of a trade-off in county classifications, with accompanying explanation, see *Huang ch'ao ching shih wen hsü pien* (Additional Ch'ing essays on improving the world; Shanghai, 1901), ch. 17, 8a-b. Other changes can be found by comparing officials lists for different years. Details on the formation or alteration of local jurisdictions are in the *Ch'ing ch'ao wen hsien t'ung k'ao* (hereafter CCWHTK; Compendium of Ch'ing period writings; Shanghai: Shang wu yin shu kuan, 1935), geographical chapters, p. 7263ff. See also TCHTSC 1818, ch. 30-31, which lists changes in jurisdictional status and distribution of offices.

For distribution of jurisdictions by classification, see TCHT 1818, ch. 6, 36a-38b, ch. 7, 2b; TCHT 1960, ch. 8, 11a-14b, ch. 9, 2b. For overall distributions of local officials in the eighteenth and nineteenth centuries, see TCHT 1767, ch. 4, 11b-15b; 1818, ch. 4 and ch. 5; 1899, ch. 4 and ch. 5; *Ch'ing ch'ao t'ung tien* (hereafter CCTT; General statutes of the Ch'ing dynasty; Shanghai: Shang wu yin kuan, 1935), pp. 2210-2211; CCWHTK, pp. 5589-5590.

5. Ch'ing commentators were well aware of this situation. A noted county director of education, Hsieh Chin-luan, wrote "There are only two really important positions in the empire, grand secretary and county magistrate.... The actual government and administrative control is in effect with the magistrates." Hsieh Chin-luan (1757–1820) in Hsü Tung, comp., *Mu-ling shu* (Writings for prefects and county magistrates, 1838), ch. 1, 51b. Many of his essays are included in this mid-nineteenth-century handbook of writings for local administrators; they are often commented on with approval in the imperially sponsored MLSCY. Liu Heng (1776–1841), a distinguished magistrate who later held higher provincial offices, pointed out that the department and county magistrates were close to the people; even prefects were sufficiently distant so that all they could do was manage their subordinates. *Ch'ing-shih kao* (The history of the Ch'ing), 5122.6. Fang Ta-chih (1821–86), a magistrate who rose to be provincial treasurer of Shansi, said that although administration was not limited to departments and counties, the latter were close to the people. "If the magistrates are capable men, the empire will be under control. Higher provincial officials will be merely concerned with regulating county-level administration." *P'ing p'ing yen, fan li* (Commonplace words, preface, 1887), ch. 1, 5a. He also said that higher officials could only talk about administrative objectives whereas magistrates could implement them. *Ibid.*, ch. 1, 10a–b, cited in Ch'ü 1962, p. 14. Many similar opinions exist. The statement "the county magistrate is the official close to the people" is found throughout Ch'ing administrative writing.

6. CCTT, ch. 34, 2211.2.

7. CCWHTK defines the duties of county magistrates simply as "personally managing all judicial and fiscal affairs" (ch. 85, 5619.2). Li Wei (1687?–1738), who rose to be governor-general of Chihli, wrote that county-level responsibility did not extend beyond law and taxation. T'ien Wen-ching and Li Wei, *Ch'in pan chou hsien shih i* (Imperial proclamation of advice on *chou* and *hsien*, preface, 1859), ch. 42b, cited in Ch'ü 1962, p. 211, n. 12. This work was commissioned by the Yung-cheng emperor.

8. TCHT 1899, ch. 25 and 99; TCHT 1732, ch. 33 and 138.

9. TCHTSL 1818, ch. 80.

10. These are the *Li pu* or *Liu pu ch'u fen tse li*.

11. Under the *ta-chi*, the evaluation of the integrity of provincial officials (held every three years throughout the empire), the senior official of each jurisdiction sent an evaluation of his subordinates to his immediate superior. Magistrates sent their evaluations to prefects, who sent theirs to circuit intendants (if any), who in turn sent theirs to the provincial treasurers and judges, as so on. TCHT 1899, ch. 11, 10b. The CCTT defined the function of the prefect as "controlling the counties subordinate to him," adding that he was in charge of all subordinate officials of the prefecture and investigated and assessed them. CCTT, p. 2210.1. Senior officials also could impeach subordinate officials and examine and assess their administration. CCTT, p. 2209.2, 2205.3.

12. For a partial translation of the Sacred Edict, see Kung-chuan Hsiao, *Rural China: Imperial Control in the Nineteenth Century* (Seattle: University of Washington Press, 1960), pp. 187–88. For official texts, see TCHT 1732, ch. 77, or TCHTSL 1818, ch. 397.

13. Cf. HCIS, ch. A, 12–13. Wang Feng-sheng (1776–1834), a county magistrate and later acting Liang-huai salt controller, who was an admirer of Wang Hui-tsu, also emphasized the close connection between legal administration and Confucian role playing. Wang Feng-sheng, *Hsüeh chih t'i hsing lu* (in *Yüeh chih ts'ung ch'eng lu*, preface, 1824), ch. A, 14b–15a. By contrast, governor Ch'en Hung-mou (1696–1771) (see *Eminent Chinese of the Ch'ing Period* 86–87), who wrote extensively on local administration, stressed the imperial view that education should precede punishment and urged officials to promote education through the Sacred Edict and the *hsiang-yüeh* rural pledge system. See MLSCY, ch. 6, 13–16. Hsiao 1960, chap. 6, indicates that Ch'ing magistrates disliked and neglected this system. They were tied to the yamen in any case by the great amount of litigation, criminal hearings, and documentary and informal business.

14. Yüan Shou-ting (1705–82), a magistrate and later junior metropolitan official, who wrote from a strongly Mencian viewpoint, held that a minor (i.e., local) official could achieve loyalty (*chung*: the more basic Confucian meaning is integrity, and is complementary to *shu*, reciprocity) by working for the people; it was not necessary to be an associate of the royal hall. *T'u min lu* (Planning for the people; 1839 ed.), ch. 1, 1b. Ch'eng Han-chang (1762–1832), another Mencian and a magistrate who rose to be a provincial governor, urged "all *chün-tzu* to work hard over government and become close to the people, in order to communicate feeling between above and below." MLSCY, ch. 1, 21b–22b. Wang Hui-tsu, who was more of a straight Confucianist, reminded local officials that they must not dote on office or hope for favors. He urged them not to be careerists, and not even to take pleasure in merit. HCIS, ch. A, 7–8.

15. On this compare Ch'ü 1962; Chung-li Chang, *The Chinese Gentry: Studies on Their Role in Nineteenth Century Chinese Society* (Seattle: University of Washington Press, 1955); and Hsü Ta-ling, *Ch'ing tai chüan na chih tu* (The system of purchasing official titles and offices during the Ch'ing period; Peking: Yen-ching ta hsüeh *with* Ha-fo Yen-ching hsüeh she, 1950). The present writer is compiling data on the effect of the appointment system on gentry careers.

16. Cf. Hsiao 1960, chap. 5; Wu Ching-tzu, *The Scholars* (Peking: Foreign Languages Press, 1957). For gentry and litigation, cf. also CCWHTK, 6619.1; F. W. Baller, trans., *Sacred Edict* (Shanghai: China Inland Mission 1921), commentary to article 6, page 66; HCIS, ch. B, 24. On their use of hostels, cf. *Fu hui ch'üan shu*, Huang Liu-hung (Complete book of good fortune and benevolence; 1893 ed.), ch. 11, 18a.

17. Cf. Ch'ü 1962, p. 272, n. 1; CCWHTK, 6597.3. The time limits were set in 1810. LPCFTL 1827, ch. 47, 15a–16a.

18. Hui-chen Wang Liu, *The Traditional Chinese Clan Rules* (Locust Valley, N.Y.: J. J. Augustin, 1959), pp. 154–58. On the accumulation of cases, see remarks made in 1812 by the Chia-ch'ing emperor, TCHTSL 1899, ch. 112. Many administrative writers stressed the need for magistrates to keep up with cases and detailed the social evil caused by their accumulation. Cf. Muhan, *Ming hsing kuan chien lu* (Humble views on criminal justice, preface, 1845), ch. 27b–29b.

19. Cf. the Sacred Edict, Articles 3, 8, and 12.

20. E.g., Liu Heng, *Yung li yung yen* (Simple words of a simple official; 1827), ch. 58, 2–b; and Li Yüan-tu, comp., *Kuo ch'ao hsien cheng shih lüeh* (Biographies of leading statesmen of the Ch'ing; 1866), ch. 54, 82–89b.

21. See below, pp. 44–45.

22. Officials waiting in provincial capitals for appointment as county magistrates received monthly allowances of three or four taels. The expenses involved in appointment to office were noted in HCIS, ch. A, 2.5.

23. For an emphatic account of these conditions by Chou Hao (1754–1823), a magistrate and prefect, see HCCSWP, ch. 16, 5bff.

24. Cf. Meadows 1847 (p. 168): "I believe ... that all mandarins take money exclusive of their salary and anti-extortion allowance, and that the grand difference between what the Chinese call the "good" and the "bad" mandarin is, that while the former makes people *pay for justice*, the latter *sells injustice* to the highest bidder." Ch'ü 1962 discusses at length the fund-raising procedures of local yamen functionaries.

25. For terms of service of magistrates, see TCHT 1899, ch. 10, 4b–8b; Ch'ü 1962, p. 32. For those of clerks, see TCHT 1732, ch. 21, 18a; TCHT 1899, ch. 12, 13a. Ch'ü 1962, p. 63, gives the term of service of runners as three years; a search of TCHT has so far failed to produce a source to confirm this figure.

26. Magistrates assuming office were often pressured by other officials, friends, and relatives to accept nominees for appointment to their personal staff; some people paid fees to obtain these recommendations. Although this practice was punishable by dismissal for all officials involved, it was sufficiently widespread for Wang Hui-tsu to warn both that magistrates not take in such nominees carelessly and that they might have to accept the nominees of their superiors. HCIS, ch. A, 2–4; LPCFTL 1827, ch. 15, 30b–31a. According to an early-nineteenth-century censor, magistrates were also pressed by aides of senior officials to accept their nominees as personal assistants (see HCCSWP, ch. 16, 1ff). Under these circumstances, magistrates found it hard to trust their assistants. According to Wang, "not four or five secretaries in ten seek to be upright. ... As for personal servants, none of them knows justice or propriety. All they scheme for is profit, ... not one or two in a hundred are sincere and dependable." HCIS, ch. A, 3; and *Hsueh chih hsü shuo* (hereafter HCHS; More advice to administrators; Ts'ung shu chi ch'eng ed., reissued Shanghai: Shang wu yin shu kuan, 1939), ch. 12. See also Ch'ü 1962, p. 271, n. 202, for the views of Wang Chih.

27. For sales of offices by clerks and runners, and for appointment of those who had already served their time or been dismissed, see LPCFTL 1827, ch. 16, 6a, 10a. Numerous sources speak of clerks and runners scrutinizing the incoming magistrate for signs of weakness in order to find out how to compromise him and secure their own positions.

28. For detailed findings, see John R. Watt, *The District Magistrate in Late Imperial China* (New York: Columbia University Press, 1972), chaps. 2–4.

29. For Sung, see *Tu shu chi ch'eng*, ming-lun, kuan-ch'ang, 645 hui-k'ao/1b–8a; 656 hui-k'ao/6a–7a. For Ming, see *ibid.*, 641 hui-k'ao/8b; *Ming hui yao* (Institutes of the Ming, 1887), pp. 233, 734–35. For early Ch'ing, see TCHTSL 1899, ch. 30–31.

30. Shen Shao-ts'an in MLSCY, ch. 1, 24b–25b; Chang Hsüeh-ch'eng,

comp., *Yung-ch'ing hsien chih* (Gazetteer of Yung-ch'ing *hsien*), 1779, ch. 9, 3b. Cf. also Ch'ü 1962, pp. 39–40, which draws on Huang Liu-hung *Fu hui ch'üan shu*. Norms for official county quotas are stated in TCHT 1732, ch. 21, 16a. Each county gazetteer indicates the quota for that particular county.

31. For commoner status of clerks, see TCHT 1899, ch. 12, 13a. For degradation of the office of clerk, cf. Chang Hsüeh-ch'eng 1779, ch. 9, 4b; and Ch'üan Tseng-yu, "Ch'ing tai mu liao chih tu lun" (The Ch'ing system of private secretaries), *Ssu hsiang yü shih tai*, 31 (Feb. 1944): 30–32. For Ku's findings see his *Jih chih lu* (Shanghai: Shang wu yin shu kuan, 1933), ch. 3, 78; and T'ang Ching-kao, ed., *Ku Yen-wu wen* (Essays of Ku Yen-wu; Shanghai: Shang wu yin shu kuan, 1928), pp. 11–12. The proliferation of administrative regulations was also held to have magnified the power of clerks. Cf. Li Chih-fang (1622–94), in HCCSWP, ch. 15, 32.

32. The Ming and Ch'ing governments permitted some variation in quotas for clerks, according to the complexity of administrative business. TCHT 1732, ch. 21, 1a; Ch'üan Tseng-yu 1944: 31–32. The Ch'ing government also established a nominal administrative punishment for officials exceeding the permitted quota of clerks. LPCFTL 1827, ch. 16, 1b. For numbers, see Ch'ü 1962, pp. 38–39.

33. Ch'ü 1962, chap. 4. Hsiao 1960, pp. 113–39. For official salaries, see *Hu pu tse li* (Regulations of the Board of Finance; 1833); ch. 78, 79ff.

34. For responsibility of secretaries with regard to *li* and *fa*, see Hsieh Chin-luan in MLSCY, ch. 2, 14a–b; and HCIS, ch. A, 1. Cf. also Ch'ü 1962, chap. 6.

35. Ming military administration provided the immediate precedent for the Ch'ing secretarial system. Sources indicate that because military officials were unskilled in documentation, subordinate Board officials were sent out by the Hung-hsi administration (1425–26) to the regional military commissions to assist the regional commanders in managing documentation and confidential communications. Later, other regional and frontier administrators with responsibility for military concerns instituted the practice of "inviting" officials and scholars to assist them in administrative management. Those preparing for this service studied such subjects as military methods, laws and regulations, taxation, and river administration over and above the classics and history. The informal and ad hoc secretarial administration thus established spread down to local administration in the early Ch'ing period. Ch'üan Tseng-yu 1944: 29–35, citing the *Ming shih*, "Chih kuan chih," ch. 4, and biography of Hu Tsung-hsien; and Shen Te-fu, *Wan-li yeh huo pien* (Notes on the Wan-li period; preface, 1607), ch. 22. For examples of late Ming secretarial aides, see *Shan-yin hsien-chih* (Gazetteer of Shan-yin *hsien*), 1936, ch. 14, 20b, 21a, 39a; ch. 15, 5b, 10b. See also Miao Ch'üan-chi, "Ch'ing-tai mu fu chih tu chih ch'eng chang yüan yin" (Reasons for the development of private secretariats during the Ch'ing period), *Ssu yü yen*, 5, no. 3 (Sept. 1967).

36. Ch'ü 1962, ch. 6. Although secretaries were not part of the official establishment, the Court admitted their need to help in managing the "complex tasks" of provincial administrators. It pressured officials to prevent secretaries from utilizing their administrative functions to establish personal liaisons through which to capture decision-making influence. Sources indicate that if they chose to do so, secretaries had little trouble in circumventing this policy of containment. TCHTSL 1818, ch. 76, 13a–14b; LPCFTL 1827, ch. 15, 30a–31a. See also Ch'ü 1962, pp. 110–11, 113–14.

37. Ch'ü 1962, chap. 5; Meadows 1847. For functions and behavior of personal servants, cf. Ho Keng-sheng in MLSCY, ch. 1, 42b–43a, ch. 2, 21b–22a; HCIS, ch. A, 3–4. As of 1736, a magistrate was required to report to his superiors the name, age, native place, and functions of each of his personal servants within three months of arriving at his post (TCHTSL 1818, ch. 70, 22a).

38. For central government regulations, cf. LPCFTL 1827, ch. 15, 33a, and TCHTSL 1818, ch. 70, 21b–22a. For an example of regulations drawn up by a magistrate for control of family retainers (*shu-kuei*, office rules), cf. MLSCY, ch. 2, 20bff.

39. Amitai Etzioni, *Modern Organizations* (Englewood Cliffs, N.J.: Prentice-Hall, 1964), p. 3.

40. Ch'ing administrative writers consistently referred to county magistrates as father and mother officials, an appellation associated originally with the *chün-tzu* of the *Book of Odes*, the Son of Heaven of the *Book of Documents*, and the Princely Ruler of Mencius. *Shih-ching*, odes 172, 251; *Shu-ching*, "Hung fan" 24, "T'ai che" 21 (a spurious chapter); *Mencius*, 1A4, 3A3.7. Hsü Tung (1792–1865), the influential compiler of the *Mu-ling shu* and the *Pao chia shu*, characterized the empire as a large *pao-chia* and the county as a small empire. "Their scope is different but their affairs are the same. Their regulation is different but their way is the same." Compiler's introduction to the *Pao chia shu* (Works on the *pao-chia* system; 1848), and *Ch'ing shih lieh chuan* (Biographies of Ch'ing personages; Shanghai: Chung-hua shu chü, 1928), ch. 2, 76, 17a–b.

41. Many sources urged incoming magistrates to treat the local gentry with respect and courtesy. According to one source, when fellow officials, students, and degree-holders came to welcome the new magistrate, he should descend from his chair and thank them for troubling to come. He should not, said another official pointedly, disturb the major lineages. The mid-Ch'ing novelist Wu Ching-tzu, satirizing the association of incumbent officials with local gentry, had a magistrate acting as "go-between" for influential families and doing whatever the latter told him (*The Scholars*, chaps. 44–46). For examples of official viewpoints, see MLSCY, ch. 2, 10ff., ch. 4, 1a–b, ch. 7, 4b, ch. 16, 25a–26b. For a general treatment, see Ch'ü 1962, pp. 180–92.

42. Hsiao 1960, pp. 454–66. Cf. also HCIS, ch. A, 12; and Wang Hui-tsu, *Tso chih yao yen* (Essentials of administration, 1786; Ts'ung shu chi ch'eng, ed.; reissued Shanghai: Shang wu yin shu kuan, 1937), p. 8.

43. Wang Chih-i, an early-nineteenth-century governor-general of Fukien and Chekiang, argued that under the tax laws currently in force it was impossible for officials to avoid breaking the regulations and sooner or later losing their posts. "Obstinate" households would exploit this situation by resisting payments, and clerks and runners would refuse to press for payments and would "indulge in malpractices" (HCCSWP, ch. 16, 4a–5b). Chou Hao, who served throughout the Chia-ch'ing reign, listed numerous informal expenses exacted from local administrators. He said bluntly that if time permitted, they took from the people; if not, they took from the treasury (HCCSWP, ch. 16, 6a ff).

44. Despite the overall lightness of Ch'ing taxation, the fact that tax collection was invariably associated with ruthless exploitation—through "pressing," "shouting," "fleecing," and "flogging," and especially through the ma-

nipulation of the currency and exchange systems to exact the maximum profit from each payment—speaks eloquently of the impact of informal financing on all levels of local administration, and through them on the weaker elements of society. In due course the pressures of informal financing precipitated a massive financial scandal in Shansi, which led the pragmatic Yung-cheng emperor to establish the *yang-lien* "nourish honesty" salary for local administrative officials.

45. Cf. Ku Yen-wu, Chün-hsien, no. 8, in *Ku Yen-wu wen*, pp. 11–12, or *T'ing-lin wen chi* (Collected essays of Ku Yen-wu), ch. 1, 6a–11b; LPCFTL 1827, ch. 16, 5aff; Ch'ü 1962, p. 52.

46. The ensuing criteria largely follow those of Weber, as found in H. H. Gerth and C. Wright Mills, eds., *From Max Weber* (New York: Oxford University Press, 1946), chap. 8.

47. On spying by subordinates, see Ku Yen-yü in MLSCY, ch. 1, 33a; Ho Keng-sheng in MLSCY, ch. 1, 42b–43a. Ho cautioned incoming magistrates to look over the yamen premises, block up side doors, and increase the height of low street walls. "If one cannot prevent the outside from coming in, one can at least prevent the inside from going out." He also warned magistrates not to let anyone but themselves break open the seals and examine the contents of incoming letters and documents (MLSCY, ch. 2, 21a). For clerical control of documentation, see Ch'ü 1962, p. 38.

48. Some regulations specifying diminishing punishments for senior officials state that if a certain offense was committed without the knowledge of provincial governors-general and governors, the case of the latter should not be deliberated. In a personal introduction to the regulations, the Chia-ch'ing emperor specified that public offenses should not be taken into account in assessing local officials for promotion to "important" posts. LPCFTL 1827, ch. 1, 1a–2a.

49. As Ch'ü points out, secretaries were not allowed to make direct contact with clerks, and it was up to personal servants to maintain and control (and to manipulate) communications within the yamen. Ch'ü 1962, pp. 77–86. Family retainers were also specifically prohibited from consorting with clerks and runners. MLSCY, ch. 2, 23b.

50. See Yeh-chien Wang, *Land Taxation in Imperial China, 1750–1911* (Cambridge: Harvard University Press, 1973).

51. Ch'ü 1962, pp. 45–49, 64–67, 87–88.

52. For income of magistrates, see Chung-li Chang, *The Income of the Chinese Gentry* (Seattle: University of Washington Press, 1962), pp. 26–28; for income of secretaries, see Chang 1962, chap. 3, and Ch'ü 1962, p. 112; for income of personal servants, see Meadows 1847.

53. See Watt 1972, pp. 280–83; and Ch'ü 1962, pp. 65 and 240, n. 89.

54. The central government's experiences with the *li-chia* system had shown that it lacked the resources to review the annual, or even decennial, fluctuations in the tax-paying economy and to adjust taxation to household income. Since wide fluctuations were inevitable in a traditional agricultural economy, the central government preferred to limit its own responsibility by establishing moderate fixed levies capable of supporting its needs, leaving it up to local administrators more cognizant of specific conditions to negotiate their require-

Notes to Pages 383–88   731

ments with the local economy. As compensation for this devolution of power the government had recourse to moral and legal sanctions and surveillance systems in hopes of checking the acquisitiveness of local officials. For further details on the vicissitudes of early Ch'ing fiscal policy, see Watt 1972, chap. 14.

55. For examples of popular rewards and punishments, see Evariste-Régis Huc, *L'empire chinois* (Paris: Gaumes Frères, 1854), vol. 2, pp. 86–92; Joseph M. Callery and Melchior Yvan, *History of the Insurrection in China* (London: Smith, Elder, 1853), pp. 77–78; John Francis Davis, *The Chinese: A General Description* . . . (London: Charles Knight, 1840), p. 99; and HCIS, A12–13. See also Chung-wen ta tzu-tien, *Encyclopedic Dictionary of the Chinese Language* (Taipei: Chung-kuo wen-hua hsüeh-yüan, 1963–69), entry 2737.7.

56. This is especially so of the *k'ao-ch'eng* review. For an analysis of Ch'ing systems of administrative review and their impact on local officials, see Watt 1972, chap. 12.

57. For details on the evolution of Ming systems of local administration, see Watt 1972, chaps. 8–10.

58. Ku Yen-wu drew attention to the adverse impact of the Single Whip reforms (and in particular the monetization of the tax levies) on rural economies in his essays on taxation ("Ch'ien-liang lun"), to be found, among other places, in HCCSWP, ch. 29, 2b–4b.

59. For Ch'ing imperial attitudes toward the Single Whip reforms, see TCHT 1690, ch. 20, 7b. For changes in social policy, compare the emphasis on social values in the six maxims of the Ming founding emperor with the sixteen maxims (Sacred Edict) of the Ch'ing K'ang-hsi emperor. These latter maxims included injunctions against concealing fugitives and against false suits, and exhortations to pay up taxes and unite the *pao-chia* security system—all of which directly related to governmental objectives. For translations of the Sacred Edict and the lengthy "Amplification" further justifying Ch'ing social policy, see Hsiao 1960, pp. 187–88, or A. Theophile Piry, *Le Saint Edict* (Shanghai, 1879); the latter includes the original text and translations of the Edict and Amplification.

60. See *Yang-ming ch'üan shu* (Complete works of Wang Yang-ming, 1925 ed.), pieh-lu, kung-i, 305–8, 396–99, 410–11. For translations of regulations setting forth Wang's organizational reforms, see Wing-tsit Chan, *Instructions for Practical Living* (New York: Columbia University Press, 1963), pp. 293–309.

61. For other late Ming *hsiang-yüeh* regulations, see Lü K'un, *Shih cheng lu* (1868), ch. 5, 1–13b. These regulations defined bad behavior as behavior contrary to the preservation of property. Watch-groups were to be organized with the object of "protecting the wealth of the rich." Ch'ing imperial *pao-chia* and *hsiang-yüeh* policies are set out in TCHT 1732, ch. 77 and 138, and TCHTSL 1899, ch. 158 and 397.

62. See the regulations of Yeh P'ei-sun and Wang Feng-sheng in *Pao chia shu*, ch. 2, 1aff. and 12aff. I have treated early Ch'ing rural administrative policies at greater length in Watt 1972, chapter 13. For an extended review of the *pao-chia*, see Hsiao 1960, chap. 3.

63. Cf. the distribution of watch-groups and *ti-pao* in Yung-ch'ing county as recorded by Chang Hsüeh-ch'eng:

	natural villages	p'ai (formally 10 households)	ti-pao
city streets			
eastern		21	
southern		17	1
western		13	
northern		11	1
suburban districts			
eastern		2	1
southern		2	1
western		4	1
northern		18	1
rural districts			
eastern	78	785	66
southern	74	1,522	61
western	63	1,362	60
northern	63	668	61

Chang noted that *ti-pao* were established according to the size of the natural villages. Their job was to "search out evildoers contravening the law." *Yung-ch'ing hsien chih*, ch. 13, 2a–5a. The imperially sponsored *T'ung k'ao* described the *ti-fang*'s functions more comprehensively as running a certain number of villages and sharing responsibility for management of tax collection, disputes over property, litigation, and investigation of robbery and homicide cases. If he was at all late or in error in supplying necessary materials or manpower, he was to be promptly beaten. CCWHTK, 5045.2.

64. Writers who complained that yamen subordinates were encroaching on the magistrate's local authority included Ku Yen-wu (see note 45 above), Shao Chin-han (1743–96; cited by Wang Hui-tsu in HCHS, ch. 12), and Feng Kuei-fen (1809–74; cited in Ch'ü 1962, p. 43). See also the statement by Han Chen (early nineteenth century) on the growth of an "invisible government" by private secretaries cited in Ch'ü 1962, p. 93.

65. On official respect for the gentry, see note 41 above. For an account of the trial of a village "thug," see Huc 1854, vol. 2, pp. 282–89. Village thugs (*ti-kun* or *kuang-kun*) were associated both with wicked gentry and notaries (*sung-shih*) who promoted law suits, and with thieves and bandits. See Mu-han, *Ming hsing kuan chien lu* (preface, 1845), ch. 30a–b; HCIS, ch. A, 18; Baller 1921, translation of commentary to articles 1 and 15, pp. 40–41 and 160; TCHTSL 1818, ch. 90, 3aff. Security-minded officials saw the *pao-chia* as a means to expose all such enemies of law and order. See above, note 62.

66. Consequently, one writer urged officials to accept no presents from gentry and to interview them only in the presence of witnesses. MLSCY, ch. 1, 34a. In fact, under the disciplinary regulations new officials accepting presents from gentry resident in the capital but registered in the jurisdiction to which they were appointed, were subject to dismissal, as were those who on arrival at their post accepted gentry as "students." LPCFTL, ch. 15, 15a–b.

Perverse lower gentry who fomented litigation were attacked as a "disgrace to the schools" and ordered to be given double the punishment of commoners. See Baller 1921, commentary to article 6, pp. 66; CCWHTK, 6619.1.

Ningpo and Its Hinterland

1. See Fujita Toyohachi, "Shina kōwan shōshi" (Short history of ports in China), in Ikeuchi Hiroshi, ed., *Tōzai kōshōshi no kenkyū, Nankai hen* (Studies on cultural intercourse between East and West: Southeast Asia; Tokyo: Oka shoin, 1932), pp. 637–41.

2. See Kuwabara Jitsuzō, "Rekishijō yori mitaru Shina no nanboku" (Interrelations between North and South in Chinese history), in Ikeuchi Hiroshi, ed., *Shiratori hakushi kanreki kinen tōyōshi ronsō* (Studies in East Asian history in honor of the sixtieth birthday of Dr. Shiratori Kurakichi; Tokyo: Iwanami shoten, 1925), pp. 387–480.

3. For discussions of T'ang and Sung maritime trade, see generally Kuwabara Jitsuzō, *Tō Sō jidai ni okeru Arabu jin no Shina tsūshō no gaikyō; Kotoni Sōmatsu no teikyoshihakushi seiikijin Ho Jukō no jiseki* (General description of the development of Arabian trade in China during the T'ang and Sung dynasties: Especially the life of P'u Shou-keng, Commissioner for Arabian Trade in the late Sung period; Tokyo: Iwanami shoten, 1935); Edwin O. Reischauer, "Notes on T'ang Dynasty Sea Routes," *Harvard Journal of Asiatic Studies*, 5, no. 2 (Jan. 1940); Shiba Yoshinobu, *Sōdai shōgyōshi kenkyū* (Commercial activities during the Sung period; Tokyo: Kazama shoten, 1968), pp. 51–78. See also Joseph Needham, *Science and Civilization in China, Vol. 4. Physics and Physical Technology. Part III. Civil Engineering and Nautics* (Cambridge: Cambridge University Press, 1971), pp. 459–77.

4. See the chapter on Sung-period shipping in Chekiang in the *Meng liang lu* of Wu Tzu-mu, and Shiba 1968, p. 61. The ocean-going junks were known as *nan-ch'uan* (later *nan-hao* or *nan-pang*); the luggers were *hu-ch'uan* or *pei-ch'uan* (later *pei-hao* or *pei-pang*). On the distinction between *pei-yang* (north-coast service) and *nan-yang* (south-coast service), and on differences in the construction of ships designed specifically for one or the other service, see D. G. MacGowan, "Chinese Guilds or Chambers of Commerce and Trade Unions," *Journal of the North China Branch of the Royal Asiatic Society*, 21 (1886): 149; Tuan Kuang-ch'ing's autobiography, *Ching hu tzu chuan nien p'u* (hereafter CHTCNP; Shanghai: Chung-hua shu chü, 1960), pp. 91–92; Negishi Tadasha, *Shanhai no girudo* (Guilds of Shanghai; Tokyo: Nihon hyōron shinsha, 1951), pp. 31–32; Shiba 1968, pp. 61–62.

5. On the Shih-po Ssu, see Fujita 1932, pp. 281–398.

6. See Chi Ch'ao-ting, *Key Economic Areas in Chinese History* (London: Allen and Unwin, 1936), chaps. 6 and 7.

7. See the map "Yin chi lin hsien yen ko t'u" (A historical map showing the development of prefectural demarcations centering around Yin *hsien*) attached to *Min-kuo Yin hsien t'ung chih* (hereafter MKYHTC; Republican gazetteer of Yin *hsien*; 1935); *Ch'ien-tao Ssu-ming t'u ching* (Ch'ien-tao gazetteer of the Ning-po region with maps; 1169), ch. 1; *Sung-shih* (History of the Sung), ch. 88, 3 a–b.

8. *Ch'ien-tao Ssu-ming t'u ching*, ch. 2.
9. *Pao-ch'ing Ssu-ming chih* (hereafter PCSMC; Pao-ch'ing gazetteer of the Ning-po region; 1227), ch. 3.
10. For post-T'ang water-control projects, refer to the map "Yin hsien ching t'u" (Map of Yin *hsien*) at the beginning of PCSMS; and see Tamai Zehaku, "Sōdai suiriden no ichi tokuisō" (A peculiarity of dike land during the Sung period), in Tamai Zehaku, ed., *Shina shakaikeizaishi kenkyū* (Essays on Chinese socioeconomic history; Tokyo: Iwanami shoten, 1942), pp. 394–99; and "Li tai chün chih Tung-ch'ien hu kai k'uang" (A historical record of the dredging of Tung-ch'ien Lake), in MKYHTC, *Yü ti chih* (Geographical treatise), pp. 94–103.
11. PCSMC, ch. 3, ch. 12; *K'ai-ch'ing Ssu-ming chih* (hereafter KCSMC; K'ai-ch'ing gazetteer of Ning *hsien*; 1259), ch. 3.
12. PCSMC, ch. 4.
13. Mori Katsumi, "Nihon Kōrai raikō no Sō shōnin" (Sung merchants trading with Japan and Korea), *Chōsen gakuhō*, 19 (Apr. 1961).
14. Idem, *Nissō bōeki no kenkyū* (A study of the trade between Japan and Sung China; Tokyo: Kunitachi shoin, 1948), pp. 189–279; Fujita 1932, pp. 493–504.
15. Shiba 1968, pp. 72–74, 102–3, 301–5; PCSMC, ch. 4; KCSMC, ch. 6, ch. 7.
16. PCSMC, ch. 13; Shiba 1968, pp. 379–80; *Chia-t'ai K'uai-chi chih* (Chia-t'ai gazetteer of K'uai-chi *hsien*; n.d. [ca. 1201–4]), ch. 7; Katō Shigeshi, *Shina keizaishi kōshō* (Studies of Chinese economic history; Tokyo: Tōyō bunko), vol. 1 (1952), pp. 322, 324; vol. 2 (1953), p. 405; Sogabe Shizuo, *Chūgoku oyobi kodai Nihon ni okeru kyōson keitai no hensen* (The development of villages in ancient Japan and China; Tokyo: Yoshikawa kobunkan, 1963), pp. 447–97.
17. *Ning-po fu chien yao chih* (Concise gazetteer of Ning-po *fu*; ca. 1477), ch. 5; PCSMC, ch. 13.
18. Katayama Seijirō "Mindai kaijō mitsubōeki to enkai kyōshinsō" (Smuggling in the coastal trade of the Ming dynasty and its relationship with the gentry class), *Rekishigaku kenkyū*, 164 (July 1953); Ch'en Mao-heng, *Ming tai wo k'ou k'ao lüeh* (A study of Japanese pirates in the Ming period; Peking: Jen min ch'u pan she, 1957); Tanaka Takeo, "Jūshi-go seiki ni okeru wakō no katsudō to kōsei" (The activities and composition of Japanese pirates during the fourteenth and fifteenth centuries), *Nihon rekishi*, 26 (July 1950).
19. Katō 1953, pp. 595–616, 688–99; Negishi 1951, pp. 31–32; Tōa dōbunkai, ed., *Shina shōbetsu zenshi* [13], *Sekkō shō* (hereafter SSZS 13; Provincial gazetteer of China, Vol. 13, Chekiang; Tokyo: Tōa dōbunkai, 1919), p. 245; Kobayashi Sōichi, *Shina no janku* (Chinese junks; Tokyo: Yōsukōsha, 1942), p. 122.
20. Liang Fang-chung, "Ming tai kuo chi mao i yü yin ti shu ch'u ju" (Overseas trade and the export and import of silver during the Ming dynasty), *Chung-kuo she hui ching chi shih yen chiu chi k'an*, 6, no. 2 (Dec. 1939); Momose Hiroshi, "Mindai ni okeru Shina no gaikoku bōeki" (Chinese overseas trade during the Ming period), *Tōa*, 8, no. 7 (July 1935); Obata Atsushi, "Nihon no kin gin gaikoku bōeki ni kansuru kenkyū" (A study of Japanese

overseas trade in gold and silver), *Shigaku zasshi,* 54, nos. 10 and 11 (Oct./ Nov. 1933).

21. *Ch'ien-lung Yin hsien chih* (Ch'ien-lung gazetteer of Yin *hsien;* 1788), ch. 4, *Shui li* (Water conservancy); *Hsien-feng Yin hsien chih* (hereafter HFYHC; Hsien-feng gazetteer of Yin *hsien;* 1856), ch. 3–4, *Shui li; Min kuo Chen-hai hsien chih* (Republican gazetteer of Chen-hai *hsien),* ch. 5, *Shui li.*

22. *Tz'u-ch'i Lin shih tsung p'u* (Genealogy of the Lin family of Tz'u-ch'i), ch. 1; *Kuang-hsü Tz'u-ch'i hsien chih* (Kuang-hsü gazetteer of Tz'u-ch'i *hsien;* 1899), ch. 10.

23. The total number of villages in Yin *hsien* in the Chia-ching period was 169. It increased to 726 by the end of the Ch'ing period. *Chia-ching Ning-po fu chih* (hereafter CCNPFC; Chia-ching gazetteer of Ning-po *fu;* 1560), ch. 9; MKYHTC, *Yü ti chih,* pp. 234–92.

24. MKYHTC, *Yü ti chih,* pp. 600–602, *Shih huo chih,* pp. 6–8; John Lossing Buck, *Chinese Farm Economy* (Chicago: University of Chicago Press, 1930), pp. 15, 40.

25. Nishijima Sadao, *Chūgoku keizaishi kenkyū* (Studies of Chinese economic history; Tokyo: Tōkyō daigaku, Bungakubu, 1966), pp. 783–84; *Min kuo Yü-yao liu ts'ang chih* (Republican gazetteer of Yü-yao *hsien;* 1920), ch. 17; Buck 1930, p. 184.

26. See Sasaki Masaya, "Kampō hachinen Kin ken gyomin no hanran" (The rebellion of fishermen in Yin *hsien* in 1858), *Sundai shigaku,* 16 (1953); and Himeda Mitsuyoshi, "Chūgoku kindai gyogyōshi no hitokoma—Kampo hachinen Kin ken no gyomin tōsō o megutte" (One aspect of the history of fishery in modern China—An analysis of the rebellion of fishermen in Yin *hsien* in 1858), in Tokyo kyōiku daigaku, Tōyōshi kenkyūshitsu, Ajiashi kenkyūkai, with Chūgoku kindaishi kenkyūkai, jt. eds., *Kindai Chūgoku nōson shakaishi kenkyū* (Studies in the history of rural society of modern China; Tokyo: Daian, 1967). See also *Kuang-hsü Yin hsien chih* (hereafter KHYHC; Kuang-hsü gazetteer of Yin *hsien;* 1877), ch. 2, *Feng su* (Customs). According to *Min-kuo T'ai-shan chen chih* (Republican gazetteer of T'ai-shan *chen*), vol. 3, boats fishing the waters off T'ai-shan island were composed of Tung-hu *pang* (from the vicinity of Tung-ch'ien Lake in Yin *hsien*), T'ung-chao *pang* (from the marketing system centered on T'ung-chao, a town in Feng-hua *hsien*), Hsiang-shan *pang* (from the *hsien* of that name), Chen-hai *pang* (from the *hsien* of that name), T'ai *pang* (from T'ai -chou *fu*), and Wen *pang* (from Wen-chou *fu*).

27. On the Hui-chou merchants, see generally Fujii Hiroshi, "Shin'an shōnin no kenkyū" (A study of the activities of Hsin-an merchants from Hui-chou in Anhwei), *Tōyō gakuhō,* 36, nos. 1–4 (June 1953–Mar. 1954). On the Shansi merchants see Kao Shu-k'ang, "Shan-hsi p'iao hao ti ch'i yüan chi ch'i ch'eng li nien tai" (The origins and years of formation of Shansi banks), *Shih huo,* 6, no. 1 (July 1937); Ch'en Ch'i-t'ien, *Shan-hsi p'iao chuang k'ao lüeh* (Researches on Shansi banks; Shanghai: Shang wu yin shu kuan, 1937); Saeki Tomi, "Shinchō no kōki to Sansei shōnin" (The rise of the Ch'ing dynasty and its relationship with Shansi merchants), in *Chūgokushi kenkyū* (Researches on Chinese history; Kyoto: Tōyōshi kenkyūkai, 1971), vol. 2,

pp. 263–322; Terada Takanobu, *Sansei shōnin no kenkyū* (A study of Shansi merchants; Kyoto: Tōyōshi Kenkyūkai, 1972). On Fukien and Canton merchants, see John King Fairbank, *Trade and Diplomacy on the China Coast* (Cambridge: Harvard University Press, 1964); Liang Chia-pin, *Kuang-tung shih san hang k'ao* (The thirteen *hong* at Canton; Shanghai: Shang wu yin shu kuan, 1937); Negishi 1951, pp. 31–32; KHYHC, ch. 2, *Feng su*.

28. It is notable that exogenous developments gave a boost to Ningpo's entrepôt functions during the first half of the eighteenth century. In 1715, new Japanese regulations respecified the number of Chinese ships permitted to trade with Japan by port of origin; they assigned 37 percent of the quota to Ningpo ships, an increase from 17 percent in 1689. In 1743, the Ch'ing government made Ningpo the chief port for the import of copper from Japan by licensing a limited number of Chekiang and Kiangsu merchants, most of whom were based in Ningpo. See Yamawaki Teijirō, *Kinsei Nicchū bōekishi no kenkyū* (Studies in Sino-Japanese trade in early modern Japan; Tokyo: Yoshikawa kōbunkan, 1960), pp. 23–37; and Ōba Osamu, "Hirado Matsuura shiryō hakubutsukanzō 'Tōsen-no-zu' ni tsuite, Edo jidai ni raikō shita Chūgoku shōsen no shiryō" (On "The scroll listing Chinese vessels trading with Japan" in the possession of the Matsuura Museum of Historical Sources in Hirado: A study of the ports of origin of Chinese vessels visiting Japan during the Edo period), *Kansai daigaku tōzai kenkyūsho kiyō*, no. 5 (Mar. 1972): 14–19.

29. See Susan Mann Jones, "Finance in Ningpo: The 'Ch'ien Chuang,' 1750–1880," in W. E. Willmott, ed., *Economic Organization in Chinese Society* (Stanford: Stanford University Press, 1972), pp. 47–77.

30. Yü Ch'e-ming and Cheng Hsüeh-p'u, eds., *Che-chiang ti i ko chang fu Ning-po* (Ningpo, Chekiang's leading port; Hangchow: Jen min ch'u pan she, 1958).

31. *Ning-po fu chien yao chih*, ch. 5; CCNPFC, ch. 9; HFYHC, ch. 1; KHYHC, ch. 2.

32. KHYHC, ch. 2; Tsur 1909, pp. 5–6.

33. G. Smith, *A Narrative of an Exploratory Visit to Each of the Consular Cities of China and to the Islands of Hong Kong and Chusan* (New York: Harper, 1847), pp. 196–97; also refer to MKYHTC, *Yü ti chih*, pp. 218–34.

34. Nyok-Ching Tsur (Chou I-ch'ing), *Die gewerblichen Betriebsformen der Stadt Ningpo* (Tübingen: Verlag der H. Laupp'schen Buchhandlungen, 1909), p. 17.

35. *Ibid.*, p. 71; MKYHTC, *Po wu chih*, pp. 84–85.

36. Tsur 1909, pp. 47–48.

37. *Ibid.*, pp. 78–94.

38. KHYHC, ch. 2, *Feng su*; MKYHTC, *Shih huo chih*, pp. 84–85.

39. Himeda 1967, pp. 79–96.

40. HFYHC, ch. 1; KHYHC, ch. 3; MKYHTC, *Shih huo chih*, pp. 70–71, 85, 88–106.

41. Mantetsu, Shanhai jimusho, Chōsashitsu, ed., *Ninpō ni okeru shōgyō chōbo chōsa* (An investigation of commercial bookkeeping in Ningpo).

42. See Nishizato Yoshiyuki, "Shinmatsu no Ninpō shōnin ni tsuite" (Ningpo merchants during the late Ch'ing period), *Tōyōshi kenkyū*, 26, no. 1 (June

1967): 1-29; and no. 2 (Sept. 1967): 71-89. See also Himeda 1967, pp. 90-92; MKYHTC, *Shih huo chih*, pp. 83-85.

43. On the origins of *hang*, *t'uan*, and *tso* see Katō 1952, pp. 422-60; and Negishi Tadashi, *Shina girudo no kenkyū* (Studies of Chinese guilds; Tokyo: Shibun shoin, 1932), pp. 197-209.
44. Gt. Brit. Public Record Office, F. O. 228/913.
45. Katō 1952, pp. 453-54.
46. KHYHC, ch. 12.
47. *Ch'ien-lung Chen-hai hsien chih* (Ch'ien-lung gazetteer of Chen-hai *hsien*; 1752), ch. 4.
48. Negishi Tadashi, *Chūgoku no girudo* (Chinese guilds; Tokyo: Nihon hyōron shinsha, 1953), pp. 109-11.
49. MacGowan 1886: 149; MKYHTC, *Shih huo chih*, pp. 217-18; *Yü ti chih*, pp. 727, 737; SSZS 13, p. 41.
50. MacGowan 1886: 145-49; CHTCNP, pp. 97-98; MKYHTC, *Shih huo chih*, p. 91.
51. SSZS 13, p. 41, map; Ho 1966, p. 44.
52. On guilds, see Tsur 1909, pp. 56-57; MacGowan 1886: 138-51.
53. On property tenure, see generally Taiwan [Sōtokufu], Rinji Taiwan kyūkan chōsakai, eds., *Taiwan shihō* (hereafter *Taiwan shihō*; Private law in Taiwan; Tokyo: 1910), vol. 1; Shiba 1968, pp. 321-27; HFYHC, ch. 1; Niida Noboru, *Chūgoku hōseishi kenkyū* [2], *Tochihō* (Studies in Chinese legal history, vol. 2, Land laws; Tōkyō: Tokyo daigaku shuppankai, 1964), pp. 164-203; Mantetsu, Chōsabu, ed., *Shina toshi fudōsan kankō shiryō* (Survey data on Chinese urban real estate), *Hoteiken* (Usufruct of houses; Tientsin: Tenshin jimusho, Chōsashitsu; Shanghai: Shanhai jimusho, Chōsashitsu, 1942); MKYHTC, *Shih huo chih*, pp. 356-58. Mantetsu, Shanhai jimusho, Chōsashitsu, ed., *Ninpō ni okeru shōgyō chōbo chōsa* (A study of Ningpo account books; Shanghai: Shanhai jimusho, Chōsashitsu, 1942), pp. 50, 70, 111; *Min-kuo Ting-hai hsien chih* (hereafter MKTHHC; Republican gazetteer of Ting-hai *hsien*), "Fang su chih," ch. 2, "Feng su"; Chou Tung-pai, *Chung-kuo shang yeh hsi kuan ta ch'üan* (Compendium of Chinese commercial customs; 1923), Part 6, "Shang tien tsu wu" (House lease customs of commercial firms); Katō 1952, pp. 261-82; 1953, p. 245.
54. Sasaki Masaya, "Ninpō shōnin no rikin keigen seigan goshu" (Petitions of Ningpo merchants for lightening likin taxes), *Tōyō gakuhō*, 50, 1 (June 1967): 96.
55. HFYHC, ch. 6; KHYHC, ch. 8; *Taiwan shihō*, vol. 3, part 1, pp. 138-39.
56. Katō 1952, pp. 299-421; Denis Twitchett, "The T'ang Market System," *Asia Major*, 12, no. 2 (1966).
57. Tsur 1909, p. 41.
58. MKYHTC, *Yü ti chih*, pp. 136-48.
59. The *chieh-hsiang* system in Peking was discussed by Imahori Seiji in his book *Hokuhei shimin no jichi kōsei* (Autonomy of city people in Peking; Tokyo: Bunkyūdō, 1947).
60. MKYHTC, *Yü ti chih*, pp. 725-27, 729; Negishi 1953, pp. 109-11.
61. CCNPFC, ch. 4; MKYHTC, *Yü ti chih*, pp. 725, 729, 732, 735.

62. MKYHTC, *Shih huo chih*, pp. 52–67; Gt. Brit., Parliament, House of Commons, Sessional papers, vol. 92: Annual series of trade reports, no. 2421 (1900); Tsur 1909, pp. 47–94; SSZS; Tōa dōbunkai, ed., *Shina kaikōjō shi* (hereafter *Shina kaikōjō shi*, 1922; Treaty ports in China; Tokyo: Tōa dōbunkai, 1922).

63. *Kuang-hsü Feng-hua hsien chih* (hereafter KHFHHC; Kuang-hsü gazetteer of Feng-hua *hsien*), ch. 1, Markets; *Min-kuo Hsiang-shan hsien chih* (Republican gazetteer of Hsiang-shan *hsien*), ch. 13; *Che-chiang sheng ching chi chi lüeh* (hereafter CCCL; Economic overview of Chekiang; 1929), sections on Feng-hua *hsien* and Hsiang-shan *hsien*.

64. Himeda 1967, pp. 98–100.

65. MKYHTC, pp. 227–92; KHFHHC, ch. 1, ch. 36; *Kuang-hsü Yen-yüan hsiang chih* (Kuang-hsü gazetteer of Yen-yüan *hsiang*); CCCL, sections on Yin *hsien*, Feng-hua *hsien*, Yü-yao *hsien*, Ch'eng *hsien*, Hsin-ch'ang *hsien*, and Ning-hai *hsien*; SSZS, p. 327; Sudō Yoshiyuki, *Sōdai keizaishi kenkyū* (Studies of the economic history of the Sung period; Tokyo: Tōkyō daigaku shuppankai, 1962), p. 339.

66. Tōa dōbunkai, ed., *Shina keizai zensho* (Compendium on the Chinese economy; Tokyo: Tōa dōbunkai, 1907–8), vol. 8, pp. 607–11; SSZS 13, pp. 439–50.

67. Gt. Brit., Parliament, House of Commons, Sessional papers, vol. 82: Misc. series of trade reports, no. 22 (1886).

68. MKYHTC, *Shih huo chih*, p. 60; *Yü ti chih*, pp. 242, 246, 795; KHFHHC, ch. 3, p. 2a, ch. 36. See also Kawakami Chikafumi, *Nimpō chiku jittai chōsasho* (Report on conditions in Ningpo; Tokyo: Kōain, Seimubu, 1941), p. 222.

69. CHTCNP, p. 97; SSZS 13, pp. 41–44, 242–45, 321–26; MKYHTC, *Yü ti chih*, pp. 696–703, 714; KHFHHC, ch. 3, pp. 2b–3b; Gt. Brit., Parliament, House of Commons, Sessional papers, vol. 89; Misc. series of trade reports, no. 330 (1894). See also the discussion of Ningpo in *Shina kaikōjō shi*, 1922.

70. See generally CCCL and SSZS.

71. MKYHTC, *Shih huo chih*, pp. 84–85; MacGowan 1886: 145; CCCL, pp. 226, 276.

72. Shiba 1968, pp. 239, 416.

73. Himeda 1967, pp. 71, 101.

74. On the marketing of cotton, see Tōa dōbunkai, ed., *Shina keizai zensho*, vol. 8, pp. 558–59, 608–9; SSZS, pp. 439–49; *Min-kuo Yü-yao liu ts'ang chih*, ch. 17, 18; MKYHTC, *Shih huo chih*, pp. 89, 100.

75. Tsur 1909, pp. 85–86.

76. Also refer to Himeda 1967, pp. 92–97.

77. *Ch'ing pai lei ch'ao* (Categorized fiction of the Ch'ing; 1920), ch. 44.

78. CHTCNP, pp. 173, 182.

79. Negishi 1951, p. 59.

80. Tōa dōbunkai, ed., *Shina keizai zensho* (Compendium on the Chinese economy; Tokyo: Tōa dobunkai, 1907–8), vol. 6, pp. 100–101, 175–76.

81. CHTCNP, pp. 34, 122–23; *Kuang-hsü Ting-hai t'ing chih* (Kuang-hsü gazetteer of Ting-hai *t'ing*; 1879), ch. 15, *Fang su* (Local customs), Part 2,

Feng su (Customs); KHYHC, ch. 2, *Feng su*; MKYHTC, *Shih huo chih* (Economic treatise), p. 72.

82. See Jones 1972 and Susan Mann Jones, "The Ningpo *Pang* and Financial Power at Shanghai," in Mark Elvin and G. William Skinner, eds., *The Chinese City Between Two Worlds* (Stanford: Stanford University Press, 1974), pp. 73–96.
83. See Nishizato 1967.
84. KHYHC, ch. 2, *Feng su*.
85. Negishi 1951, pp. 51–52.
86. Jones 1974, p. 82.
87. *Ibid.*
88. Chung-kuo jen min yin hang, Shang-hai shih fen hang, *Shang-hai ch'ien chuang shihliao* (Historical materials on native banks in Shanghai; Shanghai: Jen min ch'u pan she, 1960), p. 742.
89. *Ibid.*, pp. 733–38.
90. Negishi 1951, p. 32; Ho Ping-ti, *Chung-kuo hui kuan shih lun* (A historical survey of *Landsmannschaften* in China; Taipei: Tai-wan hsüeh sheng shu chü, 1966), p. 32; Negishi 1932, pp. 111–12.

Market Towns and Waterways: The County of Shang-hai from 1480 to 1910

1. Okazaki Fumio and Ikeda Shizuo, *Kōnan bunka kaihatsu shi* (History of the development of civilization in Kiangnan; Tokyo: Kōbundō shogō, 1940), pp. 29, 154.
2. *Ibid.*, p. 186; Chiang Shen-wu, "Shang-hai hsien tsai Yüan Ming shih tai" (Shang-hai county in Yüan and Ming times), in *Shang-hai shih t'ung chih kuan ch'i k'an*, 2, no. 1 (1934): 86.
3. (British) Naval Staff Intelligence Division, *A Handbook of China Proper* (n.p., 1917), vol. 2 (Kiangsu), p. 13.
4. E.g., the "Map of the old town of Shanghai when it formed part of Hua-t'ing county" in Chu Hua, *Hu ch'eng pei k'ao* (Notes on the city of Shanghai [18th century]), in Shang-hai t'ung she, comp., *Shang-hai chang ku ts'ung shu* hereafter SHCKTS; A collection of historical records concerning Shang-hai; Shanghai: Chung-hua shu chü, 1936), ch. shou, pp. 1b–2a.
5. Naval Staff 1917, vol. 2, pp. 51, 65, 69, 535.
6. Okazaki and Ikeda 1940, p. 303; Chiang Shen-wu 1934: 109; Wang T'ao, *Ying juan tsa chih* (A record of the coastal lands; Hong Kong, 1875), ch. 1, p. 2a.
7. Terada Takanobu, "Mindai Soshū heiya no nōka keizai ni tsuite" (The farm economy of the Su-chou plain in Ming times), *Tōyōshi kenkyū*, 16, no. 1 (1957): 10.
8. Ku Yen-wu, ed., *T'ien hsia chün kuo li ping shu* (Documents relating to the advantageous and disadvantageous characteristics of the commanderies and principates of the empire, 1639–62; Ssu k'u shan pen edition; Shanghai: Shang wu, 1936), ts'e 6, p. 29b.
9. Nishijima Sadao, *Chūgoku keizaishi kenkyū* (Studies in the economic history of China; Tokyo: Tōkyō daigaku shuppankei, 1966), pp. 822–23.
10. Nishijima 1966, p. 825.
11. Hoshi Ayao, *Mindai sōun no kenkyū* (Studies on the Ming tribute

grain transport system; Tokyo: Nihon gakujutsu shinkōkai, 1963), appendix 2, "Mindai no tōchō ni tsuite" (The dike administrators of the Ming dynasty), pp. 495–512; Morita Akira, "Mimmatsu ni okeru tōchōsei no henshitsu ni tsuite" (The deterioration of the dike administrator system toward the end of the Ming dynasty), *Tōhōgaku*, 26 (1963): 85–94. The exception was Hsing-hua in northern Kiangsu, and the passage referring to this (Ku Yen-wu 1639–62, ts'e 16, 105b) stresses the importance of the dike administrators for transport. The map is based on H. B. Morse, *The International Relations of the Chinese Empire, Vol. II, The Period of Submission 1861–1893* (London: Longmans, Green, 1918), p. 80; and (British) Naval Intelligence Division, "Agriculture and Forestry," in *China Proper, Vol 3, Economic Geography, Ports and Communications* (London: His Majesty's Stationery Office, 1945), p. 30.

12. Terada 1957: 3–8; Nishijima 1966, pp. 811–12; Mori Masao, "Minsho Kōnan no kanden ni tsuite—Soshū Shōko fu ni okeru no gutaizō" (Government-owned fields in Kiangnan during the Ming dynasty—A concrete picture of them in Su-chou and Sung-chiang prefectures), *Tōyōshi kenkyū*, 19, no. 3, Part I (1960): 5; and 19, no. 4, Part II (1961): 1. On the level of taxation, see also R. Huang, *Taxation and Governmental Finance in Sixteenth-Century Ming China* (Cambridge: Cambridge University Press, 1974), pp. 155 and 161.

13. Ku Yen-wu 1639–62, ts'e 7, p. 27a.

14. Fujii Hiroshi, "Shinan shōnin no kenkyū" (The merchants of Hsin-an), *Tōyō gakuhō*, 6, no. 1, Part I (1953): 19.

15. Nishijima 1966, pp. 835, 874, 884; Fu I-ling, *Ming tai Chiang-nan shih min ching chi shih t'an* (An inquiry into the economy of the urban population in Kiangnan under the Ming dynasty; Shanghai: Shang-hai jen min ch'u pan she, 1963), p. 84.

16. Nishijima 1966, p. 847.

17. *Ibid.*, pp. 822–23, 877–78.

18. Yeh Meng-chu, *Yüeh shih pien* (hereafter YSP; A survey of the age [late seventeenth century]) in SHCKTS, ch. 1, pp. 11a-b.

19. *Ibid.*, ch. 7, p. 5b.

20. Cited in Nishijima 1966, p. 849.

21. Chu Hua, *Mu mien p'u* (The cotton manual [eighteenth century]) in SHCKTS, p. 11a.

22. Wang T'ao 1875, ch. 1, p. 8.

23. Yü Yueh, ed., *T'ung-chih Shang-hai hsien chih* (Gazetteer of Shang-hai county for the T'ung-chih reign; Shanghai: 1871), ch. 4, p. 12a.

24. YSP, ch. 1, pp. 7b, 9b.

25. Morita Akira, *Shindai suiri shi kenkyū* (Water control under the Ch'ing dynasty; Tokyo: Aki shobō, 1974), p. 427.

26. *Ibid.*

27. Kawakatsu Mamoru, "Mimmatsu Shinsho, Kōnan no uchō ni tsuite" (Polder administrators in Kiangnan in late Ming and early Ch'ing), *Tōyō gakuhō*, 55, no. 4 (Mar. 1973): 8.

28. *Ibid.*: 10.

29. Ku Yen-wu 1639–62, ts'e 8, pp. 74b–76b. There is some sketchy evidence for an origin earlier than that suggested here: the dike administrators in

Hsing-hua, mentioned in note 11 above, functioned in the late fourteenth and early fifteenth centuries. A late Ch'ing gazetteer for Hua-t'ing, quoted in Hoshi 1963, p. 496, gives 1387 as the date when dike administrators were established there. In Yen Hung-fan and Chang Chih-hsiang, eds., *Shang-hai hsien chih* (County gazetteer for Shang-hai; comp. 1588), ch 4, p. 4b, there is a passage describing the canton administrators, the grain tax administrators, *and* the dike administrators as "the old system of the present dynasty." Against this must be put the fact that there is no mention of dike administrators in the earlier T'ang Chin, ed., and Chu Yao, rev., *Hung chih Shang-hai chih* (Gazetteer for Shang-hai in the Hung-chih reign; preface 1504), and that they only appeared in Hai-yen county in Chia-hsing in the mid-sixteenth century (Morita 1963, p. 2).

30. Kawakatsu 1973: 5–12.
31. *Ibid.*: 11.
32. YSP, ch. 6, p. 12b.
33. Yü Yueh 1871, ch. 4, p. 20b.
34. *Ibid.*, pp. 13a–16a.
35. *Ibid.*, pp. 18b, 21b–22a.
36. Hoshi 1963, p. 509; YSP, ch. 6, pp. 16a-b; Morita 1974, pp. 456–65.
37. Yü Yueh 1871, ch. 4, p. 24a.
38. Morita 1974, pp. 466–67.
39. *Ibid.*, p. 468.
40. YSP, ch. 6, p. 18a.
41. *Ibid.*
42. Yü Yueh 1871, ch. 4, pp. 24b, 26b.
43. Okazaki and Ikeda 1940 discuss the drainage problem at great length (see esp. pp. 96 *et seq.*). See also YSP, ch. 1, p. 7b.
44. E.g., Yü Yueh 1871, ch. 4, pp. 16b–17a.
45. Mori 1960: 1–4.
46. Morita 1974, pp. 433–37.
47. Li Wen-yao, ed., *Shang-hai hsien chih* (County gazetteer for Shanghai; Shanghai, 1750), ch. 5, pp. 5a-b (emphasis added).
48. For interesting details on the command economy, see Kawakatsu 1973: 66.
49. Fu I-ling 1963, p. 65.
50. Oyama Masaaki, "Mimmatsu Shinsho no daitochishoyū—toku ni Kōnan deruta chitai no chūshin ni shite" (Large landownership in the late Ming and the early Ch'ing—with special reference to the Kiangnan delta), *Shigaku zasshi*, 66, no. 12, and 67, no. 1 (1957 and 1958): part 1, p. 28, n. 9.
51. *Ibid.*: Part 2, pp. 52–53, 64.
52. Mori Masao, "Jūroku-jūhachi seiki ni okeru kōsei to jinushi tenko kankei" (Famine relief and landlord-tenant relationships from the sixteenth century to the eighteenth), *Tōyōshi kenkyū*, 28, no. 4 (1969): 446 (emphasis added). On the "new regulations" see *ibid.*: 453.
53. *Ibid.*; 441–42; Mark Elvin, *The Pattern of the Chinese Past* (Stanford, Calif.: Stanford University Press, 1973), pp. 235–50.
54. Kawakatsu 1973: 12.
55. *Ibid.*: 18–22.
56. Koyama 1957–58: part 2, p. 59.

57. *Ibid.*: part 1, pp. 2, 7; Fu I-ling 1963, p. 50.
58. Koyama 1957–58: part 1, p. 1.
59. *Ibid.*
60. Ku Yen-wu 1639–62, ts'e 11, p. 58b.
61. Koyama 1957–58: part 2, p. 61.
62. Kawakatsu 1973: 13.
63. Koyama 1957–58: part 1, p. 16.
64. *Ibid.*: part 2, pp. 55–57, 68–70; Yūji Muramatsu, "A Documentary Study of Chinese Landlordism in Late Ch'ing and Early Republican Kiangnan," *Bulletin of the School of Oriental and African Studies*, 39, no. 3 (1966): 570, 574, 582, 590, 594.
65. Koyama 1957–58: part 2, p. 61.
66. Kawakatsu 1973: 18–20.
67. Morita 1974, p. 344.
68. Adam Lui, "The Practical Training of Government Officials under the Early Ch'ing, 1644–1795," *International Conference on Asian History* (Hong Kong: University of Hong Kong, 1964), paper 53, pp. 4–9.
69. Yü Yueh 1871, ch. 4, pp. 30a, 32a.
70. *Ibid.*, p. 26b.
71. *Ibid.*, p. 27b.
72. *Ibid.*, p. 29a.
73. *Ibid.*, p. 34a.
74. *Ibid.*, p. 35a.
75. *Ibid.* (emphasis added).
76. *Ibid.*, pp. 37a-b, 38b–39a. *Tung-shih* appears about the same time in passages relating to charitable foundations. See *ibid.*, ch. 2, pp. 21b, 23a-b. For an eighteenth-century citation see Morita 1974, p. 302.
77. Yao Wen-nan, ed., *Shang-hai hsien hsü chih* (A continuation of the Shang-hai county gazetteer; Shanghai: 1918), ch. 5, pp. 4b, 11a-b, 23b.
78. The eminent official T'ao Chu, writing in 1834, observed that "in the most densely populated places (*ch'u*) there may be up to 300 *sheng-yüan* and *chien-sheng*." Cited in Nakahara Teruo, "Shindai ni okeru sōryō no shōhinka ni tsuite" (The mercantilization of the tribute grain under the Ch'ing dynasty), *Shigaku Kenkyū*, 70 (1958): 50.
79. Morita 1974, p. 302.
80. *Ibid.*, p. 327.
81. Yao Wen-nan 1918, ch. 5, pp. 12b–13a.
82. *Ibid.*, pp. 15a-b.
83. Morita 1974, pp. 266, 339.
84. Yü Yueh 1871, ch. 4, p. 43a.
85. E.g., *ibid.*, p. 40b; Yao Wen-nan 1918, ch. 5, p. 27a; Yang I and Ch'ü Ch'ing-p'u, eds., *Shang-hai shih tzu·chih chih* (Shanghai municipality self-government gazetteer; Shanghai: 1915), Document A, pp. 38b–41a.
86. Yao Wen-nan 1918, ch. 5, p. 16a.
87. Yü Yueh 1871, ch. 4, p. 42b.
88. Morita Akira, "Kanton shō Nankai ken Sōen'i no chisui kikō ni tsuite" (The structure of water control in Sang-yüan-wei, Nan-hai county, Kwangtung), *Tōyō gakuhō*, 44 (1964): 76–77.
89. Yamaguchi Michiko, "Shindai no sōun to senshō" (The tribute grain

transport and shipping merchants under the Ch'ing dynasty), *Tōyōshi kenkyū*, 17, no. 2 (1958): 57

90. L. Audemard, *Les jonques chinoises* (Rotterdam: Museum voor Land- en Volkenkunde, 1957), vol. 1, p. 76.

91. Yamaguchi 1958: 57.

92. *Ibid.*: 58; Hoshi 1963, pp. 9–12, 22, 25, 376, 380.

93. Yamaguchi 1958: 62.

94. Yü Yueh 1871, ch. 4, pp. 42b–43a.

95. In addition to the gazetteers edited by T'ang Chin, Yen Hung-fan and Chang Chih-hsiang, Li Wen-yao, Yü Yueh, and Yao Wen-nan for Shang-hai county, and referred to above, I have also utilized Shen Ch'eng-t'ao et al., eds., *Ch'ing-p'u hsien chih* (A gazetteer of Ch'ing-p'u county; Ch'ing-p'u: 1897) and Chang Wen-hu et al., *Nan-hui hsien chih* (A gazetteer of Nan-hui county; Nan-hui: 1879). One market town, located somewhere in present-day Nan-hui, has been omitted from Maps 2 and 4. It is not known if it was functioning in the period covered by Map 3; but it is stated to have disappeared by the nineteenth century. Its precise whereabouts are a mystery. In Map 5 one market that was created and disappeared between 1750 and 1860 has been omitted; and in Map 6, six markets that appeared and perished between 1750 and 1910 within the portion of Nan-hui shown on the map have also had to be left out, as it proved impossible to locate them. The locations of twelve of the markets in Map 6 are very approximate.

96. Fu I-ling 1963, p. 39.

97. An example is Chang-chiang-chia *chen*, otherwise known as Ku-t'ung-li, whose military station may be located a little to the west of Ch'uan-sha on the manuscript map reproduced as Figure 1. Chang Wen-hu et al. 1879, ch. 1, p. 12a, asserts that the market was founded in the Lung-ch'ing reign (1567–72) but the earliest appearance of the town in a gazetteer is in Li Wen-yao 1750, ch. 1, p. 8a. In accordance with the standard procedure adopted, it has therefore been entered first on Map 4, not on Map 3.

98. For recent views, see Shiba Yoshinobu, "Sōdai Kōnan no sonshi to byōshi" (Markets and fairs in Kiangnan during the Sung dynasty), *Tōyō gakuhō*, 40, nos. 1 and 2 (1961); and Sudō Yoshiyuki, *Chūgoku tochi seido shi kenkyū* (Studies in the history of land tenure systems in China; Tokyo: Tōkyō daigaku shuppankai, 1954), pp. 273–77.

99. Examples of cases in which these causes are explicitly stated to have been the origin of market towns will be found in the gazetteers listed in note 95 above, in the sections on "Towns."

100. Ch'üan Han-sheng, "Ya p'ien chan cheng ch'ien Chiang-su ti mien fang chih yeh" (The cotton textile industry in Kiangsu before the Opium War), *Ch'ing hua hsüeh pao*, 1, no. 3 (1958): 28. Cf. Naval Staff 1917, vol. 2, p. 36.

101. Yü Yueh 1871, ch. 4, pp. 37b, 38b.

102. Yao Wen-nan 1918, ch. 5, p. 6b.

103. *Ibid.*, p. 29a.

104. E.g., Ku Yen-wu 1639–62, ts'e 6, p. 15b; and Yü Yueh 1871, ch. 4, pp. 27b, 35b.

105. Yao Wen-nan 1918, ch. 5, pp. 15b, 16b, 27b, 28a, 30a.

106. Morita 1974, pp. 76–78, 93–101, 109–12, 269–72.

Academies and Urban Systems in Kwangtung

1. There is a chapter on *shu-yüan* in Tilemann Grimm, *Erziehung und Politik im konfuzianischen China der Ming-Zeit (1368–1644)* (Hamburg: Gesellschaft für Natur- und Völkerkunde Ostasiens, 1960). See also Sheng Lang-hsi, *Chung-kuo shu yüan chih tu* (Shanghai: Chung-hua shu chü, 1936); Chou Ch'uan-ju, *Shu yüan chih tu k'ao* (Shanghai, 1939); Hayashi Tomoharu, "Gen Min jidai no shoin kyōiku" (Education in academies during the Yüan and Ming periods), in *Kinsei Chūgoku kyōikushi kenkyū* (hereafter KCKK; Education in China in recent dynasties), ed. Hayashi Tomoharu (Tokyo: Kokutosha, 1958): 3–23; Ogawa Yoshiko, "Shindai ni okeru gigaku setsuritsu no kiban" (The basis for the establishment of free schools in the Ch'ing period), in KCKK: 273–308; John Meskill, "Academies and Politics in the Ming Dynasty," in *Chinese Government in Ming Times: Seven Studies*, ed. C. O. Hucker (New York: Columbia University Press, 1969): 149–74; for the present study especially valuable was Liu Po-chi, *Kuang-tung shu yüan chih tu* (The academy system in Kwangtung; Canton: Shang wu yin shu kuan, 1938 [reprinted Taipei: Shang wu yin shu kuan, 1958]).
2. Sheng Lang-hsi 1936, pp. 7–12, 18.
3. See, for example, references cited in Grimm 1960, p. 109.
4. See under "seisha" in Mochizuku Shinkō and Tsukamoto Zenryū, comps., *Bukkyō daijiten* (Encyclopaedia of Buddhism; rev. and enl. ed., Tokyo: Sekai seiten kankō kyōkai, 1955–63, 10 vols.), and under "arama" in *Pali-English Dictionary*, comp. T. W. Rhys Davids and William Stede (London: The Pali Text Society, 1921).
5. *Shu-yüan* did not systematically take over Buddhist places of study, but the spiritual influences of Buddhism and the Ch'an movement—as exemplified in the Yang-ming movement in Ming times—resulted in the founding of many new *shu-yüan*. See Grimm 1960, Meskill 1969, and Hayashi 1958.
6. Many academies got their start as memorial halls for renowned Neo-Confucian scholars and teachers. Cf. Liu Po-chi 1938, pp. 20 ff. and 79.
7. This is brought out indirectly in *Ch'uan hsi lu*, pt. II, sects. 197 and 198, quoted in W. T. Chan's translation (*Instructions for practical living and other Neo-Confucian writings by Wang Yang-ming*; New York: Columbia University Press, 1963), p. 185.
8. Grimm 1960, pp. 139–44.
9. *Ibid.*, pp. 143–44.
10. See Grimm 1960, pp. 113–14, for a discussion of Ming usage of these and related terms.
11. Tai Chao-ch'en et al., eds., *Kuang-chou fu chih* (hereafter KCFC; Prefectural gazetteer of Kuang-chou; n.p.: Yüeh hsiu shu yüan, 1879). Lin Shu-hsiu et al., eds., *Shao-chou fu chih* (hereafter SCFC; Prefectural gazetteer of Shao-chou; n.p., 1874). Liu Kuei-nien et al., eds., *Hui-chou fu chih* (hereafter HCFC; Prefectural gazetteer of Hui-chou; n.p., 1881).
12. See Ho Shao-chi and Wu K'un-hsiu, eds., *An-hui t'ung chih* (Gazetteer of Anhwei; n.p., 1877).
13. See C. B. Cressey, *China's Geographic Foundations* (New York: McGraw-Hill, 1934); and Saeki Tomi, *Shindai ensei no kenkyū* (Studies of the Ch'ing salt administration; Kyoto: Tōyōshigaku kenkyūkai, 1962).

14. In another case (that of Ch'ao-chou prefecture), of 29 academies, eighteen were within the walls, five were in suburbs, four were in or near market towns, and only two were putatively in rural areas. See *Ch'ao-chou fu chih* (Prefectural gazetteer of Ch'ao-chou; 1893), ch. 24, 46b ff.

Of 50 *shu-yüan* in Kao-chou prefecture, to the southwest of Canton, thirteen were in administrative centers, seven were in suburbs, twelve were in market towns, and eighteen were putatively rural. See Yang Chi, ed., *Kao-chou fu chih* (Prefectural gazetteer of Kao-chou; 1889), ch. 14, 1a ff.

15. KCFC, ch. 66, 17a ff.
16. SCFC, ch. 18, 1a; for a memorial inscription of 1246, see 1b ff.
17. HCFC, ch. 10, 1a ff.
18. HCFC, p. 59 (modern pagination).
19. SCFC, ch. 18, 16a ff. The degree results of Lo-ch'ang county were middling—only one *chü-jen,* eleven *en-kung* (honorary degrees), and five *kung-sheng* (senior licentiates) for the period 1820–74. Thus Lo-ch'ang ranked fourth in terms of degrees received among the six counties in Shao-chou prefecture. (By comparison, first-ranked Ying-te had six *chü-jen,* sixteen *en-kung,* and ten *kung-sheng.*)
20. See SCFC, ch. 18, 9a–14a, and HCFC, ch. 10, 1b–2b.
21. See Article 3 of the regulations *Kuei t'iao,* dated 1862. The Hui-chou regulations of 1819 are much shorter, but quite similar; since the two are widely separated in time, we may take them as fairly representative for the greater part of the nineteenth century.
22. Hai-feng county took third place behind Kuei-shan and Po-lo with 85 degrees (HCFC, ch. 21).
23. SCFC, ch. 7, ch. 8.
24. Po-lo county, adjoining the metropolitan county Kuei-shan on the downriver side, had proportionately more arable land. Weng-yüan and Ying-te counties in Shao-chou prefecture lie to the south away from the hills; the income of their *shu-yüan* was derived largely from capital rent, with more donors from market places than in any other county. See HCFC, ch. 10, and SCFC, ch. 18.
25. For example, in *Shun-te hsien chih* (Gazetteer of Shun-te county; 1929), *P'an-yü hsien chih* (Gazetteer of P'an-yü county; 1871), and KCFC, ch. 129.
26. For sketches of the lives of these scholars see Arthur W. Hummel, ed., *Eminent Chinese of the Ch'ing Period* (Washington, D.C.: U.S. Government Printing Office, 1943 [reprinted, Taipei: Ch'eng-wen, 1972]).
27. This may be deduced from the printing endeavors of Juan Yüan himself, and from the curriculum of the Hsüeh-hai T'ang, which stressed the classics in particular. See Liu Po-chi 1938, pp. 346–47.
28. KCFC, ch. 66, 18b, and ch. 72, 13a; Liu Po-chi 1938, pp. 124–28.
29. See Liu Po-chi 1938, pp. 124–28, where the memorial of Chang Chih-tung is reproduced with interesting details on the situation.
30. *P'an-yü hsien chih* (1871), ch. 16, 40b–41a.
31. KCFC, ch. 72, 12b–13b.
32. Ibid., 13a.
33. Ibid., 13a–13b.
34. SCFC, ch. 18, 7b ff.

35. HCFC, ch. 10, 2a–2b.
36. HCFC, ch. 10, 2b; SCFC, ch. 18, 9b.
37. KCFC, ch. 72, 12a.
38. *Ibid.*, 12a ff.
39. The case of Sheng Hsüan-huai, which is contemporary to our period, is most telling. See Albert Feuerwerker, *China's Early Industrialization* (Cambridge: Harvard University Press, 1958).
40. See Liu Po-chi 1938, pp. 161–203, with annexed tables (pp. 203–6).
41. Four prefectures stood out in this regard: Kuang-chou and Kao-chou, each with thirteen cases of academies with income from capital investment, Ch'iung-chou (i.e., Hainan) with eleven, and Ch'ao-chou with seven. KCFC, ch. 72; *Kao-chou fu chih* (1889), ch. 14; *Ch'iung-chou fu chih* (Prefectural gazetteer of Ch'iung-chou; 1886), ch. 7b; *Ch'ao-chou fu chih* (1893), ch. 24, 42b ff.
42. SCFC, ch. 18, 7b ff.
43. *Kao-chou fu chih* (1889), ch. 14, 1b ff.
44. KCFC, ch. 66, 18a (but as an entry for the year 1755).
45. See Article 3 of the regulations issued in 1862 governing the Hsiang-chiang Shu-yüan, given in SCFC, ch. 18, 9b.
46. *Ibid.*, Article 5.
47. *Ibid.*, 9a, attached to the document.
48. See Liu Po-chi 1938, p. 304. It would appear that the *chiao-kuan*, "director(s) of study," were not included in the *hsien-kuan*.
49. See James T. C. Liu, *Reform in Sung China* (Cambridge: Harvard University Press, 1959).
50. Liu Po-chih 1938, pp. 316–18.
51. I follow here Liu Po-chi 1938, pp. 222–90.
52. *Ibid.*; note again the importance of the Yüeh-hsiu Shu-yüan.
53. *Ibid.*
54. Figures are from the *hsüan-chü* lists in KCFC, ch. 41–46; HCFC ch. 21; and SCFC, ch. 8.

Extended Kinship in the Traditional City

1. Olga Lang, *Chinese Family and Society* (New Haven, Conn.: Yale University Press, 1946), p. 14.
2. Maurice Freedman, *Chinese Lineage and Society: Fukien and Kwangtung* (London: Athlone Press, 1966), p. 49.
3. But for an apparent exception see Marion J. Levy, Jr., *The Family Revolution in Modern China* (Cambridge, Mass.: Harvard University Press, 1949), p. 48 and footnote.
4. See Han-yi Feng, "The Chinese Kinship System," *Harvard Journal of Asiatic Studies*, 2, no. 2 (July 1937): 182.
5. Maurice Freedman, *Lineage Organization in Southeastern China* (London: Athlone Press, 1958), pp. 27–30.
6. See Hugh D. R. Baker, *A Chinese Lineage Village: Sheung Shui* (Stanford, Calif.: Stanford University Press, 1968), chap. 4; and Freedman 1958, chap. 6.
7. Freedman 1966, pp. 20–21, 27–28.
8. *Tz'u hai: ho ting pen*, Min-kuo 36, ch'ou 14.

9. Hui-chen Wang Liu, *The Traditional Chinese Clan Rules* (Locust Valley, N.Y.: J. J. Augustin, 1959), p. 26.
10. Jacques Amyot, *The Manila Chinese: Familism in the Philippine Environment* (Quezon City: Ateneo de Manila University, Institute of Philippine Culture, 1973), p. 83.
11. But see, for instance, Hu Hsien-chin, *The Common Descent Group in China and Its Functions* (New York: Viking Fund, 1948), p. 67, for an exception.
12. J. H. Gray, *Walks in the City of Canton* (Hong Kong: De Souza, 1875), p. 168. There is a further description on pp. 76–80.
13. Ch'ü Ta-chün, *Kuang-tung hsin yü* (New discussion of Kwangtung; 1700), ch. 17, p. 5a.
14. Hu 1948, p. 10.
15. Lang 1946, p. 180.
16. Morton H. Fried, "Some Political Aspects of Clanship in a Modern Chinese City," in Marc J. Swartz et al., eds., *Political Anthropology* (Chicago: Aldine, 1966), p. 292.
17. See Baker 1968, pp. 113–15.
18. Hu 1948, p. 10.
19. See Jack M. Potter, *Capitalism and the Chinese Peasant* (Berkeley: University of California Press, 1968), pp. 167–68.
20. See Kung-chuan Hsiao, *Rural China: Imperial Control in the Nineteenth Century* (Seattle: University of Washington Press, 1960), p. 323. Also Margery Wolf, *The House of Lim: A Study of a Chinese Farm Family* (New York: Appleton-Century-Crofts, 1968), p. 24: "In Taipei and in the larger market towns there have always been houses designed for rental income, houses for transients who may stay a month or ten years, but they are barren houses designed only for the present occupants and not looking toward the future."
21. F. L. K. Hsü and J. H. Hu, "Guild and Kinship Among the Butchers in West Town," *American Sociological Review*, 10 (1945): 357–64.
22. Hsiao 1960, p. 662.
23. Freedman 1966, p. 29n, summarizing from Ernest W. Burgess and Harvey J. Locke, *The Family, from Institution to Companionship*, 2d ed. (New York: American Book, 1953), pp. 33–34.
24. Hsiao 1960, p. 353.
25. Lawrence W. Crissman, "The Segmentary Structure of Urban Overseas Chinese Communities," *Man*, 2, no. 2 (1967): 202.
26. Freedman 1966, pp. 165–66.
27. Edgar Wickberg, *The Chinese in Philippine Life, 1850–1898* (New Haven, Conn.: Yale University Press, 1965), p. 174.
28. Amyot 1960, p. 104. He does not give any documentation to his assertion that the principle has existed for many centuries, nor do we know to which *basic* principle he refers.
29. Tsien Tche-hao, "The Social Life of the Chinese in Madagascar," in L. A. Fallers, ed., *Immigrants and Associations* (The Hague: Mouton, 1967), pp. 87–102.
30. Fried 1966, p. 293: "The clan temples in Taiwan in their present forms date back about 75 years or so." I hope I do not misrepresent his meaning:

"clan temples" is ambiguous in the context, so that it is not clear whether the physical buildings or the organizations are intended.

31. Ch'en Ta-t'ung, *Hsiang-kang hua ch'iao t'uan t'i tsung lan* (Overview of Chinese organizations in Hong Kong; Hong Kong: Kuochi hsin wen she, 1947), chap. 4, pp. 6, 13–14. The names, but no details, of two more such associations are given at Addenda, p. 3.

32. E. H. Parker, "Comparative Chinese Family Law," *China Review*, 8 (1879): 71f., fn. 26; quoted by Freedman 1966, p. 166n, as substantiation for his remarks on the origin of the overseas clan associations. See note 26 above.

33. *Kuang-chou chih nan* (Guide to Canton; Shanghai: Hsin hua shu chü, 1919).

34. Kuang-chou shih cheng fu, *Kuang-chou chih nan* (Guide to Canton; Canton, 1934), pp. 442–43.

35. Fried 1966, pp. 289–90. *T'ung-ch'in hui* would seem to be the same as *tsung-ch'in hui*.

36. District of origin associations (*t'ung-hsiang hui* and more official *hui-kuan*) were of course very common in Chinese cities, and were probably the earliest and most universal form of grouping among the overseas Chinese. Indeed, the principles of geographical and linguistic affinity were often the determinants of the extent of common surname groupings, making the latter virtually segments of groupings formed in accordance with the former.

37. *Ch'ien ch'eng hou tz'u ch'üan shu* (Complete records of the Ch'ien-ch'eng-hou Ancestral Hall; hereafter CCHT; 1920), ch. 1, pp. 2b, 5a; ch. 2, pp. 24b, 29a.

38. Canton was divided between the two *hsien* of Nan-hai and P'an-yü, so that this land was not necessarily at a great distance from the Nan-hai base of the lineage.

39. *Nan-hai Liang shih chia p'u* (Genealogy of the Liang clan of Nan-hai *hsien*; hereafter NHLS; 1911). All details above are taken from ch. 3.

40. NHLS, ch. 3, pp. 28b, 32b.

41. *Lu-chiang shu yüan ch'üan p'u* (Complete genealogy of the Lu-chiang Academy; hereafter LCSY; 1916), ch. 1, p. 11a.

42. *Wu-kung shu yüan shih p'u* (Genealogy of the Wu-kung Academy; hereafter WKSY; 1900), ch. 2, p. 1a.

43. *Ling-nan Hsien shih tsung p'u* (Genealogy of the Ling-nan Hsien clan; hereafter LNHS; 1910), ch. 1.2, p. 7a.

44. CCHT, ch. 1, pp. 2a, 4a.

45. *Yüeh-tung Chien shih ta t'ung p'u* (Combined genealogy of the Kwang-tung Chien clan; hereafter YTCS; 1928), ch. shou, p. 1b.

46. WKSY, ch. 1, pp. 9b–10a, 29a, and 32b.

47. LCSY, ch. 1, p. 26b; CCHT, ch. 2, p. 25b.

48. *Nan-hai Lo ko K'ung shih chia p'u* (Genealogy of the K'ung clan of Lo-ko, Nan-hai *hsien*; hereafter NHKS; 1864), ch. 2, pp. 1a–2b.

49. LCSY, ch. 1, p. 70a.

50. LNHS, ch. 2. shou, p. 1b; ch. 2.1, pp. 3b, 4b; ch. 3.39, pp. 1a–1b.

51. LCSY, ch. 1, pp. 70b–74b.

52. LNHS, ch. 2.2, pp. 1a–7a; ch. 3.39, p. 1b.

53. Gray 1875, p. 581.

54. LCSY, ch. 1, pp. 5b–6a, 7b; ch. 2, pp. 71a–90a. WKSY, ch. 1, pp. 30b, 47a–48b. LNHS, ch. 2.1, p. 4b.

55. LNHS, ch. 1.3, p. 12b; ch. 2.3, p. 3a. CCHT, ch. 1, p. 5a. WKSY, ch. 1, p. 27a; ch. 2, p. 1a.
56. See Gray 1875, p. 581; LCSY, ch. 1, pp. 26a–b; CCHT, ch. 2, pp. 25b–26b.
57. WKSY, ch. 1, p. 39b; LCSY, ch. 1, pp. 24a–b; NHKS, ch. 2, pp. 9a–11b.
58. WKSY, ch. 2, p. 37a.
59. CCHT, ch. 2, p. 27a; WKSY, ch. 1, p. 33b.
60. LCSY, ch. 1, p. 24a; WKSY, ch. 1, p. 27b; CCHT, ch. 2, p. 27b.
61. YTCS, ch. shou, p. 3a.
62. LCSY, ch. 1, p. 24a.
63. WKSY, ch. 1, pp. 27b, 28b.
64. LCSY, ch. 1, pp. 11a, 30a. LNHS, ch. 1.2, p. 7b; ch. 1.3, p. 12b.
65. NHKS, ch. 2, pp. 1a–2b.
66. LCSY, ch. 1, pp. 16a, 70b–74a.
67. CCHT, ch. 2, p. 24b; LNHS, ch. 2.2, pp. 1a–7a; WKSY, ch. 2, pp. 39b–40b; YTCS, ch. shou. 2, pp. 1a–2b.
68. *Nan-hai Chiu-chiang Kuan shu te t'ang chia p'u* (Genealogy of the Shu-te T'ang of the Kuan clan of Chin-chiang, Nan-hai *hsien*; 1897), ch. 15, pp. 44b–45b.
69. LNHS, ch. 2. shou, p. 1b; YTCS, ch. shou, p. 1a; LCSY, ch. 1, p. 16a.
70. WKSY, ch. 1, p. 33a; ch. 2, pp. 33a, 33b–34b; CCHT, ch. 2, p. 28a.
71. Freedman 1966, p. 28.
72. YTCS, ch. 6, p. 12a–b; ch. 13, pp. 53a–57b.
73. Freedman 1958, p. 105.
74. LNHS, ch. 2.1, pp. 4a–b.

Introduction: Urban Social Structure in Ch'ing China

1. Sen-dou Chang, "Some Aspects of the Urban Geography of the Chinese Hsien Capital," *Annals of the Association of American Geographers*, 51, no. 1 (Mar. 1961): 38.
2. C. K. Yang, "Some Thoughts on the Study of Chinese Urban Communities" (Paper prepared for the seminar on Problems of Micro-Organization in Chinese Society, sponsored by the Subcommittee on Research on Chinese Society of the ACLS-SSRC Joint Committee on Contemporary China, Bermuda, Jan. 1963), p. 16.
3. The quotation is from one of the earliest syntheses, Chauncy D. Harris and Edward J. Ullman, 'The Nature of Cities," *Annals of the American Academy of Political and Social Science*, 242 (Nov. 1945): 15.
4. For a map of Tainan as of 1874 and some relevant description, see Camille C. Imbault-Huart, *L'île Formose: histoire et description* (Paris: Ernest Leroux, 1893), pp. 174–79.
5. F. W. Mote, "A Millennium of Chinese Urban History: Form, Time, and Space Concepts in Soochow," *Rice University Studies*, 59, no. 4 (Fall 1973): 55.
6. Winston Hsieh, "Peasant Insurrection and the Marketing Hierarchy in the Canton Delta, 1911," in Mark Elvin and G. William Skinner, eds., *The Chinese City Between Two Worlds* (Stanford, Calif.: Stanford University Press, 1974), pp. 127–30.
7. C. P. Fitzgerald, *China: A Short Cultural History* (London: Cresset Press, 1935), p. 530.

8. Mote 1973: 59.
9. Yang 1963, p. 17.
10. Gideon Sjoberg, *The Preindustrial City: Past and Present* (Glencoe, Ill.: Free Press, 1960), pp. 97–98.
11. For a summary of relevant empirical studies, see Walter F. Abbott, "Moscow in 1897 as a Preindustrial City: A Test of the Inverse Burgess Zonal Hypothesis," *American Sociological Review*, 39, no. 4 (Aug. 1974): 543. Abbott's study of Moscow in 1897 found that the percentage of the population in the upper and middle estates declined with distance from the Kremlin, the historic city center, whereas the proportion of the working population in manufacturing increased. Levels of literacy and education also declined with distance from the city center.
12. Chang 1961: 36.
13. For a pioneering treatment of cross-societal differences in urban population gradients (which, however, makes its points in terms of an inappropriate contrast between "Western" and "non-Western" cities), see Brian J. L. Berry, James W. Simmons, and Robert J. Tennant, "Urban Populations: Structure and Change," *Geographical Review*, 53 (July 1963): 389–405. For subsequent general treatments of the problem, see James H. Johnson, *Urban Geography* (London: Pergamon,, 1967), pp. 52–56; and Brian J. L. Berry and Frank E. Horton, *Geographic Perspectives on Urban Systems* (Englewood Cliffs, N.J.: Prentice-Hall, 1970), pp. 276–93.
14. China, Nei wu fu, Tsao pan ch'u, Yü t'u fang, *Ch'ien-lung ching ch'eng ch'üan t'u* (Comprehensive map of the imperial capital in the Ch'ien-lung period [Photographic reproduction of a map drawn ca. 1750 at a scale of 1:650 on 442 leaves]; Peking: Ku kung po wu yüan, 1940).
15. Sidney D. Gamble, *Peking: A Social Survey* (New York: Doran, 1921), pp. 100, 412–13, 486.
16. Chang 1961: 37–38.
17. Edward J. M. Rhoads, "Merchant Associations in Canton, 1895–1911," in Mark Elvin and G. William Skinner, *The Chinese City Between Two Worlds* (Stanford, Calif.: Stanford University Press, 1974), pp. 101–2.
18. The statistics in question are *pao-chia* registration figures published in Camille C. Imbault-Huart, "La population de Canton en juin 1895," *T'oung Pao*, 7, no. 2 (1896): 58–59.
19. Lien-sheng Yang, "Government Control of Urban Merchants in Traditional China," *Tsing Hua Journal of Chinese Studies*, n.s. 8, nos. 1/2 (Aug. 1970): 196. Professor Yang also notes that in the mid-eighteenth century inns and theaters were not allowed in the Inner City of Peking.
20. Abbott 1974.
21. A particularly clear description of this pattern may be found in Shen Ju-sheng and Sun Min-hsien, "Ch'eng-tu tu shih ti li chih yen chiu" (The urban geography of Chengtu), *Ti li hsüeh pao*, 14, nos. 3/4 (Dec. 1947): 20.
22. The relative proportion of all transport coolies in the urban population varied, of course, with the city's position in the transport network, and the relative importance of different types of transport workers varied according to the availability of navigable waterways. In Chengtu, a great metropolis largely dependent on overland transport, it was estimated around 1920 that at least one-fifth of the city's male population were human carriers of one

kind or another. In Tientsin, a port metropolis on the Grand Canal, transport coolies associated with the waterborne trade may have totaled one-tenth of the entire population in 1846; their heaviest concentration was in peri-urban areas. See George D. Hubbard, "The Geographic Setting of Chengtu," *Bulletin of the Geographical Society of Philadelphia*, 21, no. 4 (Oct. 1923): 23; Momose Hiromu, " 'Chin men pao chia t'u shuo' ni tsuite Shindai Tenshin ken no nōkōshōko ni kansuru tokei shiryō" ("Explanation of Tientsin's *pao-chia* scheme": Statistical materials concerning the households of farmers, artisans, and merchants in T'ien-chin *hsien* in Ch'ing times), in *Tōyōnōgyō keizaishi kenkyū ono takeo hakushi kanreki kinen ronbunshū kankōkai* (Tokyo: Nihon hyōronsha, 1948), pp. 125–34.

23. Every service that a housewife might provide was available from itinerants in Chinese cities with large numbers of male sojourners. The *feng i-fu* "mend-coat woman" is a case in point. "Planting herself at some spot where the coolies and labourers will no doubt be resting awhile, she produces her work-basket and an assortment of odd patches, and offers to mend anything, from the cloth facing of slippers to a yard-wide rip in a coat. She is in great demand for sewing strong cardboard ... to the soles of socks in order to make them last longer." H. Crozier Faulder, "Chinese Hawkers," *China Journal*, 21, no. 6 (Dec. 1934): 276.

24. Chengtu was a case in point. See Shen and Sun 1947: 20.

25. Teng-shih-k'ou district in Peking, situated just east of the Imperial City, about halfway between the districts depicted in Figures 1 and 2. Gamble 1921, p. 327. Shop-houses were naturally concentrated along major streets, such as those that delineated the Teng-shih-k'ou district, whereas residences were concentrated along the alleys and side streets within. This general pattern also prevailed in Chengtu, where two-story shop-houses lined the streets that defined blocks and one-story residences faced the interior alleys. The result, as noted by Shen and Sun (1947: 21) was a "basin-like" module.

26. Mote 1973: 59.

27. Quoted in Niida Noboru, "The Industrial and Commercial Guilds of Peking and Religion and Fellow-countrymanship as Elements of Their Coherence." *Folklore Studies*, 9 (1950): 200.

28. Quoted in Ping-ti Ho, "The Salt Merchants of Yang-chou: A Study of Commercial Capitalism in Eighteenth-Century China." *Harvard Journal of Asiatic Studies*, 17 (1954): 144.

29. Frederick D. Cloud, *Hangchow, the 'City of Heaven'* ... (Shanghai: Presbyterian Mission Press, 1906), p. 9.

30. *Baron Richthofen's Letters, 1870–1872* (Shanghai: North-China Herald Office, 1872), p. 117.

31. Cf. n. 138 of Golas's paper; D. J. MacGowan, "On the Banishment of Criminals in China," *Journal of the North China Branch of the Royal Asiatic Society*, 3 (1859): 299.

32. Cloud 1906, pp. 9–10.

33. Ho Ping-ti, *Chung-kuo hui kuan shih lun* (An historical study of *hui-kuan* in China; Taipei: Hsüeh sheng shu chü, 1966), pp. 24–33.

34. The manuscript is now in the collection of the Institute of Oriental Culture, Tokyo University. I am grateful to James H. Cole for directing my attention to it.

35. Niida 1950: 197–201. See also Katō Shigeshi, "Shindai ni okeru Pekin no shōnin kaikan ni tsuite (Merchant *hui-kuan* in Peking during the Ch'ing period), *Shigaku zaishi*, 53, no. 2 (Feb. 1942): 1–31.

36. Cf. Lawrence W. Crissman, "The Segmentary Structure of Urban Overseas Chinese Communities." *Man*, 2, no. 2 (June 1967): 190.

37. G. William Skinner, "Mobility Strategies in Late Imperial China: A Regional-Systems Analysis," in Carol A. Smith, ed., *Regional Analysis, Vol. 1: Economic Systems* (New York: Academic Press, 1976), pp. 327–64.

38. Ping-ti Ho, "The Geographic Distribution of *Hui-kuan (Landsmannschaften)* in Central and Upper Yangtze Provinces." *Tsing Hua Journal of Chinese Studies*, n.s. 5, no. 2 (Dec. 1966): 131.

39. D. J. MacGowan, "Chinese Guilds or Chambers of Commerce and Trade Unions," *Journal of the China Branch of the Royal Asiatic Society*, n.s. 21, no. 3 (1886): 181.

40. A common pattern of accommodation in this regard is illustrated by the Cantonese Guild in Foochow, which designated separate managers for the three major lines in which Cantonese sojourners specialized, including one for the tea trade. See "Regulations of the Canton Guild at Foochow," trans. by C. F. R. Allen, in *A Vocabulary and Hand-book of the Chinese Language*, by Justus Doolittle (Foochow: Rozario, Marcal, 1872), vol. 2, p. 401.

41. Niida 1950: 201.

42. Ping-ti Ho 1966 ("The Geographic Distribution . . ."): 132.

43. Cf. Niida 1950: 200.

44. Ping-ti Ho 1966 ("The Geographic Distribution . . ."): 132.

45. Hosea Ballou Morse, *The Gilds of China* (London: Longmans, Green, 1909), p. 36.

46. Cf. Fredrik Barth, ed., *Ethnic Groups and Boundaries* (Boston: Little, Brown, 1969); and Abner Cohen, ed., *Urban Ethnicity* (London: Tavistock, 1974).

47. Niida 1950: 199–200.

48. Ping-ti Ho 1966 ("The Geographic Distribution . . ."): 131.

49. Isabelle Williamson, *Old Highways in China* (New York: American Tract Society, 1884), p. 108.

50. Morse 1909, p. 40.

51. A classic example is the Yung-sheng ssu outside the north gate of Canton, laid out in the form of a "city of the dead" with 194 houses. Here were deposited "coffins which contain the remains of persons who, either as officials, or merchants, or travellers, have . . . come to Canton and have, during their sojourn in the city . . . died. The burial of the remains of such persons at Canton would, of course, deprive their departed souls of the worship which . . . they ought . . . to receive. The coffins, therefore . . . are lodged in this place until the arrival of convenient seasons for their removal to the places whence the departed ones, respectively, came." John Henry Gray, *Walks in the City of Canton* (Hong Kong: De Souza, 1875), p. 541.

52. Morse 1909, pp. 39–40.

53. A cemetery for sojourners from Ning-po and Shao-hsing prefectures (Chekiang) had been established in Canton by the 1620's. Ho Ping-ti 1966 (*Chung-kuo hui-kuan* . . .), p. 40.

54. For data on Shanghai's population attesting the high proportion of so-

journers, see Peng Chang, "The Distribution and Relative Strength of the Provincial Merchant Groups in China, 1842–1911" (Ph.D. dissertation, University of Washington, 1957), p. 103; and Tōa Dōbunkai, ed., *Shina keizai zensho*, vol. 7 (Tokyo, 1907), pp. 159–60.

55. Taiwanese cities were exceptional because of the extreme violence of interethnic strife during the greater part of the nineteenth century. A high proportion of all settlements, from villages to towns and even cities, were by the 1870's completely dominated by a single regional group, either by Hakkas from the upper Han Basin of the Southeast Coast region, by natives of Changchou *fu*, by natives of Ch'üan-chou *fu*, or by natives of particular subdivisions of the last prefecture. The "ethnic purity" of Lu-kang, as described by DeGlopper, does not distinguish it sharply from other Taiwanese cities, such as Meng-chia, whose economic fortunes were improving.

56. The term is used by Gerhard Lenski in a generic treatment of inequality in agrarian societies. See his *Power and Privilege: A Theory of Social Stratification* (New York: McGraw-Hill, 1966), pp. 281–84.

57. C. K. Yang 1953, p. 22.

58. John G. Kerr, *A Guide to the City and Suburbs of Canton*, rev. and enl. ed. (Hong Kong: Kelly and Walsh, 1904), p. 10.

59. Niida Noboru, "Shindai Konan no girudo māchanto" (The guild merchant in Hunan during the Ch'ing period), *Tōyōshi kenkyū*, 64 (Feb. 1958): 78–79.

60. Edward J. M. Rhoads, "Merchant Associations in Canton, 1895–1911," in Mark Elvin and G. William Skinner, eds., *The Chinese City Between Two Worlds* (Stanford, Calif.: Stanford University Press, 1974), p. 104.

61. Tou Chi-liang, *T'ung hsiang tsu chih chih yen chiu* (Native-place associations; Shanghai: Cheng chung shu chü, 1946), pp. 35, 76.

62. *Ibid.*, pp. 73–78.

63. Niida 1958: 74–85.

64. China, Tsung li ya men, Hai kuan, *Decennial Reports on the Trade, Navigation, Industries, etc. of the Ports Open to Foreign Commerce in China . . . , 1882–91* (Shanghai: Tsung shui wu ssu shu, T'ung chi k'o, 1893), pp. 635–36; Ho Ping-ti 1966 (*Chung-kuo hui kuan . . .*), pp. 112, 131; Mark Elvin, "The Administration of Shanghai, 1905–1914," in Mark Elvin and G. William Skinner, eds., *The Chinese City Between Two Worlds* (Stanford, Calif.: Stanford University Press, 1974), p. 240.

65. *Decennial Reports . . . 1882–91*, pp. 537–40.

66. See in particular Lawrence W. Crissman, "The Segmentary Structure of Urban Overseas Chinese Communities," *Man*, 2, no. 2 (June 1967); Maurice Freedman, "Immigrants and Associations: Chinese in Nineteenth-Century Singapore," *Comparative Studies in Society and History*, 3, no. 1 (Oct. 1960); G. William Skinner, *Chinese Society in Thailand: An Analytical History* (Ithaca, N.Y.: Cornell University Press, 1957); G. William Skinner, *Leadership and Power in the Chinese Community of Thailand* (Ithaca, N.Y.: Cornell University Press, 1958); Ju-k'ang T'ien, *The Chinese of Sarawak: A Study of Social Structure* (London, Department of Anthropology, London School of Economics and Political Science, 1953); Edgar Wickberg, *The Chinese in Philippine Life, 1850–1898* (New Haven, Conn.: Yale University Press, 1965); Donald E. Willmott, *The Chinese of Semarang: A Changing Minority Com-*

munity in Indonesia (Ithaca, N.Y.: Cornell University Press, 1960); and W. E. Willmott, *The Political Structure of the Chinese Community in Cambodia* (London: Athlone Press, 1970).

67. Skinner 1957, pp. 294, 318–19, 331; Skinner 1958, pp. 23–24, 152–56.
68. Rhoads 1974, p. 104.
69. Crissman 1967: 200.
70. Niida 1958, 72–74, 83.
71. Tou Chi-liang 1946, pp. 35, 73, 76–78.
72. Elvin 1974, pp. 240–46.
73. *Hsin hai ko ming ch'ien shih nien chien shih lun hsüan chi* (A selection of discussions of current affairs in the ten years before the Revolution of 1911; Hong Kong: San lien shu tien, 1962), vol. 1, p. 174. The quotation is translated in Elvin 1974, p. 240.
74. Elvin 1974, p. 251.
75. C. K. Yang 1953, pp. 24–25.
76. Rhoads 1974, p. 104.
77. Tou Chi-liang 1946, pp. 28–32.
78. For a number of hints suggesting a role for the gentry in the Ten Guilds, see Niida 1958: 88–90.

Early Ch'ing Guilds

1. Katō Shigeshi, without going into very much detail on the period after the Sung, wrote as though there were a straight-line development of guilds from Sung to Ch'ing: Katō Shigeshi, "On the Hang or the Associations of Merchants in China, with Especial Reference to the Institution in the T'ang and Sung Periods," *Memoirs of the Research Department of the Toyo Bunko* 8(1936), pp. 45–83. Ch'üan Han-sheng seems to have held the same view; see his *Chung-kuo hang hui chih tu shih* (A history of the Chinese guild system; Shanghai: Hsin sheng-ming shu-tien, 1934). Two recent Japanese articles on Sung guilds are Furubayashi Morihiro, "Sōdai shōgyō girudo no sobyō" (A rough sketch of Sung commercial guilds), *Zenrekiken kiyō* 2 (1966): 20–29; and Onodera Irio, "Sōdai ni okeru toshi no shōnin soshiki *kō* ni tsuite" (The urban merchant associations [*hang*] in the Sung), *Kanazawa daigaku, Hōbungakubu ronshū, shigaku hen* 13(1966): 42–74.

2. Niida Noboru, "The Industrial and Commercial Guilds of Peking and Religion and Fellowcountrymanship as Elements of their Coherence," trans. M. Eder, *Folklore Studies* 9(1950): 200.

3. Ho Ping-ti, *Studies on the Population of China, 1368–1953* (Cambridge: Harvard University Press, 1959), p. 197.

4. Niida Noboru, *Chūgoku no shakai to girudo* (Guilds and Chinese society; Tokyo: Iwanami shoten, 1951), p. 148.

5. D. J. MacGowan, "Chinese Guilds or Chambers of Commerce and Trades Unions," *Journal of the North China Branch of the Royal Asiatic Society* 21 (1886): 136. MacGowan gives no date for this excerpt, though it may be from the late eighteenth century. In any case, the problem was one often faced by alien merchants. See also "K." (J. G. Kerr?, G. Kleinwächter?), "Chinese Guilds and their Rules," *China Review* 12 (1883–84): 5–6; and for the early-eighteenth-century example of the Canton merchants at Peking,

Katō Shigeshi, "Shindai ni okeru Pekin no shōnin kaikan ni tsuite" (The *hui-kuan* of merchants at Peking in the Ch'ing), in Wada Sei, ed., *Shina keizaishi kōsho, vol.* 2 (Studies in Chinese economic history; Tokyo: Tōyō bunko, 1953), pp. 578–79.

6. Ho Ping-ti, *Chung-kuo hui kuan shih lun* (hereafter Ho 1966a; A historical survey of *Landsmannschaften* in China; Taipei: Hsüeh sheng shu chü, 1966), especially pp. 37–40.

7. This term, first used by MacGowan, has been adopted by Ho.

8. Ho 1966a, p. 17; Katō 1953, pp. 576–77.

9. MacGowan 1886: 135; Ho 1966a, p. 38; Chiang-su sheng po wu kuan, ed., *Chiang-su sheng Ming Ch'ing i lai pei k'o tzu liao hsüan chi* (hereafter CSPKTL; A collection of Ming, Ch'ing, and twentieth-century stone inscriptions from Kiangsu province; Peking: Hsin Hua shu tien, 1959), p. 24. Not within the scope of this paper are the large number of rural *hui-kuan* (especially in the central and upper Yangtze area provinces) that grew up as a result not of interregional trade but of interregional peasant migrations. See Ho Ping-ti, "The Geographic Distribution of *Hui-kuan* (*Landsmannschaften*) in Central and Upper Yangtze Provinces, with Special Reference to Interregional Migrations," *Tsing Hua Journal of Chinese Studies n.s.* 2 (Dec. 1966): 120–52 (hereafter Ho 1966b).

10. Katō 1953, p. 580. Francis L. K. Hsu, drawing on Ho's work on *hui-kuan*, states that "their purpose was the twofold one of lodging and contacts, and no other." "Chinese Kinship and Chinese Behavior," in Ho Ping-ti and Tsou Tang, eds., *China's Heritage and the Communist Political System* (Chicago: University of Chicago Press, 1968), p. 589. This is certainly incorrect unless one stretches the meaning of "contacts" to include mutual aid and religious activities as well as the extensive economic activities of those *hui-kuan* that became guilds.

11. CSPKTL, pp. 24–26.

12. An explicit statement of this change of policy was made by the Wu-lin Hang-ch'ien Hui-kuan of Soochow, which decided that it would be better to open the guild to people from Soochow than to try to keep the membership restricted. CSPKTL, p. 167. On this point see also Ho 1966a, chap. 6; Niida 1951, p. 87; Imahori Seiji, *Chūgoku no shakai kōzō* (Chinese social structure; Tokyo: Yūhikaku, 1953), p. 251; and Liu Yung-ch'eng, "Shih lun Ch'ing tai Su-chou shou kung yeh hang hui" (A draft discussion of handicraft guilds in Soochow during the Ch'ing), *Li shih yen chiu* (1959): 25.

13. CSPKTL, p. 203.

14. The terminology is not consistent, however. Sometimes *hui-kuan* and *kung-so* are virtually synonymous. For example, at the beginning of the Ch'ien-lung period in Soochow, merchants from Ning-kuo *fu* "established a public hall (*kung-so*), the Hsüan-chou Hui-kuan." CSPKTL, p. 383. For a similar usage, cf. *ibid.*, p. 25, where Soochow cloth merchants even used, among other terms, *kung-kuan.*

15. Liu 1959: 23.

16. Sylvia L. Thrupp, "The Gilds," in *The Cambridge Economic History of Europe, Vol.* 3 (Cambridge: Cambridge University Press, 1965), p. 230.

17. Liu 1959: 22, 23.

18. Imahori Seiji, "Girudo shi" (A history of guilds), in Chūgoku kenkyūjo, ed., *Gendai Chūgoku jiten* (The contemporary China encyclopedia; Tokyo: Chūgoku kenkyūjo, 1954), p. 607.

19. After writing this, I discovered that Ira Lapidus uses essentially the same point of view when discussing whether guilds existed in medieval Muslim cities. "Guilds must be distinguished from the more inclusive category of fraternal societies. Only associations which restricted their membership to a single or allied crafts and trades and existed to serve the economic as well as the social interests of their members were, properly speaking, guilds." Ira M. Lapidus, *Muslim Cities in the Later Middle Ages* (Cambridge, Mass.: Harvard University Press, 1967), p. 97.

20. Throughout this paper, I use the term "association" instead of "organization" to refer to Chinese guilds since they do not qualify as organizations in the sense in which this term is used in contemporary social science theory. Cf. Amitai Etzioni, *Modern Organizations* (Englewood Cliffs, N.J.: Prentice-Hall, 1964), p. 3, where he presents a definition of organizations (not *modern* organizations!). The Ch'ing government fits this definition very nicely; Ch'ing guilds do not. This is not to say, however, that Etzioni's and other writers' analyses of organizations have no use for this study. Ch'ing guilds were in many ways more similar to organizations than the "tribes, classes, ethnic groups, friendship groups, and families" that Etzioni gives as examples of social units that are not organizations.

21. The end of the Ming must also be considered a part of this formative period but our documentation is too scanty to allow us to elaborate on developments at that time.

22. MacGowan 1886: 146, 147, 151, 159, 171.

23. *Ibid.*: 149, 166–70, 176, 179–80, 183.

24. Imahori Seiji, *Chūgoku hōken shakai no kikō* (Chinese feudal society; Tokyo: Nihon gakujutsu shinkōkai, 1955), pp. 701–837. Many of these materials, however, appear only in edited form.

25. This work, abbreviated for convenience to CSPKTL, is fully cited in note 9.

26. Niida 1951, pp. 118, 144.

27. *Ibid.*, p. 148.

28. Thrupp 1965, p. 233.

29. CSPKTL, p. 71.

30. Niida 1951, pp. 149–50.

31. Imahori 1955, p. 786.

32. John S. Burgess, *The Guilds of Peking* (New York: Columbia University Press, 1928), p. 124.

33. Niida 1951, p. 151.

34. Important as they were, one must not overestimate the numbers of geographically based guilds. Though most of the Soochow *hui-kuan* from the late Ming on had specific geographical ties, there is clear evidence for such ties only in about one-fifth of the *kung-so*. Ho 1966a, p. 101; Liu 1959: 22.

35. Niida 1951, p. 88.

36. For other examples, see Niida 1950: 198–200; Niida 1951, p. 94; Ho 1966a, p. 104.

37. Ho 1966a, chap. 1.

38. *Ibid.*, pp. 102–3.

39. *Ibid.*, p. 107. It might be well to stress here that, whatever their original intent, guilds and less economically oriented *hui-kuan* played an important role in facilitating interregional economic and social integration in China. *Ibid.*, p. 4 of the English summary.

40. Some geographically based guilds opened their doors to outsiders, only to find that the outsiders were not interested in joining. Imahori Seiji, "Kindai ni okeru Kai-hō no shōgyō girudo ni tsuite" (Merchant guilds at Kaifeng in the modern period), in Hiroshima bunrika daigoku, Tōyōshigaku kenkyūshitsu, ed., *Tōyō no shakai* (1948), p. 379.

41. Their control of capital, together with their accumulated skill, enabled people from Shao-hsing to preserve a monopoly over the dyeing of *fu* cotton. Ho 1966a, p. 104.

42. *Ibid.*, p. 104.

43. *Ibid.*; Imahori 1953, pp. 251–52; Imahori 1955, p. 225.

44. In some cases, this animosity was codified in the rules. The 1828 rules of the Leather Box Guild of Kan-chou-fu, Kiangsi refused natives of the city entry into the guild because of the bad treatment guildsmen had received from them. Niida 1951, p. 171. See also MacGowan 1886: 181.

45. Imahori Seiji, "Shinchō ikō no totei keiyaku to girudo kisei" (Apprenticeship contracts and guild regulations from the Ch'ing onward), in Tōhō gakkai, ed., *Tōhō gakkai sōritsu jūgo shūnen kinen tōyōgaku ronshū* (Collected essays in commemoration of the fifteenth anniversary of the oriental society; Tokyo: Tōhō gakkai, 1962), p. 14.

46. CSPKTL, p. 152.

47. Even where the length of apprenticeship was not stated clearly in the rules of the guild, custom tended to standardize it. See, for example, Imahori Seiji, "Shindai ni okeru minatomachi no shakai taisei" (The social structure of a Ch'ing harbor town), *Hōsei shi kenkyū* 16 (1966): 1–29. In the river port of Ho-k'ou-chen in Shansi, the term of apprenticeship was not fixed but usually lasted three or four years. This was perhaps owing mainly to custom rather than, as Imahori suggests, to the amount of time required before an apprentice could do the work expected of a full-fledged laborer.

48. Apprentices sometimes received small amounts of spending money. CSPKTL, p. 71; Imahori 1955, p. 459.

49. CSPKTL, p. 71.

50. With the exception of the apprenticeship system, which was on the fringe of guild concerns, family ties seem to have played a rather small role in guild organization. One looks in vain, in this early period at least, for evidence of kinship requirements for entry into the guild, for privileges reserved for sons and close relatives of members, and so forth. It is of course possible that family ties played a far greater role than is apparent from the regulations. Shopowners would surely have preferred to hire relatives where possible, and sons must ordinarily have followed their fathers into the same trade. On the other hand, the continuing flow of people from the surrounding countryside into the cities must have resulted in a constant infusion of new blood into the trades, and hence into the guilds.

51. Imahori 1962, on the basis of the *Shang ku pien lan*, a commercial manual of 1792. We have in the apprenticeship system an extreme example

of the kind of vertical patronage relationships that pervaded traditional Chinese cities and that were ordinarily far more important than horizontal class ties. He who would rush in to analyze this society with a ready-made class interpretation borrowed from modern Western experience will likely emerge with a skewed understanding of how it really functioned.

52. In the 1829 regulations of the building craftsmen of Kuei-sui, an apprentice who completed his term was required to pay the equivalent of two days' salary to the guild. Shopkeepers were expected to enforce this rule and were fined double the fee if they did not. Imahori 1955, p. 786; see also p. 744, the regulations of the Fine Hides Guild, which demanded a fee from apprentices both when they began and when they finished their apprenticeships. In Soochow, a woodworker who had finished his apprenticeship and wished to open a shop paid half as much for the privilege as an outsider. CSPKTL, p. 108.

53. Niida 1951, p. 117.

54. For instance, the Peking Waiters' Guild had 30 officers in the 1920's. Burgess 1928, p. 134. The Kuei-sui Fine Hides Guild might have anywhere from ten to over twenty officers. Imahori 1955, p. 470.

55. Niida 1951, pp. 148, 149; Imahori 1955, p. 786.

56. As quoted in Kung-chuan Hsiao, *Rural China: Imperial Control in the Nineteenth Century* (Seattle: University of Washington Press, 1960), p. 273.

57. Niida Noboru, "Girudo" (Guilds), in Heibonsha, ed., *Ajia rekishi jiten*, Vol. 2 (An encyclopedia of Asian history; Tokyo: Heibonsha, 1959), p. 442.

58. Niida 1959, p. 442; Imahori 1953, pp 259–60.

59. Burgess 1928, p. 140.

60. Niida 1951, p. 119.

61. *Ibid.*

62. Imahori 1953, p. 259.

63. Niida 1951, pp. 148–49.

64. Imahori 1955, p. 786.

65. Niida 1951, p. 148. Serious matters regularly had to be settled in a full and open discussion by the members even if this required the calling of an extraordinary meeting.

66. Imahori 1955, p. 471.

67. *Ibid.*, p. 786.

68. Niida 1951, p. 148.

69. Niida 1950: 191.

70. Niida 1951, p. 151.

71. Ho 1966a, pp. 14, 17.

72. CSPKTL, p. 24. See also Niida 1951, p. 152.

73. The Peking Dyers' Guild explicitly stated that this was the only expense of the guild. Niida 1951, p. 150.

74. Imahori 1953, p. 265.

75. Niida 1951, p. 151; in Peking, new drug shops had to pay one percent of the capital invested as an entry fee into the guild. Katō 1953, p. 570.

76. Niida 1951, p. 149. Contributions over a ten-year span by 26 shops to buy the Ch'ien-chiang Hui-kuan ranged from a maximum of 887 taels, 7 mace, 3 candareens from one shop to a mere 5 taels, 8 mace from the lowest contributor. (The latter may have been a newly opened shop, since it occurs at

Notes to Pages 569–74

the end of the list, which is not arranged according to the size of the contributions.) CSPKTL, pp. 26–27.

77. Imahori 1955, pp. 473–74, 744, 786. A detailed picture of guild finances in Soochow could be assembled from the materials in CSPKTL, with its wealth of information on fees and membership.
78. Ho 1959, p. 205.
79. The same attitude persisted into the twentieth century. Burgess 1928, p. 211.
80. Imahori 1955, p. 744.
81. Niida 1950: 201.
82. Imahori 1955, p. 786.
83. Niida 1951, pp. 167, 173; Imahori 1955, pp. 225ff.
84. Katō 1953, pp. 564–66.
85. *Ibid.*, p. 568.
86. "There are no laws [i.e., guild regulations] respecting the hours of labour of those who work by day; custom adjusts that." MacGowan 1886: 178. For an exception from the very end of the Ch'ing, and one that spells out working hours in some detail, see Niida 1951, p. 186.
87. Imahori 1953, p. 280.
88. Niida 1951, p. 149.
89. MacGowan 1886: 180. For other mentions of the fixing of prices, see CSPKTL, pp. 203, 217.
90. R. K. Douglas, *Society in China* (London: 1901), p. 146.
91. Niida 1951, p. 179.
92. *Ibid.*, p. 36.
93. *Ibid.*, p. 96.
94. *Ibid.*, p. 149.
95. *Ibid.*, p. 150. Morse has also pointed out the role of guilds in standardizing weights and measures. Hosea B. Morse, *The Gilds of China with an Account of the Gild Merchant or Co-hong of Canton* (London: Longmans, Green and Co., 1909), p. 25. Imahori, however, feels that the standardization of weights and measures was mainly carried on by brokers' guilds rather than by the guilds in general. Imahori 1953, p. 281.
96. Niida 1951, p. 96.
97. *Ibid.*, p. 194.
98. Burgess 1928, p. 198.
99. MacGowan 1886: 180–81.
100. Burgess 1928, p. 293.
101. See, for just a few examples, CSPKTL, pp. 5–6, 13–14. 33–36, 40–42, 67–68.
102. Ch'üan Han-sheng, "Ya p'ien chan cheng ch'ien Chiang-su te mien fang shih yeh" (Cotton spinning in Kiangsu before the Opium War), *Ch'ing hua hsüeh pao*, n.s. 1, no. 3 (Sept. 1958): 35–36.
103. Cf. the references in note 101.
104. CSPKTL, pp. 69–72.
105. Burgess 1928, p. 130.
106. CSPKTL, pp. 40–42, 72–73, 504.
107. Imahori 1954, p. 611.
108. CSPKTL, pp. 28–29, 299–300.

109. Niida 1951, pp. 223–24.
110. *Ibid.*, p. 148.
111. CSPKTL, p. 375.
112. Niida 1951, p. 148; CSPKTL, pp. 299–300.
113. Morse 1909, p. 49.
114. Following the usage of certain European historians, these guild federations have often been referred to as "guild merchants." The term is obscure, and best avoided. For more on these federations, see Imahori 1953, pp. 295–327; Imahori 1955, pp. 28–111; Imahori 1966; and Niida Noboru, "Shindai Kōnan no girudo māchanto" (A guild merchant in Hunan during the Ch'ing) Tōyōshi kenkyū 21 (1961), pp. 315–36.
115. Etzioni 1964, p. 14.
116. Imahori 1953, p. 263.
117. For example, *miao, an, tz'u,* and *kuan*.
118. Niida 1951, pp. 148–49.
119. *Ibid.*, p. 125; Imahori 1955, p. 724.
120. Niida 1951, p. 149.
121. Imahori 1955, p. 473.
122. Niida 1951, p. 152. Imahori 1953, p. 289, notes that many of the same deities worshiped by the guilds were also worshiped in the villages.
123. Imahori 1953, p. 253.
124. Niida 1950: 196; see also Burgess 1928, pp. 89–90, 171.
125. Katō 1953, p. 568.
126. Niida 1950: 201; Niida 1951, p. 148.
127. Burgess 1928, p. 183.
128. Ch'ü T'ung-tsu, *Local Government in China under the Ch'ing* (Cambridge, Mass: Harvard University Press, 1962), pp. 164, 166.
129. Niida 1951, pp. 149, 150.
130. *Ibid.*, p. 149.
131. Imahori 1953, pp. 247–48; Niida 1951, pp. 245ff.
132. Burgess 1928, pp. 209–10.
133. MacGowan 1886: 138.
134. Even when a clear dispute did arise between members, the goal was to reach a decision satisfactory to both parties. Niida 1951, p. 148.
135. Imahori 1954, p. 609.
136. Niida 1951, pp. 150–52.
137. MacGowan 1886: 184.
138. Even when the officials supported the merchants in their struggles with the workers in Soochow, the most severe punishment they ordinarily decreed was to send a "trouble-making" worker, after flogging, back to his native area (*ti-hui yuan-chi*), a punishment that deprived him of his chance to make a living. CSPKTL, pp. 41–42, 72–73.
139. Niida 1951, p. 148.
140. The same was also generally true in the clans, where "heavy fines gave the clan a set of adequate sanctions to back up their own internal organization without the trouble and expense of taking an offender to trial." Denis Twitchett, "The Fan Clan's Charitable Estate, 1050–1760," in David S. Nivison and Arthur Wright, eds., *Confucianism in Action* (Stanford: Stanford University Press, 1959), p. 117. Furthermore, in the clans, too, expulsion was

ordinarily the severest penalty. (*Ibid.*) This reminds us once again not to assume too great a dichotomy between practices in the countryside and those in the city. The style of personal relations that originated in a rural environment often changed surprisingly little when transplanted to the city.

141. Only this can account for the frequent concern shown by the guilds that their halls not be misappropriated by people who had no right to use them. In one extreme case, a guild found its hall secretly sold by an unscrupulous manager! CSPKTL, pp. 300–301.

School-Temple and City God

1. For the two prefectures I investigated (Ning-po and T'ai-wan), I have data from all eleven counties formed before 1875. Only three types of shrines of the *ssu-tien* occurred in all eleven. They were City God temples, school-temples, and temples to Kuan-ti. In ten counties there were one or more open altars to the Land and Grain (*She-chi t'an*), to Wind-Rain-Thunder-Clouds (*feng-yü-lei-yün t'an*), to Mountains and Rivers (*shan-ch'uan t'an*), and to unworshiped dead (*Li t'an*). Regional variation comes into play with the God of Literature (*Wen-ch'ang*) and the God of the Eastern Peak (*Tung-yüeh*), who are more a feature of Ning-po than of T'ai-wan, and with the God of Agriculture (*Hsien-nung*) and T'ien-hou, whose shrines were more frequent in T'ai-wan than in Ning-po.

C. K. Yang used eight county gazetteers dating from the 1920's and 1930's for his *Religion in Chinese Society* (Berkeley: University of Calif. Press, 1961). The counties were scattered throughout China—two in Hopei, two in Kiangsu, two in Kwangtung, and one each in Hupeh and Szechwan. Extrapolating official shrines from his more general survey I find that, of the open altars, Land and Grain, Wind-etc., and Hsien-nung occurred in all eight counties, unworshiped dead in six. Of the temples, those to the City God, to Confucius, to Kuan-ti, and to Wen-ch'ang occurred in all eight. But so too did temples to the God of the Eastern Peak and to Dragon Kings (gods for the control of rain, but not constituting a single cult and only marginally part of the official religion), while T'ien-hou occurred only in the four *hsien* of Kiangsu and Kwangtung.

2. The two main difficulties in compiling this list were (1) that for many temples there were no records of establishment or repair, and (2) that more than one Kuan-ti, T'ien-hou, and Wen-ch'ang temple in each county was sponsored by officials, making it difficult to know which was the one used in the annual official rites. The sources for Taiwan (all of them in the Bank of Taiwan edition) were Cheng P'ei-kuei, *Tan-shui t'ing chih*, 1872; Chou Chung-hsüan, *Chu-lo hsien chih*, 1718; *Fu-chien t'ung chih T'ai-wan fu*, 1830–69; Lien Heng, *T'ai-wan t'ung shih*, 1918; Lin Hsiung-hsiang, *T'ai-wan sheng t'ung chih kao*, ch. 2, ts'e 1, 1956; *T'ai-wan hsien chih*, 1721; *T'ai-wan t'ung chih*, 1897. For Ning-po prefecture I used *(Chia-ch'ing) Ning-po fu chih*, 1560; *(Ch'ien-lung) Ning-po fu chih*, 1733; *(Ch'ien-tao) Ssu-ming t'u ching*, 1169; *(Pao-ch'ing) Ssu-ming chih*, 1228; *(K'ai-ching) Ssu-ming hsü chih*, 1259; *(Yen-yu) Ssu-ming chih*, 1320; *(Chih-cheng) Ssu-ming hsü chih*, 1342; *(Ch'ien-lung) Yin hsien chih*, 1788; *(Kuang-hsü) Yin hsien chih*, 1876; *(Min-kuo) Yin hsien t'ung chih*, 1936, book 7, 19.

3. For examples of the *fen-hsiang* links of Taipei's major temples, and for

a general description of the process of subdivision, see my paper "City Temples in Taipei Under Three Regimes" in Mark Elvin and G. William Skinner, eds., *The Chinese City Between Two Worlds* (Stanford, Calif.: Stanford University Press, 1974).

4. Yang 1961, pp. 98–99.

5. Meng-tzu, *T'eng Wen kung*, Part II, which is *Mencius*, Book III, Part II, chap. 9, paragraph 9 in Legge's translation.

6. *Chu-lo hsien chih*, ch. 5, Hsüeh hsiao chih.

7. *Hung kung ching shih lu* (Record of paying respects in the school-temple), "Shih-tien Hsü" (The order of the rites of *shih tien*), 1686, edition of 1835.

8. This is the phrase used in John K. Shyrock's translation in *The Origin and Development of the State Cult of Confucius* (New York: Appleton-Century, 1932), p. 225.

9. Lien Heng, *T'ai-wan t'ung shih*, ch. 4, "Shen-chiao." This history of Taiwan was published in 1918 after ten years of preparation. Lien was a patriot writing under Japanese occupation, and he had obviously had a traditional classical education. His story is much like an extended gazetteer, like traditional Chinese historiographic writing. I think I am justified in taking it as a product of late Ch'ing China.

10. See the *Tz'u hai* dictionary's entry on *t'ien* for quotations from the *Shih ching* and the *Hsiao ching*.

11. Yūji Muramatsu, "Some Themes in Chinese Rebel Ideologies," in Arthur F. Wright, ed., *The Confucian Persuasion* (Stanford, Calif.: Stanford University Press, 1960), p. 255, suggests the broad outlines of a middle class of priests, monks, jobless lower degree-holders, fortune-tellers, and sorcerers that fell between the emperor and officials above and peasant farmers, merchants, and artisans below.

12. The description of the worship at the Altar of Heaven is taken from my own reading of the K'ang-hsi edition of the *Hui tien* and from E. T. Williams's reading of various other editions and his personal observation of the ceremony during the closing days of the dynasty reported in "The State Religion of China during the Manchu Dynasty," *Journal of the North China Branch of the Royal Asiatic Society*, new (2d) series 44 (1913): 11–45.

13. The magistrate of Wei *hsien* in Shantung, a noted calligrapher, poet, scholar, and wit, in 1752 wrote a commemoration of his repair and extension of the City God temple. He drew attention to the substance and brilliance of the new images and the contents of the temple. "Moreover, outside the principal gate of the temple a stage for theatrical performances has been erected. . . . Can it be that there are *shen* who delight in theatrical performances? Of course not. . . . It is simply because people wish to give expression to their feelings of gratitude that they are led to pay court to the great *shen* in these multiplied acts of love and worship. Now, as to the city god, since it is sacrificed to as though it had a personal existence, why should not such things as songs and dances be employed to give it enjoyment. But let the plays be about ancient times so that they be instructive and prohibit the low, clandestine, vulgar, and grosser passions. Fu Hsi, Shen Nung, Huang-ti, Yao, Shun, Yü, T'ang, Wen-wang, Wu-wang, Chou-kung, and Confucius [the whole line of legendary sage-kings] having been men were later deified. It is proper to sacrifice to them

as those who had a personal existence. But Heaven, Earth, Sun, Moon, Wind, Thunder, Hills and Streams, Rivers and Mountains, Soil and Grain, Walls and Moats [= Ch'eng-huang, the City God], the Impluvium, and the Stove [this is the full range of nonhuman deities in the official religion], although deified, have no personal existence and should not be sacrificed to as if they had. Yet from ancient times even the sages have all sacrificed to them as though they had a personal existence" (translation by the Reverend McCartee in *Journal of the North China Branch of the Royal Asiatic Society*, 1869-70, article XI). I take this to be typical of the agnostic Confucian official line, didactic and paternal in the rationalization of popular religion and perplexed by its similarity to the official rites.

14. This is the shortest of the oaths I have found and comes from the 1788 *Yin hsien chih*. The oath given from an inscription of 1810 in the *Chang-hua hsien chih, I wen chih*, as cited in *T'ai-wan sheng t'ung chih kao*, pp. 207-8, has the newly appointed magistrate declaring confidence in himself as the imperial delegate to look after the people. But his family might be unprincipled. He cannot control what is beyond his ears and eyes and knowledge. The god and his assistants can, however, so the magistrate asks the god to lend him power to fortify his virtue.

15. Kung-chuan Hsiao, *Rural China: Imperial Control in the Nineteenth Century* (Seattle: University of Washington Press, 1960), chap. 6, makes this quite clear—see particularly notes 193 and 197 to that chapter.

16. John H. Gray, *China: A History of the Laws, Manners and Customs of the People* (London: Macmillan, 1878), vol. 1, pp. 118-19.

17. J. J. M. de Groot, trans. by C. G. Chavannes, "Les fêtes annuellement célébrés à Emoui," *Annales du Museé Guimet*, 11 (1886): 68-72: 12 (1886): 586ff.

18. The prayer of Hu Ch'eng-kung, appointed subcircuit military intendant of Taiwan in 1824, is to be found in *T'ai-wan wen hsien*, 11, no. 2 (June 1960): 256.

19. The limits of the official religion as a matter of rank and dignity, and the official interpretation of the people's religion below it as an extension of it, are well demonstrated in an account by Magistrate Wang of Ning-yüan *hsien*, Hunan, in 1789, quoted by Hsiao 1960, chap. 6, note 204. Wang relates how it was the custom in the rain ceremony for images from all the local temples to be carried in procession to the yamen where the officials were to bow to them—a ritual similar to that described for Amoy by De Groot. When the rain ceremony occurred in 1789, Magistrate Wang refused to bow, despite the urgings of the clerks of the Division of Ritual. He explained that the local temple gods were only the equivalents of local elders, and since his office was superior to that of local elders he should not be expected to bow to their images.

20. Hsiao 1960, pp. 226-29.

21. See especially J. J. M. de Groot, *Sectarianism and Religious Persecution in China* (Amsterdam: Johannes Müller, 1903, 1904; 2 vols.; reprinted Taipei: Ch'eng-wen, 1971), pp. 102-9, 113-18, 244-48. See also Yang 1961, pp. 187-91, 308.

22. For histories of Kuan-ti and Wen-ch'ang and their canonization, see A. S. Goodrich, *The Peking Temple of the Eastern Peak* (Monumenta Serica, Nagoya, 1964), pp. 120ff and 128ff. This temple seems to have been to the

imperial capital what the Ling-ying miao was to Ningpo and the Lung-shan ssu was to Taipei—the most important popular temple, and bordering on the official religion. The gods enshrined in it ranged from those worshiped by scholar-officials for luck in the examination and related areas through almost every kind of god worshiped for luck in northern China. This admirable book documents them all.

23. The Ch'ing emperors also had an exclusively Manchu official religion that came under the Department of Ceremonial of the Imperial Household. I am indebted to Jonathan Spence for informing me of this.

Urban Social Control

1. Vilhelm Aubert, *Sociology of Law; Selected Readings* (Harmondsworth, Eng.: Penguin Books, 1969), Intro. p. 12.

2. See, for example, Martin C. Yang, *A Chinese Village: Taitou, Shantung* (New York: Columbia University Press, 1945), chap. 13.

3. See especially the seventh maxim of the Sacred Edict (*Sheng Yü*), which magistrates were supposed to read aloud periodically to their assembled subjects. English translation in F. W. Baller, *The Sacred Edict: with a translation of the colloquial rendering, notes and vocabulary* (Shanghai: American Presbyterian Mission Press, 1892). See also Derk Bodde and Clarence Morris, *Law in Imperial China Exemplified by 190 Ch'ing Dynasty Cases (Translated from the Hsing-an Hui-lan with ... commentaries)* (Cambridge: Harvard University Press, 1967), chap. I, "Basic Concepts of Chinese Law," pp. 3–51. Cf. note 8 below. As C. K. Yang has observed, Weber's statement that Chinese statutes were codified *ethical* rather than *legal* norms is fully validated in T'ung-tsu Ch'ü, *Law and Society in Traditional China*. See Yang's Introduction to *The Religion of China*, transl. by H. H. Gerth (New York: Macmillan, 1964), p. xxvii.

4. The Chinese text of these statutes is in "Hu lü: Ko ch'eng" section, under the heading "Yen fa" (salt laws, including also evasion of duties on other commodities), seven statutes; under "Ch'ien chai" (money-lending and debt), three statutes, and "Shih ch'an" (markets and marketplaces), five statutes (in most editions and compilations of *Ta Ch'ing lü li*, ch. 13–15). The relevant sections of *Hsing an hui lan*, transl. in Bodde and Morris 1967, are 80, 82, 86, and 87. On driving another to commit suicide (*wei-pi jen chih ssu*), see P. Guy Boulais, *Manuel du code chinois* (Shanghai: Impr. de la Mission catholique, 1924; Variétés sinologiques, 55): 577–79. See also sect. 172.4 of *Hsing an hui lan*, transl. in Bodde and Morris 1967, though the cases selected involve crimes of passion only.

5. For example, see S.F.C. Milsom, *Historical Foundations of the Common Law* (London: Butterworths, 1969), especially chaps. 10 and 12; Emile Durkheim, *Professional Ethics and Civic Morals* (1st Eng. ed.; London: Routledge and Kegan Paul, 1957), chap. XV, "The Right of Contract."

6. Review of *Legal Institutions in Manchu China*, by Sybille van der Sprenkel, *Pacific Affairs*, 35, no. 4 (1962–63): 396–97. Ch'ü agrees, however, that a large area of life was regulated by unofficial organization or by unwritten custom, and that people preferred extrajudicial mediation to litigation.

7. On the salt merchants generally, see Ping-ti Ho, "The Salt Merchants

of Yangchou: A Study of Commercial Capitalists in Eighteenth Century China," *Harvard Journal of Asiatic Studies*, 17, no. 1/2: 130–68. On the legal status of salt merchants, Ho quotes the following description by a Censor in 1723: "A salt merchant, being from a well-to-do family, participates in the collection of taxes for the state. His profession should not be compared to that of an ordinary lowly merchant, nor can his position be filled by one from a small household. He should consider himself important rather than insignificant." They were said to be merchants who could afford to pay taxation in advance and bear certain economic losses without being materially affected. The way some reached this enviable state by evading the law is illustrated in Bodde and Morris 1967, pp. 260–61.

8. If proper allowance is made for differences due to later developments, Morton H. Fried's study of Ch'u-hsien (Anhwei) in the 1940's may perhaps be taken to illustrate the intermeshing of relationships based on kinship, friendship, occupation, and business in one town. *Fabric of Chinese Society: A Study of the Social Life of a Chinese County Seat* (New York: Praeger, 1953).

9. Y. K. Leong and L. K. Tao, *Village and Town Life in China* (London: Allen and Unwin, 1915), pp. 86–87.

10. John Stewart Burgess, *The Guilds of Peking* (New York: Columbia University Press, 1928), p. 31. Hosea Ballou Morse, *The Gilds of China* (London: Longmans, 1909 [Reissued Taipei: Ch'eng-wen, 1966]), p. 3. Cf. Frank W. Walbank, "Trade and Industry Under the Later Roman Empire in the West," in M. Postan and E. E. Rich, eds., *Cambridge Economic History of Europe, Vol. II, Trade and Industry in the Middle Ages* (Cambridge: Cambridge University Press, 1952), chap. 2; and Steven Runciman, "Byzantine Trade and Industry," in *ibid.*, chap. 3. On comparable organization in Africa, see Peter Lloyd, "Craft Organisation in Yoruba Towns," *Africa*, 23 (Jan. 1953): 30–44.

11. Daniel J. MacGowan, "Chinese Guilds or Chambers of Commerce and Trade Unions," *Journal of the China Branch of the Royal Asiatic Society*, n.s. 21, no. 3 (1886): 141, 175.

12. *Ibid.*: 136–37; and George Jamieson, *Chinese Family and Commercial Law* (Shanghai: Kelly and Walsh, 1921), p. 115.

13. Some guild rules appear to be at variance with general trading custom that accounts should be settled three times a year—evidence perhaps of changes being introduced at this period, and no doubt another reason for the "reformulation" of rules or for the adoption of rules in cases where they were not previously explicit.

14. Sidney D. Gamble, *Peking: A Social Survey* (New York: Doran, 1921), p. 194; see also Charles F. Remer, *A Study of Chinese Boycotts, with Special Reference to their Economic Effectiveness* (Baltimore: Johns Hopkins Press, 1933 [Reissued Taipei: Ch'eng-wen, 1967]), chap. II.

15. MacGowan 1886: 184.

16. This has recently been suggested about the Protestant ethic by Thelma McCormack. See "The Protestant Ethic and the Spirit of Socialism," *British Journal of Sociology*, 20, 3 (Sept. 1969): 269.

17. Peter J. Golas, in his paper elsewhere in this volume, mentions petitions to approve rules and to forbid workers to organize. MacGowan 1886 (p. 158) reports that at a time of financial crisis the Ningpo bankers at

Shanghai petitioned the magistrate for a proclamation against the brokers, who had organized a guild of their own.

18. "A.C.D.," "Chinese Commercial Law," *China Review*, 2 (1873–74): 123–30; Justus Doolittle, *Social Life of the Chinese* (London: Sampson, Low, Son, and Marston, 1868), p. 464; Thomas R. Jernigan, *China in Law and Commerce* (New York: Macmillan, 1905), chap. 10.

19. Jernigan 1905, p. 260.

20. "A.C.D." 1873–74: p. 147; Jamieson 1921, pp. 122ff.

21. Doolittle 1868, p. 451.

22. *Ta Ch'ing lü li*, ch. 14, "Hu lü: Shih ch'an" section, under Statute, "Ssu ch'ung ya hang." See Boulais 1924, pp. 349–51; Jamieson 1921 translates the statute and summarizes the substatutes at pp. 112–13. Abram Lind, *A Chapter of the Chinese Penal Code* (Leiden: Brill, 1887) gives the Chinese text, with a translation and annotation; but in the conference to which this paper was presented Professor Lien-sheng Yang warned that it is not always reliable. George T. Staunton, *Ta Tsing Leu Lee* . . . (London: Cadell and Davies, 1810), sect. 153, p. 163, omits substatutes.

23. Burgess 1928, pp. 200–263.

24. Jamieson 1921, pp. 126–27.

25. Jernigan 1905, p. 239. On such processes of transition generally, cf. Michael Banton, "The Restructuring of Social Relationships," in Aidan Southall, ed., *Social Change in Modern Africa* (London: Oxford University Press, 1961), pp. 7–8.

26. Especially Bodde and Morris 1967. Dr. David Buxbaum presented similar conclusions, drawn from documentary and field study of Taiwan, to a conference on Chinese Legal Tradition sponsored by the Subcommittee on Chinese Law of the ACLS-SSRC Joint Committee on Contemporary China, August 1969.

27. See Sybille van der Sprenkel, *Legal Institutions in Manchu China* (London: Athlone Press, 1962; London School of Economics, Monographs on Social Anthropology, 24), p. 109, especially the translated quotation from Niida Noboru. On nonpayment of debts, see the discussion on pp. 612–13 above. Official Chinese courts had not developed any special law or doctrine of bankruptcy. One might suggest a parallel between the settlements here described and modern Western practice in the field of family law, where divorce, separation, and maintenance settlements are based on a consideration of the whole relationship, all the resources and obligations of the parties coming under review. The Chinese seem to have developed long ago a similar type of machinery in the commercial area as a form of customary procedure. Indeed, there is said to have been chaos in Hong Kong when Chinese customary mechanisms were replaced by statutes (the Hong Kong Bankruptcy Law of 1864 and the Hong Kong Partnership Amendment Ordinance of 1867). See *China Review*, 11 (July 1882–June 1883), p. 52.

28. Jamieson 1921, pp. 116–19, 126.

29. Cf. Fried 1953, chap. 5, "Non-kin relationships in an urban milieu."

30. It would seem not implausible to suggest that the guarantor-mediator's role, at one or two removes, may have been a point of entry to the commercial scene for the gentry. Doubtless many merchants who obtained rank by purchase remained merchants at heart. Further research in this area might

yield interesting results. At present one cannot go much beyond speculation. Chung-li Chang's study of the sources of gentry income contains two quite suggestive cases. Chang Kuang-tsu (ca. Chia-ch'ing period) purchased a title and became active in local affairs in Chekiang. He is said to have solved many disputes that could not be solved by the magistrate (possibly a cliché for skill as a mediator), and it is reported that he held overdue loans amounting to 10,000 taels (another cliché for large sums) and that he cancelled the loans of needy debtors. His brother, who purchased his rank after many examination failures, became an assistant magistrate in Kiangsi. Hsia Fang-yü, who had a varied career which involved being a salt merchant, an imperial student, and a businessman opened a native bank and made a name for settling disputes. See Chung-li Chang, *The Income of the Chinese Gentry* (Seattle: University of Washington Press, 1962), pp. 180, 182.

31. Gray mentions one such society formed in 1886 exclusively by women. See John Henry Gray, *China: A History of the Laws, Manners, and Customs of the People* (London: Macmillan, 1878), vol. 2, p. 86.

32. See Gray 1878, vol. 2, pp. 79–86.

33. Doolittle 1868, p. 467.

34. Jernigan 1905 (pp. 225–26, 237, 257–58) refers to a general willingness to meet obligations and to a general long-term interest in the success of transactions. He also speaks of the reliability, from the point of view of a traveler in the interior needing to change money, of pawnshops in prefectural and county-level cities, where no bad money was given and both silver and copper currency were always genuine. One cannot tell from this whether the stress is on the fact that the places mentioned were administrative centers or that they were located in the interior. In either case they were probably more typical of traditional China than the coastal cities better known to Westerners would have been, so the statement has good evidential value.

35. Donald R. DeGlopper, "The Origins and Resolution of Conflict in Traditional Chinese Society" (Unpublished master's thesis in Anthropology, University of London, 1965). I should like to express my appreciation of this work and indebtedness to it. My own point of departure in writing this conference paper was the question whether economic development had not invalidated the premises of the dominant Chinese ethic. His was dissatisfaction with the "consensus model" of Chinese society and its exclusion of all conflict. A convergence has resulted, which leaves me in some doubt about who originated some of the ideas.

36. International Sociological Association, in collaboration with Jessie Bernard et al., *The Nature of Conflict* (Paris: UNESCO, 1957), p. 111. Lewis A. Coser's distinction between social processes that are of their nature finite or transitory and those that continue until explicit provision is made to bring them to an end is relevant here. See "The Termination of Conflict," *Journal of Conflict Resolution*, 5 (Dec. 1961): 347–53.

Social Structure in a Nineteenth-Century Taiwanese Port City

1. Max Weber, *The City* (Glencoe, Ill.: Free Press, 1958; originally published in 1921), p. 119.

2. See Lawrence W. Crissman, "The Segmentary Structure of Urban Over-

seas Chinese Communities," *Man*, n.s. 2, 2 (1967); Maurice Freedman, "Immigrants and Associations: Chinese in Nineteenth Century Singapore," *Comparative Studies in Society and History*, 3, 1 (1960); G. William Skinner, *Leadership and Power in the Chinese Community of Thailand* (Ithaca, N.Y.: Cornell University Press, 1958).

3. Fieldwork in Lu-kang from April 1967 to October 1968 was supported by a grant from the Foreign Area Fellowship Program; subsequent work was made possible by a grant from the Cornell University China Program.

4. For a complete account of sources, see Donald R. DeGlopper, *City on the Sands: Social Structure in a Nineteenth Century Chinese City*. Doctoral dissertation in Anthropology, Cornell University, 1973.

5. See Chou Hsien-wen, *Ch'ing tai T'ai-wan ching chi shih* (An economic history of Taiwan during the Ch'ing period; Taipei: T'ai-wan yin hang, 1957); and Wang Shih-ch'ing, "Lu-kang k'ai kang shih" (History of the opening of Lu-kang as a port), *T'ai-wan wen hsien*, 19, 1 (1968).

6. Wang Shih-ch'ing 1968, p. 7.

7. *Chang-hua hsien chih* (Chang-hua county gazetteer [1831]; Taipei: T'ai-wan yin hang, 1964), vol. 1, pp. 40–41.

8. Taiwan (Sōtokufu), Rinji Taiwan kyūkan chōsakai, Dai nibu, ed., *Dai nibu chōsa keizai shiryō hōkoku* (Report and materials of the Second Section [of the Taiwanese Customs Research Commission] on the economy; Tokyo: Sōtokufu, 1905), vol. 1, p. 581.

9. A copy of the inscription may be found in *T'ai-wan chung pu pei wen chi cheng* (Complete collection of stone inscriptions from Central Taiwan; Taipei: T'ai-wan yin hang, 1962), pp. 78–79.

10. Quoted in Wang Shih-ch'ing 1968, p. 9.

11. Jacques Amyot, *The Manila Chinese: Familism in the Philippine Environment* (Quezon City: Ateneo de Manila University, Institute of Philippine Culture, 1973), p. 35.

12. William A. Pickering, *Pioneering in Formosa* (London: Hurst and Blackett, 1898), p. 204.

13. Amyot 1960, p. 51.

14. I have discussed the question of neighborhood definition in present-day Lu-kang in "Religion and Ritual in Lukang," in Arthur P. Wolf, ed., *Religion and Ritual in Chinese Society* (Stanford, Calif.: Stanford University Press, 1974), pp. 64–65.

15. For the relation between territorial units, temples, and incense burners, see my paper and those by Stephan Feuchtwang and Arthur P. Wolf in Wolf 1974, and Stephan Feuchtwang, "City Temples in Taipei Under Three Regimes," in Mark Elvin and G. William Skinner, eds., *The Chinese City Between Two Worlds* (Stanford, Calif.: Stanford University Press, 1974).

16. Chou Hsien-wen 1957, p. 8.

17. Pickering 1898, pp. 204–5.

18. On the rebellion of Shih Chiu-tuan, see William M. Speidel, *Liu Ming-ch'uan in Taiwan: 1884–1891* (Doctoral dissertation in History, Yale University, 1967), p. 231; and *T'ai-wan t'ung chih* (General gazetteer of Taiwan, 1893; Taipei: T'ai-wan yin hang, 1962), vol. 4, pp. 885–86.

19. See Skinner 1958, and William E. Willmott, *The Political Structure of the Chinese Community in Cambodia* (London: Athlone Press, 1970).

20. Edmund R. Leach, *Political systems of highland Burma* (London: G. Bell, 1954), p. 8.
21. Georg Simmel, *Conflict and the Web of Group Affiliations* (Translated by K. Wolff, Glencoe, Ill.: Free Press, 1955); Max Gluckman, *Custom and Conflict in Africa* (Oxford: Blackwell, 1956).

Neighborhood Cult Associations in Traditional Tainan

1. In the same period, the town of Chia-i had about 4,500 households and 52 temples. Chang-hua had even more: some 60 temples for a population of about 3,000 households.
2. These were mostly of mediumistic origin or dedicated to a local saint, e.g., Ku-fu-jen ma, a virtuous widow. Cf. *T'ai-nan hsien shih ssu miao ta kuan* (Temples in Tainan and T'ai-nan *hsien*; Kaohsiung, 1963), p. 56.
3. See, for instance, Suzuki Seiichirō, *Taiwan kyūkan: Kankonsōsai to nenjū gyōji* (Taiwanese customs: Coming-of-age, marriage, funerals, and the annual round of festivities; Taipei: Taiwan nichinichi shimpōsha, 1934), p. 48.
4. In 1928, the number of *chi-ssu kung-yeh* for the entire island was estimated at 11,491. Cf. Kajiwara Michiyoshi, "Taiwan nōmin seikatsu kō" (An examination of the life of Taiwanese peasants), *Taiwan jihō*, nos. 236–41 (Aug. 1939–Jan. 1940).
5. The *poe*, as they are called in Hokkien, are two blocks made of split bamboo roots with one rounded and one flat side. The learned character used is *kao*. Even if a member did not take part in the throwing of the divining blocks, the others would throw for him and he might still be selected. This device was often used when a certain group of people wished to keep the incense burner to themselves. They simply threw for all their absentee friends, thus enlarging their chances of hitting the highest score.
6. One *chia* equals 2.39 acres.
7. In a few instances, supporting associations built houses on land belonging to the temple they helped.
8. Shih Po-erh [Chinese name of Kristofer M. Schipper], "T'ai-wan chih tao chiao wen hsien" (Bibliography of Taoism in Taiwan), *T'ai-wan wen hsien*, 17, no. 3 (Sept. 1966): 173–92.
9. There were many temples and associations in different quarters for the worship of the same saint, e.g., four temples to Ma-tsu, two to Kuan-yü, and so on. Because of this, and also because the list gives temples as well as associations, I have adopted the term "cult."
10. Tainan City has two Ch'eng-huang miao, one for the *fu* of which the city was the capital, the other for the *hsien*. The first was built in 1673, the second in 1886.
11. *Tainan shū shibyō myōkan* (Temples in Tainan *chou*; Taipei: Taiwan nichinichi shimpōsha, 1933).
12. These *kuan-li-jen* were appointed by the Japanese authorities and were responsible for the activities of the association as well as for the payment of taxes. Formerly neither the associations nor the temples had had such an institution, everything having been in the hands of the yearly *lu-chu*. The *kuan-li-jen* were permanent, and many continued in office after the departure of the Japanese, there being no law or statute that could deprive them of their function. Many profited, too, from the years of confusion that followed the

war to have the common property registered in their own names in order to enrich themselves. In many places the *kuan-li-jen* or their offspring are now the only authorities in charge of the temples and do what they please with them, the institution of *lu-chu* being nearly extinct. This sorry state has led to many abuses.

13. Actually, the total might be slightly more. In several instances it was impossible to identify the exact neighborhood, and in these cases *miao* or *hui* have not been included. A certain number of associations reported by informants but not verified by any record have also been left out. As a whole, the associations were fairly evenly distributed over the city, with no quarter being either particularly favored or left out.

14. Shih Yang-sui, "T'ai-nan shih chieh hsiao chih (Short study of the streets of Tainan), *T'ai-nan wen hua*, 1, no. 1 (Oct. 1951): 53–55.

15. These apartment houses were one room deep and three, five, or seven rooms long. The rooms on either side of the central one were let as separate units, with adjoining courtyard. Since there was but one central roof beam, each apartment house counted as a single *tung*. The central room, with its altar table and chairs for visitors, served as a common reception hall and cultural center for all the inhabitants.

16. This explanation, given by several informants, alludes to the period when the island was being colonized: T'u-ti-kung played an important role as the first cult established by new settlers to protect them against demons and aborigines alike. See Liu Chih-wan, *Nan-t'ou wen hsien ts'ung chi* (Collected literature on Nan-t'ou; Taipei: T'ai-wan feng wu tsa chih she, 1961), vol. 9, p. 117. The explanation does not mention the building of a shrine as a logical consequence of the development of the community.

17. Another cap often found is the *hsia-ku*. This may represent a connection with the locust cult.

18. See Chiang Chia-chin, *T'ai-nan shih chih kao*, *Tsung chiao pien* (Draft gazetteer of Tainan municipality, Section on religion; 1959), p. 21.

19. Ibid.

20. Ibid. The cult of Hou-t'u originated with Han Wu-ti in 133 B.C. Cf. Marcel Granet, *La Pensée chinoise* (Paris: Renaissance du livre, 1934), pp. 286–97. Today Hou-t'u represents the guardian spirit of the grave, and is in all aspects similar to T'u-ti-kung. Note that a grave is called a *fu-ti*, "hallowed ground," just as temples are.

21. This story, very current and reported with variants by all informants, can be found in Tseng Ching-lai, *Taiwan shūkyō to meishin rōshū* (Religion and superstitious practices in Taiwan; Taipei: Taiwan shūkyō kenkyūkai, 1938), pp. 262, 268.

22. This remarkable variant of the Meng Chiang-nü story is widespread in Taiwan and is found in popular ballads. It is also cited in Chiang Chia-chin 1959, p. 20.

23. Many examples from folklore, such as the story of the White Snake, can be cited to confirm this.

24. See Henri Maspero, "Les Procédés de nourrir le principe vital dans la religion taoïste ancienne," *Journal asiatique*, vol. 229 (1937): 403–13.

25. Cf., for instance, the movement of the *T'ai-ping ching*. For a general discussion of all questions related to these movements, see R. A. Stein, "Re-

marques sur mouvements du taoïsme politico-religieux au IIe siècle ap. J.C.," *T'oung-Pao*, 50, no. 1–3 (1963): 1–78.

26. See Stein 1963: 13 and *passim*.
27. *Ibid.*: 42–59, "les Tsi-tsieou."
28. *Ibid.*: 59–76, "les t'ing."
29. The *p'u-tu* is the Buddhist festival of Avalambana, in principle held on the fifteenth day of the seventh month, but actually celebrated during all thirty days of the month from the opening of the gates of Hell on the first day until their closing on the last. The enormous importance of the *p'u-tu* in Chinese folklore, ancestor worship, and community life has not yet been fully appreciated in the West. It is second only to the Chinese New Year, of which it is the counterpart: it falls exactly half a year after the New Year cycle and represents the holy period of the Earth in contrast to the New Year period consecrated to Heaven.
30. Today's *chiao* are the continuation of the Taoist *chai*, "retreats," of medieval times. *Chai* and *chiao* are held for the consecration of newly built or restored temples, for purification (in the case of epidemics), for the ordination of Taoist priests, and so forth. The *chiao* require the collaboration of the entire community and are unique as a total religious expression.
31. The confiscation of the corporate assets of these associations by the Japanese government during the war years severely curtailed the activities of the *hui*. Even more important, the destruction of the city and the subsequent reshuffling of its population, the entire new administration, whose interference in the lives of the people is without precedent in Chinese history, and the far-reaching social change that has occurred have all but given a death blow to the neighborhood associations.
32. The name Taiwan is derived from *Ta-yüan*, an early name of a little island not far from the coast of Formosa on which the Dutch built their first and most important stronghold. Named An-p'ing after the victory of Koxinga in 1662, the former island is now a suburb of Tainan City, as the water strip separating the two has long since silted up. Because of the peculiar history of An-p'ing, it has not been included in the present survey.
33. See Yen Hsing, "T'ai-wan shang yeh ti yu lai yü san chiao" (The Three Guilds and the origins of commerce in Taiwan), *T'ai-nan wen hua*, 3, no. 4 (Apr. 1954): 9–15.
34. How and why these trading corporations came to be called *chiao* is unclear. In the religious realm, the word refers to the Altar of Heaven, opposed to and complementing *she*, the Altar of the Earth. *She* has long been used to designate a corporate enterprise, and the term *chiao* may have undergone a comparable semantic drift. *Chiao* also means suburban, and the usage in question may have arisen from the fact that the major trading corporations had their headquarters in the commercial suburbs. The chief organization for trading corporations located within the walls of Tainan was the Liu-ho T'ang, whose headquarters were in the Great Temple of Kuan-ti. Liu (the character for six) refers to the six *chüeh-t'ou* of that temple, all T'u-ti-kung *hui*.
35. The rank was modest, but it did entitle the three *chiao* to a degree of self-government. It seems that the San-i T'ang disposed of only one seal, which might indicate that after 1808 there was only one *lu-chu*.
36. The holdings of the San-i T'ang were confiscated and sold for the joint

benefit of Japanese officials and a few Tainan merchants in the last year of World War II. For some details on this, see Yen Hsing 1954. Although it might be possible to locate the inventory of the sale, memories attached to this transaction make it advisable to tread softly.

37. The revised charter, on rose-colored paper, was printed in 1937. One side has the accounts and the membership list of that year, and the other side reproduces the Record of the Statutes of 1907.

38. The expression here is *ch'ing-chu*, an allusion to the Auspicious Congratulatory Service, the Taoist ritual performed on T'u-ti-kung's birthday.

39. I have asked friends in Tainan why a street without a T'u-ti-kung might be subject to ridicule. The answer obtained from a majority was that "there would be nobody to guard the money!" T'u-ti-kung is indeed called Shou-ts'ai-nu, "the slave who guards the money," as I illustrate in a story on p. 661. One is reminded of the funeral ritual tied to the notion of *t'ien-k'u-ch'ien*, "filling the treasury." It is thought that at burial a large sum of money is due the treasury of Hades to compensate the deceased for his loss of life and of earthly assets. In order to prevent the escape of this fortune, the magnitude of which is determined by fate, the entire family, from the youngest to the oldest, sits in a circle around the pyre of burning mock money holding hands. The common interest and joint action of the entire family in preventing financial depletion has its counterpart in the common interests and corporate activity of all residents of an urban neighborhood in warding off the loss of its fated share of wealth.

40. All members were indicated by their shop name, *tien-hao*.

41. The majority of associations and temples celebrated T'u-ti-kung's birthday at the Mid-Autumn Festival on the fifteenth day of the eighth month. But according to Tainan tradition, this is in reality the birthday of T'u-ti-kung's wife. This saint is generally not worshiped in Tainan (for reasons explained in the story on p. 661), though she was in many other parts of China. The other birthday of T'u-ti-kung is in the spring, on the second day of the second month.

42. The account book belongs to Mr. Chuang Sung-lin, a great scholar of old Tainan to whom I am deeply indebted.

43. "Yüan" refer to the silver dollars known as *ta-yüan*. Until 1915, the fineness of the silver is indicated in the account book. In 1923 the accounts switched from yüan to yen.

44. There follows a full translation of the accounts for one year.

Account of ritual expenditures as of the eighteenth day of the sixth month of the year *chia-yin* (1914), anniversary of the Lord of the Fire Star. This has been a year in which a *chiao* was held.

Total income from 24 members, each contributing 4.20 yüan: 100.80
Expenses:
(1) One day of mandarin (*kuan-yin*) theater by the Hsiao-lo-t'ien troupe, including the extra fee at the beginning of the play (*chia-kuan-li*), the oil, and the *pan-hsien* (introductory ritual play) 9.00
(2) Half a day of marionette (*k'uei-lei*) theater 1.80
(3) *Chia-kuan-li* for the preceding 0.80
(4) "Oil and incense money" for the monastery 1.20
(5) 24 sedan chairs with bearers (one for each of the members) 14.40

(6) Four helpers for the day 1.40
(7) Two gong beaters 0.20
(8) Procession music (two *so-na* [a kind of oboe] and one drum) 1.00
(9) A whole hog, of 93.90 *chin* 10.70
(10) A whole goat, of 6 *chin* 4.00
(11) Two grass mats 0.37
(12) Two stacks of "flower money," three pairs of decorated candles, two stacks of "demon money," two stools, four boxes of small candles, one stack of mock money 2.83
(13) Melon seeds and betel nuts 0.60
(14) Bananas 0.72
(15) Fresh flowers (50), two baskets of charcoal, twelve packs of tea leaves 0.37
(16) Three sets of the Three Offerings (meat, fish, eggs) 0.90
(17) Two paper flowers (to be fastened on the incense burner), twenty packs of cigarettes, five reams of yellow paper 0.95
(18) Eight bottles of wine, ten bottles of beer 5.40
(19) Fee for the Taoist priest (*tao-shih*) 8.50
(20) Cost of erecting the theater stage 0.80
(21) *Man-Han* feast with roast suckling pig and one set of the Five Offerings (pig's head, duck, chicken, fish, eggs) 27.00
(22) Noodles (40 bowls) 2.00
(23) Small towels (6) 0.30
(24) Four packs of incense, one piece of sandalwood, one pair of lanterns 1.40
(25) Pastry (for the feast) 1.40
(26) Pastry dough (to make cakes to take home), one catty 4.51
(27) Cost of transferring the incense burner, with firecrackers and candles 0.10
        Grand total: 101.72

The deficit of 0.92 shall be provided by the [outgoing] *lu-chu*.

The association on this day possesses the following items: one yellow embroidered tablecloth (to be hung before the offering table); one yellow banner (with the images of the Eight Immortals, to be hung over the door); one bronze gong from Soochow; and one pewter incense burner. These items have been transferred to the new *lu-chu*.

45. The temple is the Fa-hua ssu, which dates from the second half of the seventeenth century. The Fire King sanctuary, though built on the temple grounds, is an independent structure that dates from 1764.

46. T'ai-wan yin hang, Ching chi yen chiu shih, ed., *T'ai-wan nan pu pei wen chi ch'eng* (Collection of inscriptions from southern Taiwan; Taipei: Ching chi yen chiu shih, 1966), p. 195. (T'ai-wan wen hsien ts'ung k'an, 218.)

47. *Ibid.*, p. 162.

48. *Ibid.*, p. 122.

49. For instance, in the case of another landmark temple, the P'u-chi tien, an inscription of the year 1819 forbids loitering, dumping garbage, and making disturbances (e.g., gambling or holding shadow-puppet plays) within the temple precincts. *Ibid.*, p. 211.

Character List

Character List

Entries are categorized as follows: places (P); physical features (F); terms and titles indicating status, official position, ethnicity, and occupation (S); particular associations, agencies, firms, and other organizations (A); organizational types and categories (O); deities (D); temples and altars (T); urban landmarks (U); written sources (W); and miscellaneous terms (M). Names of county- and higher-level administrative units are excluded, as are the names of major cities; location data are provided for other place names and for physical features. Associations, temples, and urban landmarks that are associated in the text with a single city are so identified. The only written sources included are those named in the text; titles of complete works are italicized and those of chapters or sections are enclosed in quotation marks. No personal names are included.

Ai-yü Shan-t'ang (A) 愛育善堂
a-la t'ung-hsiang-che (M) 阿拉同鄉者
an (M) 菴
an-lu (M) 安爐
An-p'ing (P) 安平
   [one-time port of Tainan]
ch'a-lu-chin (M) 插爐金
chai (M) 齋
ch'ai-chu (M) 差助
ch'ai-i-chuang (O) 拆衣莊
chan (O) 棧
chan-ssu (S) 棧司
chang (M) 丈
chang-fang (S) 帳房
chang-t'ou (S) 長頭
Ch'ang-an Men (U) 昌安門
   [Shao-hsing-fu, Chekiang]
ch'ang-kuan (M) 常關
ch'ang-lu hang (S) 長路行
ch'ang-tien (O) 廠店
Chao-ch'iang (U) 照墻
   [Shao-hsing-fu, Chekiang]
Chao-jih (D) 昭日

Ch'ao T'ien kung (T) 朝天宮
   [Nanking]
Ch'ao-yang Men (U) 朝陽門
   [Peking]
Che Tz'u Hui-kuan (A) 浙慈會館
   [Peking]
Che-chiang Hui-kuan (A) 浙江會館
Che-Ning Hui-kuan (A) 浙寧會館
Che-tung yün-ho (F) 浙東運河
   [canal connecting Ningpo with Hangchow]
chen (M) 鎮
chen-tung (S) 鎮董
cheng (M) 正
cheng men (M) 正門
Cheng-i Hsüan-t'an Ts'ai-shen (D) 正乙玄壇財神
Cheng-i Tz'u (A) 正乙祠
   [Peking]
Cheng-i-chiao (A) 正乙教
cheng-k'an (S) 正看
cheng-tz'u (M) 正祠
Cheng-yang Men (U) 正陽門
   [Ming Nanking; Peking]
ch'eng (M) 城

ch'eng-hsiang tung-pao (S) 城鄉董保
Ch'eng-huang miao (T) 城隍廟
Ch'eng-huang-yeh (D) 城隍爺
ch'eng-kuo (M) 城郭
Chi (P) 薊
 [Shang-dynasty city in the vicinity of present-day Peking]
Chi-ch'ing (P) 集慶
 [Yüan-dynasty name for Nanking]
"Chi-fa" (W) 祭法
"Chi-i" (W) 祭義
chi-i kung-chü ling-pan (M) 集議公舉領辦
"Chi-ssu" (W) 祭祀
chi-ssu kung-yeh (O) 祭祀公業
chi-ti (M) 基地
chi-ti-chu (S) 基地主
ch'i (M) 氣
ch'i-chang (S) 耆長
ch'i-hsiang (M) 氣象
ch'i-lao (S) 耆老
ch'i-min (M) 耆民
Ch'i-nien tien (T) 祭年殿
 [Peking]
ch'i-shen (S) 耆紳
ch'i-shui (M) 契稅
Ch'i-t'ien kung (T) 啟天宮
 [Taipei]
ch'i-yeh (S) 耆業
chia (M) 家 [family]
chia (M) 甲 [first of the ten stems; tithing; unit of land measure]
chia miao (M) 家廟
chia-chang (S) 家長 [family head]
chia-chang (S) 甲長 [tithing head]
chia-kuan-li (M) 加冠禮
Chia-ling chiang (F) 嘉陵江
 [river flowing into the Yangtze at Chungking]

chia-t'ing (M) 家庭
chia-tsu (M) 家族
Chiang-chün miao (T) 將軍廟
 [Taipei]
Chiang-hsia (P) 江廈
 [district in the eastern suburbs of Ningpo]
Chiang-k'ou (P) 江口
 [market town in Feng-hua *hsien*, Ning-po *fu*, Chekiang]
Chiang-lan Chieh (U) 槳欄街
 [Canton]
Chiang-pei (P) 江北
 [suburb northeast of Ningpo]
chiang-p'ing (M) 江平
chiang-sung (M) 講誦
chiao (M) 教 [education]
chiao (M) 郊 [guild]
chiao (M) 醮 [community rite]
chiao-i-so (O) 交易所
Chiao-she (T) 郊社
chieh (M) 街
chieh-hsiang (M) 街巷
Chieh-hsiao tz'u (T) 節孝祠
 [Hsin-chu, T'ai-pei *fu*, Taiwan]
chieh-shou (S) 結首
chieh-tu shih (S) 節度使
chien (M) 薦 [introduction]
chien (M) 間 [room]
Chien Pang (A) 建幫
 [Ningpo]
Chien-ch'ang Kung-ssu (A) 建昌公司
 [Taipei]
chien-chiao (M) 鑒醮
chien-fan (S) 肩販
chien-fu (S) 肩負
Chien-k'ang (P) 建康
 [capital of the Three Kingdoms state of Wu, Nanking area]
chien-sheng (S) 監生

Character List

Chien-yeh (P) 建業
  [capital of the Three Kingdoms state of Wu, Nanking area]
chien-yüan (S) 監院
ch'ien (M) 乾
"Ch'ien chai" (W) 慊債
ch'ien-chang (S) 千長
Ch'ien-chia tz'u (T) 千家祠
  [Hsin-chu, T'ai-pei fu, Taiwan]
Ch'ien-chiang Hui-kuan (A) 錢江會館
  [Soochow]
ch'ien-chuang (O) 錢莊
Ch'ien-hang Chieh (U) 錢行街
  [Ningpo]
Ch'ien-t'ang (F) 前塘
  [canal east of Ningpo]
Ch'ien-t'ang chiang (F) 錢塘江
  [river near Hangchow]
Ch'ien-yeh Kung-so (A) 錢業公所
  [Ningpo]
chih (M) 志
chih chien-sheng (S) 職監生
chih-hang (O) 紙行
chih-li chou (M) 直隸州
Chih-li Men (U) 植利門
  [Shao-hsing-fu, Chekiang]
chih-li t'ing (M) 直隸廳
chih-nien hui-shou (M) 值年會首
chih-nung kuan (S) 治農官
Chih-t'ang (U) 治堂
  [Shao-hsing-fu, Chekiang]
chih-tien (O) 紙店
chin (M) 斤
Chin-i Wei (A) 錦衣衛
  [Ming Nanking]
Chin-ling (P) 金陵
  [Chou-dynasty name for Nanking]
chin-lung-chi (M) 進籠雞

Chin-sha chiang (F) 金沙江
  [upper course of the Yangtze]
chin-shen (S) 縉紳
Chin-shen ch'üan shu (W) 縉紳全書
chin-shih (S) 進士
chin-yeh (S) 衿業
Chin-yüan (U) 禁園
  [Han Ch'ang-an]
Ch'in-huai ho (F) 秦淮河
  [river near Nanking]
ching (M) 境 [neighborhood subdivision of temple-support group]
ching (M) 敬 [respect]
ching man (M) 荊蠻
Ching-k'ou (P) 京口
  [former name of Chen-chiang-fu, Kiangsu]
ching-she (M) 精舍
ching-shih (O) 靜室
Ching-shih (P) 津市
  [nonadministrative city in Li chou, Hunan]
ching-shou (S) 經手
Ching-te-chen (P) 景德鎮
  [nonadministrative industrial city in Fou-liang hsien, Jao-chou fu, Kiangsi]
ching-t'ien (M) 井田
ching-ts'ui (S) 經催
ch'ing (M) 頃 [unit of land measurement]
ch'ing (M) 情 [emotions]
ch'ing chu (M) 慶祝
Ch'ing-an Hui-kuan (A) 慶安會館
  [Ningpo]
Ch'ing-chiang-p'u (P) 清江浦
  [nonadministrative center in Ch'ing-ho hsien, Huai-an fu, Kiangsu]

Ch'ing-i chiang (F) 青衣江
  [tributary of the Min River in western Szechwan]
Ch'ing-lung chiang (F) 青龍江
  [river near Shanghai]
Ch'ing-lung-chen (P) 青龍鎮
  [market town in Ch'ing-p'u hsien, Sung-chiang fu, Kiangsu]
ch'ing-ming chieh (M) 清明節
Ch'ing-ming Men (U) 清明門
  [Han Ch'ang-an]
Ch'ing-Ming shang ho t'u (W) 清明上河圖
ch'ing-p'u (O) 清舖
Ch'ing-shan-wang miao (T) 青山王廟
  [Taipei]
ch'ing-shih (O) 清室
Ch'ing-shui tsu-shih-kung miao (T) 清水祖師公廟
  [Taipei]
chiu-fang (O) 酒坊
chiu-fei (M) 舊廢
chiu-hang (O) 酒行
chiu-lou (M) 酒樓
chiu-tien (O) 酒店
Cho-shui ch'i (F) 濁水溪
  [river near I-lan, Taiwan]
chou (M) 州
Chou kuan (W) 周官
Chou li (W) 周禮
Chou-chia-k'ou (P) 周家口
  [nonadministrative city in Huai-ning hsien, Ch'en-chou fu, Honan]
Chou-hsüeh (U) 州學
chu (M) 主 [host; "sacrificial tablets"]
chu (M) 柱 [pillar; "minimal agnatic group"]
Chu I-kuei luan (M) 朱一貴亂
chu shen (M) 諸神

Chu-ch'iao Men (U) 朱雀門
  [T'ang Ch'ang-an]
Chu-ch'ien (P) 竹塹
  [original name of Hsin-chu, T'ai-pei fu, Taiwan]
Chu-ch'ien ch'i (F) 竹塹溪
  [river near Hsin-chu, Taiwan]
Chu-hang Hsiang (U) 竹行巷
  [Ningpo]
Chu-hsien-chen (P) 朱仙鎮
  [nonadministrative center in Hsiang-fu hsien, Kai-feng fu, Honan]
chu-hung-ch'i (M) 硃紅漆
ch'u (M) 廚
ch'uan-t'ien (M) 轉佃
ch'uan-shang (M) 船商
chuang (S) 莊 [commission merchant]
Chuang (S) 壯 [non-Han ethnic group]
chun che (M) 準折
chung (M) 忠
Chung shan (F) 鍾山
  [mountain near Nanking]
Chung Shih (U) 中市
  [Ningpo]
chung-ch'iu chieh (M) 仲秋節
Chung-kang (P) 中港
  [port town in Miao-li hsien, T'ai-wan fu, Taiwan]
Chung-kuo chien-chu shih (W) 中國建築史
Chung-nan shan (F) 終南山
  [old name for Ch'in-ling mountains, Shensi]
chung-pen i-mo (M) 重本抑末
chung-ssu (M) 中祀
Chung-t'ang (F) 中塘
  [two canals of the same name,

Character List

one east and one west of Ningpo]
chung-yüan (M) 中元
ch'ung (M) 衝行
chü-jen (S) 舉人
Chü-po Ching-she (A) 菊坡精舍
 [Canton]
chü-tung (S) 局董
ch'ü (M) 區
Ch'ü chiang (F) 渠江
 [tributary of the Chia-ling River, Szechwan]
Ch'ü-chiang Shu-yüan (A) 曲江書院
 [Canton]
ch'ü-fang (M) 取房
Ch'üan Pang (A) 泉幫
 [Ningpo]
ch'üan-chuan (M) 勸捐
Ch'üan-k'ou (P) 泉口
 [market town in Feng-hua *hsien*, Ning-po *fu*, Chekiang]
chüeh-t'ou (S) 角頭
chün (S) 君
chün-t'ien chün-i chih fa (M) 均田均役之法
chün-tzu (S) 君子
ch'ün-ssu (M) 羣祀

en-kung (S) 恩貢
Erh-ssu-t'ang (U) 二思堂
 [Shao-hsing-fu, Chekiang]

fa (M) 法
Fa-chu-kung kung (T) 法主公宮
 [Taipei]
Fa-hua (P) 法華
 [market town in Shang-hai *hsien*, Sung-chiang *fu*, Kiangsu]
Fa-hua ssu (T) 法華寺
 [Tainan]

Fa-lien ssu (T) 法蓮寺
 [Hsin-chu, T'ai-pei *fu*, Taiwan]
fan (M) 繁
Fan-ch'eng (P) 樊城
 [nonadministrative city in Hsiang-yang *hsien*, Hsiang-yang *fu*, Hupeh]
fang (M) 房 [house]
fang (M) 坊 [ward]
fang-chang (S) 放賬 [chief accountant]
fang-chang (S) 坊長 [ward chief]
fang-chang p'ao-chieh (S) 放賬跑街
fang-chu (S) 房主
fang-fu (S) 坊夫
fang-k'o (S) 房客
Fang-li (P) 房裏
 [nonadministrative walled town in Miao-li *hsien*, T'ai-wan *fu*, Taiwan]
Fang-ti (D) 方帝
fang-tsu (M) 房祖
fen-fang (M) 分房
fen-hsiang (M) 分香
fen-ling (M) 分靈
fen-tsu (M) 分租
Feng (P) 豐
 [early Chou-dynasty capital]
feng i-fu (S) 縫衣服
Feng-hu Shu-yüan (A) 豐湖書院
 [Hui-chou-fu, Kwangtung]
Feng-hua chiang (F) 奉化江
 [river near Ningpo]
Feng-shen yen-i (W) 封神演義
feng-shui (M) 風水
Feng-yü-lei-yün t'an (T) 風雨雷雲壇
Fo-shan-chen (P) 佛山鎮
 [nonadministrative industrial city

in Nan-hai *hsien*, Kuang-chou *fu*,
Kwangtung]
Fou chiang (F) 涪江
[tributary of the Chia-ling River,
Szechwan]
fu (M) 符 [charm]
fu (M) 府 [prefecture]
fu (M) 咈 [type of cotton]
Fu-hsi (D) 伏羲
Fu-hsüeh (U) 府學
fu-hu (S) 富戶
fu-k'an (S) 副看
Fu-lao (S) 福老
Fu-li-chen (P) 甫里鎭
[market town in Wu *hsien*, Su-
chou *fu*, Kiangsu]
fu-mu hui (O) 父母會
fu-pang (S) 附榜
fu-shou (S) 副手
fu-te (M) 福德
Fu-te Cheng-shen (D)
福德正神
fu-te she (O) 福德舍
Fu-te Tz'u (T) 福德祠
Fu-te-yeh Hui (A) 福德爺會
fu-ti (M) 福地

Hai-k'ou (P) 海口
[nonadministrative outport of
Ch'iung-chou-fu, Hainan,
Kwangtung]
hai-kuan (M) 海關
Han chiang (F) 漢江
[river flowing into the Yangtze
at Hankow]
Han chiang (F) 韓江
[river in northeastern Kwangtung]
Han-chiang (P) 蚶江
[port town in Chin-chiang *hsien*,
Ch'üan-chou *fu*, Fukien]

Han-Huang-Te (P) 漢黃德
[circuit in eastern Hupeh]
hang (O) 行
hang t'u (M) 夯土
hang-chan (O) 行棧
hang-shui (M) 行稅
hao (M) 號
Hao (P) 鎬
[early Chou-dynasty capital]
Hao-t'ien (D) 昊天
Hao-t'ien Chin-kuan Yü-huang
Shang-ti (D)
昊天金闕玉皇上帝
Heng Men (U) 橫門
[Han Ch'ang-an]
ho-ch'uan (M) 河川
Ho-i Men (U) 和義門
[Ningpo]
Ho-k'ou-chen (P)
河口鎭
[river port in T'o-k'o-t'o *t'ing*,
Shansi]
ho-ku (M) 合股
Ho-ning Men (U) 和寧門
[Southern Sung Hangchow:
Palace City]
Ho-tung (P) 河東
[circuit in southwestern Shansi]
Hou Shih (U) 後市
[Ningpo]
Hou-lung (P) 後龍
[nonadministrative walled town in
Miao-li *hsien*, T'ai-wan *fu*, Taiwan]
Hou-t'ang (F) 後塘
[canal east of Ningpo]
Hou-t'u (D) 后土
Hou-yüan (U) 後園
[T'ang Ch'ang-an]
Hsi Ta-lu (U) 西大路
[Ningpo]

Character List

Hsi-chih Men (U) 西直門 [Peking]
Hsi-shih ta-ch'i (F) 西勢大溪 [river near I-lan, T'ai-pei fu, Taiwan]
Hsi-t'ang (F) 西塘 [canal west of Ningpo]
Hsi-yüeh (D) 西月
Hsia Pang (A) 廈幫 [Ningpo]
Hsia hai (P) 霞海 [nonadministrative center in T'ung-an hsien, Ch'üan-chou fu, Fukien]
hsia-ku (M) 蝦蛄
hsiang (M) 鄉 [rural township]
hsiang (M) 廂 [suburban ward]
hsiang (M) 象 [symbol]
Hsiang chiang (F) 湘江 [tributary of the Yangtze in Hunan]
hsiang-chen chih pu-chuang (O) 鄉鎮之布庄
Hsiang-chiang Shu-yüan (A) 相江書院 [Shao-chou-fu, Kwangtung]
hsiang-jen (S) 鄉人
hsiang-lu (M) 香爐
hsiang-shen (S) 鄉紳
hsiang-tz'u (O) 鄉祠
hsiang-yüeh (M) 鄉約
hsiao (M) 孝
Hsiao Ma-tsu Chieh (U) 小媽祖街 [Tainan]
hsiao yü-chang (S) 小圩長
Hsiao-ch'i (P) 小溪 [market town in Yin hsien, Ning-po fu, Chekiang]
hsiao-fei (M) 小費
hsiao-nan pi hsiang; ta-nan pi ch'eng (M) 小難避鄉大難避城
hsiao-tsu (M) 小租
hsiao-tsu hu (M) 小租戶
hsiao-t'ung hang (O) 小同行
hsieh (M) 邪
Hsieh-chung miao (T) 協忠廟 [Ningpo]
Hsieh-p'u-chen (P) 澥浦鎮 [nonadministrative city in Chen-hai hsien, Ning-po fu, Chekiang]
hsieh-tou (M) 械鬥
hsien (M) 縣 [county]
hsien (M) 仙 [Taoist immortal]
hsien-ch'eng (S) 縣丞
Hsien-hsüeh (U) 縣學
hsien-huo p'u (S) 鮮貨鋪 [fresh-fish retailer]
hsien-huo p'u (S) 鹵咸貨鋪 [salted-fish retailer]
Hsien-i (D) 先醫
hsien-k'o (S) 鮮客
hsien-kuan (S) 憲官
Hsien li-t'an (T) 縣厲壇
hsien-nien hui-shou (M) 現年會首
Hsien-nung (D) 先農
Hsien-shih Ta Tsung-tz'u (A) 洗氏大宗祠 [Canton]
hsien-tan (M) 鹹單
Hsien-t'ang (F) 鹹塘 [canal near Shanghai]
Hsien-yang (P) 咸陽 [Ch'in-dynasty capital]
hsien-yü hang (S) 鮮魚行 [fresh-fish guild]
hsien-yü hang (S) 鹹魚行 [salted-fish guild]
hsin (M) 信

Hsin Shui-hsien miao (T) 新水仙廟
[Ningpo]
Hsin-an Hui-kuan (A) 新安會館
[Ningpo]
Hsin-ch'ang (P) 新場
[market town in Nan-hui hsien,
Sung-chiang fu, Kiangsu]
Hsin-chuang (P) 新莊
[district in Tan-shui hsien, T'ai-pei
fu, Taiwan]
hsin-fang (S) 信房
Hsin-hsing kung (T) 新興宮
[Taipei]
hsing (M) 姓
Hsing-an hui-lan (W) 刑案滙覽
Hsing-ching kung (U) 興慶宮
[T'ang Ch'ang-an]
hsing-fan (S) 行販
Hsing-hua Pang (A) 興化幫
[Ningpo]
hsing-kung (M) 行宮
"Hsing-pu" (W) 刑部
Hsing-shih Kung-ssu (A) 興市公司
[Taipei]
hsing-tsai (M) 行在
hsü (M) 墟
Hsüan-chou Hui-kuan (A)
宣州會館
[Soochow]
hsüan-chü (M) 選舉
Hsüeh Kung (U) 學宮
Hsüeh-hai Shu-yüan (A) 學海書院
[Taipei]
Hsüeh-hai T'ang (A) 學海堂
[Canton]
hsüeh-t'u (S) 學徒
hsün (M) 旬
hsün-chien (S) 巡檢
hu (M) 戶
"Hu lü" (W) 戶律

"Hu pu" (W) 戶部
Hu-ch'eng pei-k'ao (W) 滬城備考
hu-ch'uan (M) 湖船
hua-chuang (O) 花莊
hua-hang (O) 花行
hua-hung (M) 花紅
Hua-lou miao (T) 華樓廟
[Ningpo]
hua-tien (O) 花店
Huai-chou-chen (P) 淮州鎮
[market town in Chin-t'ang hsien,
Ch'eng-tu fu, Szechwan]
Huai-nan-tzu (W) 淮南子
huang-ch'eng (M) 皇城
Huang-kung-lin (P) 黃公林
[market town in Yin hsien, Ning-
po fu, Chekiang]
Huang-p'u chiang (P) 黃浦江
[river flowing through Shanghai]
Huang-ti (D) 黃帝
Huang-t'ien Shang-ti (D) 皇天上帝
Huang-yüeh I-hsüeh (A) 黃岳義學
[Ningpo]
hui (O) 會
hui-kuan (O) 會館
Hui-tien (W) 會典
Hui-t'ung Kuan (U) 會同館
[Ming Nanking]
Hung-chiang (P) 洪江
[market town in Hui-tung hsien,
Ching chou, Hunan]
Hung-shui ho (F) 紅水河
[tributary of the West River in
Kwangsi and Kweichow]
Hung-wu Men (U) 洪武門
[Ming Nanking: Imperial City]
Huo-shen (D) 火神
Huo-shen miao (T) 火神廟
Huo-wang (D) 火王
Huo-wang Hui (A) 火王會

Character List

i-fang (S) 衣房
i-hsüeh (O) 義學
I-li Ssu (A) 儀禮司
 [Ming Nanking]
I Men (U) 儀門
 [Shao-hsing-fu, Chekiang]
i-min (S) 義民
i-pang (S) 乙榜
i-she (O) 義舍
i-shen (S) 邑紳
i-shih i-fu (M) 易失易復
I-t'an (T) 邑壇
i-ting (S) 役丁

jang-tu chieh-lien (M) 攘度解連
je-nao (M) 熱鬧
jen-ch'ing hsi erh kung-ssu pu jao (M)
 人情習而公私不擾
ju chu (M) 入主
Ju-hsüeh (U) 儒學
ju-yüan (O) 儒院

kai-nien (S) 該年
kai-ti-chi (M) 蓋地基
Kan chiang (F) 贛江
 [tributary of the Yangtze in Kiangsi]
K'an-hsi Chieh (U) 看西街
 [Tainan]
kao (M) 笞
Kao-chia-hang (P) 高家行
 [market town in Shang-hai *hsien*, Sung-chiang *fu*, Kiangsu]
K'ao-cha (U) 考柵
 [Taipei]
k'ao-ch'eng (M) 考成
"K'ao-kung chi" (W) 考工記
ko (M) 格
"K'o ch'eng" (W) 課程

k'o-chang (M) 客長
K'o-chia (S) 客家
k'o-pang (S) 客幫
k'o-shang (S) 客商
k'o (*shih*) (M) 科 (試)
Ku-fu-jen Ma (D) 孤婦仁媽
ku-lou (M) 鼓樓
Ku-lou Ta-chieh (U) 鼓樓大街
 [Ningpo]
Ku-wang miao (T) 穀王廟
 [I-lan, T'ai-pei *fu*, Taiwan]
kuan (M) 觀
Kuan Ch'iao (U) 貫橋
 [Ningpo]
Kuan-hai-wei (P) 觀海衛
 [walled garrison town in Chen-hai *hsien*, Ning-po *fu*, Chekiang]
kuan-hsi (M) 關係
kuan-hua (M) 官話
kuan-li (M) 官立
kuan-li-jen (S) 管理人
Kuan-ti (D) 關帝
Kuan-ti miao (T) 關帝廟
Kuan-yin (D) 觀音
kuan-yin (M) 官音
Kuan-yin t'ing (U) 觀音亭
 [Hsin-chu, T'ai-pei *fu*, Taiwan]
Kuang-Chao Hui-kuan (O)
 廣潮會館
kuang-kun (S) 光棍
Kuang-te hu (F) 廣德湖
 [onetime lake to the west of Ningpo]
Kuang-tung hsin-yü (W) 廣東新語
Kuang-ya Shu-yüan (A) 廣雅書院
 [Canton]
k'uang-kung (M) 曠工
kuei (M) 鬼
kuei-shen (M) 鬼神
Kuei-t'iao (W) 規條

k'uei (M) 魁
k'uei-lei (M) 傀儡
k'un (M) 捆
k'un-tung (S) 捆董
k'un-yeh (S) 捆葉
kung (M) 宮
kung-chi hui (O) 共祭會
kung-chü (M) 公舉
kung-kuan (O) 公館
kung-lu (M) 公路
Kung-pu kung-ch'eng tso-fa tse-li (W) 工部工程做法則例
kung-she (M) 公社
kung-sheng (S) 貢生
Kung-shu Hsien-shih miao (T) 公輸先師廟 [Ningpo]
kung-so (O) 公所
kung-ts'ao (S) 功曹
kuo (M) 國 [country]
kuo (M) 郭 [outer wall]
kuo-chang (M) 過帳
kuo-shui (M) 過稅
Kuo-tzu-chien (A) 國子監 [Ming Nanking; Peking]

La-chu Kung-so (A) 蠟燭公所 [Soochow]
Lan-ts'ang chiang (F) 瀾滄江 [upper course of the Mekong River in Yunnan]
Lao-ho-k'ou (P) 老河口 [nonadministrative city in Kuang-hua *hsien*, Hsiang-yang *fu*, Hupeh]
lao-jen (S) 老人
lao-ta (S) 老大
lao-ti (S) 老弟
li (M) 里 [measure of distance]
li (M) 理 [reason]
li (M) 禮 [rite]

Li No-ch'a (D) 李哪吒
"Li pu" (W) 禮部
li-chang (S) 里長
li-cheng (S) 里正
Li-cheng Men (U) 麗正門 [Southern Sung Hangchow: Palace City]
Li-chi (W) 禮記
li-chia (M) 里甲
li-hao (S) 裏號
li-hsü (S) 里胥
li-jen (S) 里人
li-lao (M) 里老
li-shen (S) 里紳
Li-tai Ti-wang miao (T) 歷代帝王廟 [Peking]
Li-t'an (T) 厲壇
liang-chang (S) 糧長
Liang-Huai (P) 兩淮 [salt-administration district in east-central China]
Liang-Kuang Hui-kuan (O) 兩廣會館
liang-min (S) 良民
liang-pang (S) 兩榜
Lien hu (F) 漣湖 [lake near Shanghai]
Lien-shan Hui-kuan (A) 連山會館 [Ningpo]
lien-tsung (M) 聯宗
lin (M) 臨
Lin Shuang-wen luan (M) 林爽文亂
Lin-huai-kuan (P) 臨淮關 [nonadministrative city in Feng-yang *hsien*, Feng-yang *fu*, Anhwei]
lin-sheng (S) 廩生
ling (M) 靈
Ling Ch'iao (U) 靈橋

Character List

[Ningpo]
Ling-ch'iao Men (U) 靈橋門
  [Ningpo]
ling-ch'ü tsung-ts'ui (S) 頭區總催
Ling-hui miao (T) 靈惠廟
  [I-lan, T'ai-pei fu, Taiwan]
Ling-nan Hui-kuan (A) 嶺南會館
  [Ningpo]
Ling-t'ai (U) 靈臺
"Ling-t'ai" (W) 靈臺
Ling-ying miao (T) 靈應廟
  [Ningpo]
Liu-ho T'ang (A) 六和堂
  [Tainan]
liu-min (S) 流民
Lo (P) 洛
  [early Chou-dynasty capital]
"Lo kao" (W) 洛誥
lo-ch'eng (M) 羅城
lo-ti-shui (M) 落地稅
Lo-tung (P) 羅東
  [nonadministrative center in I-lan hsien, T'ai-pei fu, Taiwan]
lou (M) 樓
lou-erh (S) 樓二
lou-san (S) 樓三
Lou-tien Wu (A) 樓店務
  [Hsiang-shan hsien, Ning-po fu, Chekiang]
lou-t'ou (S) 樓頭
lu (M) 路
lu-chu (S) 爐主
lu-hsia (S) 爐下
Lu-kang (P) 鹿港
  [port city in Chang-hua hsien, T'ai-wan fu, Taiwan]
luan-t'an (M) 亂彈
lung p'an hu chu (M) 龍蟠虎踞
Lung-ch'ang Mao-shan Pai-huo-tien (A)
  隆昌帽扇百貨店

[Ningpo]
Lung-ch'üan shan (F) 龍泉山
  [mountain range in Szechwan]
Lung-shan ssu (T) 龍山寺
  [Meng-chia, later Taipei; Lu-kang, Chang-hua hsien, Taiwan]
Lung-shan-so (P) 龍山所
  [walled garrison town in Chen-hai hsien, Ning-po fu, Chekiang]
Lung-shen (D) 龍神
Lung-shen tz'u (T) 龍神祠
Lung-wang tz'u (T) 龍王祠
  [Hsin-chu, T'ai-pei fu, Taiwan]
lung-yen (M) 龍眼

ma-t'ou (M) 碼頭
Ma-tsu (D) 媽祖
mai-hsien-che (M) 賣鮮摺
Mai-mien-ch'iao (P) 賣麵橋
  [market town in Yin hsien, Ning-po fu, Chekiang]
mai-tung (M) 麥冬
Man-Han ta-hsi (M) 滿漢大戲
Mei shan (F) 煤山
  [artificial hill in Peking]
Mei-chou tao (P) 湄洲島
  [island in P'u-t'ien hsien, Hsing-hua fu, Fukien]
Mei-shih Chieh (U) 煤市街
  [Peking]
men (M) 門
Meng-chia (P) 艋舺
  [port city in Tan-shui hsien, T'ai-pei fu; now incorporated in Taipei]
meng-tung (M) 孟冬
mi-chan (O) 米棧
mi-tien (O) 米店
miao (M) 廟
Miao-feng shan (F) 妙峰山
  [hill west of Peking]

"Mien" (W) 綿
mien-sha ch'uan (M) 棉紗船
Min chiang (F) 岷江
  [river flowing into the Yangtze at
  Hsü-chou-fu, Szechwan]
Min chiang (F) 閩江
  [river on which Foochow is sited]
Min Pang (A) 閩幫
  [Ningpo]
Min-shang Hui-kuan (A) 閩商會館
  [Ningpo]
ming (M) 命
Ming Hsiao-ling (U) 明孝陵
  [Ming Nanking]
Ming-chih Shu-yüan (A) 明治書院
  [Hsin-chu, T'ai-pei-fu, Taiwan]
Ming-lun T'ang (U) 明倫堂
Ming-t'ang (U) 明堂
Ming-tao Shu-yüan (A) 明道書院
  [Taipei]
Ming-te Men (U) 明德門
  [T'ang Ch'ang-an]
Mo-ling (P) 秣陵
  [Ch'in-dynasty name for Nanking]
Mu-fo ssu (T) 木佛寺
  [I-lan, T'ai-pei fu, Taiwan]
mu-yu (S) 幕友

na-k'uang (M) 納曠
nan (M) 難
Nan Chiao (A) 南郊
  [Tainan; Lu-kang, Chang-hua
  hsien, T'ai-wan fu, Taiwan]
Nan Ta-lu (U) 南大路
  [Ningpo]
Nan-an (A) 南案
  [Peking]
nan-ch'uan (M) 南船
Nan-fan Hsiang (U) 南飯巷
  [Ningpo]

nan-hao (O) 南號
Nan-hao Hui-kuan (A) 南號會館
  [Ningpo]
Nan-ho Chieh (U) 南河街
  [Tainan]
nan-kuan (M) 南管
Nan-kuo Shih (U) 南郭市
  [Ningpo]
nan-pang (O) 南幫
Nan-pei Hai-shang Kung-so (A)
  南北海商公所
  [Ningpo]
Nan-t'ang (F) 南塘
  [canal southwest of Ningpo]
Nan-t'ien (P) 南田
  [nonadministrative center in
  Hsiang-shan hsien, Ning-po fu,
  Chekiang]
nan-yang (M) 南洋
Nei T'ien-hou kung (T) 內天后宮
  [Hsin-chu, T'ai-pei fu, Taiwan]
Nei T'u-ti-kung miao (T)
  內土地公廟
  [Taipei]
Nei-shih (U) 內室
  [Shao-hsing-fu, Chekiang]
nei-tsai (S) 內宰
ni-t'ou (M) 泥頭
Nu chiang (F) 怒江
  [upper course of Salween River
  in Yunnan]
nu-li (S) 奴隸
nung-ku (S) 農賈

Pa-sheng Hui-kuan (A) 八省會館
  [Chungking]
Pa-shu Hui-kuan (A) 八屬會館
  [Swatow]
pai-chang (S) 百長
pai-huo hsien-pei (M) 百貨咸備

Character List

Pai-lung-wang miao (T) 白龍王廟
  [Ningpo]
Pai-tu ho (F) 白杜河
  [river south of Ningpo]
p'ai (M) 派
p'ai-fang (S) 牌房
p'ai-nien (S) 排年
Pan-ch'iao (P) 板橋
  [market town in Tan-shui hsien,
  T'ai-pei fu, Taiwan]
pan-hsien (M) 班仙
pao (M) 保 [bonding for
  apprentices]
pao (M) 報 [report]
pao (M) 堡 [rural administrative
  subdivision]
pao (M) 保 [wards, as in pao-chia
  system]
pao tung-shih (S) 保董事
Pao-an kung (T) 保安宮
  [Taipei]
pao-chang (S) 保長
pao-chia (M) 保甲
Pei Chiao (A) 北郊
  [Tainan; Lu-kang, Chang-hua
  hsien, T'ai-wan fu, Taiwan]
Pei Ta-lu (U) 北大路
  [Ningpo]
Pei-an (A) 北案
  [Peking]
pei-ch'uan (M) 北船
Pei-hai (P) 北海
  [port city in Ho-p'u hsien, Lien-
  chou fu, Kwangtung]
pei-hao (O) 北號
Pei-hao Hui-kuan (A) 北號會館
  [Ningpo]
Pei-kang (P) 北港
  [port town in Yün-lin hsien,
  T'ai-wan fu, Taiwan]

pei-mu (M) 貝母
pei-pang (O) 北幫
pei-yang (M) 北洋
pen-chou (M) 本州
pen-t'ing (M) 本廳
pen-yen (M) 本業
P'eng-ch'eng-chen (P) 彭城鎮
  [an important Han-dynasty city,
  by Ch'ing times a market town in
  Tz'u chou, Kuang-p'ing fu, Chihli]
p'eng-ch'iao (M) 碰橋
pi (M) 璧 [jade symbol of rank]
pi (M) 晶 [ward]
Pi-hsia-yüan-chün (D) 碧霞元君
Pi-yung (U) 辟廱
p'i (M) 疲
piao-wen (M) 表文
p'iao-fang (S) 票房
p'iao-hao (O) 票號
pieh (M) 別
ping-k'an (S) 並看
p'ing (M) 平
P'ing-chiang t'u-pei (W)
  平江圖備
P'ing-Li Kung-so (A) 萍醴公所
  [Hankow]
P'ing-shui (P) 平水
  [market town in K'uei-chi hsien,
  Shao-hsing fu, Chekiang]
P'ing-tien T'ung (U) 餅店衕
  [Ningpo]
po (S) 伯
po-chuang (O) 箔莊
po-p'u (O) 箔鋪
pu (M) 補
p'u (M) 浦
P'u-chi tien (T) 普濟殿
  [Tainan]
p'u-ti (M) 舖底
p'u-ti-ch'üan (M) 舖底權

p'u-ts'ung (M) 僕從
p'u-tu (M) 普度
P'u-tung (P) 浦東
  [market town in Shang-hai hsien, Sung-chiang fu, Kiangsu]

san chou (M) 散州
San I (P) 三邑
  [the "three counties" of Chin-chiang, Hui-an, and Nan-an in Ch'üan-chou fu, Fukien]
San I Kung-so (A) 三邑公所
San-chiang Hui-kuan (A) 三江會館
San-chiang-k'ou (P) 三江口
  [district of Ningpo]
san-chien (S) 三肩
San-ch'ing kung (T) 三清宮
  [Taipei]
san-chou (M) 散州
san-chüeh li (M) 三爵禮
San-fu huang-t'u (W) 三輔黃圖
San-huang miao (T) 三皇廟
San-hui (P) 三滙
  [market town in Ch'ü hsien, Sui-ting fu, Szechwan]
San-i T'ang (A) 三益堂
  [Tainan]
san-lao (S) 三老
San-lin-t'ang (P) 三林塘
  [market town in Shang-hai hsien, Sung-chiang fu, Kiangsu]
San-men hsia (F) 三門峽
  [gorge through which the Yellow River flows into North China]
San-shan Kuo-wang (D) 三山國王
san-t'ing (M) 散廳
Sang-yüan-wei (P) 桑園圍
  [nonadministrative center in Nan-hai hsien, Kuang-chou fu, Kwangtung]

sha-ch'uan (M) 沙船
Sha ho (F) 沙河
  [river flowing through Chou-chia-k'ou, Huai-ning hsien, Ch'en-chou fu, Honan]
Sha-kang-t'ang (F) 沙岡塘
  [canal near Shang-hai]
Sha-shih (P) 沙市
  [nonadministrative city in Chiang-ling hsien, Ching-chou fu, Hupeh]
shan-chang (S) 山長
Shan-ch'uan t'an (T) 山川壇
shan-huo-hang (S) 山貨行
Shang-hai Ch'ien-yeh Kung-so (A) 上海錢業公所
  [Shanghai]
shang-hu (S) 上戶
Shang-lin (U) 上林
  [Han Ch'ang-an]
shang-min (S) 商民
Shang-ti (D) 上帝
shang-tsang (M) 上蒼
Shang-yüan Hui-kuan (A) 上元會館
  [Hankow]
"Shao kao" (W) 召誥
shao-lao (M) 少牢
she (O) 社
She-chi t'an (T) 社稷壇
she-hsüeh (O) 社學
she-huo (M) 社夥
shen (S) 神 [deity]
shen (S) 紳 [gentry]
shen-chin (S) 紳衿
shen-hsiang (M) 神像
shen-ling (M) 神靈
shen-ming (M) 神明
shen-ming hui (O) 神明會
Shen-nung tz'u (T) 神農祠
  [Hsin-chu, T'ai-pei fu, Taiwan]
shen-p'ai (M) 神牌

Character List

shen-shih (S) 紳士
shen-tung (S) 紳董
shen-wei (M) 神位
sheng (S) 生
sheng-ch'i (M) 生氣
sheng-fan (S) 生番
Sheng-wang-kung miao (T)
　聖王公廟
　[Taipei]
sheng-yüan (S) 生員
shiang (M) 鄉
shih (S) 史 [clerk]
shih (M) 實 [reality]
shih (S) 師 [teacher]
"Shih ch'an" (W) 市廛
Shih-ch'i (P) 石碶
　[market town in Yin hsien, Ning-po fu, Chekiang]
shih-chih (M) 市制
shih-ho (M) 市河
shih-kun (S) 市棍
Shih-po Ssu (A) 市舶司
　[Ningpo]
Shih-po t'i-chü-ssu (U)
　市舶提舉司
　[Shanghai]
Shih-p'u (P) 石浦
　[port town in Hsiang-shan hsien, Ning-po fu, Chekiang]
shih-tien (M) 釋奠
shih-ts'ai (M) 釋菜
Shih-tzu shan (F) 獅子山
　[hill in Nanking]
shou-hsien (S) 首縣
shou-ts'ai-nu (M) 守財奴
Shou-tu chih (W) 首都志
shu (M) 恕 [benevolence]
shu (M) 束 ["bundle"]
shu (M) 署 [yamen building]
shu-chou (M) 屬州
shu-fan (S) 熟番

"Shu-kuei" (W) 署規
Shu-te Shu-she (A)
　樹德書舍
　[Canton]
shu-t'ing (M) 屬廳
shu-yüan (O) 書院
Shui-hsien kung (T) 水仙宮
　[Taipei; Tainan]
shui-k'o (M) 水客
shui-kuan (S) 水官
shui-men (M) 水門
Shui-t'ien fu-ti (T) 水田福地
　[Hsin-chu, T'ai-pei fu, Taiwan]
Shun-hu (P) 蓴湖
　[market town in Feng-hua hsien, Ning-po fu]
so-na (M) 嗩吶
ssu (M) 司
"Ssu ch'ung ya-hang" (W)
　私充牙行
ssu ta-chen (M) 四大鎮
ssu-ch'in (M) 私親
ssu-li (M) 私立
Ssu-ming Kung-so (A)
　四明公所
　[Shanghai]
ssu-shu (O) 私塾
"Ssu-tien" (W) 祀典
Su-ao (P) 蘇澳
　[port town in I-lan hsien, T'ai-pei fu, Taiwan]
Su-Hu Kung-so (A) 蘇湖公所
　[Hankow]
su-i (M) 疏意
Su-Sung-T'ai (P) 蘇松太
　[circuit in southern Kiangsu]
sui (shih) (M) 歲 (試)
sung-shih (S) 訟師

Ta Ch'ing hui-tien (W) 大清會典
Ta miao (T) 大廟

[Ningpo]
Ta Shih (U) 大市
　[Ningpo]
Ta T'ien-hou kung (T)
　大天后宮
　[Tainan]
ta tsung-tz'u (M) 大宗祠
Ta Wu miao (T) 大武廟
　[Tainan]
ta-chi (M) 大計
Ta-chia (P) 大甲
　[nonadministrative center in present-day T'ai-chung hsien, Taiwan]
Ta-chia ch'i (F) 大甲溪
　[river in northern Taiwan]
ta-chiao (M) 大醮
Ta-ch'iao (P) 大橋
　[market town in Feng-hua hsien, Ning-po fu, Chekiang]
Ta-chung miao (T) 大眾廟
　[Hsin-chu, T'ai-pei fu, Taiwan]
ta-fang (M) 大房
Ta-hsing-ch'eng (P) 大興城
　[Sui-dynasty name for Ch'ang-an (Sian)]
Ta-hsüeh (W) 大學
Ta-k'uei T'ang (A) 大魁堂
　[Fo-shan, Nan-hai huen, Kuang-chou fu, Kwangtung]
Ta-liang shan (F) 大涼山
　[mountain range in Szechwan]
Ta-lung-t'ung (P) 大隆同
　[town in Tan-shui hsien, T'ai-pei fu: now incorporated in Taipei]
Ta-ming hu (F) 大名湖
　[lake in Tsinan]
Ta-ming kung (U) 大明宮
　[T'ang Ch'ang-an]
ta-shih (S) 大史

ta-ssu (M) 大祀
Ta-sung chiang (F) 大嵩江
　[river southeast of Ningpo]
Ta-sung-so (P) 大嵩所
　[walled garrison town in Yin hsien, Ning-po fu, Chekiang]
Ta-tao-ch'eng (P) 大稻埕
　[town in Tan-shui hsien, T'ai-pei fu, Taiwan; now incorporated in Taipei]
ta-tsu hu (M) 大租戶
Ta-tu (P) 大都
　[Yüan-dynasty name of Peking]
Ta-tu ho (F) 大渡河
　[tributary of the Min River in western Szechwan]
ta-t'ung hang (O) 大同行
Ta-yu-feng Pai-huo-tien (A)
　大有豐百貨店
　[Ningpo]
ta-yüan (M) 大元
Ta-yüan (P) 大員
　[one-time island near Tainan, now incorporated in the city]
T'a-shan yen (F) 它山堰
　[dam on the Feng-hua River south of Ningpo]
tai shih-p'u (M) 帶世譜
T'ai miao (T) 太廟
T'ai-chi Tien (U) 太極殿
　[Ta-hsing-ch'eng, i.e., Sui Ch'ang-an]
T'ai-ch'u Kung (U) 太初宮
　[Chien-yeh (ancient Wu capital)]
T'ai-ho Tien (U) 太和殿
　[Peking]
T'ai-hsüeh (U) 太學
t'ai-i (M) 太乙
t'ai-lao (M) 太牢
t'ai-p'ing (M) 太平

Character List

T'ai-tsu shih-lu (W) 太祖實錄
t'an-fan (S) 攤販
t'an-miao (M) 壇廟
t'an-tsu (M) 贉租
tang-nien hui-shou (M) 當年會首
tang-p'u (O) 當舖
tang-shui (M) 當稅
t'ang (O) 堂
T'ang Chiao (A) 糖郊
 [Tainan]
t'ang-chang (S) 塘長
T'ang-hang Chieh (U) 糖行街
 [Ningpo]
tao (M) 道
tao-ho chih fu (S) 導河之夫
tao-lu (M) 道路
tao-shih (M) 道士
T'ao yüan (P) 桃園
 [town in Tan-shui hsien, T'ai-pei fu, Taiwan]
Te-cheng tz'u (T) 德政祠
 [Hsin-chu, T'ai-pei fu, Taiwan]
Teng-shih-k'ou (P) 燈市口
 [district in Peking]
Teng-ying Shu-yüan (A)
 登瀛書院
 [Taipei]
ti (M) 地
ti-ching (M) 地精
ti-fang (S) 地方
ti-hui yüan-chi (M) 遞回原籍
ti-kun (S) 地棍
ti-pao (S) 地保
Ti-ts'ang an (T) 地藏庵
 [Hsin-chu, T'ai-pei fu, Taiwan]
Ti-ts'ang miao (T) 地藏廟
 [Taipei]
t'i-chuang (O) 提莊
T'i-chü-ssu (U) 提舉司
 [Shanghai]

tien (M) 殿
tien-ch'ing hang (O) 靛青行
T'ien-fei kung (T) 天妃宮
 [Shanghai]
tien-hao (M) 店號
T'ien-i Ko (A) 天一閣
 [Ningpo]
tien-jen (M) 佃人
t'ien (M) 田 [field]
T'ien (D) 天 [Heaven]
T'ien t'an (T) 天壇
t'ien-chia (M) 田甲
T'ien-hou (D) 天后
T'ien-hou hang-kung (T)
 天后行宮
 [Ningpo]
T'ien-hou kung (T) 天后宮
T'ien-hou Sheng-mu (D) 天后聖母
t'ien-k'u-ch'ien (M) 填庫錢
t'ien-mien (M) 田面
T'ien-ming (M) 天命
t'ien-ti (M) 田底 [agricultural-substratum rights]
T'ien-ti (M) 天地 [Heaven and earth]
T'ien-ti t'an (T) 天地壇
t'ien-tzu (S) 天子
t'ien-yeh (S) 田業
ting (S) 丁 [male adult]
ting (M) 鼎 [three-legged vessel]
t'ing (M) 亭 [pavilion; temple]
t'ing (M) 廳 [subprefecture]
To-min (S) 惰民
T'o chiang (F) 沱江
 [river flowing into the Yangtze at Lu-chou, Szechwan]
tou (M) 斗
tou-ch'eng (M) 斗城
t'ou-chia (S) 頭家
ts'a-ch'i (M) 擦漆

tsai-ch'eng kai-ti (M) 在城蓋地
Tsao-chia miao (T) 皂莢廟
    [Ningpo]
tsao-kuang (M) 造光
Ts'ao-o (P) 曹娥
    [nonadministrative center in K'uei-
    chi *hsien*, Shao-hsing *fu*, Chekiang]
tso (O) 作
tso-ku (S) 坐賈
tsu (M) 祖 [ancestor]
tsu (M) 族 [lineage]
tsu-chan (O) 祖棧
tsu-cheng (S) 族正
tsu-kung hui (O) 祖公會
tsu-tz'u (M) 族祠
ts'un (M) 村
tsung (M) 宗
tsung yü-chang (S) 總圩長
tsung-chia (S) 總甲
tsung-ch'in hui (O) 宗親會
tsung-fang (S) 總坊
Tsung-jen Fu (A) 宗人府
    [Ming Nanking]
tsung-kuan-fu (O) 總管府
tsung-li (S) 總理
tsung-miao (M) 宗廟
tsung-shang (S) 總上
tsung-tsu (M) 宗族
tsung-tz'u (M) 宗祠
tu (M) 都
t'u (M) 圖
t'u-chang (S) 圖長
T'u-ku Shen (D) 土穀神
t'u-pu (M) 土布
T'u-ti-kung (D) 土地公
T'u-ti-kung Hui (A) 土地公會
T'u-ti-kung miao (T) 土地公廟
t'u-tung (S) 圖董
Tuan-t'ang (shih) (P)
    段塘(市)
    [market town in Yin *hsien*, Ning-po
    fu, Chekiang]
tuan-tung (S) 段董
tuan-wu chieh (M) 端午節
t'uan (O) 團
t'uan-lien (O) 團練
tui-tien (M) 兌佃
tung (M) 棟
Tung Shao-chiu Hu-t'ung (U)
    東燒酒鋪衕
    [Peking]
Tung Ta-lu (U) 東大路
    [Ningpo]
Tung-ch'ien hu (F) 東錢湖
    [lake southeast of Ningpo]
Tung-ching Shih (U) 東津市
    [Ningpo]
Tung-kou (P) 東溝
    [market town in Shang-hai *hsien*,
    Sung-chiang *fu*, Kiangsu]
tung-shih (S) 董事
Tung-tu Men (U) 東渡門
    [Ningpo]
Tung-ying fu-ti (T)
    東瀛福地
    [Hsin-chu, T'ai-pei *fu*, Taiwan]
Tung-yüeh (D) 東嶽
Tung-yüeh Hui-kuan (A)
    東越會館
    [Soochow]
t'ung (S) 童 [child]
t'ung (M) 通 [communication]
T'ung-chao (P) 桐照
    [market town in Feng-hua *hsien*,
    Ning-po *fu*, Chekiang]
T'ung-chi Men (U) 通濟門
    [Ming Nanking]
t'ung-chih (S) 同知
t'ung-ch'in hui (O) 同親會
t'ung-hsiang (M) 同鄉

Character List

t'ung-hsiang hui (O) 同鄉會
t'ung-hsing (M) 同姓
t'ung-hsing hui (O) 同姓會
t'ung-p'an (S) 通判
T'ung-Shang (P) 潼商
　[circuit in eastern Shensi]
t'ung-shih (M) 童試
t'ung-tsung (M) 同宗
t'ung-yeh (M) 同業
tzu-ch'eng (M) 子城
Tzu-chin Ch'eng (U) 紫禁城
　[Nanking; Peking]
tzu-jan (M) 自然
tz'u (M) 祠 [ancestral hall]
tz'u (M) 詞 [word]
"Tz'u-chi" (W) 祠祭
"Tz'u-chi-ssu" (W) 祠祭祀
tz'u-chien (M) 此間
tz'u-miao (M) 祠廟
Tz'u-sheng kung (T) 慈聖宮
　[Taipei]
tz'u-t'ang (M) 祠堂

wa-tzu (M) 瓦子
wai-kuo (M) 外郭
wai-sheng-jen (S) 外省人
Wai T'ien-hou kung (T) 外天后宮
　[Hsin-chu, T'ai-pei fu, Taiwan]
Wai T'u-ti-kung miao (T)
　外土地公廟
　[Taipei]
Wan-hsi t'ung-kuei (T) 萬喜同歸
Wan-hu Fu (A) 萬戶府
　[Ming Nanking]
Wan-nien-feng (A) 萬年豐
　[Swatow]
Wan-sui shan (F) 萬歲山
　[artificial hill north of Peking]
wang-ch'i-che (S) 望氣者
wang-ch'un-ch'iao (M) 望春橋

wei (M) 衛
Wei ho (F) 衛河
　[river in North China flowing into
　the Grand Canal at Lin-ch'ing]
Wei ho (F) 渭河
　[tributary of the Yellow River in
　Shensi and Kansu]
wei-chang (S) 圍長
wei-pi jen chih ssu (M)
　威逼人至死
wei-so (M) 衛所
Wei-yang (U) 未央
　[Han Ch'ang-an]
wei-yüan (S) 委員
wen (M) 文
Wen miao (T) 文廟
"Wen wang yu sheng" (W) 文王有聲
Wen-ch'ang (D) 文昌
Wen-ch'ang ko (T) 文昌閣
　[Ningpo]
Wen-ch'ang tz'u (T) 文昌祠
Wen-chia Shu-yüan (A) 文甲書院
　[Taipei]
wen-hsi (M) 文戲
wen-sheng (S) 文生
Wen-wu miao (T) 文武廟
weng-ch'eng (M) 甕城
wo-fei (M) 挖費
Wu (P) 吳
　[name of Chou-dynasty city near
　Nanking]
wu chi-ssu (M) 五祭祀
Wu chiang (F) 烏江
　[river flowing into the Yangtze at
　Fou-chou, Szechwan]
Wu Men (U) 午門
　[Ming Nanking: Palace City]
Wu miao (T) 武廟
wu-fu (M) 五服
wu-hsi (M) 武戲

795

wu-hsing (M) 五行
Wu-i shan (F) 武夷山
 [mountain range in southeastern China]
Wu-ku miao (T) 五穀廟
 [Hsin-chu, T'ai-pei *fu*, Taiwan]
Wu-lin Hang-ch'ien Hui-kuan (A) 武林杭籛會館
 [Soochow]
Wu-ni-ching (P) 烏泥涇
 [nonadministrative center in Shang-hai *hsien*, Sung-chiang *fu*, Kiangsu]
wu-sheng (S) 武生
wu-shih t'ung-chü (M) 五世同居
Wu-sung chiang (F) 吳淞江
 [river near Shanghai]
Wu-ti miao (T) 五帝廟
 [Tainan]
Wu-wei (P) 五圍
 [village in I-lan *hsien*, T'ai-pei *fu*, Taiwan]

Ya-k'ou *hsiang* (P) 街口鄉
 [township in Chin-chiang *hsien*, Ch'üan-chou *fu*, Fukien]
Ya-lung chiang (F) 鴉礲江
 [tributary of the Yangtze in western Szechwan]
ya-shui (M) 牙稅
ya-tieh (M) 牙帖
ya-tsu (M) 押租
yang (M) 養
Yang-ch'eng Shu-yüan (A) 羊城書院
 [Canton]
yang-lien (M) 養廉
yang-mei (M) 楊梅
Yang-shan Shu-yüan (A) 仰山書院
 [I-lan, T'ai-pei *fu*, Taiwan]

Yao-chü T'ung (U) 藥局衕
 [Ningpo]
Yao-hang Chieh (U) 藥行街
 [Ningpo]
Yao-huang tien (T) 藥皇殿
 [Ningpo]
yao-p'u (O) 藥舖
yeh (M) 野
yeh-jen (S) 野人
"Yen fa" (W) 鹽法
Yen-Shao Hui-kuan (A) 延邵會館
 [Peking]
yin-fang (S) 銀房
yin-hang (M) 銀行
yin-hao (O) 銀號
yin-li (M) 陰禮
yin-ti chih-i (M) 因地制宜
yin-t'ien (M) 陰田
yin-yang (M) 陰陽
ying (O) 營
Ying-t'ien-fu (P) 應天府
 [early Ming name for Nanking]
Ying-tsao fa-shih (W) 營造法式
Ying-yüan Shu-yüan (A) 應元書院
 [Canton]
yu-chi (S) 游擊
Yu-ying-kung (D) 有應公
Yung chiang (F) 甬江
 [river near Ningpo]
Yung-sheng ssu (T) 永勝寺
 [Canton]
Yung-tung Shih (U) 甬東市
 [Ningpo]
yü (M) 隅
Yü-chan T'ung (U) 魚棧衕
 [Ningpo]
yü-chang (S) 圩長
yü-chia (M) 圩甲
Yü-huang Shang-ti (D) 玉皇上帝

Character List

yü-huo (S) 漁夥
yü-lao (S) 圩老
Yü-lu (W) 語錄
yü-tung (S) 漁東
Yü-yao chiang (F) 餘姚江
　[river near Ningpo]
Yü-ying t'ang (U) 育嬰堂
　[Taipei]
yüan (M) 園
Yüan chiang (F) 沅江
　[tributary of the Yangtze in
　Kweichow and Hunan]
yüan-chin (M) 緣金
yüan-hua (M) 元化
Yüan-k'ang Mien-pu-hang (A)
　源康棉布行
　[Ningpo]
yüan-wai-mao (M) 員外帽

yüan-yin (M) 緣銀
Yüeh-hsiu Shu-yüan (A) 粵秀書院
　[Canton]
Yüeh-hu Shu-yüan (A) 月湖書院
　[Ningpo]
Yüeh-hua Shu-yüan (A) 越華書院
　[Canton]
Yün-chang Ch'ou-pu-chuang (A)
　雲章綢布莊
　[Ningpo]
yün-chüan (M) 勻捐
Yün-liang ch'ien-hu so (U)
　運糧千戶所
　[Shanghai]
Yün-yü-feng-lei t'an (T)
　雲雨風雷壇
　[I-lan, T'ai-pei *fu*, Taiwan]

Index

Aborigines: in Taiwan, 163, 177f, 180, 750n120
Academies (*shu-yüan*), 161, 166, 198, 268, 478, 484-85, 648-49, 715n1; and regional systems, 260, 483, 487; development of, 475-77, 480-81, 744n6; location of, 476f, 479, 485-90, 745n14; and government, 478-79, 489, 493; finances, 481-93 *passim*, 745n24, 746n41; hierarchies of, 487-89; headmasters, 492-96
Agents: business, 412, 431-32, 543, 611, 621
Agriculture, 233, 281-82, 456-59; within cities, 38, 202, 529; in Kiangnan, 395-96, 444-45; commercialization of, 405, 446
Agriculture, God of, *see* Hsien-nung; Shen-nung
Altars, 50, 588; in suburbs, 36, 65, 262, 583ff, 587; of Land and Grain, 39, 48, 53, 61f, 64-65, 71f, 114, 584-91 *passim*, 595, 602-3, 761n1; to directional gods, 50; of Heaven, 41, 62, 71f, 587, 595, 600-601, 771n34; of Heaven and Earth, 65, 114, 133; to unworshiped dead, 182, 584f, 587, 591, 761n1; official, 584-90 *passim*, 601; wind-rain-thunder-clouds, 584f, 761n1; to mountains and rivers, 585, 761n1; to Sun, 586; of Earth, 587, 771n134; to Moon, 587
Amoy, 332-33, 417, 437, 634, 636
Amoy Guild (Lu-kang), 635, 644ff

An-ch'i: city, 86; county, 180, 199
Ancestor worship, 593-94; of imperial ancestors, 35, 39f, 43, 48, 51, 53, 57, 133, 600, 680n83
Ancestral halls, 505, 511, 514f, 517f, 599, 677
Anhwei, 91, 218, 267, 538, 556, 707n3; and macroregions, 218, 343; academies in, 484-85. *See also* Anking; Ching-shih; Ch'u-chou; Feng-yang; Hui-chou; Lü-chou-fu; Wu-hu
Anking, 90-91
Apprenticeship, 269, 410-11, 563-72 *passim*, 620, 757n47, 757n50-758n52
Architecture, 48-49, 51, 73, 112-17 *passim*, 141-42, 269, 287. *See also* Houses; Palaces
Artisans, 410, 423, 557, 570, 687n101. *See also* Workers
Associations: and urban government, 547-53; types of, 558-59, 653-54; regulations, 613-14. *See also* Guilds; Hui-kuan; Native-place associations
Avoidance (bureaucratic rules of), 341, 356, 363, 564, 611

Bamboo, 396f, 399, 409, 411, 426f
Banks and banking, 223, 403, 414ff, 420, 438-39, 536, 621, 626. *See also* Ch'ien-chuang banks; Money shops; Pawnshops
Benevolent institutions, 533, 535, 648
Board of Civil Office, 330, 358-59, 382

Board of Music, 600
Board of Revenues, 157, 419
Board of Rites, 582, 600, 607
Board of Works, 157, 419
Bonds, 419, 437
Breweries, 397
Brokers, 222, 420, 447, 555f, 558, 563, 570-78 *passim*, 621, 624f, 630, 635
Buddhism, 265, 268, 582-83, 596, 603, 606, 663; in cities, 57, 114-15, 123-24; temples, 114-15, 651; and academies, 476; popular, 604, 607
Bureaucracy, 270f, 382f, 605-7. *See also* Field administration; Government; Officials
Business, 413, 419-20, 438-39, 558, 620; districts, 408-9, 527-36 *passim*, 668, 672; in Ningpo, 409-16, 433; transactions, 620-21, 623-24, 767n34. *See also* Trade
Businessmen, 410, 412-13, 434f. *See also* Agents; Brokers; Merchants; Retailers; Shopkeepers; Wholesalers

Canals, 53, 95-96, 393, 395, 401, 405, 427f, 444. *See also* Water conservancy
Canton, 5, 219, 249, 482, 507-8, 544, 547, 748n38; as regional metropolis, 13-16, 281, 283; population, 29, 535; walls, 79, 99; urban ecology, 87-88, 534f; overseas trade, 234, 332, 714n42; primacy in Lingnan, 237-41 *passim*; and field administration, 302, 307, 317, 333, 343-44; Ningpo natives in, 437f; academies in, 489-90, 495f; extended kinship in, 510-17; religion in, 548, 602f
Canton Delta, 77, 247
Canton merchants, 403, 538, 543-44
Capital: investment, 233, 283; accumulation, 434f, 565
Capitals, 93-94, 96, 107, 221, 485-87, 588; and field administration, 17-22, 261-62, 270-71, 275, 325-26; and regional systems, 28, 269-71; low-level, 222, 224, 226, 244-46; high-level, 222, 224ff, 244-46; and economic hierarchy, 223, 230-31; 258-59, 301, 340; location of, 308-11, 318-19
—imperial, 46, 90, 129ff, 150-52, 222; and economic hierarchy, 30-31, 238-39, 340; as cosmic focal point, 47, 56, 73; symbolism of, 113-14; religion in, 585, 595. *See also names of administrative units*
Cemeteries, 574, 648, 752n51
Censorate, 131-32, 600
Central places, 244-45, 610, 629-30; evolution of, 22-23, 202; economic, 25, 222ff, 275, 285-91 *passim*, 296-301 *passim*, 340-51 *passim*, 359; urban functions, 25-26; numbers of, 26, 223, 229, 275, 285-86, 298, 710-11n17; and hinterlands, 203-4, 259, 261, 277, 282-83, 293, 299; and culture, 207-8; administrative, 222, 224, 275, 301, 340, 341-44, 359; population, 224f, 287; economic hierarchy of, 244-45, 258-59, 546; hierarchy of, 258-59, 277-78, 298, 341-51 *passim*, 629f; distribution of, 278-79; competition among, 280, 284; distance among, 280-85 *passim*, 299; ideal model adapted to China, 283-85; location of, 284-91 *passim*, 296-97, 299
Central-place theory, 276-81, 718n7
Centrality (economic), 220, 241-43, 337, 551-52; and field administration, 312-14, 316, 322-23, 335, 340
Ceramics, 396f, 399, 555
Chang-chou (prefecture): emigrants and descendants in Taiwan, 176-81 *passim*, 188, 199, 636, 653, 753n55; merchants from, 403, 637
Chang-hua: city, 158, 172, 193, 634f, 637, 648, 769n1; city wall, 182, 184ff, 702n58, 702n65; county, 634
—Plain, 525, 634, 636
Changsha, 249, 343-44
Ch'ang-an, 24, 30, 219; during Han, 43-44, 50-51, 53, 67; during T'ang, 55-57, 88, 90, 96, 682n45
Ch'ang-chou: city, 343-44; prefecture, 459
Ch'ang-kuo *hsien*, 393, 396
Ch'ang-p'ing-chou (city), 307n
Ch'ang-shu (city), 445
Chao-ch'ing (prefecture), 508, 513, 516, 544
Chao-t'ung-fu (city), 291
Ch'ao-chou (prefecture), 483, 516, 550; emigrants and descendants in Taiwan, 177f, 636, 653; centrality of, 241-42; academies in, 488, 745n14, 746n41. *See also* Swatow
Che-chiang Hui-kuan, 438

Index

Che-Ning Hui-kuan, 436, 438
Che-tung Canal, 392
Che-Tz'u Hui-kuan, 539
Chefoo, 437
Chekiang, 83, 91, 266, 391, 733n4; and macroregions, 218, 343. See also Ch'ang-kuo; Chen-hai; Ch'eng hsien; Feng-hua; Hangchow; Hsiang-shan; Hsin-ch'ang; Hu-chou-fu; K'uei-chi; Ningpo; Shan-yin; Shang-yü; Shaohsing; T'ai-chou; T'ien-t'ai; Ting-hai; Tz'u-ch'i; Wen-chou-fu; Yin hsien; Yü-yao
Chen-chiang (city), 86, 120, 437
Chen-hai: city, 395f, 401, 405, 416, 428; county, 393, 401, 403, 427, 434, 438-39
Ch'en-chou (prefecture), 342
Cheng-i Tz'u (Peking), 556
Chengtu, 91, 269, 271, 296, 692n24, 719n22, 750-51n22, 751n25; as economic center, 13-16, 242, 290f; and field administration, 317, 343-44; population, 682n45
—Plain, 296
Ch'eng hsien, 393, 426, 430
Chi-lung t'ing, 160, 173. See also Keelung
Chi-ning-chou (city), 218
Chi-ssu kung-yeh (sacrificial trusts), 653
Ch'i, Mt., 35
Chia-i (city), 183, 769n1. See also Chu-lo
Chia-ling River, 293
Chia-ting: city, 550; county, 445ff
Chia-ying chou, 177f
Chiang-hsia (Ningpo suburb), 427, 527
Chiang-hsia hsien (Hupeh), 93
Chiang-ning hsien, 86, 144
Chiang-pei-t'ing (city), 93, 307n
Chiao (religious ceremony), 596-600, 603, 667, 674, 771n30
Chiao-chou (city), 437
Chien Pang (Ningpo), 417
Chien-wen emperor, 150
Ch'ien-chiang Hui-kuan (Soochow), 557, 569, 758n76
Ch'ien-chuang banks, 403, 409, 413f, 430-38 passim, 543
Ch'ien-lung emperor, 157, 183, 365
Ch'ien-t'ang River, 212, 441

Chihli, 83, 91, 218, 266, 302, 343. See also Ch'ang-p'ing-chou; Hsüan-hua-fu; I-chou; Lu-lung; Pa chou; Pao-ting; Peking; Shun-t'ien; Ta-ming-fu; Tientsin; T'ung-chou; Wan-p'ing; Yung-p'ing
Chin-chiang: city, 688n15; county, 178, 638, 640
Chin-kuei hsien, 459
Chin-sha River, 212, 707n1
Ch'in Shih-huang-ti, 40, 42ff, 54, 120, 661
Ching chou (Hunan), 552
Ching-chou-fu (city, Hupeh), 335, 550
Ching-shih (no̩ ̩ ̩ ̩ ̩
Ching-te-chen (̩ ̩ ̩ 41, 555, 690n11
Ch'ing dynasty, 26-27, 301-02, 386, 401-5 passim, 634; government, 19, 21, 359, 480-83. See also individual topics by name
Ch'ing Ming festival, 586
Ch'ing-an Hui-kuan (Ningpo), 409
Ch'ing-chou-fu (city), 92
Ch'ing-i River, 291
Ch'ing-lung (town), 441
Chiu-chiang-fu (city), 217
Chiu-lung (Kowloon), 273
Ch'iung-chou: city, 94, 550; prefecture, 746n41
Cho-shui River, 180-81, 701n46
Chou, see Departments
Chou, Duke of, 36-37
Chou dynasty, 35-37, 119
Chou-chia-k'ou (nonadm. city), 82, 93, 342, 528
Chou-li, 46-50 passim, 56f, 67, 113
Chu (small agnatic groups), 638-39
Chu Fen, 192-93
Chu Hsi, 55, 66
Chu Yüan-chang (Ming T'ai-tsu), 101, 147, 357, 384, 694n47; and Nanking, 102, 123, 127f, 132-33, 138, 144-45, 149-50, 691n23, 693n37
Chu-ch'ien, see Hsin-chu
Chu-ch'ien River, 172
Chu-hsien (city), 690n11
Chu-lo: city, 182f, 701n50; county, 592, 594. See also Chia-i
Ch'u-chou (city), 722n53
Chü-po Ching-she, 490
Ch'üan Pang (Ningpo), 417

Ch'üan-chou: city, 24, 90, 333, 634; prefecture, 525, 542, 550, 715n1; emigrants and descendants in Taiwan, 176-80, 187-88, 199, 636-40, 653, 753n55; merchants from, 396, 403, 417, 636
—Bay, 634
Ch'üan-chou Guild (Lu-kang), 549, 635, 644-47 *passim*
Chungking, 271, 296, 307n, 544, 718n13, 719n22; and Chiang-pei-t'ing, 93, 307n; as economic center, 242, 283, 290f; merchants and guilds in, 437f, 550, 552
Ch'ung (post designation), 314
Chusan archipelago, 342, 396, 424, 427, 431
Circuit intendants, 302, 332-33, 334-35, 420
Circuits, 302, 369; capitals of, 306-7, 326, 332-35, 340. *See also* Field administration; Government
Cities: siting, 13, 33, 38, 46-47, 83f, 86-87, 94; spread of, 17-18; urban ecology, 23-24, 71, 94-95, 529-38; attitudes toward, 33f, 101-2, 106, 258, 268; directional alignment, 37f; planning of, 37, 110-14, 200, 690-91n16; shapes of, 37f, 47, 56, 84, 87-91, 168; as defensive bastions, 38, 104, 182-83, 203; northern vs. southern, 51f, 55, 79, 85, 107-8, 244-45, 247; functions of, 86, 106ff, 110, 155-56, 181-82, 261-62; field administration in, 92-93, 97, 106-7, 143, 222, 224, 312-14, 316, 325-32 *passim*, 343ff, 353ff, 609; multiple, 92ff; open spaces in, 94f, 688n15; sizes of, 94-95, 97; Chinese vs. Western, 101-9 *passim*, 114ff, 117; life in, 102, 268; as economic centers, 108, 110, 211, 216, 276, 283; as historical foci, 116-17, 143; and culture, 117, 181; economic centrality, 213, 216, 222-23, 293, 312-14, 316, 322-31 *passim*, 349; regional cores/peripheries, 217, 285; binucleate structure, 536-38
—administrative, 9, 21-22, 95, 107f, 218n, 318-19. *See also* Capitals
—greater, 296, 525; defined, 286; number of, 286, 298; population, 287, 300; location of, 287, 313, 328, 331; size of trading systems, 300; and field administration, 313, 328, 331, 334-35, 340, 342
—local: defined, 222-23, 286; number of, 286, 298; locations of, 287, 313, 328, 331; population, 287, 300; size of trading systems, 300; and field administration, 313, 328, 331, 340
—nonadministrative, 222, 224, 244-45, 272-73, 537-38, 588, 717n23
—regional, 428, 525; defined, 286; number of, 286, 298; location of, 287, 313, 328, 331; population, 287, 300; size of trading systems, 300; and field administration, 313, 328, 331, 334-35, 340, 342. *See also* Central places; Metropolises; Capitals; Urban development; Urban systems; Urbanization
City building: history of, 9-11, 35-44 *passim*, 51-60 *passim;* 113; and spread of government, 36, 184; construction, 47-48; and elites, 157, 176; financing of, 157, 173, 186, 190-99 *passim*, 696n1, 703n73; and merchants, 157-58, 176; and residents, 157-58, 161, 184-93 *passim*, 197-216 *passim*, 701n52, 706-7n127; and authorities, 161, 182-97 *passim*, 205; and hinterlands, 168, 170, 172-74; labor force for, 172, 192-93, 706n126
City Gods, 182, 262-63, 424, 578, 585-90 *passim*, 601-7 *passim*, 657; temples, 99, 166, 195f, 205, 583-89 *passim*, 601, 649, 715-16n6, 761n1, 769n10
Clans, 499, 501, 505-6, 638, 760-61n140; and centrality, 261; halls and temples, 505-6, 513f; and government, 506, 509-10, 518; in Canton, 512-17; membership in, 512-13, 516f; property, 514; and examination system, 514, 516f; geographical range of, 516-17; functions of, 517-18. *See also* Lineages
Classes, social, 166, 536, 576-77, 762n11. *See also* Elites; Gentry; Merchants; Peasants; Workers
Clerks, yamen, 271, 373-79 *passim*, 454, 535, 723n2, 728n31–n32, 730n49; income, 364, 369, 374, 379, 382; tenure in office, 365, 376; duties, 367-68; numbers of, 367-68, 712n25,

Index

728n30; status, 368, 370; and local interests, 369, 374ff
Cloth, *see* Textiles
Cloth Guild (Lu-kang), 645
Commercialization: and urbanization, 22, 26-27, 231, 233-34; and population, 229, 301; and rural areas, 232-33, 459; weightings for, 234-35; in regional cores and peripheries, 283
Commodities, 279-80, 350-51; production of, 148, 392-96, 405, 409-13, 416, 424, 430-31, 445-47, 459; trade in, 223, 396-99, 409, 412-20, 426-32, 446f, 467-68, 472, 555, 570, 634, 648, 713n30. *See also individual commodities by name*
Commoners, 186-87, 361-62, 363-64, 585
Confucian school-temples, 115, 262, 268, 362, 423, 585f, 588, 651-52, 761n1; location of, 99, 354-55, 533; in Taiwan, 161f, 166, 189, 196; growth of, 477; landholdings of, 491; symbolize capital status, 584; as temples, 590, 599, 607; as schools, 592
Confucianism, 112, 265, 627-28; Han, 42, 45; Neo-Confucianism, 55, 73, 476-77; and government, 356, 374-75, 382, 610-11; and official religion, 581ff
Confucius, 41, 45, 477; worship of, 584, 586, 588, 592-99 *passim*, 648
Contracts, business, 619ff
Controls: social, 618-19, 627ff; official, 618-19
Copper and coppersmithing, 396, 399, 424, 430
Cores, regional, 214, 216f, 282-90 *passim*, 296, 298, 308
Cosmology: of cities, 28, 44-50 *passim*, 56-60 *passim*, 64, 67, 72. *See also* Symbolism
Cotton, 444, 446; production, 396, 401, 403, 426, 431, 445; trade, 399, 414, 419, 426f, 431-32, 446f; processing, 405, 412, 445-47, 459; textiles, 424, 426
Counties (*hsien*), 22-23, 304, 588; capitals of, 9, 18, 83, 91, 222, 335; development of, 17-21; metropolitan, 93-94, 203, 304; and field administration, 303-4, 320f, 326, 335-36, 343-44, 360-65; locations of, 306-11 *passim*. *See also* Field administration; Government

County-level units, 19, 22-23, 303-4; consolidation of, 19, 21, 681n22; capitals of, 185, 306, 337-38, 342; and defense, 335-36; and political control, 360; finances of, 364, 720n36. *See also* Field Administration; Government; Counties; Departments; Subprefectures
Courts, 610, 612f, 616-17, 624, 630. *See also* Justice; Litigation
Craftsmen, *see* Artisans
Credit, 221, 411ff, 417, 429-30
Culture: Little and Great Traditions, 34, 264-65, 716n11; locus of, 117-18; urban-rural differences in, 118, 264-65, 269; urban, 150, 267-69
Cycles, *see* Urban development

Debts, 458, 616, 763n13
Defense: and cities, 13, 183; and regions, 308; and field administration, 314-22
Deforestation, 287
Degree-holders, 263, 266-67, 328, 363, 370, 494, 742n78, 745n19
Deities, 423-24, 582, 584, 589, 593-94, 599-607 *passim*, 761n1; patron, 583, 597, 643, 646, 652f, 665f; patron, of guilds, 556, 559f, 562, 568, 575, 577f, 617, 666; *See also individual gods by name; Kuei; Shen*
Demand, economic, 232, 234, 555; threshold, 277, 280; density, 281, 284f, 299-300; and economic centrality, 337
Departments, autonomous (*chih-li chou*), 222; capitals of, 303, 309-10, 325, 327, 340; and field administration, 304ff, 320ff, 326f, 359-60; locations of, 308-9, 320-31 *passim*; and defense, 314. *See also* Field administration; Government
Departments, ordinary (*san chou*), 222; and field administration, 303-4, 321, 326, 335-36, 360; location of, 306, 308-9, 320-31 *passim*; capitals of, 309, 311-12, 335. *See also* Field administration; Government
Deputy subprefects, *see* Subprefects, deputy
Dikes, 63-64, 395, 401; administration in Shanghai area, 445f, 450-57 *passim*, 461, 465, 740-41n29
Directional gods, 50, 586, 682-83n12

Directional orientation: of cities, 37, 47f, 56, 64, 72, 96-97, 141
Dispute resolution, 620-30, 758n65
Divination, 35ff, 38, 46-47, 50-51, 53, 56, 63, 769n5
Dragon God, 586, 603f, 606, 761n1
Dyers, 222, 757n41
Dyers Guild (Lu-kang), 645
Dyers Guild (Wenchow), 571
Dyestuffs, 196, 199, 409, 430, 570
Dyestuffs Guild (Peking), 562, 567f, 577ff

Earth: worship of, 65, 114, 133, 587, 601, 771n34
Eastern Peak, God of the, 586, 657, 761n1
Economy: of regions, 24-27, 220; urban locus of, 119, 461; development of, 219-20, 396-405; and population, 232; government control of, 611; depressions in, 681n37
Education, 117f, 161, 247, 263, 422, 480, 610, 726n13. See also Academies; Examination system; *I-hsüeh*; Schools; *She-hsüeh*
Eight Guilds (Lu-kang), 645, 648
Elites, 265, 337, 363, 478, 517, 608; and cities, 34, 102f, 117f, 265-67, 528-29; interests of, 339, 441. See also Gentry; Scholars; Degree-holders; Leaders
Embroideries, 397, 405, 412, 427
Emperors, 73, 595-601 *passim*
Erosion, 287-88, 718n17
Ethnic groups, 544; in Taiwan, 159, 175-88 *passim*, 194, 198-99, 203-7 *passim*, 636f; and city building, 159, 175, 181-88 *passim*, 194, 198-99, 203, 207; ethnic strife, 176-81 *passim*, 198-99, 637, 703n71, 753n55. See also Aborigines; Hakka; Hoklo; Manchus; Teochiu; *see under* Canton *for* Cantonese; *under* Fukien *for* Hokkien *and* Fukienese
Evaluations: of officials, 361, 376, 383, 725n11
Examination system, 163, 166, 207, 263, 341, 370, 434, 478; halls, 99, 164, 198, 533, 535; and cultural homogeneity, 265; and regional systems, 272, 339f; and government, 339f, 356; and native-place associations, 541, 559, 564; and kin groups, 516

Fa-hua ssu (Tainan), 773n45
Face, 579, 618, 628-29, 645
Families, 499-500, 502, 508, 510, 535, 556, 624
Fan (post designation), 314
Fan-ch'eng (nonadm. city), 93, 335
Fang (lineage segments), 512-13, 515ff, 638
Fang (wards), 143-47 *passim*, 695n56
Fen-chou-fu (city), 100
Feng (Chou capital), 35-36, 43
Feng-hu Shu-yüan, 488, 491
Feng-hua: city, 396, 428, 430; county, 393, 426f, 438
—River, 392f, 395, 405, 426f
Feng-shan (city), 183, 185-86, 701n50, 702n56, 706n125
Feng-shui, 53f, 619, 685n71; and cities, 42, 54-62 *passim*, 67, 71, 141, 262, 706n125
Feng-yang (county capital), 89, 93-94, 97
Feng-yang-fu (city), 89, 93-94, 97, 335
Fertility: land, 283, 287-88
Festivals, 430, 642ff, 645, 656, 666f, 771n29; Ch'ing Ming, 586; Hungry Ghost, 646, 667, 669
Field administration: consolidation of units, 19, 21, 24; and macroregions, 218n, 307, 345; and urbanization, 230-31, 235; and population, 231f; and economic hierarchy, 258-59, 276, 314, 340-44; integration of, 269-71; degree of supervision, 270, 358; subcounty-level, 273, 303, 360; Ch'ing system, 301ff, 359f; and defense, 317-22; and revenue collection, 322-23, 338-39; and control of powerful localities, 341-44; urbanization of, 353, 356-60; division of labor in, 373-75; rationalization of, 374-75; power centers in, 375-84. See also Span of control; Post designations; Government; *and administrative units by name*
Finance, private, 414-15, 436-37, 611. See also Banks and banking; *Ch'ien-chuang* banks; Money shops; Pawnshops
Fine Hides Guild (Kuei-sui), 569f, 758n52, 758n54
Fire fighting, 421-22, 549, 575

Index

Fire King (deity), 584ff, 659, 664-65, 667; associations, 671-75
First Sovereign Emperor, *see* Ch'in Shih-huang-ti
Fiscal administration, 376, 385, 419-20, 696n1, 720n36–721n37, 730n44. *See also* Revenues, Taxation
Fish and fisheries: industry, 392, 395f, 413, 424; trade, 396, 399, 413, 416, 431
Five Elements, 42, 44f, 589, 604, 690n16
Five Emperors, Temple of the (Tainan), 665
Fo-shan (nonadm. city), 241, 486, 591, 690n11
Foochow, 88-91 *passim*, 332, 343-44, 544, 634; as economic center, 241-42, 283; merchants from, 396, 403; merchants in, 437f
Foodstuffs: trade, 396, 399, 409, 419, 447f, 467-68; manufacture, 431; guilds, 570. *See also individual products by name*
Forbidden City (Peking), 71, 113
Forbidden Park (T'ang Ch'ang-an), 57, 60
Frontier areas, 18-19, 318-19, 322
Fruit, 396, 399, 409, 417, 426f
Fu-hsi (deity), 586
Fu-mu hui (funeral associations), 653-54
Fu-te Cheng-she (Fu-te-yeh), 548, 660, 664; temples, 548; associations, 661. *See also* T'u-ti-kung
Fuel, 397, 409, 426f
Fukien, 157, 708n3; and field administration, 83, 91, 178, 200; emigrants to Taiwan, 175, 177, 639; long-distance trade, 448, 634
—Fukienese and Hokkien merchants, 403, 416-17, 432, 565. *See also* An-ch'i; Amoy; Chang-chou; Chin-chiang; Ch'üan-chou; Foochow; Hsing-hua; Hui-an; Nan-an; T'ung-an
Furniture, 397, 409, 411, 416, 424, 430-41

Garrisons, 132, 139, 144, 159, 164, 421, 688n19
Gate porters, yamen, 371, 723n2
Gates, city, 35, 48, 51, 77, 79, 95, 97, 112; of Soochow, 17; of Han Ch'ang-an, 43-44; naming of, 43-44, 53; of T'ang Ch'ang-an, 56-57; of Kaifeng, 62; watergates, 62, 95f; of Hangchow, 64; of Peking, 70; location of, 79, 82, 96f; number of, 96; of Nanking, 134, 141; of Hsin-chu, 164; of I-lan, 164; of T'ai-pei-fu, 168; of Ningpo, 397, 405
Gatetowers, 43, 53, 77
Genealogies, 510, 512, 515, 517-18, 637
Gentry, 268, 465-67, 517, 533, 535, 606, 649-50, 716n15; and public works, 157, 161, 184-92 *passim*, 198-99, 401, 452-53, 455f, 462-67, 696n1; and merchants, 336, 341, 468, 553, 703-4n82, 722n53; and local government, 341, 363, 365, 375, 389-90, 422, 552f; and officials, 363, 375, 389, 478, 732-33n66; and religion, 423, 585, 666; and academies, 478, 481-83, 491; residences, 533, 535. *See also* Elites
Ghosts, *see* Kuei
Gods, *see* Deities
Gold-Beaters Guild (Wen-chou-fu), 542
Governance, informal, 336-44; of cities, 264, 547-53, 575
Government: central, 25f, 138-39, 219; views of, 267-68, 356, 362, 724n3; provincial, 302, 330, 360
—subprovincial, 132; influence of, 262-63; urbanization of, 267-68, 270, 353, 356-60, 384-80 *passim*, 455, 614; and local groups, 363, 375ff, 382, 384, 460-61, 609; bureaucratization of, 357, 374-75, 377-78, 382, 384. *See also* Field administration; Fiscal administration; Governance; Officials; Revenues; Taxation; Yamens
Governors, 185, 358
Governors-general, 185, 200, 302, 358-59
Grain, 409, 417, 444, 468. *See also* Rice
Granaries, 164, 166, 422, 550
Grand Canal, 64, 87, 392, 397, 403, 447, 468, 528, 538
Great Tradition, 34, 264-65, 716n11
Great Wall, 137, 661
Guarantors, 624-25
Guild of Building Craftsmen (Kuei-sui), 562
Guilds, 553, 558-59, 646; merchant, 223, 562f; in Ningpo, 406-7, 409ff, 415-18, 430; craft, 410-11, 417-18, 423, 563, 569f; functions, 417f, 575-76, 615-16,

649; services to members, 538, 574f; native-place ties, 542-58 *passim*, 563ff, 579, 755n12, 756n34, 757n40; membership, 543-44, 562-65, 576-77, 580, 645-46, 757n45, 757n50; and regional systems, 543-44, 757n39; and religion, 548, 577-79, 644, 646, 666; provide public services, 549, 575, 647ff; history, 558, 560, 754n1; organization, 559-69 *passim*, 577, 580, 645ff; patron deities, 560, 562, 568, 575, 577f, 583, 588, 617, 666; rules, 560-62, 571, 765n13; halls, 561, 569, 577f, 580, 761n141; officers, 561, 567-68, 758n54; federations, 564-65, 575, 646; control over members, 568, 577-80, 618f; dues, 568f, 577-78, 758n75; fines, 568, 574-75, 579-80; economic activities, 569-72, 759n95, 759n86; dispute resolution, 579, 616-23 *passim*, 647, 758n65; and government, 580, 619, 647-49; in Lu-kang, 645-49; in Tainan, 668-69, 771n34

Hai-feng *hsien*, 745n22
Hai-k'ou (town), 94
Hakka, 159, 637; in Taiwan, 175-80 *passim*, 186, 188, 204, 206, 636, 700n41, 701n42, 701n47, 753n55. *See also* Ethnic groups; *and under* Ch'ao-chou
Hami, 92
Han Chinese, 213
Han dynasty, 9, 13, 19, 21, 44-45, 52, 120
Han River, 87, 93, 212; Basin, 9, 86-87, 218, 753n55
Han Wu-ti, 43, 49
Han-chiang (town), 634
Han-Huang-Te circuit, 334
Hang (Sung merchant association), 555
Hangchow, 27, 90-91, 113, 129, 219, 392, 431; as economic center, 17, 24, 30-31, 403, 405, 555; as Sung capital, 17, 60, 63-66, 88, 90, 96; population, 30, 682n45; early history, 63-64; map, 65; and field administration, 307, 333, 343-44; sojourners in, 437, 439, 538-39, 546
—Bay, 212, 391-92, 395, 421, 426, 431
Hankow, 5, 93f, 129, 290, 542ff, 690n11; and field administration, 307n, 334; sojourners in, 437ff; guilds in, 565

Hanyang, 93f, 307n
Hao (Chou capital), 36, 43
Hao-t'ien, *see* Heaven
Hat making, 405, 409, 412-13, 558
Heaven, 40-41, 595, 601, 604; altars of, 41, 62, 65, 71f, 114, 133, 587, 594, 600-601, 771n34; worship of, 595-96, 599-601, 682n10, 686n83; Lord of, 600, 604, 659, 664-65
Hemp, 396, 399, 409, 426, 555
Heng-chou (city), 87, 516
Heng-yang-fu (city), 343-44
Hinterlands, 223, 234, 259, 393, 396, 717n3; role in city building, 170, 172ff; and central places, 203-4, 259, 261, 277, 282-83, 293, 299, 346; area of, 299-301
Ho-tung Tobacco Guild (Peking), 570-71
Hokkien, *see under* Fukien
Hoklo, 159, 544; in Taiwan, 175-80 *passim*, 186, 188, 204, 206, 637, 700n41, 707n47. *See also* Ethnic Groups; *and under* Chang-chou; Ch'üan-chou; T'ung-an
Honan, 83, 91, 218f, 267, 302, 447, 476, 707n2. *See also* Ch'en-chou; Chu-hsien; Chou-chia-k'ou; Hsin-yang; Kaifeng; Kuang-chou; Loyang; Shan-chou
Hong Kong, 228, 482, 507
Hopei, *see* Chihli
Hou-t'u, 661-62, 770n20
Houses, 115-16, 142, 166, 265-66, 529, 533, 635, 687n93
Hsia Pang (Ningpo), 417
Hsiang (rural townships), 143ff, 146f, 695n56
Hsiang (suburban wards), 143ff, 146f, 397, 421
Hsiang River, 212, 543; Basin, 9, 217, 713n30
Hsiang-chiang Shu-yüan, 487-88, 491ff
Hsiang-shan: city, 396, 419; county, 393, 426f
—Bay, 401, 405, 416, 421, 424
Hsiang-yang-fu (city), 93, 335
Hsiang-yüeh I-hsüeh (Ningpo), 409
Hsiang-yüeh system, 357, 368, 386-87, 591, 726n13, 731n61
Hsieh-chung miao (Ningpo), 606
Hsieh-p'u-chen (town), 428
Hsien, *see* Counties

Index

Hsien-nung, 584-85, 587, 601, 761n1
Hsien-yang (Ch'in capital), 43f
Hsin-an Hui-kuan (Ningpo), 417, 549
Hsin-ch'ang (town, Kiangsu), 448
Hsin-ch'ang *hsien* (Chekiang), 393, 426, 430
Hsin-chu (city), 89, 167f, 705n120; construction of, 157f, 161, 172-73, 186-92, 205-9, 702n62-n63, 703n73, 706n127; and field administration, 158, 161; history, 158-64; walls, 158, 161, 164; as central place, 161-64, 172, 181-82, 189, 202-3; religion in, 161, 164. 184; schools in, 161; population, 162, 172, 697n7; map, 163; hinterland of, 170-72, 204; ethnic groups in, 175-79, 186-92, 700n41
Hsin-yang (city), 335
Hsing-hua: city, 544-45, 637; county, 636
Hsing-hua Pang (Ningpo), 417, 543
Hsing-i (prefecture), 305n
Hsü-chou-fu (city), 86, 271, 293, 296, 718n13
Hsü-yung: city, 93, 343-44; autonomous *t'ing*, 305n
Hsüan-chou Hui-kuan (Soochow), 755n14
Hsüan-hua-fu (city), 717n23
Hsüeh-hai Shu-yüan, 489-90
Hsüeh-hai T'ang, 491-92, 496, 745n27
Hsün-chien, see Subprefects, deputy
Hu-chou-fu (city), 437, 543, 555
Hua-lou miao (Ningpo), 423
Huang-chou-fu (city), 334
Huang-kung-lin (town), 426-29 *passim*
Huang-ti, 586
Huang-t'ien Shang-ti, 600. *See also under* Heaven
Hui-an *hsien*, 178, 640, 715n1
Hui-chou (prefecture, Anhwei): merchants from, 403, 417, 432, 536, 538, 544
Hui-chou (prefecture, Kwangtung), 93, 516, 745n21; emigrants and descendants in Taiwan, 177f, 700n41; academies in, 483-91 *passim*
Hui-kuan, 349, 416-18, 423, 436, 755n14. *See also* Guilds; Native-place associations; Sojourners
Hui-tung *hsien*, 552
Hunan, 83, 91, 476. *See also* Changsha; Ching *chou;* Heng-yang-fu; Hui-tung; Hung-chiang; Li-chou; Li-ling
Hung-chiang (town), 549-52
Hung-shui River, 212, 707n2
Hung-wu emperor, 379
Hungry Ghost festival, 646, 667, 669
Huo-shen, *see* Fire King
Hupeh, 83, 431, 447, 707n2. *See also* Ching-chou-fu; Fan-ch'eng; Hankow; Hanyang; Hsiang-yang-fu; Huang-chou-fu; I-ch'ang-fu; Kuang-hua; Sha-shih; Wu-ch'ang-fu; Wuhan

I-ch'ang-fu (city), 290, 437
I-chou (city), 543, 571, 578
I-hsüeh (charity schools), 479-80, 485-90 *passim*
I-lan: city, 97, 164-65, 706n125; urban features, 89, 161-68 *passim;* construction of, 159, 174, 192-96, 205-7; religion in, 165, 195-96; as central place, 166, 181-82, 202-3; ethnic groups in, 175, 180-81; county, 160, 173. *See also* Ko-ma-lan *t'ing*
Ideological controls, 591-96 *passim*, 610
Imperial Maritime Customs, 420
Imperial University, 133, 139, 141
Industry, 220, 233, 279, 573; textile, 148, 405, 412, 445-47, 459; in Ningpo, 396f, 410-13, 430-31; metal-processing, 396, 411, 424, 611; rural sideline, 401, 405, 411-13, 459; handicraft, 405, 409-13, 424, 430-31, 446
Intermediaries (go-betweens), 620-30 *passim*, 766-67n30
Interpersonal relations, 556, 596, 620, 625, 757-58n51. *See also* Face; *T'ung-hsiang* relationships
Iron and blacksmithing, 396, 399, 409, 419, 424, 555, 611
Irrigation, 184, 393, 395-96, 401, 441, 445, 705-6n120. *See also* Water conservancy

Jui-chou-fu (city), 92
Justice: administration of, 364, 618, 726n13, 726n18. *See also* Courts; Litigation

Kaifeng, 16, 28, 60, 90-91, 219, 694; as economic center, 24, 30-31, 60, 218,

343; population, 30, 680n11, 681n39; as Sung capital, 60-63, 90, 96
Kalgan, 538, 546
Kan River, 212; Basin, 9, 11, 219, 713n30
Kan-chou-fu (city), 572,. 757n45
K'ang-hsi emperor, 361, 367, 460
Kansu, 83
—corridor, 85, 212. See also Lanchow; Ling-t'ai
Kao-chia-hang (town), 456, 469
Kao-chou (prefecture), 516, 745n14, 746n41
Kao-wen Shu-yüan, 492
Kashgar, 92
Keelung, 167, 172f
Khotan, 92
Khubilai Khan, 66-67, 111
Kiangnan, 212, 247, 266, 396-97, 555, 707n3; cotton, 444, 446f; land use in, 445; map, 446; transport in, 447-48; water-control administration in, 449-50; manorial system in, 457-59
Kiangsi, 83, 91, 476, 478-79, 538. See also Ching-te-chen; Chiu-chiang-fu; Jui-chou-fu; Kan-chou-fu; Nanchang
Kiangsu, 91, 266, 442, 447, 555, 707n3; and field administration, 83, 302; and macroregions, 218, 343. See also Ch'ang-chou, Ch'ang-shu; Chen-chiang; Chia-ting; Chiang-ning; Chin-kuei; Nan-hui; Nanking; Pao-shan; Shang-yüan; Shanghai; Soochow; Sung-chiang; T'ai-ts'ang-chou; Ts'ang chou; Wu-chiang; Wu-hsi; Yangchow
Kinship, 567, 637-38, 643; and regional systems, 259ff; forms defined, 499-502; fictive, 501-2, 566; and socioeconomics, 508-10; extended, 510-17; in cities, 541; in rural areas, 614. See also Clans; Families; Lineages; Surname associations
Ko-ma-lan t'ing, 164, 172, 174f, 180, 192ff, 704n91. See also I-lan
Kowloon, 273
Ku Yen-wu, 368, 444-45, 695n57, 731n58
Kuan-ti, 583-88 passim, 606-7, 648, 761n1; temples, 195, 423, 651, 667
Kuang-Chao Hui-kuan, 543-44
Kuang-chou (city, Honan), 92
Kuang-chou (prefecture, Kwangtung), 508, 513, 516, 544, 715n1; academies in, 483-88 passim, 492, 764n41
Kuang-hua (city), 94
Kuang-ya Shu-yüan, 490
Kuang-yüan (city), 290-96 passim
Kuei (ghosts), 594-600 passim, 605, 607, 660ff
Kuei-hua-ch'eng (city), 94, 307n, 688n19
Kuei-shan: city, 93; county, 489, 745n22, 745n24
Kuei-sui (city), 307n, 558; guilds in, 562, 565, 569f, 758n52, 758n54
K'uei-chi hsien, 354-55, 715n1
Kung-shu Hsien-shih miao (Ningpo), 423
Kung-so, 558, 755n14. See also Guilds
Kunming, 91, 241, 302, 317, 718n13
Kwangsi, 83, 218-19, 516. See also Heng-chou; Kweilin; Lung-chou; Pai-se; Ssu-en
Kwangtung, 83, 91, 218, 396, 417; emigrants to Taiwan, 175, 177; long-distance trade, 431, 448, 555; academies in, 480-85. See also Canton; Chao-ch'ing; Ch'ao-chou; Chia-ying; Ch'iung-chou; Fo-shan; Hai-feng; Hui-chou; Kao-chou; Kuang-chou; Kuei-shan; Lo-ch'ang; Nan-hai; P'an-yü; Po-lo; Shao-chou; Shun-te; Swatow; Weng-yüan; Ying-te
Kweichow, 83, 118, 218f. See also Hsing-i; Kweiyang; Shih-ch'ien; Ssu-chou; Ssu-nan; Ta-ting
Kweilin, 88, 91
Kweiyang, 88, 91, 241, 718n13

La-chu Kung-so (Soochow), 558
Labor, 409-10, 429, 449; forced, 36, 43, 51, 146-47, 157, 174, 357, 385, 401, 453f, 461-62; on public-work projects, 195, 208, 453, 456; division of, 231-33, 235, 713-14n33. See also Workers
Lacquer ware, 396f, 409ff, 424, 430-31
Lakes, 86, 395
Lanchow, 79, 91, 99
Land and Grain, worship of, 37, 39, 591, 601, 604; altars to, 39, 48, 53, 57, 61f, 64-65, 71f, 114, 584-91 passim, 595, 602-3, 761n1

Index

Landlords, 459-63 *passim*
Landownership, 357, 401, 419, 456, 460f, 511-12
Lao-ho-k'ou (town), 94
Law: customary, 571, 617, 620-21; statute, 610ff, 766n27
Leaders, local, 336-44 *passim*, 375-76
Leather Box Guild (Peking), 564, 572, 757n44
Legalism, 41, 49, 611
Li No-ch'a (deity), 665-66
Li Yü, 124, 692n31
Li-chi, 46, 585, 588, 593-94, 606
Li-chia system, 357, 368, 384ff, 449, 457. 695n56, 730n54
Li-chou (city), 335
Li-fan t'ing, 720n27
Li-lao system, 357, 384, 386
Li-ling *hsien*, 543, 555
Li-tai Ti-wang miao (Peking), 586
Li-t'an, *see* Unworshiped dead
Liang-Kuang Hui-kuan, 543
Lien-shan Hui-kuan (Ningpo), 407, 417
Lin ("near to," in city names), 85
Lin Shuang-wen, 178, 183, 185
Lin-ch'ing (city), 538, 546, 556
Lin-fen (city), 85, 588
Lin-hai-kuan (nonadm. city), 335
Lineages, 488, 499-505, 511, 516, 637-40, 653, 715n1; and rural/urban continuum, 259-60, 502-3, 508ff, 653; and dispute resolution, 364, 624, 627; and government, 395, 505, 518; and business, 434-35; and clans, 501, 508, 512-13; higher-order, 501, 509, 513; in cities, 502-3, 511-12; and property, 502-3, 511-12, 747n20; in Canton, 510-12. *See also* Clans
Ling-nan Hui-kuan (Ningpo), 407, 417
Ling-t'ai (city), 84f, 90, 96
Ling-t'ai (magic tower), 35, 49
Ling-ying miao (Ningpo), 584, 590, 764n22
Lingnan region, 5, 212, 218f, 228, 543, 707n2; urbanization of, 9, 11, 28, 227-35 *passim*; Canton as regional metropolis, 13, 16, 281, 283; subregions, 13; economy, 27, 293, 299ff; population, 213, 226, 229; rank-size distribution of cities, 237, 239-42; central places in, 298
Literature, God of, *see* Wen-ch'ang

Litigation, 363ff. *See also* Courts; Justice
Little Tradition, 34, 264-65, 716n11
Liu Ming-ch'üan, 648; and T'ai-pei-fu, 167-68, 174, 196-97, 200ff, 206
Livestock, 409, 419, 426f, 430, 558
Lo (Chou capital), 36
Lo-ch'ang *hsien*, 448, 745n19
Local systems, 271, 540-51, 721n48
Lower Yangtze region, 5, 11, 95f, 212, 219, 228, 707n2; subregions, 13, 298; economy, 16-17, 24, 27, 299ff, 431, 713n30-n31; regional metropolises, 17, 120, 283; urban system of, 26, 243-47; urbanization of, 28, 227-35 *passim;* population, 213, 226, 229, 243-46, 301; rank-size distribution of cities, 238-43 *passim;* transport in, 285, 293; central places in, 298; field administration of, 323, 342-43
Loyang, 79, 81, 129, 682n45, 686n75, 691-92n24
Lu-chou (city), 271, 296
Lu-kang (nonadm. city), 172, 273, 546, 549, 551-52; as economic center, 525, 634, 636; groups in, 549, 637-42, 645-49; religion in, 584, 643-44; administration of, 634, 649; social structure, 637-50; neighborhoods in, 642-45; gentry in, 649-50
Lu-lung (city), 79f, 96, 98
Lü-chou-fu (city), 90
Lumber, 396, 399, 409, 414, 417, 419, 426f, 430
Lung-chou (city), 334
Lung-shan Ssu, 644, 764n22
Lung-shen, *see* Dragon God
Luxury goods, 396f, 409ff, 424, 430-31

Ma-tsu, *see* T'ien-hou
Macroregions, 9, 211; as socioeconomic systems, 11-12, 16; delineation of, 12-13, 212, 282, 347, 707n2; in China, 212-13; population, 213-16, 226, 229; maps, 214f; and provinces, 215, 218-19, 343; subregions, 217-18. *See also individual regions by name;* Regional systems; Cores; Peripheries; Urban Systems; Local Systems
Magistrates, 185, 263, 366, 374, 388, 611, 725n5, 727n26; and religion, 262f, 578, 592, 601, 763n14; duties,

360-65 *passim*, 725n7, 726n14; tenure in office, 365, 382; and subordinates, 367, 386, 730n47; income, 379, 382; and gentry, 389-90, 729n41; and academies, 478-79
Magistrates, assistant, 273, 303, 358, 366-67, 648
Mai-men-ch'iao (town), 428-29
Malevolent spirits, *see* Unworshiped dead
Manchuria, 12f, 16, 213, 223, 282, 468
Manchus, 357, 370
Marine products, 399, 409, 424, 426, 431
Market towns, 24, 108, 204-5, 229, 258, 446, 485ff, 717n23; functional differentiation, 25; in Lower Yangtze area, 27, 64, 244-45, 247, 469-71; and regional systems, 28, 272-73; urban features of, 205; in North China region, 244-45, 247; as political centers, 272, 336; as economic centers, 276, 470; in regional frontiers, 281; in Upper Yangtze region, 296-97; in Ningpo area, 398-405 *passim*, 428-29
—central, 226, 428-29; defined, 222-23, 286; population, 224-25, 287, 300; number of, 286, 298; location of, 287, 313, 328, 331; size of marketing systems, 300; and field administration, 313, 328, 331, 340
—intermediate, 226, 428-29; defined, 222-23, 286; population, 224, 287; number of, 286; location of, 287; and field administration, 340
—standard, 226, 428-29, 509; population, 224, 287; defined, 286; number of, 286; location of, 287; and field administration, 340
Marketing (rural): and medieval urban revolution, 23-26; economic factors, 232, 285; systems, 259, 295, 336, 509; schedules, 350, 428; locations of, 469, 588
Marketplaces (urban), 22f, 43, 49, 53, 57, 71, 125; in Taiwan, 161, 166; specialized, 263-64, 426; in Ningpo, 396, 406-9
Mean people, 369, 371
Mediation, 616, 623-24, 628-29, 631
Medicines, 396, 399, 403, 409, 413, 416, 426f, 429-30
Mei-chou Island, 646, 652-53

Meng Chiang-nü, 661-62
Meng-chia (nonadm. city), 167, 179f, 193, 197ff, 204, 634, 640; early history, 172-73; as greater city, 525; temples in, 583; and field administration, 698n18, 706n122
Meng-tzu (city), 334
Merchants, 396, 420, 446, 468, 558, 570-71, 584, 625, 635; spread technology, 233; and urban culture, 268-69; regional groupings, 272; and gentry, 336, 341, 468, 553, 703-4n82, 722n53; and the economy, 341, 403, 429, 555f; as sojourners, 397, 399, 403, 405, 555f, 578, 636-37; levies on, 419, 465, 470, 472-73; and city government, 422, 549-51, 575; cotton, 431-32, 447; and education, 491f, 496; salt, 492, 612, 764-65n7; associations, 544, 549-51, 556ff, 645-46, 668; status, 612f, 649. *See also* Agents; Brokers; Businessmen; Middlemen; Retailers; Shopkeepers; Wholesalers
Metal industry, 411, 424. *See also* Minerals
Metropolises, 101-2, 105, 215f, 290, 300
—central, 217; defined. 286; numbers of, 286, 298; location, 287, 313, 328, 331; population, 287; and field administration, 313, 328, 331, 340
—regional, 13-16, 282-83; defined, 286; numbers of, 286, 298; location, 287, 313, 328, 331; population, 287; and field administration, 313, 328, 331, 342; and economic hierarchy, 340
Miao-li (town), 172, 179, 188
Middle Yangtze region, 9, 75, 77, 95, 212, 219, 228, 293, 707n2; subregions, 9, 13, 16, 217-18, 298; population, 213, 226, 229, 301; urbanization of, 227-35 *passim;* rank-size distribution of cities, 238, 240, 242; Wuhan as regional metropolis, 283; economy, 299ff, 430f, 713n30-n31; central places in, 298
Middlemen, *see* Agents; Brokers
Migration, 9, 33, 232, 391, 438; forced, 30, 144-45, 695n57; to Taiwan, 176-77, 637
Military, 52, 172, 194, 334-35, 421, 635. *See also* Defense; Garrisons; Militia
Militia, 647-48, 665, 668

Index

Min Pang (Ningpo), 417
Min River (Szechwan), 86, 293
Min-shang Hui-kuan (Ningpo), 417
Minerals, 396, 409, 419f, 426. *See also* Metal industry; Copper and coppersmithing; Iron and blacksmithing; Silver and silversmithing
Ming dynasty, 17, 66-73, 137, 385, 397-401 *passim*, 475-80; government, 19, 138-39, 367, 384-85; and cities, 26-27, 113; water conservancy, 449-57
Ming T'ai-tsu, *see* Chu Yüan-chang
Ming-t'ang, 49f, 57, 62, 66, 268, 592, 599-600, 686n75, 686n83
Moats, 38, 51, 71, 77, 79, 95, 164, 184, 196
Mobility: spatial, 103; social, 383, 540-41
Moieties, 644
Money shops, 222, 415, 571
Money Trade Guild (Shanghai), 436
Monopolies, 403, 419, 570, 612, 647
Moon, worship of, 587, 600
Moslem Rebellion, 219, 228
Mountains and rivers, worship of, 585f, 598-604 *passim*, 761n1
Mukden, 13, 16, 437, 715n50
Mutual-aid associations, 533, 535, 653-54
Mutual loan societies, 625-26, 628

Names and naming, 62, 85-86, 183, 261-62, 771n32; symbolism of, 43-44, 53, 56, 64, 688n7
Nan (post designation), 314
Nan-an *hsien*, 178, 640
Nan-hai *hsien*, 485n, 496f, 514, 516, 544, 748n38
Nan-hao, 409, 416, 733n4
Nan-hui: city, 442; county, 542
Nan-pang, 399
Nan-pei Hai-shang Kung-so (Ningpo), 416
Nanchang, 88, 91, 129, 343-44
Nanking, 27, 90f, 437, 542, 547, 692n24; as economic center, 17, 30-31, 122, 147ff, 343; population, 29-30, 138f, 143ff, 150; early history, 52-53, 119-25, 693n37; topography, 53-54, 113; as auspicious site, 54-55, 121-27 *passim*, 693n35; as Ming capital, 88, 90, 102, 113, 126-43 *passim*; strategic importance of, 121-22, 129; as cultural center, 123f, 129-31, 149f; religion in, 123f, 133; as secondary capital, 130, 150-52; wall, 131, 134-36, 691n23; and field administration, 131-32, 302, 317, 343-44; palace city, 131, 133-34, 139-41; gates of, 134, 141; map, 135, 140; streets of, 141, 143; administrative subdivisions, 143-47; foreigners in, 149, 696n66; compared with Peking, 151-53
Native-place associations, 221, 407, 416-18, 436ff, 545-46, 556f, 748n36; membership, 539, 543-44, 557; and examination system, 541; and business, 542-43, 557f; and guilds, 542-43, 558; religious ties, 548; types of, 557, 559. *See also* Hui-kuan
Neighborhood associations and groups, 423f, 547-48, 618, 640, 642-45. *See also* Religious associations
Nien Rebellion, 16, 228
Nightsoil, 288
Ning-hai *hsien*, 393
Ning-po (prefecture), 393, 542f, 585, 761n1. *See also* Ningpo
Ning-Shao-T'ai circuit, 420
Ningpo: description of, 89-90, 97, 391-92, 397, 405-8; religion in, 264, 422-24, 584, 590, 606, 764n22; as economic center, 332, 392-408 *passim*, 424-33 *passim*, 736n36; and field administration, 333, 393, 420; history, 392-405 *passim*; water conservancy in area, 393ff, 399, 401; commerce in, 396-99, 409-16, 427, 430-35 *passim*; marketing system of, 396-409 *passim*, 428-29; merchants in, 396, 399, 403, 544; population, 397, 399, 410; sojourners and native-place associations in, 399, 416, 542f, 556; merchants from, 403, 405, 432-39 *passim*, 538, 765-66n17; map, 406-7; business districts, 408-9, 527, 535; occupational differentiation in, 409-10; banking system of, 414-15; guilds in, 415-18; product specialization in, 424-26, 433; lineages in, 434-35; neighborhood associations in, 547

Ningpo Beancake Dealers Guild (Wen-chou-fu), 418
Ningpo Druggists Guild (Wen-chou-fu), 418, 430
Ningpo Guild (Shanghai), 418, 436
Non-Han peoples, 322
North China Plain, 213, 714n47
North China region, 95, 213, 218-19, 228, 342-43, 707n2; urbanization of, 9, 16, 26, 227-35 passim; subregions, 13, 298; economy, 24, 293, 299ff; population, 28, 213, 226, 229, 243-46, 301; rank-size distributions of cities, 237-43 passim; Peking as regional metropolis, 283; central places in, 298
Northwest region, 79, 85, 95, 212-13, 219, 228, 707n2; urbanization of, 9, 26, 227-35 passim; subregions, 13; economy, 24, 27, 216, 299ff; population, 213, 226, 229, 301; rank-size distribution of cities, 237-43 passim; Sian as regional metropolis, 283; central places in, 298
Numerology, 48, 54, 56, 65

Occupational differentiation, 220, 232, 409-10
Office of Overseas Trade, 392, 420
Officials, 233, 265-66, 359, 383, 390, 558, 698n18, 699n19-n20, 729n43; and public works, 189-90, 462-63, 703n74; appointment of, 270, 321, 336, 358-60, 366; ranks, 304; rule of avoidance, 341, 356, 363, 564, 611; and gentry, 341, 375, 462-63, 465-66, 478, 732-33n66; subcounty, 358-59, 362, 370, 374; evaluation of, 361, 376, 383, 725n11; salaries, 364f, 379, 382, 727n24; and subordinates, 364, 378, 388; terms of office, 365, 376, 382; aides, 369-73; duties, 373-74; and water conservancy, 445-57 passim, 461, 465, 740-41n29; disciplining of, 378, 723n2, 730n47; and lineages, 395; expectant, 462, 727n22; and education, 478, 481-83, 491, 493; native-place associations of, 557, 559; and religion, 583-98 passim, 602-3, 605-6, 648, 666, 763n19; and guilds, 647-49, 760n138. See also official titles by name; Bureaucracy; Field administration

Oil, 396, 424, 427
Oil Guild (Lu-kang), 645
Oil Merchants Guild (Peking), 567
Opium Guild (Lu-kang), 645
Organicism, 45, 47, 54
Orphanges, 164, 422, 550
Overseas Chinese, 506-7, 551, 748n36

Pa chou, 307n
Pa-sheng Hui-kuan (Chungking), 550
Pa-shu Hui-kuan (Swatow), 550
Pai-lu-tung Shu-yüan, 476
Pai-lung-wang miao (Ningpo), 606
Pai-se t'ing, 305n
Palace cities, 48-49, 67, 71, 113, 133-34, 139-141
Palaces, 43, 53, 57-64 passim, 71f, 131, 685n60
Palisades, city, 53, 161, 164, 166, 182, 194, 205, 707n128. See also Walls, city
Pan-ch'iao (town), 180, 199
P'an-yü hsien, 485n, 490, 497, 511-16 passim, 544, 748n38
Pao (rural division), 172
Pao (walled villages), 707n129
Pao-chia system, 360f, 368, 386ff, 420f, 451, 732n65
Pao-ning-fu (city), 293, 719n22
Pao-shan hsien, 464
Pao-ting: city, 90-91; prefecture, 543
Paper, 223, 399, 409, 426f, 430-31, 558, 562, 573
Paper Shops Guild (Soochow), 566
Partnerships, business, 411, 435, 625
Pawnshops, 296, 409, 415, 419f, 626
Peasants, 103, 106, 233, 265, 410, 429, 446-47, 459
Pei-hai (Pakhoi, town), 483
Pei-hao, 409, 416, 733n4
Pei-kang (town), 652-53
Pei-pang, 399
Peking, 16, 79, 96, 118, 148, 249, 291, 544; population, 29-30, 529-30, 682n44; as central place, 30-31, 237-39, 283; history, 66-73; as imperial capital, 67-72, 90, 111-13, 141, 151-53, maps, 69, 530-32; walls, 69, 75, 79, 99; provisioning of, 242, 713n20; and field administration, 246, 317, 333, 343-44; native-place associations in, 438, 539, 557; urban ecology of, 529-35; neighborhood as-

Index

sociations in, 547; guilds in, 556, 561-71 passim, 577ff, 758n54, 758n75
Peking Silver Guild, 556, 561, 568, 577
Pen-chou: defined, 304
Peripheries, regional, 216f, 283-90 passim, 296, 308-9
Pescadores, 648, 652-53
Phratries, 499, 501-2
Physiographic regions, *see* Macroregions
Physiography, 12-13, 282, 284, 297
Pi (wards), 421
Pi-yung (moated mound), 35f, 49, 62 73, 686n75
P'i (post designation), 317
Pilgrimages, 578, 652-53
P'ing-Li Kung-so (Hankow), 543
Pirates, 161, 185, 192-93, 399, 421, 470
Po-lo *hsien*, 489, 745n22, 745n24
Police, 421, 535, 549, 575
Poor, urban, 531-32, 536f, 546
Population, general: growth, 16, 19-20, 220; and field administration, 19-20, 225, 323-25; of Tan-shui *t'ing*, 172; of I-lan area, 174; densities, 213, 231-32, 234f, 277, 282f, 444; of macroregions, 213, 243; and the economy, 220, 229; 1893 data, 221, 225; of China, 708n4; rural, 712n23
Population, urban, 29-30, 99, 225-26, 236-43 passim, 286, 528-30, 711n18, 711-12n21-n22; growth, 16; of Soochow, 17; densities, 99, 529-30, 532; of Nanking, 138, 143-44, 150; of Hsin-chu, 162, 172, 697n7; of T'ai-pei-fu, 173, 636; and economic centrality, 224-25, 286, 337; and field administration, 224, 230-31, 246, 323-25, 421; of Ningpo, 397, 399, 409-10; of Peking, 529-30, 532, 682n44; of Lu-kang, 635-36; of Tainan, 651; of Kaifeng, 680n11, 681n39; of Shanghai, 682n44; of Wuhan, 682n44; of T'ang Ch'ang-an, 682n45; of T'ang Loyang, 682n45; of Hangchow, 682n45; of Chengtu, 682n45
Post designations: meanings of terms and frequency of occurrence, 314-16; and economic hierarchy, 316, 323-31 passim; and field administration, 316-17, 323, 325, 330, 358f; "secret" strategic component, 317, 332; deficits in, 318-19

Post offices, 221, 270, 347ff, 393, 708-9n10
Postal agencies (private), 435-36, 439
Prefects, 303, 722n50
Prefectural-level units, 312-14, 325, 327. *See also* Prefectures; Subprefectures, autonomous; Departments, autonomous
Prefectures, 304; capitals of, 91, 222, 304, 309-14 passim, 320, 325-31 passim, 340; and field administration, 303ff, 359f; locations of, 308-9, 312. *See also* Field administration; Government
Prices, 419, 432, 571f
Priests, 588f, 595-605 passim, 656
Printers, 409, 565
Private secretaries, 270-71, 363, 369-79 passim, 723n2, 728n35-n36, 730n49; salaries, 365, 371, 374, 379, 382; and state interests, 374f
Property, 500, 511, 514, 612. *See also* Landownership; Trusts
Prostitution, 222, 351
Provinces, 707-8n3; capitals of, 90-91, 222, 304, 309-10, 326, 340; and macroregions, 215, 218-19. *See also* provinces by name; Field administration; Government
P'u ("riverbank," in city names), 85
P'u-chi tien (Tainan), 773n49
P'u-chou-fu (city), 88, 335
Public services, 421-22, 548-49, 552-53, 575, 675-76. *See also* Fire fighting; Police
Purchasing power, 277, 301

Queen of Heaven, *see* T'ien-hou

Rain ceremony, 602-3, 763n19
Range of goods, 277, 279f
Rank-size relationships of cities, 236-42, 248-49, 714n39
Real estate, urban, 418ff, 655-56
Rebellions, 104, 177, 182f, 185, 648. *See also* Moslem Rebellion; Nien Rebellion; Taiping Rebellion
Red Basin, 212, 288, 719n21
Regional cycles, *see* Urban development
Regional specialization, 220, 232
Regional systems, 293, 543-44; developmental cycles, 24-28, 219-20; regional integration, 241-42, 272-73;

as analytical tool, 258-60; definition of, 281-82
—of cities, 216-18; urbanization, 226-35; rank-size distribution of cities, 236-42. *See also* Macroregions
Regions, *see* Macroregions
Religion, 114-15, 181ff, 260, 262-63, 577-79, 584-85, 588; government control of, 581, 591, 596, 605-7; popular and official contrasted, 584-85, 588, 596-606 *passim;* views of, 603-5, 762-63n13
—official, 57, 114, 423, 581, 651, 686n83; rites, 582, 589, 595-97; sources of, 584, 587; characterized, 586ff, 590, 607, 763n19; participation in, 588; hierarchy, 589-90; and social control, 591-96; views of, 594-95, 605, 607; alternatives to, 601. *See also* Altars; Buddhism; Deities; Festivals; Rites; Taoism; Temples
Religious associations: and neighborhoods, 423f, 547-48, 618, 640, 642-45; and city governance, 615; types of, 653-54; officers of, 654-56, 769-70n12; finances of, 655-56, 659-60, 770n15, 772-73n44; in Tainan, 654-75; activities of, 656. *See also under* T'u-ti-kung; Fire King
Renting, 418-19, 446, 458-62, 491-92; double-rent system, 191, 193-94, 200
Residence patterns, 533, 535, 537, 638-39
Retailers, 410-14, 430, 563
Revenues, 382, 612; and regional economies, 232, 322-23, 349; and field administration, 314ff, 323, 338-39. *See also* Fiscal administration; Taxation
Ricci, Matteo, 152-53
Rice, 397, 399, 414, 426f, 430, 634, 645-46, 713n30
Rice Guild (Lu-kang), 645
Rites, 42, 44-45, 50; and city building, 36-37; Ch'ing system, 585ff; and social control, 592f; views of, 595; description of, 597-601
Rivers, 86, 296; and macroregions, 212, 214; market, 467-73. *See also individual rivers by name;* Waterways; Water conservancy
Roads, 291, 393, 719n22

Rotating-credit societies, *see* Mutual loan societies
Runners, yamen, 263, 373-79 *passim;* tenure in office, 365, 376, 727n25; number of, 367ff, 712n25; functions, 369; and local interests, 369, 374ff; barred from office, 369, 383; wages, 369, 379, 382
Rural-urban, *see* Urban-rural continuum

Sacred Edict, 361-62, 591
Sacrifices, *see* Rites
Salaries: of officials, 364, 367, 371, 379, 382; of academy headmasters, 490-91
Salt, 395, 403, 419f, 424, 611
Sam Yap, 497-98
San I, 178ff, 700n41
San I Kung-so, 544
San-chiang Hui-kuan, 438
San-huang miao, 586
San-i T'ang (Tainan), 548, 550, 668-69, 771-72n36
San-men Gorge, 234, 334, 707n2
San-shan Kuo-wang, 636, 642
Scholars, 410, 434, 559, 584, 592, 607
School-temples, *see* Confucian school-temples
Schools, 117f, 406-7, 477, 479-80, 488, 588, 594. *See also* Academies; Education; *I-hsüeh; She-hsüeh*
Servants: of officials, 371-79 *passim,* 383, 729n37, 730n49
Service industry, 222-23, 350-51
Sex ratios, 530, 532, 535
Sha-shih (nonadm. city), 217, 335, 437, 550f
Shan-chou (city), 335
Shan-yin: city, 380-81; county, 354-55, 715n1
Shang-hai *hsien,* 444f, 470; water conservancy in, 448-57 *passim,* 470. *See also* Shanghai
Shang-ti, 40, 595. *See also* Heaven
Shang-yü *hsien,* 393
Shang-yüan *hsien,* 143
Shang-yüan Hui-kuan (Hankow), 542
Shanghai, 228, 290, 333, 441, 444, 448, 546; as economic center, 17, 24n, 283; Ningpo natives in, 403, 436f, 439; cotton trade, 431f; maps, 442f; nearby market towns, 469-71; population, 682n44
Shansi, 91, 218, 267; and field

Index

administration, 83, 302; merchants, 403, 544, 556; academies in, 476
—Banks, 403, 432, 572. *See also* Fen-chou-fu; Kuei-hua-ch'eng; Kuei-sui; Lin-fen; P'u-chou-fu; Sui-yüan; Ta-t'ung; Taiyuan
Shantung, 91, 218, 267, 417, 447, 556; and field administration, 91, 302; merchants, 403; long-distance trade, 447f; academies in, 476. *See also* Chefoo, Chi-ning-chou; Chiao-chou; Ch'ing-chou-fu; Lin-ch'ing; Te-chou; Tsinan; Tung-ch'ang-fu; Wei-hai-wei; Wei-hsien
Shao-chou (prefecture), 483-91 *passim*, 745n19, 745n24
Shao-hsing: city, 95, 343-44, 354-55, 397, 437; prefecture, 270, 426, 715n1, 757n41; in Ningpo's economic sphere, 393, 420; migrants from, 538, 542, 556
She-hsüeh (community schools), 479-80, 485ff, 488
She-huo (religious associations), 423-24
Shen (spirits), 582, 594, 596, 598, 605f
Shen-ming (gods), 590, 594, 599, 604
Shen-nung, 586
Shensi, 83, 218-19, 707n2. *See also* Ch'ang-an; Sian
Shiang (rural townships; periurban wards), 143ff, 146f, 695n56
Shih-ch'i (town), 426, 428-29, 528
Shih-ch'ien (prefecture), 305n
Shih-t'ien (religious ceremony), 596-99
Ship Guild (Lu-kang), 645
Ships, 222, 228f, 405, 427, 468, 733n4
Shipyards, 149, 396, 409
Shopkeepers, 349-50, 414, 567, 757n50
Shops, 222f, 414, 645; locations of, 408-9, 416, 537, 751n25; craft, 441, 536; and guilds, 563
Shou-ts'ai-nü, 661
Shrines, *see* Temples
Shu-yüan, see Academies
Shun-chih emperor, 367
Shun-ch'ing-fu (city), 271, 293, 296
Shun-te *hsien*, 485n, 497, 510
Shun-t'ien (prefecture), 266, 307n
Sian, 88, 90-91, 129, 132, 291; as economic center, 237-38, 240, 280; and field administration, 317, 343-44
Silk, 396f, 409, 427, 445, 472, 555, 572

Silver and silversmithing, 396, 399
Single Whip tax reforms, 151, 368, 370, 377, 385-86, 455, 460, 731n58-n59
Social-overhead investment, 220, 708n7
Sojourners, 201-2, 266, 533, 538-46, 556, 636, 751n23, 752n51, 752n53
Soochow, 5, 17, 79, 90-91, 120, 129, 249, 430, 758n52; maps, 14f; as economic center, 17, 122, 148, 555; population, 17, 29; and field administration, 302, 307, 317, 333, 343-44; sojourners in, 437; urban ecology, 527ff; migrants from, 538-39; native-place associations in, 557f; workers in, 558, 573; guilds in, 562, 565f, 569, 755n14, 756n34
South Guild (Lu-kang), 645-46
Southeast Coast region, 212, 218f, 228; urbanization of, 11, 227-35 *passim*; subregions, 13, 16, 298; economy, 24, 27, 293, 299ff, 713n30; population, 213, 226, 229f, 301; rank-size distribution of cities, 239-42; Foochow as regional metropolis, 283; central places in, 298
Span of control, 246, 270, 305, 314, 323, 325, 327; defined, 305f; and location of capitals, 309-11, 319-20, 325-33 *passim;* and economic centrality, 312, 314; and defense, 319-21
Spirits, *see* Shen
Ssu (subdistricts), 303. *See also* Subprefects, deputy
Ssu-chou (prefecture), 305n
Ssu-en (prefecture), 305n
Ssu-ming Kung-so, *see* Ningpo Guild
Ssu-nan (prefecture), 305n
State cult, *see under* Religion
Straw products, 396, 401, 411ff, 426f, 429, 555
Streets, 48, 97-98, 167; grids, 23, 43, 48, 62-67 *passim*, 72, 97f, 107, 161; of Ch'ang-an, 43, 56-57; of Kaifeng, 62; of Hangchow, 64, 66; of Peking, 67, 72; of Nanking, 141; in Taiwan, 161, 167, 635; of Ningpo, 405, 409
Su-chou (prefecture), 444-47 *passim*, 451-52, 459-60, 543, 558
Su-Hu Kung-so (Hankow), 543
Su-Sung-T'ai circuit, 333
Subcounty administrative units, 273, 303, 360

Subprefects (*t'ung-chih*), 158, 161, 273, 634, 637, 646ff
Subprefects, deputy (*hsün-chien*), 166, 273, 634
Subprefectures, autonomous (*chih-li t'ing*), 222; capitals of, 303, 309-10, 319-20, 340; and field administration, 304-5, 321-37 *passim*; location of, 308-9, 320-21; and defense, 314. *See also* Field administration; Government
Subprefectures, ordinary (*san t'ing*), 222; and field administration, 303-4; 321, 326, 334ff; location of, 306, 308-9, 320-21; capitals of, 309, 311-12. *See also* Field administration; Government
Subregions, 13, 16, 298. *See also under name of each region*
Suburbs, 485ff, 699n26; growth of, 23ff, 99; altars in, 50, 62, 65, 71, 587, 600; commerce in, 492, 536
Sugar, 396, 399, 409, 416f
Sugar-cake Bakers Association (Peking), 543
Sugar Guild (Lu-kang), 645-46
Sui dynasty, 19, 21, 56
Sui Wen-ti, 56
Sui-yüan (city), 94, 307n, 688n19
Sun: worship of, 586, 600
Sun Ch'üan, 52-53, 120
Sun Erh-chun, 186-89 *passim*
Sun Ts'e, 52, 120
"Sundries" Guild (Lu-kang), 645
Sung dynasty, 19, 90, 125-26, 367, 396-97, 475-76, 686n83; Northern Sung, 11, 13, 17, 60-63, 124; Southern Sung, 17, 26, 63-66, 124-25
Sung Hui-tsung, 62
Sung Kao-tsung, 55, 63
Sung-chiang: city, 148, 555; map, 442; prefecture, 444; agriculture in, 444-45, 468; cotton industry in, 445-47; water transport in, 447-48; water conservancy in, 449-56 *passim*, 467; manors in, 458
Surname associations, 499, 501, 506-8, 666; in Taiwan, 175, 507, 638-42; in Canton, 508, 510; in cities, 510, 653
Swatow, 228, 437, 483, 550f. *See also* Ch'ao-chou
Symbolism, 35, 37, 44, 47, 113-14, 141-42. *See also* Cosmology

Szechwan, 83, 212, 218, 302, 707n2, 719n21-n22. *See also* Chengtu; Chiang-pei-t'ing; Chungking; Hsü-chou-fu; Hsü-yung; Kuang-yüan; Li-fan; Lu-chou; Pao-ning-fu; Shun-ch'ing-fu; T'ung-ch'uan-fu; Wan-hsien; Ya-chou-fu; Yung-ning

Ta-ch'iao (town), 426, 428
Ta-k'uei T'ang (Foshan), 553
Ta-ming-fu (city), 343
Ta-sung River, 401, 403; valley, 426
Ta-tao-ch'eng (nonadm. city), 167f, 173, 180, 198-204 *passim*, 715n6, 715n16
Ta-ting (prefecture), 305n
Ta-tu (Yüan Peking), 66-67, 112-13, 142
Ta-t'ung (city), 77f, 88, 97, 100
Tablets (objects of worship), 589-90, 592, 600
Tainan, 527, 548, 550, 634; temples in, 264, 584, 651-53, 658, 769n10; as regional city, 525; neighborhood associations in, 547; official religion in, 592; population, 651; religious associations in, 654-56, 664-75; T'u-ti-kung *hui* in, 656-60; cults in, 657ff; map, 658; Look West Street, 667-75. *See also* T'ai-wan-fu
Taipei, 437, 547, 636, 764n22. *See also* T'ai-pei-fu
—Basin, 167, 172, 177, 179-80, 187, 196-202 *passim*, 701n42
Taiping Rebellion, 16f, 141, 219, 228, 559, 593
Taiwan, 159, 220, 223, 507, 702n56, 708n3, 771n32; maps, 159f; settlement of, 175-77; immigration restrictions, 176-77, 196; and field administration, 182, 200, 705n101; city building in, 183-84; seaborne trade, 426, 634; religion in, 584, 590-91, 602-3; ethnic strife in, 640, 753n55. *See also* Chang-hua; Chi-lung; Chia-i; Chu-lo; Feng-shan; Hsin-chu; I-lan; Keelung; Ko-ma-lan; Lu-kang; Meng-chia; Miao-li; Ta-tao-ch'eng; Tainan; T'ai-pei-fu; T'ai-wan-fu; Tan-shui; T'ao-yüan
Taiyuan, 79, 88, 91
T'ai, Lake, 441, 444, 446, 456f

Index

T'ai Miao, 586
T'ai-chou: city, 392, 396, 437; prefecture, 393, 420, 427
T'ai-pei-fu, 699n26; construction of, 157, 160, 167, 173-74, 196-209 passim, 701n52, 704n100; description of, 167-68, 171, 197-98; and field administration, 167, 173, 200; sojourners in, 167, 201-6 passim; maps, 169, 171; temples, 171, 583; as central place, 173, 181-82, 204; population, 173; ethnic groups in, 176, 180
T'ai-shan, Lord of, see Eastern Peak, God of the
T'ai-ts'ang-chou (city), 344n
T'ai-wan-fu (city), 182f, 525, 585, 634f, 648, 701n50, 761n1. See also Tainan
Tan-shui: city, 437, 634; county, 160, 167, 196; autonomous t'ing, 159, 164, 172, 179, 182, 187, 204, 207
—River, 172
T'ang dynasty, 75, 392-96; and cities, 13, 17, 122; counties, 19, 21, 24; market system, 22-23, 25, 419-20
Taoism, 41, 45, 265, 582, 606; and cities, 34, 57, 62-63, 114-15, 123; and academies, 476; and official religion, 594-95; popular, 597-607 passim, 644, 662-64
T'ao-yüan (town), 172, 179, 205, 702n56
Taxation, 360-61, 364, 382, 385, 729n44, 730-31n54; Ch'ing system, 29, 419; for public works, 51, 173-74, 191, 193-94, 201, 203, 464, 472-73; in cities, 146-47, 151; and economic centrality, 308, 322-23; Ming reforms, 385-86, 455; land taxes, 397, 419; and industry, 446; grain taxes, 449-52; of trade, 612, 634. See also Field Administration; Revenues; Single Whip tax reform
Te-chou (city), 342
Tea, 419f, 426f, 431, 570
Teachers, 492-96, 596
Technology, 12-13, 29, 231-35, 570, 712-13n26, 713-14n33
Temples, 57, 124, 585, 591, 606, 635, 642, 763-64n22, 769n1; to imperial ancestors, 61-66 passim, 71f, 114, 133; location of, 99; and cities, 114-15, 614-15; in Taiwan, 161, 165f, 189, 195ff, 651-53, 657f, 667; territories of, 264, 548, 590-91, 643; and markets, 397, 469, 588; in Ningpo, 406-9 passim, 422ff; sponsorship of, 423-24, 583-84, 648, 666; usage of, 577, 675-76, 773n49; popular, 583; official, 586; networks of, 590-91, 652-53; Buddhist, 644; finances of, 655-56, 688-69. See also individual temples by name and under names of gods
Tenants, 200, 457-62 passim, 626-27
Teng-shih-k'ou (district in Peking), 751n25
Teochiu, 550
Textiles, 148; trade, 399, 409, 414, 416, 419, 634; guilds, 558, 565, 569, 571. See also Cotton; Dyestuffs; Hemp; Silk
Three Guilds of Tainan, see San-i T'ang
Ti-pao (constables), 263, 387-88, 731-32n63
Tientsin, 228, 332, 437, 565, 751n22
T'ien-hou (Ma-tsu), 416, 423, 583ff, 590, 606-7, 646, 666, 669, 761n1; temples of, 195, 636f, 640, 645, 651-57 passim, 665f; Great Temple of the Queen of Heaven (Tainan), 652, 657f, 665, 669
T'ien-t'ai hsien, 393
Ting-hai: city, 322, 396; county, 393, 430
T'ing, see Subprefectures
T'o River, 293, 296f
Tobacco, 419, 426, 472, 558
Towns, see Market towns
Trade, 110, 232, 276, 396-97, 447-48, 556, 576, 611, 624; government regulation of, 24ff, 43, 468, 611; taxation of, 25, 419, 634; extraregional, 27, 217, 241, 432, 713n32; foreign, 27f, 31, 228f, 234, 239ff, 396-97, 399, 482-83, 559; and macroregions, 212, 220, 233-35; in commodities, 223, 396-400, 409-19 passim, 426-32 passim, 446f, 467-68, 472, 555, 570, 634, 648, 713n30; and the economy, 349, 555; maritime, 392, 403
Trading systems, 555, 721n48; size and location, 284-85, 300; in Upper Yangtze region, 290-98
Transport, 122, 233, 392, 397, 426-27, 444; and regional systems, 12-13,

212f, 216-17, 233f; and central places, 23, 277-85 *passim*, 293, 332, 469; overhead, 13, 212, 293, 719n22; mechanized, 167, 220, 222, 228, 247, 405; costs, 232, 277, 283, 301; workers, 558. *See also* Roads
—water, 13, 216-17, 233f, 403, 405, 719n21; and regional systems, 282, 293; in Ningpo area, 395f, 403, 426-27; maritime, 396, 403, 733n4; in Shanghai area, 441-48 *passim*, 465-57, 468; and water conservancy, 448, 456-57, 470. *See also* Ships
Treaty ports, 221, 403, 405, 482ff
Trusts, ancestral, 502-3, 511ff, 648f, 653, 655-56
Ts'ai Ch'ien, 161, 185, 192
Ts'ang *chou*, 550
Tsao-chia miao (Ningpo), 423
Ts'ao-o (town), 392, 427
Tsinan, 79, 91, 95, 99
Tso (Sung craftsmen's association), 555
Tsu-kung hui, *see* Clans; Lineages
T'u-ti-kung, 262, 423-24, 548, 660-64, 770n16, 772n39, 772n41; shrines, 164; associations, 548, 656-60, 664, 667-76 *passim*, 771n35
Tung-ch'ang-fu (city), 343
Tung-yüeh, *see* Eastern Peak, God of the
Tung-yüeh Hui-kuan (Soochow), 558
T'ung-an *hsien*, 178ff, 187, 640, 700n41, 715n6
T'ung-chou (city), 307n, 431, 570
T'ung-ch'uan-fu (city), 98, 719n22
T'ung-hsiang hui, *see* Native-place associations
T'ung-hsiang relationships, 175-76, 270, 435, 437f, 541-42, 564-65, 579
T'ung-hsing, *see* Surname associations
T'ung-Shang circuit, 334
Tz'u-ch'i: city, 395f, 405, 428; county, 393, 434, 438-39

Unworshiped dead, 594, 601; altars to, 182, 548f, 587, 591, 761n1
Upper Yangtze region, 77, 212, 218, 228, 707n2, 719n21; urbanization of, 9-11, 226-35 *passim*; subregions, 13; Chengtu, 13, 16; population, 213, 226, 228, 299, 301; rank-size distribution of cities, 238, 240, 242; economy, 271, 288-99, 713n30-n31; Chungking as regional metropolis, 283; map of, 289;

central places in, 290-301 *passim*; trading system, 290, 293, 300f; transport in, 291-93
Urban development: regional cycles of, 16f, 24, 26-28, 31, 219-20
Urban-rural continuum, 103ff, 116ff, 119, 258-61, 508-10, 609
Urban systems, regional integration of, 13, 28, 269-71; and regional analysis, 216-18, 276, 281; functional differentiation of, 243-47
Urbanism, 125-26, 219
Urbanization, 219, 247, 273; rates of, 28, 218, 225-27; and field administration, 29, 230-31; regional variations in, 212, 226-36 *passim*, 243-46; in 1890's, 220-29 *passim*; in 1840's, 228-30; theories of, 236. *See also* Urban development
Urumchi (Ti-hua), 92
Usury, 612

Vegetables, 396, 409, 427
Villages, 223, 258, 462, 509, 591, 735n23

Waiters' Guild (Peking), 758n54
Walls, city, 35, 43, 47-48, 137, 221, 706n125, 707n128, 723-24n3; Soochow, 17; construction of, 38, 67, 75, 77, 79, 90, 113, 136, 183-84, 702n53; Ch'ang-an, 43, 67; Kaifeng, 60; Hangchow, 64; Peking, 67, 69; define cities, 75; for defense, 77, 184, 691n23; shapes of, 89-90; around suburbs, 99-100; significance of, 107, 132f, 184, 208-9; Nanking, 113, 131-38 *passim*; in Taiwan, 159, 161, 168, 182-83, 196, 702n56, 702n58, 703n65; outer, 164, 189; financing of, 185, 188; cost, 198; Shanghai, 444. *See also* Palisades, city
Wan-hsien (city), 90, 271, 290, 293, 296, 342
Wan-nien-feng (Swatow), 550
Wan-p'ing *hsien*, 307n
Wang Mang, 50-51, 686n75
Wang Yang-ming, 357, 380, 479
Wards, 43, 56, 125, 143, 360; intramural, 143-47 *passim*, 421, 695n56; suburban, 143-47 *passim*, 397, 421
Warehouses, 417, 431-32, 555-56, 668
Water conservancy, 393, 395f, 399, 401,

Index

460; financing of, 401, 464-66, 470, 472; and transport, 448, 467-72 *passim;* administration of, 449-56 *passim,* 462-67; labor on, 461-62. *See also* Canals; Dikes; Irrigation; Waterways

Water Immortal; temples of, 407, 423, 667ff, 675

Water supply, urban, 94-95, 395, 410, 422, 430

Waterways, 60, 84ff, 290-91; and commerce, 441, 448; dredging of, 448. 450, 464. *See also* Rivers; Water conservancy

Wei River (Shensi), 13, 35, 43

Wei-Fen crescent, 247

Wei-hai-wei, 273

Wei-hsien (city), 342

Weighing Scales Guild (Wuhan), 572

Weights and measures, 417, 562, 572, 759n95

Wen miao, *see* Confucian school-temple

Wen-ch'ang, 584, 592, 594, 606, 761n1; temples of, 161, 423, 586, 607

Wen-chou-fu (city), 392, 437, 542, 556, 571

Wen-wu miao, 584, 648-49

Weng-yüan *hsien,* 745n24

West River, 87, 212, 516-17

Wind-rain-thunder-clouds, worship of, 584f, 598-604 *passim,* 761n1

Wine, 414, 419, 427, 431

Wharves, 409, 427

Wholesalers, 412ff, 426, 429f, 563, 635, 645

Wood carvings, 410f, 424, 430-31

Workers, 410, 536; wages, 465-66, 562, 574-75; associations of, 558, 562f, 567, 570, 574, 576; and employers, 572ff. *See also* Artisans

Wu miao, 586

Wu River (Szechwan, Kweichow), 212, 707n2

Wu-ch'ang-fu (city), 91, 93, 302, 307n

Wu-ch'i (town), 640, 648

Wu-chiang *hsien,* 450

Wu-hsi: city, 89-90, 241, 342; county, 495

Wu-hu (city), 119, 335

Wu-lin Hang-ch'ien Hui-kuan (Soochow), 755n12

Wu-ni-ching (town), 469f

Wu-sung River, 441, 453, 456, 470

Wuhan, 93, 249, 307n, 572; as economic center, 16, 217, 219, 242, 281, 283; population, 29, 682n44. *See also* Hankow, Hanyang, Wu-ch'ang-fu

Ya-chou-fu (city), 291, 719n22

Yamens, 161, 166f, 196, 221, 270, 649, 722-23n1; locations of, 57, 99, 141, 354-55, 406-8, 533, 535; and cities, 92-93, 230, 343-44; urbanization of, 353, 356-60; bureaucratization of, 356, 377-78; functions, 360-65; and gentry, 363; income of, 364; structure of, 365-75; local interests of, 372-73, 375; power centers in, 375-84; layout of, 377-81
—personnel, 270-71, 421, 461, 727n27, 732n64; and rural areas, 353, 356; objectives, 360; income, 364f, 369, 374, 379, 382; tenure in office, 365, 376, 382, 384; rules on, 374; vocationalization of, 377. *See also* Clerks; Gate porters; Servants; Runners

Yang: in city names, 87

Yang T'ing-li, 193-94, 207

Yang-ch'eng Shu-yüan, 490

Yangchow, 120, 343-44, 529, 694n47; as economic center, 17, 24, 27, 122, 148; sojourners in, 538, 546

Yangtze corridor (subregion of Middle Yangtze), 9, 217-18, 242, 441-42

Yangtze Gorges, 234, 707n2, 713n31

Yangtze River, 87, 212, 234, 291-96 *passim,* 441, 707n2; valley, 52. *See also* Lower Yangtze; Middle Yangtze; Upper Yangtze

Yao-huang tien (Ningpo), 407, 423

Yellow Emperor, *see* Huang-ti

Yellow River, 13, 82, 212-13, 707n1, 707n2

Yen-Shao Hui-kuan, 539

Yin: in city names, 87

Yin *hsien,* 393-99 *passim,* 420, 426, 438, 593, 602, 735n23

Yin-yang, 41-42, 44f, 54, 589, 604

Ying-te *hsien,* 745n19, 745n24

Ying-yüan Shu-yüan, 490, 496

Yü (urban quarters), 421

Yü-yao: city, 92, 392, 395; county, 393, 401, 403, 426, 430, 438
—River, 392, 401, 405, 427

Yüan dynasty, 11, 19, 66-67, 75, 125, 131-32, 475-76

Yüan River Basin, 9, 212, 549
Yüeh-hsiu Shu-yüan, 486, 492, 494
Yun-Kwei region, 96, 212f, 219, 228, 323, 707n2; urbanization of, 11f, 226-35 *passim;* subregions, 16; population, 213, 226, 229; rank-size distribution of cities, 237, 239ff; economy, 282, 293, 299ff, 718n13; central places in, 298

Yung River, 391ff, 395, 401, 405, 424, 427; basin, 426
Yung-cheng emperor, 183, 361
Yung-lo emperor, 67, 71, 130, 146, 150
Yung-ning (city), 93
Yung-p'ing *hsien,* 317n
Yung-tung (Ningpo suburb), 408-9, 527
Yunnan, 83, 118, 144. *See also* Chao-t'ung-fu; Kunming; Meng-tzu

The City in Late Imperial China

編 著 者	G. Willliam Skinner
發 行 人	魏德文
發 行 所	南天書局有限公司
地　　址	台北市羅斯福路3段283巷14弄14號
電　　話	(02)362-0190（代表號）
電　　傳	(02)362-3834
郵　　撥	01080538（南天書局帳戶）
登 記 號	行政院新聞局局版台業字第1436號
國際書號	ISBN 957-638-310-2
版　　次	民國八十四年十月台一版
印 刷 者	國順印刷有限公司
廠　　址	板橋市中正路216巷2弄13號

台灣地區・著作權所有

KEY TO ENDPAPER MAPS

The endpaper maps show the cities of China in 1894. North China is shown on the front endpaper, South China on the back. Seven city symbols are used:

- ★ National capital
- ■ Provincial capital
- ▲ Capital of prefecture (*fu*)
- △ Capital of independent department (*chih-li chou*)
- • County-level capital of unexceptional economic importance
- ◉ County-level capital of exceptional economic importance
- ○ Nonadministrative city

County-level capitals consist of capitals of counties (*hsien*), dependent departments (*chou*), and subprefectures (*t'ing* and *chih-li t'ing*).